LABORS OF INNOCENCE
IN EARLY MODERN ENGLAND

LABORS OF INNOCENCE
IN EARLY MODERN ENGLAND

Joanna Picciotto

HARVARD UNIVERSITY PRESS

Cambridge, Massachusetts
London, England
2010

Library of Congress Cataloging-in-Publication Data

Picciotto, Joanna.
    Labors of innocence in early modern England / Joanna Picciotto.
        p.   cm.
    Includes bibliographical references and index.
    ISBN 978-0-674-04906-2 (alk. paper)
    1. English literature—Early modern, 1500–1700—History and criticism.
2. Intellectuals in literature.   3. Labor in literature.   4. Great Britain—Intellectual
life—17th century.   5. Literature and science—England—History—17th century.
6. Religion and science—England—History—17th century.   7. Science—England—
History—17th century.   I. Title.
PR438.I67P53   2010
820.9'004—dc22   2009052648

For Geoffrey

CONTENTS

Contents

LABORS OF INNOCENCE
IN EARLY MODERN ENGLAND

INTRODUCTION

The Intellectual's Two Bodies

Reflexivity takes on its full efficacy only when it is embodied in collectives which have so much incorporated it that they practise it as a reflex. In a research group of that kind, the collective censorship is very strong, but it is a liberating censorship, which leads one to dream of the censorship of an ideally constituted field that would free each of the participants from the "biases" linked to his or her position and dispositions.
—Pierre Bourdieu, *Science of Science and Reflexivity*

What an absurdity it is to pretend men are "other," to try to convince them that their deepest desire is to become "themselves" again!
—Jean Baudrillard, *The Mirror of Production*

The concept of objectivity suggests that we place our trust in the perspective of the innocent eye. Those who seek to expose objectivity as a myth usually insist that such a perspective is inaccessible; rarely do they challenge its claim to authority. Yet that claim is hardly an intuitive one. Our trust is straightforwardly compelled by experts; the authority of an innocent observer is less easily explained. The question raised by objectivity is how innocence, traditionally understood to be a state of ignorance, ever came to be associated with epistemological privilege. I suggest that this association results from the seventeenth century's conversion of the original subject of innocence, Adam, into a specifically intellectual exemplar.[1] Used to justify experimental science, an emergent public sphere, and the concept of intellectual labor itself, the innocent Adam generated two originary myths of modernity: the state of nature from which popular sovereignty was derived and the assumption of a visible and palpable nature ontologically prior to—and radically different from—humanity's "fallen" experience of it.[2] One of the aims of this book is to demonstrate how these two myths worked together in seventeenth-century England to reorganize collective life around intellectual production. I will argue that the figure of the innocent observer distributed intellectual authority rather than concentrating it: first, by privileging the perspective of humanity prior to its fall into social difference, and second, by offering people a perspective to which their own persons provided no access. Even now, the myth of a rationally reconstructed "view from before" seems too useful to surrender; the fiction of historical priority provides the ground for constructions of *ontological* priority on which modern efforts to describe the real depend.[3]

As an intellectual model, the innocent Adam embodied a new ideal of estranged and productive observation. According to this ethos, it is by performing the work of defamiliarization that contemplation becomes productive, a means of working on and transforming the world. The figure of the cultural worker who serves the public by exposing the blind spots of normative perception continues to shape our concept of intellectual labor, a concept no more intuitive than that of objectivity. Flattening the distinction between work and labor that, as Hannah Arendt pointed out long ago, most languages mark, the very term strains to reconcile oppositions long held to describe the inevitable poles of human existence: action and contemplation, *negotium* and *otium,* things and ideas, and, above all, the laborer and the thinker.[4]

Today, of course, to defend intellectual life as one form of productive work among others is a powerful means to sustain the illusion of its exclusivity, identifying intellectual pursuits as the province of a specialized class of producers rather than as the work proper to "the common."[5] But if the modern concept of intellectual labor promotes an unduly exclusive conception of intellectual life, its early modern ancestor did exactly the reverse, redefining that life to include people who were traditionally considered incapable of it.[6] Intellectual labor was first conceived not as the province of a restricted class of people but as an ideal encounter between the self and the world. The inclusive character of this ideal was determined by the figure that personified it, the man from whom all people descended and in whom all were represented. This ideal image of the intellectual was really an image of the whole social body: "*Adam* in Paradise was but our nature personated; and we out of Paradise are but his Person multiplyed."[7] This at once universal and impossibly remote object of identification upheld a vision of intellectual life as a collective progress toward the restoration of innocent insight.[8] The distance between self-styled heirs of Adam and the first man himself— with whom all could identify but to whom none could be identical—

sustained the asymptotic progress of a calling, something both more and less than a career.[9] The demands of this calling, unlike those of a job, were provocatively ill-defined (hence infinite) and they excluded no one. One could participate in this general calling without being aware of it; reciprocally, some who thought they were engaging in it stood accused of impeding its progress.

The reason for this ambiguity was that such labor was conceptually grounded outside the world of fallen experience, and indescribable within the familiar oppositions that structured life inside it. The figure of the innocent observer integrated traditionally distinct, even contradictory, images of Adam himself: the laborer, the namer of the creatures, and the sovereign. As the delver, Adam had long served as the proper name of an undifferentiated humanity prior to the distinctions of rank: the state of nature personified. But if social difference disappeared in Adam the digger, it originated in Adam the sovereign. In the seventeenth century, however, the basis of the first man's sovereignty was theorized anew: the notion that Adam was the first king *because* he was the first worker brought the delver, the namer, and the sovereign into new relation. As the king was expanded into a "royal society" whose sovereignty was to be exercised over creation itself, the corporate digger became an intellectual laborer, and the *corpus mysticum* became a public: a body whose members were united by their shared participation in the labor of knowledge production—a labor that could confer on each of its agents the character of a "public person."[10]

It was largely experimentalists—intellectuals who drew inspiration from Francis Bacon's promotion of what was variously called "active philosophy," "the experimental philosophy," or "the mechanical philosophy"— who integrated the stooped figure of the delver with the nominating Adam of Genesis 2:19.[11] By transferring the primal scene of discovery from Eve's eating of the fruit to Adam's naming the creatures—and by linking the act of naming to the work of experiment—Bacon redeemed curiosity from its association with original sin: associated with investigative labor rather than appetite, the first sin became the first virtue. Understood as the exercise of innocent curiosity, labor ceased to refer exclusively to the production of items for consumption to become something like the natural and free exercise of "the activity of man": a productive undertaking so delightful, experimentalists insisted, it was not like work in the fallen sense at all.[12] While Hans Blumenberg's seminal account of curiosity's rehabilitation stresses the theoretical character of what he calls "the cognitive appetite," experimentalists stressed its physical aspect. Leaning heavily on the supposed etymon *cura,* they insisted on the willingness of the curious to invest *care,* to take physical pains, in the production of knowledge of "things themselves."[13] The exercise of curiosity modeled an ideal integration of the higher and lower parts of the social as well as the individual body.[14] For the experimentalist, the fallen division into ranks corresponded to a compartmentalization of knowledge; both stood in the way of restoration, and both disappeared in Adam. The disappearance of social difference in this corporate subject made it an ideal model, perhaps the only possible model, for a knowledge-producing public.

Jürgen Habermas's claim that the public sphere came into being only at the end of the seventeenth century has few remaining adherents among English historians; sources on the midcentury public sphere are now legion.[15] Yet there is more to say about the role that experimentalism played in shaping this virtual space. What J. G. A. Pocock famously described as the emergence of the individual's "awareness of himself as a political actor in a public realm" depended on a more primitive awareness of the self as a potential intellectual authority within that realm; by identifying productive laborers as privileged generators of knowledge, experimental philosophy distributed this awareness more widely across the social body than any other intellectual movement had.[16] The mechanical philosophy really was what it claimed to be: a philosophy based on the experiences of "mechanicks." The celebrated rise of "mechanick preachers" in the period can hardly be understood outside the context of the spread of experimentalism as a popular ideology.[17] I suggest that the common ground between Puritan "experimental faith" and the Baconian faith in experiment was a shared Adamic epistemology, predicated on a new understanding of how innocence and experience might be related through productive labor and the literacies associated with it.[18] As the original reader of God's first book, Adam was constructed as the first Protestant, applying the principle of *sola scriptura* to nature itself.[19] Yet the productivity of his engagement with creation (ambiguously confirmed by Genesis 2:15) suggested that this literatus of nature had also been its author. The moral was clear: to become natural authors in their own right, university-educated gentlemen had to cultivate an alternative form of literacy. While working experimentalists adapted artisanal techniques to restore creation to legibility, "experimental Christians" adopted an artisanal approach to the works of faith, identifying the defining practices of the godly life—Bible-reading, "good conference"—with the production of new truths. Rejecting the scholastic given or "datum" as the basis of trustworthy knowledge, the promoter of experimental truth was defined by his willingness to subject familiar doctrines, and cherished private beliefs, to open trial.[20]

Although we tend to think of the public sphere as a marketplace of opinion, many of its early cultivators identified it with the production of facts: literally, things made. The factual grounding of the public sphere was the very basis of its sacred character as a transcendental artifice, an ongoing collaborative construction.[21] In making this assertion, I am suggesting that the public sphere was not initially imagined as a space for debate in which rights-bearing individuals argued on behalf of their interests. To be sure, there were many models of the public in seventeenth-century England, and in the minds of some contemporaries it is clear that the mystical body, the marketplace of opinion, and the republic of letters form a kind of unity.[22] But a more primitive idea underlies all these constructions: that of a corporate body engaged in the labor of truth production; even explicitly polemical claims were presented as the disinterested products of this work.

The image of the mystical body being torn apart by the centrifugal forces of dissent (a mainstay of early modern attacks on "schismaticks") shapes many of our most celebratory treatments of the seventeenth-century public sphere, organized as they often are around narratives of heroic self-assertion.[23] According to such accounts, the emergence of a public coincides with the individual coming into his own as the proprietor of his conscience and self, establishing possessive individualism as the basis of modern secular society.[24] For Habermas, a public composed of private people is a crucially secular phenomenon, predicated on the individual right of religious freedom: what John Milton famously celebrated as "all this free writing and free speaking" finally resulted in religion becoming a "private affair."[25] The story is so familiar it feels like knowledge: exposed to the free market of opinion, religion lost its links to corporate ritual and became a solitary possession, the private property of faith. But rather than defending freedom of opinion, Milton was protecting the sacred work of truth production. Diversity of opinion was only tolerable to the extent that it offered a means toward ultimate consensus; opinion was valued as, and only as, "knowledge in the making." William Walwyn was similarly confident that "by liberty of discourse, and liberty of writing," people would be "brought to be of one mind"; the realm of mere opinion worked toward its own vitiation.[26] If the goal of public intellectual life was to knit "every creature together into a onenesse," to participate in this process was to gain an anticipatory experience of that oneness. Such participation is associated throughout the period with an expansion of the self that entails a loss of the self "in its particular."[27] When explaining his public defense of the collective author known as Smectymn-uus, Milton described his new sense of himself, as he participated in a new experience *of* self, a self at once diminished and dilated by the demands of a public office: "I conceav'd my selfe to be now not as mine own person, but as a member incorporate into that truth whereof I was perswaded." Radical thinkers now praised for their "rugged individualism" constantly describe their incorporation into a body where "respect of persons" disappears.[28] The frequency with which the biblical phrases "without respect of persons" and "no respect of persons" appear in such contexts suggests that in order to understand the changing character of public life in the period we must look not just forward but also backward, to the *corpus mysticum* itself.[29]

Within the terms of secularization theory, to assert that the mystical body became the public is to claim that the mystical body was "killed," since in these transformations of religious substance, as Blumenberg complains, it is always supposed that the vital essence is extinguished, leaving only an empty form. Blumenberg accuses secularization theorists of trading on the term's association with the expropriation of ecclesiastical goods; modernity is "illegitimate" because its contents are stolen, and in the process of the theft, something has been lost; the alienation of substance originally housed in a Christian framework results "neither in an intensification nor a clarification" of that substance. In contrast, the term's canon-law use, referring to the release of a cleric from the obligations of an order into the status of a secular priest, gains no purchase in secularization theory at all.[30] A counternarrative of secularization might take this instance as its background metaphor, describing the progressive publication of sacred offices from the cloister through the church and into the world, resulting precisely in their intensification and clarification. One might argue that the Reformation produced no end of such accounts, that the ideal of the priesthood of believers could generate nothing else, and that the effort to sacralize worldly engagement was precisely the process by which the world's desacralization occurred. In this view, eighteenth-century England did not stand in need of an "enlightenment" since the anticlericalism unleashed by reformers made it unnecessary; the process of secularization had already been carried out under the name of primitive religion.[31] Without utterly rejecting this claim, I will argue against its apparent corollary: that the relationship of the mystical body to the public was merely one of causal succession—in other words, that the body metaphorics made no substantive contribution to the emerging public at all. On the contrary, the topos provided a more functional model of the public than any that came after. It was not a "phenomenologically thin" space of debate between rights-bearing individuals that enabled the formation of an intellectual commons; it was the idea of a sacred corporate person.[32]

Although the execution of Charles I was explicitly defended as a restoration of the mystical body he had failed to represent, scholars following Carl Schmitt have often treated the topos as if it were inseparable from sacerdotal kingship.[33] This conviction informs Schmitt's philosophy of "concrete life": the social totality can never be sensuously grasped as one except under exceptional conditions and by means of a charismatic representative who condenses the energies of his subjects into material form. Political power finds its purest expression in sacramental presence, making the sovereign's power to decide the exception analogous to the miracle of transubstantiation.[34] It stands to reason that Schmitt approved of Thomas Hobbes's description of the sovereign as an idol or *"Mortall God"* in whom individuals see themselves "personated" or "represented" but before whom they become a passive audience. This image of civil idolatry in action conjures up Protestant caricatures of dazed popish congregations: the migration of the Pauline term for the body of believers, *Corpus Christi,* to the consecrated elements of the host becomes a paradigm for political representation, predicated on an absolute division between public and private persons.[35] For Hobbes, the corporate body is artificial *by definition;* it is because ontological priority is given to man in the plural that equality in the state of nature leads ineluctably to conflict. Since his sovereign is essentially an artifice without subjectivity, Hobbes makes no effort to imagine the public person from the inside.[36] Many of Hobbes's contemporaries, however, assigned ontological priority to the corporate body, to the single "man in the creation," and in their writing it is this man who tries to speak. While the experience of the Hobbesian individual can result only in "private opinion," this other "I" is comprehensive: the product of a laborious effort to restore the first person to the first person.[37]

I will suggest that this person was constituted by a productive sacrament, identified with the progressive production of Adam rather than the ritual consumption of Christ. On this understanding, the source of the priestly miracle was always "concrete life": the productive power of the *corpus mysticum* on display. As traditional motifs like the labors of the months already suggested, the Eucharist "that bestowed identity and dignity on so many" was the product of the labor of those who worshipped it; this dignity was already theirs.[38] Once the priestly appropriation was recognized, it had only to be reversed. Robert Boyle declared that "Men were born with a Right to Priesthood; so Reason is a Natural Dignity, and Knowledge a Prerogative, that can confer a Priesthood without Unction or Imposition of Hands": the ideal of the priesthood of believers is realized in a sovereign priesthood of knowledge producers. This priesthood was an Adamic inheritance.[39] Affording an experience of self as at once the one and the many, the intellectual commons restored Corpus Christi to its original, promoting what Amos Funkenstein has called a "secular theology": a sacralization of creation and the collective subject of humanity's productive engagement with it.[40] The galvanizing power that Schmitt imputed to the exception was embodied for the experimentalist in the discovery, in the mystical body's continuous transubstantiation of things into facts. This nonmiraculous conversion was predicated on another. The communion of the productive sacrament was constituted not by Christ's vicarious sacrifice but by a bloodless sacrifice of the private self; it was this sacrifice that enabled the translation of personal experience into public truths. If, as Debora Shuger observes, the figure of "the crucified Jesus slips to the margins of English Protestantism," it is largely because the doctrine of substitutionary atonement had no natural place in this process.[41] Congregants were the agents, not just the beneficiaries, of the sacrifice that made productive communion possible.

In the experimentalist etiology of sin, the fall occurred when innocent curiosity degenerated into idle curiosity—when, instead of investing *cura* to produce knowledge for the body of humanity, the first couple attempted to consume it. The distinction between the private body—appetitive, fallen—and the public body—productive, innocent—lay at the very heart of curiosity's rehabilitation.[42] By reinventing the innocent Adam as an agent of innocent curiosity, experimentalists made him a model member of the knowledge-producing public of which he was also the embodiment. Adam's distribution across two bodies modeled the relationship between the private and public selves that ideally characterized every working member of the public. The corporate agent of innocent curiosity was conjoined to its fallen members not by means of a political fiction but through constantly renewed effort, of which Adam modeled both the means and the ends. Throughout the century, this corporate worker materializes under a variety of names, and as a variety of collectivities—the Diggers, the invisible college, the Royal Society, the Athenian Society—all of which seek some degree of incorporation into the greater body of the public. Even the "I" of seventeenth-century spiritual autobiography registers the displacement of the personal voice by another, impersonal one. The circumstantial details that characterize the genre serve less to individuate the subject than to locate him in the concrete physical realities of shared experience; it is in the public person of Samson, not in "his particular," that John Bunyan addresses his readers in the preface to *Grace Abounding*. As Christopher Hill observed long ago, the protagonists of Milton's major poetry are all public persons, and their arduous labors of self-cultivation reprise those of the public celebrated in *Areopagitica*.[43] To this self, Gerrard Winstanley is a better guide than Hobbes; indeed, the towering originality of the more famous philosopher illuminates the comparatively representative nature of the other. I am not suggesting that most of Winstanley's contemporaries cheered on the Digger experiment, but the assumptions and figures of which it was a concrete expression did organize new forms of corporate personhood in the period. When describing the virtual space in which all could "come together," many contemporaries, like the Diggers, imagined not merely an agora or marketplace of ideas but a recovered space of communion: a paradise under cultivation.

The story of the emergence of the public sphere, then, is also the story of how production became the ruling figure for intellectual life. Baudrillard complains that, because of the modern idolatry of production, "it is no longer a question of 'being' oneself but of 'producing' oneself"; but for the intellectuals explored in this book, the labor of self-production—of "becoming themselves again"—was a very different undertaking, since the person to be restored was necessarily a corporate one. By the same token, they employed the figure of production to sever the concept of labor from the idea of its division; the most valuable product of their labor was precisely the idea of an intellectual collective in which social differences might be rendered irrelevant.[44]

I have suggested that what made it possible for experimentalists to imagine the thinker as a worker was their discovery that workers were thinkers. This was more of an admission than a discovery, and they were not the first to make it. Medieval scholars like Albertus Magnus and Roger Bacon closely followed the work of alchemists and artisans. These philosophers lived in a period of great artisanal creativity and self-assertion; as Lynn White demonstrated, it is possible to speak of a medieval industrial revolution.[45] Understood strictly as the collaborative pursuit of scientific and technological knowledge rather than as a general model for intellectual life, "Baconianism" long predated Bacon.[46] But the progressive success of the crafts did not set up a model of empiricism for natural philosophy to imitate: philosophers generally ignored Roger Bacon's plea for experiment, and the natural magic and alchemical traditions developed independently of philosophy so defined.[47] The ancient distinction between the slave and the freeborn had long segregated the productive toil of the laborer, which altered the physical world, from the *ataraxia* of the contemplative man, which did not. Prior to the experimentalist revolution, this distinction remained largely undisturbed.

It was left to seventeenth-century Baconians to rescue the concept of intellectual labor from the oxymoronic. They did so by inventing the intellectual as an interventionist spectator, a spectator whose observations were themselves interventions, not figurative interventions but physical ones. Bacon declared that it would "dignify and exalt Learning; if contemplation and Action were more neerely and straitly, than hitherto they have bin conjoyn'd and united together": the active life and the contemplative life would come together again in the experimental life.[48] The natural philosophers who worked to fulfill Bacon's prophetic declarations did not hope to shatter the dichotomy of thinking and doing by fiat; they developed procedures to integrate the two, constructing an intellectual life in which mind and body both participated. Scientific practitioners made words depend on deeds in a very literal sense: by cultivating "maker's knowledge" they tried to link representing the world to acting upon it, to move knowing *that* into knowing *how*.[49] Involving more than feats of language or imagination, their intellectual practice was not restricted to reading, writing, or talking; experimentalists—or virtuosi, as they often called themselves—were extremely proud of this difference.

The social provocation of experimentalism lay in how it proposed to combine the active and contemplative lives: by incorporating *techne* into the category of *praxis*. The mechanical arts—referred to variously as the *artes illiberales, serviles, vulgares,* or *sordidae*—were supposed to render man unfit not only for contemplation of truth, but for virtuous action. Classical writers frequently describe maker's knowledge as a kind of unthinking experience, "a mere knack for manual dexterity."[50] It is easy to understand such degrading constructions of maker's knowledge as the philosopher's defense against the threat posed by the artisan's ability to make knowledge productive, and, more fundamentally, by the evidentiary authority of sensuous experience itself, the basis of artisanal epistemology. Such resistance is suggested by Plato's counterintuitive insistence that it is the actual bed made by the carpenter, rather than the philosopher's idea of it, that is a "shadowy thing," only a step removed from a painterly representation.[51] In experimentalist discourse, the charge of ontological deficiency is finally reversed: words and ideas are the shadowy images of "things themselves." It seems paradoxical that a nation obsessed with extirpating idolatry should have fostered such reverence for material things, but such reverence was an expression of piety, an effort to encounter the living word of nature as it had been revealed to its first reader.[52] In the wake of Reformation iconoclasm, such visually fixated devotion filled a vacuum, and it was easily justified. As William Perkins argued in *A Warning Against the Idolatrie of the Last Times,* "the sunne, moone, & stars, are the workemanship of God, whereas images are but the workmanshippe of man." In attaining "a cleerer prospect into this greate frame of the visible world, & therein of the power & wisedome of its great maker," the "Christian virtuoso" helped to restore the most primitive church of all: the religious service of Genesis 2:19, when the gift of creation was first "magnified" and declared by man.[53]

The identification of Adam as the only genuine representative of the human species—compared to whom, as John Donne put it, "we are not men"—defined fallen human beings as deficient, amputated creatures in need of prosthetic support.[54] Such assistance was traditionally supplied by the mediations of sacramental religion. However, once innocence was identified with insight and the aims of magnification or praise were joined to those of discovery, prosthetic help could be sought in new technologies and working collectivities. In his notes for a tragedy based on the fall, Milton observed that people "cannot se[e] Adam in the state of innocence by reason of thire sin": to see Adam it was necessary to see *as* Adam. The provisional identification with Adam was what Nelson Goodman would call a calculated category mistake, or a metaphorical identification. Goodman reminds us that to see *x* as *y* entails the notion that *x* is not *y:* to try to identify with Adam entails admitting that you are not he. But with repetition, "a transferred application of a schema becomes routine, and no longer requires or makes any allusion to its base application . . . metaphor fades to mere truth."[55] In this way, the experimentalist mapping of Adam's innocent eye onto productive and "unprepossessed" perception was so successful that the connection between objectivity and the innocent eye became a truism. Through an effort of conceptual integration that was as much physical as intellectual, experimentalists managed to transfer attributes from the world they sought to recover to the mundane world, and bodies, they inhabited.[56] As a term in a whole series of metaphors that people in seventeenth-century England lived, worked, and wrote by, the experimentalist paradise generated new physical spaces in which to pursue these activities, such as the laboratory and the coffeehouse.[57] Existing in dialectical relation to the church, alehouse, court, and theater, these spaces bred experiential and discursive equivalents, like the "paradise within" and the periodical, while benefiting from the dissolution of other spaces, most notably the antechamber to heaven consecrated to progress: purgatory. Providing a model for his laboratory or workroom, Eden, now a place of pains and trial, provided the intellectual laborer with the conceptual room to work. Cleansed of idolatrous attachment to concrete externals of place and time, paradise was regained through the work of estrangement, or discovery: the production of alien experiences of the known world.

Restored as the field for the exercise of innocent curiosity, creation looked very different; indeed, it became visible in radically new ways. Recent historians of science have argued that acceptance of a new theory depends not only on internal inconsistencies in the old theories it supplants but on its association with new physical experiences, preferably dramatic ones. It was not by accident that the resurgence of atomism coincided with the widespread use of the microscope, which, by exposing the intricately particulate structure of matter, revealed the visible world for the first time as the product of material operations beneath the threshold of visibility.[58] It was largely by playing with microscopes that members of the public gained hands-on experience in the messy habits of experimentalist observation, the combined discipline of eye and hand that Robert Hooke described so painstakingly in *Micrographia* and that popular manuals like Henry Baker's *The Microscope Made Easy* rehearsed for the benefit of the public: slicing specimens open, pinning them down, and contriving various lighting conditions in order to coax the things within things themselves into visibility. Through these so-called *"artificial Organs"*— which were widely figured as instruments of incorporation—contemplation became both interventionist and productive: a means to expose the material substrate of the visible world and open it up to new kinds of cultivation.[59] A process of excavating the things behind fallen appearances, contemplation could now be understood as a kind of Adamic delving.

Part I of this book is organized by a few basic questions: given the obvious theological difficulties posed by an ethic of *imitatio Adami,* how did it emerge? What new devotional and intellectual practices did it encourage, and how did these practices shape an image of the intellectual as public worker? Finally, how did this new concept of the public person—and the public it sustained—survive the restoration of monarchy? Part II documents how the experimentalist effort to bring together thoughts and acts, words and things, influenced intellectuals who worked exclusively with words. Scholars who explore the relationship between early modern literature and science sometimes treat connections between them as near-inevitabilities. Such an approach is congenial to the comparative study of the thematic or propositional *content* of literature and scientific theories, and it is with the influence of particular scientific theories—above all, theories of matter—that most of this scholarship has been concerned.[60] But while one can discern commonalities in the attempts of William Harvey and Phineas Fletcher to represent nature, a comparison of the actual practices required by their tasks of representation would reveal much less common ground. Involving more than feats of the discursive imagination, experimentalist labor demanded the combined discipline of body and mind, making it, in many ways, a preposterous model for literary authors. The ideal of innocent observation posed an enormous challenge to intellectuals who had only words at their disposal; experimentalist authors had to employ remarkable ingenuity to reinvent themselves as laborers engaged in the work of truth production, turning their readers into virtual witnesses and "co-curators" of the art of making truth visible.[61] In considering the literary output of the seventeenth century, with its space journeys and poetic anatomies, we should not underestimate the catalyzing shock of the virtuosi's success in making physical phenomena visible whose existence had previously never been imagined.[62] I will suggest that this shock led authors to reimagine the task of mimesis itself. The Renaissance imagined mimesis as a mirror held up to nature; experimentalist authors transformed the inert looking glass into a penetrating lens. In appropriating the technology most associated with the virtuosi, pamphleteers, poets, and periodical writers fashioned a new image of the author as a productive spectator: one who serves the public by extending the realm of the visible.

As the Horatian dictum that literature should delight and instruct suggests, the notion that the author exerts an impact on the world he represents by transforming his readers has a venerable history, but this traditional understanding of the author's function has always been in conflict with the equally conventional understanding of literary pursuits as gratuitous leisure activities, for writers and readers alike. Prior to the experimental revolution, what claim the literary text had to reforming power was likely to be exerted under the sign of idleness. Philip Sidney flaunted the leisure that was the enabling condition for his literary pursuits, notoriously referring to himself as one "who (I knowe not by what mischance) in these my not old yeres & idelest times, having slipt into the title of a Poet." Content to regard literary products as luxury items, he referred to the *Arcadia* as "this idle work of mine" and advised his sister to "read it, then, at your idle times." Although this flip courtly attitude seems to trivialize the "unelected vocation," it also opens up the possibility of an independent justification for poesy.[63] By upholding an absolute distinction between literary composition and applied forms of knowledge like the law, Sidney stresses poetry's irrelevance, and thus its independence: "freely ranging onely within the Zodiack of his owne wit," the poet disdains "subjection" to nature, to which other human activities remain bound. It is by luxuriating in his irresponsibility with respect to the world of masculine action that the poet reveals his own peculiar "vigor," his power to represent things that "never were in Nature," and indeed to "growe in effect, another nature." As we will see, experimentalists who attacked the schoolmen shared an identical view of the fruits of idleness; because the writing of the schoolmen did not originate in physical engagement with real objects, it bore no relation to them. For Sidney, however, idleness and effeminacy were siblings of potency; the distance of the literary text from the world of affairs was a measure of its reproductive potential, its ability to give birth to a new world.[64]

The dream of the experimentalist author is different. Rather than insist on the reproductive potentiality of the literary, in which the description of what is not might one day mysteriously cause it to be, these writers suggest that new worlds inescapably follow from a transformed perception of the present one. Instead of ushering their readers into a new world, they present their texts as technologies through which to see into—and through—this one. In contrast to the architectural frontispieces of many sixteenth-century books that invite the reader inside a dwelling or palace, pamphlets of the 1640s feature spectacles on the cover, announcing their utility as instruments: to read these texts is to see better, to find visual manifestations of what had previously been invisible. These "instruments of truth" enable both their inventors and users to see themselves anew, as intellectual laborers engaged in the excavation of truth.[65]

Of course, for all his talk of idle toys, Sidney also lent poetry a role in promoting "the end of well dooing and not of well knowing onely," and Spenser famously presented *The Faerie Queene* as an attempt "to fashion a gentleman or noble person in vertuous and gentle discipline." Poetry could be an instrument of discipline by offering "lively" examples of well-known precepts; this was a defense of literature as suasion, and as fable. On this understanding, literature proves its relevance to the world not by revealing anything new about it but by reproducing known truths in a vivid manner, with virtues and vices "ensampled" in fictional characters.[66] But the Baconian identification of knowledge production with the production of new experiences offered a different way to conceive of literature's relation to the world—as an instrument of discovery.[67] The literature I call experimentalist is organized by a research question: what would an experience of creation *prior* to the distortions introduced by the corrupted mind and body be like? In this connection, it is crucial to note that not one the successes of literary experimentalism examined in this book was presented to the public as a fiction (the single failure I examine, William Davenant's much-ridiculed *Gondibert,* was). The experimentalist text offered itself as an instrument with which to *escape* fiction, to purge perception of the false images generated by custom, idols of the mind, and the fallen body itself.

The dominant use of the literary lens is as an instrument of empirical demystification to be applied to the fallen world. A related category of text attempts to represent a world in which seeing into the nature of things is the normal mode of being; it opens into a world that is the end of penetration, a world already seen through and so no longer fallen. While texts of the first type treat the lens as a prosthetic analogue to the "paradise within," recovering paradise through and as a perspective, these latter texts employ the garden itself as a lens. In aligning themselves against literature conceived of as fiction, experimentalist authors joined literary experience to the interventionist aims of what we now call critique, and it is in their performances that we can find the ancestral body of modern intellectual ambitions. Unlike many of his descendants, however, the experimentalist author gained power by giving it away; it was because his authority did not reside in his own person that it could form the basis for a public experience of truth. As I will argue, precisely because his readers were virtual witnesses to his interventions as well as their objects, these textual experiments depended for their success on the author's ability to replicate the crucially prosthetic, collective, and processual character of experimentalist insight.

The specimens of literary experimentalism examined in this book are linked by a unity of intention rather than an identity of tactics, but they are all characterized by what I call sensuous iconoclasm, the collectivization of authorship, and a refusal to conclude. In their attempt to reveal a world that must be *made* visible, experimentalist texts recruit the reader as an active co-curator of an objective perspective under permanent construction and revision. To guarantee the instability of their products, many adopt a processual approach to imagery, invoking hierarchies only to invert or level them and employing constantly changing methods of mediation, often through perspectival metaphors. The reluctance to terminate the open-ended space of authorial inquiry can be formally realized at the level of the sentence or through a processual mode of publication, as in periodical literature or the sequential paradisal restorations that constitute Milton's continuous oeuvre. By seeing through, and reforming, earlier models of their genres—and earlier versions of themselves—experimentalist texts are able to redescribe the cumulative character of literary culture as a condition of truth production; they declare their fitness to "make a progresse," and they enlist the reader in the work of advancing that progress.[68]

The tendency to treat all "looking glasses" as equivalent has made it hard for the ambitions and techniques of literary experimentalism to be recognized.[69] The difficulty has been compounded by the assumption that the institutionalization of the new science in England—the founding of the Royal Society of London for the Improving of Natural Knowledge—marked the beginning of the "two cultures" famously described by C. P. Snow.[70] Perhaps because many first encounter the Royal Society virtuosi through Part III of Jonathan Swift's *Gulliver's Travels* (where, to avoid ambiguities caused by speech, philosophers in the kingdom of Lagado communicate through the literal exchange of things themselves), critics have traditionally regarded the virtuosi's major contribution to literature as providing fodder for satire.[71] Associated with the dubious-sounding cause of "language reform" and the "plain style," the virtuosi have often been treated as if they were in fact Lagadoans, openly hostile to the resources of language.[72] Yet experimentalist rhetoric is saturated with figures, employing metaphor after metaphor to attack the idolatrous fancies of the mind. These apparently self-imploding statements of purpose may indicate a tension at the heart of experimentalist ambition, but such a glaring discrepancy between theory and practice invites us to reconsider whether the theory existed at all.[73] In fact, virtuosi and the authors who followed their lead were not engaged in a campaign against figurative language; they were attempting an innocent critique of ordinary language. Their quarry was restricted to metaphors that did not announce themselves as such, an analogical discourse through which unverifiable ideas about creation had been long been disseminated as truth. To a great extent, the virtuosi's attacks on figurative language were directed at scholastic terms of art: at "figures of speech" that were mistaken for things themselves, relics of a time when language was philosophy's only instrument.[74] This targeted purge did not result in an idiom cleansed of rhetorical figures; experimentalist style had a number of characteristic features, but plainness was not one of them.

Yet the myth of the plain style has survived. Rejecting the old dichotomies of Ciceronian/Attic, Scientific/Rhetorical, Puritan/Anglican, and Commonwealth/Restoration, Stanley Fish concedes that the new scientific writing and the literature influenced by it was not necessarily plainer than writing in the so-called rhetorical tradition, but he preserves the old distinction on a new basis. The difference is real, he insists, but it is a difference in epistemology rather than style. The crucial distinction is between "self-consuming" and "self-satisfying" texts:

On the one hand there is the assumption that the mind, either in its present state or in some future state of repair, is adequate to the task of comprehending and communicating the nature and shape of reality; and on the other, the assumption that the mind is a prisoner of its inherent limitations, and that the apprehension, in rational or discursive terms, of ultimate truth, is beyond it.

For the former group, "understanding is assumed to be easy"; it is not their style, then, but their thought that lacks complexity:

Now we see through a glass darkly, asserts the Apostle, and with him Augustine, Donne, Herbert, Milton, Bunyan, and, in a limited sense, Bacon; but for many in the Restoration the glass has been made clear by the power of reason, whose workings are believed to yield a direct and undistorted access to the order of things as they have been disposed by God. This is certainly the case with the propagandists of the Royal Society.[75]

The statement that "the glass has been made clear by the power of reason" should not be in the present tense; Fish has forgotten his own qualifier about the mind being adequate to comprehend and communicate things as they are "in some future state of repair." The way in which Fish handles the case of Bacon—one in which the epistemological divide runs through "the corpus of a single author"—reveals the awkward consequences of this collapse of the present and the imagined future. Although in *The Advancement of Learning,* Bacon is sufficiently "naive and optimistic" for Fish to consider him a self-satisfying author, in the *Essays* "he is concerned to disabuse his readers of beliefs they already hold" and "deliberately withholds" from the reader "present satisfaction." Rather than reflecting opposite sides of an epistemological divide, these passages clearly imply one another. It was crucial to "trouble the understanding, to displace, and to discompose, and disorder the judgment" in order to repair it. Behind the perky assertions of reason's power to gain "a direct and undistorted access to the order of things" is the certainty that such reason is no longer a natural human endowment: this is why experimentalist authors and readers were able to experience their struggle to escape the "darke dungeon of blindnesse," "the groveling and limited Reason of man," as a heroic one.[76]

However novel their techniques, experimentalist texts are driven by the motive of Protestant allegory: the dread of the idolatrous power of fiction.

The Faerie Queene is overrun with figures that pervert the proper subordination of the copy to the original, the appearance to the essence, and the sign to the thing signified, and Spenser kills them off one by one. This ritual sacrifice of the Archimago within has no stopping mechanism. Exploiting the idolatrous potential of literary forms and energetically denouncing that power, Spenser makes iconoclastic anxiety serve a compositional logic. A rhythm of doing and undoing is sustained as we are exposed to truth and all of its delusive doubles: we know that Una is real and the temptress Duessa (who calls herself Fidessa) is a fake, but we are also aware that both are fabrications; this fosters a compulsion to multiply episodes in which they will be distinguished once and for all.[77] Iconoclastic anxiety provides the impetus for narrative, which becomes a perpetual effort to fix, and exercise control over, the moment at which representation inclines toward idolatry. In staging the continual failure of this project, authors like Spenser and Godfrey Goodman succeed in making their writing the site of the most important struggle there is, but they are not able to present that struggle as productive, much less progressive.[78]

It might be said that, for the experimentalist intellectual, "the structure of allegory" characterized every instant of sensory experience.[79] Yet the iconoclastic desire to break through the illusions of sense assumed an entirely new character once Copernicanism, the epiphany of a microworld beneath the threshold of visibility, and the resurrection of the ancient atomists' distinction between primary and secondary qualities extended semiosis into the realm of perception.[80] In an inescapably new relation to the physical world, the senses were suspect not because they reflected the merely material aspects of creation, but because they *failed* to do so. The challenge to the observer was no longer to see through creation to the Creator, but to see through the false images of perception onto creation itself. The iconoclastic assault on false images was now to be waged through an *expansion* of the visible world. The stock of things themselves rose as they joined the prestigious category of what was hidden from immediate view, and the effort to defeat the seductions of sense assumed strangely sensuous (yet studiously noncarnal) forms.

The project of constructing an Adamic body, a body adequate to a real experience of the things God made, reprised the old conflict of body and soul as a dialectical tension between the fallen, "sensitive" body with which the experimentalist was saddled and the spectatorial body toward which he strived. In practice, the spectatorial body was recovered as his own body, improved by artificial enhancements, disciplined by new evidentiary canons, absorbed into a collective subject of knowledge production, and directed to spiritual ends. The contemplative became an intellectual laborer when he started identifying with a body he did not have and acting in ways it was impossible for any natural person, burdened with a sensitive body and private interests, actually to be. He was, for one thing, innocent— "unprepossessed," uncontaminated by fallen dogmas and opinions—and he was able to see things no fallen human being ever could. But the experimentalist was only an aspirant to the identity that defined him; the authority conferred by the spectatorial body to which he stood in prosthetic relation was not naturally anybody's to claim. To put off the old man and put on the new was to become a reformed, artificial man, but, unlike the artificial man of the Hobbesian sovereign, this man could not be decisively embodied by any single person. The experimentalist's performance was consequently a paradoxical one, in which modesty was the sign of superhuman ambition; personal humility provided the occasion and the means for the corporate development of prosthetic insight. The determination to pursue this restorative project combined with an awareness of all that deferred its ultimate completion produced the mixed mode of self-aggrandizement and self-abasement that became the intellectual laborer's signature. As the means and ends of paradisal recovery were rendered strategically indistinct, the labors of innocence came to characterize an asymptotic progress; the gap between the author's personal and spectatorial bodies describes the space of this progress. The closing of this gap depended on the work not of one reader but many. Just as the restoration of the subject of innocence required its repopulation, so the restoration of what Milton called "the body of Truth" depended on the growth and continual self-reformation of a working public.[81]

An account of how intellectuals came to regard themselves as workers must address this new understanding of work as the proper expression of the human essence, an understanding that pushed knowledge production to the center of public life. This understanding made possible an expansive and inclusive conception of the task of knowledge production that was in principle separable from the professionalization that it also enabled. It is often remarked that in the seventeenth century science stopped being a kind of knowledge one had—one possessed *scientia*—and became something that one did. Equally familiar is the claim that religion in this period became less identified with doing particular things than with believing particular things, as reformers elevated faith over the old forms of ritual participation.[82] But the decline of particular works as instruments of salvation corresponded with a moral elevation of work in the singular. The really crucial difference between the works entailed by a primarily sacramental religion and the work enjoined on the Protestant faithful is that the latter could not be determined in advance. The labor involved in "working out one's salvation" began with determining the iterable forms such work should take.[83] The ideal of a popular priesthood made everyone a potential intellectual laborer, engaged in the work of faith that, like the unelected vocation of the intellectual—or the exercise of innocent curiosity—was undetermined and open-ended.

The thinkability of intellectual labor did not, then, derive exclusively from experimental science; it followed from Protestant ideas of which Baconian ideology was itself a product. An important consequence of the moral reevaluation of work undertaken by reformers, for example, was an expanded role for thinking, as distinct from meditation or prayer, in conceptions of the life of the nonidle believer. Intellectuals like John Locke and Milton denied that an individual could claim to be truly in possession of his ideas or the tenets of his faith if he did not invest the necessary pains in reconstructing them from the ground up; without this effort, "the very truth he holds, becomes his heresie."[84] Having invested such care, however, the individual was qualified to undertake productive "experimental" engagements with God's word (in both its forms), wrenching new experiences out of common doctrine, and common things, for "the public good."[85]

Of course, during the century of revolution, Protestant identity was not a unitary entity. We know that England's political revolution coincided with the revolution in knowledge brought about by the new philosophy, but we are far from reaching a consensus about how these two revolutions interacted (or, indeed, whether either should be called a revolution).[86] It has been a long time since any scholar could share Christopher Hill's confidence that "on the whole the ideas of the scientists favoured the Puritan and Parliamentarian cause." Charles Webster's *The Great Instauration* presented the Royal Society as a straightforward extension of "puritan experiments in intellectual organisation," and in keeping with scholarly rhythms, the recent trend has been to overturn this assumption completely, as the wide currency of the phrase "Restoration science" suggests.[87] We have been repeatedly reminded that the Society was not comprised exclusively of frustrated Parliamentarians, and that it strove to disassociate itself from the "heady enthusiasms" of midcentury Baconians like Theodore Haak and Samuel Hartlib.[88] The Society was in fact an amalgamation of intellectual collectivities that took shape during the Interregnum, and attempting to locate even a single member of any one of them along the ideological spectrum on a purely political or doctrinal basis is a thankless task.[89] The difficulty is multiplied exponentially when determining the affiliations of the Society as a whole, not to mention the intellectuals its activities influenced. When looked at closely enough, each person seems to change beyond recognition: Boyle has been called a closet dissenter and a loyal Anglican and, in a sense, both are true. Our understanding of the complex inner life and social performance of a figure like John Evelyn, officially a high-church Anglican and royalist, is poorly served by thinking of him as either.[90] As far as doctrinal commitments go, Milton and Archbishop Laud can both justifiably be called Arminians, while Winstanley's freewheeling treatments of scripture are more reminiscent of Neoplatonist church fathers than they are of Luther or Calvin. Given this untidiness, it is not surprising that people who are "for" and "against" the new science do not align themselves conveniently along doctrinal or political lines.

One is tempted to say that the "Puritanism and new science" thesis is most persuasive if one adopts Ernst Bloch's notion of Puritanism in its most "comprehensive sense—reaching back to Bernhard de Clairvaux."[91] Michael Finlayson has argued that what we think of as radical Puritanism is itself simply a form of anticlericalism extending back at least to Wycliff (as we will see, many contemporaries believed the same thing).[92] For our purposes, what matters is not doctrine but "discipline" in the very broadest sense: what people chose to spend their time doing and what they fantasized about doing—the different imaginative and practical uses, in other words, to which they put common doctrine.[93] In this regard, the categories of Anglican and Puritan, and even royalist and Parliamentarian, can be poor sorting mechanisms, with little predictive value for determining someone's daily habits or intellectual style. This stands to reason, since what Hill called a three-handed struggle between royalist, Parliamentarian, and radical often raged within a single person.[94] Finlayson complains that there is something fishy about accounts of the seventeenth century in which the concept of Puritanism is used to explain almost everything up until 1660, after which it almost disappears, active only in circles of "dissent"; the problem, however, is not that *Puritanism* is too broad a term, but that it is not broad enough.[95] The originary ideologies that shaped the culture of early modern England—from the movement of humanism to the ancient constitution to the primitive church—powerfully shaped Protestant English and experimentalist identity and the emergent concept of intellectual labor as well.[96]

Having declared that the opposition of Interregnum "experiments in intellectual organisation" and "Restoration science" is a spurious one, I should confess my own bias. I believe that in many ways the Interregnum offered a more receptive climate to experimentalism than the England of Charles II; certainly, it is difficult to imagine a member of the invisible college like Hartlib being on the government's payroll after 1660, paid to pursue an open-ended experiment in being useful to the commonwealth.[97] Despite the hopes with which the Royal Society adopted the royal name, the state-funded commonwealth of science that Bacon had prophesied in his *New Atlantis* never materialized; Evelyn found it "impossible to conceive" how the Society "should have found so few *Promoters,* and so cold a welcome in a *Nation* whose *eyes* are so wide open."[98] Precisely because it was a self-supporting institution, however, the Society was able to maintain its integrity as a *hortus conclusus* in Restoration culture (though one with roots extending beyond its walls), in which many of the most vital aspects of "the good old cause" could be sustained.[99]

"Till about the yeare 1649," John Aubrey observed, "'twas held a strange presumption for a man to attempt an innovation in learning; and not to be good manners to be more knowing than his neighbours and forefathers. Even to attempt an improvement in husbandry, though it succeeded with profit, was look't upon with an ill eie."[100] The casual hyperspecificity with which Aubrey identifies the year of the king's execution as the start of England's Baconian progress begs for some explanation, which the field of Restoration science is ill-equipped to provide. In other words, as Michael Hunter has asserted, to be convincing, accounts of science's role and appeal have to account for its success before and after 1660. Such accounts must also explain why, as I Iill put it, "Bacon was a prophet with little honour in his own country before the 1640s."[101] This book treats experimentalism as the primary medium through which the "culture of the losers" shaped mainstream life during the Restoration and eighteenth century. The royalism of many Restoration figures would have been unrecognizable to supporters of Charles I; I will suggest that the culture of experimentalism had something to do with the change. To take Joseph Addison and Richard Steele seriously as experimentalist authors alongside such writers as Milton is to challenge the literary history given to us by the Restoration victors, whose coordinated campaign to deny all continuity with the Interregnum period provided the basis for the scholarly myth of "the long eighteenth century."[102] This book returns Restoration and Augustan culture to the context of a long seventeenth century. The practical efforts to restore paradise that convulsed England during the civil war years would continue to bear fruit for several generations, not least in the shaping of literary ambitions and expectations.

The experimentalist model was clearly not the only means of authorial self-definition in the period. Although the social and authorial performances of libertinism required considerable effort, what Alexander Pope called the "Mob of Gentlemen" surrounding Charles II did not figure this effort as work; poets like Lord Rochester presented themselves as wits, not laborers, identifying themselves firmly (and to great comic effect) with their sensitive bodies, whose insatiable appetites were modeled on those of Charles himself.[103] And because the new oppositions through which curiosity was rehabilitated and knowledge production organized were firmly gendered, women did not have a straightforward route to this identity. But then again no fallen person did. The public face of experimentalism was a masculine one, but the openly artificial nature of experimentalist masculinity provided the condition for its performance without respect of persons. As the cases of experimentalist intellectuals like Dorothy Moore and Celia Fiennes demonstrate, the basic strength of the experimentalist model of intellectual labor lay in the conviction that anyone who took sufficient pains could become part of the restored Adam, even a daughter of Eve.[104]

To argue that the Adamic public emerges during and as a result of England's revolutionary moment is not to claim that the promoters of that public were on the side of the revolutionaries. The revolutionary nature of the experimentalist model of knowledge production exceeded the political programs of most (though not all) of the individuals who promoted it; its egalitarian vision was often at odds with the personal loyalties and prejudices of individual experimentalists, particularly those who had faced the prospect of property loss and death during the civil wars. It does not after all require much digging to unearth nonegalitarian aspects of any part of early modern culture, and it is not my aim to describe experimentalist culture as unaffected by a society that was obsessed with protecting the privileges of rank and sex. But in their capacities as intellectuals or public persons, experimentalist intellectuals exhibited social imaginations at least as capacious as our own. Social levelling was the very mechanism of experimentalist knowledge production, and it lay at the center of experimentalism's self-understanding (where, to be sure, it was associated less with the redistribution of property than with the growth of knowledge). Slavoj Žižek has urged that "the 'concrete' definition of a historical epoch has to include its crushed potentials"; it is in this spirit that I emphasize a particular strand in experimentalist thought and practice that never found successful political expression in the legislative arena and that found only fitful expression outside it.[105] In exploring the "radical" ideas of people who sometimes spoke with contempt of those who did not own property, who pursued religious speculations well beyond the pale of orthodox theology but who could be made nervous by the menace of schism, we should not feel compelled to reveal the "radical" strain as the "conservative" strain in disguise, or insist on their mutually implicating character (which comes to the same thing). Locke's defense of property shares the rationale of Winstanley's attempt to abolish it, but in the experimentalist culture from which both drew inspiration it is possible to glimpse a working utopia—a utopia of work—that has existed, in some form, for centuries, in the effort to imagine a working life that reflects the original state of creation rather than its corruption.

It will be evident that this book does not treat the "rhetoric of self-abstraction" through which private persons turned themselves into public workers as a resource whose availability is *necessarily* differential, since this rhetoric creates the domain outside of which, as Michael McKeon observes, "the question of inclusiveness is not even askable." I see no reason why fantasies of self-abstraction should privilege "the male, the white, the middle class, the normal," although historically, of course, they have. If the opportunities created by such fantasies have been made unequally available, so has every resource on this planet; the fault may not lie with the resources themselves.[106] This does not make close reading of these fantasies a pointless exercise. Ethan Shagan has remarked that "while philosophers use terms to define and delineate ideals, historians use them to comprehend and taxonomize the decidedly non-ideal behaviour of real human beings"; literary scholars have the license to do something else still: analyze articulations and symbolic enactments of these ideals as generators of meaning in their own right.[107] Simply to see through (that is, to identify) a fiction, or to expose its instrumentalization by individual, group, or class interests, is not to analyze it. A full analysis demands some examination of the emancipatory potential—what Bloch called an "anticipatory" dimension—that resides in all fictions, even in the mystifications of ideology itself. The notion that there could be a social fiction so cleverly constructed as to make its co-optation by power impossible is itself a fantastical assumption, and a restrictive one, limiting our engagements with cultural products to the (by now fairly routinized) critical operations permitted by a hermeneutics of suspicion. Rather than ignore the instrumentalization of the paradisal fiction altogether, however, this book focuses on its utility in fostering a "culture of fact."[108] The constructive fiction that first sustained the idea of a participatory "reality-based community," a collective organized by a responsiveness to evidence, is worth the attention of literary scholars, who in recent years have largely ceded the defense of this necessary fiction to others.

My aim is not to offer a "thick description" of intellectual life in England during the seventeenth and early eighteenth centuries, much less a systematic analysis of the institutions and social networks that sustained it.[109] I offer instead an analysis of an "ideal type" and an ideal space.[110] The term *experimentalist,* which I have extended to Baconian practitioners, experimental Christians, and authors as different from one other as Andrew Marvell and Daniel Defoe, is not intended as a marker of uniformity, but I believe it has as much analytical power as dozens of terms already in use in the historiography of this period, such as "the godly," which admit of considerable internal diversity.[111] I will be tracing family resemblances on the understanding that the family under consideration here was a fractious and divided one. A commitment to collaborative empiricism could accommodate any number of metaphysical commitments; I will be focused less on what individual virtuosi believed than on the mythology that shaped their efforts to work together. Some of the people who appear in this study would be horrified to be grouped under a common label, but scrutinizing the physiognomy of the imaginary person in whom they all glimpsed their idealized self-images has seemed to me a useful way to illuminate their relationships to one another and to their historical moment. Finally, I do not stress the complicity of experimentalism with the nightmares of modernity—its embrace of an instrumental logic that ultimately joined the concept of progress to ecological devastation, for example—because this ground has been amply covered by others, and because the grounds experimentalism opened up for an alternative understanding of its key terms—progress, man, restoration—have received less consideration.[112]

The spectatorial persona unearthed in this study is perhaps most recognizable to us now as the professionalized agent of ideology critique. It stands to reason that Jacques Larrain's history of the concept of ideology begins with Bacon's idols: empiricism's reinvention of sensory experience as a type of distortion that needed to be diagnosed and corrected to yield knowledge turned "the study of ideas" toward a meaning emphasizing distortion, as in the famous *camera obscura* passage in *The German Ideology*.[113] The organizing figures of experimentalist labor—the figures through which intellectual life first threw off the dichotomy of action and contemplation and defined itself as productive—have been preserved almost unchanged in the arena of cultural criticism. By performing critical interventions that transform images into (open, rewritable) texts, and interrogating spectacle to reveal its conditions of production (thereby restoring the link between cause and effect that spectacle is said to erase), modern intellectuals confer on themselves something like the early modern experimentalist's cultivated immunity to the deceptions of custom and the fallen body.[114] To uncover the origin of these figures in early modernity's programs of paradisal recovery invites us to imagine this work extended beyond the minimal task of demystification and restored to its properly collective agent.

I believe that the people explored in this book were not unaware of the utopian thrust of their own thought and practice, however skilled most of them were at controlling its subversive potentials. In its ideal aspect, the restored Adam was the product of an effort to recover a state in which all people were workers, and all workers, intellectuals. It now requires some work on our part to appreciate how strange a space experimentalists made out of Eden, a space reconciling past and present, nature and artifice, primitivism and technophilia, innocence and knowledge, pleasure and work, and, most ambitiously, the thinker and the laborer. Imagining and then creating a space in which such fallen oppositions disappeared, experimentalists made them seem less inevitable and, above all, less real. The intellectual's attempt to create himself in the image of innocent humanity coincided with the project of remaking the English public in that same image: a fully restored England would be a paradisal state in which every inhabitant participated in the innocent labor of truth production. Had the success of this project been complete, it would have produced an unrecognizable world, one made all the stranger for being composed entirely out of traditional materials.

If in one respect the ambition to develop an experimentalist literary practice was impossibly far-fetched—language being an inadequate medium for the autoptic authority of the experimental demonstration—in another respect writing was a fitter medium for "the Great Instauration" than an embodied experimentalist collective could ever be. The task of sustaining the collective forms of belonging required to restore Adam was one that literary technologies were particularly well-equipped to perform.[115] Describing the impressions of a foreign visitor to the Royal Society, Henry Oldenburg reported that the foreigner was very taken "with our sedate and friendly way of conference, as also with the gravity and majesticknes of our order," but a more perspicacious observer would have seen cause for "concern for our prosperity, that nothing is done with the king for us; that our meetings are very thin; and that our committees fall to the ground, because tis not possible, to bring people together."[116] As the Society's own *Philosophical Transactions* demonstrated, however, print could always bring people together, in perpetually revisable forms. An innocent collective could be gathered together, and a creation prior to the respect of persons perpetually restored, in the virtual spaces opened up through writing. Here people could undertake the lessons in innocent observation, and innocent authorship, through which they believed the world could be written again.

PART I ||| CONTEXTS

1 ||| DIGGING UP THE *HORTUS CONCLUSUS*

Lost, lost it is; for at the guarded gate
A flaming Sword forbiddeth Sin
(That's I,) to enter in

I now dread not the thought
Of barracado'd Eden, since as good
A Paradise I planted see
On open Calvarie.
    —Joseph Beaumont, "The Gardin"

That bare and simple working in the Earth, according to the freedome of
the Creation, though it be in the sweat of mans browes, is not the curse.
    —Gerrard Winstanley, *An Humble Request to the Ministers of both Universities*
      and to all Lawyers in every Inns-a-Court

The same spot of Ground, which some Time since was nothing but
Heath and Desart, and under the Original Curse of Thorns and Bryers,
after a little Labour and Expence, seems restor'd to its Primitive Beauty
in the State of Paradise . . . the familiar and easie Productions of
Industry and Ingenuity.
    —Timothy Nourse, *Campania Fælix*

Any attempt to represent the state of innocence endangers the very distinction between created and corrupted humanity; to be capable of imagining paradise suggests you belong there. Paradise is thus conventionally represented under the sign of its loss. Our reward for being denied imaginative entry into the garden is the supreme reassurance of the *felix culpa:* "Ne hadde the apple take ben, / The apple taken ben, / Ne hadde never our Lady / A ben Hevene Quen. / Blissed be the time / That apple take was."[1] Contracted to an apple, Eden becomes a happy emblem of the human frailty that fosters our dependence on the Savior. Typological representations of Eden open out onto the "paradise" conferred by grace, turning the first

garden into a paradoxical symbol of humanity's release from paradise and
its demands. In the Ghent altarpiece, Adam and Eve appear on opposite
panels, each encased within a narrow border marking them off from their
native surroundings; only when the panels are opened are we able to see the
earthly paradise, now transformed into the domain of the lamb. Eden's
original inhabitants are actually barriers to our view of the garden, to which
we may gain access only by separating them from it and each other. The
base of the trumeau of one of the portals on the west façade of Notre Dame
in Paris offers another instance of the conventional iconography of paradise: here, Adam and Eve flank the tree around which the serpent is already
winding itself; as the eye traces these vertical figures upward, it encounters
a massive Virgin—sin is the literal foundation for the Mother and Son. In
depictions of Eden as a *hortus conclusus,* the crossing of the garden with the
body of the Virgin renders paradise invisible except as seen through the
perspective of the fall and its happy consequence. Point-by-point comparisons performed the conceptual integration that filled out the mixed space
of the Mary-garden: like the bride in the Song of Solomon 4:12, Mary was
an enclosed garden into which God descended like dew, where "the white
lily of virginity grows without fading, the inviolable violet of humility spreads
its perfume, and the rose of tireless love glows red."[2] Within a church whose
"highly articulated sacramental system" had come to be regarded as the
"eternalizing of the Incarnation," identifying Eden's enclosed fertility with
the Virgin Mother of the Savior was a means to control its *conceptual* fertility as a field of independent human agency.[3]

By opening up a proleptic perspective onto the garden and restricting
us to it, such representations of paradise reenact the word's transformation
in the gospel itself. In the Septuagint, *paradise* refers to the garden of Eden;
it is in the New Testament that its referent migrates to the afterlife, as in
Christ's assurance to the crucified thief: "Today shalt thou be with me in
Paradise."[4] As an antechamber to heaven, as the world under the future
reign of the saints, and even as the monastery garden, paradise retained an
association with Eden while shedding the primary association with its first
inhabitants.[5] In this tradition, paradise is only truly paradise when the second Adam takes the place of the first, revealing Eden's four rivers, for example, to be the four evangelists, spreading the gospel to the four corners of
the earth.[6] The relation of the two Adams is zero sum: to recognize Christ
as the second Adam is to reduce the first to "him that first produced sin."[7]

The need to identify the first human exclusively with the first sin did not simply disappear after the Reformation. In John Bale's *Tragedie or Enterlude, Manifesting the Chiefe Promises of God Unto Man,* "Adam Primus Homo" appears in order to present himself as an exemplum of the truth that without grace "We must needes but fall" and promptly withdraws, it would seem with good reason: what more could the *primus homo* possibly have to say to us? The intuitive analogy between the individual life and the life of humanity as a whole makes growing up into sin inevitable; understood as humanity's childhood state, innocence is not susceptible to temporal expansion. Long after reformers excluded the *necessarium Adae peccatum* from the liturgy, the paradoxes of cavalier wit continued to deliver its message. John Donne's joke, "And that this place may thoroughly be thought / True Paradise, I have the serpent brought," provides the formula for countless lyrics that enact the fallen imagination's inability to grasp innocence as anything but a projection of corrupt desire. The "witty" reduction of knowledge to carnal knowledge places the first age beyond the "thorough thought" of any knowing adult.[8] In such poems, prolepsis does the work of litotes, suggesting that we can only imagine innocence negatively, by taking the measure of its loss. Paradise may then assume ironic form, as the state of nature. When, in "Love Made in the First Age," Richard Lovelace describes the "golden Age" as a time when "Lads, indifferently did crop / A Flower, and a Maiden-head," he suggests that primitive perfection was no more than a state of insensibility to moral law (reflecting the easy commingling of scriptural and pagan myths of origin in the period, these golden-age lovers woo "in *Hebrew*"). Abandoning the notion of original perfection, Lovelace deprives his readers of the hedonistic fantasy they might have expected to find in its place by extending this insensibility to prehistoric sex, suggesting that "cropping" in the original state of creation was, like Hobbes's state of nature, nasty, brutish, and short.[9] Such reductive redescriptions of paradisal bliss are above all proud demonstrations of the poet's own loss of innocence; paradise is only a negative image of perfection designed to throw into relief a present so complacently fallen that it can hardly take the idea of innocence seriously. Relentlessly and predictably surprising us with sin, this poetry locks us into the "discovery" that any attempt to reconstruct the state of innocence can only enhance our awareness of its inaccessibility. Were Eden representable, it would no longer be Eden, a place "Unfit for man to see with sinfull eyes."[10]

In Baconian constructions of paradise, the stiff oppositions on which cavalier wit depends simply collapse. Once the cause and effects of the fall—curiosity, knowledge, and labor—become the stuff of innocent experience, the master figures of conventional paradisal representation, prolepsis and litotes, lose their moorings. The scrambling of pre- and postlapsarian frames of reference is no longer a source of easy irony, a witty demonstration of our inability to imagine innocence, but a straightforward attempt to open the border between the two states. In 1633, it was left to a Jesuit to celebrate Mary as "the Soveraigne and *Mystical* GARDEN itself, the Paragon of Gardens." Having narrowly escaped a tryst with a demon after entering a garden that seemed a "Copy of old *Paradise*," Beaumont's Psyche finds what she was seeking in Mary—"Behold Her face, and read all Paradise"—but this stubborn substitution of Mary for the garden was the construction of an unrepentant Laudian forced into retirement.[11] All around them, intellectuals were engaged in practical efforts to restore paradise, a project that began with destroying the idol of a "barracado'd Eden."

Luther's lectures on Genesis provided the framework for this project. Identifying innocence with insight rather than ignorance, Luther dwells with vengeful relish on the gulf separating Adam's knowledge from ours: despite the vast libraries that have grown up since the fall, we do not know how to call the creatures by their right names, as Adam did. Although Luther was partly concerned to police the borders of paradise, his speculations ended up making the boundary between paradise and the known world more porous. For just as consequential was his assertion that Adam would have tilled the earth even if he had remained innocent, since man was "created not for leisure but for work, even in the state of innocence." These were the two images of Adam that seventeenth-century experimentalism brought together. The hexameral tradition had long accepted the naming of the animals as a sign of man's dominion over them; now this dominion could be imagined as the product of knowledge gained through cultivation of the garden. By extolling the first man's "most dependable knowledge" of astronomy as well as his expertise in the properties of trees and herbs, Luther effectively provided a job description for practitioners of the new philosophy, who made Adam's innocent labors of naming the creatures and "dressing" the garden (Genesis 2:19–20 and 2:15) a paradigm of their own efforts.[12]

Luther's identification of Eden as a specifically epistemological paradise, a place where man could discover the real names of things, challenged

traditional models of knowledge and of literacy. Where names correspond
to natures, language is knowledge; where natures can be forced to correspond to the "names" that humanity imposes, it is power.[13] Francis Bacon
declared that "the first Acts that man perform'd in *Paradice,* comprehended
the two summary parts of *knowledge;* those were the *view of Creatures, and
the imposition of names,*" but it was not through language schemes that experimentalists managed to impose new names on creation. Literacy in the
language of nature—the ability to discern and harness the physical processes that governed creation—demanded not reading or writing but "exercise": the extension of working hands into the visible world.[14] Extending
the propriety of a linguistic intervention to include the material, experi
mentalists transformed the scene of naming into a mineable metaphor for
the physical interventions through which nature's book could be coaxed
into legibility and even recomposed. In hermetic circles, the concept of
Adam's nominative and creative power over creation led to his being regarded
as a sort of magus, but, through strategic redescriptions of this scene, Baconian intellectuals turned a magical relationship into an experimental one.[15]
Their Adam was not a magician but a laborer: "After the creation was fin-
isht, we read that *Man was plact in the Garden to worke therein;* which work
so appointed to him, could be no other than the *work of Contemplation,*
that is the end hereof, was not for necessity, but for delight and exercise."[16]
Against the classical tradition that identified ideal contentment with leisurely contemplation, Bacon presents paradisal bliss as consisting in "the
work of Contemplation . . . for delight and exercise," weaving together conventionally opposed terms as if they were synonyms. Made up of two collapsed oppositions, Bacon's conceptual chiasmus puts contemplation and
delight at the heart of work and exercise; so did experimentalist practice.
Experimentalists worked to imitate the Adam they praised, philosophizing
in a way that integrated physical and intellectual exertion. Extending the
Protestant call of *sola scriptura* to God's first book, they tried to engage
creation without the mediation of fallen texts, reinventing innocence as
objectivity.[17]

The restoration of knowledge to paradise set into motion a realignment
of images of the world in its created and corrupted states, with the result
that paradise became identified with the defining feature of human existence under the curse: work. Reimagined as a spur to exertion, curiosity was
redeemed from its primary association with original sin.[18] When Bacon

asserted that the fall was caused by a "proud and Imperative Appetite" to define good and evil independently of God's commandment, he further suggested that humanity sustained this revolt by yielding to the temptation of wishful anthropomorphism, which prevented it from undertaking the work necessary to make God's works legible:

> . . . we copy the sin of our first parents while we suffer for it. They wished to be like God . . . we clearly impress the stamp of our own image on the creatures and works of God, instead of carefully examining and recognising in them the stamp of the Creator himself. Wherefore our dominion over creatures is a second time forfeited, not undeservedly.[19]

Rather than taking a lethargic delight in creation as revealed to the senses, innocent curiosity had sought satisfaction through exercise. Uncontaminated by the lust of the eyes that Augustine identified with the cognitive appetite, Adam had excavated the material *causes* of the visible. In the new etiology of sin, paradise was lost when, instead of working to produce knowledge, Eve attempted, "while at leisure," to consume it. Once innocent curiosity degenerated into idle curiosity, the paradise of "exercise and experiment" ground to a halt.[20] The curse, on this understanding, was not a punishment to be borne but an opportunity to be seized. Bacon actually called it a charter, stipulating that, through exertion, humanity could recover its original command over creation.[21] As the laborious program of *imitatio Adami* rendered paradise an attribute, not of a lost place or time, but of a subject engaged in the progressive work of recovery, the means and end of paradisal return became indistinct. Paradisal restoration became coextensive with knowledge production, and the vocabulary of return began to yield a discourse of progress.

Musing a generation later on "the first service, that *Adam* perform'd to his *Creator,* when he obey'd him in mustring, and naming, and looking into the *Nature* of all the *Creatures,*" Thomas Sprat grew wistful: "This had bin the only *Religion,* if men had continued innocent in *Paradise,* and had not wanted a *Redemption.*"[22] This counterfactual conventionally served as a preamble to rehearsals of *felix culpa;* here, it concludes a line of thought that would have ended in heresy had Sprat pursued it much further. In describing the most primitive church a Protestant could hope to restore, he comes close to elevating the state of nature over the state of grace, daydreaming about a hypothetical humanity that would not require saving and for whom religion, as distinct from "looking into nature," would not be necessary at all. For created humanity, divine worship was indistinguishable from working to satisfy the cognitive appetite; whether corrupted humanity could gain a virtual experience of innocent religion by the same means was a question that called for further research. As if to promote this program, Sprat's description quietly extends the first religious service into the present by evoking experimentalist aims and methods: his Adam does not simply survey and name the creatures, he looks into their very natures; through techniques like dissection and the use of optical instruments, modern experimentalists did the same. Revealing to his readers the "stupendious Mechanisms and contrivances" characterizing "the smallest and most despicable Fly" when viewed under a microscope, Robert Hooke wondered, "Who knows but *Adam* might from some such contemplation, give names to all creatures?" The shift into the present tense is telling: the lenses that Hooke called *"artificial Organs"* were prosthetic replacements for parts of the first man's body.[23] By "disciplining" the senses with these instruments of restoration, fallen humanity was regaining that body's lost powers. To claim, as Joseph Glanvill did, that Adam had not yet needed *"Galilaeo's* tube" in order to contemplate distant planets, and that "he had as clear a perception of the earths motion, as we think we have of its quiescence" was to celebrate *contemporary* discoveries. As William Rabisha declared, "we are *Adam* as well as he, it is to us God brings the creatures, to see what names we will call them": Adam's body was being restored as the collective subject of science.[24]

Sprat was specifically concerned to identify the revival of Adam's innocent labors with the activities of the Royal Society of London for the Improving of Natural Knowledge, the institution founded in 1662 to advance the aims of the Baconian philosophy. Its Fellows, drawn from various networks that took shape during the Interregnum, thanks in part to state encouragement, looked to Sprat's *History of the Royal Society* to project a public image of their activities that would secure the patronage of the king; they were disappointed.[25] In the eyes of many contemporaries, such disappointment was well-deserved; some of the Society's critics were convinced that the Society posed a threat to the newly restored monarchy. Although the *History* is an open invitation to the Merry Monarch to refashion himself as the national overlord of experiment, it identifies the actual practice of experimental philosophy with the restoration of another king, one who was traditionally imagined as a laborer. The notion that the first monarch could be revived as a working collective resuscitated a very different myth of restoration associated with "the good old cause."[26]

As Ernst Kantorowicz's seminal study *The King's Two Bodies* showed, the identification of the monarch as a corporate personality, distinct from the king's physical body, could legitimize not only absolutism but regicide: it was in the name of the king that Parliament had declared war on the king. Transferring to themselves the sovereign authority of the king's ideal character, the regicides presented themselves as defending the monarch although *"his own Person oppose or interrupt."*[27] (As a supporter of the Restoration ironically explained, "the Kings Personal and Politique Capacity are distinct, and so they fought for his Crown, when they shot at his Person.") Members of the Army in turn declared Parliament a "degenerate Representative body," and assumed the task of representing the people themselves.[28] Soon the distinction between the individual body and the public office could be claimed by any pamphleteer who involved himself in the "public controversy": as Richard Overton declared against his accusers, what "I am in my self in respect to my own personall sins and transgressions" had no relevance to what "I am in relation to the Common-wealth." Overton was speaking in the style of an MP, but he fulfilled the demands of his office from *"the infamous Goale of Newgate,"* where he stood *"for the Liberties and Freedomes of England."*[29] Although he was not a political representative, Overton was no longer a private person; he represented a corporate body under construction.[30]

In experimentalist practice, this topos permitted the creation of a collective body that, like the old doctrine of the king's two bodies, made each of its members of "another Degree than it should be if it were alone by itself." The collective body of knowledge production was "conjoined" to the fallen bodies of its members not by means of a legal fiction but through constantly renewed effort. If the magus identified the first philosopher's powers with his own, the experimentalist assimilated his knowledge-producing powers to a body whose capacity for spatial and temporal extension was infinite. The king was famously described in Edmund Plowden's *Reports* as "a Name of Continuance, which shall always endure . . . as long as the People continue"; as the proper name of the corporate subject of knowledge production, Adam became that name of continuance, the agent of human progress.[31]

Traditionally, Adam designated an undifferentiated humankind prior to the distinctions of rank. For the experimentalist, these two identities implied one another. The Great Instauration depended for its success on the pursuit of knowledge across occupational and social divisions—above all, on uncovering and cultivating the knowledge of those who worked with "things themselves." The ongoing labor of mending the gap between fallen name and thing was continuous with the project of mending gaps in the social body. Working experimentalists laid claim to a body that was "void" of the "natural Defects and Imbecilities, which the Body natural is subject to" through a variety of means, explored in these opening three chapters, but they began by imitating those with the power to understand and shape the material conditions of existence: productive laborers. The distinction between the body and the office became the attribute not of the political representative but of the knowledge-producing subject who learned to think of himself in representative terms, as an agent who united the higher and lower parts of the social body. The restoration of innocent curiosity thus required specifically *social* experiments, fostered by the slide of the Adamic subject from the singular to the plural and back again. "To make way for what follows," Glanvill proclaimed, "we will go to the root of our antient happiness"; our inquiry into "what followed" from the attempt to reverse the fall through experiment thus begins with the restoration of Adam as a laboring collective—with the "happiness" conferred by the first person plural.[32]

To recover the context of Sprat's fantasy, this opening chapter focuses on the prehistory of its central figures—Adam, the garden, trial—as they shaped the religious and political imagination and, primarily, intellectual life before 1660. Much work on "Restoration science" presents a severely foreshortened view of the Society, many of whose active members were in regular contact before the Restoration. They engaged in precisely the same activities after Charles returned from exile in which they had been engaged before: prosecuting the work begun by creation's first sovereign.[33] In doing so, they took up a native tradition of collective Adamic self-fashioning that stretched back to the Middle Ages. After a brief look into this history, I will explore how the working Adam reemerged as a revolutionary historical agent during the Interregnum. Gerrard Winstanley, who chose not to distinguish sharply between the fall of man and the descent of the Norman yoke over England, imagined Eden as serially lost, and thus as serially regainable; his attempt to restore paradise in England is filled with citations to Adam's prior collective incarnations, particularly the delving Adam appealed to by the 1381 peasant rebels.[34] But now the delving Adam has become a specifically intellectual laborer, and the mystical body has become a public: a body whose members were united not by "custom" and "long usage"—the sacraments, intercessory rites, and the festival year, with all of its sanctified "sports"—but by their shared participation in the labor of truth production. The second half of this chapter investigates how shifts in sacred time and sacred geography—the Puritan assault on the festival year and the dissolution of purgatory—eased the transformation of the *corpus mysticum* into a *corpus laborans*. I will argue that paradise and purgatory were released into the world together: the effort to restore creation as a commons of knowledge production, an open field in which innocent curiosity could assert itself, and evolve, converted the *hortus conclusus* into a purgatorial paradise of pains. The language of trial common to Protestant "experimental faith" and the Baconian faith in experiment provided the conceptual ground of a restored paradise, to be dressed and redressed by a public determined to try all things.

The Sacrament of Production

My account of how Eden became a "workroom" or laboratory is straightforward: the doctrine of the curse of labor was overpowered by a conviction in the paradisal origins of work once Adam's sovereignty over creation became identified with the labor he invested in it. This is not to say that experimentalist constructions of innocent labor were *sui generis*. Church fathers maintained that Adam had not been idle in the garden (though they were somewhat vague about the degree of work required to "dress" it), but until a newly rehabilitated curiosity linked labor to knowledge production, Adam's investment of *cura* in creation could not be identified outright with the force of progress. Yet representations of the first laborer had long provided an occasion to give expression to the value of work, as penance and as theophany. Experimentalists thus drew on an image repertoire that was centuries old even as they redefined its central figure. Throughout the Middle Ages, the image of the first worker condensed a range of ideas about the original state of creation that the *hortus conclusus* could not accommodate.

Most importantly, the motif of Adam delving and Eve spinning was a sign of equality in the original state that God ordained. Humanity's common descent from Adam could be used to explain the mechanism of original sin and the human capacity for empathy, but assertions of this common ancestry could also be deployed to contest the natural status of social distinctions. The thirteenth-century abbot Alexander Neckham maintained that if "man had not sinned there would be no difference of degree for a degree is a lapse from the norm."[35] Again and again, the image through which the "norm" finds expression is Adam the digger. In the proverbial couplet "When Adam delved and Eve span, / Where was then the pride of man?" Adam performs with his spade the same "levelling" work as Death with his scythe.[36] John Ball, one of the leaders of the Peasants' Revolt of 1381, devoted his Blackheath sermon to expounding a pugnacious variant of the proverb: "Whanne Adam dalfe and Eve span, / Who was þanne a gentil man?" In Ball's hands, a conventional rebuke to aristocratic pride becomes a means to expose the unnatural status of social differences. The labor interests represented by the rebels were various, since many artisans joined the cause, but they find unified expression in the figure of the innocent delver.[37] By stretching the boundaries of this figure to accommodate themselves (along with up-to-date counterparts like Piers the Plowman), the rebels were able to participate in his representative character; the names they assumed, occupational markers like Miller and Carter, themselves promoted a generalized identification, enabling them to gather together many kinds of laborers into the first.[38] According to the chronicler Thomas Walsingham's account of the sermon, Ball argued that "all were created to be equal by nature [*a natura*] from the beginning [*a principio*], and that serfdom had been introduced . . . against the will of God." If that had been his intention, "he would have fixed from the beginning who would be a serf and who a lord." The speculative argument Ball fashions from this saying makes the crucial moves of social contract theory's attempt, over two centuries later, to recover what John Rawls calls humanity's "original position" (a position glimpsed through the crucially deindividuated perspective provided by "the veil of ignorance"—a perceptual medium capable of restoring what the seventeenth century would call the insights of innocence).[39] The identification of a truth as "primary" or "original" or "primitive" in the historical sense, characteristic of our first stage of development, is a means of expressing its foundational status in a synchronic sense, its identity with deep structures of present knowledge and action. In fusing "by nature" and "from the beginning," this originary mode of thought performs revolutionary work.

Chroniclers asserted that the rebels raided the abbey at St. Albans to destroy archives "so that the memory of ancient things would vanish," but this looting party was a research mission—the rebels were searching for documentary evidence of a prehistory of custom, with roots in the created rather than the corrupted order.[40] If the rebels' desire to restore this order was scandalous, their vision of what it had been was thoroughly orthodox. Bishop Thomas Brunton preached that "God from the beginning did not create one man of gold from whom sprang the rich and also the noble, and another of clay from whom are descended the poor and the ragged, because with a certain spade Adam dug the earth."[41] In such formulations, we can see how for many the image of the first laborer could be a source of pride rather than its rebuke. Adam's digging is the proper expression of his own humble material origins—linking *humilitas* and *humus*—but it also declares his resemblance to the Creator: the material on which Adam works is the material from which God made him.[42] Brunton's sentence begins with God's work and ends with Adam's; by defining one in terms of the other, it recalls images of the Creator as an artisan, molding Adam out of clay or working with a compass. In the Hebrew Book of Jubilees, God is himself a master delver, who takes on Adam as an apprentice: "we gave him work and we instructed him to do everything that is suitable for tillage." This instruction was given while Adam was in Eden; once expelled, "he tilled the land as he had been instructed in the Garden."[43] Something like this suggestion of continuity between Adam's pre- and postlapsarian vocations informs the conventional representations of primitive labor that adorned medieval churches and books of hours.

These representations offer opportunities to see the first humans unobscured by Marian camouflage; compared to the decorous and static imagery of the enclosed garden, they seem positively boisterous, with angelic overseers casting a sacred aura on the scene of labor and even providing the necessary tools. Scenes of angels giving tools to Adam and Eve, or instructing them in the arts of digging and spinning, were an English speciality; art historians have pieced together a coherent tradition in which the spade (and sometimes a hoe or mattock) is given pride of place.[44] The angels encourage us to regard the scenes they grace as independently celebratory images of the laborers from whom all human beings descended and in whom they were all represented. The motif blends the ontological prestige of the original order with the most prominent feature of the fallen world; the first laborer in his humility and lack of pride merges with Adam in the state of blameless innocence, seeming to suspend him between his fallen and un-fallen state. A medallion on the entrance arch of the south porch of Malmesbury Abbey does so in a quite literal fashion: disregarding the Genesis text, the Adam and Eve depicted receiving a spade and distaff from an angel are actually naked.[45] In these unique yet representative figures, innocent nudity and labor come together, each a sign of the other.

The tilled earth presents a stark contrast to the Mary-garden that *"was never sowne,"* which the Holy Spirit pervaded like *"a subtile wind."*[46] If Mary's erect passivity models the proper mode for the reception of divine grace, the stooping delver would seem to figure miserable humanity's need for it. But if these images look forward to Christ at all, it is by suggesting a continuity with him in his kenosis as *homo pauperrimus.* Michael Camille suggests that the original viewers of the elegant, and surprisingly erect, Adamic delver in the north window of Canterbury Cathedral would have seen a "Christ-like figure,"

> with the long hair and even the facial type of the one who will eventually redeem him . . . The idealization of this figure, the softly rippling green earth and the blue water alongside that suggest irrigation and fertility, the nearby tree (the tree of Life that will become the tree of crucifixion), which provides a convenient hook for Adam's other tool [an axe], all suggest that this is a complex typological image.

Camille interrupts himself at this point, remarking "I have strayed too far from the perceptions of the 'lewd' folk," but this seems unlikely. Here, typology works in reverse, lending dignity to the first Adam rather than diminishing him, to suggest a brotherhood, even an identity of sorts, between the first and second Adams.[47] The tiller of the garden was in fact a conventional manifestation of the Son; Mary Magdalene's mistaking the resurrected Christ for a gardener in John 20:15 justified depictions of Christ *as* a gardener, holding the attribute of Adam: a spade.[48] Allegories of Christ as gardener stress the arduousness of tilling, even invoking the sweat of the brow; Julian of Norwich describes how the Father sent his son to undertake "the grettest labour and the hardest traveyle that is"—to "delve and dike and swinke and swete and turne the erth up and down" in order to produce "nobille and plentuous fruite." Such "traveyle" is registered in the window at Canterbury, which, as Camille suggests, registers the muscular strength and effort necessary to penetrate the earth, and does so in contemporary terms: the silvery blue handle and shoe are clearly made of metal, Tubal-cain's invention (Genesis 4:22).[49] The anachronism secures the image as an object of contemporary identification without in the least disturbing its Christological resonance; Christ suffered in his physical body, he suffers daily in his mystical body.

The implied analogy of the crucifixion to the life of the laborer, who bears the brunt of the curse for society as a whole, becomes explicit in a motif that the early twentieth-century art historians Tancred Borenius and E. W. Tristram called the "Christ of the Trades." Usually located in the lay space of the nave, this was an image of Christ displaying his wounds while surrounded by working tools "arranged so as to form a halo or glory."[50] Often local specialties are represented, confirming the image as an object of popular identification. Athene Reiss argues that this figure should instead be called "The Sunday Christ"; she contends that these representations are "aggressively sabbatarian, no matter how quaint they now seem" and that contemporary viewers would have drawn from them a very clear message: "working on Sunday injures Christ, is therefore sinful, will result in damnation, and would best be avoided." But in England, concern about the Sunday habits of parishioners focused overwhelmingly on leisure activities.[51] Reiss's case thus must rest primarily on the "pathos, rather than the glory, of the image" as militating against a positive representation of labor, but of course Christ's sacrifice is his glory.[52] The tools surrounding the Christ of the Trades indeed correlate with the tools of the crucifixion as they are arranged around the Man of Sorrows; in doing so, they identify the working life as a consecrated sacrifice, one that redounds to the giver after death. In the Christ of the Trades at St Mary Church in Purton, the subject is continued on the other side of the door, as Saint Peter receives the laborers in heaven; women carrying distaffs lead the procession. Such representations make it hard to accept Reiss's dismissal of the consecration of labor as a relic of a Middle Ages existing only in the imaginations of John Ruskin and William Morris.[53] In Ju-

lian's allegory, one cannot help but notice, alongside the sacrificial emphasis, an appreciation of the gardener's mastery over his materials in
the transformative work of turning "the erth up and down." The image
of a God laboring to produce fruit unites the role of Creator to that of
Redeemer and identifies both with the "delving and dyking and sweating" existence of those who undertake "the grettest labour and the hardest traveyle that is."

The life inherited from Adam is celebrated less lugubriously in the labors
of the months, a familiar motif in public buildings and books of hours.
Here the focus is not on pain but on the happy results of pains taken. As
Bridget Ann Henisch argues, these conventional images of workers engaged
in seasonally appropriate activities express neither contempt nor pity. In
this tradition, "men and women seem to have exchanged one paradise for
another," a working world in which forethought and skill are rewarded by
a receptive nature. The working life seems to consist in endless opportunities for the confident display of expertise; the "disciplined grace" of these
figures—robust and trim, of median age—expresses a pleasure in execution, an absorption in the tasks that "maintain the state of the world" (Ecclesiasticus 38:34). Athough they are crammed with carefully observed
details, these are heavily symbolic, not realistic, images: a late fifteenth-
century book of hours made for the English market shows a man collecting
acorns for the pigs that root around by his feet; standing incongruously
beside him is a woman with a distaff and thread in the same posture as the
spinning Eve, her presence conferring on the acorn-gatherer some of the
prestige of his "original."[54]

The selection of labors represented, moreover, is iconologically precise.
While images of beer and cider production are absent, each stage in the
cultivation of grape and wheat to make wine and bread receives detailed
presentation: pruning vines, crushing grapes, breaking ground, winnowing
the grain from the chaff. While machinery is not often represented in the
calendar tradition, the wine press is, no doubt in allusion to the most popular of all late medieval prayers, the final prayer in the Fifteen Oes of Saint
Bridget, in which Christ by turns "treads the wine press alone" and is the
wine press, his blood flowing out to redeem the faithful. The cultivation
of grain evokes Christ's identity as "the bread of life" (John 6:35) and the
allegorical linkage of the crucifixion to milling or grinding (as we will see,

this figure strongly inflected experimentalist propaganda).[55] These mimetic conventions gain a startling significance in light of the fact that these self-sufficient workers are never depicted turning for help or consolation to the Virgin Mary or a local saint.[56] While they do not evoke Christ's suffering, neither do they seem to figure a humanity laboring under the curse and in need of his mercy. Instead, these images of work well done point more immediately to its tangible products: the items of the liturgical feast. In the thousands of images of productive labor that form the calendar tradition, the work that produces the items central to the liturgy almost seems a sufficient sign of its power. Displaying the work necessary to turn seeds, fruit, and earth into bread and wine—the transformative labor that precedes and enables the priestly miracle—the labors of the months tradition appears to be an alternate means of representing Christ's mystical body, not in its victimage but in its strength. The Pauline term used to designate the community of the faithful—*Corpus Christi*—finds graphic expression in images of a community of producers engaged in mutually sustaining labors. The grounds for the opposition that Baconian experimentalists would draw between the sacred production and idolatrous consumption of "fruit" are plainly visible here.

Of course, the Feast of Corpus Christi, instituted in 1264 to honor the daily miracle of the Eucharist, identified the *corpus verum* not with the community of the faithful but with the consecrated elements of the host. Members of the congregation were not agents of this transformation but spectators to it. But through the weekly ritual of "holy bread," parishioners were able to perform a mild reassertion of the unity of the *corpus verum* and *corpus mysticum*. Taking turns to provide the weekly loaf, which was blessed but not consecrated and then shared at the church door, they formalized the links that made the working community a community of companions, bread-sharers. For some, this moment was extended by the communal guild feast, which followed upon the mass and became a "paraliturgical" institution in its own right (and a target of clerical attacks): the link between communion and labor asserts itself in the institution of a "love feast" that began at the church doors and continued into the guild hall.[57] (Of course, the distribution of holy bread, like the kissing of the pax, was an occasion not just for the affirmation of community but the reinforcement of social hierarchy, and parishioners often "fell at varyaunce" over the issue of precedence: in 1522, an Essex parishioner smashed the pax over the head

of a clerk who had offered it to another man first.[58]) Guilds and craft fel-
lowships also provided a vehicle for the Adamic language of equal fellowship: in the corporate idiom of the guild, all members were united by oath
to form a collective body.[59] Pains were taken to protect this unity through
rules that prevented guild members from being "out of charity" with one
another; bricklayers in Chester, for example, were forbidden "to call any of
the brothers worse than his proper name in wrath or anger."[60] At feasts,
guild members gave themselves over with abandon to the language of
love, affective bonds for which industry formed the matrix. Guests from
neighboring trades were frequently invited to these feasts; because of the
collective conditions of artisanal labor, good relations across the trades
were essential. Like a sown field, the construction of an everyday object
like a saddle was a collective achievement, the product of the coordinated
efforts of saddlers, joiners, lorimers, and painters. Love feasts were occasions to consecrate the cooperative labor that held the *corpus mysticum*
together.[61]

As Steven Justice has shown, it was no accident that in 1381 the rebels
selected the Corpus Christi Feast as the occasion to gather their forces: the
raid on St. Albans culminated in a liturgical celebration. Breaking the confiscated millstones the abbot had used to pave his doorway (to produce a
design of repeated crosses), the rebels distributed the fragments among
themselves as if the broken stones were pieces of holy bread.[62] In John
Cleveland's disgusted description, "Milstones before the doore of the Parler,
These *John* the Barber with others tooke away, as a token of victory over the
Law; these they break into small pieces, and distribute amongst the worthies, as the sacred Bread is given in the *Eucharist.*"[63] This ritual imputed
divinity not to bread but to the collective labor that produced it—labor
that the rebels associated as much with the first Adam as the second. In
choosing the Feast of Corpus Christi as an occasion to consecrate their
labor formally and to assert demands as workers, the rebels made explicit the
assertion we find diffusely suggested throughout the labors of the months
tradition. One is moved to say that the rebels dispersed the priestly miracle
into the daily transformations of matter that make up the working life, but
their inversion of the eucharist did more than that: it suggested that the
routinized miracle was parasitic on and parodic of the work performed by
the priest's own flock. Locating the *corpus verum* in their own collective
labor power, they identified the sacrament with production itself.[64]

Certainly, contemporary chroniclers grasped the rebellion in terms of a dispute over Corpus Christi's true place of residence, and thus the nature of his collective being. Walsingham interpreted the uprising as divine retribution for eucharistic heresy; during the preceding year, the Wycliffite challenge had focused precisely on the host.[65] The contemporary perception that the Lollard threat and the rebel threat were one and the same may have been mistaken, but the perception was hardly unmotivated. Ball was first arrested for preaching as a layman, and the research raid on St. Albans was an act of intellectual as well as political self-assertion; by delving into the archives, the rebels extended the challenge posed by the vernacular Bible itself.

Protestants looked back to the Lollards for evidence of a native tradition of dissent that predated Luther; Edward Coke maintained that *Lollard* was only another name for *Protestant*. If Wycliff had only been embraced by the church establishment, Milton lamented, "the glory of reforming all our neighbours had bin compleatly ours." In Wycliff's assertion that theological discussion should take place among the laity, not just in the universities and pulpits, Milton could recognize his own vision of a regenerate public.[66] In Milton's lament, the counterfactual becomes hortatory, as in Sprat's evocation of a religion based on Adam's innocent labors. Through a sort of systematization of regret, lost opportunities are revived as present ones. When Milton presented "our Chaucer" as far more timely reading than the writings of "popish" contemporaries, he probably had a Lollard writer in mind: two of the three Chaucer references in *Of Reformation* are to *The Plowman's Tale,* an anonymous Wycliffite work that became attached to the *Canterbury Tales* in the sixteenth century.[67] When a seventeenth-century parishioner suggested that a good substitute for the Bible was "the book called Chaucer"—which he might well have identified with *The Plowman's Tale,* or with any number of other Lollard works attributed to Chaucer—and asserted that he would never believe in miracles that he could not see with his own eyes, he was at once tapping into a long tradition of anticlericalism and expressing a thoroughly current mood.[68] As his comment on scripture suggests, such sentiments express an attachment not to Lollardy per se but to the idea of a subterranean tradition that can be traced back to an original order, now ready to be excavated. In broad terms, this is the vision that drove the 1381 rebels themselves. All radical in the root sense, these speculative reconstructions share the fundamental assumption that the view from *outside* normative and limited views is the view from *before*.

Milton's tactically wistful reflections may have had grounding in fact; Puritans to whom predestinarian theology seems oddly irrelevant might have been heirs of a native tradition that preceded Calvinist influence.[69] In recent decades, the notion that the so-called premature Reformation contributed in any direct way to the formation of a Protestant national culture has been rejected as part of a "bloated model of Protestant triumphalism," yet since fissures in traditional religion generated opportunities for repeated challenges to priestly authority—challenges that, as Ethan Shagan has shown, shared at least a family resemblance—a continuous tradition was easy for reformers to back-form, inhabit, and extend.[70] This is a tradition in the sense most familiar to literary scholars: a real artifice constructed by those who wish to be its heirs. Still, it is suggestive for our purposes that, with the decline of upper-class support after the rebellion, Lollardy drew most of its strength from artisans, like the goldsmith John Barret who put up poorer Lollards in the 1520s and evangelized his apprentices; Lollard gatherings were sometimes even disguised as trade meetings.[71] Such dissenting subcultures may have provided the matrix from which Adam emerged as a model not just for an egalitarian spirituality but for an intellectual culture organized around the knowledge-producing powers of "the industrious sort," enabling humble lay divines like the illiterate Whitechapel bricklayer John Harrydaunce to preach to crowds a thousand strong.[72] It was a commonplace among the sects that "Learned men were the cause of grete errors." Through their appeals to the probative value of shared experience, Puritanism's "experienced" or "experimental Christians" (analogues, if not actual descendents, of Lollardy's "true men") extended artisanal epistemology into zones of intellectual authority once restricted to "the schools."[73] These appeals to experience in turn constitute a common language between Puritan promoters of "experimental faith" and experimentalists, a language in which Adam is a key term. Even the popularity of names like *Experience* and *Takeheed* among the godly suggests the spread of what we might call an Adamic epistemology, predicated on a new understanding of how innocence and experience might be related.[74] As we will see, it is labor and the experiential literacies associated with it that provide the medium for their interaction.

Adam probably would not have emerged as an exemplar of productive and experimental knowledge in the absence of a continuous tradition associating the delving Adam with the self-assertive claims of laborers. To make the case for such a continuity one can appeal to dozens of Renaissance texts that employ Adam in just this way. "There is no ancient gentlemen but gardeners, ditchers, and gravemakers," says the gravedigger in *Hamlet;* "they hold up Adam's profession."[75] Condensing the delving Adam and Death the Leveller, the gravedigger here offers a *reductio* of the proverb that not only deprives gentlemen of any claim to natural nobility but locates this nobility exclusively in those who delve; Adam becomes a model for the world turned upside down.[76] William Basse's *Sword and Buckler, or, Serving-Man's Defence* reminds his reader of the common ancestry of all men in Adam ("we had all one father") and asks, "Pray who was *Adams* man when *Cain* was borne? / Or in what scripture doe we reade or finde, / That ever God created *Adams* two? / Or we proceeded of worse stocke then you?" The undifferentiated unity of humanity in the figure of Adam promotes his identity not as the first king but as the people's representative. The speaker goes on to describe the inequality of estates as the result of "discentious striving" after the fall in which "some gain'd, some lost, / And who got least serv'd him that gained most." The bland assurance that this unity will be restored at the end of time—"that we were all one, and shall agen, / Appeares in the good minds of Serving-men"—gains historical immediacy in the author's declaration: "I have begun this combat for them all."[77]

The delving Adam merely embodies the radical potentials of Christian doctrine, but the suspicion that each successive instantiation of this figure owed something to previous ones is confirmed by his tendency to materialize through his medieval avatars, the 1381 rebels. In his *Survay of the Pretended Holy Discipline* (1593), for example, Richard Bancroft critiqued the use to which Adam was put by a "certaine writer for reformation" who employed the premise that *"all men came of one man"* as an occasion to thunder against aristocratic vice. Bancroft complains that the apparently orthodox use of the proverb to humble the pride of the wellborn had the potential to endanger their very status:

> We live in a worlde (you know) that crieth out: the *firste institution, the first institution:* every thing must be brought to the *first institution.* The wordes

be good, if they be well applied. But something was amisse in the Priestes application of his text, being such a like saying, amongst a multitude of rebelles: vz: *When Adam digged, and Eve spanne, who was then the Gentleman* . . . noblemen and gentlemen . . . lift themselves above the rest of the children of God, to whom indeede the inheritaunce of the world doth equally appertaine; by the same right, that all true Christians are fellow heires together of the kingdome of heaven. Call they this the bringing of thinges to the first institution? Surely such and the like conceits do tend to nothing, but to bloud and confusion.[78]

To use the old proverb of Adam delving, even for the traditional purpose of attacking aristocratic luxury and pride, was "like saying [it], amongst a multitude of rebelles." To make his meaning clear, Bancroft adds a note in the margin: "John Wall, or Ball in the time of Jacke Cades rebellion, in Rich 2. daies" (following Shakespeare, he lumps 1381 and 1450 together).[79] After Ball, this once unexceptionable saying could not be cleansed of revolutionary contagion. A generation after the publication of this text, civil war had begun in England and Ball's ideas were once again news. In 1642, Charles I warned that the demands of "the common people" would "end in a dark, equal chaos of confusion . . . in a Jack Cade or a Wat Tyler"; the official case of the House of Commons against Lilburne traced his *"levelling fury"* to "your *Predecessors, Jack Straw* and his *Associats.*"[80] *The Just Reward of Rebels, or the Life and Death of Jack Straw* (1642) concludes with Straw's penitent ghost bringing bad news to "my brother Rebells": as he has discovered in the afterlife, Adam's descendants cannot be agents of humanity's restoration; they can only wait in patience for the second Adam to effect it. Straw urges his heirs to escape the pangs of a "horrid Conscience" by loving and fearing the king: "So shall your soules without disturbance rest, / Till Christ shall come to make you fully blest."[81] Christ is the first line of defense against the "disturbance" threatened by Adam's resurrection.

In 1654, John Cleveland saw fit to produce a 155-page account of the 1381 uprising. *The Idol of the Clownes, Or, Insurrection of Wat the Tyler* was republished four years later as *The Rustick Rampant or Rurall Anarchy Affronting Monarchy: in the Insurrection of Wat Tiler:*

The beginnings of the Second *Richard*'s reign are turmoiled with a Rebellion, which shoke his Throne and Empire: A Rebellion, not more against

Religion and Order, than Nature and Humanity too; A Rebellion never to
be believed, but in the Age it was acted in, and our owne, in which we finde
how terrible the overflowes of the common people (ever delighted in the
calamities of others) untyed, and hurryed on by their own wills, and beastly
fury, must prove.[82]

Before the end of its first sentence, an account of the rebellion written in
the historical present ("The beginnings of the Second *Richard*'s reign are
turmoiled with a Rebellion") becomes a reflection not just on "the Age it
was acted in," but "our owne." Cleveland wants to make anachronism prophetic, to suggest that the current assault on "Religion and Order" will
meet the same end that the rebels did almost three hundred years ago (thus
Milton's famous Ovidian description of books as "Dragons teeth" becomes
a symbol of doomed rebellion: "They had risen like those Sons of the Dragons teeth, in tempests, without policy or advice").[83] In Cleveland's allegory,
each fourteenth-century figure predicts a contemporary: Wycliff is "Pres-
byter *Wycliffe*"; Wat Tyler, Cromwell, "*Protectour and Captaine Generall* of
the *Clownes*"; and the rebels, "new Common-wealthsmen."[84] Cleveland
faithfully replicates Walsingham's account of the raid on St. Albans, down
to the detail of the breaking of the millstones as "sacred Bread," but their
leader speaks like a Cromwellian, warning the abbot not "to exasperate
the *godly party,* the righteous *Commons*" and to "consider our strength,
and the happinesse of the new *Modell,* the eminency of the Commons . . .
visible to every eye." Ball's couplet—a "levelling leud Text"—becomes a
rallying cry for the Levellers themselves. Cleveland's Ball exhorts the
clowns to turn their agricultural implements on the state: "now was the
time appointed them by God to cast off the yoake" and, "like good Husbandmen, who love their field, pluck up the weedes which over run it . . .
lopping off the Heads of those which were too tall, which over-topped too
much." Rather than being identified with sacramental production, the
labor of cultivating the earth becomes the grounds of "divelish ambition":
delving becomes deviling, raising "*Tylers* and Sons of the Earth" to a
"height which God (as some love to speake) never called them to"; popular
identification with the first son of earth evokes the revolt of the Titans,
men sprung out of "slime and dirt."[85] Cleveland's depiction of the mob
exploits the deep-seated disgust with soil as a medium where distinction
disappears; the risen Adam is a "promiscuous," hence unclean, mixture of

elements. Paradise erupts into the postlapsarian world as dirt: "matter out of place."[86]

Even as they seek to raise the reader's disgust by associating an undifferentiated commons with dirt, these texts also try to dissipate the threat of "that many-headed monster, the multitude being drawne together" by exposing this filthy unity as a fictitious one. The Adamic collectivity is actually an illusion, a vehicle for the individual ambition of "self-seeking" opportunists—"Mechanicks" who are envious of their superiors.[87] Samuel Rowlands employs a version of this strategy in *Hell's Broke Loose,* whose very title affirms the dogma that any attempt to restore the created order reenacts the fall in miniature. Here the descendants of the "good Com mons Wealths men . . . *Jacke Straw, Watt Tyler, Tom Myller, John Ball,* &c. in the raigne of *Richard the 2*" are the German Anabaptists. As the resurrected "Ghost of Jacke Straw," Leyden spreads the message received from *"Parson Ball"*:[88]

Affirming wee ought Kings apeece to bee,
And every thing be common unto all:
For when old *Adam* delv'd, and *Evah* span,
Where was my silken velvet Gentleman?

Wee *Adams* Sonnes; Hee Monarch of the Earth,
How can wee chuse but be of Royall blood?
Beeing all descended from so high a birth?
Why should not wee share wealth, and worldly good?
. . .
Why, Kings are made of Clay; and so are wee.
Wee are the men will make our Valours knowne,
To teach this doting world new reformation . . .
Let's turne the world cleane upside downe, (mad slaves)
So to be talk'd of, when w'are in our Graves.[89]

The humor of this speech is supposed to be generated by its self-cancelling character—a tailor can no more be a king than a politics based on the equality of dust and ashes can be "cleane." The concluding rhyme effects the separation of king from slave required to bury the latter in the grave, blending him back with the earth from which he came. In this passage, the reintroduction of postlapsarian distinction requires the intervention of the narrator's voice ("mad slaves"), but in Rowlands's analysis of rebel psychology, Leyden is in fact no more capable than any other fallen subject of integrating king and slave. His identification with Adam the worker is only a stepping stone to a far grander identification with the first sovereign that, once attained, excludes any other. Leyden was "a *Taylour*, / But all my minde was Kingly eve'ry thought," and although he consoles himself with the thought that "Old Father *Adam* was a *Taylour* too," he cannot integrate the working Adam and the royal Adam. Rather than becoming a tailor-king, he merely abandons his trade to become one of the silken velvet gentlemen he once outfitted, loading his body with the finery he now refuses to make. His identificatory choice predicts his failure: although he cites Ball's couplet, Leyden takes his model not from the naked delver but from the sinner who labored to make "Fig leave Breeches."[90] By placing the innocent laborer beyond the reach of possible identification, Cleveland and Rowlands dissolve the unclean mixtures that serve as fertile ground for Adamic popular rebellion—the blends of high and low, of innocent existence and the life of labor enjoined by the curse—and protect the principle of distinction, predicated on that most basic divide between created and corrupted humanity.

Early modern responses to the threat of Adamic popular rebellion register awareness of another mixture: the revolution in knowledge that muddled the spheres of the learned and unlearned by conferring philosophical respectability on the knowledge of "mechanicks." In Cleveland's retelling, the raid on St. Albans has a distinctly Baconian inflection: "we come not hither for words but things."[91] In one respect, Basse's *Sword and Buckler,* an attempt by a retainer in the Wenman family to "combat" the charge that servants were idle and unskilled, is a thoroughly conventional check to upper-class pride; but the work—Basse's first published piece of poetry—also functions as a testimony to the *intellectual* capabilities of social inferiors: the intellectual authority he claims, moreover, is based entirely on his own experience. And in *Histrio-Mastix* the menace of mob rule encodes a very different threat, one that, in the decades to follow, would result in the elevation of "the mechanicks' philosophy" to the mechanical philosophy.

At first, the threat to order seems familiar enough: a group of *"Mechanicalls . . . crying confusedly,"* led onstage by an allegorical figure called Fury, crying "Liberty, liberty, liberty":

4. All shall be common.
1. Wives and all: what, *Helter, skelter.*
2. Slid, we are men as well as they are.
3. And we came all of our Father *Adam.*
2. Goe to then, why should we be their slaves?
Omnes. Liberty, Liberty, Liberty.[92]

These mechanicals, obviously, have none of the wit of Shakespeare's grave-digger. Only the first and fourth lines are free of slang, and they are mirror images of one another; in contrasting future and past tenses, they are locked in an epanaleptic relation—"all shall be . . . and we came all"—that expresses the tight relationship between speculative histories of Adam and a prophetic social vision of a decidedly "common" sort. Marston portrays these men as unable to imagine what communal property rights would free them to do, aside from putting their wives—the only property to which they can lay any claim—on the open market.[93] At the end of the play, however, the threat to social order is banished by the restoration of a less tangible form of property to its rightful owner, in the procession of the liberal arts to the throne of Astrea; Marston invokes the august philosophical tradition that identified the mechanical arts with the slave and the liberal arts with the freeborn. This distinction was the first and most important casualty of the experimentalist revolution.[94]

When the virtuoso John Aubrey remarks that gravediggers tend to provide "a much better account" of the qualities of soil than most landowners, he describes delving as a labor that can produce knowledge—an implication entirely absent from the speech of Shakespeare's gravedigger, and even from traditional celebrations of productive labor as a consecrated sacrifice.[95] The description in Ecclesiasticus 38 of the various trades that "maintain the state of the world" registers the diligence and skill of those who perform difficult tasks "perfectly . . . All these trust to their hands: and every one is wise in his work," but it presents that very dedication as the grounds for the laborer's exclusion from learning—the "wisdom of a learned man cometh by opportunity of leisure"—and so from the realms of political and religious discussion: "They shall not be sought for in public counsel, nor sit high in the congregation: they shall not sit on the judges' seat, nor understand the sentence of judgment: they cannot declare justice, and judgment, and they shall not be found where parables are spoken." The work of "maintaining" the world is inconsistent with exerting intellectual authority within it. For a worker to hanker after such authority can only indicate his unwillingness to work. Experimentalist thought turns such formulations on their head. In Bacon's scientific utopia, *The New Atlantis*, it is those who actually shape the material conditions of existence that inspire the awe and obedience of the populace; and, in the revolutionary period, manual labor becomes an actual medium of political agency, grounded in a new form of intellectual self-assertion.

The Working Sovereign

Gerrard Winstanley claimed that the Digger project had its origins in a trance, during which he heard the words, "*Worke together. Eat bread together;* declare this all abroad."[96] The blending of labor and bread-sharing that had been a traditional feature of popular piety, and popular rebellion, now assumed a startling new form: "my mind was not at rest, because nothing was acted . . . I tooke my spade and went and broke the ground upon *George-hill* in Surrey, thereby declaring freedome to the Creation."[97] Winstanley urged his fellows to assert their collective right to "dig, plow, plant and dwell upon the commons, without . . . paying rent to any" by going ahead and doing so, turning labor into an innocent form of battle: "stand up for your freedom in the Land, by acting with *Plow* and *Spade* upon the *Commons*." Literalizing Shakespeare's pun on Adam's arms, this form of action was predicated on a new understanding of what the first laborer's work had "declared," an understanding that required a new method of declaration: a continuous stream of print keyed to an ongoing physical demonstration.[98]

Winstanley argued that Adam's sovereignty over creation was expressed in his custodial work upon it; kingly sovereignty resided in labor power itself. "The Earth in the first Creation of it, was freely given to whole mankind, without respect of Persons"; the "word of Command" was imparted "to whole mankinde (not to one or a few single branches of mankinde)" to "take possession" (357, 451). From this primal unity Winstanley excavated the birthright of every individual to stake his or her claim to the earth; "an equal freedom in the Earth to every one" was given to "every man in his creation": the personal pronoun migrates easily from Adam to his progeny.[99] Declaring that "the Virgine-state of Mankinde . . . this Innocencie . . . was not an estate 6000. yeare agoe onely . . . you need not looke back six thousand yeares to finde it," Winstanley asserted the corporate identity of all workers in God's garden, seeming to confer, at the same time, a multiple existence on the innocent Adam himself: "before were all one, and looked upon each other as all one . . . whole mankinde walked in singlenesse" (480, 482, 489). Winstanley identified innocence as the freedom to work, to exploit "the free content of the fruits and crops of this outward Earth, upon which their bodies stand: this was called The mans innocency, or pleasure in the Garden before his fall" (377–378). Not just a means of paradisal recovery, the Diggers' delving was paradise itself, an Eden of labor restored on actual physical ground. Like the naked working couple in the window at Malmesbury, these "naked Spademen" labored under the sign of innocence, not the curse (380).

This dynamic interpretation of the original state implied an equally dynamic interpretation of the fall, which was enacted daily by people "enslaving those who in the Creation are their equals" (354). Indeed, "the whole world of mankinde, generally at this day, through all the nations of the world, is eating of this Tree of knowledge, of good and evill, and are cast out of themselves, and knowe not the power that rules in them" (453). To such people, and to those who sought to suppress the Digger project, Winstanley declared, "I look upon you as part of the creation who must be restored" (391). The contraction of the events of sacred history into a single space is familiar to us from the *hortus conclusus* tradition: now, however, the space is not enclosed by any wall, and the play of forces within it is determined by human effort. The leap from historical into sacred time is no longer a means to blend the original creation with the reassuring image of its corruption; it is a sacralization of the opportunities afforded by the present moment to the reforming will. Winstanley warned his contemporaries that the agent of this will was "now rising in Husbandmen, Shepherds, Fishermen"—anyone who was able not only to speak but "to act their words," for "words cannot try all things" (475, 101). In this labor power lay both innocence and divinity. For the first and second Adams merge in this effort; Winstanley has a disarming habit of running them all together: Adam's "work of digging, being freedom, or the appearance of Christ in the earth, hath tried the Priests and professors to the uttermost, and hath ripped up the bottom of their Religion."[100] The inspired work of physically "unearthing" the corrupt institutions of church, state, and private property was as powerful a theophany as humanity was likely to experience.

These Adamic spademen did more than dig. What excited the fury of some of their countrymen was their felling of trees. John Rogers has argued that this toppling of trees was an attack on the royalist mythology that surrounded trees (particularly the oak, sacred to the royalist cause after Charles had been forced to hide in one).[101] The Diggers were engaged in symbolic recapitulations of Charles's execution, an event only two months old, and insisting on the appropriate interpretation of that event: having dispensed with the false sovereign, the nation could create a level landscape (Winstanley also referred to his collective as the "true Levellers") and relocate sovereignty in the people themselves.[102] Of course, this toppling of trees was not only a form of symbolic action; the Diggers were trying to grow food. They did not expect a miraculous deliverance to issue from a merely ritual performance. Organized human effort was not only necessary to their vision, it was constitutive of that vision; the providential intervention they believed that digging would set into motion was one of which they were both the agents and the instruments.[103] The Diggers were clearing ground on which to test new agricultural methods, "introducing fallow crops into regular field rotations and using the same land for arable and pasture" (up and down husbandry).[104] Using innovations in applied knowledge to "quietly improve the Waste and Common Land" in the Baconian confidence that it would soon be "increased with all sorts of Commodities," the Digger experiment was not merely analogous to Baconian instauration but an instance of it (356). Winstanley's assertion that the spirit was to be found in "words performed in action" rather than in "Schoole learning succession" was a declaration of both experimental faith and faith in experiment: the ongoing labor of bringing *res* and *verba,* working and declaring, together (353, 475). The restoration of paradise is identical to the formation of a cumulative culture of works and words, organized around the production and cultivation of facts: things made.

The Adam that had "risen up" through the Diggers was not the resurrected Adam of John Ball's sermon, but rather his heir. In the period that intervened between these collective incarnations of the delver, a working culture that had endured for half a millennium had been publicly redefined as a source of knowledge, with the result that the figure of the first worker could now be appealed to as an intellectual authority, not just a moral one.

Productive laborers were recognized as graduates of an educational process that, rather than "producing a 'lettered man' . . . had the goal of making knowledge productive"; those who made their living by working with things themselves possessed an alternative form of literacy, and a powerful one.[105] For Winstanley, delving has become a figure not just for physical labor but for an intellectual mastery that, unlike the digging of the 1381 rebels, does not have to be extended into the archives to gain legitimacy. Such digging can, however, provide the basis for new texts, "written by the experimentall hand."[106]

Winstanley had been a freeman in the Merchant Taylors when he lived in London; his writings extend the corporate and sacramental rhetoric of the guildhall to describe a national apprenticeship that will result in the entire citizenry of England becoming a (single) freeman.[107] Until everyone in "this Land of our nativitie" lived *as if they were but one,"* the land could not "properly be called a Common-Wealth" (326, 337, 323). The force guiding history toward the restoration of the original commonwealth—the land of humanity's nativity—was "Reason, which I call God." Winstanley imagined this God in the same way he imagined man: as "the Maker" (105). The source of insight into creation's moral and physical order, reason was a productive force: generating the maker's knowledge through which creation would be restored, it was also the means by which "we are made to see our Priviledges, given us in our Creation." The process of excavating "the secrets of the Creation" that had been buried under fallen learning— "locked up under the traditional, Parrat-like speaking, from the Universities, and Colledges for Scholars"—made visible the privileges of Adam's progeny, which consisted above all in the right to continue the Maker's work (271).

The Diggers were not merely "demonstrating" or voicing their opinions as rights-bearing individuals; as truth producers publicizing their collective discoveries, they were demonstrating in a specifically experimental sense: excavating ontologically prior truths concealed by custom. For digging also describes the process by which the individual probes beneath the false images produced by the vitiated senses and "unexperienced Imagination"—a "blinde Imagination"—to reveal the ground of true religion in creation (452). Digging could thus take many forms, such as the rotating Sabbath lectures on natural philosophy, or "experimental knowledge in the things which are," that Winstanley recommended to Oliver Cromwell as the basis of devotion in the reformed commonwealth (564). Offering findings about crops that grew or failed to grow, the mechanisms of heat and cold, or newly discovered features of animals and the planets—all of which Winstanley described as "practical knowledge of God"—congregants would revive the first religious service, when Adam surveyed, looked into, and named the creatures. "God manifests himself in actual knowledge," and only those who engaged physically with the creation were qualified to declare that knowledge.[108]

Constructing an innocent Adam who labored by the sweat of the brow, Winstanley linked tillage to the labor that was unambiguously innocent: the labor of Genesis 2:19. Running the digging hand together with "the experimentall hand," he cultivated the productive eye, an eye capable of seeing new things. Although medieval treatments of the scene of naming suggest a link between Adam's power to name the animals and his rule over them, this link is characterized not as the cause or effect of knowledge or cultivated discernment but rather as a chain of obedience: if Adam is obedient to God, the creatures will be obedient to him.[109] But now that Adam's sovereignty over the creatures was "artificial," the product of pains taken, to act with plow and spade was to restore that sovereignty, planting paradise as a field of productive knowledge on the grounds of industry, observation, and trial. The comprehension of all these pursuits under the sign of digging is justified by the assumption that Adam's nominative and material powers over creation were the products of the *cura* he invested in it. If labor was the foundation of sovereignty, the working philosopher king was no longer an unassimilable paradox, as it is in Rowlands's portrayal: Adam was the first king *by virtue of* being the first worker, and the naming of the creatures was itself a form of digging, a productive labor.

Figured as delving, discovery becomes processual; it is not merely a matter of unearthing truth but of continuously cultivating it. Winstanley thus decreed that anyone "who speaks of any Herb, Plant, Art, or Nature of Mankind, is required to speak nothing by imagination, but what he hath found out by his own industry and observation in tryal" (564). Only information produced in this manner could be trusted and passed onto others in consolidation of the collective subject that was "rising" throughout the land.[110] This rising up was an interior event, but also a public one: it occurred "when the five Sences acts [*sic*] in their owne light . . . Hearing, Seeing, Tasting, Smelling, Feeling, which is called the body of the living soule, that is, very good" (485, 468). The living soul rises up when the body is restored to its use as an instrument of knowledge production, rather than seeking personal (hence "imaginary") gratification in "selfish" and "fleshly" consumption.[111] As the breeding ground of "words performed in action," the working senses are in fact humanity's best defense against the flesh, identified with the vagaries of covetous imagination—the false images produced by the carnal mind and body enthralled to "this Lust of the eye" (482). When used to produce common knowledge, one's body ceases to be flesh, because it ceases to be merely one's own. It was a commonplace among Digger sympathizers that private property emerged from "man following his own sensualitie."[112] No longer the necessary consequence of humanity's moral failure in Eden, private property is a fallen illusion to be seen through.

Winstanley described "our cause of digging" as one that "knits every creature together into a onenesse" to "make but one body perfect," and his experience confirmed this claim (321, 105, 261; see also 323). The vision he had first received continued to "sound" in him—"This Trumpet is stil sounding in me, *Work together, Eat bread together, declare this all abroad*"—and in the course of trumpeting this vision, he literally incorporated others into it: the first-person plural is used to relate the exact same vision in *The True Levellers Standard Advanced,* signed by fifteen people, as if they had originally experienced it together, as a single dreaming subject.[113] In the formal "Declaration" of the Diggers' desire "to eate our bread with the sweat of our brows . . . working together, and eating together, as one man," the tendentious scrambling of working and eating subsumes the sacramental feast within the productive labor that provides it, a process of compression that also results in its agents becoming "one man" (256–257). They soon "knitted together" with others; declarations sprouted up in print from "commons" all over England by people using Winstanley's exact words as their own.[114] Although the host had also expressed a "onenesse," this unity was repeatedly shattered by the rules of social precedence that required its uneven distribution; the Diggers' sacrament of production was part of a historical process that would restore this unity in fact.[115]

In the command to "declare this all abroad," the ambiguity of *all,* working at once as an adverb and a direct object, is the point: Winstanley was declaring an all to an all. But to do so effectively, he had to declare that all *as* an all. This was made possible by the change he underwent during his "sweet Anointing," effecting his transformation from a private person into a public one. His testimony to this experience has rightly been praised for its "rich disclosure of interiority"; the interior richness results not from a personal psychology but from its surrender. As he explained, he did not speak in "a spirit of private fancie" but rather in light of experience, registered inwardly as a mortification of the private self.[116] His description of the experience conveys the hard labor required to restore the first person to the first person: as he confesses, "I myself could not at first bear" the truths it revealed. These truths would compel him to bind his own demands, and his own satisfactions, to those of every other person in the commonwealth. The subject that survived this trying but sweet experience was one cleansed of "covetous Kingly power": a "corrupt bloud, that runs in every man, and womans vaines, more or lesse, till reason . . . cast him out." Monarchy, understood as the foundation of private property, had to be ripped up inside as well as out: "before you be bound up into one universall body, all your particular bodies and societies must be torne to pieces."[117] Winstanley's anointing was the result of that self-cultivation; as he believed, his resulting incorporation into one universal body enabled him to see and know things that the private imagination suggested were impossibilities.

As a result of his anointing, it was not Winstanley alone but "the poor Diggers" who "have got the Crown, and weare it"; to assume this consecrated office was to share it with others (434). The translation of corporate personhood from one person to another is enacted through Winstanley's writing, whose most striking feature is its relentless synonymizing. Alonzo Church credits synonymy with giving us a notion of semantic content "independent alike of any particular expression in words and of any particular psychological act of judgment or conception"; it is "not the particular judgment, but the objective content of the judgment which is capable of being the common property of many."[118] In Winstanley's hands, synonymy becomes a powerful instrument of transformation: digging is freedom, God is reason, and the restored Adam is all of these. Sometimes the work of "is" is performed by "or," or the phrase "which I call," but the effect is the same. The "I call" is not a demonstration of priestly power, but a teaching-by-example, and it often comes with an explanation: "I am made to change the name from God to Reason; because I have been held under darknesse by that word, as I see many people are . . . this I hope will be a sufficient accompt why I alter the word . . . that people may rest no longer upon words without knowledge."[119] In these conversions of linguistic substance, synonymy becomes the eucharist of experimental faith, but the semantic transubstantiation it effects is antimiraculous: unlike the priest of the old religion, Winstanley does not turn his back on his witnesses while converting one thing into another; he turns into them. The priest's hocus pocus becomes the proffered "is": enabling a metonymic passage across equivalence, destroying difference and revealing the prime substrate, the verb is an invitation into a form of being that reverses humanity's fall into individuation.

This reversal required sacrifice. However natural the office of this corporate king was, to live in accordance with the demands of that office could not come naturally to individuals accustomed to the rule of covetous imagination. Winstanley's language shows the reader how to go about it; his renovating equivalences convey a methodological lesson. When Winstanley declared freedom to the creation with his spade, his intent was to plant a paradise of production, of which knowledge would be the fruit. To wear their crown, Diggers had to cultivate knowledge, not "rest . . . upon words," and this required them to transubstantiate themselves: no private man who "worships his owne imagination" was equipped to make discoveries (107). Surrendering the habits of the covetous "imagination of flesh" was not just a spiritual and moral exercise but an intellectual one: an apprenticeship to a new use of the body, geared toward the excavation of truth and gradual effacement of personal difference (105). Winstanley specifically identifies the proper functioning of the senses with the state of innocence, a state that enables knowledge to grow: "the mighty Creatour may at length be known, in the clear sighted experience of one single creature, man, by seeing, hearing, tasting, smelling, feeling." Rather than offering instant illumination, the senses of any particular individual can only "at length" be made to yield knowledge worthy of the "one single creature, man" (165). To investigate and testify to creation as a "universall body," the individual had to continually submit his imaginations to open trial, revealing the grounds of the truths he asserted in things themselves. The body of the living soul gained through the proper use of the senses is not a personal possession but a shared substance, producing knowledge whose redemptive power lies in its impersonality. From this grounding in circumstantial particulars emerges a subject unqualified by contingency, ready to be incorporated with others: a mysterious transformation, but not a miraculous one. The "mysteries" or craft secrets that held together the body of a guild were the products of a similar translation, of individual bodies into organs of deindividuated and productive knowledge.

If the Diggers' actions were scandalous, their philosophical justification for these actions, and the figures they used to express it, soon faded into common sense. Indeed, as far as many of their contemporaries were concerned, the Diggers' assumptions already constituted common sense. Winstanley's habit of conflating the fall of man with the fall of the Norman Yoke over England was no mere idiosyncrasy: John Cook, the author of *Monarchy no Creature of God's Making*, was confident that if "*Adam* had not sinned in Paradice all the world should have been governed by the Common Law of *England*" (provided that such law was itself congruent with "pure naturall principles").[120] The Diggers' vision of a paradise of labor was no less widespread. Although the Fifth Monarchist Mary Cary believed that the lifting of the curse would result in radically altered human bodies, she was equally certain that these bodies would continue to engage in what they were created to do: work. The New Jerusalem would be characterized not by the disappearance of labor but the expansion of it. The poor would not "toyl day and night" to maintain others in "idleness, drunkenness, and other evil practices"; instead, all the saints together "shall comfortably enjoy the work of their hands."[121] The ideal of the priesthood of believers is realized as a priesthood of producers.

More influentially, John Locke would employ the concept of the state of nature to describe property as supervenient on labor invested, reading Genesis as conferring proprietary rights upon all men over all things, according to "the Original Community of all things amongst the Sons of Men."[122] As a world "belonging to nobody but available for the appropriations of all," Locke's "infinitely exploitable" earth is also Winstanley's (though one assumes in each case that such exploitation must eventually take into account nature's limits and needs, if only to protect the future of improvement).[123] Of course, Locke took this insight in a different direction by atomizing the Adamic subject: "*As much Land* as a Man Tills, Plants, Improves, Cultivates, and can use the Product of, so much is his *Property*," for "God, when he gave the World in common to all Mankind, commanded Man also to labour."[124] And yet, as the following chapter will show, Locke also entertained a Winstanleyan scheme to distribute the blessing of labor more evenly throughout the social body, elaborating a vision for society that John Dunn calls "almost Maoist." If, as Dunn observes, Locke found the doctrine of original sin uncongenial and "embarrassing," this was in large part because labor for him was the central fact of the state of nature, understood as the "continuing moral order within which human beings live and make their history." The "gift of the world to Adam" imposed strenuous demands on all his descendants, leaving no room for "a leisure class."[125] My point is that Winstanley has as much a claim as Locke to being a representative seventeenth-century thinker, and for many of the same reasons. Even as it continued the movement of squatters onto wastelands that had been going on for over a century, the Digger project was a concrete expression of the assumptions and figures that shaped the emerging public sphere as a field of arduously cultivated experimental knowledge and a recovered space of communion: a paradise under restoration.[126] As my account of Winstanley's thought suggests, these two aspects of the public sphere—its factual grounding and its status as a commons in which respect of persons could disappear—implied one another. The productive sacrament at the center of Winstanley's imagination was predicated not on Christ's vicarious sacrifice but on the bloodless sacrifice of the private self. It was this sacrifice that enabled the translation of personal experience into public truths, turning individuals into public workers—workers capable of incorporation as a single productive agent.

Of course, as a space whose mode of existence was virtual, the public sphere could be, and was, figured in all kinds of ways. But the vision of a public life organized around the collective conversion of things into facts—and an associated understanding of intellectual life as a productive labor—required a particular concept of public space to realize itself, one that could not be fully captured by the figure of a marketplace or even the commonwealth of letters. The tendency to imagine public intellectual life in terms of a creation restored is the common thread between Winstanley, Locke, and other seventeenth-century thinkers we might call experimentalist. Locke even playfully presented himself as an Adamic delver at the beginning of *An Essay Concerning Human Understanding*, an attempt to dig beneath philosophical language of the falsities of "Schoole learning," with its "uncouth, affected, or unintelligible Terms," so that a language reflecting "the true Knowledge of Things" could take root: "'tis Ambition enough to be employed as an Under-Labourer in clearing Ground a little, and removing some of the Rubbish, that lies in the way to Knowledge"—a "way" with which he believed "ingenious and industrious" workers were already famil-iar.[127] Philosophers only had to follow them, and a language that described "things themselves" could once again form the basis of philosophical thought, now geared toward physical rather than syllogistic "demonstration." Names would again relate to the creatures, and human agents would engage creation more directly.[128] But while Locke famously styled himself as an under-laborer in relation to builders like Isaac Newton and Robert Boyle, Boyle *himself* claimed to be nothing more than an "Underbuilder" and "a homely Digger."[129] Digging his "way to Knowledge," the distributed agent of sov-ereign reason clears the ground for the conversion of experience into under-standing: the first sovereign is put back to work.

The Ingenious Gardener

The difference in the meanings that the Adamic collectivities of 1381 and 1649 attached to their labor can be gauged by the history of a single word: *ingenuity,* a word that came to signify a state of virtual innocence. Begin-ning as a loan word from the French, *ingenious* originally meant showing talent, cleverness, or genius, but in the second half of the sixteenth century, its primary meaning shifted to denote handiness in particular: the *Oxford English Dictionary Online's (OED)* examples of its usage include "The labori-ous care of an ingenious and industrious artificer"; "According to my Obser-vation and common Consent of the most ingenious Workmen" (def. 3). The words that accompany *ingenious* in these examples are typical and indicate the connotational cloud that has begun to gather around it: care, industry, artifice, observation. In the second sentence, taken from Joseph Moxon's *Mechanical Exercises,* the care invested by skilled workmen forms the basis of their consensual and trustworthy truth claims. This is important, for by the seventeenth century, *ingenious* also started to be (as the *OED* puts it) "used by confusion for *ingenuous* or L. *ingenuus*" (II): having the qualities of a free-man, of free or honorable birth, honest, candid, open, of a noble disposition. Reciprocally, the editors remark that *ingenuous* was "In 17th c. frequently misused for *ingenious.*" A word that had been a class marker to distinguish the trustworthy from the common was now interchangeable with a word that denoted the knowhow of "mechanicks." Through a constant shuffling of the *i* and the *u,* an experimental hybrid was created that utterly inverted the relationship between trustworthiness and gentlemanliness.[130]

What the *OED* calls the "confusion" was noted by contemporary critics: "*Ingenious and Ingenuous,* are too often confounded," the lexicographer Elisha Coles complained in 1676.[131] The confusion was strategic; it enacted the union embodied by Adam himself, the first sovereign who was also the first laborer. In particular, it expressed the idea that the sign of his free and honorable birth was his skillful investment of care in creation, care that was also the source of his authoritative insight into it. For Adam's ingenious heirs, what inspired trust was not rank or a gentleman's education, but a humble receptivity to the testimony of things themselves. The sign of innocence restored, ingenuity was the foundation of *"Real Philosophy,"* a philosophy founded on the cultivation of experience.[132]

More generally, ingenuity provided the foundation for the concept of intellectual labor. The word, in both its forms, was employed by experimentalists, preachers, and self-styled heirs of Adam to announce who they were: it conveyed a mind freed from the power of dogmas and received traditions, characterized by a receptivity to the lessons of experience rather than "the schools." It was the sign of a trustworthy knowledge producer, designating the intellectual laborer, as distinct from—usually in opposition to—the scholar.[133] The constant companion of *curious* in its positive designation, *ingenious* presented innocence as the sign of innovation. The word conveyed the new understanding of innocence, not merely as the absence of knowledge, but as a means to gain it. Through a model of intellectual life that located authority in those uncontaminated by scholarly expertise, innocence became a method. Promoting what would become the canons of modern scientific objectivity and collaboration, Sprat would describe the ingenious man as "rather innocent, and vertuous, then knowing"; a "plain, industrious Man . . . willing to be taught," was the real "Character of a True Philosopher," not "the high, earnest, insulting Wits, who can neither bear partnership, nor opposition" who normally went by that name.[134] Sprat stresses the lowly modesty of the ingenious as the condition for partnership, a willingness to work collectively: it is not just Adam's innocence, but his corporate identity, that the exercise of ingenuity restored.

Benjamin Whichcote—friend of Samuel Hartlib and John Wilkins, tutor of John Wallis, and one of Locke's favorite preachers—tirelessly invoked the word, in both its spellings, to praise the "ingenuous-spirited Christian" who was prepared through a "diligent use of meanes to finde out truth." The ingenious, he explained, were "Humble and Modest" enough to "converse to mutual edification" instead of engaging in furious clashes of opinion: this modest open-mindedness provided the grounds for truth production.[135] The "Heroick Vertue of the Ingenuous," this "Ingenuity and Modesty of Nature," was the essence of man's created as opposed to his corrupted nature. The absence, in many Christians, of *this Ingenuity of Carriage* did not arise from an inbred *"Disability* of Mens Natures" due to original sin, but simply from *"their Neglect* and *Abuse"*: this aspect of human nature could be recultivated. Whichcote invoked ingenuity so often that it became a source of conflict with his former tutor, Anthony Tuckney. "I doe not fancy, as some others," Tuckney complained, "this affected word *Ingenuous;* and I wish, the thing itself were not idolized; to the prejudice of *Saving Grace.*" He went on to deplore those who "cry up ingenuity" in sermons attacking his former pupil: "all this brag *of ingenuity*" led Christians to the vainglorious belief that they could think or work their way into heaven, all the while congratulating themselves on their modesty. (Whichcote responded, as one might expect, ingenuously, expressing his innate "Modesty of Nature": "If I have done prejudice to saving grace, by idolizing natural ingenuity; the Lord reprove itt in me.") But the new "prejudice" in favor of "impartial Consideration" had spread. Wilkins insisted that it was the ingenious who were the *"truly noble."* Nobility resided in "submitting to sufficient evidence," in the modest disinterest that formed the proper state of preparation for *"the Entertainment of Truth."*[136]

In pursuit of the insights of innocence, the ingenious truth-seeker had to divest himself of the fallen preconceptions imbibed through education and custom, adhering to Glanvill's austere directive: "we must endeavour to estrange our assent from every thing."[137] Such a commitment could not be expected from most of the learned. Reporting on the burning of Milton's *Defensio* in Paris, the *Mercurius Politicus* remarked that the book was "liked and approved by the ingenuous sort of men" there; Walwyn referred *The Vanitie of the Present Churches* to "the ingenious Reader, for satisfaction of what *they call Religion among them.*"[138] Even as John Bond's sermon preached before the House of Commons proclaimed England's future as one of "ingenious *Liberty,* or Norman *Slavery . . .* according to your *standing* or *falling,*" Milton was extolling ingenuity as a "willingnesse to avouch what might be question'd, or to be better instructed" in one of his attempts to open his countrymen's minds to the high "doctrine" of divorce. Through the efforts of the ingenious, the nature of religion and institutions like marriage could now be considered as if for the first time, their foundations made newly visible as they had been manifest in the original state of creation (it is of course the marriage of Adam and Eve that is Milton's constant touchstone in the *Doctrine and Discipline of Divorce*).[139] Similarly, Cook insisted anyone with "but a dram of ingenuitie" could discern that kings were "strange creatures" not of God's making. Again and again, ingenuity is identified with the insights of innocence: with the ability—and the willingness—to dig past fallen appearances in order to bear witness to and engage the actual state of creation. In *The Readie and Easie Way*, Milton declared that "I doubt not but all ingenuous and knowing men will easily agree with me, that a free Commonwealth without single person or house of lords, is by far the best government, if it can be had"; ingenuity naturally locates freedom and what is "best" not in the "single person" but in a commons.[140]

The Royal Society's *Philosophical Transactions* would identify itself as an "ACCOMPT of the Present Undertakings, Studies, and Labours of the INGENIOUS in many considerable parts of the WORLD," but well before the Society was founded, *ingenious* had become the sobriquet by which its future members identified themselves and each other, almost like a password: in 1655 Robert Boyle wrote Hartlib about a visit to "our Ingenious Freind Dr Wilkins" at Oxford, which, since its Cromwellian purge, had become "a Knot of Such Ingenious & free Philosophers," utterly untouched by "their Predecessors failings."[141] After the Restoration, John Evelyn described a visit where he found "Dr *Wilkins*, Sir William Pettit [Petty], & Mr. *Hooke* contriving Charriots, new rigges for *ships*, a Wheele for one to run races in, & other mechanical inventions, & perhaps three such persons together were not to be found else where in Europ, for parts and ingenuity." Fans of ingenuity piously expounded the theme of the intellectual laborer's humility, but, by virtue of this humility, the ingenious laborer accrued power that a mere scholar could not hope to attain. Wilkins was certain that a device enabling humans to fly would be "easily effected by a diligent and ingenious artificer."[142]

This brings us back to the primary meaning of *ingenuity:* the receptivity to new truths was displayed most powerfully by those who involved their bodies in the process. What Evelyn called "an experienced hand & ingenuous spirit" were mutually reinforcing. Walter Blith, a one-time captain in Cromwell's army who introduced himself as "a lover of Ingenuity" on the title page of his *The English Improver Improved,* declared that England "might be made the paradise of the World, if we can but bring ingenuity into fashion." The treatise argues that God, "the Originall, and first Husbandman," had created a precedent for man, a "Paterne . . . for his incouragement," by bringing "that old Masse and Chaos of confusion into so vast an Improvement, as all the world admires, and subsists from . . . [A]fter that . . . *Adam* is sent forth to till the Earth, and improve it."[143] Such formulations fold the space of paradise into the process of improvement. Arguments built on this foundation could be used either for or against enclosure, but what all these arguments share in common is the assumption that God's "Improvement" must itself be improved: in investing the care necessary to achieve this end, the ingenious laborer—like the delving Adam—joined Christ's humility to the Creator's power.[144]

Ingenious and *ingenuous* alternate throughout the writings of Evelyn; the word, in both its forms, attaches to those who engage with what is "*Mechanically* curious and usefull" in the world, as distinct from those who "have only minded the sensuality and satisfaction of a private *Gusto.*"[145] To be ingenious for Evelyn is above all to engage the senses productively, in a curious and public rather than sensual and private manner. While distinguishing the truth producer from the mere scholar, ingenuity thus also offered a means to distinguish between innocent and carnal uses of the body. The distinction between public-spirited and selfish uses of the body is predicated on the basic opposition between created and corrupted humanity; indeed, the function of this new distinction is to make that once absolute opposition dialectical.

Although no one could mistake Evelyn for a Digger sympathizer, it is no exaggeration to say that his efforts to be ingenious were geared toward the resurrection of Adam's body in his own. Assuming the role of the ingenious gardener in his own garden, which he explicitly likened to Eden as "a place Consecrated for sober Discipline," he made an effort to turn this discipline and this place into collective possessions, using print to extend both into public space. In his *Kalendarium Hortense,* he remarks,

> As *Paradise* (though of *Gods* own *Planting*) was no longer *Paradise* then the *Man* was put into it, to *dress it and to keep it;* so, nor will our *Gardens* (as neer as we can contrive them to the resemblance of that blessed Abode) remain long in their *perfection,* unless they are also continually *cultivated.*

While such pains characterized the most "laborious life" the world had to offer, they also generated a far keener delight than that which "*Fools* derive from sensual objects." Physical without being sensual, the gardener's pains were the source of innocent pleasure.[146]

These breezy formulations conceal a complex act of conceptual integration. Throughout the 1650s Evelyn struggled to integrate Bacon's georgic paradise with the conventional notion of the original state as one in which the dressing of the garden was performed without the sweat of the brow. The field for this struggle was the rambling *Elysium Britannicum* (the source for many of his published works) whose proem is worth quoting at length:

> When Almighty God had exiled our Fore-fathers out of Paradise, the memorie of that delicious place was not yet so far obliterated, but that their early atempts sufficiently discover'd how unhappily they were to live without a Garden: And though the rest of the World were to them but a Wildernesse, and that God had destin'd them this employment for a sweete & most agreable purition of their Sinns Adam instructed his Posteritie how to handle the Spade so dextrously, that in processe of tyme, men began, with the indulgence of heaven, to recover that by Arte and Industrie, which was before produced to them Spontaneously; and to improve the Fruites of the Earth, to gratifie as well their Pleasures and contemplations, as their necessities and daily foode. for doubtlesse even in the most innocent state, though ther was no individual in itselfe imperfect, yet these perfections were to be discovered by Industry, & perhaps were not actualy existent & exerting their natures, & productions, till by his ingenuity they should afterwards be cultivated by such applications, marriages combinations & experiments as his deepe knowledge in nature should prompt him to. True it is, that it was somewhat long before they had arrived to any considerable perfection in this Arte the first and noblest part of Agriculture . . . [and] were by Contemplative men, and *Philosophers* refined to their successive improvement, and present magnificency. So that to define a Garden now, is to pronounce it *Inter Solatia humana purissimum*. A place of all terrestriall enjoyments the most resembling *Heaven,* and the best representation of our lost felicitie. It is the common Terme and the pit from whenc we were dug; We all came out of this parsly bed.[147]

We can untangle this passage by starting with its remarkably condensed final sentence: abstracted to a "common Terme," the garden assumes the functional role of Adam himself in denoting humanity's common origin. As a pit from which "we" have been dug, presumably by the delving God, the garden is the ground from which Adam was made. The sentence also suggests a link between the paradisal "pit" and the grave, perhaps the one from which Christ emerged as a gardener. There is a long tradition of images of Christ lifting Adam out of the pit of hell, and Evelyn is doing something like that here, raising up Adam together with our "lost felicitie" and planting them in an actual garden: "no phantasticall *Utopia,*" as he insists later, "but a reall place" (97). At the start of the passage, Evelyn explains that it was through the spade, handled "so dextrously" by Adam, that Adam's descendants began a "most agreable purition" of their sins and, by this means, "began . . . to recover" gifts nature once yielded without labor. But the implication that Eden was a garden of ease is unacceptable to Evelyn, so he undoes the statement: "even in the most innocent state . . . yet these perfections were to be discovered by Industry." Having already run together the pleasures of paradise with the "agreable purition" of sins through work, he now describes paradise as a place where perfection was the aim, not the starting point, of "Industry." The progressive vision of history Evelyn wants to promote could be most straightforwardly established by identifying the arts of civilization as postlapsarian developments, "not actualy existent" in Eden until "they should afterwards be cultivated," yet Evelyn cannot bear the association of the arts with sin; postlapsarian progress must therefore have been enabled "by his [Adam's] ingenuity." The labor enjoined by the curse cannot finally be distinguished from Adam's innocent labors, since its fruits are paradisal. The labor that constituted "our lost felicitie," the labor enjoined by the curse, and the progress of the arts after the fall are thus all the unfolding expression of Adam's ingenuity—a word that had become a virtual container for paradise as experimentalists were reinventing it. It is this word that enables Evelyn to present the progress of the arts just as Winstanley did: as the ongoing exfoliation of Adam's innocence.

An experimental hybrid itself, ingenuity provided the conceptual ground for the kinds of "marriages" and "experiments" that Evelyn celebrates throughout *Elysium.* Unsurprisingly, Evelyn declares that the gardener's primary qualification is that "He be of an ingenious and docile spirit, diligent and patient" (not wanting to neglect the *u,* he then extols the gardener's "experienced hand & ingenuous spirit"). As Glanvill put it in his

book addressed to "the Ingenious Reader"—the only sort who would
understand—in order to regain humanity's original power over creation,
gentlemen had to unlive their former lives, divesting themselves of the
usual markers of their social difference.[148] Evelyn conveys the anxious thrill
generated by this surrender: "We now produce the hardy Gardners Tooles.
And truely, we are not asham'd to bring them forth." He goes on to defend
himself anyway: although "possibly this may seeme a low & ignoble Subject," yet indeed "the plough is of more dignity then the Scepter" (83). This
is not merely tossed off as a georgic commonplace; Evelyn not only admon-
ishes "the *Gentlemen* of our Nation" to consider the "Title of a *Good-
Gardiner* . . . none of the least of their *Encomiums*," he proposes that those
who have "invented some usefull thing" should be immediately elevated to
the ranks of the nobility.[149]

Inevitably, "Amongst all the Instruments belonging to our Artist, the
Spade is the principall"; declaring at once the Adamic gardener's humility
and his resemblance to the Creator, the spade separates the idle noble from
the ingenious gentleman—and, by the same logic, the beast from the man
(84). The good gardener is "not as a Beast to looke and feede them [plants]
onely; but to contemplate and to applie" them. No longer a matter of mere
looking (which, lazily done, is just a form of feeding), contemplation bears
fruit in applied knowledge: "To comprehend the nature of the *Earth*, and
her productions: To be able to discourse of the *Elements* and to penetrate
into the energie and reason of things with judgment and assurance. In a
word, What is our Gardiner to be, but an absolute Philosopher!"[150] As
in Winstanley, the far-seeing, spade-wielding philosopher restores the second Adam in the form of the first. It is no accident, Evelyn goes on to explain, that Christ should have returned from the grave in a garden in the
person of a gardener; he will probably choose a similar place to "appeare
againe, & leade us from this terrestriall ~~Paradise~~ Elysium to his heavenly
~~Elysium~~ Paradise" (199; see 202). The recently published transcription of
the manuscript reveals the chiasmus underlying this celebration of "the ingenious gardener": if humanity would exert itself in the properly ingenious
spirit, the names of heaven and earth might be made into virtual synonyms. Evelyn laments the devil as a "most dreadfull adversarie of Mankind & of Gardens" because he made Adam "loose Paradise, and the innocent delights of what this chapter has so much celebrated," but since the
chapter, like every other, has described laborious delights that Evelyn has

himself enjoyed, it becomes clear that this paradise of pains was not lost at all; as in Winstanley, the state of innocence and the fall describe potentialities of the present moment. Were "due culture & Industry applied," all of England could be a restored heaven on earth, each of its citizens a "Brother of the Spade."[151] The power of work to produce a regenerate self extends well beyond the sphere of "vegetable productions," for just as gardening work is revealed to embrace everything from statuary to medicine, so reciprocally any ingenious activity can be understood in terms of the master figure of the garden, as a form of digging (69). The ingenious subject becomes functionally identical to his first representative, a permanent resident of the paradisal scene of innocent agency, now inclusive of every art and craft.

As Winstanley and Evelyn urged their contemporaries to become brothers of the spade, another ingenious truth-seeker, tried by "exercises" and in search of "experience," roamed all over England and, in doing so, found himself in "the Paradise of God."[152] From an outsider's perspective, George Fox's experiences consisted in being beaten and imprisoned for his preaching and refusal of the "hat custom" as he went from town to town. From the perspective of the estate he inhabited, however, he was restored to creation, having acquired Adam's ability to relate name to thing. Even Fox's refusal of the hat custom, which became an essential part of Quaker discipline, can be understood in these experimental terms. A means of exposing material truths behind fallen appearances, this was a public and replicable demonstration of the equality of all people as "being the Sons of Adam by nature."[153] Where others saw a church, Fox perceived a mere "steeple-house"; reciprocally, he could see the creatures as they really were: the "creation was opened up to me and it was showed to me how all things had their names given them according to their nature and virtue." Indeed, he found himself "at a stand in my mind whether I should practice physic."[154] The digging eye asserts itself again, penetrating false exteriors and excavating truth. This is a new, modern kind of perceptual transcendence, for when these surfaces fall away, what "rises up" is not a transcendent dream vision, but things themselves. This is the scene not of the soul's triumph over the body, but of the emergence of an Adamic spectatorial body. Like Evelyn's ingenious gardener, and Winstanley's naked spademen, Fox can "comprehend the nature of the *Earth*" and all of its productions because he allows "the body of the living soule" to do its work.[155] Of course, Fox's intuitive approach to knowledge production would have struck Winstanley and Evelyn, not to say Boyle, as too "imaginative" by half, and as the Quaker movement gathered strength and numbers—including, some historians think, Winstanley himself—their more idiosyncratic and enthusiastic forms of testimony were increasingly subjected to the collective discipline of consensus by the "church" of believers.[156] Creation would only be "opened up" through protocols capable of transforming private illuminations into public knowledge. This is why the "several Paradises" under construction had to take textual as well as physical form and be entered into the commons of print, where they might be "knitted together" by the public. The state of nature could only be restored by the state of England as a whole.[157]

The First and Second Adams

The test of England's identity as a Protestant nation might be said to depend on how many restorations it could produce. The myth of the English constitution was as important to this mania for restoration as England's role in the international restorative movements of Protestantism and humanism. Although the ancient constitution was often identified with "long usage," this "ancient birthright" could also overturn historical precedent by claiming earlier precedents more ancient than any written record; on this understanding, Magna Carta itself was merely a "restoring and confirming" of older liberties.[158] But just as the republic's great seal proclaimed 1649 as "the First Yeare of Freedome by God's Blessing Restored," so England's primitive freedom was reestablished once again by the restoration of monarchy in 1660. No one could afford to be against the cause of restoration: the signifier remained while its signified passed back and forth between interested parties.[159] Thomas Peyton praised James I as "A royall King derived from the race, / Of *Edens* Monarch in her greatest grace, / Within whose face true Majesty doth shine." Protecting the "*Naturall* power of Kinges" against the "Unnatural Liberty of the People," Robert Filmer's *Patriarcha* defended this inheritance of "true Majesty" despite the fact that the innocent Adam had had dominion only over the creatures, a position that uncomfortably identified the king's subjects with beasts.[160] Defenders of divine right would continue to trace monarchy back to Adam well into the eighteenth century, but they stressed the role of the second Adam in "annointing" him, as they had to. The first sovereign was safe for royal use only when Adam was understood as an individual from whom a line of inheritance could be traced. If, however, he was understood as a representative of humanity—as the doctrine of original sin and common sense demanded—he was transformed into a collective subject. If the monarch could declare himself Adam's heir, so could everybody else.[161]

The question is why so many felt compelled to do so. Clearly, there was no doctrinal necessity at work in Adam's conversion into an object of Protestant infatuation; on the contrary, it posed an inescapable theological problem. The turn to Adam was partly a reaction to the intense fixation on the body of the Son characteristic of the old religion, as if Christ's body were itself contaminated by the idolatrous worship to which it had been subjected. With the zeal of a convert, the reformed recusant John Salkeld almost seems to assign ontological priority to Adam in his *Treatise of Paradise* (which he dedicated to Bacon) when describing how God created Christ using the first man as his model. The Catholic ideal of *imitatio Christi* found its "new-model" counterpart in the ethic of *imitatio Adami*.[162] In light of the theological difficulty posed by such an ethic, however, some better explanation is needed for how this extension of the originary impulse was even possible—how, to paraphrase Tuckney, so many Protestants adopted disciplines that put them at risk of idolizing ingenuity over saving grace. Throughout the century, in fact, critics across the Protestant spectrum would thunder against the ingratitude of those who turned the first man into an idol. To such critics, Adamolatry was actually as pernicious as popery in undermining the fundamentals of Christianity. Samuel Pack spelled out these fundamentals as plainly as he could in *The Mystery of the Gospel Unvail'd: Wherein is Plainly Shewed and Proved, that the Man CHRIST JESUS has honoured all the Perfections of God more than Adam and all his Posterity could have done, had they continued in their Primitive State of Innocency;* the treatise is a reiteration of its title.[163] These critics actually bother to argue at length for the superiority of the second Adam to the first; the fact that one of them was God now had to be pointed out, the case for Christ's elevation over Adam argued on the merits. But despite complaints about contemporary efforts to "turn the *Bible* backward," Adamolatry retained its grip on the national consciousness: writing after the Restoration, John Eachard snidely remarked that "his present *Majesty* much wondred to what *Nation* he was restored, when the Rhetorical *Mayor* welcom'd him to his *Corporation* with a long Complement deriv'd from *Adam*," while his satirical character of the modish clergyman singles out the preacher who takes his preface "from *Adam*, though his business lie at the other end of the *Bible*" and who would not deliver a sermon on the Savior even if his parishioners were to bribe him.[164] Although high and low Protestants alike made efforts to remind their contemporaries of the religion to which they belonged, they were not contending with an innovation in doctrine; they were engaged in a much more nebulous struggle over the religious imagination.

But doctrine played a role, through covenant theology. Even this was less a doctrinal innovation than a ruling metaphor for understanding the states of sin and grace. Asserting what Victoria Kahn calls "the constructive power" of the contract, covenant theology replaced the traditional emphasis on the supernatural efficacy of Christ's sacrifice with an emphasis on human agency, corresponding to a new understanding of the role of the governed in the political sphere: passive assent became active consent.[165] An eagerness to disown a mechanical understanding of substitutionary atonement, in other words, coincided with a challenge to political representation as brute substitution; representation now required the participation of the represented. What I wish to stress is how this whole approach to redemption could steer devotion away from its traditional focus on the suffering of the Redeemer and toward his "original." Because of the weight placed on human agency in securing the new covenant, the labors enjoined by the state of grace were easily (if not always consciously) run together with the labors of innocence—especially because, unlike the works enjoined by the old religion, these labors were provocatively undefined. No longer the beneficiaries of grace as dispensed through the traditional ritual channels, the regenerate were actively engaged in accepting and even "improving" on it. Thus Evelyn could celebrate "A *Garden*" as "a Consecrated place, / Where the first *Covenant of Grace* / Was with our *parents made*, 'Til sinn did chace / Them hence."[166] The medieval Mary-garden saturated paradise in the imagery of Christ's sacrifice; here, the process occurs in reverse: unmoored from the redemptive sacrifice of the incarnate son, the state of grace is "paradiz'd." Evelyn, along with other aspirants to ingenuity, consented to the new covenant of grace by electing to reenter the paradise of pains.

To understand the logic behind this doctrinally unauthorized use of Adam requires us to examine more closely his identity as a public person. It was this identity that placed Adam at the very center of contemporary debates about political representation and popular sovereignty, debates that spilled into the devotional register as experimental Christians across the ideological spectrum tried to wrench new experiences out of the old doctrine of original sin. That doctrine made identification with Adam compulsory at the moment of the first disobedience; when he sinned, all of humanity sinned. Some sought to turn this compulsory identification to account, exploiting the identificatory opportunity offered by sin to see their own potential mirrored in an Adam who not only fell, but "stood (as a Parliament man doth for the whole country) for all."[167] They may have felt justified in doing so because, rather than describing original sin as an organic inheritance, theologians of all stripes were now illustrating the transfer of guilt using what would seem to be the unnecessarily cumbersome model of political representation: "*Adam* was no private person, but represented all mankinde"; he was "a publick Person," who could impart "*legal Guilt*" to those he represented.[168] Adam and Eve "must not here be *personally* considered, but as *parts* and representatives of mankind"; it was in this quasi-legal sense, Robert Harris explained, that "*We are Adam.*"[169] The concept of Adam as a public person was not new; what was new was the suggestion that original sin, a contagion by inheritance, was actually *contracted* in the primary sense, "established by mutual agreement." Anthony Burgess stressed that Adam was our representative "by way of delegation, as if we had chosen him."[170] Under the old patriarchal model, the concept of a public person carried no such implication. When James I warns his heir that "any sinne that ye commit, not being a single sinne procuring but the fall of one; but being an exemplare sinne, and therefore drawing with it the whole multitude to be guiltie of the same," there is no sense that the multitude has any agency in the transfer; the emphasis is on the responsibility of the "exemplary" person.[171] Covenant theology made the represented "multitude" an agent in the drama.

As Christopher Hill noticed long ago, it was just as "election to the House of Commons was being stressed, when constituencies were refusing to accept M.P.s nominated by their betters . . . [and] when contractual theorists were challenging Filmer's patriarchalism" that accounts of Adam's identity as a public person began increasingly to appeal not to the king but to the House of Commons.[172] Once the Adamic inheritance was inflected by the concept of consent, the limitations imposed by original sin became, as it were, elective (and in the case of a thinker like Locke, dispensable), enabling a dynamic understanding of the state of nature and the fall as potentialities of an ongoing present.[173] If *"Adam* in Paradise was but our nature personated; and we out of Paradise are but his Person multiplyed," one might choose which Adam to attempt to "personate." In identifying with Adam, one could become a public person, "one who represents, personates, and acts the part of another."[174] Taking up permanent residence in the scene of paradisal choice, one might impersonate—assume the office of—a subject equal to the rigors of innocent existence. Such efforts generated novel ways to experience the traditional doctrine of humanity's actual physical incorporation in Adam, for, even when shaped by the concept of consent, Adam's identity as a public person could not finally be separated from his substantial identity as a corporate subject.

As the analogy between Adam and Parliament itself suggests, the first sovereign was a model not just for the individual but for a community under the new covenant, such as that within which Nehemiah Wallington developed his "means to keep me from falling."[175] As the condition for representation, consent was the mechanism through which single people could be made many, and many could be made single. When the Levellers of the Army declared that they represented the people better than the "degenerate Representative Body" of the Commons, they became, in the words of a contemporary, "one Lilburne throughout."[176] Adam similarly contracts and multiplies; while Thomas Hooker suggests that the innocent Adam stood "as a Parliament man," Thomas Tuke's Adam is the entire assembled Commons, monarch included: "As the King, his Nobles, Knights and Burgesses doe represent the whole realme in the Parliament: even so did *Adam* represent the person of his whole posteritie."[177] By turns shrinking to an individual "Parliament man" and expanding into the whole assembly, Adam embodies the numerical ambiguity of representative identity itself. This ambiguity now became a feature of *intellectual* identity, and a shaper of intellectual aspirations. Just as the ingenious sought to embody the intellectual strengths of social body as a whole, so attempts to recover the epistemologically privileged view from paradise were attempts to reconstruct the perspective proper to the social body rather than the private person, to created humanity rather than the corrupt individual.

That the epistemological privilege of innocence was in part conferred by its corporate character is confirmed by the figure of the Adamite, a contemporary bogey so convinced of his own innocence that he was freed from all sense of personal shame. This contemporary (and no doubt strictly imaginary[178]) incarnation of Adam represented everything that the innocent Adam was not: as the pronounced *I* and *my* in *Adamite* proclaim, it was in his personal rather than public capacity that the Adamite identified with his original.[179] Defined by precisely the kind of identification that royalist avengers like Cleveland insisted was the only one available to corrupt humanity, the Adamite used the noble aim of paradisal restoration to sanctify fallen desire. Anti-Adamite pamphlets are uniformly concerned with the bestial lusts of these pretenders to innocence. Sometimes brandishing woodcuts of naked women and men with erections, these pamphlets self-consciously appeal to fallen salacious appetites themselves, encouraging the reader himself to "bring in the serpent." The antinomian might go naked "for a sign," to demonstrate publicly that he was clothed in the robes of righteousness; onlookers who saw only a person without any clothes could then experience their own entrapment by fallen lusts. But *The Adamites Sermon: Containing their Manner of Preaching, Expounding, and Prophesying* suggests that no such experimental demonstration is possible, or even intended; for the Adamite, to inhabit paradise is simply to be naked.[180] Introducing himself to a Brownist as "the Sonne of *Adam,* who begot me in his innocencie," the group's leader goes on to explain that he prefers to prophesy and expound scripture while naked, "that is to say, free from sin, as our Father was whilst he was naked"; his attacks on clothes as "superstitious weeds and coverings . . . ragges of ungodlinesse, and prophane Relicks of sin" suggest merely an idolatrous attachment to nudity. His favorite biblical passage to expound is of course "And they were both naked." The common charge was that whenever Adamites convened to worship, their prophesizing and testifying degenerated into orgiastic free-for-alls: John Taylor claims that "Adamites . . . labour to increase and multiply in the world . . . in their societies, they are so overcome with lust, that they cannot pray." As the plural suggests, Adamites identify Adam not with the working body of the faithful but with the carnal body of each of its members.[181] Their attempt to come together "as one" results in endless division; the splintering of the Adamic body into crowds of fornicating couples reenacts humanity's division into male and female and its descent into sensuality prior to redemption by the Son: a derangement of the *corpus verum.*

It is clear that the accusation of carnality was an attempt to discredit claims being made for a physicality grounded in work, not sex. The extension of artisanal epistemology into theological matters lent intellectual distinction, and public authority, to the wrong sort of people. In the same pamphlet, after matching the Adamite's boast of personal innocence, the Brownist adds, "Moreover, I am by trade a weaver."[182] Setting aside the joke that these worshippers of nudity work in the cloth trade, no "Moreover" could be more provocative: it suggests that membership in the trades is a sign of worth on par with, and possibly greater than, the distinction of being Adam's prelapsarian son. The word gestures toward the existence of an entire underground in which the normal signs of worth and status are either ignored or inverted. Adamites inhabit an entirely different world; what most would read as bathos, they see the opposite way. The Adamite gains a convert in his new acquaintance, moreover, on the basis of their shared contempt for the written word; the idolatry of church worship, they agree, extends to the alphabet in hornbooks, both linked by the sign of the cross (3). These artisans cultivate a religiosity based on a different kind of literacy, deriving their representation of paradise not from books or windows but directly from their own experiences in Marylebone park.

The descriptions of the Adamites' nudity and uninhibited sexuality are spiked with a predictable mixture of revulsion and envy, but they register the Adamite's freedom from fallen hierarchies with less legible emotions, documenting the existence of a new set of intellectual priorities in a class that had never been identified with having any at all. Of course, the Adamites' claim to an alternative, experiential literacy is swiftly made ridiculous; these figures are not permitted to engage in the work by which they proudly identify themselves (and as a result this work can never be integrated into the paradisal image repertoire they construct). Given the aim of Adamite satire, this is a necessary omission. The threat of the ingenious collectivity can only be neutralized if the labor with which it is associated degenerates into a "labour to increase."[183] Physical productivity must be despised under the sign of carnal reproduction; the serpent must be brought in through the sensuality that the ingenious, at least, explicitly excluded from the paradise of pains. The concept of labor had become so interwoven with the concept of the regenerate life that no attempt to satirize paradise fever could afford to depict its protagonists at work. When imagined as a paradise of carnal delights, the garden was the province of the fallen. Imagined as a site of labor, the garden inexorably became Edenic: a field for the productive and collective exercise of ingenuity.

Just as the corporate person of ingenuity was not invoked every time Adam was mentioned, so this corporate person did not always brandish the proper name Adam. Some writers derided "the pompous vanity of the first creation" in what can only be considered a Winstanleyan spirit—as a means to protect the growth of ingenuous and ingenious collectives. The army chaplain and alchemical dabbler Henry Pinnell, for example, offered his countrymen *A Word of Prophesy, Concerning the Parliament, Generall, and the Army. With A Little of the First Adam* in order to remedy "confusions that are in the world, or in your owne heart, concerning the first *Adam.*" Pinnell was specifically determined to refute the doctrine that Adam was *"at first endowed with a spirituall understanding, knowledge, righteousnesse, holinesse, and every way like God, Immutability only excepted; for he knew the nature, property, and use of every thing, and was able to give names to every creature."*[184] If this were the case, Pinnell argues, a believer who put off the old man and put on the new could hope for nothing more than to become *"the first* Adam *recovered from his fall, and reduced to his pristine and primitive state"*—a "Naturall Jew." As it turns out, however, what Pinnell most resents is the image of an Adam who was passively endowed with divine knowledge: an Adam deprived of ingenuity. Moreover, because Pinnell understands Adam's naming of the creatures as a *linguistic* feat, he treats Genesis 2:19 as a paradigm of what he calls "humane learning," the learning of the universities, the province of those "who live and lurke like Dorres and Drones in a Common-wealth, without care and calling and have no cloake or covering for their sloth and idlenesse." In exemplary contrast to the university drones who simply *inherit* knowledge as a legacy are those who invest care in producing it: the "active and industrious" sort, whose way of life makes them less afraid than literate men to bring questions to "open tryall." "To deal plainly and ingeniously with you, when I was under the teaching of men I got more from simple countrey people, husband-men, weavers, &c." Having followed the example of such ingenious men and subjected himself to the rigors of experience, he is no longer "under the teaching" of any man.[185] Such independence from authority, if multiplied across individuals, could serve as the basis of a different kind of godly community, organized around the open-ended cultivation of experience.

Pinnell makes the possession of grace indistinguishable from the active exercise of ingenuity, so that it almost ceases to matter which of the two Adams is invoked to sponsor it. The new man Pinnell urges us to put on, in other words, resembles the first man as Winstanley had reinvented him, and even as the Fellows of the Royal Society would try to embody him.[186] The Society's motto "nullius in verba," from Horace's First Epistle, employed Latin learning against the schools, and against the authority of Aristotle in particular: "And lest by chance you ask by which leader, by which household god I am sheltered, I, bound to swear according to the words of no master, am carried off as a guest, whithersoever the storm takes me."[187] So was Pinnell; *A Word of Prophesy* records how God "pursued me with a strong winde," raising "a continuall tempest in, and round about me"; the tempest drove him from London to Windsor, landing him at Cromwell's door. There, and in the pamphlet that testified to the meeting, he "layd down nothing but my experiences" (3, 73). In rehearsing how he was "carried off as a guest" by the tempests of experience, Pinnell provides a model—an "occasion"—for others eager to learn how to "exercise" their faith. He opposes this experimental faith, in which, "every dayes experience" should bring fuller "testimony" of truth, to the undemanding religious discipline of those who "finde a little plaine, smooth, faire-promising plat of ground in the first *Adam*, and they dwell there" (13, sig. A4ᵛ). But the experimentalist effort to restore the insights of innocence did not dwell in an idolatrous fixation on the first man. Like Pinnell, those who sought to recover these insights did not seek to restore paradise as a place of rest, but rather as a range of processes designed to produce experiences, more occasions for care.

To readers worried that such open-ended pursuit of experience in search of the truth would result in the overturning of all social order, Pinnell had this response:

These may goe to the plow-man for their answer and satisfaction: He will tell them that by the continuall motion of his Cart and Plow wheeles, he hath his businesse done, whereas if they stood still, he could have no seed sowne, no crop reaped, nor any profit at all made of his land; yet in the revolution of the wheel, no spoke therein is always fixed either upward or downward . . . the spirit of life within keeps this wheele in motion: God will have his people make a progresse; He will carry them from dispensation to dispensation; from strength to strength, and never let them stand still (in any forme) till they appear in the perfection and beauty of the Spirit. (sig. A6)

The Langlandian plowman getting "his businesse done" becomes an exemplum for the whole nation. The "spirit of life" is captured in the movement of his cart and plow; by perpetually returning to their starting point, the wheels move the vehicle, and his labor, forward. Revolution, a constant turning back to the first point, is the very mechanism of progress.[188]

The at once originary and progressive vision of time embodied by Pinnell's plowman was, as John Bradshaw said of the ancient constitution, no new thing: it is expressed by the traditional craft idea of maker's knowledge as cumulative, with each pupil attempting to improve upon the technique taught him by his master as he turns back to its source in the materials, a process of progressive return that moves the arts forward.[189] The realm of *techne* has always depended on the "disposition of the subject . . . to take part in a process that generates knowledge in a transsubjective manner" that Hans Blumenberg identifies with modern science. The iterability of the artisanal secret would become the Baconian standard for "public" knowledge; replicability provided the conditions for progressive refinement. Bacon complained that philosophy and science "stand like statues, worshipped and celebrated, but not moved or advanced . . . In the mechanical arts we do not find it so; they, on the contrary, as having in them some breath of life, are continually growing and becoming more perfect."[190] The generalization of craftsman's time to society as a whole is what enabled the renunciation of "anthropological egoism" that underlies the modern scientific project, understood as an investment of human energy in a necessarily imperfect and accretional activity whose ultimate goal—complete understanding of the natural world—no individual participant will survive to reach.[191] In joining "a progress" that stretched beyond any individual life, seventeenth-century promoters of ingenuity helped give birth to the collective subject of science, a massive subject that adheres to no particular perspective, time, or place, but aspires to all. Cook declared that "when the wheels of Reformation are well oyled, and in a true motion, no man thinks himselfe a looser, though he suffer in his particular, because the publique is a gainer." It was by putting his shoulder to the wheel that the ingenious subject expanded beyond "his particular" and participated in the representative identity of his original. Adamic ingenuity and representativeness

implied one another, the former providing the basis for the latter. By producing testimonies of experimental knowledge, intellectual laborers declared
their independence from "selfe ends" and their membership in a corporate
agent of progress or "improvement," a word that was just beginning to
move beyond its primary association with the land, following the lead of all
those working to extend the labors of innocence to new grounds.[192]

It might be asked how the doctrine of predestination fit into this ongoing spectacle of human effort. In what R. T. Kendall calls the "experimental predestinarian tradition" believers had to infer their possession of grace
from the activities they undertook; even antinomians like John Eaton believed that the justification accompanying conversion initiated a process of
sanctification that testified to the change. As Weber argued long ago, the
doctrine created an incentive to fix the evidence, to produce the testimonies.[193] But Weberian accounts of the Protestant work ethic have perhaps
overemphasized the merely probative value of works as indications of regeneration rather than its mechanism. It is not merely that such a distinction
was difficult to observe in practice, although this was certainly the case. In
keeping with the old joke that the pressures of pastoral care turn Calvinists
into pulpit-Arminians, by the end of the century bishops and dissenters
alike were essentially preaching a theology of works (and, as David Como
has shown, repeatedly inviting the antinomian challenge in the process).[194]
But, given that predestinarian theology was rejected by some sectarians as
far back as the sixteenth century (conventiclers in Bocking and Faversham,
for example, called predestination a "doctryne . . . for divilles"), it might be
that the habits under consideration here owe little to strict Reformed orthodoxy.[195] Paul Seaver has suggested that "preparationist thought" as elaborated by such divines as Thomas Hooker had in any event largely "eroded
orthodox predestinarianism among the laity by the 1640s." Indeed, as Tim
Cooper observes, divines like Richard Baxter "constantly employed the
nickname of Antinomian or Libertine to describe what was really the doctrine of justification by faith alone without works." The figure of the Adamite was an ideal symbol of the dangerous temptations lurking in the
doctrine of justification by faith alone; his negative example helped to assert
the compulsory status of work in the regenerate life. At the same time, the
Adamite's idolatrous relationship to the particular (and easily performed)
work of being naked also provided a handy caricature of the old belief in
salvation through works. It was the habit of gauging one's spiritual status

by the accomplishment of *particular* works that, more than anything, hindered the endless work of faith.[196]

The trend I am trying to track thus cannot be reduced to an enthusiasm for the person of Adam, or even to his use as an object of devotional identification. The Adam of George Herbert's "The H. Communion" who "did not know / To sinne," for example, offers precisely the kind of identificatory opportunity that the ingenious rejected, for it was only as long as his state of enchanted ignorance held that Herbert's Adam "might to heav'n from Paradise go, / As from one room t'another" (lines 33–36). In Herbert's construction of the state of innocence, paradise and heaven are different rooms in a continuous domestic space which, no matter how literally expansive, could not be more snug; an Adam characterized by what he does not know does not have to "smother" sin because he is enclosed by his own limits. Although humanity could not remain swaddled in this infant state forever, Herbert suggests that we have been "restor'd . . . to this ease" by Christ's sacrifice (lines 34, 37). Remade into a humble beneficiary of a mystery beyond rational understanding, humanity is returned to a state of dependency, characterized by the surrender rather than the exercise of reason or choice. "Inclose me," Herbert begs in "Paradise"; the poem's iconic shape seems to suggest that paradise could not be imagined any other way.[197] Such a construction of the first state produces little of the "confusion about Adam" to which Pinnell addresses himself; such confusion is proper only to a culture in which the concept of the earthly paradise is losing its enclosing wall.

Contemporary visual representations of Eden are characterized by broad, expansive spaces, almost inviting groups like the Diggers to step into the open "commons." No longer a fenced-in garden defended from the world, the Eden depicted on the title page of the apothecary and gardener John Parkinson's *Paradisi in Sole Paradisus Terrestris or A Garden of all sorts of Pleasant Flowers which our English Ayre will Permitt to be Noursed Up* reveals a riot of flora and fauna from both the old and new worlds, with sunflowers and cyclamen as tall as Adam and Eve themselves. Rather than flanking the tree of knowledge, Adam and Eve are busily engaged on opposite sides of the garden: under the eyes of an approving parrot, Adam shakes fruit from a tree as Eve leans over to pick a flower, and what look like snakes curling up the trees turn out, on closer inspection, to be vines.[198] No "little plat of ground," the paradise pictured in Joseph Fletcher's *Historie of the Perfect-Cursed-Blessed Man* is a teeming safari park.[199] The unrecognizable image repertoire of paradise is the most powerful evidence of its restoration: "opening up" to the eyes and hands of its sovereign, creation was once again a place of discovery.[200]

We can gauge how far the culture had drifted from conventional devotional uses of Adam by comparing attitudes toward the substance from which he was made. In Donne's sermons, the redness of the earth

> amounts to a shamefastnesse, to a blushing at our own infirmities . . . imprinted in us, by Gods hand. For this rednesse, is but a conscience, a guiltinesse of needing a continuall supply, and succession of more, and more grace. And we are all red, red so, even from the beginning, and in our best state.

In "being earth, we are equall," but this equality is one of sin: "that was all *Adams* patrimony, all that he could give."[201] Ingenuity transformed this blushing earth into unembarrassed paradisal ground. Describing how he often "us'd a spade in a Garden" to chase away "that Grand Beel-zebub of Idlenesse," Boyle explained that through this "Corperiall Employment," he enjoyed the satisfactions God had bestowed on Adam "as a Part of his Deliht in Paradise": "our first Father ev'n in Paradise it selfe, had Handywork enjoyn'd him in that Comand hee receav'd to till that Ground of which he was compos'd." Like Boyle's, Adam's body was created outside of the garden; but when sanctified by innocent labor, it became the very ground of "Paradise it selfe."[202] Regarded as an attribute, not of a lost place or a time, but of a regenerate laborer in the making, paradise had begun its journey into the present.

Festival and the Ground of True Religion

However novel, this particular devotional use of Adam had long roots. As I have suggested, the idea of the working life as an ongoing sacrament of production can be traced all the way back to the medieval calendar tradition. By the seventeenth century, however, the demands of production overran the calendar itself.[203] As seasonal production was subjected to the linear logic of improvement, and the meaning of improvement was itself extended to the progressive cultivation of creation in all its forms, production followed suit to become the ruling figure for intellectual life. Truth production was a labor so incessantly demanding, and indiscriminately demanded, as to require the elimination of the festival year and all the "sports" traditionally associated with it. Patrick Collinson finds "few events of more importance between the Middle Ages and modern times" than the attack on seasonal festivities, which represented the "obliteration of the established rhythm of life itself."[204] I would like to explore this attack not merely as a negative campaign but as a positive one, as an effort to reform Christian community into a public: a corporate body consecrated to the progressive (and crucially vague) labor of cultivating truth. What I am calling a campaign was as much a "bottom-up" phenomenon as it was a program of indoctrination that had begun with the so-called complaint literature of the sixteenth century—for, by the seventeenth century, "popular" festivity had itself become a largely "top-down" affair.[205]

In the cheap printed books of hours of the late fifteenth century, stuffed as they are with material having nothing to do with the festival year—practical knowledge like recipes, along with idealized images of people putting such knowledge to use—Eamon Duffy glimpses the beginnings of a "'bourgeoisification' of time . . . the smoothing and regulating process which would ultimately seek to abolish the festival calendar altogether in favour of the regular weekly observance of the sabbath." Duffy's terminology implies that the loss of distinction between days correlates with a regrettable loss of *social* forms of distinction.[206] Seventeenth-century critics were less oblique. In his defense of festival pastimes, John Howson described "the meanes which God useth in advancing some daies before their fellows" in explicitly social terms:

> God hath dealt with daies as with men: for men are al of the ground, and Adam was created out of the earth, but the Lord hath distinguished them by great knowledge, & made their waies & reputations diverse: some of them hath he blessed and exalted, as kinges and princes: & some of them he hath sanctified, and appropriated to himselfe, as Prophets and Priestes: but some hee hath cursed and brought lowe, and put them in meane estate, and place of base calling.[207]

Although Howson goes on to make further distinctions, mapping high and lower feasts onto the greater and lesser nobility, his basic strategy is to fold his defense of festival into a defense of the three estates, a construct uneasily erected on the common "ground" of the undifferentiated material of which time and humanity are made. Although "men are al of the ground, and Adam was created out of the earth," their callings and reputations vary; so with days, and the levelling of one threatens to result in the levelling of the other. It is not immediately obvious what these two forms of distinction have to do with each other, but Howson soon makes the motivation behind his analogy clear. The sermon is directed at the industrious sort, born to bear the burden of the curse ("cursed and brought lowe"), who not only refuse to give festival days the recognition they deserve but celebrate the Sabbath incorrectly. Seeking to make Sabbath observance an "exercise," they "gad up & downe to heare the word preached"; pretending to turn "Churches into Schooles," they reveal their basic incomprehension of the very nature of worship, which is a "vertue morall, & not intellectual." Although the topic of Howson's sermon is the distinction between days, its *aim* is to maintain the distinction that kept the industrious sort from gadding about in the realm of learning, attempting to gain a "reputation" of "great knowledge" from which their callings disqualified them. Charles I's campaign to legislate a Merry England into existence had much the same motivation; the main appeal of the activities he defended against Puritan criticisms—"jolly pastimes" like dancing, bear-baiting, and shin-kicking contests—was that they excluded others.[208]

So cleverly did the defenders of state-enforced sport weave their defense of "honest recreations" into an anti-Sabbatarian agenda that it has taken scholars centuries to untangle the two. Although scholars were long persuaded that Puritans were strangely attached to Sabbath observance (with some going so far as to call Sabbatarianism a "Puritan invention"), Kenneth Parker has demonstrated that Puritans calling for stricter Sabbath observance were simply representing the mainstream Protestant, and even the mainstream medieval Christian, position. In the late sixteenth and early seventeenth centuries, Parliament was almost unanimously in favor of stricter Sabbath observance; it was not until the 1630s that an "anti-sabbatarian campaign was launched by a small group of Laudians."[209] This stands to reason, since it was clearly not the *fact* of Sabbath observance but its changing nature—its metamorphosis into a "vertue . . . intellectual"—that explains Laud's simultaneous insistence that the Sabbath be observed less "precisely," and that holidays be more strictly observed through the playing of games. As Bishop William Piers fretted in a letter to Laud, with the decline of "honest and lawfull recreations," parishioners "would goe either into tipling houses, and there upon their ale-benches talk of matters of the church or state; or els into conventicles." Laudian criteria for what constituted a conventicle were not exacting. Almost any independent gathering that fell outside the canons of "good fellowship" fell under suspicion, especially those organized around what Thomas Hall pointedly called "good conference."[210]

What worried many observers was that strict Sabbath observance in its newfangled "intellectual" form was spilling into the workweek. Put differently, people's callings were no longer filled by their jobs; they had additional work to do. "Exercises" and "prophesyings," for example, which had started out as closed, clerical exercises, had evolved into public "combination lectures," which Collinson describes as "a kind of open university"; and, by the mid-seventeenth century, "prophesying" assumed forms that its early facilitators could never have imagined.[211] At the end of the century, the Royal Society Fellow John Wallis looked back proudly on the "numerous auditory" drawn to his father's "Week-day Lecture" on market-day. (Reciprocally, William Cavendish told Charles II that lectureships had been "one off the greateste Causes off our Late Miseries."[212]) Sermons and lectures had become what Susan Brigden calls a "popular spectator sport" for youths; local authorities were particularly worried about the participation of apprentices in the "contraversy" lectures generated. Naturally, their expressions of concern seized on the threat of social disorder, but the toleration extended to rowdy festival sports suggests that the perceived threat posed by these crowds lay in their hankering for controversy itself. This appetite was the inevitable result of the godly's refusal of Howson's distinction between worship and intellectual exercise. John Earle's character of the "She precise Hypocrite" who finds "the Weeke dayes Exercise farre more edyfying then the Sundayes" because they offer occasion for "Gossipings" is only a hypocrite from the perspective of one who identifies genuine worship with the administration of the sacraments rather than with the discoveries facilitated by public speech.[213]

Baxter saw evidence of the Reformation's success in the fact that the "poor men" of his parish at Kidderminster now "did competently understand the body of divinity, and were able to judge in difficult controversies." Identified with the spread of knowledge, the progress of reformation was the strongest evidence that history was moving forward; it was this palpable sense of a progress underway—"a perennial source of perpetual motion to something yet to come"—that served as Evelyn's ultimate proof of God's existence.[214] Such a conviction jarred against a very different experience of time promoted by the festival calendar. The work of scholars such as Ronald Hutton and Leah Marcus has shown us how deeply the traditional Christian calendar impressed a cyclical pattern of seasonal festivity on daily life; well into the early modern period, Christianity was "lived as a cosmic liturgy."[215] An experience of religion as an eternal repetition of ritual observances had been linked for most people to the boon of periodic respites from labor: maypoles and bonfires during Midsummer, fiddling and dancing at Candlemas, football at Shrovetide, and so on. As moralists from William Prynne to Henry Oldenburg liked to point out, many Christian festivals were survivals of pagan celebrations of the divinity incarnated in cosmic rhythms or objects, the sacred dimension of vegetation and other theophanies of nature—in other words, relics of idolatry.[216] Whether such critics were correct in producing pagan precursors for every festival, they were certainly correct in their assessment that festivity was implicated in the old religion's sacramental character, which Charles and Laud hoped to sustain in the reformed church.[217] Baptism, marriage, and final absolution had been predictable markers of the stages of the individual life story, while the sacrament of confession imposed on the individual's daily life a cyclical rhythm of sin, repentance, atonement, and release followed by renewed sin, which Weber described as promoting a "hand to mouth" spiritual existence that replicated the subsistence rhythms of traditional agrarian society itself.[218]

Fortification for these cycles of sin and repentance came in the accumulation and periodic discharge of energy in "festival liberties." As Marcus has shown, these were treated by their supporters and detractors alike as virtual extensions of church ceremony. Against mounting popular criticism, James I defended these recreations in his 1618 *Declaration to His Subjects, concerning lawfull Sports to be used on the Sabbath Day*, which was reissued by Charles I in 1633; clergymen were instructed to read the King's Book of Sports, as it came to be known, to their parishioners.[219] When the speaker of Robert Herrick's "Corinna's Going A-Maying" urges Corinna to "obey / The proclamation for May," he is alluding to the Book of Sports, which made it "a sin" not to "take the harmless folly of the time."[220] As the very existence of this royal "proclamation" suggests, royal and ecclesiastical powers were relying on traditional holiday pastimes as a mechanism of repressive desublimation to keep some semblance of the old order together. It is no accident that Milton's Comus identifies festival riot with "the canon laws of our foundation"; as Cavendish put it to the king, "wee feaste In our Defense."[221]

Among the "common opinions" that William Perkins held responsible for hindering reformation was the belief that "drinking and bezeling in the ale-house or taverne is good fellowship, & shews a good kinde nature."[222] Ale-drinking is what one is free to do when not at work, and it figured heavily in the Laudian attempt to decouple Christian fellowship from intellectual labor. Aubrey's observation that in Yorkshire it was the "custom for the Parishioners after receiving the Sacrament, to goe from the Church directly to the Ale Hous and there drink together" is a concise expression of the link between sacramentalism and so-called alebench Anglicanism: the image of the faithful washing down the host with ale suggests that the moment of communion can only be extended through further consumption.[223] Festival days were often used to make collections for the maintenance of church buildings through church ales or "Whitson-ales"; it was perhaps in honor of such an occasion that Herrick taught his pig to drink out of a tankard.[224] The church house, where ales were often held, was sometimes sold off for funds and transformed into an actual alehouse, literalizing the link between church and ale; and in the aftermath of attacks on church-oriented games and rituals, the alehouse developed as a rival center for festivities, where critics argued their true nature was revealed; supporters of the Book of Sports actually concurred with this diagnosis.[225] These passionate defenses of "the king's laws" are also the most cynical, inviting comparison with Hobbes's defense of a state religion or our own "steam valve" explanations of festival. As Herrick put it with his inimitably malignant sentimentality, "the anger ends all here, / Drencht in Ale, or drown'd in Beere." Marcus observes that Herrick's concept of mirth is inextricable from "the 'drowning' of individual consciousness"; I suggest that what Herrick symbolically drowns in beer is also a *public* consciousness, and the work required to achieve it.[226] Good conference offered opportunities for self-cultivation as a public person that good fellowship did not.

To blame the commercialization of leisure on the Puritan suppression of traditional festive culture is to overlook the fact that fiddlers, players, and bull- and bear-baiters made a brisk business from the "good fellowship" they brought to different parishes. Money changed hands at church ales; that is why they were held. At wakes and ales, as Herrick put it, "the businesse is the sport."[227] Much less were festivals occasions for the spontaneous overflow of good fellowship and "neighborliness"; Thomas Hall pointed to events in his own parish as testimony to the truth of the "common saying" that "'tis *no festival unless there bee some fightings*."[228] Cavendish described the purpose of festival pastimes as keeping the industrious sort "In harmles action," but he did not mind them harming each other. The traditional relaxing of punishments for assault on holidays was in response to an expectation. When May Day celebrations broke out in Halifax after the Restoration, it was not simply a killjoy spirit that led Oliver Heywood to lament that "hell is broke loose."[229] As Žižek observes, it is the conformist who periodically feels like an outlaw, in obedience to the superegoic command to enjoy himself; such conformity was often perhaps *most* on display during those occasions when festival liberty escalated into violence. When confronted with London riots during the May of 1640, Lord Conway dismissed them as a harmless overflow of festival liberty: "the prentices will make but a Shrove Tuesday business of it."[230] But throughout the century, the king repeatedly commanded the people to enjoy themselves, and many refused.

Some festival "rioting" could challenge the naturalizing power of festivity by retaining a deliberate focus on the work that filled the year between holidays. The eucharistic ceremony staged at St. Albans was an attempt to restore a prehistoric liberty before custom, and perhaps it produced a countertradition of its own: Jack Cade's Rebellion also broke out during the Whitsun holidays. The Inns of Court were notoriously rowdy during the Christmas holidays, but during the legitimized disorder of the Twelve Days in 1516, Lincoln's Inn would not tolerate, even in jest, a reveller who called himself "Jack Straw," who was prohibited from entering the premises again.[231] Rather than feeling like outlaws as the spirit of festival demanded, some rioters took the opportunity afforded by festival not to escape the demands of work but to assert their demands as workers, honoring those who had done so before them with a citation. In their provocatively innocent and nonviolent "acting with plow and spade," the Diggers did the same, referring their activities at once to a distant past and an imminent future.

Winstanley compared the agents who destroyed the Diggers' crops to "hollowing and shouting" good fellows "dancing at a whitson Ale . . . that they might hinder the work of freedome."[232] If the Diggers' activities were informed by a positive vision of a society in which labor was a celebration that obviated holiday, so were early modern denunciations of festival. Often represented as prigs and curmudgeons, critics of festival bear eloquent testimony not just to a horror of disorder but to a fervently held alternative model of sociability. Exerting interpretive pressure on the discourse used by defenders of "good fellowship, as they call it"—the contemporary equivalent of scare quotes, the phrase "as they call it" (or "as they term it") is a constant refrain in the literature—such critics offered their countrymen an opportunity to inspect the discourse on which they were raised with alien eyes. A Mrs. Yarde of Wells, offended by a maypole that had been erected in front of her church, explained her absence from services with the comment that "shee could not goe to the Churche" because "the paynted caulf stoode in her waye." She saw something different than many of her neighbors did, and although her perspective exposed her to mockery (good fellows "would cry ba, like a Calf" at her door), her vision was not an idiosyncratic one; it was the result of an effort to *see through*, undertaken with the help of others.[233]

John Northbrooke called attention to the general insult contained in the very word *pastime;* the idea that one's allotted time was simply to be lived or passed through rather than progressively used was actually a means of "restrayning men," a strategy to "traine up the people in ignorance and idlenesse." Although, as many have observed, there is a palpable concern with getting people back to work in this literature, such industry could take many forms. Attacks on "exercises" in fact leaned heavily on the accusation that people were neglecting their callings, by which they meant their jobs; the insistence with which critics of festival harp on the theme of ignorance, in contrast, suggests an interest in a kind of labor that goes well beyond putting in a day's work.[234]

Hugh Roberts, minister of Aberffraw, urged his parishioners "by reading & exercise [to] seeke the ground of true religion." He described with approval how the conventiclers under Mary's reign made a habit of "assembling together at co[n]venient times in woodes and solitarie places" to bear witness to one another about their experiences—these were "witnesses for our example." It was Satan who said "let not artificers, husbandmen, and menne without learning, busie themselves with holy scriptures, and with matters of faith and religion"; God, in contrast, was "no accepter of persons."

In fact, "what calling, what trade of life, or what condition soever we be of," each person had the responsibility to shoulder the "duetie of mutuall exhortation . . . that none might perish for lacke of knowledge." Appealing to his parishioners as potential knowledge producers, he asked them to engage in the mutually sustaining—and endlessly sustainable—calling of articulating and refining their beliefs. Rather than manifesting itself as assent to doctrine or through ritual participation, faith is the infinitely receding goal of the search for "the ground of true religion," a collective work of uncovering and cultivating "the ground." Roberts presented himself as a fellow worker in this ongoing labor, describing his pamphlet as an "exercise" undertaken by one of God's "workmen that neede not to be ashamed."[235]

Roberts explained that it was not enough merely to undergo baptism, like one's fathers: we are "ingrafted into his [Christ's] misticall body according to the meaning of our baptism" (50). Optimistically scolding the older members of his congregation because they had "not yet learned" this meaning (35, misnumbered as 36), he urged his parishioners not only to attend his sermons and read scripture but to exhort *each other* so that all could be "*made partakers* of all the merits of Christ," "*annexed with Christ*" and "made *one flesh*" with Christ—and to partake of "his innocency": only when transformed into the occasion for mutual edification does the sacrament truly become operative, effecting the mystical union (50–51). In place of the concept of a mystical body that connected the living to the dead through ritual, "custom," and "long usage," Roberts offers an image of the mystical body as a body under construction, a body not merely constituted by its members but actively improved by them: a body at work on itself, like Boyle's Adam, tilling the soil from which he was made. The attempt to see the subject of innocence in the figure of the worker goes back for centuries, as does the notion of the mystical body as a working collective. But the work that Roberts enjoins is now a progressive undertaking; it is the work of truth production. This is why defenses of festival that "alleadge antiquity, & custome" incensed him. In his attack on May games as a "custom of sin," it soon becomes apparent that this custom is sinful simply because it *is* a custom: jolly pastimes literally trapped parishioners in past times (sigs. K5ᵛ, A2ᵛ). "There is nothinge so common," he scoffs, as praise of "*forefathers,* and of the dayes that are past; as it were inough for us, if we could but follow the example of our *fathers;* never examining how they beleeved . . . examples of *fathers* can be no ground."[236] Real primitive truths were discovered, not inherited: although papists appealed to "the multitude of people, and nations, which have followed the church of Rome, and receyved their traditions," this very fact "proveth not the truth to be of their side, but rather the contrarie" (17). The very continuity of the old religion exposes its unfitness to sustain the labor of a properly functioning mystical body. Roberts presents the old religion much the way Bacon described scholasticism, as a monolith; the supposed lack of any radical alterations in its substance, offered by papists as proof of its strength, was in fact proof of its weakness; it was unfit to "make a progresse."

When the residents of Stafford converted their maypole into fire-fighting ladders, or when the residents of Bury transformed part of St. James Church into a library for communal use, they established community in the destruction of custom.[237] Under the direction of John White, the godly town of Dorchester organized a cooperative brewing operation to fund systems of charitable giving, education, and vocational training. This miracle of ingenuity, a true sacrament of production, transubstantiated ale itself into an instrument of improvement. David Underdown has explored this experiment in relation to an emergent ideal of "a different kind of community . . . united by belief and mission, sometimes formally by covenant in a 'gathered church', as a substitute for the territorial parish community."[238] Such communities were defined by the investment of human energy toward the all-embracing goal of reformation. The very vagueness of the aim linked the "callings" that defined these communities to "the unelected vocation" described by Sidney: intellectual labor is the kind of work that resists definition, whose rules one must make up as one goes. It is also work with no natural end. The search for the meaning of one's baptism can start anywhere, but it can never stop.

Roberts's insistence that, in subjecting the beliefs of one's fathers to critical scrutiny, one must examine *how* they believed lays the groundwork for a procedural definition of heresy as obedience to authority, a resistance to undertaking the work of truth production.[239] Such work was described in increasingly Baconian terms. Stephen Denison suggested that those who had no "peace of conscience" about their election were suffering because of their exclusion from this productive labor: "It is because they do not grow and increase in saving knowledge: for if they grew in knowledge, they should also grow in all other graces. Knowledge is the first wheele in this clocke, it moveth all the rest . . . we must take great paines in seeking of it, and in digging for it."[240] The wheel (now capable of moving other wheels) comes together with the spade to cultivate "graces"; although grace is prudently put in the plural, the state of grace is clearly being run together with the labors of ingenuity. For Denison insisted that simply reading the Bible did not qualify as true productive labor: since "the grounds and principles of true religion" had to be empirically grounded, it was necessary to "labour that your knowledge in Religion may be experimentall." No one, he explained, ever mistook the color of snow for black; to attain a similar degree of certainty in matters of faith, the godly had to contrive new experiences to submit their beliefs to trial, and perhaps to develop new ones: they had to conduct experiments to transform their faith into knowledge.[241] Like artisanal knowledge, "true knowledge of Christ" was, as Thomas Taylor insisted, *"experimentall,"* not acquired "out of books . . . but by experience."[242]

The effort to integrate the principle of *sola scriptura* with artisanal epistemology, with its associated contempt for book learning, inevitably bred tensions, but, as the case of John Bunyan shows, they were quite manageable ones. In the opening of *Grace Abounding,* Bunyan seems almost embarrassed by the fact of his literacy, insisting that although his parents taught him to read and write, "I did soon loose that little I learned, even almost utterly, and that long before the Lord did work his gracious work of conversion upon my Soul."[243] Since any notional textman can read, he rarely describes himself doing so; instead, he bears witness to physical encounters with the incarnate word—moments at which a scriptural passage claps him on the back and so forth.[244] Those who opened themselves up to such experience could "speak of the things of the Law, and of the Gospel, experimentally," and he urged his readers to experience the truths to which he testified for themselves: "these things . . . do absolutely concern thee to know, and that experimentally too."[245] In the absence of such active cultivation on the grounds of one's daily life—in the "Close, the Milk-house, the Stable, the Barn, and the like"—scripture was "but babbling."[246] By virtue of his strenuously cultivated experimental expertise, Bunyan even develops a remarkable ability to "predict" scriptural passages long before he encounters them as a reader.[247]

Bunyan's mentor Mr. Gifford "pressed us to take special heed, that we took not up any truth upon trust, as from this or that or another man or men, but to cry mightily to God, that he would convince us of the reality thereof," but a solitary sifting of the word was not sufficient (117). Experience had to be cultivated collectively; Bunyan's experience of the word required a commons in which to unfold itself.[248] Thus it is only after Bunyan has encountered members of the Bedford congregation—the "three or four poor women sitting at a door in the Sun, and talking about the things of God"—that the door of the gospels is opened to him.[249] He came upon these congregants when "the good providence of God did cast me to *Bedford,* to work on my calling"; it is when he enters into this collective that another calling—that of a preacher, and more broadly, an intellectual laborer—becomes available to him (37).

Experimentalist protocols could thus be applied to Bible study itself. John Goodwin appealed directly to Bacon's interpretation of Daniel 12:4 ("many shall go to and fro, and knowledge shall be increased") in support of an artisanal approach to the works of faith. Just as "the visible world" had been expanded by modern discoveries, so the Bible was a *terra incognita* waiting to be mapped: there was an "unknown abysse of truth there." Those who testified and prophesized needed to be evaluated by a new standard: whether they made "som new discoverie," or were content merely to dwell in "common and received truths." The author of *A Glimpse of Sions Glory* adds an intervening step to the biblical passage: "many shall runne to and fro, and take paines in finding it out, and Knowledge shall be increased"; a greater willingness to take pains itself becomes the object of excited prophecy.[250] These formulations do not just figure devotion as artisanal labor; they are attempts to redefine it, as Bacon redefined philosophy, according to the model that such labor provides.

To understand how the subordination of custom to painful progress played out on the national scale, it is instructive to consider what holidays the Commonwealth did permit. In addition to the Sabbath and a monthly fast, the 1645 Directory for Public Worship had allowed for fast days in response to national disasters and days of thanksgiving for triumphs; thus the old ritual of bell-ringing could now serve as a "progress report" on government. The Commonwealth funneled festivity into occasions that were, precisely, occasional, commemorating particular events rather than sacralizing an unchanging natural (and social) background against which those events unfolded.[251] In doing so, it intensified a trend that had begun under Elizabeth and the early Stuarts, of marking exemplary occurrences of providence through specifically memorial holidays.[252] The progress of history became a theophany; like the garden itself, history was a medium in which human and divine agency were blended together. The entertainments that Underdown describes the inhabitants of the Puritan town of Norwich enjoying, such as shows representing the Creation and waxworks of Protestant worthies like King Gustavus, celebrated the continuing progress of sacred history and the role of human agency in it.[253]

This sacralization of history could make piety look a lot like simple curiosity: a receptivity to worldly events, a willingness to reflect on them, and the occasions they offered for the reforming will. Wallington followed every step of this unfolding progress, copying for posterity the petitions sent up to Westminster in support of "the removing of those great obstacles that lie in the way [of] the blessed Reformation both of Church and Commonwealth . . . This is the work of the Lord, and it is marvelous in my eyes." (Even Joad Raymond, the historian of the English newspaper, thinks that Wallington was "a little obsessed with news.")[254] The increasingly popular practice of daily meditation on "such of the divine attributes as appeared . . . in the new occurrances of providence" could barely be distinguished from an interest in the world—from something like an intellectual life as we would now understand it.[255] In a sermon registered with the Stationers' Company five days after Charles I's execution, John Wilkins made the rather pointed suggestion that every "particular event is most seasonable in that time which God appoints" and went on to explain that, through such observations, each individual might make "an experimentall divinitie of his own": these "confused times" offered "a rich treasury of experience" that could be "improved by observation," permitting the individual to study "the wisdom of Providence" without any ecclesiastical assistance at all.[256] For the "experimentall," keeping abreast of the news could be improved into a form of devotion.

Such study could be extended to "many common things"—especially the tangible things of creation. In his *Book for Boys and Girls,* Bunyan sought to wean children from sin through "Meditations upon an Egg" and the like.[257] Among the papers confiscated by the authorities, Overton most regretted the loss of his "Meditations upon the works of the Creation, intituled, *Gods Word confirmed by his Works,*" in which he proved the essentials of Christianity from "the consideration of things visible and created," a work he felt would "prove usefull to many." Although he could not excuse or clear his own "personal Infirmities" and "personall sins," he could offer the pains he had invested in this scriptureless divinity as proof of "my Integrity and uprightnesse to the Common Wealth." However corrupt the private man, his public labors were innocent. Overton's system of divinity was part of his larger program to persuade his countrymen to "remove their eies from persons to things" and become "un-interested, unprejudiced," entering on new ways of truth "without respect of persons"—an appropriately Adamic religion for an increasingly ingenious public.[258]

In a similar vein, Boyle worried that Christians were too inclined to let "God's mercy . . . ingrosse our thoughts," given that they were all "honor'd with the Priesthood of so noble a Temple" as "the Common-wealth of Nature."[259] Since an exclusive focus on the divine gift that "most advantages us"—grace—"may relish a little of selfishnesse," he stressed the importance of devoting at least some part of the Sabbath to making "Theologicall Use" of "the Contemplation of the Creatures." Such use did not consist merely in gazing on the things of creation, but in attempting to expose what "their obvious Appearances and Qualities" concealed.[260] Through this labor of seeing through, the investigator could gain a virtual experience of innocent religion while helping to restore it. Instead of a devotion organized around ritual repetition, Boyle offered one based on progressive discovery and invention (for such contemplation inevitably raised "thoughts of Improving the Creatures").[261] This form of religious observance is constructed around worship of the Creator, not the Redeemer, and it proceeds through the excavation and cultivation of facts. When Hooke claimed to find in Wilkins "an evident Instance, what the true and the *primitive unpassionate Religion* was, before it was *sowred* by particular *Factions*," he was no doubt celebrating Wilkins's latitudinarian leanings, but the experimental divinity that he and other virtuosi promoted approximated the most primitive religion of all.[262] Henry Oldenburg's "Admonitions and Directions of a good Parent to his Child, especially a Son" urged his unborn child not only to pray and read the Bible every day, but to seek out the company of persons helpful "in acquiring knowledge of the works and creatures of God . . . or in Artificial good things and Mechanical Ingenuities [since] all good is of God . . . and therefore we are to discern it and make use of it." Since God had "scattered" good "up and down through the Creation," too broadly for any single individual to gather together, his ingenious saints had to work together to try all things.[263]

By resisting the legislation of fallen appetite, the godly paved the way for the ingenious to seize on Donne's "true Paradise" as the ongoing invention of those who worked to inhabit it. The decline of state-enforced sport fostered a Protestant ethic of laborious re-creation: sanctified attempts to continue the Creator's work through internally and externally directed programs of improvement. In contrast to Herrick's efforts to intoxicate his pig, for example, William Petty proclaimed his conviction that pigs could be taught to labor. Although most did not choose such recalcitrant material on which to concentrate their reforming efforts, they found other means to imitate Adam's labors, the "voluntary effect of his well disposed minde."[264] Idleness had always been attacked by moralists; now, however, ever-escalating cycles of improvement introduced the demand of *making progress* not only in one's work but in one's chosen sphere of recreation. The rejection of festival liberty went along with the invention of new spaces promoting "sober recreation" like the coffeehouse, the cultivation of elective affinities, and a civil society that did not depend on the alehouse (or church) to flourish: the epistolary networks fostered by Hartlib, discussion groups like James Harrington's Rota (40 percent of whose members would become Royal Society Fellows), the Gresham College group, and the Oxford Philosophical Club, collectivities that met weekly while sustaining themselves on the future tense.[265] For many Baconian intellectuals, there was no meaningful distinction between recreation and labor: all was comprehended under vocation or calling, understood not in terms of the profit motive but as a dilation of the self, a new-modeling of the individual to be a better servant and representative of the larger mysterious body of the public. The willingness to regard human existence in general as an ongoing work of re-creation depended on a progressive experience of time rather than the cyclical one that the liturgical calendar, the sacraments, and old agrarian ways had fostered for centuries. There is no particular time, place, or season more conducive than any other for forcing the fallen world closer to its created perfection; and there is no sacrament that corresponds to efforts to recapture a state prior to the need for grace.

This progressive vision did not simply die out at the Restoration, though William Cavendish, the Marquis of Newcastle, urged Charles II to revive "Merrye Englande" through

> Maye Games, Moris Danses, the Lords off the Maye, & Ladye off the Maye, the foole—& the Hobye Horse muste nott bee forgotten.—Also the whitson Lorde, & Ladye,—Thrashinge off Hens att Shrove-tite,—Caralls & wassells att Christmas, with good Plum Porege & Pyes . . . & affter Eveninge Prayer

Everye Sundaye & Holedye,—The Countereye People with their fresher Lasses to tripp on the Toune Greene aboute the Maye pole, to the Louder Bagg-Pipe ther[e] to bee refreshte with their Ale & Cakes, Kinge James off Blessed Memorye writt a litle Booke nott onlye In defence off dansinge, butt comanded thatt his good People Shoulde reioyce them selves with dansinge after Eveninge Prayer.[266]

The image of country people seeking refreshment from cake, ale, and "fresher Lasses" after a good hen-thrashing is thoroughly secular in spirit; the social historian in search of the roots of the modern concept of leisure as consumption might begin here—the Marquis's repetition of *fresh* even manages to run the women together with the food. This was a Merry England Charles was happy to restore. He made no effort, however, to tighten the slackening links of festival culture to religious observance. Dispensing with the Platonic frippery of masques, the court of the Merry Monarch celebrated the Twelve Days by drinking, gambling, and whoring. Games were again permitted in towns and villages, where the aggregated power of the faithful yielded to the imperative to "riot," earning the disdain not just of the dissenting godly but "the sober sort":

> . . . those *Royotous* Assemblies of *Idle People,* who under pretence of *going a Maying* (as they term it) do oftentimes *cut down,* and *carry away* fine straight *Trees,* to set up before some *Ale-house,* or *Revelling-place,* where they keep their drunken *Bacchanalias* . . . occasioning so much *wast* and *spoyl* as we find is done to *Trees* at that *Season,* under this wanton pretence, by *breaking, mangling,* and *tearing* down of *branches,* and intire *Arms* of *Trees,* to adorn their *Wooden-Idol.*[267]

This passage comes not from an early seventeenth-century screed against jolly pastimes but from the most famous treatise on trees ever written: *Sylva,* which Evelyn dedicated to Charles himself. (As an expression of "Ingenuity Learning & publick spirit," the book, according to Thomas Browne, had "given large satisfaction unto the Ingenious world," if not to the king.) Evelyn's upset over the waste of "fine straight *Trees*" was not just the hobby-horse of an oak enthusiast; Roberts had also attacked revelers who cut down "flourishing trees," which "if they were suffred to grow, would in time be good timber for necessary uses," in order to "sette them up to bee drye and unfruitfull like them selves." The maypole was a perfect emblem for the deadening power of the festival year: halted in the midst of its "progress" toward usefulness, the dead tree became the center of whirling revelry, an objective correlative for the cyclical festival year itself—the very opposite of the plowman's wheel, whose revolution enabled the people to "make a progresse."[268]

In *Areopagitica*, Milton had associated the cyclical rhythms of festival with an "obedient unanimity":

> Another sort there be who when they hear that all things shall be order'd, all things regulated and setl'd; nothing writt'n but what passes through [the licensers] . . . will strait give themselvs up into your hands, mak'em, & cut'em out what religion ye please; there be delights, there be recreations and jolly pastimes that will fetch the day about from sun to sun, and rock the tedious year as in a delightfull dream. What need they torture their heads with that which others have tak'n so strictly, and so unalterably into their own pourveying. These are the fruits which a dull ease and cessation of our knowledge will bring forth among the people. How goodly, and how to be wisht were such an obedient unanimity as this, what a fine conformity would it starch us all into? doubtles a stanch and solid peece of frame-work, as any January could freeze together.[269]

Contrasting the fertility of the natural world, the focus and organizing principle of festivity, with the spiritual sterility of its inhabitants who, measuring each year "from sun to sun," are rocked to sleep, he leaves them frozen into a "solid . . . frame-work," delivered "strait . . . up into your hands."[270] Milton need only make a passing allusion to "jolly pastimes" that confer on the people an "order'd," "regulated," and "setl'd" style of life, knowing that his readers will fill in the rest with their common knowledge of festival as an obstacle to reformation. The connection between cyclical festival time and historical decline due to the dulling effects of error and custom has become a commonplace. In the second edition of *The Readie and Easie Way to Establish a Free Commonwealth,* written practically on the eve of the Restoration, Milton used this understanding of festival liberty with pyrrhic irony: "If thir absolute determination be to enthrall us, before so long a Lent of Servitude, they may permitt us a little Shroving-time first, wherin to speak freely, and take our leaves of Libertie."[271] With the restoration of monarchy, any attempt to "speak freely" would only be understood as an unsustainable "Shrove Tuesday business," a taking leave rather than an assertion of liberty, of what Winstanley called the work of freedom.

But during the Interregnum another culture had taken root that would extend further in time, and more deeply into the imaginations of its citizens, than the culture of festival, which after 1660 was in any case a feeble one, incapable of raising funds for church maintenance.[272] The culture that defined itself against state-enforced sport was, in 1660, the culture of the losers, but in some ways it would prove to be the more influential. In the 1650s, Boyle everywhere saw evidence of "Lesse Licentious" times approaching; the culture ushered in by the Restoration was not the kind of restoration he had anticipated.[273] But throughout the Restoration period, the efforts of the ingenious to "redeeme the tyme that has been lost" continued to evolve.[274] Henry Bell, an Interregnum mayor of King's Lynn, supported an attempt to replicate the Dorchester brewhouse experiment in his city, and his efforts were revived by his son, an acquaintance of Robert Hooke who sought to "inlighten" the city with street lamps and a charity school. Groups like the Society for the Reformation of Manners did their part to form the sober public so familiar to Restoration and eighteenth-century scholars, a public characterized by rational interest in intellectual exchange and "improving" entertainments, such as the celebrated public lectures in physico-theology funded by Boyle's estate.[275] This public was the fruit of a collective intellectual self-assertion that the challenge to traditional pastimes helped make possible.

Purgation and Progress

We have seen that extravagantly dilated descriptions—and virtual reenactments—of life in Eden managed to fill a once brief and thin existence with a fullness, and a degree of dynamic activity, it had never had before. It was through these imaginative recoveries of innocent life that paradise came to accommodate process, and, indeed, to require the ongoing efforts of the fallen. At once a space for progress and its goal, paradise had acquired a systematically ambiguous nature; this was the source of the "confusion" that Pinnell had attempted to resolve. Yet it is likely that the newly ambiguous paradise helped work out a confusion caused by an earlier upheaval in sacred geography; in their efforts to restore a paradise of pains, the ingenious were also recuperating the lost space of purgatory.

Although the reformed experience of time as a linear progression defined itself against the festival year, many of the rituals of the old religion had centered on a space consecrated to progress. Duffy has called purgatory the "defining doctrine of late medieval Catholicism." Monasteries were purgatorial institutions, established to offer intercession for the souls of their founders and benefactors. The parish church was itself an antechamber to purgatory, filled with memorials to those who had made donations in exchange for the prayers that would help them through the space of "dyverse paynes."[276] Compared to the traditionally static regions of heaven and hell, purgatory had offered the devotional imagination a space for narrative: the "temporary fire" told the story of the soul's journey toward salvation.[277] Reformers pointed out that the doctrine of purgatory discouraged this painful progress from beginning at birth, confining the trials that should characterize the regenerate life to a postmortem chamber. I suggest that the dissolution of purgatory created imaginative pressure to reintroduce this lost sense of process into other sacred spaces, to reserve a place in sacred geography that, being more susceptible to penetration, could perform the function of a "Heavenly Spiritual School" on earth.[278] Such a space needed to be fermenting, incomplete, yet sanctified all the same. Having once simply marked a site of origin, the earthly paradise took on the newly evacuated function, marking a now moveable terminus of human potential. By releasing the purifying ordeal from the fiery chamber, reformers brought into being a purgatorial world, the grounds on which the ingenious could cultivate a paradise.

It might be said that the dissolution of purgatory was really its restoration. Peter Brown describes purgatory as emerging from the tradition of Augustine, which suggested that spiritual growth after the fall was "a prolonged and painful process. It might, indeed, take more than a lifetime to become worthy of the presence of God."[279] Many details of this "third place" remained murky, but fire was a constant feature, in keeping with the doctrine's proof text: "we are labourers together with God . . . Every man's work shall be made manifest: for the day shall declare it, because it shall be revealed by fire; and the fire shall try every man's work of what sort it is" (1 Corinthians 3: 9 13).[280] The dissolution of a place whose borders were porous to begin with took an appropriately vague form: Henry VIII commanded only that people "abstain from the name of purgatory." One clergyman remarked that "I wold not care thoughe I nevver called it Purgatorye, but let A. be his name." In fact, although the place disappeared, the "name" remained, assuming the form of a hortatory verb. When Harris urged, "let us now look forward, and see what is to be done," the response was clear: "Purge self, fear self, guard self, fortifie self, gage self."[281] As Brown suggests, it was through such imperatives that the doctrine of purgatory had originally come into being.

Perkins declared that "by this Purgatorie we understand the afflictions of Gods children here on earth . . . *the fierie triall* wherby men are clensed from their corruptions, as gold from the drosse by the fire."[282] The case was still being made a century later. William Gibson's *Election and Reprobation Scripturally and Experimentally Witnessed unto London* warns against those who "preach up IMPERFECTION and SIN for Term of Life," stressing that justification through faith does not mean that those who receive grace cannot lose it; through "Neglect, Sloth and Unwatchfulness," people do all the time. It is only by working to purge and fortify themselves that the faithful can become—and keep becoming—"new Creatures." There is no other opportunity to do so: "neither is there any Purgatory (as some do falsly teach) to purge people from their sins after they are dead and put in their Graves": the time to enter "the Heavenly Spiritual School" is now.[283] The world itself had to become the place of "dyverse paynes":

> Now here are two wayes set before thee, Yf thou wilt go to hell; Follow the multitude . . . But if thou wilt enter into life . . . Christ saith to thee, *strive* . . . If the heart be not purged by grace, all outwarde holynesse is but as painted sepulchers . . . For while the heart is not purged . . . He is carried from one vanitie to another . . . The time to exhort, and likwise to learne, is, *while it is called, today.*[284]

Learning and mutual exhortation have become the new medium for the purgatorial fire. But although Roberts urges his parishioners toward an immediate experience of purgatory, collapsing the imaginary place into the present sensations of striving, exhorting, and learning, the release of purgatory into the world of mundane experience was not sufficient; the imagery of the garden was required to sanctify these verbs.

A fifteenth-century manuscript illumination explored by Stephen Greenblatt suggests how the proof text's statement that "we are labourers together with God" enabled purgatory and paradise to merge. It depicts a lone peasant raising a hoe above his head; he is either working the field or digging a grave.[285] In either case, he is an Adamic delver. Although the ground he is tilling seems solid to him, our cross-section view reveals it to be paper-thin: alarmingly close to the earth's surface is a cavern containing two chambers, hell and purgatory, into which the unsuspecting delver is clearly digging his way. An unsentimental sense of the trajectory of fallen life is contracted into an efficient little emblem: a life of incessant work abruptly concluding in either damnation or the further work of redemption. Hell and purgatory appear to be almost identical; both are filled with naked people in flames, but the purgatorial flames are graced by the presence of an angel and the torments of hell are presided over by a demon. An unmistakable visual link is established between purgation and labor, between the trial by fire and the trial of work. The link could almost be a variation on the motif of the angel handing Adam his working tools.

A seventeenth-century book of spiritual exercises provides another clue: it is called *Adams Garden: A Meditation of Thankfulnesse and Praises Unto the Lord, for the Returne and Restore of Adam and his Posteritie: Planted as Flowers in a Garden, and published by a Gentle-man, long exercised, and happilie trained in the schoole of Gods afflictions.*[286] Presenting spiritual meditation and exercise as a method of replanting Adam's garden, it elaborates the themes of return and restoration in horticultural terms. The writer explains that just as Adam's guilt is shared by his posterity, "so his returne descendeth unto them . . . This exercise therefore I call *Adams Garden*." He asks God to "helpe mee, to plant, to square, and frame everie quarter . . . [to] undergoe my calling, to digge and delve still, by penaltie from the first *Adam*." This figurative delving is not just a penalty for sin but a way to purge oneself of it; yet the action of purgation is undertaken in a conceptual space very like the one that this action is supposed to restore. Shot through with the purgatorial language of trial, the treatise weaves into its garden frame the conventional motifs of purgatory as both a fiery chamber and a school to prepare for heaven. This Adamic delver thanks God for "instructing and nurtring mee in thy owne most holy schoole of discipline"; even as he expresses fear of being "shaken with the rods of thy schoole and academy," he is grateful to be made "sweete and acceptable, by the often scowring and purging of that inherent corruption." It is not merely that labor and purgation are associated: labor *is* purgation, and, more strangely, it is somehow also paradisal.[287]

The mixing of bliss and pains had been a feature of purgatory itself; in addition to being located between heaven and hell, it was the space that blended them. In mapping that space onto paradise, *Adams Garden* reveals this blend to be constitutive of innocent existence and the regenerate life at once. John Salkeld suggested that it was "not likely that man should have beene confined there onely, untill the time of his translation into a more happy estate, which should have bin after his sufficient triall in the terrene Paradise." Understood as a place of trial to prepare for heaven, paradise was functionally equivalent to purgatory and continuous with the terrain of earthly existence. The state of innocence collapses into the state of regenerate belief; both are dynamic, processual, pervaded by pains. Greenblatt notes that in *Paradise Lost,* Milton does not feel compelled to go out of his way to refute the doctrine of purgatory: in Milton's epic, and the culture it reflects, "there is no purgatorial space at all"; another way to put this idea is that, in this culture, there is no escaping purgatory. The banishment of purgatory has permitted an expansion of its functions.[288]

It was above all the artisanal imagery of the proof text that offered itself to the devotional imagination of the ingenious. The "prudent, discerning fire," a symbol of God's ability to transform his own creation, became a central feature of the paradisal workrooms set up to foster humanity's open-ended renovation.[289] As Bacon put it, "natural philosophy proposes to itself; as its noblest work of all nothing less than the restitution and renovation of things corruptible." The doctrine of purgatory had gathered strength from the linkage of the holy paradise to Eden, whose gates were guarded by the cherub's flaming sword; in both cases, the holy place was separated from the dross of the fallen world by a space of fire. Now the fire was located inside.[290] More precisely, it was the medium through which the fallen world was refined or "sublimed" into that place, now conceived in temporal terms, as the future. When the nonclassical Latin noun *laboratorium* first began to take on its modern meaning in the late sixteenth century, it referred exclusively to a place with a furnace, a place with fire. In two medieval instances, it refers to a workshop and a task or labor. It was alchemists who combined this signification with the purifying and transforming fire whose power they sought to master. Experimentalists extended the metaphor to characterize all investigative manipulations of natural phenomena.[291]

For rather than allowing the purgatorial metaphorics of fire to die out, experimentalists actively tended to it. Evelyn went so far as to inscribe the word *Purgatorium* over the outer door of his garden laboratory. After successfully setting up his first laboratory at Stalbridge, Boyle wrote to his sister that "Vulcan has so transported and bewitch'd mee, that as the Delights I tast in it, make me fancy my Laboratory a kind of Elizium," he could now consider himself familiar with "those seates of Blisse" celebrated by the poets.[292] The fires of Vulcan could not be distinguished from the blessed garden, a space where purgatorial pains and pleasure intermingled. Without these fires, Elysium was a barren wilderness. When an earthen furnace was delayed due to the "unluckly & unexpected lingring of the Waggon which is to bring me all my Vulcanian Implements," Boyle's "necessitated Idlenesse" left him disconsolate: he could only "sadly walke up & downe in my Laboratory"; without his Vulcanian implements, the book of nature remained closed, unimproved.[293] Boyle even conferred on his nephew and protégé the honorary name of Pyrophilus, lover of fire.[294] The closer we look into articulations of the value of work undertaken by Adam's self-styled heirs, the more this purgatorial strand of paradisal imagery becomes visible: even William Basse's worker is "strongly tride" in "fornaces of care"; under this pressure, he acts with "truth and serviceable skill." What made the purgatorial paradigm so valuable was this oscillation between subjective and objective senses: in trying all things, the Adamic laborer was himself tried. In his famous attack on the universities, John Webster complained that instead of being "idlely trained up in notions, speculations, and verbal disputes," students should "learn to inure their hands to labour, and put their fingers to the furnaces . . . so they may not be sayers, but doers, not idle speculators, but painful operators . . . which can never come to pass, unless they have Laboratories as well as Libraries, and work in the fire." Those who were "too proud to put their hands to the coals and furnace" would never "produce effects that would be beneficial to all posterities."[295] The matter tried by fire includes the body of the scholar himself, who emerges from this purifying trial as a public-spirited intellectual laborer. Hobbes's famous mistrust of experiments "forced by fire" went along with his rejection of an entire model of intellectual labor; as Steven Shapin and Simon Schaffer have shown, the sheer effort required to make a fact was for

Hobbes a self-evident demonstration that experimental trial could never serve as a stable foundation for knowledge.[296] Experimentalists positively embraced the instability of knowledge produced by trial as the defining condition of progress.

Just as crucially, trial enabled the desired tangling of divine and human creativity: the Adamic laborer's power to "refine" creation was itself an expression of the "Makers Power Divine," which "does, like Grace, the Fallen Tree restore / To its blest state of Paradise before." Purgatorial burning also ran through Winstanley's paradisal labors, cleansing the "corrupt bloud" of "covetous Kingly power": a corruption "that runs in every man, and womans vaines, more or lesse, till reason the spirit of burning cast him out."[297] In Winstanley's theology, Christ's ascension was no more or less than his entrance into creation as a purgative force. The "burning" and "casting out" of pride from the garden was set into motion by reason and expressed through tilling the earth and the literal burning or "devonshiring" of crops: in this innocent labor, through which creation was "purged and delivered from the curse," spiritual and physical trial went hand in hand.[298] "For by our hands truth is declar'd," went one of the Diggers' songs; their trial of the things of creation was a means of subjecting the nation to the trial through which they had already passed, as they recomposed their surroundings in accordance with the paradise they now inhabited: "This tryal may our God see good, / to try, not us but you; / That your profession of the Truth, / may prove either false or true." It was through this trial that the Lord was "burning up the dross of our flesh and shaking down corruption in kingdoms and churches," enabling contemporaries to witness the "drosse and Tin of Monarchy being happily purged away" before their eyes.[299]

Many artisanal applications left the metallurgical imagery of Corinthians 3 behind altogether; writers wanted to weave purgatory directly into vegetation. Purgatory inflected the rhetoric of weeding so prevalent in Protestant devotional literature—weeding out backsliders from a regenerate society, rooting out temptations from the individual soul—which drew motivation from the collective attempt not only to sever the link between the awareness of nature's fertility and a festival consciousness, but to set oneself against the matter of creation as an opposing creative force that would dress and redress it. Winstanley figured those who resisted the restoration of common property as weeds in "the Garden of *Eden*" that had to be uprooted: "outlandish men; for they are not the true native Inhabitants" but rather "strangers" to the restored state of England. Evelyn's ingenious gardener must also dedicate himself daily to "clensing & exactly purging it [the garden] of all noxious weedes, rubbish and impediments whatsoever"; "there is nothing more pernicious to young plants, then the neglect of purging them"; through "prompt purging," Evelyn declares, the very "ground" itself could "be altered from its former nature." Such purging required "incredible paines," even "infinite paines."[300] For regenerate gardeners like Evelyn or Ralph Austen, horticulture is no mere metaphor for spiritual discipline, it is one of the highest forms of that discipline[301]; their gardening treatises attempt to endow the act of weeding with some of the vigor and energy, if not the hilarity, associated with traditional holiday pastimes, and it is purgatorial rhetoric that does the trick. Rather than pulses of energy that fluctuated with the seasons, the Creator demanded a constant expenditure of energy geared toward a distant end. The purging of the garden becomes a master figure for all improvement: having subjected his own library and commonplace book to "many tryals and reformations," Evelyn told his grandson that a library "should be weeded out to give place to better till it were thro'ly purged."[302] Once purgation is introduced, even a library can be "paradiz'd" into a garden in chronic need of an Adamic custodian.

The purgatorial paradise of pains offered an ideal template for the regenerate life: just as the Protestant embraced work as a preferable option to idleness, so he pressed recreation into the service of progressive trial. Accordingly, John Pettus praises Adam's "harmless industry" as one of the greatest "pleasures of *Paradise.*"[303] Salkeld insists throughout his treatise on Adam's labor as a "recreation, and rejoycing of the will and minde." Innocent man would not have been happy living an idle life; hence, as Joseph Hall put it, "mans store-house was also his work-house": "Man therfore is no sooner made, then he is set to work," so that "hee working might keepe paradise, and paradise by the same worke might keepe him from idlenes, from sinne." Idleness is assimilated to sin, and work not only to innocence, but to bliss. If Adam "must labor, because he was happy; how much more we, that we may be? . . . how much more cheerfully we go about our business so much nearer we come to our Paradise." This asymptotic program of *imitatio Adami* renders work a continual source of comfort and recreation, and a means to make and keep the self holy.[304] In Adam's labor, Salkeld finds an object lesson for the idle rich:

God would not have man idle: not an ill item for our lazie gallants, who thinke their gentilitie to consist in idlenes, and a point of honour to live of other mens labour: but even in this (I am of opinion) that God doth punish them, that they have more griefes, and more discontent in their idle pleasures, then others in their most wearisome toiles, and labours, which though it be a most voluntary bondage, yet is it likewise the most base, and cruell slaverie to the base appetites; a tyranny of Satan, a double bondage to a double tyrant, to Satan, to sinne . . . an intolerable slavery, and an infinite misery; the beginning miserable, the proceedings damnable, the end, as which hath no end, intolerable.[305]

Like the delver digging his way into purgatory, Salkeld suggests that the only choice that humanity has *ever* had is between damnation and the trial of work. In this redescription of the high life as a condition of intolerable slavery, the surrender of the working, reforming will becomes its own punishment, one that, extending into the torments of hell, "has no end," like a nightmarish parody of reformation: "wearisome toiles, and labours," in contrast, become the stuff of paradise. Linking pleasure to the demands of recreation, Adam opened up the possibility of extracting festival mirth from work itself; the curse of labor, like the purgatorial experience of temporary damnation, becomes a permanent, reliable, and sanctified source of pleasure. Like Dante's purgatory-dwellers who cut short their conversations with the pilgrim in their eagerness to leap back into the saving flames, so the Protestant laborer aimed to "cheerfully go about his business."

I have suggested that the concept of ingenuity linked intellectual labor to participation in a collectivity capable of transforming private experience into public knowledge. I will now suggest that, once dissolved, purgatory forged an indissoluble bond between such labor and the concept of a public. That it promoted works of an open-ended rather than ritual nature is clear enough. Reformers complained that the doctrine of purgatory had encouraged a complacent deferral of spiritual labor until after death, demanding nothing but "lippe labour" from the living, a pantomime of effort that, like the fallen learning propagated in the universities, could never perform the task of purgation. As Bacon asserted, those who preached up intercession "propound those noble effects which God hath set forth unto man to be bought at the price of labour, to be attained by a few easy and slothful observances"—observances that enabled "purgatory rakers," the clergy supported by chantries, to live "without any labour, paine, or travaile," as Thomas Becon put it.[306]

What was most insidious about intercessory prayer, however, was its role in focusing attention on the progress of single souls rather than the restoration of humanity as a whole. Becon mocked the popish mass for atomizing the mystical body into a hodgepodge of individuals:

> yee pray for *Philip* and *Cheny* . . . for the soules of your great grand Sire, & of your old Beldame *Hurre,* for the soules of father *Princhard,* and of mother *Puddingwright,* for the soules of goodman *Rinsepitcher,* and goodwife *Pintepot,* for the soules of Sir *John Husgoose,* and Sir *Simon Sweetlips,* and for the soules of all your Benefactors, Founders, Patrones, Friends and well-willers.[307]

The comic names that Becon assigns the dearly departed evoke carnivalesque consumption and its aftermath—pudding, goose, sweet lips, rinsepitcher— suggesting by association the heathen "bread god" itself.[308] The constant repetition in intercessory prayer of the names assumed by souls when still alive effects the same reduction of the spiritual to the material as the popish mass. It was precisely the individual bonds linking "friends" that purgatory had sustained; the social cohesion fostered by purgatory was predicated on an identification of the mystical body with the local community, and thus the social hierarchy, into which one was born.[309] Reformers cultivated an alternative vision: of a purgatorial refinement of individuals *into* a mystical body, one in which the accidents of birth might really be irrelevant. Although Galatians 3:28 described the community of the faithful in Christ as just such a body, purgatory had permitted social difference to extend beyond the grave; the notion that God did not distinguish between rich or poor did not sort very well with the wide array of intercessory options that made "the purchase of paradise" the privilege of the wealthy.[310] While defenders of the doctrine complained that the proscription of purgatory deprived souls of "that Christian charitie," through which "by mutuall affection the members of one bodie helpe one another," Andrew Willet pointed out that promoters of purgatory were actually inimical to charity since "they doe make great difference betweene the rich and the poore," thereby undoing the work of Death the Leveller (and Adam the digger). Willet maintained "the scripture saith plainly, that God is no accepter of persons," yet those who could afford it could have chantries up and running before they were even dead: under this system, the first did not become the last, they remained the first.[311]

The banishment of purgatory is often blamed for having fractured the mystical body, forcing its members to bear sole responsibility for their post-mortem fate while surrendering their own dead to an undifferentiated heavenly host.[312] As Perkins explained, the faithful could now pray only in a "general manner for the faithfull departed . . . To pray for particular men departed: and to praie for their deliverance out of purgatorie, we thinke it unlawfull." (The insult was apparently returned from beyond the grave, as the dead sent blessings to the living in an equally "generall" manner.[313]) But it was precisely by learning how to conduct spiritual business "in a general manner," without "respect of persons," that members of the mystical body were made into a public. Purgatory had been a powerful tool of individuation, operating discretely and variably on each of the faithful even as it sustained "particular" relationships beyond the grave. Theoretically, chantries were supposed to profit all the faithful departed, but in fact prayers were believed to be most effective when offered for "particular persons"; to spread intercessory prayers too thinly across the mystical body diluted their power. And while patrons were free to name all Christians as beneficiaries rather than focusing on themselves and their immediate family in their mortmain licenses, they almost never did.[314]

Once released into the world, purgatory strengthened the idea of a mystical body as a body that could not be "seen or handled." The way to alleviate the pressure of bearing exclusive personal accountability for one's fate after death was to cultivate an identification, a sort of impersonal intimacy, with the body of humanity as a whole. The progress once identified with the individual soul's purgatorial ascent to heaven could now characterize that larger body; describing the trial of reformation itself, purgatorial process characterized history's movement toward a final restoration. "Dyerse pains" became general ones. During prayers for the dead, Perkins did find it lawful to desire that "God would hasten their joyfull resurrection, and the full accomplishment of their happinesse." Wills, funeral sermons, and funeral monuments reflected this new emphasis, and the general resurrection became "the great religious theme" of all three.[315] The dead and the living would be restored in perfect, agile, luminous bodies, fulfilling the hope expressed in Job: "in my flesh shall I see God" (19:26). This almost reduced the postmortem heaven to "a waiting room," where souls "rested" in anticipation of their glorious restoration, one that depended on the prosecution of reformation on earth.[316]

Rather than fostering an atomization of the mystical body, the new finality of death—an impermanent finality, after all—only made mutual assistance and exhortation more important; the restoration of humanity as a whole was at stake. A highly personalized culture of benefaction gave way to legacies promoting what W. K. Jordan calls "social rehabilitation and municipal betterment" that would speed improvement along. While, as Joel Rosenthal argues, philanthrophy "directed toward social reform was singularly absent from the late medieval world, both in theory and in practice," Jordan offers evidence of "a notable and a very rapid quickening of charitable giving" in the decades after the Reformation, and between 1601 and 1640, London's generosity became "prodigal," accounting for over half of the total of benefactions for the entire period from 1480 to 1660.[317] Most importantly for our purposes, the increase of spending on social rehabilitation, poverty relief, and education corresponded to a sharp decline in offerings to the church itself.

It is perhaps in the realm of education that the influence of the purgatorial paradigm is most apparent. Since the promise of a restored paradise on earth lay in the possibility of cumulative culture, what I described above as the extension of craftsman's time to history as a whole, the single community embracing the dead and the living once provided by intercession could be reconstituted through the transfer of knowledge. As paradise and purgatory were both released into the mundane world, conceived of now as a field of progress, the work of restoring the body to its original (and future) perfection became one of the central cares of the intellectual laborer, for the revived fascination with the restored body now focused on its capacities specifically as an instrument of knowledge.[318] The "final epiphany of deified humanity must await the resurrection of the transfigured body": in the meantime, humanity had to work toward that general restoration through rehabilitative efforts of its own.[319] Such projects were for "the public good"—a phrase whose relentless repetition by members of the Hartlib circle made it almost "a party slogan," as Paul Slack puts it. Hartlib himself was, as Cowley put it, so "publick-spirited" that he offered his very body as raw matter for discovery, forgoing a grave so that he could provide himself "for an anatomy. And then was seene all the effects of his medicines upon his stone, bladder, &c." This was the ultimate absorption of the body into the office, a literal incorporation of the person into the ongoing labor of an intellectual commons.[320]

The Invisible College

Hartlib had been equally absorbed by his office when alive. The phrase "the Hartlib circle" is so naturalized a part of our mental geography of seventeenth-century culture that it is easy to overlook the accomplishment it represents. Contemporary epithets for Hartlib recall the metaphors we use to describe the Internet today: Hartlib was a "conduit-pipe," the "hub of the axletree of knowledge," "the Great Intelligencer of Europe."[321] Coined to describe an office network, the Internet soon described an office extending across the world; this "living laboratory" sought a similar destiny, one in which "all the world would become a divine college"—a purgatorial heavenly school.[322] Hartlib sought not to be a teacher in this college but its infrastructure, and his effect was viral; satellites of Hartlib were communicative networks in their own right.

In a 1658 letter to Thomas Browne, Evelyn expressed the hope that a group of *"Paradisi Cultores,"* a society of "ingenuous men," might "redeeme the tyme that has bin lost, in pursuing vulgar errours, and still propagating them." Something very like this hope sustained gatherings at Gresham College that an alarmed Laud referred to as "conventicles." It was out of these conventicles that the Royal Society eventually emerged.[323] The group of future Fellows gathered, Wallis later recalled, in "the *Bull-head* in *Cheap-side;* and (in Term-time) to *Gresham*-Colledge, where we met weekly at Mr. *Foster*'s Lecture, (then Astronomy-Professor there) and, after the Lecture ended: repaired, sometimes to Mr. *Foster*'s Lodgings, sometimes to some other place not far distant, where we continued such Inquiries; and our numbers encreased." What is so striking about this description of the meetings is how it keeps sliding from one place to the next, from Gresham to "some other place"; the meeting ground of truth producers, "Persons, studiously Inquisitive," is continuous with social space in general.[324] The man behind these meetings was Theodore Haak, one of Hartlib's closest associates.[325]

First appearing in Boyle's correspondence in 1646, the term *invisible college* was understood by Boyle's eighteenth-century editor, Thomas Birch, to refer to the London group described by Wallis; scholars now associate the term with promoters of a "chymical utopianism" who initially did not include Hartlib but later came to be associated with him (Boyle's final reference to the invisible college explicitly describes it as a society in which Boyle and Hartlib are both involved).[326] While scholarly discussion of the term has focused quite tightly on the issue of membership,[327] I am more interested in exploring the figure of the invisible college than in determining its membership. Since the term appears nowhere except in Boyle's correspondence, it may not refer to anything as determinate as a club, especially since Boyle seems to be describing an ever-expanding network. Yet the fact that so many candidates for the invisible college have been proposed tells us something important about this historical moment.

The term first appears when Boyle assures his former tutor, Isaac Marcombes, that he will be "extremely welcome to our *invisible college*" if he sends "good receipts" concerning husbandry as it is "practised in your parts," since "our new philosophical college . . . values no knowledge, but as it hath a tendency to use." Subsequent references to a college in Boyle's letters to Hartlib suggest the same entity (e.g., "that *college,* whereof God has made you hitherto the midwife and nurse"). Thus when Boyle speaks of laying "some few stones towards the building of your *college,*" his rhetoric sustains Hartlib's own description of his scheme for the propagation of learning, to which, in accordance with "the Counsell and Designe of the Lord *Verulam* . . . every yeare some stones should bee added."[328] Sometimes these stones are individual people, other times they are pieces of information, but the college is always described as a plant in a state of permanent construction.[329] It found expressions through epistolary networks, print, and schemes like the Office of Address, a clearinghouse for correspondence among the learned (as that category was now being redefined). This "office" combined the functions contained in the double signification of *address,* linking the primary sense of preparation to the action of sending written messages, primarily "receipts" containing "matters of ingenuity"; the work undertaken by this office was in a sense all preparatory, laying the foundation for future work.[330]

The scheme was outlined in Hartlib's *Considerations Tending to the Happy Accomplishment of Englands Reformation,* where it is described as "the greatest Worke of Charity, which can bee bestowed upon the whole Nation." Combining an Office of Communications with an Office of Accommodations, it was to have served as "a combination patent office, employment agency, commodities exchange, spiritual counselling centre and public library . . . in short, a clearing-house of information"—one that required a "rewriting of older notions of the state in which information was hierarchically distributed and controlled."[331] Here one can glimpse something like Winstanley's vision of the "Land of our nativitie" after its restoration: "men will knit together in one body and will cease to teach, for everyone will be taught of the Father."[332] Since the father was for Winstanley a synonym for reason, this was a vision characterized less by an absence of teachers than by an absence of any distinction between teachers and pupils: a field of learning characterized by a horizontal rather than vertical organization of knowledge production. If guilds were defined by their exclusive possession of secrets, Hartlib was dedicated to transforming the "secrets of nature"— specialized knowledge of God's creation—into public property.[333] The Office of Address was a potential incarnation of Winstanleyan reason, which "hath a regard to the whole creation; and knits every creature together into a onenesse; making every creature to be an upholder of his fellow; and so everyone is an assistant to preserve the whole."[334]

I have been tracing the emergence of the concept of the public throughout this chapter, but the literature of the Hartlib circle offers perhaps the first self-conscious articulation of this concept. Given the inordinate frequency with which Hartlibians refer to the public and its "good," the case for identifying their projects with a seventeenth-century public sphere is almost too strong to require making. The interesting question is why scholarship on the public sphere in England, when it has turned to the Interregnum period, has so often focused on the realm of political polemic rather than on the projects undertaken by intellectuals who were defined almost entirely by their obsessional concern with the public.[335] The answer may lie in their interest in promoting *applied* knowledge, in areas from medicine to beekeeping, which from a modern perspective suggests a proto-scientific community, or a group of policy wonks, rather than a group of what we would now call public intellectuals. It is paradoxically their concern with matters that were of genuine practical concern to the public welfare, such as street sanitation, as opposed to strictly constitutional or doctrinal matters, that has excluded them from consideration as creators of a public sphere.[336] But of course the spread of ingenuity provided the very basis for extra-parliamentary politics; political authority depends on intellectual authority, and the Hartlib circle extended it to people, particularly members of "the industrious sort," who in other circumstances may never have risen to public attention.

Many members of this circle seemed happy to work with almost any form of government, as demonstrated by John Dury's efforts on the Continent to realize his scheme for the reconciliation of Protestant churches. When Hartlib served as a witness in Laud's trial, his testimony focused narrowly on the obstacles Laud posed to Dury's plans: Laud had committed the crime of hindering "good conference" on a global level.[337] To be sure, some members of this network gained support from the government; Hartlib was even paid a salary.[338] Hartlib's protégé, Henry Oldenburg, was confident that "the continued success of the Protector is an evident sign that Heaven has some extraordinary task for him"—one that would entail equally extraordinary tasks for his ingenious subjects. For Hartlibians were no accepters of persons; they celebrated every useful member of the public on the same terms. After meeting with an artisan who expressed willingness to have some of his secrets published, Hartlib described him as "a man raised up by God in a peculiar manner for the advancement of the Publick Good." All who were willing to exert themselves to "discern and make use of" creation were to be "raised up" as public servants.[339]

Boyle described members of the invisible college as instruments of "so extensive a charity, that it reaches unto every thing called man, and nothing less than an universal good-will can content it . . . they take the whole body of mankind for their care"; in doing so, they "put narrow-mindedness out of countenance." In reaching "unto everything called man," the invisible college reached deeply into individual men, invisibly refashioning them on the model of the public they served. What Evelyn would call "that incomparable fruition of a mans selfe" depended on the coming to fruition of this larger body.[340] Hartlib implored Christians not to become "*straitned within themselves*":

> I Find by Experience, that it is nothing but the *Narrownes* of our *Spirits* that make us miserable; for if our Hearts were enlarged beyond our selves, and opened to lay hold of the *Advantages* which God doth offer, whereby we may become joyntly serviceable unto one another in *Publicke Concernments;* we could not be without *Luciferous Employments* for our selves; nor *Unfruitfull* to our neighbors.[341]

When Eve fed the fruit to Adam, she neither consumed nor offered up the product of her labor; in contrast, the bonds uniting members of Hartlib's Christian community are forged entirely out of labor; fruit becomes processual fruitfulness, harnessing the individual appetite for knowledge to the innocent production of public knowledge. On this understanding, the taking up of *"Employments"* is the very condition of involvement in *"Publicke Concernments";* if many statesmen and political controversialists-for-hire did not meet this standard of public service, many of the industrious sort did. Adam's working body and his representative body are revived in these mutually reinforcing aspects of ingenuity. For Hartlib describes a body whose members each embody a collective, even a representative, consciousness, expressed in efforts to be "jointly serviceable unto one another."[342] The "enlargement" of their hearts "beyond themselves" permits them to have an expansive concept of their neighborhood. When Hartlib refers to "our neighbors," he is not referring to members of a parish but to a more amorphous concept of Christian community, sustained through flexible associations extending well beyond national borders.[343] This model of Christian commmunity—of individuals engaged in open-ended labors of intellectual, religious, and political discovery—fosters individual pursuits of "experience" while identifying the ultimate end of these independent endeavors as a collective one. Even when pursued alone, Boyle's devotions in the laboratory were a collective activity; they bore fruit in public truths.

The French correspondence of André Rivet and Dorothy Moore (a member of the Hartlib circle, familiar to us as the sister of Edward King or *Lycidas*) on the subject of women's role in the Christian community is a virtual explication of this expansive notion of a public.[344] Moore writes, "I do not see how it is possible to serve God other than as his members . . . the female sex must not be idle in the Lord's work but work for the good of the public in the mysterious body, which is now militant on the earth." To be sanctified, such work must "achieve the effect of a truly public service." When Rivet suggests that Moore perform local charitable works and care for her family, she bristles, stressing again the importance of undertaking work that relates to "the whole spiritual body" rather than a few individuals. Rivet's response is strategically nonresponsive: "I cannot find anything whatsoever to suggest that your sex had the duty to carry out or actually carried out any public service in the Church." Although in "days gone by" there were nuns and widowed deaconnesses, their offices are no longer required. They are talking at cross-purposes: Moore keeps describing "the body" while Rivet keeps referring to God's work in the church. Moore's final letter articulates the underlying semantic difficulty:

> Sir, after meditating on and rereading your letter I find that we refer to the word *public* in a different sense for it seems that you understand nothing by the public except that which is apparent to all in an ecclesiastical and political office but I understand the public to mean all that directly involves the state of the entire body, considered in itself to be an entirety, which ought to give you a clearer impression of my meaning.[345]

The tone of polite exasperation reflects Moore's disbelief that she must reacquaint the celebrated theologian with the meaning of the term *corpus mysticum*. In fact, she is subjecting the hoary topos to a revision, describing a body that required a continual but provocatively undefined labor from its members: the amorphous task of spreading truth. A tireless producer of information for the public, Moore worked on schemes for female education and wrote letters to procure governmental support for Hartlib, while sending him a steady stream of receipts from her own attempts to distill medicines (an appalled contemporary commented that "Mistresse Durey . . . cowld farre lesse have stooped . . . to have taken up a publick shop for selling of spirirts & oills"). And, after a long and agonizing bout of self-analysis, she eventually recognized marriage to Dury as a valuable "Instrument" for her huge and shapeless, hence infinitely demanding, "calling."[346]

The correspondence of this circle registers the excitement of personal contacts that are also general ones: as Boyle wrote to Hartlib in 1647, "you interest yourself so much in the *Invisible College*, and that whole society is so highly concerned in all the accidents of your life, that you can send me no intelligence of your own affairs, that does not (at least relationally) assume the nature of *Utopian*." The invisible college was a utopian no-place because it was located everywhere, transforming even private "lodgings" into spaces for public knowledge production.[347] Any accidents undergone by Hartlib's own person were "at least relationally" implicated in the "whole society" because his very person was constitutive of the utopia under construction. Although not a political representative, neither was he a private person.

Much of the literature associated with Hartlib's name thus consists in letters or "relations" conveyed to him by others. Milton's *Of Education,* like many other educational treatises of the period, was addressed "To Master *Samuel Hartlib*"—though Milton, observing the distinction between the private person and the public office, took care to stress that he was not "prevail'd" to write it by "lawes of any private friendship" but rather for "love of God, and of mankinde."[348] Boyle's first published essay appeared in a 1655 volume entitled *Chymical, Medicinal, and Chyrurgical Addresses Made to Samuel Hartlib;* like Milton's treatise, it was really an address made *through* Hartlib to a much more dispersed recipient: *"An Epistolical Discourse . . . inviting all true lovers of Vertue and Mankind, to a free and generous Communication of their Secrets and Receits in Physick."*[349] Boyle's first entrance into the sphere of print took the form of a demand for others to join him there.[350] "I must ingeniously confess," he declared, that hoarders of nature's secrets appeared to him as "Usurers and Hogs," since, like the sinner in the parable who "folded up his Talent in a Napkin," they kept to themselves what should be freely extended to their neighbors. God intended knowledge of creation to be gained "through labor," yet he intended the fruits of such labor not for "some single person," but rather for "all Mankind."[351]

Given the size of the ingenious truth producer's "neighborhood," it is not surprising that the distinction between a private letter and an epistolary essay went unrecognized by the most active prosecutor of "Our Publike Interest in Christs Universall and Communicative Kingdom." As Moore expressed it, using Hartlib's own language, Hartlib had so "enlarged his heart to serve his Sonne in his Members" that he lived entirely "without respect to privatte ends," and he ingenuously expected his associates to do the same.[352] When Moore and John Dury wrote a series of letters to Moore's best friend Katherine Boyle, Lady Ranelagh (Boyle's sister), about their decision to marry, he got hold of the letters and, finding them so filled with improving reflections, had them printed, as if they, too, were secrets of nature deserving of public scrutiny:

> Good mr Hartlib
> I thought I could never have received from you a just grownd of quarell . . . how doe you thincke I am able to beare your printing of that rude indigested paper written to the Lady Ranalaugh?, which I profess I had not time

to read once over before I sent it: alass! it must needs discredit the matter which might convincingly and powerfully be handled concerning the intention of Christans in maryage: for when these unknowen principles (for soe I may justly call them in regard of most men) come first under the consideration of men, if they be not found cleerly and substantialy exprest and opened, they give a prejudice [to] the truth, and sett men in a wors capacitie to receive information, then they were in before they heard of them, and this is the service you have done the publicke; treuly mr. Hartl: I have noe pardonne for you, that is the worst Languag I will give you, but I am in zeal of publick hurt hartily angry with you which I should more full express, but that time calles upon mee to tell you, that we heare nothing of the Covenant.[353]

Rather than dwelling on the invasion of her privacy, Moore declares that "I am in zeal of publick hurt hartily angry": the six words between *am* and *angry* change everything. It is a "publick hurt," and she is merely zealous on its behalf. A humiliating public exposure is lamented as a lost opportunity for the spread of truth. Like Milton, Moore regards the institution of marriage as one predicated, for "most men," on entirely "unknowen principles," which the ingenious are just beginning to reveal for the first time; what was once a sacrament is now an object awaiting discovery. Moore's worry is that a publication of a "rude indigested" piece of personal correspondence on the subject might hinder the research program by sparking "prejudice," which will "sett men in a wors capacitie to receive information . . . this is the service you have done the publicke." But public hurt is short-lived—other public business calls, and Moore cannot put off asking him about the Solemn League and Covenant.

It is clear that the attempt to live in relation to this mysterious body made awkward but exciting psychological demands on its members. When the Irish patrimony of Boyle's family was in doubt, he reflected on the difficulty of not being a respecter of persons when the person in question was oneself: "We cannot without regret mention or call to mind the losse of our Estates, & yet we can remember without Sorrow, the Losse (in Adam) of our first State of Innocency."[354] In imagining what it would be like to experience the fall as a personal loss, Boyle articulates an ambition to identify, not with himself or his "friends," but with his neighbors that is, with humanity as a whole; and he takes himself to task for not being able to do so. But as a reader of the book of creation, he could fill out this Adamic subject position nicely. "Heroical Men ar more frequently observ'd (for the most part) in Common-welths then in Monarchys," he reflected; as an investigator who labored in "the Common-wealth of Nature," he could embody this depersonalized form of heroism, assuming the role of a truth producer whose bodily experiences were matters of public record.[355] He hoped that "Lesse Licentious and More Discerning Times, (which may be, perhaps, approaching)" would enable everyone to do the same. The nation's political upheavals portended a "Revolution, whereby Divinity will be much a Looser, & Reall Philosophy flourish, perhaps beyond men's Hopes."[356] Loose rather than licentious, this new divinity would sustain a bloodless revolution in knowledge, resulting in a philosophy that was "Reall," and therefore fruitful.

It must have seemed to many that what Boyle called the invisible college would soon extend its reach not just across the country but the world, embracing "the whole body of mankind." The work of agents abroad like Dury persuaded Boyle's sister (who was responsible for his introduction to Hartlib, Oldenburg, and Wilkins) that Cromwell was God's agent in building a Protestant union that would destroy Antichrist, making the world safe for truth production. As might be expected from a woman who chose Milton to tutor her son, she regarded the proliferation of sects as a sign of "ye cleerer breaking forth in this age than formerly of that light of truth, which shews liberty of conscience to be one of the most unquestionable rights belonging to men as men."[357] This was not an argument for diversity of opinion as an end in its own right; rather, it was the sign of progress being made. Walwyn concurred that the only possibility of men being "brought to one mind" was "by liberty of discourse, and liberty of writing." To facilitate mutual enlightenment, it was essential that none "pretend to more infallible certenty than other men"; uncertainty was to be cultivated as a public good because of its productivity: ingenuous "indifferency" offered fertile ground for future findings.[358] Public edification occurred on precisely the same model as scientific progress, through the sharing of results. Katherine Boyle was confident that the repeated assertion of this right of conscience would bring about the apocalypse: "this old frame of heaven & earth" would pass and "a new one be sett up in Its place." In the reunion of the body of humanity with the body of truth, God would again be "all in all."[359] The arena of representativeness moves toward its own vitiation;

when expressed through print, the "no-place" of the invisible college was filled with bodies working toward their own dissolution.

The ingenious employed productive labor as the master figure for intellectual life because they believed it was the best basis for it. But intellectual labor "improved" on its model by making the knowledge that had always been generated by productive labor its desired end-product. This was the central insight of Baconianism: artisanal methods could be used for the exclusive purpose of generating new facts. The unrestricted nature of this production in turn linked intellectual labor to the nebulous work of faith. The Westminster divines had explicitly made faith itself a matter of the will; faith was both an active decision and an ongoing labor. While the demand to "work out one's salvation" was not ambiguous, the means could not have been more so.[360] Thomas Taylor urged "experimental Christians" to "Labour to get Faith": out of the deterioration of particular works such as intercessory prayer came a working life that was scrupulously ill-defined, hence infinitely time-consuming.[361] Thus Baxter, who insisted that "I live only for *Work,*" confessed in 1681 that "I have these Forty years been sensible of the sin of losing time: I could not spare an hour"; and Boyle deplored the hours lost during the "Necessary Idlenesse" enforced by "that slavery of sleepe."[362] The desire to reduce time spent in purgatory had evolved into a determination to squeeze as much purgatory into one's time on earth as possible. As exemplified by the ingenious, the Protestant work ethic in these decades was less concerned with the profit motive than it was to meet the crushing demands of being faithful—which included being serviceable to the larger body by means always to be improved upon, or yet to be discovered. On this understanding, the slothful observances of the old religion were slothful precisely because they could be easily identified; investing the effort to discover, or invent, one's service was part of fulfilling it.

This calling inevitably distracted people from their jobs. Between Wallington's calling as a member of the London godly community and his calling as a wood turner there was simply no contest; measured by his investment of time and energy, the former always prevailed (more evidence, if any were needed, that, as John Rumrich puts it, our "view of the Puritans is literally preposterous when articulated through the 'Protestant ethic'" as generally understood).[363] The same demand that led artisans like Wallington to pursue callings once considered above their social station led gentlemen like Boyle and Evelyn to descend beneath it, laboring to discover new ways to be ingenious; the same principle that led Wallington to have new experiences not yielded by his artisanal work led his social superiors to seek those laborious experiences out. Ingenuity had the potential to restyle the social body into an undifferentiated "onenesse."

Baxter wrote to Boyle that, while the "search after *Truth*" was a "meanes to *Goodnes*," it was essential that the seeker distinguish between mere contemplation, "a pleasant easie *dreame*," and "a waking working knowledge." To qualify as waking and working, the search for truth had to be active, which now meant it had to be fruitful. Anxiety over the ease with which the innocently delightful search after truth could slide into fruitless dreaming was inevitable, and strategic. There was no explicit definition of "working out" that would enable the believer to distinguish between the two states; hence the participial nature of the endeavor. It stands to reason that Boyle, who was haunted by "scruples," found so much comfort in artisanal pursuits; these could produce solid "fruits" or testimony, in the form of material effects, far more easily than the work of faith in its more general designation.[364] Evelyn's daughter Mary worried that she had "mis-spent a great part of that pretious tyme allowed for the working out my salvation, In vain, unnessecary, sinfull Actions, nay Sometymes in Absolute Laziness & sloth"; but she had to develop, not merely implement, "Rules for spending my precious tyme well."[365] This initial and provocative lack of definition assimilates the work of faith to the "unelected vocation" of intellectual labor, and compels it toward ingenuity.[366]

We are familiar with the thesis that the decline of traditional religion atomized the mystical body that had figured Christian community for centuries.[367] Equally familiar is the history that discovers, near the beginning of the long eighteenth century, the emergence of the public sphere. This chapter has tried to show how the idea of a sacred corporate person itself contributed to the formation of the public sphere, understood as an intellectual commons rather than as a "phenomenologically thin" space of debate between rights-bearing individuals. J. G. A. Pocock blamed the topos of the mystical body for England's delay in embracing the notion of the state as a polis maintained by the active efforts of its members, but, reimagined as an agent engaged in the innocent and productive work of discovery, the mystical body provided the very framework for this ideal, opening up the space in which the intellectual laborer could prosecute his endless calling.[368] The ideal of a productive *corpus mysticum* that had made the delving Adam a traditional object of popular identification also inspired seventeenth-century intellectuals to refashion themselves in the image of that sovereign worker, while compelling them to extend intellectual authority to workers themselves. Once its ties to ritual practice were loosened, the mystical body became identified less with the shared experience of sacramental presence than with a shared participation in a sacramental process: the corporate body's continuous transubstantiation of experienced things into facts.

In his eloquent defense of the "indispensable" nature of the concept of the public sphere to historical understanding, Michael McKeon has crucially emphasized its "fundamentally metaphorical" nature: "what's new about the public sphere is that it is a virtual space, a discursive realm of imagined collectivity where people 'come together' in a sense far different from their traditional assembly in the *agora,* the public square, the meeting hall, or the like." In obvious ways, Boyle's metaphor of the invisible college fits the bill; its resistance to absorption by any particular institution, practice, or place—and its corresponding ability to pass through the borders of all three—is proclaimed by its name. But in the seventeenth century it was the original state of creation, and the original person, that provided the archetype for this and other structures of collective and open-ended production, structures whose largely notional or "ideal" character did not render them altogether unreal. In this connection, McKeon credits the public sphere's imaginary form of existence with its ability to sustain the sense of progress: as "an imagined collectivity that is all the more compelling for not being limited by actuality," it becomes the field of "a virtual and collectivized sort of knowledge in perpetual process of formation."[369] He also recommends that eighteenth-century scholars concerned with this entity should become acquainted with its roots in the previous century—a welcome suggestion. As he puts it, the "killing of the king in 1649 also killed the doctrine of the king's two bodies by showing that the death of the natural or private body of monarchy—its separation out from the political or public body of monarchy—did not result in the death of the state." With the abandonment of "esoteric doctrines of public kingship," political discussion could now appeal to "commonsense experience of private citizens" and the "intimate impulses of private conscience."[370] I would tell this story slightly differently, since it was this esoteric doctrine that justified the king's execution: in exemplary contrast to public servants like Hartlib, Charles had perverted his office to serve "privatte ends." Once severed from sacerdotal kingship, this doctrine proved capable of transforming private individuals into public laborers, each of whom might serve and even "stand for" the body of which he or she was also a part. Above all, it was this doctrine that was able to pair a virtual space—a paradise under restoration—to a real sovereign body requiring repopulation and care. Throughout this period, the ingenious sought to identify with and serve a body that would be under improvement until the end of time, when God and all his servants would be "all in all." For those working toward the restoration of this body, the restoration of monarchy could be used as any other occasion for the exercise of the reforming will.

2

A UNION OF EYES AND HANDS

The Royal Society of London for the Improving of Natural Knowledge

Therefore let all men rest in this contented,
For they in ADAM are all represented.
—William Rabisha, *Adam Unvailed, and Seen with Open Face*

Each thinks his Person represents the whole,
And with that thought does multiply his Soul . . .
—Andrew Marvell, *The Last Instructions to a Painter*

The blending of purgatorial labor with the pastoral retreat of the garden made a muddle of the means and ends of paradisal recovery; this was the point. Francis Bacon's call to regain paradise through experiment was brazenly circular: paradise was blissful because it was the ideal place to practice active philosophy. At once the space of progress and its goal, the purgatorial garden also scrambled the concepts of "advancement" and return, giving spatial expression to the logic of reformation itself. The Great Instauration, which meant both a restoration and a founding or institution, explicitly took the Reformation as its model; like the ideal of the primitive church, the labors of innocence projected the crushed potentials of humanity's past onto an imminent future. But in the sphere of maker's knowledge, as opposed to church discipline, progress did not correlate with primitive simplicity; this was the sphere of "Artificial good things and Mechanical Ingenuities."[1] Although artifice had its ultimate origin in the Creator, who used the ingenious as his instruments, this did not change the fact that the restored nature of the experimentalists was a transformed nature, while the image repertoire of the primitive state of creation was indeed primitive. To reopen the field of innocent agency, experimentalists had to reconcile the imagery of Eden to the technological progress of fallen history.

Cain and Abel provided the terms for this operation; Bacon famously suggested that their rivalry figured the postlapsarian divergence of virtues that had formed an ideal union in their father. The innocent shepherd and the founder of a great city, whose descendant Tubalcain was the ancestor of metalworkers in bronze or iron, were handy personifications of a familiar opposition.[2] As Joseph Hall put it, the innocent Adam could play the role either of "an Actor or Spectator"; ever since the time of Cain and Abel, fallen humanity had had to choose between these roles. John Pettus explained that in Cain "Industry, Art, and Nature do concur," while "the pastoral life of *Abel*" affords "all the varieties that Contemplation can afford or administer to us": like a servant catering to an idle master, contemplation "administers" pleasures to the observer, while prestigious nature, aligned with art and industry, is on the side of Cain. In Pettus's remarkably even-handed dramatic reenactment of the conflict, Cain grouses to Abel, "you lead a meer Lazy life" as compared to his own "sweating Labours"; Pettus almost seems concerned to provide a reasonable motive for the fratricide.[3]

Debates over the relative superiority of these traditionally opposed but complementary virtues were an old parlor game that had assumed many forms, and since neither side was actually supposed to win, the suggestion that the ideal life consisted in a judicious blend of the two felt like a fashionable restatement of a familiar idea, a formulation of a truth that had always been implicit. But these innocuous formulations concealed and enabled a profound alteration of their constitutive terms. In urging a union of the active and contemplative lives, experimentalists were widening the meaning of the "active life" beyond the martial, beyond even the political, to embrace the arts that shaped the material conditions of human existence. John Wilkins declared that the "best and most divine knowledge is intended for action, and those may justly be counted barren studies, which doe not conduce to practise as their proper end."[4] The way to distinguish between innocent and fallen curiosity, ingenious and barren pursuits, was that the first bore fruit in productive knowledge, knowledge that produced material effects. This was the traditional distinction between high learning and mechanical know-how, the province of the villain or "rascal." Experimentalists reconsolidated the patrimony that had been distributed across Cain and Abel by taking up the work Aristotle had consigned to natural slaves.

The signature of pastoral is a speaker's provisional identification with a social inferior. By turning this rhetorical performance into a physical apprenticeship, gentlemen virtuosi transformed what William Empson called the pastoral pretense into an investigative art.[5] Like the herdsmen of pastoral who live in nature's bosom and have an insight into nature that their refined betters lack, working-class practitioners could lend their superiors the power to repair a terrible loss. But the knowledge experimentalists sought from workers was not the homely wisdom that the pastoral mode conventionally imputes to them. The belief that workers skilled in the mechanical arts were ahead of idle theorists on the path "back" to nature employs the pastoral assumption that to descend the social scale is to go back in time, but experimentalists had mapped onto humanity's point of origin the concept of progressive knowledge, not primitive simplicity. The blending of pastoral and georgic elements in the new paradise of pains used sacred geography to integrate a degenerate model of history with a progressive one; to complete this integration, experimentalists had to unravel and expose the contradictions of the pastoral mode itself: the mode that made the working man an ironic representative of the gentleman's contemplative ease. In doing so, they invented a new kind of gentleman.

The Royal Society of London for the Improving of Natural Knowledge was a veritable factory for the production of such gentlemen. By attaching nobility to this process of manufacture, Royal Society propaganda offered Restoration society an alternative vision of royalty itself—an Adamic counterterrestoration. This chapter explores the Royal Society virtuoso as the product of a distinctly Adamic ideal of representativeness. The Society existed in order to repair the intellectual losses caused by humanity's fall into social difference; Fellows sought to reconstruct and represent the knowledge proper to the social body as a whole. The Society thus projected a very different image of a well-functioning social body than that suggested by the old metaphor of the body politic, which presented social distinction (the differentiation of the head from the hands) as the basis of social cohesion. Simply put, the Society's self-understanding as a new kind of representative body required its members to engage in behaviors that subverted traditional justifications for social difference. Because it was predicated on access to productive knowledge, the representative identity to which the virtuoso aspired could not be asserted through the kind of mystical substitution that made all of England "representatively present" in the king or Commons, which meant it could never serve as the stable basis for a representative monopoly.[6] One of the large-scale developments of the seventeenth century is the spread of representative identity to those who were not political representatives: by making productive work the foundation for "meeting by representation," the Royal Society played a role in that story.[7] The aims of the Society required an intellectual commons to be realized, and the Society projected a particular image of that commons, as a corporate body in which each strived to be a representative of all.

Michael Hunter has observed that the Royal Society "can only be properly understood if the interplay of ideals and realities is appreciated"; my perspective in this chapter will be decidedly "ideal."[8] If recent scholarship on the Society has been dominated by any theme, it is the discrepancy between the Society's idealized self-representation and its actual workings. Promoters of the "gentlemanly thesis" associated with Steven Shapin and Simon Schaffer rightly point out that, despite its egalitarian rhetoric, privileges of rank were asserted in the Society; as we might expect, the intellectual prestige accorded to productive laborers in experimentalist circles could coexist with rank snobbery toward social inferiors in practice.[9] But if the Society's failure to live up to its protestations of social openness is by now widely recognized, the fact that such openness actually formed the basis of its representative claims has received less attention. If the intellectual commons imaginatively realized in Society propaganda was largely a fiction, it was one that virtuosi nonetheless made some effort to inhabit. Moreover, this working fiction had real cultural effects: elaborating an understanding of intellectual labor as both production and representation, the Royal Society visibly institutionalized an ideal of the intellectual as a public worker. The mythology that the Society elaborated around itself was arguably its most influential product, inspiring genuinely popular imitations like John Dunton's Athenian Society, while practically shaping the aspirations and behavior of virtuosi themselves. To take this mythology seriously is not to suggest that the gestures to social levelling made by gentlemanly virtuosi should be read straight (whatever that would mean). The very fact that these gestures took ambivalent and reversible forms suggests how awkward they must have felt to make, evidence that they cannot be read in purely "functionalist" terms. The Fellow who acted in accordance with the prestige of his office was required to deviate quite radically from gentlemanly behavioral norms; this demand generated social performances that were contradictory, often cringeworthy, and totally novel. If the representative authority of the Society Fellow was distinct from that of the monarch or the MP, it was also distinct from the intellectual authority of the artisan, whose possession of "secrets" proclaimed his access to a carefully guarded source of specialized insight. The Fellow distinguished himself from both of these models of authority by working to integrate them; the result was a union of high and low utterly alien to the pastoral mode.

Ironizing the Golden Age

The myth of pastoral innocence relies on a degenerative understanding of history. In the seventeenth century, this model of history was itself diagnosed as a fiction, as the concepts of historical degeneration and the decay of nature were subject to more intensive debate than ever before. Both concepts trade on an intuitive analogy between history and the individual life, suggesting that the world grows old the way that people do.[10] Donne devotes much of his *First Anniversarie* to describing the world as a putrefying corpse; his poems and sermons return again and again to the contrast between the longevity and massive size of men who lived during the world's youth and the debilitated men of today who are, in fact, "not men."[11] In the wake of George Hakewill's massive refutation of these and other commonplaces associated with the world's "pretended decay," other Baconians rushed to the defense of fallen nature.[12] Modeling the power of ingenuity to discern blessings in apparent curses, Pettus spends two pages singing the praises of the thorns and thistles the fallen earth brings forth; John Beale made the extraction of medicine from thistles the center of an ambitious research program. But while virtuosi like Henry Oldenburg were persuaded that "the world has not grown so old, nor our age so feeble, that nothing memorable can again be brought forth," those convinced that the world was in its dotage enlisted technological innovation as *proof* of nature's decayed state.[13] For moralists like Godfrey Goodman and William Bloys, all arts of civilization are shameful evidence of our need to depend on artificial means for what God was once willing to provide naturally. Even so humble a technology as fertilizer is a mortifying reminder of "how barren we have made the earth by our sins"; humanity must look inward and concentrate on "amending the barren heart, rather than the barren earth."[14]

Although the link between a pessimistic anthropology and the decay of nature was articulated through the doctrine of original sin, it did not originate there. The association between technological progress and moral degeneration is the premise of Hesiod's myth of the four ages: the decline from the gold and silver ages to the bronze and iron ages marks a progression from the natural to the man-made, and thus, by primitivist logic, from harmony to discord.[15] What George Boas calls "hard primitivism" stuck eulogists of primitive virtue with the task of extolling a diet of nuts and acorns. While primitivism could be softened by suggestions that nature once gave more liberally of its crude and wholesome gifts, this did not alter the picture much. Church fathers who mapped the myth of the four ages onto Christian history fostered an association between the spread of sin and the rise of the civilized arts, providing a reason to be grateful to sin for having made life more comfortable; thus the doctrine of *felix culpa* could be securely grounded in a hedonistic motive. The connection of the innocent Adam and Eve with the primitive golden age was irresistible and widespread: when a rector in Essex in 1630 delivered a sermon about Adam and Eve making coats of fig leaves, a parishioner demanded to know where they got the thread to sew them.[16] A golden age or paradise conceived in terms of the absence of such conveniences suggests that the freedom from want enjoyed by our primitive counterparts was a subjective rather than an objective state, aligning humanity's original perfection with the morally prestigious state of contented poverty.

One of the functions of the pastoral mode is to play with the fiction that envy of such a state is possible. The faith that the world of social inferiors offers access to a more desirable, because simpler, past creates Arcadias but cannot survive outside them, and usually is not entertained very seriously within them. Richard Brathwait's plodding "First Satyre of Degeneration" braids the Hesiodic myth with the Genesis account to produce a thoroughly unappealing image of primitive innocence:

> It was a good time when Eve spun her threed,
> And Adam digg'd to earne his food thereby:
> But in this time Eves do their panches feed,
> With daintie dishes moving luxurie.
> That was the golden age, but this is lead.[17]

Most people still lived in this "good time," and those who did not were glad to be spared. Against the labored simplicity of the lines around it, the polysyllabic burst that propels us back to the comfortably fallen present feels altogether welcome.[18] Confirmed in "daintie . . . luxurie" and sin, we can admire a paradise as safely out of reach as that evoked in Donne's "Twicknam Garden."

On this understanding, the consolations of pastoral and the fortunate fall are the same: both represent primitive nature (poverty) under the reassuring sign of its loss. In the seventeenth century, however, the thread connecting this familiar doctrine to that most familiar of all literary spaces, Arcadia, snapped, and caused that space to change. Seventeenth-century pastoral spaces increasingly resemble the landscape of Virgil's fourth eclogue, in which the first and last ages come together. This poem famously envisions humanity returning to its golden origins by iron means: humanity will no longer be driven by dissatisfaction with what nature provides to violate the boundaries between sea and land, or art and nature, because the natural world will itself abound with manufactured goods and services.[19] Sheep will spontaneously dye themselves while at pasture, enabling Romans to wear brilliant clothes without being guilty of manufacturing or trading for them.[20] Like most of Virgil's optimistic prophecies, this one may disguise a discreet reproach; the sheep are blushing, whether out of pride in their gaudy coats or in shame over humanity's need for them it is hard to tell. Posing as an emblem of the reconciliation of the first and last ages, the image only makes the discrepancy between them more pronounced; flamboyantly colored sheep are gifts of nature for which our golden age counterparts would have felt no need. Fulfilling Virgil's prophecy, they bear the traces of the modernity from which they promise to deliver us. Virgil describes their transformation using *mutabit*, the same word he uses for overseas trade: the navigation, commerce, and artifice eradicated by goldenness reemerge in the fleece of literally outlandish animals.[21] Composites of nature and artifice, past and present, these sheep would seem to embody the compromises necessary to provide even imaginary satisfaction to originary longing. Unsettling the primitivist fantasy he initially pretends to promote, Virgil has staged an aggressive intervention into nature's laws, recuperating the technology he has suppressed by a sleight-of-hand that makes artifice natural. Of course, in this simultaneously primitivistic and futuristic piece of science fiction, the craftsman's labor of coercing nature is sublimated into purely literary art: in place of craftsman's knowledge that intervenes in nature, we get art that does violence to its own primitivistic premise.

It is the newborn infant that provides the excuse; through an innocent figure that matures and evolves, the poem is made to accommodate all that it is supposed to exclude. Interpreted syncretically as the infant Jesus by later commentators, this innocent could model as well another kind of "second Adam," a paradisally restored humanity. For Christian readers, the crux lay in *scelens vestigia,* which Augustine identified with original sin, but the sheep bearing the traces of deceitful modernity remain stubborn mascots of the technological impulse (often associated with Virgil in his supposed sideline as a magician). It is "for the relief of man's estate," as Bacon puts it, that Virgil wrenches nature from its regular course, weaving maker's knowledge into the very nature it works upon.[22]

Paul Alpers has called the fourth eclogue a poem that consciously tests "the limits of pastoral expression"; it does so through a landscape that exposes the logic of the mode.[23] We know that we read pastoral in order to encounter, in disguised form, all that it is supposed to exclude. This insight has been a generative one for criticism that presents the shepherd as an ironic instrument of political criticism or self-advancement, and it was popular among Renaissance theorists, who habitually associate the pastoral mode with a cloak or other form of disguise; George Puttenham regarded pastoral as a technique of using "rude" exteriors to "glaunce at greater matters."[24] Similarly, Empson taught us to see pastoral as the "trick" of putting "the complex into the simple": the rustic who speaks like a courtier can thus easily be replaced by Lewis Carroll's Alice, the child who speaks like an adult; the important thing is that the "effective elements" of society be given expression in a single speaker. But the trick of putting courtly speeches into a worker's mouth is more cunning than that; it ironically imputes to the worker knowledge he does not have in order to efface the knowledge he does have. What Michael Drayton called "speeches in Verse, fathered upon Heardsmen," creates opportunities for those who lack productive knowledge to feel more intensely their knowledge of other things, to be freed from a potentially humiliating awareness of their dependence on rude knowledge over which they have no personal mastery.[25] Thus personal ignorance is projected outward as the "innocence" of someone else. By turning labor into idleness, pastoral drives away from the scene of work the knowledge production that, under preindustrial conditions, inevitably accompanies productive labor. The concentration of all the labors entailed by agricultural production into the single task of digging is, in this respect, a pastoral reduction, equivalent to the reduction of animal husbandry to passing time in the company of sheep.[26] Experimentalists like Winstanley resisted this reduction by dilating the meaning of digging to include the rational penetration of creation; Virgil penetrates the pretense by revealing the processes of *techne* on the sheep's very body.

It is when maker's knowledge is divorced from its agents and given mythic or generalized expression that the classical tradition acknowledges its power, imputing to it something like the heroic daring and moral complexity of the Faust myth. The dyeing of wool, in particular, is a frequent emblem in Roman poetry for luxury and decadence; dyeing gave visual concreteness to the coupling of technology with deceitful cunning suggested by Prometheus's theft of fire from Zeus. These acknowledgments of the power of maker's knowledge suggest how much effort must have gone into upholding the pretense that genuine knowledge could, as Seneca put it, have nothing to do with tools or anything else involving a bent body and a mind gazing upon the ground. Such acknowledgments continually erupt within the philosophical tradition itself. Plato describes the agents of maker's knowledge as occupants of a subphilosophical realm: knowledge of the ephemeral and the particular is not "certain" knowledge; it cannot be demonstrated syllogistically, only physically. But when he needs to demonstrate the human capacity for rationally guided action, he constantly repairs to examples from the crafts. His insistence on the base and degrading nature of any activity that brings man into intimate contact with matter is constantly belied by this tendency, which at one point in the *Gorgias* leads Callicles to complain that he never stops talking about cobblers, fullers, cooks, and doctors as if his argument were actually about them. Once extracted and removed from the actual body of the worker, such productive knowledge can be extolled and employed as a philosophical model; it can even be feared.[27]

As the fourth eclogue suggests, this productive knowledge is contained within and disguised by pastoral's mascot. The imagined whiteness of the sheep, proclaiming the creature's identity as a blank canvas, is a furtive sign of its colorful destiny; the artificial image of the perfectly white sheep not only implies Virgil's purple sheep, it is their disguise. It is because we imagine sheep as being natural clones that counting imaginary sheep is supposed to make us drowsy, and the thought of purple sheep, nervous, but the unnatural image is anticipated by the equally artificial image it violates.

(The name of the most famous sheep of the twentieth century, Dolly, itself evokes the innocence of childhood, but it does so by evoking the child's first encounter with the replica.) Similarly, when we call someone a "dyed-in-the-wool conservative," we mean that the person is ineradicably that way, almost as a matter of her essence or nature; referring to the process of dying raw wool right off the sheep's back, the idiom enacts the naturalizing power of culture that it describes. Giving the lie to this fantasy of laying hands on nature in the raw, Virgil peels away the disguise of pastoral to reveal the plain old white domesticated sheep for what it already is: second nature, the product of human pains. The image repertoire of pastoral is always the ground of georgic care.

If Virgil playfully attempts to "gild" this space where nature and the human crafting of it meet, experimentalists attempted to subject that space to infinite expansion, casting themselves as the artists and authors not of an ambivalent fantasy but of a changed world. Suggesting that the dominion Adam had over the creatures might be regained, and even exceeded, Boyle expressed gratitude that God had granted man "the power to introduce so many Formes . . . and work such changes among the Creatures." Virgil's sheep have biblical siblings in the speckled, streaked, and spotted sheep Jacob was able to cultivate by art with green- and-white-striped rods, in which seventeenth-century commentators discerned the remnants of a paradisal technology.[28] Boyle's friend Thomas Vaughan was convinced that Jacob's "*Art* to *Multiplie* his own *Colours*" that enabled the "*Propagation* of his *speckled Flocks*" was derived from Adam. Brandishing the marks of art, these sheep testify to the interventionist power of their custodians. Pettus's Adam is thus not only a metallurgist but a genetic engineer, creating a "Diversity of *Species* by Transplantations, Ingraftings, Inoculatings, and other various Cultivations."[29] This understanding of Genesis 2:19 transforms semiosis into the law of pure convertibility; semantic proliferation is fused with the sense of a "proper name," the name through which one can take possession of an object, as when one lays claim to a piece of land as *Virginia* and begins to "improve" it. Such a speech act sublimates the impropriety of naming: each named thing can be made into anything that one desires, and intervention becomes natural, creating something like the second golden age Virgil wished on posterity.

The philosophical tradition at once acknowledged that imposing new forms on matter was a defining human endowment, even a privileged instance of rationally guided action, while consigning the actual execution of such tasks to brutes and slaves. The result of the hard division between philosophical knowledge and maker's knowledge was that the scholar lacked the very traits that were conventionally invoked to distinguish humans from beasts. Of course, the priest of the old religion combined university learning with the power to miraculously transform matter; the reformed clergy lacked even this opportunity. The powers that Boyle celebrates as God's most precious gifts to humanity were powers scholars were just beginning to discover. The brilliant Sir William Petty was almost overwhelmed by the task of explaining all the steps involved in transforming wool into cloth: having "curiously" looked into every stage of the process and produced a lengthy report for the Royal Society, he concluded that, especially when it came to the "great and subtil work" of shearing, "the sight itself cannot scarce apprehend it, much less can words describe it; for it is only the touch of the workman's hand, that can understand it." To gain access to all these "secrets," scholars really did need to learn a new language. In doing so, they had to divest themselves of their university training and even the marks of their social status—to "unlive our former lives."[30] This entailed a surrender of the pastoral mode, the primitivist mythology that identified innocent humanity, and the rugged virtue of the laborer, with simplicity (Hakewill's remark that the decay of nature was an "*idle tale* and *vaine fancie* forged by *Poets*" reflects an awareness that it was largely a literary tradition they were fighting).[31] In declaring their humble willingness to learn from their social inferiors, experimentalists sometimes pretended to take up the pastoral pretense, but they were doing something quite different. In attempting to embody the "innocence" of the humble laborer, they were trying to gain intellectual sophistication, not escape its burdens.

Even our most critical accounts of pastoral, such as Raymond Williams's critique of pastoral's reduction of primary activity to mere form, do not focus on its containment of the specifically intellectual threat posed by working knowledge.[32] Indeed, most accounts do not acknowledge that any such threat exists. Defining pastoral as a mode devoted to the lives of "herdsmen or their equivalents," in which he includes not only Andrew Marvell's Mower but a wide variety of workers, Alpers's account of pastoral, like Empson's, invites broad application, requisitioning what looks like georgic territory, but without drawing the implications that the fourth eclogue does. Like Empson, Alpers focuses not on any particular image repertoire but on a particular motive: the attempt of intellectuals to identify with people who work for a living. But neither he nor Empson identifies the basic motive behind the pastoral motive: an awareness of worker's knowledge and a desire to drive that awareness away. Both accounts are predicated on the assumption that whatever admiration one might feel for a social inferior, intellectual esteem is unlikely to play a large role in it. As Alpers puts it, pastoral concerns people who are "traditionally considered 'simple'" and who have a diminished strength relative to the world. Such speakers can endure but never overcome their lot; they derive their dignity, in other words, from being noble losers.[33] As long as labor was regarded simply as a curse it would be hard to imagine any other way to understand a persona modeled after those who bore the brunt of it. Puttenham expresses the point with refreshing directness:

> the actions of meane and base personages, tend in very few cases to any great good example: for who passeth to follow the steps, and maner of life of a craftes man, shepheard or sailer, though he were his father or dearest friend? yea how almost is it possible that such maner of men should be of any vertue other then their profession requireth?

But experimentalist intellectuals did copy "meane and base personages" (and, as we will see in subsequent chapters, other intellectuals copied their copying), drawing on the experience and testimony of what Sprat called "extraordinary men, though but of ordinary Trades."[34]

Alpers concedes that pastoral and georgic "merge in various ways" during the seventeenth century because "in Christian thought ideas of humility are connected with the curse of labor," but this is not an adequate description of the seventeenth-century intellectual climate.[35] Alastair Fowler has objected that the "recent blurring of pastoral and georgic does not exactly help us to understand the history of English literature in the seventeenth century. For one of the largest and most significant changes during that period was the displacement of pastoral by georgic."[36] I suggest that the reason for the change was that the assumption behind the pastoral pretense was no longer possible to entertain even provisionally. What Empson describes as the quintessentially pastoral sentiment of the high regarding the low—"I am in one way better, in another not so good"—lost its disingenuous character.[37] Rueful condescension had fluctuated into its opposite, for the knowledge of people "traditionally regarded as simple" did not turn out to be simple. By the measure Alpers employs, the speaker's strength relative to the world, the worker came out ahead of the scholar once the world was identified with the physical forces that constituted it. What was once a disingenuous pretense had become an entry into ingenuity.

Robert Hooke suggested that there was much knowledge to be gained "scattered up and down" the social scale of "Mens Practices"; men who labored with their hands held "many excellent Experiments and Secrets." Locke argued that "a Smith, or a Jeweller" has more accurate complex ideas about the substances he deals with than the scholastic philosopher, "who, whatever substantial forms he may talk of, has no other *Idea* of those Substances, than what is framed by a collection of those simple *Ideas* which are to be found in them." But, by adding together such ideas, the mind could extend itself even to infinity, approximating the perceptual knowledge of an angel; it is by acquainting oneself with the ideas of the smith that one moves toward the angel.[38] Experimentalists assumed the identities of workers in order to realize their own intellectual ambition. In doing so, they moved out of the realm of "allegorical travesty and satirical mask," as Renato Poggioli describes pastoral, and into a genuinely hybrid identity.[39]

This new species of person required a new habitat. I have argued that experimental space was expressed through sacred geography as a purgatorial paradise of pains; in sublunary geography, it was mapped onto the New World. The journeys of discovery served as Bacon's dominant figure for experimental philosophy, but experimentalists used purgatory and America to figure an equally exotic space: the sphere of lower-class work. As an anonymous Royal Society memo put it, the "enquiring of persons of all Professions, Trades, & Occupations . . . might Lead us into an unknown world."[40] It was through the actual journeys of discovery that the mixed space of the fourth eclogue first acquired physical reality, which is why Bacon places his scientific utopia, the New Atlantis, at the end of such a journey. In their descriptions of America as a newfound Eden, explorers made Virgilian concessions to iron-age appetites, assaulting the paradise they sought to restore most flagrantly by employing "impious boats" to get there. The frontispiece of the *True Pictures of the People in . . . Virginia*, appended to Thomas Harriot's *Briefe and True Report of the Newfound Land of Virginia*, shows Adam and Eve about to eat the apple: the image of a world suspended between innocence and the fall provides the template for the uneasily mixed space the reader is about to enter. The colonization of America is figured as England's incorporation of Eden, a swelling of the nation to include that paradisal terrain literally and conceptually. Harriot celebrates Virginia as a recovered Eden where the golden age still reigns (involving himself in some difficulty, since the Iroquois whom he describes as fishermen and gatherers of wild fruit were also farmers, a fact he admits with some reluctance), all the while insisting to potential investors that it abounded with "marchantable commodities." Blended into this investors' report is a checklist of golden age motifs: while the modest diet of the Iroquois preserves them from the diseases of civilization generated by gluttonous luxury, their country is well-adapted to cultivating crops that will cater to it.[41] Documenting Harriot's restless search for commodities in paradise, the *Report* shows Virgil's *reductio ad absurdum* becoming a self-evident assumption: the recovery of paradise depends on tailoring it to meet fallen demands. A century later, in *Magnalia Christi Americana,* Cotton Mather, the first native-born American to be a member of the Royal Society, introduced the founding of the Massachusetts Bay Colony with the fourth eclogue's opening words—"paulo maiora"—without any sense of having brought in the serpent at all.[42]

Bacon suggested that the discovery of America fulfilled the first part of the prophecy in Daniel 12:4: "Many shall run to and fro; and knowledge shall be increased"; the great instauration would fulfill the latter part. Both opened up new worlds in which originary longings could be reconciled to progress. Just as journeys across the ocean were journeys back to the future, so scientific discoveries were *re*coveries of prehistoric wisdom that could reveal "an *America* of secrets, and unknown *Peru* of Nature." Without sailing beyond "the *Land* of gross and vulgar Doctrines . . . we are not likely to reach the Treasures on the other side the *Atlantick:* The directing of the World the way to which, is the noble end of true *Philosohpy* [*sic*]." An America could be found closer to home, under artificially contrived conditions that were even more alien than those created by mere change of place.[43] Coding the space of the university as a "*Land* of gross and vulgar Doctrines" while identifying the knowledge of the vulgar as the shore of a soon-to-be-recovered paradise, experimentalists inverted class-based modifiers to expose the pastoral pretense—the identification of workers, and humanity's originals, with a primitivist past—as a fallen illusion.

Thus one of the testimonials prefacing the 1640 edition of Bacon's *Advancement of Learning* praises Bacon as one who "*may seem to have learn'd his knowledge* even in the Schoole of the First Man," while the frontispiece provides a graphic expression of the first school's curriculum: William Marshall's engraving depicts a ship sailing beyond the pillars of Hercules, labeled Oxford and Cambridge. The two parts of the Daniel prophecy (reproduced on the title page: "*Multi pertransibunt & augebitur scientia*") are contracted into a single image as the commonwealth of learning's ship of state sets off to found new worlds. In the sky sit two globes, labeled the *Mundus visibilis* and the *Mundus intellectualis,* from which two arms extend and lock hands. This handshake, an emblem of the original commerce of the human mind with things, reveals that the journey being symbolized here is the thinker's journey into the working world. The discovery it proclaims is that thinkers had to become workers, because workers, it turned out, were thinkers. As my account of pastoral suggests, this was more of an admission than a discovery.

If the pastoral pretense was a reaction against the impenetrability of the scene of labor—a means to exercise symbolic mastery over, and establish elite community in, a site of knowledge that excluded the learned—print provided the means to treat the underlying condition.[44] In the first century of printing perhaps the most common printed matter aside from religious material dealt with the realm of "secrets" known only to workers. Some of these were, or pretended to be, guild secrets. This strategically inexplicit literature, which often merely hinted at the skills involved, lent the artisan some of the mystery that once surrounded the priest.[45] The realm of guild knowledge was mysterious, secretive, and unsystematized primarily for economic reasons—guildmembers' exclusive possession of this knowledge insured their livelihood—but also because there was often little point in trying to spell it out.[46] Apprentices learned these techniques through experience, by doing. Paracelsus was able to impute a mystical and magical character to artisanal knowledge, calling carpenters alchemists of wood and so on, because for most of his readers this knowledge really was profoundly mysterious. "Chiromancy" must have seemed as good a word as any for the unfailing ability of some carpenters and joiners, for example, to select wood that was resistant to warping.[47] The distinction between the magician and the artisan was in fact a porous one; a 1561 arrest for magical offenses rounded up a merchant, an ironmonger, a salter, a goldsmith, and a miller.[48] As Paracelsus suggested and as many experimentalists believed, to some degree all artisans were magicians, though their transformations of matter, unlike the priestly miracle, were the product of pains.

The belief that the worker's life was one of epistemological privilege was not projected exclusively onto artisans. The phenomenal culture of rustics and commoners, whose intellectual life had evolved for centuries in isolation from the Latinate culture of the university, was rich in what experimentalists called receipts or relations, often delivered in the form of "folk wisdom." More diffuse and less reliable than the knowledge of skilled craftsmen, this knowledge was also the product of centuries of discourse and experience, of collectively undertaken trial and error. Within working communities, medical practitioners without formal training, along with so-called wizards and wise women, had an enormous store of knowledge, particularly of herbs; the superiority of "kitchen physic" to the care of university-trained practitioners was a commonplace. "Old women" are mentioned by almost every early modern botanist, but old women's knowledge extended unpredictably in all directions. Extolling the "laborious Bee," Charles Butler observed that "the contemplation thereof may well beseeme an ingenious nature," but he went on to warn that the scholar steeped in bee lore extracted from Aristotle, Pliny, and the "grave fathers of the Church" (who said "little out of experience") was not as "throughly instructed in these mysteries" as he might imagine. When such an inkhornist tries to put his knowledge into practice as a bee-keeper, "every silie woman is ready to deride his learned ignorance." It was from these silly women that the scholar had to learn.[49] Henry Power thus declared himself ready to accept tutelage from "any shee-empirick";[50] Thomas Vaughan violated both masculinist and class norms when he asserted that women might be "fitter" for natural investigations than men, "for in such things they are more *neat* and *patient,* being used to a small *Chimistrie* of *Sack-possets,* and other finicall *Sugar-sops.*"[51] Through the "finicall" habits of the kitchen, real knowledge was produced. Evelyn's decision to share his discovery that stale bread could be improved by being warmed gives some idea of just how alien this space was to some gentlemen.[52]

Bishop Jewel complained that ignorant wizards boasted they had inherited their cunning from Moses, the Archangel Raphael, or Adam; in some way experimentalists believed this was true. By virtue of their very isolation from centers of scholastic learning, and their necessary immersion in "things themselves" in order to make a living, such knowledge producers were closer than most university men to "the flourishing Universitie of Eden."[53] The repository of "working knowledge" was capable of travel over chronological and geographical distances, by which, John Aubrey believed, it was no doubt corrupted: in other words, it was much like the *prisca theologia,* the ancient philosophy stretching back to Adam, believed to have had an underground existence throughout the centuries through such figures as Moses.[54] Rather than vainglorious displays of rhetorical brio, the intellectual performances that made up this tradition were the fruits of labor undertaken by the collective subject of humanity in traffic with nature; in this sense, they were indisputably the fruits of Adam's labor. Ancient "vulgar" knowledge was created within a true *universitas,* a "collection in one body of a plurality of persons."[55] Corruptions of the knowledge produced by this Adamic body could often be traced to the fallen universities themselves. As Thomas Browne observed, many of the "vulgar errors" he sought to correct could be traced to "some good Author"—to Pliny, or medieval chroniclers, whose "fabulous" inventions priests and schoolmen had disseminated among the vulgar. The testimonies of antiquity were often contradicted by "common and Country observation"; while Aristotle "did not understand a muscle," working butchers did.[56] Aubrey wondered whether printing itself was responsible for making "Old-wives Tales" less "ingeniose," as if the university of ingenuity had been corrupted by the written and printed word; the technology that opened up access to this world also made it susceptible to adulteration. Indeed, the "First and Father-cause of common Error," the fall, could itself be traced to Eve's dependence on a "secondary narration."[57] Relations had to be tried to warrant belief; those who sought to redeem vulgar knowledge from vulgar errors had to test it by vulgar means.

One might say that virtuosi simply announced what everybody already knew: to find out about things, one had to ask people who knew about them. A seventeenth-century shopkeeper used the utmost "importunacie" to extract a secret from a customer for stanching blood "which is privatly usd amongst countrie persons, and not publickly knowen"; virtuosi merely systematized these efforts at knowledge extraction and elaborated the moral: that the *terra incognita* of worker's knowledge had remained unexplored, its very existence denied, because of upper-class pride.[58] The classificatory schemes sixteenth- and seventeenth-century people used to describe their society were in fact studiously vague about the lower orders; beneath the threshold of the minor nobility, chaos reigned. Sir Thomas Smith distinguished between yeomen on one hand and citizens and burgesses on the other and used the designation "rascall" for everyone else, from day laborers to merchants. William Harrison was particularly confused as to the location of artisans in his scheme: he distinguished yeomen from "laborers and the common sort of artificers," explaining that they are "gentlemen . . . or at the leastwise artificers"; on the very next page, however, he places "all artificers" in the category of the "fourth and last sort of people in England." Such vagueness provided further protection from the *terra incognita* of productive knowledge, that "America of secrets" separating gentlemen—all those who could "live without labour"—from everyone else.[59]

In an attempt to penetrate this culture for the benefit of "the curious," virtuosi like Aubrey and John Ray recovered as many "vulgar Proverbs" as they could, "for proverbs are drawn from the experience and observations of many ages; and are the ancient natural philosophy of the vulgar, preserved in old English in bad rhythmes, handed downe to us"; Aubrey thus set them down as *Instantiae Crucis* for our curious moderne philosophers to examine."[60] Aubrey's interest in popular superstitions has less in common with Herrick's condescending affection for them than modern readers may assume. His famous declaration that printing and gunpowder had scared away "Robin-good-fellow and the Fayries" had a corollary: history's next phase consisted in the extraction of experimental truths from "old Fables"; his argument that fables often disguised "the profoundest natural Magick" appealed to Bacon's *Wisdom of the Ancients*. This project of recovery is the very opposite of the preservation effort undertaken in *Hesperides*. When, in "Another to Bring in the Witch," Herrick wryly describes the cake of cornmeal and piss that "will bring / The old Hag in. No surer thing," we are supposed to chuckle at the superstitious gullibility of country people even while approving of it.[61] As experimentalists found, however, even unpromising genres like doggerel verse—the "bad rhythmes" Herrick imitates here—turned out to be vehicles of knowledge; practical wisdom was often expressed in couplets to aid retention by the illiterate: "In June and August, as well doth appeere, is best to mowe brakes, of all times in the yeere." As John Norden observed, partly because of their use of such methods, the illiterate seemed to have "more retentive" minds: they could not depend on "the use of the pen," but "the memorie only . . . fed with continuall pondering the things they delight in."[62] Norden idealizes the working life as one of "continuall pondering," rich in the contemplative delights that Baconians insisted had characterized the world of Genesis 2:19, that "unthorny place of knowledg." This illusion signals the surrender of another: such idealizations of the working life were part of an effort to redefine "the simple folk," a sloughing off of the pastoral pretense.[63]

Nourishing the Body Politic

For those eager to navigate the Atlantic of secrets that lay just beyond the gates of Oxbridge, Gresham College was a natural starting point. Laud had charged the institution with fostering criminal gatherings or conventicles; in 1636 he requested that articles be drawn up for an archiepiscopal visitation.[64] A center for practical adult education founded in 1598 by the merchant Sir Thomas Gresham (who was related to Bacon by the marriages of his aunt and half-brother), Gresham allowed its instructors to abandon the university practice of instruction through textual commentary. Wilkins supported public lectures in the vulgar tongue to inspire "every unlettered ingenious Artificer," and this is what Gresham provided: its classes were in English, on practical matters geared toward the public at large; its course in astronomy, for example, was customized to "the capacity of mariners." Its approach to instruction and openness to all who cared to attend made it almost the opposite of a university. Bacon had imagined endowed lectureships in applied fields that would free the universities from Aristotle's grip; what Gresham created was even more visionary—an institution that served the general population.[65]

Bacon's plan for university reform was implemented, however, when John Wilkins, John Wallis, and Jonathan Goddard were installed at Oxford as part of the program to "Greshamize" the universities. (The members of the Oxford Philosophical club with any connection to the university were all "intruded" there in place of dismissed royalists).[66] At that point, as Wallis recalled later, the Gresham group divided. The new Oxford lecturers convened with "the most inquisitive Persons" there—not indeed in the university itself, but at the house of an apothecary where Petty had moved, in order "to view, and make use, of Drugs and other like matters, as there was occasion." Others met in London, as before: "In the mean while, our

Company at *Gresham*-Colledge being much again increased, by the accession of divers Eminent and Noble Persons upon His Majesties return; we were (about the beginning of the Year 1662) by His Majesties Grace and Favour, *Incorporated* by the Name of *The Royal Society*."[67] A seamless continuity is suggested here; Wallis is making clear that "our Company" did not owe its existence to the king's "Grace and Favour."

In common speech, the Society was still referred to simply as "Gresham."[68] The activities of those who gathered there remained the same; Hooke and Boyle worked on making their air pump more "staunch," those qualified to do so made astronomical observations, and all the Fellows pored over "curiosities." Hartlib's work was carried on through the Society's prodigious international correspondence, coordinated by his protégé and occasional roommate, Henry Oldenburg, who became the Society's first secretary. (Hartlib died the year the Society received its charter.)[69] Correspondents could simply use the address "Mr. Oldenburg, London" and have their letters delivered to the Society, perhaps even published. It was as impossible to have a private correspondence with Oldenburg as it had been with his mentor, and correspondents like John Beale (whom Oldenburg inherited from Hartlib) regularly had their letters read out loud to the Fellows.[70]

Charles did not involve himself much with the affairs of the Society, unless his decision to lock Oldenburg in the Tower for two months counts as involvement.[71] As we will see in Chapter 4, Charles also attempted to close down coffeehouses, where Fellows regularly met. Much less did he fund its projects as had been hoped. As Samuel Pepys famously reported, "Gresham College he mightily laughed at, for spending time only in weighing of ayre, and doing nothing else since they sat." Although Charles was happy to place bets on the outcome of their pneumatic experiments, he was not willing to pay for them.[72] Of course, he identified himself as the founder of the Society in its charter-book and declared his "readiness to give them all due encouragement." The hope that such "encouragement" might be material, and that "as his majesty being their founder, might also be their chief benefactor," was relinquished only slowly. By 1665, it seems, reality had sunk in: "It was resolved, that the business of procuring benefactors, and the manner of well managing the same, should now be begun to be seriously considered of."[73] Foreign visitors who assumed that the Royal Society was the equivalent of continental academies were surprised by the lack of seriousness with which the king treated a body that bore the royal name. One Italian visitor, Lorenzo Magalotti, secretary of the Accademia del Cimento, patronized by the Medici, was stunned when he heard that Charles called the Fellows his "fools." Having gleaned that, in Britain, the virtuoso was not "the most advantageous role in which to find favour in courts," he initially sought to make his visit there as brief as possible.[74] It might be said that the Fellows did not even rise to the status of fools or court jesters, since, far from treating the Society as an extension of the court, Charles seems never to have visited the Society, despite its anxious preparations for such a visit.[75] The author of an anonymous Society memo worried that the king was teaching the whole court "to despise us" and that the city and country might follow suit, "And at last perhaps [we] shall be ready to despise ourselves."[76]

Remarking on Charles's lack of support for the Society, Mario Biagioli concludes that its "'Royal' was an almost empty signifier," but a very useful one all the same; Oldenburg used it to insinuate to overseas correspondents that the Society enjoyed more royal support than it did. Even as he sought to enhance the Society's prestige in the eyes of contemporaries accustomed to patronage-based science, Oldenburg was solidifying a correspondence network that was as instrumental as the *Philosophical Transactions* themselves in effecting the transition of science from a patronage system to what Biagioli calls "corporate infrastructures" based on "peer-based protocols."[77] In this sense, the "Royal" predicate was systematically ambiguous rather than empty. To foreigners Oldenburg was happy to claim that "our king bestows remarkable favor upon us and has resolved to endow generously this, his Royal Society," but the possessive pronoun often goes missing when he is addressing Fellows themselves. When he complains that there are not "performances enough" for "a R. Society," or warns that, unless more Fellows "putt their shoulders to the work," their "Noble Institution will come far short of its End," it is clear that predicates like *royal* and *noble* have become honorifics that the Fellows must earn through their labor.[78]

Charles did provide the Fellows with some regalia. As Evelyn proudly reported, the king was "pleas'd to give us the armes of England, to beare in a *Canton,* in our *Armes,* & send us a Mace of Silver guilt of the same fashion & bignesse with those carried before his Majestie to be borne before our

President on Meeting-daies."[79] The kingly mace was as big as Charles's, but it was held up before someone else; in this space, the royal prerogative shifted from the king to the collective that gathered there to produce knowledge out of, and declare their sovereignty over, things. The Society's antagonist Henry Stubbe protested that not even the general councils of the Catholic church aspired to be "*Sovereigns* to determine of *new truths*," but this is exactly how the Fellows presented themselves.[80] In doing so, they met with the same resistance that the Levellers had. As *A Declaration of some Proceedings of Lt. Col. John Lilburn* insisted, "you can represent your *own pressures,* but not those of *all the Kingdom,* for *you are not all the Kingdom* . . . remember this, and be modest for once, act not as if you were *all.*"[81] At the time, of course, such objections only underscored the tenuous nature of the Parliament's own representative claims. But rather than representing "pressures," the Fellows saw themselves as representing the knowledge-producing strengths of the whole realm; indeed, with its charter, royal mace, and coat of arms, the Society attempted to conduct itself as a superior sort of representative body. The authors of the 1604 Apology of the Commons had warned James I that the "voice of the people in things of their knowledge is said to be as the voice of God": the Royal Society brought a new inflection to this statement, identifying the people's practical knowledge of "real things" as knowledge of public importance.[82] By insisting on their identity as public servants, gentlemen members defended life choices that were, to say the least, unusual for members of their class.

The royal charters of 1662 and 1663 ratified the Society's permanent constitution, ensuring the "perpetual succession" of its *"Immortal"* body: a president, a treasurer, two elected secretaries, and an elected decision-making council of twenty-one Fellows, ten of whom were replaced through yearly elections.[83] (When he was nominated to the council, Evelyn excitedly wrote in his diary that he was now empowered to make "Laws & statutes.") At meetings, the president sat at the head table with the secretary at his side, the Fellows on benches "as they think fit, and without any Ceremony." The Fellows were to "form an *Assembly* . . . whose privileges shall be the same; whose gain shall be in common; whose *Members* were not brought up at the feet of each other."[84] But they all together showed deference to the president, formally addressing speech to him rather than to each other, and removed their hats when speaking.[85] As Shapin has suggested, the Fellows were imitating procedures from the House of Commons.[86] Members of the House were also supposed to occupy any available seat, without regard to precedence, "no difference being there held of any degree," and to keep their hats on; when speaking, they were to remove their hats and address their remarks to the Speaker (before whom the Sergeant at Arms carried a mace).[87] Observing that all visitors to the Society remarked on its mace, Shapin suggests that the mace indicated that the ultimate source of its authority was royal: "its authority flowed from, and was of the same quality as, that of the king." I believe these two claims are separable (indeed, they are hard to square with one another), and there is evidence to suggest that Fellows (like the MPs they imitated) resented their conflation. When Samuel Sorbière, a French visitor to the Society, published an admiring account of the Society that laid great stress on the king's sponsorship of the body, Sprat took issue with almost everything he wrote. Sorbière's suggestion that Charles "gave them *Gresham Colledge*" elicited the testy response that the Fellows met in Gresham "by the Permission of the Professors of the Foundation of Sir *Thomas Gresham,* to whom that House does belong. We are beholden to him for this Noble Bounty."[88] Given that Sorbière found the English Parliament "a bizarre body" (a phrase removed from the English version of his account),[89] it stands to reason that he treated the Society as a virtual extension of the court, and that, accordingly, he emphasized the ceremonial aspect of its meetings. This emphasis infuriated Sprat: after quoting a long passage filled with the Frenchman's "Tittle-tattle" about the mace and other "mean Circumstances," he exploded, "Can you, Sir, indure to read all this Stuff with any Patience?" Was it not a "shameful Weakness" to dwell on the forms rather than the "Noble Matter" of the Fellows' meetings "when the *Royal Society* itself is so careful that such Ceremonies should be just no more than what are necessary to avoid Confusion?" Sprat's touchiness regarding the true nature and source of the Society's "nobility" gains further significance in light of Hunter's suggestion that its proceedings may have been modeled on the Rota: parallels between the two organizations include the use of a secret ballot to reach decisions, contributions levied from members, dependence on a committee structure (which, however, was shared by Parliament), and, for a brief time, the monthly rotation of the chairmanship. These parallels are particularly suggestive in light of the fact that eleven of the Rota's twenty-seven known members became Fellows.[90] If it is clear that the Fellows were collectively laying claim to a representative identity, it is equally clear that this identity was to be rigorously distinguished from that of political representatives like the king, or indeed the MP, representatives whose authority depended on the "mean" trappings of office. The Fellows' identity as public persons was grounded in the "Noble Matter" of their work.[91]

While the parallels between the Society and Parliament are striking, they only become meaningful when interpreted against the backdrop of the two bodies' differences. As Oliver Arnold has shown, early modern accounts of Parliamentary representation matched the mysticism that attended sacramental kingship.[92] Confirming Bacon's argument that every person in England was present in the Commons "representatively," Sir Thomas Smith in *De Republica Anglorum* declared that "everie Englishman is entended to bee there present . . . from the Prince (be he King or Queene) to the lowest person of Englande. And the consent of the Parliament is taken to be everie mans consent."[93] Coke arrogated the power of representation to the Commons alone: while the monarch and the nobles "represented but themselves . . . [the] Commons though they were but inferior men, yet every one of them represented a thousand of men."[94] Such statements are clearly to be understood by analogy to the eucharistic doctrine of real presence. At other times, however, MPs articulated their representative powers in virtually prosthetic terms, arguing from the limitations of the monarch's body natural: the monarch could not "be in every corner of his kingdome and dominions at one instant," and the Commons could supplement this deficiency; its members had "many eyes to se, many feet to go, and many hands to labour withall, and so sircumspect they are for the government of the commonwealth."[95] Although the claim about eyes and feet sounds reasonable, since most MPs must have visited their home districts at least occasionally, the laboring hands are distinctly odd. Evidently, neither the magic of sacramental substitution nor their willingness to confer with their constituents was sufficient to perform the trick of representative presence; that required the trick of pastoral. MPs felt compelled to impersonate the people they represented, adopting clownish exteriors to "glaunce at greater matters."

Proudly supporting a bill that would not suit his "perticular" financial interests in 1601, William Hakewill elaborated a theatrical understanding of his role, entering the pastoral space of "allegorical travesty":

> We must laye downe the respectes of our owne persons, and put on others'
> and their affections ffor whome wee speake, ffor they speake by us. If the
> matter which is spoken of touche the poore, then thincke me a poor man.
> He that speakes, sometymes, he must be a lawyer, sometymes a paynter,
> sometymes a marchante, some tymes a meane artifycer.

Hakewill suggests that the representative cannot be a respecter of persons;
with each new piece of legislation he considers, he must lay down his own
person and take on the characters of those he represents. But, as Richard Martin's speech against monopolies that same year reveals, Hakewill's model of
the MP as a stage actor is a simplification:

> I doe speake ffor a towne that greyves and pynes, ffor a countrye that
> groneth and languisheth under the bur-then of monstrous and unconscio-
> nable [monopolies] . . . of starche, tynne, ffyshe, clothe, oyle, vinegar,
> salte and I know not what . . . Yf these blood-suckers be still lette alone to
> sucke up the best and principallest commodities, which the earth there
> hath given us; what shall become of us, whom the fruits upon our own
> soil, and the commodities of our own labor, which with the sweat of our
> brows (even up to the knees in mire and dirt) we have labored for, shall be
> taken by warrant of supreame authority, which the poor subject dares not
> gainsay.[96]

The speaker of this speech that "speaks for" others is a far more unstable
agent than an actor playing a role. The singular first person in which the
speech begins soon swells into the first-person plural, assuming the "person" of all who work by the sweat of the brow, but after lingering on some
picturesque details of that misery, it directs itself back to the "us" of the
Commons. Although the cowed subject "dares not gainsay" supreme
authority, its collective voice—which is that authority—can. The impact of
this speech could only be felt as legislation, imposed "by warrant of supre-
ame authority," and to which the people (having spoken) automatically
gave their consent. The mixed space of the Commons generated impossible
subjects, subjects whose birth and death coincided with the duration of
speech—subjects that could not exist outside the House. Like Arcadia, the
space of political representation could not be mapped onto the world
outside.

Royal Society Fellows attempted to give these sorts of mixed subjects a worldly existence. Sprat's metonymic description of the Society as a "*union of eyes,* and *hands*" recalls the Commons' self-justification, but the laboring hands were no longer a mere figure. The high seriousness of Society proceedings must have struck some visitors as incongruous with the business conducted: "Sir ROBERT MORAY, Dr. WILKINS, and Dr. GODDARD were appointed to try the producing of maggots with old cheese and sack." Appointments in the public service had never taken such a form. The compassionate but one-dimensional portrayal of the working life in Martin's speech could not be more different from the vision of that life entertained by the Society, which sought "the *Pleasure* of Contemplative minds, but above all, the *ease and dispatch* of the labours of mens hands"; note how aristocratic "ease" migrates from pleasure to manual labor.[97] Sprat excitedly informed his readers that "Of our *Nobility,* and *Gentry,* the most *Noble* and *Illustrious* have condescended, to labour here with their *hands*": such men elevated themselves above the learned ignorance of textual authorities through their exemplary willingness to slum. These intellectual workers whose "*hands* are open, and prepar'd to *labour*," were fit to engage in "a painful digging, and toiling in *Nature*," undertaking the "*drudgery* and *burden* of *Observation*" and "tedious tryal of Experiments" for the public good.[98]

Richard Martin, like Empson's pastoral speaker, seeks to combine the "effective elements" of society in a single voice: those who suffer nobly and those who exert *noblesse oblige* on their behalf. The MP's impersonation of the victim of the curse is the very inverse of the Society's attempts to perform the working life and testify to the results—through experimental demonstrations and "relations"—within a space that they, with some justice, identified as public; unlike the proceedings of the Restoration Parliament, the *Philosophical Transactions* were actually published by official order.[99] In this mixed space, conceptual integration took physical as well as discursive forms. With Fellows gathering together to perform experiments in the living quarters of its members, the Thames, and even in coffeehouses while receiving correspondence from people about their experiences in other parts of the country and abroad, the project through which the "minds, and labours of men of all Conditions, are join'd" was carried on through space after space.[100] Sprat declared that "we find many Noble Rarities to be every day given in," not just from "Learned and profess'd

Philosophers," but from "the Shops of *Mechanicks; from the Voyages of Merchants; from the Ploughs of Husbandmen*": the predicate *noble* attaches to the findings of anyone willing to work as a truth producer.[101]

Rather than representing themselves as the voice of laborers, Fellows attempted to find out what laborers did, to imitate rather than merely impersonate them; this required interacting with them. The aims of this representative body required it to do what representative bodies rarely do: invite the "vulgar" in to represent themselves.[102] The Baconian revolution had "shew'n to the World this great secret, That *Philosophy* ought not only to be attended by a select company of *refin'd Spirits*. As they desire that its productions should be *vulgar,* so they also declare, that they may be promoted by *vulgar hands.*" Sprat wittily presents the Fellows' interest in craft secrets as a sign of their possession of the greatest secret of all. All this talk of collapsing the higher and lower parts of the social (and individual) body was not just propaganda; the Society's activities brought together people who, as Barbara Shapiro observes, "in ordinary circumstances would not have been likely to interact socially," and certainly not in this manner.[103] While traditional demonstrations of lordly hospitality had always required the wellborn to rub shoulders with the throng, they had never required the lord to work alongside or take instruction from the vulgus.

The Society also admitted members of the professions as Fellows.[104] Hooke, whose father was a curate and whose brother was a grocer's apprentice, began his career as an apprentice to portrait painters in London; with the exception of Boyle, he was the Society's most important active member until his death. As Shapiro points out, many of the clergymen, government officials, and physicians who were Fellows had at best an ambiguous claim to gentlemanly status.[105] When judged against Restoration standards, the Society's membership was remarkably mixed, and like Parliament, it required occasional purges: in the first round of expulsions of members who were in arrears, examples were made out of such distinguished figures as Sir John Denham, Lord Lucas, John Dryden, and the physician to Charles II, Charles Scarburgh.[106] Many of the Society's most active members were not of gentle birth: Michael Hunter has found that 75 percent of the merchants and tradesmen who joined were active members, compared to 56 percent of the aristocratic members, whose memberships often just revealed a "passing curiosity"; some of these members were expunged from the rolls in the 1670s and 1680s.[107] (Hooke's letters to Boyle on occasions when Boyle missed a meeting suggest the demands such members put on the patience of active members, as well as some fun at their expense: "Some things about the growth of salmons were handed to and fro, some flatly contradicting others.")[108] Often, it was not gentlemen, but "*men of no reading*," as Stubbe complained, who were considered most worthy of credit by the Fellows. One foreign visitor remarked that the Society was filled with "none but apothecaries and other such people who know scarce a word of Latin."[109] Wilkins described the ingenious as "ready to follow the Banner of truth by whomsoever it shall be lifted up," and, to a surprising extent, this is what the Society did. Regardless of their social status outside of experimental space, within it the Fellows worked as a collective of "equal observers," with every member being held to the same evidentiary canons, subjecting the opinionated singularity of the person to the collective discipline that formed the Fellow.[110]

This is not to say that aristocrats were not eagerly sought after as Fellows, and even fawned over; the Society needed patrons. It was decided early on that anyone of or above the degree of baron could be admitted to the Society "without scrutiny." Social rank was the quickest route to membership, with the result that a core of active workers had to carry the weight for a number of "well-off dabblers."[111] But Fellows hoped that such members would permit the Society to hire more salaried members, since those who could afford to be dues-paying volunteers tended to be, as Richard Waller put it, "unwilling to be too much confined and obliged to strictness in some particulars." And within this meritocratic subculture, to be admitted by privilege could be something of a stigma: Sir Charles Howard particularly asked to be "rather admitted by scrutiny, than by the privilege of his birth."[112] To be admitted without scrutiny was to be exposed as a mere gentleman, something less than a Fellow.

Some scholars have found evidence that the dignities of rank were observed in the Society in a manner that permitted members such as Hooke to be regarded as "paid servants," unworthy of the respect accorded to gentlemen Fellows.[113] Yet assertions that the Fellows "ignored the ideas of hirelings like Hooke" fly in the face of overwhelming evidence of Hooke's enormous power in the Society, both as its Curator of Experiments and a guardian of its public image.[114] Although Hooke performed a disproportionate amount of what Sprat called the "laborious" part of experimental investigations, as indicated by the etymon of his title, he also exerted a disproportionate influence on the philosophical questions addressed by the Society as a result of these labors. In 1665, Christopher Wren wrote to him, "I know you are full of employment for the Society wch. you all-most wholy preserve together by your constant paines," but Hooke demanded that other Fellows do their part—not merely by ponying up money for assistants, but by submitting themselves to the same evidentiary standards that he observed.[115] It is finally hard to square a servant status with Hooke's intellectual self-assertion and his control over the high-profile *Micrographia,* which did so much to create the Royal Society's public image; no servant could exercise the kind of control over his employer that Hooke did.

Pepys's diary entry on the day he was admitted into the Society offers a striking registration of the clash of hierarchies enabled by experimental space: "Above all, Mr. Boyle today was at the meeting, and above him Mr. Hooke, who is the most, and promises the least, of any man in the world that ever I saw." The Honorable Robert Boyle may be "above all," but Hooke is nonetheless "above him," his unpromising exterior a badge of innate nobility. Evelyn's admiring description of the most ingenious collection of men in Europe, glanced at in the previous chapter, is striking in a different way: there is no impulse at all to single Hooke out from this group of men of "parts and ingenuity"; he is simply one of their number.[116]

Many Fellows must have been intellectually intimidated by the brilliant and moody Hooke, as they were by the other artisans from whom they were supposed to learn. With diffident optimism, Oldenburg touted the Society's publications as aids to enable bashful "Gentlemen and Schollars to converse with Tradesmen . . . or at least, it will qualify them to ask questions of Men that converse with things; and sometimes to exchange Experiments with them" (note the movement of conversation from words to things and back again). The timorousness Oldenburg seeks to assuage is the result of intellectual intimidation: a felt lack of "qualifications," not just to exchange experiences with working people, but even to "ask questions" of them.[117] Compare the words of the late sixteenth-century minister Samuel Bird, advising his upper-class parishioners on how to comport themselves when offering hospitality to their poor neighbors: "when we see them and talk with them," it should "be done warily without upbraiding of them by their poore estate . . . for because they were not brought up as we have beene, they cannot tell howe to apply themselves in their speech unto us, therefore should we apply ourselves unto them."[118] Such applications were now being made in reverse. Describing the new hybrid gentleman the Society was engaged in breeding, Sprat explained that while the *"Ancestors"* of members of this new breed of aristocrat "convers'd with few, but their own Servants . . . now they are ingag'd in freer rodes of *Education:* now the vast distance between them, and other orders of men is no more observ'd: now their *conversation* is large, and general."[119] If gentlemen could be persuaded not to observe "the vast distance" separating them from the lower orders, they might learn to observe things whose existence was real. By conversing with people who conversed with things, they could compensate for the intellectual deprivations that accompanied social privilege, receiving a "freer . . . *Education*" than that to which their position had hitherto entitled them.

Proudly exhibiting the reverse snobbery that was becoming the new token of belonging, Evelyn sniffed that a lack of familiarity with the mechanical arts was itself a mark of bad breeding, diagnosing the "naturally slavish" disposition of the French as a result of the fact that "no *Gentleman* will in *France*" raise his sons "to any *Trade* or *Mechanique Calling* whatever"; even physick and the law were "despised." This refusal bred bad intellectual habits: they "imagine to comprehend all upon an *instant*" and display both gullibility and idolatry in their conversation. It stood to reason that France was the only nation in Europe to "*idolize* their *Soveraign*."[120] In these patriotic reflections we can discern an almost Miltonic definition of slavishness as spiritual and intellectual impoverishment, here betokened by a lack of familiarity with the *artes serviles* themselves, an ignorance that leaves the subject unschooled in the habits of intellectual patience and care that such arts foster. Through provocative inversions of class-based modifiers like *vulgar* and *slavish,* virtuosi struggled to close the gap that separated them from their socially inferior teachers. The Ballad of Gresham praised Petty for having "describ'd att full / The Philosophie of making Cloath," from his explication of "what grasse doth make coarse wooll" to the processes of carding and dyeing: "Great learning is i'th' Art of Cloathing / Though vulgar people thinke it nothing."[121] The vulgar and the learned have switched places, recapitulating the social challenge effected by the redefinition of *ingenuity* itself.

Sprat idealized the laboratory as a site of social hybridization where a productive confusion between classes would be assiduously cultivated in order to engender social and intellectual half-breeds exhibiting the supposed strengths of each: "the weak minds of the *Artists* themselves will be strengthen'd, their low conceptions advanc'd, and the obscurity of their shops inlighten'd . . . the flegmatick imaginations of men of *Trade,* which use to grovell too much on the ground, will be exalted." Correspondingly, "the conceptions of men of *Knowledge,* which are wont to soar too high, will be made to descend into the *material World.*"[122] The passage erects a familiar vertical axis of value, associating the celestial realm with soaring "men of *Knowledge*" and the ground with "*Artists*" and "men of *Trade*" who, weighed down by phlegm, grovel in obscurity. Sprat imagines a "middling" process that will instill the conceptions of men of Knowledge with matter and infuse the groveling classes with spirit. But through this flattering portrait of soaring university-trained men of Knowledge, Sprat is clearly attempting to redefine genuine knowledge. The clear implication is that the "conceptions" of the aristocratic intellect have no relationship to the world at all. And in many fields of inquiry explored by the Fellows, the exchange of information across class divisions benefited the high-flying men of knowledge far more than it did the phlegmatic artisans. The truth is that artisans had never deviated from what Bacon called the "true and lawful marriage of empirical and rational faculties," and philosophers had to set about learning from them. Such learning often took the form of begging; artisans unwilling to part with their secrets could sometimes be prevailed upon to toss the virtuoso a few "good hints," as Boyle put it.[123]

To impose a pastoral framework on the frequently hapless, humiliating, and expensive intellectual dependence of virtuosi on artisans and workers is to obscure its basic motivation: a longing to partake of their authority. There is little evidence to suggest that steeping oneself in the discoveries of vintners and welders was an especially good way to get ahead in courtly and aristocratic circles. The idea that it might *become* one inspired real anxiety among the Society's contemporary critics; at stake was the very distinction between the learned and the vulgar. I am not suggesting that experimentalist identity could not be assimilated into gentlemanly identity, but such assimilation was riddled with contradictions. If curious pursuits were *primarily* a way for gentlemen to shore up a distinction between themselves and the vulgar, it remains a mystery why the Royal Society insisted so loudly (and in such exaggerated terms) on its social openness. Indeed, when compared to other contemporary sources, experimentalist discourse is noticeably lacking in insults directed at the lower classes. Rather than striving to define themselves against the vulgar, gentlemen like Boyle seem most concerned to distinguish themselves from foppish, idle, and profligate members of their own class. A good gauge of the distance separating experimentalist norms from courtly ones is the virtuosi's use of *gallants* as an abusive epithet.[124] So heavily did virtuosi lean on this term that Beale eventually decided to replace it in his own writing with terms like *Hobbian*, *Stubbian*, and *atheist*; as he explained to Boyle, he did not want to "reflect upon . . . *Whitehall*" too overtly.[125] It has been argued that, although he dealt with "potentially utilitarian subjects," the virtuoso transformed the data he gathered into "signs of his superior social status by draining them of their original usefulness," yet the Fellows stressed the utility of such information rather relentlessly.[126] Despite his infatuation with tulips and hot-house flowers, Evelyn declared that without "some tincture in Medicine, Gardening is a voluptuous and empty Speculation." He invested enormous effort in trying to invent a new method of brick-making and to extract more efficient fuels out of loam to minimize pollution, and he was convinced that his program to make every citizen a beekeeper would make the commonwealth rich: this was what real public service looked like.[127]

Boyle observed that "titular Greatnesse is ever an impediment to the Knowledge of many retir'd Truths, that cannot be attain'd without Familiarity with meaner Persons, & such other Condiscentions, as fond opinion in greate men disapproves & makes Disgracefull"; but by unliving their former lives, aristocrats could rejoin a collectivity from which distinctions of rank had alienated them and reclaim their birthright as sons of Adam.[128] Not content with identifying themselves as the products of a preexisting conceptual integration like that performed by traditional pastoral, they sought to produce a new mixed space inside of which their work was not gratuitous but necessary, and they tried to map this space onto the world.

And yet virtuosi scattered pastoral motifs freely throughout their writings. Opting for fidelity to the pastoral code rather than the English climate, Boyle's *Sceptical Chymist* frames a dialogue between philosophical approaches as the story of how one Carneades (a proponent of innocently carnal knowledge), on "one of the fairest dayes of this Summer," retires with friends to "one of the Arbours in his Garden, to enjoy under its coole shades a delightful protection from the yet troublesome heat of the Sun."

Careless *otium* fluctuates into pastoral *débat,* which results in the haughty Themistius getting his comeuppance (along with the "vulgar spagirists" scolded on the title page).[129] Naturally, he argues on behalf of the "vast and comprehensive Intellect" of Aristotle, whose followers are "capable of a Nobler Conviction" than "petty Philosophers" who require physical evidence for their beliefs. He insists that Aristotelian doctrines need no more evidence "then that which their mutuall Coherence gives them"; scholasticism could not receive a more damning defense. As each participant gets to have his say in what has now evolved into a "Philosophical conference" rather like that between Milton's Adam and Raphael in *Paradise Lost,* the debate becomes like a pastoral contest of songs in which the innocent and unassuming figure of Carneades triumphs.[130] In this friendly contest, withdrawn from the world of affairs and in the bosom of nature, we can discern the open-ended character of natural investigation characteristic of the "flourishing Universitie of Eden," in which all of society might have been included had humanity remained innocent.

But the move that would interest Empson the most is in the preface, where Boyle speaks in *propria persona* of his "good Fortune" in having "illiterate Persons" as his teachers—they taught him to notice things that learned philosophers had overlooked. Following their example, Boyle claims it was "not uneasie for me" (the double negative a marker of the experimentalist's aggressive humility) to "Take notice of divers *Phaenomena,* overlook'd by prepossest Persons," particularly phenomena that "seem'd not to suite so well" with hermetic doctrines (213–214). Boyle is careful to make no claims for his intellectual endowments, expressing his disagreement with other philosophers in purely perceptual terms. It is not a matter of greater or lesser intellectual ability, he seems to suggest, but merely of visual awareness, of "taking notice" of rather than "overlooking" phenomena. The claim to virtual illiteracy only seems to perform Empson's trick of pastoral, for Boyle actually took very close notice: in devising his experiments, he drew extensively from the information accumulated by metallurgists, dyers, and distillers.[131]

The ingenuous lack of prepossession Boyle celebrates in deceptively pastoral terms was given graphic expression in the Society's coat of arms. Evelyn produced a charming series of sketches for designs to be blazoned on the shield held up by the hunting dogs (proper emblems of the *venatio* of scientific discovery) which included telescopes, a vessel under sail, and even a hand emerging from the clouds dropping a plumb line (the artisanal God), but the Fellows decided on a shield bearing a canton and nothing else: a tabula rasa, declaring their determination to be innocent and "unprepossessed."[132] What Charles bestowed on the Society as a privilege, they attached to the subject of innocence, evoking their allegiance to the first sovereign in whose efforts their work had begun. The motto—*nullius in verba*—declared the Fellows' independence of any authority but the evidence produced through their experience of things. As the Ballad of Gresham put it, "These men take nothing uppon trust."[133] Just as those outside the Society could be enlisted as what Shapin and Schaffer call virtual witnesses, so the Fellows could be virtual witnesses of experiences cultivated elsewhere, but so-called "relations" had to contain circumstantial particulars to be deemed useful; rather than taking the traditional form of general assertions, claims had to be rooted in discrete events.[134]

The Society did not succeed in establishing an egalitarian space, but it was one in which social rank was an unstable indicator of intellectual worth or "credit." Although some scholars have stressed the degree to which such reports were credited on the basis of the social standing of the reporter, this consideration could go either way; credibility and gentility were often inversely related.[135] Boyle was convinced that an account about ambergris was "sincere, and on that score Credible" because it was "not written by a Philosopher to broach a *Paradox,* or serve an *Hypothesis,* but by a Merchant or Factor for his Superiors, to give them an account of a matter of fact."[136] As a rule, the Fellows did not credit statements made by people who "neither themselves ever took the pains to make trial" of statements nor received reports from those who had, and in general, anyone who was an eyewitness was better than anyone who was not.[137] As a result, "reports of different classes were mingled together" in the relations that Boyle produced, while his accounts of laboratory work everywhere conveyed the collaborative nature of that work, with assistants, "laborants," and servants indicated by names, initials, or at least the use of the first person plural.[138] If individual assistants were sometimes acknowledged only minimally, gentleman witnesses were often not acknowledged at all—a point observed by Stubbe, who complained that readers could not "judge what *repute* they *deserve.*"[139] The dispersal of personal "repute" put the burden on the fact itself, a thing made and remade by indifferent persons both within and beyond the Society (so Boyle offered his experimental relations to "excite" his readers "by the delivery of matters of fact, such as you may for the most part try with much *ease*").[140] Similarly, those who had come upon a noteworthy physical curiosity needed to send the thing itself to be confidently believed. The experimental demonstration, an adaptation of artisanal productive labor, was the ideal against which all other forms of knowledge production were now to be judged. This new form of demonstration was not the syllogistic demonstration of the schools, but a shared experience: an occasion for the collective construction of truth.

Cowley's ode "To the *Royal Society*" (examined in more detail in Chapter 3) allegorizes this occasion as the recovery of a paradisal opportunity.[141] The poem offers a first-person-plural narration of the band of philosophers reentering Eden: once inside, they turn away from the temptation of eating the fruit and drink wine instead, pressed in "the Mechanic way" by Bacon himself; the messiah who treads the winepress incorporates them all. The miracle of this rational sacrament resides in the philosophers' freedom to drink the fruits of human labor—and in their liberty to call this wine by its true name. Understood in these sacramental terms, the experimental demonstration was the descendent of the Corpus Christi feast orchestrated by the 1381 rebels, or the "love feasts" of the guilds. (Indeed, Fellows explicitly compared themselves to the "Love-Brothers" of guilds and companies.)[142] But here, the sacrament not only honors the scene of labor, it is that scene. In the moment of demonstration, God's works and the works of his servants came together to produce a shared—and representative—experience of consensual truth.[143] The sacrament of production has been revived as experiment, offering the most innocent fruit of productive processes: knowledge. As Oldenburg put it to a skeptical Hobbes,

> this demonstratif knowledge stayeth and satisfieth the mind as much as food doth an hungry stomach: and the same diffusing itself through and to ye good of all ye parts of ye body politique, as good meat well concocted doth to all ye limmes of ye body naturall, & must needs beget ye greatest contentment yt any sublunary thing can doe.[144]

Playing on the double meaning of *concoct*—to produce or prepare and to digest or assimilate—Oldenburg celebrates the conversion of "things themselves" into *facts:* things made and then digested by the "body politique."

This body could not be nourished by knowledge it merely received, it had to concoct such knowledge for itself; the Fellows were both the agents and public representatives of this process, whose products were diffused beyond the Society through painstakingly circumstantial reports enabling the virtual participation of the public at large.

As with the church sacrament, however, there was always the risk that Fellows would be content to be mere spectators to the exploits of Hooke and his assistants, on whom the burden of producing experiments often fell.[145] Efforts were thus made to engage everyone in experiment: at an early meeting, "It was resolved, that every member of the society shall consider against the next meeting of some experiment, which he will undertake himself." When the Lord Viscount Brouncker offered thoughts on how the velocity of bodies might be measured, "His lordship was desired to be curator of that experiment."[146] Nonetheless, as Hunter observes, some aristocratic members who joined the Society in the early years seemed to regard experimental science as a kind of performance art, an opportunity to attend spectacular demonstrations. Active Fellows put up resistance against this tendency; the repeated insistence that experimental philosophers were not "wonder-monger[s]," "maker[s] of gimbals," or "Juglers" extends into this new space the reformers' critiques of the priestly miracle as a piece of theater performed by "conjurers" before a dazed congregation.[147] As one early Fellow complained,

> If the members of the R. S. do nothing seldome come to Meetings and when they come tis only as to a play to amuse themselves for an hour or so, tho they never think of promoting the Ends of the Institution, yet if they pay their Contributions which by their subscriptions they are unavoidably obliged to do, they take themselves to be (and indeed in respect of those who scandalously refuse payment are) good Members.[148]

Such complaints reproduce those of reformers describing ignorant commoners' opinions of the minimal requirements of the Christian faith: tithes-paying and attendance. As Magalotti was distressed to discover, the Society did not admit any visitor "simply as a curious passer-by": "they do not want to permit me to go and be a mere spectator without being obliged to give opinions like all the others."[149] Such participation was how consensus on truth claims was achieved. When Fellows demurred about the interpretation of an experiment, Hooke insisted that they articulate the cause of their doubt so that it might be resolved; he was not putting on demonstrations for their entertainment.[150] As Sprat encouragingly put it, to bring one's eyes and mind uncorrupted by "false Images" was itself a contribution, but one had to commit to being a responsible member of the truth-producing community, annexing oneself to the "*union* of *eyes, and hands.*"[151]

Hooke hoped to extend the principle of communal reciprocity that defined the Society's "fellowship" even to the readers of the *Philosophical Transactions,* requiring all who intended to reap its benefits to contribute something to its store (this scheme for a participatory periodical would to some extent be realized by Dunton's question project).[152] This suggests that Hooke's very real desire to gain fame for the Society (and personal "credit" by means of the Society) was in the end weaker than his determination to extend its reach and productivity; he wanted to extend fellowship to readers by enlisting them in its duties. All opportunities for the merely passive consumption of knowledge were to be systematically excluded from the experimental life, whose dominion would be extended into the space of reading itself. This desire to break down the boundary between production and consumption is inextricably bound up with the non-zero-sum economy of "credit" the Society hoped to establish. But while the *Philosophical Transactions* played a role in collectivizing knowledge, it also provided a medium for the establishment of priority claims. Fellows were in fact heavily invested in preventing "philosophicall robbers" from depriving inventors and discoverers of credit, yet the premium placed on "communicativeness" almost invited such robbery, so that, as Adrian Johns puts it, virtual witnesses became "*actual* pirates." Indeed, as Johns observes, the fact that almost every prominent virtuoso of the period was at some point accused of intellectual theft only underscores how difficult it was to reconcile experimentalist practice with the ethos of possessive individualism; "the sheer ubiquity of concern that intellectual 'propriety' in general was under seige" resulted from the experimentalist production of knowledge itself, in which an individual's ideas could be "used as 'hints' from which others would then perfect their own 'inventions.'"[153] The contrast with Galileo is instructive in this connection. As Biagioli argues, Galileo crafted his reports "so as to minimize the chance that his readers would try to replicate his claims and then turn into his competitors." Rather than treating his readers "as colleagues in an emerging philosophical community," he regarded them as "remote, credit-giving consumers." In contrast, Boyle's and Hooke's circumstantial relations of what they achieved with their instruments sought to stabilize a community of real and virtual experimenters.[154] These detailed relations at once enabled replication and made it unnecessary, so that findings might be put by readers to further use. Rather than styling itself as a monopoly, the Society would be a clearinghouse or refinery, where local findings were converted into universal knowledge, enabling the progressive incorporation of the public around "the body of Truth."[155]

The University of Eden

By locating innocent habits of investigation in their social inferiors, gentlemen held up the educations they had received to ingenious scrutiny. The Ballad of Gresham expresses a juvenile delight in tearing down the ancient seats of learning: "Thy Colledg, Gresham, shall hereafter / Be the whole world's Universitie, / Oxford and Cambridge are our laughter; / Their learning is but pedantry"; the ballad goes on to call Aristotle "an asse." More solemnly, it suggests that the Society embodies the original meaning of the university: a "noble learned Corporation" that "Not for itselfe is thus combyn'd / But for the publique good oth'Nation / And generall benefit of Mankynd."[156] A representative space in which unelected public servants worked to embody, refine, and apply the knowledge-producing power of the social body as a whole and a temple consecrated to reviving the first religious service, the "house of experiment" was also a new kind of school:

> Seats of Knowledg, have been for the most part heretofore, not *Laboratories*, as they ought to be; but onely *Scholes*, where some have *taught*, and all the rest *subscrib'd*. The consequences of this are very mischievous . . . It being onely the *Master's* part, to examine, and observe; and the Disciples, to submit with silence, to what they conclude. But besides this, the very inequality of the Titles of *Teachers*, and *Scholars*, does very much suppress, and tame mens Spirits . . . [and] is by no means consistent with a free Philosophical Consultation . . . scarce any man's mind, is so capable of *thinking strongly*, in the presence of one, whom he *fears* and *reverences*; as he is, when that restraint is taken off.[157]

At first Sprat's protest against the "inequality of ... Titles" is securely articulated within a pedagogical frame: it is the master's demand for the submission of the student, not the commoner, that is deplored as depressing men's spirits. But as Sprat goes on to extend this program of reform beyond the sphere of formal education, the critique of inequality takes on a broader application. While knowledge producers on whom Sprat confers the Baconian epithet of "first men" are made "meek, and gentle" by the pains they have taken in the labors of discovery and invention, those whose schooling consists merely in submission to authority become "positive, and Tyrannical" themselves. In the laboratory, however, men who are "*insolent* to their inferiors" can find their "cure"; in learning how to "think strongly" through vigorous traffic with things, they will cease to abuse their social inferiors out of fear, as "we always find *cowards* the most *cruel*."[158] Rather than simply moralizing about the poor treatment of social inferiors, Sprat offers a novel diagnosis of its cause, identifying the roots of such behavior in intellectual intimidation and shame. Aristocrats were not used to *"thinking strongly"* about things themselves; normally, they did not have to. For gentlemen to take instruction from their inferiors would require a thoroughgoing moral rehabilitation; this alternative seat of knowledge was really a reform school.

The Society realized many of the aims of the educational schemes produced by members of the Hartlib circle in the 1640s and 1650s, the most famous of which is John Milton's prose attempt "to repair the ruins of our first parents," *Of Education*, addressed "To Master *Samuel Hartlib*."[159] The treatise begins by announcing, with disarming matter-of-factness, that the aim of education is to reverse the fall and regain paradise. To expunge the traces of original sin, students will need to acquire "universall insight into things"; and Milton has a practical suggestion as to how they will do so: field trips. Sweeping through "all the quarters of the land," they will discover working knowledge as it is made: "what hinders, but that they may procure, as oft as shall be needfull, the helpfull experiences" of workers, from "Hunters, fowlers, Fishermen, Shepherds, [and] Gardeners" to *"Apothecaries," "Architects,"* "Engineers," "Mariners," and *"Anatomists."*[160] To keep students indoors, studying words rather than the things they represent, is a "sullennesse against nature" that only trains them to produce "babblements"; this coinage suggests the entrapment of England's youth in fallen language, as they are condemned forever to rehearse its paradigmatic scene.

Milton suggests that those with languages but no practical knowledge of "solid things" (that is, most teachers) are actually less learned than "any yeoman or tradesman competently wise in his mother dialect only," an astonishing assertion coming from England's legendary polyglot. The subordination of words to things fosters a deeply practical model of education as apprenticeship to productive action—action of all kinds, for this progressive curriculum will also reveal "the beginning, end, and reasons of politicall societies." The study of nature will become relevant to civics through systematic study of England's systems of production, but the most important political lesson here lies in Milton's handing over the reins of instruction to working-class practitioners. To distinguish such "helpfull" teachers from conventional pedagogues, Milton describes their very instruction in artisanal terms, as if they would soak the students' minds with dye: giving them "such a reall tincture of naturall knowledge, as they shall never forget, but dayly augment with delight." While Milton's students may "easily" learn "at any odde hour the *Italian* tongue," their effort "to enlarge experience, and make wise observation" of the physical world will require daily augmentation, extending indefinitely—and delightfully—into the future.[161] Milton's ideal curriculum joins together the means and ends of paradisal recovery, making it worthy of the Baconian Eden it honors: not a lost place or time, but a process of continual investigation into God's first book.

Milton's bitterness over the very different education he had received at Cambridge never faded. He expressed his feelings without inhibition while still a student; in one prolusion, he urges his fellow students to stop doing their homework and take their education into their own hands, developing their own experiential curriculum based on the study of nature. Decades later, after surrendering his pupil Richard Jones, Katherine Boyle's son, to Oldenburg (who worked as a tutor before becoming the Society's secretary), he was aghast that Oldenburg was taking little Pyrophilus to Oxford: "what that retreat contributes except plenty of books, I do not know," he fumed; he went on to lament that scholars dedicated to "empty quibbling" were still being "supported at grievous public expense."[162] Oldenburg insisted that their intent in going to Oxford was to study nature "really closely." Although he conceded that some "still tread the customary path, and never stop brawling over both divine and natural subjects," he had found an alternative to the university in Oxford itself, in the community formed by future members of the Royal Society.[163]

The insistence on experiential learning is a constant feature of all these educational schemes; Aubrey's *Idea of Education of Young Gentlemen* even finds a place in the curriculum for cookery and a "noble Bassin" in which to "learn the Art of Swimming." Like Milton, Aubrey wants to subordinate the study of words to the study of things, but he cannot bear for his imagined students to be without the languages he has; as in Milton, wishful thinking solves the dilemma: "Greeke will insensibly steale upon them" while they read Euclid. He concludes his "idea" by imagining his old tutors barging in on the scene to thrash his pupils: "About now (me thinkes) I see a black Squadron marching from Oxford led up by a Crosier Staffe . . . to discomfit this pretty Flock: and so my pleasing Dream is at an END."[164] The contrast between his school and Oxford could not be starker. The university was where the gentleman was made; the ideal of an experiential curriculum Aubrey elaborates, with all its "noble" instruments, took as its positive model the educational process of apprenticeship, a process of learning by doing. Aubrey imagines his "dream" as a pastoral one (the squad of "hirelings" that disturb his "pretty Flock" seem to have marched out of *Lycidas*), but the pastoral ideal under threat here is a thoroughly georgic curriculum, predicated on the nobility of labor rather than contemplative leisure.

Although apprenticeship was widely considered to "extinguish gentility" in those who took it up, many virtuosi seem to have attempted, while growing up, to supplement their formal schooling with what were virtually lay apprenticeships.[165] In reminiscing about his childhood, Aubrey claimed that it was his "greatest delight to be continually with the artificers that came there [to his father's estate] (e.g. Joyncrs, carpenters, coupers, masons) and understood their trades . . . I was wont (I remember) much to lament with my selfe that I lived not in a City, e.g. Bristoll, where I might have accesse to watchmakers, locksmiths, etc." He brags that he "cared not for play, but on play-dayes" went instead to visit "the shop, and furnaces of Old Harding, the only Country-glasse-painter, that ever I knew." By the time he was eight, he flattered himself, such extracurricular pursuits had transformed him into "a kind of Engineer," making him a fit roommate for the ingenious Hooke.[166] Boyle urged gentlemen who had not spent their childhood as wisely to make up for lost time, filling their "vacant houres" by learning a skill like limning, watchmaking, gardening, "or som manuall Vocation, or other":

I know this will be spurn'd at by all our Gallants as a Proposition fit to be made rather to blue Aprons then to skarlet Cloakes. But sure it is not so much below a gentleman to do somthing, as it is below both a Man and a Christian to be Idle . . . Neither indeed is it reasonable that those Drones shud participate of the Benefits of Society, that will contribute nothing (that is theirs) to it's Good.[167]

Henry Pinnell's exemplary opposition between the university's buzzing idlers and ingenious workers reemerges in the reflections of the Honorable Robert Boyle. The sarcastic assertion that "it is not so much below a gentleman" to take a break from being useless and unworthy of human society completely collapses the praiseworthy active life with the life of the mechanic. It is as if the conventional forms of the active life for gentlemen—politics, warfare—barely register on the ingenious mind.

Boyle took the occasion of praising Adam's laborious delights to attack every aristocratic pastime he could think of: gaming, hunting, the reading of plays and romances, excessive sleeping, and "uninstructive Visits" that consisted entirely in "fruitless kinds of Chattings." Confessing that it was one of the great "miserys of Greatnesse, to be forc't to make and to receave these sencelesse Visits," he railed against "Custome (in the disguise of Civility)" that forced him to interact with those whose "Idleness is Infectious." He went so far as to confess that he "liked" the idea of killing a napping idler, knowing that he could always say in his own defense that he had merely left the man as he found him.[168] As one who took hold of a spade and went into his garden when he felt pursued by the Beelzebub of idleness, Boyle clearly took to heart Evelyn's suggestion that gentlemen should learn to consider the title of gardener as "none of the least of their *Encomiums*." Indeed, he declined every other title offered him; in addition to refusing the position of provost of Eton, he refused a bishopric and a peerage, so that he was the only male member of the Boyle family to die without a title.[169]

As Barbara Benedict has shown, attacks on the character of "the curious man" stressed the socially useless character of his knowledge, its alienation from the forms and ends of human life. But the curious man's knowledge, as the product of ingenuity, was only socially useless in its failure to uphold social distinctions between the noble and the common, the learned and the unlearned. In severing curiosity from idleness, the identification of curious looking with doing opened up a sphere of action to the gentleman that had nothing to do with the performances that conventionally justified his social status. Stubbe snidely asked "which *Studies* deserve the *most encouragement* by the *publick*": that which bred men for *"Employments* in *Church* and *State"* or *"Aphorisms of Cider, planting of Orchards, making of Optick Glasses, magnetick* and *hortulane Curiosities*[?]"[170] The gentleman virtuoso was ridiculous because he exerted the power of his birthright over inappropriate subjects. Nathaniel Highmore extolled Boyle as "a pattern and wonder to our Nobility and Gentry . . . you have not thought your blood and descent debased, because married to the Arts"; he had shown the world that the "nobler choice" was a life of "industry," and did not disdain to offer the world his "most intricate" knowledge, "though with your own sweat and treasure obtained."[171] This blending of sweat and treasure is a perfect emblem of the hybrid identity Boyle sought to make for himself.

To perform ingenuity as well as Boyle did naturally required some dis-ingenuity. Despite his fabulous wealth, Boyle tried to present himself as one of the middling sort, free from the temptations specific to both high and low status; he was, by his own description, neither "high enuf to prove a Temptation to Lazinesse; nor low enuf to discourage him from aspiring," a claim that was flatly ridiculous, but one that he defended by stressing that he was not the eldest son: being middling, it seemed, was a state of mind. He also liked to point out that his father, like Evelyn's grandfather, had built his fortune from "very inconsiderable Beginnings" (he was known as "the Upstart Earl").[172] Many socially prominent experimentalists were products of upward mobility: Evelyn was the grandson of a tycoon in the gunpowder industry; Wilkins, who ultimately became a bishop, was the son of a goldsmith; Petty's father was a clothier; and John Ray's father was a blacksmith. As products of social hybridization themselves, such men might have sought to dilate the space in which they felt most at home: a space between the social ranks of a contemporary taxonomy that was scarcely a more accurate reflection of social realities than the three estates. According to these bald divisions, the distinction between the noble and the common was still congruent with that between the lettered and the unlettered (where literacy denoted knowledge of Latin).[173] Experimentalists turned the identity of rationality and literacy upside down. Adam, after all, had "read no book but the volume of the world." Facts generated by innocent eyes and working hands would replace what Boyle, scrupulously inverting social markers, dismissed as the "common" knowledge recorded in books. Sprat proudly stressed the Fellows' horror of "falling into *talking,* instead of *working,*" figuring the scholar's dependence on mere words as a lapse into sin.[174] The belief that the unlettered were free of philosophical prejudices, possessed of a special ability to "take notice," was a key article of experimentalist faith; accordingly, many experimentalists strove to present themselves as virtual illiterates.

Modest illiteracy was an extension of epistemological "innocence," and it offered the same rewards. Richard Waller's biography of Hooke, appended to the edition of Hooke's works published after his death, depicts him as almost untouched by literate culture. Although his father "took some pains" to force him to learn "his Grammar by Heart," Hooke had "but little understanding"; the more he applied himself to his books, the more he became "subject to the Head-ach," with the result that his father soon "laid aside all Thoughts of breeding him a Scholar, and . . . wholly neglected his farther Education." The termination of Hooke's formal education was the start of his experimental career: "being thus left to himself, [he] spent his time in making little mechanical Toys." (Hooke claimed to have invented "thirty severall wayes of Flying" before he dropped out of Westminster.)[175] In this coming-of-age narrative, the willingness to resist authority (the father) and a lack of verbal facility permit the young virtuoso's escape from the world of what Boyle called "prepossest" language to a world of activity and experience. Characterized by an inveterate distaste for the books of men—indeed, made sick by them—Hooke turns to the book of nature, gaining knowledge through traffic with objects. Waller's endearing evocation of "little mechanical Toys" encourages the reader to regard experimental work as an unassuming and harmless activity, a literal extension of child's play. But in these mechanical toys, readers familiar with Hooke's career could foresee the compound lens microscope and air pump that he would design for Boyle: the pastoral space of childhood innocence opens out into a "nature" much like that of Virgil's fourth eclogue.

Given his humble origins, Hooke could actually afford to be well-read. Other experimentalists were under pressure to produce continual evidence of their virtual illiteracy, along with autobiographical recollections documenting their determined failure to develop into proper aristocratic subjects.

Aubrey proudly confessed that as a boy with "an inventive and philosophi-call head" he "did not very much care for Grammar," which made him unfit for conventional gentlemanly accomplishments: his "witt was alwaies working, but not adroict for verse."[176] Boyle's public account of his youth, *An Account of Philaretus during his Minority* (related in the third person), describes his own initiation into literacy as an unmitigated trauma. His caretakers compelled him to read "the stale Adventures" of romances, whose "Fabulous & wandring Storys" incited his "restlesse Fancy" to a "Habitude of Raving" that plagued him ever after: "so great an Unhappinesse it is, for Persons that are borne with such Busy Thoughts, not to have congruent Objects propos'd to them at First." He found solace in the "more laborious Operations of Algebra" which kept his raving under control by "exacting the whole Man." It was against heroic odds that, being born a nobleman, he managed to attain full humanity. Boyle is almost unwilling to admit that he ever succeeded in learning Latin, insisting that "Philaretus" "forgot much of that Lattin he had gott: for he was so addicted to more reall Parts of Knowledge, that he hated the study of Bare words, naturally," thinking it was "much nobler . . . to learne to do things" than to learn "the Gowne-men's Language."[177] Entranced by the fantasy of replacing the scarlet cloak with the blue apron, Boyle radicalizes the humanist topos of innate nobil-ity; such nobility is now betokened exclusively by a natural propensity for artisanal work.

Boyle declared that "I could be very well content to be thought to have scarce look'd upon any other Book than that of Nature." His extraordinary claim to have "purposely refrain'd" from reading Descartes, Gassendi, and even Bacon—"though not altogether from transiently consulting about a few Particulars"—so that "I might not be prepossess'd with any Theory or Principles," was calculated to link him to his illiterate teachers; such absti-nence freed him to think "what Things themselves would incline me to think."[178] Sir Peter Pett confirmed that, after his youth, Boyle "totally for-bore reading bookes of poetry & never saw any Play, nor read either Play or Romance," even those written by his own brother, so "that he might . . . devote his thoughts with the greater Purity to the Divine Life," dedicated to the study of God's creation.[179] Boyle's eagerness to reveal that he really did get his hands dirty led him to insist on the "mutilated" character of his writings, blaming their failings on laboratory accidents that were con-tinually destroying his notes. In 1688, he issued what Michael Hunter has called "one of the oddest publications of the seventeenth century": a freestanding broadsheet announcing the destruction of his writings which contained a lengthy account of how a manuscript was destroyed by laboratory chemicals. It is as if he wanted to testify more directly than language ever could to the living presence of things themselves in the knowledge he produced.[180]

The attempts of experimentalists to demonstrate, and back-form, their fitness for inhabiting the university of Eden were ways of conjuring up and exorcising its fallen opposite: the actual university, the haunt of the detested schoolman, a figure in bondage to useless study, at once physically and mentally inert and crazed by a fixation on imaginary metaphysical entities such as essences and substantial forms. This grotesque figure of uncontrolled speculation was a perverted foil of his "unfallen *Protoplast*," for whom the concerted labor of disciplined hand, eye, and brain had been a source of knowledge, power, and bliss.[181] Identifying their own knowledge practices with this ideal of physical and mental fitness, experimentalists diagnosed the "learned ignorance" of the schoolmen as a hallucinatory fixation on ideas and words that had no reference to things themselves.[182] Like Eve, whose dependence on "secondary narration" caused the fall, the "gownman" preferred to consume knowledge while at leisure, imbibing false doctrine and succumbing to the tempter's voice by poring over fallen texts and producing more. The "crimes" that had "stain'd . . . the Purple Gowns of Learning" were the fruit of the first. The blending of botanical and bibliographical *folia* and the pun on *codex* and *caudex* had long linked texts to both the forbidden fruit and the leaves that signalled the first couple's shame; this understanding of the fall as a fall into rhetoric (and textuality) is revived in satirical treatments of the schoolman's "Impertinency in *Folio*" and "laborious idleness."[183] But what had once served as a generalized warning against the deceptions of rhetoric and the pride of the learned was now a targeted, and gendered, attack on traditional learning as a kind of pathology; the frenzied notions of scholasticism were the symptoms of lazy bodies that were unwilling to labor.

The schoolman represented the seductions of fallen textual learning, but his mastery of learned languages, flat refusal to work, vested interest in tradition, and haughty indifference to things themselves also made him a handy (and plausibly deniable) objective correlative for the aristocrat. Through this figure, experimentalists lamented the existence of an entire class of people to whom labor was as alien as paradise. As an object of the experimentalist's ritual abuse, the schoolman embodied the intellectual deprivations, and the psychological disorders, that accompanied social privilege. The project of remaking society in Adam's image depended largely on promoting disgust with aristocratic codes and values (hence Boyle's provocative allusion to Aristotle as one of the "great Wits"); the lampooned schoolman, far more repellent than a perfumed fop, was an instrument of social as well as intellectual reform.[184]

The schoolman's real-world counterpart had had good reasons to identify natural philosophy with textual commentary rather than physical investigation. The object of his investigation was form, the invisible source of all essential qualities and changes in natural bodies. But many virtuosi construed the impossibility of ever perceiving the operation of form as evidence of form theory's *irrationality*. The scholastic approach, reduced to armchair philosophizing, was not merely mistaken; it fostered mental derangement. Through the figure of the schoolman, gentleman virtuosi reminded themselves that while fallen humanity was fundamentally unwell and in need of healing intervention, some were more sick than others. By pathologizing scholastic error—refusing to distinguish it from hallucination and rational failure—experimentalists were able to identify their own knowledge practices with a *healthy* as well as an innocent curiosity. The concerted discipline of hand, eye, and brain was also an ongoing therapeutic regimen through which the defective natural man could be gradually restored to full humanity, becoming paradisally "fit" in every sense. This program for the intellectual and social rehabilitation of the upper classes thus had an explicitly medical dimension.[185]

There is some evidence that Boyle took up dissection as part of a therapeutic regimen. By 1649, Boyle had successfully set up his alchemical laboratory at Stalbridge, but from 1652 to 1654 estate matters kept him "prisoner" in Ireland, where because of the difficulty of obtaining chemicals and equipment, he was spending twelve hours a day reading; as if on cue, he succumbed to ill health.[186] After studying Boyle's case, William Petty, then working as a medical practitioner,[187] advised him to read less, since reading "weakens the brain" (Petty credited his own talent for "Discoveries and improvements" to his abstention in this regard),[188] to focus less on the thoughts of others and more on his own—and to write up his own experiences as an investigator.[189] Soon thereafter, Boyle was assisting Petty in dissection. In a letter to Hartlib's son-in-law, he remarked that he had seen "(especially in the dissections of fishes) more of the variety and contrivances of nature, and the majesty and wisdom of her author, than all the books I ever read in my life could give me convincing notions of." Things he had merely read about became objects of actual experience; in addition to confirming the existence of the thoracic duct, he "satisfied myself of the circulation of the blood."[190] As Boyle's recollections of his raving youth suggest, mental health was the product of laying hold—physical hold, if possible—on "convincing notions," overcoming an alienation from the physical world; experimentation becomes the scene of the gentleman's triumph over the solipsism fostered by aristocratic breeding.

In his essay on labor, Locke accordingly represented aristocratic ignorance of "useful and mechanical arts" as a public health crisis. It is "a mark of goodness in God that he has put us in this life under a necessity of labour"; this blessing needed to be distributed more equally. The "studious and sedentary part of mankind as well as the rich and noble," he laments, "have been deprived of that natural and true preservative against diseases": bodily labor. Locke briskly assimilates the "lazily voluptuous" and the "busily studious"—the voracious Eves and the bookish schoolmen—as equally "deprived" because they "sit still," it makes little difference whether it is "at their books" or "their pleasure"; once again, gown-wearers are all the same. Gleefully inverting social markers, he describes those who live in luxurious estates as impoverished inhabitants of a "languishing estate of a broken health," the spleen or gout "rob[bing]" them of their thoughts as well as their limbs; they in turn rob the commonwealth by languishing uselessly. The language of dispossession was not merely a witty reversal: if lower classes were deprived of capital, the upper classes were dispossessed of knowledge which useful work might have provided them. In contrast, "the sober and working artisan and the frugal laborious country man performs his part well and cheerfully goes on in his business to a vigorous old age."

Since it was social hierarchy that had "brought honest labour in useful and mechanical arts wholly into disgrace," Locke imagines a total eradication of "idle and useless employments" promoted by "the luxury of Courts" (and the "inferior grandees" who imitated them), proposing a scheme whereby every single member of society might invest six hours a day "in the constant exercise of some laborious calling." Such "constant exercise" would "supply the inhabitants of the earth with the necessaries and conveniences of life" while preserving "mankind from the mischiefs that ill men at leisure are very apt to do." Redescribing the opportunity to perform useful labor as a privilege, the birthright of all Adam's sons, Locke imagines restoring it to all: "if the labour of the world were rightly directed and distributed there would be much more knowledge, peace, health and plenty in it than now there is. And mankind would be much more happy than now it is."[191] Again, the paradisal counterfactual becomes hortatory. The rebels of 1381 had never formulated a program for dissolving the three estates; as Steven Justice observes, despite their critique of "gentlemen" as a postlapsarian category, they left largely untouched the assumption that the estates lived differently because they had different jobs. The pursuit of natural investigation across class divisions now enabled utopia to assume a new form: the well-run society was one in which each member embodied the strengths and functions that were currently distributed across (or as Hooke put it, "scattered up and down") the social body. Reconciling the higher and lower parts of the social and individual body at once would result in a reformed, healthy body, a body in which each member would act not just in relation to but *as* the larger body—a state in which each would be a representative of all.[192]

It was this state that the Royal Society Fellow prefigured and represented. Although metonymic descriptions of the Society as a union of eyes and hands can create the impression that the Fellows strove to be laboring bodies, untouched by the corrupting influence of thought, celebrations of active knowledge were not merely ways to valorize the bodily exertion required to pull knowledge out of things themselves. While experimental looking required such "exercise," it did not end there; it was, as Hooke explained, "to *begin* with the Hands and Eyes," only to be "*continued* by the Reason," and "to *come about* to the Hands and Eyes again," in a "*continual passage round* from one Faculty to another."[193] This constant movement, recalling the revolutions of the ploughman's wheel, was what moved knowledge forward. Hooke locates the wheel inside; the image is of the functioning of a healthy body according to the model of Harveyan circulation, with data replacing blood in a "continual passage round." It is the integration of the higher and lower parts of the body that enables this continual passage, producing health and knowledge at once. Removing impediments to data's circulation in the body politic—bringing together the higher and lower parts currently separated by a "vast distance"—would restore individual bodies to health as well.

The assault on textual knowledge in favor of the knowledge that had been cultivated in the university of Eden finally reshaped university culture itself. Wallis recalled that as a student at Cambridge interested in the new science,

> I had none to direct me, what books to read, or what to seek, or in what method to proceed. For Mathematicks, (at that time, with us) were scarce looked upon as *Accademical* studies, but rather *Mechanical;* as the business of *Traders, Merchants, Seamen, Carpenters, Surveyors of Lands,* or the like; and perhaps some *Almanak-makers in London* . . . For the Study of *Mathematicks* was at that time more cultivated in *London* than in the Universities.[194]

By the end of the century, partly through the efforts of intruded men like himself, the universities had changed to accommodate fields of knowledge that just a few decades before were considered beneath respectable notice.[195] The overthrow of the book by the thing is dramatically evident in Robert Plot's praise of Elias Ashmole for donating to the University of Oxford "the best History of Nature, Arts, and Antiquities . . . not in print . . . but in a generous donation of the real things themselves." When the Ashmolean Museum was finally completed, university finances were so depleted that for some years the Bodleian was unable to purchase any books at all.[196] In exemplary contrast to the ancient seat of learning in which it was housed, the museum was accessible to anyone who could afford the small entrance fee; a foreign visitor complained that visitors "impetuously handle everything in the usual English fashion . . . they run here and there, grabbing at everything."[197] One could hardly hope for a more concise emblem of the shuffling of elite priorities that experimentalism had promoted.

The Histories of Trades

The pastoral pretense and artisanal secrecy had long reinforced one another: the wildly divergent images of worker's knowledge as bestial gruntwork and superhuman magic conspired to place such knowledge at once beneath and beyond the perception of the educated. By exposing the relationship between physical exertion and intellectual mastery, the labor and the magic, experimentalism revealed maker's knowledge as knowledge in the making: a progressive process that would require the effort of many eyes and hands. Of all the crushed potentials of this effort, the Histories of Trades project was the most tragic. An extension of the lay apprenticeships that many of the Fellows had pursued on their own, this project was supposed to register discoveries workers had already made in fields such as tanning, iron-making, and fermentation. The Society's role was to coordinate these discoveries so that they might be applied between "arts" and developed further.[198] "I look upon a good History of Trades," Boyle wrote, "as one of the best means to give Experimentall Learning both growth and fertility, and like to prove to Natural Philosophy, what a rich Compost is to Trees, which it mightily helpes, both to grow faire and strong, and to bear much fruit": from a collection of such histories, a fertile ground for a restored paradise of knowledge might be concocted.[199]

Of course, the effort to consolidate this knowledge threatened the foundation on which this orchard was to be planted: the labor itself. Guilds, especially those that worked with the same material, like tanners and shoemakers, themselves made provisions for separating labor so as not to encroach on one another—thereby ensuring their livelihoods, and, from the Society's perspective, inhibiting the progress of knowledge, that *continual passage round*" of data through the social body.[200] The openhanded appeals to the commonwealth of learning that Fellows made to working practitioners were assaults on their economic survival. This may not have been immediately clear to the Fellows. In anticipation of government funding, Sprat declared that "the *Royal Society* will be able by degrees, to purchase such extraordinary inventions" and "bring them into one common Stock, which shall be upon all occasions expos'd to all mens use"; Sprat imagined a future near at hand in which *"all conditions of men"* would work together to subject these technologies to further refinement. Bowing, as he thought, to economic realities by appealing to workers' self-interest, he declared the Society's intention to share with inventors "the *greatest part of the profit*," cheerfully anticipating the *"solid honor"* the Fellows would bring to all of England's ingenious and impecunious subjects.[201] Sprat was freely offering money the Society never had to give. The Ballad of Gresham predicted that the Society would be granted 1,000 pounds a year, but although Charles granted the Society, as a corporation, the legal right to buy property and employ as large a staff as it wanted, he provided it with no means to do so. The Society had to make do with the fees and annual subscriptions of Fellows and the occasional generosity of individuals, under pressure from the designated "Committee of Beggars," as some Fellows "merrily" called it.[202] Far from being able to afford the large staff it envisaged, it could barely support its most hard-working member. But the ubiquitous metaphors of appropriation and colonization in accounts of virtuosi's use of craft knowledge obscure the frankly Winstanleyan spirit in which this program of knowledge-sharing could be imagined.

Fellows had faith in an essential difference between the possession of matters of fact and pieces of land: to take ownership of a fact from another person did not leave that person without it, nor did it leave that person without power. If anything, they imagined that it extended to him greater power, what Locke would call "credit," authority or intellectual capital. But in the absence of any government initiative to make it economically feasible for working inventors to come forward with their secrets, this plan to make truly common knowledge out of practices that were separated not just across social classes but across the trades could not get far off the ground. (Within a century, the consolidation of worker's knowledge would take a much less innocent form, under the figure of the industrial manager.) A recurring feature of the Society's minutes is the mention of tantalizing hints dropped by skilled workers of various Fellows' "acquaintance" concerning secrets, from techniques for softening steel to the best soil for apples, about which the Fellow is invariably instructed to find out more. But as the watercolor painter Alexander Marshall pointed out when asked about his secrets for preparing paints, his knowledge consisted in "pretty secrets, but known, they are nothing. Several have been at me to know how; as if they were but trifles, and not worth secrecy. To part with them as yet I desire to be excused."[203] These trifling secrets were "worth secrecy," because their economic worth lay in secrecy.

The conflict of interest between the virtuoso and the artisan could even play out within the breast of a single person.[204] In his capacity as a Fellow, Hooke complained that "the *Arts* of life have been too long *imprison'd* in the dark shops of Mechanicks . . . *hindred from growth,* either by ignorance, or self-interest"; yet, as Rob Iliffe has shown, during the extended priority dispute over the lucrative invention of the balance-spring watch,

Hooke behaved exactly like a craftsman protecting his secret. Hoping to circumvent the Society altogether, Hooke sent the king progressively improved versions of the timepiece he was developing with Thomas Tompion, in the hopes that the controversy might be placed within the jurisdiction of the court. When private interest took precedence over the public good, the counterrestoration effected by the Society was reversed, making the king the sovereign decider.[205]

An "Advertisement" Evelyn appended to his *Sculptura* registered a public protest against such churlish secrecy: "I could wish with all my heart, that more of our *Workmen,* would . . . impart to us what they know of their several *Trades,* and *Manufactures.*"[206] But although he wanted such information for his history of engraving, he was finally unwilling to reveal all the secrets he had gathered, and even delayed publishing the text, for fear he would "dissoblige some, who make those professions their living; or at least, debase much of their esteeme, by prostituting them to the Vulgar": the vulgar reader was not simply a socially common reader, but an uninformed or unscrupulous one, a dilettante or opportunist who would be indifferent to their philosophical and public value.[207] Motivated by the original meaning of *prostituere* (to make public or to disclose), the metaphor of prostitution suggests an erotic relation to the craft secret, as if it were a mistress one could not abandon to the open market, and a triangular affective bond with, as well as a reverence for, the artisans themselves, whose contributions to the generation of knowledge could not be cheapened or dishonored. The metaphor also furtively registers Evelyn's awareness that what for him could be a disinterested love of nature's secrets was for artisans an economic arrangement; they prostituted their secrets for money precisely by refusing to expose them. This asymmetry was awkward for both parties. While the expense of Evelyn's brick-making project exposed him to his wife's ridicule, artisans who participated in the commonwealth of knowledge did so at their own economic risk.[208] Reciprocally, Evelyn confessed to Boyle that he found the "many subjections" to "mechanical capricious persons" required to produce a history of trades difficult to bear (a complaint Boyle found "Childish, and too unworthy of a Philosopher to be worthy of a solemne Answer"). And though he hopefully declared that the *Elysium Britannicum* was intended "for persons of all Conditions whatsoever," in many cases he was sharing knowledge that working gardeners already had.[209]

Despite these difficulties, however, the attempt to articulate tacit artisanal knowledge produced results, most notably in a literature organized
around moments of "taking notice." Here, as if celebrating the long delayed
gratification of an ontological hunger, experimentalists revel in their intimacy with the things of creation, approaching these things as potential cultivators and producers rather than mere consumers. In passages that strive
toward what Lorraine Daston has called an "epidermal language," all the
hidden dimensions of things themselves, and through them, the crowded
but heretofore invisible sphere of the working life, are revealed to the senses
as if for the first time.[210] In his *History of Clothes,* as Petty tries to make explicit all the knowledge about cloth-making comprehended in the "understanding" of the workman's hand, a new world swims into view. Petty
anatomizes what Locke would call the compound idea of dexterity into all
the operations required to force "curled, complicated, and entangled hairs
to lie parallel" and to "bind a thousand several threads together with one
single thread, so as to make a tela beautifully variegated in its superficies."
Almost all the modifiers he uses are participles, emphasizing each feature
he brings to our attention as the product of physical actions, taken first
by the Creator and subsequently his servants (the first curls, complicates,
and entangles hairs, the second smooths them down and binds them). The
manual operations through which new forms are imposed on matter are
reenacted through commanding gerund-streams—"burling, scowring,
milling, tentering, rowing, sheering, cottoning, and pressing, and even to
the folding and packing of the cloth"—that render the discrete steps of
production a continuous material surface, like the cloth being manufactured. As Petty unfolds each of these implicated operations, his point of
view becomes progressively more minute, until he has abstracted himself
into a virtual atom, describing how the "abstersives" applied to cloth "serve
as ten thousand little scraping knives." Revealing the intricacies of this
"great and subtil work" requires a corresponding subtlety of perception; it
is as if, in order to bring the implicit knowledge of the artisan into view,
Petty must avail himself of a microscope. The most familiar animals of the
English landscape, along with the most familiar items of clothing, "as common, and as cheap as these are," become like objects seen under the lens:
totally "new Creatures."[211]

If Adam dressed the garden, Petty innocently undresses clothes, seeing
through their material surface to the labor that produced them.[212] As we

will see in Chapter 3, for the experimentalist, to undress appearance in this manner *was* to dress the garden. Petty defends the exhaustive detail of his account by recovering this present labor's primal scene, when these techniques were first invented, and operations discovered, as they were now being discovered for the first time by "the public":

> I have been perhaps too long in describing the minutiae of very ordinary and small operations; but I hope no philosopher will despise this, no more than he would the anatomy of a mouse or frog; for as small, and as common, and as cheap as these are, I do not doubt but the invention of them was very difficult and curious at the first . . . I say, to perform all these compounded operations with some one simple regular motion, as that of carding, and spinning, and weaving are, is not contemptible, nor easy for a very inventive wit, without deep and long meditations to excogitate.[213]

A "history" was a complete description of something; as the effort to make knowledge productive came to privilege knowledge of material causes, a complete description could not help but become historical. Here, however, the history of clothing becomes historical in another sense, triggering a form of retrospection that combines rational reconstruction with prehistorical speculation, in an effort to imagine the insight that characterized the first moment of discovery, and the subsequent labor of invention, which the foregoing account has just reenacted: an extensive "history" now compendiously contained in "one simple regular motion" of the workman's hand.[214] Petty insists that his anatomy of manufacture is analogous to an anatomy of one of God's creatures, and thus something no philosopher can afford to "despise"—for the sake of his soul if for no other reason: Petty believed the modern anatomy theater "to be (without Metaphor) a Temple of God."[215] These anatomies are not just analogous but continuous, since the work Petty is revealing is merely an extension of God's, part of the endless work of dressing and redressing creation. In his participle-packed "deep and long meditations" on these operations, Petty attempts to "excogitate" or think out—not merely ponder but reconstruct—each step of this labor. Such intricate excogitation presses out into the world, finding satisfaction in construction, as when Evelyn describes the brain that "excogitates new *Arts*."[216] The process of revealing work that the pastoral mode and artisanal secrecy had long conspired to keep hidden provided a "rich Compost" for excogitation of all kinds.

The systematizing of vulgar knowledge through histories also bore fruit in efforts to expand humanity's capacity for prediction. Hooke's project for creating a history of the weather was an attempt to systematize an ability widely attributed to country people, who were renowned for their skill in the "prognostics" of the weather, with their knowledge of the "signes and tokens of every particular season." (Others could consult the meteorological information contained in the *Georgics,* still being recommended to "the learnid" in the period.)[217] Hooke sought to reconstruct this ability from the ground up. He kept a log of daily weather observations, employing primitive technology like the oat beard, which curled in humid weather, as well as more newfangled instruments and his "baroscopical index." As the beards of oats become hygroscopes, the wheel barometer transforms the rise and fall of mercury into a measurement of air pressure; mastering the grammar through which different parts of nature's book relate to one another enabled all of nature to become "artificial," making every object a potential instrument.[218] Hooke hoped that such efforts would

> help us one step towards the raising a theo[re]tical pillar, or pyramid, from the top of which, when raised and ascended, we may be able to see the mutations of the weather at some distance before they approach us, and thereby being able to predict, and forewarn, many dangers may be prevented, and the good of mankind very much promoted.[219]

This theoretical pillar is the cognitive equivalent of the telescope, which makes distant things available "before they approach," extending the reach of the eye well beyond the skin. To raise worker's knowledge to the threshold of public visibility, both Petty and Hooke take virtual hold of the lens, the technology through which fallen sight was to be restored to its original power.

In different registers, the trade history and technologically assisted observation teach the same lesson: the restored paradise resides not in an alien world but in an alien experience of the known one. This labor of estrangement was also a means to domesticate the strange: when using his telescope to make observations of the lunar crater Hipparchus, Hooke hazarded the opinion that it

> seems to be some very fruitful place . . . I am not unapt to think, that the Vale may have Vegetables *analogus* to our Grass, Shrubs and Trees; and most of these incompassing Hills may be covered with so thin a vegetable Coat, as we may observe the Hills with us to be, such as the short Sheep pasture which covers the Hills of *Salisbury* Plains.[220]

The homely image of sheep grazing on the moon brings the lunar landscape into the known world. It does so by offering a view of that world, Salisbury plains, from above: "I am apt to think, that could we look upon the Earth from the Moon, with a good *Telescope*, we might easily enough perceive its surface to be very much like that of the Moon." The result is an image at once more and, just as startlingly, less exotic than Virgil's sheep. Projecting pastoral and golden age imagery onto the newly "maculate moon" became an irresistible habit; through such projection, contemporaries enacted the experimentalist reinvention of the pastoral mode itself. The new image of the moon was the product of georgic effort, and it now became a "paradiz'd" image of that effort: so Francis Godwin described the moon as "another Paradise," populated by long-lived inhabitants who regard work as "playing, and with pleasure."[221]

But the intellectual component of the so-called georgic revolution posed an actual danger to workers. In adapting artisanal epistemology and techniques, virtuosi threatened their more traditional applications: for example, although the thermometer would have been useful to early modern brewers, they resisted the technology precisely because it threatened to render a master brewer's judgment useless.[222] Work with the new visual technologies, however, offered a means to reveal the world of things themselves and to promote "the good of mankind" without hurting individuals. Similarly, developing error-free weather prediction would not compete with agricultural labor; no one scraped together a living on a talent for weather prognostication alone. And, far from encroaching on the sphere of craftsmen, the research program in assisted observation was a boon for lens makers. In addition to the Fellows, members of the curious public wanted these new tools.[223] By producing material effects in the form of new experiences of creation, experimental work could retain a link to productive labor without posing an immediate menace to it. Alongside the experiments with the air pump (which were also efforts to give visual manifestation to the invisible), experiments in assisted observation were the activities with which the Society became most identified. The labor of making truth visible became the Society's signature work.[224]

The Society's effort to restore creation as a common field of knowledge production, a guild of guilds, like Winstanley's effort to found paradise on the soil of the commons, could only be realized within an economy organized around collective ownership. While Fellows entertained the idea of amassing all potentially profitable knowledge into a "common Stock," they made no effort to bring such a society into being. Indeed, many members were reluctant to part with their money to help keep the Society going, a reluctance Oldenburg could hardly understand. As he wrote to Boyle, the Society could be "a mighty and important Body . . . if all the members thereof could but be induced to contribute every one their part and talent for the growth, and health and wellfare of their owne body": for Oldenburg, such "remisse and carelesse" treatment of the corporate body is hardly distinguishable from an abuse of one's own.[225] That members resisted the private sacrifices required for incorporation is perhaps less remarkable than the fact that, in the early years of the Restoration, a motley group of gentlemen and members of the professions sought to publicly formalize their links as "Love-Brothers," and to extend this fellowship to the public at large. That the radical potentials of this effort were never practically realized does not suggest that they were unthinkable; on the contrary, they could never be fully repressed. Since access to productive knowledge provided the basis of the Fellows' identities as public servants, it might be said that until and unless the Society represented—and admitted—everyone, its members could not even properly represent themselves. The Fellows' integration of the opposed values of Cain and Abel did result in a dramatic levelling of social hierarchy as it shaped the theory and practice of intellectual life. This levelling depended on a historical vision of restoration that, like the Reformation itself, reconciled originary longings to a mythology of progress. Extolling the unelected representatives that were redefining "the unelected vocation," Glanvill declared that the "*Constellation* of Illustrious Worthies, which compose *The ROYAL SOCIETY*, is enough to strike dead the opinion of the Worlds decay, and conclude it in it's [*sic*] *Prime.*"[226] The goldenness of the new age experimentalists hoped to bring into being was a specifically paradisal alloy, the synthetic product of skills that should never have been separated in the first place. Through an experimental reunion of the working life and the contemplative life, Fellows tried to repair the intellectual damage caused by a social order that was alien to the creation.

3 ||| THE PRODUCTIVE EYE

Seek not out the things that are too hard for thee, neither search the
things that are above thy strength. But what is commanded thee, think
thereupon with reverence, for it is not needful for thee to see with thine
eyes the things that are in secret. Be not curious in unnecessary matters:
for more things are shewed unto thee than men understand.
 —Ecclesiasticus 3:21–23

If therefore there be any humility towards the Creator, any reverence for
or disposition to magnify His works, any charity for man and anxiety to
relieve his sorrows and necessities, any love of truth in nature, any hatred
of darkness, any desire for the purification of the understanding, we
must entreat men again and again to discard, or at least set apart for a
while, these volatile and preposterous philosophies . . . and to approach
with humility and veneration to unroll the volume of Creation, to linger
and meditate therein, and with minds washed clean from opinions to
study it in purity and integrity.
 —Francis Bacon, *Historia Naturalis et Experimentalis*

I, remaining astonished, said to Galileo that this was another Creator,
given that it makes things appear that until now one wouldn't know that
they had been created.
 —Johannes Faber, after using the microscope for the first time

Artisanal laborers were the most important of Eden's human emissaries—
they modeled the union of rational and physical energies to which virtuosi
aspired—but to lay claim to the powers of unfallen perception, virtuosi re-
lied on instruments like the microscope and telescope. Engaging the working hand, these tools made contemplation laborious; as the sexed rhetoric
surrounding their use suggested, they also made it fruitful. Unlike the barren disputes of the schoolmen, technologically assisted observation could
generate *"Off-spring"*: new discoveries.[1] The lens served as a kind of spade, a
tool with which to excavate the material causes of the visible and open the

world up to new kinds of cultivation. Rather than celebrating the lens as a simple work tool, however, virtuosi figured optical instruments as *"artificial Organs."*[2] In doing so, they linked the productive labor of innocent observation to the project of incorporation, which began with putting off the old man and putting on the new.[3] For Royal Society Fellows, the power of artificial organs to make contemplation productive was a function of their power to produce a certain kind of user: a public person, working through and on behalf of a body greater than his own.

The lens itself was not a new invention. Eyeglasses had been in use since the thirteenth century, and by the early seventeenth century the spyglass— combining concave and convex lenses to correct defective vision—was a familiar device. The invention of the telescope, and the microscope that evolved from it, was largely a matter of adapting the technology to a new use: to extend vision rather than simply to mend it.[4] Even this aspiration wasn't new; medieval and Renaissance authors had elaborated an extensive lore around telescopic mirrors known to the ancients. Symbols of spectatorial agency as well as spectatorial privilege, mythic mirrors like the Pharo of Alexandria could act on what they revealed—for example, by setting fire to distant ships. As Eileen Reeves has shown, the Dutch invention was initially confused with its legendary ancestor, lending the discovery the feel of a recovery.[5] By the later seventeenth century, the association of the lens with the so-called imperial mirror had loosened, but its association with a recovered potential had not. English virtuosi identified this potential with the collaborative protocols surrounding the technology's use—protocols that many continental practitioners (notably Galileo) did not share.[6]

The encumbering of philosophy with these newfangled instruments irritated many contemporaries: what could be "more Absurd and Impertinent," John Norris asked, than "a Man who has so great a Concern upon his Hands as the Preparing for Eternity, all busy and taken up with *Quadrants,* and *Telescopes, Furnaces, Syphons* and *Air-Pumps?"*[7] By figuring the spiritual preparation for death as a concern on the believer's hands, Norris is able to draw a pointed contrast with the proudly busy hands of the virtuoso, laboring to transform great concerns into little ones: focused so intently on the works of the Creator, the virtuoso loses sight of the Redeemer. In fact, the Christian virtuoso carried away by his investigative paraphernalia was engaged in a new form of devotion, geared less toward his own personal salvation than humanity's restoration. The sacraments and intercessory rites of the old religion had secured the redemption of individuals, but the end of reformation was to restore the whole body of the faithful; "Mechanical helps" were central to this effort.[8] Optical instruments in particular seemed to literalize the traditional metaphors for the transformative power of grace, which could now be used to support the role of technology in completing what the Reformation began.

Arguing that paradise was not "*lost* or destroyed, but *hid* beneath the ruins of the fall," Cromwell's chaplain Peter Sterry had celebrated the "awakening by reason of the primitive Image of pure Nature raising it self by degrees, and sparkling through the *Rubbish,* the confusions of the present state."[9] If paradise was not lost but merely hidden beneath a veil of false appearance, its restoration might be achieved through the gradual disclosure of "pure Nature." A devotional life once organized by ritual repetition might become one of progressive revelation. Writing on behalf of the Society, Thomas Sprat made a similar suggestion:

> This will teach him to *Worship* that *Wisdom,* by which all things are so easily sustain'd, when he has look'd more familiarly into them . . . he will be led to admire the wonderful contrivance of the *Creation;* and so to apply, and direct his praises aright: which no doubt, when they are offer'd up to *Heven,* from the mouth of one, who has well studied what he commends, will be more sutable to the *Divine Nature,* than the blind applauses of the ignorant.[10]

A religion in which the operations of nature and providence occupy the place once held by routinized miracle is one in which worship and understanding, wonder and familiarity, are no longer opposed terms; knowledge production has become the matrix of prayer. Of course, the intimacy with divine wisdom Sprat celebrates is projected, not attained; the future thrust of the passage—"will teach him . . . will be led . . . will be more"—suggests that the praise most "sutable" to God lies ahead, as the fruit of work undertaken in the present ("has look'd . . . has well studied"). The asymptotic progress from blind applause to suitable worship is the progress from ignorance to knowledge—a progress that is also a return, for this call to look "more familiarly into" the things of creation is Sprat's introduction to the first religious service, the scene of naming in Genesis 2:19. Physico-theology, the experimentalist strain of Christian apologetics that instructed the public in how to observe the Creator in every leaf and insect, restored the faithful to this scene.[11] But to play his part, the investigator had to suit his perceptual apparatus to "the *Divine Nature*" he studied. Celebrations of the lens as an instrument of worship thus constellate around the command to *magnify,* or praise, as in Job 36:24: "Remember that thou magnify his work, which men behold."[12] To render more of God's work visible was to multiply opportunities for such praise.[13]

Speculative anatomies of an original human body capable of sensing what now took labor to make visible revived a very different conception of the first man than the humble laborer we have encountered in earlier chapters. This Adam was a sort of demigod, appearing, for example, in the rabbinic tradition that the first man had extended from the earth into the firmament, a giant stature to which Israelites would be restored in the messianic time.[14] This image of the original human body also evoked the perfect bodies to which humanity would be restored in the final resurrection, as well as the mystical body of the king in its more extreme formulations, a superbody devoid of imbecility or weakness, a body incapable of erring. This body now symbolized the aspirational identity of any member of the commonwealth of knowledge who laid aside the fallen body of the natural man in order to take on a spectatorial body, a body proper to the truth producer's office. But in keeping with the first man's ability to model the means of experimental labor as well as its ends, the effort required for incorporation into this body could itself be figured as innocent labor, for, in addition to being imperfect, these instruments of office were not easy to use.

In their mythic capacity, artificial organs purified vision of the carnality identified with the first disobedience, fallen sexuality, and idolatrous religion, offering their users prosthetic access to a body capable of seeing through the "false Images" of fallen perception and onto creation itself.[15] If the popish mass compelled the worship of what scholasticism had called accidents, the microscope provided the means to look through them. As we will see, the lens was the virtuoso's most potent weapon against the philosophical underpinning of the old priestly miracle, the scholastic doctrine of form. In providing the means to see through that "empty" name, this "instrument of truth" provided the medium for an alternative communion, based on Adam's labors of discovery.[16] The old sacrament had linked visual temptation to idolatrous consumption; in contrast, artificial organs incorporated all "lovers of truth" into a body of truth production.[17] Humanity's descent from godly production to sinful consumption (from Adam to Eve) was reversed through the technology that restored discovery's—and religion's—primal scene. The productive sacrament long associated with the delving Adam was revived in the labor of innocent observation.

By imputing to the lens the power to reverse the effects of the fall, virtuosi seemed to confer on the lens a function once reserved for Christ.[18] The distinction between created and corrupted humanity identified the fallen person as a subject in need of prosthetic assistance; the lens provided that assistance. And like the body of the Son, the lens threatened to inspire an idolatrous attachment. John Eachard mocked the "*Ingenioso* or *Experimenteer*" who, regarding the lens as a literal instrument of salvation, asks "the *Aristotelian Parson*" how he can "*preach* to *people,* and go about to *save* them, without a *Telescope,* and a *glass* for *Fleas.*"[19] But if what Milton called the "unactive blindnesse" of idolatry expressed itself in an inert dependence on priestcraft as a dispenser of grace, this mediator offered a labor-intensive model of prosthetic dependence, one that, through a process of trial at once purgatorial and experimental, remade its user into a fit inhabitant of the state he sought to restore.[20]

The stupendous powers that experimentalists attributed to their instruments thus inevitably accrued to their persons. Indeed, through the mythology they elaborated around their "artificial helps," experimentalists managed to confer on themselves some of the attributes of the priest in the old religion.[21] Aubrey suggests as much when he calls Boyle an "excellent Divine, I had almost sayd Lay-Bishop"; Beale described an "operative, practical, and experimental" religion in whose "priesthood" Boyle might be "consecrated a chief."[22] The priest had a monopoly on the Bible and the tradition of commentary in ancient languages; he had a unique power to transform matter through a ritual that was widely understood as magical and beyond the powers of other men; he was further set apart from the common run of humanity by his official virginity. The experimentalist "priest of nature" embodied each of these attributes in a properly reformed manner.[23] An expert user of technology that manifested God's word in the creation, he was a literatus of nature, with special access to scriptural knowledge that lay beyond the scope of both fallen literacy and mortal sight: what the fallen observer experienced as a visual percept, he could read as text. The investigations he pursued figuratively transformed natural bodies into "testimonials" while literally transforming them beyond recognition. And in exemplary contrast to the "hocus pocus" of the Catholic mass, his interventions into creation had visible physical results for all to see. In December 1650, William Petty and Thomas Willis became famous when they revived an apparently dead woman on a dissecting table; experiments in assisted observation produced equally wonderful results on a regular basis, revealing life where it had never been seen before.[24] Finally, refining his sensitive body into a spectatorial body, the chaste virtuoso cultivated an erotic life beyond the carnal, gaining satisfaction in the "innocent" ravishment of Dame Nature. The very mark of the virtuoso's humility—his exemplary willingness to get his hands dirty in things themselves—gained him access to a garden of delights closed to "sons of Sense."[25]

But because of the crucially prosthetic character of the insight and power he claimed, the superhumanly ambitious virtuoso was able to keep the most valuable commodity in his possession intact: his modesty. By displacing all the powers to which he aspired onto his methods and instruments, even figuring himself as a mere appendage to these prosthetic helps, this priest of nature was able to preserve his blameless posture of pious humility—and to protect its privileges. But the Christian virtuoso differed from the priest in one crucial respect: he presented his work, along with his very body, as a medium through which these privileges, and the duties they entailed, could be extended to others.

The Monstrous Representative

The gentleman virtuoso made personal humility the medium of demiurgic ambition. In condescending to learn craft secrets, he aspired to learn God's. Using artificial means to create more finely textured experiences of natural structures than nature made possible, he exposed God's handiwork, revealing to the "eyes, the things that are in secret" that Ecclesiasticus asserted should remain hidden. Virtuosi loudly insisted on the piety of this activity because it could not be taken for granted. As Henry Stubbe pointed out, nobody had "ever taught, that *Adam's* fall (which was a breach of his *religious duty towards God*) was a deficiency from the study of *Experimental Philosophie*," or that he was expelled from Eden "for not minding the *cultivation of the Garden,* and *natural curiosities.*" Indeed, the tradition that God made Adam after the creation was finished in order to shield its secrets suggested that to pry into the hidden mechanisms of creation was to

challenge divine omnipotency.[26] On this understanding, productive laborers charged with "maintaining the state of the world" had to cultivate experimental knowledge, but to pursue such knowledge for its own sake, extending the search into nature's hidden parts, was to perpetuate the first
sin. Against this objection, virtuosi insisted that such knowledge was not
gratuitous but necessary if "the state of the world" was to be restored rather
than merely maintained. Pursued, as Bacon put it, "for the relief of man's
estate," the cultivation of experimental knowledge was an ongoing work of
charity. But the work of restoring humanity to its original strength as
an agent of knowledge production was not traditionally numbered among
the works of mercy; such "charity" was hard to distinguish from prideful
invention. Locke's fantasy of a society in which labor was divided not across
classes but across a day, like Winstanley's program of true levelling, was not
a charitable vision but a revolutionary one. Social levelling was the very
mechanism of experimentalist knowledge production, and it was the core
of experimentalist identity. While the cultivation of craft, agricultural,
and medicinal knowledge had manifest utility for traditionally charitable
ends, in many ways experimental labor was a perfect inversion of charity.
Traditional demonstrations of lordly hospitality and the postmortem be-
quests of the great had long enforced respect of persons within the mystical body; this depersonalized form of charity took as its object humanity
as a whole.

   But although technologically assisted observation employed craft techniques, all that it actually produced was new experiences. Its distance from
the traditional scene of productive labor—its lack of resemblance to work
whose utility was not in doubt—made it particularly vulnerable to traditional attacks on curiosity. In this respect, the groundwork for attacks on
the lens-obsessed virtuosi was laid down centuries before these technologies
were invented. Attacks on curiosity had long focused on astronomers, conventionally described as more interested in the heavens than in heaven itself. As Carlo Ginzburg has shown, in their eagerness to associate astronomical curiosity with pride, translators of the Bible consistently rendered
Paul's command in Romans 11:20, "be not highminded" as "do not seek to
know high things."[27] Exploiting the double meaning of *altus* as high and
deep, Augustine attacked the temptations that would later be associated
with the telescope and microscope, declaring that the proud could not find
God even if they had the skill to count all the stars and grains of sand in

the universe.[28] Straining against the limits of human perception, the curious only mired themselves further in the body's deceptions.

Rather than condemning intellectual life in general, traditional attacks
on curiosity tended to focus on the pursuit of knowledge available to the
senses. Next to *concupiscentia carnis,*

> there is conveyed into the soul by the same senses of the body, a certain vain
> and curious itch; not of delight taking in the flesh, but of making experi-
> ments by help of the flesh; which is masked under the title of knowledge and
> learning. Which, because it is seated in the appetite of knowing, and that
> for the attaining of knowledge the eyes be the principal of all the senses, is
> in Holy Writ called the lust of the eyes.[29]

The appetite for experiential knowledge was seated in the highest of the
senses, on the border of what is flesh and not flesh. Attempts to scratch this
vain and curious itch masquerade as *scientia,* but they are appetitive, all
the more perniciously so because they engage the higher faculties. This urge
can have no discharge, no release; for this reason, the pursuit of knowledge is more terrifyingly addictive than the more easily satisfied, and so
more easily despised, pleasures of the flesh. Yet lust and curiosity are siblings; visually fixated eroticism, the hankering for spectacle, and the empty
longing for information available to the senses are all of a kind, since none
provokes the self-transformation that characterizes conversion; the externally directed gaze of the curious leaves them indiscriminately spellbound
and thus unchanged. Denouncing his own susceptibility before so trivial a
spectacle as a rabbit hunt, Augustine declared that unless God through the
sight itself or "by some contemplation" permitted him "to raise myself towards thee, or wholly to despise and pass it by; I dully stand besotted with
it." For medieval writers, the hunt became a figure not only for venery but
for the promiscuity of the curious mind chasing after worldly knowledge
(virtuosi would reform the *venatio* into a ruling figure for natural investigation).[30] On this understanding, the thirst for experiential knowledge could
be at least temporarily sated with a minimum of trouble, through mere
"busyness."[31] But the redefinition of an experiment as an elaborately contrived and controlled experience of nature made the identification of busy
curiosity with idleness, sensuality, and caprice comically inappropriate.
Through experimentalist discipline, curiosity, once identified with the sur-

render to aleatory experience, became the quintessential expression of self-mastery, extending to the painstaking and labor-intensive shaping of experience itself.

The case for identifying the exercise of curiosity as a labor rather than the indulgence of an appetite or an expression of pride did not, then, rest exclusively on the appeal to immediate utility or analogies to the humble and necessary trades. In the context of technologically assisted observation, it hardly could. But *curious* and its cognates carried many meanings, not all of which could be easily assimilated to *concupiscentia oculorum* or Faustian pride, such as meddlesome, gossipy, trifling, fault-finding, nitpicky, finely made, industrious, mechanically skilled, and careful. By taking advantage of this large semantic range, experimentalists were able to present a richer and more contradictory picture of curiosity in action than Augustinian critiques allowed. A "curiosity" could be something on which great pains or care had been invested; it might also be a trifle, the product of useless pains. When used to refer to the investigative urge, *curiosity* and other words in its semantic orbit, such as *discovery*, embraced both objective and subjective senses: just as an object could be "curious" if it elicited the investigative urge, so nature's laws "discovered" themselves to the attentive viewer.[32] Curiosity's defenders benefited from the word's infinitely tractable nature: the same writers who celebrated natural investigation as godly could attack the semantic disputes of the philosophers as curious—trivial distractions from solid investigation. By attacking curious disputes, they were able to insinuate themselves into a long tradition of attacks on curiosity even as they wrenched this polemical tradition away from its original objects.[33]

Far from reflecting an aporia at the heart of the experimentalist project, the systematic ambiguity of its key terms served strategic ends. So, for example, the curious were uniquely well equipped by their ingenuity in mechanical matters to appreciate God's workmanship, works of nature so curious that the deeper one delved, the more curiosities one found. Such careful probing into nature's secret contrivances was anything but reckless; rather, it invokes the root meaning of care expressed in the proverb, "Care Will Kill a Cat," where excessive feline caution rather than overweening inquisitiveness is at issue.[34] The virtuoso could never be too careful, too curious, in his attempt to read nature's book accurately; such effort repaid the curiosity displayed by the Creator himself. This flexible usage eased curiosity's metamorphosis from the first sin into the first virtue, proof that man was made in God's image. In this way *curiosity* was able to ride the coat tails of *ingenuity* to achieve its modern, positive designation, evoking the disposition of the "unprepossessed" and unassuming truth-seeker; Sprat's Adam explicitly sought knowledge in obedience to the Creator's command. By the time William Derham published *Physico-Theology* in 1713, the conviction that God's works were to be *"sought out, enquired after,* and *curiously* and *diligently pryed into* by us" had passed into common sense: "the *Creator* doubtless did not bestow so much Curiosity, and exquisite Workmanship and Skill upon his Creatures, to be looked upon with a careless, incurious Eye." God's curiosity was meant to elicit curiosity, which entailed a responsibility: those who sought to "admire [God's] Handy-work" had to "set it forth to others, that may see, admire and praise it also."[35]

Bacon had argued that

> the Psalmes, and other Scriptures doe often invite us to consider, and magnifie the great and wonderfull workes of God: so if we should rest onely in the contemplation of the exterior of them, as they first offer themselves to our sences; we should do . . . injurie unto the Majestie of God.[36]

To praise God's works, one had to work to restore them to legibility; merely to look at them as they appeared to the fallen senses was to "rest . . . in contemplation." Thomas Browne declared that the "wisedome of God receives small honour from those vulgar heads, that rudely stare about, and with a grosse rusticity admire his workes; those highly magnifie him whose judicious enquiry into his acts, and deliberate research of his creatures, returne the duty of a devout and learned admiration."[37] At once a work tool and an instrument of worship, the lens could transform the acts of staring and admiring into "deliberate research," reforming "vulgar heads" into "judicious" ones. The discipline required to fulfill this duty distinguished experimentalist curiosity from experience-mongering, demanding an inquisitiveness that was not careless and idle but arduous and introspective—enabled by the body's focus on its own nature, on what it can and cannot know by itself. The curious individual was still driven by an unappeasable hunger, but the nature of this insatiability could be newly understood. Rather than a ravenous gathering of knowledge across the plane of worldly experience, curiosity impelled a perpetual and disciplined ascent up a phenomenological hierarchy. Experimentalist curiosity thus *methodized* the yearning for sensory transcendence. Once virtuosi had redefined curiosity as the means by which individuals might distinguish between truth and appearance, material cause and effect, meditations on the deceptive appeal of sight could be used to vindicate what Abraham Cowley called "curious Sight."[38]

"*God* never yet left himself without witness in the *World*," Sprat declared, but by the time he wrote his *History*, Copernicanism, the epiphany of a microworld, and the resurrection of ancient atomism had all revealed humanity's natural unfitness for its supposedly natural role.[39] While Copernicanism traced the source of observed movements back to the spectator, who turned out to be the origin of error, the microscope confirmed corpuscular theories of matter by revealing the powers and perceptible properties of natural substances to be the products of actions occurring beneath the threshold of normal perception. Atomism, with its distinction between primary and secondary qualities, was as important as heliocentrism in promoting the certainty that "the sensitive body" was not fit to read the "vast book" of the universe. In his famous formulation that provided the basis for Boyle and Locke's, Galileo explained that smell, color, sound, and taste "so far as their objective existence is concerned, are nothing but mere names for something which resides exclusively in our sensitive body [*corpo sensitivo*], so that if the perceiving creatures were removed, all of these qualities would be annihilated and abolished from existence." It was a rational failure to conceive of names like red or white as though they pointed to anything beyond our own sensitive bodies; it was merely because our reason is "escorted by our physical senses" that we arrived at such notions.[40] The reason and understanding of Adam, many conjectured, could not have been thus escorted. The experimentalist theodicy for the recently "fallen" senses made it possible to trace an apparent design flaw to the fall itself.

Although, in explicating the failures of the sensitive body, Galileo appeals to venerable oppositions between the senses and reason, carnal blindness and spiritual insight, he also reveals their inadequacy. As atomism suggested and the lens revealed, the world as shown to the senses was the immediate result not of immaterial causes but *material* ones that, rather than being invisible, were simply invisible to the human eye.[41] Genuine insight was no longer simply a matter of looking beyond the material world; one could not look beyond what one had never even laid eyes on.

The knowledge-seeker's traditional point of departure was now a distant goal, to be reached not by repressing the body but by refining its powers. Thomas Vaughan explained that thus far philosophers had sought only to improve "their *immortal parts*," but their *"Corruptible bodies"* stood in much greater need of assistance; without such improvement, the corrupted body remained incapable of experiencing the world God made.[42] Constructing and inhabiting this spectatorial body became the aim of "True learning"; rather than simply indulging his senses, the rationally curious observer worked to reconstruct the phenomenology of the "body absolute."[43]

The effort to restore "Originals" thus included not only attempts to circumvent limits on the thinkable imposed by fallen traditions (like the division of knowledge across classes) but attempts to understand how and why the fallen body responds to the world the way it does. Similarly, what Locke called his "Historical, plain Method" was based on the assumption that one arrives at the truth about something by revealing its origins. By giving an *"Original"* of human understanding, for example—an "Account of the Ways, whereby our Understandings come to attain those Notions of Things we have"—we elucidate both the structure of our thinking and the world that conditions this structure; the aim of this introspective project is to build our ideas back up from the basis of an original purity or epistemological innocence such as Adam was often used to represent. It is easy to see how, in keeping with the double meanings of words like *primitive* and *primary*, the *"History of the first beginnings of Humane Knowledge"* could become the occasion to study how *we ourselves* "come by any Knowledge." Constructs like the state of nature and the first man offered a way of talking about the origins and first beginnings, the causal mechanisms and deep structure, of our own intellectual (and, of course, political) life as it might operate under both actual and ideal conditions.[44] Such heuristic fictions promise to restore us to the originary perspective of their protagonists: the perspective of the innocent observer. The search for originals in this more metaphysical sense relates to the most abstract constructions of epistemological priority of the period. Adam became so freely generalized that it came naturally to Walter Charleton, for example, to refer to the atom as *"the Adam or Radical and Primary Cause of all motion"* (Petty pushed the analogy further by extending the text *"Male and Female created he them"* to "the smallest parts of the *first Matter*").[45] It is not far-fetched to suppose that the homophone of *Adam* and *atom* reinforced the link between historical and ontological "originality." The pun suggests that the search for the radical and primary cause of all experience terminates at once in the atom and in the original witness of creation who first discerned its qualities. Described by alchemists as what remained after "reductions to the pristine state," atoms were implicated in the experience of nature's first and best observer.[46]

Though they paid due respect to Adam's luminous beauty, supernatural strength, and sexual self-control, seventeenth-century writers were entranced, in a way that the patristic and scholastic writers had never been, by his imperviousness to perceptual distortion, by the notion that "the circumference of our *Protoplast*'s senses" was "the same with that of natures activity."[47] When imaginatively filling out an existence shaped by such epistemological privilege, they drew on the evidence produced by new investigative technologies, permitting an identification of the innocent "body absolute" with the extant body of knowledge producers and its battery of artificial helps. Thus Glanvill's Adam perceived phenomena that could now be rationally reconstructed, such as the earth's movement around the sun and the operation of magnetism.[48] Detaching technology from history, Glanvill makes it possible to understand recently invented prosthetic devices iconologically as Adam's body parts. The Adam that he imagines, a man with telescopes and microscopes for eyes, is as grotesque a hybrid of past and present, nature and artifice, as anything in Virgil's fourth eclogue, but this version of the originary myth opens up a more optimistic perspective on paradise by suggesting that it *is* a perspective: Eden was no longer to be sought in a foreign landscape but in a different experience of the familiar. The use of the lens was predicated on the surrender of the assumption of a natural coordination between human perception and its objects, but in making use of this technology, the observer recovered an identity that, however alien, was "by nature" his own.

Although the idea of a fall into sensory deception preserved for created nature a reassuring fit between human perception and its objects, the notion that created humanity was "other" could be disconcerting; Adam's perceptual and cognitive perfections evoked an original creation that, far from being a more perfect version of the known world, was a monstrous deviation from it. When pondering the innocent Adam's radical difference from the humanity he represented, seventeenth-century commentators seem to oscillate between admiration and horror. John Salkeld appears to have been tormented by the thought that Adam was a monster, a sentiment he takes every opportunity to condemn. Even Adam's probable possession of a "super-abundant" rib out of which Eve was created elicits his concern: "it may bee thought that this was rather monstrous, then agreeable to nature." He suggests and discards the possibility that, in lacking this extra rib, we are "monstrous by defect," concluding that while in another person this skeletal excess would be monstrous, in Adam it was "most naturall." Adam's size prompts a similar worry; if we imagine Adam to have been too large, "hee might rather seeme a monster in regard of us, then a man." Salkeld struggles with the conflict posed by Adam's bodily difference for several pages before blandly concluding that, whatever size he was, it was most fitting to him. He finally declares that, if anyone is monstrous, it is us: compared to our progenitor, we "may justly bee deemed in a manner maimed, imperfect, and monstrous."[49] As monstrosity floats back and forth across the division between created and corrupted nature, the categories of the "most naturall" and the unnatural are utterly evacuated. Such lessons in perceptual relativity are perfectly tailored to a research program dedicated to restoring innocence by producing alien experiences of the known world.

Since, as we found in Chapter 1, covenant theology's emphasis on the contractual nature of original sin generated novel ways of experiencing the old doctrine of humanity's actual physical incorporation in Adam, it could also justify collective efforts to assume the monstrous attributes of our first representative.[50] Salkeld recommends as a rule of thumb that, when considering potentially disturbing discrepancies between created and current humanity, we ought not to "consider *Adam,* as one particular man" at all. The trick of representation rationalizes the existence of difference where equivalence needs to be asserted; it also provides a mechanism for the progressive eradication of that difference. The traditional notion that humanity inherited sin in the way that one inherits hair color offered the most straightforward explanation of humanity's perceptual limitations, but it failed to offer any justification for amending them. Once this inheritance was inflected by the concept of consent, these limitations became, as it were, elective. When accounting for Christ's ability to assume the burden of our sins, Thomas Bradley suggests that such a transfer of guilt requires "the consent of all persons concerned": we must consent to accept Christ as our savior if his sacrifice is to redound to our benefit. The implication is that we must have somehow consented to the initial transfer of guilt from Adam to us. It was this consent that the virtuoso withdrew.[51] As I will suggest, he did so within the terms provided by the doctrine of original sin itself, taking up permanent residence in the scene of temptation.

In his anonymously published *The Reasonableness of Christianity*, Locke queried the notion that "all *Adam*'s Posterity [are] doomed to Eternal Infinite Punishment for the Transgression of *Adam*, whom Millions had never heard of, and no one had authorized to transact for him, or be his Representative," but of course the same objection could be leveled at the social contract itself, as well as at the coerced consent that often characterized Parliamentary elections.[52] The issue of consent raises a stifled protest from Salkeld: "we never gave any consent by our own willes unto the foresaid disobedience," but he retains the plural to describe the agent of sin: "yet did we both taste and eat in *Adam,* who was our head." The redoubtable Robert Harris instructs his readers to admit that "'tis sin, my sin in *Adam* that hath forfeited mine honour, undermined my Authority over creatures": he urges them to admit not just the gravity of the first sin but their agency in it: "It is an *universall apostasie,* and it is *from your selves,* you were *Adam* . . . legally, naturally considered, you can blame none but your selves."[53] He goes so far as to insist that we are responsible "chiefly for the *first sin,*" since other sins are partial and can always plead extenuating circumstances: the sins we have personally committed are nothing compared to the sin we consented to commit in Adam. A common platitude was that the first sin contained within it all other sins; Harris extends the logic to identify Adam's sin lurking in every minor sin we commit, and compared to the first one, they are all minor. He lards his text with objections (e.g., "What's this to us?" or *"It is long of Adam. What can they help it?"*): the solution is always *"We are Adam."* Although "men shift it off," in fact *"Adam is every man:* the whole species mankind is in that pair": note how Adam already expands to include another person before the transfer of guilt is even effected. As he explains, the first couple "must not here be *personally* considered," but as *"parts* and representatives of mankind."[54] As Bradley put it,

> *Adam* in Paradise was but our nature personated; and we out of Paradise are but his Person multiplyed . . . we are not onely guilty of Originall sin derived from him . . . but even of that Actuall sin . . . for *Adam* stood not there as a single Person, but a representative of us all.

When we reflect on original sin, it is therefore incumbent on us to feel as if we were "personally present at the *transacting* of it." The stress on personal agency in the initial contraction of sin implied that one had a choice as to what part one might "personate" in this scene. For Bradley insists that although our corrupted nature prevents us from being able to fathom our created state, God nonetheless requires that "we should live up to the Principles of our Created Nature . . . when he first Created us in *Adam*." He concedes that we have no experiential knowledge of that standard:

> Oh that we had but one dayes experience of what we were at the first, as God Created us in *Adam* . . . if it were but for one day, or houre, that Image of God, which was stampt upon us in our Creation, that we might compare it with this our present estate.[55]

As Harris lamented, "We see, we feel what he is, but what he either was or shall be we can rather guess then judge, as blind men do of colours." Salkeld remarks that it would be easier to number all the stars in the firmament than to develop clear ideas about the state of innocence, since "of these we have some sight, some experience, some naturall ground; but of this of Paradise, we have no view, no experience, nor any naturall foundation." Yet he devotes hundreds of pages to the project: for by "ignoring" our prehistory, "we become desperately sicke, and of our selves and nature, without remedy."[56] But by working to "understand your *Originall*," and working at feeling "personally present" at the original scene of choice, one could become a virtual inhabitant of paradise and "learn to be thankfull for this first estate." This required the individual to become, like Adam, "A *Common person*," defined by Thomas Goodwin as "one who represents, personates, and acts the part of another."[57]

Experimentalist labor implemented this effort so rigorously as to produce physical results. Harris urged his flock: "say, I have not the understanding that once I had, *Prov.* 30. and therefore must beg eye-salve," and this is what experimentalists did. Construing humanity's identity with Adam in terms of a shared potential provided a structure of identification with our "unfallen *Protoplast*" while providing continuing impetus for radical self-transformation, the means by which this identification might be transformed into identity.[58] In this way virtuosi exploited the identificatory opportunity offered by sin to see their potential mirrored in an Adam who not only fell, but "stood" for all. It might be thought that the challenge of assimilating all of humanity's agency to Adam's in the moment of sin was almost trivial compared to the challenge of identifying with him at any time before that moment, but Adam's status as the people's representative permitted both at once.

The more the habit of Adamic personation became entrenched, the less alien Adam could seem. Salkeld argued that we were still invested with Adam's power over the creatures, "though not in the same act, or actuall exercise of his power and dominion . . . *non actu, sed potentia,*" another way of saying that fallen humanity simply had to work to realize its natural powers.[59] But perhaps this was all Adam had done himself. Before elaborating at length on his famous assertion that Adam did not need spectacles, or any other investigative aids, Glanvill admits that it is "somewhat hard, to verifie my *Hypothesis* of the *literal Adam.*" He even expresses worry that "the Ingenious" will "take offence at the seemingly disproportionate excess, which I ascribe to *Adam's senses.*" The ingenious reader, Glanvill suggests, might prefer to imagine the Adamic body as a "vehicle" he could "form," a passive instrument entirely susceptible to the manipulation of the rational will; such control is "almost as impossible to be conceiv'd, as to be regain'd." In fact, merely to conceive of this will puts one on the path to regaining it; the artificial helps at the experimentalist's disposal were also "vehicles" subject to human control. And, as it turns out, the actual "constitution of *Adam's* Organs" might not have been different from "those of his *fallen* self"—and therefore ours—after all. His "*Organical* defects" might have been compensated for by the "vast perfections of his *Animadversive*" powers, since data make more of an "impression" on people with "a greater degree of the *Animadversive* ability."[60] Contemporary meanings of *animadvert* include both to take cognizance of and to chastise after examination: as the ingenious reader would have known all along, it is not how one naturally sees but how one mediates and interprets visual data that makes the difference.[61] Although Glanvill leaves open the possibility that Adam's perceptual powers were less vitiated than ours, he stresses the "active" nature of Adam's mind above all, representing the first man less as a passive recipient of divine illumination than as a model for working philosophers: a self-made man, for whom the painful cultivation of ingenuity was its own reward.

Adam plays a similarly dual role in Power's paean to contemplation as a priestly calling incumbent on all men: the "homage due to their Creator," who "though he hath disclaimed all Brutal, yet still accepts of a Rational Sacrifice . . . a Tribute we ought to pay him for being men." Even as Power presents the labor of magnification as a means for men to "obey the prescript of their Natures," he declares that it "transpeciates our Natures": what was sacrificed through such homage was fallen nature. Men who neglected to make this sacrifice could not "justifie their titles to Rationality," and hence could not "justifie their Parentage": "*Pugs* and *Baboons* may claim a Traduction from *Adam* as well as these." Yet in trying to imitate "our Primitive father Adam," who was "more quick & perspicacious in Apprehension," investigators were merely recovering the experience of a man who engaged the world "ingeniously." The repeated realization that, for all its "primitive Strength," "the Constitution of *Adam*'s Organs" was perhaps not so "diverse from ours" after all made the most ancient constitution of all available as common property. It is not that creation's first sovereign and priest is continually elevated only to be cast down, but that, like Winstanley's Adam, he is "raised up" by being levelled—recovered as a royal, and priestly, society of the ingenious.[62]

When glimpsing his idealized self-reflection in Adam, the experimentalist thus saw a systematically ambiguous figure, one identified with both the complacent possession of knowledge and the dynamic and humbling process of obtaining and applying it. Understood as a condition of perfect *knowledge,* Eden was rather like the forbidden fruit in *Areopagitica:* "a provoking object" ever before the virtuoso's sight, whose impossible possession guaranteed its permanence as an object of desire, organizing the progressive knowledge production of a collective. Understood as the condition of *discovery,* paradise offered a methodological model for the activities of the single Adamic investigator striving to serve, and incorporate himself into, this larger knowledge-producing body. By turns a hard-working truth producer, engaged in "a painful digging, and toiling in *Nature,*" and a man with microscopes for eyes who could simply perceive all that was left to be laboriously rediscovered, Adam was a crucially elastic object of identification.[63] Indeed, he embodied the personal elasticity that was the experimentalist's signature.

It was this elasticity that enabled the virtuoso to assume the office of a subject equal to the rigors of paradisal investigation. With his instruments of discipline, the experimentalist maintained "a *watchfulness over the failings* . . . of the Senses," making his own sensory experience the object of critical scrutiny. While watching over, diagnosing, and correcting the frailties of the sensitive body, he also strived to correct for the distorting effects of "breeding and converse with men," which made him "subject to slip into all sorts of errors."[64] As the figure of slipping suggests, the original fall into sensory deception was ongoing; the subject's watchfulness over his own defects had to be constant. The experimentalist's anxious self-monitoring reflects an almost paralyzing awareness of the slips and errors to which the fallen mind is susceptible and of the strength of the forces, organic and cultural, that keep it in bondage to the known world. But this intensely dynamic—essentially continual—experience of the fall implies a dynamic experience of paradise as well. Constantly checking to determine whether he is genuinely working in and on the real "state of nature," the curious investigator reveals that he is already engaged in the labors of innocent subjectivity.

Of course, the theodicy for the fallen senses could also be used to discourage a repeat performance. Because assuming responsibility for the apparent design flaw in creation made the moral dimension of human blindness all the more pronounced, it was easy to argue that efforts to redress the frailties of fallen perception were attempts to evade just punishment. On this understanding, the investigator who sought to check humanity's ongoing fall into the world of appearance conflated the results of the fall with original sin itself, which could only be washed away by grace. In *The Fall of Man,* Godfrey Goodman lamented, "Who can patiently endure, that the soule being quick sighted and piercing, for want of perspective glasses, should be imprisoned within the bounds of our sense, mewed up in a darke dungeon of blindnesse; here is the torture of error." Although the result of original sin is that we are "imprisoned within the bounds of our sense," Goodman suggests that only a perspective glass for the *soul* can release us from our sensory dungeon; only "faith, sanctified by grace . . . purgeth and cleanseth the eye." Experimentalist rhetoric drew much of its force from literalizing such figures, but to invoke such a perspective glass as this could also make the improvements afforded by lenses seem rather inconsequential. Although sensory frailty was the consequence of the fall, to try to avoid this punishment through technological means was to ignore its moral meanings, to exhibit spiritual blindness. Moreover, such effort was pointless. Since we can never have the understanding that "the Angels have," to the extent that we indulge our "immoderate thirst" and "curiositie of knowledge," we only condemn ourselves to being further "perplexed and tormented with [our] ignorance." Depending on its own efforts, humanity will be "brought into a fooles paradise," not "true paradise."[65]

Similarly, while William Bloys conceded that in the first state of creation "Mans speciall vocation was the study of the creatures, wherein hee might discerne the wisedome of the Creatour," he represented postlapsarian natural philosophers as fools who misunderstood their place in history: "It was the employment of *Adam* in the estate of innocency, to dresse and keep the garden of Eden," but we must tend to ourselves. Rather than trying to regain paradisal sovereignty over creation, fallen humanity must tend to the soul in order to keep it "blameless"; this is a more difficult "inward labour."[66] But experimentalists showed that the arts that *testified* to human defects could actually *correct* them; and rather than contrasting technological advancement, or improving the "barren earth," with the tending of the self, they made the one depend on the other.[67] Experimentalist rhetoric encouraged a spiritual understanding of these twin processes of cultivation, as if, by using their instruments of discipline, they were precisely attempting to keep their "soule and body blameless," mending their "intellectual blindness" along with their bodily defects.[68] Goodman asked "who can endure" not having the sight of an angel, and it was precisely of their own endurance that virtuosi boasted. They tended to the damaged, fallen body in a spirit of humble self-mortification. By speaking of chastising and censuring their senses, they fostered the impression that taking pains in the production of knowledge was literally painful. Trying to overcome the errors generated by prejudice was hard enough; as Hooke ruefully put it, they left "so deep an impression upon the fancy, that they are not without great pain and trouble obliterated."[69] And when enumerating the deficiencies of our sensory apparatus that require mending, virtuosi express an almost crushing awareness of human inadequacy. Charleton describes humans as "grovelling Moles, uncessantly labouring for light," which only reveals to them "their own native Blindness." Glanvill describes the fallen mind as "naturally amorous of, and impatient for *Truth,* and yet averse to, and almost incapacitated for, that diligent and painful search, which is necessary to its discovery"—a "blind *Bat*" compared to the "perspicacious *Eagle*" that Adam was.[70]

But these self-abasements have a ritual function. They are calls to enter the purgatorial paradise of pains, to undergo the trial—"that diligent and painful search"—required to disengage natural investigation from specifically human (or "fallen") perspectives. These generalized expressions of self-contempt proclaimed the necessary rather than gratuitous nature of the experimentalist's labors; those who worked to correct the perceptual symptoms of inbred corruption collectively assumed the role of "good physician" to the mystical body.[71] Human liabilities were the experimentalist's assets; they were the basis of prosthetic insight. Lapsing into the first-person plural, as if he were speaking for humanity as a whole, Charleton declared that "contempt of our own nature" was enough to "put us to a stand," had not the "inhaerent Curiosity of our Genius sharply spurred us on again."[72] The spiritual subject of scripture becomes the collective subject of science, ready to avail itself of a vast array of "Mechanical helps." The dichotomy of blindness and insight that structures the pessimistic anthropologies of Goodman and Bloys is laid along a temporal axis, revealing a series of steps connecting present blindness to future insight. The rationally curious individual eager to mend his blindness does not remain at "a stand" but begins to take these steps; the groveling mole begins to dig.

It "lies in the *Natural Philosophers* hands," Sprat insisted, "best to advance that part of *Divinity:* which, though it fills not the mind, with such *tender,* and *powerful contemplations,* as that which shews us Man's *Redemption* by a *Mediator;* yet it is by no means to be pass'd by unregarded." What reads like an uneasy admission is also a provocation. The generalized reference to Christ as *a* mediator seems calculated to inflame critics of the Society, suggesting that these new mediators failed to *show* man's redemption by a mediator because they were actually effecting one. Among Stubbe's (many) religious objections to Sprat's *History* was the threat that physico-theology posed to a Christ-centered worship: so much emphasis on God as Creator threatened to make his incarnation as savior ancillary. In the *Reply* to Stubbe, Sprat's defender ingenuously protested that he had never denied that "Christ is our Mediator," going on to joke that their exchange was itself providing a "pritty *Medium*" for readers to discern experimental philosophy's religious value.[73] As this pun suggests, the work of mediation was now being undertaken through new mediums, with print and lens technologies consolidating a corporate body capable of serving as a middle term between humanity in its created and corrupted states.

When employing the artificial organs of this common body, even the virtuoso who worked alone did not work as an individual. The virtuoso whose powers were "magnified" and "multiplied" was able to produce insights at a remove from his individual sensitive body. A working member of an improved Corpus Christi, the user of optical instruments was no longer his own person. Describing the "scientific habitus," Bourdieu describes "an incorporation of the constraints of the instrument so perfect that one is corporeally bound up with it, one responds to its expectations; it is the instrument that leads"; such incorporation enables the practitioner to abandon his "singular originality," to be inhabited instead by a "collective super-ego." As Barbara Shapiro points out, instrument-based testimony was deemed more trustworthy by the Society than the testimony of technologically unenhanced persons: knowledge producers who employed artificial helps consented to being represented by this larger body, a body they in turn tried to represent when working alone.[74] Experimentalists thus co-opted Adam's identity as a public person to establish the virtuoso's right to perceptual experiences that were not his to have. If no single individual had a claim to the privileged perspective of humanity's representative, the collective subject of knowledge production did.

Referring to the "many faults and inequalities the naked eye and unmachined hand do commit," Hooke presented the reformed body as a futuristic blend of nature and artifice, a representation that did not in the least disturb his identification of its powers with those of humanity's original: what Charleton calls humanity's natural "Genius" required unnatural conditions to be expressed. Imagining a whole panoply of sense-enhancing instruments, Hooke speculated that "the adding of *artificial Organs* to the *natural*" would one day result in a wholly reconstructed body through which the philosopher might radically extend the reach and scope of every sense (as J. A. Bennett observes, given Hooke's mechanical view of heat and cold, even the thermometer could be understood as an artificial organ of touch).[75] As experimentalists never tired of stressing, the disappearance of colors under powerful magnification rendered many colored objects "pellucid"; this phenomenon suggested that the improved lens technology of the future would raise the atomic constituents of all qualities to the threshold of visibility. Regarding color as a sort of imposition, or *"Phantasm,"* Power predicted that "artificial Eys" would soon enable humans to perceive its causes, along with the operation of magnetism and the spring of the air.[76] As Hooke's ideal of the "machined hand" suggests, the promise of intensity is paradoxically accompanied by a loss of intensity; as percepts are incomprehensibly abstracted from mere human sensation, the sensitive body is left behind altogether.[77]

Virtuosi who developed expertise with prosthetic technologies seem to have enjoyed their role prefiguring the artificially enhanced humanity of the future. Hooke clearly took pleasure in convincing others that he had personally undergone such a metamorphosis already, telling Pepys, for example, that he was "able to tell how many strokes a fly makes with her wings (those flies that hum in their flying) by the note that it answers to in Musique during their flying." (Pepys was politely skeptical: "That, I suppose, is a little too much raffined; but his discourse in general of sound was mighty fine.") At a 1668 meeting of the Society, "Mr. HOOKE gave a hint of making glasses, by which one might see and read in the dark"; he also dropped hints about an otacousticon.[78] Hooke created as much mystery around his sensory refinements and inventive powers as the proverbial priest who pretended to make God from bread with his back turned. Alluding to flying machines he had invented, described variously as a "flying chariott by horses," artificial muscles, and a "module," he presented himself as a sort of cyborg.[79] Unlike a magus, however, he had no interest in being thought of as a recipient of gifts from demons or spirits.[80] The Christian virtuoso was a son of Adam, the curious product of curious labors. At once less and more than a man, this self-made representative of humanity's knowledge-producing potential was also—like Adam himself, or Hobbes's *Mortall God"* and "Artificiall man," the Leviathan—something of a monster.[81]

This representative was the very opposite of the charismatic sovereign or eloquent statesman. The condition of virtual illiteracy to which he aspired could even be signaled by an inability to speak (a trait Joseph Addison and Richard Steele made sure Mr. Spectator inherited). Contemporaries described Boyle as "constrained by an internal force to swallow his words," in exemplary contrast to the garrulous schoolmen and chattering members of the beau monde whom he held in such contempt.[82] Evelyn was persuaded that Boyle's stutter was in some mysterious way the product of "his frequent attendance on Chymical Operations," as if the Christian virtuoso's speech was inexorably constrained by his efforts to make things themselves speak.[83] Eulogies of virtuosi tirelessly stress their lack of all the attractions desirable in a gentleman: Richard Waller remarked that Hooke was nothing to look at, but he had "a sharp ingenious Look"—an "eie full and popping," as Aubrey put it. The image of an ingenious Hooke is strengthened, not weakened, by the remark that "As to his Person he was but despicable, being very crooked," for his strengths did not inhere in his own person.[84] Even Hooke's curvature of the spine was traced to his labors, as if his dedication to the things of the earth had transformed him into a prosthesis of his own technology, a living "instrument of truth." At Westminster, Hooke was "very mechanicall," and it was at this time that "he first grew awry, by frequent practicing, turning with a Turn-Lath, and the like incurvating Exercises."[85] Experimental investigation literally perverts the body, turning it "awry" from its naturally fallen destiny, to transform it into the spectatorial body: a working prophecy of a posthuman future, modeled on humanity's irreducibly alien, yet "common," past. But if the virtuoso enjoyed a privileged access to that future, he also offered himself as a medium of access for others: the work Hooke published under the auspices of the Society was designed to permit the reader to replicate or at least virtually experience his results, and thereby to be incorporated into the spectatorial body under construction. Members of the experimentalist priesthood imagined by Beale were "bound to offer sacrifices" in order to effect "the grace of reconciliation"; what the virtuoso sacrificed was his person.[86]

The Natural Literatus

Renaissance experiments with perspective had already taken views and their relation to the world as their object, but perspectivism offered liberation only from a single vantage point, not from the constraints of human perception itself.[87] Imagining a world stripped of secondary camouflage involved precisely such transcendence. Experimentalists sought to see through the visible to its temporally remote material causes: in plumbing the depths of the visible world, the virtuoso sought to see through time. Indeed, early uses of the term *prospective glass,* a term that became synonymous with the telescope, often refer to a magic glass or crystal in which it was supposed that past or future events could be seen.[88] As we will see, virtuosi actually imputed to the lens the power of conquering time, but they made this power dependent on the work of rational reconstruction. It was by attaching itself to a collective rather than individual, sensitive body that curiosity was reformed: to uphold the ideal of progressive discovery through the cultivation of facts, it was essential that the effort to see through time *take* time, that optical instruments not offer instantaneous illumination to their users.

Boyle was once tempted by a glass that he believed could impart such instant gratification. In one of his many agonized casuistical consultations with Bishop Burnet, he confessed that he had once had the opportunity to look through a magic perspective glass. According to Burnet's notes, "he had the greatest Curiosity he ever felt in his life tempting him to look into it and said if a Crown had been at his feet it could not have wrought so much on him but he overcame himselfe which he accounted the greatest Victory he had ever over himselfe."[89] Of course, the glass *was* a crown, an instrument that would have enabled him to merge completely with the powers—but not the practice—that defined his kingly (and priestly) spectatorial office. In resisting this temptation, he respected the genuinely public nature of that office, subordinating his personal gratification to the needs of the collective subject of science, which was nourished by knowledge gained through regulated and replicable rather than magical means. The sacrifice of the private man was a redemptive one; by refraining from taking this shortcut, Boyle overcame the temptation to which Eve had succumbed. Boyle also relayed the testimony of an anonymous colleague who encountered a magic glass that could only be used by a virgin; a nine-year-old girl who looked into it reported that she was able to see events from his own past.[90] The refusal to look through such a glass protected a different kind of virginity. When Evelyn compared Boyle to "a Chrystal or Venice-Glasse . . . as cleare, and candid; not a bleb, or spot to tarnish his Reputation," he repurposed a compliment conventionally applied to chaste women (and to the Virgin Mary above all) to figure a new kind of chastity, one that made its subject into a trustworthy perceptual medium for others.[91] The virtuoso's personal restraint and internalized discipline made him a reliable public worker, a dependable instrument of truth in his own right. For Boyle clearly did not doubt the efficacy of such tempting glasses; the temptation they extended was not a surrender to seductive illusion but the opportunity to gratify his curiosity without undertaking the requisite labor. It was this labor that really crowned the investigator (and his coworkers), marking his victory over "selfe ends."

The virtuoso who forswore "unlawful Magick" organized his life around a satisfaction he would never personally experience. Since "the full discovery of Natures Mysteries, is so unlikely to fall to any mans share in this

Life," the virtuoso was like one who had "to live upon Sallads," which "excite more appetite than they satisfie." By restricting himself to what Evelyn called "paradisian fare"—a diet that left him in a state of chronic hunger—the virtuoso guaranteed the innocence of the knowledge he produced.[92] Describing the bittersweet pleasures of natural investigation, Boyle observed that the success of his best "Toils" only engaged him in new ones,

> either to free himself from his scruples, or improve his successes. So that, though the pleasure of making Physical Discoveries, is, in it self consider'd, very great; yet this does not a little impair it, that the same attempts which afford that delight, do so frequently beget both anxious Doubts, and a disquieting Curiosity.[93]

It was essential that the making of physical discoveries, however delightful, remain uneasy. A truly innocent curiosity was insatiable; the anxious doubts fostered by the disquieting passion only spurred the investigator on to be ever more "scrupulous." As Michael Hunter has argued, the word *scruple* was as crucial to Boyle's repeated observational trials in the laboratory as it was to his casuistical consultations with Burnet and Stillingfleet. The identity of the Christian virtuoso was predicated on his continual investment of *cura* to resolve scruples of both kinds.[94]

Such investment was time-intensive; discoveries were always imperfect, because further perfectible. If optical instruments revealed the organic imperfections that encumbered the fallen body's powers of discovery, imperfections in the tools themselves testified to its debilitated powers of invention. Galileo's correspondence with contemporaries who were eager but unable to see what he saw through his telescope reveals the extent to which early modern telescopic vision was, in Milton's phrase, "less assur'd" than a modern reader might assume: lens-images were distorted, had colored fringes, and frequently appeared in places different from the place of the object, while optical after-effects were the source of considerable confusion. The first usable telescope that Kepler received from Elector Ernst of Cologne, who had in turn received it from Galileo, seemed to him to show the stars as intensely colorful *squares* (Ernst had been unable to see anything at all through the instrument). Other users of the telescope complained that they saw three suns instead of one; some frustrated users asserted that Galileo could only have seen the moons of Jupiter if he had put them in the telescope himself.[95] The fact that the telescope did not offer a quick visual fix only underscored the necessity for combining rational reconstruction with perception and undertaking repeated observational trials. It was by relinquishing the demand for sensual immediacy that the laborer became a philosophical observer, distinguished by his animadversive powers.

The fact that they were not easy to use—requiring patient application and a type of visual "literacy" to produce reliable knowledge—helped to make optical instruments the most celebrated emblems of *reading* nature as opposed to merely gazing at it.[96] As I have suggested, the most important use to which virtuosi put the topos of nature's book was to brand scholastic philosophers as illiterates in the language of nature: Sprat declared that "those who have the best faculty of *Experimenting,* are commonly most averse from reading Books"; they were engaged in acquiring real literacy in nature's grammar.[97] Hooke's *Micrographia* sums up an entire metaphorics of reading, from the atomized letters to the words and syntax that constitute nature's language. Henry Baker, the eighteenth-century popularizer of the microscope, declared that whoever wanted to read "Nature's mighty Volume . . . with Understanding, must make himself Master of the *little Letters,*" not just the "CAPITALS"; Cowley's "To the *Royal Society*" celebrates the ability of the microscopist, not the natural man, to read Nature's "smallest Hand."[98] By representing optical instruments as necessary aids to this process, experimentalists were able to distinguish themselves from the schoolmen while at the same time wresting nature's book away from its most confident readers: Paracelsians, whose doctrine of signatures offered a competing model of experiential literacy. R. F. Jones's appealing description of Paracelsus as "that remarkable Swiss genius who burned his Galen and turned to the study of nature" discourages us from appreciating the residual scholasticism that informed this study. If, as Pamela Smith argues, Paracelsus styled himself as a spokesman for artisanal epistemology, his campaign to locate philosophical authority in "the body of the artisan" nonetheless appealed to philosophical categories recognized by the schoolmen. Like the scholasticism it threatened to replace, Paracelsian natural magic was predicated on the subordination of matter to form.[99]

The schoolmen had had good reasons to identify natural philosophy with textual commentary rather than physical investigation. As Peter Dear explains, the definition of experience among scholastics was common experience, expressed in universal statements about the way things are: "Heavy bodies fall." To provide an authoritative source for a statement was to render it trustworthy; such data were literally givens. The scholastic focused on general cases as recorded in authoritative texts because the objects of his investigation were not things themselves, but their forms, the source of all qualities and changes in natural bodies. In addition to providing a basis for natural kinds or species, the doctrine of form provided an explanation for transubstantiation as a formal change that did not affect perceptible accidents of matter. For the operations of form did not merely lie beyond the scope of fallen perception; they were immaterial. To understand the nature of an acorn one had to look to general cases and the "experience" recorded in books, not at any particular acorn, since the accidents of matter could in any particular instance interfere with the fulfillment of its essential nature.[100]

Paracelsians also believed that true knowledge of an object focused on its form, but they believed that these indwelling essences were betokened by signatures. Oswald Croll insisted that these "exemplary Notes . . . and Symbols of Internal Invisible things," while "Visible," required unusual penetration to see—a "higher ingenuity, and more subtile Inquisition, then can be obtained by sight of the Eyes only." Although Croll was stern toward the "*Plebeans* destitute of internal Eyes" who considered only "the external face of things," his analysis of the "Internal Form" of each herb is almost exclusively concerned with externals, the "exteriour Signatures" of the forms contained within.[101] This was the key to popular Paracelsianism's allure: intimations of arcane knowledge known only to adepts coexist with an emphasis on nature's easy legibility to those who regard it with any attentiveness. Nature's book of "common Hieroglyphicks" was at once invitingly open and deeply mysterious, individual signatures plainly visible yet somehow inscrutable.[102] The "Archeus or chief Workman" that controlled the development and functioning of each body organ, plant, and animal suggested an artisan who would only reveal his secrets to other artisans; the appeal to artisanal expertise encoded in personifications of form—the "inward worker . . . Master-Workman . . . the Vulcan or Smith of generations"—reproduced the clergy's privileged relation to form in the priestly miracle even while appealing to a popular priesthood.[103]

This secret knowledge that was at the same time common knowledge reflected the origins of the doctrine of form itself. As Michael Ayers points out, form theory and the notion of innate knowledge were introduced into

Western thought at the same time, through Plato's suggestion that entities called forms were directly apprehended before birth; on this understanding, we grasp truths by recalling them.[104] The connection between form theory and the faith in the innate powers of the human intellect to grasp essences conditions Paracelsus's belief that man had knowledge of creation and the creator already within him. The power to "think God's thoughts after him" was not pieced together through rational reconstruction; it was merely reawakened by *experientia*. Knowledge of the macrocosm was already contained within "the little world"; the process of acquiring natural knowledge was intuitive, as easy to claim as it was difficult to explain or systematically replicate. Paracelsus told his followers to try to overhear nature; this state of alertness was at once pious and self-regarding.[105] "Plants do speak," Croll insisted; in overhearing the murmurings of plants, stars, and stones, the observer could gain access to a vast system of signs in which he was also described, for the scientific, philosophical, medical, and political lore to be gleaned from signatures related directly to the ends of human life.[106] Within this "semantic web of resemblance," visual similarities between objects betokened common indwelling forms or essences (the source of natural kinds or species) that enabled things of like shape (and therefore of similar essences) to exert sympathetic power over one another. Signatures on leaves and fruits bore an analogical likeness to human organs that they might cure: the walnut rind bore "an entire Signature" of the pericranium and was therefore good for head wounds; hairy moss offered a cure for baldness.[107] While the appeal to privileged intuition was intimidating, it was also inviting; such analogies harmonized well with early modern habits of thought. On the basis of the principle that the "world consisteth of marriage and the uniting of couples," for example, Goodman uses the invisible marriage of form and matter as hard evidence for the model relationship between husband and wife: "the one is active, the other passive; the one apt to give, the other apt to receive impression; the one giving beautie and splendor, the other supporting and upholding the action."[108]

From the perspective of most virtuosi, romances about "*prime Matter courting Form*" were not evidence on which arguments could be based.[109] Hooke curtly announced that the "two general and (unless further explain'd) useless words of *Matter* and *Form*" were better explained by the material "composition of Bodies" and "the instruments and manner of their inward motions." The first epigraph to Locke's *Essay,* from Ecclesiastes

11:5, rebuked the confidence of those who discussed the operations of form in the absence of having clear and distinct ideas about them: *"As thou knowest not what is the way of the Spirit, nor how the bones do grow in the Womb of her that is with Child: even so thou knowest not the works of God, who maketh all things."* While Charleton brusquely dismissed the "stupid admirers of that Fanatick Drunkard, *Paracelsus*," John Ray patiently explained that "Signatures of Plants, or the Notes impressed upon them as *Indices* of their Virtues" were "rather fancied by men, than designed by Nature to signifie or point out" any thing.[110] Paracelsians thought they were reading God's word; they were only stamping their own signatures on everything they viewed. Baker thus finds it necessary to console beginning users of the microscope who may possibly "cry out, *What is all This to us?*" Posing the same question Harris asks and answers with respect to Adam's experience, Baker reveals such painful lessons of estrangement to be the microscopist's lifework. Although the decipherment of nature was not an operation the sensitive body was fit to undertake, Baker nonetheless insisted that "it is really our Duty."[111]

Thus the lazy refusal to undertake the labor necessary to make nature legible could be laid at the door of the signature-reader and scholastic alike. In relating his discovery that green powder under the microscope resolved into blue and yellow grains "confusedly enough Blended together," Boyle is careful to exploit the multiple associations of the term *mechanical* to stress the roots of technologically assisted observation in real artisanal work. Taking his cue from "the Mechanical use of Colours among Painters and Dyers" who created green from blue and yellow pigments, Boyle offered a microscopic demonstration of how green was "Mechanically produc'd" by nature—a demonstration that left no excuse for invoking "I know not what incomprehensible Substantial Form" to describe color as an "Inherent Quality." Modestly following in the steps of Adamic mechanicks, the microscopist revealed an atomic mechanics invisible to readers of signatures.[112] Henry Power asserted that without "Mechanical assistance, our best Philosophers will but prove empty Conjecturalists, and their profoundest Speculations herein, but gloss'd outside Fallacies; like our Stage-scenes, or Perspectives, that shew things inwards, when they are but superficial paintings." To endow speculations about the natural world with genuine rather than illusory depth, it was necessary to regard nature as a document indeed: "true universal Characters legible to all rational Men," provided they equipped themselves to read it.[113]

Signatures were among the "wilful and superstitious" doctrines Hooke denounced as the result of "negligence, and intemperance" stemming from original sin: "a deriv'd corruption, innate and born with him [man], and from his breeding and converse with men." Against this ongoing fall into custom and wishful anthrocentrism, he offered his *"artificial Instruments and methods,"* revealing essences to be "the meer products" of the motion, figure, and size of tiny particles of matter, the true constituents of nature's *"Orthography."*[114] Signatures were ostensibly legible only to those touched by God's *"Incarnate Word,"* yet it turned out that signatures were merely deceptive doubles of the word, this holy reading corrupt.[115] Indeed, what purported to be a reading practice actually worked to enforce a kind of il- literacy: focusing on manifest resemblances between shapes reduced nature to a collection of reified images, "Pictures for Children to admire and be pleased with." Whereas "Gazing" at nature merely raised "Wonder," which suppressed the viewer's analytical faculties, *reading* nature enabled rational penetration.[116] Such penetration began with seeing through the spurious scriptural unities available to the naked eye.

Drawing on Lucretius's analogy between letters and atoms, virtuosi dissolved signatures to refigure the book of nature as an open text—a book in the making.[117] Shifting focus away from the teleological develop- ment of form to "the *ABC* of Nature's working," the atomization of signa- tures resulted in the *alphabetization* of nature, redefining qualities as the visible result of "Transpositions and Metamorphoses" occurring beneath the threshold of human perception. As Charleton explained, qualities de- pended not on formal "Principles" reflecting "absolute and entire Reali- ties," but rather on "various transient Accidents." Aside from atoms and space, "nothing in the Universe stands possessed of a Real or True Nature"; nothing "doth constantly and invariately hold the praecise Quale, or Suchness of their particular Entity, to Eternity." As natures were tradition- ally understood, nature had no real nature. In scholastic terms, "First Matter" was all there is, so that "all the mysterie of those reciprocal meta- morphoses amounts to no more, than a meer putting of the parts of the same common and indifferent matter into different modes," which, after existing as one natural body, can obtain another "Disposition, and Forme, and so exhibit the species of a New body."[118] As Grew declared, "For the *Form* of a *Body,* we can conceive of no otherwise, than as of the *Modifica- tion* of a *Body.*" If a form is simply a moment in an ongoing metamorphosis, it has assumed its modern denotation: it is simply a shape, a temporary configuration of matter.[119] The dynamic sense of nature as an open text leads Hooke to anticipate the theory of evolution: if "we see that there are many changings both within and without the Body, and every state produces a new appearance, why then may there not be the same progression of the Species from its first Creation to its final termination?"[120] The reduction of natural forms to a single moment in an ongoing process of decomposition and reassemblage suggested the susceptibility of nature's text to editorial intervention. Because the virtuoso aimed at such intervention, he actually *depended* on an alphabetized rather than scripted nature to perform his function.

The Lucretian alphabetization of natural bodies permitted what Boyle called "more Fontal explications" of nature's book. On this understanding, to read nature was not to extract ready-made semantic content from it but rather to reconstruct the causal narrative that produced it. The visible was defined as an effect of a material cause; to read and understand the visible world was to excavate this cause.[121] While "sons of Sense" and "Notional Speculators . . . onely gaz'd at the visible effects and last Resultances of things," virtuosi were able to turn false images into historical records—transforming the visible world into a testimonial of its own production.[122] Hooke looked forward to a natural dictionary that would lay out the *"Orthography, Etymologia, Syntaxis,* and *Prosodia* of Natures Grammar,"* enabling the curious to "turn to and find the true Figure, Composition, Derivation and Use of the Characters, Words, Phrases and Sentences of Nature written with indelible, and most exact, and most expressive Letters." To "peruse, and turn over, and spell, and read the Book of Nature" was to discern not just the "Figure" and "Composition" of its letters, but their "Derivation" and "Use." Having grasped the derivation of natural sentences, the structure of their components, and how their grammatical parts fit together, the *"Literatus* in the Language and Sense of Nature" could find new uses for these parts.[123] Understanding the composition of the world enabled him to recompose it in turn.

By presenting his instruments as the real agents of his work, the modest virtuoso was free to attribute to himself, through praise of his reading aids, powers bordering on the fantastic. Hooke speaks of the ability of optical instruments to foreshorten, perhaps to conquer, time and so to confer a sort of immortality on the user:

> However it were desirable by the Experience and Inquiry of a short time to dispatch and hasten the Growth and Ripenings of the Productions of Nature, since the Experience and Duration of a Man, whether he looks forward or backward, is very short in comparison of what seems requisite for this Determination; his Sight is weak and dim, his Power and Reach much shorter, yet may it be worth considering (tho' he cannot lengthen or prolong his limited time either past or to come), whether by Telescopes or Microscopes he may not see some hundreds of Years backwards and forward, and distinguish by such Microscopes and Telescopes Events so far-distant both before and behind himself in time, as if close by, and now present? And whether by Instruments he may not extend his Power, and . . . lengthen his Life and increase the injoyments thereof by a multiply'd and condens'd knowledge of times past, and of times also yet to come.[124]

Obviously such superhuman powers did not emanate from optical instruments; Hooke is describing the observer's ability to reconstruct past events and predict outcomes on the basis of the visual evidence these instruments provided. The lens conquers time in two ways: it enables its user to "see" causes across time, and in doing so, it enables him to reverse fallen history (the passage leans heavily on the theme of fallen blindness: man's sight is "weak and dim," and his powers even weaker).[125] Hooke is really celebrating the virtuoso's intellectual ability to think beyond his own corporeal limits, yet the phrase "by Microscopes and Telescopes" or a variant accompanies each claim, mitigating its audacity. Without this crucial deflection, Hooke's boasts would appear alarmingly immodest and even delusional, since the scientific observer's exemption from bodily limitations places him beyond the absolute limit of death. But by displacing his intellectual as well as his visual capabilities onto his instruments, the virtuoso could exult in his superhuman powers without overtly abandoning his humble bearing.

The context of Hooke's celebration is the interpretation of fossils. Rocks sporting images of animal and vegetable substances—"that easily raise both the Attention and Wonder"—were widely regarded as especially conspicuous examples of the signatures that proliferated everywhere in nature (280). Rejecting as "fantastical and groundless" the suggestion that these apparent signatures indicated "a secret Vertue whereby they do at a distance work Miracles on things of the like Shape," Hooke heaped scorn on the notion that Nature sought to "play the Mimick in the Mineral Kingdom" (288, 289). How much more reasonable to assume that these similitudes were produced by means of "moulding" rather than by virtue of "any internal or substantial Form" (292, 289). Instead of interpreting these similitudes as "the effects of Nature idely mocking herself," a literatus would read in these "Testimonies . . . small" the "History of the World before *Noah's* Flood," when some species were perhaps spelled differently than they were at present (318, 412). Rather than regarding the images imprinted on fossils as permanent and absolute inscriptions, the natural literatus sought to understand the grammatical laws governing their production. Under the gaze of such a literatus, fossils, like ancient "Records," became annals of the past; in deciphering them, the virtuoso saw—and read—across time (321).

This iteration of the topos of nature's book no longer calls attention to nature's meaning. There is no sense in the combinations of nature's letters; their fluid arrangements do not testify directly to an immanent authorial intention; they have to be invested with sense, with relevance, for the uses of human life. The vanishing of an immanent order was the occasion for its human construction. Indeed, the undertaking of this labor was what providence had intended all along: the "*Stenography* of Providence" extended itself to the judicious reader as a potential writer. The "Causes of things from . . . Originals in Nature," Power said, "are producible by Art"; "discoveries" led providentially to "works."[126] There was no matching textual paradigm to guide the assemblage of its constituent letters into new arrangements. Rather, to this end, Hooke explained, the virtuoso had to subject natural bodies to alterations just as nature had,

> by Fire, by Frost, by Menstruums, by Mixtures, by Digestions, Putrefactions, Fermentations and Petrifactions, by Grindings, Brusings, Weighings and Measuring, Pressing and Condensing, Dilating and Expanding, Dissecting, Separating and Dividing, Sifting and Streining; by viewing with Glasses and Microscopes, Smelling, Tasting, Feeling, and various other ways of Torturing and Wracking of Natural Bodies, to find out the Truth or the real Effect as it is in its Constitution or State of Being.[127]

This passage portrays humble artisanal procedures like straining and sifting, along with apparently noninvasive investigations like smelling, as methods of asserting a tyrannical rule over natural bodies, "ways of Torturing and Wracking" them to get them to reveal their secrets. It is not simply that Baconian melodrama seethes beneath the conventions of modesty; rather, modesty is its catalyst. It is by virtue of his abject dependence on his instruments that the virtuoso is permitted to metamorphose into a ruthless inquisitor once he has them in hand. In celebrating the labor through which artisanal power is exerted, the passage recapitulates it: the recompositional flow of nature's alphabet in the hands of an assured literatus is enacted here through alliteration, which decomposes and reassembles itself across the passage (pulled together by the repetition of "ing," the verbal sign of continually refreshed activity). Although the passage ends with the comparatively stable phrase "Constitution or State of Being," the placement of the last "ing" after the long series of participial action phrases suggests this last state as one of present flux—a flux, however, now under the creative control of the experimentalist. This trajectory is contained in the compendious subtitle of Hooke's most famous work: *Some Physiological Descriptions of Minute Bodies Made by Magnifying Glasses with Observations and Inquiries Thereupon*. The ambiguous syntax suggests that his book of descriptions was actually made by his magnifying glasses: the microscope has become a pen. By making visible nature's secret grammar, these reading aids enabled their user to become an author in his own right.

Power argued for the necessity for artificial aids to vision by explaining that "our Eyes were framed . . . as might best manage this particular Engine we call the Body, and best agree with the place of our habitation (the earth and elements we were to converse with) and not to be critical spectators, surveyors, and adaequate judges of the immense Universe."[128] The virtuoso had no special gift enabling him to be a critical spectator or adequate judge; it was his "mechanical helps" that enabled him to elude the sensory limitations imposed by what Power, with self-conscious detachment, refers to as "this particular Engine we call the Body." Once equipped with these helps, however, the virtuoso no longer "agreed with" his appointed place in the chain of being and was able to gain knowledge that lay beyond the body's reach. There was a lack of agreement—a breakdown of consent—between the virtuoso and his limited natural endowments, both because he saw things that did not accord with his naked sensory experience and because he actively strived to see such things. No longer merely unlettered in intellectual norms, less confident and "prepossest" than dogmatic philosophers, he could not only "converse" with nature but begin to rewrite it.

Such a literatus had experiences that were quite foreign to those of the rest of the species. As Hooke declared, the world as seen through the lens was one to which the bulk of humankind were "utterly Strangers." Disciplining his body to extend its naturally "narrow sight," Baker saw each "hated Toad, each crawling Worm" with "Reason's piercing Eye." Through this eye, he could discern that the admiration elicited by an apparently flawless work of human artifice, a well-executed engraving or piece of Venetian lace, "arises from our Ignorance of what it really is": in fact, "the utmost Power of Art is only a Concealment of Deformity, an Imposition upon our Want of Sight." Seen from the perspective opened up by this "valuable Discoverer of Truth," the "most boasted Performances of Art" appeared "ill-shaped, rugged, and uneven . . . disproportionate and monstrous."[129] As in Salkeld's ruminations about Adam's body, the categories of the monstrous and proportionate are emptied out.[130] For the same instrument reveals in a dissected frog "a beauteous Landscape, where Rivers, Streams, and Rills of running Water are every where dispersed," since the circulatory systems across creation were "established on one and the same Plan"—governed by the same grammar.[131] In his eagerness to overturn naturalized hierarchies of beauty, the microscopist is not content to lavish the same attention on the guts of a frog that the connoisseur invests in the appreciation of a fine engraving; he must also expose the engraving as a fallen deformity. Whatever anxiety is introduced by the artificiality of the microscopist's own perspective is recuperated by its exposure of the cheats of artifice that seek to impose on the viewer: having gained an artificial liberation from sensory limits, he is now free to resist the imposture of artifice everywhere else.

To demonstrate one's exemplary alienation from the sensory and cognitive experience of dumbstruck sons of sense, it was not enough merely to extol beauties that were invisible to the fallen eye. Baker's appreciation of the frog's innards is not limited to what the lens reveals; what is "beauteous" is the manifestation of "Nature's constant Law," apprehended in a mode of sight that renders the frog's circulatory system a network of rivers in a landscape.[132] But this "seeing as" is not justified by Paracelsian resemblance. Like the virtuosi's comparisons of the universe to watches, clocks, and automata, it is homologous, directing our attention to structural correspondences across dynamic systems. Rather than analogizing the entities of nature we habitually see, virtuosi dissolved them into structurally similar and curiously wrought machines that could be peered into, tinkered with, and transformed. To "give a satisfactory Account" of natural operations required the observer to be "an Artificer indeed, and one well skill'd in the Wheelwork and Internal Contrivance of such Anatomical Engines." Although divine workmanship was superior to human workmanship, they operated on identical principles: as Hooke explained, the principles for understanding "instruments" of nature are no different from those we use to understand "the productions of Art," which are "manag'd by Wheels, and Engines, and Springs, that were devised by humane Wit."[133] The dissolution of signatures enabled divine writ to be scrambled with human wit.

Like the homologies suggested by social contract theory, these analogies almost seemed to defeat the whole point of analogy: rather than fostering a sense of the inevitability of any particular form (like the analogies that once linked roses, dolphins, and lions together as monarchs of their respective realms) they destabilized all forms.[134] As atomistic natural explanations described a world devoid of natural hierarchies, the quibble on "Democrit-al" and "democratic" became an organizing pun.[135] Examining his own urine under the microscope, Hooke found the "working of some of the parts of the Urine upon others, and thereby a setting others at Liberty." The "Putrefaction" of his urine bore testimony to Charleton's politicized account of the *"perpetual Commotion"* amongst atoms, commotions that led to "intestine war," with even the "lasting peace" of a "compaction" eventually dissolving as particles "attained their liberty, and flye off": the forces governing England's recent history are replicated at the atomic level.[136] Where the sensitive body saw urine, the spectatorial body saw the mutations of matter from which the operation of laws governing creation at all levels of matter—perhaps even laws relevant to the "science" of politics— might be derived. It was on the basis of homologies like these, not visible resemblances between individual bodies, that nature's book—and the dispensations of providence in human history—could be read and understood.[137] The indifferent matter that assumed various forms could also serve as a metaphor for selfless membership in the transsubjective subject of science: in their representative capacity, investigators were also "common matter" in different modes. And indeed, the more personal "indifferencie" they exhibited—the harder they worked to extract their personal and sensitive selves from their investigations—the more powerful they became.

The hermeticist John Webster lamented "all the treasury of those *ideal signatures*" lost with Adam: these "preaching *Symbols*" had elucidated connections between the macrocosm and the microscosm, imparting revelations of the "mysteries of their own secret and internal vertues and qualities" for human use—knowledge that "the dead paper idols of creaturely-invented letters" could never convey.[138] In contrast, when Power employed God's signatures as a conceit, he referred simply to "how curiously the minutest things of the world are wrought . . . inrich'd and embellish'd." Placing the wing of a butterfly under the lens, "you may see the very streaks of the Cœlestial pencil that drew them," streaks that excel even the "strip'd bravery of the Tulip." Such celebrations of God's text not only violate Samuel Johnson's warning against numbering the streaks on the tulip; they suggest that such numbering is not nearly close enough.[139] But this close reading is not a hermeneutics; there are no emblems in which humanity can see its own ends and purposes reflected. This mode of reading equipped the natural literatus to pick up God's celestial pencil and restore the scene of naming as a scene of authorship, applying maker's knowledge to its source. The virtuoso thus emerged from his identification with the unlettered artisan—ignorant of textual authority, devoted to physical exertion in the service of truth—to assume the identity of a superhuman, wellnigh bodiless author of nature. The disintegration of nature's book into textuality, a work in the making, created imaginative pressure to reconsolidate nature as a coherent body. With the same eagerness with which they tore natural forms apart, virtuosi reassembled them into the singularly beautiful form of Dame Nature—a form invisible to sons of sense.

Keeping a Virgin Mind: The Temptation of the Visible

The microscopist's almost literal ecstasy proclaimed his detachment from the sensitive body of the fallen man, susceptible to superstitious "Wonder, and Gazing." When Baker urged his reader to "Bring forth thy Glasses: clear thy wond'ring Eyes," he drew on an established identification of the lens as a weapon against superstitious wonder—an identification that was enhanced, not threatened, by his raptures over the beautiful landscapes that lay hidden in a toad or "stinking fish."[140] Technologically assisted observation substituted the pleasures of self-diagnosis and rational recon-struction for direct knowledge of the thing-in-itself for oneself that Eve had naively sought through "Degustation." On this understanding, the tempta-tion represented by the forbidden fruit was the urge to identify knowledge with mere sensory stimulation—in the words of Milton's Eve, to "feed at once both Bodie and Mind."[141] But the pressing demands of the sensitive body could at any time cause curiosity to degenerate into a carnal appetite, tipping godly production back into disobedient consumption.

To fully inhabit the Baconian paradise of exercise and experiment, it was not enough to identify with Adam; the experimentalist investigator also had to define himself against Eve. Her association with sensory stimu-lation and carnal knowledge, intensified by the stubborn association of the first sin with some form of sexual temptation, made her prelapsarian iden-tity difficult to accommodate in constructions of Eden that identified para-disal bliss with the innocent pleasures of discovery. Although traditional representations of the delver often feature his helpmeet working alongside him, in most experimentalist representations of Adam as an intellectual laborer Eve is nowhere to be seen, and original sin is firmly associated with feminine error. Experimentalists did not imagine an Eve who had investi-gative successes before she gave in to the temptation to cut methodological corners; as soon as she tried to participate in Adam's labors of discovery, the paradise of exercise and experiment ground to a halt. By removing Eve from what could have been a collective labor of understanding, experi-mentalists were able to protect the image repertoire they were busy con-structing around the first man from being tainted by his status as "the first Criminal."[142]

But Eve proved remarkably useful as an object lesson in the pitfalls of experimental investigation. Her association with carnality was subjective as well as objective; she was tempted by the very thing she was. Extending the carnal allure of appearances to superficially plausible theories, Charleton described Eve as a zealous but incompetent investigator whose "Desire of Science" resulted in hasty theoretical commitments on the basis of some-thing that merely seemed "to promise a satisfaction of that desire." Eve be-lieved what she heard and what she saw; when confronted by sensory evidence she had been unable to maintain the "indifferencie, or aequilibration" of the "Will" necessary to suspend judgment. The urge to link knowledge of nature to sensuous contact with it, to gain rational and physical satisfaction at once, is now an "inseparable Annex to our Nature." Our raging desire of science instills us with *"Impatience"* and *"Praecipitancy,"* goading us on to constant error and sin. Charleton regards every temptation to sin as at bottom a temptation of knowledge; the ultimate motivation behind every "Vicious inclination" and action is that it "seem[s] to promise an encrease of *Knowledge* in some kind or other." These virtually Augustinian sentiments are directed not toward curiosity itself but toward the *"Irregularity of our Curiosity."*[143] Curiosity becomes irregular when it seeks to be satisfied instead of exercised:

> If either the discourse, or writings of some Person, in great esteem for Learning or Sagacity, or our own meditations furnish us with one plausible and verisimilous [explanation], such as seems to solve our Doubt: how greedily do we embrace it, and without further perpension of its solidity and verity, immediately judge it to be true, and so set up our rest therein.[144]

Charleton here exposes gullibility as a weakness of the flesh. The uncritical acceptance of a merely plausible explanation is a greedy embrace, the desire for certainty, an indolent desire to "set up our rest" without having earned it. Since a truly innocent curiosity was insatiable, such rest could never be earned.

Experimentalist rhetoric most often described the *"precipitancy of concluding"* in quasi-sexual terms, as a sort of sluggish promiscuity. Here Eve appears in the habit of the great whore of Babylon, as temptation's object rather than its subject. The connection of idolatry to adultery in the Old Testament and the topos of the marriage of the regenerate soul to Christ provided a basis for describing the dead image as whorish display; this temptation could now be identified with undiagnosed sense perception— the threat of secondary qualities to the recovery of primary, authentic knowledge—along with the false mediation of custom, opinion, and the dead letter. Thus Evelyn lamented the *"Tyranny* of *Opinion,* delusory and fallacious Shews" that had "sadly *debauch'd* the *Minds* of Men."[145] Glanvill describes the fallen mind as liable to

> please it self in the possession of imaginary appearances, which offering themselves to its embraces in the borrowed attire of that, which the *enamour'd Intellect* is in pursuit of, our impatient minds entertain these counterfeits . . .

For as the *Will*, having lost its true and substantial *Good*, now courts the shadow, and greedily catches at the vain shews of *superficial* bliss: so our no less degenerate *understandings* having suffered as sad a divorce from their dearest object, are as forward to defile themselves with every meretricious semblance, that the variety of opinion presents them with.[146]

The sorceress-temptresses of Christian allegory flit through this passage, which is conditioned by a strange feature of Protestant romance. In Spenser's *Faerie Queene*, the temptress must be stripped to be resisted; in obedience to the prophesy that the Lord will expose the "secret parts" of the daughters of Zion, her naked body inspires only scorn.[147] Here, however, the mind, divorced from truth, its "dearest object," embraces the "meretricious" clothes themselves, "the "borrowed attire" of "imaginary appearances" and counterfeit charms. A truly curious investigator, who took pains to maintain an "indifferencie," refused to defile himself with such embraces. Such attacks on irregular curiosity make *regular* curiosity—steady, recurring, never failing—a precondition for spiritual regeneration, to which the necessarily false prospect of immediate satisfaction was a constant threat.

As a modifier of curiosity, *regular* evokes, and redefines, the ecclesiastical sense—subject to or bound by a religious rule or belonging to an order. Identified with the project of chastening the senses, chastity becomes a quintessentially masculine, intellectual, and quasi-priestly virtue: "No man so fit to receive and retain the impressions of *Truth*, as He, who hath his Virgin mind totally dispossesed of *Praejudice*."[148] By chastising their senses with mechanical helps, experimentalists transformed their bodies into more supple instruments of their own "animadversive power" while protecting their virgin minds from the blandishments of superficial appearances and plausible theories. Bookish philosophers could thus be scorned as latter-day Eves, philosophers of the "FEMAL Sect": "as women constantly retain their best affections for those who untied their Virgin Zone; so these will never be alienated from immoderately affecting those Authors who had the Maiden head of their minds." A masculine philosopher never surrendered this maidenhead, to Aristotle or even to Gassendi. What distinguished the rationally curious investigator from the intellectually promiscuous "degenerate" was his ability to cultivate detachment from all experience. Those who constructed rickety theoretical structures on the basis of undiagnosed sense experience and inherited dogma were "sonnes of *Eve*": instead of remaining content to cultivate "experimentall" knowledge, they had inherited the "saucy appetite of their Grand-mother" for "speculative knowledge."[149] Speculative knowledge was now understood as an accomplice of naive empiricism, the easy acceptance of undiagnosed empirical evidence that always turned out, on closer inspection, to be the projection of the observer's fallen desire.

By publically excluding Eve's female descendents from the laboratory, virtuosi protected the ideal of the paradisal workroom: like Evelyn's Eden, "a place Consecrated for sober Discipline." The homosocial camaraderie that characterized the experimental "conventicles" in Interregnum Oxford and London equally characterized the Royal Society, as the notorious disruption presented by Margaret Cavendish's visit suggests (Pepys worried that "the town will be full of ballets [ballads]" over the visit). On the occasion of a purely social call, Evelyn had been "pleasd" with the Duchess; in contrast, when she visited the Society, he dismissed her as "a mighty pretender to Learning": the contrast between the attitudes of the sociable gentleman and the Society Fellow proclaims the distinction between Evelyn's body natural and the virtuoso's office.[150] Although some virtuosi worked alongside women in their private capacities, this did not change the public construction of experimental labor as a masculine activity (though one could argue that the emphatically artificial character of experimentalist masculinity in principle created a space for female participation). A year before the Society received its charter, Evelyn proposed that he and Boyle design a Solomon's House on the model of a "kind of Lay-monastery."[151] Abraham Cowley's *Proposition for the Advancement of Experimental Philosophy* gives detailed shape to this monastic fantasy, which confirms the sentiment, expressed in his ode "To the *Royal Society*," that philosophy is a "Male Virtu." In this cloistered Philosophical College outside London, "no Professor shall be a Married man," so that each could live with a young male scholar. Visitors would be permitted only rarely, "nothing being more vain and unfruitful than numerous Meetings of Acquaintance," and the only women on the premises would be four maids; he specified that they should be "old." Analogously, Salkeld finds it "most probable" that if humanity had remained innocent in paradise, there should have been more men than women there; such women as existed would have been "necessary" women, required for propagation and domestic labors.[152]

The degree to which Eve was excluded from Adam's rational bliss became an obsessive theme in literary re-creations of the first man's experience. That paradise was most truly paradise before Eve was created was a common joke: Cowley quips that "As soon as two (alas!) together joyn'd, / The Serpent made up Three"; Evelyn concurred that Adam "could not live innocent a day" after Eve appeared; Marvell's garden enthusiast famously remarks that "Two Paradises 'twere in one / To live in Paradise alone."[153] The casually misogynist wit testifies to a genuine imaginative difficulty. It stood to reason that experimentalists linked the perspicacity of the innocent Adam to his continence: as Robert South explained, Adam could not desire "such things as he saw through." Eve's beauty would have distracted the first philosopher from his aim of penetrating the causes of the visible; and, Augustine's theory of voluntary arousal notwithstanding, it was difficult not to assume that sexual desire would have unsettled Adam's bodily self-mastery, the absolute subjection of the "passive vehicle" of the body to the animadversive power. The overdetermined identification of sin with cupidity sometimes makes it difficult for commentators to keep Eve and the serpent straight.[154] As we will see in the following chapter, the virtuosi's troubled relationship to the theatrical culture of the Restoration, widely regarded as feminine and feminizing, provided steady fodder for the ongoing drama of the virtuoso's threatened chastity. Some virtuosi extended this Adamic bodily self-mastery into their own private lives. Bacon had counseled philosophers to marry only "things themselves"; as the speaker of *The Masculine Birth of Time* tells his protégé, only this "chaste, holy and legal wedlock" can "restore you to yourself."[155] Boyle took pride in never having been "hurt by *Cupid*"; he recommended a similar renunciation of "unmanly Sensualities" to other philosophers. Although Hooke exposed himself more readily to the related temptations of books and women, he exhibited an impressive detachment from both, recording orgasms in his diary in the same fashion as the rest of his findings—and, as far as his colleagues were concerned, he led a "Monastick Life."[156]

Yet virtuosi eroticized natural investigation, often to absurd lengths. In doing so, however, they were describing the exploits of a spectatorial body that was virtually a signifier of the conquered and chastened sensitive body. Praising Boyle for his chastity, Burnet's eulogy declared that he was one of those rare persons who "have used their Bodies only as Engines and Instruments to their Minds, without any other care about them, but to keep them in good case, fit for the uses they put them to." Boyle's physical fitness was of a sort that raised his soul to a height of purity that, to ordinary people, would "scarce appear credible." Presenting the experimentalist body as one of the instruments it used to discipline itself, Burnet's tribute to the quintessential Christian virtuoso seeks to stamp out all thought of the carnal body of the private man. Hooke's praise of Christopher Wren—"there scarce ever met in one man, in so great a perfection, such a *Mechanical Hand,* and so *Philosophical a Mind*"—identified him at once with the admired "mechanick" and with the prosthetic devices through which the virtuoso's hands and eyes extended their powers.[157] The idea that real men had mechanical eyes and hands redirected erotic energy from women to Nature, a female figure that could only be penetrated using mechanical means. The experimentalists' rigorously repressed eroticism returns with a vengeance in their accounts of intercourse with a partner who requires the superhuman vigor of an "Engine" rather than a man.

Having effaced the disturbing presence of Eve from "true Paradise," experimentalists reintroduced the feminine display they had banished by projecting it onto an alternately coy and wanton Nature, as if she were Adam's true consort and helpmeet. Sometimes, Nature appears as an idealized maternal figure, a mother who cannot stop feeding her sons; the "Degustation" for which Eve is blamed is now embraced with gluttonous abandon. The frontispiece to Evelyn's partial translation of *De Rerum Natura,* for example, features a Nature whose breasts pour milk over Lucretius's head. Such scenes also permit frank expressions of sibling rivalry. A dedication to Edmund Waller, a Royal Society Fellow, calls him "Nature's Darling, free to tast / Of all her Store; The Master of the *Feast:* / Not like old *Adam,* stinted in his Choice, / But Lord of all the spatious *Paradise*": this invidious comparison presents the virtuoso as a son of Nature more beloved than the first-born. The near rhyme of "choice" and "paradise" echoes Milton's declaration in *Areopagitica* that "reason is but choosing": the renovated subject of paradise is imagined as even more unfettered than his original, a spoiled child, "Nature's Darling," free to eat anything he wants.[158]

More often, however, experimentalists described their encounters with nature as voyeuristic intrusions and rapes, personifying her as a coquette who was asking for it. Bacon offered a gendered account of experiment that linked it to respectable marriage—nature was to be regarded not as a "Courtezane for Pleasure, or as a bond-woman for gaine; but as a spouse for generation, fruit and honest solace"—but he had also bequeathed to the virtuosi an extensive metaphorics of torture; the mixing of these codes induced a kind of sexual vertigo.[159] Sprat described the laboratory as the site where the "Beautiful Bosom of *Nature* will be Expos'd to our view"; unlike the daughters of Zion, Dame Nature would remain beautiful even when stripped. But in accordance with the *venatio* paradigm, such exposure lay in the future, after a long and arduous pursuit; Nature is best seized, Hooke declared, "when she seems to be put to her shifts to make many *doublings* and *turnings,* and to use some kind of art in indeavouring to avoid our discovery"; nature's provocatively artful doublings and turnings "naturally" elicit the arts of discovery, as if she demanded "the adding of *artificial Organs* to the *natural*" to make submission worth her while.[160]

Figuring discovery in sexual rather than alimentary terms enabled experimentalists to present their knowledge not only as active but as productive. Cowley refers to horticulture as Evelyn's "Wife," but, "you have hundreds of other Arts for your Concubines . . . you know them," and by means of an "*Extraordinary Application* . . . beget Sons upon them all"; this libertine compliment relates Evelyn's wide-ranging competence as an investigator to sexual profligacy and his useful discoveries to the breeding of bastards.[161] But these productive erotic engagements were undertaken at a remove, mediated through artificial organs, and dispersed throughout a series of discrete and partial investigations. The ongoing "conversation" with nature was suspended between arousal and abstinence, externally focused attention and diagnostic introspection, pervaded by a diffidence born of modest probabilism and acceptance of uncertainty. This brazen but teasing mistress required a courtship that extended to the end of time, as the progressive structure of scientific inquiry demanded, though in her wanton capacity, nature did not mind breeding bastards in the meantime. Even the fantasy of nature's ultimate submission was an ambivalent one since the ultimate perfection of maker's knowledge would render nature an unrecognizable hybrid of nature and artifice, a union that could hardly be imagined before it was attained. The comforting impossibility of the union in the present, which guaranteed the permanence of the romance, was evident in day-to-day experimental practice; nature could never be spied on without being utterly defamiliarized—wracked, dissected, and so forth—which

made her ravishment a (redemptively) alienating affair. The rigors of intimacy might have dissipated the initial attraction, as virtuosi worked to expose nature's "Beautiful Bosom" by dissecting dogs, suffocating birds in air
pumps, and anatomizing corpses; but the language of courtship and rape,
or, much less commonly, of a quasi-incestuous relationship with an indul-
gent mother, conferred a single name on the object of investigation, imputing a bodily integrity to the whole, an integrity that actual investigative
procedures repeatedly shattered. Recomposing nature through the language of sexual pursuit reconstituted her as an object of desire, enabling the
chase to begin again.

I have suggested that the chase after nature was also a flight from nature's
secondary camouflage. "Together with the Knife it will be necessary to joyn
the Microscope": the knife and the lens implied one another, instruments to
tear through the veil of appearance. But in the enduring romance of experimentalist investigation, ripping away nature's veils only seemed to uncover
more "Gay outside[s]."[162] The space consecrated to penetrating appearances
also multiplied them: peeled back, the surfaces of creation revealed more
surfaces, putting the investigator at risk of being ravished by nature's secondary enchantments. "Ocular demonstration" was often the occasion for scopic
pleasure, though not of a sort that fans of Nell Gwynn would have recognized. Although the Christian virtuoso might have been expected to obey
John Corbet's mandate, "Never terminate in the sensitive Pleasure, but make
use of it to raise thy Heart to God," the strikingly unfettered experimentation
with various insect species using the microscope, needles, and other tiny tools
sometimes seemed to terminate precisely there.[163]

Power's mesmerized pleasure in viewing insects—particularly their
"vibrassant eyes"—is so intense as to seem illicit:

[The horsefly's] eye is an incomparable pleasant spectacle: 'tis of a semi-
sphaeroidal figure; black and waved, or rather indented all over with a pure
Emerauld-green, so that it looks like green silk Irish-stitch, drawn upon a
black ground, and all latticed or chequered with dimples like Common
Flyes, which makes the Indentures look more pleasantly: Her body looks
like silver in frost-work, onely fring'd all over with white silk . . . After her
head is cut off, you shall most fairly see (just at the setting on of her neck) a
pulsing particle (which certainly is the heart) to beat for half an hour most
orderly and neatly through the skin.[164]

The description of a female body "fring'd all over with white silk," along with the allusions to lace and emeralds, transforms this anatomy of the horsefly into the stuff of romance. Power's enumeration of each body part, combined with the slide from lush description to sadistic torture, even suggests the blazon. The literary form devoted to the enumeration of the beloved's body parts could only perform a figurative dismemberment; Power is able literally to fragment his subjects while paying them the courtliest of compliments. Throughout his accounts, he endows his subjects with charisma and personality so that they achieve a certain star quality. He attributes to them flatly emblematic personality traits—nobility to the louse, on account of her purple blood, or virtue to the ant, who, he says, "excels . . . most men"—and grants them affective states, as when he affectionately remarks on the mite's gusto for food. Although he makes references to the wisdom of the Creator throughout, it is the "theater of the creatures" that dominates the scene. While he dismisses the secondary enchantments of color as cheats of fancy, nature's lurid spectacle inspires him to paint his specimens with the colors of rhetoric, even quoting Donne's "The Flea"—"so great is the mechanick power which Providence has immur'd within these living walls of Jet." As the creatures go about their business, he refers like a stage manager to the "incomparable pleasant spectacle" their mundane lives and even their death throes provide when viewed under the lens. Power heaped insult on those who would not quit bodily pleasures for the sturdier joys of natural investigation, but at times this lofty program seems to demand no more than the ability to draw a voyeuristic pleasure from a scene "pleasant to behold": mites eating cheese.[165]

Although virtuosi attempted to distinguish dumbstruck wonder from rational investigative desire, identifying the lust of the eyes with the former, wonder percolates throughout early modern natural investigations; it would boil over in the literature of physico-theology. But even though the awe-struck testimonies of the intricacy and beauty of the meanest insect when viewed under the microscope are suffused with wonder, these appeals to pleasure are always rationally recuperated within a broader program of penetrating appearances. When examining sand "of noe alluring color" under the microscope, Beale discovered "rubyes, emeralds, every Jewell, not one sand of dull hue. I pounded the blacke shining sand, & it was full of staring eyes," from which "I seeme to receive many hints, & much ayde towards the discovery of the Originall of colours." However captivating these glittering eyes, it was the prospect of uncovering the origins of sense experience that most "inflamed" his "desires."[166]

This did not stop promoters of the experimentalist project from making abandoned appeals to the sensory stimulation and pleasure of discovery. Attempting to enlist public support for the Society, Hooke dangles before his readers the prospect of expanding the dominion of hearing, smelling, tasting, and touching, and continues:

> I do not only propose this kind of *Experimental Philosophy* as a matter of high *rapture* and *delight* of the mind, but even as a *material* and *sensible Pleasure*. So vast is the *variety of Objects* which will come under their Inspec tions, so many *different wayes* there are of *handling* them, so great is the *satisfaction* of *finding* out *new things* that I dare compare the *contentment* which they will injoy, not only to that of *contemplation,* but even to that which most men prefer of *the very Senses themselves.*[167]

Recognizing that "most men" prefer sensory to intellectual pleasure, in this passage Hooke bases his pitch on the former, though he stretches his descriptive capacity when he attempts to convey the sensuous joys of handling a vast *"variety of Objects."* Hooke "dares" to compare the "high *rapture* and *delight*" he feels when working to an erotic pleasure, which "most men prefer." Sprat reiterated this suggestion, describing experiment as a means for men to enjoy "the *pleasures* of their *senses* . . . without guilt or remors."[168] Though there may have been a *"material* and *sensible Pleasure"* to be had in physical investigation, it required a curious refinement to identify sensory satisfaction so closely with "the *satisfaction* of *finding* out *new things"*; even as Hooke makes his case, he seems content to allow that such "high" enhancement of the sensual drive is beyond "most men." The distinction between physical knowledge and merely carnal knowledge reserved the thrill of penetrating nature's secrets for the truly discerning, who found in the theater of nature pleasures that simpler men could only derive from the actual theater or bawdyhouse. Applied to nature's garden of delights, such erotic rhetoric is less reminiscent of libertine constructions of the first age than of Browne's temperate fantasy that "we might procreate like trees," participating in a diffuse eroticism in which genitality seems to disappear. Libertine rhetoric becomes the very sign of the virtuoso's absention from "this triviall and vulgar way of coition"; like the garden itself, the fertile and chaste virtuoso *"produces* and *nourishes* . . . and *generates* . . . without violation of *Virginity."* [169]

Balanced between attention and indifference, the virtuoso treated Dame Nature as an assiduous yet detached lover. Even when he seemed to be gazing directly at her naked glory, he had to retain a virgin mind, to abstain from the embraces of superficially plausible explanations that she threw up through successive veils of meretricious appearance; his reward lay in the experience of a continual apocalypse or unveiling. The surrender of direct, unmediated experience through the use of mediating paraphernalia, which paradoxically enabled a more intimate view of nature's interior, had its affective counterpart in the virtuoso's refusal to commit when attempting to interpret what he saw. Remaining innocently poised between alternatives provided a continual pretext to keep looking.

Cowley's ode "To the *Royal Society,*" a bricolage of experimentalist cliches printed at the beginning of Sprat's *History,* [170] reproduces the paradoxical combination of distance and closeness generated by experimentalists' simultaneous insistence on the mediated character of rational vision *and* its capacity to permit physical intervention. Cowley's procedure in the ode is to jumble together contemporary motifs of spectatorship to create revealing juxtapositions between them—experimenting, then, with different models, in visually jagged lines that flaunt the organized rebellion against fastidious art encouraged by the ode form itself. Cowley first attempts an aesthetic translation of the experimentalist ideal of "exact" imitation, by implication associating his own mimesis with precise draughtsmanship rather than the detested "paint of Art" (line 187). Of all the poem's experiments, it is the least compelling:

> Who to the life an exact Piece would make,
> Must not from others Work a Copy take;
> . . .
>   No, he before his sight must place
>   The Natural and Living Face;
>   The real Object must command
> Each Judgment of his Eye, and Motion of his Hand.
>   *(lines 79–80, 85–88)*

Phrases like "The real Object" and "The Natural and Living Face" straightforwardly announce the independence of the "exact Piece" from secondary effects like color, reinforcing the distinction between rational representation and "Painters Fancy" that structures the poem as a whole (line 6). As Cowley returns to the scene of copying later in the poem, however, the aesthetic of visual immediacy gives way to a more complex and mediated model, characterized by an insistence on what is hidden from view. Nature is no longer a lively visual surface but something hidden and "imperceptible" behind a surface that conceals:

> Natures great Works no distance can obscure,
> No smalness her near Objects can secure.
>   Y'have taught the curious Sight to press
>   Into the privatest recess
> Of her imperceptible Littleness.
> She with much stranger Art than his who put
>   All th'*Iliads* in a Nut,
> The numerous work of Life does into Atomes shut.
>   Y'have learn'd to Read her smallest Hand,
> And well begun her deepest Sense to Understand.
>
>   *(lines 141–150)*

Agitation of the viewer's senses by an object that "commands" them is no longer sufficient; as nature's futile attempt to "secure" herself from her pressing observer suggests, the relation of command has reversed. This is because the "real Object" is no longer the "Natural and Living Face" but something hidden in nature's "privatest recess" that must be read (the line's descent from capital to lower-case letters registers the observer's sharpened focus). Rather than placing a flamboyant object "before his sight" and drawing it, the copier must read and understand nature's "deepest Sense," which requires him to "press" further and deeper than the draughtsman; the face as object of imitation is replaced by the pudendum as object of penetration. Yet just as Philosophy is ready to exhibit his potency, at the moment of entry, nature becomes a book, and physical penetration is replaced by close reading: Philosophy asserts its power by means of "curious Sight," through a *rational* penetration. As nature becomes a text, the probing body of Philosophy undergoes a corresponding abstraction, becoming an instrument of rationalized sense. For, as the allusion to Hooke's *Micrographia* makes clear, the invasion of nature's interior that brings to light her "deepest

Sense" is accomplished through a prosthetic device—the artificial organ of the lens. The body of which Philosophy can now boast is a purely spectatorial one, created in the interaction between technology and the mind of the observing subject.

Prior to this climactic scene of close reading, Cowley has described the process by which the "Male Virtu" of Philosophy, a sort of man *in potentia,* requiring "solid meats" and "vigorous exercise" to grow, developed into a man indeed (lines 7, 22, 23). While he was still only an heir of "hopeful parts," Authority resided in his place, who "did a Body boast, / Though 'twas but Air condens'd" (lines 13, 41–42). In this allegory, when knowledge ceases to be merely authoritative, it produces physical results: it gains a body that can act as well as look. Ceasing to be a "Scar-crow," Philosophy may take possession of nature rather than ineffectually gazing at her with a "curious but not covetous Eye"; when it is later joined to curiosity, covetousness will assume a new meaning as active and rational (lines 59, 29). After the gates of paradise are reopened by Bacon, Philosophy's long-awaited savior, all are urged to gather their "Fill" of the fruits of real knowledge (line 61). Cowley, however, pulls back at the last moment and stops short of permitting the "injur'd Pupil[s]" to eat from the tree: as Charleton explained, paradise cannot be regained by straightforward "Degustation" (line 40). Although the mature Philosophy now casts a rigorously "covetous" eye on nature's body, he cannot get overstimulated; he must "press" for a mediated form of satisfaction from her. The escape from "painted Scenes, and Pageants of the Brain" to "Things, the Minds right Object" occurs not through direct physical experience but disengaged decipherment (lines 30, 71).

Far from suggesting a virgin mind, however, Cowley's passage seems almost lewd: by placing the paradisal fruit under strict taboo and making curious prying occur across a distance, he places the curious reader of nature in the pornographic situation of suspended arousal. Pricking the superficial exterior of the temptress appearance with a phallus that was rigorously distinguished from his sensitive penis, the masculine investigator may have proven his chastity, but in doing so, he transformed distance and mediation into independent sources of stimulation. Although the artificial organ held by "machined hands" was supposed to be a rational phallus, Leeuwenhoek's famous observations of the "animacules" in his semen reinforced the ignoble link of the instrument to masturbation, a

linkage the public never forgot.[171] In the case of telescopes, enormous length
did indeed correlate with increased power, which may have strengthened
the comic association (inconveniently long telescopes, however, also provided protection to their users, reducing their susceptibility to ravishment
by the deceptive shows of spherical aberration). In her *Emperor of the
Moon*, Aphra Behn represents the virtuoso as a peeping Tom in the creepy
figure of the Doctor Baliardo, obsessed with catching the man in the
moon in his "secret closet." Even as he prides himself on his "abstinence
from carnal thought," Baliardo becomes obsessed with spying on extrater-
restrial nymphs and making his daughter the moon-emperor's wife.[172] Alexander Pope and William Pulteney's notorious ballad about Mary Toft,
who claimed to have given birth to rabbits, depicts a virtuoso peering
through a telescope he has plunged into her vagina.[173] In such satires, the
observer poised between intimacy and rational distance is supposed to
withstand the enticement of appearances as he penetrates them, but in the
process, he becomes fetishistically attached to the instruments of mediation themselves, the artificial organs through which he imagines he extends his body's powers.

The rationally mediated distance that paradoxically permits penetration of nature's interior is charged with the thrill of the fetish. As a constitutive feature of the fetish in the "anthropological" sense, William Pietz has
singled out its active relation to the living body of an individual, its status
as a kind of external controlling organ.[174] As a prosthetic device, the optical
instrument was an extension of its user's body, an artificial organ that enlarged the scope of the viewer's sight and power while alienating both from
his physical self. The self-directed quality of fetishistic enjoyment, which
detains desire from its ultimate aim by deferring, and even abstracting, the
physical drive to possess, characterizes the relationship of the user of optical
instruments to the things he views, which under his scrutiny cease to be
themselves, becoming evidence or "testimonies" of something else. Like the
Freudian fetish, which emerges as a substitute pleasure when satisfaction of
the primary drive is deferred, in mediating the subject's relation to the primary object the lens could become a repository of erotic investment in its
own right. In Cowley's ode, when Philosophy's corrupt tutors seek to distract him with "Painted Scenes," it is primarily to distract him from the
sight of his own "Natural Powers," and only secondarily from the sight of
nature herself (line 17). Kepler famously apostrophized his telescope, not

the objects it revealed; the thrill of discovery pales before the fascination of the viewer with his own instrument.

Experimentalist rhetoric was often so hyperbolic that it was hardly possible to exaggerate it further for comic effect. The extremity of experimentalists' self-presentations as stooping illiterate workmen and rapists of Dame Nature granted them a virtual immunity to satire. But by appropriating a libertine rhetoric whose practitioners they despised, virtuosi revealed, at least to their own satisfaction, the virility and purity of their desire; those who saw obscenity in their activities simply revealed themselves to be sons of sense. The gratuitously eroticized rhetoric of assisted observation was itself a version of "going naked for a sign," a performance of innocent chastity that could be distinguished from its fallen opposite by those who had eyes to see.[175] It is in fact easy to forget when reading descriptions of the virtuoso's sadistic sexual mastery over Dame Nature the humble nature of the objects that were actually under his dominion: cork, thyme seeds, ants, bacteria in water or urine. As I have suggested, one purpose of this insistent personification was to unite the objects of all these discrete and partial investigations of particular bodies, themselves dissected and anatomized, under the single proper name Nature, just as virtuosi could be united under the proper name of Adam. To confer a single name on each of these complex entities was a remarkable feat of abstraction, enabling a single erotic union of two "multiplied" agents. The rhetoric that described the beauty of nature seen as a coherent but false image invited the process of anatomy, stoking the investigator's desire to peel back the surface and uncover the underlying processes that produced it. Thus decomposed into a strange and swarming multiplicity, nature's body was repeatedly recomposed through the rhetoric of romance, ensuring that the chase after Nature's secret parts would be a permanent one.

The most important work performed by this sexual rhetoric was to identify the spectatorial body as the agent of this chase; no man enthralled to his sensitive body would see a beautiful bosom in a stinking fish. Although the satiric transformation of the masculine instrument of truth into a sex toy expressed the suspicion that the apparently pure desire to become Adam disguised the perversity of the Adamite, satirists like Pope actually had to bring the lens into proximity with the objects of the sensitive body's temptation in order to make the accusation stick. In fact, the Adamic investigator was the very inverse of the Adamite: rather than perverting godly rhetoric to carnal ends, he used libertine rhetoric, and even masturbated, as the progress of knowledge demanded; rather than merely spilling his seed, he turned it to chastely productive ends. The eroticization of natural investigation stressed productivity over all: nature's ravishment was not the work of the flesh; it was only the spectatorial body that could "seize" her.

Just as Adam embodied both a condition of perfect knowledge and the dynamic condition of discovery, so the wooing of nature unfolded on two registers; while coy nature's surrender to *total* rational mastery lay at the end of an interminable courtship, wanton nature could be impregnated constantly. Thus the old devotional topos of the soul as bride of Christ assumed innocent form in the spectatorial body's erotic "conversation" with God's female creation. If a sacramental understanding of technologically assisted observation sounds stretched, it did not seem so to Cowley. As we have seen, when the gates of Eden are thrown open, the Fellows can "Behold the rip'ned Fruit" and "gather" their "Fill," but this temptation, successfully resisted, sets into motion another conceit:

> Like foolish Birds to painted Grapes we flew;
> He [Bacon] sought and gather'd for our use the Tru;
> And when on heaps the chosen Bunches lay,
> He prest them wisely the Mechanic way,
> Till all their juyce did in one Vessel joyn,
> Ferment into a Nourishment Divine,
>   The thirsty Souls refreshing Wine.
>
> *(lines 72–78)*

The allusion to Pliny's birds pecking at painted grapes extends the earlier denunciation of scholastic terms as empty images that bear no relation to things themselves; these grapes are also an oblique reference to the idolatrous mass, which has been triggered by the threat of "Catching at the Forbidden Tree" (line 63).[176] The priest, in this construction, entices his flock with a feast at once carnal and imaginary, in which the sensitive body is by turns tempted and frustrated. But here, word and thing are brought together in a genuine sacred union through "the Mechanic way," the productive body providing the "thirsty Souls refreshing Wine." Described in suggestively "representative" terms, this gathering of "all . . . in one" enacts the abstraction of multiplicity that produces both Dame Nature and the

Adamic brotherhood. Although Eden has been described in appropriately georgic terms as an "Orchard," this is not just an approving image of productive labor. Cowley is alluding to the devotional image that appears throughout the labors of the months tradition and whose meaning is explicated in one of late-medieval England's most popular prayers, the final prayer of the Fifteen Oes of Saint Bridget, glanced at in Chapter 1, which describes Christ as both the savior of Isaiah who treads the wine press alone and the grapes themselves. Bacon has taken Christ's place at the wine press, and the meaning of the image has changed accordingly. The new second Adam has led the experimentalist faithful out of a painted world and into creation, which means that the items of the feast of love can be enjoyed under their proper name: the wine is enjoyed as the product of human labor; the Adamic brotherhood is extracting "Nourishment Divine" from facts they make. Assuming their role as coauthors of God's creation, Bacon's brethren consecrate their homosocial marriage with things themselves.

Losing Perspective: Anti-virtuoso Satire and *An Essay Concerning Human Understanding*

Since the following chapters will explore how the virtuosi's activities reverberated across seventeenth- and eighteenth-century culture as a whole, it is worth considering how the project of assisted observation looked to contemporaries. As we have seen, some critics simply revived traditional teachings against curiosity; Norris bluntly insisted that the "reputation of *Innocence*" enjoyed by those who "turn *Vertuoso*" was unfounded: "our Curiosity is impertinent, our study immoderate, and the *Tree* of *Knowledge* still a *forbidden Plant*." The Augustinian critique was applied with brutal force by the "Laudian avenger" Robert South.[177] South is a fascinating figure for our purposes: an admirer of John Locke who held rather extreme views about the extent of Adam's epistemological privilege (and whose speculative reconstructions of that experience were as sensuous as any virtuoso's), he was nonetheless a ruthless critic of the Society. The Society seems to have represented a double threat to him: promoting a dangerously rationalist approach to religious matters, it also served to promote ignorant mechanics he associated with the sects. He described its members as "a set of fellows got together and formed into a kind of diabolical society, for the finding out new experiments of vice . . . obliging posterity with unheard of inventions and discoveries in sin; resolving herein to admit of no other measure of good and evil, but the judgment of sensuality."[178] The Fellows' effort to produce new and "unheard of" sensory experiences is just a newfangled version of the scopic lust denounced by Augustine. South's wholesale rejection of the distinction between the sensitive and the sensuously cultivated spectatorial body enables him to dismiss as absurd any notion that these experiments could be intended for posterity—any notion that the Fellows were engaged in a progressive enterprise. Hobbes famously accused the virtuosi of trying to establish themselves as a new priestly caste; his determination to raise doubts about their investigative technologies, in particular, suggests that he well understood the central role these instruments played in the virtuoso's identity as a priest of nature.[179] Yet Cowley's ode, like all experimentalist propaganda, suggests that to be in paradise is simply to experience things themselves—to inhabit the world God made. This conviction was quite difficult to ridicule as religious enthusiasm. Satirists who did not want to make the impious suggestion that God's creation was not worthy of being magnified were stuck defending the discarded teleology which held that what was worthy of sight was available to it. To mock the humble nature of the virtuoso's toil or ridicule his estrangement from normal perception was to risk underscoring his proudest accomplishment.

This was a risk that satirists did not mind taking. Identifying users of the microscope with the lowly specimens they examine, they count on the reader's ready acceptance of the premise that small things are disgusting things. Often they merely provide lists of such things, hoping to carry their point by sheer enumeration (thereby unwittingly duplicating experimentalist canons of style); the author of *An Essay in Defence of the Female Sex* (probably Mary Astell) describes a virtuoso that has "sold an Estate in Land to purchase one in *Scallop, Conch, Muscle, Cockle Shells, Periwinkles, Sea Shrubs, Weeds, Mosses, Sponges, Coralls, Corallines, Sea Fans, Pebbles, Marchasites* and *Flint stones;* and has abandon'd the Acquaintance and Society of men for that of *Insects, Worms, Grubbs, Magots, Flies, Moths, Locusts, Beetles, Spiders, Grasshoppers, Snails, Lizards* and *Tortoises.*" Such men are able to "amuse themselves continually with the Contemplation of those things, which the rest of the World slight as useless, and below their regard." While some contemporaries might have found these catalogues amusing, their satiric bite could not have been very deep. Satiric motifs like the curious man crouching over a chamber pot only reproduce the emphasis in experimentalist writing on the lofty secrets contained within repugnant matter: the curious man who peers into chamber pots without shame inhabits a world in which the distinction between what is worth knowing and what is a matter of indifference is not evident to the naked, or fallen, eye. It was because the curious man, like Adam, saw *through* the merely visible that there was, as Sprat declared, nothing in it "too mean" for his "consideration."[180]

Thomas Shadwell's play *The Virtuoso* seems to suggest that the virtuoso's dignity is lessened by his association with the specimens he drags out of puddles and swamps, and the filthy activities, such as dissection, in which he engages. When Hooke went to see the play, he felt put under the microscope himself: "Damned Doggs. *Vindica me Deus.* People almost pointed." He was brooding over the text a month later, as his rhyming entry for July 1 suggests: "Virtuoso play. Sick with drinking whey."[181] Shadwell's Gimcrack is described as having "broken his brains about the nature of maggots"; he has "studied these twenty years to find out the several sorts of spiders, and never cares for understanding mankind." Rather than mocking Hooke's empiricism, however, the play attacks its perversion by an aristocratic dilettante. In the play's most famous scene, when Gimcrack chooses to swim in theory but not in water, he declares as he performs his strokes face-down on his study table that "I content myself with the speculative part of swimming; I care not for the practic. I seldom bring anything to use; 'tis not my way."[182] This announcement reveals Gimcrack to be an incompetent impostor; we are supposed to laugh at him because he *refuses* to get his body fully involved in his investigations. (Hooke, in contrast, did not hesitate to put his own arm in the air pump to see what would happen to it.)[183] Gimcrack's immersion in trivia does not reflect a commitment to intellectual labor, but a cultivated eccentricity in which he takes an antisocial delight; he adopts alien views solely to alienate himself from other people. Gimcrack's very name denotes both a scientific instrument and a gaudy, insubstantial thing; the clear implication is that, rather than being an instrument of truth, he pretends to be one for show. Although the suggestion that Royal Society Fellows did not live up to their own ideals was potentially damaging, Shadwell had to invoke ideals internal to the experimental project in order to inflict this injury. This after all is a play whose hero of "wit and sense" is a lover of Lucretius.[184]

There was no more dedicated critic of the virtuosi and their technologies in the seventeenth century than Samuel Butler, but, as William Horne has suggested, his energetic attacks on the new science employ its norms. *The Elephant in the Moon* tells the story of a mouse squashed between the lenses of a telescope that credulous scientists take to be an elephant. Rather than calling the lens a deluding glass, Butler suggests that those who use the lens are easily deluded, content to "judge with mere imagination" and to "explicate appearances / Not as they are, but as they please." Assisted observation is not presented as itself a perverse, outrageous act. Indeed, Butler's preoccupation with human error and its causes, the intentness of his focus on the conditions under which assisted observation could go awry, make his satires virtual extensions of Royal Society propaganda. His cautionary fable recalls the virtuosi's admonitions to exercise intellectual restraint when using optical instruments, as he dramatizes the consequences of what Hooke described in *Micrographia* as "the uncertainty, and mistakes" arising from "the narrowness and wandring of our *Senses,* from the slipperiness or delusion of our *Memory,* from the confinement or rashness of our *Understanding.*"[185] The poem reaches its climax when a member of the group tries to convince his colleagues to suppress the truth that the elephant is a mouse: what we thought was an attack on science becomes an attack on those who pervert its noble aims. By the same token, *Hudibras*'s attacks on crazed philosophers whose "Speculations tend / Above their just and useful end" suggest Hooke's expressions of irritation with dilettantes who attempted to engage the Society in harebrained speculation while ignoring findings of use. The scope of Butler's satire is in the end surprisingly modest, restricted to grotesque distortions of experimentalist aims.[186]

In fact, Butler's notebooks reveal his abiding fascination with the microworld the virtuosi had uncovered:

The smallest Sands in the River Sein appear in a Microscope to be all Snayl-shels. As the Egs in the Rows of Fishes to have little fishes in them. And the Blew Tarnish upon Plums, to be Animals. So in the Bloud of men in Fevers, and in vinegar, little Animals are discoverd by the same instrument.[187]

The little animals are everywhere, and are even responsible for the color of plums. The exotic underpinnings of familiar sights form a hidden zoo that extends from the Seine to the veins of "men in Fevers." While the satirist mocked the demented Whachum who "would an *Elegie* compose / On Maggots squeez'd out of his Nose," the author of the notebooks seems quite capable of such a performance; *Hudibras* ridicules the effort to determine "How many different *Specieses* . . . live in *Vineger* and *Wood*," precisely the question that concerns Butler in the passage quoted just above.[188] In addition to their role in producing the visible world, Butler is intrigued by the visible world these smaller animals themselves inhabit, writing that "Snayles and Fleas are reported by Virtuosos to see through Naturall Tubes and perspectives. For their eies grow on the ends of their Hornes." As Svetlana Alpers observes, to focus on the eyes of organisms under the microscope intensified the experience of looking through a lens twice over; one looked through an optical instrument only to find another. Alien perceptual apparatuses intensified the observer's awareness that "the world is known not through being visible, but through the particular instruments that mediate what is seen." (Beale, we recall, had managed to discover "staring eyes" in sand itself.) By calling the organic perceptual equipment of snails and fleas "Naturall Tubes and perspectives," Butler makes this lesson in perceptual relativity explicit. Such reflections became the staple of physico-theological lectures and popular experience, for, by the eighteenth century, microscopes had become an affordable luxury for many, their use extolled as an improving pastime in popular venues like *The Female Spectator*.[189]

Butler's character of the virtuoso describes a man who "bends all his Forces against the hardest and most improbable," who "delights most in attempting Things beyond his Reach" and makes "Men wonder, how 'tis possible for *Art* to put *Nature* so much out of her Play"; the deflationary remark that "His Industry were admirable, if it did not attempt the greatest Difficulties with the feeblest Means" is easily tweaked into a paean to the virtuoso's industry and ambition, which depended for its fulfillment not on the subject's innate endowments but on his elasticity. While in principle the experimentalist was vulnerable to the criticism that his modest bearing cloaked demiurgic ambitions and Faustian pride, the criticism usually leveled at him was that he was absurd, not dangerous. Exploiting *curiosity*'s suspension between grammatically objective and subjective senses, satires of the virtuoso rehearse the theme that those obsessed with viewing curiosities became curiosities themselves at tiresome length. In doing so, they actually promote the notion of experimental investigation as an innocent activity, a wholesome if eccentric extension of child's play; the virtuoso was not too proud to manifest the wisdom of the child.[190]

Yet these satires do suggest the moral and social hazards of transforming the obsessive pursuit of nonnormative perspectives into an end in its own right. What did it mean to become immersed in a sensuous world to which most people were "utterly Strangers"? What purpose was served in alienating oneself from one's own perceptual experience? Such questions are really challenges to the project of knowledge production itself. They received a powerful reply in Locke's *Essay Concerning Human Understanding.* Throughout the *Essay,* the lens continually sets into motion ocular fantasies that provide an occasion for the introduction of a satirical or religiously wary perspective on experimentalist ambition, from which the attempt to aspire beyond human sight appears either as an absurdity or a sort of sacrilege.

Locke begins one of these meditations with the speculation that if we had "Senses acute enough to discern the minute particles of Bodies, and the real Constitution on which their sensible Qualities depend, I doubt not but they would produce quite different *Ideas* in us . . . This Microscopes plainly discover to us." The microscope reveals blood to be not consistently red but rather a "pellucid Liquor" with "some few Globules of Red." If lenses could magnify them "1000, or 10000 times more" how these globules would appear "is uncertain," but Locke implies that they would appear pellucid as well since he suggests that, if we had eyes that were stronger than microscopes, the color of gold would disappear altogether; in its place we would see "an admirable Texture of parts of a certain Size and Figure" (2.23.11). Locke then pushes down the lid of the Pandora's box he has thrown open. Although the hidden textures of things of which colors are symptoms might be "admirable," the "infinite wise Contriver" is even more admirable for having hid them from us behind a veil of color. Rather than magnify creation, we should magnify the creator for having hidden his contrivances from us: He "fitted our Senses, Faculties, and Organs, to the conveniences of Life, and the Business we have to do here," giving us just "insight enough" into the "admirable Contrivances" that create the visible world to "magnify the Wisdom, Power, and Goodness of their Author . . . But it appears not, that God intended, we should have a perfect, clear, and adequate Knowledge of them: that perhaps is not in the Comprehension of any finite Being" (2.23.12). The rhetoric of resignation, along with the pious acceptance of limits it advises, is clearly disingenuous, as the pun on *magnify* suggests. Three divine nouns associated with the Author are balanced by three matching modifiers of the knowledge humanity would like to have of his works, the symmetry conveying a sense of rightness to their union: why should we not have perfect, clear, and adequate knowledge of our Creator's wisdom, power, and goodness? Of course, Locke has only said that it "appears" that God wanted to keep his works from our view; his entire discussion is devoted to revealing the inadequacy of appearance to the scope of creation's plan.

Having explained that our senses are conveniently adapted to "the Business we have to do here," Locke goes on to pursue the implications of this word quite literally, suggesting that our social and economic well-being depends on surrendering any effort at perceptual transcendence. More acute senses, he cautions, might very well be "inconsistent with our Being, or at least well-being,"

> Nay, if that most instructive of our Senses, Seeing, were in any Man 1000, or 100000 times more acute than it is now by the best Microscope, things several millions of times less than the smallest Object of his sight now, would then be visible to his naked Eyes, and so he would come nearer the Discovery of the Texture and Motion of the minute Parts of corporeal things; and in many of them, probably get *Ideas* of their internal Constitutions: But then he would be in a quite different World from other People: Nothing would appear the same to him, and others: The visible *Ideas* of every thing would be different. So that I doubt, Whether he, and the rest of Men, could discourse concerning the Objects of Sight; or have any Communication about Colours, their appearances being so wholly different . . . And if by the help of such Microscopical Eyes, (if I may so call them,) a Man could penetrate farther than ordinary into the secret Composition, and radical Texture of Bodies, he would not make any great advantage by the change, if such an acute Sight would not serve to conduct him to the Market and Exchange. (2.23.12)

The man with "Microscopical Eyes" "would come nearer . . . penetrate farther" than "the rest of Men": the description of the possessor of this phallic or digging eye reads like a discreet series of come-ons to the reader. Locke dangles before the reader the prospect of penetrating "farther than ordinary into the secret Composition, and radical Texture of Bodies": to read this "secret Composition" would be to read a novel indeed, experiencing the mundane world from an entirely fresh perspective by engaging a flood of heretofore unimagined circumstantial particulars. But the fantasy of a "wholly different" experience of the familiar world is brought up short by the concluding rhyme: instead of being the beneficiaries of such a miraculous change, we must conduct our business at the Exchange.

Locke goes on to awkward problems of scope that anticipate the misadventures of Gulliver, detailing the social costs and burdens such "acute sight" would entail. Since the man with "Microscopical Eyes" would be "in a quite different World from other People," he would not be able to communicate with them. While he could provide a satisfactory account of the internal contrivance of a clock, he would be unable to tell the time by it. This fable inverts a cherished experimentalist topos, articulated here by Henry Power:

> [To discover] the management of this great Machine of the World, must needs be the proper Office of onely the Experimental and Mechanical Philosopher. For the old Dogmatists and Notional Speculators, that onely gaz'd at the visible effects and last Resultances of things, understood no more of Nature, than a rude Countrey-fellow does of the Internal Fabrick of a Watch, that onely sees the Index and Horary Circle, and perchance hears the Clock and Alarum strike in it: But he that will give a satisfactory Account of those *Phaenomena,* must be an Artificer indeed, and one well skill'd in the Wheel-work and Internal Contrivance of such Anatomical Engines.[191]

Here, the university-educated dogmatist is the "rude Countrey-fellow," while the proponent of the mechanical philosophy—the philosophy of "mechanicks"—is the one with the skill to understand the contrivances of Creation. In Locke's reinterpretation, the elastic identity of the "rude Countrey-fellow" seems to snap back: it is not the man who cannot figure out how a watch works but rather the man who is immersed in its "Internal Contrivance" who exposes himself as a rude fellow; he has lost sight of the instrument's social use. His eagerness to describe a mechanical universe stripped of Aristotelian ends and purposes prevents him from being able to appreciate even the most modest ends of everyday life. The result of his alien perspective is social isolation; inhabiting a world that is a clock, the observer who is "well skill'd" in "Wheel-work" lives in a clockless world.

Locke thus appears to entertain the assumption that rationally penetrating the visible world is inversely related to the ability to live in it comfortably. The man who "penetrates farther" is a social monstrosity.

But then Locke elaborates a new fantasy, of being able to alter the scope of perception at will. Speculating that this ability must be what angelic superiority consists in, he explores this idea using the pious terms provided by the scale of being:

> Spirits can assume to themselves Bodies of different Bulk, Figure, and Conformation of Parts. Whether one great advantage some of them have over us, may not lie in this, that they can so frame, and shape to themselves Organs of Sensation or Perception, as to suit them to their present Design, and the Circumstances of the Object they would consider. For how much would that Man exceed all others in Knowledge, who had but the Faculty so to alter the Structure of his Eyes, that one Sense, as to make it capable of all the several degrees of Vision, which the assistance of Glasses (casually at first light on) has taught us to conceive? What wonders would he discover, who could so fit his Eye to all sorts of Objects, as to see, when he pleased, the Figure and Motion of the minute Particles in the Blood, and other juices of Animals, as distinctly, as he does, at other times, the shape and motion of the Animals themselves. But to us in our present State, unalterable Organs, so contrived, as to discover the Figure and Motion of the minute parts of Bodies, whereon depend those sensible Qualities, we now observe in them, would, perhaps, be of no advantage. God has no doubt made us so, as is best for us in our present Condition. (2.23.13)[192]

The wistful statement that acute sight "would, perhaps, be of no advantage" to humanity pulls hard against the detailed elaboration of the "one great advantage" that angels have over humans: it is impossible to believe that it would "be of no advantage" to have "one great advantage." The language Locke uses to urge us to resign ourselves to our limitations is once again strategically ineffective: *perhaps* and *no doubt* express a barely controlled longing for less pitiful sensory capacities. Locke in fact is only making a limited admission; it is only "unalterable Organs" that "would, perhaps, be of no advantage." The assertion that "God has no doubt made us so, as is best for us in our present Condition" prompts the realization that it *is* possible in our present condition to alter the scope of our perception; the fantasy he is describing has already been realized, since prosthetic versions of "Microscopical Eyes"—microscopes—can be employed and withdrawn at will, enabling the human observer to "alter the Structure of his Eyes, that one Sense." Indeed, it is actually "the assistance of Glasses" that "has taught us to conceive" of this angelic condition; by referring to sight as "that one sense," Locke invites Hookean speculations about future prostheses that might alter the structure of other organs. The prosthetic nature of optical instruments offers a liberating and, above all, reasonable compromise between the extremes of a frustratingly deficient and horrifyingly excessive visual acuity. A man who had microscopical eyes would indeed have lost perspective, but "the assistance of Glasses" has only "taught us to conceive" of his perspective, enabling humanity gain access to it without being subject to its limitations. In fact, optical instruments seem to catapult their users to the very pinnacle of politeness, enabling them to become supremely decorous beings that can "frame, and shape" themselves to suit various circumstances, exhibiting the adaptability on which discovery and sociability equally depend.

Locke's provisional employment of a satiric perspective on lens technology thus fluctuates into a powerful defense of the experimental project: the intermittence of assisted observation enhances not only our knowledge but our identity as social beings who can "adapt" themselves freely to the various circumstances of human life. This intermittence is enacted by Locke's rhetoric: proffering a world of "secret Composition[s]" only to withdraw it with a textual frequency mimetic of assisted observation itself, Locke also hints at the improved lenses of the future through longer and longer trails of zeros. Earlier in the *Essay*, Locke had employed the rhetoric of modest resignation to discourage the promiscuous use of concepts like infinity and the universe, terms which evince the fact that our language outstrips our ability to imagine what we are talking about. The identification of natural perceptual limits is now revealed as the condition for stretching them. Locke suggests that the pain produced from straining our eyes is designed to persuade us to keep our bodies "confin'd within certain bounds," and to remain content with "Satisfaction in a quiet and secure Possession of Truths, that most concern'd us" (2.7.4, 1.1.7). But this confinement only describes the sensitive body of the private man, not the "us" who have discovered what the microscope reveals. The disproportion between our "narrow Capacities" and our desire to understand can actually be corrected through the artificial expansion of the realm of simple ideas; by adding these ideas to one another, "the Mind comes to extend it self even to Infinity" without the body undergoing any change at all. Locke's meditations on the improved lenses of the future suggest that the body might yet teach the mind to conceive far more than it has (2.17.21, 2.18.1). Earlier Locke had spoken of infinity as "a growing and fugitive *Idea,* still in a boundless Progression, that can stop no where"; the cautionary warning now seems like a triumphant prophecy (2.17.12).

Through the fable of the man with microscopical eyes Locke introduces a crucial distance between sensory transcendence and its beneficiaries. We might regard the man with microscopical eyes as a caricature of an enthusiast of the lens—a man who, having refused to regard a watch as simply a time piece, would eventually lose the ability to do so. Locke suggests, however, that to aspire "Beyond the reach of eye, or hand" and escape the limitations of one's place on the scale of being is not to be grasping, but rather to be modest, to refuse to regard oneself as the measure of all things.[193] It is those who take for granted that they see all there is to see who "boldly quarrel with their own Constitution" by pretending they have clear and distinct conceptions when they do not (1.1.5). By incorporating and then inverting antiexperimentalist ridicule, Locke makes it serve the ends of modesty; technological self-enhancement, it seems, can coexist with good breeding, and even with knowing our place. Sociability is not threatened by the expansion of the visible world, he assures us, because our newfound "angelic" insights are not really *ours.* And thus they are no one's private property. It is a mark of the experimentalist philosopher's modesty that he can integrate reductive caricatures of lens-users into his own more capacious perspective, defusing their power in the process; he can even make comedy out of the imagined burdens of microscopic sight, showcasing his detachment from the very insights to which he aspires.

If the reasonableness of experimentalist insight was guaranteed by its prosthetic character, the epistemology elaborated around the exemplary scene of assisted observation assumed, and exacerbated, an internal conflict in the investigator between the natural man and the spectatorial man. In this division we can see a new intellectual type taking shape, characterized at once by extreme modesty and extreme ambition—a "groveling mole" that strives to see like a Lockean angel, and who, by dint of extraordinary effort, under carefully controlled conditions, and with a great deal of strain, achieves imperfect and partial successes. The artificial angel is nothing other than the body of the mole-like digger's office.

Bacon had argued that science discouraged superstitious wonder, but by redefining science as an open-ended pursuit of new powers, he permitted human potential itself to become the focus of wonder: as living embodiments of that potential, virtuosi, as Butler put it, made "Men wonder." But if the virtuoso's quasi-angelic perception declared the powers of his office, so did his humility. Locke asserts his own right to the truth producer's office when he appears in the humble habit of a Digger in his "Epistle to the Reader," declaring his intention to dig up what Winstanley called "imaginary" knowledge so that "the true Knowledge of Things" can take root: "'tis Ambition enough to be employed as an Under-Labourer in clearing the Ground a little, and removing some of the Rubbish, that lies in the way to Knowledge" ("Epistle to the Reader," 10). The virtuoso's identity was as systematically ambiguous as that of the experimentalist Adam: at once a hard-working truth producer, even a mole, perpetually "digging and toiling in Nature," and a man with lenses for eyes.

Reformers had regarded the superstitious elevation of the priest above his parishioners as an affront to the ideal of a priesthood of believers; Hobbes hoped to make this accusation stick to the virtuosi, but he never managed to do so. It is true that the virtuosi's attempts to reconstruct the experiences of the first man set them apart as people with special bodies and minds, and their rhetorical self-presentations did little to make them seem normal. We have noted the relentlessly rehearsed cliché that the virtuoso became a curiosity by indulging his curiosity on curiosities: this was not a hazard of experimentalist work but rather its goal. Making sexless (yet somehow aroused) innocence a token of intellectual sophistication, experimentalists developed a new personal style in which Socratic skepticism, Christian humility, and mental virginity came together; and through their identification with artificial organs, these humble laborers assumed quasi-superhuman attributes. Yet they only had intermittent access to the spectatorial body that defined them and were entirely dependent on their instruments for this access. Even their cultivated detachment from bodily experience and rigorously repressed eroticism were the products of artificial helps, a battery of protocols through which they attempted to subjugate the sensitive body. Despite its association with humble labor—indeed, by means of it—curiosity retained its traditional link to prideful self-assertion, but experimentalist pride, like experimentalist charity, was no accepter of persons. Rather than a personal attribute, it characterized the self-assertion of transsubjective knowing, predicated on the reiterated sacrifice of the private man. The powers that defined the virtuoso adhered not to his own person but to a corporate body spread across time and space, united by common technologies and methods and the medium of print; this body filled out the subject position occupied by humanity's first representative in the original state of creation. As experimentalism entered the mainstream, the division between the body and the office of the truth producer became available to every member of the rationally curious public. For, far from remaining exiles from the polite world, these human curiosities were the heart of an expansive intellectual culture their own labors had helped bring into being.

4 ||| THE CULTURE OF CURIOSITY

> . . . doubtlesse the best way to perfect knowledge, is, and will be, by
> endeavouring after meetings of people to conferre and discourse together
> (in a discreet, quiet, and well ordered way) . . . it would be happy, that all
> wel-meaning people would seriously set themselves to procure frequent
> and full meetings, for increase of knowledg in all sorts of people, and no
> longer to depend, either on the publique, or congregationall Sermons, for
> information of their understandings.
> —William Walwyn, *The Vanitie of the Present Churches*

> The late times of *Civil War,* and *confusion,* to make recompense for their
> infinite calamities, brought this advantage with them, that they stirr'd
> up mens minds from *long ease,* and a *lazy rest,* and made them *active,*
> *industrious* and *inquisitive.*
> —Thomas Sprat, *The History of the Royal Society*

> And in luxurious Cities, where the noyse
> Of riot ascends above thir loftiest Towrs,
> And injury and outrage: And when Night
> Darkens the Streets, then wander forth the Sons
> Of *Belial,* flown with insolence and wine.
> —John Milton, *Paradise Lost*

Curiosity's redemption was so successful that the mid-seventeenth century
might be said to have marked the start of a curiosity craze in England.[1]
Having fabricated his identity using the models provided by artisans, new
investigative technologies, and humanity's first representative, the virtuoso
offered himself as a model for the nation. Thomas Sprat elaborated a national
myth around curiosity as "the present prevailing *Genius* of the *English*
Nation" that was transforming the country into "a Land of *Experimental*
knowledge," a paradise regained:

> . . . even the position of our climate, the air, the influence of the heaven, the
> composition of the English blood; as well as the embraces of the Ocean,

seem to joyn with the labours of the *Royal Society,* to render our Country, a Land of *Experimental knowledge.* And it is a good sign, that Nature will reveal more of its secrets to the English, than to others; because it has already furnish'd them with a Genius so well proportion'd, for the receiving, and retaining its mysteries.[2]

Adam and his environment had been perfectly "proportion'd" to facilitate the labor of knowledge production; the people of England were now the beneficiaries of a similarly providential fit. Running the virtues of the English people together with "the labours of the *Royal Society,*" Sprat makes the first-person plural, like the ocean, "embrace" both: apparently, every English citizen had the capacity to express the national "Genius." It is not clear how many of them were moved to do so. Sprat's portrayal of England as a nation of intellectual laborers, like Milton's depiction of ingenious Londoners in *Areopagitica,* is clearly an attempt to coax into existence the nation it purports to describe. Both national portraits, however, had some basis in the changing character of intellectual life in the second half of the seventeenth century. At no prior time did so many sectors of the population pride themselves on their peculiar susceptibility to the investigative urge; curiosity distinguished the journalist as well as the aristocratic collector, the coffeehouse autodidact as well as the modern divine.

The elevation of the virtuoso's defining trait into a national virtue may seem unaccountable, since virtuosi did so little to make themselves seem normal. The experimentalist priest of nature would seem beyond imitation, yet precisely because his defining traits were the products of laborious cultivation, they could be cultivated by others. Just as the lens bestowed on its users an authority that was not naturally theirs to claim, the privileges of the spectatorial body were not the exclusive property of anyone, least of all the gentleman or the genius. Whether the intellectual laborer chose to identify with the first public person or the public itself, the capacity of this identification to subordinate the body he was born with to its own greater and transsubjective aims remained constant. Elevated above all bodies, noble and common, the spectatorial body could in principle be inhabited by anyone willing to undertake the necessary work of incorporating artifice into the self. As previous chapters have suggested, this figure was not a Restoration novelty but an Interregnum survival: in the 1640s and 1650s, experimental Christians and Hartlibians had cultivated ingenuity as a public service. The ingenious public was almost wholly defined by the taking of pains; its model was the innocent delver himself. The emergence of a *curious* public can be seen as part of a feedback loop and a further stage in a proselytizing effort. One can still glean from Sprat's language the old godly vision of the public as a priesthood of knowledge producers; even his shrouding the secrets of nature in the language of "mystery" is evocative of the productive sacrament.[3] Those who participated in this ongoing sacrament were only aspirants to the identity that collectively defined them: like the epistemology elaborated around the scene of technologically assisted observation, curious agency was constructed on the fault line of corrupted and created humanity, the line that distinguished the private person from the public worker.[4]

With the return of Charles II, this division became a national one. The "Merry Monarch" placed his sensitive body at the center of the body politic, joining with his court to present aristocratic profligacy as a revival of native festival traditions, embodied in his own public identity as a "carnival lord of misrule."[5] At the same time, he revived the practice of touching for the king's evil, a custom predicated on the monarch's identity as Christ's anointed (his proclamation on the subject boasted of his "great success" in the "great work of Charity," made operative by his "sacred touch").[6] In an effort to secure its monopoly on the king's two bodies, the court even resuscitated Robert Filmer's ideas during the Exclusion Crisis, overseeing the publication of *Patriarcha* in 1680.[7] Those who prosecuted the labors of a public person as experimentalists defined it now had to contend with a monarch for whom this concept of a public person, and the concept of intellectual labor that supported it, had no currency. "Since the King was restored," Anthony Wood observed, "it was looked upon as a piece of pedantry . . . to be earnest or zealous in any one thing . . . all, forsooth, must be gentile and neat—no paines taken, Bantring."[8] Pitting gentility against the taking of pains, the Restoration court had a very different image of the public life; the conflict between these two visions was largely what public life during the Restoration consisted in.

Jonathan Scott observes that "attempts to legislate forgetfulness" were a feature of the Restoration from the very beginning; chief among the objects to be driven into the cultural unconscious were the earlier meanings and projects of restoration that defined the Interregnum period. As Melissa Mowry has argued, political pornography—constructing the "liberty of the subject" in reductively sexual terms—was mobilized throughout the period to dissolve the threat of popular corporate identity, refiguring public space as the terrain of merely private "compacts"; the strategy is familiar to us from the Adamite pamphlets of the 1640s.[9] Of course, many institutions associated with the monarchy were not restored, such as Star Chamber and the Court of High Commission.[10] Imprisonments and executions aside, the reopened theaters were perhaps the most powerful cultural expression of the restored monarchy's power. Here members of the culture of the victors could gather together before larger-than-life projections of themselves; Milton's strenuous effort to imagine Satan's experience from the inside found its theatrical foil in the rakehell, now elevated to a sardonic national symbol.[11] The identity of the court with the stage was an old commonplace, but now this trope was literalized, as actual prostitutes and actresses were put on display at court, prosecuting their service as royal mistresses. Disgust with what James Grantham Turner calls the "pornotropic" spectacle emanating from "the great bawdy-house at White hall" spread well beyond the ranks of the self-defined godly: as Andrew Marvell joked, there was "so general a depravation of Manners, that even those who contribute towards it do yet complain of it."[12] The court's effort to organize public life around fallen appetite only offered the "curioso" ubiquitous objective correlatives for everything he sought to resist, creating ideal conditions for the flourishing of an experimentalist counterculture.[13] As in any culture war, the battle lines could be drawn inside a single person.[14]

The culture of curiosity ensured that the restoration of monarchy did not result in the restoration of Merry England. The space of free and methodically innocent inquiry was as elastic as its subjects: like Milton's "paradise within," it could expand to fill public space and contract to fit the contours of the individual mind.[15] The various instantiations of experimental space fortified one another, as the mind consecrated to the exercise of curiosity sought reinforcement in places geared to the same end, such as the laboratory, the curiosity cabinet, and the coffeehouse, spaces that existed in dialectical opposition to court and theater. The constitutive conflicts of intellectual identity thus played out in competing models of public space, but these struggles began in the mute recesses of what Locke called "the mind's Presence-room," where, through holding "Audience" with ideas, reason worked to exercise its kingly prerogative over "things themselves."[16] Through therapeutic regimes designed to strengthen the mind's powers of reflection, the vicissitudes of experimentalist identity became public property. Extensions of Sprat's proselytizing effort to promote the spirit of curiosity in the lay public, these regimens of self-improvement encouraged people to reform themselves into knowledge producers. This effort bore fruit in John Dunton's so-called question project, with which this chapter concludes; one of the most innovative publishing experiments of the period, *The Athenian Mercury* consolidated the identity of the curious public. Elevating "good conference" over the old bonds of "good fellowship," members of this public gathered, often virtually, to exercise their collective rights as knowledge producers, natives of a land of experimental knowledge.[17]

The Laboratory of the Mind

The mystical union Sprat posits between "the composition of the English blood" and the Royal Society's labors suggests a bloodline stretching back to the sovereign of the first land of experimental knowledge, a royal lineage to which anyone willing to express the national genius was an heir. Circulating throughout the body politic, this nature was expressed in the act of being constructed; it was, in fact, literally a "composition," for the experimentalist attack on innate ideas had extended the atomistic reinterpretation of form even into the mind.[18] As essences and species dissipated, so did the defining human essence; rational man became curious man, characterized not by the complacent possession of reason but by an ability to develop it. The curious man, like his traditional predecessor, gained strength from his identification with the godliest part of human nature, the thinking part. This godly part, however, was now characterized by lack, often described as a hunger or a thirst, which goaded him to undertake improving exertions, by dint of which he became something extraordinary: an artificially improved human.

The very sense of deficiency that provided the impetus for this labor was also, it turned out, an acquired trait. Contemporary celebrations of curiosity celebrate it both as a universal disposition and a quality that must be coaxed into existence; the insistence on the innate character of the desire for knowledge competes with an equally powerful conviction that, despite the insatiability of this desire, people will do nothing at all to satisfy it if left to their own devices. Humanity's defining trait was also, it seemed, the most inaccessible to the conscious will. This paradox recalls all the others

associated with the distinction between created and corrupted humanity
that have concerned us in previous chapters. While this distinction provided
the ground for curiosity's moral rehabilitation, the celebration of intellectual exertion, and its impetus in curiosity, was finally detached from any
specific moral end to become an end in its own right. It was driven by a
sense of wonder both at what humanity might make of itself through "minds
that can wander beyond all limit and satiety," and at the fact that humanity
could cultivate and act upon this "singular Passion" at all.[19]

Thomas Bradley found some traces of humanity's created nature in
that "insatiable desire, and thurst of the minde after Knowledge, in the in-
defatigable industry and study in the disquisition of high things." These
were remnants that needed to be "worked up" to approach their former
strength; adapting Revelation 3:2, Bradley urged his readers to exert themselves in cultivating this desire, to *strengthen the things that remaine.*"[20]
Thomas Vaughan also identifies the Adamic remnant with the soul's "most
fervent Desire to *know*," but although infants are born with this desire,
which is "the *Best*, and most *mysterious part* of their *Nature*," they soon lose
it; by the time they are adults they have learned to be ashamed of what they
do not know and only exert themselves to defend their ignorant errors. So
difficult was it for corrupted humanity even to recognize its own innate
desires that "ignorant Nurse[s]" interpreted the drive of babies toward
experimentation—looking, feeling, and even tasting everything with
which they came into contact—as a trifling desire "to *play*" with these objects. In fact, as soon as the baby has learned all he can about the qualities
of a given object, he casts it aside as being of no further use: the *"mysterious"*
and holy innocence of the child is evinced not by wonder, pliability, or
trusting obedience but by cool intellectual ambition.[21]

Henry Power complained that few men

> obey the prescript of their Natures . . . There is a world of People indeed,
> and but a few Men in it; mankind is but preserv'd in a few Individuals; the
> greatest part of Humanity is lost in Earth, and their Souls so fixed in that
> grosser moity of themselves (their Bodies) that nothing can volatilize them,
> and set their Reasons at Liberty.

To "obey the prescript" of human nature was not to express one's nature
but to modify it, "for it is Reason that transpeciates our Natures": the man

distinguished himself from his person by refining the body's powers and setting the reason "at Liberty" to instrumentalize them. Power describes the soul of the rationally curious subject as "an excellent Chymist" in the "internal Laboratory of Man" which even in sleep is busy preparing the workshop for the next day's labor, "augmenting, repairing, and regenerating all the Organs and Utensils within." Rather than clogs of the soul, the organs of the human body are properly regarded as its "utensils," with which the soul becomes "volatilize[d]." The soul reinvents itself as an "excellent Chymist" by laboring in the body's workroom, turning it into the very vehicle for the soul's liberation.[22]

The image of the mind fit for such progressive labor was not the traditional tabula rasa, a medieval topos that made God the imprinter, author, and origin of ideas. Throughout the *Essay*, Locke reworks this analogy to suggest that, while the senses receive impressions, the mind lays claim to them and does things with them. The mind is a space where inscriptions made by objects, taking the form of simple ideas, are looked at, deciphered, and diagnosed, becoming the raw material for what Locke calls the mind's "compositions": acts of authorship. Locke's analogy of the mind to a presence chamber quietly transfers the royal connotation to reason itself, imagined as a worker. As William Walker points out, Locke most often uses the figure of a storehouse of ideas to portray the mind not as the storehouse itself, but as an agent inside it, working to transform the site. Constantly returning to words like *work, employ, industry, application, exercise,* and *pains,* Locke presents the mind as the object as well as the scene of transformative labor. Rather than a merely receptive organ, the well-used mind is a productive one—like Eden, the realm of a hard-working sovereign.[23]

Locke thus suggests that we can choose what kind of epistemological space we inhabit. The images of the mind's *camera obscura* can range from the "dim and obscure" to the "very vivid and sensible"; it can be a space for genuine enlightenment or revert to being a *"dark Room,"* "a Closet wholly shut from light," a sort of tomb (Locke even compares the fading inscriptions of sense data on the memory to the faded letters on a tombstone).[24] The mind of the man who does not "exercise" himself in vigorous traffic with objects is a "Sanctuary of Vanity and Ignorance," which it is the philosopher's duty to "break in upon," like an idol smasher (Locke was perhaps sublimating his father's participation in the 1643 attack on Wells Cathedral).[25] Paradoxically, the iconoclast's aim is to *restore* the role of sensuous data in this sanctuary, saving the mind from the dangerous power of "unintelligible Terms" that sink the mind into darkness: the work of the "illiterate and contemned Mechanick" generates this sort of enlightenment.[26]

The mind is most like a well-functioning laboratory, however, when it "turns its view inwards upon it self" to discover the "Original" of its own ideas (2.19.1, 1.1.2). The attempt to "examine our own Abilities, and see, what Objects our Understandings were, or were not fitted to deal with," sets up interior observational conditions that, like those of technologically assisted observation, are unnatural, designed to shake both nature and the viewer out of settled habit, for usually the "Understanding, like the Eye . . . takes no notice of it self: And it requires Art and Pains to set it at a distance, and make it its own Object."[27] Like the laboratory, the presence chamber of the mind, where phenomena are observed and theories constructed, is both the world outside represented in miniature and the site of ongoing paradisal renovation. Reciprocally, the laboratory theater was a model of the well-functioning mind expanded into a public space. Locke claimed that "we may as rationally hope to see with other Mens Eyes, as to know by other Mens Understandings," but in witnessing an experimental demonstration, one saw with other men's eyes in the act of seeing through one's own (1.4.23). Having collectively witnessed a demonstration, itself the product of repeated trials, Royal Society Fellows entered their signatures in a log that testified to what they had experienced; the mind's solitary composition of a complex idea was reenacted collectively through a "composition" achieved by consensus.[28]

If the reflecting mind is an experimental space capable of producing knowledge, the mind ruled by habit is the product of external powers, an inert lump of undiagnosed sensory stimuli and received dogma. Habit has the power "to *produce actions in us, which often escape our observation*": the man who lets nature take its course is dominated by motions of external objects, represented internally as seemings, to which he responds inertially and mechanically (2.9.10). To exert creative control over these internal motions was to harness one's faculties as instruments for the sovereign will of reason. The self-possession of the rationally curious individual was thus, like Winstanley's commons, a species of ownership gained through the investment of labor. Since one can truly be said to possess only the knowledge that one constructs for oneself, minds in which these improving labors are absent become the property of others.[29] By treating himself as raw material to be ordered, diagnosing and disciplining his ideas, the rationally curious individual could construct a stable and integral self out of the matter that naturally constituted him. But the individual did not have unlimited freedom to create himself however he pleased, and genuine self-possession did not result in a private kingdom: the self was not privately owned property. Just as humanity cannot create matter *ex nihilo,* so it cannot create ideas independently of experience, and without collective evidentiary protocols governing its interpretation and use, no individual can turn his experience into knowledge.

Locke uses the Lucretian analogy between letters and atoms to describe the foundational status of simple ideas, the atoms of our conscious life: "Nor will it be so strange, to think these few simple *Ideas* sufficient to employ the quickest Thought, or largest Capacity; and to furnish the Materials of all that various Knowledge, and more various Fancies and Opinions of all Mankind, if we consider how many Words may be made out of the various composition of 24 Letters" (2.7.10). This analogy implies that the matter of the world should be the matter of our thoughts; it also suggests that the matter of our thoughts might literally be made up of the matter of the world.[30] The decline of form theory enabled the literatus of nature to decompose and recompose nature's book, yet the newly atomized world did not stop where the self, the source of these compositions, began. In the same way that atoms have only physical extension, so Lockean personal identity consists only of temporal extension: a series of discrete, if causally related, motions produced by the impact of external bodies on the "different Particles of Matter, as they happen successively to be united to that organiz'd living Body" (2.27.8). However we choose to conceptualize the manner in which life is "communicated" to these particles which "happen . . . to be united" into an "organiz'd" person, it is clear that Locke makes human superiority over mere matter something other than a necessary given. As I have suggested, prosthetic insights like those provided by the lens seem to have been Locke's model for how, with the feeble materials of simple ideas, humanity might lay claim to the resources to escape its own limitations. Although the matter of thought is naturally "confused," and there is no inborn intuition to guide attempts to order this matter, the reflecting mind can evaluate the perspicacity of its own ideas, determine if they are clear and distinct enough to build upon, and contrive unnatural situations in which to produce new ones. It can gain rational understanding of how it comes by its ideas through self-diagnosis, even if a subjective distance separates it from the insights gained by these means. Striving to catch up with these insights, the reflective individual slowly illuminates, and alters, the presence room of the mind to accommodate them. The image of the mental laborer who works to improve his mind is also an image of the technologically enhanced self, with refined and heightened powers.

Locke makes the individual's feeling of elevation over matter—even his feeling of having complete possession of his own sensory experience—depend on the imposition of an artificial order. The self's constructed nature posed a mortification to human dignity comparable to Copernicanism itself: if the individual did not rationally reconstruct his mental content, he remained in a sort of mental state of postlapsarian nature, in which his consciousness was disaggregated, the epiphenomenon of obscure and unexamined ideas with tenuous connections to the world and to one another. Locke suggests that this disorder characterizes the mental life of other animals, who have ideas but cannot control them. Although he admits this difference between humans and other animals as an empirical matter of fact, he prevents it from fostering human complacency: a man who could not discourse, reason, and philosophize would still be a man, and a philosophical parrot would still be a bird.[31] Merely to be a human, in other words, was not a rational accomplishment. Urging his reader to "trust not any, try all things, hold fast that which thou art made one in, without learning from another man as a *Parret*," William Rabisha had suggested that parroting authority was what most men did.[32] One could only distinguish oneself from the beasts by the desire for intellectual self-mastery, a desire satisfied—and even produced—by "Art and Pains." Humanity reinvented itself as rational by taking such pains, entering into a purgatorial subjectivity of continuous trial. A distant goal rather than an indwelling essence, rationality was the fruit of a struggle against fallen nature. The rationally curious individual affirms the strength and resistance of his active, "animadversive" powers (whatever ontological status such powers were granted) in the act of exercising them, decomposing and recomposing himself anew.

The artificiality of the distinction separating humanity from beasts— the fact that it has to be created and maintained—pressures the individual to choose a cultivated cognitive life as a pleasure and a good. Locke does not state, as Aristotle would, the natural good or end served by thus tending to the self; indeed, he shies away from defining good and evil in terms of anything but pleasure and pain: "Things then are Good or Evil, only in reference to Pleasure or Pain . . . however caused in us" (2.20.2–5). In light of the newly unsettled foundations of personal identity, however, the inability to satisfy the cognitive appetite has a redemptive function. The *inde-fatigability* of the inquisitive urge, as opposed to other physical urges, endows it with the capacity to sustain the mind's unity over time. Hobbes, too, celebrates curiosity merely for lasting longer than the "short vehemence of any carnall Pleasure." The unity of the self is filled out temporally, by "a perseverance of delight," an inquisitive persistence that continually informs the self, providing it not only with knowledge, but with the ends and purposes that nature does not.[33] Curiosity not only protects human exceptionalism with respect to other species, it perpetuates the integrity of the self, by continually promoting the labor of active contemplation. A thread of intentional unity binds perceptions together in the desire to know: "still searching what we know not, by what we know, still closing up truth to truth as we find it," the curious subject strings together a continuous identity.[34] This identity is stabilized not by any particular ideational content but by the temporal unfolding of the drive to acquire it, a desire that receives only provisional satisfactions and requires constant stoking to be sustained.

Personal identity in this model is not finally personal; it resides in no "singular originality" of character or personal attribute, nor is it rooted in a private "inner light" inaccessible only to the self. It is rooted in a process that includes others, generating transsubjective knowledge. Locke complained that "the whole stock of Human Knowledge is claimed by every one, as his private Possession, as soon as he (profiting by others Discoveries) has got it into his own mind," but such possession could never be "properly" private, since it was never the product of anyone's "own single Industry": the man who "studies . . . and takes pains to make a progress" had always to consider "how much he ows to their pains, who cleared the Woods, drained the Bogs, built the Bridges, and made the Ways passable; without which he might have toiled much with little progress."[35] The personal identity of the intellectual laborer was a public works project.

As N. H. Keeble observes, John Howe seems to imply that if enthusiasts privately experienced the instant and total illumination some of them claimed, God had deprived them of a great pleasure. Unless one educates oneself in this pleasure, one can "scarce understand" in what it consists:

> To the altogether unlearned it will hardly be conceiveable; and to the learned it need not be told, how high a gratification this employment of his Reason naturally yields to the mind of a man: When the harmonious contexture of truths with truths; the apt coincidence, the secret links, and junctures of coherent notions are clearly discerned; When *effects* are traced up to their *causes; Properties* lodg'd in their native *subjects:* Things sifted to their Principles. What a pleasure is it when a man shall apprehend himself regularly led on (though but by a slender thred of discourse) through the Labyrinths of nature; when still new discoveries are successfully made, every further enquiry ending in a further prospect; and every new Scene of things entertaining the mind with a fresh delight! How many have suffered a voluntary banishment from the world, as if they were wholly strangers, and unrelated to it; rejected the blandishments of sense, macerated themselves with unwearied studies for this pleasure; making the ease and health of their bodies, to give place to the content and satisfaction of their minds![36]

Howe speaks of the "continual exercise" of the investigative faculties as both "pleasant" and "Soul-rectifying." Such rectification admits of no completion since its ultimate aim—the sifting of things "to their Principles"—is pushed forever forward; it is the purgatorial process of self-rectification that constitutes the bliss. Howe celebrates the activity of sifting itself, of being "regularly led on," with "pleasure," by "a slender thred" to successive discoveries. The consecutive nature of inquiry, which, as Boyle observed, makes the end of every inquiry the start of a new one, does not press toward any climax. As the mind moves through the labyrinthine structure of nature's secrets, "every new Scene of things" entertains it "with a fresh delight." The passage thus leads the reader on, through rapidly shifting rather than statically "mixed" metaphors, opening out into a progressively more complex "prospect," but "macerates" the scene before it becomes a fixed image. The stress on the continuous, progressive nature of investigation attests to the desire to thread together the continuity of the thinking self through progressive investigation; the escape of Theseus from the labyrinth is here expanded into a lifelong project which lasts until death enables one to rise above matter's maze. This internal landscape is an experimentalist paradise within—a paradise whose bliss consists in piecing the landscape together.

To inhabit this space is to be intimate with creation and one's own capacities, but alien to "the world"; such shared experiences of alienation could form the basis of ties with other "strangers." Rather than fixing the self, this paradise offers it a wandering continuity, shaped by the open-ended process of truth production. Genuine progress could be made only when one was uncommitted to a particular destination: sure of one's methods of proceeding, but innocent, like George Fox or Milton's Son, of where one was going. In a similar spirit, John Smyth appealed to the sanctity and rigor of his continual search for truth to justify his frequent conversions; the "secure Possession of Truths" that most directly concerned him was clearly not the point of the practice.[37] To take the pains to be born again was to commit to infinite rebirths.

Curiosity creates the ground of freedom on which the mind, by means of discipline, can erect a protective boundary between the self and the material world in the very act of investigating that world, even while creating a common space of "Employment" with other subjects of discipline. It was on the basis of this "active Principle" that the Cambridge Platonists finally rested their arguments for the existence of an immortal soul.[38] How particular individuals came down on this metaphysical question concerns us less, however, than the fact that the encroachment of corpuscularian explanations into psychology created an imperative to celebrate the distinctively human possession of wandering minds, even if, left to their own devices, many fallen minds preferred to stay put. Since to possess one's own ideas, and thus oneself, one had to invest care in the labor of reconstructing them as one's own, the decision to follow the thread of curious investigation was motivated not just by pleasure but by a fear of becoming unstitched. As the foundations of personal identity were unsettled, curiosity became a means to protect the integrity—but not the singularity—of the self that pains produced.

Composing a Self: Shaftesbury's Regimen and Boyle's *Occasional Reflections*

Comparing the fall to textual error, Robert South urged his readers to work to "re-print . . . a second, and a fairer edition" of human nature.[39] The difficulty was that, although the text of nature was no longer "about" him, it included him: once the critique of scholastic form was extended into the mind, the literatus of nature became part of the meaningless alphabetical machinery in which he sought to intervene. He became a literatus of the self, perpetually preparing and publishing "fairer" editions of himself in order to exert the power that, though supposedly his birthright, was not naturally his possession. In the absence of this effort of self-recomposition, he degenerated into a text written by others. The experimentalist model of human understanding stressed the ease with which individuals might succumb to the literally self-destructive pleasures of being deceived. Insight into the psychological strains created by this epistemology can be gleaned from contemporary examples of what we would now call the literature of self-help. In the world described by this literature, the ability to exert even a minimum of control over one's own mental life is freighted with affective significance. As specimens of the genre, I offer the "regimen" of Locke's private pupil, Anthony Ashley Cooper, Third Earl of Shaftesbury, and Robert Boyle's *Occasional Reflections.* Whereas the first occupies a middle region between the diary and a self-help book, Boyle's is a systematic manual of instruction in how to refashion one's inner life by cultivating an experimentalist orientation toward everyday experience. Both therapeutic regimens pit the carnal body with which the subject is born against the spectatorial body he must labor to construct in the mind's presence chamber. By publishing the experiments he undertook in this mental space, Boyle affirmed the mind's identity as a laboratory; inviting members of the public in as virtual witnesses to his own thought experiments, he brought together individual and collective subjects of knowledge production to found another version of the invisible college.

A product of Lockean psychology, Shaftesbury's regimen for the management of "the *visa*"—mental imagery or "things seen"—is in the broadest sense a pursuit of truths behind appearances, but it is also an attempt to stave off a breakdown of the self associated with being "deceived."[40] He called his regimen a *counter-discourse;* as the term suggests, he regarded it as a program to invert or subvert normative views, from simple sensory deception to the more complex snares of imbibed prejudice. The regimen is a declaration and enactment of experimentalist faith, expressing the certainty that the procedures of the experimental life can be made into a "lifestyle." Shaftesbury pursued this mental discipline as if his life depended on it. Continually urging himself to apply "The discipline, the inversions as before," he makes artificial self-improvement the stuff of his daily existence:

"To thy work then, thy art, thy life . . . make it right then here [in the mind] as it is there; make things here accord with things there." He undertakes his discipline with the combined effort of mind and hand, which lends the notebooks a Richardsonian immediacy; as he scribbles into his notebooks, he writes himself anew.[41]

The first step in this process is visual atomization. To liberate himself from common opinion, Shaftesbury fixates on precise visualizations of its constituent ideas. Sharpening the mental sight is not an end in itself; like virtuosi who atomized signatures into discrete letters in the hopes of rewriting natural sentences, he wants to take apart compounded ideas in order to build them back up again in new combinations. Such mastery is attained through the second stage: "inversion, change, and transforming of the fancies or appearances, and the wresting of them from their own natural and vulgar sense into a meaning truly natural and free of all delusion" (168). The word *natural* here does double duty, first referring to the naturalized perceptions that organize what Locke called civil life and then, attached to the intensifier *truly*, to perceptions of nature itself. The natural man is alienated from nature; it is the artificially cultivated man who can live in accordance with her.

Why Shaftesbury associates his discipline with inversion is worth considering. Kepler's model of the brain—an optical device that inverts the retinal image to produce a representation of reality—associates looking with inverting; to invert the image-as-seen yet again might have struck Shaftesbury (as it later struck Marx and Engels) as a plausible metaphor for the labor of seeing through.[42] More obviously, the discovery of a heliocentric universe depended precisely on inverting the roles of the observer and the observed. Shaftesbury clearly associates reclaiming mastery over his own ideas with a revolutionary seizure of power: a "world turned upside down." The driving assumption here is that to perceive an object accurately is to overcome false wonder, to remove oneself from the field of its influence, and indeed to reverse the power relation. To banish identification with the objects of one's observation was to create the possibility of a new relationship to them, beginning in detachment, proceeding through understanding, and ending in mastery: creative recomposition.

Shaftesbury's flustered attempts "to hinder all confusion," however, unfold as a florid psychomachia. In order to set his ideas in their "due light," he interrogates his mental content—"Idea! Wait a little"—and stages violent confrontations with it, talking back to each idea and thereby showing "the impostress Fancy . . . what she is herself, and whom she has to deal with" (172, 167, 177). In working to see what his "Fancy" is composed of, he affirms his tutor's claim that it requires "Art and Pains" to make the mind its own object while giving dramatic expression to the process, stripping and shaming his female parts. Having made the imaginary daughter of Eve his slave, he exults, "This it is to be a man" (177). Now an instrument of masculine rationality, he is able to establish an intimacy with the real, to see "things themselves" as they really are. Analyzing his jealousy of a man who owns "a prodigious estate," for example, he refuses to interpret his envy as natural or to take the owner's good fortune as a given, as is the "common way" (166). Decomposing his apparently "sensible" mental content, he reveals it to be "confused." He reconstructs the series of clear and distinct ideas compounded by the phrase "prodigious estate" in order to give a fixed and controllable form to all its vaguely enviable associations, compelling his "imaginations" about the gentleman to declare themselves explicitly. Images of tables, horses, gravel, and dishes march across his introspective field of vision, and Shaftesbury, astounded to discover that, scrutinized individually, they are all trivial, concludes that the purported happiness of which they are the sum must be trifling as well. It is by allowing our mental images to whisper "imperfectly, indistinctly, and confusedly," he explains, that we become "slaves" to their "sly" insinuations (166, 177, 176). By forcing his fancy to "speak out" audibly and disciplining her, Shaftesbury liberates himself from the miseries that torment the grossly "deceived."[43]

We may object that this victory lacks the unbanal character of a discovery, but it could be said to loosely follow experimentalist procedure. Experimental observation was a contrived experience of a fragment of nature, wrested from its natural and conventional discursive contexts, in order to be seen anew. Performing this operation on his own ideas, Shaftesbury alienates objects from standard frames of reference and associations; he sees the "Originals" of his complex ideas, and puts himself in control of the process by which they are constructed. When he shatters the image of a successful man and finds in its place horses and a tea service, he anatomizes a unity and dissipates a mystique; the same operation could be performed on such complex ideas as "justice, faith, honesty, the public" (103). The constant clashing of conventional precept with particular percept anticipates the zeugmatic procedures of Augustan satire. This use of simple ideas to chastise complex ones can be seen as a sort of sanitized fantasy version of experimentalist labor, in which by pure mental strain, in obedience to Freudian condensation, the imposition of a corrective focus *on* the *visa* magically results in the correction *of* the *visa*, without any need for low meddling with things themselves.

But Shaftesbury's language in fact suggests the opposite wish, a desire to engage in vigorous traffic with things. The insistently physical terms in which he relates his struggle to "be a man" suggest that brute force is required to expel from his soul and mind "the incitements, commotions, and disorders of sense" (58). The "inversion, change, and transforming" stage of the regimen tends to degenerate into wrestling matches between reason and fancy in her various personifications (implying that fancy was the ultimate victor). It is as if Shaftesbury were fighting the abstraction of language itself, along with the deceptive camouflage of secondary qualities, in order to tussle directly with its referents and the material grounds of his experience. He occasionally suggests that the regimen is not simply a means of escaping the body's deceptions, but of submitting the body to rigorous discipline, as an athlete would. Leaning hard on the experimentalist association of intellectual and physical exercise, he even compares the discipline to Olympic training. Lax heterosexuality is replaced by disciplined homosociality, which—as in experimentalist practice—is the means toward a more lasting and productive bond with nature herself:

> Remember the Isthmian and Olympic exercises and what resembles this within . . . Grant it be hard to deny what seems so natural, so inviting and alluring; but remember how much more solidly pleasing, how much more satisfaction, the consciousness of such a victory. Not only this, but remember withal the agreeableness of the very exercise itself after a certain way when once a strong habit is established, and the mind in a good station, a good bent. Nor is this only proper to philosophy; but amongst the other sorts of mankind, those who can advantageously command themselves in any particular, or are used to hardiness and labour, take not a little delight in this sort of exercise and love to try their strength. (116–117)

The regimen is physical training that occurs "within"—making Shaftesbury's "habit," not his body, strong—but the satisfaction he derives from victory over his imaginary opponents permits a fantasy of solidarity with brawny athletes who exhibit their self-command in more muscular fashion. The notebooks are rife with complaints about the "tedious and burden-some" nature of "application" of the regimen; these protests recall Sprat's proud insistence on the drudgery and burden of experimental labor, rein-forcing the association of physical and mental exertion (113). It was one thing for Shaftesbury to relate the pains he took to manage his mental im-agery to those taken by a Greek athlete, and quite another to relate them to those taken by the "other sorts of mankind . . . used to hardiness and labour." His tutor presented himself in the *Essay* as a doughty "Under La-bourer," working to clear the way for the labors of men like Boyle (who himself declared his contentment to be an "Underbuilder"); the male bond-ing Shaftesbury enjoys with phantom athletes and workers at the expense of the fair impostress within can be understood in similar terms.[44] In a case of mimetic desire run wild, Shaftesbury attempts to identify with the kind of men famous for identifying with laborers by doing so himself. This suspi-cion is confirmed by the wishful analogies he draws between their disci-pline and his, as when he reenacts major scientific events like the Coperni-can revolution at home: "The house turns round—No, but my head turns, that's all" (174). His private victories over "inviting and alluring" fancies that come naturally and seem natural but do not reflect nature are domestic reenactments of experimentalist victories. Thus he compares his regimen to a corrective lens: as opposed to the deceptive "glass" of fancy which "crooks and distorts the objects," the regimen "straightens and redresses what is amiss, and sets everything in its due light, so as to hinder all confusion" (117, 172).

Shaftesbury's attempt to live in a state of alienation from his own men-tal content recalls Joseph Glanvill's austere demand that we "estrange our assent from every thing."[45] But Shaftesbury does not succeed in coming up with a method by which any of his hypotheses could be falsified, and he always knows what he will end up discovering. Seeking reassurance in re-staging victories that have already been achieved, he comforts himself with examples of deception overcome, but rehearsing the Copernican revolution in his living room can only get him so far. It was easy to imagine one's own reason endowed with all the instruments that made up the "body absolute"; how to put these imaginary tools to use was less clear.[46] The virtuoso had technologies and coworkers assisting him in the separation and coordina-tion of his sensitive and spectatorial selves; behavioral protocols protected his discourse from the fallen realm of opinions and dogmatizing. Shaftesbury attempted to attain this nobler, abstracted body in solitude, and by dint of pure mental effort. His attempts to establish a subjective distance from his own fancy by personifying it as a woman who needed to be kept in line did not confer a similarly concrete existence on the *agent* of discipline; his effort to identify this disciplinarian with his own reason produced only a vicious cycle of self-accusation and chaotic infighting. Taken as a whole, this extension of experimentalist ambition into the context of human life, with its imaginary interventions, its brittle assertions of superiority, and its ritual declarations of victory over the detested cheat Fancy, recapitulates the anxious rather than the productive aspect of experimentalist discipline, its worried self-monitoring rather than its results. It is not surprising that Shaftesbury's solitary attempt to recompose himself by fiat through a negative hermeneutics of suspicion rendered his newly composed self a chaotic amalgamation of self-images, by turns threatened, impotent, and grandiose. As Glanvill explained, because of "the excursions of our roving *phancies* (which cannot be kept to a close attendance); it will be found very hard to retain them in any long service, but do what we can, they'l get loose from the Minds *Regimen*."[47]

Boyle's *Occasional Reflections Upon Several Subjects* presents another strategy for the disciplined management of the stuff of conscious life. Calling on his readers to abandon the "unskilful, and ill govern'd self-love" that drives them to squander their free time drinking in taverns and worse, Boyle offers them a program for a more laborious and satisfying form of recreation that also serves as a form of devotion. Boyle does not paralyze readers with the accusation that they are cheats of fancy; he engages their interest in actively reconstructing the simple ideas with which the world presents them. This scheme of "Persuading and Teaching men to Improve their Thoughts" was clearly an attempt to extend his interventions into nature to the improvement of other people: those employed in improving their thoughts would learn how to "Husband their Time" instead of simply trying to pass or "get ridd" of it. Boyle is extending Puritan arguments from earlier in the century against jolly pastimes. But far from treating his readers as raw material for his reforming efforts, Boyle placed the burden of self-improvement on them. As in experimentalist practice, the demands of the work would help practitioners acquire the skills necessary for ultimate success.[48]

The project consists of a series of experiments with an observational and discursive component: the individual forces himself to "reflect" on discrete events, then writes up his reflections. Boyle calls these compositions "Composures," and, like Shaftesbury's regimen, they are a means to self-composure (5, passim). Through such compositions, the curious individual takes possession of both his body and the world as sites of his own ongoing self-renovation. Like Shaftesbury, Boyle compares this regimen to physical exercise: just as limbs that are exercised become stronger, so the faculties of the mind are improved by exercise, made "more vigorous and nimble" (33). In fact, the exercise and improvement of the mind *is* physical exercise: Boyle's highly physical understanding of cognitive exertion suggests that such activity "excites good motions" in the mind, understood as a body part (41). For benefits to accrue, the regimen must be "a frequent and regular Practice"; as with any exercise regimen, one must "addict" oneself to receive benefits (34, 31). Boyle was clearly confident that his "way of thinking" would lead to habits conducive to discovery in the public at large; the "exercise and improvement of divers of the faculties of the mind" worked to "dispose men to an attentive frame of mind (32). This was a program to create a nation of people who knew how to "take notice," like the artisans praised in *The Sceptical Chymist* (28, passim).

The brisk spirit of exercise stands in righteous contrast to traditional forms of Christian meditation, most famously the exercises developed by Saint Ignatius Loyola.[49] These exercises were developed to exploit rather than to expose or diagnose the weakness of the visual imagination, its parasitic dependence on fading memories of actual percepts. Imitating the visual iterations, the saccades and fixations, of the sensitive body's eye, this program of guided mental imagery fostered intense concentration on precise details through a redundant descriptive language, language dedicated almost entirely to the repetition of particular images.[50] Meditative manuals provided highly particularized guidance for readers to fashion inward constructions of episodes from Christ's life, leading readers through graphic descriptions of the Passion, or of tender scenes between the Madonna and Child. For a penny, the illiterate could purchase ready-made *compositio loci* in broadsheets before which they could kneel. These images—distributed through holy cards or *estampitas*—were crucial to the evangelization of the Americas. In Europe, profusely illustrated books of meditations were widely available. Antonius Sucquet suggested that they especially help simpler folk to concentrate their attention and to meditate more usefully. For he who uses this method will easily overcome those two things which tend to make meditation difficult and even fruitless. The first is the instability of the imagination: after the sin of Adam it became wholly unbridled; the unstable mind was made to wander over the whole course of the earth, and was not allowed to stick to pious thoughts. In order to restrain it, it seemed appropriate to fix it, as it were, by means of pious cogitations and by images. The blessed Ignatius approved of just this . . . and the Holy Church, which makes considerable use of images, confirms this by its authority.[51]

Wandering minds are not remnants of the state of innocence but products of the fall; the fallen mind must be fixed to particular images. Boyle's practice replaces this fixation on prescribed imagery with a call to reflect on things encountered at particular times and places. Pitting errancy against error, he pushes his readers into the world to undertake the very wandering that these manuals sought to curb. The matter for these meditations is, precisely, occasional; the individual exercises himself on whatever objects providence makes available. The open-ended and highly circumstantial character of these meditations carries a religious as well as intellectual lesson. Rather than the state of stability sought by the Ignatian, the occasional reflector seeks to "make a progress."

Protestant controversialists derided devotional images in the same terms that virtuosi derided Paracelsian signatures: by calling them pictures for children. William Sherlock objected that "a Picture informs a Man of nothing, but what he was informed of before"; it certainly could not teach a man anything of "the History of Christs Sufferings" (Sherlock even seems unpersuaded that the actual sight of Christ on the cross could teach a Christian anything of importance). Although "Children may be taught by Pictures . . . a Picture cannot teach; and at best this is but a very childish way of learning."[52] Beneath this sputtering contradiction we can discern the basic opposition between the idol and the living word, carnal image and textual history, that conditioned experimentalist celebrations of optical instruments. Keeping up the crusade against this form of visually fixated worship, Boyle fought the flood of *estampitas* to the New World by paying to have translations of scripture shipped to the colonies. Rather than promoting converts by means of prescribed imagery, he would extend to them the "liberating" power of the Word.[53] The experimentalist export of occasional meditation to a lay audience provided another field for the conquest of fallen image by regenerate text. Instead of offering the "composed places" of images drawn from scripture, this devotional tool empowered its user to engage the book of the world as a reader and a potential author.

To this end, the meditator, like the lens user, has to penetrate it. Boyle is keen on comparisons between occasional meditation and various types of "Looking-glasses" (24). Idle moments are like ashes and grains of sand: useless when scattered, worthless particles of experience can be fashioned into glass by "a vehement Fire" under the control of a "skilful Artificer." The glass is a mirror in which to see the self and its "Blemishes"; it is a telescope, with which to discern "Celestial objects"; it is "a magnifying glass, [which] shews us, even in common Objects, divers particularities, undiscerned by those who want that advantage"; and it is a burning glass, with which to "kindle" objects, setting them aflame with meaning (24, 32–33, 24). The opportunity to manipulate a figurative glass gives Boyle an excuse to invoke all the legends surrounding the telescopic mirror or imperial glass.[54] Boyle also endows this glass with the ability to conquer time. As we have seen, Hooke extended this ability to actual optical instruments; it was precisely the capacity of the lens to turn visible exteriors into "chronicles" of their own production that led him to claim that optical instruments conferred a sort of immortality on their users. Boyle describes the observer's mastery over time in microscopic terms: like a magnifying glass for the attention, an occasional reflection magnifies or multiplies moments and is thus a "compendious way to Experience," permitting the observer to gain the wisdom of age "without grey-hairs" (33). By packing instruction into all his idle moments, the "Occasional Reflector" extends his life by extracting disproportionate intelligence from each "small compass of time," magnifying creation and himself at once (26, 33). Occasional meditation offered a systematic means to extend the textual metaphors of reading and rewriting the world into the self to make a "fairer edition": there are many "uncertain Parentheses" between "the more solemn Passages" of life, but by filling up these parentheses with cultivated matter, one could bring substance to and even lengthen all the passages in one's life story (24).

Boyle makes writing a personal book of the self synonymous with reflecting on nature's book; and indeed it is the latter's fate to be rewritten according to the dictates of the former. At first Boyle suggests that the competent reader of nature's book is distinguished simply by an openness to the lessons of experience: "our Instructions are suddenly, and as it were cut of an Ambuscade, shot into our Mind, from things whence we never expected them" (27). But despite their apparent violence, these ambuscades escape the notice of the "ordinary regardless beholder"; it takes effort and skill even to put oneself in the line of fire (33). Whereas to take instruction from books is merely "docile," it is truly "ingenious" to take it from "the Book of Nature": indeed, it takes a "Dexterousness and Sagacity that is not very ordinary" (27–28). The reverse snobbery that shaped celebrations of experimentalist literacy asserts itself here: the truly "skilful Contemplator" can wrench instruction from the "very Mean, and Trivial"—the more trivial the better (24, 9). Like a microscopist, Boyle proudly occupies himself with "Trifles." By bragging about "how low I can stoop" in search of instruction, he made Swift's satiric task in *Meditation on a Broom-stick* almost redundant (10). In addition to meditations on a horseshoe and eating an oyster, there are meditations *"Upon his Coaches being stopt in a narrow Lane"; "Upon ones Drinking water out of the Brims of his Hat"; "Seeing a Child picking the Plums out a piece of Cake his Mother had given him for his Breakfast."* (61, 141, 167). The attentive reader will understand that to extract instruction from such common objects reveals the degree to which one has trained oneself out of "the common" way. As Cowley piously put it in his celebration of microscopic vision, "The things which these proud men despise, and call / Impertinent, and vain, and small, / Those smallest things of Nature let me know." Going further, Locke praises Boyle as a recycler of garbage: "there is nothing so slight or barren, which you cannot force to yield you something, and make an advantageous use of poor common things, which others throw away."[55] It was through such reversals of normative views of the despicable and the great, the high and the low, that the judicious observer distinguished himself from sons of sense.

Boyle's artisanal shaping and reshaping of glass is a demonstration as well as a figurative description of the practice, for the occasional reflector does not aim merely to passively reflect the world presented to the senses. The occasional reflector, Boyle claims, always has his library with him; he does not have to attend school, he needs only to "take notice"; this open-handed appeal to a form of knowledge available to everyone suggests an ideal of natural or experiential literacy, but one that requires practice to master. The contrast between fallen and innocent literacy inevitably generates the figure of nature as an open text awaiting recomposition; as he elaborates on this skill, Boyle makes clear that such reading is really a productive labor. Encouraging readers to "take the pains to try their skill in making Meditations," he stresses their artificial, made quality as products of *cura* (8). For the point of the practice, it turns out, is to force things to trigger thoughts that are "extremely distant" from "natural Thoughts": the ambuscade goes in both directions. Boyle speaks of how "Thoughts can be made to have a Relation to such remote Subjects"; the world must be coerced into becoming the raw material for this reforming process (27). Innocence becomes aggressive as he extols the satisfaction obtained by "compelling senseless Creatures to reveal Truths to us" (28). As in experimentalist accounts of Genesis 2:19, observing becomes rewriting, for one way "to make the Objects we consider informative to us" is by "framing Comparisons out of Dissimilitudes" (39). Such reading seems as willful and misleading as Paracelsian reading, but the occasional reflector does not pursue his craft with any trust that the book of the world is really a semantic web of knowledge designed for his lectorial convenience.[56] As Rabisha suggested, God had given us the creatures precisely in order to see and to judge how we name them. The creatures do not brandish their names; rather the creatures are there to be studied, named in obedience to our needs, and rewritten accordingly. Contemplation reveals its innocent character by enabling this productive work.

The wondrous God-given capacity of the mind to operate on the world is the real object of Boyle's celebration: "the mind of a rational man, vers'd in Meditations, may compound and disjoyn Notions so many ways" (51). To become versed in meditations is to become an artisan of compounding and disjoining; it is to become acquainted with one's own inventive capacity. This approach to observation represents the world as raw material for the experimenting mind, a substratum for the operation of "humane Wit"; objects that have been reflected on are left with few of their naturally given qualities intact.[57]

Boyle provides a long series of examples of his scheme in action that it would be cruel to rehearse, but his overdetermined encounter with a piece of fruit occasions a meditation worth quoting in full:

> *Upon his Paring of a rare Summer Apple*
> How prettily has curious Nature painted this gawdy Fruit? Here is a green that Emeralds cannot, and *Flora's* self might boast: And *Pomona* seems to

have affected, in the fresh and lively Vermilion that adorns this smooth Rind, an Emulation at Rubies themselves, and to have aim'd at manifesting, That she can give her Vegetable productions, as Lovely, and Orient, though not as lasting, Colours as those that make Jewels pretious Stones; and if, upon the hearing the Praises this Scarlet deserves, her Blushes ennoble her own Cheeks with so Vivid a Colour, perhaps such a Livery of her Modesty might justifie her Pride. In a word, such pure and tempting Green and Red dye this same polish'd Skin, that our Vulgar boldness must be no longer question'd, for rendring that Fruit an Apple, that inveagled our first Parents: But though these winning Dyes delight me strangely, they are Food for my Eye alone, and not my Stomach; I have no Palate for Colours, and to rellish this Fruit well, and know whether it performs to the Taste what it promises to the Sight, and justifie that Platonick definition which styles Beauty *the Lustre and Flower of Goodness;* all this Gay out-side is cut and thrown away, and passes but for Parings. Thus in Opinions, though I look with Pleasure on that neat fashionable Dress, that smoother Pens so finely Cloath them with, and though I be delighted with the pretty and spruce Expressions, that Wit and Eloquence are wont to trick them up with; yet when I mean to examine their true Rellish, that, upon liking, I may make them mine, I still strip and devest them of all those flattering Ornaments (or cheating Disguises rather) which so often conceal or mis-represent their true and genuine Nature, and (before e'r I swallow them) after they have been admitted by the more delusible faculty we call Fancy, I make them pass the severer scrutiny of Reason. (60–61)[58]

Identifying the apple with the fruit "that inveagled our first Parents," Boyle prepares us for a reenactment of the first temptation, though the sensually alluring fruit suggests a "vegetable production" much less than it does a bejeweled and painted woman. Boyle has caught nature out being curious, as if she had invested care in fashioning what Milton, referring to the forbidden fruit in *Areopagitica,* called "a provoking object." Words like *emulation, affected,* and *adorns* all suggest the artifice of "the curious maid," one who has undertaken the "curious Toil" of Pope's Belinda.[59] Although the mention of scarlet suggests the whore of Babylon, the fact that this scarlet adheres to her "Livery of . . . Modesty" suggests a mixture of modesty and prideful exhibitionism that might be particularly seductive to the unwary Protestant.[60]

Boyle is not "inveagled." Having "no Palate for Colours," he counters these curious and cunning erotic manipulations with the exercise of rational curiosity. Like Red-Crosse Knight faced with a temptress, he strips the apple of its ornament: "all this Gay out-side is cut and thrown away, and passes but for Parings." Boyle establishes an experimental relationship to the first object of our temptation and to temptation itself: with the assistance of a paring knife, he puts the apple on trial, to "know whether it performs to the Taste what it promises to the Sight." As the surfaces of creation are peeled back, colors that have the power to "delight me strangely" disappear. Unlike Eve, Boyle eats the fruit grimly. To have no palate for false images means that you can engage with them without danger; so powerful is innocent curiosity that it can reform the first disobedience in the act of reprising it.[61] Had Eve eaten the apple in a more skeptical frame of mind, he seems to imply, the fall might not have occurred. The fall occurred when the spectatorial body surrendered to the pressing demands of the sensitive body; subordinating the latter to the former in the very act of consumption is the ultimate spectatorial victory. Boyle's makes his very "Degustation" of the fruit an exhibition of his ability to keep intact a virgin mind; true sapience makes tasting itself an expression of "severer scrutiny of Reason," a virtual pun for dissective observation. Boyle's innocent encounter with the apple transforms consumption into processual discovery; rather than seeking instant gratification, he undertakes an act of penetration that suggests strategies for consecutive inquiries, an asymptotic progress toward satisfaction.

Iconoclasm thus works through sensuous response itself. As Boyle put it in *The Christian Virtuoso,* aside from the "Impresses" of God's goodness on the "Surfaces" of creation,

> there are a great many more curious and excellent tokens, and Effects, of Divine Artifice, in the hidden and innermost Recesses of them; and these are not to be discovered by the perfunctory looks of Oscitant or Unskilful Beholders; but Require, as well, as Deserve, the most attentive and prying Inspection of inquisitive and well-instructed Considerers.[62]

The oscitant observer is either a yawning or gaping one; the fruit entering the open but uninquisitive mouth is a different object than the fruit that is sliced open, cut apart, pried into, and put on trial by a "prying" observer before being consumed. It is the investment of care in the apple that renders it nourishing, the lack of care that renders it mortal.

Boyle makes his victory of rational penetration over carnal sight relevant to language, explaining that he performs the same operations on texts
as he does on apples. Though "I look with Pleasure on that neat fashionable
Dress" of "pretty and spruce Expressions" (of which his own reflection offers plenty), he is above all concerned to "examine their true Rellish." Before he makes any opinion his own he strips it of its "flattering Ornaments
(or cheating Disguises rather)" and inspects it with his reason. If opinions
pass the test of reason, "I may make them mine" (rather than pursue the
eroticization of the knowledge-by-acquaintance theme further, however,
Boyle has the woman metamorphose back into food). This is a reading lesson that applies both to the world and to books, and there is an embedded
composition lesson here too: fallen language becomes Adamic when it serves
the end of penetrating exteriors. Boyle consistently conflated the functions
of books and lenses, inviting his readers to think of writing itself as primarily a medium for making things visible: those who "affect needless Rhetorical Ornaments in setting down an Experiment," he declared, might as well
"paint the Eye-glasses of a Telescope, whose clearness is their Commenda-
tion." Decorative rhetoric obstructs the mind's eye, like the apple skin:
"even the most delightful Colours cannot so much please the eye as they
would hinder the sight."[63]

Boyle gestures to the tradition of meditation he is trying to overturn at
the end of his introduction by alluding to Bonaventura's famous defense of
religious icons: "A devout Occasional Meditation, from how low a Theme
soever it takes its Rise, being like *Jacob*'s Ladder, whereof though *the foot
lean'd on the Earth, the top reach'd up to Heaven*" (53). The curious man
stoops only in order to rise up and conquer. For Boyle, it is not an image
but its shattering that raises a ladder to heaven, offering the reconstructive
opportunities that permit an integration of human and divine creativity.[64]
Even though the flame-throwing "skilful Artificer" razes the world in order
to build it anew, such productive destruction constitutes the highest praise
of creation, which exists for improvement and use rather than indolent consumption: the curious mind, like that of Marvell's Adamic garden-dweller,
honors creation most when "Annihilating all that's made."[65]

Boyle's pride in stooping recalls Hooke's legendarily curved back and
the stock figure of the curious man with his nose in a chamber pot, peering
into the lofty secrets contained in human waste. When considering this
perversity, we might think of it etymologically—as an "addiction" to "turning

about" in thought and in act. By perverting visual data, the rationally curious man turns himself around. What appears as viciously circular self-torment in Shaftesbury—the terror that one is not Adam producing a manic insistence that one is indeed Adam—is expanded by Boyle into a paradigm of Protestant selfhood and an intellectual identity based on the project of becoming progressively more Adamic, slowly turning one's fallen nature inside out.

Boyle's acquaintances treated occasional meditation with great seriousness as a form of religious observance; they constituted the pious Robert Moray's dominant mode of worship. Goaded on by Evelyn, Margaret Blagge pursued her occasional meditations with such zeal she had fits.[66] Boyle's sister Mary Rich produced a whole series of meditations occasioned by sights whose lack of intrinsic interest offers impressive testimony to her faith in the practice—"Upon the phyllerea hedge that grew before the great parlour door"; "Upon seeing a fine Carpet taken off a dusty Table."[67] Although the practice seems innocuous enough, its lineage was anything but. This was the "experimental divinitie" that Wilkins had extolled only days after Charles's execution, when he urged members of the public to discover "the Beauty of Providence" in "the publick confusion" about which some were complaining. What appeared to the casual eye as "disturbed confused times," he had suggested, could be "improved by observation." With some digging behind appearances, the spectator could become sufficiently "well read" in the book of experience to discern the "excellent contrivance" operating behind contemporary events. What seemed like "rude and uncomely" developments were beautiful, or could yet be made so: as "they that have experimented the use of Microscopes" could attest, there was "excellent beauty" even in "common things." Through the analogy to microscopic specimens, Wilkins was describing the rising up of the "rude," "uncomely," and "common" to the threshold of social and political visibility as a development for which the truly "observant" would be grateful. Boyle was writing up his meditations during just this period.[68] He now extended this simple technology to the public in user-friendly form—a volume replete with examples of applications through which any reader could be apprenticed to the practice—and encouraged the common reader to assume his office as a fellow contemplative laborer. Wilkins's experimental theology has been domesticated, largely restricting itself to hat brims and dusty carpets, but there was no telling where the work of taking notice might lead. In the labor of penetrating exteriors, there was ample opportunity for topical reference; in one of her reflections, Rich seized on the occasion provided by Lord Rochester, one of the "sparks" of the court who was lighting his way to hell.[69]

Boyle's proselytizing on behalf of his scriptureless divinity made some of his colleagues anxious; Beale brooded that "experimental theology" alone could never provide a firm basis for the Christian faith. Richard Baxter's response to Boyle's sensuous iconoclasm was almost perfectly ambivalent. While observing that application of the technique offered a sensual delight, he also claimed that Boyle's own efforts "make me put off my hatt, as if I were in the Church"; Laudian beauty of worship had found an innocent, because occasional, form. Baxter was even hopeful that such meditations would render "women & weake persons" capable of "frequent profitable worke." The very "innocency" of the "manly worke of *Meditation*," however, was perhaps itself a problem: "Doubtlesse in our *Innocency this* was the Booke which man was made to learne & read," but while urging the public to this manly labor, Boyle might keep in mind that Christians must first love God "as our Redeemer, that we may Love him againe as our Creator."[70] Beale was blunter, and begged Boyle to "acknowledge God's mercy to be his great and most obliging attribute." Still, Baxter reasoned, God himself began the scriptures "with the doctrine of Physicks," and the fact that we only see him through a glass darkly should not lead us to "despise the glasse."[71]

The Theater of the World

The potentially curious public to which Boyle recommended this regimen was the audience of an ongoing spectacle of a very different kind, the most theatrical reign since Elizabeth's. These godly programs for spiritual and intellectual self-improvement were not easily integrated into the agenda to make England merry through a hard-core application of Herrick's doctrine of "cleanly wantonnesse."[72] Just as the primitive vision of the new Adam had to be defended against Eve-like appearances, so the space of innocent inquiry required protection from the corrupt theatricality of Restoration culture. Sprat, as we have seen, described the Fellows of the Royal Society as men who "bring their hands, and their eyes uncorrupted: such as have not their Brains infected by false Images."[73] As a space consecrated to the rational penetration (and multiplication) of natural appearances, the laboratory offered itself as a refuge from theater and court.

Decades earlier, opponents of Anglican ceremony had represented the cultures of church, court, and theater as unfolding on a vast undifferentiated stage: as a result of Laudian innovation, Peter Smart complained, "the Sacrament itself is turned wel neere into a theatricall stage play." In 1643, *Mercurius Britanicus* accused royalists of desiring "some *Religious Masque* or play instead of Morning and Evening Prayer; it has been an old fashion at Court amongst the Protestants there, to shut up the *Sabbath* with some wholsome Piece of *Ben Johnson* or *Davenant,* a kind of *Comicall Divinity*"—a concise *reductio* of the Laudian attempt to baptize "honest" traditional pastimes as extensions of sacred ritual.[74] In *The Rehearsal Transpros'd,* Marvell revived these criticisms, comparing the "secular grandure of the Church" to "Princely garb and Pomp." Employing ornate costumes and props ("*Candles, Crucifixes, Paintings, Images, Copes*"), the choreography of worship was so elaborate—"*bowing to the East, bowing to the Altar,* and so many several Cringes & Genuflections"—that "a man unpractised stood in need to entertain both a Dancing-Master and a Remembrancer." By persecuting those "unpractised" in these performative arts, Laud had forced all England's people to become stage players. Identifying pageantry throughout the pamphlet as feminine and the "cringing" before it as feminizing, Marvell extends this antitheatrical critique of the Laudian service to contemporary attacks on Dissenters, treating defenders of the persecution as if they were actresses that graced the royal bed. By giving Samuel Parker the name Bayes, Marvell implied that Parker's priestcraft and Bayes's stagecraft (as made ridiculous in Buckingham's play satirizing Dryden) were of a piece.[75] In contrast to the "Majesty and Beauty which sits upon the Forehead of masculine Truth and generous Honesty," Parker's prose paraded "the Deformity of Falshood disguised in all its Ornaments," so "bedawb'd with Rhetorick" as to be "part Play-Book and part Romance": "There is no end of his Ostentation and Pageantry."[76] Marvell clinches his attack on Parker by comparing him to the pornographer Aretino: the literary forms associated with the dominant culture descend from plays to romances to pornography. Against such whoredom stood the power of ingenuity. For even as he hurled anti-papist rhetoric at high-flying Anglicans, Marvell was happy to concede that an actual papist, if invested with sufficient "ingenuity of spirit," might well attain salvation.[77] Marvell was engaged in more than a struggle over the discipline of the national church; he was defending a particular vision of public intellectual culture.[78]

The culture of spectacle created challenging but not, as it turned out, entirely hostile conditions for the cultivation of curiosity. While it was dedicated to excavating the truth behind appearances, the everyday life of experimentalism pursued inside the Royal Society was suffused with ambivalent concessions to theatricality. Hooke's career was the product of this productive tension: having started out as an apprentice to the painter Peter Lely and the miniaturist Samuel Cooper before heading off to Oxford to join Boyle in his laboratory, Hooke brought together his aesthetic and investigative talents in the art of experimental demonstrations, of which he performed three to four a week during his career as Curator.[79] Hooke was essentially the creative director of the Society; particularly in the early days, most Fellows had "little experimental skill," and were "disconcerted if on any occasion he failed to be present at a meeting": they counted on the curator and his assistants to, as Sprat put it, "carry the eyes, and the imaginations of the whole company into the *Laboratory* with them."[80] Richard Waller praised Hooke's ability to contrive "easy and plain, not pompous and amusing Experiments," but he was not above abandoning the pious contrast between the laboratory and the stage when necessary; visits from important personages outside the experimental community elicited all Hooke's talents for showmanship.[81] Experimental demonstrations for the public depended for their effect on the pleasure afforded by mere vision, as shown by the anxious preparations for the king's promised visit in 1664. Since Charles was already familiar with Boyle's air pump, the Fellows were at a loss as to what he could be shown. Wren fretted:

The solemnity of the occasion, and my solicitude for the honour of the society, make me think nothing proper, nothing remarkable enough . . . [I]f you have any notable experiment, that may appear to open new light into the principles of philosophy, nothing would better beseem the pretensions of the society; though possibly such would be too jejune for this purpose, in which there ought to be something of pomp. On the other side, to produce knacks only, and things to raise wonder, such as KIRCHER, SCHOTTUS, and even jugglers abound with, will scarce become the gravity of the occasion. It must therefore be something between both, luciferous in philosophy, and yet whose use and advantage is obvious without a lecture; and besides, that may surprise with some unexpected effect, and be commendable for the ingenuity of the contrivance . . . In the few chemical experiments I have been acquainted with, I cannot tell whether there will be any, that will not prove too dirty or tedious for an entertainment. Experiments of anatomy, though of the most value for their use, are sordid and noisome to all, but those whose desire of knowledge persuadeth them to digest them . . . The key, that opens treasures is often plain and rusty; but unless it be gilt, the key alone will make no shew at court.[82]

Wren is alert to the likelihood that what might best "beseem the pretensions of the society" might strike Charles as merely pretentious—and insufficiently "amusing." It is not sufficient for the experimental demonstration to "open new light into the principles of philosophy," particularly if a lecture is required to indicate how; moreover, such luciferous demonstrations often appear to sons of sense as "dirty" and "sordid." For a royal audience, philosophical light must be accompanied by the "gilded" splendor of a "show"; a demonstration fit for a king perhaps does not need to demonstrate much beyond itself. But although Wren is anxious to please, the attempt to stage an event for a spectator who might well consider most of their philosophical interests "jejune" makes him edgy; while the demonstration had to be "remarkable," have "something of pomp," and "surprise with some unexpected effect," it also had to demonstrate that, offstage, the Fellows were engaged in more than juggling.

How Hooke set about training his assistants is revealing in this connection. When he took on the obscure commoner Harry Hunt who arrived from "out of the Country" in January 1673, he "Set Harry about painting"; later entries in the diary proudly record Harry's experiments "painting on silver" and combining pigments to make "a most orientall colour for flowers."[83] These artistic pursuits had philosophical value: the discovery of the distinction between "primitive" and secondary colors came out of the observation not just of dyers' work but from the discoveries of artists in mixing pigments and using varnishes to layer colors.[84] Hunt went on to have a brilliant career in the Royal Society, gaining an appointment as an Operator in 1676 (after which Hooke referred to him as "Mr. Hunt") and becoming Keeper of the Repository in 1696 (even lending it large sums, at interest, to help pay off its mortgage when it moved to Crane Court).[85] Hunt's last appointment seems to have been the fruition of a long-lived hope, since Hooke "Shewd Harry his charge of repository" within two weeks of his arrival in 1673; he later "Set Harry about Repository" with a host of books and "1 quire of paper" on the same day that he spoke to Sir John Laurence about "salary for repository," perhaps with his protégé in mind.[86] The Repository provided another sphere for the competing claims of wonder and philosophy. The curiosity cabinet presents "the theater of the creatures" in miniature; it might also be said to contract the magical landscape of the fourth eclogue into a tiny space; here, nature and art, creation and the maker's knowledge that works upon it, become mingled together. The tense but fruitful marriage between wonder and investigation under the rubric of curiosity bore fruit in artfully disorganized and "surprising" collections that filled curiosity cabinets across Europe; as I will suggest, the Repository was at once an extension of this craze and its rebuke.

Both as an aristocratic habit and a Society project, the collecting of curiosities cautiously welcomed back curiosity's maligned sibling into the repertoire of acceptable experimentalist dispositions, presenting it anew as a pious susceptibility to the glory of God's creation. As in the literature of microscopy, however, wonder was best showcased as having been triggered by humble or even ugly objects rather than aesthetically ratified ones. The collection of curiosities has been described as a form of conspicuous consumption designed to showcase the owner of curiosities himself as a wonder, a glittering luxury item.[87] This view is hard to sustain without some qualification when we consider the actual contents of curiosity cabinets and the museum collections to which they gave rise: the Royal Society boasted among the collection it amassed "A TOOTH taken out of the Testicle or Ovary of a Woman, and given by Dr. *Edward Tyson*"; "A piece of a BONE voided by Sir *W. Throgmorton* with his Urine. Given by *Thomas Cox* Esq."[88] If the culture of collecting reaffirmed traditional genteel identity, it could not have been through the collector's identification with objects like these. If collecting brought prestige to their owners and appreciators, it was not by virtue of their analogical relation to the objects on display but by their use of the platform it offered to demonstrate their ability to see the Creator's power working variously and indifferently through the matter of creation. As Hooke declared with some defensiveness, the "use of such a Collection is not for Divertisement, and Wonder, and Gazing, as 'tis for the most part thought and esteemed, and like Pictures for Children to admire and be pleased with, but for the most serious and diligent study of the most able Proficient in Natural Philosophy."[89] To provide the basis for a "cleer and full Description of Things," it was essential that the Society's collection of

"Things strange and rare" embrace "the most known and common amongst us," for, in fact, to the innocent eye, there was no difference. As Marjorie Swann shrewdly observes, the catalogue of the Society repository provides a graphic sense of how the practice of collecting (like atomistic metaphysics) could flatten accepted hierarchies of importance in the natural and social worlds at once, erecting a hierarchy of discernment in their place.[90] Stripped of any explanatory framework that would impose order, much less hierarchy, on its motley arrangements, the curiosity cabinet promoted a Democritean levelling of nature.

The identification of objects that were not intrinsically valuable as collectibles prepared the ground for the conquest of elite households not just by objects which held antiquarian or natural interest but by the men who could procure them. The traffic in teeth, feathers, and the odd root became central to curious identity in the period, presenting opportunities for the collector to pride himself on the careful contemplation he lavished, or was thought to lavish, on even apparently inglorious objects, including the mundane anomalies produced by human bodies. But by investing such care, the collector only imitated the behavior of those who did the actual physical collecting. If collectors exhibited their refinement most impressively by seeing *through* traditional hierarchies of value, discerning the wondrous variety of creation where the rude observer might see only a kidney stone, such refinement was by no means restricted to the wellborn. The *cura* invested in these objects, whether in procuring, tending to, or contemplating them, was perhaps more important than the brute fact of possession. If the artisanal identity promoted by collecting extended to aristocratic collectors, it was the primary possession of men like John Tradescant. The etymon *cura* motivates John Parkinson's praise of Tradescant as a "painfull industrious searcher," one who "wonderfully laboured" on behalf of his elite clients; Tradescant's investment of care inspires as much wonder as the curiosities themselves. As Swann observes, Tradescant established an "artisanal propriety over the objects" through his labor; Parkinson's praise reflects a specifically "non-elite homosociality that is rooted in an expertise."[91] His investment of care and skill created a proprietary relationship to the objects even when he no longer owned them; regardless of its owner, Tradescant's collection stubbornly retained its name.[92] It could even be argued that more prestige accrued to him than to his elite patrons, for the spectacle *behind* the spectacle of the cabinet was the pains that produced it.

The Royal Society sought to liberate curiosities from individual ownership altogether, reforming private collectors into public servants: Fellows were urged to contribute their curiosities to the Repository, where they would be better used "than in their own private Cabinets." Michael Hunter observes that "it seems to have been felt that the transference of the collection from private to institutional ownership would somehow alter its character and make it more worthwhile," in part because of "the sense that institutions had a collective life beyond that of individuals."[93] As one of London's great tourist attractions, the Repository was a public space consecrated to collective acts of naming, offering "a great abundance of matter for *any Man's* Reason to work upon" (my emphasis). Nehemiah Grew's catalogue—which likely drew on the work of Hunt, Hooke, and Aubrey—got the process started: "As to the Names, where they were wanting, (which in our own Language were many) I have taken leave to give them." Pliny's natural history had offered merely a *"Nomenclature";* the Society's Repository would generate "a History," with every name serving as "a short Definition," being "declarative" of the thing's "Nature." In this Adamic project, as we would expect, reading nature served the ends of authorship, since through the work of naming "many Particulars relating to the Nature and Use of Things, will occur to the Authors mind, which otherwise he would never have thought of."[94] As a public space dedicated to fostering such acts of authorship, the Repository promised to acquaint visitors with creation and their own capacities at the same time.

Generalizations about the "gentlemanly" character of collecting and other curious pursuits, however, are best tested against particular case studies. I will thus conclude this section with a look into the diary of the reluctant courtier John Evelyn, who spent the early years of the Restoration careening between theatrical and experimental spaces. Evelyn's diary exposes the rifts in Restoration cultural geography as they conditioned the activities and inner life of an individual who moved through all of its purlieus.

A May 1659 entry is a harbinger of trouble to come. Pressured by aristocratic acquaintances to attend one of William Davenant's stage pieces, Evelyn spends an evening at an *"Opera* after the *Italian* way . . . I being ingag'd with company, could not decently resist the going to see it, though my heart smote me for it."[95] This inaugurates the rhetoric of inversion through which Evelyn registers the instability of "high" and "low" throughout the Restoration period: decency requires that he bear witness to indecency; he is smitten, not with the beautiful spectacle, but by his own heart for having gone to see it. He finds it "prodigious" that "such a Vanity should be kept up or permitted"; the hated usurpers were not, it seems, puritanical enough. After his initial jubilation on the occasion of the king's return, Evelyn begins to discern a decline in manners among his aristocratic acquaintances; encountering Lord Aubigny in 1662, he observes that he was once "a person of good sence," but is now "wholy abandon'd to Ease & effeminacy."[96] The most consistent thread in the diary during these years is Evelyn's mortification at aristocratic revelry, sustained by the presence of actresses and the performance of plays at court. Expressions of generalized disgust with the theatrical self-presentation of foppish courtiers constantly flow back into criticism of the "lewd" plays acted "before his Majestie," and the "monstrous excesse . . . countenanc'd in a Court, which ought to be an example of Virtue." Sometimes Evelyn expresses such sentiments through pained understatement: walking in the royal garden with the king, he "saw and heard a very familiar discourse betweene—[the king] & *Mrs. Nellie,* as they cal'd an impudent Comedian . . . I was heartily sorry at this scene"; "I saw acted the 2d part of the Seige of *Rhodes*: In this acted . . . the E[arle] of *Oxfords* Misse (as at this time they began to call lew'd women)."[97] Evelyn was particularly discomfited by the use of "*Misse*" as a title, used "with solemnity": the provocation was not merely that Whitehall more resembled "a luxurious & abandon'd rout, than a Christian Court," but that, here, abandon wore a decorous face.[98]

To combat these courtly arts, Evelyn composed a pamphlet, *Tyrannus,* against the fashions that led the gentleman to venture into public "dres't like a May-Pole." Given that Evelyn left for the Continent in order to avoid declaring for either side during the wars, he had every incentive to demonstrate his loyalty to the king, yet in attacking courtly fashions, he seems to tap a secret fountain of antimonarchical zeal: "*Mode* is a Tyrant," he declares, "and we may cast of his Government, without impeachment to our Loyalty."[99] Evelyn's response to the fire of 1666 might have been taken from a dissenting sermon: the fire was a "highly deserved" punishment for the "burning Lusts" and "profane & abominable lives" of members of the "disolute Court" who "ought to walke more holilie"; what John Dryden tried to celebrate as the "Annus Mirabilis" Evelyn figures as apocalyptic punishment. When Margaret Blagge quit her service at court, he claimed not only that she "was come out of Egypt," but from "a certaine

Citty the Scripture speaks of"—yet "there was no danger of her lookeing back."[100]

After one evening spent watching "a lewd play" with the king, Evelyn decides to come "home to be private a little, not at all affecting the life & hurry of Court"; the following entry finds him embracing the company of "our *Society*."[101] On the occasion of another morning after, he seeks out Browne, whose "Garden being a Paradise . . . did exceedingly refresh me after last nights confusion" (3: 594). Evelyn's references to "our Society," so different from his references to the "disolute Court," suggest a longing for *civil* society which high society could not provide. While Glanvill had declared the necessity of unliving one's former life, Evelyn took refuge in experimental space in the hope that he might unlive his current life; he wanted to take some pains.[102] A particularly striking contrast is presented by two consecutive entries in April 1661. On the twenty-fourth, Evelyn, in the presence of "many great persons," presents the king with a panegyric of his own composition in the Privy Chamber (the king, in keeping with his preference for "Bantring," had expressed the hope that it "would not be very long"); he spends the following day struggling with Boyle's air pump: "I went to the *Society* where were divers Experiments in Mr. *Boyls Pneumatique* Engine. We put in a *Snake* but could not kill it, by exhausting the aire, onely made it extreamly sick" (3: 284–285). Unable to stem the tide of corruption at court, he could still subject Satan's instrument to the ingenious instrument of Robert Boyle. On another occasion, he goes "to *Chelsey* to visit Mr. *Boyle,* & see his *pneumatic Engine* performe divers Experiments"; the following week finds him confronted by a very different spectacle, with "all the Court" at "St *Margarites* faire," looking at an *"Italian Wench"* dance on the "high rope," along which *"Monkyes* & Apes daunce, & do other feates of activity . . . They were galantly clad *alamode,* went upright, saluted the Company, bowing & pulling-off their hatts: They saluted one another with as good grace as if instructed by a Dauncing Master" (3: 255–256). Evelyn is clearly identifying the gallant, dancing monkeys with the bestial, "a la mode" courtiers who watch them. Evelyn's low tolerance for the degradations of high culture—which led him into the theater, street fairs, and the company of prostitutes—is balanced by his prideful descriptions of his own artisanal pursuits.

Reflecting this instability through his politics, Evelyn takes stands whose apparent inconsistency, in historical hindsight, only reveals the inadequacy of the crude dichotomies we employ to make sense of individual minds in this period.[103] A staunch Anglican, he nonetheless refers to Samuel Parker as a "Violent, passionate haughty man"; he is offended by the "phanatic" Quakers but proud to report his pious son's approval of their fasts; he makes the remarkable choice of employing Edward Phillips, the nephew of the man "who writ against *Salmasius's Defensio,*" as his son's tutor, and some years later engages in a correspondence with Beale on the improving reflections to be gained from Milton's *History of Britain.*[104] And of course, he finds himself edified by discourse about the "model of the Christian Society" with the "honest & learned Mr. *Hartlib,* a Publique Spirited, and ingenius person."[105] In the 1650s he admits to enjoying Independent sermons on occasion to hear "sound doctrine," a "liberty" not licensed by festival; he even managed to extract profit from a sermon on Genesis he considered *"Rabinical."*[106] The liberties now taken in the religious services attended by members of court, in contrast, incensed him, particularly the innovation of violin music "betweene every pause, after the *French* fantastical light way, better suiting a Tavern or a Play-house than a Church" (3: 347). During the Interregnum, the Christmas festivities of Evelyn's family were disturbed by major-generals who cited him for celebrating "the superstitious time of the *Nativity*"; fifteen years later, he was railing against the Easter "fopperies of the Papists" permitted by Charles at York House.[107]

An interesting decision Evelyn made as a young man anticipates his later career as a reluctant member of this culture of "foppery": having been elected as one of the comptrollers of the Middle-Temple-Revellers, he "got leave to resigne my Staffe of Office."[108] This resignation prefigures his response to honors and appointments offered to him by the king later in life. At the coronation, he declined the apparently much-sought-after honor of participating in the ancient ceremonial bathing of knights in the painted chamber, a ritual that in Charles's court was doubtless an occasion for "revels" (3: 276). Indeed, he regarded even the most trivial services Charles requested of him as intolerable burdens; when Charles asked him to write a short memo concerning some hostilities between two ambassadors, Evelyn found himself "indisposs'd & harrass'd, with going about, & sitting up to write, &c." (3: 300). Having "got most dextrously off" having to accept a knighthood, he spoke slightingly of the post he was offered as Latin Secretary to the king in 1670, a post Milton had proudly accepted under the Commonwealth; he only wrote a history of the naval war with Holland for Charles because (as with his trips to the theater) he "could not decently refuse."[109] Yet Evelyn was forever conducting dignitaries, like the Danish ambassador, to view the experiments *in vacuo* and doggedly attempting to distract Charles from his "lewd" recreations by engaging him in what may have been one-sided discussions, in discourse "Concerning *Bees*" on one day and "severall particulars relating to our *Society, & the Planet Saturne*" on another.[110] These activities reveal him trying out a more socially hybridized and laborious concept of public life, to which the Royal Society offered him a means of entry.

Evelyn's activities in the years just before the Society received its royal charter reveal that the Society elicited from him demonstrations of administrative capacity and an enthusiasm for public service that the court could not. The very name Royal Society seems to have started out as Evelyn's hopeful wish, since he started referring to the Society by that name before the fact. The entry for December 3, 1661 reads,

> By universal suffrage of our Philosophic Assembly, an order was made, & registred, that I should receive their Publique Thanks for the honorable mention I made of them by the name of *Royal Society*, in my Epistle Dedicatory to the Lord Chancellor, before my Traduction of *Naudeus*: Too greate an honour for a trifle.[111]

This is one honor that Evelyn did not refuse. He wants to make clear that this occasion is sufficiently splendid to elicit the false modesty he displays so cumbersomely in the final sentence. Using political language to make this "public thanks" appear as public as possible—"By universal suffrage," "an order was made, & registred"—Evelyn exhibits both the talent as a publicist for which he was being thanked and his desire to participate in a society in which honor accrues through reciprocally sustaining labors rather than in the individual prestige bestowed by status or libertine exploits. His decision to give the Society an "honorable mention" by a name which lent it the appearance of public stature was a tactical move that paid off: less than a year later, Evelyn reports that Charles is "constituting us a Corporation under the Name of the *Royal-Society*" (3: 330).

In many ways, this name was the closest connection this corporation ever had to the king.[112] Although the "Royal" prefix of the Society makes the cultural distance between the court and the virtuosi surprising, the politically charged rhetoric of Evelyn's diary entry—particularly the startling phrase "universal suffrage"—suggests why. The Society enacted the transfer of kingly prerogative from Charles to things themselves as observed by sovereign reason. Under these conditions, *royal* became something of a floating predicate, furtively modifying the Society's mission. On January 30, 1661, a day of "fast and humiliation for the death of king CHARLES I," the Fellows did not meet, but so anxious was Evelyn to be worthy of "the honour to serve this noble society" that he did not hesitate to discharge the duties he had been assigned the previous week: "Though I suppose it might be a mistake, that there was a meeting appointed (being a day of public solemnity in the church) yet because I am uncertain, and that I would not disobey your commands, I here send you those trivial observations of mine concerning the anatomy of trees."[113] When a conflict arose between sovereigns, the royal commands of the Society prevailed; the labor of "looking into the *Nature* of all the *Creatures*" had to go on regardless of the calendar.[114]

Given the tensions Evelyn negotiated, it stands to reason that he fantasized with Cowley about retreating to a lay monastery.[115] But although experimentalists often drew on the motif of retirement to characterize their activities, their "exercise and experiment" made retirement a laborious affair, and a public one; it is fair to say that the Society offered Evelyn a way to retire from the court and into the public. In the pattern of doing and undoing that marked his dual career, we can see Evelyn trying to carry on the tradition of Hartlib, imagining and working toward a society in which "the active life" might be redeemed as a productive one. He provided a polemical defense of this effort in his treatise *Publick Employment and an Active Life,* a response to George MacKenzie's *Moral Essay, Preferring Solitude to Publick Employment.* When Cowley expressed his surprise that Evelyn should have praised the active over the contemplative life, Evelyn defended himself with a hysterical insistence that he was really the contemplative sort:

> You had reason to be astonished at the presumption, not to name it affront, that I who have so highly celebrated *Recesse,* and envied it in others, should become an advocate for the enemie which, of all others, it abhors and flies from. I conjure you to believe that I am still of the same mind . . . But as

those who prays'd dirt, a flea, and the gowte, so have I public employment
in that trifling essay . . . it will appear, *I neither was nor could be serious,* and
I hope you believe I speak my very soul to you.[116]

The tone of Evelyn's reply implies that he is trying to clear his name of some
awful wrongdoing, an astonishing "presumption" and "affront." But the
suggestion that he wrote "that trifling essay" as a spoof is unconvincing.
Rather, he had tried to distance himself from the traditional view of what
an active, public life entailed; seeing that he failed to do so, he is prepared
to disown the conviction.[117]

The treatise is clearly an attempt to redefine the active life in experimentalist terms. Although it begins by treating the active life as one that
unfolds in the company of kings, the manner in which it praises participation in court life is guarded, to say the least: "Let it be confess'd the *Court*
is a Stage of continual *Masquerade,* and where most men walk *incognito*";
and, like the stage, it exposes the individual to constant temptation. To be
"*chast* amongst such *licence,*" Evelyn argues, is the crowning achievement of
the active man.[118] On this understanding, the active man proves his merit
by defining himself *against* the court rather than as an integral part of it; by
keeping his sensitive body in check at court, he warily guards the productivity of his virgin mind. Evelyn then turns to the *"Country life"* as a version
of the active life: "You will say it is not *publick:* If it contribute and tend to
it, what wants it but the name?" Innocently exposing the gap between
fallen name and thing, he points out that many men are "full of *businesse* in
their *Villas.*"[119] The frame of reference shifts as the concept of action begins
to take on a purely Baconian cast; behind the walls of buildings throughout the country, the collective subject of science is asserting its rights. Declaring that "Action is the proper fruit of *Science,*" Evelyn implicitly rings
the theme of the schoolman-as-aristocrat: it is the "most superstitious of
men" who choose retirement; such "*letter-struck* men" are not able to "converse with *living Libraries,*" to learn from men who have knowledge of useful activity.[120] Since one can be "active" in retirement, it is clear that Evelyn
is not attacking retired men in any conventional sense. He is describing the
intellectual retirement promoted either by superstition or courtly dissipation—
the schoolman and the foppish gallant are once again blended together to
produce the retired gentleman, a grotesque victim of self-imposed exile
from the useful, curious pursuits engaged in by working members of the

general public. The dichotomy between active and passive modes of living becomes a matter of intellectual style, describing different approaches to knowledge as well as different ideas about its function: "'tis a grand mistake to conceive, that none are employ'd, but such as are all day on horse-back, fighting Battels, or sitting in Tribunals: What think you of *Plow-men* and *Artificers?* nay the labours of the *brain* that excogitates new *Arts . . . ?*" The essay concludes with a celebration of Boyle as the epitome of active virtue: "I am confident, there lives not a *Person* in the *World,* whose *moments* are more *employ'd* then Mr. *Boyles . . .* if it be objected, that his employments are not *publick,* I can assure him, there is nothing more *publick,* than the *good* he's always *doing.*"[121]

According to this definition, the "Publique Fruit" Evelyn presented to the king in the form of *Sylva*—the first book printed by order of the Society—is the genuine product of an active life, not the idle hours he spent in the company of the great.[122] Writing to Cowley, Evelyn had expressed the "envie" he felt for those who could enjoy "recess," which "abhors and flies from" the public life as it was conventionally understood; it was Evelyn who abhorred and flew from this life as much as he was able, regarding it as the "enemie" not only of recess, but of his own ambitions as a public servant.

Evelyn's self-invention as an artisanal-aristo was an experimental effort to live out the conjunction Bacon imagined between Saturn, the planet of rest and contemplation, and Jupiter, "Lord of Civill society and Action." When in middle age he attended the dedication of the Sheldonian Theatre at Oxford, he entered a mixed space in which this integration failed to occur. His identity as an innocent truth producer was contaminated by the "sarcastical rhapsodie," the "licentious lying, & railing" of the *terrae filius:* "In my life was I never witnesse of so shamefull entertainement." The crowning humiliation was the speech delivered by the University Orator Robert South berating the Society Fellows as underminers of the university who cared about nothing but "fleas, lice, and themselves."[123] But when Evelyn entered other kinds of public space, he felt transported to Elysium. Describing a garden he visited in Paris, he wrote enthusiastically that it was a "Paradise" where persons of quality mingled with jolly citizens "without the least disturbance." Rosemary Kegl has remarked that "Evelyn's paradise depends upon an exuberant conjunction of classes which renders class struggle invisible," but his enthusiasm is certainly amenable to a less pastoral interpretation. What Kegl calls Evelyn's "garden logic" or "logic of conjunction" may be a "depoliticizing strategy," but it also identifies paradise as a place in which "accesse is freely permitted" to all.[124] That Evelyn, against the grain of his gentlemanly breeding, tried to see value in uncoerced and intellectually productive associations between people across the social spectrum reflects a specifically experimentalist idealization of the possibilities of public life, of a life conducted in public, alongside other working members of the public. The connection of experimentalist intellectual style to this social preference—which, particularly in Evelyn's case, often conflicted with the unreconstructed preferences of the private man— suggests counterparts in the orderly disorder of cabinets of curiosities and the space most identified with the public sphere, for what Kegl calls garden logic was also coffeehouse logic.

"There's No Respect of Persons There": The Coffeehouse as a Paradise Restored

Although virtuosi like Evelyn sought to redefine gentlemanly identity around experimental pursuits, social levelling was the mechanism of experimentalist knowledge production, and the core of its (always unstable) self-definition. Sprat hopefully remarked that while the *"Ancestors"* of the nobility "convers'd with few, but their own Servants," their curious descendants were "ingag'd in freer rodes of *Education:* now the vast distance between them, and other orders of men is no more observ'd: now their *conversation* is large, and general"; the freer roads of education that led through the laboratory and artisanal workshop also passed through the "penny university."[125] As we saw in Chapter 2, Sprat idealized the laboratory as a site of social hybridization; here, a productive "confusion" between classes would be assiduously cultivated to enhance the knowledge-producing powers of the social body as a whole. It might be said that Sprat was describing the laboratory as a coffeehouse, for contemporary celebrations of this new space describe it in precisely the same terms. This novel space was as intensely mythologized as the laboratory; as I will show, it was described by its defenders (and even its detractors) as a *historically prior* space: at once a pre-Restoration oasis and a paradise restored. This paradise was not attached to any particular place; multiplied and distributed all over the city, it could be wandered through.

The first coffeehouse opened in Oxford in 1650; by the end of the century, the number of coffeehouses in London alone had exceeded 2,000, so that there was one "almost in every street," according to a contemporary observer; most provincial towns had at least two.[126] It is well known that defenders of coffeehouses identified their socially diverse clientele with a new style of discourse, characterized by both sobriety and freedom. The former depended on the latter: the sobriety of this space paradoxically flowed from the absence of restraints, which put the burden of self-control on the individual if he hoped to participate in the "free discourse" on offer. Like "the flourishing Universitie of Eden," the coffeehouse was "a place Consecrated for sober Discipline"; here, one could impersonate the sober public of which one wanted to be a part.[127] Habermas famously identifies the public sphere with the coffeehouse; the obligatory skepticism about the status of coffeehouses as "democratic and rational utopias" fails to take into account what preceded them: nothing of the kind.[128] Given the absence of any precursors to this space, it makes sense to take seriously what contemporaries actually said about them. Early pamphlets about the coffeehouse offer valuable evidence of how the public saw itself and sought to see itself; reflecting on this new space in print provided contemporaries with an occasion for collective self-idealization that functionally and substantially parallels Royal Society propaganda.

As one writer asked, "*wh[i]ther* shall a person wearied with hard study or the laborious turmoils of a tedious day repair to *refresh* himself, or where can young *Gentlemen* or *Shop-keepers* more Innocently and advantagiously spend an *hour* or two in the Evening, then at a *Coffee-house*," where they could be surrounded by a wide variety of people "all expressing themselves on divers subjects according to their respective Abilities?"[129] The writer efficiently outlines all the needs met by this new space. Alehouses and taverns had been the traditional gathering places for the humbler and middling sort; many coffeehouses were in fact converted taverns, a renovation that matched the renovation undergone by the concept of leisure time itself: refreshment from "laborious turmoils" might consist not in more tumults and turmoils, but in "innocent" and advantageous discourse, to which each participant might contribute according to his ability. The clear implication is that those "expressing themselves" are not already known to one another; they are experiencing a Hartlibian expansion of their neighborhood—and acquiring the character of a *"Curioso"* in the process.[130] The author presents the coffeehouse as a place where citizens could congregate to "restore their *senses*" that had been *"Brutified"* in alehouses; if they could be "perswaded to play the *Good-fellows* in this wholesome wakeful Innocent drink," they would find that it was "Incentive of Ingenuity."[131] To be persuaded to play the good-fellow in coffee is to leave good fellowship behind, to seek communion instead through an innocent and sense-sharpening medium. Curiosity's constant companion word *ingenuity* appears once again as the double sign of innocence and innovation, while coffee itself is described as something in which innocence somehow inheres, partly because it is not alcoholic and partly because it stimulates thought and speech, an experimentalist fuel.

Contemporary commentary on these new haunts place particular stress on their capacity to facilitate interchange between classes. To one critic, the coffeehouse was a *"Lay-Conventicle,"* where "each man seems a Leveller"; here, "Good-fellowship" was "turn'd *Puritan*." As the "Rules and Orders of the Coffee-House" put it, "Gentry, Tradesmen, all are welcome hither, / And may without Affront sit down Together."[132] Modestly attributing the knowledge that enabled him to write his *Brief Lives* to his "generall acquaintance," Aubrey explained that he had

> lived above a halfe a Centurie of yeares in the world, but have also been much tumbled up and downe in it which hath made me much knowne; besides the moderne advantage of Coffee-howses in this great Citie, before which men knew not how to be acquainted, but with their owne Relations, or societies.

To be a "moderne" knowledge producer, it helped to be "tumbled up and down" the social scale.[133] *The Character of a Coffee-House* (1665) describes the coffee house as a Winstanleyan utopia where social hierarchy seems to dissolve, removing any need for personalized forms of address:

> Now being enter'd, there's no needing
> Of complements or gentile breeding,
> For you may seat you any where,
> There's no respect of persons there.[134]

The absence of "respect of persons" creates the conditions for different forms of respect that are indifferently extended and enjoyed, since every coffee-drinker enjoys the right to the best seat in the house. Addressing all readers as "you," the pamphlet extends this space of equality to the scene of reading: "Now being enter'd," if only virtually, we are entitled to this familiar but respectful form of address, one that does not distinguish between the one and the many.

M. P., the author of *A Character of Coffee and Coffee-Houses*, describes this lack of social differentiation as generating "a meer Chaos." The metaphysical levelling of matter in a world not yet endowed with form by God— or this world as redescribed by atomistic metaphysics—figures a social levelling that threatens to return society to the primitive equality of the first state of creation. Here, the visitor "cannot prefer even Light before Darkness, not being here separated . . . amidst confusion it self," as citizens "bold[l]y" pull up seats for themselves in the presence of their betters; as M. P. acidly notes, this "great privilege of *equality* is only peculiar to the *Golden Age,* and to a *Coffee-house.*" The practice of indiscriminate seating was also suggestive of Parliament: here was a place for members of the public to conduct public business, a Commons for commoners. M. P. thus advises other gentlemen (and presumably other MPs) not to risk "exposing" themselves, "by conversation, to the open view of the Society" of coffeehouses; frequenting such places would render them "familiar" and, ultimately, "contemptible." In a coffeehouse, as Butler put it, "gentleman, mechanic, lord, and scoundrel mix, and are all of a piece, as if they were resolv'd into their first principles."[135] M. P. suggests that by boycotting the coffeehouse, gentlemen might prevent this society of "first principles" from extending beyond its boundaries; otherwise, the state of nature might leak into the world.

Commentators on coffee noticed that after imbibing this "Potion, not yet understood," people tended to "go out more *sprightly,*" but contemporaries primarily stressed its tendency to stimulate discussion; the ingenuity that flowed freely in the coffeehouse was partly chemically induced, and these pamphlets describe volubility itself in liquid terms.[136] M. P.'s description of the "Garrulity and Talkativeness" fostered by this novel beverage, however, evokes nightmarish free-for-alls: "In this confused way of gabbling the Coffee-drinkers fondly imagine, that they make a better Consort, than four and twenty Violins." Such conversation, restrained by "neither Moderators, nor Rules," inevitably degenerates into anarchy. Yet, as one critic of coffee observed, "men do vent their minds more quicker" when under the influence of "*Ale-house* liquor"; sippers of coffee tended to dole out their speech in a more measured manner.[137] According to the author of

Coffee-Houses Vindicated, the coffee-drinker was surrounded everywhere by "*sage* and *solid* Reasonings" of "able *Physitians,* Ingenious *Merchants,* and understanding *Citizens*": "observing their *Discourses* and *Deportment*" could not help but "Inlarge our *understandings.*" Elaborating a characteristically seventeenth-century understanding of the logic of repressive desublimation, the author contrasts the expansive liberty enjoyed in the coffeehouse with the restrictive license fostered by tyranny: the "mayhem" on offer in alehouses and the *"Billingsgate Rhetorick"* of a recent coffeehouse critic, who "will needs take upon him to be dictator of all Society."[138] Replicating the reversal of high and low endemic to experimentalist discourse, the vindicator presents the snobbery against coffeehouses as evidence of a vulgar understanding, more fit for the brutifying atmosphere of the alehouse than the ingenuity of the coffeehouse. Blinded and degraded by social prejudice, such critics were not fit to perceive the free yet rationally managed discourse the coffeehouse had spawned.

In a sense, critics discerned it all too clearly. Charles's 1675 *Proclamation for the Suppression of Coffee-Houses* attempted to "put down" coffeehouses, threatening anyone selling "Coffee, Chocolet, Sherbett or Tea" with the "utmost perils."[139] Charles's statement that "Tradesmen and others . . . mis-spend much of their time" in coffeehouses, "which might and probably would otherwise be imployed in and about their Lawful Callings and Affairs" evokes caricatures of Puritans attempting to put down holiday pastimes. But as this attack on a whole series of trades makes clear, Charles's worry was not economic; he believed that "the Multitude of Coffee Houses of late years set up and kept within this Kingdom" threatened "the Peace and Quiet of the Realm." The threat posed by "the Multitude" of coffeehouses was the threat of the multitude itself. Since the window-smashing gangs who menaced Londoners with "injury and outrage" in this period were as likely to be members of court as apprentices or commoners, it is clear that Charles was interested in securing a particular kind of "Peace and Quiet."[140] As his proclamation against "Riots" issued the same year and directed against "Assemblies of Weavers" made clear, when it came to the humbler and middling sort there was no important distinction to be made between assembling and rioting.[141] The "disturbances" fostered by alehouses and taverns did not worry Charles; sobriety did.

It is no coincidence that the lord replaced the beggar as "proverbially the drunkest member of the community" in the seventeenth century. Alehouses and taverns had a reputation as royalist-friendly spaces: during the Interregnum, Anti-Cromwellian tracts had been dispatched from London alehouses, where loyalists to the king were notorious for drinking rowdy healths to the exiled monarch, and they were often the sites of traditional games on Sundays.[142] Coffeehouses, in contrast, bred "Scandalous Reports": not merely private scandal, but the scandal created by public discussion of public matters. Queen Elizabeth had told the House "that she heard how parliament matters was the common table-talk at ordinaries, which was a thing against the dignity of the House," and the Commons were constantly admonished not to permit public matters to be "used as table-talk." Although such tables were then to be found in "taverns and tippling houses," now a sober space had been invented precisely to facilitate such talk.[143]

Such scandalous talk was famously generated by groups like the Commonwealth club and James Harrington's Rota, which met in coffeehouses; it was also generated by scriptoria and print.[144] *A Cup of Coffee* represents coffeehouse patrons as imbibing "Books of News" along with their coffee; as the broadsheet's title suggests, the two go together. We recall Aubrey's observations on the custom of promoting good fellowship by repairing to the alehouse after church; writing in the 1660s, a Cambridge man reported on a new "custom": "after chapel," townspeople tended "to repair to one or other of the coffee houses (for there are divers), where hours are spent in talking and . . . reading."[145] The "Dialogue between the Two Horses," possibly by Marvell, accordingly treats Charles's edict against coffeehouses as an attack on the press. Asserting the coffeehouse freedom to "publish" and "prophesy," the poet compresses the coffeehouse and the printing press into a single medium for public utterance. Identifying coffee-drinkers as those who "Conquered the Father" and "won't be slaves to the Son," the poet identifies the coffeehouse as a pre-Restoration zone; its present domination over public life suggests that the good old cause has managed not only to survive but to flourish within its walls. *The Character of a Coffee House* (1665) makes the connection between coffee and the commonwealth explicit:

> *Coffee* and *Commonwealth* begin
> Both with one letter, both came in
> Together for a *Reformation,*
> To make's a free and sober *Nation.*[146]

Coffee and the commonwealth both "came in / Together"; one of them, at least, has survived to promote the identity between England and reformation proclaimed by the final rhyme.

If the coffee-news nexus was what worried Charles, the frequent association of the institution with a (newfangled) university makes clear that it was not only, perhaps not even primarily, a place for "news": "So great an University, / I think there ne'r was any; / In which you may a Scholar be, / For spending of a penny. / Here men do talk of every thing . . ."[147] When Milton famously declared that "opinion in good men is but knowledge in the making," he identified what we think of as the realm of public opinion as a factory of knowledge; the public made itself through the collective making of facts. John Houghton's "Discourse of Coffee," read at a meeting of the Royal Society, thus took it as a given that "Coffee-houses have improved useful knowledge very much." *Coffee-houses Vindicated* describes "a *well regulated Coffee-hous*" as "An *Accademy* of *Civility*" as well as a "*Free-School* of *Ingenuity*."[148] As M. P. complained, "A School it is without a Master." These "tattling Universities" were really Offices of Address: horizontally organized cells of knowledge production.[149] When the *"Curioso"* in *The Character of a Coffee-House* (1665) declares that "liberty / Of speech and words should be allow'd / Where men of differing judgements croud," and that place is the coffeehouse, for "where / Should men discourse so free as there?" the rhyme of *allowed* and *croud* suggests not the tolerated misrule of Charles's court but the unruled toleration of a curious public.[150]

This public lies at the center of *The Transproser Rehears'd*, a richly incontinent attack on Marvell's *The Rehearsal Transpros'd*.[151] Picturing Marvell as a "Street-walker" marching "in state" with "a full Cry of *Boys* and *Women* at his heels" (to which he responds with "a sober remark or two"), the pamphlet charts his progress from the booksellers (where he pauses to admire his own pamphlets) into the coffeehouse, where he is mistaken for the man pictured on the sign of the establishment. Here, amid "a continued Noise of *Arcana Imperii,* and *Ragioni di stato,*" this representative man of print and coffee begins to hold forth on the Popish plot, at which point the author shifts without transition or warning to an extended critique of the invocation to Book Three of *Paradise Lost*. Milton's internal "vital Lamp"—the figure that launches the poem's first image of the paradise inside the poet—is sarcastically identified with Marvell's own liquid source of inspiration.[152] As Sharon Achinstein has observed, this pamphlet is fundamentally concerned with the problem of inspiration, but rather than being identified solely as the domain of private enthusiasm, inspiration here provides the basis for a porous kind of subjectivity, conducive to the formation of corporate persons.[153] Having ironically commended Marvell for having obliged the "Coffee-men" by "demonstrating to the world the wonderful effects of an Education in their Academies," the author warns that "there are many *Miltons* in this one Man." First Milton's internal garden is mapped onto Marvell's "academy"; we briefly imagine the coffeehouse habitué in Milton's internal garden, basking in the blind poet's vital lamp, only to discover there are multiple Miltons inside him. The impossibility of determining which man is in which man is of course the point. Marvell dilates and contracts throughout the pamphlet; an active member of the public he also represents, he continually bleeds back into it; his identity as a magnified or multiplied Milton is the very sign of that ability.[154] Like Milton, Marvell stands accused of attempting to "personate *Mankind*"—"(which in the *Malmsbury* Stile is but *Artificial man*)"—in his rage to restore England to something like "the *Hobbian State* of *Nature*," only "wilder."[155] As the portrait of Marvell "in state" at a coffeehouse suggests, the "wild" form of sovereignty on display here is that of a man who seeks to "personate" a collective *in which he also participates*—an aim to which I suggest every self-identified member of the ingenious public aspired. There is only one artificial man under construction in this imagined coffeehouse, a public engaged in paradisal self-cultivation.

As one would expect, the author makes the accusation that it was in establishments like this that "our late Forms of Government were model'd," and he repeatedly denounces the revolutionary understanding of the doctrine of the king's two bodies—"This Doctrine of *killing Kings in their own Defence.*"[156] But the constitutional threat associated with the coffeehouse is rooted in a more basic threat; it is the distribution of *intellectual* authority that threatens to disperse political authority across the kingdom, refashioning it on the model of the commonwealth of coffee. The author therefore expresses the hope that, "the People," out of respect for "Royal and Sacerdotal Dignity" (which "have the same Original") will be "so civil as to forego their *uncontroulable* Power in Language (which they have by a *Natural Right, antecedent to Christ*)" (96, 125). The snide parenthetical concession indicates the state of nature most feared: not a Hobbesian state of nature but an Adamic one, a sovereign state of knowledge.

In showing how it came to be that coffeehouses came to enjoy broader support than either King or Parliament in the period, Steven Pincus argues that the coffeehouse offered contemporaries a space in which disagreement did not lead ineluctably to violence; like the Royal Society itself, it stood as a public declaration that such a space was possible.[157] The heterogeneity of metaphysical beliefs entertained by the Fellows was matched by the spectrum of opinion on display in the coffeehouse; here disagreement, like uncertainty, could be cultivated toward productive ends.[158] I am not suggesting that it necessarily was. I am describing a shared aspirational identity, based on a collectivist discipline—a discipline enabling a coincidence of diversity and incorporation—that used this new space as an occasion to articulate itself. Nor am I suggesting that taverns and alehouses were incapable of accommodating the *"Ingenuous Tryal of Opinions."*[159] The "brotherly dissimilitudes" Milton celebrated in *Areopagitica* seem to have been a constant feature of the nonconformist Roger Lowe's experience in alehouses, where he often sought out defenders of episcopacy for "discourse": one late-night drinking session even found him in "Controversie" with a papist, but "We ware in love and peace in our discourse."[160] The point is not that such habits of argumentation depended on the coffeehouse but rather the reverse. The coffeehouse was clearly grasped by contemporaries as a space deliberately created to foster such exchange: an academy of ingenuity for congregations of the curious.

In addition to being figured as an "innocent" (and somehow prehistoric) zone for the production of knowledge, the coffeehouse was a literal extension of experimental space.[161] Hooke convened his philosophical clubs at coffeehouses like Garaway's and Jonathan's (where he was present for the opening night), and coffeehouses like Button's provided a platform for the popular lectures on physico-theology later supported by Joseph Addison and Richard Steele; Don Saltero's in Chelsea even had an extensive curiosity cabinet.[162] M. P. goes so far as to append an "Apology" to the "several *Virtuosi* and *Ingenuosi*" who regularly make coffeehouses their meeting place, and whom he claims to know personally; his attempt to disengage the "Society" of the coffeehouse from the Royal Society only underscores their continuity.[163]

That the coffeehouse was Hooke's favorite haunt is not surprising given its identity as a space where "differing judgements" could proliferate with dialectical vigor rather than violent conflict. His diary reveals that he made a daily stop at some coffeehouse or other in search of "good discourse," patronizing over sixty of them over the course of 1670s; the coffeehouse was such a regular part of his daily routine that it served for him as a marker of the time: "At home til Garaways" is a typical entry.[164] We find him there one morning, where he "taught quaker to make cantilevers," a sociable alternative to preaching the millennium. On the day that he takes note of the king's proclamation against coffeehouses, he is undeterred from spending the better part of the afternoon sitting in one, talking to a Mr. Wild and "3 strangers" about his plans for a flying machine. The "potion" on offer clearly whetted his ingenuity: "At Garways. Drank 4 dishes of coffee. Slept not all night. Meditated much upon quadrants."[165] Hooke's diary sometimes reads like a parody of Adam's existence as experimentalists imagined it: "Invented flying chariott"; "Writ Universall character"; "could not sleep. Meditated upon motion of Planets"; "Spent most of my time in considering all matters."[166] Wherever he goes, Hooke inhabits an experimental space, impermeable to contamination even as it admits the presence of others: one day, after conferring with a carpenter, he stops at the lensmakers and the booksellers, where he enjoys discourse about printing technologies and explains the mechanics of a clock to an acquaintance; he then attends a Society meeting to hear Dr. Croon lecturing on the muscles of birds ("I discoursd much of it. Declared that I had a way of making an artificial muscule and to command the strength of 20 men").[167] Experimental labor blends easily into coffeehouse discussion; stretches of solitary and collective experimentation alternate with free discourse in different places all devoted to the same end.

Hooke's style of sociability depends on the open-ended character of speculative discussion that is rambling without being rowdy; rather than furious clashes of opinion, free discourse consists of a series of discursive experiments. The intellectual style associated with experimental space was characterized above all by a provisional attitude toward belief. The reconquest of "unprepossessed" and virgin minds was an attempt to recover the lost space in which the mind had once pursued its play through creation, unhampered by state-enforced doctrine or aggressive "dogmatizing." Exercising the freedom not to be certain was a crucial part of this innocent pleasure.[168] Just as the virtuoso protected his innocence by resisting the urge to make hasty theoretical commitments, so he protected the freedom of other investigators by detaching the findings he shared with them from his own metaphysical commitments. This required a rigorously abstemious approach to debate: Hooke's life was filled with episodes in which he "bit his tongue" (most notably at a lens-grinder's shop when he bumped into Hobbes, who immediately launched an attack on optical instruments as useless gimcracks).[169] Experimental space had to be a safe space for disagreement, where schism could be tolerated so that truth might be reconstructed dialectically and collectively. In 1663, Hooke even tried to pass a resolution forbidding "hypothesizing" in the Society, demanding that members indulge this vice in private; overconfident assertion of hypotheses posed a constant menace to the "philosophical liberty" of others. But when "confident men" made themselves too noisy without humbly submitting their claims to evidence (as when Oliver Hill dominated discussion with what Hooke considered "Strange whimsys about the salt or soule of Corn"), Hooke could always convene a meeting of his philosophical club at the coffeehouse to enjoy good discourse.[170] Despite Charles's proclamation (which public pressure forced him to reverse within the month), an experimentalist culture pulsed underneath the dominant theatrical and courtly culture of the Restoration and long outlived it, a culture organized around good discourse rather than good fellowship.[171] One can easily imagine an eighteenth-century "progress" poem tracing the movement of English culture from the church and alehouse to the laboratory and coffeehouse. A social space of ingenious inquiry, however, could also be brought into being through purely discursive means.

The Athenian Mercury and Discursive Experimental Space

The fortunes of the periodical, a text that appeared on a daily, weekly, biweekly, monthly, or quarterly basis, were tied up with those of the coffeehouse; it was there that periodicals were distributed and torn apart, figuratively and literally, by the public. This was the most important new form of literature to emerge in the later seventeenth century, accounting for about a fourth of all titles published from 1641 to 1700.[172] The periodical's processual mode of publication was analogous to the diurnal rhythms of the coffeehouse; one could dip into either one at regular intervals to "refresh" oneself with news, tracking the progress of its "quotidian current" along one's own. If periodical form registers the historical transition by which politics became "a suitable object for discussion by private people," John Dunton's *Athenian*

Mercury helped to confer this status on other "occasional" forms of knowledge; in this sense, it was an extension of occasional meditation itself.[173] Published twice a week on a folio sheet and sold for a penny from 1691 to 1697, it was one of the century's most successful periodicals, with a readership into the thousands. Appropriately, many of its subscribers were coffeehouses rather than individuals; like the coffeehouse, the *Athenian Mercury* offered the curious public the chance to represent itself.[174]

This readership was, as Dunton insisted, a "Society." Like the collectivity of humanity, it first assembled in one man. In his account of its "original," Dunton declared that "the *Athenian Society had their first meeting in my Brain*," when he was reflecting mournfully on the fall:

> The Humane Mind, tho it has lost its Innocence, and made Shipwrack of the Image of GOD, yet the Desire of *Knowledge* is undestroy'd . . . Now under this Condition, what *Project* cou'd be more agreeable, than that which promises, at least, to open the *Avenues,* raise the Soul, as 'twere, into DAY-LIGHT, and restore the Knowledge of *Truth* and *Happiness,* that had wandered so long unknown, and found out by few?

By satisfying the "Desire of *Knowledge*" that the fall had not managed to destroy, the *Mercury* would be nothing less than an instrument to "restore the Knowledge of *Truth* and *Happiness*" to the human mind, a means to build up and improve the "undestroy'd" remnant of created humanity. Hooke articulated similar hopes for the instrument he called "my faithful *Mercury,* my *Microscope.*"[175]

The *Mercury* might be more accurately described as an opportunistic scheme to exploit contemporary excitement about experimental science, to make curiosity profitable; given this aim, it did not need to be written by experts. Throughout the *Mercury,* excited references to experiments that disprove superstitious errors jostle against references to the four elements, while vaguely Aristotelian explanations are presented as the latest in cutting-edge "natural speculations."[176] This does not alter the fact that Dunton's periodical succeeded in identifying experimentalist ideals and practices with the public sphere. It did so by placing itself squarely within the space where the public congregated:

> *All Persons whatever may be resolved* gratis *in any Question that their own satisfaction or Curiosity shall prompt 'em to, if they send their Questions by a*

Penny Post letter to Mr. Smith *at his Coffee-house in* Stocks Market *in the* Poultry, *where orders are given for the Reception of such Letters, and care shall be taken for their Resolution by the next Weekly Paper after their sending.*[177]

The public, prompted by curiosity, sent questions to the coffeehouse; they received responses (on which "care" was taken), in the form of a publication that was circulated, consumed, and discussed in the fora provided by coffeehouses. Those who did not find satisfaction in the answers they read in the paper were invited to apply again, specifying "in what particular" they were still curious: the trajectory of curiosity extends from the individual to the coffeehouse to the text and back again. The public clearly had an appetite for this kind of participation. While the second issue tells readers to "Continue to send your *Questions* as directed in the first *Gazette*," by the thirteenth issue, requests to "forbear sending" have become a constant refrain.[178] By changing the title of the series from *The Athenian Gazette* to *The Athenian Mercury,* Dunton stressed the importance of this flow to his scheme. As he explained, "*Gaza* signifies a Treasury," making it appropriate to retain "*Gazette*" as the general title of collected issues, but "*Mercurius* signifying a Messenger, 'tis the more proper Title for the single Papers, which run about to Coffee houses and elsewhere, to seek out *Athenians.*"[179] Dunton wants us to imagine the *Mercury* in active intercourse with its polis of readers, its papers running to and fro like the knowledge seekers of Daniel 12:4; rather than being an inert repository of erudition, it *moves*—a sprightly member of the rationally curious public, darting around public spaces in search of people who, through their queries and acts of witness, not only read it but bring it into existence and sustain its survival.[180]

Dunton encourages his readers to help create the product they are consuming. Inviting them to send in "Objections," to talk back to their messenger, he promises to devote whole issues to these objections if he receives an adequate number. He even gave over an issue to a satirical poem, christened "The *Doggerel Mercury*," to demonstrate to its author "how *reasonable* a *Society* he has met with."[181] In addition to talking back, readers were encouraged to test what they read for themselves. To support his claim that rain is produced by a spout of water which disperses into rain drops in transit, for example, Dunton tells readers to "experience this Truth by emptying a Cup or Glass of Water out of your Chamber Window" and witnessing the spout separate into drops as it falls.[182] Dunton wants to blur the line between reading and acting, passive consumption and active experimentation: by tossing water out their windows, readers can "experience the truth" and give Dunton's report credit. Rather than simply consulting the Athenian Oracle for truths, readers are urged to contribute their own findings to the treasury:

> *If any Person whatever will send in any New* Experiment, *or* curious Instance, *which they know to be truth, and matter of fact, circumstantiated with Time and Place, we will insert it in our Mercury . . . and if it wants a* Demonstra-tion *. . . we will endeavour to find one, for the satisfaction of them as well as of all other Ingenious Enquirers into* Natural Speculations.[183]

Readers seeking satisfaction can gain it from each other, with "our Mercury" acting as both medium and go-between. Although where demonstrations are wanting the *Mercury* offers to supply them, the line of authority from text to reader is reversible. Imbricating the roles of readers and writers, the "question project" aims to bring a curiosity collective into being, one in which experimentalist canons are strictly observed—matters of fact must be "circumstantiated." (The abyssality of the process of questioning that so impressed the Society's Italian visitor is suggested here by the reference to enquirers into "Speculations" themselves.) Dunton wants his readers to imagine this dynamic interchange as sufficiently powerful to knock down national borders. Since the aim is not just to answer questions, but *"also to give Accounts of most Books transmitted to us from* Forreign Parts," Dunton enlists an overseas correspondent (or claims to). Moreover, he will *"insert the Transactions and Experiments of several* English Virtuoso's, *and what ever else is* CURIOUS *that shall be sent us from time to time."*[184] Readers send in their questions, transactions, and experiments to this messenger and are in turn sought out by it; this circuit of curiosity creates a space of inquiry that levels geographical and social barriers along with the distinctions between writers and readers, producers and consumers. What Sprat celebrated as the land of experimental knowledge becomes an empire of knowledge extending across classes and nations, whose capital is a *"Coffee-house in* Stocks Market *in the* Poultry."

A few contemporaries suspected that the "we" of the *Mercury*'s editorial board was not a learned society but a group of Grub Street hacks who met above a coffeeshop—or even, as J. Paul Hunter puts it, "a lonely figure pretending to be legion."[185] Makeshift attempts by this group to keep the personal identities of its members vague became occasions to suggest a dependence on—and thus a resemblance to—the Royal Society itself: "For further satisfaction, consult the Opinion of the Royal Society in this matter."[186] This editorial voice makes bold overtures to scholars of Cambridge and Oxford, asking that they *send us all the Questions they can possibly think on in ten days time"*: the most exclusive institutions in the country are invited to request the assistance of coffee house curiosos.[187] Jonathan Swift's first published poem, the fulsome "Ode to the Athenian Society," revealed the success of the imposture, causing Swift such mortification that he spent the rest of his career taking his revenge on the denizens of Grub Street.[188] Yet even the "civilian," doctor, and surgeon who formed the fictitious core membership of the Society as it projected itself to the public were exciting symbols of the advancement of knowledge beyond Oxbridge and into the world at large.[189] Gallantly extending invitations to women, the Society revealed that the Athenians sought out by the *Mercury* were self-chosen; merely the desire to participate was ample qualification: "*The Ladies pleasant question about* Fleas, *&c. shall be answered as soon as we have opportunity to make* Experiments necessary, *to decide the doubt proposed.*"[190] Dunton abandoned a scheme for a special *Ladies Mercury,* since he realized that it would divert too many readers from the *Mercury,* which had elevated itself beyond such respect of persons (the paper was specifically addressed to "the Ingenious of either Sex").[191] Respectability was not the function of any particular background, education, or gender; any questioning citizen could be an Athenian. Indeed, the English people already were Athenians; they only needed to recognize their own citizenship in the commonwealth of knowledge.

Membership in this curiosity commune had its responsibilities; the circulation of curiosity and satisfaction was free but not lawless. The sobriety that was the constant companion of coffeehouse freedoms found its counterpart in this discursive space. In the second number, breaches of propriety have already arisen that need to be managed: "We have receiv'd some *Questions* which we think not proper to take any notice of, our Design being to answer only what is a *fitting Entertainment for the Ingenious,* or what does consist with *Faith and good Manners.*"[192] The propriety observed here conforms not to the codes of the profligate aristocracy but to those under construction by sober citizens of all backgrounds. Members of this public were characterized by a mental discipline of which civility was an outward manifestation; to inhabit experimental space comfortably, one's mind had itself to be an experimental space, where discipline and *"Entertainment"* were compatible terms. Readers who make queries into occasions for raillery are thus swiftly rebuked: the querent who sends in the question, *"Who is the Author of the last Query?"* receives a cool response—"The design of this Paper is not amuzement but Satisfaction," and gentlemen who are "disposed to be *Merry*" should not attempt to participate.[193] By permitting this outburst into the text and disciplining it, Dunton offers an object lesson to his readers in how "the rules and orders of the coffeehouse" can be extended into print.

The disciplining of this "merry" questioner demonstrates something else: that print is no place for fellowship between persons. The disruption caused by the questioner lies in his unwelcome assertion of the private identities of individuals that make up Dunton's curiosity collective. The question project depends on the absorption of individuals into a corporate subject that this particular question threatens to dissolve; during debate, MPs did not address one another by name either.[194] The *Mercury* existed to scratch the "Athenian itch" of the collective body of the public; it was by attaching itself to a collective rather than to an individual, sensitive body that Augustine's "curious itch" had been reformed. By enlisting its readers and writers into an anonymous process of discovery in which no single person was privileged, or even visible, the *Mercury* could transform even the private "scruples" of casuistry into the kinds of disinterested "scruples" with which Boyle contended as an experimenter.[195]

The very germ of the question project had been *"a confus'd Idea of concealing the Querist and answering his Question."* While Dunton's larger aim, as he presented it, was to restore innocent knowledge, the occasion of his public-spirited inspiration had been personal: "a very *flaming Injury*" he had received from a *"Wretch."* Although he considered consulting a clergyman about the matter, to do so would have revealed his identity and the wretch's as well. It was this perplexity that enabled him to imagine print performing the function that the clergy could not: addressing personal problems without respect of persons.[196] Within the space afforded by the *Mercury,* such problems could become matters of public record, occasions for disinterested instruction. Because questions and answers were exchanged between people without names, the personal benefit received by the individual reader was separate from the public benefit she offered as a querist: the division between the public office and the private person characterized every member of the curiosity collective. We recall that the Athenians first met in the presence chamber of Dunton's brain before materializing as a public; the representative identity suggested by this numerical ambiguity now adheres to each Athenian, by virtue of the rhythmically identical, and thoroughly Adamic, title "Anonymous."[197]

The curious Athenians of Acts 17:21 were not obvious exemplars of a rationally curious public: "For all the Athenians and strangers which were there spent their time in nothing else, but either to tell, or to hear some new thing." But by detaching the notion of a "new thing" from the ephemera of news, the *Mercury* transformed what some found a debased appetite into a civic labor. The substantive of the title, *Mercury,* is a probable allusion to the slew of periodicals produced by Marchamont Nedham, who was so ingenious and impartial an observer that, during the course of the 1640s and 1650s, he produced propaganda for both the royalists and the Parliamentarians. Swapping sides three times, he renamed his periodicals accordingly; whereas the sequel to his parliamentarian *Mercurius Britanicus,* the *Mercurius Pragmaticus,* was a royalist periodical, *Mercurius Politicus* was the later Commonwealth version, produced under the Protectorate.[198] Nedham continually insisted that his intent was to "undeceive the people"; his special section on intelligence in *Britanicus* used "Quaeries," rhetorical questions designed to arouse anxious interest in possible goings-on about the country. Even as he presented himself as a noble promoter of truth, Nedham leaned on the Augustinian association of curiosity with a carnal itch: "Since the *mad Scabs* have such an *Itch* after *News,* Ile see they shall not want *Mercury* to cure them." Reducing his curious readers to the symptoms of their own disease, Nedham drolly figured his paper as a "cure" that left its recipients more addicted to the degrading appetite.[199] By making queries the basis of the *Athenian Mercury,* Dunton lifted curiosity and its constant companion, the dread of being deceived, out of the sphere of strictly political speculation and directed them to impersonal and timeless ends. In keeping an ostentatious distance from political news, Dunton broadened the realm of what could be considered public business: the political importance of Dunton's question project lies in its promotion of a concept of the citizen or "Athenian" as an adjudicator of truth claims in all areas. Such distribution of intellectual authority was politically significant in its own right, providing a potentially stronger basis for extra-parliamentary political authority. (And, as one would expect, the redirection from news was not complete; the paper was at one point briefly shut down on account of an insulting reference to James II).[200] It is of course in Acts 17 that Paul is brought into the Areopagus; if Dunton was identifying the *Mercury* with Paul, he was also invoking *Areopagitica*'s portrait of an ingenious, truth-producing London. In doing so, he revived Milton's vision of the public as a congregation, implicitly declaring that the holy spirit did not "dwell in temples made with hands"; it dwelled where people gathered, often virtually, to learn new things.

Even as he detached the hunger for mere news from the noble aim of discovering new things, Dunton retained Nedham's image as an ingenious, disinterested, and therefore (by experimentalist logic) ever-changing arbiter of truth; he did so, as we have seen, by openly subjecting himself to the correction and objections of his readership. The provisional character of his truth claims was reinforced by the form of the periodical itself; the absence of any order in the queries, which were not even thematically related, suggests the stylized disorder of the curiosity cabinet—the reader of the *Mercury*, like the visitor to the Society's Repository, was invited "to find likenesse and unlikenesse of things upon a suddaine"—as well as the coffeehouse's motley clientele, imparting a piecemeal character to the project in keeping with experimentalist canons (as well as the procedure adopted by Milton's "sad friends of Truth," who piece her body together part by part).[201] To have imposed any order on the contents of the *Mercury* would have stripped them of their atomized character, directing them toward predetermined ends rather than flexible ones. Alienated from any explanatory context that might determine beforehand the scope of their use or relevance, these factual bits were available for open-ended use.

The organization of the *Mercury* invites comparison with the formal features of Royal Society literature. Boyle defended these features as devices to link the aims of demonstration to the protection of the reader's liberty. The necessarily provisional character of experimental truth entailed a particular discursive method:

> . . . when a Writer acquaints me only with his own Thoughts or Conjectures, without enriching his discourses with any real Experiment or

Observation, if he be mistaken in his Ratiocination, I am in some danger of erring with him, and at least am like to lose my time, without receiving any valuable Compensation for that great loss: but if a Writer endeavours, by delivering new and real Observations or Experiments, to credit his Opinions, the Case is much otherwise; for let his Opinions be never so false, his Experiments being true, I am not oblig'd to believe the former, and am left at liberty to benefit my self by the later.[202]

The experimental writer extends to his readers the freedom to master for themselves the causal sequence by which he has reached his conclusions. Using an economic metaphor that stresses rules for fair exchange, Boyle suggests that authors who appeal merely to their own authority shortchange their readers, causing them to lose their time and energy without receiving any solid compensation for the expenditure. The experimentalist author, in contrast, reveals his collateral so that his readers are justified in crediting his accounts. Currency and goods are literally exchangeable in this metaphor, since all findings serve as currency for more. By "enriching his discourses" with "new and real Observations or Experiments" that have led him to embrace certain opinions, a writer enables his readers either to "credit his Opinions" or to put this enriched discourse to their own profitable uses, perhaps in support of other opinions. Thus, although *Micrographia* was filled with speculations, these were carefully flagged as hypotheses the reader could take or leave; the Society was particularly concerned that such "modesty" be maintained throughout the volume. The trustworthy information Hooke provided was free of dogmatic conjecture; rather than offering propositional certainty, he engaged his reader in virtual observation and conversation.[203] The experimentalist text thus presents itself as a point of departure for further inquiry: an invitation and a prelude to further exertions on the part of both writer and reader within a labor-intensive economy elevated above zero-sum principles. This style discouraged the reader from assuming that responsibility for his beliefs rested on the work of others; it pointed the reader beyond the text into the discoverable world where he could "experience the truth" for himself. By creating a space in which readers are left at liberty, experimentalist style put them to work, but the products of such labor went back to the common store. As readers subject findings to further improvement, the borders between author and reader, labor and thought, text and world, become porous, creating a continuous space of

observation and experiment. Opening this space to many thousands of
people, Dunton enabled the common reader to become "as it were, a new
kind or species": an Adamic truth producer engaged in public work.[204]

Clarendon identified the danger of the coffeehouse with its power to
bring together "people who knew not each other," granting them "a charter
of privilege to speak what they would without being in danger." This charter, unlike that of the Royal Society, was not granted by any king.[205] El-
kanah Settle's *The New Athenian Comedy* seeks to revoke it. Assigning the
men behind the Athenian Society the belittling names of Obadiah Grub,
Jerry Squirt, Joachim Dash, and Jack Stuff, Settle places them in a *"Coffee
Cockloft,"* a phrase derived from the space over a barn into which fowls ascend by a "hen ladder."[206] The identification of the humbly born with barn-
yard fowl goes back at least as far as Chaucer's treatment of those other
self-styled heirs of Adam, the peasant rebels; here, Settle suggests that a
chicken coop is as high as these Grub streeters, elevated by "the sublime
Spirit of Coffee," will ever get. The tradition of warning against knowledge
that was *altus* is now mapped onto the social scale, exposing the efforts of
the humbly born to advance knowledge as mere social climbing. They employ anonymity to disguise their humble origins, yet in the act of covering
their faces with *"Mosaic Veils,* very magisterially intimating that they are
Persons that daily converse so near with *Divinity,* that their *shining Faces*
are too dazling for humane View,"* the Athenians somehow manage to fool
themselves. Even while their speech is larded with low colloquialisms like
"d'ye see," they appropriate the ceremonious rhetoric of heads of state, receiving "Embassy" and delivering "Commands." The Royal Society Fellows
adopted procedures from the House of Commons to proclaim their identity as public servants; the Athenians do the same here. Stuff declares "A
whole House Gentlemen; not a member wanting"; and Dash tries to prevent Squirt from speaking until "Mr. Chair-man" is seated.[207] The hybrid
rhetorical register of Settle's Athenians is perfectly suited to their socially
humble but pretentious readership; one query they vet concerns the relative
nobility of the louse to the flea, sent by a reader who describes the louse as
*"a constant Attendant of my present Retirement and Studies, and therefore not
improperly some part of my speculations."* The querist presents the obscurity
of poverty as if it were elective gentlemanly retirement, describing the para-
site as a servant or footman; the double negative of "not improperly" apes
polite discourse even as it reveals its own lack of propriety. The play concludes

with Mr. Freeman, "a worthy gentleman of the town," venting his fury that those who have pretended to be "Sons of *Helicon*" should turn out to be "Sons of *Paddington*" by kicking them down the stairs.[208]

Although this conclusion feels decisive enough, Settle has as much difficulty as the coffee-hating M. P. keeping his satiric norm distinct from its butts. In the opening scene, Mr. Freeman is shooed out of a room in the coffeehouse since the Society is about to convene there; when he asks "Poll" if she means Gresham, we are supposed to roar with laughter at the discrepancy between these two societies. But the implications of Settle's reactionary satire target both; Settle's Athenians share too many assumptions in common with the Fellows for the suggestion of incongruity to convince. Like the Fellows, they belittle the value of traditional university education, which Dash declares would have rendered him "incapable of my present post of Honour" (11). They are doggedly determined to wrench edification from each moment, even while eating supper: "we *Athenians* must improve all our minutes in pushing on the *Great Work,* the *Cultivation of Learning,*" a resolve that summons a tortured disquisition on beef pudding so lacking in irony it recalls Boyle's improving meditations on cake and oysters; a satire of social upstarts ends up alluding to the *Occasional Reflections* of the Honorable Robert Boyle.[209] Most importantly, the Athenians acknowledge their limited abilities as individuals but assert their intellectual might as a collective, exhibiting the mixture of humility and grandiosity in which the virtuosi specialized: "we pretend not to Infallibility *Ex Cathedra.* As men or so, in our severall private Capacityes we may have our over sights and Faylings; but as the whole Body of *Athenians,* in full *Sanedrim,* in General Council assembled, we defy the whole world to overreach us." The scope of this critique inevitably extends to include the sons of Gresham. Perhaps this was why, as Dunton put it, the "poor Performance . . . [written] to expose us . . . fail'd so far in the Design of it, that it promoted ours."[210] Named after the indifferent matter of creation, Jack Stuff was in fact a congenial representative of the levelling of social and metaphysical hierarchies that gave curiosity room to exercise itself.

Settle's focus is above all on the potential for social evasion permitted by the self-identification of the curious individual with the universal and immortal subject of truth production—a subject so eminent, and so bodiless, that it renders the accidents of birth characterizing any of its constituent members irrelevant. In contrast, Mr. Freeman's sole qualification as the representative of the play's satiric norm is that he is a gentleman; the prerogative to kick Grub and his crew downstairs is simply his birthright. Unlike the satires of Shadwell and Butler, *The Athenian Comedy* is not devoted to exposing frauds who only pretend to the successful self-renovation undertaken by the virtuosi; the brutality with which it finally reinstates class hierarchy makes clear that it is the social provocation of curiosity, the opportunities for self-improvement it extends to every son of Paddington, that is its real object of attack. It is the anonymity of the Athenians that rankles him: "'tis pity the world should be so vastly indebted, and know not where to pay their Acknowledgments" (sig. a). Settle wants to acknowledge the person so that he may disacknowledge the distinction between the person and the office invoked in Grub's *"Ex Cathedra"* speech. The capacity of curious identity to assimilate individuals of all ranks and backgrounds is a violation of decorum, an ethos of social "decencie" as well as a rule of rhetoric. The rhetorical equivalent of sumptuary laws, the rules of decorum applied not just to fictional characters but to real ones; the principle of adequation presupposes that different modes of speech and behavior correlate with social station.[211] Although Settle can only regard the opportunities curiosity opened up as occasions for the proliferation of false and secret identities, the culture of curiosity placed the principle of decorous adaptability on a new footing; rather than adhering to an exclusive set of "public persons," politeness was now a feature of sober public life.

We recall Evelyn's suggestion that particularly ingenious subjects should be elevated to the ranks of the nobility; Dunton improved on this suggestion, asserting that "every *Smith, Carpenter, Mason,* &c. that makes an Improvement in his Craft or Mystery, deserves the Title of *Virtuoso,* and to be number'd among the Philosophers." Now the title of virtuoso alone is sufficient to confer the privileges of Adamic sovereignty. Dunton took every opportunity to identify himself with the virtuosi on the title page of his *New Practice of Piety:* declaring that it was "Writ in Imitation" of *Religio Medici,* it bore the alternative Boylean title of "The Christian Virtuoso" and was dedicated to "the Learned Mr. JOHN LOCK, Author of the Essay upon Humane Understanding." But just as importantly, it was written by "a Member of the New Athenian Society."[212] It stands to reason that his occasional meditations were also published under the title of *Religio Bibliopolae:* the religion of a bookseller. The identity of the curioso had become as consitutive of the society of print as it was of the society of the virtuosi.

Despite its freedom from traditional models of decorum, the identity of the curious man was a highly restrictive one, requiring its bearer to become a self-interrogating literatus of the self in private and a strenuously restrained interlocutor in public. Unlike Hobbes, who by Hooke's description walked the London streets freely behaving as a natural man while telling everyone else to submit to their sovereign, the sober truth producer enlisted the participation of others in his project by observing the norms of "free discourse": protecting their freedom and his own by refusing to "vent," by biting his tongue. As the attempt to rewrite the "*Stenography* of Providence" was extended from nature to the social world, authors had to reconcile their interventionist ambitions with their own tongue-biting strategies for controlling the natural self, with its sensitive body and private interests.[213] To this end, literary authors made use of the virtuosi's methods and their very instruments.

PART II | TEXTS

5 ||| INSTRUMENTS OF TRUTH

> The Liberty of the late times gave men so much Light, and diffused it so
> universally amongst the people, that they are not now to be dealt with,
> as they might have been in Ages of less enquiry . . . Men are become so
> good Judges of what they hear, that the Clergy ought to be very wary
> how they go about to impose upon their Understandings, which are
> grown less humble than they were in former times . . . the World is
> grown sawcy, and expecteth Reasons, and good ones too, before they give
> up their own Opinions to other Mens Dictates.
>   —Sir George Savile, *The Character of a Trimmer*

> Is it not evident, in these last hundred years (when the Study of
> Philosophy has been the business of all the *Virtuosi* in *Christendome*) that
> almost a new Nature has been reveal'd to us?
>   —John Dryden, *An Essay of Dramatick Poesie*

By turning the mirror of mimesis into a penetrating lens, seventeenth-century writers created a new image of the author as an interventionist spectator, one who served the public by extending the limits of the visible. This literary persona made its debut with what one pamphleteer held up as "A New Invention": spectacles made of print.[1] Offering itself as a means of escape from the false images produced by fallen perception, custom, and idols of the mind, this new invention sought not to reveal an exemplary reality but to render the familiar strange. By presenting novelty as the sign of truth, the "textacle" might be said to anticipate the novel, but if the novel defined itself against romance to establish verisimilitude as the mode proper to fiction, the literary lens focused on revealing the fictional character of known truths; its model was the instrument that had exposed the Ptolemaic system of the world as "the fancy of a Poet or a mad man."[2] Writers who seized on the lens as an antifictional alternative to the mimetic mirror were entirely uninterested in asserting their power to represent things that "never were in Nature" and to "growe in effect, another nature"; their aim

was to expose fictions, not to create more.[3] Paradoxically, they carried out
their iconoclastic assault on false images through an *expansion* of the visible
world; by experimentalist logic, one entailed the other.

Appropriations of the lens occur in high and low literature and across
genres, from political pamphlets to verse satire and epic. The lens was almost irresistible to writers as an emblem of their work, for it suggested that
one who contemplated the world could be a productive agent within it. The
author who holds a mirror up to nature or a magistrate is less integral to
this compound image than the user is to the optical instrument. I do not
need anyone to hold a mirror up to me since I can look into one myself, but,
without a skilled user, the optical instrument is as useless as a prosthetic
organ detached from a body. Yet it is also available for others to pick up,
and when properly used, it transforms the observer as well as the observed.
The question explored in this chapter is whether the literary lens could be
an instrument of spectatorial privilege rather than just its emblem. Used
simply as a means to assert spectatorial privilege by fiat, a lens constructed
out of words could do nothing to distinguish its inventor from hawkers of
opinion. To reproduce the impersonal nature of experimentalist authority,
the literary lens had to replicate the prosthetic character of experimentalist
insight; its author had to refrain from a complete self-identification with
the perspective he adopted, even while this perspective determined every
feature of his authorial "voice."

The dominant use of the literary lens is as an instrument of empirical
demystification to be applied to the fallen world. To be ignorant of causes,
Bacon argued, is to be frustrated in action; activist observers employed the
lens to expose hidden causes operating in the political sphere in an effort to
subject them to rational and popular control.[4] A related category of text attempts to represent a world in which seeing through to the nature of things
is the normal mode of being; it portrays a world that is the end of penetration, a world already seen through and so no longer fallen. While texts of
the first type employ the lens as a prosthetic analogue to the "paradise
within," these texts use the garden itself as a lens, an instrument to reveal not
lost truths but permanent ones obscured by fallen perception.[5]

The literary lens interposes itself between the two literary models famously contrasted by M. H. Abrams in *The Mirror and the Lamp*. Abrams's
binary argument was a historical one, identifying a late eighteenth-century

shift from a mimetic to an expressive understanding of literature, typified by Coleridge's assertion that poetic images are valuable only insofar as "a human and intellectual life is transferred to them from the poet's own spirit."[6] While admitting that Locke's account of secondary qualities already "implicitly gave the mind a partnership in sense-perception," Abrams contended that the mind's role in producing what it experiences had to wait for pre-Romantics like Edward Young to receive explicit exploration: Locke "more than any philosopher established the stereotype for the popular view of the mind . . . as a passive receiver for images presented ready-formed from without . . . a mirror."[7] Yet Locke's account of the agent within the mind working to compose the world it experiences makes plain that this partnership hardly required *Night Thoughts* to be brought to light. Popularizations of Locke's *Essay*, like Joseph Addison's in the *Spectator*, stressed the deceptive character of sensory experience over almost everything else, often using the rhetoric of romance to describe the phenomenal world as a fiction. The experimentalist doctrine that perception was a kind of unconscious composition that had to be reenacted deliberately to produce genuine knowledge made the well-functioning mind anything but a passive receiver.[8]

Abrams's account remains useful to us, however, because it underscores the irrelevance of a purely personal or "psychological" form of expressivity to the aims of most seventeenth-century authors. To be sure, the acts of bearing witness analyzed in this chapter reveal as much about what drives the observer from within as they reveal in the world without; when the lens and its user come together, assuming the form of the author's spectatorial body, observation becomes expressive: each exposure of the king, for example, is also a self-exposure. Yet it reveals nobody in particular. The literary lens reaches into the world bearing real but impersonal traces of its creator and first user; this impersonality conditions its reception, and subsequent use, by the reader. The transfer of lens technology from nature to the human world collapsed the object of discovery and intervention with the virtual witness; as part of the world undergoing alteration as he reads, the reader-as-virtual witness becomes annexed to the "instrument of truth," incorporated into a collective spectatorial body under construction.[9] In this chapter, I will explore what it took for such interventions to succeed, examining how functional textual lenses worked and why the first attempt at an experimentalist epic failed. I will argue that the successful experimentalist author gained power by giving it away; it was because his authority did not reside in his own person that it could form the basis for a collective experience of truth.

The literary lens was designed for use by a public, not a patron or coterie; as I will suggest, it was a technology used to create the public. Here, as in Part I, I focus on a particular idealization of the public as a corporate agent of discovery, and a corresponding idealization of investigative technologies as instruments of public office. The new looking glasses through which the seventeenth century rediscovered the physical world were a powerful symbol of that office, inviting analogies to the medium of print itself; as we have seen, optical instruments and newspapers even shared a name: mercuries. In practical terms, print and lens technology were closely associated, each magnifying the powers of the other. Most contemporaries experienced the discoveries made with optical instruments textually, as users of these instruments published narrative recreations of their experiences. Through the virtual witnessing enabled by print, users of "multiplying glasses" were themselves multiplied. Reciprocally, print was not just a means of communication but a technology of self-magnification, a means for constituencies of all kinds to overcome limited numbers.[10]

In England, the meanings attached to actual, virtual, and figurative uses of lens technology were conditioned by the extension of Protestant iconoclasm and iconophobia into all aspects of conscious life. The dread of assenting to illusions that one did not recognize as illusions made the optical instrument a compulsory rather than a discretionary model for writers who believed, with Sprat, that seekers after truth had to "devest themselves of many vain conceptions, and overcome a thousand false Images, which lye like Monsters in their way." Although Sprat wittily uses the language of romance to warn against "vain conceptions," he is not joking. Writers who appropriated lens technology enlisted literary experience in a progressive struggle against illusion. If, as Richard Helgerson suggests, literature's surrender of an "autonomous epistemological function" in the later seventeenth century left the poet "no way of distinguishing himself from the experimentalist," it also opened up new opportunities for writers to cultivate their identities as truth producers. By seeing through, and reforming, earlier models of their genres, textacles present the cumulative character of literary culture as a condition of truth production; their authors declare their fitness to "make a progresse," and like the curator of experiments, they attempt to "carry the eyes, and the imaginations" of their readers along with them.[11]

Experimentalist literary practice depended entirely on the model of virtual witnessing; this is how the literary lens performed its interventions. However, scholars have often located the point of contact between literature and the new science in the Royal Society's ambitions for "language reform," a project often described as if it were identical in spirit to its fictional counterpart in *Gulliver's Travels*. Although the virtuosi's programmatic statements on language would seem to be an obvious starting point for any consideration of their literary influence, this approach has not been particularly fruitful. Many "pansophists" on the Continent and in England did embrace the idea of a universal language that would resolve verbal ambiguity and deliver humanity from bloody controversies. Comenius looked forward to the recovery of a *lingua universalis* that existed in the state of innocence and that followed the guidance of things themselves, but he fell short of inventing one. At the start of *Of Education,* Milton confessed that to "search" into all the improvements that Comenius had "projected" for language, "my inclination leads me not," and many experimentalist practitioners felt the same way.[12] As far as most of the Royal Society virtuosi were concerned, the essential aims of this project could be met by purging philosophical language of its papist inheritance: scholastic terminology. Some writers hoped to develop a substitute for Latin that would open up the commonwealth of knowledge to the non–university educated; these were early modern versions of Esperanto. Texts that are directly concerned with the capacity of a universal language to refer in some Adamic fashion to things themselves are rarer than scholars like Russell Fraser imply.[13] There were some thinkers who were entranced by a Cratylist understanding of Adam's naming, imagining that a nonarbitrary relationship had obtained between Adam's names and things while stubbornly conceiving of this naming as a verbal activity; they tended to be hermeticists who worked with scholastic categories.[14] On this understanding, a true grasp of form's operations resulted in magical powers: in calling a creature by its right name, a name that both identified its essence and participated in that essence, the Adamic namer could exert power over occult forces. This understanding of Adam's command over the creatures identified his naming with a sort of verbal spell, a prelapsarian "hocus pocus."

John Webster's attack on the universities seems indebted to some such understanding, and it is a very confused intellectual performance. Although Webster rehearses standard Baconian objections to the scholastic curriculum, the alternative he proposes is basically magical. Proclaiming that "ease and idleness are not the way to get knowledge," he urges the universities to go "beyond the *Herculean* pillar with a *ne plus ultra*," paying no mind to "the sloathful person" who "usually cryeth, go not forth, there is a Lion or Bear in the way."[15] But Webster does not have a clear idea of how this journey should proceed. His main complaint is that there is not enough "soul-ravishing knowledge" being taught at the universities, which have made no concerted attempt to recover the language of the *"Protoplast Adam"* who spoke, and inhabited, the language of the father: "no care is taken for the recovery and restauration of the Catholique language in which lies hid all the rich treasury of natures admirable and excellent secrets."[16] If rigorously undertaken, the pursuit of mysterious knowledge will lead back to this original language: the "all-working and eternal *fiat,* in which all things live stand, operate, and speak out." Although "sinfull man . . . hath now lost, defac't and forgotten it . . . this *Angelical* and *Paradisal* language speaks and breaths forth those central mysteries that lay hid in the heavenly *magick*." Rather than participating in a "civil war of words" with the "immodest Sophister[s]" of the universities, Webster wants scholars "practically to dive into the internal center of natures abstruse, and occult operations" and find the roots of real language there. The language Webster imagines humanity as being too lazy to reinvent is "all-working" and immediately efficacious, blending accurate representation with the power of the divine fiat.[17]

For a language to be operative, Webster suggests, it must materially *answer* the natures, virtues, effects, operations, and qualities of the creatures: if word and thing "do not to an hair correspond with, and be *Identical* one to the other . . . it is no longer verity, but a ly, and falsity" (29–30). Webster describes language as if it were a set of statements rather than a generative tool with which to make them, as if the true language would consist in nothing but descriptive utterances—which would also be performative. Such a language is knowledge itself, not a universal means of communication with which to assist its discovery; it is a language whose possession is equivalent to power.[18] Webster himself can only hint at how this original "operative" language might be recovered; he knows that "consorting and sympathizing with nature" will be a necessity, but as far as laying out a procedure for building up such an acquaintance, he can "onely wish that so much of it as is discovered, and made clear by others, might be put into practice, then would the benefit of it be better understood by use, than I can demonstrate in words" (67, 100–101). Even what Webster wants out of this universal language cannot finally be demonstrated in words; this too must await clarification by others. In the meantime, he can only pile up synonyms to refer to it: it will be "*Hieroglyphical, Emblematical, Symbolical* and *Cryptographical*"; it will contain "all . . . sorts of *Symbolisms*"; it will be "*Polygraphy, or Steganography,*" and so forth (24). The fantasy of a perfectly descriptive and operative language expresses a refusal of, and hostility to, the resources of actual language.

As I will suggest, something like this fantasy shapes the design of William Davenant's malfunctioning textacle, *Gondibert,* but it was largely irrelevant to experimentalist literary and scientific practice. Indeed, Webster was attacked by the virtuosi he thought he was defending: Seth Ward and John Wilkins retorted that "the *Universall Character* about which he smatters so deliciously" had already been invented; it was called mathematics.[19] Natural laws could be expressed mathematically, but they had to be discovered: no system of signs could provide answers to questions without being manipulated by a user. As Webster recommended, virtuosi revived the scene of naming by "diving into" nature, but they understood the scene of naming in Genesis 2:19 metaphorically, as the primal scene of experiment, not of language. Language was a necessary instrument of active philosophy, but it could not be the defining one.

The virtuosi's elevation of things over words did make it difficult for them to celebrate literature for its own sake, despite producing a prodigious amount of it themselves. In his turn as virtuoso, Abraham Cowley offered a plan for an agricultural college whose professors would be chosen not for their "Ostentation" of "Literature" but for the "solid and experimental Knowledge of the things they teach . . . so industrious and publick-spirited as I conceive Mr. *Hartlib* to be, if the Gentleman be yet alive."[20] In his celebratory life of the poet, Sprat is keen to represent Cowley as an experimentalist fellow traveler, but founders when forced to describe the art to which he actually devoted himself. Describing the poet's preference for retirement over the "Arts of Court," and the absence of "affectation" in his nonetheless "wonderfully curious" language—the natural expression of a mind "endued

with the primitive meekness and innocence"—Sprat goes on to claim that
Cowley took words "as he found them made to his hands," as if the making
of poems, when Cowley did it, were actually a form of manual labor.[21]
Cowley's confession that as a child he was "an enemy to all constraint, that
his master never could prevail on him to learn the rules without book" is
heightened by Sprat into the claim that "his Teachers never could bring it
[his memory] to retain the ordinary Rules of Grammar"—an exaggeration
that Samuel Johnson indignantly rebutted in his own life of Cowley. Johnson found in Sprat's claim "an instance of the natural desire of man to
propagate a wonder"; in fact, it was a rehearsal of an experimentalist cliché.
Aubrey eagerly agreed that Cowley "discoursed very ill, and with hesitation," imputing to him the lack of verbal facility that distinguished the best
virtuosi.[22] But it was not by assuming the stereotyped attributes of the
natural literatus, or claiming unique access to the language of nature, that
authors were able to invent an experimentalist literary practice; their success came from adapting the procedures of virtuosi themselves.

Precursors: Donne and Burton

What Hooke modestly referred to as the "rude *Draughts*" of *Micrographia*
imprinted themselves more deeply on the consciousness of the reading, and
writing, public than any other print illustrations of the period; Pepys stayed
up until two in the morning with it and called it "the most ingenious book
that ever I read in my life," praise condensing a multitude of associations
that at this point speak for themselves.[23] English literature would certainly
have developed very differently without this book. The revelatory microworld to which Hooke's illustrations gave such precise expression inspired a
native tradition of literary experimentation with scale; the achievements of
Alexander Pope, Jonathan Swift, and James Thomson in the following century are unimaginable without the instrument to which these illustrations
are testimony.[24] But literary appropriations of the lens in England long predate *Micrographia*. Early seventeenth-century writers seized on this technology regardless of whether they had seen or virtually witnessed all that it
made visible.

The space journey related in Donne's *Ignatius His Conclave*, for example, bears only a marginal resemblance to a Dantean journey across the
Christian cosmos. Donne revels in the infinite interstellar space opened

up by the telescope, and in the freedom of the mind that can travel
through it:

> My little wandring sportful Soule,
> Ghest, and Companion of my body
> had liberty to wander through all places, and to survey and reckon all the
> roomes, and all the volumes of the heavens, and to comprehend the situation,
> the dimensions, the nature, the people, and the policy, both of the swimming
> Ilands, the *Planets,* and of all those which are fixed in the firmament.[25]

Donne's *"sportful"* wandering is undertaken by a ghostly *"Companion"* of
the body that can "survey and reckon . . . volumes" closed to mortal eyes
and understanding. But this companion, identified with the soul and the
lens at once, owes as much to the medieval dream vision as to the spectatorial body associated with the new technology; this double agent serves
Donne's divided satiric focus, enabling him to correct both theologians and
astronomers as he sees fit. For he is of two minds about the technology that
has granted him this "liberty to wander." Even as his text reprises Galileo's
bold inquisition into the secrets of outer space, it subjects modern astronomers themselves to mock-heroic treatment: Galileo has "summoned the
other worlds, the Stars to come neerer to him, and give him an account of
themselves," while Kepler declares that he has received the universe *"into
his care, that no new thing should be done in heaven without his knowledge."*
The hyperbolic equation of surveying with commanding is of course deflationary; imputing to astronomers the belief that they have literally brought
the heavens down to earth, Donne renders the idea absurd. Indeed, although these celebrated users of the lens pride themselves on their power
and daring, they take fewer liberties than representatives of the old religion,
and Donne uses their vantage point to challenge the old sacred geography,
solemnly reporting that he found no evidence of purgatory or limbo on his
journey. Claiming the same autoptic authority as the astronomers, he
adopts the posture of a fellow investigator who responsibly acknowledges
the priority of Galileo and Kepler's discoveries before announcing his own:
"For by the law, *Prevention* must take place; and therefore what they have
found and discovred first, I am content they speake and utter first."[26]
Donne's pretense of offering an eyewitness account enables him to exult in
his own freedom from visual evidence, to which these moderns, for all their

audacity, remain tied. The poet's defense of modern truth production is above all a sly declaration of his own independence from its methods.

Ignatius reproduces this epistemological modesty in one respect: the journey into the heavens does not extend into heaven itself. It does include a visit to hell, where Donne finds that by "the benefit of certaine spectacles . . . all the inhabitants of all nations, and of all ages were suddenly made familiar to me." He speculates that popes must wear such spectacles since they can "discerne so distinctly the soules of their friends," and pretends to wonder if Robert Aquinas used a sense-enhancing instrument applied to the ear, since he was able to overhear Christ's oration on the cross and reproduce it verbatim.[27] The instruments and truth claims of modern astronomy seem positively humble when compared to such revelations, whose false or imagined percepts suggest the comprehensive marshalling of the senses required by the spiritual exercises of the text's namesake, Ignatius. Thus when Donne encounters Copernicus in the underworld, he is surprised, never having heard that the astronomer led a sinful life, until he recalls that the papists have "extended the name, & the punishment of Heresie, almost to every thing" (13). As it turns out, however, Copernicus is clamoring to get into hell's inner sanctum—reserved for dangerous innovators—and being denied entrance. Despite his loud insistence on his own Luciferian arrogance—he has "turned the whole frame of the world, and am thereby almost a new Creator"—Ignatius is not impressed:

> what new thing have you invented, by which our *Lucifer* gets any thing? What cares hee whether the earth travell, or stand still? Hath your raising up of the earth into heaven, brought men to that confidence, that they build new towers or threaten God againe? Or do they out of this motion of the earth conclude, that there is no hell, or deny the punishment of sin? Do not men beleeve?

Lucifer gets nothing out of astronomers' success in "raising" earth to heaven. Only "contentions, and schoole-combats" and the manipulative arts of visualization concocted by Ignatius himself advance the doubtful and idolatrous faith on which the expansion of Satan's kingdom depends (15, 17).

Donne's digressive narrative, whose "wandering" formally enacts the vertiginous journey into outer space, concludes with Ignatius being provided with his own colonial outpost of hell on the moon. The preposterous-ness of this narrative testifies to the lifting of restraints on the speculative urge that, despite its promiscuous wandering, poses no threat whatsoever to religious faith. As Ignatius laments, such loosening of visual and cognitive restraints results neither in "confidence" nor atheism. Modernity's expansion of the realm of the visible does, however, create the conditions for the complete spiritualization, perhaps an internalization, of sacred geography, with which the physical cosmos may have little to do. As Donne says of the astronomers, "they may vouchsafe to take from me, that they shall hardly find *Enoch,* or *Elias* any where in their circuit": mapping the physical universe will not illuminate sacred geography.[28] As the fallen world of hellish experience is extended even to the moon, the freedom to wander through the infinite worlds of space is actually used to confirm the truths of religion, even as it erects boundaries around their scope of application, leaving the new philosophy free to make whatever discoveries it will. Although Donne does not celebrate the perspective provided by the lens as innocent, exactly, he reveals it to be harmless (despite the best efforts of its champions) and a handy tool for bringing papist bigotry into focus. But to be used in this fashion, it needs to be supplemented by the "sportful" instrument of fiction, which, in reproducing the audacity of Catholic fabrications, subverts them. Asserting the poet's liberty to range "freely . . . within the Zodiack of his owne wit," Donne bests the astronomers and the papists at once, flaunting his freedom from the world of facts even while testifying to his secure possession of (Protestant) truth.[29]

The counterpart of this wide-ranging space travel is the anatomy. Donne's *First Anniversarie* and Robert Burton's *Anatomy of Melancholy* both pretend to provide a discursive equivalent of anatomy, cutting creation so finely they uncover its atomic substructure. Both anatomies also include a discursus on the new outer space, whose growing dimensions Burton's text imitated by expanding with each new edition.[30] The perspectives of the space journey and the anatomy imply one another as much as the microscope and the telescope do: each seeks to subject the realm of the visible to infinite expansion, as opposed to what Reid Barbour calls the "fear-inspired ritualism, idolatry, and popery" portrayed in the emblems on Burton's title page, where they stand for varieties of melancholic subjectivity, which for Burton is virtually continuous with fallen subjectivity as a whole.[31]

In his preface, Burton presents the *Anatomy* as an attempt "to revive againe, prosecute and finish" the project on which Democritus was embarked when Hippocrates discovered him in his garden, surrounded by "carcasses of many severall beasts, newly by him cut up and anatomized."[32] A classical counterpart of the Eden where Adam mustered and looked into the nature of the creatures, this is also an image of modern philosophy's attempt to reverse the fall by reviving that scene. Democritus is seeking the organic cause of melancholy—a disease that Burton's first chapter identifies as a product of the fall, and the near-universal condition of postlapsarian humanity. As the celebration of Democritus's garden of anatomized creatures fluctuates into a lament for the lost garden of Eden, the two gardens seem to merge. But the research problem that engages Democritus did not exist in Adam's paradise. Absorbed in labors undertaken "for the relief of man's estate," the laughing philosopher is in fact a perfect double of the Adamic experimentalist, engaged in the labor of paradisal recovery—which raises the question of what role Burton's own persona, Democritus Junior, has in the scheme. This persona, by turns as grandiose and hapless as Donne's astronomers, declares Burton's intention to finish what Democritus started, but the *Anatomy* never manages to do so. Its rambling character only becomes more pronounced with each new edition, along with explanations for the failure of the book to achieve its aims. These could recall the disclaimers of Bacon, whose plan for the *New Organon* extended far beyond what he alone could produce. But although one could argue that the progressive character of the anatomy admits of no conclusion by any single observing subject—since a complete anatomy must take into account the innumerable worlds of infinite space—in fact Burton confesses that he has made no progress toward his aim at all.

The problem lies in his tools: books. While he has "delighted" in the study of cosmography, he has not turned a curious eye, or hand, to the object of his study, and he laments at the outset that his limited experience of the world beyond the university makes him a poor authority on many of the topics he addresses. He has read many books, "but to little purpose . . . I have confusedly tumbled over divers Authors in our Libraries, with small profit," with the result that there is "No newes here" but what he has "gathered together from severall Dung-hills, excrements of Authors" (1: 4, 8, 12). To this fetid matter, Burton has added a generous helping of his own: "this I aymed at . . . to ease my minde by writing, for I had *gravidum cor, foetum caput,* a kind of Impostume in my head, which I was very desirous to be unladen of, and could imagine no fitter evacuation then this" (7). The circuit of reading and writing is a literally sick one, consisting in the transfer of waste and purulent matter. Burton's text is not only a symptom of the disease it is supposed to anatomize, it is a carrier of the contagion, a vehicle for the "evacuation" and transmission of corrupt substance. Of course, the author might turn the contagion to regenerate use by dramatizing its tragic consequences, in the manner of a Godfrey Goodman, and Burton's notion of a fit evacuation suggests that he is digging up his own head, perhaps engaged in a demented version of Bacon's "Georgics of the Mind." But, as both the preface and section on "the Misery of Schollers" argue, a sedentary life devoted to writing and reading is both the product and an exacerbating cause of the universal malady, an epitome of humanity's fallen state.[33] One might assume that, in Burton's diagnosis, almost nothing is excluded from melancholy's ambit, but in fact he casts a longing eye at "industrious Artificers," the world's "painefull inhabitants," whose soul or active mind is "placed in their fingers ends."[34] Compared to the morbid melancholics who surround them, these laborers are paragons of health, and it is on these industrious subjects that the reformation of England's "sicke body" depends.[35] Although Burton attempts to recreate Democritus's garden in his study, it flourishes only where creation is physically engaged with the eyes and hands, where "news" is discovered and facts are made.[36]

Democritus Junior is thus aptly named: a diminished successor of his original. The real object of Burton's frustrated longing—the life of the virtuoso—combines the scholar's life and the worker's life in true Democritean fashion, generating speculations and discoveries with which the ever-expanding "digression" struggles to keep pace. But while Burton honors the technology that promises to anatomize the whole universe, he does not presume to be its user; his attempt to follow the progress of astronomy is specifically marked as a digression from his own doomed enterprise. What excludes him from the modern investigation into the heavens is what excludes him from Democritus's garden: although he is a modern, he lives the life of a schoolman. In this respect, the *Anatomy* is an anti-textacle, for it exposes—and mourns—the gap between author and practitioner that the literary lens seeks to bridge.[37] While Donne and Burton make some effort to reproduce the sensory disorientation introduced by lens technology, neither identifies the lens with their own authorial powers: Donne, because he has a better technology at his disposal, fiction; and Burton, because the futility of trying to produce truth out of words alone is the very premise of his "self-consuming" satire.[38]

"A New Invention"

The first authors who sought to make the lens their own employed it as a didactic instrument. In this literature, the decision to wield the lens is invested with the significance of a weighty ethical choice. The author announces his intention to aim the lens at something or someone; he then moralizes about what he sees. The action is in the taking aim; the detailed visual elaboration of what is seen can be minimal, taken care of by largely evaluative rather than descriptive language. (As the genre comes into its own, however, description increasingly does the work of evaluation; in Andrew Marvell's *The Last Instructions to a Painter,* the instrument that enabled Nehemiah Grew to reveal "Infinite occurrences and secret Intrigues" in the vegetable kingdom is turned on the kingdom itself, and poetry takes on the function of a newsbook.)[39] Exploiting their freedom to subject the imaginary instruments they wield to continual transformation, writers focus our attention on the moral meanings of various observational postures and the agency involved in assuming them: they fashion and wear spectacles, they "seize" and "aim" the microscope or telescope. These acts of exposure are directed against speciously smooth surfaces that the writer, like Walter Charleton's microscopist, reveals to be "impolite."[40] Such performances suggest that to adopt a certain contemplative posture is to act; and in some cases—like publicly aiming the telescope at the king to expose his "spots"—it was.

In *Britannia's Pastorals,* published just two years after *Ignatius,* William Browne provides the model from which satiric uses of the lens would take their cue: proposing the telescope as an alternative to shepherd's pipes. The author's effort to extend the realm of the visible is also an attempt to see through inherited mimetic norms. Browne's "pastoral" is thus one in which a description of morning anticipates a day ringing with the labors of Tubal-Cain: "The carefull *Smith* had in his sooty forge / Kindled no coale; nor did his hammers urge / His neighbours patience."[41] The inclusion of georgic and iron-age elements transforms this pastoral space into contested territory, even, at times, into the field of a struggle against pastoral. Throughout the text, Browne's intermittent fidelity to pastoral convention grates against his determination to make contemporary England visible. The lens makes its entrance as an emblem to dramatize this effort, and then becomes its instrument:

> . . . as a man who standing to descry
> How great floods farre off run, and vallies lye,
> Taketh a *glasse prospective* good and true,
> By which things most remote are full in view:
> If Monarchs, so, would take an Instrument
> Of truth compos'd to spie their Subjects drent
> In foule opression by those high in seat
> (Who care not to be good but to be great)
> In full aspect the wrongs of each degree
> Would lye before them; and they then would see . . . [42]

The poem stands in for the good and true glass it calls for; it is "an Instrument / Of truth compos'd," and Browne offers it to James. The analogy between the poem and this instrument is prepared for by the analogy that precedes it: a man who has difficulty reading because "age hath dim'd his eyes" decides to use "his Spectacles, and as he pryes / Through them all Characters seeme wondrous faire." Reading letters from a distance was a standard method of measuring the power of optical instruments; its efficacy thus established, the instrument is put to use, and its powers of magnification intensify.[43] As the spectacles turn into a telescope, the book unfolds into the English countryside, and the "Characters" change accordingly; the king's favorites come into focus as sharply as the valleys and rivers that the lens user attempts to "descry"—to discern, reveal, or make out, but also to sketch or publish. Although the king is blind to the destruction they are wreaking on the countryside by seizing property and raising rents, Browne's instrument of truth can reveal these things—demonstrating to everyone else in the process that Britannia and the British monarch, which were represented throughout Elizabeth's reign as "virtually interchangeable," are in fact strangers to one another: "things most remote."[44] In case we have failed to notice that Browne has dropped his pastoral mask in the course of making these observations, he makes a show of reassuming it—"But stay sweet *Muse!* . . . Keepe with the Shepherds; leave the *Satyres* veine." By the end of the song, however, he has dropped it once again, urging English shepherds to "change your pleasing melody" to "rough-hewn *Satyres*"; he promises to do the same, the better to "jerke to death this infamy of men." Repeatedly putting on and throwing off his shepherd outfit as he shifts from "singing" to the labor of making visible, he demonstrates the limits of pastoral as an instrument with which to "glaunce at greater matters"; he wants not to glance but to pry.[45]

Browne does not openly take the step of aiming this *"glasse prospective"* at the king himself, much less "jerking" or hitting him with it, but implicitly, of course, he is doing just that. Reversing the Mirror for Magistrates tradition, he suggests that he is interested in getting the king to look not at himself but at the country. The focus is on the people rather than their betters; their betterment, rather than the private moral perfection of the king, is the desired end of this indecorous intervention. To imagine that the lens has the power to reform the king depends on the assumption that looking through the lens transforms the viewer as well as the world revealed. However, in the short passage that intervenes between the spectacles simile and the telescope simile, this transformation is imagined differently, through a solar metaphor:

> But let him lay his sight of grace aside,
> And see what men he hath so dignifide,
> They all would vanish, and not dare appeare,
> Who *Atom-like,* when their *Sun* shined cleare,
> Danc'd in his beame; but now his rayes are gone,
> Of many hundred we perceive not one.

It is not surprising that Browne goes on to worry that he might, like Icarus, get "scorch[ed]" if he continues in this vein; the royal sun and his telescopic instrument of truth have been brought into thrilling proximity.[46] The analogy between the king's "sight of grace" and a sunbeam invokes a common metaphor for vision to describe a kind of blindness, and Browne even goes so far as to suggest that the king's "eyes of favour" produce the oppression they fail to discern (line 849). Although Browne does not directly inveigh against the king or the solar topos, he subjects both to critical scrutiny. Having set up the conditions for a virtual experiment ("But let . . ."), he relates the results with perfect "indifferency": as he informs us not of what he believes but of what "we perceive," the royal sun is temporarily extinguished.

We recall that for Hooke, optical instruments permitted their user to turn visible surfaces into testimonials of their own production. This is the operation Browne has performed here, in his attempt to render visible the causes of Britannia's decay. It is also the operation he performs on pastoral. Adhering to and deviating from its mimetic conventions as each occasional observation demands, he produces a sensitive register of what he portrays as pastoral's limits: some things require instruments of truth to be descried. But the critique he launches in "*Satyres* veine" is crucially displaced from his person. Just as it is not wrongdoers that are "jerked" but wrongdoing, so it is not Browne himself but the instrument that reveals what he insists pastoral song cannot. When the king regards his favorites, "all their actions are / To him appearing plaine and regular," but he has only to avail himself of this instrument to see what Browne does (lines 849–850). When the speaker drops his pastoral mask and ceases to be a "singer," we encounter him as a medium for another perceptual medium.

The spectatorial body on which the author stakes his authority is superior to all bodies, noble and common, offering a denaturalizing perspective on what seems "regular"—"Subjects drent / In foule opression by those high in seat." In the 1640s, revolutionary pamphleteers would use the lens for a complementary purpose: to render alien the perspective from which revolution appeared outside the natural course of things. Positing an isomorphism between the *arcana naturae* and *arcana imperii,* a pair of 1644 pamphlets blazoning lenses on their title pages present their assertions not as the subjective certainties of faith, much less opinion, but as *findings.*[47] Recasting political argument as spectatorial instruction, these pamphlets present themselves as instruments and their readers as experimentalists in the making.

Brandishing a title that is comically lengthy even by contemporary standards, the first pamphlet compresses a mass of information into a tiny frame, resulting in ever-diminishing letters that call for the progressively sharpened sight it promises to deliver: *A New Invention; or, A Paire of Cristall Spectacles, By helpe whereof may be read so small a Print that what twenty sheetes of paper will hardly containe shall be discover'd in one; besides, they have such a speciall vertue in them, that he that makes right use of them though hee hath beene blinde three or foure yeares will recover his sight very perfectly.* Presenting the span of time since the outbreak of the conflict as a text requiring close reading, the pamphlet presents itself as an instrument to make this text legible. At first glance, however, *A New Invention* appears to be a royalist pamphlet: "Why, how now *England,* what turned Rebell now, that hast so many hundred yeares been famous through the world for thy fidelitie to thy Prince?" To make "right use" of these spectacles, the reader must invert the meaning of all its statements. The author rehearses soothing and familiar orthodoxies: "let me a little rubbe your memories with the maine Motto of the Nation, *Feare God and honour the King.*" With enough repetition, we "shall in a few yeares be as well content with our fetters as we are now with our freedomes, when wee have beene well disciplin'd and curb'd a while, we shall forget." Welcoming the return to law and order and peace, the reader will embrace the Pope along with the king's "cutthroate Councellors," who are "as free from feare as they are from honesty." The only "Reformation . . . worth talking of" will then be the existence of "no Sects nor Schismes but all of one Religion, no Preaching in houses then nor any where else."[48] To see through the pamphlet's literal meaning is to see through the pamphlet into the world; the inversion that this instrument requires its user to perform enacts the revolutionary program of turning the fallen world upside down. To see things properly is to be driven to invert them, in the same way that the dominant mottoes rehearsed by the pamphlet—fear God by loving the king—beg to be inverted. (Such inversion would continue in Shaftesbury's repeated attempts to "apply the discipline, the *inversions* again.") As Sharon Achinstein observes, by engaging the reader in "correcting a false impression, the author of the pamphlet encourages a process of reading by which a reader becomes capable of resisting propagandistic assault."[49] That the pamphlet is itself a piece of propaganda hardly matters, since the reading skills it seeks to impart could be applied to any text at all. Denaturalizing the key terms of the conflict—schisms, rebels, God's anointed, loyalty, treason, the Protestant religion—the pamphlet apprentices the reader in the labor of seeing through their customary uses, permitting her to become acquainted with her own capacities as a critical observer as she exercises them. The author concludes,

> he that hath any sight left may see enough here to informe his Judgement, how and what religion is endeavour'd to be maintained, and by that meanes put his resolution into a posture that may shew him to be a lover of the Truth so happily discovered, which is only aim'd at in the framing these new fashion'd Spectacles. (6)

He "that hath any sight left": the author pretends to address a selective audience culled from the public at large (the tiny print with which the pamphlet concludes confirms the reader's membership in this sharp-sighted group). The satire is hardly difficult to decode, but this appeal to exclusivity gestures at a spectatorial hierarchy that the writer hopes to erect in place of the existing one, a hierarchy based not on the curbing and forgetting of freedoms, but on the expansion of freedom and the vigilance that can protect it. The author is at the top of this spectatorial elite, since it is he who has undertaken the "framing" of "these new fashion'd Spectacles." These spectacles now frame the reader, who will "see enough here to informe his Judgement"; this act of virtual witnessing will commit him to a "posture": this was the goal at which the invention was "aim'd." Enjoining the reader to show himself as a "lover of the Truth," these glasses make the contemporary scene legible to the user while compelling him to adopt a role within that scene. The glass offers the reader a depersonalized role to fill, that of an ingenious lover of the truth. The glass is really the kingly scepter of the public, an instrument of the corporate truth producer's office.

The sequel is entitled *The Second Part of the Spectacles; Or, Rather a Multiplying Glass, fitted for their use, which are not able to see with Spectacles: By the helpe whereof may be discerned many things at distance, which are hardly to be seen otherwise, and not ordinarily taken notice of.* This text makes another distinction in the spectatorial hierarchy, inserting an intermediate rung between the merely imperceptive and the almost blind; the progression Browne made from spectacles to the multiplying glass is traced again. Despite the invocation of a more powerful technology, the inversions performed by this pamphlet are no more or less straightforward than before: a *"true Protestant"* is defined as a "Papist" who exhibits "an implicite faith, and blinde obedience to the Church" and so forth. The speaker baldly states that "though I have gotten a *Glass,* to discerne things which are so far off from the common capacity, yet I will not beleeve what this *Glass* helpes me to see," yet such is the power of this glass that he is finally forced to. The pamphlet offers evidence for its putative position—details about the Spanish match and the Scottish war—whose accumulated force compels a conversion. The fiction promoted by this text is a transcendental one, of opinion's supplanting by evidence—the fiction that opened up a space for a "culture of fact."[50] The pamphlet ends with an emotional plea; the author, having "come thus farre in Speculation," addresses the reader directly, and the lens conceit gives way to a testimonial: *"I* now professe my self a *Puritan,* a *Round-Head,* or any thing, so you please to call me a Convert." He has seen "what Religion is intended" by the king: "If *I* should relate what *I* have perceived . . . without so much as the helpe of a *Multiplying Glass,* it were enough to mollifie a Malignant of Marble."[51] Now the speaker is himself the glass, through which the reader can discern the real things "ordinarily" distorted and falsified by names such as *Puritan* and *Round-Head.* Although in departing from the conceit the author skirts dangerously close to expressing mere opinion, the personal appeal, itself disciplined by reference to actual experience, is a privilege earned by having come so "farre in Speculation."

Both pamphlets hold out the possibility of attaining a disinterested perspective on the conflict. Rather than openly making the case for any particular doctrine or discipline in the national church, they focus on how implicit faith and blind obedience limit the public's opportunities for "discovery"—which the lover of truth will embrace as an end in its own right. The truths "so happily discovered" by the "new invention" generated more instruments of truth, spin-offs such as the eye salve. *The Eye Cleard, or a Preservative for the Sight* even begins with a reference to the spectacles pamphlets: "What's here! another paire of Spectacles?"[52] In these texts, the appeal to experience is no longer an Aristotelian reliance on common experience, as codified by trusted authorities. Even while condemning Laudianism as a dangerous innovation, the author who sarcastically offers to "rubbe your memories with the maine Motto of the nation, *Feare God and honour the King,*" is elevating the model of natural history—the accurate description dependent on eyewitness testimony—over the appeal to history as precedent. And, as in Boyle's *Occasional Reflections,* the artisanal reshaping of the glass itself carries a lesson; the instruments used to look through false images must themselves be subjected to continual reformation.

In a rearguard action, royalist propaganda of the period is crowded with sinister illusion-producing instruments that alienate people from the natural and correct way of seeing things; so the distinctly Puritan polemic against false mediators gets turned against its best practitioners. But these pamphlets often suggest that the right way to see things is not to see them fully. While the author of *The Cuckoo's Nest at Westminster* glances at the spectacles pamphlets when he declares that "the People may now see (without spectacles) how grossly they have been disceived," the author of *The Great Assises Holden in Parnassus by Apollo and his Assessours* (in which Apollo puts journalists on trial for their desecration of letters) accuses the author of *The Spye* of using

Old Galilaeo's glasses . . .
Which represented objects to his eye,
Beyond their measure, and just symmetrie,
Whereby the faults of many did appeare,
More and farre greater, then indeed they were
                    . . . though he indeed
So blind was, that he did a leader need.
He was accus'd that (like *Aglauros*) hee
Forbidden objects had presum'd to see.[53]

Blaming the starry messenger, the author seems to suggest that the telescope exaggerates or multiplies sunspots; he also implies that the king's faults, or spots, had a certain "just symmetrie" when viewed naturally. Extending the scope of the people's vision, these "new-fashion'd Spectacles" distort the natural relationship of the people and their rulers, a relation whose apparent naturalness depends on public business remaining just beyond the scope of public—that is, popular—visibility.

The charge of exaggeration or even falsification may reflect the fact that many astronomers who tried to observe sunspots after Galileo found that they were indeed missing. As far as Galileo was concerned, the spots' lack of permanence—their patterns of change as they came together and dispersed—actually "testified to their nonartifactual nature." The credibility of the visual narratives that he made to testify to their existence thus depended not just on their detail but on "the *frequency of the sampling*"—on a periodical logic. As Mario Biagioli argues, an incorruptible, unchanging celestial body had no place in Galileo's dynamic cosmos.[54] Increasingly, it had no place in the realm of letters either; the continually changing "face of things" made serial publication a necessity.[55] Demonstrating an intimate familiarity with contemporary newsbooks, *The Great Assises* ends up testifying, against itself, to the centrality of periodical form to public life. The crimes against letters it enumerates are no longer crimes; periodical form and the public it sustains have taken up permanent residence in the realm of letters and redefined it.[56]

The effort to form an ingenious public organized around the will-to-see extended artisanal epistemology beyond its conventional bounds; Nathaniel Bernard's *A Looking-Glasse for Rebellion* redescribes this expansion as an effort to make everyone a mechanick. Forced out of his calling by

"Rebells" who told him he was an "able bodied man, and might goe *worke*," he has made himself "fit" for a new calling in *"Manuall arts"*: "And now you have, my first *handy-worke, A Looking-glasse* of Rebellion"—a glass that "discovers" rebellion to be witchcraft.[57] John Eachard complained that the example of the new science was politically dangerous; it set an example that made "every man when he pleases a rational rebel."[58] Following such examples, the people had come *too* "farre in Speculation." Indeed, the persona we see taking shape through these "new fashion'd Spectacles" was easily assumed by the readers who used them, since this persona—unlike that of the cavalier, for whom personal allegiance *was* principle, and personal style an indwelling trait (if not a birthright)—seemed to adhere to no person at all. To prove one's access to the depersonalized insight that distinguished their inventor, one had only to assent to their discoveries or confirm them by experience. Merely to use these spectacles was already to assume the flexible "posture" of "a lover of the Truth"—to become part of the spectatorial body under construction: a body empowered to produce a demythologizing revision of the world, and to subject that new world to further revision.

The Last Instructions to a Painter

After the Restoration, the lens continued to serve the aims of rational rebellion. The most important satire of the first decade of the Restoration, Marvell's *The Last Instructions to a Painter,* begins with the microscope and ends with the telescope.[59] Opening in the studio of a state painter, whom Marvell subjects to a regimen of raillery and mock-instruction, the poem enacts the experimentalist redirection of the mimetic impulse, tracking the process by which Marvell steers the painter away from an art of idealized representation to one of aggressively innocent investigation. Intervening in Lady State Britannia's last sitting for her portrait, Marvell interrupts the painter to suggest he exchange his brush for a microscope; by the poem's end, Marvell has commandeered his assistance to produce a different kind of portrait, a Galileo-style exposure. In between, Marvell elaborates a whole experimentalist politico-poetics dedicated to exposing the causes of both the Dutch naval victory at Medway and the crisis of political representation in Charles II's England.[60] For Marvell, as for Browne, the literary lens is an instrument for critical reflection on inherited mimetic norms, for behind the figure of the painter is another poet, Edmund

Waller, author of *Instructions to a Painter*. A celebration of the English naval victory at Lowestoft that pandered to the contemporary fashion for heroic portraiture, the poem elicited a series of satiric sequels offering the painter further *"Advice."* Waller's poem was reformed by multiple hands into a self-interrogating instrument of discovery, one that revealed *"the History of our Naval business"* instead of painting over it.[61] *The Last Instructions* may be the only one of the series composed by Marvell alone.[62] Although at times the "dear *Painter"* whom Marvell treats with a mixture of condescending affection and aggression is mocked simply for being a painter (as in such quips as "let some other Painter draw the sound"), he is primarily attacked as a producer of state propaganda—attacked, that is, in terms applicable to Waller himself, who, having been exposed by earlier poems, is primed for rehabilitation in this one.[63] While continuing to badger the painter with advice, Marvell widens the scope of the lesson: modeling a Baconian reformation of the active life, he apprentices the painter and the reader to the experimental life, an ongoing public work that will require the overhaul of political and literary representation alike.

The poem's ambitions are asserted through its wandering focus: like Donne's soul, Marvell's spectatorial body is granted the "liberty to wander through all places, and to survey and reckon all the roomes," to "comprehend the situation, the dimensions, the nature, the people, and the policy," not of the universe but the nation. Such vast comprehension makes the poem as onerous to read and talk about as an old newspaper; the breadth and density of its topical allusions force the critic into the confining path of line-by-line exegesis. The critic's inconvenience is Marvell's triumph: the poem's density of contemporary allusion testifies to its investigative rigor, as the pains Marvell has taken must be taken again by the reader. The privileges of the spectatorial body must be earned, not just by the investigator but the virtual witness as well. Pierre Legouis's description of the poem suggests above all a newspaper: it "tells nine or ten months of the history of England, diplomatic negotiations, parliamentary debates, naval operations, intrigues of the bed-chamber or the lobby, and his narrative seems to be written day by day, as the events impress him." Produced according to a periodical logic, the poem exposes the limits of painterly ekphrasis; its aim is progressive apocalypse, a lifting—and, ultimately, a tearing—of the veil.[64] The poem does not offer its perspective as the possession of an individual psychology; rather, the reader assumes it while it is still under construction and being put to use. Exposed to its findings in real time, the reader is enlisted in an ongoing experiment in assisted observation, and incorporated into the body that performs it.

What the experiment repeatedly uncovers is the "Gross Bodies" and "grosser Minds" of the aristocracy (line 179). Arguing that the poem is structured by an opposition between innocence and appetite, Steven Zwicker has suggested that Marvell's decision to attack political corruption by depicting aristocrats in the throes of voracious sensual appetite was a means of alluding to the king's personal fault in the Medway debacle: by implicitly addressing Charles's debaucheries through theirs, Marvell is able to link the king's inability to control his own body to his poor management of the body politic.[65] My reading supports this view—not, however, with respect to the virginal innocence of "the loyal Scot," the ephebe who plays uncomprehendingly at combat "as if in sport" and gets killed, but in relation to the investigative innocence of the virtuosi, who emerge, seemingly gratuitously, as the exemplary foil of the painter, the aristocracy, and Charles himself (line 666). The poem is indeed structured by an opposition between innocence and appetite, but it splits the first term of that binary in half. If the youthful Douglas (whom virgins can only "hope . . . is a Male") exemplifies innocence as inexperience, the virtuosi demonstrate how experience can be innocently used.[66] Marvell, in turn, demonstrates the most productive use to which their investigative arts can be put: to expose monarchy's artificial basis.

Marvell does not simply aim the lens at the country's rulers to expose their profligacy and bungling. Instead, he ironically imputes to them a passion for empirical investigation, then exposes them to be fraudulent virtuosi, too mired in the senses to make rational use of the evidence they provide. Why Marvell would go to such lengths to expose their inadequacy in an area where most never pretended expertise is worth exploring in greater depth than critics have.[67] The painter and the frenetically ineffectual aristocrats that crowd his portrait are failures in their respective tasks of representation, and it is as a labor of representation—carried out in public, for the public—that experimentalism emerges as the poem's satiric norm. As we will see, the contrast between private appetite and public work is as central to this poem as it is to Royal Society literature.

Marvell's personal connections are elusive, but we know he had a personal link to the virtuosi through Katherine Boyle, whom he may have met through Milton, since both were frequent visitors at Milton's house in Petty France; when Katherine Boyle's daughter, Frances Jones, died, it was Marvell who wrote the epitaph.[68] But although the virtuosi provide both a model for Marvell's art of testimony and a foil for its satiric butts, they do not appear in the poem as human beings with passions and interests of their own. Of course, the poem's cast of characters includes some actual Fellows (most notably, Peter Pett), but only Hooke is presented *as* a Society Fellow, and he appears through his instrument, the artificial organ that serves as the prosthetic source of Marvell's authorial power.

Like the modest virtuoso who became nature's torturer when he had his instruments in hand, Marvell's role as the poem's resident curator blends two innocent personae: a naif who marvels at the inventions of the nation's rulers and a ruthless inquisitor who labors to expose them. The work performed by this double persona arrests the painter's descent into corruption; interrupting the painter "er'e thou fal'st to work," Marvell devotes the rest of the poem to reversing that fall (line 3). He begins by ingenuously suggesting that the painter consider an approach more appropriate to his debauched subject; obscene graffiti might be more fitting media with which to "match" his "skill" to England's "Crimes" (line 13). As James Grantham Turner observes, Marvell presents these indecorous forms of expression as enabling a decorous adaptation of manner to matter.[69] Thus begins the theme of the aristocracy's riotous submission to fallen nature, in which the painter-as-propagandist is obliged to collude. As a falsely idealizing mimetic "mirror," the state painting (in either its graphic or textual forms) is a literal work of collaboration. Thus when we encounter Lady Castlemaine, one of the king's most visible and powerful mistresses, "Poring within her Glass" as she "re-adjusts / Her looks," *looks* is degraded from an action to a surface, and the two face-painters become co-conspirators; the painter must paint "Her, not her Picture, for she now grows old" (lines 87–88, 80). Having painted over her defects like a makeup artist, he might as well benefit from his work: Castlemaine worries that she has lost her seductive power; Marvell suggests that the painter, with the king's blessing, undertake a trial of that power. Alternatively, he might attempt a more innocent form of penetration, and "With *Hook* then, through the *microscope,* take aim" (line 16). Marvell makes the microscope a weapon; perhaps by imitating the rage in which Protagenes hurled his sponge at the canvas, the painter might achieve "by a lucky blow, / What all thy softest touches cannot do"; an exposé of the debauched state would itself be a blow to it (lines 27–28). For such a testimonial art, the microscope is far more suited than the brush; it can "score out" its subject, just as Marvell's "compendious" poem will (line 15).

He first takes aim at Lord Clifford, revealing him to be a louse that, like the insect in Hooke's *Micrographia,* is smaller than the staff he carries as Comptroller (a human hair in Hooke's engraving), unequal to and dwarfed by his office.[70] By the end of the poem, this instrument will reveal how the "smallest Vermin"—"scratching *Courtiers*"—can "undermine a *Realm*" (lines 981, 978). But these vermin are presented as perverted experimentalists from the start. Thus Henry Jermyn, Earl of St. Albans, "full of soup and gold" (a pun on bullion) appropriately shares his name with Bacon, since "never *Bacon* study'd Nature more" (lines 29, 36). Marvell's St. Albans studies nature only in the sense that he pays practical regard to its demands; as the references to animals that clutter his description make clear, he resembles "bacon" only in being a pig. As Henrietta Maria's "Stallion," he is also "Member'd" like a mule (lines 30, 34): as Zwicker observes, "the language conjoins sexual and physical appetite; ingestion and copulation are one."[71] Anne Hyde, the Duchess of York, is also an assiduous conductor of mock-experiments, a better philosopher than Margaret Cavendish because, in a twist on the example set by Archimedes, she conducted her "Experiment upon the *Crown*" in the nude, angling for the throne by seducing the Duke (line 52). Whereas Archimedes was so excited about his discovery he forgot he was naked when he ran into the street to proclaim it, getting naked was the very aim of this experiment, an Adamite rather than Adamic one, elevating the "rare Inventress" to the *"Highnesses Royal Society"*—a society here identified entirely with the sensitive bodies of its rulers (lines 57–58). Her savvy, Marvell notes admiringly, has resulted in the perfection of an "Engine" for shortening the term of pregnancy, enabling her to give birth two months after marriage, as well as a new poison, which she poured into Lady Denham's cocoa (line 53). Marvell directs the painter to represent this attempted murder innocently—as another experiment:

> Express her studying now, if *China*-clay,
> Can without breaking venom'd juice convey.
> Or how a mortal Poyson she may draw,
> Out of the cordial meal of the *Cacao.*
>
> *(lines 65–68)*

Obviously, such investigation permits her not to control fallen nature but to give in to it; as we leave her, she is still at work on her final invention, an unbreakable dildo (line 60). Similarly, Castlemaine has "Discern'd Love's Cause" in her lackey's drawers (lines 81–82). Driven by animal passions and selfish interests, these investigations into causes are clearly perversions of innocent inquiry, attempts to secure carnal relief and individual estates rather than "the relief of man's estate" as a whole.

Ironically, it is when the focus shifts from the boudoir to the floor of Parliament that the painter can stop for a "rest"; the House is "thin" and the "small Arts" on display make few demands on his own (lines 117, 235, 118). But this declaration shows Marvell's art of exposure at its most hardworking. The Royal Society adopted the procedures of the House to declare itself as a representative body; Marvell brings that body's observational arts to bear on its "degenerate" original. When he observes that the House is thin he is revealing something important: absenteeism undermined claims to representation.[72] It was taboo to publicize Parliamentary proceedings; how statutes were produced was not supposed to be public knowledge. Because of texts like Marvell's, however, it could be. By exposing backstage machinations behind England's naval defeat through scribal publication, *Last Instructions* reveals causes that were supposed to remain invisible: Marvell "fills in the parliamentary background to the Chatham disaster by relating it to the issue of Supply," revealing that funds that should have been spent on the war were spent maintaining the court.[73] In doing so, he restores to the body of the state its inherent spectatorial privileges, improperly arrogated by the House.

However dire in its consequences, what Bacon called "Civil action" appears comically inactive, as members of the court party prosecute their roles in various states of distraction and undress; "having lost the nation at *Trick track*," they wonder what they are going to do to get their credit back (line 109). In his *Account of the Growth of Popery*, Marvell compared the House to an alehouse, complaining that MPs "live together not like Parliament men, but like so many Good-fellows, met together in a Publick House to make merry"; in contrast to the coffeehouses, the House was not interested in conducting the public business. Charles famously joked that Parliamentary debates were "as good as a play," and Marvell turns the joke to account here.[74] The country's leaders treat Parliamentary business and the war effort itself as theater—or indeed, as a state painting, in which one

may "awe" with one's "Coife" (line 181). "No Troop was better clad," he says
of the king's "Procurers"; Sir Richard Powell is late because " 'twas so long
before he could be drest"; the king later waits "as at a Play" for the speaker of
the House to get dressed (lines 176, 173, 216, 854). And the "feather'd *Gallants*" who come down on the day of the great loss to be "Spectators safe of
the *new Play*," run away at the sound of gunfire when the spectacle becomes
real.[75]

   We get a heroic pictorial of sorts with the entry of the Dutch, but the
only truly martial-seeming English figure in the painting will be the soldier
who ran away from his post.[76] Marvell asks the painter to depict him as
ferociously as possible: "Mix a vain Terrour in his Martial look, / And all
those lines by which men are mistook"; the man who rowed away "unsing'd"
will be depicted in the commemorative painting as a war hero (lines 637–
638, 647). The quibble on *lines* glances back to the corrupt original of the
poem, Waller's *Instructions,* now being disassembled before the reader's eyes.
Michael Gearin-Tosh suggests that Ruyter's arrival moves the poem "to a
higher level of style and thought . . . [into] a world alive with nymphs and
gods. The court seems even more sterile by contrast. This is the right milieu
for Ruyter, a hero who hacks through Stuart subtleties and evasions like
Alexander at the Gordian Knot."[77] There are certainly gods present in the
scene, Aeolus "Puffs them along," but the effect is not quite that of a martial
victory (line 548). Marvell has wittily placed the Dutch fleet inside a state
painting come alive, a painting of which the Dutch are the subjects: a "sudden change" for sailors expecting to do battle (line 531). Having searched in
vain for an enemy, the men "sit and sing," while Ruyter begins preparing for
a sexual rather than military conquest: the sight of topless nymphs "Swells
his old Veins," inspiring him to shave, as "am'rous Victors" do before taking
the field, and an effeminate nation is "ravish'd" (lines 541, 532–533, 744).

   The nation's leaders, with their passion for penetrating causes, will seize
upon the shipwright and naval commissioner Peter Pett as the one responsible: "*Pett,* the Sea Architect, in making Ships, / Was the first cause of all
these Naval slips" (lines 785–786). An old republican who had served as an
MP in Richard Cromwell's Parliament (and whose supporters were now
smeared as sectaries), *"Phanatick Pett"* was a handy scapegoat, but the logic
that held him reponsible would blame God for the fall: "Had he not built,
none of these faults had bin; / If no Creation, there had been no Sin."[78]
Like the other causal histories produced by these counterfeit virtuosi, this is

a parody of Baconian ideology, identifying creation not as the medium (and final end) of paradisal restoration, but as the matter and cause of corruption. It is fitting that the attack on Pett assumes the form of a perverted Baconianism; this scapegoat of Restoration society was a founding Fellow of the Royal Society. Represented not in the capacity of an active virtuoso but as a threatened ideal in need of defense, Pett provides an occasion for Marvell to assume the mantle of the *political* scientist who can predict—and even shape—outcomes.

Although the poem was written after Clarendon's fall, Marvell gives us only the king's train of thought that led up to his disgrace. Remarkably, he presents himself as *directing* this train of thought. His belittling treatment of the "dear *Painter*" fluctuates into complete mastery as the scene shifts to Charles's own bedchamber, which becomes the stage for a wholly different kind of authorial performance. Ordering the painter to "Raise up" an image of a naked virgin in bondage, Marvell creates the conditions for the king to expose himself: naturally, Charles tries to force himself onto the allegorical figure (line 891). England has reassumed the form of Lady Britannia, but now the painterly emblem serves the purpose of an experimental demonstration; the tense shifts into the past as Marvell offers his relation of what occurred: her touch was "cold," and she "vanisht from his hold" (lines 903–904). The body of England cannot be held by, much less identified with, the sensitive body of its monarch (whose scepter and prick, as Rochester famously put it, were "of a length"). The portrait of the king resonates with that of St. Albans, "a priapic portrait of the contemporary public man that shrinks him in proportion to his swollen member." Exposed as its ravisher, the king is firmly distinguished from, then abandoned by, the country he is supposed to represent.[79] "Shake then the room, and all his Curtains tear," Marvell then commands, as he terrifies the king with the prospect of execution (line 915). The ghost of Charles I materializes like Hamlet's father, turning down his collar to reveal the "purple thread" around his neck—the seam between the head of state and its body—and advising his son that "who does cut his Purse will cut his Throat" (lines 922, 938). Once subjected to this vision, the king resolves on "*Hyde*'s Disgrace" (line 926). The scene underscores the wholly contingent nature of Charles's reign over a country that can dispose of its kings. There is a threat of violence here, but the real threat has already been carried out: to kill the king's mystical body, one only has to see through it.

Having compelled the painter to become an accomplice in this expo-sure and intervention—a spectatorial regicide—Marvell now dismisses him. Instead of "matching" crimes, the painter has exposed them: now "our Arts agree."[80] More strikingly, Marvell has imaginatively imposed his will on the king, who has received as much instruction as the painter. The poem's structuring contrast between private appetite and public labor begins to bear fruit, as Charles—now equipped to look through deceptive exteriors himself—is encouraged to undertake the "great work" of being his own *"Poet"* and *"Painter"* according to the model Marvell has provided (lines 931, 945, 948). Marvell has forced painterly celebration to yield to the arts of discovery and intervention, redefining the king as a public servant in the process: rather than a monarch invested with divine right, he is an office holder under scrutiny by a body he can never incorporate or "hold." We have had a glimpse into the state of mind that makes the "great work" of representation possible, during the mock-epic debate over the Excise. Among the MPs who resist the court party, representative identity is not merely a privilege of office but an aspiration that generates a discipline: "Each thinks his Person represents the whole, / And with that thought does multiply his Soul" (lines 269–270). As in experimentalist discipline, to mul-tiply (or magnify) oneself is to act *as* the social body, not merely in its name, while making one's perspective available to every other member of that body for further correction. Waller thus redeems himself in this scene not simply by resisting the court's demands but by swearing to "write / This Combat truer than the Naval Fight" (lines 263–264). As Waller's vow and the example of Marvell's own poem demonstrate, this labor of representa-tion cannot be contained within the House; it must be extended through perceptual mediums made available for public use.

After bidding "adieu" to the painter, Marvell takes a step back from his poem and, in an epilogue addressed "To the King," describes what he has done: "So his bold Tube, Man, to the Sun apply'd, / And Spots unknown to the bright Star descry'd" (lines 949–950). The intervention we have just witnessed is framed anew. As the sun, Charles is the object of scrutiny, whose spots can be descried—discerned, revealed, sketched, and published. As evidence of the identity of sublunary and celestial matter, spots reveal that the monarch is made of the same stuff as his subjects; the apparently natural institution of monarchy is a construction that the spectator might see through—and, in doing so, radically alter. The spectatorial regicide has exposed Charles as a fumbling private man in his bedchamber, vulnerable and under threat. Marvell's next step is to subject another "restoration" to innocent scrutiny: the ideologically potent symbolic identification of the king with the sun, which restored the monarch to the very residence from which the rest of humanity had recently been exiled.[81] The introduction of the king into the center of the solar system and relegation of his subjects to obsessed orbits, always in the sun's light or sight, combined the latest scientific findings with a discarded teleology to promote idolatry of the monarchy, and fear of its powers of surveillance. Marvell takes what is already a fulsome metaphor when addressed to the king and deforms it into a relationship of reciprocal identity, so that the sun becomes the Charles of the solar system (line 956). But Marvell's possession of a "bold Tube" turns this piece of flattery into a warning; Charles is being watched; he is being investigated. When Marvell graciously identifies Charles's spots with his advisors, the results are immediate: "Through Optick Trunk the Planet seem'd to hear, / And hurls them off, e're since, in his Career" (lines 953–954). Turning the contemporary scarcity of visible sunspots to account, Marvell presents it as evidence of the power of the lens as an interventionist tool.[82] Through a blending of modalities enabled by the puns on *descry* and *trunk* (telescopes were sometimes called "perspective trunks," but a trunk could also be a speaking tube or ear trumpet), Marvell suggests both that Charles receives this message through his optic nerve and hears it.[83] It is print that can be both seen and heard, read silently or aloud; the bold tube is the poem itself.

But the poem does not just convey instructions to the king. If the sun occupies the center and thus the privileged vantage point of the universe, Marvell's use of the bold tube has recovered that privilege for the marginal viewer. The metaphysical necessity of kingship, which it is the purpose of the painterly emblem of the sun-king to establish, is annulled as Marvell shows how kings pursuing the wrong "Career" are brought back in line: kings "oft have gone astray" and should not be ashamed to "learn the way," even from a "Peasant" (lines 959–960). Because of its strangely moving sun, some critics have argued that the poem is geocentric in its assumptions, even as it registers an awareness of the controversy surrounding the missing sunspots, which seems unlikely.[84] The metaphor of the sun-king, it becomes clear, has been used *only* to sustain the analogy of the poet to the user of a bold tube; once the topos has served this purpose, it is seen through and discarded. The "bright Star" that wanders lost through space is not the sun but merely a comet, whose "Career" may be extinguished at any time (Clarendon himself was compared to one at line 348). Reforming kings into the proper objects of popular observation and control, Marvell associates his instructional program with a toppling of the political hierarchy and the erection of a spectatorial one. This was a hierarchy keenly felt by actual lens-users, as Kepler's apostrophe suggests: "O telescope, instrument of much knowledge, more precious than any scepter! Is not he who holds thee in his hand made king and lord of the works of God!" The elevation of the optic tube over the kingly scepter itself reprises the lens-as-spade topos, an assertion, in the spectatorial register, that "the plough is of more dignity then the Scepter" (and certainly of more dignity than the priapic monarch's fleshy member).[85] By aiming this instrument at the powerful and *their* works, Marvell effects the transfer of power from the kingly scepter to the latest optic invention, his own poem. Pathetically trying to seduce a symbol, the king himself is an enfeebled, passive figure in his bedchamber; Marvell is the aggressive agent who terrorizes him into taking the proper career, a career whose success has been demonstrated to depend on the consent of others.

When Marvell orders the king to "Blame not the *Muse* that brought those spots to sight," he affirms that he is not imputing flaws and motives to the butts of his satire, only revealing them (line 957). The fact that he makes such objective claims for his art of discovery does not deprive the performance of expressive power. Having removed the virtuosi from their instruments, Marvell fills the space left by their personal absence with his own majestic but bodiless presence. Registered only as a series of imperatives directing an experimental demonstration, the spectatorial body protects its privileges while extending Marvell's authorial reach into the king's very bedroom. In Cowley's ode "To the *Royal Society*" as we have seen, as nature becomes a book, the body of philosophy undergoes a corresponding abstraction, finding an intangible but potent incarnation as the product of the instrument and the observing subject. The reader of nature is composed of the lens and the one who uses it; it is in this compound identity that we may find the "body absolute" of the experimentalist author, attempting to represent (and coax into being) a sovereign public.

Prior to this experimental demonstration, the poem's rapid shifts of focus have prevented the reader from focusing on any single character for long. As the painter's canvas has blended with the show of politics beyond its borders, Marvell has directed our attention to various corners of the political scene; prying into hidden motives here, accusing there, he has been the focus of our attention and admiration. His labors of observation and exposure seem heroic because of the span he has to cover and the depths he has to probe—and the names he has to name, at no small danger to his person. But this person is nowhere to be found in the poem. Authorial invisibility, reinforced by anonymous composition, acquires methodological import within the experimentalist frame. The authority of the textacle's author rests less on his personal signature than on what he can make visible; the heroic labor he invests in dragging remote objects and hidden process into public view *is* his signature. His authorial presence impresses itself on us purely through this labor; here, attention comes to *stand for* the self, which means that others can stand for, and as, that self as well.[86] Unlike the revelations of the lyric voice, the knowledge produced by this performance is presented as the rightful property of the public, even though it is first the product of the author's work of discovery; the poem's imperatives issue from an empty subject position, into which the reader—"with *Hook*"— can step. Rather than merely asserting or demonstrating the action inherent in the labor of contemplation, Marvell reforms his readers into the agents of such action, offering a Boylean relation, in real time, of the spectatorial arts that make the people a public: a corporate body that can "descry" the actions of those who claim to represent it.

Toward the end of the poem, Marvell relegates the allegorical personages that would be likely to populate a state painting to a formulaic couplet, enclosed in dismissive parentheses: "(But *Ceres* Corn, and *Flora* is the Spring, / *Bacchus* is Wine, the Country is the *King*)" (lines 973–974). This apparently innocuous couplet conveys the message of revolution: lining up the parts of the analogy, we find that the people or "Country" are in the position reserved for gods while the fleshly king is on the side of material objects with the tangible reality of corn and wine. The people of England are the royal society; the subjects of divine right, they constitute the true monarch. To restore that right, they must represent themselves, making their representatives the objects of innocent scrutiny and intervention. There was no excuse for "a Rational people" to stop working; printshops, scriptoria, and coffeehouses were filled with instruments to help them meet the demands of their office.[87] It is this king to whom the bold tube, Marvell's starry messenger, is being offered.

Instrumentalizing the Garden

The Last Instructions has never been praised for its lyric economy, but this apparent failure is a gauge of Marvell's success in extending empirical investigation into the domain of politics; instead of passages that are visually synoptic, we get passages compendiously crammed with names and events. The poem is the political equivalent of *Micrographia,* "scoring out" the events beyond the realm of popular visibility that result in public scandal. Elsewhere, however, instead of ostentatiously wielding the lens as a weapon, Marvell silently assumes its powers to focus on the natural world. In this less strenuously journalistic mode, he does more than any poet before him to reproduce the sensory disorientation and richness of experimentalist insight. The division of Marvell's oeuvre between the satires and the "garden poetry" reflects the adaptation of his instrument to its subject: the fallen world and creation itself.

Much of what we expect to find in nature poetry is purged from Marvell's, or rather reformed beyond recognition. Mythological allusions are turned against themselves to support a Baconian protest against the anthropomorphizing habits of nature's fallen observers, while plaints that one would expect to be sung by lovesick shepherds become the work songs of a modern independent contractor: the mower, whose economic self-assertion in the period reflected radical changes in the life of the countryside.[88] Examining nature as it is actually lived in and worked on, as the grounds of historical as well as seasonal change, these poems see through, and reform, the genres to which they belong; as in *Last Instructions,* the process of discovery begins with decomposing "all those lines" by which truth is "mistook." Following the example of Ben Jonson's *To Penshurst,* countryhouse poems focus relentlessly on festive consumption; *Upon Appleton House* directs the reader's gaze to the processes of production.[89] While Herrick's countryhouse poems figure agricultural labor as an extension of festival mirth, the accounts in *Upon Appleton House* of harvesting hay and grazing the stubble are shot through with references to the Leveller insurgency, as well as to the "true Levellers" or Diggers, blending an awareness of seasonal rhythms with a historical alertness occluded by the ritual year.[90] And in "The Garden," Marvell engages, and subverts, the lyric tradition of "self-consuming" paradisal representation that had been reinvigorated by the cavalier poets. Rather than celebrate a paradise safely lost, or contained within the *hortus conclusus,* the poem releases the garden into the world.

Although space does not permit a full reading of what Turner calls the most complicated topographical poem in English, it is worth noting that this countryhouse poem is also a textacle, whose shifts of scale suggest the elastic perception of a Lockean angel. It is largely because of these shifts that so many of its images stand, as Legouis suggests, "in the disputed territory between the serious and the burlesque."[91] T. S. Eliot famously complained that *Upon Appleton House* abounded in "conceits, distended metaphors and similes," images that were "immediately and unintentionally ridiculous," "absurd," "undesirable," "over-developed or distracting," images that "support nothing but their own misshapen bodies," symptoms of the mid-seventeenth-century erosion of wit that permanently "injured the language." As R. I. V. Hodge points out, these often seem less like images than "meticulously managed optical illusions, with all the necessary equipment provided."[92] Thus instead of simply seeing cattle in the distance, we see them as fleas waiting to be magnified into cows, making Davenant's "Universal Heard" at once less recognizable and more startlingly perceptible than we will find it to be in *Gondibert:*

> They seem within the polisht Grass
> A Landskip drawn in Looking-Glass.
> And shrunk in the huge Pasture show
> As Spots, so shap'd, on Faces do.
> Such Fleas, ere they approach the Eye,
> In Multiplying Glasses lye.
> They feed so wide, so slowly move,
> As *Constellations* do above.[93]

The "polisht Grass" is a "Looking-Glass" on which the cows are painted (landscape paintings on glass being a contemporary fashion), but the glass we have been looking at suddenly becomes a glass we are looking through, first at fleas and then at slowly moving constellations. As in Browne and the

spectacles pamphlets, the looking glass must be subject to continual transformation; as a polished mirror becomes a microscope, and then a telescope, the cows are seen as pimples, fleas, and stars.[94] This alien experience
of the familiar world is, as Hodge says, meticulously managed and curated,
but it is not an illusion. Here, as in the other analogies Eliot calls over-
developed, it is the conditions of observation themselves that are exposed: x
is not compared to y; rather, x as seen from point p is compared to y as seen
from point q. As Marvell's dig at Davenant suggests, the experimentalist
poet does not treat any concrete noun "universally"; each thing is apprehended at a certain moment and place, under particular perceptual conditions which themselves become the object of scrutiny. Each thing, in other
words, is appreciated and cultivated as a fact, a thing made.[95] What Eliot
called the dissociation of sensibility, the fatal split between thought and
sensation, Marvell apprehended as a feature of the nature he sought to represent. The experimentalist author's first duty is to represent a world that
must be *made* visible. Rather than being pursued for their own sake, then,
novelty and strangeness function as indices of experiment. We do not recognize this countryside because we are in the process of discovering it.

   Marvell's attempt to reveal the grounds of the visible extends in a very
literal sense to the ground itself. As Legouis observes, Marvell is "the poet
of grass": no nature poet before Marvell, from Theocritus to Spenser, lavished so much attention on the actual grass on which their pastoral flocks
grazed. After having been "flower-enamelled" for centuries, in *Upon Appleton House,* it never appears the same way twice; after being "vext" by the
sun and "levell'd" by the mowers, "the Abbyss . . . Of that unfathomable
Grass" through which men seem to dive becomes the "Table rase" of the
meadows, appearing again later in

> . . . the Meadows fresher dy'd;
> Whose Grass, with moister colour dasht,
> Seems as green Silks but newly washt.[96]

Rather than merely comparing the appearance of grass to green silk, Marvell figures the grass after the flooding as having been dyed—"with moister
colour dasht." And rather than imagining the grass splashed with a more
vibrant green, he makes the dye moistness itself, so that the artisanal effort
of dyeing becomes continuous with the laundering of silks by human

hands. Running together these actions through the medium of water, he uses the analogy between grass and silk to make visible both the processes that produce the appearances and the frames of reference that condition their reception by the spectator (clearly accustomed to clean silk garments). Each instant of perception is infused with an awareness of the pains spent to produce it.[97] This awareness includes the pains taken by the observer himself; to become an organ of such compendious awareness, the eye must be constantly exercised in observing itself. Marvell is continually engaged in grafting the artificial percepts of the spectatorial body onto those of the natural body, so that the eye is subjected to as much cultivation as the land it observes: a field of grass seen from a distance so great that the men in it appear like grasshoppers must in the following line be magnified so that the grasshoppers can dilate into giants. This famous passage clearly reflects on Richard Lovelace's use of the grasshopper as a royalist symbol. Here, however, the grasshoppers' elevation to the status of "squeaking, contemptuous overlords" is an accident enabled by the "temporary luxuriance" of the grass; exposing the conditions for their temporary (and doomed) elevation, Marvell's spectatorial body rises above them.[98]

The effort to reveal as much of the world in the grass as possible finds satisfaction in the effort to transform grass into a perceptual medium, which can be done with the alteration of a single letter; grass becomes glass. The treatment of grass as a reflecting surface, like water ("a green Sea") or glass, is of course a signature habit, as in "The Mower's Song" when Damon recalls how

> My Mind was once the true survey
> Of all these Medows fresh and gay;
> And in the greenness of the Grass
> Did see its Hopes as in a Glass.[99]

The grass once reflected not the mower's body but the green hope of his mind. In *Upon Appleton House,* however, grass becomes "unfathomable," not just an objective correlative of the observer's interior state or a "*Chrystal Mirrour* slick," but a looking glass of infinite depth that extends the realm of the visible (line 636). The transformation of grass into glass correlates with the reformation of the fallen, sensitive body into a spectatorial one. Since "all flesh is grass" (Isaiah 40:6), the poet's effort to transform the things of creation into instruments of truth begins with his own body—a body that, in the meadows sequence, expands to include others. We recall that, for the virtuoso, the sensitive body undisciplined by instruments and collaboration could only "rudely gaze" at the "Pictures" produced by fallen perception, pictures that were fit only for "children to admire and be pleased with." The observer who "greedily catches at the vain shews of *superficial* . . . imaginary appearances" was merely a consumer, not a cultivator, of the visible world.[100] Marvell draws the contrast between the productive observer and gazing consumer just as boldly when he imagines the grass that he uses as a lens actually being masticated by Davenant.

For before Marvell gets to work cultivating his percepts of the cows, he simply sees them on the razed field. Compared to "The World when first created . . . rase and pure," the field becomes a blank canvas stretched for Lely "to stain."[101] The sin that stained the original purity of creation assumes the form of paint, and painted cows in particular: "Such, in the painted World, appear'd / *Davenant* with th' Universal Heard" (lines 455–456). In *Gondibert,* as we will see, God's act of creation is described as perfectly captured in a painting: to render the original creation through painterly means, Marvell implies, is simply to reenact its corruption.[102] Marvell mocks Davenant's attempt to convey creation in a "painted World" by placing him inside it, as one of the cows that "rase" the grass "closer" than even the mowers did: "And what below the Sith [scythe] increast / Is pincht yet nearer by the Beast."[103] A painterly art of surfaces pinches—limits, constricts, shortens—occasions to make nature's depths legible. But what Davenant bestially consumes, Marvell vitrifies. Looking at, seeing through, and transforming it, he cultivates the land alongside the laborers.

These two registers of cultivation are not merely parallel; they come together. The laborers at work in the meadows sequence do not go about their business in decorous ignorance of the fact that they are being talked about.[104] When Thestylis cries out "he call'd us *Israelites,*" she does not merely break the frame of the poem, she expands it, responding with her own scriptural allusion not to mock Marvell but to "make his saying true" (lines 406–408). Unlike Montrose's pastoral speaker, Marvell does not establish elite community with his reader against the backdrop of rural labor, nor does he represent a laborer simply "talking back" to him. Rather than merely "reversing the gaze," she participates in it and subjects it to further cultivation. As Marvell establishes literate reciprocity with its agents, the scene of labor expands to comprehend a learned exchange, and for a moment, even the labor of authoring his textacle is gloriously shared.[105] The customary distinction between those who work on the landscape and those who wrench meaning from it falls away in this scene, whose central location in the poem is essential to the meaning of the whole. In the meadows sequence, we have stumbled into a world in the process of being restored to its paradisal model—a world being turned upside down. Our perceptual disorientation signals our entrance into a world prior to "the respect of persons." It is here, where personal identity seems most threatened, that the first person singular finally appears, for the first time in the poem: the "we" becomes an "I" only when its eye is collectivized.[106] The author "discovers" himself when he is entered into the company of others, his perspective shared and improved in a "levell'd space."

Thestylis is a fellow author not simply because she contributes some lines to the poem but because she is a co-curator of Marvell's perspective. Such is not the case with Prioress Langton, whose speech is responsible for many more lines (generating most of stanzas 13 through 25). The Prioress does not speak to Marvell or to the reader; her speech is part of a narrative set piece of historical retrospection, enclosed within and corrected by the poem. By recontextualizing her lines, Marvell decomposes them, just as the Fairfax family reforms the nunnery into a *"Religious House"* (line 280). She insists that the nuns "Live innocently"; among their tasks is the preparation of "mortal fruit" that they "pull" into candy—"Baits for curious tasts" associated with "sweet Sins." The nuns invest *cura* in the perversion of curiosity, turning the doctrine of *felix culpa* itself into a confection.[107]

The poem enacts a reversal of this fall. When Marvell describes the "naked equal Flat" of the meadows as the model that the *"Levellers* take Pattern at," he himself becomes a Thestylis, testifying to and building on the symbolic, and literally disorienting, use the "true Levellers" had already made of the land while they worked it (lines 449–450). Marvell has been extending the Diggers' experiment all along, replicating their effort to "temper" the perceptual and physical cultivation of the country into a single process. His ironic description of the changes of the meadow as scene-changes in a court masque plunges the trappings of kingship into the productive labor of those who until recently were the king's subjects.[108] In his description, this labor symbolically embraces not just the civil war (with agricultural equivalents of "Massacre" and "Pillaging") but the Digger program to reconstitute the English people as a single agent of innocent labor. Rather than a vengeful murder, the killing of the rail—"the king of quail"—is revealed as a mere side effect of the productive labor that forms a public. The contemptuous grasshoppers, the astonished cattle, and the slaughtered rail—Lovelace, Davenant, and Charles—are strangers to the paradise of pains under construction here, degraded to the status of onlooking beasts surrounded by producers.[109]

Of course, it is only after Marvell heads for the forest and becomes a "great *Prelate of the Grove*" that he adopts the full-fledged persona of an Adamic reader of *"Natures mystick Book,"* gleaning God's word from the "light *Mosaick*" in the trees and speaking the original language to call, and command, the birds (lines 592, 584, 582, stanza 72). But Marvell can only adopt this role ironically; rather than a witty conceit that gathers force and seriousness as it is developed, as in "To his Coy Mistress" or "The Garden," his performance as the first priest of nature becomes increasingly comic, climaxing in the sado-masochistic sequence in which he begs brambles and "courteous *Briars*" to "chain" and "nail" him, so "That I may never leave this Place" (stanza 77). As this popish reenactment of the crucifixion suggests, rather than restoring the world of Genesis 2:19, he has fallen into the ersatz paradise once inhabited by the nuns on the estate. "How safe, methinks, and strong, behind / These Trees have I incamp'd my Mind," he pretends to imagine, while actually "languishing with ease"; the nuns who sought to "restrain the World without" the convent also thought they saw in "holy leisure" the opportunity to "Live innocently" (lines 601–602, 593, 97–99). In assuming the posture of a "car[e]less . . . *easie Philosopher*," Marvell revives priestcraft as Hermetic mystery, parading his ability to read nature's book while keeping its contents secret.[110] The expansive first-person of the meadows is "pincht," and privatized. The spectatorial privilege Marvell ironically assumes here has not been collectively cultivated through a prosthetic source; it is asserted by fiat, and, since it has not been earned, it cannot be shared. The surges of perceptual energy that characterize the stanzas describing, and enacting, the cultivation of the land are therefore absent; we see him, not what he claims to see. In assuming the mantle of a great prelate, Marvell is most concerned with making an entertaining—and satirically instructive—spectacle of himself.[111]

A paradise this easily restored is just as easily abandoned, because it is an abandonment of everything paradise is to Marvell. As if forgetting his

desire to be nailed to the spot, he abruptly casts off his cope and leaves the
"Labyrinths" of the forest to take up the posture of an angler by the river
(line 622). Although Izaak Walton's *Compleat Angler* identified "the contemplative man's recreation" as "innocent," Marvell clearly disagrees, guilt-
ily doing away with his "idle Utensils" and "Toyes" when Maria walks by.[112]
The poem's image of a restored paradise is appended to her as a gallant
compliment, but it stands on its own. If the play-acting of the Hermetical
easy philosopher and the idle utensils of the angler fall comically short of a
paradisal and productive union of action and contemplation, Maria seems
to drag along behind her a trail of figures for that union, of cultivated fields
and purgatorial flames, of a looking glass and the purged eye that looks
through it. In her presence, "loose Nature . . . doth recollect" itself; the serious pun on *recollect* suggests that, in being restored, nature remembers
what it is (lines 657–658).

The restored state evoked through Maria is of a nature recollected
through purgatorial pains: "by her *Flames,* in *Heaven* try'd, / *Nature* is
wholly *vitrifi'd*" (lines 687–688). Marvell is probably riffing on James
Howell's occasional reflection on the art of glassmaking in *Epistolae Ho-
Elianae,* a collection of "familiar letters" on "emergent occasions" which we
know was a source for the poem:

> when I pried into the Materials, and observ'd the Furnaces and the Calci-
> nations, the Transubstantiations, the Liquefactions that are incident to this
> Art, my thoughts were rais'd to a higher speculation; that if this small
> Furnace-fire hath vertue to convert such a small lump of dark Dust and
> Sand into such a specious clear Body as Crystall, surely, that gran Universall-
> fire, which shall happen at the day of judgment, may by its violent-ardor
> *vitrifie* and turn to one lump of Crystall, the whole Body of the Earth.[113]

When folded into this scene of labor and "violent-ardor," the doctrine of
transubstantiation itself is reformed. As one who worked as a manager of a
glass factory, Howell's reflections on this art of conversion were not idle
ones. The artisanal labor that transforms dust, identified by the burial service with flesh, into "a specious [i.e., beautiful] clear Body" of crystal is continuous with the transfiguration of creation at the end of history. Observing
these transformations, Howell's thoughts are raised "to a higher speculation";
he is himself refined. The close association between the refining fire, the glass,

and the eye that employs it in turn shapes Marvell's figuration of Maria. A purgatorial fire whose flames have themselves been tried by a heaven as "pure, and spotless as the Eye," she is also the agent of nature's transformation into an equally spotless glass, the vitrified nature of Revelation.[114]

The heaven referred to here, however, is the *"Domestick Heaven"* of the family's discipline, of which she is the product (line 722). If Maria is now the agent of purgatorial vitrification, it is because she has been its object. The invidious comparison between Maria and women in general thus blends the imagery of cultivation into this fiery repertoire: other women whose only study is their faces are afraid to knit their brows at vice for fear of wrinkles, "When *knowledge* only could have fill'd / And *Virtue* all those *Furrows till'd*" (lines 735–736). Subjected to such cultivation, and *"Discipline* severe," Maria figures the purgatorial paradise of pains that served as the model for the experimentalist Eden and the experimentalist laboratory—and the paradise under construction in the meadows (line 723). A fit descendent of William Fairfax, for whom "Religion . . . dazled not but clear'd his sight," Maria is the agent, object, and now the instrument of innocent perspicacity, the product of a paradise of knowledge and tillage (lines 227–228).

This welter of figures does not, of course, settle securely on her person; she is simply the occasion for Marvell to articulate the labors of innocence enacted by his poem: the labor of refining sight into insight.[115] But since the comparison of a chaste and beautiful woman to a glass vessel was proverbial, boasting a long history in representations of the immaculate Virgin—free from the spot of original sin herself, yet central to the devotion that celebrated sin as the occasion of Christ's vicarious sacrifice—it is worth dwelling for a moment longer on how Marvell has transformed it here.[116] Marvell is reworking the figure in order to present glass as a perfectible (rather than already-perfect) substance—an object as well as an agent of improvement.

Howell's text is in fact deeply concerned with the improvement of glass. Traditional "forest glass" was characterized by a greenish color; but in the sixteenth century, English glassmakers had begun to use the ash of a marine plant called *barilla* (glasswort) as a fluxing agent, to produce fine transparent cristallo, often referred to as "Venice glass," suitable for use in lens-making. (In fact, the highest priority of Howell's superior, Sir Robert Mansell—a brother-in-law of Francis Bacon—was to improve and expand the production of crystal plates for lenses.) In the case of glass, increased transparency and perfection literally had a "green" cause—further motivating Marvell's association of glass with grass, since *grass* often referred to herbage in general.[117] This technological advance is registered at the very start of Howell's text. Explaining that he has been relieved of his duties as steward and sent to Italy in search of workmen and new materials, he jokes that if he had remained at the factory, he would have "melted away to nothing, amongst those hot *Venetians,* finding myself too green for such a Charge": Howell compares his unsuitability for the work to the unsuitability of the old product (3–4). In a later letter, Howell proves his usefulness as Mansell's Italian agent, securing for him a "commodity call'd Barilla" for making a "resplendent and cleer . . . Crystall Glasse" (40–41). It is possible that the sharp contrast Howell draws between mere forest glass and crystal glass relates to the difference between Marvell's forest and meadow "speculations"; it certainly strengthens the identification of the "Chrystal-pure" Maria as the product of laborious effort (line 694). An old figure for the immaculate virgin has been "Adamized": made to figure the progressive "transubstantiations" and improvements effected by labor.

Howell's text is suffused with wonder at productive knowledge and artisanal practices (and shot through with Baconian prejudices),[118] but as we progress through the letters and arrive at the 1640s, the connections between productive labor, spiritual purgation, and Adamic restoration become increasingly tight. He complains that "us poor Adamites" have "a kind of cloud upon our intellectualls that they cannot discern the true essence of things with that clearnes as the protoplast our first Parent could, but we are involved in a mist," but during his imprisonment in the Fleet for his (uncertain) loyalty to the king, this mist starts to lift.[119] The artisanal imagery of purgatory's proof text and his own factory experience come together to condition his experience and discovery, in his own experience of trial, of

> a chymicall kind of quality to refine the dross and feculency of a corrupt nature, as fire useth to purifie metalls, and to destroy that *terram Adamicam* in them as the chymist calls it . . .'tis fire can only rectifie, and reduce them towards such a perfection. This *Fleet* hath bin such a *furnace* to me . . . I have been heer time enough in conscience to pass all the degrees and effects of fire, as *distillation, sublimation, mortification, calcination, solution, descension,*

dealbation, rubification, and fixation . . . I who have so much dross and corruption in me, that it will require more paines and much more expence, to
be purg'd and defecated: God send us both patience to bear the brunt of
this *fiery* tryall . . . through a prison to Paradise.[120]

Thus purged, the corrupt Adamite makes his way back to the home of
Adam, "the protoplast our first Parent." If we characterize them purely by
their allegiances, Howell and Marvell might be said to be looking at the
same events through different ends of a perspective glass; but, as far as
Marvell was concerned, both were bearing witness to the same necessary,
natural, and productive process. If Marvell associated Restoration culture
with theatrical corruption, he (as Dzelzainis and Patterson observe) identified "the good old cause" with natural causes: the process of nature being
restored, or "recollected," to itself.[121] If the world outside the Appleton estate
is a creation "overthrown," the world within it is not a paradisal retreat
fenced off from the "rude heap," but rather *"Paradice's only Map,"* pointing
the way, through *"Discipline* severe," to the world's restoration—a restoration that in fact requires a world overthrown.[122] And in true experimentalist
fashion, the ends and the means of restoration prove hard to distinguish; the
productive labor of cultivating innocent perception, a labor now being undertaken by England's "Israelites," is constitutive of the state to be restored.

In "The Garden," the dreamy but active contemplation that Marvell
pursues in Nun Appleton's productive fields (and temporarily abandons for
easy philosophy) is presented even more explicitly as providing a virtual
experience of paradise as experimentalists imagined it: "that happy Garden-
state, / While Man there walk'd without a Mate" (lines 57–58). The beginning of the poem reworks George Herbert's "Redemption" to suggest that
"sacred Plants" from which redemption is to be sought actually grow
"among the Plants" themselves.[123] Consisting of "all Flow'rs and all Trees,"
the garden celebrated in this poem does not exclude any part of the created
world; the grounds of a restored paradise await cultivation everywhere (line
7). Marvell elaborates a millennial vision that consists largely in the prosecution of vision itself, conceived not as a mere metaphor for spiritual illumination but as a means for the world's restoration. The poem is directly
concerned with retrieving the concept of paradise from the dogma of its un-
representability, which again involves Marvell in the effort of decomposing

and recomposing "the lines" by which paradise has been "mistook." For "The Garden" is above all a rewriting of cavalier paradisal poetry; what we now know to be a Restoration poem offers us a counterrestoration.[124]

The notion that paradise cannot be imaginatively recovered, only glimpsed under the sign of its loss, is ideally suited to lyric, the form least equipped to take narrative responsibility for its subject.[125] Among the cavalier poets, the paradox that any effort to represent paradise reenacts the fall became a defining obsession. In Thomas Carew's "A Rapture," however, the self-consuming representation of paradise acquires a newly ambiguous character: using the garden as a lens with which to see through the sham of fallen existence, this poem attempts not merely to provide a view of paradise but the view *from* paradise. Undertaking an innocent critique of ordinary language, the poem is an instrument to reveal gaps between word and thing in fallen usage, but this experiment in Adamic renaming employs a strategy of reductive redescription; Carew restores innocence as mere disillusionment even as he makes disenchantment a condition of bliss. Marvell seems to have read this poem carefully, and reformed it in "The Garden."[126]

Carew describes a new world that is also the first world, characterized by freedom from Baconian idols of the tribe and mind, a world that one can enter simply by reforming one's perception of the present one: "be bold, and wise," the speaker urges Celia, "And we shall enter." The idol "Gyant, Honour, that keepes cowards out" cannot prevent the journeys of exploration undertaken by the valiant explorers who "daily sayle betweene / The huge Collosses legs" in order to reach "the blissfull shore." Recasting the Baconian motif of sailing beyond Hercules's pillars as a brave journey between the legs (the Colossus of Rhodes, also associated with Hercules), Carew folds the landscape of Elysium into the geography of the female anatomy; paradise becomes the body of "free woman" writ large. Reworking the Marian symbolism of chastity that shaped conventional representations of Eden as a garden enclosed, Carew maps paradise onto a sexually responsive female body, and "free woman" becomes the paradise she agrees to enter.[127] The imperatives and descriptions of a promised future state with which the poem begins fluctuate into present tense description, so that we witness the restorative discovery as it occurs.

In properly Baconian fashion, Carew's projected garden frolic incorporates technology into its vision from the start. As Celia's "rich Mine" of "virgin-treasure" is "to the enquiring eye / Expos'd," her body fills the land-scape, a hybridized expanse of snow and "polish'd Ivory" that nonetheless remains vegetal (lines 32–34, 30, 28). Fruits pop up everywhere in the "curious Mazes" of this paradise, including the "warme, firme Apple," topped with a berry, which he can taste without danger.[128] Just as Boyle responded to this curious fruit by subjecting it to an investigation that made its "degustation" redemptive, so Carew can fully relish his paradise without losing it. Like the virtuoso who allowed himself to be provision-ally seduced by the nature he then ravished, Carew puts his own sexual arousal and performance to curious ends. His "Chimmique skill" in culti-vating the sweets of paradise renders them benign; rather than simply fall-ing prey to natural impulses, he refines them, distilling the sweets of "Loves Alimbique" into a "great *Elixar*" (lines 76, 78). Through such cultivation, the fallen names that have clustered around the act of intercourse are jet-tisoned and idols like honor smashed. Baconian iconoclasm serves the cause of free love:

> . . . there, the hated name
> Of husband, wife, lust, modest, chaste, or shame,
> Are vaine and empty words, whose very sound
> Was never heard in the Elizian ground.
> All things are lawfull there, that may delight
> Nature, or unrestrained Appetite;
> Like, and enjoy, to will, and act, is one:
> We only sinne when Loves rites are not done.
> *(lines 107–114)*

Unlike Lovelace, who imagines golden age sex as mere rutting, Carew braids the refined arts of love into nature's fabric, just as Milton would do when celebrating "the Rites / Mysterious of connubial Love" in Adam and Eve's bower. The discovery that the names inhibiting sexual experimenta-tion are "vaine and empty" launches a true Baconian restoration, elevating the dweller of Love's Elysium above what Hobbes called "meer Nature" and fallen civilization at once.[129] Recovering a landscape of unfallen sexuality in which, by "sacred right," nature is assiduously cultivated to serve "unre-strained Appetite," Carew restores not a primitivist paradise but a georgic one, for love's rites turn out to be remarkably laborious (lines 155, 112).

We might imagine that "free woman" cannot become the subject of the freedom she represents, that the woman who is identified with paradise is effectively barred from it, as, passing through the legs of honor, she parts her own and disappears into topography. But in this mixed space, as in Milton's Eden, a feminized landscape can be the grounds of tireless female agency. Instructed by the "artfull postures" of the pornographer Aretino that are carved on every tree by "learned hands," each woman here studies "how to move / Her plyant body in the act of love" (lines 121, 123, 117–118). Like the books at Democritus's knee as he pores over the creatures, the texts are absorbed into a circuit of practice, but here texts literally inhere in the material of which they are made: trees.[130] Like a good experimentalist relation, these living texts are both the product and the source of active performance. Nature is obeyed here only after it has been rewritten, but such rewriting must follow the laws of its own production. Lucrece, Penelope, and Laura all make use of the lessons of experience, exercising their artisanal skill with the tempters they once shunned. Even Daphne

> . . . hath broke her barke, and that swift foot,
> Which th'angry Gods had fastned with a root
> To the fixt earth, doth now unfetter'd run
> To meet th'embraces of the youthfull Sun . . .
> Full of her God, she sings inspired Layes,
> Sweet Odes of love, such as deserve the Bayes,
> Which she herselfe was.
>
> *(lines 131–139)*

Thus unfastened, Daphne is free to chase after her erstwhile rapist and sing "inspired Layes" about her experience at his hands (filled with the spirit of her god, Daphne in fact is free to do anything but escape rape). The wound of division between lover and beloved is healed in an image of self-identity, with Daphne deserving the plant that she also is. Daphne's singing prevents the entire lyric tradition, which now unravels along with the "endlesse webb" of Penelope, who once "toyl'd for a name / As fruitlesse as her worke."[131] As Penelope takes up dancing before the Ithacan suitors, Petrarch permits Laura to dry the eyes whose tears once "did in such sweet smooth-pac'd numbers flow" (line 141). While the spring of the Petrarchan love lyric dries, art flourishes as embodied performance and curious cultivation.

Carew's dream of an "original" nature improved by art literally decomposes fallen literature while healing the rift between word and thing.

Fallen language rudely intrudes at the end of the poem, where, after railing against dueling as a custom imposed by honor against God's commandment, Carew concludes the poem with the question, "Then tell me why / This Goblin Honour which the world adores, / Should make men Atheists, and not women Whores" (lines 164–166). This question puts its addressee in a double bind: if she refuses to accompany him on his journey of exploration, Celia will reveal herself to be a craven idolator of "empty" custom, but if she demonstrates the philosophical valor required for the journey, she will expose herself as a natural whore (line 109). To conclude that everything we have read may be comprehended under the bare name of whoredom is to annul the poem; the reader is left to choose between the poem and the word. If the reader decides to see through Elysium as a false paradise, he, like the reader of the spectacles pamphlet, commits to a "posture"; he must defend the institutions of honor against the sixth commandment. But if he looks through Elysium, using it to see through custom (and its hidebound concept of innocence), he is faced with the imaginative task of envisioning how humanity's "sacred right" to experiment freely on the matter of creation can be restored. This was the right asserted by the Diggers when they acted with plow and spade (these projects of restoration share an identical structure and even issue in the same activity—tilling the female earth). But, as the self-delighted bravado of the final rhyme of *adores* and *whores* suggests, perhaps to assert that right is merely to embrace prostitution; and it is not clear whether, once mined, virgin treasure can remain paradisal ground. As its binary critical reception suggests, the poem remains ambiguously poised between opposites, modeling either an arduous Adamic journey of discovery into new conceptual territory or an Adamite pursuit of familiar fallen pleasures, a mocking seduction that presents "Deflowring the fresh virgins of the Spring" as if it were a labor of ingenuity.[132]

Marvell's rewriting of the poem tips the balance. "The Garden" expresses the Diggers' Baconian vision more closely, even though its speaker never lifts a spade. Like "A Rapture," the poem is a call to experiment. But if for Carew, innocent bliss is a condition enabled by clear-sightedness—a series of pleasures one is free to enjoy, or rather, work indefatigably at, after having seen through the laws of custom—in Marvell's poem, bliss consists in nothing but the innocent pleasures of clear-sightedness itself. Such clarity of sight results in "quiet"—a quiet presented not as passivity but as the continual apocalypse or unveiling that innocent observation is.[133] The poem's opening rejection of "busie Companies" does not elevate solitary contemplation over a life of action (line 12). Like Evelyn's treatise, Marvell renders the active life innocent by redefining it in experimentalist terms. All plants reproach men who strive for the palm, the oak, or the bays by "upbraid[ing]" such efforts, because the virtues these plants represent can be braided together, just as, together, all plants "weave the Garlands of repose" (lines 6, 8). The spiritual repose of these plants, like that of Marvell's garden enthusiast, expresses itself in productive activity.[134]

Marvell begins by repairing the bark from which Carew's Daphne "broke," insisting that Apollo and Pan desired not women but the plants into which they changed. Rather than attempting to prevent the tradition of love lyric by undoing its originary figures as Carew did, Marvell subjects those figures to a re-vision, making metamorphosis the goal of the chase.[135] Literalizing the laurel as an object of erotic desire, he treats the Petrarchan tradition as a lengthy gloss on a vulgar error: a misconstrual of "vegetable Love" as it originally flourished and is now revived in the famous vines, fruits, and grass in which the solitary Adamic wanderer can become ensnared and fall without sin or danger (stanza 5). In "A Rapture," words like *wreathes, entwine, unwreathe, twisted,* and *winding* run together the arms and legs of lovers with the vegetation that surrounds them, but here, rather than a garden sexed by man—and literally inscribed by Aretino—human sexuality is sublimed into the vegetable love that in his earlier, cavalier mode Marvell could only offer as a *reductio ad absurdum*.[136] Since he has conquered the temptation to personify the garden as woman, his stubbornly erotic attraction to it becomes evidence of his purity; his idyllic intercourse with nature is only made possible by the exorcism of "Passions heat" (line 25). This encounter recalls Thomas Browne's chaste wish to copulate without coition, like vegetation, yet it also evokes the sexed rhetoric of experimentalist investigation, and serves the same end.[137] Although fruits seem to be the aggressors in this encounter—dropping, crushing, reaching, and ensnaring while he merely stumbles, passes, and falls—the "curious Peach" declares that human cultivation has prepared this scene of ravishment. The trees may be inscribed with their own true names, but they are nonetheless inscribed. What seems like an assault undertaken by "meer Nature" has been curated as an experiment: a contrived experience of nature designed to yield knowledge.

It is easy to overlook the fact that it is not after the tussle with the melons and grass, but during it ("Mean while") that the mind "Withdraws" from these lesser pleasures (lines 41–42). The apparent contradiction noted by Robert Ellrodt—of "sensuous pleasures supposed to be free from sensuality"—vanishes, though the paradoxical energy remains; it is the paradox of empiricism itself.[138] In the act of immersing himself in, and being ravished by, the spectacle of nature, the Adamic garden-dweller looks right through it. His insusceptibility to sexual temptation extends to secondary qualities themselves; the one implies the other. In obedience to the experimentalist coding of percepts themselves as temptresses, the exclusion of the feminine terminates in the transcendence of appearance, as the speaker penetrates the world behind the visible one. The mind withdraws,

> Yet it creates, transcending these,
> Far other Worlds, and other Seas;
> Annihilating all that's made
> To a green Thought in a green Shade.
> *(lines 45–48)*

Being green, his thought partakes of the creation in which he is immersed, but annihilates it as well. Green thought would seem to resemble nothing green we have seen. It is green in the sense of being newborn, innocent, because deceiving color has itself been reduced to shade, with its ghostly overtones: what remains after annihilation. Hodge has made the indispensable suggestion that Marvell is drawing on Hooke's idea that all colors might be reduced to green's constituent colors, and the latest dating of the poem confirms the likelihood of the allusion. If Marvell is indeed referring to a green of this kind, the word acquires, as Hodge puts it, "a precise, even technical meaning" as an "atomic or ultimate green," the foundation of all color, perceived by a vision that has "contracted in an instant from an infinite universe to the ultimate constituents of matter."[139] We are granted a vision of nature that is brought forth by nature, as Geoffrey Hartman puts it, and in a very literal sense: this is a vision of nature that nature itself would recognize, a vision rationally reconstructed from the insufficient images generated and consumed by our sensitive bodies.[140] Green thought denotes the observer's ability to excavate, contemplate, and "see" the physical causes of color in the very act of reconstituting it again. The delving Adam and the Adam of Genesis 2:19 are once again contracted in the digging eye.

Hooke himself found this contraction a thrilling one, confessing as he shared his theory of color's origin that to his mind there was "nothing comparable to the ravishing pleasure with which a curious and well tempered *Green* affects the eye." The normally opposed operations of seeing and sensing come together here, as the ontological priority of green, discovered by a curious and well-tempered observer, provides an innocent basis for the "ravishing pleasure" it brings him.[141] Hooke and Marvell transform color into a testimonial of its own production, enjoying a rational and above all productive erotic union with nature, a union that spawns new experiences, and new facts. In contrast to Lely and Davenant's attempts to "stain" creation with artificial color, we recall that in *Upon Appleton House* Marvell reversed the process, "refreshing" dye itself into water, a clear medium through which the green of the grass was magnified. The transformation occurred figurally as well, as the flesh that grass figures was purified into glass, itself presented as an infinitely improvable perceptual medium—a sensuous renovation of the sensual. "The Garden" offers us the fruits of this transformation.

What at first seems to be a pastoral poem about recreational retirement becomes an experimentalist one about the re-creation of the world and the self through interventionist spectatorship. Rather than reproducing the effects of the lens, as in the perceptual dilations of *Upon Appleton House,* Marvell leads the reader through a rational reconstruction of the moment of innocent insight, as Petty did in his *History of Clothes.*[142] What he unfolds for us are the stages of the labor of looking through. The innocent observer's simultaneous commitment to physical engagement and sensory detachment is here anatomized into its discrete parts, as Marvell takes a tumble with the tempting fruits in the very act of annihilating their perceptual existence. Like a virtuoso, he describes that annihilation as a creative act of destruction: a spectatorial alchemy or "reduction to the pristine state" of green. When undertaken by the artificial organ and machined hand, the labor of observation "makes things appear that until now one wouldn't

know that they had been created."[143] Like Boyle in *Occasional Reflections,*
Marvell has taken the scene of the first disobedience, and all of its associations with sexual, intellectual, and gustatory temptation, and reformed it
into a scene of innocent knowledge production. In doing so, he combines
the aims of discovery and intervention into a single image of spectatorial
power that annihilates the difference between them. The result is an ecstasy, but when the soul takes flight from the body, it does so merely to land
in a tree just above: perched on a branch, it continues to work on itself,
whetting and combing its wings in preparation for a "longer flight."[144] This
staggered flight is less a figure of the soul's separation from the body than
their continued dialectical relation in and as the spectatorial body, engaged
in its own self-renovation in a paradise of pains.

Carew's rapture is thus redescribed as a progress. Rather than consisting in a single decisive movement from one place to another, the reformed
rapture is an ongoing Baconian "advancement," a necessary sensory disorientation that disorients paradise itself, distributing it across processual discoveries. While the following stanza makes explicit that this "wond'rous
Life" restores the "happy Garden-state" before humanity's division into
multiple subjects, the last stanza of the poem descends into an entirely different mimetic register, depositing the reader into a local garden with a local
feature, a floral sundial (lines 33, 57). Legouis articulates the feeling of
many readers when he remarks that the poem ends on a nonchalant note,
without "a real conclusion."[145] The sundial may be an ingenious piece of
work by a "skilful Gardner," but it can hardly carry the burden of emblem-
atizing nature's ultimate submission to rational and physical mastery in a
restored paradise; it is too particularly rooted in a contemporary place and
time for that (line 65). But the analogy of creation to a clock was a cherished experimentalist commonplace, and the figure of the skillful gardener,
like the "ingenious gardener" of Evelyn and Blith, suggests the tangling of
divine and human creation on which experimentalist mythology was
based.[146] The anticlimax is a necessary one, another version of the experimentalist text's refusal to end, since it implicitly tasks the reader-observer
with more to do: the poem's settling down into a locality suggests that the
purgatorial paradise consists in the work that awaits the ingenious gardener
in whatever garden lies to hand. Marvell concludes the poem by praising
the arrangement of flowers to reckon the "sweet and wholsome Hours" (line
71) as both ingenious and appropriate: how else should they be reckoned

in paradise? The garden, now a space consecrated to progress, is also an instrument with which to gauge that progress. It is a clock, as Nun Appleton is a map. The insistence in both poems on the instrumentality of cultivated land in a larger program of paradisal recovery justifies the poet's choice to make it the site of his own self-cultivation as an instrument of truth: a lens.

As in Cowley's ode "To the *Royal Society*," the rationally mediated distance that permits penetration of nature's interior enlarges the scope of the viewer's sight and power while alienating both from his actual physical self. Accordingly, under his gaze things themselves cease to resemble themselves, becoming evidence or testimonies of something else. The open-ended metonymic progression of *Last Instructions* and *Upon Appleton House,* in which each exposure occasions another, characterizes this investigative sequence nicely; what the observer is discovering is the reach of his own spectatorial agency.[147] But in Marvell's poetry, as in experimentalist rhetoric, the observer's self-regard adheres not to a private person but to the human observer in his iterable, Adamic capacity. A spectatorial self-assertion that adheres to nobody finds an appropriate tonal register in Marvell's coolness, the almost inhuman combination of immersion and detachment that characterizes both his satiric and garden modes.[148] This coolness characterizes even his garden ecstasy, which stands to reason, since the pleasures offered by the garden state are precisely those enabled by depersonalized sensory experience. Reciprocally, Marvell's satiric mode is divorced from any hint of personal vengeance, even when he threatens Charles with assassination. Whatever indignation *Last Instructions* arouses is proper only to the royal society of the public. In all these poems, rather than representing an expressive lyric self, Marvell offers us a demonstration of his experimental attempt to inhabit the subject position of the innocent observer. The immersive annihilation he models for us is the work of the Adamic body we have seen variously inhabited by Winstanley, Fox, and the virtuosi, the body whose excavating gaze causes fallen surfaces to fall, revealing things themselves—and the "indifferent matter" that constitutes both them and their observers.[149]

When Allan Pritchard identified "The Garden" as a Restoration poem, he also identified its prompt: Cowley's death and the posthumous publication of his *Works* after his highly publicized rural retirement. (It was Cowley's misunderstanding of Evelyn's celebration of the active life, we recall,

that led Evelyn to so much cowardly backpedaling.) Pritchard demonstrated that the poem is filled with echoes of Cowley's *Essays* and Katherine
Philips's *Poems,* a book prefaced by a commendatory poem and an elegy by
Cowley and featuring a poem about his retirement.[150] *Upon Appleton House*
and "The Garden" are both, then, occasional reflections on famous retire-
ments, seizing the opportunity to reform retirement into an active effort of
estranged contemplation—just as, working from the opposite direction,
Last Instructions enacts a form of detached, interventionist observation that
utterly redefines the active life in the political sphere.[151] Like Evelyn, Marvell engages in a Baconian redefinition of the relationship between action
and contemplation; he does so by locating production in the act of perception. Among the images offered by Cowley's "The Garden" is the virgin tree
who "blushes" in her fruit to discover she is a mother; Marvell locates this
virgin productivity in the interventions of the "occasional" experimental
observer.[152]

To paraphrase Marvell, by explicitly setting out to decompose and recompose the lines by which truth has been mistaken, the literary lens enables the project of mimesis to be seen anew, as a means to chart a progressive escape from fallen illusions. No longer suspect as a sign of literature's
deviation from a familiar, exemplary truth, the novel "news" revealed by
the textacle authenticates the author's possession of an instrument of discovery. The prosthetic and processual relationship to truth makes its flight
from falsehood to the original facts of creation interminable, but not unproductive. We recall that what sets the whole lens conceit into motion in
Browne's pastoral is the image of the bespectacled reader who "pryes." Rou-
tinely invoked in the context of occasional reflections and microscopy, this
word condenses all the ambitions of interventionist spectatorship—the
power that the author seeks to extend to his readers. The literary lens seeks
to transform the mediated character of the reader's experience of truth into
a source of strength. The virtual spectatorial body of a readership gains
satisfaction that no individual body could achieve; by rationally penetrating the object-as-seen, this corporate body might exert a cognitive mastery
over the object that could indeed culminate in dominion. Merely by looking, this human instrument of truth could menace the identity of every
object it viewed as an inevitable feature of the world, a process Marvell
dramatizes through his remarkably uninhibited experimentation on Charles
and the annihilating power of green thought. While the virtual witnessing

enabled by the textual lens obviously lacks the immediacy of a visual experience, the temporally extended character of verbal representation—in contrast to the paintings Marvell loves to lacerate—enables readers to become acquainted with the strategies of "taking notice" as they are adopted. Through reading, we see observation in action, and as action, and are remodeled into its agents. Following the process of discovery as it unfolds, we become virtual participants in the work of making truth visible.

The knowledge that Marvell cultivated his satiric and garden modes alongside one another during the Restoration—pursuing the arts of interventionist observation in a generalized garden as well as on the floor of the House—suggests a progress aimed at bringing these two spaces together. If *Upon Appleton House* is, among other things, a stifled protest against the retirement of Fairfax, the man who might have restored England as the "*Paradise* of four Seas" (line 323), it also marks the beginning of the poet's prosecution of that restorative labor by spectatorial means, a labor in which he is joined by others—the laboring poor, and even those who might be considered political adversaries (Howell). The most tangible benefit of this labor is its creation of a commons, the virtual witnesses and co-curators that constellate around the instrument of truth. Marvell seeks to improve the vision of others, but that process of improvement is reciprocal; as the meadows sequence suggests, and his collective authorship and distribution of satires confirms, trustworthy prosthetic insight is generated by many pairs of eyes and hands working to discipline each other. If we, along with the poet, feel the grounds of observation shifting underfoot as a result, this is the surest sign that progress is being made.

Dryden's Modest Inquisition

Further confirmation that the lens had become an inescapable metaphor to read and write by can be found in the most famous work of Restoration literary criticism, *An Essay of Dramatick Poesie,* a work whose author, John Dryden, could hardly be accused of ideological sympathy with Marvell. Like *Last Instructions,* the essay deposits an exploration of literary experimentalism in the seemingly arbitrary context of the Anglo-Dutch wars. The participants in this dialogue make the unusual decision to debate literary questions in a boat on the Thames, in spitting range of the cannon fire between Dutch and English ships. As it turns out, they are waging their own war with France, prosecuting the battle between the ancients and the moderns. Yet, like Boyle's *Sceptical Chymist,* the *Essay* is an object lesson in the management of disagreement, recasting the seething conflict of the ancients and the moderns as a civil chat—so well-mannered, in fact, that the character who is in the wrong has the good grace to argue against his own opinions. In his defense of the *Essay,* Dryden declared that its "Discourse was Sceptical, according to that way of reasoning" of Socrates and the ancients, which had been recently revived in "the modest Inquisitions of the Royal Society," the discourse sustained by "persons of several opinions, all of them left doubtful, to be determined by the Readers in general."[153] As Peter Pett himself had hopefully remarked, "The old way of arguing about speculative points . . . with passion and loudness . . . is grown out of use," having been succeeded by "that moderate temper that men use in debating natural experiments."[154] Dryden's experiment in extending the "modest" and "moderate temper" of natural investigation to criticism reveals his own faith in the idea of literary progress. As Northrop Frye has remarked, the *Essay* conveys the sense that "Dutch fleet or no Dutch fleet, English literature is entering an intensely progressive period."[155]

It is Crites, "the ancient," who articulates the view that antiquity handed down a "perfect resemblance" of nature that modern authors, "like ill Copyers, neglecting to look on, have rendred monstrous and disfigur'd." His position is unsettled by the recognition of a "new Nature" when he asks, "is it not evident, in these last hundred years (when the Study of Philosophy has been the business of all the *Virtuosi* in *Christendome*) that almost a new Nature has been reveal'd to us?"[156] Seizing the opportunity, Eugenius observes that "your instance in Philosophy makes for me," and goes on to elaborate the analogy between drawing and writing to suggest that modern deviations from classical models are more accurately regarded as discoveries: "We draw not therefore after their lines, but those of Nature; and having the life before us . . . it is no wonder if we hit some airs and features which they have miss'd." Modern authors copy the lines of a living body, revealing a new nature in the process. Eugenius complacently concludes that "if Natural Causes be more known now then in the time of *Aristotle,* because more studied, it follows that Poesie and other Arts may with the same pains arrive still neerer to perfection" (22). As in Cowley, however, the appeal to direct apprehension proves insufficient to capture "the business of all the *Virtuosi.*" If the "new Nature" the virtuosi have revealed consists of newly discovered causes of "the life before us," then the methods used to discover the "Noble Secrets in Opticks, Medicine, Anatomy, Astronomy" (which Crites, the champion of the ancients, so incongruously celebrates), would seem to provide more fitting models for the modern author's work (15). Lisideius comes to Dryden's assistance with the needed analogy by objecting to another deviation from classical models, Shakespeare's violation of the unity of time. He complains that by condensing the events of forty years into several hours, Shakespeare's plays do not "paint Nature" but rather "draw her in miniature" and "take her in little," as if Shakespeare had attempted "to look upon her through the wrong end of a Perspective" (36). Lisideius faults Shakespeare's works for being too much like "Chronicles," a complaint that reproduces the central features of experimentalist *celebrations* of the new visual technologies. The "lines" of nature celebrated by Eugenius metamorphose into lines of text again and again in experimentalist propaganda as virtuosi celebrate the ability of the mechanically assisted eye to transform objects into chronicles, enabling the observer to begin to "read" the whole "History of the World in miniature."

Yet Dryden agrees with Crites that so comprehensive a view of nature cannot be gained by regarding her directly. Neander, the "new man," does not suggest that Shakespeare drew nature "to the life," as the more simplistic modern Eugenius does: he claims rather that Shakespeare "needed not the spectacles of Books to read Nature; he look'd inwards, and found her there" (55). Linking the two analogies, we find that the perspective glass the modern author uses to create his synoptic visions are located inside himself. Dryden associates Shakespeare with the experimentalist who can read nature without the aid of books, and without staring directly at her either. If copying the outward forms of "things themselves" is as an aesthetic extension of simply staring at sensuous surfaces, undertaking imitations that transcend what is immediately given to the eye is a requirement of a modern aesthetic experimentalism. Such a representation reveals objects in an unfamiliar light, in ways not normally available to "mortal sight," while at the same time approaching Coleridge's ideal of poetry that embodies "a human and intellectual life . . . transferred . . . from the poet's own spirit."

That Dryden is celebrating Shakespeare concerns us less than the terms in which he does so. Even as he defends his own essay on the "originals" of literary value as the disinterested product of Royal Society method—which, having reformed the opinionated into the "doubtful," sets into motion a progress to be carried on by "Readers in general"—he defends the quintessential modern on experimentalist grounds. Crites, to the detriment of his own position, offers the lens as a model for modern literary composition, and Neander relates this assisted sight to introspective vision. Almost simultaneously, Milton was uniting these two models in practice, joining the Puritan inner light of inspiration to Galileo's telescope in order to lay claim to a vision that was his own, but not only his—replicating the prosthetic and trustworthy power of experimentalist insight in a way that an enthusiastic claim of divine inspiration alone could never do.[157] That he required the space of paradise to exercise his vision should come as no surprise. In Dryden's essay, it is the defender of the ancients that ends up making the best argument for the "new man": as Bacon insisted, the new philosophy was in fact the ancient philosophy, and the experimentalist author, like the virtuoso himself, was modeled on the first man of all.

As it turned out, however, Milton was not the first English writer to attempt a Baconian epic. That distinction belongs to William Davenant, whose *Gondibert* provides an ideal test case for my account of literary experimentalism. The last two sections of this chapter are dedicated to this famously botched effort. If Dryden's modest inquisition reflects an awareness that experimentalist literary practice depended on a technology of virtual witnessing, Davenant's attempt to produce the literary equivalent of the *Novum Organum* was predicated on a magical faith in the power of the right words to compel matter.

"Accus'd of Innovation": Davenant as Natural Philosopher

Born only two years apart, Milton and Davenant were mirror images of each other, one serving the regicides' cause, the other fighting for the king and then joining the exiled court in Paris.[158] Each poet worked on his epic while the other poet's side was in power, and each employed the new philosophy not just as a source of content but as a model for their own efforts. While, for Milton, the new philosophy modeled both paradisal subjectivity and the inspired effort to restore it, for Davenant, it modeled the modern victory over superstitions, starting with the dangerous idol of inspiration itself. It was under the tutelage of Hobbes, not Hartlib or any of the virtuosi, that Davenant became aware of the new philosophy, which as a result meant something very different to him than it did to Marvell and Milton. As a member of a displaced court that could no longer afford masques, Davenant enlisted the philosopher to assist his self-reinvention. In addition to providing a *Reply* to Davenant's preface, Hobbes regularly read installments of the poem and satisfied the poet's appetite for constant discussion about it. Davenant pursued his task with such voluble dedication that members of court complained that "to ply it," he sacrificed "thy sleep, thy diet . . . and what's more, our quiet." Such mockery may have contributed to Davenant's decision to leave France for the New World. Accepting a commission to replace William Claiborne as the treasurer of Virginia and, if possible, to oust Lord Baltimore as governor of Maryland (whose loyalty to the monarchy was in doubt), he set out for America, from which he intended to send Hobbes his completed poem.[159] A Parliamentary fleet intercepted his ship, landing him in prison, where he managed to complete half of the third book and the confessional postscript, written when he expected to be executed. His release may have been assisted by Milton himself, who was perhaps also responsible for the announcement in the *Mercurius Politicus* of the publication of an epic "commended by Mr. *Hobbs.*"[160]

Milton may even have been behind the tacit understanding that Davenant was not to be molested as he began putting on the performances he was careful not to call plays at Rutland House. On May 23, 1656, *The First Days Entertainment at Rutland-House, By Declamations and Musick: After the manner of the Ancients,* was attended by a government spy, who reported that the newfangled entertainment, a mixture of "Declamations and Musick," had concluded with a song in praise of the Protector.[161] Two years later the public was treated to *The Cruelty of the Spaniards in Peru. Exprest by Instrumentall and Vocall Musick, and by Art of Perspective in Scenes, &c.* Of these performances, Aubrey remarks that "because Playes . . . were in those Presbyterian times scandalous, he contrives to set up an Opera *stylo recitativo* . . . It did affect the Eie and eare extremely."[162] Davenant's theoretical defense of these entertainments, *A Proposition for Advancement of Moralitie, by a New Way of Entertainment of the People,* describes their aim: stunning the people into obedience by the "surprisall of their Eyes and Ears." Songs and speeches, driven home by the spectacular effects created by "ingenious *Mechanicks,*" would render the people "civiliz'd" and "subdued";

ingenuity would be pressed into the service of ingenuity's suppression.[163] Intended to ingratiate its author with Cromwell's government, Davenant's *Proposition* instead conveys *Leviathan*'s pragmatic understanding of culture and even religion as props to state power. Davenant's commitment to this understanding led him to place a superstitious faith in the power of the right words to "move" people—a power that he understood in literal, even materialist, terms.

Although it was shaped entirely by Hobbes, Davenant's concept of true philosophy looks rather like Webster's. Of course, Hobbes disdained popular hermeticism and took on the scholastic doctrine of form in the very title of *Leviathan: The Matter, Forme, and Power of a Common-Wealth,* whose appositives imply the equivalence of matter with forms and powers. Thomas Spragens has persuasively argued that just as form theory informs Aristotle's teleological political model, in which it is man's perfection to be social within a political structure, so inertial motion provides the foundation for Hobbes's science of politics: "When a Body is once in motion, it moveth (unless something els hinder it) eternally."[164] The vital motion of man begins in the embryo and does not end until death; as long as the inertial force of "meer Nature" operates unchecked, individuals either form unstable compactions or violently collide. According to Davenant, the author's task in the face of this chaos is to assist in the imposition of order, to construct a literary Leviathan. The "Mindes of Men," he explains in the *Preface,* are like "the Bodies of Whales," requiring "space for agitation." If not directed in orderly ways, such agitation will necessarily introduce more conflict into the already tempestuous element of nature, in which "active motion . . . is as necessary as the motion of the Sea." Since "Images of Action prevaile upon our mindes," it is the poet's task to represent actions that will produce only the kinds of "agitation" that conduce to order and peace.[165] His poem, like Hobbes's government, is an artificial monster designed to keep natural monsters in line. It is this faith in the power of the right names to compel matter that constitutes the common ground between Webster's unhinged Paracelsianism and Hobbes's own system.

Blending a loose Baconianism with an unbounded faith in the power of the right words, Davenant became embroiled in the same difficulties that bedeviled Webster's attempt to conceive of a language that was an "all-working . . . *fiat.*" If the rigor of Samuel Butler's parodies—the intentness of their focus on the conditions under which investigation went awry—

made them virtual extensions of Royal Society literature, Davenant's lax approach to adapting experimentalist canons tipped imitation into parody. As obsessed as any experimentalist with exerting causal impact on the world, he failed to include his reader as a virtual witness in the project of rendering that world the object of observation. It is *Gondibert,* the colossal failure of literary experimentalism, that displays the "self-satisfying" episte-mology that Stanley Fish attributes to the virtuosi, and it failed to satisfy anyone.[166]

Davenant's account of how the modern epic poet should proceed falls into two parts that are never satisfactorily related to one another. First, the poet must portray nature as it really is: this entails abjuring supernatural machinery (which Davenant does not manage to do) and representing characters not as personifications of good or evil but as machines driven by physical drives, morally neutral in themselves, which can be directed to socially beneficial or destructive ends. Second, the poet must impose be-havioral norms on his readers as forcefully as possible. On one hand, *Gondibert* seeks to provide an anatomy of human behavior that can serve as a guide to the state and clergy; on the other, it seeks to stun its reader with "force." Davenant wants both to convey to his readers what he regards as a modern understanding of the mechanisms governing human motion or ac-tion while also seeking, on the basis of this understanding, to determine the motions within them. Translated into a literary practice, this double aim makes inconsistent demands on writer and reader alike.

Davenant's faith in the power of the text, not to make things happen, but to make *particular* things happen by compelling the reader's assent sug-gests Hobbes's fetishization of the geometric proof. The famous occasion of Hobbes's secular conversion to modern philosophy was his accidental glance at a book of geometry; overwhelmed to find that his assent had been compelled, he had a revelation of what philosophy, modeled on this proce-dure, could accomplish. Boyle's conversion experience, in contrast, was triggered by a violent thunderstorm: a sensuous experience of the Creator's power.[167] The contrast predicts their future careers, and their ongoing con-flict. As Shapin and Schaffer have shown, the dispute between Hobbes and Boyle about the possibility of a vacuum did not merely reflect a method-ological difference, it concerned nothing else. Dismissing appeals to sen-sory evidence, Hobbes asserted the impossibility of a vacuum based on a set of premises from which he derived conclusions; Boyle "modestly" refused to talk metaphysics and kept providing relations of the physical results he and his coworkers had achieved with the pump.[168]

Davenant sought to produce in his readers something like the epiphany Hobbes had experienced: "by the strict survay and Goverment that hath been had over this Poem, I shall think to governe the Reader" (24). Hobbes no doubt believed that his conversion experience, like everything else, could be described materially, and Davenant provides a reductionist account of the influence he intends to wield through writing. The "feaver of the minde, which insensibly dispatches the Body," can be manipulated and controlled by representations; the impressions of language work upon the reader's body, insinuating themselves into it and redirecting its motions through the physical power of suggestion (33). But even the geometric epiphany is not an adequate model for the scenario Davenant envisages: through compelling consent, he wants to compel behavior, much as the Hobbesian social contract was intended to do. In contrast, the covenant of witnessing in experimentalist practice (and competing versions of contract theory) reprised assent as ongoing and freely given by ingenious subjects, not compelled once and for all in some lost originary moment.[169] Davenant's faith in the power of the right words to force matter's hand is in this sense reminiscent of the magical interpretation of Adam's naming as a specifically linguistic event: a form of "calling" that was also a form of commanding. The connection was not lost on Marvell. Ridiculing Samuel Parker's suggestion that religious matters, and even definitions of contested linguistic terms, should be fixed by the monarch, Marvell remarked that such "Arrogance and Dictature . . . surpasses by far the presumption either of *Gondibert* or *Leviathan*," so thoroughly did it entangle "the matter of Conscience with the Magistrates Power."[170] A sovereign dictator who extends his personal rule to language evokes the power-hungry Davenant and his master Hobbes. While arrogating to himself the identity of an all-powerful magus, Davenant figured his readers as obedient creatures susceptible to re-creation by the names he imposed on them; such creatures were animals to his Adam, or more accurately, Adam to his God. Nothing suggests the divergence of Davenant from the experimentalist sensibilities of a Marvell or Milton as much as his decision to invoke Adam as a model of submission: "till his disobedience," Adam exhibited "a willing and peacefull obedience to Superiors," a trait which is "more needful and advantagious then liberty," since it carries the "reward of pleasant quietnesse"; it was his unquestioning submission to this delightful yoke that made his "Paradise." This was the paradise that Davenant's "Dominion of Poesy" would restore (30).

Davenant wanted to stand "accus'd of Innovation" alongside other modern offenders, and he wanted to show that it was his "method" that was responsible (18). Placing himself at the forefront of a revolution in literary method that was to overturn the "Errors" of every epic author from Homer to Spenser, he envisioned himself in the preface as the father of modern literary progress, casting earlier poets as the schoolmen to his Bacon (7). He even presents the unfinished state of his masterwork, as Bacon presented his *Novum Organum,* as the necessary result of its ambition. For *Gondibert* was first introduced to the public as a freestanding preface, or, in the words of a contemporary, as "a Porch to no house."[171] Although the full title of this volume is *The Preface to Gondibert, An Heroic Poem Written by Sir William D'Avenant: With an Answer to the Preface by Mr Hobbes,* the epic was in fact not yet written, and the volume did not contain even a canto of the projected poem. The first two books, and part of the third, were published the following year. This unfinished state is not an instance of an experimentalist refusal to conclude, because Davenant's project was anything but open-ended.

The advance for which Davenant claims credit in the preface is methodological: unlike other poets, he writes without being inspired. Blaming Homer as the first to have identified the source of poetry as a *"Familiar"* rather than the author's "rationall Spirit," he explains that subsequent writers, out of a lazy "humor of imitation," did the same (3, 7). Inspiration itself is exposed as a vulgar error. The literary tradition produced by this mistaken methodology resembles "a continuance of extraordinary Dreames," such as the "overstudious may have in the beginning of Feavers," while its frightful visions seem composed "out of the Dreames of frighted Women" (7, 6). (As in experimentalist accounts of popular superstition as a prop to scholastic error, women and "gownmen" are partners.) Davenant's gendered description of the imaginative process is closer to Hobbes's etiology of popular superstition in *Leviathan* than Sidney's *Apologie;* Hobbes had assigned a prominent role to "old wives" in forming a popular consciousness that was hopelessly unfit to engage in collective rational decision making.[172] In contrast to these victims of superstition, the self-consciously modern author regards writing as work—he takes pains. People object to "painfulnesse in Poets" because they assume that a willingness to take pains is an admission of a want of "force," a claim Davenant assures his readers is ridiculous (21). Redefining *force* in ostentatiously modern terms as mere physical momentum, he asserts that possessing force is nothing to brag about, since all force is natural force, and nature is characterized by motion throughout all its parts: nature "hath not any where, at any time, been respited from action (in her, cal'd motion) by which she universally preserves and makes Life" (14). Davenant's description of force as inertial momentum majestically hints at an entire materialist system.

Davenant's freedom from the "melancholy mistakes" of the old philosophy empowers him to deliver readers and future writers from the seductive power of chimeras like inspiration (6). Unencumbered by this fever, such an author is also someone who works well with others; solitary inspiration is superseded by progressive inquiry within a rational male community. For Davenant's "painfull" method of writing requires such "great labour in managing" that it cannot be shouldered by him alone; by depending so heavily on men like Hobbes, "I shall not so much attest my owne weaknesse, as discover the difficulties and greatnesse of such a worke." Just as the building of Solomon's temple required the contributions of "Fellers of Wood, and Hewers of Stone" in addition to "learned Architects," so Davenant is "oblig'd to men of any science, as well mechanicall, as liberal" (22). Drawing on Bacon's favorite metaphors—Solomon's temple, the journeys of discovery—Davenant flounders to find a vocabulary with which to redescribe writing not as leisure or fever but active labor, a way of bringing "comprehensions into action" (19). The interrelated themes of withdrawal, idleness, and solitude that protect the specialness of literary language in Sidney's *Apologie* must be reversed if literary authorship is to be brought into line with other forms of rationally motivated, goal-directed, and knowledge-producing activity. Davenant's defense of his slow progress on the poem similarly evokes the conditions of scientific research: one must be "long and painfull in watching the correspondence of Causes" before attempting to "foretell effects" (21). Hobbes's opening remark in his *Reply*— that the subject of poetry is not natural causes but the manners of men— seems to have been a gentle reminder to his protégé that just because Davenant had, in his own words, "forborne . . . posting upon *Pegasus*" did not mean he had become a natural philosopher (45, 21). But although Davenant presents literary composition as an attempt to intervene in the world outside the text, he makes no attempt to dramatize this experiment as an effort to answer a problem of knowledge. Like his mentor, Davenant is content with a vague physical reductionism that substitutes metaphysics for investigation. Since it is known in advance that everything comes down to matter in motion, the details of nature's "smallest Hand" do not actually concern him. His interest in assuming control over real processes far outweighs any interest in observing those processes, which are always sufficiently transparent in accordance with a prior understanding about the way nature works; Davenant is no more "unassuming" than Hobbes. Given that he has no real research question, he is drawn to the experimentalist ideal purely as it represents a model for the demonstration of power. What is missing from his account, despite the talk of observing cause and effects, is any sign of curiosity.

Of all the Baconian motifs, it is the journey of discovery that Davenant leans on the hardest: ancient models "serve not those who have the ambition of Discoverers, that love to sayle in untry'd Seas"; such ambition requires the author to sail along "unfrequented and new ways" by "fantastick and uncertaine windes" (3, 20, 8). Rather than pressing this imagery into service as a model for investigation, he employs it to distract the reader from his actual literary practice. His concluding announcement that he is off to America, where he will write the last three books of his poem, is a self-conscious extension of the seafaring imagery beyond metaphor, an attempt to suggest an unbroken continuity between his actions within and beyond the text. It underscores the idea that the new "rational" species of literary composition is an extension of what he calls "painfull activenesse" and a prelude to further exertion (14). This sense of writing as a progressive activity is supposed to guard him against the risk of failure; if readers find that he has not yet reached his goal, they can rest assured of his "continu'd Sayling" towards it (8). But he gives the reader no means to connect this brave voyage to the task of writing, much less their own experience as readers.

It is not surprising that, having made a boast of his lack of inspiration and willingness to depend on the help of others, Davenant was mocked for his "laboured lines"; contemporaries remarked that his work ethic suited him to "some good trade" rather than the "riming rage."[173] In fact, writing *Gondibert* was so painful that he finally gave up trying, though he maintained his faith in Gondibert the project to the bitter end. As his freestanding preface suggests, it was really the statement of intent, not the process of its realization, that had interested him all along. A year later, the preface and Hobbes's reply were reissued along with some commendatory verses, a fragment of the projected poem, and a postscript in which he announced his decision to abandon his epic. He seems to have hoped that his reader might tactfully overlook the stillborn poetic fragment at the work's center and regard his project not as a simple failure but as a pioneering attempt to open up new literary possibilities. It was to be expected that the establishment of a "Dominion of Poesy," like dominion over nature, lay beyond the limits of any single trial.[174]

Like Davenant, Cowley ended up publishing only a portion of his modern epic, presenting the fragment as an "essay" to be carried on by others:

> I am farre from assuming to my self to have fulfilled the duty of this weighty undertaking: But sure I am, that there is nothing yet in our *Language* (nor perhaps in *any*) that is in any degree answerable to the *Idea* that I conceive of it. And I shall be ambitious of no other fruit from this weak and imperfect attempt of mine, but the opening of a way to the courage and industry of some other persons.[175]

Cowley here imagines the reformist task of poetry in Baconian terms, applying the craft principle of *techne* as a progressive project coordinating human effort across time. Unlike Davenant, however, Cowley invites future authors to grapple with a problem, not merely with a frustrated will to power. Convinced that there "is not so great a *Lye* to be found in any *Poet,* as the vulgar conceit of men, that *Lying* is *Essential* to good *Poetry*," he wants to adapt poetry to the ends of magnifying truth—and particularly scripture. Lamenting the dependence of poets on fabulous tales of knights errant and pagan machinery, he prophetically asks, "Why will not the actions of *Sampson* afford as plentiful matter as the *Labors* of *Hercules?*"[176] In contrast, Davenant's assumed identity as a modern makes him seem embarrassed that he is writing poetry at all. If Davenant's boast of being uninspired left him vulnerable to satire, his attempt to reproduce experimentalist attacks on the schoolmen is positively self-defeating. Righteously opposing immersion in texts to his own immersion in a rational collective of "men of any science" and "right Masters," he models a positive disdain for books. Writers who are "more in Libraries, then in company" are both lazy and benighted: books, unlike the secrets of nature, are "easily open'd," but they are not where real "Treasure" is to be found (22, 23, 8).

The Desperate Cure of Verse

My autopsy of the poem will be brief. Like *Leviathan,* Davenant's preface is filled with reductive redefinitions of complex ideas: "indefinite Love is Lust; and Lust when it is determin'd to one, is Love" (15). These continue throughout the poem. While providing his reader with a heroic narrative about love and war, Davenant also provides a running philosophical commentary on their causal underpinnings in the same "vital heat," which is motion. "Man's loose rage" normally finds expression in the disputes of "the schools," political power struggles, sex, and war. Since the poem is set in medieval Lombardy, whose inhabitants, Davenant pretends to believe, were alternately crazed by lust and aggression, the poem has many opportunities to impart this lesson.[177] The heroic narrative is stuffed with philosophical asides, attempts at "mechanical" explanations of events or Hobbesian critiques of ordinary language. So, for example, in addition to reminding us that each plot twist is simply another morally neutral effect of heat's motion, Davenant provides, alongside an account of the character Laura's passion, an analysis of its effects on her liver. It was such reductive redescription that, among Hobbesians, passed for Adamic naming. Thus the same behavior we call cruelty in "Beasts untam'd" is in humans "courage nam'd"; hereditary aristocracy is also a sham: "Soules are alike, of rich and ancient Race; / Though Bodies claim distinctions by descent."[178]

Even while constantly tearing apart word and thing to reveal the arbitrariness of custom, Davenant addresses his reader as if she were powerless to resist its force. Though his scientific asides reveal his own detachment from the conventional fare he serves up, he announces to the reader that "thou shalt weep to read" of Gondibert's adventures, even apologizing for the pain they are certain to cause (1.2.2). Though the reader will "wish it all unread, or else untrue," she will, he is confident, "With a hot Reader's haste, this Song pursue" (3.1.44). In spite of his own renamings of the concepts of martial valor, aristocratic nobility, and love, he describes the dignity of kings and splendor of courts in terms that are supposed to awe, and expects his reader to weep at the shedding of "noble blood" and the vicissitudes of courtship (2.4.4). It is as if he were writing two poems that have become scrambled together—one that addresses the reader as a potential philosophical peer and the other that treats her as brute matter on which to work.[179] Rather than fashioning a narrative voice to integrate these registers, he figures the reader as infinitely adaptable to the shifting ends of his dominion of poesy. Having attacked courtly society for deforming the characters of its members, he in the next moment presents these courtly paragons for the reader's admiration and emulation, predicting that a future reader's bride will confess to him on their wedding day that she modeled the character with which he fell in love on patterns she read in *Gondibert:* "my Laws / Did teach her how by Nature to perswade, / And hold by Vertue whom her beauty draws" (3.3.10).

Davenant seems to have grown aware of this conflict and to have attempted a resolution by suspending the epic plot for a long sojourn in an experimentalist paradise, the kingdom of Astragon ("*Astragon* the Apothecary," as the poem's detractors called him).[180] The inhabitants of "great Nature's Court" are "Recov'rers of time past," for they, like Adam, not only live in accordance with nature's laws, but spend all their time studying them. To satisfy the "curious Eie," they have even managed to preserve the very bodies of Adam and Eve in the "Cabinet of Death" (2.7.84, 2.5.9, 35, 33). This idolatrous embalming of Adam's body is almost a perfect foil to the attempt of Baconians to resurrect and reinhabit it; Davenant seems doomed to reproduce the letter rather than the spirit of experimentalist faith. The princess of this restored paradise, appropriately named Birtha, does not gather flowers merely for pleasure; she is an expert horticulturalist. Thus, when she is cynically wooed by ambitious suitors, it is not for her access to state secrets, but her knowledge of the secrets of nature. That Davenant permits corrupt intrigue in the paradisal court of nature again suggests that he simply could not imagine this place.[181] Yet he gamely goes on to describe a happy collectivity in which all are as "busy as intentive *Emmets*," with "Impatient *Simplers*" running from "flowry Fields to weeping Stills" and others "as in a pleasant shade, retir'd," engaged in "Toyles which their own choice desir'd" (2.5.9, 29, 10, 21). Pastoral shade provides a space, not for songs of love, but dissections and astronomical observations; this innocent retreat is the site of free but incessant labor.

The warrior heroes who wander into this kingdom are instantaneously reformed. Before, they had felt compelled by duty to participate in any fight they witnessed; they "esteem[ed] it an unpleasant shame / With idle Eies to look on busie hands" (1.3.51). Now they gain a different sense of what busy hands can accomplish:

> The noble Youths (reclaim'd by what they saw)
> Would here unquiet war, as pride, forsake;
> And study quiet Nature's pleasant Law;
> Which Schools, through pride, by Art uneasy make.
>
> (2.6.1)

His wounds cured thanks to Birtha's expertise in medicinal herbs, Gondibert finds that he has also gained back "my healthfull Minde (diseas'd before)" (2.7.59). He would happily "Leave shining Thrones for *Birtha* in a shade" (2.8.46). Although Gondibert feels "reclaim'd" by the activity that surrounds him, he remains an observer rather than a participant. Davenant clearly identifies with Gondibert, who, torn between this realm and the court, cannot thrive in either place. Just as Gondibert's retirement in this philosophical paradise removes him from his heroic destiny, so Davenant's respectful catalogue of the activities of these intellectual laborers requires him to suspend the action of his heroic poem. These laborers do not seek any more than Davenant does to post upon Pegasus—rather, like him they want to "climbe" to truth "by the wings of diligence" (2.5.8)—but Davenant does not manage to identify his work with theirs. Although he peppers the poem with technical-sounding modifiers (*abstersive* was singled out for special ridicule), when he describes experimental activities in any detail, our sense of the distance between their work and his own only widens.[182]

This episode does enable Davenant to deliver some peremptory truths about human nature, with which these subjects, unseduced by custom, always act in full accordance. Although Birtha is momentarily shamed by her passion for Gondibert, she reasons herself out of this conventionally ladylike response. Addressing heaven and its "Disciple, Nature," she asks, "Why should I hide the passion you have given, / Or blush to shew effects which you decree?" (2.7.37). Although her anxiety about losing his love causes her to pray, she recovers from this uncharacteristic lapse of reason after being scolded by her father (3.5.30–39). Strict Hobbesian determinists, the inhabitants of this kingdom take a dim view of penitence, regarding it as "unnaturall." Through regret, "we our selves forsake," and "repent what Nature did perswade"; they are loath to "Accuse what Nature necessary made" (2.6.10, 86, 10). It is because penitence is "A summons Nature hardly understands," Davenant surmises, that churches have to use "lowd Bells" to compel "the persecuted Eare" to perform the custom. Although Astragon's kingdom has such a church, "few, and slow are those who enter here"; its seats are "thinly fill'd" because "none this place by nature understood" (2.6.14, 22).

However, the House of Praise, a nearby house of physico-theological worship, is packed. Here, instead of praying for the fulfillment of their desires or repenting their sins, these intellectual laborers convene to celebrate their own discoveries; praise of their maker blends with self-congratulation ("indeed," Marvell jovially remarked in the course of his attack on Parker's vision of the Anglican church, "all Astragon appear'd to me the better *Scheme of Religion*").[183] On the day that Gondibert arrives, the House shakes with shouts and noise because the navigational use of the loadstone, "so long conceal'd," and which "so oft Made Nature's spies to pine," has just been discovered (2.6.29). It is in describing this temple that Davenant attempts his single literary experiment in making truth visible, which, had he undertaken it more rigorously, might have enabled him to identify his project more closely with that of the intellectual laborers he celebrates. On the walls of this temple, the "great Creation" is "by bold Pencils drawn," and Davenant describes it in detail. What pretends to be a description of a painting is a hexameral poem in miniature (a "flip ekphrastic hexameron" as John Rogers calls it), but one in which "a feign'd Curtain does our Eies forbid" the sight of Chaos that preceded creation.[184] In *Paradise Lost,* Milton will lift this curtain and search into the ontologically and temporally prior realm of first matter; Davenant leaves it untouched.

Compressed into the frame of word-painting, this reconstruction of creation is characterized by an odd confusion of the spatial with the temporal; instead of relating temporally distant causes to objects of immediate perception, it conflates them. The painting "starts" in darkness, "Till the Sun's Parent, Light, first seems to dawn / From quiet *Chaos,* which that Curtain hid" (2.6.53). A description of some of the highlights of creation follows:

Then this all-rev'renc'd Sun (God's hasty Spark
Struck out of *Chaos,* when he first struck Light)
Flies to the Sphears, where first he found all dark,
And kindled there th'unkindled Lamps of Night.

Then Motion, Nature's great Preservative,
Tun'd order in this World, Life's restless Inn;
Gave Tydes to Seas, and caus'd stretch'd Plants to live . . .

(2.6.54–55)

The infusion of motion into "stretch'd" and lifeless creatures suggests the stretched-out corpses of the anatomy theater. Once transformed into "Life's restless Inn" by the indwelling *conatus* of matter, this dead space explodes into the teeming and lively nature we know. Creation then follows in its several stages, including the "universal Herd" made famous by Marvell.[185] Although we can imagine a sequence of panels representing this chain of events, the obtrusive *thens* and the constant reference to causes testify to a struggle between time and space, depth and surface, cause and effect, that we can only register as a series of conflicting commands. The sequence is designed "To shew how Nature thrives by Motion's heat," but the urgency of exposition vastly outweighs any sense of ocular demonstration. Parentheticals like "(For light ne'r warm'd, till it did motion get)" straightforwardly instruct us, rather than revealing anything (2.6.56). And Davenant's careless confusion of the modalities of sight and sound by having the painting somehow represent the voice of God leaves the reader nonplussed. Davenant describes God slurring his commands in order to move on to create the next world, his voice seeming "to denote the Speaker was in hast, / As if more worlds were framing in his thought" (2.6.59). Inserted to reveal his modish belief in the plurality of worlds, the detail does not relate to any percept a viewer of the painting could experience, which makes its virtual experience by the reader an empty set; she just has to take Davenant's word for it.[186] Davenant's insistence on revealing everything at once rather than going through the process of experimental demonstration leaves the reader blind and deaf, and distinguishes him from the patient "diligence" of Nature's courtiers he presents for our admiration.

In the preface, when casting about for ways to imagine the direct impact his epic would have on readers, Davenant confessed that he had so much "pride" as to "presume they might . . . be sung at Village-feasts" as part of some kind of civic celebration (17). It is precisely on the surrender of pride that the investigative spirit of Astragon's subjects is predicated. Astragon, Davenant informs us, invented the science of optics and made the Copernican thesis public in order to discourage pride: "Man's pride (grown to Religion) he abates, / By moving our lov'd Earth; which we think fix'd" (2.5.19). His humble subjects have surrendered the fantasy that those "vaste bright Globes" were made "to attend our little Ball" (2.5.20). They are rewarded for their humility with dominion: Davenant represents their observational work as if it were actually a means of controlling outer space. Those in charge of observing heavenly changes do not merely observe but "censure Meteors" (2.5.15). And

> Others with Optick Tubes the Moons scant face
> (Vaste Tubes, which like long Cedars mounted lie)
> Attract through Glasses to so neer a space,
> As if they came not to survey, but prie.
>
> *(2.5.16)*

The magnifying power combined with the vast length of the telescopes (whose "trunks" encourage the comparison to trees) seems to bring outer space near, permitting them to "prie" rather than merely "survey," just like Browne's telescope user.[187] They "attract" the matter of the heavens to earth in an almost magnetic way, as their users seek not only to "reach with Optick Tubes the ragged Moon" (3.2.55) but even to gain access to "the Maker's Throne" (2.5.17). In describing the activities and attitudes of these virtuosi, Davenant displays an experimentalist understanding of how individual humility served the ends of collective empowerment, which makes his own difficulties in managing this paradox all the more apparent; the virtuoso's careful weaving of spectatorial ambition with personal modesty finds no correlative in his own strictly alternating self-presentation.

Davenant cannot afford such a demonstration of humility; his own philosophical authority is too thinly grounded. When he turns his attention to Astragon's library, "The Monument of vanish'd Mindes" (2.5.36), he engages in a bit of anxious projection. Less like Prospero's library than a penitentiary, this "Monument" contains books by "talking" philosophers who tried to "disguise" truth. "[L]ong since read, / And shut by *Astragon*," they are punished by being housed in a crypt, where they lie neglected and covered by spider webs as "Subtle, and slight, as the grave Writers were"; having been "Truth's Tormentors," they are now justly "lost in dust" (2.5.44, 51, 49, 51). Opportunizing the homophone of *tombs* and *tomes*, Astragon suggests that these tormentors of truth deserve to have their books "lie un-visited," like dishonored graves (2.5.51). But later verbal echoes link the description of this library-prison-crypt to Davenant's fantasies about the treatment of his poem by posterity: his fantasy of the newlyweds whose wedding fluctuates into a celebration of *Gondibert* concludes with a command that the couple leave the churchyard where his body is buried to re-visit the place his mind is buried: "Then in the Temple leave my Bodies Tomb, / To seek this Book, the Mon'ment of my Minde" (3.3.11). Coming in the middle of an extravagant articulation of authorial power, this fune-real imagery, in recalling the monument of vanished minds, implies his awareness that his epic may have a very different fate than the one he is de-scribing. Rather than the active source of a dominion of poesy, Davenant's poem might be simply an inert "tomb" of his thoughts that will gather dust instead of compelling the obedience of the living.[188] His reference to his poem as "this Book" sounds like a melancholy admission.

There are occasions when Davenant openly compares the operation of "this Book" to the instruments and practices of the new philosophy, but these images tend to self-destruct. When he boasts that his poetry has "Chymick pow're," a productive heat that will revive in the world the vir-tues it formulates on paper, he employs the figure of the alchemical resus-citation of the ghost of a rose, an image that fuses observation and interven-tion in a magical and possibly illusory way (1.4.4). Hobbes would tweak this image as a courtly compliment at the end of his *Reply*, where Dav-enant himself becomes both the flower and the perspective glass that unites the scattered virtues of all the characters of his poem (55). The trick per-spective gathers together scattered parts in a synoptic whole, but this syn-thesis is not a tangible event, only an optical effect. Like the anamorphic or catoptric devices explored by Ernest Gilman, the glass Hobbes describes only works on the specially prepared "trick-picture" designed to fit it, rather than making visible features of the world beyond.[189] In the stanza following his "Chymick pow're" boast, Davenant makes the latent pessimism of his own image explicit, lamenting that "reviv'd Patterns us no more improve, / Then Flowres so rais'd by Chymists make us sweet" (1.4.5). But he will not be deterred from making the attempt: "Yet to this desp'rate cure I will proceed." Thus emboldened, he seems to regain his confidence; he promises to show us "patterns" such "as shall not fail to move" (1.4.9). His readers, like Gondibert, are also products of a diseased culture bred on "Books and Batails," and they stand in need of his examples. Although other poets have "long / Forborn" to participate in this project, he refuses to believe that his contemporaries are so sick as to be "past cure of verse" (2.8.20, 1.4.8). But this self-assertion is itself riddled with uncertainty. While he refers to the cure of his verse as "desp'rate," he will later describe Astragon's physical ministrations as "certain cures" (1.6.65).

Elsewhere, Davenant urges us to "study more in Nature, then in Schools," bolstering this precept with another optical figure:

> Let Nature's Image never by thee pass
> Like unmark'd Time; but those unthinking Fools
> Despise, who spie not Godhead through her Glas!
> *(3.6.23)*[190]

The way Davenant handles this figure sums up his approach: the glass urged on the reader is less an instrument than it is an "Image" of nature, and it precludes the use of any other. Whereas Marvell deepens the mirror of grass into a lens—which he then uses to transform color into a testimonial of its own production—Davenant has the lens lapse back into a mirror, offering an image in which truth may be found. Modeling an authoritative certainty about what Nature was and how it worked, Davenant regarded his own metaphysical beliefs and found truth there, dispensing his conclusions in peremptory asides. With the exception of the half-hearted attempt in the House of Praise, where the source of data is a painting, he did not reproduce the prosthetic nature of experimentalist insight in a manner that might engage his readers as virtual witnesses. Rather than participating in the virtuosi's labors of making truth visible, he could only narrate them. Davenant was able to conceive of telescopes as instruments with which scientists might "prie" into the secrets of the heavens while remaining free of pride themselves, but when he relates optical technologies to his own project, they cease to be invested with the same power; they do not function properly. Parasitic on the work generated by "busie hands" rather than continuous with it, *Gondibert* could not integrate its celebration of the Baconian realm of Astragon with the Hobbesian principles that directed the project as a whole.

Davenant's desire to claim a kinship with the experimental laborer comes to seem as delusional as any schoolman's, as he mistakes the word *power* for the thing it represents. The knowledge that he was in prison when he wrote the final book of the incomplete manuscript makes the gap between his visions of domination through poetry and the fate of Astragon's books all the more pathetic. In the postscript he calls attention to the conditions under which he tried to finish the poem:

> I intended in this POEM to strip Nature naked, and clothe her again in the perfect shape of Vertue; yet even in so worthy a Designe I shall ask leave to desist, when I am interrupted by so great an experiment as Dying: and 'tis an experiment to the most experienc'd; for no Man (though his Mortifications may be much greater then mine) can say, *He has already Dy'd*. (250)

In dying he can feel like he is conducting an experiment, and even assume the role of a pioneer, charting a new course that no one living has yet taken; he seems undisturbed by the fact that everyone else will do the same. The seafaring imagery from the preface is revived as he announces his intention to "strike Sail, and cast Anchor" in search of death, "a Harbor in a Storm." Although "a common Spectator" might find this tragic, a wise one will foresee a happy ending, for his poem if not his person, since so "severe a representation of Vertue (undressing Truth even out of those disguises which have been most in fashion throughout the World)" must one day "arrive at fair entertainment"; the topos of a stripped nature reveals Davenant once again bravely projecting an experimentalist persona (250, 251). He goes on to defend the immodesty of his preface:

> I appeal to thy Conscience, whether it be more then such a necessary assurance, as thou hast made to thy self in like Undertakings? . . . [S]uch inward assurance (me thinks) resembles that forward confidence in Men of Armes, which makes them to proceed in great Enterprise; since the right examination of abilities, begins with inquiring whether we doubt our selves. (252)

Davenant suggests that his "great Enterprise" was a means of waging war. The only possible targets of his hostile campaign were his own readers, to whom he now appeals for sympathy: it was the greatness of the undertaking that required him to demonstrate a "forward confidence." The last clause implies that behind this assurance lay doubt in his own abilities, a self-doubt of which the inaccessible chaos behind the curtain stands as both symptom and symbol. Although the "right examination of abilities, begins with inquiring whether we doubt our selves," such inquiry does not lead to self-diagnosis here. The experimentalist's strength was to turn his weakness and deficiency into an asset, to make his want of power the occasion for prosthetic self-enhancement. Here, the only remedy for authorial insecurity is symptom management, in the form of bravura: a majestic denial of doubt, which can be retracted, as it is here, when the "great Enterprise" has failed.

I have argued that this literary leviathan sought to impose truths on its readers instead of revealing anything, but Davenant's difficulty in adapting experimentalist protocols to literary authorship also resulted in large part from his dutiful sense that, as a spokesperson for the new philosophy, it fell to him to heap scorn on texts themselves. In one of his didactic asides Davenant remarks "How vain is Custom, and how guilty Pow'r" (2.1.75), and although he claimed to impose his laws in "spite of Courts," his poem aspired to the same kind of power, even as he worried that his labored verse was failing to exert it (3.3.10). Yet the fantasy of a compliant readership eager to use *Gondibert* as a conduct manual proves to be self-defeating, since those who seek instruction from books—scorning "experience from th'unpractis'd Cell—are "but dead Heads," unqualified for membership in the modern rational collective idealized by the poem (2.2.58, 3.5.47).

Reminiscing about the occasion when he introduced Cowley and Davenant to Boyle, Pett remarked, "I remember when I went away with them from him, they gave their Judgment of Mr Boyles being equall in the talents of Wit to any of the first-rate men of the Age."[191] It is intriguing to speculate on what would have come of their efforts to produce modern philosophical epics had exile not left them dependent on Hobbes as their tutor during the formative decade of the 1640s. When Davenant left prison, he abandoned his epic ambitions and reinvented himself yet again. Cowley, in the meantime, was already undergoing the conversion that would eventuate in his ode to the Royal Society and membership in that body. Cowley's elevation of collective labor over individual genius and concern for poetry as an instrument of discovery, a vehicle for truth claims rather than fictions, were perhaps the values which made both Milton and Boyle number him among their favorite English poets, but it was Milton himself who revived Davenant's experiment.[192]

6 ||| MILTON AND THE PARADIZABLE READER

The Minister and the people cannot so sever their interests, as to sustaine severall persons; he being the only mouth of the whole body which he presents. And if the people pray he being silent, or they ask one thing & he another, it either changes the property, making the Priest the people, and the people the Priest by turnes, or else makes two persons and two bodies representative where there should be but one . . . I know not what to name it . . . the *schisme* of a slic't prayer . . . a continuall rebounding nonsense.
—*An Apology Against a Pamphlet Call'd A Modest Confutation of the Animadversions upon the Remonstrant against Smectymnuus*

[Adam] signifies in Greek the whole world, for there are four letters, A, D, A, and M. But as the Greeks speak, the four quarters of the world have these initial letters . . . Adam therefore has been scattered over the whole world. He was in one place, and fell, and as though broken small he filled the whole world; but the mercy of God gathered together the fragments from every side, and forged them by the fire of love, and made one what was broken.
—Saint Augustine, Exposition on Psalm 96:15

Truth indeed came once into the world with her divine Master, and was a perfect shape most glorious to look on: but when he ascended, and his Apostles after him were laid asleep, then strait arose a wicked race of deceivers, who . . . took the virgin Truth, hewd her lovely form into a thousand peeces, and scatter'd them to the four winds. From that time ever since, the sad friends of Truth, such as durst appear, imitating the carefull search that *Isis* made for the mangl'd body of *Osiris,* went up and down gathering up limb by limb still as they could find them. We have not yet found them all, Lords and Commons, nor ever shall doe, till her Masters second comming; he shall bring together every joynt and member, and shall mould them into an immortall feature of lovelines and perfection. Suffer not these licencing prohibitions to stand at every place of opportunity forbidding and disturbing them that continue seeking, that continue to do our obsequies to the torn body of our martyr'd Saint.
—*Areopagitica*

To make the state of innocence accessible to the fallen imagination is to threaten the distinction between created and corrupted humanity on which the idea of paradise depends. This double bind confines traditional representations of paradise to a proleptic mode; as the breeding ground of sin, Eden becomes a symbol of humanity's release from paradise and its demands. In the seventeenth century, this mimetic constraint begins to loosen; it is destroyed by Milton's career. As a subject of serious art, so is Eden; in the eighteenth century the first state of creation loses its proper name to Nature. As previous chapters have suggested, some credit for this shift belongs to experimentalist intellectuals who turned Bacon's paradise of exercise and experiment into a working model for their own activities, restoring the first man as a corporate producer of knowledge. Milton's career was an extension of this project. In this chapter I argue that, for Milton, the recovery of paradise and the reformation of public life were not separate things: to release paradise from its idolatrous identification with the first garden was to create the conditions for the emergence of a productive public.

While the *felix culpa* also promises a paradise severed from its Edenic roots, it is a paradise gained through the human frailty that fosters dependence on the Savior, a dependence traditionally satisfied through the mediations of sacramental religion.[1] Milton's restored paradise, in contrast, relies entirely on inspired human agency. His projected play, "Adam Unparadiz'd," made paradise into a verb, if one negated and banished to the past tense; *Paradise Lost* and *Paradise Regain'd* attempt to realize corrupt humanity as the present subject of this verb.[2] This is the project of his continuous oeuvre: from his prose writings to his major poems, Milton applied the principle of *imitatio Adami* as universally as he could, describing the reformed life as a process of setting human existence against its created model and taking progressive steps to eradicate discrepancies between them. According to *The Doctrine and Discipline of Divorce*, for example, if a marriage did not "in some measure" restore the original happiness enjoyed by the first couple, God and nature had not joined the couple in matrimony.[3] Marriage is by nature what it was in the beginning; unions that did not partake of this nature were not what canon law called them. In order to assess whether one's marriage adequately restored the first, one had to rely on "experience," not "conjecture" or "Church-rites."[4] What was once a sacrament becomes an experiment, with knowledge gained from a failed union becoming the basis for a new one. There is no vantage point untouched by the contingencies of fallen experience from which to judge that experience and find it wanting, and the ad hoc character of Milton's various campaigns of paradisal restoration has often been remarked. John Eachard assured his readers that he was not one of "those occasional Writers, that missing preferment in the University can presently write you their new ways of Education; or being a little tormented with an ill chosen Wife, set forth the Doctrine of Divorce to be truly Evangelical." Turning every personal struggle into public business, Milton's reforming efforts were as "occasional" as Boyle's reflections.[5] Far from being a disinterested intervention in the controversy over book licensing, for example, *Areopagitica* was an effort to defend against the censorship of his own writings.[6] In *Samson Agonistes,* after Samson has destroyed the temple, Manoa expresses the hope that the Israelites will "Find courage to lay hold on this occasion"; for Milton, fallen existence was filled with occasions on which to "lay hold."[7] Milton offered his writings as such an occasion: our opportunity to imagine paradise not as a permanently foreign world but as an alien experience of the world we already know. Conferring the ontological prestige of the original order on the defining features of fallen life—work, sex, the daily experience of imperfection and failure—*Paradise Lost* enables us to perceive them all from the estranging perspective of innocence. Revealing paradise as the fruit of a project that can be undertaken now, in this world, the poem challenges the reader to resist both tragic and comic accounts of the fall—to imagine it rather as a "thing indifferent," a stage in an ongoing process of experimental self-cultivation that demanded no more from the first couple than it now demands from their progeny. To a people committed to cultivating a "paradise within," it matters little where this process begins: the project of paradisal existence was once undertaken in Eden; it now proceeds along the paths providence makes available.[8] While this process unfolds, as we would expect, the means and ends of restoration collapse.

We are poorly prepared for *Paradise Lost* by the tradition of paradisal representation that precedes it, but it is this tradition that has shaped the poem's critical legacy. The most influential twentieth-century account of Milton's Eden, that of Stanley Fish, drives a wedge between fallen and unfallen experience that baldly contradicts the poem's commitment to the work of bringing paradise to the world beyond the garden. For Fish, the fall

marks a rigid boundary between two states of being whose incommensu-
rability provides the mechanism for readerly self-correction. The process
turns out to be strangely pointless, consisting in the repeated recognition
that "we cannot understand innocence at all."[9] I will suggest that Milton's
famous dips into fallen language when describing Eden are just what they
seem to be: efforts to disrupt an at once naïve and corrupt understanding of
innocence as a reassuringly lost state of perfection to which no "fallen"
modifier could ever be applied. Like any other experimentalist collective,
Milton's prelapsarian people work on a world in urgent need of "reform."[10]
It is to the innocent labor of reformation that Milton seeks to restore us.

We generally move in and out of fictional worlds aimlessly, without
subjecting our readerly identifications to a progressive logic, but Milton's
paradisal narratives are not presented to us as fictions, and they stipulate a
much less casual approach to identification. As sequences in a progression,
Paradise Lost and *Paradise Regain'd* move the reader from an identification
with the damned toward an identification with a son of God who restores
paradise in the desert of fallen existence simply by existing as a paradisal
subject. Contemporaries would have expected a poem called *Paradise
Regain'd* to be about the Passion, but Milton makes a strictly Adamic use of
the Son.[11] Described in *Paradise Lost* as a perpetually recurring subject position, the identity of the "one just Man"—the single subject in which regenerate humanity is deposited, as it was originally deposited in Adam—is
in principle available to any son of God.[12] As I will argue, it is the model for
the Miltonic public: a corporate worker on whom Milton's final poem confers the name Samson.

Milton's restorative project inevitably has some purely constructive
aspects. In order to "score out" to epic length the handful of sentences with
which Genesis describes the first state of creation—and to extend that
length across the life of humanity—Milton had to make things up.[13] In
assuming narrative responsibility for innocent existence, he engaged not in
fiction but experimentation: an ongoing effort of rational reconstruction.
The distinction was lost on many of his contemporaries. Lucy Hutchinson's
hexameral epic *Order and Disorder,* clearly written as a corrective to *Paradise Lost,* is prefaced by the disclaimer, "I tremble to think of turning Scripture into a romance"; the poem consists largely of pious refusals to fill in
gaps in the Genesis account.[14] The experimental speculation that Hutchinson strives at all costs to avoid was for Milton a necessary condition of

regenerate art and the regenerate life. While Hutchinson lards her margins with biblical citations,[15] Milton's epic interposes itself between scripture and the reader as an instrument of magnification, to help us see further into the world Genesis describes. It could be regarded as even more dangerous than "romance" for this very reason. In his dedicatory poem, Marvell worries that the epic infringes on its readers' freedom to look at scripture with their own eyes, as Milton the prose writer had repeatedly urged them to do. As Kenneth Gross observes, Marvell's censure of Dryden's dramatic adaptation of the epic—an attempt to "excell" Milton's text through "ill imitating"—clearly reflects on the relationship of Milton's poem to *its* primary source, the Bible. If Dryden's efforts seem merely foolish, Milton's attempt to "improve" on scripture inspires real anxiety; Marvell fears not its failure but rather its success in "o'rewhelming" God's word.[16] Marvell's own paradisal restorations were abstracted from scriptural narration and designed for generalized and open-ended application; Hutchinson's *Order and Disorder* was a straightforward versification of Genesis. Milton's prelapsarian narrative seemed to be neither thing. *Paradise Lost* does not merely model itself after Genesis; in presuming to offer detailed knowledge of the original creation, it appears to present itself as a possible replacement.

It is the contention of this chapter that Milton's poem assumes and exercises this privilege experimentally. The experimentalist conviction that to live in paradise is simply to inhabit the world God made depends on a concept of that world as alien, needing to be discovered; *Paradise Lost* offers itself as an instrument for that discovery. The poem redeems fallen perception and reveals paradise not through any single decisive insight but by offering itself as a medium for a collective revisionary effort. This is not to say that Milton makes no assertions about innocent existence, but he does so through a language that reproduces the prosthetic, processual, and perpetually revisable character of experimentalist insight.[17] The poem is not a scriptural surrogate for literal application by the "Carnall textman."[18] Rather than petrified idols for the mind's eye to stare at, the poem provides materials for the mind's eye to see with; instead of colonizing the reader's mind with fictions about paradise, it exercises her ability to see through fictions into paradise—and, ultimately, I will argue, through it. Experimentalist practitioners cultivated innocence as a method; aligning himself with Galileo, the only named contemporary in the poem, Milton recovers it for us as a perspective. Turning paradise itself into a perceptual medium, the poem becomes an instrument with which the reader works to cultivate a vision adequate to creation.

To unpack this claim requires us to analyze what *Paradise Lost* is like to read, as Fish advises us to do. Like the technology on which it is modeled, the poem provides evidence of the recently discovered maladaption of human perception to the scope of creation, with results that centuries of complaints have made famous: it lacks "the freshness, raciness, and energy of immediate observation" (Johnson); it is "incompatible with sharp, concrete realization" (Leavis); it severs thought from sensuous perception, exhibiting a "dissociation of sensibility" (Eliot).[19] While Milton provides a very solid sense of the physical reality of the observational conditions he sets up, he leaves what is seen under these conditions largely up to us, literally making *Paradise Lost* a trial to read, its images only as vivid as the reader works to render them. Like the optical instrument of truth whose powers it assumes, this technology for extending the limits of "mortal sight" requires a user willing to invest care in making truth visible. By taking steps to reform its reader into such a user, *Paradise Lost* fulfills the ideal of "sensuous" writing espoused in *Of Education*.[20] Milton invented this reformed variant of *sensual;* the coinage condenses a whole experimentalist aesthetics. The sensuous text is not merely a means to delight the sensitive body (responsive to the "jingling sound of like endings" censured in the note on the verse), nor is it pure nourishment for thinking substance; it is an instrument to be engaged in the dialectical struggle between the intellectual's two bodies. Taking seriously the embodied nature of the reading experience, Milton sought to subject the mind's eye to the same discipline to which working experimentalists subjected the body's eye, expanding the private experience of reading into the necessarily collective labor of seeing through the world and into creation. In undertaking this work, Milton and his readers continue the experiment that innocent humanity began.

The Making of an Experimentalist Author

The development of this technology was a protracted process. Milton's experimentalist aims are evident early in his career, but they are manifested largely as aims; rather than being formally realized, they are associated with values asserted or scenes represented. Of his attraction to Baconianism there can be no doubt.[21] During his "studious retirement," Milton reported that he often went into the city "to become acquainted with some new discovery in mathematics or music, in which I then took the keenest pleasure." As David Masson and Barbara Lewalski both point out, there is nowhere he could have gone but to the only center in London for lectures on each of these subjects: Gresham College.[22] Some of Milton's mathematical observations, like his contention that the prelatical pyramid is "the most dividing, and schismaticall forme that Geometricians know of," suggest that he may not have learned a great deal there.[23] But although Milton was no virtuoso, he went on to forge close ties to the experimentalist community. In addition to being friends with Samuel Hartlib and Henry Oldenburg, he was an intimate of Katherine Boyle: "to me," he wrote, "she has stood in the place of all relations."[24] After the Restoration, John Beale thought it worthwhile to ask Evelyn's help in persuading Milton to take up some "honest argument," directing "every potent Inspiration" to the "glory of the R Soc"; casting about for an "Argument . . . worthy of his force," Beale came up with *De Vitris Opticis* and *De Machina Pneumatica* as candidates.[25] The proposal almost makes sense. Had it not been publicly linked to the king, the Gresham of the 1660s might have been as congenial to the "clubbable" Milton as its earlier counterpart, or even as the Italian academies: from his university schoolwork to his major poems, Milton's career was a sustained effort to make literary experience an instrument of Baconian "advancement."[26]

The young Milton had as much grounds as any virtuoso to complain about the schoolmen; as his Cambridge prolusions make clear, he held them personally responsible for his miseries as a university student. On one occasion, he calls for a strike, declaring that he will have attained "the height of my ambition for the present" if he can persuade his fellow students to stop doing their homework. Railing against scholastic debates as "useless and barren controversies," he heaps ridicule on the "expert ignorance" and "blind Barbarity" of the schoolmen: mistaking words for things themselves, they make the student believe himself to be blind when there is, in fact, "nothing for him to see." Immersion in their writings actually *causes* blindness: "my mind has been dulled and my sight blurred by continued reading." He urges his classmates to put down their books and "let your eyes wander" over maps and the physical world, gleaning real knowledge of the nature of stones, herbs, stars, and meteors; the study of maps, history, and nature all come together in an ocular "wandering" ("oculis peramubulare"). Describing observation as a form of movement, Milton clothes contemplation in the language of action. He then tries to present literary study as a natural extension of such action: unlike barren controversies that leave the student unequipped for any "new situation," eloquent speech and divine poetry provide a means to engage the world, moving the soul and inciting it to glorious deeds.[27]

Of course, this was a humanist commonplace. Literature was supposed to link "well knowing" to "well dooing" by providing "lively examples" of trusty precepts; this was how Spenser proposed to "fashion a gentleman."[28] But the identification of the progress of knowledge with the artificial production of new experiences offered a different way to conceive of poetry's relation to the world, as an instrument of discovery. Years later, in support of the unsurprising claim that the author should be virtuous, Milton did not suggest that the author should resemble an exemplary hero, but that he "ought him selfe to bee a true Poem"; such an author was a "composition, and patterne" of the "experience" the poem embodied.[29] Rather than the expected mimetic (imitative) correspondence between the reader and fictional character, Milton posits an isomorphism between the author and the text. Both are mediums for experience that can be incorporated and subjected to further cultivation by the reader; the experience of the artist forms the foundation of a literary practice devoted to truth production through virtual witnessing.

Milton's movement toward such a practice is already evident in his final prolusion. As if speaking from experience, he relates the joys of transcending "the crass perceptions of the senses" to penetrate the causes of the visible. Although Milton's sense of science seems almost magical, he presents it as a georgic antidote to superstition. In understanding "all the movements and changes of the atmosphere" and "the hidden virtues of plants and metals," the "spirit of man, no longer confined within this dark prison-house, will reach out far and wide." A prophetic observer who could "perfectly . . . understand" creation would regard events like comets merely as instances of nature's predictable "chances and changes"; from such a perspective, "hardly anything can happen . . . which is unforeseen or fortuitous." Rather than being cowed by the majesty of thunder, this spectator would himself be a king, as if "some god had abdicated the throne of the world and entrusted its rights, laws, and administration to him as governor." Milton suggests that the escape from the prison house of the senses begins by using those senses—letting one's eyes wander over creation and beyond their fixed abode on earth. Through what Balachandra Rajan aptly calls "a progressive apprenticeship to the visible," the secrets of nature are revealed.[30] Not having learned any of these secrets, Milton does not impart them; instead, he seeks to represent the total experience of discovery, which he does in suitably "wandering" prose. The agent of discovery is identified not with himself or any particular person but with a general human potential; in wandering away from its author toward the subject position inhabited by an ideal spectatorial body, the text points the reader toward that vantage point. So, Milton suggests, would a real education.

Over a decade later, Milton filled out the details of this daydream in more sober fashion. Presented as a redaction of observations made to Hartlib in the course of "incidentall discourses which we have wander'd into," *Of Education* is also described as a blossom, what "flowr'd off" many years spent in search of knowledge. The imagery is precise. Milton presents his "*Idea* . . . of a better Education" through what we will find to be central figures for paradisal life, wandering and cultivation, because his idea is to restore that life:

> The end then of learning is to repair the ruins of our first parents by regaining to know God aright, and out of that knowledge to love him, to imitate him, to be like him . . . But because our understanding cannot in this body found it selfe but on sensible things, nor arrive so cleerly to the knowledge of God and things invisible, as by orderly conning over the visible and inferior creature, the same method is necessarily to be follow'd in all discreet teaching.[31]

The "discreet" or prudent method of "orderly conning" fits grandiose ambitions to modest means; like experimentalist practice, it proceeds discretely, by steps.[32] To con over is to peruse or commit to memory, as one would with a prayer book or lesson to be learned by rote, and Milton makes the book of creation the lesson: students of his ideal academy will be "fraught with an universall insight into things." If in his student years he was somewhat vague on how such insight would be gathered, the mature Milton (as we saw in Chapter 2) is able to offer the commonsensical suggestion of roving apprenticeships with working-class practitioners, and field trips. Students will visit "all the quarters of the land: learning and observing all places of strength, all commodities of building and of soil, for towns and tillage, harbours and Ports," all the while engaging in "constant exercises."[33] The coordination of physical and mental energies that underlies the virtuoso's discipline of mind, eye, and hand forms the basis of Milton's restorative curriculum.

While he was an enthusiast for experimentalist education, Milton was not its beneficiary; he happily recommends Pliny as an expert in natural history, while suggesting that the practical knowledge of anatomists and gardeners will unlock difficult classical texts, making them "facil and pleasant."[34] Nonetheless, the Baconian vision of paradisal restoration organizes the entire treatise. Like Boyle's Adam, tilling the soil from which he was made, Milton's students will cultivate themselves as paradisal ground. In defense of the claim that forcing children with "empty wits" to compose orations is "an old errour of universities not yet well recover'd from the Scholastick grosnesse of barbarous ages," Milton declares that extorting performances from pupils who have not cultivated "preparatory grounds" through experience is the "plucking of untimely fruit," resulting only in "babblements."[35] Evoking the paradigmatic scene of corrupted language, Milton's coinage associates the hasty plucking of compositional fruit with the fall itself, and this premature harvest is indeed a fatal one, breeding a "hatred and contempt of learning" that actually compels students into sin. Starved for experience, those whose education consists in "meere words" are driven to learn "such things chiefly, as were better unlearnt," surrendering to the carnal enjoyments of "ease and luxury" and the worldly ambition that can secure them; the rest fly to the opposite extreme of an "ignorantly zealous Divinity" and its civic counterpart, "conscientious slavery" (375-376). In contrast to these pathologies of the undisciplined body and undernourished spirit, Milton's "happy nurture," a dialectical cultivation of body and mind, lays the grounds for an existence in which labor and delight are mutually supportive, and pleasure need not be chased through "feast and jollity" (377, 376).

Milton depicts himself leading Hartlib and England's youth on a path that is "laborious indeed at the first ascent, but else so smooth, so green, so full of goodly prospect, and melodious sounds on every side, that the harp of *Orpheus* was not more charming." The phrase "goodly prospect" occurs one other time in Milton's corpus, to describe paradise—"this World"—as "First-seen" by Satan and the reader.[36] Orpheus, who appears in Bacon's *De*

Sapientia Veterum as the personification of active philosophy, here models both the power of Milton's curriculum to revivify the "dullest and laziest youth" and the kind of eloquence in which the youth are to be trained, for the study of mere words can also offer a portal into experience, through the "simple, sensuous and passionate" language of poetry.[37] In *Of Reformation*, Milton had described the soul's "sensuous collegue" as capable of sinking the soul into "sensuall Idolatry," but education could train the sensuous body to be a good colleague; sensuous language provides a reformed alternative to the "trifling at Grammar and *Sophistry*" which, failing to engage the senses, leaves them open to corrupt uses.[38] In the *Apology Against a Pamphlet,* Milton had argued that "art is most eloquent, which returnes and approaches neerest to nature from whence it came; and they expresse nature best, who in their lives least wander from her safe leading, which may be call'd regenerate reason." Writing that expresses regenerate reason cannot simply reflect nature but must *return* to it, retracing the wandering path out of the original creation and back to things themselves. Milton's students must do the same. In spring, "it were an injury and sullennesse against nature not to go out, and see her riches, and partake in her rejoycing with heaven and earth." In contrast to targeted field trips, such wanderings represent the "opportunity of gaining experience to be won from pleasure it selfe."[39] What began as a figurative "goodly prospect" of a restored paradise is now literalized as the actual English countryside, through which youths innocently roam in search of experience.

Body and mind are sensuously blended everywhere in Milton's language, as in the experiential curriculum it describes; even Latin class is described in unusually calisthenic terms, leaving students "enflam'd," "stirr'd up," and eager to perform "manly, and liberall exercises." Milton concludes *Of Education* declaring that the educator able to impart this curriculum "will require sinews almost equall to those which Homer gave Ulysses," uniting intellectual muscle to physical brawn as he later would when idealizing the English as "sinewy to discours" in *Areopagitica.*[40] In such passages, Milton's attempts to link literary pursuits to the active life can seem strained, as if a rhetoric of athletic physicality were being offered to compensate for the lack of the thing itself. The modified dualism that celebrates the sensuous body as an agent of production rather than consumption vies with the stark oppositions the seventeenth century inherited between action and contemplation, body and mind. This friction between an emerging

ethic of productivity and one of brute action can be felt throughout the
prose, as in the blending of horticultural and martial rhetorics in his famous Ovidian description of books as "Dragons teeth" that, when "sown,"
can spring up as "armed men."[41] At times, the perfect union of action and
contemplation seems achievable only through metaphor, one that obscures
the sedentary conditions of reading and writing.

Acknowledging the wishful nature of this analogizing between contemplative and conventionally "active" pursuits should not distract us from
the synthetic, experimentalist ideal of the *productive* subject that such
analogizing serves. This ideal is the cornerstone of Milton's pedagogical
theory. As if to retroactively assert the relevance of that theory to his evolving literary practice, Milton included *Of Education* in the 1673 edition of
his poems: read with this intertext, the most familiar passages of his early
poems take on an unexpectedly Baconian dimension. The pensive man of
"Il Penseroso," for example, comes to us as an expert in "conning over the
visible and inferior creature." Presented in the first person, this figure, like
the privileged spectator of Milton's final prolusion, exists in the future tense,
as the embodiment of an as-yet-unrealized human potential. In the poem's
penultimate image, Milton imagines this self being dissolved "into exta-
sies" at a church service, but then the church itself dissolves, and with it the
fantasy of an ecstatic separation of soul from body. Conventional ecstasy is
reformed by innocent embodiment: the poem's final scene is one of sensuous contemplation in a "Mossy Cell," an excrescence of vegetable nature
that, like Marvell's "green Shade," opens back out onto creation. At once
removed from nature and an extension of it, this "peacefull hermitage" re-
fashions the monkish cell as a paradisal workroom

> Where I may sit and rightly spell
> Of every Star that Heav'n doth shew,
> And every Herb that sips the dew;
> Till old experience do attain
> To something like Prophetic strain.[42]

Like the laboratory, this space is consecrated to the cultivating and ripening
of experience so that it may mature into prophecy or prediction. Roy Flannagan glosses *spell* as "to make out, understand, decipher, or comprehend,
by study," and most commentators agree.[43] Clearly, Milton employs the

word to evoke the topos of nature's book, but the *of* suggests that he is using an older meaning of *spell*, to discourse or preach.[44] Although alone, he is preaching, and the text of his sermon is the created world. As Milton argued in *The Reason of Church Government*, preaching occurred "not only in Pulpits." It was through print that Milton entered into his famous "covnant," not with any particular godly community, but with "any knowing reader": through this covenant, Milton made clear that the reading public was the only godly community he cared about.[45]

By the end of "Il Penseroso," the opposition of action and contemplation that structures the companion poems has been reinvented; the pensive man alone embodies both virtues, integrating them through productive contemplation: a sacred labor, and a public one, as the virtual congregation of his readers reconstitutes the church he has left behind. It is in this poem that we encounter Orpheus in his strength; at once the personification of efficacious song and the arts that compel matter, his revival here corresponds to the revitalization of literature by an experimentalist poet-preacher who, having learned to spell the book of nature, can spell of it rightly.[46] As in the Baconian experiment, it is experience itself that speaks, not the experimenter; the pensive man is only the medium for its prophetic strain. But it is a strain to imagine what this strain will be. A "sensuous" literary practice that aspires to the force of the physical while elevating itself above the carnal presents the same paradox as the cultivation of physical experience toward godly ends propounded in *Of Education;* this is the animating paradox of empiricism itself. For working experimentalists, as we have seen, the solution was prosthetic. The paradoxical combination of attitudes toward the body and sensory experience could be resolved through collective and technologically mediated observation—a way of seeing with one's own eyes that extended what the eyes could see. "Il Penseroso" sets the scene for a literary adaptation of such labor, but does not enact it. The prophetic poet who can spell of creation will be embodied decades later as a speaker who can "see and tell / Of things invisible to mortal sight" by relying on a prosthetic source of insight, but here that source is thinly imagined, obscurely associated with a personification of melancholy whose gifts are anticipated rather than known. The poem is a statement of intent: he will choose to live with (but, crucially, not simply as) the source of insight that will make the sacred labor possible.[47]

When Milton laid hold on the occasion of the Bridgewater household's Michaelmas festivities to model a progressive alternative to state-supported holiday mirth, he returned to this scene and populated it.[48] *A Maske,* of course, centers on the conflict of Comus—the son of Bacchus and Circe, a bestial, castle-dwelling aristocrat who takes cover in rural weeds and customs, much like Herrick's jolly parson—and the bearer of Milton's college nickname, the Lady, whose virtue is signaled by her disgust with the "Riot, and ill manag'd Merriment" of "Wassailers" who "thank the gods amiss."[49] They are led on by the "hellish charms" of festival itself: "Joy, and Feast, / Midnight shout, and revelry, / Tipsie dance, and Jollity"—freedoms on which, Comus admits, "the canon laws of our foundation" depend.[50] Milton handles the paradox that the wassailers seem to be enjoying themselves by delivering it straight: "so perfect is their misery" that they "roule with pleasure." At the same time, he saps festival fun of its associations with charitable fellowship—reduced to beasts, the revelers "all their friends, and native home forget." Against this backdrop, Milton presents his captive aristocratic audience with a very different image of thanksgiving, and of humanity's "native home," through the Spirit's description of

> . . . a certain Shepherd Lad
> Of small regard to see to, yet well skill'd
> In every vertuous plant and healing herb
> That spreds her verdant leaf to th' morning ray,
> He lov'd me well, and oft would beg me sing,
> Which when I did, he on the tender grass
> Would sit, and hearken even to extasie,
> And in requitall ope his leather'n scrip,
> And shew me simples of a thousand names
> Telling their strange and vigorous faculties . . . [51]

The pastoral motif of the exchange of songs is expanded to accommodate the sharing of "strange" horticultural and medicinal knowledge, generating an "extasie" absent from Comus's revels. Comus insists to the Lady that nature's "bounties" are "all to please, and sate the curious taste"; but here, a thousand plants elicit the exercise of curiosity as *skill*.[52] This sociable showing and "Telling," on "tender grass," of "every vertuous plant and healing herb" is a productive form of thanksgiving, like the rightly spelling song of "Il Penseroso"—or the first thanksgiving of Genesis 2:19, for the shepherd assigns names to the plants whose qualities he unfolds.

Among the plants explicated by this experimental demonstration is "a small unsightly root . . . of divine effect": *"Haemony,"* an herb Milton concocted using etymons relating to blood and knowledge or skill. Following Coleridge, critics often gloss *haemony* as a symbol of grace.[53] Its sacramental resonance is clear enough, but rather than evoking blood sacrifice, this "unsightly root"—only one of thousands of simples with "strange and vigorous faculties"—serves merely as a synecdoche of an ongoing sacrament of knowledge production: the sacred process by which small and unsightly things are made to disclose divine ones, often by people of equally "small regard."[54] Offering a means of escape from the survivalist logic that underlies the festival cycle (Comus's "Refreshment after toil, ease after pain"), the progressive disclosure of nature's secrets opens out into the paradisal curriculum elaborated in *Of Education:* an academy planted on English soil.[55] The academy originally designated a garden; as an institution that made its members "more industrious, more ingenuous," as he later put it, the academy restored what for Milton was the essential, and recoverable, feature of the first garden.[56]

In both poems, Milton's experimentalist ambition is expressed in hybrid terms, associated with an Orphic magus-preacher-poet or located in the exchange of a shepherd-simpler and spirit-singer; these efforts at conceptual integration show their seams. The elusive ideal is expressed most vividly through its opposite: "Blind mouthes." Classically associated with "blind bellies," the eye that cannot see anything new is also the mouth that won't shut up: associated with a bulemic cycle of gluttonous consumption and corrupt verbiage, this mouth is a constant presence in the antiprelatical tracts.[57] The corrupt, usually prelatical mouth—the mouth that seeks to be "the only mouth of the whole body"—was an essential foil for Milton's evolving vision of the one body representative, to paraphrase the first epigraph of this chapter: a productive *corpus mysticum* rooted in an alternative physicality, an alternative sense of time, and an alternative sacrament. The blind mouth conjured up its opposite, the eloquent and productive eye, an organ that forms the basis of the corporate spectatorial body at the center of *Areopagitica* and the major poems: a paradisally restored body that binds together the emergent concepts of intellectual labor and the public. As a source of negative inspiration, the prelatical mouth stimulates Milton to develop counterfigures for a calling enjoined on "the people" as well as the priest: intellectual labor. Conceived of as a progressive undertaking, such labor will restore a unity to the mystical body that can never be achieved through ritual means.

Milton famously contended that any gifted craftsman could preach more soundly than most clergy; accordingly, he tends to reserve the pejorative use of the term *mechanicks* for schoolmen or monks, while figuring Laudian worship and the knowledge practices of the university as a grotesque combination of unthinking drudgery and corrupt consumption.[58] In *Of Reformation,* he compares the soul "over-bodying her selfe" with the "customary ey-Service of the body" to a broken-winged bird that has given up "the labour of high soaring" to "plod on in the old rode, and drudging Trade of outward conformity."[59] Here Milton does not identify soaring with high contemplation and trudging with low labor: what in another writer might serve as a means to distinguish between the learned and the laboring sort becomes a means to distinguish labor—progressive, elevating— from the drudgery of underemployment. The bird soon reappears on the plate of a clergyman, through the overstuffed rhyme of the "many-benefice-gaping mouth of a Prelate" and his "canary-sucking, and swan-eating palat."[60] Sucking up individual souls along with benefices, the prelate consumes his parishioners precisely by turning them into consumers; incorporating them into a regime of carnal worship, he renders them unfit for the "labour of high soaring." Milton's concept of what such labor entails has little to do with learning as conventionally defined. In *The Reason of Church Government* he complains about being forced

> to club quotations with men whose learning and beleif lies in marginal stuffings, who when they have like good sumpters laid ye down their hors load of citations and fathers at your dore, with a rapsody of who and who were Bishops here or there, ye may take off their packsaddles, their days work is don, and episcopacy, as they think, stoutly vindicated. Let any gentle apprehension that can distinguish learned pains from unlearned drudgery, imagin what pleasure or profoundnesse can be in this, or what honour to deal against such adversaries.

Milton's association of gentility and honor with the taking of pains, along with the reduction of university-educated gentlemen to beasts of burden, recapitulates the experimentalist inversion of high and low learning: displays of Latin erudition and learned appeals to authority are here figured not merely as the "unlearned drudgery" of day laborers but as activities unworthy of the human animal.[61] Without the investment of pains, literate activity is reduced to clubbing, intellectual matter to "stuffing," and publication itself to a delivery of a "hors load of citations." The pun on *hoarse* completes the insult, as learned disputants are reduced to street cryers, or even whores, having prostituted their minds to authorities, even as the figure of textual engorgement redefines what true learning consists in: not the consumption and disgorgement of authoritative texts but the "painful" cultivation of experience.

The imagery and argumentation of the antiprelatical tracts, along with their organizing oppositions—bestial drudgery and manly labor, idolatrous and reformed religion, cyclical degeneration and progress—are structured less by a dualism of body and soul than by a distinction between two corporeal modes: carnal passivity and sensuous productivity. The opposition is tailor made to promote an experimentalist understanding of intellectual labor as productive contemplation. It is only in the context of civil or religious idolatry that observation of mere things becomes diabolical, an obsessive feeding of the corporeal eye that results in "an unactive blindnesse of minde." Approving descriptions of vigorous physicality, and sensuous engagement with things themselves, suggest a very different attitude toward the body as a source of knowledge. Throughout the prose, Milton employs a rhetoric of strapping athleticism to present truth as something that is produced and "exercised" rather than imbibed.[62] *Areopagitica* makes the analogy explicit: "our faith and knowledge thrives by exercise, as well as our limbs and complexion . . . as in a body, when the blood is fresh, the spirits pure and vigorous, not only to vital, but to rationall faculties." Although he consistently associates the exercised and cultivated body with spiritual refinement, Milton sometimes conveys the summons to exercise in such unconditionally calisthenic terms that it can be hard for the reader to visualize its "spiritfull" analogue.[63] It is when Milton imagines contemplation *as* action, rather than merely constructing hopeful analogies between the two, that he can present the exercise of faith as something more than the stepchild of muscular exertion—as a productive activity in its own right.

At such moments he makes use of the rhetoric of experimentalist spectatorship. In his description of the ministers known collectively as Smectymnuus, whose "strong and sinewy force in teaching and confuting" made them "the eyes of their Country, and the prospective glasses of their Prince," sinewy force enters the domain of "teaching and confuting" by means of the art that made contemplation productive.[64] The intellectual laborer who publicly offers himself as a prospective glass is a body capable of incorporating others. As Milton explained, he was moved to defend Smectymnuus because he felt himself becoming a part of them: "I conceav'd my selfe to be now not as mine own person, but as a member incorporate into that truth whereof I was perswaded," As in experimentalist discourse, the topos of the *corpus mysticum* and spectatorial rhetoric sustain one another, for Milton describes Bible-reading as a kind of assisted observation as well. By aligning the study of scripture with experimentalist investigation, he identifies the defining practice of the godly life as a progressive one. In *The Reason of Church Government*, he describes the power of words like *schism* to lead "the blinder sort of people" to "deride sound doctrine and good christianity under two or three vile and hatefull terms"; he hopes that "the people of England will not suffer themselves to be juggl'd thus out of their faith and religion by a mist of names cast before their eyes": they should "look quite through" this mist and "search wisely by the Scriptures . . . into the things themselves."[65] Scripture is not an inert repository of truths but a perceptual medium, enabling its user to disperse the "mist of names" that everywhere camouflages the real things of creation. Elsewhere, Milton encourages warfaring Christians to perform involuntary eye surgery on Laud's defenders, heaving up the gospel in order to "hold it ever in their faces like a mirror of Diamond, till it dazle, and pierce their misty ey balls."[66] Here the mist is an inherent feature of the carnal eye, which must be lanced in order to provide the soul an organ with which to work. Scripture is the instrument with which to perform this operation: shining into the eyes like a burning glass, it pierces through an ocular mist, purging the sensitive body from the spectatorial body. The sharpened glass suggests the trope of the lens-as-spade, digging into the carnal eye so that the eye of what Winstanley called "the body of the living soule" can do its work of digging past fallen perception and dogma.[67]

Scripture could offer an estranged perspective on the false names and images promoted by custom and fallen perception, exposing the real things beneath them; but to serve this purpose it had to be made the subject of estranging scrutiny, and even improved, by reformed readers. Thus Milton's

own experimental exegesis—which subjected the letter of scripture to
the lessons of painful "experience" and the heuristic principle of charity—
resulted in a complete inversion of Christ's words against divorce. The satirical author of *Little Non-Such: or, Certaine New Questions Moved out of
Ancient Truths* ("Newly published with intent to finde out the truth") indicated the extremes to which such a lavish application of Baconian "charity"
might lead by using Genesis to defend incest.[68] The effort to "move" new
truths out of old ones was easily satirized: the phrase "new truths" was practically a motif in the literature against the sects; in Cleveland's scornful
depiction, the peasant rebels "wonder at the new truths" revealed by their
ringleader John Ball. But of course the ability to produce new truths was
the very measure of the experimentalist's worth. Boyle suggested that one
could arrive at a "dis-interess[t]ed" evaluation of a philosopher's merit by
considering "what new Experiment or matter of fact" he had produced,
"what new Truths he has discovered."[69] Milton transfers this criterion to
Bible study: to be reformed, it must be productive; rather than simply confirming known truths, it must always be generating new ones.

By describing the Bible as both an object and instrument of discovery,
Milton subjects the doctrine of *sola scriptura* to reform. In doing so, he follows the lead of experimental Christians, but he goes considerably further
than Stephen Denison ever would. England's release from the idolatrous
bondage of Laudian innovation turns out to have been only the beginning
of its restoration; to complete the process, England must throw off the yoke
of the Reformation itself:

> The light which we have gain'd, was giv'n us, not to be ever staring on, but
> by it to discover onward things more remote from our knowledge. It is not
> the unfrocking of a Priest, the unmitring of a Bishop, and the removing him
> from off the *Presbyterian* shoulders that will make us a happy Nation, no, if
> other things as great in the Church, and in the rule of life both economicall
> and politicall be not lookt into and reform'd, we have lookt so long upon the
> blaze that *Zuinglius* and *Calvin* hath beacon'd up to us, that we are stark
> blind.

The light of the Reformation becomes an idol if it is not immediately put to
use as an occasion for more reformation; the instruments of reformation

must themselves be "lookt into and reform'd."[70] Milton writes as if reformation had less to do with establishing purity of worship than with prosecuting a Baconian program of discovery: reformation consists not in "ever
staring on" the truths that have been attained, but in using them "to discover
onward things more remote from our knowledge." There is no distinction
to be made between reformation and intellectual labor at all.[71]

In *Areopagitica,* Milton projects his experimentalist image of the
reformer—the laborer who demonstrates his "sinewy force" by publicly offering himself as a "prospective glass"—onto the English public itself. The
spectatorial body materializes as "a Nation of Prophets," whose labors have
"enfranchis'd, enlarg'd and lifted up our apprehensions degrees above
themselves."[72] In *Areopagitica,* print is virtually celebrated *as* an optical
instrument—a technology with which to restore fallen "apprehensions" by
expanding and collectivizing them. Identified with magnification—the
exposure of the causes of the visible—iconoclasm becomes a progressive
labor, the calling proper to a magnified or multiplied agent of curiosity.
Although *Areopagitica* is arguably the most important exploration of assisted observation in Milton's prose, it makes no mention of the lens, only
its most celebrated user: "the famous *Galileo.*" (Needless to say, this Galileo
is not the scientist working in a patronage-based model of science who concerned us in Part I but rather the idealized figure English experimentalists
constructed—"a Protestant hero of free thought.")[73] In one of the most
powerfully understated sentences he ever wrote, Milton recalls meeting the
astronomer in Italy: "There it was that I found and visited the famous *Galileo* grown old, a prisner to the Inquisition, for thinking in Astronomy otherwise then the Franciscan and Dominican licencers thought." Rather than
a chance encounter, this meeting was the end of a pilgrimage; Milton set out
to find and visit the "famous . . . prisner," a martyr to the cause of speculative freedom.[74] Milton presents Galileo's astronomical instrument as
"thinking," the more easily to present his cultivation of vision as a general
public right, for while the intellectual liberty asserted in *Areopagitica* is
imagined in thoroughly spectatorial terms, it attaches to the ideal of unli-
censed printing. Anticipating the grand textacle of his epic poem, *Areopagitica* transfers the power to enlarge apprehensions from the perspective
glass to print, the technology through which "friends of Truth" are
"enfranchis'd" into a public.[75]

"Every Joynt and Member": Molding the Body of Truth

The "Speech of Mr. John Milton for the Liberty of Unlicenc'd Printing, to the Parlament of England" has a feature that sets it apart from other Parliamentary speeches: as a printed pamphlet sold to the reading public, it addresses members of Parliament through the England that was only "representatively present" in the Commons. The Commons might well have posed the same question to Milton that it did to Lilburne: "If it be a Petition to the House, why is it Printed and Published to the *people,* before the presenting of it to the *House?* Is it to get the approbation of *multitudes?* What need of that? . . . The *whole Judgment* of the Kingdom, is in the *Judgment* of the *Houses.*"[76] As I discussed in Chapter 2, the identity of the representative with the represented was a fiction that enabled a "pastoral" substitution of the latter by the former. Milton exposes the sacramental fiction of political representation by pretending to take it seriously; treating the identity as reciprocal, he addresses Parliament through the people.[77] Milton's assault on Parliament's representative monopoly is undertaken on behalf of the "Nation of Prophets" that, in the sphere of truth production, claims the right to represent itself. To place the exercise of this right under the power of twenty licensers, Milton contends, is an "undervaluing and vilifying of the whole Nation. I cannot set so light by all the invention, the art, the wit, the grave and solid judgement which is in England, as that it can be comprehended in any twenty capacities how good soever."[78] The "whole Nation" cannot be "comprehended"—either understood or contained—by a handful of its members. Thus comprehended, England is no more England than Parliament itself is.

Although Milton gamely addresses MPs as if they were indeed interchangeable with the people of England—"they who counsell ye to such a suppressing, doe as good as bid ye supresse your selves"—he draws the line at extending this fiction into the "Commonwealth of learning" (559, 529). The everyday insult of political representation becomes intolerable when extended into the commonwealth of print, presented as the real foundation of England's identity as "a place of *Philosophic* freedom" (537). It is in this sphere of truth production that the "enfranchis'd" subject exercises his liberty as a public person. The transformation of the private man into a public one is enacted even as it is asserted: Milton begins by praising England's Parliament for accepting the advice of "private persons"; two pages later, books are described as "the living labours of publick men."[79] It is such labor, collectively undertaken (since any "industrious" author "consults and conferrs" with others), that authorizes Milton's own exercise of "freedom": his liberty to come forward as a public person to represent not "a particular fancie" but "the generall murmur," one based on a "common grievance" (532, 539).

The odd thing about Milton's appeal to a specifically English ideal of freedom is that its martyred representative is an Italian. And rather than appearing in solitary splendor, as a glorious exception to his countrymen (with the potential to be claimed as an honorary Briton), Galileo is only one of the company of "lerned men" who included Milton among their number during his time in Italy, counting him "happy to be born in such a place of *Philosophic* freedom, as they suppos'd England was" (537). They were of course mistaken, Milton hastens to add, since "England then was groaning loudest under the Prelaticall yoak, neverthelesse I took it as a pledge of future happines, that other Nations were so perswaded of her liberty" (538). How surprising then, with the yoke thrown off, to hear the same "words of complaint" that he heard against the inquisition in Italy now being uttered against Parliament at home (539). Milton offers this bit of personal history in order to ward off the objection that his arguments against licensing are "meer flourishes, and not reall," and he presents it without any metaphorical embellishments at all: unlike Smectymnuus, Galileo does not need to be figured as his optic glass in order to evoke it. But the astronomer provides the occasion for Milton to pull off a perspective trick of his own: Milton's eyewitness account of "what I have seen and heard in other Countries, where this kind of inquisition tyrannizes," has, by the end of the paragraph, become a description of his own country (537).

By making dual use of Italy, identifying Florence as a site of resistance to Rome, Milton challenges England actually to *be* what, to those languishing under papal domination, it represents: a place of philosophic freedom. Aligning the English ideal of freedom with disaffected Catholics from an enemy state, Milton reveals such freedom as alienable from England, as it is in fact alien to its current "rule of life" (550). The imprisoned Galileo becomes the occasion, and the instrument, for Milton to pry apart word and thing, to expose the distance separating "English liberty" (which all asserted) from liberty itself. Of course, as Susanne Woods has argued, Milton is engaged in a stealthy redefinition of that ideal. Rather than the

Tudor "freedom to participate in affirming public order under the law"—
the traditional privilege of freemen—Milton posits an English tradition of
freedom that incorporates the experimentalist ideal of disciplined and
open-ended truth production, a freedom whose exercise requires "the liberty of unlicenc'd printing." [80] This ideal entails a particular image of the
public as the agent of such production, of which Galileo becomes a representative. As the only named member of Italy's company of learned men, he
is both member and symbol of a truth-producing collective, not a solitary
genius but a public person, isolated (like Lilburne) only by imprisonment.

In claiming that it was an "honor" to sit among Italy's learned men,
Milton plants English liberty, as he has redefined it, in enemy territory
(537). The trip to Italy was widely understood as a journey into temptation.
As William Harrison complained, "the gay booty" brought back by "noblemen's and mean gentlemen's sons into Italy" consisted merely in coming
back "far worse men than they went out"; hardly any returned from a
visit to the "Courtesan of Rome" an "earnest Protestant." Visitors warned
against the dangerous beauty of the art that adorned Italian churches,
where the whore displayed herself "in the most tempting fashion."[81] But, as
Michael O'Connell points out, what is striking about Milton's various remarks on his extended stay in Italy is "his utter silence about the art we
presume he must have seen."[82] What he did talk about, in all his public
recollections of his journey, were the Italian academies. It was within these
intellectual collectivities devoted to ingenious inquiry that he could pursue
"that freedom of discussion which I loved."[83] Milton's presentation of his
provocatively innocent experience of Italian "freedom" is not just a means
of inverting its popular construction as the errant opposite of England so as
to expose corruption at home; it also exemplifies his argument against guard-
ing the soul from contamination by "the matter of sin." As the Italian example confirmed, "Good and evill . . . in the field of this World grow up
together almost inseparably"; truth-seekers had to go out into the field
where "the windes of doctrin were let loose to play."[84]

Most importantly for our purposes, Milton's Italian sojourn offered
him an extended experience of intellectual life as collaboration. Because his
construction of the public in *Areopagitica* was conditioned by this experience, it is worth pausing here briefly to consider in what it consisted. As the
only seventeenth-century English visitor to Italy to become an active participant in the academies, Milton took the Accademia degli Svogliati by

storm, his contributions, as he modestly put it, finding "acceptance above what was lookt for," leading the academy to take the unusual step of electing an Englishman as an official member. The academy's protocols made literary production into a collective enterprise: a rotating group of censors read anonymous contributions and produced line-by-line critiques that became the basis of discussion during meetings, after which the piece was returned to the author for revision, and ultimately transcribed into the academy's permanent book.[85] (This sealing of the collective effort suggests the registering of signatures in the Royal Society's book, testifying to experimental results, after demonstrations.)[86] Although Milton may have witnessed such collaboration at Gresham, the contrast with the conditions of his post-collegiate "studious retirement" could not have been starker; these were truly "Pastures new."[87] Milton was also present for at least one meeting of the Accademia degli Apatisti, which is perhaps where he met Galileo's student Carlo Dati, a poet and classicist as well as a virtuoso, and through him, Galileo.[88] Galileo was himself a member of the Accademia Nazionale dei Lincei—known for grinding lenses "with the sharpness of lynxes' eyes." In his poem to Manso, Milton fantasizes about taming the lynxes with the power of his "novo . . . carmine," suggesting his desire to match wits with the most famous lynx of all.[89] The mingling of literary and scientific pursuits in the academies clearly encouraged Milton's self-cultivation as an experimentalist author. It was certainly reflected in the praise he received: Dati celebrated Milton as a Ulysses who, using astronomy as his guide, had perceived all areas of the world; the language seems lifted straight out of Milton's own prolusions.[90] Despite his association of Italian flattery with "fustian," in this case Milton chose to believe it; as he famously remarked, this encouragement confirmed his own "inward prompting" to "leave something so written to aftertimes, as they should not willingly let it die." The values encoded in these panegyrics, and translated into practice in the life of the academies, shaped Milton's ideal vision of himself and the public he hoped to work with.[91]

Upon his return to England, Milton imagined recreating this collegiality in his native land on a large scale. As a reformed alternative to "publick sports, and festival pastimes" that promoted only "drunkennesse and lust," Milton proposed (alongside "martial exercises" to "inure and harden our bodies") a nationwide effort to "civilize, adorn and make discreet our minds by the learned and affable meeting of frequent Academies." The suggestion that festivals be replaced by "frequent Academies" extends the implications of his intervention into the Bridgewaters' holiday celebrations; the "discreet" method of instruction advocated in *Of Education* becomes the basis of civil society.[92] In this sentence *learned* and *affable* slide from a substantive to an adjectival use; rather than a designated group of learned men gathering to better the nation, the nation is bettered by learned and affable meeting. As a modifier of academies, *frequent* can mean both crowded and recurring; the word disperses the academy into the assembled crowd.

In *Areopagitica,* Milton embraces print as the medium that enables such affability, transforming the contemplative life into a collective and productive undertaking. "When a man writes to the world," if he is "industrious," he "likely consults and conferrs with his judicious friends"; but it is through his "publisht labours" that the conversation becomes "generall," since "writing is more publick then preaching."[93] The freedoms enjoyed in the "privat Academies of *Italy*" now constitute the freedom of public life in England, envisioned as one big academy—a "mansion house" in which all can "joyn, and unite into one generall and brotherly search after Truth," if not barred by licensers. Milton always stressed the privacy of Italian academies: the academy is "Englished" by being made public.[94]

I have suggested that Milton's faith in knowledge production as a means to recover paradise prevented him from making any strong distinction between reformation and intellectual labor. In *Areopagitica,* this faith drives him to present the multiplicity of opinions as a progress toward unity—toward humanity's reconsolidation as a single paradisal subject. According to the experimentalist model of intellectual labor that Galileo, and then the English people, are made to represent, "much arguing, much writing, many opinions" in the present predicts future unanimity. Since "opinion in good men is but knowledge in the making," "brotherly dissimilitudes" are the only possible means toward communion:

> They are the troublers, they are the dividers of unity, who neglect and permit not others to unite those dissever'd peeces which are yet wanting to the body of Truth. To be still searching what we know not, by what we know, still closing up truth to truth as we find it (for all her body is *homogeneal,* and proportionall) this is the golden rule in *Theology* as well as in Arithmetick, and makes up the best harmony in a Church; not the forc't and outward union of cold, and neutrall, and inwardly divided minds.[95]

Like the piecemeal procedures of experimentalist investigation, the work of "closing up truth to truth as we find it" draws together the "dissever'd peeces" of truth and brings together her "friends" in the process. That story is told by the second epigraph to this chapter. Ever since Christ's ascension, the "sad friends of Truth" must go "up and down," gathering her scattered parts "limb by limb." Milton's description of these efforts as the "obsequies to the torn body of our martyr'd Saint" conjures up the worship of saints and relics, but, like the analogy to the pagan myth of Isis and Osiris—or the ritualistic, two-bodies rhetoric he uses to describe publication—this seemingly idolatrous rhetoric is purified by its referent: Milton is describing the work of "reforming of Reformation it self."[96] Associated with fertility and wisdom, Osiris personifies knowledge as a productive force, recalling the allegories of Bacon's *De Sapientia Veterum* as much as Plutarch.

But the passage is also a rewriting of Augustine. In the first epigraph, Augustine figures the fall as a breaking of Adam's body, whose pieces were scattered to the four corners of the earth; Christ gathered these fragments and together and "forged them by the fire of love, and made one what was broken." Thrusting this unity out of the ritual present and into the historical past, Milton presents it as a goal to be reattained through human effort. Even more boldly, he transforms the topos of a broken and scattered humanity into a figure for the state of human knowledge: humanity's postlapsarian fragmentation becomes a specifically epistemological problem. Describing the body of truth as Augustine described the body of Adam, and presenting it both as a product of labor and an object of veneration, Milton dissolves Adam into the sacred work of discovery, through which humanity's *"homogeneal"* unity will be restored.

The sacrament of truth production, through which the remains of Christ on earth are gathered together, will continue until the end of time, but the certainty that Christ himself will one day finish the job justifies those who "continue seeking" rather than rendering their efforts needless: "We have not yet found them all, Lords and Commons, nor ever shall doe, till her Masters second comming; he shall bring together every joynt and member, and shall mould them into an immortall feature of lovelines and perfection" (549). Augustine also looks ahead to the second coming, but he focuses on the Last Judgment, when the elect will gather together at Christ's right hand. In contrast, the focal point of Milton's image is not Christ, or even the separation of the elect from the damned; it is the "lovelines and perfection" of truth's restored body, the combined product of divine and human labor. Christ's return is the occasion for the ultimate experimental demonstration, made possible by the "carefull" efforts of its future witnesses and co-curators. Since Milton's truth is a "practice" into which the faithful are "inur'd," the body of truth cannot be separated from the corporate body of her "friends": the restoration of one is the restoration of the other. The molding of the body of truth molds and perfects the spectatorial body that constructs and beholds it. A body that makes itself through collective making of facts, the *corpus mysticum* is itself a thing made.

The reconstitution of this body is the perfection of the body of the public. Milton goes on to describe the purgatorial transformation currently being endured by that body:

> not degenerated, nor drooping to a fatall decay, but casting off the old and wrincl'd skin of corruption to outlive these pangs and wax young again, entring the glorious waies of Truth and prosperous vertue destin'd to become great and honourable in these latter ages. Methinks I see in my mind a noble and puissant Nation rousing herself like a strong man after sleep, and shaking her invincible locks: Methinks I see her as an Eagle muing her mighty youth, and kindling her undazl'd eyes at the full midday beam; purging and unscaling her long abused sight at the fountain it self of heav'nly radiance. (557–558)

Through the free exercise of ingenuity, the nation will slough off the "skin of corruption" and "wax young again." The oddly snakelike image that Milton uses to figure the restoration of humanity evokes the Baconian redefinition of knowledge, as what was once thought to be the cause of corruption becomes the means to cast it off, and indeed to "unscale" or deserpentify the sight. Presented as visions of his mind's eye, the figures in this passage enact the extension of paradise beyond the garden that they describe, and are thus paradisal visions in two senses: demonstrating the author's own Galilean triumph over "degenerated" carnal sight, they reveal the English public undergoing the same restoration.

"So soone as the minde frames unto it selfe any forme of God . . . an idol is set up in the minde," William Perkins warned, and Milton applies this insight to his attempt to "frame a form" of the restored public.[97] Subjecting whole symbols to the transformative operations of Winstanleyan

synonymy, Milton runs the concept of paradisal restoration through a series of figures that extend paradise into new territory, focusing on objects
of collective Adamic identification that are not Adam without letting any
settle into a fixed form. He first takes up the contemporary identification of
the English nation with Samson.[98] That Milton is invoking Samson in his
representative capacity is signaled by the female pronoun: shaking "her invincible locks," this "strong man" comprehends both genders, all people.
Erik Gray points out that a single strand of hair is lifeless, but, when gathered together, hair is "the crowning, most freely-moving and lively part of
the body"—a fitting emblem for a crowd or commons, which replenishes
itself across the lives of its constituents.[99] The phrase looks ahead not only
to *Samson Agonistes* but to the hair-intensive lines that introduce us to
Adam in *Paradise Lost,* where the first man's sovereign dignity is declared
by the crown or crowd on his head, also made of locks, which Milton elsewhere compares to the binding force of laws that constrain political representatives.[100] As the source of Samson's strength, these locks suggest a
diffusion of power across a multitude.[101] The body politic made social differentiation the mechanism of association; Milton seizes on the head of hair
as an image of collectivity that refuses hierarchical organization, a body in
which any can be a representative of all.[102]

The iconoclastic strong man was often used as a figure for popular sovereignty in the period, but his long-standing association with the calling
(due to his status as a Nazarite) is just as essential to Milton's use of him to
figure a working public—a public engaged in the iconoclastic, progressive,
and productive labor of enlarging apprehensions.[103] Perkins's famous treatment of Samson as a vocational figure in *Treatise of the Vocations* begins
with Adam, "called & appointed to dresse the garden of Eden"; in *Areopagitica* Milton makes the object of the worker's labor the faculty of vision
itself.[104] Accordingly, the strong-haired man morphs into a sharp-sighted
eagle, who is herself undergoing a transformation, entering the purgatorial
paradise of pains. Here Milton draws on the Douai Bible commentary on
Psalm 103:5 ("so that thy youth shall be renewed like the eagle's"), in which
the eagle "burneth her fethers in the elemental fire, & new fethers growing
she becometh fresh, as in her first youth."[105] Although "muing" describes
molting, what permits the "labour of high soaring" here are not new feathers but new eyes. Milton's eagle uses the fire as "kindling" not to burn away
her old feathers but to purge the scales from her eyes and restore her "long

abused sight": the fall is reversed through a specifically spectatorial transformation. An eagle gazing into the sun was the *impresa* of the Accademia
degli Oziosi, whose members defined themselves by an ethos of "active
otium"—an oxymoron that, like Bacon's "active philosophy," erected itself
on the ruins of the opposition of action and contemplation; Milton makes
the bird a mascot of the productive and ingenious English people, engaged
in the work that makes it a sovereign public.[106]

The Samsonian eagle purging her sight at "the fountain it self of
heav'nly radiance" is not an image of stillness or peace; Milton's earlier account of truth as "a streaming fountain" explicitly rules out such stasis: "if
her waters flow not in a perpetuall progression, they sick'n into a muddy
pool of conformity and tradition" (543). The image counters Calvin's denunciation of the "immense flood of error with which the whole world is
overflowed," like "water gushing forth from an immense and copious
spring . . . every man giving himself full license, and devising some peculiar form of divinity, to meet his own views."[107] Calvin's "flood of error" is
famously disgorged by Spenser's Error as a stream of vomit and printed
matter. Here, the flow of "arguing" becomes a "streaming" progress, and a
sacred one, associated with the purged and cultivated eye rather than the
consuming and disgorging mouth. The contrast between the productive
spectatorial body of the public and the appetitive body of the private self is
vividly evoked here, since Milton surrounds the corporate eagle with birds
that "flutter about, amaz'd at what she means, and in their envious gabble
would prognosticat a year of sects and schisms" (558). Outsiders to the can-
tankerous communion they are witnessing, they cannot comprehend it as
the progressive refinement of a single body. Refusing incorporation into
this process, they are responsible for the very schism they prognosticate,
for they cannot even perceive the eagle as the corporate incarnation of
themselves. *Gabble* signifies gibberish but, paired with selfish envy, conjures up *gobble* (and *babble*); these unincorporated selves are blind mouths
flocking around a corporate eye.[108]

Left to their own devices, few readers would associate an eagle purging
her eyes at the fountain of heavenly radiance with the pamphlet wars that
sustained London's booming print market, but Milton makes sure they do,
glossing the fountain in the very next sentence as "this flowry crop of
knowledge and new light sprung up and yet springing daily in this City"
(558). Having lifted our apprehensions of a restored paradise far above the

first "academy" of Eden toward an image of heavenly light, Milton now grounds it in an "ingenious" urban public, "enfranchis'd" as a collective paradisal subject.[109] Superimposing garden imagery on the fountain of heavenly light, Milton presents paradisal print as the purgational source of this subject's continual illumination: in contemporary London, "all this free writing and free speaking" has borne fruit in a "flowry crop of knowledge" and a "new light" that, like flowers in a garden of eternal spring, has "sprung up" and continues "springing daily" (559, 558). The serious pun on *spring* as both season and fountain identifies the recovery of paradise with the production of knowledge: paradise is regained through an instrument of truth that has "enfranchis'd, enlarg'd and lifted up our apprehensions degrees above themselves" and even "rarify'd and enlightn'd our spirits like the influence of heav'n" (559). A seizure, *apprehension* denotes the actions both of laying hold with the senses and of grasping with the intellect, much like Galileo's "thinking in astronomy"; action and contemplation are integrated through a sensuous dialectic that expands the body's perceptual powers beyond its physical limits. But it is the technology of print, not the lens, that lifts up "apprehensions degrees above themselves," purging fallen perception by collectivizing it.

Paradise is cultivated in London, through print; the "perspicacious *Eagle*" to which Glanvill compared Adam is the reading and writing public—the corporate refinement of thousands of gabbling and gobbling selves.[110] The suppression of this agent's ingenious labors, Milton warns, will result in "the fall of learning," bringing to a halt "the triall of vertue, and the exercise of truth" (520, 528). Between the feared "fall of learning" and the fall itself there seems to be no difference, since paradise is recovered as a purgatorial progress toward a heavenly goal.[111] The eagle staring at the light of heaven is imagined as purging her sight, not as having attained a consummate vision of heavenly truth; like the public she represents, she is advancing toward it "by degrees," and by means of productive disagreement. The means and ends of restoration are scrambled here, restoring the public to the state of being continually reborn: a state as purgatorial as it is paradisal. It is the collective participation in a sacramental process, not a shared experience of sacramental presence, that constitutes innocent communion.

Milton's effort to extend paradise beyond the precincts of Eden does not prohibit him from mentioning Adam altogether. Both times he does so, however, it is to insist on the continuity between the first man and the contemporary public. In his effort to defend the reading of "bad books," even pornographic books, Milton describes the condition Adam "fell into" of learning good by evil, which now makes virtue dependent on "triall . . . by what is contrary."[112] But, lest this reference to the fall suggest a radical difference between the innocent Adam and the Adamic public, Milton reforms it in his subsequent attack on "foolish tongues" who hold God responsible for Adam's transgression.[113] Here, Milton not only makes the expected argument for Adam's "freedom to choose," without which he would have been a puppet ("a meer artificiall *Adam,* such an *Adam* as he is in the motions"), he goes on to describe humanity as occupying this same paradisal situation of choice, as if the fall had made no real difference:

> God therefore left him free, set before him a provoking object, ever almost in his eyes; herein consisted his merit, herein the right of his reward, the praise of his abstinence. Wherefore did he creat passions within us, pleasures round about us, but that these rightly temper'd are the very ingredients of vertu? . . . This justifies the high providence of God, who though he command us temperance, justice, continence, yet powrs out before us ev'n to a profusenes all desirable things, and gives us minds that can wander beyond all limit and satiety. (527–528)

Rather than a rehearsal of *felix culpa,* this is an account of the fall as a thing indifferent; humanity's condition is identical in and out of Eden. The continuity between pre- and postlapsarian existence makes the transgression itself easy to overlook, as in fact this passage does. We have wandered through appetite past satiety back to innocence, without ever having to pay obeisance to the redemptive possibilities afforded by human helplessness before sin. Like Adam, we are provoked by passions and pleasures, and possessed of minds "that can wander beyond all limit and satiety," but these very appetites, "rightly temper'd," are what constitute virtue itself. As the "provoking object" of the apple expands into the world of sensuous experience, "abstinence" softens into "temperance," just as, in the earlier discussion of Adam, the call to "abstain" is quickly modulated into an admonition to "distinguish" (514).

As mediators of experience, it is books, we might imagine, that enable the subject to "see and know, and yet abstain" (516). Yet Milton goes out of his way to deny any essential difference between reading and other modes of sensuous experience: "what ever thing we hear or see, sitting, walking, travelling, or conversing may be fitly call'd our book, and is of the same effect that writings are" (528). Milton's reading is Winstanley's digging. In reading, as in assisted observation, the difference between sensuous and sensual experience, knowledge production and carnal consumption, is a product not of the medium used but of the user's skill (and motive) in cultivating it. Accordingly, Milton describes "discreet and judicious" reading as if it were an artisanal secret, even while presenting that secret as a public one (512). Hartlib sought to make nature's secrets the basis of public knowledge; Milton represents the public's practice of knowledge production—the determination to try all things—as the greatest craft secret of all. Books are "usefull drugs and materialls wherewith to temper and compose effective and strong mcd'cins"; it requires "art to qualifie and prepare these working mineralls" (521). Rather than gaining insight or nourishment directly *from* books, the "discreet and judicious Reader" has to "compose" it *out of* books; reading is thus as constructive an art as "the labour of book-writing" (532). The skilled reader subjects himself to these "working mineralls" only after he has invested curatorial skill in qualifying and preparing them. The ability to refine these sometimes hazardous materials is an art that is itself gained through experience, by reading "promiscuously" (517). Rather than a merely negative virtue, temperance is the active art of tempering and composing what, to those who are "not skilfull considerers of human things," appears merely as "the matter of sin" (527). Innocent temperance actually *requires* promiscuity.

Reader and author, like the virtual witness and experimental curator, are thus joined together through the sharing of artisanal expertise. The ability to refine the "drossiest" material and turn it to godly ends—"to cleanse a scurrilous vehemence into the stile of a rousing Sermon"—is only one aspect of this art of "concoction," in which discovery plays as important a part as invention.[114] Since "our eyes [are] blear'd and dimm'd with prejudice and custom," the truths revealed by some books will not be immediately apparent to all; as in microscopy, what can seem "slight and contemptible"—even "unsightly"—may be demonstrated by a more experienced reader to illuminate "truth it self" (565–566). This labor is as essential to the defense of the commonwealth as the military. Alongside "instruments of armed Justice in defence of beleaguer'd Truth," there must also

be pens and heads there, sitting by their studious lamps, musing, searching, revolving new notions and idea's . . . others as fast reading, trying all
things, assenting to the force of reason and convincement . . . disputing,
reasoning, reading, inventing, discoursing, ev'n to a rarity, and admiration,
things not before discourst or writt'n of. (554, 557)

Where there are instruments of war, there must be instruments of truth.
Milton presents contemplative pursuits as a form of action, but rather than
figuratively mapping the space of study onto the field of battle, he unleashes strings of participles that anticipate Hooke and Petty's celebrations
of artisanal labor.[115] Of course, instead of bodies sifting and straining,
these "heads" are "sitting," yet they are active, even "fast," actually performing the work of revolution by "revolving new notions." *Reading* is first
an escort of *trying,* then of *inventing:* experimentalists redefined the shaping of sensuous experience as a form of action, and Milton describes reading as experimental testing. The pursuits of truth's sedentary defenders are
active because they are productive, resulting in new truths: "things not before discourst or writt'n of." By eliding the distinction between the written
and spoken word (*disputing, discoursing*), Milton gathers these truth producers into a virtual congregation. The metonymic reduction of its members to heads and pens, like the Royal Society's eyes and hands, creates a
"homogeneal" image of the body of truth at work: this is the real source of
truth's "streaming fountain."

Perfected in Weakness

As is frequently pointed out, Milton's faith that truth production would
very shortly "bring together every joynt and member" of the public was itself short-lived. Throughout his prose career, he tended to address his reader
as one of "the more discerning sort," and he even tried to imagine that the
mass of English people were of that sort: "no rabble sir Priest, but a unani-
mous multitude of good Protestants."[116] But after the publication of *Eikon
Basilike* and the outpouring of public sympathy for the king—from people,
Milton suspected, who did not read the book and were simply struck by the
frontispiece's "new device of the Kings Picture at his praiers"—he found it
increasingly difficult to address readers who "live and dye in such a strook'n
blindness" in such respectful terms. The "fools and silly gazers" the king

had managed to "catch" with his "device" seemed to include almost everyone; Milton now regarded himself as the one just man battling the blind
superstition of the mob. No longer crowing to sir Priest, he found himself
haranguing, and then insulting, the very people whose truth-producing
abilities he had once passionately defended, now dismissed as "an incon-
stant, irrational, and Image-doting rabble."[117] So "fatally stupifi'd and
bewitch'd" as to "give to bare words more credit then to op'n deeds," the
English people combined an idolatrous susceptibility to the deceptions of
the carnal eye with a tendency to confuse "bare words" (the king's plausible
utterances) for things themselves. Perhaps such a people could never be
"rationally evinc'd and perswaded"; he could only urge them "to bethink
themselves, and recover."[118]

As the Restoration loomed, Milton continued his efforts, sometimes
adopting a kindly tone suitable to children ("kingship, though looking big,
yet indeed . . . [is] full of fears") and sometimes appealing over their heads
to his fellow learned republicans. Although he regarded himself as a fount
of spectatorial instruction for an easily deluded public, he had not developed a pedagogy. In the pamphlet he reissued on the very eve of the Restoration, under the pathetically upbeat title *The Readie and Easie Way to
Establish a Free Commonwealth,* he sighs, "Thus much I should perhaps
have said though I were sure I should have spoken only to trees and stones."
Invoking not just Ezekiel but Orpheus, whose eloquence could move both,
he implies that a "madd or strangely infatuated" people enthralled to a
"blinde and obstinate beleef" might be more immovable still.[119] Milton's
changing constitutional preferences arguably reflect this pessimism, but his
political vision had never been firmly rooted in any particular constitutional form; it was rooted in the idea of a collective discipline that would
produce subjects capable of politics and capable, above all, of industrious
communion.[120] In the midst of a constitutional crisis, Milton therefore finds
it appropriate to press for the establishment of a national network of schools,
to render the people "more industrious, more ingenuous": "communicating
the natural heat of government and culture more distributively" throughout the national body, direct instruction would accomplish what print had
so far failed to achieve: the formation of a working public.[121]

That Milton was completely blind by this time in one sense only
strengthened his credentials as a spectatorial guide to fools and silly gazers;
Tiresias and Homer were obvious identificatory objects, and Milton made

use of them, presenting himself as a prophetic bard "recompensed" for his loss of sight with deeper insight. Rather than drawing a stark contrast between outer and inner sight, however, he made this opposition dialectical. Milton had not been "struck" blind, as his enemies charged; he had gone blind gradually, and he presented this progressive deterioration as, precisely, a progress. As his eyes started to fail, he adopted a modified quotation from 2 Corinthians 12:9 ("my strength is made perfect in weakness") as his personal motto: "I am made perfect in weakness." In doing so, he figured his blindness as the necessary condition of prosthetic, and paradisal, insight, for the passage recounts, in tantalizingly cryptic fashion, the experience of a subject "caught up into paradise"—Paul himself, describing his experiences in the third person. (Paul was privileged with a visit to heaven's antechamber—for this "paradise" is also called "the third heaven" at 12:2— but Milton drags that antechamber down to earth.)[122] Paul's ecstasy had long been likened to that of Enoch and Elijah, but the interpretive framework Milton imposed on Paul's experience was that of a spectatorial progress: "There is a certain road which leads through weakness, as the apostle teaches, to the greatest strength . . . an inner and far more enduring light." Milton's wandering progress down that road had become a matter of public record. Attacks on his *Defensio pro Populo Anglicano,* and thus on the "English people," focused on his blindness as a sign of divine judgment; against this charge, he explained his loss of sight in the same way that virtuosi explained Hooke's physical decline, as a work injury. His doctors had warned that if he undertook the task of "replying to the royal defense," he would lose both eyes: "I was not in the least deterred by the warning . . . You see what I chose, what I rejected, and why." At the end of a life devoted to refining corporeal sight into insight, Galileo, too, had gone blind. Indeed, rather than losing his eyes, he had left them behind as he entered more deeply into the "waies of Truth."[123] Milton insisted that he certainly preferred his own blindness to that of Alexander More, which, "deeply implanted in the inmost faculties, obscures the mind, so that you may see nothing whole or real. Mine, which you make a reproach, merely deprives things of color and superficial appearance." What he could no longer see fell under the heading of secondary qualities, which many were confident would soon be dissolved by the power of improved lenses. Milton presented himself as one of the Linceans, who, according to their motto, could "look out at and look into" *(auspicit et inspicit)* nature, for rather than asserting that he could see *beyond* things themselves, he claimed that he was better able to focus on them, and indeed, to see through them into their natures: "What is true and essential in them is not lost to my intellectual vision."[124]

Milton's model of reading as spectatorial "enlargement" had involved him in a perplexity. As he himself argued, ocular demonstration exercised an irresistible force on "convincement" that mere words could not, yet outward appearances were deceiving; as an author, he could only point to his more trustworthy visions through words, or urge his readers to open their eyes and look for themselves. His simultaneous exhortations to look at things themselves and to see beyond them left him at an impasse, for while the analogy to experimental prosthetic technology offered a conceptual resolution to the paradox, it had not yet yielded him a model of spectatorial instruction.[125] Even if a text presented itself as an instrument of truth, it could not reveal anything to the reader who was unwilling or unfit to use it; the account of reading in *Areopagitica* for the most part assumes a "discreet and judicious Reader," already well advanced in the art of cultivating experience. Perhaps because the Restoration suggested that the public required a spectatorial instruction more radical than any he had yet provided, and perhaps because, in a very practical sense, vision had become a collective and distributed undertaking for him, Milton elaborated the relation between reading, writing, and incorporation into a spectatorial "body representative" with renewed vigor in his later career. By this time, his daily life had become a continuous rehearsal of the scene of assisted observation; he required amanuenses and readers to help him shoulder the "labour of book-writing" and reading, labors he had always imagined in strongly spectatorial terms. The collaborations necessitated by his blindness may have offered him an existential correlative to his authorial identity as an inspired medium, dependent on a prosthetic source of insight, and "incorporate" with a body greater than his own.[126]

In his Restoration epic, Milton set about inventing an instrument of truth that was also an instrument of spectatorial education, an instrument that would instruct the reader in its own use. Seizing on the "Optic Glass" of Galileo, he trained it on an image of paradise that even an "Image-doting rabble" could recognize: the garden of Eden itself.[127] The poem begins with a false image—the lost paradise of its title—and proceeds to look through it, transforming the idol of Eden itself into a perceptual medium.

More than any other literary work we have examined, *Paradise Lost* attempts to reproduce through formal means the conditions of experimentalist insight; in this sense, the poem is the "spring" of innocent insight that *Areopagitica* only describes. Identifying himself with Galileo, Milton enacts the astronomer's labors through language, integrating his experimentalist self-presentation with a model of paradisal labor that includes his readers.[128]

Although the bulk of my discussion of the poem will explore its use of the garden as an instrument to extend perception, *Paradise Lost* is shaped by the lens in a more obvious way. As Marjorie Nicolson pointed out long ago, it is the first English epic whose action is played out against the outer space opened up by the telescope; its whole setting and vision depend on Galileo's glass.[129] Milton combines its use with "thinking," not only "in astronomy," but in terms of the atomic substrate out of which the book of creation was first written, for he grounds the cosmos of his poem in Chaos.[130] The combined product of astronomical observations and atomistic speculations, integrating the insights associated with the telescope and the microscope, Chaos is at once infinite interstellar space and an ontologically prior space pregnant with the "Ancestors of Nature": the "original" of Eden itself (2.895). In opening this space up to exploration, Milton continues the efforts of his own Adam to "magnifie his [God's] works" (7.97). By extending the labors that defined paradise into a space in which the concept of place has no meaning, Milton reveals that paradise cannot consist in the attachment of a privileged body to a privileged place. In a universe where "one first matter all" forms the matrix of both divine and human creativity, it is by ceasing to privilege—by working to see through—the apparent ontological separateness of bodies and places that humanity again becomes worthy of paradise and empowered to construct it.[131] For Bacon, this labor begins with the effort "to unroll the volume of Creation" with "humility and veneration," and with a mind and body "washed clean . . . to magnify [God's] works"; Milton's Adam echoes the sentiment, and Milton's poem acts on it.[132]

Paradise Lost provided proof that Milton's inner illuminations—his *"Strenuous, Inward Speculations"* as an early reader called them—were productive, exposing readers to things they had never seen before.[133] But Milton also proved himself to be Galileo's literary equivalent through his method of revealing these sights—or rather, by barely revealing them. Even the reader who rejects outright the idea of paradise's accessibility through and as a perspective cannot escape a reading experience that confirms it; Milton's method of "scoring out" innocent insight compels her participation in the work of "purging and unscaling her long abused sight." Throughout the poem, Milton asks us to envision what we could not possibly see. This opacity disturbed Johnson, who blamed it on Milton's blindness and pedantry, portraying Milton much as Milton portrayed the schoolmen:

> His images and descriptions of the scenes or operations of Nature do not seem to be always copied from original form, nor to have the freshness, raciness, and energy of immediate observation. He saw Nature, as Dryden expresses it, *through the spectacles of books;* and on most occasions calls learning to his assistance . . . his great excellence is amplitude, and he expands the adventitious image beyond the dimensions which the occasion required. Thus, comparing the shield of Satan to the orb of the Moon, he crouds the imagination with the discovery of the telescope, and all the wonders which the telescope discovers.[134]

Johnson imagines the blind Milton forced to regard nature through the spectacle of books and learning, unable to convey the "freshness, raciness, and energy of immediate observation." But what Johnson describes here is actually a perceptual expansion, though one that is unnecessary: as Milton throws a telescope into the already crowded verse, our imaginations are filled quite "beyond the dimensions which the occasion required." Like the opponents of the lens, Johnson suggests that we do not *need* to see this way; such sight is unnatural, exorbitant, and above all disorienting.

Johnson's critique was revived throughout the twentieth century. F. R. Leavis accused Milton's style of being "incompatible with sharp, concrete realization," revealing the poet's lack of "interest in sensuous particularity"; Eliot famously complained of the dissociation of thought from sensuous perception in the epic.[135] In levelling those charges against Milton, these critics show no awareness that they are employing his own coinage. Fowler's introduction to his edition of the poem offers eloquent rebuttals of these criticisms:

> Whenever you move your eye over one of these vistas, or follow out any of the poem's innumerable flights through space, or trace out its chartings of the movements of heavenly bodies, you are constantly astonished by the

power of spatial realization and by the sustained inventiveness with which natural phenomena are imaged more fully than ever before . . . Everything we see in his poem tells us that . . . T. S. Eliot [is] wrong: Milton had a strong spatial imagination.[136]

But one cannot be mistaken about one's experience of a poem; Eliot and Leavis, and many of their followers, were clearly not lying when they claimed to find something seriously wrong with Milton's approach to image-making, to which Fowler's defense of Milton's strong spatial imagination and sustained inventiveness does not seem an adequate response. Milton's innovative use of space accounts for the complaints of Leavis and Eliot as well as Fowler's praise; like the presence chamber of Locke's well-functioning mind, the often obscurely lit spaces of *Paradise Lost* require the labor of an agent inside, working to transform the site. As Milton moves us through the successive spaces of Hell, Chaos, Eden, and Heaven, we are never allowed to forget that we are provisionally inhabiting internal states whose shaping assumptions provide particular *perspectives* on the world. Each space we move through is the site of an experiment—a contrived experience of the created world demanding diagnosis—that we cannot help but perform.

What guidance we get in carrying out our work is provided by extended perspectival metaphors. The poem everywhere calls attention to the constructed nature of the perceptual experiences it records. Rather than representing completed images or perceptions, the poem recreates the conditions of viewing, engaging the reader's conscious effort to complete the task of perception. The poem's perspectival metaphors recruit the reader as co-creator of each scene: x is never merely like y; almost always, x as seen from point p is like y as seen from point q. Since such metaphors provide only the conditions of perception, they cannot be processed easily; what is seen must be rationally reconstructed by the reader willing to project herself into the observational conditions that Milton, like a Hookean curator of thought experiments, is continually arranging for her to submit to trial. After conducting the experiments he has set up for us, we must interpret the stimuli produced as the contingent response of our somatic, cognitive, and spiritual equipment, requiring diagnosis to yield knowledge.

Milton's syntax is designed to extend this labor indefinitely: the length of the sentences, about a fourth of whose clauses are inverted, diffuses the sense through a much larger mass of words than we are accustomed to; ambiguities proliferate through double syntax (as when Satan and Adam share a pronoun), while delayed exposure to crucial information creates the conditions for surprise "discoveries" that demand repeated acts of re-reading and re-seeing, literally retarding our movement down the page.[137] In contrast, the epistemological uncertainties conveyed by Marvell's per-spectival metaphors in *Upon Appleton House* do not extend to the mechan-ics of the reading experience itself, since they are not forcefully enacted syntactically or metrically. Marvell's handling of the line participates only mildly in "occasional" response to the percepts under cultivation; his fre-quently closed couplets represent confusion but rarely produce it (except at the interpretive level). Our physical reading experience thus unfolds in a separate register from our experience of "enquiring into speculations," to adapt John Dunton's phrase; the reader's sensitive and spectatorial bodies are not placed in direct sensuous relation. In *Paradise Lost,* however, our virtual ocular wanderings are keyed directly to our embodied experience as readers. It can require many lines for the conditions to be set for us to begin to get a perceptual "read" on each new environment and dramatic situation; by the time we do, the setting is usually in the process of changing again and we are moving on. Throughout the poem, long blocks of steeply en-jambed lines provide a sense of headlong forward momentum while stav-ing off a complete representation of what is happening. This paradoxical progress is a formal manifestation of experimentalist progress, combining the copious accumulation of experimental results with a modest deferral of certainty about their meaning.[138] The autoinquisition forced by Milton's repeated invitations to perceptual self-consciousness intensifies the sense of retarded movement, prompting us to hesitate, to reexamine, like vic-tims of a checking compulsion (a reformed alternative to the repetition compulsion Angus Fletcher associates with allegory).[139] Instead of recreat-ing the immediacy of spectacle, or Ignatian meditation, Milton has cre-ated a literary counterpart to experimentalist observation, contriving un-familiar observational conditions and demanding repeated trials to resolve Boylean "scruples," even as the propulsive verse compels us to "make a progresse."

We recall that Antonius Sucquet extolled the art of meditation as a technique to "restrain" and "fix" the imagination to pious imagery, a con-trivance made necessary by the fall: "after the sin of Adam [the imagination] became wholly unbridled; the unstable mind was made to wander over the whole course of the earth."[140] In contrast, Milton's poem impels the mind to wander the infinite universe. Ignatian meditation was designed to exploit rather than expose or diagnose the weakness of the visual imagination, its parasitic dependence on fading percepts, actually encouraging such dependence through a redundant descriptive language, rehearsing the visual iterations, the saccades and fixations, of the sensitive body's eye. Milton's poem does precisely the opposite. Its attempt to recover paradise begins not with *compositio loci* but with the decomposing of place. Identifying paradise with the labor of seeing through and intervening in the visible world, Milton creates the conditions for the reader to see through place as a thing indifferent.

If our sense of the vividness of *Paradise Lost* depends on how we respond to the meticulousness with which Milton arranges the conditions, rather than the contents, of each perceptual moment, it is also shaped by our sense of being on the move, like the scouts or explorers with whom his perspectival metaphors often compare us. We are constantly engaged in virtual motion across new spaces, sometimes three in a single book, and the shifts can occur at lightning speed. The reader is always on the alert in this poem, never at rest and never "at home." The disorientation that characterizes much of our experience of the poem results from our awareness of a potential plenitude of detail that is often only barely indicated in its broad sweeps across space—detail that must be supplied by the reader, using data that illuminate the ever-changing conditions, but not the final results, of observation.

Of course, the reader must have some solid matter on which to perform her curatorial labors, and Milton in fact employs many of the mimetic techniques Elaine Scarry has described in order to provide material for the mind's eye. But he always combines their use with a summons to perceptual self-diagnosis. One example will suffice to conclude this introductory overview of the poem's strategies. What Scarry calls "radiant ignition" pairs moving agents with light: a running figure might be compared to lightning, or attention drawn to the flashing of armor in the sun.[141] Milton avails himself of this technique almost every time an angel takes flight, as, for example, when Uriel flies into Eden to warn its other guardian angels that Satan has infiltrated the garden:

Thither came *Uriel,* gliding through the Eeven
On a Sun beam, swift as a shooting Starr
In *Autumn* thwarts the night, when vapors fir'd
Impress the Air, and shews the Mariner
From what point of his Compass to beware
Impetuous winds . . .

                        (4.555–560)

Uriel is paired with two light sources, a sunbeam and a shooting star. The sunbeam here is actually a means of locomotion; once Uriel delivers his message, he "Returnd on that bright beam."[142] Milton even uses the word *lighted* to describe the angel's landing so that light suffuses the scene of movement from beginning to end (4.570). Richard Bentley famously objected to the angel's gliding through a period of time, but in the absence of any watch or clock, the evening can only be marked by the gradual fading of the sky into imperceptibility, against which Uriel's radiant flight becomes all the more salient.[143] This technique capitalizes on the visual phenomenon known as the motion parallax, which makes near objects seem to move past us more quickly than distant ones. Christopher Collins has argued that because we associate the apprehension of speed with closeness, a swiftly moving object in our imaginary visual field will push other images into the background. (When the eye tracks a particular object in motion, engaging in what psychologists call "pursuit," the background against which such motion takes place becomes a blur or "retinal smear"; this lends the backgrounds of our perceptual experiences the fuzziness that makes them backgrounds.)[144] All this suggests that radiant ignition is part of a redundancy system, a means to call attention to, and thus enhance, the "well-lit," foregrounded nature of the moving object under description. But Milton's use of this technique is combined with a second-order comparison that compels us to reflect on our perceptual stance in the act of adopting it. As we see Uriel, so the mariner sees the star. Drawing on the meteorological wisdom according to which falling stars were thrust down by winds from the upper atmosphere, Milton presents the mariner inferring from a star's fall the direction of dangerous winds, just as Uriel's blazing flight brings warning of Satan's "impetuous" presence in the garden. As the rhyme of *air* and *beware* suggests, the mariner, though armed with a compass, is "with dangers compast round"; the danger represented by Satan is similarly ambient (7.27). The gliding angel momentarily "thwarts the night," delaying the victory of darkness over light that we know is inevitable; night will fall and Satan will succeed, for a time, in extending his kingdom to earth, but the motion parallax makes the ultimate victory of enlightenment over darkness a matter of the reader's sensuous experience. Nonetheless, as Johnson would put it, the mariner "expands the adventitious image beyond the dimensions which the occasion required"; lifting us out of the immediate scene, the perspectival metaphor enhances our sense of the contingency of our perspective. The sense that we are only getting a partial view, rooted in a particular time and space, of the dangers to and sources of enlightenment is essential to the uneven and asymptotic progress that structures both the poem and regenerate subjectivity as Milton imagined it. Again and again, it is Milton's mimetic techniques themselves that define our task: to piece together imperfect views from particular, partial perspectives in an effort to construct the view from everywhere.

In this sense, the spaces of Hell and Eden operate no differently than the perspectival metaphors do. Susceptible to geographical descriptions but not contained by them, these spaces are most stably identified with perspectives that determine how God's creation is seen, judged, deformed, and reformed by its inhabitants. The functional equivalence of the poem's actual and metaphorical spaces places the author, along with the reader, side by side with the poem's characters. But within these spaces, Milton always offers the reader a prosthetic source of insight with which to diagnose and reform the perspectives they provide. By continually exposing the grounds on which the reader creates his identification with its unfallen, fallen, and falling protagonists, Milton constructs the reader as the subject of ongoing paradisal choice. *Areopagitica* famously defined reason as "choosing" and celebrated Eden as the primal scene of that choice; placing before us perspectives that we must construct, compare, and submit to correction ourselves, Milton restores us to our original work from which, he insists, the fall never freed us.

Hell, Chaos, and the "Cleer Spring"

The first sentence of the poem charts the typical movement of Milton's mind, the radical movement from a point of origin to the future, a move-

ment that has already been sketched in the note on the verse.[145] Combined
with the invocation's parenthetical treatment of the expulsion ("With loss
of *Eden*"), the cascade of *or*'s works to construct us as paradisal agents of
choice.[146] Suspending us across a series of sacred places, the choice-stream
ends with the reenactment of God's first creative act, the shaping of Chaos,
in the poet's body, of which we become a "member incorporate." It is in entering this site of work, rather than any particular place hallowed by God's
presence, that the reader finds her first (and only) "place of rest."[147] Work on
Chaos—the matter of choice, and the matter of the first garden—is what
the labor of innocence consists in, and the poem is a fruit of that labor, a
labor in which divine and human agencies (and authorial and readerly
agencies) are inextricably confused.[148] Such confusion contains conflict
rather than precluding it. This is a poem in which the first "trial" of man's
obedience actually requires him to argue with his maker, thereby demonstrating that he can "judge of fit and meet" with respect to creation and
become a maker himself.[149] No external authority, not even the outward
physical manifestation of God, is permitted to obstruct the innocent and
necessarily tentative effort to bear testimony to what "Light after light
well us'd" seems to reveal about the nature of things (3.196): Adam must
therefore testify to the fact that it is not good for man to be alone, addressing a Creator who seems to be unaware of it. The struggle to cultivate an objective perspective on the work that remains to be done in the
world continues to make up the drama of paradisal existence after Eve's
creation.[150]

The poem's opening books induct the reader into this labor, carried out
on the seemingly unpromising materials of Hell and Chaos. Long before
we set foot into Eden, Milton puts us to work cultivating the "preparatory
grounds" for our identification with its inhabitants.[151] In Milton's universe
of undifferentiated substance, paradise is not simply created, it must be
constructed by a collective subject, the single laborer, "Homeward returning," that figures Adam and Eve as they leave the garden (12.632). The
"solitarie way" pursued by the laborer on his wandering pilgrimage to a restored paradise leads through the purgatorial middle space of Chaos, the
raw material of "His own works and their works," matter waiting to be revealed and reformed by God's inspired agents (12.649, 3.59). This way also
leads through *Paradise Lost,* whose reading is an act of experimentalist introspection, a collective activity pursued alone.

The poem's first explicit image of the extension of innocent subjectivity beyond the garden—the "paradise within . . . happier farr"—opens out into this scene of reading (12.587). It is occasioned by Milton's lamentation over his blindness. Instead of "the Book of knowledg fair" he is

> Presented with a Universal blanc
> Of Natures works to mee expung'd and ras'd,
> And wisdome at one entrance quite shut out.
> So much the rather thou Celestial light
> Shine inward, and the mind through all her powers
> Irradiate, there plant eyes, all mist from thence
> Purge and disperse, that I may see and tell
> Of things invisible to mortal sight.
>
> *(3.47–55)*

Milton effectively invokes nature's book to proclaim its illegibility to him, but as he draws the reader's eye from one divine text to another—from creation to the poem she holds in her hands—lamentation fluctuates into self-assertion.[152] The ability to extend perceptual horizons through writing—to "see and tell / Of things invisible to mortal sight"—seems to depend on organic failure. Physical insufficiency creates the conditions for prosthetic insight; Milton's strength is perfected in weakness. In his notes on the poem, the seventeenth-century commentator Patrick Hume observed that the spelling of *blank* as *blanc* suggests not darkness but "a piece of white Paper," and indeed a *"carte Blanche."*[153] Hume's insight is a useful one, for the blank page is an invitation to authorship; as in "The Garden," the perceptual annihilation of the book of nature creates the conditions for its recomposition. This inspired labor generates the poem we are reading; as I will suggest in this section, it also provides the basis for the poem's theodicy.

Milton does not suggest that the book of nature was created merely to be seen beyond; the visible world retains its honored status as the book of knowledge.[154] The contrast is between two instruments used to read it: the sensitive body and the spectatorial body. It is to the latter that nature extends a *carte blanche.* The contemplative labor Milton dramatizes for us is a refinement of sight rather than an abandonment of it—the poet's spectatorial triumph over Satanic gazing. *Gaze,* which appears throughout the poem in connection with Satan, becomes obtrusive in the scene of the fall, where, as we would expect, it is associated with the idolatrous consumption of creation rather than its cultivation.[155] There, Satan promises Eve that the fruit will "cleere" the eyes of her sensitive body; but here, Milton asks God to "plant eyes" in his mind and purge *it* of mist. Incorporated into the body without "degustation," these floral eyes are objects as well as instruments of paradisal labor.[156] Paradise is a garden of prosthetic insights, planted by God, but cultivated and harvested by Milton and his readers.

Milton affirms his sensuous engagement with the created world by lingering forlornly on the rich sights that his blindness blocks out, but wisdom is only shut out "at one entrance." Seasonal fluctuations, conventionally described as a consequence of the fall, are invisible to him; he is so much the rather able to see—and see through—a permanent spring he carries inside him.[157] Although he can no longer see the creatures Adam once named or the "human face divine," his vision embraces their source, for the "ever-during dark" that engulfs him also brings forth the nocturnal visits of his muse Urania, during which, he has just informed us, he can "wander where the Muses haunt / Cleer Spring, or shadie Grove, or Sunnie Hill," and chiefly, *"Sion,"* where his muse washes her feet in "flowrie Brooks" (3.44–45, 27–28, 30). This permanently "Cleer Spring," like that imagined in *Areopagitica,* can "irradiate" the mind; Milton accentuates the pun on *spring* as source and as season by placing flowers, and the body of his muse, directly in the water.[158] Out of this testimonial of personal inadequacy, comparable to the experimentalists' expressions of disgust for the deficiencies of the sensitive body, the spectatorial body triumphantly emerges, for as soon as the invocation concludes, Milton is able to "see and tell" of creation from the vantage point of heaven. Under the guidance of the muse of astronomy, and "Cut off" from the "wayes of men," Milton wanders into a world to which most men were, as Hooke put it, "utterly Strangers."[159] With this image of an internal garden blooming with "artificial Eys," Milton has managed not only to update the topos of the blind bard but to accomplish what would seem an impossible feat: to present his blindness as the condition for a flowering of prosthetic insight analogous to Galileo's technologically assisted eye.[160]

It was not Milton's claim of divine inspiration but this apparent assertion of superhuman epistemological privilege that rankled early readers. Writing after Milton's death, Daniel Defoe wondered how it was that he was able to tell us about events in heaven: "Mr. *Milton* here takes upon him to give the History of it, as particularly as if he had been born there, and came down hither on purpose to give us an account of it; (I hope he is better inform'd by this time)." The notion that Milton could lay claim to a vantage point from which the problem of evil could be solved struck Defoe as the height of presumption: "Here we must bid Mr. *Milton* good night; for, in plain terms, he is in the dark about it, and so we are all."[161] But it was by making plain how much he was in the dark that Milton persuaded his readers that he could see things they had not. By presenting himself as a deficient appendage to external sources of insight, he insists, as Janet Adelman suggests, on his own "instrumentality," an observation I will pursue as literally as Milton himself did.[162]

Incorporated into this instrument, Milton's body, we gain entrance to a "paradise within" and gain a new vantage point onto creation, following the steps of the progress that Adam will chart out for the humanity he represents: "In contemplation of created things / By steps we may ascend to God" (5.511–512). As Milton rises up to the vantage point from which God, in return, "bent down his eye, / His own works and their works at once to view," we recover an appropriately paradisal perspective on creation as the joint product of human and divine labor (3.58–59). This is the fruit of Milton's extension of innocent subjectivity beyond the garden, our formal introduction to the paradise within and around us. Yet it retroactively "paradizes" an earlier spectatorial performance, undertaken in very different surroundings.

We have already seen Milton's spectatorial labors, and our own, merge with those of Galileo in the famous analogy between Satan's "massy, large and round" shield and

> . . . the Moon, whose Orb
> Through Optic Glass the *Tuscan* Artist views
> At Ev'ning from the top of *Fesole,*
> Or in *Valdarno,* to descry new Lands,
> Rivers or Mountains in her spotty Globe.
> *(1.285, 287–291)*

Homer had seen a whole world engraved on the surface of the shield of Achilles. The artistry Milton invokes here is different, as is the world he sees. He sees another world, not our own; and the art that makes its rivers and mountains visible is Galileo's art of discovery. *Descry,* to discover by observation, to sketch, or to publish, places Milton alongside the "*Tuscan Artist*"—where he would soon be joined by Marvell, who, we recall, used the word to describe his own accomplishment with the "bold Tube."[163] This spectatorial brotherhood is an open one, for we too are implicitly being compared to Galileo: the moon as seen by him is the shield as seen by us. We have been seeing along with Satan; now, the art that reveals the newly maculate moon permits us to make him, the bearer of our own corrupted perspective, the object of diagnostic scrutiny.[164] For it is Galileo's glass that makes Hell another world: with its help, we become alienated from the perspective of Hell and begin to descry this new land from a vantage point outside it. A poem that, after the first invocation, we might have worried was morphing into the *Sataniad* seems to be restored to itself, but it is we who are undergoing the restoration.[165]

This step toward objective insight is not a step toward stability; the introduction of the glass with which Galileo made earth a wandering planet has a dizzying effect on the verse. The strangely multiple locations provide a wandering view of the whole Italian countryside, as if from above the earth looking down. This view gives us a prospect rather like the one Galileo sees in the moon, with the "Mountain" of Fiesole, the river Arno, and the lands of its valley region doubled a few lines later as Vallombrosa with its brooks.[166] In the rush of similes that follow we are forced to refocus our vision repeatedly, performing radical shifts in scale appropriate to the introduction of Galileo's optic glass: one minute we are looking at the rebel angels as falling leaves, the next as drowning soldiers. It is our job to reconstruct the perspective from all these vantage points. Virtuosi described the lens as an instrument to see across time, and, here, the lens occasions an expansion of the temporal frame of reference as well; the passage integrates present, present perfect, and past tenses to embrace events from humanity's prehistory through Biblical times to Milton's own European trip, as he specifies actual locales that he visited as a young man and wrote about in recent memory. Both forms of comprehensiveness are equally associated with Galileo's thinking in astronomy, but the necessary corollary of such an ambitious scope is uncertainty and vacillation; we are not even sure if we are looking "down" at Fiesole or Valdarno.

The description of Satan's spear, "to equal which the tallest Pine / Hewn on *Norwegian* hills, to be the Mast / Of some great Ammiral, were but a wand" alludes to Galileo's instrument as it was invoked in the only English experimentalist epic before *Paradise Lost*.[167] Davenant, we recall, had compared telescopes to pine trees that seem to reach up to the moon, attempting to "prie" into the heavens; he also made the pine tree telescopes the property of a vaguely un-Christian experimentalist collective. Rescuing the hypervisual from such misuse, Milton not only separates the pine trunk from the optic trunk, he places the pine in Satan's hand and subjects it to Tuscan spectatorial art. Flaunting the power of magnification to shape our perspective, this obtrusively curated view of Satan's spear "in perspective" introduces us to the art that, at the end of the book, will miniaturize the fallen angels to insects. Satan uses this spear to support his "uneasie steps" through unfamiliar terrain; Milton's reader depends on an instrument of truth (1.295).

Milton does not lend us virtual access to Galileo's glass until he has made us aware of our need for it. As theorists of mental imagery tell us, when we project ourselves into the inevitably underdescribed environment of a narrated space, our mind's eye engages our experiential memory and our "conventional memory" to supply images that will serve to hold us in place; a few anchoring images from the text are enough for us to fill in the perceptual gaps.[168] The beginning of *Paradise Lost* utterly disables this process. Contemporary readers would have brought to the poem a rich store of conventional "memories" of the tortures of the damned, but Milton does not trigger them, and his few concessions to convention raise more questions than they answer. Even the hellfire he provides is provocatively deviant: far from inflicting unbearable physical agony on the demons, it is surprisingly easy for them to acclimate to. Nor is it the kind of fire that the mind's eye knows how to work with, emitting "No light, but rather darkness visible."[169] Milton deviates so radically from the standard image repertoire of Hell that we are unable to anchor ourselves by drawing on a preexisting mental store; we are forced into the adoption of an innocent perspective. Disabling our habitual techniques for adapting to the limitations of the mind's eye, Milton puts us to work to strengthen it in weakness.

Milton undermines our trust in the habitual procedures of the mind's eye not just by denying it the raw material it is conditioned to expect, but by delaying exposure to crucial information—most famously, by revealing almost 200 lines too late that Satan delivered his first two speeches prone and in bondage. No sooner are we informed of his prone position, "Chain'd on the burning Lake," than Satan "rears from off the Pool" without any apparent trouble (1.84–124, 157–191, 195, 210, 221). In this, the poem's first perspectival metaphor, Satan is compared to Leviathan, fatally mis-identified as an island by "The Pilot of some small night-founder'd Skiff" who fixes anchor on his body; rising up, Satan drowns the pilot that had mistaken his bulk for a safe shore (1.204). A cascade of *or*'s finally deposits the reader on the "Sea-beast," then into the sea: as many readers have noted, the pilot of a little boat lost in an open dark sea is as fit an emblem as any for the reader at the start of the epic (1.200). This is because, prior to the introduction of Galileo's vantage point, no virtual space is provided for her from which to descry the Leviathan.[170] We find our anchoring perspec-tive in Satan, since he is all we have (thus when Satan steps on "dry Land," Milton's aside—"if it were Land"—causes us to lose our footing yet again; the Fishian reader will find in his necessary dependence on Satan satisfying evidence of his own fallenness).[171] The perspectival metaphor, however, suggests the existence of a hitherto unidentified vantage point from which to descry the Leviathan; it is the reader's job to construct the perspective from that point, and, as we have seen, she is soon given the technology with which to do so.

Through the whale-island, Milton may have been accessing some gar-den lore to suggest a false paradise, perhaps even the icon of lost paradise itself: Thomas Browne wrote of "gardens upon great fishes . . . extraordina-rie & Anomalous gardens."[172] The false opposite and functional equivalent of lost paradise is the brutal state of nature offered by *Leviathan,* a text with which Satan shows some familiarity during the great consult. Hobbes's state of nature was driven repeatedly into the garden's interior throughout the century, resulting in the ironized paradise, which preserved the most reassuring image of paradise there was: the always-already-fallen paradise that slips out of reach the moment we try to imagine it.[173] The slippery paradise extends the same invitation to us as a conventionally hellish Hell—the temptation of setting up residence in the familiar space of cor-ruption, shrugging off the burden of innocent agency through surrender to a sovereign: a Leviathan (which Satan becomes) or a mechanically effica-cious Redeemer.[174] The cozy familiarity with Hell we are currently being denied is felt in its absence, but by extending to us the "artificial help" of Galileo's subject position, Milton offers us access to a perspective on corrup-tion just beyond the perspectives that corruption provides. In the process, he identifies our cultivation of that perspective as a productive labor—an art in the contemporary sense. Our induction into this art hardly results in smooth sailing, but the disorientation experienced by our imagined sensitive bodies, projected into the space of narration, provides the very grounds for the spectatorial body to orient itself.

For, like the moon on which Hooke dreamed he saw the grazing sheep of the Salisbury plains, Hell is finally rendered familiar, but not in the way we expected. The interposition of Galileo's glass estranges us from the perspective of the damned, but in the act of doing so, it reveals Hell to be a disconcertingly familiar environment. As we look more closely into Hell, we begin to see through it, and find ourselves the butt of the same perspective trick Milton played in *Areopagitica,* where what began as an account of "other Countries" mutated into an alienated portrayal of his native land. As the pattern of repetition in Satan's speech suggests (hail, hail, hell, hell . . . reign, hell, reign, hell), to submit internally to monarchy is already to enter Hell's kingdom (1.250–263). By seeing into and through Hell, Milton transforms it into an instrument of innocent insight, offering an alien perspective on the contemporary scene. In the dazzling city of Pandemonium, distinguished from our world only by the superiority of its inhabitants and quality of life, the reader sees the culture of the victors as it tried to see itself, and sees it as Hell. In providing this perspective on the Restoration, Milton offers his readers a way out of it, into a genuine restoration.

I am not suggesting Milton believes that all of London's citizens are stuck in hell, or that Hell is nothing more than a symbol of England under Charles. Rome, specifically St. Peter's and the Vatican, are palpably present here as well (though London was often bitterly described as papal Rome after 1660). The devils' consult is described as a "secret conclave," the council by which the Pope was elected; it is also called a "Synod," a meeting of Presbyterians, and a meeting of "peers," members of the Parliamentary House of Lords; the room into which extruded MPs were herded during Pride's Purge was also popularly known as "Hell."[175] The invitations to link Hell to the known world lead us in multiple directions, but, like the choice between Oreb and Sinai presented by Milton's "or" at the start of the poem, these are distinctions without a difference; Hell is simply the most impressive civilization that could come into being in the absence of inspiration. Aside from its technological wonders and architectural achievements, Pandemonium provides a synopsis of pagan culture: there are Olympic games, philosophical fora in which issues such as free will are debated, and contests of epic song, whose "harmony / (What could it less when Spirits immortal sing?) / Suspended Hell, and took with ravishment / The thronging audience" (2.552–555). Employing a mimetic line break before "Suspended," the poem takes up a momentary identification with demonic epic: what could it less? The always alert Defoe was disturbed by the activities of the fallen angels, finding Milton's desire to uncover "places of Retreat and Contemplation in *Hell*" suspicious.[176] It is certainly striking: even the fallen angels seem surprised by the comfortable lifestyle; as Belial asks during the consult, "is this then worst, / Thus sitting, thus consulting . . . ? . . . our present lot appears / For happy though but ill, for ill not worst . . ." As he reasonably points out, the burning lake "sure was worse."[177] In arguing against further struggle, he warns that God might "plunge us in the flames," that Hell might "spout her Cataracts of Fire": Belial tries to frighten his peers into submission, in other words, with images of Hell (2.172, 176). But as their own experience proves, such torments are not what Hell consists in. Milton leaves open the possibility that at "certain revolutions" God may see fit to visit these conventionally hellish punishments upon the fallen angels, but he reveals a submission to God rooted in the terror provoked by Hell as the piety of those who are already living there (2.597).

If Galileo is the only named contemporary in the poem, Belial, the most "lewd" of all the spirits, qualifies as a contemporary too, albeit one with a floating referent (1.490). Milton describes "the Sons / Of *Belial,* flown with insolence and wine" sweeping through the streets of "luxurious Cities" in the present tense, and in terms that clearly suggest the rowdy gentlemen associated with Charles II, who, along with their less ambitious expressions of libertine behavior, often aspired to a sophisticated intellectual libertinism, showcasing the ability to extend the implications of the new philosophy to materialist and nihilistic—and Hobbesian—limits; Beale, we recall, treated *Hobbesians* and *gallants* as virtual synonyms. Belial is present in "Courts and Palaces," and he is also present "when the Priest / Turns Atheist."[178] (The word *lewd* reemerges only once more in the poem, to modify church "Hirelings," underscoring the figure's contemporary resonance).[179] The identity of Belial and his sons was in fact a long-standing subject of contemporary controversy: Charles I's chaplain Thomas Bradley had defined *"Sonnes of Belial"* as "sonnes of disobedience" who refused to submit to the government under which they lived. Naturally, the king's opponents disagreed: in the opinion of the author of *Light Shining in Buckinghamshire,* to defend the king was to hold "fellowship with Belial."[180] Even as the official Restoration prayer book reassigned Belial's name to the late regicides, Thomas Hall insisted that defenders of May-games were "sons of *Belial,*" "*Libertines,*" "the *Belialists* of the Time" (whose ultimate defeat would "delight" the "ingenious"). Arguing from etymology, Robert Harris had explained that "a Belialist" was "yoke-less," refusing "dependence upon God."[181] From Milton's perspective, of course, to be yoked to this monarch was to be unyoked from all others.

Belial extends the contemporary dispute over competing styles of yokelessness into the challenge posed to the concept of place by the new philosophy. One of the most moving passages in the poem is that in which Belial finds the words to describe what makes life worth continuing, even in Hell. Arguing against further confrontation with God, for fear that such war, undertaken a second time, will "end us," he muses like Hamlet on the prospect of utter extinction:

> To be no more; sad cure; for who would loose,
> Though full of pain, this intellectual being,
> Those thoughts that wander through Eternity,
> To perish rather, swallowd up and lost
> In the wide womb of uncreated night,
> Devoid of sense and motion?
>
>   *(2.145–151)*

In celebrating the freedom of thoughts to "wander through Eternity," Belial ventriloquizes Milton's own celebration in *Areopagitica* of the mind's power to "wander beyond all limit and satiety."[182] Though "full of pain," the liberty of "this intellectual being" makes even a damned existence worth protecting. It is worth asking why, Satan excepted, Milton reserves his most explicit denunciations for the demon who speaks so movingly on behalf of an untethered "intellectual being," and who alone counsels against further rebellion, going so far as to claim that their punishment cannot be considered unjust. Of all the fallen angels, only Belial seems to grasp that they have well and truly fallen; he just does not care that much. His yokelessness paradoxically expresses itself in a kind of obedience—a casual submission to a law he has no part in fashioning, to which he has no real objection, and in which he has no stake.

It is through Belial that we are first exposed to Chaos as a psychological and intellectual state: a fall into Hobbesian "meer Nature," and disincorporated privacy.[183] Although his speech ostensibly *opposes* intellectual wandering through infinite space to the physical fall into "the wide womb of uncreated night," it actually makes them hard to distinguish. In their fall through interstellar space, into which we will soon be cut loose—

> . . . the hoarie deep, a dark
> Illimitable Ocean without bound,
> Without dimension, where length, breadth, & highth,
> And time and place are lost—

Belial and the other fallen angels experienced with a jolt the infinite space revealed by Galileo's glass (2.891–894). Falling, in Alexandre Koyré's famous phrase, from the closed world into the infinite universe, they were subjected to the radical implications of modern "thinking in astronomy," entering a space whose existence Aristotle did not recognize.[184] Belial's entrancing description of what it is like to fall suggests that to wander even intellectually through the newly expanded universe is to risk falling in the worst sense possible.

Milton's own flight into Chaos (it is "my flight" in the subsequent invocation) reverses this fall (3.15). As I have suggested, Chaos is the infinite interstellar space described by the new science, and it is also a space hollowed out in the middle of the poem for the substratum of all creation, the prime matter that preexisted God's creative acts, and the material remnant of that labor. But for quite a long stretch it feels like the physical correlate of the political state of nature as Hobbes imagined it: matter in a state of aimless unrest, expressed in atomic collisions and constant war. As John Rogers observes, Chaos serves as a "laboratory" in which Milton can reveal "the metaphysical foundations of the state"; Milton crafts its "spiritless collision of atoms" to engage, and reform, Hobbes's mechanistic materialism.[185] Belial introduces us to this laboratory, but it is Milton who makes it our workroom.

That Belial appeals to the hellish Hell of conventional piety while turning us toward the disorientation of Chaos stands to reason; his "sons" are at once hireling priests and atheist freethinkers. Belial counsels obedience, but the *content* of that obedience is to him, a thing indifferent; like one of Hobbes's atomized contracting subjects (subjects of private interest, capable only of "private opinion") his only interest is self-preservation. Using "reasons garb," Belial turns *Areopagitica*'s celebration of a wandering progress toward truth into an argument for "ignoble ease": his wandering is inertial motion along the path of least resistance.[186] In the Chaos episode, Milton makes wandering "beyond all limit" a collective work, and the occasion for the poem's most astonishing experimental demonstration: the erection of a theodicy on the grounds of "ill chance" itself (2.935). Wandering becomes the condition of obedience, expressed in the effort to "magnify," and continue, the maker's work. As a virtual witness and participant in this process, the reader learns how to "hold dependence on God" in the very act of wandering, abandoning both a stable place in creation and a place from which creation looks stable. Unyoked from place, Milton's paradisal subject is placeless, but not yokeless.

While Satan is indeed threatened "with utter loss of being" as he wanders into the abyss, it is here that the spectatorial body finds its philosophical bearings (2.440). Habituated to continual perceptual disorientation and reorientation by the first two books, the reader is weaned from a dependence on place, her experiences in Hell and Chaos training her to approach the fetishized barrier around Eden as only one of many crossable conceptual thresholds. It is in Hell itself that the reader gains access to a perspective from which Hell can be escaped; reciprocally, it is on earth that Satan discovers that "a lower deep / Still threatning to devour me opens wide, / To which the Hell I suffer seems a Heav'n" (4.76–78). If Satan's discovery that "my self am Hell" replicates that of Marlowe's Faustus, his fear of a still lower deep that threatens him with nonbeing registers the flight through nature's "vast vacuitie" he has just undertaken, the vacuity dreamily evoked in Belial's speech (4.75, 2.932). In this experimental space, the natural causes of the created garden itself are laid bare, if never exactly "seen," in the atomic structure of the matter that composes it; here, the raw matter of paradise becomes the raw material for our own *"Strenuous, Inward Speculations"* and compositions. There is little stock religious imagery with which the reader might domesticate this space; Milton's negating descriptions deprive us of anything tangible to hold on to. And yet the matter with which this historically and ontologically prior space confronts us cannot finally be distinguished from the stuff of creation as we now encounter it, and not just because Satan's journey literally paves the way for the entrance of Chaos into creation. Walter Curry's rumination on the logical difficulties posed by the construction of this highway offers useful guidance here: as he notes, substances like asphalt that Sin and Death use to construct this pathway are themselves "actualized products of God's creation of the Mundane Universe" which should be "impossible existences in the chaos frame of reference."[187] Once again, a space to which we should have no access is rendered indistinct from a space filled with things we recognize. By blurring the boundary separating the created world from the realm of matter in a perpetual purgatorial state of becoming, Milton engages us in constructing another path from Chaos to creation.

As we know from the first invocation, the "dark materials" of Chaos reside in the poet's own body; the matrix of the world is also the matrix of the poem (2.16). Other hexameral poets in English compared God's creative work on Chaos to his ability to inspire and order the chaos of the author's mind, but none pursue the implications of the parallel they suggest: that there is uncreated matter within God's creatures on which work remains to be done. It is most interesting that Hutchinson, who translated Lucretius, declines this task. Linking God's creative work on Chaos to his work on the chaos within her, she calls her own compositional acts "outgoings," a clear echo of the "outgoings" she attributes to God in the act of creation.[188] Yet, just as her fiercely end-stopped couplets keep her syntax in check, so she abstains from going into the matter that preceded God's creative efforts. In the poem's preface, she declares that she undertook the epic in order to "fortify my mind," deranged by reading and translating the poet she elsewhere called a "Lunatick." She attributes the indiscretion to "the vain curiosity of youth," which "had drawn me to consider and translate the account some old poets and philosophers give of the original of things." Hutchinson did not trust herself to integrate these two "originals": Genesis and the "Irrational dance of Attomes." Conceiving of her epic effort as an "antidote," an "occasion to vindicate my self from those heathenish authors," she used poetic composition as a means to "reclaim" her "busy roving thought from wandering."[189] For Milton, in contrast, it is the "cloister'd" subject, not the wandering one, that is "fugitive"—fleeing the demands of "trial," without which, as Eve declares, *Eden* were no *Eden*,"

Where Eve is mistaken, of course, is in her insistence that such trial must be undertaken "Alone, without exterior help sustain."[190]

The closest equivalent to Milton's "outgoing" into Chaos was written by Galileo himself. Galileo attempted his own speculative rewriting of Genesis, focusing on the divine speech act by which light was created. He launches this experiment by elaborating on the distinction between primary and secondary qualities, which reduces most of our visual experience to mere symptoms or "tickling." But the very next sentence expounds on the "excellence" of vision, which throws him into a pious reverie:

> I believe that the sense of sight, most excellent and noble of all the senses, is like light itself. It stands to the others in the same measure of comparative excellence as the finite stands to the infinite, the gradual to the instantaneous, the divisible to the indivisible, the darkness to the light. Of this sense, and all that pertains to it, I can pretend to understand but little . . . Therefore I shall ponder it in silence.[191]

Galileo associates sight, in neo-Platonic code, with the attributes of divinity, and even the divine light itself. But he immediately inverts this rhetoric and the metaphysical hierarchy it implies by using the very terms in which he celebrated the excellence of light—instantaneous, indivisible, infinite—to describe the "tiny particles" that constitute our universe: atoms. The valorization of atoms comes during a consideration of heat, which Galileo claims "can finally be analyzed as motion," which he again pursues to the ultimate constituents of matter:

> Perhaps while this pulverizing and attrition continue, and remain confined to the particles themselves, their motion will be temporary and their operation will be merely that of heating. But once we arrive at the point of ultimate and maximum dissolution into truly indivisible atoms, light itself may be created, with an instantaneous motion or (I should rather say) an instantaneous diffusion and expansion, capable—I do not know if by the atoms' subtlety, rarity, immateriality, or by different and as yet unspecifiable conditions—capable, I say, of filling vast spaces.[192]

He leaves off here, concerned about giving birth to a "hundred doubts," but the direction of his reasoning is clear. Motion generates heat, a word that describes the experience of a sensitive body; in the absence of such a body, in the idiom of primary qualities, heat is the dissolution of bodies caused by friction. When such motion reaches the atomic level, it creates light capable of "filling vast spaces," as in the Genesis account of creation. Genesis has been translated into the language of science, the language of creation itself.[193] Galileo's meditation on the excellence of sight has led him into the investigation of temporally remote causes residing in atoms, recreating a temporally distant event that lay well beyond his visual capacity. By "looking" in the idiom of primary qualities, he sees without sensing the origin of the universe in the indwelling *conatus* of particulate matter.[194] The sight whose nobility Galileo celebrates is a kind of vision that can penetrate the causes of the visible, discerning how they have operated across time; the observer who can decipher the text of nature is able to bear witness to what he could never have seen. Milton performs an even more ambitious experiment, for his comprehensive perspective on the "Ancestors of Nature" comprehends natural and human worlds at once (2.895). Incorporating the reader into a spectatorial body that, like Hooke's, discloses a "multiply'd and condens'd knowledge of times past, and of times also yet to come," he offers us a revisionary experience of Hobbes's state of nature as a paradise *in potentia*.[195]

When Satan asks "what art can then / Suffice" to guide the traveler on a journey "through the palpable obscure" of Chaos, we inevitably contrast his journey through space with the intellectual and imaginative wanderings of Milton, following in the steps of the "*Tuscan* Artist," for the art that frames Satan's journey is of a very different kind (2.410–411, 406). Just before Satan leaps into the "wild Abyss," the poem seems to take a literary historical step backward, in the encounter with Sin and Death (2.917). The contrast between this allegorical episode and the utterly modern space of Chaos is diagnostic: it calls attention to—and demonstrates the necessity for—the enormous technological advance that Milton is making. As Catherine Gimelli Martin argues, Milton here enacts for us a "transformation of the traditional sacramental 'world picture' that underlies the entire system of magical pictorialism informing most normative allegory." Satan's fall into allegory is our opportunity to diagnose the "external process of symbolic displacement" that generates "iconic and sacramental 'realities'": the real experience of "false consciousness."[196] The scholastic doctrine of form had made divinity available *as* idolatrous form, and allegory had performed the same operation on literary form, with truths made flesh in pictorially rendered icons (hence the association of Sin and Death with "wondrous Art /

Pontifical").[197] Allegory's promise of easy visibility is made as problematic and vexing as possible as we enter into the space of a new kind of "Art," and a new kind of vision. Psychologized as an eruption of symptoms, Sin and Death are revealed as Winstanleyan imagination, expressing what Stephen Fallon calls a "deficient ontology" as well as a "deficient epistemology"; projections of Satan's diseased consciousness, these are shapes that "shape had none."[198] The Chaos episode is in fact bracketed by allegorical set pieces, the second one a literal throwaway: offering us a Dantean Limbo of Vanity, a Paradise of Fools pictorial, Milton then trashes it; after describing the souls undergoing their emblematically appropriate punishment, he then informs us that in fact there is no one there.[199] Milton also sets some allegorical figures adrift into Chaos itself, where they self-destruct. Chaos cannot support its own personification, a Mr. Chaos; he is thus wittily lent a "visage incompos'd" (2.989). These personifications—Rumor, Discord, "Sable-vested *Night*," and so on—will soon be released into creation, where they will disappear into naturalism (2.962–967).

Predictably, Addison disapproved of the allegory, but was delighted with "that immense Waste of Matter" in which these "Imaginary Persons" were deposited.[200] This immense waste elicits his approval not just because it is sublime, but because it asserts the poem's identity as an instrument of truth rather than fancy. Satan's leap out of Spenserian allegory and into Chaos dramatizes intellectual history's leap from one representational scheme to another: from a static and hierarchical model of nature in which analogies are drawn across bodies to a dynamic one in which homologies are drawn across systems, understood in corpuscularian terms. It is a leap Satan barely survives. For Milton and his reader, it is a leap from false images into the material conditions of unreifiable processes, the grounds of inspired labor. Many contemporaries were unable to imagine that the new atomistic analogies could be used to represent anything but the breakdown of order. From the perspective of the closed world, the political analogies suggested by the new science defeated the whole point of analogy: rather than fostering a sense of the inevitability of any particular political form, they destabilized all forms. But in revisiting "Matter's teeming bodies" that "scoot / Across the great void," Hobbes had found the "matter and forme" of the commonwealth at once.[201] Here, speaking as an apparent Hobbist, Milton quotes directly from Lucretius—"The Womb of nature and perhaps her Grave"—to dramatize the "endless Warrs" of "embryon Atoms," whose victors are decided by the "warring Winds" of chance, by whose laws each "Faction . . . rules a moment."[202] The eclipse of Book One that "with fear of change / Perplexes Monarchs" suggests the worldview abandoned by this sort of speculation.[203] Subjects of a superstitious belief in their own analogical identity with the sun, such monarchs necessarily regard heavenly changes as objects of credulous "fear" rather than "bold" investigation.[204] Doubles of the gaping fools of Milton's prolusion, these perplexed kings are the foil of the Galilean spectatorial brotherhood, their abject gazing another instance of the kingly scepter's supersession by the optic tube.

Amazingly, in a poem that purports to be a theodicy, Milton here permits the Lucretian clinamen to determine sacred history. Lucretius described the clinamen as a spontaneous and unimaginably small swerve in the atom's downward fall. Without such swerves, no collisions that create compound bodies would take place; atoms would just fall downward in infinite space.[205] So, we discover, would Satan, had it not been for a cloud of nitrous matter scooting across the space beneath him: leaping into the "vast vacuitie," Satan "to this hour / Down had been falling" but for the "ill chance" of the nitrous cloud that "hurried him / As many miles aloft" (2.932, 934–938). Rather than the unfolding of a providential design—a divine plot arching toward humanity's redemption through Christ—Satan's success in reaching the earth (and, evidently, the political defeat of the Restoration after "endless Warrs") was simply the result of "ill chance."

What would seem to be a radically unprovidential worldview is given a sensuous correlate: the journey across Chaos plays heavily on our fear of falling. Even though Satan's first movement in hell unsettled our attempt to "anchor" ourselves in him, his continued motion only invites us to keep on trying: when he leaves hell and flies through infinite space, we feel close to him because of the motion parallax; in "the wide womb of uncreated night," there is nothing else to feel close to (2.150). But we have access to a perspective on this experience that Satan lacks. Milton's first invocation located the "dark materials" of Chaos inside him, awaiting divine shaping into the poem we are now reading (2.916). Representing God as impregnating these materials, Milton identified this creative process with his own: "What in me is dark / Illumin, what is low raise and support" (1.22–23). The incomposure or "faultring speech" associated with the anarch of Chaos "retire[s]" under "the sacred influence / Of light," openly equated with God, who appears in the subsequent invocation to Book Three as an artisanal shaper of chaotic matter.[206] Although Milton admits atomic randomness into the world, he does not present human agency as powerless before it; contingency provides the very grounds of inspired creativity. Redescribed as resistant potentiality, all the matter of the world indifferently serves the project of restoration, through which God's instruments—Christ, Milton, and the reader—may generate "new Worlds" (7.209). As Walter Blith argued, God had created a "president" for man by bringing "that old Masse and Chaos of confusion into so vast an Improvement, as all the world admires, and subsists from . . . after that . . . *Adam* is sent forth to till the Earth, and improve it."[207]

If in *Paradise Lost* the imposition of form upon the dark materials of Chaos by the "Author of all being" is paralleled by the divine illumination and ordering of all that is dark and chaotic in the author's mind, on what then can the divinely illumined author impose his will, in what chaos can he intervene? Milton shows us when he compares the war of "embryon Atoms" to "the noise / Of endless Warrs" when "*Bellona* storms . . . Som Capital City."[208] If paradise adheres to human exertion on the chaotic matter of the world, this is the stuff of paradise. Looking into the nature of creation, Milton sees through the matter at hand and makes visible the unity of natural causes, not only across time and space, but across natural and political contexts, as the spectacle of embryon atoms merges with that of warring citizens. If we demand to visualize how Chaos can be both at once, Milton's poem will present us with "a Universal blanc." But by shutting wisdom out "at one entrance," Milton asks us to read his poem as he reads the world. As with the experimentalist revival and extension of Adam's innocent labors among the creatures, the labor of seeing through the world generates the means to recompose it. Revealing the processes he spent his life trying to shape, Milton reproduces the observations of contemporary experimentalists who saw England's recent history replicated at the microscopic level: the "order Democraticall" was an oxymoronic one of "chance and Atomes," into which inspired agents had to intervene perpetually.[209] Milton's view into Chaos offers insight into the processes connecting the present to the past and future; by focusing our attention on the observational art that submits these processes to what Boyle called the "severer scrutiny of Reason," Milton crowds out the immediate spectacle of warring bodies and inducts us into an experimental art—the "steps" by which the world will be read and written again.[210]

Before we have even reached Eden, the poem has already delivered on its promise as a theodicy. Providence is justified as providing the conditions for its own recomposition, a recomposition to be undertaken by God's inspired agents; in the final lines of the poem, double syntax will thus permit "Providence" to be both Adam and Eve's "guide" and the direct object of their choice (12.647). If working to impose forms on matter was first undertaken by Christ, God's effectual might during the Creation, it is now left to the care of humanity, as fit instruments as any for God's creative power.

Milton proves his own fitness as such an instrument through Galilean self-fashioning, and he extends that identity to the reader in her capacity as virtual witness and co-curator: the shaping of all things begins with seeing into them. But although he associates Galileo's technologically enhanced sight with his own sensuously grounded and cultivated insight, neither "artist" attains the body of an angel; their mutual project of revealing things invisible to mortal sight proceeds fitfully and leaves room for hesitation and uncertainty. When Milton returns to the telescopic moon a second time, he addresses this condition of doubt, comparing the archangel Raphael's vision to that achieved through Tuscan art, "when by night the Glass / Of *Galileo,* less assur'd, observes / Imagind Lands and Regions in the Moon" (5.261–263). (Galileo is so lacking in assurance here that, like Hooke, he is not even the grammatical agent of his own observations). Blending projection and discernment, this art of discovery is necessary rather than perfect; as Hooke found, it is difficult to keep seeing or "descry[ing] new Lands" strictly separate from imagining these lands (1.290). Disorientation is generated not only by what the glass seems to reveal, but by the fact that it only seems to reveal it. Milton's relationship to this uncertainty is less anxious than many critics have allowed. As Judith Scherer Herz rightly asserts, this art "depends upon the tension between certainty and doubt . . . the problematizing of knowledge is not an unfortunate result but the essential condition of the poem's undertaking."[211] The spectatorial body that wanders innocently must wander, as Adam tells us, "By steps" (5.512).

To enhance our perplexity, Milton's poetic testimonial is filled with references to results that have not yet come in, showcasing the "indifferencie, or aequilibration" that Charleton identified as the mark of a virgin mind by suspending judgment on what exactly Satan might have seen in his flight across space: "undetermind square or round," "Uncertain which, in Ocean or in Air."[212] Milton even takes pains to contrive his descriptions of the universe to fit both geocentric and heliocentric models, displaying an almost exaggerated commitment to "innocency" since by this point the dominance of the heliocentric hypothesis was almost total.[213] By multiplying occasions for such demonstrations of intellectual forbearance, Milton reveals the extent of his intellectual ambition. The provisionality of his results testifies to the boldness of his experimental project: the frank admissions of ignorance as he attempts to make the mysteries of space and matter visible, like his lamentations over his blindness, are proud assertions of his commitment to an innocent investigative style. Unlike Donne, who in a similar "wandering" space journey flaunted his freedom from scientific canons of evidence, and unlike Hutchinson, who refused to wander into "things uncertain," Milton puts himself and his reader to work to make uncertainty productive, and therefore redemptive.

The dynamic nature of experimental inquiry opens up the opportunity for rivalry between artists engaged in it to test their results, and their progress, against one another. When describing Satan's appearance on the sun, Milton sees a sunspot "like which perhaps" Galileo "Through his glaz'd Optic Tube yet never saw" (3.588–590). Milton's poem, like Galileo's tube, is also glazed—that is, fitted with lenses; as Fowler's note suggests, Milton is bragging that "no astronomer has seen comparable signs of corruption" on the sun as Milton sees here. And immediately following the declaration that Galileo's perspective is "less assur'd" than Raphael's, Milton adopts Raphael's perspective, assuming the angel's voice to tell the story of creation, the war in heaven, and the secrets of the "one first matter." Such assertions of spectatorial bravado do not efface Milton's own less assured moments, such as his striking request after representing the war in heaven that he be returned to his "Native Element" before he falls, like Bellerophon—or Eve—"Erroneous" (7.16–20). Godfrey Goodman, we recall, could hardly "endure" being deprived of angelic sight, but by proudly insisting on their blindness, experimentalists asserted their capacity to speculate beyond their mortal—and individual—limits; Milton does the same. Continually announcing his awareness of the possibility of error, he demonstrates the methodological divide that separates his investigation from Eve's attempt to wrench wisdom directly, and personally, from undiagnosed "experience."[214]

To accompany Milton in this process of discovery and invention is to inhabit the subject position of Milton's Adam, whose physical exertions on creation keep pace with his labors to understand it. Adam is an astonishingly eager and hard-working reader of nature; having started at year zero in "the progress of the arts and sciences," he easily deduces evidence of monotheism from the landscape within his first moments of existence, then works through astronomical speculations lifted out of Galileo's *Dialogue Concerning the Two Chief World Systems* over the following day. We might wonder why Adam would need to speculate about anything, since we are told that when he named the creatures, he was endowed with "sudden apprehension" of their natures (8.354). Adam was able to deduce the essence of each species from the creature's outward form, identifying the "Parsimonious Emmet" and housewifely bee with the ease of the reader of an emblem book (7.485–492). Like the practice of reading signatures, this naming suggests an emblematic concept of natural kinds. Milton does not suggest that Adam's "apprehension" was false—in this field of natural knowledge the stakes are sufficiently high that Milton becomes tendentious, using Adam's eyes to confirm that ants are commonwealthsmen. But in the context of the contemporary reduction of politics to natural laws of matter and motion, such analogies were certainly not "proof of deeper learning," as his nephew and pupil had haughtily claimed.[215] Any student of Milton's would be aware that it was no longer sufficient to read one's social destiny in the outwardly visible behavior of insects; the structuring terms of relevant analogies were not individual bodies but the "indifferent matter" that constituted them and the forces that traversed them.[216] Self-consciously modern observers of the contemporary scene were aware that the principle of social order was not to be found in exterior forms—or in the instantly recognizable, exemplary difference of a metaphysically ordained ruler from his subjects. Similarly, since natural types no longer emanated from indwelling forms betokened by signatures, but were simply "modes"—atomic motions and arrangements—identifying the species of a creature was only the first step in a deep physical description. Adam does not regard the object-as-seen as the "thing itself"; he recognizes it as the product of material causes behind the sensuous surfaces of his "apprehension." Thus, when he grills his angelic instructor Raphael, it is the causal relation of all the life forms he sees to their temporally and ontologically prior "embryon Atoms" that he longs to understand; although he has named the visible creatures, he cannot see how natural kinds relate to the "one first matter." The investigation into the secrets of first matter that Adam begins is continued by Milton and the collective reader of *Paradise Lost*. In this scrupulously innocent labor, illumination comes through the inspired work of rational reconstruction—a wandering, productive, and collective progress through uncertainty.

Growing up to Godhead

Milton beleaguers his reader with scruples, but he creates just as much insecurity by seeming to remove them. Once she enters the garden in Book Four, the reader is almost paralyzed by scruples; the opportunities for missteps seem so much greater given what tradition has taught us to identify as the alien character of the territory. Entering a familiar natural world that we are overprepared to find "made strange," we make the far more disorienting discovery that this setting is much less weird than we would ever have anticipated. Paradoxically, we would feel far more at home during our sojourn in paradise if paradise did not feel so much like home: like Paul in 2 Corinthians, the reader is "caught up into paradise" before she can remind herself that she does not belong there.

The reader determined to find a means of escape may seize on the "mazie error" of the river and "wanton growth" of the garden to reassure herself that she is indeed encountering the breeding ground of sin. To enter a paradise swarming with anticipatory hints of the fall is to ready oneself for the familiar consolations of *felix culpa*.[217] A related prophylactic against the psychic threat of Eden is to locate the always-already-fallen paradise in the reader, not as a heuristic choice but as an ineradicable feature of fallen subjectivity. On this understanding, there is a poem behind the poem that we cannot read, a poem to which we will never gain access: Milton's provocative modifiers carry a radically alien meaning in the context of unfallen existence, whose present unavailability provides the reader with a comforting reminder of his helplessness before his own corruption.[218] Both strategies introduce opacity into our experience of Milton's Eden, fending off its disconcerting continuity with our world.

But, like the suburb to which Milton compares it, Eden is no more alien to us than Pandemonium. Confronted with Milton's homely description of Adam and Eve sitting "Under a tuft of shade . . . on a green," Bentley snorts, "*On a green* is poor stuff indeed. He seems to have fansied himself in some Country Village, and to have forgot that the Scene was Paradise."[219] And of course it gets worse. Literally imperfect, Eden is an unfinished, fermenting space of growth with "unsightly" as well as beautiful features, which, like many objects of reforming efforts, "mock[s]" and "derides" attempts to improve it. No other early modern paradise stands in such urgent need of reform as Milton's; he is at least as insistent as any of his contemporaries on the garden's "wild," "wanton" character. (Other entities with which wildness is associated are Chaos and fancy, all matter requiring subjection and improvement.)[220] That the first garden should have stood in such desperate need of reform as soon as it was created is not a proposition the reader can register casually. When describing the object of their "pleasant labour," Adam and Eve use not only equivocal modifiers like "wilde," but morally loaded ones like "Luxurious."[221] Soon after our introduction to the first couple, Adam observes to Eve that the plants "mock our scant manuring, and require / More hands then ours to lop thir wanton growth" (4.628–629). The next day, Eve picks up on the suggestion of mockery, complaining to Adam that "what we by day / Lop overgrown, or prune, or prop, or bind, / One night or two with wanton growth derides / Tending to wilde" (9.209–212). Chiasmus, made into a figure for getting nowhere, enacts the endlessly repeated cycle of the garden's growth: "Thir growing work: for much thir work outgrew / The hands dispatch of two Gardning so wide" (9.202–203). Their endless work is to subject this cycle to the linear logic of improvement.

If fallen man works by the sweat of his brow, Milton's depiction of Adam wilting under the "fervid Raies" of the noonday sun suggests that innocent man did too (5.300–302). But despite the nuisance and aggravation that attend their hapless attempts, renewed daily, to restrain the unbridled fertility of their surroundings, Adam and Eve never succumb to the temptation to hate their jobs, and what would be called the curse of labor Adam experiences as a relief: "what harm? Idleness had bin worse" (10.1055). As he explains to Eve when we first encounter them, their difference from the creatures that "Rove idle unimploid . . . unactive" is the defining privilege of their happy state; the curse ensures that this crucial difference, like the torments of Satan's hell, will survive a "change of place" (4.617–621, 23). Although the fall disrupts their work schedule (rather than marking the start of it), the saving power of labor reenters the poem in a final simile, which suggests that what the first couple has experienced is all in a day's work. As they leave to establish their new paradise, the angels glide behind them like "Ev'ning Mist / Ris'n from a River" that "gathers ground fast at the Labourers heel / Homeward returning" (12.587, 629–632). The open-ended wandering of this laborer tends homeward without leading any-where in particular. "God attributes to place / No sanctitie, if none be thither brought / By Men"; just as the physical borders of Eden are easily crossed by Satan, so its spiritual and conceptual borders may be extended to encompass human experience in the physical world outside the garden (11.836–838). If the first couple is able to carry an innocent perspective on labor out of Eden, their offspring must be capable of recovering it. *Paradise Lost* is the instrument of that recovery, with which the reader has been working long before setting foot into Eden. As far as the reader's experience is concerned, the curatorial demands of paradise extend from Hell to Heaven; through the experimentalist discipline imposed by Milton's in-strument of truth, she has been meeting them. Now, however, she can see her labors narrated and "multiplied" as the labors of her originals.[222]

She encounters them engaged in the exercise of curiosity, investing custodial and investigative care in creation. We recall that Satan actually has to *pretend* to an appreciative curiosity of God's works in order to gain entrance into creation; Uriel admits him precisely because Satan claims to be filled with "Unspeakable desire to see, and know / All these his won-drous works" (3.662–663). Curiosity is a precondition of entrance into this paradise, guarded by an angel whose stout Baconianism rivals Browne's. Reviving the latter's criticism of the corruptible mind's dependence on "sec-ondary narration," Uriel extols Satan's desire to "witness with thine eyes what some perhaps / Contented with report hear onely in heav'n," insisting that the more seemingly excessive this desire is, the better (3.694–701). Uriel is deceived because the emotion Satan expresses is precisely that to which faith, among Milton's regenerate, is always linked; Milton's villains invariably pretend to the virtue of curiosity and plead excuse on that basis, but they are strangers to this unspeakable desire of the disciplined and in-nocent body, merely speaking of it.[223]

By giving innocent curiosity free rein in paradise, Milton integrates primitivist and progressivist Edens, much as Evelyn did when he figured human progress as the unfolding expression of Adam's ingenuity. (Such integration does not preclude concessions to paradise and Golden Age lore, as when Milton refers to Adam and Eve's gardening tools as "Guiltless of fire," but such concessions are ironized by their context.)[224] Milton's Adam is clearly poised to make rapid progress in the "contemplation of created things" from the moment he is created, and his knowledge base expands exponentially during the lunchtime symposium with Raphael (5.511). Even when Adam probes into the sensitive area of astronomy—"Led on, yet sinless, with desire to know"—the angel explicitly reassures him that his speculations are innocent and part of his appointed work: "To ask or search I blame thee not, for Heav'n / Is as the Book of God before thee set" (7.61, 8.66–67). It is a reassurance Adam hardly needs. Raphael does caution Adam about the tendency of the "Fancie" to "roave / Uncheckt" (8.188–189, Adam's paraphrase). Having issued this caution, he encourages Adam to speculate about heliocentrism, gravity, and the possibility that the spots on the moon might be rain clouds that permit agriculture. Such speculation, of course, is not fancy. Cribbing generously from Wilkins's *Discovery of a World in the Moone,* Adam and Raphael's exchange also incorporates language from attacks on Wilkins levelled by Alexander Ross in *The New Planet no Planet: or, The Earth no wandring Star;* like Locke, Milton incorporates objections to modern experimental inquiry in order to produce a stronger defense of it.[225] Raphael warns Adam against pursuing knowledge for the sake of pride and, like Ross, consistently elevates moral knowledge over knowledge of the physical world, but Adam is in no danger of misunderstanding the role of natural knowledge. His hunger to learn what "Mov'd the Creator . . . to build / In *Chaos*" is stimulated by a desire to expand upon the work God started: "the more / To magnifie his works, the more we know."[226]

Raphael dangles before Adam the prospect of gaining angelic insight into matter's secrets even while urging him to accept his epistemological limitations: "Mean while enjoy / Your fill what happiness this happie state / Can comprehend, incapable of more" (5.503–505). He is addressing two Adams. Adam's modest acceptance of his limits as an individual is compatible with his participation in the intellectual progress of the humanity he represents; indeed, the personal modesty that expresses itself in an individual contentment with "this happie state" is a necessary condition of that progress. As in the "amorous delay" Milton deems necessary for erotic bliss, the gradual and cooperative striving toward fulfillment brings its own plea-sures (4.311). Such delay, as we have seen, dominated experimental procedure; by striving to remain indifferent in the heat of investigation, forestalling the subjective satisfaction of certainty for as long as possible, the investiga-tor safeguarded his innocence and imparted it to the knowledge he pro-duced. Only data produced by such discipline were fit to be assimilated by the collective of which he was both a member and representative. The sys-tematically ambiguous identity of Adam, suspended here between his indi-vidual and collective instantiations, prefigures the very dialectic between the intellectual laborer's two bodies that propelled experimental progress.

As a paradigm for this progress, Raphael provides a tableau of the transformation of "one first matter" from vegetable material to thinking substance through the processes of human consumption and digestion. He first blazons the plant, beginning with a stalk that "Springs lighter" from (and than) the root: the two components of Milton's cultivated inward sight—*spring* and *light*—appear again here (5.480). Once ingested, "flours and thir fruit / Mans nourishment, by gradual scale sublim'd / To vital Spirits aspire, to animal, / To intellectual . . ." and so on up to the angelic summit (5.482–490). Although this passage describes human consump-tion, it does not describe an individual's appetitive act of "degustation": the act of degustation is reformed by being magnified—temporally extended and multiplied (in seventeenth-century usage, as we have seen, *magnify* encompassed all these meanings). Raphael is restating Eve's fantasy of "growing up to Godhead" in collective and incremental terms (9.877).

Here, it is not the eater but rather the matter eaten that "aspires" to a higher place by becoming nourishment. Raphael compares this undifferen-tiated first matter to the undifferentiated humanity that Adam represents; the one first matter becomes the one first man. Addressing Adam in his representative capacity, Raphael explains that in exactly the way vegetal matter is refined by becoming "Mans nourishment," so "Your bodies"—using "corporal nutriments"—may be "Improv'd by tract of time," may even "at last turn all to Spirit" (5.496–498). History had borne out the first part of the prophecy; the human body had indeed been improved as an organ of knowledge in Milton's own time, as prosthetic technologies ex-panded its sensory powers beyond mortal limits. Raphael's fable suggests that this progress is driven not by the desire to consume nourishment but rather to *become* it—a desire that is itself nourishing, as the energy humanity invests to satisfy its intellectual hunger itself becomes the food. Humanity is nourished and "sublim'd" by Adam's body—the same innocent body that *Areopagitica* had identified with the public and then dissolved into the work of truth production. As the medium and symbol of humanity's perceptual expansion, this sublimed matter figures the sacred transformation of human substance: the private person's progressive incorporation into the public.

Raphael has explicated the theology of the productive sacrament. There is no other reason why "transubstantiate"—a word that has "much disturbed the World," as Hume complains in his commentary—should appear in this context, or indeed in this poem.[227] Understood within the framework Raphael provides, the verb describes the productive transformations that accompany the digestion and incorporation not just of food but of knowledge, both drawn from the one first matter of creation. Compared to the transformations produced "by fire" and the skill of "the Empiric Alchimist" on the "drossiest Ore," the "concoctive" processes of digestion suggest the artisanal skill praised in *Areopagitica,* of extracting precious material from the "drossiest" volumes; here the drossy volume is creation itself (5.437–442). This artisanal tempering is conveyed to us through the by now familiar imagery of the purgatorial paradise of pains. The phrase "concoctive heate" condenses purgatory and the garden: to concoct is to prepare by heating or boiling, but it is also to ripen or mature, as in a fruit (5.437). The phrase achieves the systematically ambiguous agency on which purgatorial discourse thrived, since to concoct can mean both to assimilate and to compose. This is the sacrament Oldenburg celebrated when praising "demonstratif knowledge" as "good meat well concocted" to nourish "the body politique"; Milton renders the figure using what Evelyn called "paradisian fare."[228]

Adam grasps the object lesson, assimilating and composing the parable. If, as he later declares, "Knowledge is as food," it is up to him to concoct it: "Well hast thou taught the way that might direct / Our knowledge . . . In contemplation of created things / By steps we may ascend to God." Here, I believe, Adam alludes to John Salkeld's claim in his *Treatise of Paradise* that it was not by "the curious searching of God in externall things" but by "seeing himselfe, hee [Adam] may ascend by contemplation unto God."[229] In place of such purely introspective illumination, Milton's Adam substitutes an external orientation toward "created things," puts the comment in the first-person plural, and adds the crucial phrase "By steps," restoring collectivity and process to the sudden enlightenment Salkeld describes, or the sudden "high exaltation" that Eve craves (5.90). For Adam truly to "see himself," in other words, is to see himself magnified and multiplied—prepared to seek satisfaction not by consuming knowledge but by producing it for the body of humanity. This communion is impelled by "real hunger"—not imaginary (private) appetite (5.437). As Regina Schwartz points out, "real hunger" substitutes for the sacramental phrase "real presence," but I would suggest that rather than suggesting a tragic lack, this hunger is a productive force, expressing the longings while enabling the satisfactions of a distributed subject.[230]

What John Rumrich calls "nutritional communion" describes the process of collective induction.[231] Adam interprets the different levels of the natural hierarchy Raphael has described as levels in a phenomenological ladder to be climbed, not by any single person, but by the corporate agent of innocent curiosity. As Locke insisted in *The Reasonableness of Christianity,* knowledge was best understood as the product of collective "pains," not a "private Possession."[232] The collective and progressive nature of such knowledge production poses an exemplary contrast to Satan's solitary and regressive journeys of discovery, just as this extended lunchtime colloquy, which raises more questions than it answers, provides an innocent alternative to the forbidden snack. Chastened by gradualism and the collectivist discipline required for incorporation, the first disobedience is reformed by being magnified, temporally extended and collectivized. In contrast, Eve's solitary consumption of "intellectual food" is an attempt to terminate once and for all the collective process of cultivating knowledge through uncertainty. Eve wants to eat rather than cultivate a "Wisdom-giving Plant," but in the sphere of knowledge, such cultivation, it turns out, *is* "Mans nourishment" (9.768, 679).

It is fitting that the poem's figure for the productive sacrament is itself the fruit of that sacrament, gradually ripening through the progressive stages of a conversation; collectively pieced together, it is a "thing made." Thus, in addition to addressing the first man as a public person, Raphael forms a public with him; like the coffeehouse patrons imagined by the author of *Coffee-houses Vindicated,* Adam and Raphel sit together, "expressing themselves on divers subjects according to their respective Abilities."[233] By introducing this "affable Arch-Angel" into the garden, Milton has made

Eden the scene of the "affable meeting" that, earlier in the century, he had hoped to foster in England through "frequent Academies"; the public that could make England a paradise now makes Eden seem like heaven.[234] Anxious to keep Raphael with him, Adam tries to arouse his curiosity, jovially remarking, "How suttly to detaine thee I devise":

> For while I sit with thee, I seem in Heav'n,
> And sweeter thy discourse is to my eare
> Then Fruits of Palm-tree pleasantest to thirst
> And hunger both, from labour, at the houre
> Of sweet repast; they satiate, and soon fill,
> Though pleasant, but thy words with Grace Divine
> Imbu'd, bring to thir sweetness no satietie.
>   (8.207, 210–216)

Here is the homosocial philosopher's paradise of which experimentalists dreamed.[235] By means of Raphael's tutorial, which he requites with his own historical relation, Adam virtually wanders to heaven and is "Imbu'd" by its knowledge—and its grace. Adam distinguishes physical hunger, sharpened by labor and easily satisfied during workbreaks, from an appetite that, seeking satisfaction *through* labor, the exercise of curiosity, admits of "no satietie," like the minds celebrated in *Areopagitica* that wander past its limit.[236] Rigorously distinguished from carnal consumption and identified instead with lengthy and inconclusive cognitive experimentation—since Raphael refuses to give Adam certain answers about anything outside the moral realm—this insatiable and productive appetite is the very engine of progress.[237] Adam's curiosity, like that of Boyle's occasional reflector, lays hold on circumstantial occasions to exercise itself; it is he who transforms Raphael's visit, whose stated purpose is to warn Adam of Satan's presence, into a scientific conference: "sudden mind arose / In *Adam,* not to let th' occasion pass / Given him by this great Conference to know / Of things above his World," though he is discreet enough to begin diffidently, with "wary speech." This "Conference" is a modest step toward the findings that will one day transform humanity's body into an angelic organ of knowledge.[238]

Adam's identity as a public person fundamentally shapes his characterization: as one who realizes his nature in and as a collective, Adam calls out for an interlocutor the moment he is created, addressing questions about creation to no one.[239] Like the virtuoso, Adam realizes his identity in conference with others. The spectatorial body with which the Adamic investigator sought to identify was composed not just from a battery of "mechanical helps" but human helps: the other members of the corporate body who cultivated and digested the fruits of his labor and whose labor in turn fed his own production. In *Paradise Lost,* the subject of prelapsarian labor is already a "Person multiplyed," both because Adam embraces his public identity as humanity "personated" and because he submits his own person to collectivist discipline through his ongoing collaboration with Eve.[240] It is not merely that Adam and Eve work together, but that working together is the most important part of their work. As Satan sees, Adam and Eve are "Imparadis't" by their very union, and Milton's analogies frequently treat them as a single (masculine) agent, even as Samsonian England itself.[241] Their desire for children is primarily expressed as a longing to "magnify" the scope of this agent's activity: their desire for "More hands then ours" expresses the corporate vocational identity of the experimentalist community as a "*union* of *eyes,* and *hands*" far more than it does anything we could characterize as family feeling.[242]

In order to model the distributed subjectivity that enables innocent progress, the first couple's characterization is flexible; Eve is by turns Adam's doughty coworker and a near-personification of the allurements of the individual sensitive body, requiring the "Subjection" of publically exercised reason so that she may "to realities yield all her shows" (4.308, 8.575). Eve's fitness for innocent labor is magnified (or multiplied) by Adam's ability to magnify (or see through) her "outside . . . fair" rather than being subjected to it, a spectatorial accomplishment that requires the "subjection" of his own sensitive body in turn (8.568, 570). As Raphael's warnings make clear, Adam must work to shore up the distinction between innocent sexuality and the merely carnal "delight . . . voutsaf't / To Cattel and each Beast" (8.580–582). In the act of cleaving to Eve's fair outside, he risks cleaving the subject of innocence into two separate sensitive bodies that unite as "one Flesh" only.[243] In Milton's Eden, the division of the corporate subject of innocence into discrete sensitive bodies—whether through carnal attraction or a division of labor—coincides with that subject's fall from paradise.

As previous chapters have argued, the Adamic investigator worked to integrate faculties that in fallen humanity worked at cross-purposes, healing the rift caused by the "divorce" of Cain and Abel, or the disconnection of the sensitive and spectatorial bodies. Milton alone among experimentalist authors relates this synthetic ideal to the separation of Adam and Eve. Yet it cannot be asserted without qualification that in *Paradise Lost* innocent psychology is equally distributed between two people, male and female. *Pace* Johnson's observation on the "want of human interest" in Eden, Milton's Adam is manifestly a person, albeit a newly created one, who displays the spectrum of recognizable human emotions.[244] Eve is in many ways even more of a person, yet her relentlessly exteriorized presentation is designed to discourage our identification; Milton insistently makes us look at her from the outside, and often, even *as* an outside. As readers often notice, her nakedness is repeatedly insisted upon, if not actually to disguise the nakedness of Adam, then certainly to naturalize it; only through Adam do we experience life without clothes from the inside.[245] And although Eve participates in the life of Eden, Milton deprives crucial moments of that existence of narrative exposition; her naming of the flowers and her dream vision of fallen history never become objects of the reader's virtual experience.[246] They remain private. This is appropriate to her mode of existence in the poem, where she lives both as a historical personage—a recalcitrantly individual one—and as a signifier of sensory knowledge in all its forms: "good," necessary, to be used with care. These two aspects of Eve are mutually reinforcing, since her user (and improver) is the public person, the intellectual laborer comprised by Adam, and by Adam and Eve together. It is with the public, not the person, that Milton's poem (often against our will) compels us to identify.

To impose this schematic model on two characters who are also historical people feels like a sort of violence. Yet if we analyze their relationship in purely personal terms, we will fail to capture the intense political and intellectual stakes for Milton of innocent humanity's public form of being, a mode of being that confers innocence on all the knowledge it produces. Even as Milton bravely weaves Eve into the homosocial philosopher's paradise of the virtuosi, he relies on the basic experimentalist contrast between masculine rational penetration and feminine identity with (and susceptibility to) appearances—public reason and private fancy—in order to construct that paradise. In his account of Adam and Eve's separation, Milton imagines a more subtle loosening of the paradisal union of faculties than virtuosi's portrayals of Eve would ever allow, but it is still the disjoining of the higher and lower parts of the human intellect that occasions the (temporary, but unfortunately iterable) disintegration of paradise.

However off-putting this schematic account of their characterization may feel, it is no more so than the gloss Milton provides on the fall and Eve's role in it: "Understanding rul'd not, and the Will / Heard not her lore, both in subjection now / To sensual Appetite, who from beneathe / Usurping over sovran Reason claimd / Superior sway" (9.1127–1131). The appetite associated with Eve implies self-sovereignty; as Georgia Christopher observers, for many reformers, the two ideas come together in and as flesh. (Such an understanding shapes Winstanley's suggestion that, after the fall, "In our present experience, The darkness or self-love goeth before; and light or universal love follows after; the flesh runs hasty and quick, and loses himself in unrational excessive action; the true Spirit comes slowly after, and takes the Crown.")[247] Adam's diagnosis of Eve's dream serves as a heavy-handed gloss on their respective natures: during waking hours, reason supervises fancy's work in constructing mental images on the basis of data gathered by the senses, but during sleep, when reason "retires," fancy attempts to do this work herself, and "misjoyning shapes, / Wilde work produces oft" (5.108, 111–112). It is of course Adam who retired into the privacy of sleep, and Eve who attempted through her dreamwork to imitate him in his absence. Adam is "sovran Reason," and Eve "mimic Fansie," whose daytime "office" is to form imaginations of "external things" as revealed to the senses—the raw material for the construction of humanity's spectatorial body (5.110, 103). Eve is literally made out of fancy, since she is Adam's dream girl (while he slept, God "op'n left the Cell / Of Fancie" so that its phantasmata informed her "glorious" shape). Eve's connection to external appearance is evident both in her presentation by Milton and in Raphael's disapproval of Adam's captivation by her: "what admir'st thou, what transports thee so, / An outside?" (Such frankness is made possible by her withdrawal from the public they have formed).[248] Raphael advises Adam to take more seriously the governance of reason that he after all represents: "Oft times nothing profits more / Then self esteem" (8.571–572). Rather than encouraging Adam to cultivate a personal self-regard, Raphael is advising him to place esteem in the collective possession of "sovran Reason"—what Boyle called humanity's "Natural Dignity" of office. Only then will Eve acknowledge him as "her Head" and "to realities yield all her shows" (8.574–575). The latter statement is almost nonsensical if we assume that Raphael is *simply* talking about a woman; a person with a beautiful outside can't just knock it off and yield up the show of her appearance. Raphael is counseling Adam in the management of sensory experience, in the disciplining of his own sensitive body and private fancy.

Because Eve is associated with undiagnosed sensory ideas, she is also, by experimentalist logic, associated with false ones.[249] It stands to reason that Eve is a zealous but incompetent natural philosopher. As Karen Edwards observes, rather than test or "'make experiment' of the serpent's claims," Eve chooses simply to "accept the experience he offers."[250] It is the capacity "to discerne / Things in thir Causes" with which Satan tempts her; she hopes to understand the laws that govern creation and so rise to godhead herself (9.681–682). As her symbolic identity dictates she must, Eve behaves like a naïve empiricist, convinced that she can obtain knowledge of things through direct experience of things, regardless of the methods she employs.[251] The temptation represented by the fruit in *Paradise Lost*, as in experimentalist accounts, is that of conflating sapience and experience outright in the desire to "feed at once both Bodie and Mind" (9.779). The frequently noted synesthesia of Satan's description of the fruit (combining smell, taste, and sight) identifies Charleton's purely sensual "Desire of Science" as the basis of the temptation; under its influence, "hunger and thirst" and "sharp desire" seize reason's sovereign position as "Powerful perswaders"; it is the sensitive body that thinks, decides, and acts (9.586, 584, 587).

What that body hungers for above all is to rest in certainty; Eve hopes to consume "intellectual food" without having to cultivate it. Although induction can produce either "knowledge or opinion," she identifies the "Mother of Science" with sensual "Experience" alone, and she appeals to Adam accordingly: "On my experience, *Adam*, freely taste" (5.108, 9.680, 807, 988). The "sapience" of carnal knowledge produces no knowledge of causes, but without Adam to inform her of this, she might never have known the difference. Her "sad experiment" ends with her bowing and praying to the divinity contained in a food source (10.967). Without any means to penetrate appearances, she becomes an idolatress. Her sacramentalizing of consumption is predicted by the idolatry of works that led to her separation from Adam; her desire for quick results is a perfect inversion of the experimental discipline by which trustworthy results are procured.[252] Just as she expects to work faster alone, she is eager for trial "Alone, without exterior help sustain"; her apparent workaholism is a refusal of innocent employment, which sacralizes corporate productivity rather than its individual products.[253] Thus in her "uncouth dream," she is abruptly lifted, without dint of labor or the coordinated application of method, to a "high exaltation" from which she beholds "The Earth outstretcht immense," like God when he regards his creation "In prospect from his Throne."[254] He can see creation from this perspective because it answers "his great Idea," but Eve has not worked with Adam to reconstruct God's thoughts after him; she has no ideas to structure or explain her sensitive body's experience, and she descends from her sudden elevation. It is through the disciplining of such private fancies that private persons are refined into public ones. If humans are to grow up to godhead through "contemplation of created things," they have to ascend together, "By steps."

Floral Spectacles

Raphael's floral tableau is ideally adapted to its subject: the slow, incremental growth of flowers and their responsiveness to cultivation make them fit emblems for the progress of knowledge according to an experimentalist understanding. Not only objects of but figures for paradisal work, involving physical and intellectual exertion in equal measure, flowers are also the medium through which the reader sees this work as it happens. After gently chastising Eve for her dream of solitary flight, Adam announces the start of their work day in language that, by reprising this ascent in floral code, inflects it with the discipline of collective gradualism: "let us to our fresh imployments rise / Among the Groves, the Fountains, and the Flours / That open now thir choicest bosom'd smells / Reservd from night" (5.125–128). Their "fresh imployments" recall the fresh flowers on which they are employed. As they open their eyes and "rise" to their daily work, the flowers "open now" and release their odors that float heavenward, garden and gardeners linked in a rhetoric of rising. The efforts of the first couple to restrain Eden's "wanton growth" and "lop" its excesses suggest that this blameless striving, like Eve's fantasy of "growing up to Godhead," requires continual "Subjection" to be kept under control (4.629, 9.877, 4.308). Eve's dream, a "Wilde work" of the fancy—which evokes the rebels' "Wild work in Heav'n"—finds its vegetal correlative in the garden's "Tending to wilde," but the ongoing drama of vegetable rebellion requiring continual "reform" is itself disciplined by a competing strain of imagery of incremental floral progress—and, at the meta level, by the use of flowers as lenses to "open" the reader's sight in the very act of chastening it.[255]

Rendering concepts that are conventionally opposed to innocence—such as curiosity, ambition, and labor—florally, Milton uses flowers as a medium of conceptual integration. Perhaps most saliently, he weaves floral imagery into our perception of Adam and Eve's sexuality: we first see them kiss through a shower of petals, and the climax of "the Rites / Mysterious" of innocent intercourse brings down the flowery roof (4.742–743). Presenting innocent sexuality through a floral perceptual tissue, Milton literally makes flowers into spectacles, his curatorial artistry identifying the reader's perspective with the object of the innocent couple's reforming efforts. Adam and Eve are the custodians of the vegetation through which we view them: their labor is to reform the eyes "planted" in us, to help us see them not just in paradise but through paradise—through a reformed rather than an "unsightly" or "wanton" garden. Milton loses no opportunity to underscore the moral meanings that his culture attached to gardening when describing Adam and Eve's daily renewed attempts to "reform" the "flourie Arbors"; these are the labors we must perform on our own sight (4.625–626). By helping us sharpen the prosthetic insights harvested from Milton's internal garden and our own, Adam and Eve make it possible for us to imagine ourselves—sexual creatures condemned to work—as paradisal subjects. Dunton enabled Londoners to reimagine themselves as Athenians by providing them with a model of this identity and an opportunity to assume it; Milton does the same in his representation of the state of innocence.

Scarry has shown that writers frequently exploit what she calls "floral supposition" to lend perceptual vivacity to their fictional worlds.[256] Her analysis of this technique helps to explain why we use the predicate "flowery" to describe writing that flaunts its literariness, or why, throughout the Renaissance, lyric poems are referred to as posies and flowers, so that

Herbert chooses "The Flower" to title a poem celebrating his revived "relish" for "versing."[257] Flowers provide a handy objective correlative for the productions of the imagination, Scarry suggests, because they are easy to imagine. Because of the inverse relationship of extension to intensity that characterizes mental images, it is much harder to fill in a landscape that encompasses the imaginative equivalent of the whole visual field than it is to fill out the face of an imagined flower. Because of their size, we are able to imagine flowers as close to us, hence easier to "see" in detail; we have to imagine an elephant at a greater distance than we do a flower in order to see it whole. Like swiftly moving objects, then, flowers seem close. Most importantly, flowers duplicate the gauzy rarity of all our mental images; flower petals actually resemble the only kind of objects that the imagination is fit to make with ease. To these perceptual reasons we could add analogical ones; flowers are fitting emblems for the products of the imagination because they reappear after disappearing, like Herbert's inspiration. Scarry does not extend these qualities to all vegetation; her analysis privileges petals. The face of a flower is most vivid to us, she says, as a liquid pool of color. Milton spills these pools liberally in our imaginations by describing the garden as "pouring forth" flowers, but he is equally confident in the imaginability of the filaments of the stem and the vine.[258] He consistently pairs them with adjectives or verbal phrases that, by stressing the ramifying nature of their vectors and arcs, instruct the motor capacities of the mind's eye in how the body's eye would actually track these lines and curves: this natural tracery which "gently creeps / Luxuriant" engages our sense of movement.[259] Admittedly, Milton could not have avoided including plants and flowers in his depiction of the first garden, but plants show up everywhere, even when they are not physically present, most famously in Eve's hair, which waves "As the Vine curles her tendrils," their sinuous curling recalling the luxuriant vine described just above (4.307).

Milton links the concept of innocence with specific percepts to make innocent existence imaginable to us, but he is not interested in exploiting the hypnotic power of literary illusion using hidden means. He shares his "craft secrets" with their beneficiaries, his readers, in order to enlist them as co-curators of his art of rendering visible. As I have suggested, his usual procedure is to follow up moments of assisted sight with invitations to perceptual self-consciousness, often by means of a perspectival metaphor in which we can see our own sensuous response dramatized, an objective correlative for our subjective response that renders it susceptible to diagnostic scrutiny. Our sojourn in Eden (and in every other space) is in this respect an extended perspectival metaphor, one subject to continual correction by others. In the case of floral interpolation, however, Milton's exposure of the mimetic technique comes only after it has enabled an extended virtual experience of innocent sexuality: after the fall, this representational strategy becomes part of the action, as the Genesis account demands. On the other side of the verdant wall they dressed in their innocence, Adam and Eve attempt to reconstruct it by inventing floral clothes—a curtain of vegetation through which neither they nor we can see. The needed perceptual scrim is finally restored by Michael, who performs on Adam the "original" of the surgical operation executed on Milton's inmost sight; purging Adam's vision with herbs, he reintegrates the purgatorial garden of pains with the cultivated eye.

If Raphael and Adam celebrate intellectual labor in vegetal terms, the labor required to keep innocent sexuality innocent is instantiated in the "verdant wall" around Adam and Eve's bower (4.697). The constructed analogue to the created "verdurous wall" over which Satan hops into Eden, the verdant wall of the bower marks the separation between cultivated, innocent sexuality and its fallen counterpart, the lust that ranges among "bestial herds" and "adulterous" lovers (4.143, 753–754). The contrast between the conventional walled garden of the earthly paradise and a paradise identified with the project of cultivating that wall could hardly be starker: Adam and Eve's bestial rutting after the fall occurs on the other side of the wall, inside Eden and outside paradise. Although it is easy to assume that God created the bower, Milton specifies only that God chose its location "when he fram'd / All things to mans delightful use" (4.691–692). We get an image of the sort of use "the sovran Planter" had in mind twenty lines later when we see Eve at work decking the bed with flowers (4.691, 708–710). It is by serving as a platform for human labor that the bower's "delightful use" is fulfilled. The verbal phrases describing the bower's artfully arranged vegetation—"inwoven," "Fenc'd," "Broiderd," "wrought / Mosaic"—overlap with those in a subsequent description of the garden under the shaping "hand of *Eve*": "thick-wov'n," "Imborderd" (4.693–702, 9.437–438). God has merely created a stage for the first couple's art; his work is magnified by their work. There are enough indications of floral impetuosity in the passage, as plants "higher grew" and "Rear'd high thir flourisht heads," to remind us that it *is* work, carried out on recalcitrant matter (4.694, 699). Milton identifies the discipline of innocent sex with the collective work of rationally penetrating, praising, instrumentalizing, and "dressing" the beautiful but unruly matter of the garden; he identifies fallen sex with idolatry and consumption—with eating rather than cultivating fruit. In paradise, prayer (undertaken, like Adam's philosophical labors, to magnify the creator) serves as foreplay; Milton famously uses the word *Rites* for both prayer and intercourse, with one work of faith blending seamlessly into the next (4.736, 742). But this is all still within the realm of propositions: it must become a matter of perceptual experience for us to know it "experimentally." The eyes that have been planted in Milton must become our perceptual medium.

It is often remarked that we first see Adam and Eve kiss through Satan's eyes, but our perspective, unlike Satan's, is mediated through the floral spectacles God planted in our author. Having no access to these instruments, Satan cannot see what we see:[260]

> [Adam] Smil'd with superior Love, as *Jupiter*
> On *Juno* smiles, when he impregns the Clouds
> That shed *May* Flowers; and press'd her Matron lip
> With kisses pure . . .
>
> *(4.499–502)*

What pretends to be an analogy is really the occasion for floral interpolation. The analogy's parts do not line up: Jupiter smiles on Juno as he impregnates not her but the clouds, which release a cascade of flowers as a result. Telescoping cause and effect, Milton transforms the rain into the vegetation it nourishes. Against the cloudy background, the falling flowers emerge all the more sharply; Milton has taken advantage of the motion parallax. Milton has "reformed" the Homeric analogy between Zeus's ejaculations and rain into a storm of flowers—one that characterizes not Adam, Eve, or their Olympian counterparts, but the first couple's relation, actually blending with the "kisses pure." Although the filminess of flower petals makes them an unobtrusive perceptual medium through which to view the scene, they actually succeed in obscuring the kiss in a sort of floral smear (were it not for the semicolon, a reader might for a moment imagine that what presses against Eve's lip are the floral clouds themselves).[261] The flow-

ers into which the kiss all but disappears make the superimposition of sexuality and innocence a matter of vivid perceptual experience for the reader,
who discovers the overlap of these normally opposed concepts in and
through the literal stuff of paradise. As instruments of paradisal discipline,
floral spectacles extend the limits of the reader's mortal sight even as they
chasten it.

This brief floral interpolation prefigures the floral explosion to come in
the bower, where perceptual salience attaches to flowers as objects of innocent labor. As I have suggested, the verdant wall Milton erects with flowers
marks a line of separation between paradisal sex and its bestial and fallen
counterparts, a separation fortified by phrases like "Fenc'd up" and "thickest covert" (4.697, 693). Here, after Milton enumerates "each beauteous
flour" that constructs both the verdant wall and the bower it protects, he
informs us that "other Creature here / Beast, Bird, Insect, or Worm durst
enter none; / Such was thir awe of Man" (4.697, 703–705). The context
suggests rather an awe of flowers, since the assertion is nestled between a
ten-line catalogue of the flowers and an image of Eve decking the "nuptial
Bed" "With Flowers, Garlands, and sweet-smelling Herbs" (4.709–710).
Milton narrates a steady progression from work to prayer to intercourse
while floral tissue performs its connective work: the wall Milton erects with
flowers exists to be passed through by the reader's eye as flowers extend the
"workhouse" of paradise even into the boudoir. Our image of Eve's domestic labor fluctuates into a scene of prayer and finally resolves into an image
of Love waving his purple wings, wings that evoke what Scarry calls the
fluttering petals of a butterfly.[262] The obvious purpose of Love's reign here
is to obstruct our view of the sex scene we have been waiting to see, but in
doing so, he makes its difference from any sex we are likely to have a matter
of vivid perceptual experience, far more vivid than an exhaustive and literal
Aretinian display of "postures" could have made it.[263]

We are in fact barely aware that Milton has covered our eyes during the
act since the purple film, illuminated by the "golden shafts" of Love's lamp,
imprints itself so easily on our imaginary visual field, much like the shining, irradiated plants of Milton's internal seat of vision with which our
discussion of the poem began.[264] (As Fowler's note points out, since *pur-
pureas* means *shining*, the word releases a pulse of light and floral burst of
color simultaneously.) Even Edenic ejaculation appears to us as floral; the
moment of climax releases a storm of flowers like that through which we saw

their first kiss: "And on thir naked limbs the flourie roof / Showrd Roses, which the Morn repair'd" (4.772–773). Although we might have assumed that it would be ruptured beyond repair by such "enormous bliss," the roof, like Eve's chastity, survives intact: it is the wall between innocent sexuality and corrupt vision that has fallen here, becoming the agent of our view into paradise (5.297). The line concludes with Milton calling to the first couple to "Sleep on" while the roof repairs itself. This serendipitous result of the garden's excessive fertility, which in their waking hours Adam and Eve must work incessantly to control, pulls the focus back to the ongoing work required to cultivate paradise, along with fallen humanity's perception of it. The pun on *re-pair* extends coupling through sex and prayer into the labor of the following day.

There is an implied lesson in sexual technique here, a "Puritan art of love" that links slow vegetal striving to the pleasures of extended "amorous delay" through the application of *techne*.[265] The floral catalogue, of course, is itself a specimen of *cura* invested in patient "close reading" of the particulars of the natural world.[266] Such care distinguishes paradisal sex from carnal "Casual fruition" and the cold agitations of thinking substance that form the sum of the Petrarchan lover's satisfaction (4.767). Neither sensual nor "Platonic," paradisal sexuality is as sensuous as experimental labor itself. In contrast to bestial rutting or the sudden exaltation of Eve's satanically inspired orgasmic flight, the "sweet reluctant amorous delay" that we are told characterizes Adam and Eve's erotic life suggests a slow and stately wandering progression towards a goal, a progressive cultivation that "when properly practiced . . . will discipline and eventually replace" human sexuality altogether, as Thomas Luxon suggests.[267] The contrast between the character of movement and change in the vegetable and animal worlds protects our sense of paradisal eroticism's radical difference without making it unattractively alien. If, like Satan, the reader is envious of this bliss, it is not a bliss that is out of his reach. The cultivated, constructed character of the distinction between unfallen human sexuality and its bestial counterpart is made explicit when Raphael reminds Adam that God gave the same "dear delight" to "Cattel and each Beast" (8.580–582). If Adam subordinates his reason to his uxorious obsession, Raphael intones, he will soon become "sunk in carnal pleasure," in which case God might as well have selected him a mate from "Among the Beasts."[268] The verdant wall that separates Adam and Eve's bower from the copulating animals beyond it is their own creation; it is an artificial separation, requiring disciplined upkeep to sustain.[269]

In addition to employing an optical technology that actually intertwines our perception of "naked limbs" with the objects of this innocent labor, Milton also relies on litotes, the reflex of seeing paradise through its opposite familiar to us from the lyric tradition; it is here love reigns, not in the bought smile of harlots and so on. But this default mimetic technique is supplemented and revivified by a *positive* virtual experience of paradisal sex in all its radical but approachable difference, an experience enabled by the interpolation of an innocent perspective using a technology literally constructed out of Eden, in both senses. The continued existence of flowers in postlapsarian nature underscores that there is no quality intrinsic to their created nature that makes them what Milton calls "Flours worthy of Paradise"; such worth is conferred by the care invested in them as objects—and in Milton's hands, instruments—of human labor (4.241). As the poem's preferrred spelling, *flour,* suggests (a spelling that appears nowhere else in Milton's poetry), matter worthy of paradise is still in our collective possession.[270]

The systematically ambiguous characterization of flowers as both the objects and instruments of innocent labor draws strength from their celebrated identification with Eve. From a cavalier perspective, Milton's sexualized garden would offer an always-already-corrupt, because enticingly corruptible, paradise; but for Milton the alternative to the Mary-garden enclosed is an Eve-landscape open for improvement and "use." I have suggested that, as a personification of the individual sensitive body, Eve is the raw, even resistant material of Adam's rational labors, while, in her capacity as Adam's helpmeet, she shares in the agency of this inspired work. The famous analogy between Eve's "wanton ringlets" and a "Vine" requiring "Subjection," reinforced by a series of punning descriptions (including the hairy-sided "mound" and "Bush with frizl'd hair implicit"), is capped by an explicit identification of Eve, just before the fall, as one of the "drooping" flowers she must stoop to support (4.306–308, 134–135, 7.323, 9.430). The technique of floral interpolation becomes increasingly conspicuous at the very moment that the labor of cultivating fallen perception is about to become part of the story; we start to become aware of the spectacles we are wearing. A flower working on flowers, Eve is also enclosed in a floral haze: "Veild in a Cloud of Fragrance . . . so thick the Roses bushing round /

About her glowd."[271] As Milton sinks the human body at work into paradise itself, subsuming all under a floral veil, he abbreviates *handiwork* to suggest an outright equation of Eve's hand with the flowers it tends: "thickwov'n Arborets and Flours / Imborderd on each Bank, the hand of *Eve*" (9.437–438). As Satan sees Eve both through and as her handiwork ("This Flourie Plat, the sweet recess of *Eve*"), he becomes for a moment "abstracted . . . From his own evil": the floral veil has a transformative effect on his perception, but a limited and temporary one. Unlike the reader, Satan is an unwitting beneficiary rather than a co-curator of this experiment in assisted sight, which thus can only render him "Stupidly good" (9.456, 463–465).

When Eve encounters Satan in the snake "on his reare," the penis that flowers have occluded suddenly appears without the floral veil: "Circular base of rising foulds, that tour'd / Fould above fould . . . erect . . . pleasing was his shape, / And lovely" (9.497–504). This sight, followed by a shower of "faded Roses" that Adam releases when he sees that Eve has been "deflourd"—a gloomy reprisal of the first floral shower we see in Eden—is a fitting preface to humanity's first experience of bestial sex (9.893, 901). In witnessing this act, we get to experiment with the fall, the dropping away of "innocence, that as a veile" has mediated our vision of curiosity, work, and sex in paradise (9.1054). Instead of seeing the act through a tissue of cultivated flowers, we see bodies copulating on top of wildflowers ("Flours were the Couch"), on an as yet uncultivated patch of ground they come across fortuitously. Eve has not "bedeckd" it; although a "verdant roof" is above them, it is not theirs, and the pathetic fallacy is conspicuously inoperative: no flowers fall on their limbs when their now "Casual fruition" reaches its climax (9.1038–1039). The amorous delay that distinguished Adam and Eve's erotic life and aligned it with their productive work is now merely "amorous play," associated with the frenzied consumption that characterized the first sin: once they take "thir fill of Love," they are "wearied," then "Oppress'd" by sleep, like satiated gluttons (9.1042–1045). To mark the decline from delightful work to joyless play, from production to consumption, Milton unleashes the rhetoric of hellish carnality he had honed in the divorce tracts: "Carnal desire enflaming"; "in Lust they burne"; Eve's eyes dart "contagious Fire" (9.1013, 1015, 1036). These destructive flames are what Milton called "that other burning," rooted in "venom" rather than "inbred" in man. They may be contrasted with the *tempered* flame: the "coequal & *homogeneal* fire," the "rationall burning" associated with Love's lamp, innocent conversation, and the production and digestion of knowledge in the productive sacrament.[272] Like the nonpurgatorial flames of hell in which we encountered "darkness visible," these flames do not enlighten the scene, as did the light that illuminated the petals through which we glimpsed Adam and Eve's innocent union. The wall that distinguished the first couple from the beasts has been consumed by what *Doctrine and Discipline of Divorce* calls an "irrationall heat," which is destructive to the cultivation—the continual construction—of paradise.[273]

From an innocent, dialectical understanding of the relationship between body and soul, Adam and Eve have fallen into a dualistic one, according to which the sensitive body is by turns gratified and deprived rather than progressively cultivated. Thus when they awaken into consciousness of their "op'nd" eyes and "dark'nd" minds, their first impulse is to mortify the sensitive eye, rather than to purge and improve it (9.1053–1054). No longer eager to work by steps toward angelic insight, Adam seeks rather to prevent himself from ever seeing the "heav'nly shapes" of angels or God again, crying aloud for

> . . . some glade
> Obscur'd, where highest Woods impenetrable
> To Starr or Sun-light, spread thir umbrage broad
> And brown as Evening: Cover me ye Pines,
> Ye Cedars, with innumerable boughs
> Hide me, where I may never see them more.
> *(9.1082, 1085–1090)*

The veil of translucent foliage thickens into solid arboreal vegetation that obscures sightlines and spreads shade—"Woods impenetrable." On the same side of the verdant wall as Adam and Eve, we can no longer see them through it. The perceptual medium becomes the inert object of our gaze, much like the couch of wildflowers. This is the reader's final invitation to perceptual self-consciousness; as the veil becomes obtrusive, its function becomes clear. As the floral glass becomes opaque, we become retrospectively aware of how the cultivated vegetation of paradise has been working

to cultivate and expand our own perception, providing the necessary medium for us to experience sexuality innocently so that we can register the
difference once this artificial help is removed.

It is from this "thickest Wood" that Adam and Eve find materials from
which to make the first set of clothes—coverings for the eye as much as the
human form (9.1100). The bower that once "Fenc'd" innocent sexuality off
from its fallen perversions is parodied by the "broad" leaves which "fenc't,
and as they thought, thir shame in part / Coverd" (9.1111, 1119–1120).
Since the collective subject of innocence is itself "in parts," the floral veil of
innocence, the porous mediator through which sight could pass and be
"multiplied," disintegrates into a mere multiplicity of leaves, flimsy barriers
to sight gathered from "thickest shade" (9.1110). Adam and Eve's "alterd
stile" marks the altered style in which we view them (9.1132). That Adam
first names pines and cedars as possible hiding places in this speech is not
fortuitous; cedar and pine are among the very trees that initially blocked
Satan's entry into the garden and which then served as his hiding place as
he prepared to tempt Eve (4.139, 9.435). Adam's spiritual departure from
paradise is assured as he reaches out for the very landmarks that Satan
passed when he first entered it, also believing that he could not be seen. We
recall that Milton compared Satan's spear to a pine tree—severing it, in the
process, from its Davenantesque association with the telescope, and prim-
ing it for its present (re)association with "loftiest shade," a barrier to light
and sight (4.138). An extended metaphor compares Eden to America and
the clothed Adam and Eve to its native inhabitants; the ground on which
we find ourselves is officially part of our world. Surrounded by "black Air"
like that through which Satan traveled to reach the garden, Adam also
echoes Satan's thoughts as he prepares to make the same journey in reverse—
"O Conscience, into what Abyss of fears / And horrors hast thou driv'n me;
out of which / I find no way, from deep to deeper plung'd!"—for "a passage
broad" now connects that abyss to the created world; Hell, Earth, and Chaos
are now "one Realm, one Continent / Of easie thorough-fare" (10.847, 842–
844, 304, 392–393).

But Eden was always a little chaotic. Just as the matter of Chaos exists
to be given forms and ends by inspired agents, so the garden continually
confronted its custodians with its need to be shaped.[274] As Eve's exasperation with their "growing work" indicates, the decisive difference introduced
by sin lies in the recalcitrance of the subject rather than in the objects of

human labor. Adam is ultimately able to orient himself within this chaotic world by means of the very artificial helps he has prefigured. These open up a diagnostic glimpse into what "thy original crime hath wrought / In some" of his descendants (not all of them, again suggesting the functional equivalence of the state of nature with a state of grace), to create the world we know:

> *Michael* from *Adams* eyes the Filme remov'd
> Which that false Fruit that promis'd clearer sight
> Had bred; then purg'd with Euphrasie and Rue
> The visual Nerve, for he had much to see;
> And from the Well of Life three drops instill'd.
> So deep the power of these Ingredients pierc'd,
> Eevn to the inmost seat of mental sight,
> That *Adam* now enforc't to close his eyes,
> Sunk down . . .
>
>   *(11.424–425, 412–420)*

Perceptual assistance comes in the form of garden herbs, infused with the power of grace (made available without any need for the Crucifixion). The purgative powers of these herbs pierce into "the inmost seat of mental sight," forcing the sensitive eyes to close; once again, the eye is dug into, so that it can start to dig. The acquisition of grace marks not the end but merely the initial condition of this spectatorial labor.[275] "Soon rais'd" up by the angel, Adam opens his eyes, now prosthetically assisted, to "behold / Th' effects" of sin, just as Milton was able to do once eyes were planted and mists purged within him (11.422–424). Between his use of Galileo and these herbs, Milton has incorporated into his poem the technology invoked by the pamphlet literature examined in the previous chapter—the "eye salve" as well as the "spectacles." We must "purge with sovrain eyesalve that intellectual ray which *God* hath planted in us" Milton had declared in *Of Reformation;* to cultivate vision is to purge what is planted.[276]

    The conditions of Miltonic inspiration are distributed across Adam and Eve in this episode, though, as we would expect, only Adam's are given detailed narration. The labor of "reparadizing" shared between Milton and his reader sustains the collective working conditions that defined life in paradise: Adam assumes the role of the active observer engaged in perceptual self-correction, refining his capacities of rational penetration with "artificial Eys," while Eve's access to Adam's vision through sleep corresponds to the private nocturnal conditions of Urania's visits to Milton (her slumber now an emblem, as well as an instance, of the shutting of the sensitive eye). With the interpenetration of vegetation and "sight" that enables Adam to survey and look *through* the pageant of fallen history, the work of rebuilding the paradise within has already begun.

Rather than a show of outsides, the pageant is a vehicle of spectatorial instruction. Adam now joins us in using his body and the products of the garden as we have been using them. Driven into his eye as purgative vegetation, the matter of the garden becomes an instrument to render the fallen world, and true paradise, legible. As Adam trains his sight on the postlapsarian world, he is able, with prosthetic assistance and direction, *not* to gaze, for in this realm what is merely visible to the naked eye is hardly worth seeing. As the pageant comes to its premature conclusion, Michael dismissively tosses off, "the rest / Were long to tell, how many Battels fought, / How many Kings destroyd, and Kingdoms won . . ." (12.260–262). The perspective that would take these human kingdoms as its proper focus is the perspective proper to Hell. Such gazing links Satan to the beasts even before he assumes the form of one. When we first entered Eden, we found the animals that "Coucht, and now fild with pasture gazing sat, / Or Bedward ruminating" (4.351–352). Sandwiched between eating and sleeping, gazing is the occupation of the "unemploid." Four lines later, we encountered Satan "in gaze" as he uttered the first words we hear him say in paradise: "O Hell!" (4.356–358). Satan is frenetically active, but, like the animals, he has no proper employment. Gazing is at the center of the temptation, which is above all the temptation of unemployment; unlike gazing, which is fixed and absorptive but never penetrating, innocent vision wanders and deepens. Like the ocular wandering celebrated in the prolusions, wandering sight prevents the subject from developing a parasitic relation to any particular image while providing the experience necessary to begin penetrating the causes—the enabling conditions—of every sight one has.[277]

Rather than a single decisive insight, Adam, like Milton, achieves moments of prosthetic penetration. Sharing the fruits of his inward eye as he harvests them under the spectatorial discipline exerted by Michael, he cultivates a vision that can penetrate exteriors. It stands to reason that the final book begins with a prosthetically assisted Adam seeing instantly through the false image of monarchy. His vision at once purged and paradized, the man long misperceived as the first king sees through himself to the corporate subject he really is. But when properly seen through, the spectacle of history yields another royal lineage, in the reappearing figure of "the one just Man": human subjects employed in the work of reformation, the same labor that organized paradisal existence. Through these figures, a model and a lineage of heroism emerges that is separable from any single idolatrous embodiment of it.[278] The modifiers of one apply easily to another, so that Enoch can reappear a hundred lines later, in different surroundings, with the proper name of Noah.[279] In this experimental demonstration, as in Milton's strategic substitutions in Chaos, the bodily identities of the matter under view—whether they are atoms, regenerate citizens, or kings—are constantly displaced and replaced. This principle of substitutability is an essential part of the poem's spectatorial strategies in which we have been trained from the start of the poem, when we learned to see Pandemonium as Restoration London. But it is also a feature of the public person under consideration. This "seeing as" is the most important instrument of paradisal restoration, for it enables us to see ourselves as Adam multiplied—to enter into the porous subjectivity of the paradisal subject.[280] The final exchange of Adam and Eve further wears down our "respect of persons," as "me" spills over again and again into "thee"; the "here" of paradise is located in that spillage, identifying the "paradise within" as a continuous commons.[281] Our own experience as readers confirms that the "paradise within," like Lockean knowledge, is not simply "a private Possession"; as "members incorporate" of Milton's internal paradise, we have been cultivating the eyes planted there for the duration of the poem.

In these final books, Adam strains to see the subject of innocence through the veil of fallen history, and so do we. The poem ends with Adam's two bodies regarding one another—an ingenious, because multiplied, version of Eve's admiration of her own reflection in the lake. Engaged in a common task, the two bodies begin to converge, along with their perspectives.[282] The collapse of subject positions had already begun when Adam crowed over his good luck upon hearing the terms of the curse: "with labour I must earne / My bread; what harm? Idleness had bin worse; / My labour will sustain me" (10.1054–1056). Speaking as humanity in this moment, Adam ranged across all tenses: the initial present tense turned retrospective, as if spoken from a future point in a fallen history that could have been worse, and then shifted into the future, toward the work remaining to be done. Adam then turned to anticipate the invention of fire, not as a Promethean discovery but as an inspired invention (10.1060–1084). The innocent artisanal flame that, during the extended love feast, was the agent of the "transubstantiation" of experience into knowledge, now returns— first as technological progress, then as purgatorial process. Adam's successors will be "Tri'd in sharp tribulation, and refin'd / By Faith and faithful works, to second Life" (11.63–64); this purgatorial process will be the very medium for the progress of knowledge. Just as Boyle blended the fires of Vulcan into his Elysium, so Adam prepares to extend purifying and productive trial beyond the garden. After providing an extensive catalogue of the fruits of both of these progresses (or rather the moral and intellectual dimensions of the same progress), Michael declares, "then wilt thou not be loath / To leave this Paradise": the use of "this" suggests infinite paradises that can be mapped onto or substituted for one another (12.585–586). Ernst Gombrich suggests that "all art is image-making, and all image-making is the creation of substitutes"; by forcing the reader to assume some of the imaginative burden of creating and diagnosing those images, Milton has kept his paradisal art from consisting of *petrified* substitutes, idols for the mind's eye to gaze at, and has made them images for the mind's eye to see things through, just as he imagined the Bible itself did.[283] Michael's art serves as the raw material for an Adamic art of observation, the art that made Milton's own art possible.

As readers we have been both the objects and co-curators of Adam's labor of paradisal construction, a labor that begins with diagnostic self-scrutiny. The progressive "steps" Adam takes while in paradise are continued by the "wandring steps and slow" with which the collective laborer makes his way back to paradise; they are the steps taken by the user of the sensuous instrument of *Paradise Lost* (12.648). Milton's own artful reformation of Eden's growth into lenses through which we can discipline and expand our fallen vision invites us to identify the vegetation's recalcitrance with our own resistance to taking these steps. The vegetation that derides and mocks the efforts of the first couple to subject it to control, in other words, has its counterpart in our own refusal of paradise and its demands. As Milton suggests in the invocation to Book Seven, it is against the derision expressed by the objects of his own reforming efforts—other people— that he must guard this paradise, his poem. If Adam and Eve can rebuild the verdant wall through work even after the fall, so Milton, "Cut off" and "with dangers compast round," can erect boundaries to protect the floral lenses planted in him (3.47, 7.27). This image is of course a solitary one: Milton is in darkness, under house arrest, receiving inspiration, as he implies, while in bed. But this is not an image of withdrawal. The garden, while guarded, is not fenced; its fruits are cultivated, harvested, and incorporated by the body of his readers.[284] It was from the "wayes of men," not men themselves, that Milton cut himself off, to reveal to them what "waies of Truth" he could make out, and make up, by "Light after light well us'd" (3.46, 196). As Adam suggests, such labor sustains the agent of innocence through postlapsarian history (10.1056).

It is to promote this extension and generalization of the subject of paradisal labor that Milton restricts narration of its primal scene—Adam's naming of the creatures—to a few lines.[285] Given the lengths to which Milton went to portray Adam as a struggling "improver" and budding astronomer, it is striking that he seemed to show so little interest in the scene on which the experimentalist paradise was based. But instead of merely representing this scene, Milton magnified it, dilating the work of Genesis 2:19 almost beyond the scope of the poem's narrative ("we are *Adam* as well as he, it is to us God brings the creatures, to see what names we will call them").[286] Conventional rehearsals of the topos of nature's book still assimilated the words and letters to the outwardly visible creatures, but Milton, like Hooke, sought to render nature's book through its "orthography" and "grammar," extending reading into the processes that form the substrate of the visible world. By presenting such acts of bearing witness as the grounds of paradisal humanity's custodial care of creation, he provided a model of innocent labor for the generation of authors that succeeded him.

Comparing the ending of *Paradise Lost* to that of the *Paradiso*, where the poet stands speechless in his contemplation of the light of God, Max Weber remarked that "one feels at once that this powerful expression of the Puritan's serious attention to this world, his acceptance of his life in the world as a task, could not possibly have come from the pen of a medieval writer."[287] For Milton's Adam, man's "daily work . . . declares his Dignitie" (4.618–619). But the labor-intensive economy described here, unlike that described by Weber, is not zero-sum. As Karen Edwards observes, Eden's richness "cannot be inscribed in an economy of ownership"; its economy runs on work and praise.[288] To work is to declare one's "Dignitie" as a conscious participant in God's work and to ensure that God is conscious of you, taking account of your "doings" and "waies" on a regular basis. Heaven and earth are already joined through the rhythms of labor; while the first humans work the garden and angels dart around on unnecessary errands, God repays them with approval; they repay God with praise. God derives bliss from looking at his works and their works; angels look at his work and praise it, and he returns the compliment. When Eve asks Adam why the stars shine even when they are asleep, Adam, assuming that Eve is anxious that God will "want praise" for his celestial handiwork during the night, assures her that spiritual creatures "with ceaseless praise his works behold / Both day and night" (4.676, 679–680). Satan is the first to introduce a zero-sum principle of gain (and "counterfet") into this economy of mutually sustaining work and magnification.[289] As a participant in this economy, Adam is unable to regard the curse of labor as a curse; it is a comfort and a relief that he can still build the verdurous wall through work. Through such work, as Michael prophesies, humanity will discover the "secrets" of "all Natures works," and, uniting this knowledge with a working faith, attain the paradise "happier farr" (12.578, 587). The destruction of the garden is insisted upon, less as a punishment than as the necessary destruction of an image: Eden will become a barren rock "To teach thee that God attributes to place / No sanctitie" (11.836–837). The indifference of place, and of persons, informs the paradisal consciousness of the poem's conclusion. Inducted into the open subjectivity of the paradisal subject, the reader is included in the laborer of the poem's final simile, whose steps are continued at the beginning of the epic's sequel. The expulsion, a walk home after a day's work, opens into a paradise that is invisible to mortal sight, but one that provides the pattern for the world's collective and material recreation. Adam and Eve's wandering pilgrimage out of the frame is to nowhere specific. At the end of human history, the divine indifference to place will be the only feature of place, "Whether in Heav'n or Earth, for then the Earth / Shall all be Paradise, far happier place / Then this of *Eden,* and far happier daies." (12.463–465). Grace has already been granted them; happier days will result from the progress they labor to make.

Entering on the Work

It is not, then, a question of getting back to the garden. Although experimentalism provides a contemporary context for understanding Milton's project, we might also think of the Kafka of Gilles Deleuze and Felix Guattari: the aim is not to reterritorialize experience into the garden but to deterrorialize paradise into the world, and to push this deterrorialization until nothing remains but the "intense and barren world," a world much like that of *Paradise Regain'd*. The quotation from Kafka's diary that Deleuze and Guattari regard as the apothegm of the "minor" author describes the wandering steps taken by Milton's paradisal subject in a purgatorial world of undifferentiated substance: "I must just take my walks and that must be sufficient, but in compensation there is no place in all the world where I could not take my walks," for the laborer's journey that leads beyond the frame of *Paradise Lost* is continued by the Son at the start of *Paradise Regain'd*.[290]

The sequel to Milton's endless epic offers the reader no more images of the garden.[291] We are told at the outset of the poem that Jesus "rais'd" Eden "in the wast Wilderness," but the poem exclusively concerns a hero being "exercise[d]" in the wilderness (1.7, 156). We owe this restoration to George Fox's amanuensis Thomas Ellwood, whose notorious response to *Paradise Lost* occasioned the "brief epic": "Thou hast said much here of *Paradise Lost;* but what hast thou to say of *Paradise Found?*" According to Ellwood, this challenge plunged the poet into a "Muse"; Milton may have been wondering how his friend could think that his pointedly anticlimactic poem, which contains fairly explicit instructions on how to extend paradise beyond the garden, was about anything else. The poem Milton later presented to Ellwood with the words *"This is owing to you,"* however, is the fruit of a radical revision.[292] The poem describes a second Adam remarkably like the Quakers' leader, a seeker who, in "Wandring the Wilderness" of the fallen world, "step by step," finds himself in the Paradise of God.[293]

The poem may be owing to Ellwood, but its title corrects him; here the paradise wandered into is neither lost nor found, but actively regained. The poem's first line, however—"I Who e're while the happy Garden sung"— seems to enact a self-correction, beginning with the statement *I who err.* From the reader's perspective, Milton seems to err rather drastically here, reducing *Paradise Lost* to a pastoral poem about the first garden, but in reprising Ellwood's interpretive error, Milton seizes on the insight that must have prompted it. To see through the idol of Eden is still to be engaged with it. Once seen through, Eden must be found where it does not appear to be: in the waste wilderness. We might object that Milton had already done exactly what Ellwood wanted, uncovering the matter of paradisal labor in Chaos itself. But the experiment had not succeeded with at least one reader, and Milton now wanders toward new means for another trial.

Notwithstanding his resemblance to the community of Quaker friends, the Son also comes to us as the young Milton. We encounter him as the subject of a vocational crisis, "revolving in his brest" how he might "Publish" his "mighty work": how is it possible for him to achieve "What might be publick good"? The Son is "Private, unactive, calm, contemplative, / Little suspicious to any King" (1.185–188, 204, 2.81–82). How a private, contemplative man can rescue his country from "the *Roman* yoke" (and the Norman yoke) is soon made clear (1.217). As many readers have noted, Satan is the source of the poem's *dramatic* action: picking up on what he imagines are cues in the Son's refusals to stage each subsequent temptation, Satan is the improvisational artist, continually putting on performances in which the Son refuses to participate. The Son's vocation is realized, and published, as he undertakes the work of magnification: the labor of seeing through.

The poem enacts the strategy of paradisal recovery it narrates: Milton had revealed paradise to and in the fallen world by writing *Paradise Lost;* the next step was to see through and move beyond the strategies that enabled that experiment. Severing his own personal dependence on the outward symbol of his spectatorial privilege, Milton hands his instrument of truth over to Satan before it can become an idol, another inert exterior.[294] In *Areopagitica* Milton had called for the reforming of the Reformation itself; so here, the instruments Milton invented to extend mortal sight beyond fallen limits must themselves be transformed into the raw material for successive interventions. Thus it is the adversary who employs an instrument called both a "Telescope" and an "Aerie Microscope"—which, like Milton's, supposedly penetrates appearances, revealing "Outside and inside both" (4.42, 57–58). Satan uses his "Optic skill" to present gratifying images of paradise regained: false images of a world restored through the personal achievements of its savior and king, and the Son sees through them all.[295] His spectatorial counter-art renders him vigilantly *inattentive* to the tempting surfaces and "majestic show" to which Satan hopes to restrict his gaze; these visions do not "allure mine eye, / Much less my mind" (4.110, 112–113). Performing a hostile takeover of Satan's experiment in assisted observation, the Son assumes the character of Boyle in his confrontation with the apple, processing each image and scene into "parings" as the reader looks on. In undoing Satan's pseudo-experimental artistry, the Son reverses Satan's own hostile takeover of the strategies of *Paradise Lost,* and the earlier poem is restored even as it is transcended (for the Son reprises, and improves upon, the spectatorial performance turned in by a prosthetically assisted Adam). This labor of penetration has no end; there can be no climax, hence, as Fish has argued, no plot to this story.[296] A plot would conflict with Milton's aim: to render alien and decompose the plot of the story he had just written, so that he could sing and "spell" of creation restored once again.

As Fish suggests, the poem reveals to us the extent of our own appetite for narrative by frustrating it. Readers often remark that they share Satan's impatience for something to happen, for Jesus to do something; but again and again nothing happens, he is always "unalter'd," "unmov'd," "untroubl'd" (1.493, 3.386 and 4.109, 4.401). All of Satan's rhetoric and spectacular effects "in froth or bubbles end" until, seemingly arbitrarily, he is "smitten with amazement" and falls from the pinnacle, never to appear in Milton's verse again (4.20, 562). Of course, Satan's amazement is not arbitrary. Having subjected the Son to temptation, Satan finally subjects him to a different sort of trial, to discover what he is made of, not morally, but substantially: to determine whether he is really "more" than "meer man" (4.535–536). The poem's final simile discloses the experimental result, invoking the "riddle" of the "*Theban* monster," the riddle whose answer is man: "For as many as are led by the Spirit of God, they are the sons of God."[297] The "rock / Of Adamant" to which Satan has compared the Son has already enacted the handoff of the subject position of "Adam" to "man" in his iterable capacity, the terminal letter of one name marking the start of the other (4.533–534). Occuring thirty-eight times in the poem, "the Son of God" is the title with which the Son is most identified. The word that attached the messianic office and work of salvation to a single proper name—Christ—does not appear at all.[298] Fish has rightly called attention to the "temptation of plot" in this poem, but he has not identified its source: it is the singular hero of the redemption plot that the Son needs to see through—to magnify and multiply.

Some early readers of *Paradise Regain'd* were indignant that a poem bearing this title did not treat the doctrine of atonement, but no one is more disappointed by this incarnation of God than Satan.[299] As he reasonably protests, "All men are Sons of God" (4.520). It is Satan himself who expresses impatience for Christ's reign, Satan who, "inly rackt," and complaining that the Son said he was going to reign, urges him to "Raign then" (3.203, 180). As Milton's orthography suggests, Satan associates "thy raign" with rain, or as he puts it, "A shelter and a kind of shading cool / Interposition, as a summers cloud" (3.216, 221–222). The temptation once contained in Satan's kingdom now materializes as a rain of grace. Even the Son feels compelled to point out the absurdity of Satan being impatient for this reign, but, as always, Milton's double syntax offers us a clue. There is a good reason that Satan and the Son share a pronoun after the fall from the pinnacle; Milton has been demonstrating the temptation of Christ in both senses.[300] It is not just the temptation of Christ by Satan, but the Satanic temptation that Christ represents, which sons of God must work to resist: the hope for a "shelter" from the demands of innocent agency that might justify a surrender of that agency—the temptation of a Redeemer. For Jesus, the temptation of plot is the temptation of the first-person singular; for the reader, the temptation of Christ is the temptation of the third person. This spiritual temptation is not separated from its political expression: the urge to surrender the kingly office to a third party rather than working to share it. To be sure, Satan's question as to whether Christ's reign is "Real or Allegoric" is not easily dismissed; if this kingdom is never to be established, "What dost thou in this World?" But the question expresses a refusal of the paradisal duties of corporate sovereignty.[301] The cooling rain of "interposition" that Satan describes in such appealing terms as a soothing "shade" from "fire" figures the temptation of unemployment, of being spared the pains of purgatorial process.[302] Milton makes the withholding of this consolation permanent, for while Satan does not appear in Milton's final poem, neither does Jesus.

The purgatorial pains Satan wants to spare the world are the pains proper to a public. In *Areopagitica* and *Paradise Lost,* Milton had presented Adam's body as both the agent and the matter of the sacrament of truth production: *Paradise Regain'd* identifies this progressive labor—the work of all sons of God—with the reign of Christ. To become paradized is to wander into the "glorious work" of this ongoing sacrament, not to complete it.[303] At the end of the poem, we find ourselves once again at the beginning of the work, at the start of an experimental process that will last as long as time. Having thus restored paradise as labor in the indifferent wilderness, the Son, like the laborer at the end of *Paradise Lost*, goes home, ready to "begin to save mankind": "on thy glorious work / Now enter": entering into work rather than a place, he resumes a continually renewed process of redemption in which any son of God, or Adam, can participate (4.634–635). To be an "imparadis't" Son of God is to find oneself forever at the start of a process of refining sight into insight and insight into intervention, a process that will take until the end of history to complete itself. The agent of this labor is a community under construction, an assemblage of which the Son, like Milton, is only a part; the working collectivity that Adam was identified with, but not yet identical to, is taking shape throughout his oeuvre, coaxed into existence by Milton's changing style itself. The work will be completed when its agent is fully constituted, when paradisal discipline finally breaks down the barriers of individual subjectivity to make a single and continuous subject, an "All in All."[304]

It is this goal of repopulating the corporate subject of innocence that explains the altered style of the poem. *Paradise Lost* had revealed paradise where it did not appear to be, but the experimental demonstration required an intense investment of care to virtually witness. If the reader could not be a witness, the experiment lacked an object; it did not happen at all. To readers who invest the necessary care to curate *Paradise Lost*, what is wounding about its sequel is its shocking accessibility. Paradise is straightforwardly identified with the experience of being persecuted and harrassed wherever one goes and continuing to wander along anyway; the lesson could hardly be simpler, or more plainly delivered. It is a generalized biography of Ellwood himself and his friends during the Restoration. The verse itself seems to aspire to statuary; this is a poem in which a book can end with the brute statement, "So fares it when with truth falshood contends" (3.443). There seems to be no work left for us to do. But Milton's conditional embrace of a poetry of statement, and even his dismissal of sensuous description—the wilderness is now a desert, now a wood—enabled him to gather into the agent of innocence those readers who had been excluded from his earlier poem: readers currently being "try'd in humble state, and things adverse, / By tribulations, injuries, insults, / Contempts, and scorns, and snares, and violence" as they tried to carry out the work of testimony

(3.189–191). If the experiential basis of experimental faith—its grounding in artisanal epistemology—linked it to the processual character of the insights that *Paradise Lost* opened up for the reader's cultivation and improvement, the "preparatory grounds" for much of the reader's work was nonetheless provided by a literary education. The labors of ingenuity in such communities as Ellwood moved were carried out on different grounds, with different tools and materials. Milton does not altogether exclude classical materials from *Paradise Regain'd;* its object is to exclude no one from the project of recovery it enacts.

If Adam represented a humanity without respect of persons, it was necessary to represent him through means that accommodated different persons; tracking the progress of the corporate person's steps, "a little further on," from one work to the next, this is what Milton did.[305] Extending paradise across a series of texts, he made the style of its delivery a thing indifferent. The incorporation of readers into the "homogeneal" body of truth would be achieved not through a monumental masterpiece but by progressive and piecemeal "handywork" capable of reaching all whom Quakers called (interchangeably) sons of Adam and sons of God. It is a difficult accommodation Milton attempts to make in this poem, creating a Son that manifestly incorporates the likes of both Ellwood and himself, but the labors of innocence were the fruit of an even more difficult union. In Milton's account, the first marriage had come remarkably close to ending in divorce, and even the sacramental feast with an affable angel incorporates disagreement, just as Adam's first conversation with his maker generates a very productive argument. Milton's effort to reform his own paradisal restorations required changing tactics, and a shifting gallery of virtual witnesses: the publication of this "mighty work," to use the Son's terms, would be serial; naturally, it would require successive authors. Like any experimentalist, Milton was participating in a process whose completion he would not live to see.

Milton's final literary performance throws the reader on his own resources to carry on the work, extending it into the space of civil idolatry itself. For members of the culture of the losers, as N. H. Keeble observes, the world was "the adversary, as well as the field of combat"; Milton's last gesture is to push the reader back into that field as a potential author in his own right. In the process, the concept of authorship itself undergoes further revision, expanding well beyond the sphere of letters.[306]

Samson Agonistes achieves its climax in the destruction of an idolatrous structure that is both a theater and a temple, housing a Laudian blend of "Sacrifice" and "sports."[307] Milton could not have chosen a more legible symbol of Restoration theatrical culture and its persecuting church: it is Charles's theatrical reign that Milton's drama—which, as his prefatory note proclaims, "never was intended" for the stage—symbolically levels or "evens."[308] The ironic self-references with which Milton litters Samson's speeches suggest that this was a much-rehearsed fantasy. Samson's acute sense of the embarrassment of political defeat, his awareness that everyone says he has come upon his just "deserts," along with his father's comment, "I cannot praise thy Marriage choises, Son," all invite us to identify Samson with Milton, as indeed Marvell had already done in his poem on *Paradise Lost*.[309] A favorite personification of the English people during the Interregnum now figures the public servant Milton, the one just man of Restoration England who was "no private but a person rais'd . . . To free my Countrey."[310] Funnelled through this representative person, Milton's biography becomes a national one.

For this translation to be effected, the personal lament must be progressively refined, along with its person. Like Milton in *Paradise Lost,* Samson employs a lamentation over his blindness as artistic self-preparation. This generates the fantasy of a visual faculty that, like the sense of touch, is "diffus'd" throughout his body (line 96). When Samson analogizes between such sight and light, we know that his identity as one "separate to God" will reveal itself in a demonstration of this diffuse power—that Samson's sight will not be "confin'd" to "such a tender ball . . . So obvious and so easie to be quench't," anymore than Milton's is.[311] When Harapha comes to "survey" Samson, Samson mutters that he should "take good heed my hand survey not thee"; the bitter joke turns out to be a prophecy (lines 1089, 1230). Samson's grasp of truth is finally expressed through an ideal union of eyes and hands: of insight and intervention, of spectatorial and physical agency, of sight with the power of touch. Manoa's prophecy that "God will restore him eye-sight to his strength" is borne out, since Samson's vision and his strength turn out to be identical (line 1503). I will suggest that, like Smectymnuus, Samson combines "sinewy force" with the power of a perspective glass, whose powers magnify the public that identifies with it and uses it. For buried in one of Manoa's laments is another inadvertent prophecy: "So *Dagon* shall be magnifi'd, and God" (line

440). To see through one is to praise the other; it is through being "compar'd with Idols" that God and his creation are revealed (line 441). The play permits us to witness Samson's self-refinement as a human instrument of truth capable of performing this demonstration. His final encounter with the self-seeking strong man Harapha offers him the occasion to see through a carnal incarnation of himself.[312] In distinguishing himself from this "bulk without spirit," Samson apprehends the nature of his own "diffus'd" spirit and lays hold on what he really is: "no private . . . person" (lines 1238, 1211). Samson's judgeship is not mentioned in the play; his status as a public person is organic, and it is grounded in Milton's own corpus. It is as an Adamic corporation that Samson is "rais'd." When he finally offers "public proof" of his strength, his demonstration well exceeds the limits of martial action, and even of individual action (line 1314).

The poem meets festive culture on its own grounds; Samson enters the theater to make "sport" for the assembled Philistines, just as Milton has entered into what is now an enemy genre. The result in both cases is a transformation. Samson turns a "spacious Theatre" into a space of public testimony, a space of magnification and publication (lines 1328, 1605). In reprising the whole history of the word *agon,* from games to combat to interior struggle, the poem withdraws it from the realm of spectacular visibility. Critics often invoke Johnson's complaint about the play's missing middle to describe its radical internalization of the action: the anagnorisis is located in Samson's breast—in the "rouzing motions" that propel him to the theater.[313] But this is the breast of a corporate person, whose internal revolutions open out into public space.

The *agon* that occupies Samson for most of the play consists in the abandonment of personal allegiances, a taking leave of the private person. Just as Winstanley's anointing restored his corrupted self to a corporate one, so this purifying struggle enables Samson to "quit himself"—acquit himself, and quit himself—"Like *Samson*" (lines 1709–1710). The Samson who quits himself like Samson is not "like" the biblical Samson at all; the poem's deviations from its source are so many, and so drastic, that what is most salient to us is his status as an ongoing construction, a "thing made" by and for the public he embodies. His final performance is accordingly not the fulfillment of a prayer for personal vengeance, as in Judges 16:28, or an expression of "spight," as in Marvell's poem (line 9). It is the impersonal work of "inward eyes illuminated." After modifying "inward eyes," *illuminated* becomes a verb, acting on—and, indeed, rouzing—"fierie vertue" (lines 1689–1690). It is through this "vertue rouz'd" that Samson's "rouzing motions" roll outward into public space, levelling the ritual structure erected to contain it. Within this public space, one vision of the public confronts another: the populated unity of Samson faces members of an ungathered multitude, "in order rang'd," separately assembled to consume a spectacle (line 1694). They are annihilated, not by a spectacle, but by an inward yet interventionist vision that decomposes spectacle and divulges man in the creation: a sovereign public.[314]

The violence in this play is virtual, and emphatically so, for Milton enables this bloody act to be read as a spectatorial annihilation, a catastrophic seeing-through. Excavating the public beneath the image of the subjected multitude, Milton makes the means and ends of his experimental demonstration match, for Samson's haptic visual faculty is rooted in his hair; his "diffuse" power is literally rooted in the power of self-diffusion. The Chorus's shock at his "diffus'd" state at the start of the play can be seen retroactively as the necessary condition of his regeneration as a public person rather than a heroic individual or "petty God" (lines 118, 529). As Rogers has argued, the alignment of Samson's strength with the length of his locks identifies this power with an immanent process working through a body, one that refuses all hierarchical organization. In the tangling together of Samson's bodily faculties, Rogers even glimpses the "body without organs" imagined by Deleuze and Guattari.[315] Such a body is proper to the Adamic public, in which each member works to be a representative of all. It is this body that is restored here, for in what is surely the most important deviation from Judges, Milton ensures that the public itself emerges unscathed from the event. If Samson's physical body remains "tangl'd in the fold" of sacrificed individuals, his living body dwells in the public that escapes—the singular "throng" that stood in the "op'n," under the sky rather than the triumphal arch, as "aloof" from the festival as the strong man brought in to be its star performer (lines 1665, 1609, 1611). (The "Lords, Ladies, Captains, Councellors, or Priests" can be understood as the architects and supporters of the Restoration settlement, which requires a multitude of subjects rather than a public to remain stable [lines 1653].) Talal Asad's claim that in Milton's final poem "mass killing is translated into a story of redemption" is true only in a qualified sense; as I will suggest, It Is a distributed sacrifice of the private person that constitutes the sacrifice, hence the redemption.[316]

From this site of personal wreckage, Milton's reader, like the messenger, has to chart his own course. It is up to the public, like the Israelites, "to lay hold on this occasion" (line 1716). But we are made to understand that even an appreciative response to this authorial performance must be thoroughly scanned and diagnosed for error. The response of Manoa, who hopes to fetch his son's corpse and bring it "With silent obsequie and funeral train / Home to his Fathers house," would seem to be the inauguration of a disheartening reception history:

> . . . there will I build him
> A Monument, and plant it round with shade
> Of Laurel ever green, and branching Palm,
> With all his Trophies hung, and Acts enroll'd
> In copious Legend, or sweet Lyric Song.
> Thither shall all the valiant youth resort,
> And from his memory inflame thir breasts
> To matchless valour, and adventures high:
> The Virgins also shall on feastful days
> Visit his Tomb with flowers, only bewailing
> His lot unfortunate in nuptial choice,
> From whence captivity and loss of eyes.
> *(lines 1732–1744)*

Placed at the center of a deadening festival cycle, Samson's body will do what Samson swore he never would: "sit idle"—as an idol—"to visitants a gaze," as a "Vain monument" in his father's house.[317] Manoa's bathetic final line offers confirmation, if any were needed, of the permanent nature of the struggle between the spectatorial body and the carnal eye, the restored first person and the alienated third (as we would expect, it is a *they,* not a *we,* that Manoa hopes will "lay hold" of the occasion). Milton is laying bare the impulse to "cluster around a single representative of the original victim"— the basis of sacramental kingship as well as the idolatrous mass.[318] The tomb draped with palm and laurel is also, of course, Milton's monument. Concluding with a misreading of the performance to which his poem is a testimonial, Milton pushes his readers to find another use for the "true

experience" contained in his corpus, which, like the body of Samson, cannot be confined to a monument, or even to itself.[319]

In the phrase "Home to his Fathers house," readers like Ellwood would
have heard an echo, inaudible to another class of Milton's admirers, of
James Nayler's attempt to turn Genesis 12:1 to experimental account: "I
was at the Plow, meditating on the things of God, and suddainly I heard a
Voice, saying unto me, *Get thee out from thy Kindred, and from thy Father's
House.*"[320] But almost any reader familiar with Milton's earlier works would
have recognized, in the final simile, the return of the Samsonian eagle—
still in the throes of purgation decades after the publication of *Areopagitica,*
and still surrounded by a multitude of atomized birds. The gabbling birds
are now "tame villatic Fowl," individuated by their separate coops, and they
are still struck with "amaze" by their own corporate incarnation (lines
1695, 1645). In the Samson "who pray'd, / Or some great matter in his
mind revolv'd," Milton's fellow citizens might have apprehended the grounds
of this incarnation in the peaceful work of revolution—the ongoing work
of "revolving new notions."[321] They might also have seen, in these two lines,
the return of "the Miltonic or" from *Paradise Lost.* If this *or* seems to assert
the exchangeability of prayer and intellectual labor, the command to magnify creation (like the homophone of *prays* and *praise*) asserts nothing less.
It is by collectively undertaking this work of magnification that the public
discovers and magnifies itself.[322]

The carnal emblem of the dragon is given to us first. As the forced cel-
ebrant of Dagon, the eagle is an "ev'ning Dragon"—a levelling adversary.[323]
To a king who threatened public assemblies with "the utmost perils," the
public was indeed an adversary, and he used every means at his disposal to
dissolve it into a multitude of subjects.[324] But if we dig into this false image
to excavate its material cause (the word that generates it), we can lay hold
on *dragon*'s etymological root—*the seeing one*—and bear witness to the
grounds of the public person's Adamic sovereignty even as we participate in
it.[325] The contrastive relation of the dragon to Samson is indicated by the *but*
that precedes his unveiling as the eagle, whose continuing purgation now
results in a sacrificial transformation: the transubstantiation into the phoenix, releasing the "fame" of a "secular bird."[326] In witnessing this substantial
transformation, we bear witness to the very process of secularization—the
continuous release of the sacred from the corporate body, perpetually killed

and perpetually resurrected, revived by the very purgatorial trial that seems to be killing it.[327] The "fame" of this body, divided as it had been throughout the century, is inevitably "double-mouth'd" (as Dalila reminds us at line 971); at the moment the play concludes, Samson's "rouzing motions" have yet to be taken up as public property by Milton's fellow citizens. As the occasion slips through the hands of the Israelites, it becomes available to us.

In arguing that the final simile contains, and releases, the revolutionary public, I am not suggesting that the public is defined solely by its agreement with Milton's constitutional preferences. The public celebrated in *Areopagitica,* and in all the major poetry, is merely a *functional* public, engaged in the work of processually unveiling creation, and thus itself: a reality-based community constituted by collective responsiveness to the evidence of "experience," rather than a collection of private persons united through obedience to an individual sovereign will. The work of restoration—what *Areopagitica* celebrated as the "healthfull commotions" of a "generall reforming"—begins in the work of an intellectual commons, whose corporate self-assertion had provided such fertile ground for popular sovereignty decades before.[328] This may seem like an absurdly pacificist reading of what appears to be a very bloody play. But *Areopagitica* had in fact already reformed the "patron saint of the revolutionary army"—an iconoclastic hero, but also a bloodthirsty maniac—into a figure for an Adamic, knowledge-producing public, grounding the work of revolution in the iconoclastic labors of ingenuity.[329] The transformation is upheld here, in the spectatorial body of a risen Samson. It is with "head erect" that this populated unity unveils creation and itself.

Samson's work of "revolving new notions" into public space is also carried on by the Son, who first appears to us "much revolving in his brest" how to "Publish his God-like office," a state that retroactively we may identify as Samson's before his unveiling in public as the public.[330] The conclusion of *Paradise Regain'd* enjambs onto the Son's earthly ministry, the endless work of using "words to conquer willing hearts" (1.222). Far from suggesting withdrawal, his return home "unobserv'd" and "private" at the end of the poem is a stunning assertion of the public power that resides in the private person, operating in the same way as "private persons" in the opening pages of *Areopagitica.*[331] Like those other sons of God, the Son is entering on the "glorious work" of productive communion—a communion that will open out into the world of print and other collectivizing technologies of truth production. The individuals who refuse incorporation into this process—*Areopagitica*'s envious gabbling birds, Satan at the pinnacle, and Samson's spectators—are all struck with amaze; like the fallen angels, they are stuck in a maze.[332] The "wandring mazes" of self do not open out onto the creation that can be progressively wandered through, for the agent of the "step by step" progress of testimony, through constructed facts and toward truth, cannot be individual.

In different ways, all of Milton's major poems enact a version of the spectatorial regicide performed by Marvell in *The Last Instructions to a Painter*. Turning Galileo's "bold Tube" on the king, Marvell revealed that Charles was made of the same matter as his subjects and extracted the moral: "the Country is the *King*."[333] Milton's objects of magnification—the first sovereign, heaven's anointed king, and the Samsonian multitude—turn this technology on themselves. In doing so, they reveal the ontological priority of the corporate subject of humanity, the "one first matter" that is the agent and object of its own sacred transformation. The instrument that Milton and Marvell adapted to the purpose was often identified by working experimentalists with the perception of Adam, but ingenuity's most active promoters also made Samson into an object of Adamic identification, seizing, as Milton had, on the hair-hero's association with iconoclasm, the idea of the calling, and England itself. Hooke exulted that, in "setting our shoulders" to the work of improving lens technology, "we have removed the Herculean Columns" and "plucked up and carried of the Posts Gates and barrs of those Gates of Gaza" where others "would have us believe we were imprisoned . . . I am not therefore for limiting or stinting the boundaries of Art and the industry of Man."[334] The marriage of the singular and plural first persons in this passage is fostered by the very instruments it celebrates. The posts in Samson's hands are now those of Judges 16:3, the gates of the city of Gaza (where his would-be assassins are gathered), which he heaves onto his shoulders as he walks out to extend the city limits. By expanding the city of his confinement, Samson extends his own life. The pillars in Samson's hands necessarily evoke those of the idolatrous temple he tore down, but they are also the Herculean pillars—here not just sailed beyond but physically moved, declaring the expansion of human perception beyond mortal—and individual—limits. Describing the posts being plucked up, almost like flowers, Hooke strikes what seems an inappropriately gentle note considering the Biblical context, but one that is altogether appropriate to herald an ongoing and bloodless revolution in knowledge. The constitutional losses of 1660 did not preclude cultural gains for those still working to dig up and topple a world of false appearance. This work found partial expression in the political sphere through the revolution of 1688, but it found an unsettled, hence permanent home, in the public space consecrated to the collective cultivation of fact.

This space included the sphere of print, but experience could be cultivated through other mediums and by other means. Indeed, Milton's final works point magisterially to the limits of the page, pushing their readers to prosecute the labors of innocent observation, and innocent authorship, beyond its margins. Taking up the experimentalist critique of fallen literacy, Milton brings it to bear on literary experience itself, insisting that the experiments carried out in the sphere of print not be contained there. Demanding the surrender of the hope that one might derive all truth from a book, the Son tells us that one who reads

> Incessantly, and to his reading brings not
> A spirit and judgment equal or superior,
> (And what he brings, what needs he elsewhere seek)
> Uncertain and unsettl'd still remains,
> Deep verst in books and shallow in himself,
> Crude or intoxicate, collecting toys,
> And trifles for choice matters, worth a spunge;
> As Children gathering pibles on the shore.
>
> *(4.323–330)*

Areopagitica had already rendered moot the distinction between books and other vessels of experience. Books could not be fetishized as privileged sources of knowledge; like all things, they had to be worked up to generate light, or else remain "trifles."[335] Testing could not be enclosed within the scene of reading, since all things had to be tried. Refusing complete resolution within themselves, Milton's final poems thus cast their readers into the world, toward the open spaces and real things that innocent discipline requires to exert itself fully. My concluding chapter will explore a literary practice dedicated to documenting such engagements. The literature of professional observation picks up where Milton's work leaves off. It is a steep descent from the works of Milton to the circumstantial observations of critical spectators, but this descent into the world of experience is also a sort of progress, anticipated by the messenger's journey away from the theater and the Son's own descent from the pinnacle to the path that leads back to town.

7 ||| THE PROFESSIONAL OBSERVER

There is not that thing in the world of more grave and urgent importance throughout the whole life of man, then is discipline . . . So that whatsoever power or sway in mortall things weaker men have attributed to fortune, I durst with more confidence (the honour of divine providence ever sav'd) ascribe either to the vigor, or the slacknesse of discipline. Nor is there any sociable perfection in this life civill or sacred that can be above discipline, but she is that which with her musicall cords preserves and holds all the parts thereof together . . . it is not for every learned, or every wise man, though many of them consult in common, to invent or frame a discipline, but if it be at all the worke of man, it must be of such a one as is a true knower of himselfe, and himselfe in whom contemplation and practice, wit, prudence, fortitude, and eloquence must be rarely met, both to comprehend the hidden causes of things, and span in his thoughts all the various effects that passion or complexion can worke in mans nature; and hereto must his hand be at defiance with gaine, and his heart in all vertues heroick . . . observation will shew us many deepe counsellers of state and judges to demean themselves incorruptly in the setl'd course of affaires, and many worthy Preachers upright in their lives, powerfull in their audience; but look upon either of these men where they are left to their own disciplining at home, and you shall soone perceive for all their single knowledge and uprightnesse, how deficient they are in the regulating of their own family; not only in what may concerne the vertuous and decent composure of their minds in their severall places, but that which is of a lower and easier performance, the right possessing of the outward vessell, their body, in health or sicknesse, rest or labour, diet, or abstinence, whereby to render it more pliant to the soule, and usefull to the Common-wealth: which if men were but as good to discipline themselves, as some are to tutor their Horses and Hawks, it could not be so grosse in most housholds.
—John Milton, *The Reason of Church Government Urg'd Against Prelaty*

Many shall run to and fro, and knowledge shall be increased.
—Daniel 12:4

The heroism of the early modern professional observer is asserted through acts of attention much like the Son's in *Paradise Regain'd*.[1] The refusal of more spectacular forms of heroism is the product of a hostility to spectacle itself; this specialist in the work of seeing through transforms every sight he encounters into a testimonial of its own production. Such methodically innocent observation provided a template for the reformation of sons of the letter as well as "sons of Sense," for the literature of professional observation offered itself as a means of escape from literature; some authors actually depict themselves running away from books into the streets. Ned Ward turns into the London Spy when he abandons his "old calf-skin companions" to wander through the "living library" of the world. In an epiphanic moment, he realizes he has been transformed by years of sedentary study into "Aristotle's sumpter-horse," burdened with as many "whimsical" and "frenzied" notions as an "old astrologer." It is then that he resolves to quit his library and go to London, armed with a new goal: "observation." No longer a schoolman, he has become an empiricist, and the reader-as-virtual-witness can follow him on his "ramble."[2] After the Restoration, the dissenters to whom the Son bears a resemblance could be imprisoned for their acts of bearing witness; the writers explored in this chapter put their bodies on the line in another way. Marvell's *Last Instructions to a Painter* invokes regicide and revolution as threats, but its actual intervention depends on the tools and methods of experimentalist observation; professional observers throw themselves headlong into this work. In the literature of professional observation, the hopeful analogies between literary and physical labor long made by experimentalist authors gain a kind of reality; these writers take field trips and produce testimonies to create a new authorial regimen in which "contemplation and practice" are "rarely met" and a spectatorial "discipline" is framed. Calling attention to the physical demands and frequently sordid conditions of their labors, professional observers flaunt their arduous pursuit of experiential literacy; they are literate in "the Book of the World" because they have journeyed through it, and they compulsively call attention to the discrepancies between their experience and the mistaken accounts recorded in books. The professional observer's acquisition of literacy originated in physical expenditure—"a great deal of elbow-labour and much sweating," as Ward put it—but ended in corporeal transcendence, tracing a progress from "traveling through" to *seeing* through.[3]

I have suggested that once experimentalism redefined innocence as objectivity, the physical world itself could become an object of originary desire. As instruments of innocent perception, these observers seek to restore their readers to the world in which they already live. Revealing the streets, shops, docks, farms, and factories of England "in *Perspective,*" they expose the causes behind what is given "to the eye."[4] It was by claiming to see what could only be rationally reconstructed that the working investigator became a spectatorial author. The professional observer provided a public service that, prior to his emergence, no one had imagined was necessary. He had to demonstrate the public's need for his apparently useless services: he performed this task positively, through his adherence to a particular spectatorial etiquette, and negatively, by offering evidence that the public was being imposed on. Going well beyond the "mad tricks" exposed by cony-catching pamphlets, the imposture he labored to expose could extend to the entire realm of the visible.[5]

The virtuosi's elevation of spectatorship to the status of a vocation was a necessary but not sufficient condition for the emergence of this new intellectual type. It was largely lens technology that had enabled this elevation, and writers who sought to perform contemplation as an active and productive labor had been appropriating this technology for decades. In the literature of professional observation, the use of the lens is less emblematic and more integral; the author tries to *embody* this technology—not mystically but literally, presenting his very physical self as an instrument of truth composed. To become fit for such use, he had to become fit indeed. I will suggest that the literature of professional observation was an extension of contemporary therapeutic regimes designed to transform the body into a more reliable conduit for ideas of "things themselves." These exercise regimes, athletic counterparts of the self-improvement programs explored in Chapter 4, launched the professional observer's "rambles" while paradoxically enabling him to remain, like Abdiel or the Son, "unmov'd"—"Unshak'n, unseduc'd," among "innumerable" deceived.[6] But just as the Son provided the pattern for the recurring subject of the one just man—an identity available to any son of God—so the professional observer offered himself as a model for the public at large. Despite the exceptionalist character of his persona, the professional observer embodied a heroism that was strengthened by being shared.

Milton had argued that the fate of any nation was decided by "the vigor, or the slacknesse of discipline" of those who inhabited it; the discipline that "with her musicall cords preserves and holds all the parts thereof together" began with each member's "right possessing of the outward vessell . . . to render it more pliant to the soule, and usefull to the Commonwealth." Invoking a key metaphor of the medical literature on nervous disease, Milton presents the relation of the fit body to a fit nation as not merely analogical but causal. By the end of the century, the "musicall cords" that held the nation together were increasingly identified with the nerves of its citizens. The healthy functioning of the social body depended on the nervous systems of its members: the coordination of efficiently operational nervous systems would result in an informed and harmoniously functioning citizenry. The fit spectator could play a crucial role in the general tuning process; his "right possessing" of his own "outward vessell" fostered his conversion into a "pliant" and "usefull" tool available for general use.

Of course, the more superhumanly fit the spectator, the more potentially ridiculous. His alienation from normative views could render him a comic figure, like Locke's man with microscopical eyes. In his attack on John Wilkins, Alexander Ross had ironically informed his readers of "a namelesse man come down from the Moone, who brings us strange newes of a late discoverie . . . This man of the Moone goeth about to perswade us . . . that the world, ever since *Adam,* hath been in a dreame, in thinking that the heavens move, and the earth rests." Ross tried to deprive Wilkins of authority by imputing the strangeness of his perspective to his person, reducing him to one of the moon-men about whom he speculated; but in this battle, it was the virtual alien, to whom common sense seemed a dream, who had triumphed. The risible figure of the "namelesse man . . . who brings us strange newes" had the power to define the *sensus communis* anew; his strangeness was the very source of his authority.[7] It was by inhabiting this position of radical innocence and personal absurdity that the "namelesse man" of Mr. Spectator became one of early eighteenth-century England's most powerful public persons, a spectator who was able to exert causal force on his primary object of observation, the public itself.

The periodical through which Joseph Addison and Richard Steele set out to reform popular perceptions was an unprecedented literary technology.

John Dunton's *Athenian Mercury* was the most influential early periodical that was not a newspaper, but the *Spectator* was the first daily of this kind, and the degree of influence it attempted to exert over its readership exceeded that exercised by any text before it.[8] Mr. Spectator sought not merely to offer moral instruction to his readers, but to interfere with their lives in extremely concrete ways: to determine what they wore, what else they read, even what flowers they cultivated. However trivial each of these social directives may seem when considered singly, together they acquired considerable accumulated force. Indeed, it is in their very modest specificity that these directives reveal the unbridled ambition of their authors; these daily and petty interventions could literally reform readers, imposing new forms upon their outward behavior and inward thoughts, in a way that general exhortations never could.

Yet these directives were presented as observations rather than commands. This modestly factual presentation made Mr. Spectator's "dictatures" all the more irresistible. While Dunton's Athenians were members of a collective in which the lines of authority were reversible, readers of the *Spectator* were encouraged in a one-way dependence on a prosthetic source of spectatorial privilege.[9] As a product of collective and open authorship, the *Mercury*'s question project had enabled the ingenious public to read and compose itself as a "Society"; Mr. Spectator offered an ideal image of the public contained in a single person. In his inhumanly objective and cool responses, readers could discern their own idealized collective self-image: this was a rational public "personated." But while his spectatorial penetration and disinterest suggested an interiority that nobody could share, his responses could be publicly performed by anyone.

In their circuits around the nation, observers like Celia Fiennes and Daniel Defoe strain to perform the function of hands, eyes, and nerves for the social body, conveying ideas drawn from direct physical experience while subjecting these ideas to continual diagnosis and refinement. Neither wants to be thought "an idle Spectator, or a careless unobserving Passenger in any Place"; they perform the "laborious" part of observation, and, like the Royal Society's Curator of Experiments, they hope to "carry the eyes, and the imaginations" of their readers with them.[10] In contrast, Mr. Spectator's precepts are delivered almost directly as percepts, relaying sensory experiences no human body could have. To track the professional observer's progress toward such perception is to witness the ingenious public becoming the *polite* public.[11] If the public had first taken shape as the corporate body of innocent curiosity, its evolution into what Lawrence Klein calls "the polite zone" occurred through the dematerialization of that body—a dematerialization paradoxically embodied by Mr. Spectator.[12] Within the nervous mythology that arose from experimentalist practice, the perfectly fit body was one that nearly refined itself out of existence.

The progressive abstraction of the spectator's body modeled changes in the public face of experimentalism itself. In the early eighteenth century, experimental science underwent a radical transformation at the hands of Isaac Newton. Hooke's model of knowledge production—of data circulating freely from the eyes and hands to the understanding and back again—was a circulatory model, but it was also a dynamic one, designed to effect an ever-closer integration of the lower and higher parts of the individual and the social body: this sensuous dialectic, like the wheel of revolution, was intended to "make a progresse." The Newtonian system redescribed such circulation as a fixed system: rather than producing the "healthful commotions" of reformation, the tensile strength and vibrations of Milton's "musicall chords" now generated a ghostly and inaudible "harmony," which sought only to produce more of itself.

"Well-Tun'd Instruments": Experimental Athleticism

In Chapter 2 we considered Locke's suggestion that if every member of society invested several hours daily "in the constant exercise of some laborious calling," humanity would be restored to health, knowledge, and happiness. Locke's critique of the leisure class doubled as a diagnosis of intellectual stagnation and disease: the mutually reinforcing pathologies of the social body and the individual body obstructed the circulation and progress of knowledge in both. As I have suggested, the identification of health and knowledge followed from the experimentalist diagnosis of scholasticism. As the example of the schoolman demonstrated, too much "close thinking" pursued without the active participation of the body resulted in "*wandering* and *delusory Images* on the Brain, and *Instability* and *Unsettledness* in all the intellectual Operations."[13] Experimentalists regarded the impossibility of perceiving the operation of form as evidence of form theory's *irrationality:* the bodily experience that could provide the reason with "clear and distinct" percepts was missing. The experimentalist claim was not merely that form theory was mistaken, but that the scholastic approach, reduced to armchair philosophizing, fostered mental derangement. So, by extension, did aristocratic leisure.

That Locke's vision of the ideal state of health was shared by his close colleague, Thomas Sydenham, "the English Hippocrates," is not surprising, for, by the end of the century, the organizing contrast of Locke's essay between a healthy natural order and a diseased, civilized one—itself predicated on the distinction between created and corrupted humanity—had generated a new medical consensus.[14] Medical writers were soon describing the leisure classes as victims of the very condition experimentalism had sought to remedy: alienation from things themselves. Victims of nervous disease suffered a second fall, a virtual expulsion from creation itself. Virtuosi had identified Bacon's paradise of exercise and experiment with a lost but recoverable state of health: by insisting that investing *cura* in the work of discovery was actually *curative,* they helped to turn a genealogy of sin into an etiology of disease. As experimentalism entered the social mainstream, the critique of idle philosophy evolved into an exercise craze: a medical and moral campaign against the deranged ideas of the idle rich. The standard account of what G. S. Rousseau has called "the nervous revolution" holds that it actually promoted the social desirability of being nervous.[15] On this understanding, the superior delicacy, taste, and irritable susceptibility of the better sort provided a medical justification for the continued existence of an aristocracy within the new commercial economy, as well as a means for the merely rich to behave like aristos. What complicates this picture is that the touted benefits of exercise—conceived throughout the literature on nervous disease as a dumbshow imitation of productive labor—were primarily intellectual. I will suggest that the therapeutic interventions outlined in texts like Francis Fuller's *Medicina Gymnastica* (1705) and George Cheyne's *The English Malady* (1733) were actually efforts to produce intellectuals among "the better sort"; in this respect, they extend the seventeenth-century effort to transform lazy schoolmen into ingeniosos. The aim in both cases is the same: to rehabilitate sedentary consumers into knowledge producers. Popular medical literature reaffirmed what among the virtuosi had long been an article of faith: knowledge and health depended equally on the cultivation of investigative fitness—on an intellectual life in which mind and body both participated.

It was the Lockean reduction of thought to "distinct perceptions" that provided the explanatory framework for the nervous subject's inability to form reasonable judgments. John Purcell described nervous disease as

> nothing but a *disorder of Reason,* and *Reason* consisting only *in the Affirmative or Negative Comparison, which the Soul makes of two or more distinct Perceptions;* it follows, that if there be renew'd at once a great many incoherent Idea's, of which the Soul has no clear and distinct, but only confus'd Perceptions, she cannot form a reasonable Judgment of them.[16]

For Locke, to have a clear and distinct idea was actually to see it with the "Eye of the Soul"; when the reason had "no clear and distinct, but only confus'd Perceptions" with which to work when constructing ideas, no such mental viewing could occur. The nerves were the "Conduits" to convey ideas "from without to their Audience in the Brain"; if they were so "disordered, as not to perform their Functions," then such simple ideas or percepts had, as Locke had put it, no "Postern to be admitted by; no other way to bring themselves into view, and be perceived by the Understanding." Under such conditions, rational thought was impossible. The belief in the faulty percepts of the nervous subject could be interpreted quite literally. Cheyne notes as common nervous symptoms such false perceptions as "*Flies* and *Atoms* dancing before the Eyes, a *Noise* like the *dying* Sounds of Bells, or a *Fall* of Water, in the Ears."[17] The nerves were also the conduits for the *association* of ideas, from which complex ideas were generated. The more disordered these were, the less relationship the individual's mental content had to real relations existing in nature.

Medical writers traced deranged ideas to the slackening of the nervous fibers, which were described in almost mystical terms as the site where that "wonderful Bond of Union" of the soul and the body "seems to terminate." In order to perform their function as the conduits through which sensory data from the outside world made their appearance in the mind—and through which the mind, the seat of the rational soul and will, exerted itself on the world—the nerves had to be taut. As the "*Medium* by which the Rational Soul exerts it self" on matter, nerves were the very essence of action. As conduits for receiving knowledge of "things themselves," they were the agents of contemplation.[18] What the image of Adam surveying, naming, and intervening in the creatures offered to the experimentalists, nerves and the animal spirits offered eighteenth-century physicians: a way to imagine how mental and physical exertion—action and contemplation—might sub-tend one another.

It was impossible for nervous fibers to remain in the requisite state of tension when the body was perpetually relaxed and at leisure:

> All Nervous Distempers whatsoever from Yawning and Stretching, up to a mortal Fit of an Apoplexy, seems to me to be but one continued Disorder, or the several Steps or Degrees of it, arising from a Relaxation or Weakness, and the Want of a sufficient Force and Elasticity in the Solids in general, and the *Nerves* in particular.[19]

Yawning and stretching, seemingly harmless signs of aristocratic lassitude, are the first hints of nervous disease, arising from a weakness that is as much moral as physical. In describing yawning "up to a mortal Fit of an Apoplexy" as the spectrum of "one continued Disorder," Cheyne translates experimentalist dogma into the language of nervous physiology, attributing a loosened grip on the world to a literal loss of strength in the "nervous parts." It is easy to assume that, though it might have provoked vague alarm, such a passage was on the whole reassuring to the genteel reader. To be accused of physical debility, "Relaxation or Weakness," and particularly of a deficiency of "sufficient Force," was to be reminded that one's style of life did not require a robust constitution, much less actual physical strength. One could afford to be an idle theorist, like Scotus. But, as we will see, ner-vous physiology confounds any straightforward mapping of the individ-ual body on the higher and lower parts of the social body. Although medical writers load their texts with flattering assurances that the better sort are endowed with finer nerves and thus a "greater Capacity for intel-lectual Functions" than the *"heavy, dull, earthy, clod-pated Clown,"* they also warn that the failure to realize this capacity through *"mechanical Force and Strength"*—such as are found in the "Employments, Trades, and Professions"—will culminate in reason's undoing, bringing on "the Destruction" of "the whole rational *Man*."[20] By casting this rational break-down in the future tense, Cheyne softens the insult, but, in the context of his alarmist report on the state of the nation, it comes through clearly enough. These medical writers take away with one hand what they give with the other: they impute to their readers virtually angelic constitutions woven of exquisitely sensitive fibers, but their accounts of the effects of the high life on those fibers focus obsessively on sluggish, morbid matter, the deceased rational man's remains.

It stands to reason that when Cheyne proclaims his intent to "try what a little more just and solid *Philosophy*" can do "to put a Stop to so universal a *Lunacy* and *Madness*" among the "People of *Condition* in *England*," the lunacy to which solid philosophy stands opposed embraces both nervous disease and the old philosophy. Throughout the literature on nervous disease, the ritual abuse of "the idle theorist" in the preface prefigures the case studies to follow: just as the idle theorist offers only "the unshapely production of a lively and wanton imagination," so we find that leisured nervous sufferers are "quick thinkers . . . of most lively imagination."[21] In both cases, idle bodies produce lively imaginations, and mistaken ones. Cheyne's autobiographical case history thus recounts his acquisition of experimentalist competence and his recovery from nervous disease as a single process. Having spent his youth first "in close Study, and almost constant Application to the *abstracted Sciences*" like a schoolman, he then indulged in a dissolute life of leisure in the city; his successive falls into the scholastic and aristocratic varieties of the idle life reduced him to the staggering state of a drunk. It was not until he forced himself to adhere to a daily exercise regimen that he gained "full, free and perfect use of my *Faculties*," which now manifests itself in "a Facility of *Study,* and of going about the Business of my *Profession; and,* in short, of every rational *Function of Life* . . . and indeed of every Thing worth living for as a *free and rational Intelligence*." In ceasing to behave like a man of leisure, Cheyne ceases to be an idle theorist; in learning to live like a free and rational intelligence, he asserts his identity as an intellectual man of action, one who is fit to *practice* medicine, and who thus has something to live for: opportunities to exercise healthy curiosity through "Observation, and Experiment."[22] The clear implication is that few of the idle rich are in a position to live as free and rational beings, since they are deprived of any calling "worth living for." These medical writers' own journeys toward health are coextensive with their entry into the professions, and they urge their genteel patients to imitate this rise. The nervous gentleman and lady of leisure actually depend for their survival on their willingness to incorporate the habits of the "employed" into their daily routines.

As Boyle insisted, to condescend was to rise again. When the medical literature probes cases where the mysterious interaction between the rational soul and the body has gone awry, the working man makes his appearance as a model to be emulated. Because "the Labour of the Poor generally secures 'em from this Distemper," Fuller suggests that the rich investigate "whether those Means which are Preservative to others, may not prove Curative to them." He calls for the replacement of passive luxury by "Active Luxury," a mode of living that, like Bacon's active philosophy, incorporates work into contemplative leisure through "that voluntary Labour which goes by the Name of Exercise."[23] Such labor is a curative, a preservative, a restorer; it recovers an original balance that differences of rank have subverted.

Roy Porter and G. S. Rousseau suggest that accounts of nervous disease as a disease of civilization made it "the cross of High Society, the distinguishing stigmata of those fine spirits, those sensitive souls singled out for excellence."[24] In this view, the literature on nervous disease spread a message that was internalized by aristocrats and pretenders to gentility alike: "Be nervous, be hyppish, be billious." Carol Houlihan Flynn suggests that in this literature melancholy becomes "a responsibility, but also a privilege, a sign of the status of its sufferer. It is not even clear that melancholy can—or should—be resisted."[25] But if we pursue to its logical end the notion that the strength communicated to the "Nervous Parts" through physical exertion "cannot be any other way procur'd," we will conclude that the dichotomy between the nervous aristocrat "whose Faculties are the brightest and most spiritual" and the *"heavy, dull, earthy, clod-pated Clown"* must be reversed in this literature, and it is, compulsively.[26]

Medical writers constantly reassure their readers and potential clients of their social and intellectual superiority—Boyle permits the scholastic disputant in the *Sceptical Chymist* to be brilliant too—but when they describe how this supposed superiority manifests itself, they communicate feelings close to disgust. Because leisure frees the person of quality to be a consumer rather than a producer of goods, idleness correlates not only with "Laziness, or Neglect of due Exercise" but with a penchant for extravagant consumption as well. Cheyne notes that *"Great Wits* are generally great *Epicures,* at least, Men of *Taste"*; the pun on *taste* introduces the shift, and soon he is attacking the "Voluptuous, and the Lazy" for being *"gross Feeders."*[27] Again and again, soothing reminders of the necessity for developing *"corpo-*

ral Sensibility, as well as *intellectual Delicacy"* fluctuate into invective against *"short and thick neck'd"* gluttons who, in Fuller's words, "can't command themselves."[28] The very sign of the aristocrat's difference from the brutish poor is reversed as men of taste metamorphose into Circean hogs before the reader's eyes. Like the laborious idleness of the schoolmen, the high life turns consumption itself into a depraved form of labor, sinking the better sort under the burdensome legacy of the curse. The "high, strong Food" that only the wealthy can afford to eat requires "more Labour to break, grind and digest" than the light diet of farmers and ploughmen; thus "crammed" with "Morbid Matter," the aristocratic body submits itself daily to grinding labor while its animal spirits languish.[29]

There being a direct correlation between "a Supine Course of Life" and "weakened and relax'd . . . Nervous parts," Fuller declares, "I take it to be no paradox, that the more a Man stirs himself, the more Animal Spirits are made in the Brain."[30] Physical "stirring" enlarges rational capacity, giving the brain more animal spirits to perform its work, while taut fibers facilitate rational thought by expediting the movement of spirits. The nerves are broken down by the "Passive Enjoyments of Sloth and Indolence," but they gain tensile strength through physical activity (186). Exercise actually *animates* the body, making it a more spiritual instrument. Just as the carnal appetite that led Eve to eat the fruit was evidence of an insufficiently rigorous curiosity, so the frayed nerves of the aristocracy were evidence that it was in fact not nervous enough—the aristocratic body was a virtual graveyard of "broke and confounded" nerves (206).

There is a punitive, even purgatorial strain in the repeated urgings to *"prompt, whip, spur, and stimulate"* the animal economy, to *"stimulate, rouze,* and *spur* the dead and languishing Solids, to push forwards the sluggish *Circulation* and *Perspiration."*[31] These exhortations to movement suggest that nervous torpor has reduced the aristocracy to the level of dead matter; the sluggish internal motions of pampered bodies testify to a missing "active principle," which must therefore be whipped into them. Such punishment is rhetorically meted out through the inversion of conventional social markers of superiority. That the nervous parts of workers were "incomparably more wound up, more tense" was evident from their "Noble" appearance and their very blood, which was "of a better Condition, and more Rich" than the "impoverish'd and Languid" blood of the sedentary.[32] Through daily exertion, the body's nervous fluids were able to "purifie and exalt themselves," becoming "rais'd" and "eminent."[33] By loading these physical descriptions with modifiers whose primary meanings are socioeconomic— *impoverish'd, of a better condition, noble,* and, most straightforwardly, *rich*—Fuller suggests that the physiological and social hierarchies as they now stand exist in a state of conflict: commoners have richer and nobler endowments than the nobility; their very blood is of a higher quality. In accounts of the briskly moving spirits of the lower orders, the near-personification of the busy nerves makes them admirable exemplars of the Protestant work ethic, even as their incessant activity asserts the sovereign power of the reason they serve. In describing the "Alterations in the Body" produced by exercise, medical writers use words like "Rarefaction," "Volatiliz'd" (the very term Henry Power used to describe experimental labor's effect on reason), and even "transubstantiated."[34] The productive sacrament reappears as the basis of exercise, the psychotherapeutic descendant of reformation. Fuller confesses that, prior to the adoption of an exercise regimen, he, like the young idle Cheyne after him (and the idle rich at all times), was so afflicted with "Giddiness" that he staggered about "like a Drunken Man." But having become an exercise enthusiast, he finds "my self as it were, *Renasci,* and all the parts of my Body gradually receive a kind of New Life." By undertaking voluntary labor, the nervous subject could put off the old man and put on the new, liberating his reason and its servants, the nerves, into productive action. The voluntary laborer was restored to an "inimitable Mediocrity": a peerless, middling state of productivity.[35]

This Pauline new man, of course, resembled the first man as experimentalists had reinvented him. "Mediocrity" describes Fuller's principle of therapeutic treatment and its result, the balance achieved through the integration of higher and lower faculties; as in Bacon, the "Active Life" is modeled after the productive one. Like experimental labor itself, voluntary labor enacted a fantasy of social reconsolidation, enabling the worker to gather together the far-flung parts of an original humanity presently "scattered up and down" the social scale.[36] These writers seem to openly yearn for such a reconsolidation; although the nervous are only being urged to exercise, medical writers describe this as being "compell'd to a sort of Labour." For the nervous aristocrat even to consider doing exercise, he needs to redefine himself as a worker: a producer rather than a consumer of his own health. Those who refused to do so were like inhabitants of a debtor's prison who have "learn'd the way, of living an Idle Life upon other Folks

Cost": obstinately refusing "the severe Conditions of Industry and Labour," they preferred to remain "supinely content" within a "sickly complaining Life," offering themselves as matter for their physicians' labors.[37] Paying doctors to "remove all their Afflictions, while they are wholly Passive," they "take it very ill" when they are told that experimentalist physicians do not "deal in Charms": it is because they take this news "ill" that they remain so. Such patients live idly upon others not just because they live off the labor of others (though this is the strong implication throughout), but because they refuse to match their doctor's investment of time and care with investments of their own; they assume that the offer of money will be sufficient. Their blind faith in the efficacy of nostrums discourages them from *"taking some Pains"*—investing care in the rational management of what Locke called their languishing estates of health.[38] A flourishing estate of this sort could not be purchased with the profits drawn from an actual estate, it could only be produced through a full-spectrum cultivation.

Belief in transubstantiation, and the doctrine of form that supported it, had long been diagnosed as a product of the mutually reinforcing conditions of idleness and superstition. This "unactive blindnesse of minde" was now projected onto wealthy victims of nervous disease: possessed by "Phantastick and Imaginary" notions, they easily succumbed to a superstitious consumerism that left them addicted to opiates and quack medicines.[39] These, Fuller sighs, "prove a meer Charm"; they "creep into the Understanding, and teach People to impose on themselves, and fansie Excuses for the use of 'em, till they come to be so blinded as to think that Health it self, is scarce an equivalent" (151–152). Viewing health as a commodity to be bought rather than a state to be earned, such consumers are already blind slaves of fancy, of which addiction is merely the confirmation and outward sign; they are charmed by everything money can buy. Fuller's diagnosis of how consumerism alienates the subject from things themselves reads like an incipient critique of commodity fetishism, but it also employs the old Protestant arguments against idolatry and implicit faith: just as knowledge could not be consumed through the fruit and truth could not be consumed through authorities (or bread), so health could not be ingested in the form of nostrums. Those who sought to consume health would be better off taking the "*Opiate . . .* of the *Day-Labourers.*"[40]

Many virtuosi seem to have elaborated their own fitness regimes based on these convictions. As Sydenham declared, it was Society Fellow Seth

Ward's "peircing Judgment, that could discern the Reason of things," that led him to take up exercise.[41] Hooke's diary contains tantalizing hints of an exercise machine featuring a pedometer (or "waywiser") and "pacing saddle" (elsewhere called an "ambling saddle" or a "springy saddle") that required the use of "Dancing Shoos."[42] Hooke was able to perform physical feats beyond what even Wren could conceive, for when Hooke "Told him of Dancing shooes and saddle. He believed it not nature having done noe such thing." On one occasion, he followed the lead of the English Hippocrates himself: "Rode to Acton with Dr. Siddenham, did me good"; on another, he "Exercised till I sweat." Milton also "delighted" in "walking and using exercise"; when he was old and blind, he made use of an exercising machine that involved a "Pully to swing and keep him in motion."[43] As we will see, Mr. Spectator availed himself of a similar contraption.

Because the aim was to agitate the spirits, promoters of exercise regarded practices that may strike us as passive, like allowing themselves to be jolted and bounced, as forms of intense exercise (so Hooke writes in his diary, "Jolted in coach agreed well").[44] The point was to be kept "in motion"; in addition to springing, the nerves were also galvanized by violent changes in temperature and "purging." Virtuosi displayed interest in such internal motions before fashionable society did, and they also frequently used chemicals for the purpose. But rather than purchasing ready-made nostrums as "charms," they experimented "occasionally" with chemicals that came to hand, often those whose properties they were already involved in investigating. Hooke's diary opens with "Drank iron and mercury"; on another occasion, he finds himself "In a new world with new medecine." The following day finds him taking "volatile Spirit of Wormwood which made me very sick and disturbed me all the night and purged me in the morning"; with the addition of a mixture of small beer and "spirit of Salamoniack" (ammonium chloride), he "purged 5 or 6 times very easily upon Sunday morning. This is certainly a great Discovery in Physick."[45] Although Hooke took the principle of gathering knowledge through physical experience to reckless extremes, his taking of "Physick" never resulted in an addiction, because he was always making new discoveries, whether through the ingestion of an "Elixir Proprietalis" or the snorting of nutmeg. His purges were really purgational, a means to make progress. Almost every page in Hooke's diary includes some observation about the result of his body's adventures, whether it is the ever-changing consistency of his mucus or the impact on his constitution of being bounced; on one occasion, to test its effects on his sinuses, he "sung much." Viewing his body as part of the natural world to be investigated, Hooke regards his disinterested self-experimentation as part of the observation and experiment that conditions his relationship to the outside world. Sometimes these parallel experimental careers form apposite pairs: on a day that he has a "supra" orgasm, for example, he also attempts an experiment with gunpowder. Other pairings are alarming: while "Guiddy" from the effects of his elixir, he experiments with a "burning glasse" and starts work on a wheel-cutting engine.[46] His reports express great satisfaction whenever a treatment has "wrought well," induced a physiological response of some sort, even if this has cost him a night of continuous vomiting (his treatments often "wrought all night"). Hooke's willingness to exercise himself, in every way, sustains his physical and mental functioning as a virtuoso, even if, from another point of view, it mostly likely hastened his death.[47] Boyle also "raised self-treatment to the level of high art," as Steven Shapin puts it, with cures that involved wearing a ring made of elk's horn and drinking rancid walnut oil.[48] The virtuoso's curb against intellectual sloth could not be relaxed at any point in his daily routine: just as Hooke did not hesitate to introduce a "stinking fish" into his private lodgings for dissection, so he never stopped conducting painful experiments on himself, for it was through such investigations that he "invincibly arm'd" himself against all the "inchantments" to which fallen humanity had succumbed—authority, custom, enthusiasm, and, above all, the errors of an undisciplined, inexperienced, and untried body.[49]

Faith in the benefits of water immersion was equally indebted to this logic. Sir John Floyer and Dr. Edward Baynard contended that "*Cold Water* contracts and strengthens all *Nervous Parts*," keeping them "*Strong* and *Vigorous*" and helping "the *Circulation*, in which Life it self chiefly consists": "Now a sudden *Plunge* and *Immersion* into very *cold Water*, where there is a great Quantity of it, must be the greatest *Alterative* in Nature, for it must give a new Motion to all the Spirits, both from its *Frigidity* as well as *Pressure*, by driving them from their *Posts* to another *Action*."[50] It is less important to move oneself than to "drive" the spirits that inhabit the body: in fact, merely to subject the body to any sort of drastic alteration is beneficial, since it gives "new Motion" to the spirits. The harmony between body and spirit generated by such driving and posting is often figured as holy music, proclaiming the body's restoration as a temple. Cheyne speaks of the soul as a musician in the brain's organ room who requires "a well-tun'd Instrument" to play.[51] If the strings were slack, it was impossible for the soul to produce music. Sometimes the nerves are to be tightened "like a *Drum*," but Floyer and Baynard shape the body into a variety of instruments, usually stringed ones, to convey the central role of the taut nerves: "Man is a Sort of Musical Instrument, and the Strings of Life and Death are tun'd or disorder'd upon more Keys than a Welsh Harp, or a Scoth Bagpipe," and they warn of the dangers that befall an "ill Fidler [who] plays upon his own Carkass." As Bruce Holsinger has shown, the metaphor of the body as a musical instrument has a long tradition, but here the pain produced by being played and the *pains taken* by the soul in playing the bodily instrument join purgatorial suffering to the production of knowledge, of which spa culture was both medium and product.[52]

Floyer and Baynard rationally reconstruct the rationale for baptism by immersion—its "Original," in Lockean terms—and propose to restore the practice under a reformed description: a "rational use of *Baths*." To make a rational use of baths is to make a statement of one's commitment to experimental faith. Floyer and Baynard mark out for particular abuse those who attacked the superstitious practice of baptism in the name of primitive religion; in their anthropological account of the origins of the practice, the superstitions that once surrounded baptism by immersion actually served a useful end, since the practice strengthened the body against hereditary diseases. The attempt of reformers to unmask the symbolic rather than miraculous character of baptism degenerated into bickering about the relative merits of "*Dipping* or *Sprinkling*," with the ultimate result that a healthy practice was abandoned.[53] The attack on baptism by immersion, in turn, created a climate of suspicion around the act of plunging into cold water. But "to be wedded to an Opinion" rather than convinced by "Demonstration" is "true Madness," and "*Physick Biggotry* is worse than that of *Popery*"— indeed, it is an act of treason within "the Commonwealth of *Health*." This impeccably experimentalist line of reasoning seems to relish its own perversity: an originally papist practice is defended for its practical rather than supernatural benefits, while the reformed attack on superstitious practice is itself revealed as a mad bigotry that ended in "mischief to *Bodies*."[54] Now it is the sectaries, rather than the schoolmen, who are accused of starting vain disputes to impede humanity's reformation. The justice of the assault on superstitious error pales in comparison to the realization that the present health crisis can be traced to the zeal with which this assault was carried out, against which their reasonable, secular defense of baptism by immersion stands in unexpected contrast.

The rational agent capable of being convinced by demonstration will baptize himself repeatedly, becoming reborn on a rational, because continuous, basis. Against the hysterical imaginations of frightened and foolish people who imagine that they can die from bathing, these judicious practitioners can only appeal to experiments, and their text is loaded with testimonies in support of their theory. These testimonies, like the text as a whole, loosely conform to the standards for an "experimental relation" as outlined by Boyle, enabling virtual witnessing: "I was lately inform'd by a Lady, whose *Lap-dog* I had seen in *Convulsions,* that 'twas cured of them by being thrown into a Tub of Water"; readers may test the usefulness of cold baths in such cases by immersing a canary in cold water if they can't find a dog (sig. B^v). They include the testimonies of epicures who, after overeating, "swam up and down for the Space of near two Hours" and felt better, and suggest that gluttonous readers replicate this experiment themselves. That

> cold Water concenters the *Spirits* and strengthens the *Nerves* and musculous *Fibres,* by bracing them, as it were, like a *Drum* when the Parchment-head is relax'd, is very evident by the Experiment of two Boys running for a Wager a hundred Yards, more or less; let the Boys be near of a Speed and Strength, take the *Boy* that loseth and dip him in *cold Water,* and then let them run a second Time, and the losing Boy shall beat the other, *&c.* (265)

The description of an experiment doubles as a set of instructions for its replication: the fit reader of this text will test its propositions out herself, as either the object or the curator of experiments, or both.

Such proofs cannot be appreciated by "People of superficial, little or no Thought, at least of such shallow thinking"; for them it is enough that "the Character of Whim or Gimcrack be labell'd unto it, 'tis for ever damn'd" (202, 198). Those who will not test a theory or even give it a fair hearing are precisely those who make it possible for bookish and ignorant doctors to "bury their Patients in a Tomb of *Book-Plunder*" (251). We have seen how medical practitioners related the consumption of "charms" to popish superstition; Floyer and Baynard also detect the specter of popery in "your

Nostrum-monger Dr. *Stew-Toad*" who "sets up for *Miracle* and *Mystery*,"
leading his patients down the road of idle superstition, away from rational
baptism (203). The assault on papist superstition and bigotry, driven out of
hiding from unlikely corners, once again enables the schoolman to be collapsed with the lazy aristocrat, addicted to Eve-like consumption. But by
dipping themselves, along with their acquaintances and pets, into water,
readers could both achieve health and participate in an ongoing experimental project. Exhibiting an innocent and healthy curiosity in the laws of nature as they operated on their own bodies, they could conduct experiments
by and on themselves. Ladies could report their eyewitness accounts of the
effect of cold water on themselves and their acquaintance, and such reports
had experimental use: such experiences *were* experiments, situations deliberately contrived by a group of investigators as a source of transmissible
experiential knowledge.

Through such practices, the virtuosi's tendentious contrasts between
health and sickness, labor and idleness, and knowledge and delusion became actively relevant to the polite public, whose leisure activities could
themselves become a form of labor. As texts dealing with nervous disease
swell with the "testimonies" of patients, writer and reader become partners
in a collective that reprises the Royal Society's united eyes and hands on
an even larger scale. Of course, the spa culture that curiosity produced did
not prove to be the most fertile ground for further experiments, at least not
of this kind; the leisurely exertions of "voluntary Labour," for most patrons,
began and ended in the baths.[55] But in Celia Fiennes's *Journeys,* these shrines
to "Active Luxury" serve as stations on an open-ended pilgrimage propelled
by sheer investigative desire.

If the point of exercise was to "drive" the spirits within the body, such
an effect was most directly achieved by actual bodily movement: being
jostled or bounced in a carriage was good; riding on horseback was even
better. Such voluntary labor created endless opportunities for the salutary
work of discovery—the replacement of confused ideas with clear and distinct knowledge. There are two corollaries to the belief that confused, incoherent ideas and idleness and go together: the rational would take care to
be physically active, and, once active, they would gain knowledge unavail-
able to the sedentary. When Fuller urges ladies to "break through the
Mode" and get on their horses, he is encouraging them not merely to exercise but to exercise curiosity: "I say, it is high time to look out, and set upon

a resolute Course of Riding . . . a Series of Journeys, continued Day after Day without intermission." Such exertion provides both a motive and the means for "looking out" into the world. Advising nervous sufferers to imitate "Travellers" obliged "upon the account of their Affairs" to go "many Miles in a Day," Fuller explains that such a traveler could "not be sollicitous as to what he Eat or Drank, or have any regard to the Weather"; he would have to "take up with whatsover he met with."[56] Though, unlike a medical practitioner, modish ladies had no pressing business forcing them to ride through inclement weather "Day after Day without intermission," they had to learn to behave as if they did. Putting up with bad weather and uncomfortable lodgings do not seem essential to exercise, but refusing to be sollicitous about food and lodgings frees the individual to be sollicitous about other things. The "freer rodes of *Education*" Sprat urged on the leisured classes lead out onto the open road itself, along which ladies can view "new Scenes" and expose themselves to a "Variety of Airs," rather than merely assuming them. Riding out into the world, they might become fit to experience it.[57]

"An Idea of England": The *Journeys* of Celia Fiennes

This is precisely what Celia Fiennes set out to do. Recording a series of trips on horseback taken around England and Scotland between the early 1680s and 1712, Fiennes's *Journeys* provides us with an insider's view of the process that, at the end of the century, joined the pursuit of knowledge to the quest for health. This text has often been mined for information about England (and perceptions of Scotland) in the period, but the intentions it registers are as historically revealing as the facts it records. Producing knowledge by the sweat of the brow, Fiennes pursued a fitness program in the spirit of public service; she labored to "be curious" in an effort "to regain my health," and she urged others to follow her example.[58] Viewed in the context of experimentalist propaganda and the literature on nervous disease, Fiennes's project offers evidence that the national myth constructed around the English as a nervous people had its origin in a campaign to reform them into a *curious* people: a people fit to understand the world they inhabited.

Little is known about Fiennes herself, but we know that her grandfather William, one of the leaders of the aristocratic opposition to Charles

I, had been among Hartlib's supporters. A house she owned was registered as a Presbyterian meeting place in 1730, which suggests that she was a prominent member of the dissenting community.[59] It would be interesting to know what her friends and family made of her decision, on the "great journey" of 1698, to ride on horseback accompanied by a single servant. Describing how Fiennes rode through rain and hail storms, Margaret Willy remarks that it is "amusing to learn from her Foreword to the *Journeys* that they were initially undertaken for the sake of her health."[60] As we have seen, however, aspirants to health could not afford to be "sollicitous" about such matters. Riding across the country on horseback, Fiennes is literally fleeing illness—a state she identifies with aristocratic ignorance, an enforced alienation from labor and its productions. Her prefatory note to the reader offers a blunt precis of the emerging medical wisdom: if, instead of indulging in idle dissipations like gambling, people of leisure would "be curious to inform themselves and make observations of the pleasant prospects, good buildings, different produces and manufactures of each place" in their native land, it would "cure or preserve" them from "these epidemick diseases of vapours, should I add Laziness?" (As we would expect, laziness and nervous disease are rendered synonyms.) To "be curious to inform" oneself and "make observations" is to invest *care* in becoming curious: representing her investigative desire as the product of pains taken rather than innate appetite, Fiennes renders it innocent, an attribute of the productive rather than the consuming body. Demonstrating an exemplary detachment from the latter-day Eves she addresses, she observes that curiosity can cure many ills to which the pampered aristocratic body is subject, such as "the evil itch of over-valueing foreign parts." By the end of the preface, she is urging her readers to exert themselves in preparation for the afterlife, to "render Suffering and Age supportable and Death less formidable and a future State more happy."[61] Their very salvation, it seems, depends on the care they invest in becoming curious now.

Fiennes's vision of a happier future state is also a vision of England. By acquainting her readers with those who work and the methods and products of their labor, Fiennes will "form such an Idea of England" as will "add much to its Glory and Esteem in our minds" (32). Here, glory attaches to the labor that actually makes the country; an idea that is not forged through direct experience of this labor does not reflect the thing itself. An anonymous Royal Society memo proclaimed that the "enquiring of persons of all Professions, Trades, & Occupations . . . might Lead us into an unknown world"; applying the "souveraign remedy" of curiosity to gain entrance into this world, Fiennes seeks to assert her sovereign rights within it. In the process, she escapes the great "reproach to the English": "ignorance and being strangers to themselves."[62] The notion that the members of England's ruling classes ("the English") will no longer be strangers to *themselves* once they become acquainted with the processes of production suggests that, conventional usage notwithstanding, the country is represented not by its statesmen but by its producers; to "make observations" is to join this class. Righteously suggesting that MPs follow her lead in order to acquire some knowledge of the counties they represent, Fiennes, like the Society Fellows, establishes a competitive identification with them; to truly represent England, she implies, one must be intimately acquainted with— and even attempt to embody—its knowledge-producing capacity. It is the England brought into being by maker's knowledge to which Fiennes is a stranger, and into which she hopes somehow to gain entry. As we will see, in her effort to "be curious," she will strive to represent England both to her readers and *as* herself.

Thus a project akin to the Royal Society's histories of trades is presented as part of a health regime whose aims dovetail with public service. It is this association of health and knowledge, combined with a faith in the power of curiosity to confer a representative character on its agent, that distinguishes Fiennes's project from the early modern tradition of descriptive chorography on which it is based. Sixteenth-century chorography sought to create a "Speculum Britanniae" that would reflect a fixed image of the country; and, as Stan Mendyk, Richard Helgerson, and Cynthia Wall have shown, by focusing on the reassuring stabilities of architecture and genealogy, it succeeded.[63] In contrast, Fiennes wants to create—and to be seen creating—an "Idea." Her observational persona as a taker of pains is the most important "manufacture" the reader encounters. While William Camden bases his examination on the archives, Fiennes bases hers on physical exertion; while Camden neglects locales that have no antiquities, Fiennes passes swiftly through areas that fail to evince signs of "progress."

Fiennes was not, of course, the first chorographer to venture into the field. William Harrison's *Description of England* (1577) is based largely on the fieldwork of John Leland, who set out "to searche all the lybraryes of

Monasteryes and collegies," but who wandered instead into "a whole worlde of thynges." Harrison displays the "passion for the circumstantial" exhibited by his predecessor; as Georges Edelen observes, his apology for not having "by mine own travel and eyesight viewed such things as I do here entreat of" would have been "incomprehensible to a monastic chronicler."[64] Where Harrison most differs from Fiennes is in his embarrassed relationship to his own curiosity, particularly when it is directed at the processes of production. Venturing on a description of native brewing methods, for example, he assures the reader that "I am scarce a good malster" and that he only mentions such details to correct the falsehoods spread by foreign writers. Belittling his "fond report of a servile trade," he apologizes for exposing the reader to "a musty malthouse": "bear with me, gentle reader (I beseech thee)." After offering a few more details, he checks himself again: "But what have I to do with this matter, or rather so great a quantity, wherewith I am not acquainted? Nevertheless, sith I have taken occasion to speak of brewing, I will exemplify in such a proportion as I am best skilled in"—though he is quick to clarify that his "skill" is actually just second-hand, having been informed of this "servile trade" by his wife and her maidservants.[65] The contrast with Fiennes's dark hints that the salvation of the gentry actually depends on their willingness to look into such matters could hardly be starker.

In contrast to Harrison, Fiennes presents her very observations as the unembarrassed products of artisanal effort; the *Journeys* is a factual relation, and *fact*, for her, retains its primary meaning as a thing made. Yet if Fiennes's idea of England is the product of pains, her *Journeys* registers little interest in writing as a craft in its own right. Norman Nicholson concludes on this basis that Fiennes "aimed her story at no one. It is purely personal, entirely without purpose—the overheard mumblings of a talkative old maid." The charge is refuted by Fiennes's address to the reader, but the question of audience is one she invites.[66] Although it is presented for elite consumption and imitation, her humble manufacture is a calculated assault on elite taste—a taste she expressly refuses to feed: "as most I converse with knows both the freedom and easyness [with which] I speak and write as well as my deffect in all, so they will not expect exactness or politeness in this book, tho' such embellishments might have adorned the descriptions and suited the nicer taste." Eschewing embellishments and adornment for "freedom and easyness," her innocently naked prose seeks not to satisfy polite readers but to agitate their spirits. The stripped-down style that Robert Southey called "bald" observes a kind of decorum, how-ever, since it is perfectly suited to the indecorous behavior it narrates.[67] Fien-nes's descriptions of being thrown by her horse onto a muddy riverbank or choking on peatsmoke in a rural cottage suggest a woman determined to divest herself, however provisionally, of gentility's trappings, to "break through the Mode"; as we will see, these unladylike demonstrations of physical fortitude are mere preparation for her attempts to break into the working life.[68]

Because she is content to pursue a seemingly haphazard descriptive strategy—she saw this and then she saw that—Fiennes has been described as "breathless," "artless," "eager as a child," and "pitifully limited"; she has even suffered the indignity of being compared to Molly Bloom and Miss Bates.[69] Her prose is indeed breathless; it is the spirit of exercise that breathes through this writing. It is hard to say where Fiennes's desire for physical exertion stops and her investigative ambitions begin; for her, the call to experiment *is* a call to exercise, and as she takes her solitary way through the country on an open-ended pilgrimage, riding seems to become her writing. Abandoning punctuation for long stretches, she favors parataxis that enacts a studious lack of "prepossession" about what should be subor-dinated to what. Her exemplary alienation from conventional canons of value results in a string of impressions that is literally nervous, rapidly reg-istering the pressure of things themselves—everything—on the receptive body and mind. In language that, as Southey complains, lacks all "sublim-ity" and "conveys to the mind no ideas but simply those of the objects themselves" (an evaluation that would have delighted her), Fiennes revels in her intimacy with all the things supposed to be beneath a gentlewoman's notice. Uninterested in sublimity, she seeks to gratify a different appetite: an ontological hunger for contact with the things of creation. In this re-spect, the apparent aimlessness of her curiosity is deceptive. If we look be-yond the superficial diversity of its objects, we will find that it is fixated on the very experience of investing care and pains in the material creation. The "symptom[s] of pleasure" for which Southey searched in vain are every-where in the *Journeys,* but they are not of a kind that he would have recog-nized: Fiennes's language registers a pleasurable struggle against an alien-ation from productive labor.[70]

Fiennes's scenic overviews of towns and the countryside are only pre-ludes to a suitably celebratory exploration of the care that has created these appearances. The transition from descriptions of panoramic views to accounts of local manufacture is so frequent that we may assume it follows her own associative train, reflecting her ambitions as an observer. At Nottingham Castle, for example, she enjoys "a prospect more than 20 mile about shewing the diversityes of Cultivations and produce of the Earth" (87). This comprehensive prospect leads her to describe local farming methods, the labor that has shaped the features of the land. We return to the motif with which this book began, the labors of the months, now explicitly the grounds for the performance of intellectual labor, for Fiennes's "art prospective," like Hooke's, pierces through time as well as space. Fiennes could hardly have seen all the stages of the process that she recounts from her observational perch; she must have learned about them from questioning people in the area, but she chooses to convey this knowledge as an instant of perception; this art of observation combines perception with rational reconstruction to make economic production itself visible. The momentum of her account of rural labor leads her to zoom in on local manufacture; the synoptic vision narrows and we end up inside a glass factory, where we see a craftsman making a swan and Fiennes giving it a try (87–88). This interior becomes a metonymic expression of the wider view, providing an "idea" of England's productivity—an idea into which she can insert and then "discover" herself. Her dissertation on a hill at Toddington provides another example of this spectatorial procedure: it "gave a large prospect to the eye; I saw some of this land improved in the produce of woads which the dyers use; its ordered in this manner" (54). She goes on to describe the cultivation of woad, from repeatedly cutting the plant close to the root to grinding its leaves in a horse-powered mill and preparing the paste thus manufactured for use as a dye. The "large prospect" narrows its focus while opening out into a temporal panorama of the entire labor cycle, a series of events that is not beneath the notice of the genteel observer, for it made the "prospect" that is given "to the eye"; it is these procedures which have "ordered" the land "in this manner." The work that shapes the land provides not merely the enabling conditions but the very substance of Fiennes's enjoyment of prospects.

Fiennes brings the same concern to divulging the causes of the visible when she takes in urban prospects. Generally, if a hill overlooks a town, it "gives the prospect of the town very finely to the eye," but that is not the sole aim; to really penetrate the prospect one must have at least a vicarious, but preferably direct, experience of the processes that produced it (124). Through Fiennes, we are exposed to stocking-weaving, shipbuilding, cidermaking, silk-weaving, and paper-making, in addition to such projects as the draining of the fens. The painstaking exactitude with which Fiennes sets down the details of manufacturing processes suggests a participatory zeal in itself, but her journeys are also marked by transient apprenticeships. We have seen Fiennes trying her hand at glass spinning in Nottingham. In the York mint she not only takes note of the activities in a list of gerunds reminiscent of Hooke's and Petty's, cast in the pseudo-immediate present tense—"I see all parts of the work about, the pounding the boyling refineing and makeing Barres and cutting out in the mill and bakeing and stamping"—but she also "stamp'd one halfe crown my self," doing her part to enrich the lifeblood of England's body, and to crown herself, enacting her sovereignty over the things with which she comes into contact (92). At the Cornish tin mines she watches molten tin being poured into molds and gets "a piece poured out and made cold for to take with me," to add to her idea (204–205). In Lincoln, she even gets to try her hand at the venerable, and physically strenuous, art of bell-ringing: "its as much as a man can reach to the top of the bell with his hand when he is in the inside, its rarely ever rung but only by ringing the Clapper to each side—which we did—and that sounds all over the town" (84). Her exertion, forging a momentary unity out of herself, "a man," and a "Clapper," permeates the place. And in the printing room at the Sheldonian Theatre at Oxford, "I printed my name severall tymes" (55). The iterable impressions of her name are products of her own innocent willingness to be impressed by the labor she regards; the opportunity to reproduce her own name as its agent is her reward.

When Fiennes cannot penetrate the scene of work, she is frustrated: in Derby, for example, "I did not observe or learn any other trade or manufacture, they had only shops of all sorts of things" (149). She is not a tourist, content to consume the local wares; she came to town to learn a trade. She initially feels fortunate to have arrived at Maidstone on market day, but she "could not learn what particular thing that was their staple Commodity or tradeing in," and not being interested in making purchases, she leaves (124). Her intentions are evident from her frustration in towns and villages where the cycle of production has ground to a halt; it leaves her with nothing to do—no prospects. This flusters her, and she typically inveighs against the "sloth" of those who are content to live "in so nasty a way." Visiting

Scotland, she concedes that of all the people she saw, "I think there were one or two at last did take spinning in hand at a lazy way," but her overall impression is of massive unemployment, which repels her: "I attribute it wholly to their sloth for I see they sitt and do little." In such cases, this is all she can see, since unemployment makes it impossible for her to do her own job: "I am sure I mett with a sample of it enough to discourage my progress farther in Scotland" (174). Her progress through Britain is parasitic on the opportunities her routes afford her to witness *its* progress, to observe and make trials of productive work, and to form an idea of the country on the basis of this experience that will add to the "Glory" of all its members; Scotland seems to have no place in this idea. It might be said that observation of and participation in skilled manufacture performs the same function as sheep-tending in pastoral; Fiennes's symbolic participation in such activities generates a sense of England's harmonious unity, but her interest in how these activities are actually "ordered" by the experts who undertake them distinguishes her symbolic participation from a merely pastoral pretense. Indeed, Fiennes makes very clear that there is nothing "natural" about her participation in this labor. Her expertise in these matters, like her idea of England, is the artificial product of pains taken—pains her readers are urged to imitate.

While Fiennes violates aristocratic norms in her rebellion against the "Laziness" and "ignorance" of more fastidious members of her class who are "strangers" at home by mingling with and learning from those whom she calls "ordinary people," she is herself extraordinary, although she would somehow like her extraordinary pains to inform the ordinary course of life for all. Traveling the distance from York to Aberford she gauges the intellectual distance that separates her from "ordinary people":

> I observe the ordinary people both in these parts of Yorkshire and in the northern parts can scarce tell you how farre it is to the next place unless it be in the great towns and there in their publick houses; and they tell you its very good gate, instead of saying it is good way, and they call their gates yates, and do not esteem it uphill unless so steep as a house or precipice; they say its good levell gate all along, when it may be there are severall great hills to pass, but this account did encrease on us the nearer we came to Darbyshire, but in generall they live much at home and scarce ever go 2 or 10 mile from thence, especially the women, so may be term'd good housekeepers. (102)

Fiennes's griping covers many points of difference between herself and "the ordinary people": they speak incorrectly (in the North "they call their gates yates"); they are so physically hardy that they "do not esteem it uphill unless so steep as a house or precipice"; and their limited experience makes it impossible for them to provide reasonable estimates of the distance between the areas in which they live and the rest of the country. Although this inconveniences Fiennes, her attitude is reluctantly approving. Such people live "at home" because their proper work keeps them within a ten-mile radius of their dwellings. The domestic work that structures the lives of ordinary women, in particular, restricts their mobility; their resulting ignorance of what lies beyond their neighborhoods is a sign that they are "good housekeepers." (The mention of "housekeepers" here seems to be a conscious pun, one of Fiennes's rare attempts at "wit.") Even so, when she describes their inability to imagine their distance from the rest of England, she registers their intellectual distance from the idea of England she is trying to fashion, and from the kind of work she is herself attempting.

Fiennes's experience enables her not only to assess distances, but to keep her distance from the narrow perspectives associated with each place she visits. Inhabitants around the Wrekin, for example, boast that it is the highest in England but, having viewed higher hills, she is "full convinc'd" that this is untrue; it only appears that way to people who have not seen much of the rest of the country, and who are struck by the contrast between the Wrekin and the low hills running alongside it (186). Fiennes's distance also enables her to judge the areas she visits more reliably than their inhabitants: in Ely, she puts up with frogs and snails in her room, and concludes that the area, with its unpitched streets and unhealthy air, seems less "an habitation for human beings" than "a cage or nest of unclean creatures," but "the natives say much to the contrary which proceeds from custom and use" (141–142). She is untouched by local custom, and can see Ely as it really is. Fiennes consistently disassociates herself from the parochialism of those who have not traveled extensively through the country, showcasing her sophistication as well as her religious affiliations through a tendency to turn up her nose at popish ornamentation and local "wonders." Visiting the famous "Whispering Place" in Gloucester Cathedral, she remarks wryly that it is "not quite soe wonderfull as I have heard," for she is familiar with the phenomenon from her visit to the large room at Montague House.[71]

Fiennes's ability to perceive that apparent wonders are "not quite soe won-derfull" as those who live near them believe reflects not only her wide expe-rience but her freedom from local custom; this is finally what separates her observations from the common sort. Her idea of England, like Milton's "paradise within," is crucially not localized to any particular place.

Fiennes's effort to see the causes of what is given to the eye identifies her project as experimentalist observation. She can explain, for example, *why* the whispering wall phenomenon is not so wonderful by providing a material explanation for it: the sound is carried along the high vaulted ceil-ing (191). By the same token, her efforts at work are experimental trials; her looking, like Hooke's, requires "doing," but it does not end there. Her par-ticipation in productive labor points beyond itself, to a curious subject in the making. Arriving at Elden Hole, which was widely held to be bottom-less, she briskly sets about designing an experiment that demonstrates to her satisfaction that it merely "runns aslant," which is why a plummet and line will not pass through it. (After having someone cast a stone down which struck the sides of the hole, she put her ear to the ground a hundred yards away in the direction where she thought the hole went, and found that the stone "rang" louder there than at the mouth of the hole [109–110].) She is critical of observations that do not meet a stringent evidentiary standard, withholding her belief, for example, from "the Report" concern-ing the River Mole, which popular lore described as running straight under-ground for several miles. Noting that "Camden does credit this," she queries his account of "a tryal one made of forceing a Duck into one of those falls, which came out at the other side by Moles with its feathers allmost all rubbed off." Fiennes is not willing to reject the report outright, but the cur-soriness of the description, the absence of any explanatory details of "how they could force the Duck into so difficult a way," leaves her, as it would leave any experimentalist, suspicious of the relation, and she concludes, "whither anything of this is more than Conjecture must be left to every ones liberty to judge" (63). Learned authority and popular gullibility have con-spired to lend credibility to this story, but Fiennes succumbs to neither the authority of texts nor hearsay; she models the virtuoso's insusceptibility to both high and low intellectual temptations. Yet she leaves a final judgment to the reader's "liberty," demonstrating by example how both the dogmatic assertions of authoritative texts and folk wisdom differ from her own disin-terested and liberal-minded mode of knowledge production.

Fiennes's expressions of detachment from local wonders anticipate the comic effects achieved by later professional observers. When she visits the chamber of state at Windsor, which "looked very glorious," she remarks on its canopy having been "newly made to give audience to the French Embassadour to shew the grandeur and magnificence of the British Monarch—some of these foolerys are requisite sometymes to create admiration and regard to keep up the state of a kingdom and nation" (219). Such "glorious . . . foolerys" are the very opposite of the "Glory" to which she seeks to restore England's idea. She takes note of the various means by which "admiration and regard" are extracted from viewers while exhibiting her own insusceptibility to these emotions and so draining them of their power to impress the reader. She takes a dim view of Stonehenge as well, regarding its mystery as a fraud: "to increase the wonder the story is that none can count them [the stones] twice alike." Rather than accepting this wonderful story at face value, she tests it repeatedly, counting the stones over and over—"I have told them often and bring their number to 91"—and provides a matter-of-fact explanation for the perplexity: the stones are difficult to count because "they stand confused." (Defoe attempted the same thing and arrived at the number 72.) Fiennes makes short work of Stonehenge while others stand astounded, for she does not dwell on the sources of its mystery that she cannot plumb. The compulsion to debunk expresses itself in a conviction—that many apparent wonders are "not quite soe wonderfull" once their causes are ascertained—and in a method.[72]

The desire to experience wonder serves many needs, and the curious spectator must guard against them all in his effort to go beyond the merely visible. While some draw pleasure from wonder, others draw a misguided spiritual solace. In the *Journeys,* hot springs provide dramatic sites for the conflict between innocent inquiry and fallen superstition. The legend surrounding St. Winifred's Well, for example, was that it had sprung forth from Winifred's head after she had been decapitated by a disappointed seducer. For adherents of the old religion, its waters were invested with the power of Winifred's martyrdom.[73] Some "small stones of a reddish coullour in the Well said to be some of St. Winifreds blood" were offered by "the poore people . . . to the strangers for curiosity and relicts." Fiennes is aghast: "there I saw abundance of the devout papists on their knees all round the Well; poor people are deluded into an ignorant blind zeale and to be pity'd by us that have the advantage of knowing better and ought to be better."

The poor papists ascribe health-giving properties to the well which Fiennes is sure that it lacks. Although "they say its of wonder full operation," she can find nothing unusual in this holy water, and can only recommend it for the most mundane of uses: "the taste to me was but like good spring water which with wine and sugar and leamons might make a pleasant draught" (158–159). Such homely praise makes the agitation of the "poore people" seem grotesque by contrast.

Fiennes is convinced that certain waters do have health-giving properties, and she seeks to provide philosophically acceptable rather than wondrous reasons for their "operation." The waters of St. Winifred's Well are not useful for anything more than refreshment because they lack mineral traces, but the water at Tunbridge, "whose property is to retrieve lost limbs that are benumbed," has them in abundance, "comeing from steele should have that effect, it raiseing the blood and gives it a new circulation" (120). The difference lies not in the belief that waters can operate on the body, but in the nature of the cause ascribed to this effect. It is entirely on this distinction that the rational use of baths depends. So, although Fiennes joins the papists in jumping into the chilling waters of St. Mungo's Well, she is not doing the same thing that they are:

> Setting aside the Papists fancyes of it I cannot but think it a very good Spring, being remarkably cold, and just at the head of the Spring so its fresh which must needs be very strengthning, it shutts up the pores of the body immediately . . . some of the Papists I saw there had so much Zeale as to continue a quarter of an hour on their knees at their prayers in the Well, but none else could well endure it so long at a tyme; I went in 7 severall seasons and 7 tymes every season and would have gone in oftener could we have staid longer. (94)

It is because they are motivated by "Zeale" and "fancyes" that the papists risk hypothermia in waters whose temperature "none else could well endure." Yet she immediately goes on to brag of the frequency with which she herself dipped in and out of the well. Her displays of physical fortitude serve a different end; they are motivated by the zealously held, because experimentally grounded, belief that the waters are "strengthning." A responsible explanation of this strengthening power begins by "Setting aside the Papists fancyes of it" and excavating a material cause for this effect: the coldness of the water, she suggests, causes the pores of the body to contract. If both groups at the well suffer discomfort, in one case this is the necessary by-product of investigative trial, while in the other, it is merely purgatorial suffering without progress.

Fiennes is an avid experimenter on her body, recording the effects of different waters on her constitution with a frank attention to detail which suggests that she and Hooke would have reveled in each other's company. She drinks a quart of the water of a "Stincking spaw" and finds it "a good sort of Purge if you can hold your breath so as to drinke them down." The waters of Buxton Well were as warm as she had been told: "I was in it and it made me shake."[74] And Fiennes always attempts to support her evaluations with testimonials, if she can get them. The Canterbury Spring can confidently be said to be inferior to Tunbridge because a man complained of "a numbness in his limbs after drinking it sometyme, which is quite contrary to Tunbridge waters." Here again, Fiennes provides a physical explanation: "I like no spring that rises not quick and runs off apace; that must have most spirit and good off the mincrall it comes from" (120). She recounts a "trial" which involved carrying buckets of it down a path and weighing the bucket at various points to test the speed at which it evaporated; its speedy evaporation demonstrates to her satisfaction its "spiriteous" nature (125). Although she does not explain how waters have the "spirit and good off the minerall it comes from" or provide a definition of "spiriteous," it is clear that experiment, rather than appreciative superstition or wonder, provides the terms of reference for interpreting her experience.

Fiennes's experimental allegiances are evident even when she confesses likes and dislikes of a frankly subjective character. She is less excited by splendid country houses—of which she usually gives cursory descriptions, generously sprinkled with the all-purpose word "neat"—than she is by the treasure of Thomas Macro, an apothecary, who "shewed me a Curiosity of an Herball all written out with every sort of tree and herb dryed and cut out and pasted on the leaves . . . it was a fine thing and would have delighted me severall dayes."[75] By far the word most consistently associated with her esteem and pleasure is *curious*. While she sometimes uses the term to refer to natural objects which inspire an investigative desire, she uses it more often to refer to some happy way in which nature has been adapted to human needs or to one who is skilled in this manipulation of nature. She finds that the fruits in Herefordshire are excellent due to the efforts of persons "curious in planting" (65). Burghley House is "eminent for its Curiosity," which is evident not in its immodest paintings but rather in its well-contrived prospects and fountains (83). Henry Winstanley's house in Littlebury is a pleasure to visit, as "a house with abundance of fine Curiosityes all performed by Clockwork and such like" (77). She finds that a cannon in Dover that can propel balls with remarkable velocity is highly esteemed "for its curiosity" (123). Fiennes uses the word almost purely to convey its supposed etymon; care or pains have been invested in the object or wrought upon it. In this sense, the very impoverishment of her descriptive language carries a lesson. Since she is interested less in what is given to the eye than in the work that has produced it, her laborious reconstructions sometimes disregard the merely visible, so that her observations, like the throne in Windsor, are so "curiously wrought like needlework that you can scarce see the ground or stuff its wrought on" (219).

I have suggested that, like the Curator of Experiments who performed the "laborious" part of observation, Fiennes hopes to "carry the eyes, and the imaginations" of her readers with her. As her investigative style attests, the form of work with which she actually *identifies* is the progressive labor of the experimentalist, who delved into appearances to reveal their material causes. When Fiennes visits the anatomy theatre in Newcastle, she enters the scene of this kind of work:

> there I saw the roome with a round table in it, railed round with seates or benches for the conveniency in their disecting and anatomiseing a body and reading lectures on all parts; there was two bodyes that had been anatomised, one the bones were fastned with wires the other had had the flesh boyled off and some of the ligaments remained and dryed with it, and so the parts were held together by its own muscles and sinews that were dryed with it; over this was another roome in which was the skin of a man that was taken off after he was dead and dressed and so was stuff'd the body and limbs, it look'd and felt like a sort of parchment; in this roome I could take a view of the whole town, it standing on high ground. (177)

Here Fiennes is presented with the scene of scientific labor as well as its products. She notes that the room is where researchers perform dissections and read lectures, but when she describes the operations that have transformed the dead bodies into suitable objects of study, she does not describe the men performing them. Rehearsing the work that has produced the appearances, she places the verbs in the passive voice and thrusts them into the past tense. Having effaced the agents of this labor, she steps into their place, performing the work herself. Whereas Fiennes spun glass under the eye of a skilled worker, here the work of which these bodies are the products is closer to her own vocation; she may stand in for the absent medical men. Subjected to Fiennes's lively scrutiny, the lifeless bodies offer a foil, and a stage, for her curiosity to exercise itself. Presenting the bodies to the reader's view in a neutral, zero-degree style, she performs a verbal anatomy of them: the body that "had had the flesh boyled off"; "the skin of a man that was taken off after he was dead"; the bones that are "fastned with wires." The description, like the objects on display, is the product of hands and eyes working together to contend against ignorance. The scene of the virtuoso's work—using the domestic techniques of boiling, cutting, curing, and dressing to torture truth out of dead matter—becomes the platform for a demonstration of her own skill.

As curiosity moves her to touch the skin of one of the bodies, which feels "like a sort of parchment," Fiennes turns, without a transition or even sentence break, to "take a view of the whole town." The parchment provides the bridge: as the body under investigation becomes text, the analytic, dissective gaze, the perspective on internal organs and excised parts, merges with the familiar "prospective" view. The corpses and the town are assimilated together as part of a world laid open for a curatorial art for which there can be no unworthy object, and to which there can be no end. Claiming Adamic sovereignty over this workroom, now coextensive with the whole country, Fiennes invites her readers to join her there.[76]

Traveling in a Critical Manner: Defoe's *Tour thro' the Whole Island of Great Britain*

Defoe's travels at some point must have overlapped with Fiennes's own; although the first volume of the *Tour* came out in 1724, the work is largely based on trips made decades before.[77] What is worth stressing at the outset of our examination of the "curious" observations of the *Tour* (the modifier appears on its title page) is that Defoe is the first literary author we have encountered who was essentially trained to become a virtuoso. In the academy of Charles Morton, who had attended meetings of the Philosophical

Club at Oxford, the "pleasing dream" elaborated in Aubrey's *Idea of Education* was the daily routine. In addition to using Morton's own textbook, a digest of the writings of such virtuosi as Boyle, Hooke, and Power, they read Locke's *Essay,* still banned at Oxford, and enjoyed the benefit of teaching aids like thermometers and even an air pump, while receiving all their instruction in English. As Ilse Vickers has discussed, Defoe was defensively proud of the education he received there.[78] When John Tutchin mocked him for being an uneducated apprentice, Defoe challenged him to a translation contest "to show the World, how much *De Foe* the Hosier, is Inferior in Learning, to Mr. *Tutchin,* the Gentleman," claiming that if he had "lost the Fluency of Expression in the *Latin*" it was not his father's fault: "I freely Testifie that if I am a Blockhead, it was no Bodies Fault but my own; he having spar'd nothing in my Education."[79] Elsewhere, however, he insisted that the "knowledge of things, not words, make a schollar," describing a course of study that ran "thro' a whole course of Phylosophy" and "perfectly compass'd the study of Geography, the use of the maps and globes . . . all that Sir Isaac Newton, Mr. Whiston, Mr. Halley had said in English upon the nicest subjects in Astronomy and the secrets of Nature," enabling the student to become "a mathematician, a geographer, an astronomer, a philosopher, and, in a word, a compleat schollar: and all this without the least help from the Greek or the Latin." One could be a "philosopher" and even "a compleat schollar" without any knowledge of the classics, since real education consisted of things rather than words, the secrets of nature rather than the arcana of man.[80] Morton clearly instilled the lessons of artisanal epistemology in his pupil, who internalized its values: his blunt assertion that "the most noble Descendants of *Adam*'s Family . . . were really *Mechanicks,*" since they first cultivated the arts that "enrich" human life, firmly identifies nobility with material production rather than possession.[81] It cannot be said, however, that Defoe mastered Morton's curriculum. One can imagine how disappointed Morton would have been if he had read what Defoe had to say about fossils in the *Tour:* "Next here are the Snake Stones, of which nothing can be said but as one observes of them, to see how Nature sports her self to amuse us, as if Snakes could grow in those Stones." Defoe did, however, recall Morton's "mechanical" explanation of the whispering place in Gloucester cathedral, and he regularly poached the *Philosophical Transactions* of the Royal Society, larding *The Storm,* for example, with excerpts from Leeuwenhoek's observations on rain water.

References like these may be multiplied, as they are in Vickers's excellent book, but the impact of experimental science on Defoe was more profound and less obvious than such references reveal.[82]

Defoe was an experimentalist author in every sense: in addition to being taken with the ideal of penetrating observation, he was extremely skilled in the discourse of modesty, achieving through it a remarkable simultaneity of opposed effects. His decision to write England's history "by Inches" in the *Review* conveys both humbly microscopic ambitions and a Marvellian determination to get specific. Even his addresses to the reader combine boldness and humility in a distinctively experimentalist way: he made brazen predictions in the *Review* but openly admitted his mistakes ("I Cannot but acknowledge the last Review a little wide of the State of things"); the redemptive use that experimentalists made of error became an organizing feature of serial publication.[83] And, like the *Athenian Mercury,* the *Review* took all of knowledge for its province. Defoe considers theories concerning all sorts of material phenomena, asking for example, "Why are ladies Fatter than was known in former Years?" He evaluates various possible "natural Causes," including the fact that contemporary women consume "Modern Drinks, which our Ancestors never had, I encline to think, there may be something in that."[84] The judicious tone brought to bear on apparent trivia suggests Jack Stuff himself. But it is above all in the *Tour* that Defoe sets out to present the making of observations as both a productive labor and a public service.

Defoe offers the *Tour* for use as a Boylean relation. Although it might tempt the reader to travel over Great Britain himself, if the reader cannot conveniently confirm the account by independent testimony, it will still "qualify him to discourse of it, as one that had a tolerable Knowledge of it, tho' he stay'd at Home." Defoe insistently stresses the physical pains he has taken to see "the whole Island." His demanding scheme of "circuits," as he called them, required him to make repeated observational trials, visiting the north of England "no less than five times" and West Riding "no less than three."[85] The labor-intensive nature of such looking, he remarks, "is perhaps the Reason why . . . the other Writers of Journies and Travels this Way might not see how to go about it." This is the first and most important thing the professional observer has to see. By the beginning of the second volume, he seems exhausted and cranky, complaining that "It is not an easy Thing to travel over a whole Kingdom, and in so critical a Manner too." The emphasis on distance covered—traveling "over a whole kingdom" (like Fiennes going "7 long miles" on an average morning)—underscores the physical stamina required to make a comprehensive survey, but, as Defoe notes, it is not just a matter of displaying hustle; in order to "undeceive the World in the false or mistaken Accounts, which other Men have given of Things," he has "Travell'd critically." The *Tour* is "a full Account of Things" both because its author had the opportunity to see these things "oftner," and because of the "Deliberation I have taken in the View of them."[86]

Defoe's language is calculated to put the virtual witness at ease by closing the distance between the reader and the scene of observation. Like Pamela, he uses the present tense: "I must now leave *Yorkshire*"; "I am now at the Gates of *Edinburgh*"; "I am now come back . . . to the same Bank of the *Trent*"; there is hardly a page from which deictics such as "Here is," or "From hence, let us view" are absent.[87] And like Pamela he writes letters, in a conspicuously humble style: "Our Manner is plain, and suited to the Nature of Familiar Letters; our Relations have no Blusters, no Rhodomontadoes of our own Abilities."[88] His frequent use of the plural first person serves to make the reader his virtual companion, as she relives his perceptual experience in laborious detail. His description of London's perimeter records his walk around it with comic exhaustiveness: "about one Furlong and half to the Corner of my Lord *Godolphin*'s Garden Wall, the Line goes *North* behind the Stable-Yard Buildings, and behind *Park-Place,* and on the Park Wall behind the Buildings; on the *West* Side of St. *James*'s *Street,* to the corner in *Soho,* or *Pickadilly,* then crossing the Road," and so on for five more pages.[89] Defoe performs an ingenious inversion of the Rogation perambulation; no longer a public demonstration of parochial jurisdiction and the parish officer's "right of way," this solo beating of the bounds asserts the innocent observer's temporary jurisdiction over all he surveys. He even re-creates the experience of slowly approaching objects for the viewer: as the Severn comes into view, he notes first that "as you go on, the Shores begin to draw towards one another, and the Coasts to lye Parallel," and then moves in a cinematic progression to its view at close range as "a most raging, turbulent, furious Place" (2: 438). And Defoe is careful to canvas his own perceptual experience for error and wishful thinking, just as Hooke advised the microscopist to do. At the top of the highest of the Cheviot Hills, his guide points out the Irish Sea: "But if he could see it, knowing it in particular, and where exactly to look for it, it was so distant, that I could

not say, I was assur'd I saw it" (2: 767). Not much depends on whether the
Irish Sea can be seen from the top of this hill, but, like the expressions of
uncertainty that clutter *Paradise Lost* ("Uncertain which," "undetermind
square or round"), these equivocations provide him with an occasion to
build our trust in his observational office. Perhaps Defoe could not be
"assur'd" that he saw the sea from this vantage point because he was never
there, but his personal ignorance provides an occasion to showcase Boylean
scruples, and thus to justify the surrender of our imaginations to being
"carried along" by him.

Although Defoe records each moment with a deliberateness that borders on the overscrupulous, we do not imagine him actually jotting down
his observations as he goes. In fact, it is essential that the reader understand
that "I do not write you these Letters from the Observations of one single
Journey"; he performed repeated observational trials (2: 664). He does not
take full advantage of an aesthetic of immediacy because his concern is to
establish his credibility as a witness and "the Authority of the Relation";
spontaneity is the last effect he is after (1: 3). If his style sometimes lacks the
energy we associate with Richardsonian "writing to the moment," it is because his letters are not modeled after speech; the letters that comprise the
relation of the *Tour* are not the products of "talk[ing] upon paper," to use
Pope's famous phrase for epistolary composition; they are instruments designed to permit looking through paper.[90] This aim motivates its own conceits. He loves to fuse things seen with the relation itself; the border of
Scotland marks the termination of a letter: "But being now at the utmost
Extent of *England* on this Side, I conclude also my Letter" (2: 688). Preparing to describe the "waste" lands of Scotland, he reflects that they are "more
pleasant than the Traveller cou'd expect, or than the Reader perhaps at first
Sight will think possible" (2: 539). Here sight resides in the reader and expectations in the traveler; the reader's experience seems inseparable from
the traveler's sense impressions.

Above all, Defoe takes every opportunity to make clear that "the Accounts here given are not the Produce of a cursory View, or rais'd upon the
borrow'd Lights of other Observers"; he is "very little in Debt" to previous
written reports and oral accounts, giving "but very few Accounts of Things,
but what he has been an Eye-witness of himself" (1: 3). Although it has
been shown that Defoe in fact copied a great deal from the very sources he
pretends to scorn, particularly Camden's *Britannia,* the fact that he felt it to

be a rhetorical necessity to deny his dependence on previous writers indicates how essential to his persona this claim was.[91] Thus he refuses to dwell on "antiquities," not because he is ignorant of them, but because doing so would render his work an "Abridgment of *Stow* and his Continuators," and "would be falling into that Error, which I condemn in others, and making my Accounts be, what I resolved, from the Beginning, they should not be; namely, A Copy of other Men's Performances"; rather than imitation, Defoe is engaged in the manufacture of "Produce."[92] He is even scared to mention the cathedral of Exeter because "it has been so fully, and often Described that it would look like a meer Coppying from others to mention it."[93] He claims artisanal propriety over his ideas through a finicky insistence on performing all the labor of gaining and building them up himself. Yet he is obsessed with other texts, winnowing and sifting through the claims of previous authorities, no matter how inconsequential, to establish the superiority of his own testimony, inflating even the most trivial errors into outrages against the truth: the ships built in Ipswich, for example, can weigh up to 400 tons rather than 200 tons—contrary to Macky's "wild Observations"—and for confirmation, "I appeal to the *Ipswich* Colliers." He concludes magisterially, "but superficial Observers, must be superficial Writers, if they write at all" (1: 42). He continually expresses astonishment at the clash between his own hard-earned knowledge and what passes for received wisdom among learned authors, ingenuously remarking that " 'Tis strange" that "Error should prevail in this manner, and with Men of Learning too." Indicating his shock at the "Positive" accounts of authorities who "fall unwarily" into "unaccountable Error," Defoe demonstrates not only the greater accuracy of the *Tour* compared to earlier relations, but its independence of them (1: 148).

But the observer does not work alone; the search for credible witnesses is a constant. When Defoe does rely on the accounts of other witnesses, he provides reasons why they might be credited: the Ipswich colliers presumably would know how much their ships weighed, just as Locke's smiths know their own business. The "Country People," however, are problematic witnesses; natives can rarely see where they live properly because their relationship to their environment is mediated by fabulous traditions. Defoe can barely contain his disgust in Ellsmere, "famous for a great Lake or Mere . . . which the People pretend has in some Places no Bottom" (2: 457, 474). Country people who circulate tall tales are as shiftless when it comes

to intellectual labor as learned authorities; like Fiennes, Defoe skirts both
high and low intellectual temptations and reveals them to be the same. But
he is happy to make a rhetorical appeal to the knowledge of country natives
if by doing so he can humiliate a learned author. Describing tourists, misled by Camden, who rush to Box Hill "not doubting but they should see
some wonderful Gulph, in which a whole River should be at once as it were
Bury'd alive," he sets about to "undeceive the World" at even greater length
than Fiennes, explaining how hills block the river's passage and cause it to
separate into little channels. To confirm the existence of these hills, Defoe
is prepared to "appeal to the Knowledge of the Inhabitants of *Darking,
Mickleham, Leatherhead,* and all the Country round" without discrimina-
tion.[94] But Defoe is eager to show that he is not unwilling to believe even
the most apparently unlikely news, so long as he is provided with the right
sort of evidence.[95] And he makes tantalizing allusions to rumors he has
heard, often about local scandals, in order to demonstrate his intellectual
forbearance: "There are more particulars related of this Story, such I do not
take upon me to affirm"; "I say of it, as we generally say of improbable
News, *it wants Confirmation*."[96] Finally, he makes reference to a vast store
of prior experience to make clear to the reader that his more evaluative
judgments are not those of a parochial rube: having "seen the *Alps,* on so
many Occasions," as well as the "mighty mountains of *America, the Andes,*
which we see very often in the *South-Seas,*" he can assure his readers that
the mountains of Wales are indeed impressive; he even claims that England
can boast of plains "(far in my Opinion) excelling the Plains of *Mecca*."[97]

Defoe is not a "superficial observer," satisfied to reproduce uncorrobo-
rated reports from unreliable sources after taking a "cursory View" of the
country, but nor does he indulge in a mere looking spree; he searches for the
"original" of what he sees, "to give a View of the Difference between the present and the past" of the country (1: 332). The British landscape, like its
fossils when observed by Hooke, offers testimony of times past to the discerning viewer, whose understanding of the forces that have shaped the
country enables him to predict—perhaps even to shape—outcomes. As
microscopists peered into the causes of color, so Defoe discerns the underlying causes of the state of the towns and villages he surveys. Where a normal viewer might see a busy street, Defoe sees "the Face of Trade" made
visible; *trade* is not a simple abstraction here, but the material process that
has created the visual scene.[98] Where a visitor to Southampton might be

struck by its poverty, Defoe sees its cause: "the decay of the Trade is the real decay of the Town" (1: 141). Because causal forces operate identically at micro and macro levels, surface differences between humble and lofty instances of the same processes do not impress him: "The Ruins of *Carthage,* of the great City of *Jerusalem,* or of antient *Rome,* are not at all Wonderful to me; the Ruins of *Nineveh,* which are so entirely sunk, as that 'tis doubtful where the City stood; The Ruins of *Babylon,* or the Great *Persepolis,* and many Capital Cities . . . these, I say, are not at all Wonderful" because the processes governing the rise and fall of great empires can be understood by observing the flourishing and decline of seaport towns like Ipswich.[99] The responsible use of homology in place of old-fashioned analogy that distinguished the literature of microscopy proclaims his ability to see systems with the immediacy that others perceive bodies.

Inquiry into the causes of the visible draws Defoe irresistibly to the past and then into the future. Approaching Spitalfields Market, he seems to see what it was a generation ago—"a Field of Grass with Cows feeding on it"—and he describes the "deep dirty Road" that Brick Lane once was, when "there was not a House standing" anywhere; there are two hundred thousand inhabitants in the area now (1: 329–330). In his concern to document and explain the reasons for the "eminent Increase"—and decay—in various parts of the country, Defoe often finds it difficult to keep his eyes on what is in front of him (1: 326). The discerning observer judges things "by Rules of Mechanism," and an investigator of causes cannot remain sequestered within the limited perspective of the present or restrict his gaze to what is merely physically apparent; a complete Baconian inventory demands Hookean time-travel (1: 261). When Defoe regards Liverpool, he sees into Liverpool's future; although it had not yet overtaken Bristol in size, he sees this happening as if before his eyes (2: 665). This is why many of Defoe's observations, despite his straining for exhaustiveness, precision, and immediacy, have an abstract quality. His description of London does not vividly capture the urban environment; it focuses on the deep structure of the city, the processes that underlie fluctuations in crowds and commerce. Britain itself is a system of intricately related causes and effects that can be explained in mechanical terms; everything within it can be traced to a material cause: to the growth or decline, the concentration or redistribution, of wealth.

Wealth produces social distinctions that are widely accepted as real, but Defoe explains that the merchants and tradesmen who can afford to erect considerable estates now will be the aristocratic families of the future: so "the encrease of Wealth . . . plants Families and Fortunes, who in another Age will equal the Families of the antient Gentry" (1: 15). The metaphor of planting suggests cultivation and improvement—the experimentalist interface of nature and art—in contrast to the ex post nature of distinctions between the gentle and the common.[100] Titles, like scholastic species, signify only the most recent stage in the perpetual "Transpositions and Metamorphoses" of the matter of wealth as it assumes and puts on different forms.[101] The fact that the "fine Houses of the Citizens of *London*" in Cashalton "look rather like Seats of the Nobility, than the Country Houses of Citizens and Merchants" is in one sense a deceptive appearance, yet it attests to a more fundamental similarity: clearly, there is no essential difference.[102] Just as the atomistic reinterpretation of form unsettled the fixity of natural kinds, so here social classes are reinterpreted as mere epiphenomena of the changes undergone by matter in constant flux. The only natural fact reflected by titles is the temporary accumulation of wealth under a certain name, a concentration of matter that time will disperse, leaving only an empty name, with no more referent in things themselves.[103] The declining fortunes of the decayed nobility, whose titles no longer refer to their possession of any things, are thus documented with relish. When observing the mixture of the noble and merely famous individuals buried in Westminster Abbey, Defoe dwells happily on the work of Death the leveller: "so that in Time, the Royal Ashes will be thus mingled with common Dust."[104] The predicates of conventional language are finally conquered by the undifferentiated matter from which all of creation is made.

Defoe's "natural history" of culture reveals that even apparently inveterate features of local identities, which show themselves in styles of social intercourse and consumption patterns, are the secondary effects of systemic (economic) factors. Under Defoe's gaze, the "natural" affiliations of class, nationality, and local identity are revealed again and again as the social equivalent of secondary qualities, products of material causes invisible to the naked eye. Even the aesthetic delight Defoe takes in prospects is related to the discernment of causes, especially those that undo intellectual and social "prepossessions." Nothing, he asserts, "can be more Beautiful" than the outlying districts of London: "It is impossible to view these Countries from any rising Ground, and not be ravish'd with the delightful Prospect." Yet "few People value, and fewer understand" the "Beauty in these things . . . in *Perspective*" (1: 168, 167). To obtain this perspective, one cannot simply climb rising ground, though naturally Defoe does the required legwork; but, having reached the summit, he labors to achieve an intellectual and temporal distance from the immediate scene. Defoe presents his way of looking at beauty in perspective as an invention, and his eye actually works like a perspective glass: like Adam watching the pageant of history, he strains to look through it. Most of the residences beneath him belong to citizens who work in "the busy City; so that in short all this Variety, this Beauty, this glorious Show of Wealth and Plenty, is really a view of the Luxuriant Age which we live in, and of the overflowing Riches of the Citizens" (1: 169). Defoe enjoys a view of the productive forces that have created the visible opulence, forces that can only be grasped from a perspective that comprehends their long evolution and probable future course. Defoe's frequent pun on "prospect," which conflates the economic outlook of an area with its visual appearance, makes Hookean ambition the basis of aesthetic response. For a profound appreciation of this scene, it is necessary to have information about what created it; it helps to know, for example, that men like Josiah Child, who have great estates in this area, have "exceeded even the greatest Part of the Nobility of *England* in Wealth" and that it is "all of their own getting" (1: 169). Were these fine estates actually what they resembled, no doubt they would seem much less beautiful to him.

If the mere evidence of recently earned wealth is sufficient to send Defoe into a rapture, his rational bliss is primarily derived from a comprehensive exposure of its systemic operation. As it turns out, his rational ravishment actually consists in his *victory* over seduction by a beautiful but deceptive show. In this model of appreciation, aesthetic delight actually consists in nothing but rational penetration, for, as we shall see, Defoe soon reveals that he is being ravished by a "monster": this does not bother him, since he, like Marvell's garden-dweller, is able to requite the ravishment with a spectatorial annihilation.

He first complains that conventional appreciations of the Thames either focus myopically on its surface appearance, or are mediated by "the Humour of the ancient Poets." He announces that he will "sing you no

Songs" describing the mythic origin of the river in the couplings of pagan gods, but rather "I shall speak of the River as Occasion presents, as it really is *made glorious*": by revealing its role in a larger system, "I expect both to inform and divert my Readers, and speak, in a more Masculine Manner . . . and also more to their Satisfaction, than I could do any other way" (1: 173–174). In strict obedience to the gendered contrast between surface and depth we have encountered throughout this book, Defoe's way of looking promises the virtual witness a more masculine form of satisfaction. Rationally reconstructed as a material symptom, the splendor of the Thames is then subjected to further diagnostic scrutiny, one that reveals a disconcertingly different face of "the Luxuriant Age which we live in." Returning to consider the reasons for the sudden growth of London, particularly its outlying parts, he explains that the feature of the city "most deserving a Stranger's Observation"—and thus deserving of his own innocent sight—is "that prodigious Paper Commerce, called *Stock-Jobbing*," so extensive that taxes on transfers of stock alone annually bring thousands of pounds to the government. Because so many families are "deeply concerned in those Stocks," they find it "absolutely necessary to be at Hand to take the Advantage of buying and selling" (1: 337–338). The necessity imposed by the imaginary money form, referring to nothing beyond the paper itself, has led London and its outlying districts to attain proportions that are not merely generous, but monstrous. Defoe predicts that soon the city will subsume all of Chelsea, "which if it should once happen, what a Monster must *London* be" (1: 391). The "prodigious Conflux" of people has made London not just a large city, but an overgrown one, which "sucks the Vitals of Trade in this Island to itself." This monstrous overgrowth is responsible for the lovely London suburbs, but it is also "the chief Reason of any decay of Business" in towns like Ipswich.[105]

The beauty of the London suburbs was proverbial; Eden as first seen through the eyes of Milton's Satan prompts an extended metaphor of a day trip from the city to the suburbs that delights and refreshes the senses. It requires a perspective as innocent as that of the first couple to perceive in the midst of one's delight that "overgrown" and "luxuriant" parts of Creation need to be "lopped" in the interests of reform. By looking on the familiar suburbs of London with an estranged eye, Defoe reaches just this conclusion, for he is seeing ahead. He observes that towns that have managed to survive London's monstrous growth have "some particular Trade or

Accident to Trade, which is a kind of *Nostrum* to them, inseparable to the Place, and which fixes there by the Nature of the Thing; as the Herring-Fishery to *Yarmouth*."[106] He predicts, moreover, that the unruly semiosis of stock-jobbing will come to a bad end: then "the vast Concourse of People to *London,* will separate again and disperse as naturally, as they have now crouded hither: What will be the Fate then of all the fine Buildings in the Out Parts, in such a Case, let any one judge" (1: 339). The ruins of Nineveh appear before our eyes.

Stripping away the veneer of fabulous traditions about the country, Defoe has shown us that its real beauty resides in its "mechanism." His observational method both informs and diverts, presenting the country anew as the source of a rational delight. As rational celebration shades into diagnosis, however, the object of his gaze is transformed. Underneath his diagnostic scrutiny, the beautiful economic and cultural center of Britain, with its delightfully expanding suburbs, reveals itself to be a monster, rapaciously sucking the vitals from its neighbors and driving them to nostrums for their survival. Aesthetic pleasure attaches to the analytical pleasure of "reading" or penetrating a beguiling sensuous exterior to expose its subtext, defined as its material conditions of possibility. Appreciating the prospect "in *Perspective,*" the "critical spectator" (like the modern critic engaged in ideology critique) finds delight in the exposure of a monstrous substrate. What Defoe unveils suggests the Chaos beneath Eden, making its presence known through a riotously "wanton" growth that manages to be beautiful and "unsightly" at once, releasing the simultaneously appreciative and interventionist energies of the innocently curious beholder.[107] Of course, his opening boast that "I shall speak of the River as Occasion presents" also conjures up Boyle's reflector, who takes the occasions offered by providence to reshape it, and Defoe seeks to improve all he sees. Where some objects of speculation are concerned, however, the urge to critique makes aesthetic delight impossible: Defoe looks past the great pile of Westminster Hall ("'tis like a great Pile of something") and makes short work of the memorials in the abbey, some of which are "rather pompously Foolish, than Solid and to the Purpose," in his hurry to discourse on the social equality of ashes and dust (1: 366–367).

But in one extended section of the *Tour,* Defoe adopts this penetrating critical strategy toward material that has been specifically designed to thwart rational scrutiny. Here, he manages to perform a critical intervention that fuses looking with intervening, transforming what he sees in the very act of describing it. Defoe introduces this section with a flourish:

> And now I come to this wonderful Place, the *Peak,* where you will expect I should do as some others have, (I think, foolishly) done before me, *viz.* tell you strange long Stories of Wonders as (I must say) they are most weakly call'd . . . Now to have so great a Man as Mr. *Hobbes,* and after him Mr. *Cotton,* celebrate the Trifles here . . . as if they were the most exalted Wonders of the World; I cannot but, after wondering at their making Wonders of them, desire you, my Friend, to travel with me through this houling Wilderness in your Imagination, and you shall soon find all that is wonderful about it. (2: 566–567)

The comic repetition of *wonder,* which appears in this section in every grammatical permutation, is intended to make us snort at the fools who seek wonders in a howling wilderness. Defoe sustains the bathos throughout the section by relentless repetition of the word—referring to "the *Wonderless* Wonders of the *Peak,*" he suggests that the real wonder is that such wonderless wonders could be paraded as wonderful, contentedly parading his insight into the gap between word and thing.[108] Defoe encourages the reader to regard himself as a fellow participant in the campaign against wonder; he appeals to him—"my Friend"—in rational solidarity against the superstitious awe on which the popularity of the legendary Peak district depends. The good humor fades quickly enough as Defoe gets down to interrogating the sources of the Peak's popularity, redescribing its wonders as easily explained natural phenomena and indignantly protesting against such impositions on the public's understanding. But through laborious critique, the value of the experience is salvaged, transforming each apparent wonder into the occasion for an object lesson in true discernment. Although "*Peak* people . . . are mighty fond of having Strangers shewed every Thing they can, and of calling everything a Wonder," Defoe transforms each wonder he is shown into an object of spectatorial resistance.[109]

Defoe's immediate aim is straightforward; he intends to demonstrate that every apparent wonder in this area has a sound material explanation; the Peak is no more wonderful than the laws of nature themselves. Devil's Arse, for example, is simply a chasm; the only wonder is that "our Ancestors should give it so homely a Sirname" (2: 579). Tideswell, a spring that ebbs and flows like the sea, is just a small basin at the end of a stream with small openings on either end; water flows in, is contracted, and thus flows out "with a bubbling Noise" until the basin swells up again:

> and then the same Causes produce the same Effects, as will always be while the World endures. So that all this Wonder is owing only to the Situation of the Place, which is a meer Accident in Nature; and if any Person were to dig into the Place, and give vent to the Air, which fills the contracted Space within, they would soon see *Tideswell* turned into an ordinary running Stream, and a very little one too. (2: 581)

Defoe reveals the phenomenon to be a predictable result of unremarkable causes, and even designs an experiment that would confirm his hypothesis: one has only to "dig into the Place" to discern the influence of its situation.[110]

Throughout this section, Defoe instructs the observer in how to "dig into" wonders both physically and rationally. Having revealed the wonders of the Peak to be wonderless, he focuses on how its wondrous atmosphere might be dispelled. As one of the first tourist attractions in England, the Peak District was not just a geographical but a cultural site; the experience of visitors to the district was mediated by the legends propagated through what David Stafford has called "Restoration Peak discourse."[111] Sheer exaggeration, particularly of heights and depths, was typical of this discourse; so the arch of Poole's Hole is "far from what a late flaming Author has magnified it to," a quarter of a mile perpendicular (576). Defoe gets to work to straighten out the relationship between these words and the things of the Peak, but his project is not simply to correct vague, misleading, or exaggerated accounts; it is a crusade against a certain kind of aesthetic experience, one based on the wrong kind of "magnification." It is the manner in which these attractions are presented to unwary strangers, the incipient tourist industry itself, that Defoe wants to dig into and disable.

The microscopic examination of pictures and "gaudy trinkets" undertaken by his son-in-law Henry Baker provides the model for Defoe's critical approach to the most popular Peak attraction, Poole's Hole.[112] Baker's "experiment," we recall, demonstrated that the products of art were "a Concealment of Deformity, an Imposition upon our Want of Sight," and that our admiration for most of it "arises from our Ignorance of what it really is"; Defoe enters Poole's Hole with the same intent, to respond to what he sees not as a sentient man but as a corrective lens.[113] What he discovers is that one's eyes are dazzled in the damp cave because the guides hold candles that reflect the drops of water clinging to the cave walls, creating "ten thousand Rainbows in miniature." Rather than surrender to gaping wonder at this pleasant and purportedly mysterious effect, the future visitor to the cave is advised to "try the Experiment" he has devised: "take a long Pole in his hand, with a Cloth tied to the end of it, and mark any Place of the shining spangled Roof which his Pole will reach to; and then, wiping the drops of Water away, he shall see he will at once extinguish all those Glories," revealing them to be a "Fraud, a meer *deceptio visus*" (577). In fact the cave has no more beauty than "the Back of a Chimney; for, in short, the Stone is coarse, slimy, *with the constant wet,* dirty and dull; and were the little drops of Water gone, or the Candles gone, there would be none of these fine Sights to be seen for Wonders" (577). Rather than regard this optical effect as an opportunity for pleasure, Defoe treats it as a base attempt at deception, an imposition on the unwary visitors' want of sight. This is a critical intervention in every sense, for Defoe actually disables the spectacle in what is almost an act of vandalism. As he complains, earlier writers had compared the cave's "spangled Roof" to cathedral architecture, describing "*Fret Work,* Organ, and *Choir Work*"; Defoe is defacing a figurative church (577, 576). But this intervention instructs more than simple iconoclastic defacement ever could: Defoe imparts to his readers the tool of experiment as a means of rational resistance to those who would seek to impose upon their susceptibility to "fine sights." Penetrating the cave with his pole, Defoe shows us how to transform fine sights, as Hooke transformed fossils, into testimonials of their own production. Penetrating visible effects to make their causes visible, he aggressively insinuates himself inside the production of the spectacle and reveals its "mechanism." With a simple pole, Defoe manages to do for a moment what Power predicted would only be accomplished by lenses: liberate the senses from their thralldom to secondary effects like color altogether.

In this experimentalist retelling of the Platonic fable, physical investigation permits a rational and masculine alternative to "Women's Tales" of the Peak (579). The masculine satisfaction Defoe gains by means of his pole is an extension of his approach to observing the outlying districts of London; recognition of beauty gives way to a spectatorial penetration, and Adam the delver again turns up in the form of the digging eye. Baker articulates the assumption governing Defoe's experiment in his poem *The Universe:* "Pleasure casts a Mist" before the eyes of the unwary, but "Reasons's piercing Eye / Discerns those Truths our Senses can't descry."[114] The observer unleashes a penetrating visual faculty that is conceived of as separate from the body; by "seeing" with his reason, he confers on himself a sort of immunity to organic perceptual limitations, and is empowered to transform every "fine sight" into a discovery.

The fact that the cave turns out to be dirty and dull does not make it an unworthy object of Defoe's investigation. Sprat insisted that no matter was too mean for the virtuoso to study; as we recall from Boyle's occasional meditations, it is a source of pride to the investigator to demonstrate "how low" he "can stoop." But in permitting his experimental perspective to perform its disciplinary work on popular perceptions, the professional observer insists that it is celebrated objects of beauty that require him to stoop the lowest. Milton had had to stoop to lift the "court fucus" from the king's image, set out to "catch fools and silly gazers"; by taking apart this idol, Milton had hoped to denaturalize the institution of monarchy itself, to peel back its surface and reveal a constructed and therefore changeable nature. It was experimentalist observation that allowed this once embattled spectatorial ideal of intellectual labor to flourish: here, rather than presenting himself as an inspired image-smasher, Defoe can present himself as curator of an "Experiment."

As it turns out, Defoe's attempt to travel "in a critical manner" was a political act in a more concrete sense. Given his pretensions to high neutrality, it is shocking to discover that many of his "circuits" were undertaken as intelligence missions for Robert Harley. Defoe's self-identification as "one whose Business is Observation" has a different ring when we imagine it spoken by a Secret Service agent.[115] But it is worth considering how Defoe's private work as a spy might have shaped his public identity as a vocational spectator. It is interesting to discover, for example, that Harley also tried to enroll Addison and Steele as agents, for a letter that Defoe wrote to Harley in which he celebrated his own "circumspection" during his tour of Scotland brings Mr. Spectator to mind:

> I am Perfectly Unsuspectd as Corresponding with anybody in England. I Converse with Presbyterian, Episcopall-Dissenter, papist and Non Juror, and I hope with Equall Circumspection . . . I Talk to Everybody in Their

Own Way. To the Merchants I am about to Settle here in Trade, Building ships &c. With the Lawyers I Want to purchase a House and Land to bring my family & live Upon it . . . To day I am Goeing into Partnership with a Membr of parliamt in a Glass house, to morrow with Another in a Salt work. With the Glasgow Mutineers I am to be a fish Merchant, with the Aberdeen Men a woollen and with the Perth and western men a Linen Manufacturer . . . I am in the Morning at the Committee, in the Afternoon in the Assembly, I am privy to all their folly, I wish I Could not Call it knavery, and am Entirely Confided in.[116]

Materializing in so many contexts, Defoe seems omnipresent, talking to the "mutineers" and aristocrats by whom he is by turns surrounded with equal ease. Talking to everybody in "Their Own Way," Defoe erases his own way of talking; he becomes "privy" to the interests of every member of the public by not standing for any himself. Accompanying this lack of a firmly held personal identity is an ability to penetrate the "folly" and "knavery" in each of the identities he provisionally assumes. Through "Circumspection" in his personal address, he achieves circumspection in the etymological sense, for Defoe boasts that by such means he has produced a comprehensive anatomy of the country, uncovering all that lies beneath the notice of a superficial observer: from the West Country, for example, he is able to send to Harley "a perfect skeleton of this part of England."[117] Chicanery and investigative labor combine to produce an anatomy of the nation.

Defoe's task in Scotland was not simply to gauge the extent of popular support for the Act of Union but to increase it. He was to do this not by speaking passionately in favor of the Union but by making judicious and neutral-sounding observations to everyone with whom he came into contact. As we will see, this persuasive method, in which the art of describing converged with the art of prescribing, is very close to that employed by Mr. Spectator. Defoe employs this technique on the reader of the *Tour,* offering a neutral-sounding "mechanical" account of England that permits him to interweave policy prescriptions with seemingly objective observations of physical phenomena. Defoe had no qualms about misrepresenting himself as a visitor to Mecca as well as the South Seas in order to enhance his credibility as an experienced observer. But in addition to pretending to a neutrality and wealth of experience he lacks, he actually goes out of his way to convince the reader that he is a High Church Anglican, thus seeming to risk an affiliation that would taint his perspective with prejudice. But this pretense provides him with ample opportunities for ingenuous confessions of "surprise" at the various signs of the growing influence of dissenting faiths across the country. In Biddeford, he is startled to meet a dissenting minister who, contrary to expectation, had "nothing Soure, Cynical, or Morose in him" (1: 260). And in Southwold,

> I was surprized to see an extraordinary large Church, capable of receiving five or six thousand People, and but Twenty-seven in it besides the Parson and the Clerk; but at the same time the Meeting-House of the *Dissenters* was full to the very Doors, having, as I guess'd from 6 to 800 People in it. (1: 56)

An Anglican would certainly be "surprized" to see the dominance of dissenting faiths in town after town, and he could never be accused of partiality for remarking on it. Defoe does not insist too strenuously on his religious affiliation, because he does not want to be limited by it; he wants to retain his freedom to smirk at popish ornamentation, for example. For such commentary to have maximum impact, it must be outweighed by indications of utter aloofness from allegiances, passions, and interests of any kind. So when he passes over civil war sites at Marston Moor, he declares that "'twas none of our Business to concern our Passions in the Cause."[118] His spectatorial persona appears to us as the product of honest labor, but also as the office of a man whose only business is to be unconcerned.

Defoe's ability to provisionally adopt the perspective of each person he met, and even to ventriloquize his ideological enemies in order to stage reluctant and therefore apparently unprejudiced "admissions" of his actual beliefs, was no doubt related to his actual investigative talents. His personal elasticity permits him to be comfortable with the cave-dwelling family of a Derbyshire miner, in whose company he manages to adjust his perspective and expectations so that he is able to discern that their home is actually quite "clean and neat," a welcome alternative to Plato's cave of appearance housed in the Peak (2: 569). And despite his rabid anti-Catholicism, when he visits Durham Cathedral and inspects the vestments of the old clergy, he comments that they "are so rich with embroidery and emboss'd work of Silver, that indeed it was a kind of a Load to stand under them," which suggests that he actually tried them on.[119] Actually assuming the robes of the papist, Defoe can provide us with a report of the excesses of the old religion from the inside. Like Milton's perspectival epic, in which even the devil was ventriloquized with apparent conviction, Defoe is compelled to try all things.[120]

In his later career, Defoe disguised himself in print by writing on every side of political questions in no less than half a dozen journals, collapsing the different stages of Marchamont Nedham's career as a flip-flopping and thus disinterested observer of the contemporary scene. Having infiltrated Nathaniel Mist's *Weekly Journal,* a Tory paper, Defoe complained that he was being forced to play a role he found abhorrent,

> I am Sir for This Service, Posted among Papists, Jacobites, and Enraged High Torys, a Generation who I Profess My Very Soul abhorrs; I am Oblig'd to hear Traytcrous Expressions, and Outrageous Words against his Majties Person, and Governmt, and his Most faithfull Servants; and Smile at it all as if I Approv'd it.[121]

Even in this confession of distress, however, there is a sense of pride in a job well done. Smiling as he murmurs his assent, Defoe, like Hooke, is willing to bitc his tongue and refrain from bearing witness to his beliefs—and even to bear false witness, if by doing so he can serve as an instrument of discovery. Like the virtuoso, he forces his objects of study to reveal their true nature by refusing to act in accordance with his own. George Starr has analyzed how casuistry's exploration of context-dependent perspectives, encouraging the provisional assumption of serial identities on the part of writer (and absorbed reader), laid the foundation for the extended first-person narratives that Defoe composed; casuistry's thought experiments might look forward as well to the epistemological experiments of free indirect narration.[122] But they also conditioned the construction of the spectatorial author, offering a means for the experimentalist model of vocational observation to be extended into the realm of culture. It stands to reason that the *Athenian Mercury,* the first periodical of popular science, was also a work of popular casuistry, the first "agony column" in English literary history, as Helen Berry calls it. By considering situations from a variety of subject positions, the casuist asymptotically approached what Thomas Nagel calls the "the view from nowhere," and what a Baconian would call the view from paradise.[123] As an independent in politics as well as religion, who was proud to be neither Whig nor Tory, Defoe perhaps believed he was closer to such a view than most. But to firmly identify himself with this view, he had to strive to be a nobody. Defoe's popular biographer Richard West observes that with Defoe,

> we face the problem that no contemporaries seem to have found him worthy of note. In all the letters and journals of prominent men and women of the early eighteenth century we look in vain for a mention of him. Even the hostile lampoonists, who vilified Defoe as a turncoat and devil, never ascribed to him any particular personal characteristic . . . even if he had wished to, Dr Johnson could not have filled a page on the character of Defoe.[124]

Such social invisibility resulted partly from the fact that Defoe was not a gentleman, but he refined this spectatorial privilege through his shifting, even somewhat shifty, self-presentations. To lay claim to the status of personal nonentity was to be able to distinguish oneself almost purely through acts of witness, allowing interventionist vision to stand where a self would normally be.

For Fiennes and Defoe, such acts were a means to promote an "Idea of England"; clearly, teaching people to view things in perspective advanced the work of nation-building.[125] But the nation under construction was a special kind: what Sprat had called "a Land of *Experimental knowledge*," a land of innocent observers. Despite Defoe's near-idolatry of wealth, he is determined to help his reader "see through" both the unproductive massing of wealth under a title and the imaginary profit generated by speculation around an empty sign, going so far as to refer to stock-jobbing as a "new invented sort of *Deceptio Visus*," like the imposture of Poole's Hole itself.[126] In the Peak, his apparent willingness to admire any money-making venture meets its limit; here, he tries to "dig into" and dig up a potentially lucrative local tourist industry: the attempt to extract profit from wonder, with all the suppression of critical scrutiny that this entails, appears to him a sort of sacrilege.[127] Again and again, such acts of vision lead us through the veil of appearance and back to things themselves, the ground of productive labor, which he also, of course, presents as the ground of his own speculations. To chasten the nation's sight, Defoe even attempts to behave as an optical instrument, extending to his readers the prosthetic tool of "experiment" for the ends of critique—a pole that is at once a spade and a lens. That he was also a political instrument being manipulated by Harley reveals the fundamental tension of the literature of professional observation: the readers to whom the professional observer appealed as virtual witnesses were also his experimental subjects.

Surveying the Gaping Throng: The Observer as Cultural Critic

The *Journeys* and the *Tour* are straightforward extensions of Royal Society literature: Fiennes and Defoe's literature of testimony focuses on all the processes through which nature is transformed by art and even tries to provide material explanations for natural phenomena. But if these works draw on the models of histories of trades and experimental relations, they also extend the spectatorial model of intellectual labor beyond subjects of scientific interest, adapting the virtuosi's techniques to the scrutiny of the human world rather than creation. As professional observers turned their attention to topics even less readily identified with experimental science—street life, courting styles, fashion, and high literary culture—they made bolder and more provocative use of the virtuosi's topoi, insisting more rather than less strenuously on their experimentalist credentials. Such compensatory insistence generated comically incongruous self-presentations, particularly in the persona of Mr. Spectator. As I will show, however, the comedy generated by his misapplication of experimentalist methods merely reproduced the paradoxes of experimentalist identity itself. Addison and Steele's achievement can best be appreciated through comparison with the observational personas fabricated by Ned Ward, Tom Brown, and Steele himself, whose construction to some degree interfered with their ability to work as interventionist instruments.

As I have suggested, these observers define themselves through the topos of experiential literacy: to become literate in the world, they insist, one has to take the physical pains to travel through it; thus the London Spy refers to his rambles as his labors. Rambling provides opportunities for slumming, which, according to a by now familiar paradox, permits an elevation on the scale of being. The London Spy's conversion from schoolman to investigator is sparked by his realization that he has become Aristotle's "sumpter-horse." The reduction of schoolman to beast of burden recalls Milton's complaint in *The Reason of Church Government* about being forced to contend with "sumpters."[128] In that passage, Milton had identified true gentility and honor as the product of pains, and though these pains were not literally physical ones, those were never far from his mind; Milton persistently invoked "sinewy" muscular energy in his celebrations of intellectual labor, and, in the epigraph to this chapter, his protest against the "slacknesse of discipline" leads ineluctably to a consideration of the care of the "outward vessel."[129] It was "not for every learned, or every wise man . . . to invent or frame a discipline": such a man had to be one "in whom contemplation and practice" were "rarely met." Within the mythology elaborated around the professional observer, as in Milton, this "rare" meeting of contemplation and practice bore fruit in spectatorial privilege: an ability to "comprehend the hidden causes of things."

Tom Brown introduces his observations of London life by drawing an exemplary contrast between those "who are qualified to Read and Understand the Book of the World" and those who "have no other knowledge of the World, but what they collect from Books." While the former "may be beneficial to the Publick," the latter "are not fit to give Instructions to others." Fitness here settles on both mind and body, suggesting a fully animated, engaged, and intellectually productive observer, with the sterile, retired bookworm serving as the necessary foil. "Nothing will please some Men, but Books stuff'd with antiquity, groaning under the weight of Learned Quotations drawn from the Fountains. And what is all this but pilfering [?]" Brown will pillage the world itself; following him on his "ramble," the reader can experience what it is like to read "the Book of the World" in "the Original."[130] To read this book will scarcely be like reading at all; the reader is invited to take a journey of discovery into a new world that lies just behind the familiar one.

We are by now well acquainted with the tension generated by the observer's simultaneous insistence on bodily exertion and bodily transcendence, but in proclaiming their experiential literacy in the realm of manners, these writers had to cope with a further paradox: while the spectator had to assert his literacy in the social world, such literacy also destabilized his authority as an epistemologically privileged innocent observer. In their use of the topos of nature's book, virtuosi had promoted an ideal of epistemological parsimony, locating the authority of the virtuoso in the Adamic innocence of his eye. Hooke had advised the aspiring philosopher to regard even the most "common" phenomena as if "they were the greatest Rarity, and to imagine himself a Person of some other Country or Calling, that he had never heard of, or seen anything of the like before."[131] Defoe had accordingly focused on phenomena he considered "most deserving a Stranger's Observation," and he had impersonated that unprepossessed, hence far-seeing, stranger while observing them. But the professional observer could not claim trustworthy knowledge about the contemporary scene simply by appealing to his lack of preconceptions about it; his job was to make it legible. An innocent observer might be able to notice minute variations in dress, behavior, and speech in a crowd of people, but a spare sensory language was not adequate to describe what Locke called civil life; this domain was the product of convention and shared understandings, of words and ideas as much as things. In addition to the basic tension between bodily exertion and bodily transcendence, then, satiric professional observers had to negotiate the opposing claims of innocence and fallenness, naivete and sophistication, for they sought to claim the privileges of the outsider and the insider at once.

Although the demands of a cultural observational field made it difficult for the professional observer to emulate the distinctive combination of innocence and expertise of the virtuoso who investigated nature, these traits could be distributed across two observers easily enough. Satiric professional observers duly created literary counterparts of unprepossessed investigators—the country rube or the foreigner. They saw with "other eyes," uncorrupted by local prejudice and corrupt custom, and were equipped to make the familiar strange. Thus Tom Brown has the ultimate authority of a London insider, and for a fresh perspective he avails himself of an Indian companion, to whom everything is a surprise: "We shall see how he will be amazed at certain things, which the Prejudice of Custom makes to seem Reasonable and Natural to us." The foreignness of his associate is a purely functional characteristic rather than a source of independent interest; he is present to function as a prosthetic instrument of unprepossessed vision that Brown can use and discard at will. But Brown is not content to let each function reside in its own character; he wants to unite them somehow:

> To diversifie the stile of my Narration, I will sometimes make my Traveller speak, and sometimes I will take up the Discourse myself. I will represent to my self the abstracted Ideas of an *Indian,* and I will likewise represent ours

to him. In short, taking it for granted that we two understand one other by half a word, I will set both his and my Imagination on the Ramble. Those that won't take the Pains to follow us, may stay where they are, and spare themselves the trouble of reading farther in the Book.[132]

Brown makes a demand of his reader: she will have to "take the Pains to follow us." Adapting her style of reading to the double focalization of the narrative, she will experience her virtual ramble as the journey of two subjects at once. The imaginations of the traveler and the native are independent, yet as an instrument of truth, Brown's language will construct a perspective from which the "ideas" of both can be experienced, giving that perspective at least a discursive existence through a diversified narrative voice in which the imaginations of each can wander. The reader must take it for granted that "we two understand one other by half a word"; this intimacy justifies the near-integration of their voices and perceptions, which attain their ultimate union in the receptive (and painstaking) reader, who can now experience for herself the impossible conjunction of innocence and experience in worldly matters, gaining the objective experimental lessons that *personal* experience could never provide. Although Brown's dithering produces a disjointed effect, his attempt to convert a balancing act into a near-integration of the perspectives of the insider and outsider lays bare the mechanism that makes the spectator-as-cultural-critic work. In *The London Spy*, Ned Ward attaches these perspectives to a single observer using a strategy of temporal distribution: initially a country rube (though, as we have seen, a somewhat bookish one), the London Spy soon makes snide asides that indicate his increasingly sophisticated grasp of urban culture. The switch, however, is sudden, making the London Spy less a dynamic than an incoherent character. Moreover, this strategy excludes the possibility of an integration of these two perspectives, unlike Brown's innovative solution (which, however, is not pursued with any rigor).[133] These glitches in the self-presentations of early professional observers suggest their groping to develop a persona that could exploit an "innocent" perspective for critical purposes without being subject to its limitations.

These purposes were those of cultural criticism. The paradigm for the spectator's critical interventions is laid out in Defoe's *Tour*. Here, aesthetic pleasure is the symptom of a material cause that has to be diagnosed to yield rational satisfaction. Such diagnosis usually manages to undo the initial appreciative response without destroying it altogether. Defoe's appreciative meditation on the outlying districts of London, which he suggested could only provide a truly rational delight if analyzed as a symptom of "the luxuriant Age which we live in," finally became a diagnosis of a monstrous birth. But when Defoe invaded Poole's Hole with his pole, what he intended for the experiment to prove was never in doubt; appearances would once again be unmasked as deceiving. The cultural criticism of satiric professional observers for the most part follows the latter model: they do not bother with the appreciative interlude, and instead leap immediately to the diagnosis and condemnation of cultural products of all kinds. Like Defoe, professional observers insinuate themselves between the transmission of cultural messages and their reception, providing their readers with a viewing immunity capable of transforming what Ward called "senseless" entertainments into lessons in cultural literacy. While professional observers might attend a low entertainment, they, like Hooke's "Philosophical Historian" regarding nature's spectacle, had "somewhat else to do than admire" what they saw. The London Spy can hardly contain his disgust with members of "the gazing multitude" who regard a tin squeaker used in a puppet show as "a piece of conjuration" as great "as ever was performed by Dr Faustus," but while members of "the gaping throng" go to street fairs to feast their eyes on senseless spectacles, he attends in order to "take a survey," to "overlook the follies of the innumerable throng."[134] Like Fiennes at St. Mungo's Well, he is not doing the same thing as everyone else around him. The reader's instruction begins when she recognizes the contrast between these two perspectives, and the very different experiences they produce.

The professional observer faced a difficult challenge in coming up with convincing ways to present himself as disassociated from his own sensory apparatus, which he shared in common with the gaping throng. This Ward can barely do. He responds without detachment to his experience; he is too immersed in the objects of his scrutiny, arguing and singing in prisons and taverns with the very throng whose stupid diversions he attempts to anatomize.[135] Defoe, as we have seen, was most successful in doing so under especially contrived experimental conditions. Mr. Spectator's predecessor, Isaac Bickerstaff, was in this sense no better off than other professional observers. Although the stated aim of the *Tatler* was spectatorial instruction, Bickerstaff was not a persona whose observations inspired automatic trust.[136] At this stage, Steele still conceived of the project of spectatorial education in openly polemical terms. Indeed, the references in early numbers of the *Tatler* to "Pretenders" that needed to be exposed linked the project quite closely to Milton's exposure of Charles I.[137] The *Tatler*'s aim was "to open Men's Eyes," to promote the aim of "Discovery": "to expose the false Arts of Life, to pull off the Disguises of Cunning, Vanity, and Affectation" (1: 7, 8). Leaning on the virtuosi's opposition of words and things, Bickerstaff complained that the "Imposition of honest Names and Words upon improper Subjects, has made so regular a Confusion amongst us, that we are apt to sit down with our Errors, well enough satisfied," rather than trying to "deliver our selves from the Tyranny under which we are reduc'd" (1: 347–348). He intends to provide assistance to "ordinary Minds," which were apt to be "wholly govern'd by their Eyes and Ears" (1: 456). But rather than encouraging his ordinary readers to look for themselves through his text into the world, the gregarious Bickerstaff announced his intention to *tell* on people. Though this persona was also supposed to be sociable, his "tatling" civil and eloquent, his observations were merely the utterances of a single truth-telling man, not the products of a public instrument of truth.[138] The resolution of this difficulty began with silencing the *Tatler* altogether. Replacing the garrulous Isaac Bickerstaff with a pathologically taciturn eyewitness, Addison and Steele presented their new literary project as the embodiment not of a gossipy and at times hectoring voice, but of a curious—and crucially monstrous—eye.[139]

"One of Another Species": The Construction of Mr. Spectator

The speaker of a "diversified narration" must affect obliviousness to the contradictions posed by the hybrid of his persona, or even deny that it is a hybrid at all. The innocent observer who discourses in an implausibly sophisticated and knowing manner about what he sees bears some resemblance to Empson's hybrid pastoral speaker, but, rather than an impossible union of class positions, this speaker embodies a basically inhuman blend of epistemologies. Brown and Ward do not quite pull off the trick; in providing excuses for the doubleness of their perspective they call attention to it. To escape the liabilities of being both a man on the inside and a man on the outside, the spectator had to strive to become a different kind of being altogether. This was the achievement of Mr. Spectator, who joins innocence and experience so seamlessly as to create the effect of a unity. Most himself when humbly registering his "surprise" at some trendy absurdity his readers would probably have taken for granted, or been guilty of, Mr. Spectator seems to be at once a cosmopolitan Londoner and a perpetually startled newcomer, eliciting our amused condescension and deference at once. The world as seen through his eyes is at once alien and familiar, like a mundane object placed under the microscope. Before Addison and Steele, Samuel Johnson remarked, "England had no masters of common life"; the common life had never before been made the object of such studiously innocent observation.[140]

Mr. Spectator summed up his ambitions by stating simply that "it has been my Ambition, in the Course of my Writings, to restore, as well as I was able, the proper Ideas of Things." He would restore his readers to the world in which they already lived, but did not yet perceive. To a greater extent than any author this study has yet considered, Addison and Steele's persona was identified with an ideal spectatorial body, modeled on the artificial organs of the microscope and telescope: a walking instrument of truth, possessed of the virtuoso's insight but unencumbered by the virtuoso's body. Mr. Spectator did not meddle "with any Practical Part in Life," yet he was "a Speculative Statesman, Soldier, Merchant and Artizan."[141] There was no need for him to undertake transient apprenticeships, like Fiennes; he could pass through these callings virtually, like a Lockean angel. Initial responses to this "Looker-on" were mixed. Delariviere Manley asked, "Why chuse to be an idle Spectator, rather than a Celebrator of those Actions he [Addison] well knows how to define and adorn?" Manley seems to imply that if he were going to remain on the sidelines, he should at least do his minimal duty and *celebrate* the active life. A hostile critic who called himself "the Spy upon the Spectator" doubted that "a meer Spectator" could be capable of "any great Performances."[142] Such critics were not yet prepared to entertain the idea that "looking on" might itself qualify as a great performance. Determined to expose the man behind the spectatorial office, the Spy on the Spectator insisted that Mr. Spectator's "creeping behavior" and equally creepy ocular obsessions were unworthy of a "Gentleman." Mr. Spectator famously introduced himself as an observer of mankind rather than "one of the Species," and this critic found this self-characterization altogether accurate: the first issue seemed to him to represent "the Author as a Monster."[143] As the bearer of a spectatorial body,

Mr. Spectator did indeed place himself in an exceptional relation to the rest of the species, but his awkward and inhuman self-presentation conferred extraordinary privileges on his creators.

Following Boyle's example, Addison always liked to confound texts and lenses. In an oration in defense of the new science delivered at Oxford in 1693, he described optical instruments in suggestively textual terms: "We no longer pay a blind veneration to that barbarous Peripatetic jingle, those obscure scholastic terms of art, once held as oracles, but consult the dictates of our own senses, and by late invented engines force Nature herself to discover plainly her most hidden recesses."[144] While elevating the book of nature over books themselves, Addison alludes to Milton's dismissal of rhyme as the "jingling sound of like endings . . . the Invention of a barbarous Age, to set off wretched matter." Having likened scholastic language to rhyming blather, a "barbarous" menace to the referential function of language, he contrasts it with the plain visual evidence provided by the "late invented engines" of optical devices. Recalling the active trope of Hooke's *Micrographia,* he describes these data textually, as "dictates"—things dictated and copied down. The *OED* reveals that the scribal connotation was alive in contemporary usage: that which is uttered in order to be written down; a dictated utterance; the monitions of a written law. Paying heed to these dictates, "we" abandon an obscure scholastic language and use optical instruments to dictate to Nature, forcing her to "plainly discover" her "hidden recesses." Invoking the privatest recess of Cowley's coy nature, Addison associates these engines with phallic force; the passive voice of "held," appropriate to describe abject superstition ("terms of art, once held as oracles"), has matured into active discovery, a kind of looking that is also an acting upon. Although Addison is content to let the sexual undertone rest without elaboration—an expression of his "modesty" that so impressed his contemporaries—such bravado nonetheless seems a far cry from the *Spectator.* Yet it was Mr. Spectator's modest self-effacement, and, indeed, his bodily absurdity, that promoted his identification with the "late invented engines" whose "force" Addison so admired.[145] The *Spectator* papers were also interventionist tools, through which the book of the world and all its characters would first be made legible, then recomposed.

Explaining that his own literary tastes tended toward those authors who enable the reader to become "a kind of Spectator," Mr. Spectator claimed that "among this Sett of Writers, there are none who more gratifie and enlarge the Imagination, than the Authors of the new Philosophy." His explication of what they "authored," however, makes no mention of books; it deals exclusively with the ocular "Discoveries they have made by Glasses," which expand the realm of the visual beyond what human sight "in Conjunction with the Body" can attain (3: 574, 577). Through this strategic confusion of glasses and texts, Mr. Spectator defines the "Author" as one who extends perception. His "more than ordinary Penetration in Seeing," of course, distinguished him as just such an author (1: 20). Just as he christens users of optical instruments authors, so he refers to his own works—in which he sought "to Print my self out, if possible, before I Die"—as lenses (1: 5). To "Men of no Taste nor Learning" who dismiss his daily "Speculations,"

> I must apply the Fable of the Mole, That after having consulted many Oculists for the bettering of his Sight, was at last provided with a good Pair of Spectacles; but upon his endeavouring to make use of them, his Mother told him very prudently, "That Spectacles, though they might help the Eye of a Man, could be of no use to a Mole." It is not therefore for the Benefit of Moles that I publish these my daily Essays. (1: 508)

Those who have "no use" for "bettering their sight" have no use for the *Spectator*, for, like "a good Pair of Spectacles," it imposes corrective discipline on the perception of its readers. Virtuosi had used the figure of the curious man as a groveling mole, "uncessantly labouring for light," to motivate the trope of the lens as spade, a prosthetic help with which the natural mole might dig further into creation than nature allowed: into and behind appearances themselves.[146] Here, the digger and the subject of spectatorial privilege part ways. The mole stands for an uncomprehending reader while the pair of spectacles—an instrument that works without "labouring"—stands for the insight of the author. By looking through the *Spectator* at the theater, the latest hatwear, and even *Paradise Lost* itself, contemporary readers could see what polite entertainment consisted in, what lapses of taste required correction, and what great literature was, but such insights, for Mr. Spectator, were merely percepts.[147]

Although the source of Addison's inspiration was clearly the optical instrument—along with the topos of the lens-user as a natural "literatus"—the decision he makes in this passage to compare the *Spectator* papers to the more modest prosthetic help of spectacles is easily explained. By domesticating the virtuoso's lens, Addison expunged its association with the virtuoso's work. He engaged his readers in virtual witnessing by suggesting that it could be undertaken casually, without effort; once one gets used to them, one is barely conscious of wearing glasses. As a paper published on a daily basis, the *Spectator* could be put to automatic use. By advertising its utility as a tool to see with, and to talk with, Addison and Steele gave the *Spectator* an instrumental but unthreatening character. Even an unfriendly commentator admitted that "you shou'd scarce find a Lady dressing, or drinking Tea in a Morning with her Friends, but Mr. *St–le's Paper* made up the best Part of the Entertainment" (as I discuss below, it was strategically valuable for enemies of this persona to identify it with Steele rather than Addison). Addison's image of a family sitting down to read the *Spectator* with breakfast similarly inserts the paper between the self and the world; it is a set of spectacles one puts on in the morning in order to perceive the world one will soon encounter.[148] As an instrument of discipline, however, it also functioned reflexively, as a "looking glass" with which a reader could discover what was "amiss" in herself.

In practice, the *Spectator* sought to replicate the effects of more powerful lens technology on its users, disciplining their vision while liberating it from thralldom to secondary effects; Mr. Spectator offered himself up as a pair of spectacles for spectacles. I have suggested that professional observers created and then met a public need for lessons in cultural discernment by representing consumers as visually illiterate, susceptible to wonder— "smitten with every thing that is showy and superficial"—and thus easily imposed upon by the other kind of spectacles. Mr. Spectator did the same, while relentlessly penetrating spectacle to its source: color. Focusing on the deception that provided the material conditions for all others, he observed that women had a weakness for "perpetually dazling one anothers Imaginations, and filling their Heads with nothing but Colours" (1: 66–67). Giving over significant space in the periodical to the popularization of Locke's account of the distinction between primary and secondary qualities, he made that distinction relevant to the processing of culture, modeling a detached superiority toward art that depended on "deceptive" secondary effects. If women would be less dazzled by the phenomenon of color itself, surely they would be less likely to flock to entertainments whose "only Design is to gratify the Senses": no less than dancing monkeys, rope dancers, or tumblers, opera could only "entertain that Part of the Audience who have no Faculty above Eyesight," who craved only "the Pleasure of the Ears and Eyes" (1: 22; 2: 56). By singling out "Eyesight" as a low faculty, he made clear that the agent of his own "looking on" was not the sensitive eye. Readers were made to see paintings themselves differently after encountering Mr. Spectator's observation that the public lavished praise on those that had nothing to recommend them beyond the "Show and Glare of Colours"; such paintings were "made for the Eyes only, as Rattles are made for Childrens Ears" (2: 447). But although Mr. Spectator could not tolerate the sound of bells on his coral when he was a baby, in pursuit of his ambition to "restore . . . the proper Ideas of Things," he finds that even "The Bell rings to the Puppet-Show . . . afford Matter of Speculation" to him (1: 2, 197, 196). Anticipating the modern convergence of low culture and high theory, he explains that he can "command my Attention at a *Puppet-Show* or an *Opera*, as well as at *Hamlet* or *Othello*" (1: 331). Having looked into the highest and lowest, Mr. Spectator is in no danger of being degraded by the objects of his observation, because they are the objects of his rational penetration and intervention rather than sources of unreflective pleasure. As Mr. Spectator explains when urging his readers to adhere to a disciplinary regimen of daily exercise, the world "furnishes Materials," but "we should work them up our selves"; a truly curious observer is one whose skill in such working up emerges regardless of how trifling the material (1: 472).

But the "Bodily Labour" that Mr. Spectator deemed "necessary for the proper Exertion of our intellectual Faculties," was, when he undertook it, no labor at all, for he was not a fully corporeal entity (1: 471). When Mr. Spectator moves through the fairs and marketplaces of London, he does so as a spectatorial rather than human body. He refers to his "late Rambles, or rather Speculations" around London, using the two nouns interchangeably; in Mr. Spectator, "traveling through" and "seeing through" have literally become the same activity (1: 14). His ontologically ambiguous status enables him to transform London into a viewing chamber where he "discovers" to us the contemporary scene in a state of apparent liberation from bodily constraints on perception. The virtuoso's coordination of physical and mental energy that Hooke figured through circulation becomes in Mr. Spectator a straightforward union.

The textual realization of this union, however, is anything but straightforward. Mr. Spectator's public appearances are impossible to visualize— hence undemanding for the reader to process because during them, he barely appears at all. He is different from the rest of the species, not just because he is "a queer modest Fellow," a "disaffected Person," or "a dumb Man" who cannot "talk like other People."[149] When he is recognized as a person, he gives a confoundingly unstable impression. He is mistaken for a Jesuit, a popish priest, a wizard, a murderer, a ghost (one correspondent calls him "the SPECTER"), and a *"White Witch,"* while his landlady finds it appropriate to treat him as a "domestick Animal."[150] These identifications, of course, expose the identities of those who make them rather than revealing anything about Mr. Spectator himself, aside from confirming his uncanny strangeness. The sense that there is something pathological about his body enables him to join the Ugly Club ("he need not disguise himself to make one of us"), yet he is not a candidate of "undoubted Qualifications" either (1: 133, 205). It is not simply that Mr. Spectator is ugly or deformed; his bodily difference is both more extreme and less easily identified: he is less physically *there* than other people. People see right past him on the street, and when they do notice him, it is only to identify him as "Mr. *what-d'ye-call-him.*" When one Londoner asks another who *"That strange Fellow"* is, he receives the reply: *"I have known the Fellow's Face these twelve Years, and so must you; but I believe you are the first ever asked who he was"* (1: 19). Even the notorious "shortness" of his face testifies to a certain bodily deficiency. One correspondent writes, "I had the Honour of seeing your short Face," and "have ever since thought your Person and Writings both extraordinary" (2: 131). The extraordinary nature of Mr. Spectator's writings depends on the extraordinariness of his body, which confers on him the ultimate spectatorial privilege: that of observing others without becoming fully visible himself. But rather than behaving like a peeping Tom, Mr. Spectator compels others to reveal themselves without ever trying to; as an instrument of truth, he can't help it. His speculative rambles function both as testimonials of his virtual presence alongside his readers and as occasions for his inhuman anatomy to flaunt its special privileges. Mr. Spectator's hostile critic found *"the Clouds and Mist that he pretends to cast over his Actions"* outrageously incongruous with his pretense of politeness; his constant striving to be "invisible" was more appropriate to a "Pickpocket" than a gentleman: such exaggerated self-effacement hardly suited one who was resolved "to invade every ones *Province*" in order to establish "a Tyranny over the Sense and Reason of his Countrymen."[151] But it is essential that Mr. Spectator compromise his ontological status as a man in order that he may be used as an instrument. While he seemed to serve a purpose, he did not appear to have any of his own. Yet just as the virtuoso's rational penetration of nature was expressed in authorial control over it, so Mr. Spectator's "Skill . . . in Speculation" resulted in a "Spectatorial Authority" over his chosen domain, the culture of London and, by extension, the nation as a whole (1: 22; 4: 374). His aim was not merely to affect the reader, but to create effects in the reader's world, to intervene in, and, at his most ambitious, even to control the world he sometimes modestly pretended only to reflect. Anticipating the causal force he will soon exert on the objects of his observation, Mr. Spectator warns at the start of the *Spectator*'s run that "the World . . . shall not find me an idle but a very busy Spectator" (1: 22).

Mr. Spectator's impoverished physical presence enabled him to be the omniscient narrator of "the common life," because he was potentially everywhere: sitting unnoticed in a coffeehouse, he is even able to witness the responses of readers of the *Spectator,* coolly relating their misprisions to the public in a subsequent issue (4: 539–541). Rather than having "spied" and then "tattled" like a truth-telling man, he is merely doing what an instrument of truth does: imposing discipline on the people who use him. And, like the treatises with which we began this chapter, the *Spectator* soon produced testimonials of its own power by readers eager to announce that they had "conformed our selves to your Rules" (2: 74). When Mr. Spectator leaves town and women "know themselves to be out of the Eye of the SPECTATOR," the petticoat swells out of "Compass," but "a Touch of your Pen," writes a correspondent, "will make it contract it self, like the Sensitive Plant" (2: 5, 7–8). Mr. Spectator's female readers merge with botanical specimens, or vivisected experimental subjects, yielding to the pressure of his penetrating scrutiny. The virtuosi's metaphors of reading, copying, and revising nature's book take on a pointed character as with the touch of a pen Mr. Spectator can "rewrite" his subjects and circumscribe them within proper bounds. Although he introduced himself as an unthreatening pair of spectacles, he could sharpen himself into a demanding "bold Tube" at the slightest provocation; thus readers were slowly habituated to the discipline he demanded.[152]

It is worth asking why women, in particular, found the daily proclamations of this self-effacing dictator of fashion and manners such delightful reading. One possibility is that being transformed into a specimen to be probed and analyzed by an instrument of truth felt better than being gazed at or governed by fully incarnate men: women readers were able to feel seen, exposed, and even penetrated without actually being subject to voyeuristic assault by a sensitive body. Mr. Spectator, like Plowden's monarch, was endowed with a body that could not be "seen or handled"; one could thus be seen and handled by it while eluding all physical contact. Had Mr. Spectator been differently endowed, it is unlikely that the freedoms he took in his "dictatures" on fashion and deportment would have been so ecstatically received; if Ned Ward had issued directives to ladies based on his own experience of them, for example, he would certainly have caused offense. As we saw in Chapter 3, the extravagantly eroticized rhetoric of experimentalist investigation, through which virtuosi styled themselves marauders and rapists of Dame Nature, read as testimonials of innocence and chastity precisely because the acts of sexual aggression they describe are being carried out against an abstract entity, the sum total of objects under the auspices of natural philosophy. Even at its most intensely physical, the language of sexual pursuit was sapped of all carnality, with each penetration mediated through artifical organs and abstracted further by being figured as acts of reading. Through the mediation of print, women readers of the *Spectator* were able to become collective objects of a similarly rational ravishment. For such rational penetration to occur, Mr. Spectator required a body of some sort, but one that sat on him so lightly that it could cause him to be mistaken for a "specter." Above all, Mr. Spectator had to be desexualized, lifted out of the realm of fallen carnality entirely, not merely by being a confirmed bachelor but by existing on a different ontological register. He could be neither attractive nor repulsive; his acceptance into the Ugly Club took care of the first danger, while the dubious character of his qualifications protected him from the second. His refusal even to be ugly made him more liminal, more monstrously exceptional.[153]

Given the logic that determined his construction, any appearance of a fully incarnate Mr. Spectator deserves special attention; such appearances must have been attended to with particular interest by his original readers. *Spectator* 115 presents such a case; it concerns his exercise regimen. Suddenly Mr. Spectator is ostentatiously encumbered by a body that requires care. The incongruity created by the physicality of exercise and his own ambiguous corporeality makes this scene amusing; it also throws into relief the aptness of his use of a "dumb Bell," a reminder of his own taciturnity. As Bond's note explains, rather than a weight, this was a swinging apparatus (1: 473). Mr. Spectator refers to his routine as his "ringing": when he exercises, he becomes the clapper of a bell, but one that is dumb. His ringing, like the music of the spheres, generates sounds inaudible to human ears. Having looked into some treatises of contemporary exercise enthusiasts, we can appreciate how this unlikely demonstration of athleticism identifies Mr. Spectator with the effort to transform the human body into a more perfect organ of curious sight, even as his personal participation in this effort—silent ringing—suggests that he himself does not really stand in need of such transformation. Recommending Fuller's *Medicina Gymnastica* to his readers, he explains that "Exercise" differs from "ordinary Labour" only by its motive, which is to make the body a more "proper Engine for the Soul to work with." He goes on to describe exercise as necessary for

> the Faculties of the Mind, by keeping the Understanding clear, the Imagination untroubled, and refining those Spirits that are necessary for the proper Exertion of our intellectual Faculties, during the present Laws of Union between Soul and Body. It is to a Neglect in this Particular that we must ascribe the Spleen, which is so frequent in Men of studious and sedentary Tempers, as well as the Vapours to which those of the other Sex are so often subject. (1: 471–472)

Eve and the gownmen again make their appearance as foils to the body fit for knowledge production. Upholding the principle that exerting the body enlarges the capacity for intellectual and spiritual exertion, Mr. Spectator relates these reflections to their source in Bacon's interpretation of Genesis: God has decreed that we must gain benefits through the "Toil of the Hands and Sweat of the Brows. Providence furnishes Materials, but expects that we should work them up our selves." Indeed, those whose social station does not require them to work are likely to be "more miserable than the rest of Mankind, unless they indulge themselves in that voluntary Labour which goes by the Name of Exercise" (472). The curse of labor is again transformed into a divine gift, since happiness lies in "working up" the materials the world provides. The defense of moderate physical exertion fluctuates into a sermon on the spiritual necessity of work, one in which labor is presented, Adamically, as a pleasure—something readers can "indulge themselves in."

Although, unlike Fuller, Mr. Spectator does not transform his defense of exercise into a means of waging class warfare, he makes a characteristically modest sally in this direction. Diffidently turning attention away from himself, he spends the bulk of this issue praising the Tory squire Roger de Coverley for his addiction to hunting. If any gross associations are triggered by the thought of Mr. Spectator's bodily exertion, they can be projected onto the bloody squire. Of course, Sir Roger enjoys hunting under the name of hunting, not exercise; Mr. Spectator's gory description of this quintessentially aristocratic pastime poses a contrast with his own elegant routine, making it seem more refined, more spiritual, more nervous. Sir Roger measures his strength, we are told, by the piles of animals he has killed; and Mr. Spectator notes with mild surprise that he has indeed "destroyed many thousands of Pheasants, Partridges and Wood-Cocks."[154] Measuring his own strength by heaps of dead matter, the squire evokes the images of morbid aristocratic consumption with which exercise manuals are filled, providing a perfect foil to Mr. Spectator's at once graceful and comic home routine. In contrast, when Mr. Spectator goes abroad "in quest of Game," as he puts it elsewhere, it is in the service of a purely ocular aggression (1: 195).

This issue takes a further risk by describing the more vigorous form of exercise that Mr. Spectator preferred in his youth, but this pursuit was equally harmless and "innocent." While his present machine "does every thing I require of it in the most profound Silence," the "more laborious" efforts of his past consisted in nothing more substantial than shadow boxing, providing "all the pleasure of Boxing, without the Blows." He ingenuously recommends the practice to "Learned Men" who engage themselves in "Controversies and Disputes about nothing," since their time would be more productively spent "fighting with their own Shadows" (1: 473–474). The backstory does double duty, providing an opportunity to link the lazy rich to the quarrelsome schoolmen even as it blends the potentially disturbing image of a youthful and robust Mr. Spectator with an insubstantial and harmless shadow.

Here as elsewhere, bodily absurdity allows for the same interplay between humility and grandiosity, passivity and aggression, that we find in the writings of the virtuosi. But whereas the modest virtuoso could be deferential to his disputants while torturing natural bodies, Mr. Spectator's potential adversaries were also his objects of his study; his virtual witnesses and his experimental subjects were the same. His observational field was the realm of culture, in which his readers participated as fellow creators and consumers. The extent of his interventionist ambitions in this area made his near-dehumanization a necessity. Readers would only submit to such treatment if the instrument that worked on them made them feel feel "gratifie[d] and enlarge[d]" in the process, possessed of the same skills of the "Authors of the new Philosophy" Mr. Spectator praises.[155] Spectator's by turns ugly, invisible, and weightless body was a crucial condition of his authority and power; his extreme form of modesty provided a comic mask for, and a means of announcing, his ambitious experimental designs on the English public while making them bearable. Using the *Spectator* as a pair of spectacles, which might at any moment turn on them and transform them into specimens, readers of the *Spectator* were experimental subjects in both ways. By announcing his physical proximity to his readers while eluding their perception—exposing his readers without being seen himself—Mr. Spectator implicitly parades his ocular mastery over them, but at the same time offers his speculations and his very body for their use (since he has thoughtfully printed himself out) so they too can carry out the work of testimony. Mr. Spectator declares as much when, announcing his intention to drop his persona, he explores the uses it has served:

> That might pass for Humour, in the *Spectator*, which would look like Arrogance in a Writer who sets his Name to his Work. The Fictitious Person might contemn those who disapproved him, and extoll his own Performances, without giving Offence. He might assume a mock Authority, without being looked upon as vain and conceited.

Even Mr. Spectator's proper name was a public function whose agent could not be "looked upon" at all; his body natural *was* the *persona ficta*. Thus when he prosecutes his intention to break his fifty years' silence, he can only "pretend" to talk like other people, alternating the assumed identities of fanatical Whig and Tory (4: 491, 498–500). The experiment in being a real man is a failure.

If Addison and Steele hold a particularly privileged place in the history of professional observation, it is because they exploited most fully the comic potential of applying the conventions of experimental observation to the relationship between author and reader. And they made this humor work for them in the same manner that modesty worked for the virtuoso, to grant themselves latitude to pursue meddlesome ends.[156] When exposed to the vices of the city (or, more alarmingly, the arbitrary rule of a tyrannically hospitable country house), Mr. Spectator becomes an object of our affectionate condescension and solicitude; when his observations fluctuate into grandiose proclamations, he becomes our dictator, and often he is both at once.

If Mr. Spectator was impossible to identify with personally, his responses could be learned and imitated. One might learn to express innocent surprise when confronted with the unreasonable outbursts of a Sir Roger, killing his kind with politeness, as indeed the *Spectator* literally does.[157] One could learn to discriminate between sociability on one hand and "Jollity, and what they call Good-Neighbourhood" on the other, while learning how to defend philosophical liberty and the interests of one's party by claiming to be of no party at all.[158] By such means, Mr. Spectator helped to recompose the public life he personated, literally shaping the English character. Of course, the virtual witnesses and subjects of his experiments remained recalcitrantly free creatures. Defoe called attention to the readers' right of resistance to being rewritten when evaluating Steele's campaign against swearing: "a pretty Thought" to "tell the People here, that Swearing is Ungentlemanly," he remarked, imagining the response of a typical coffeehouse reader: "Swearing out of Fashion! Senseless rascal! G-d damn him."[159] Even the most receptive readers do not remain attached to the perspectives to which reading provides them access. Mr. Spectator was able to "touch upon" his reader's faults without manhandling them, because he permitted them to feel like they could "become a kind of Spectator" alongside him, acting as real participants in an ongoing project, in which each day brought new findings. It was by making the very discipline he imposed gratifying to his readers that Mr. Spectator was able to magnify and multiply himself. Rather than being presented as "interrogations," his cultural interventions were collective experiments and even social occasions, attempts to build a certain kind of corporate body. Precisely because people were the "things themselves" in which he sought to intervene, successful interventions in the realm of culture *required* witnesses—many of them—in order to exert any impact at all.

Even as he worried that they were "Ineffectual," Defoe confessed his envious admiration of Addison and Steele's strategies to readers of the *Review*:

> You Have had so many Authors of late to please you, by Way of Speculation, and that . . . inform you, as on your Follies to reprove you; that accordingly . . . I have left off medling with, or so much as thinking, either to Instruct or Reprove . . . The *Tattler* and *Spectator,* that happy Favourite of the Times, has pleas'd you all with . . . such neat Touches at the vulgar Errors of the Times.[160]

Reprising their pun on "Speculation," Defoe alludes to the interventionist ambitions of Mr. Spectator's creators by relating their observations to "touches," a gentler form of the "surveying" Milton's Samson threatens to perform with his fist, while confirming their experimentalist roots with the allusion to Browne. But Defoe implies that if he attempted to do what Addison and Steele do, it would only look like hamfisted "meddling." Defoe seemed to grasp that the presentation of bodily difference had become de rigueur for the observer who sought to shape popular perceptions; showcasing the labor required to excavate the causes of the visible was not enough. The inhabitants of Poole's cave did not want to hear from a man wielding a pole; they wanted to hear directly from the pole itself.

Defoe made use of this insight when, with the assistance of his microscopist son-in-law, he started the *Universal Spectator*. This periodical announced itself as "a Prosecution of the same Design" as the *Spectator,* and it features an observer who makes much of "the *Littleness of my Person*," and who, like Mr. Spectator, is barely a man at all, having by "much Pains and Application divested" himself "of all blind Attachment to *Sex, Party,* or *Opinion*." This blunt confession was his first mistake. Although he has gamely assumed the form of a dwarf, Defoe has failed to identify his bodily difference as the condition of any superhuman epistemological privilege. Instead, he presents his freedom from personal prejudice as the product of "Pains and Application"—exactly as we would expect the author of the *Tour* to do. He goes on to explain that people refer to him as "the *Strange Gentleman,* or the *Little Gentleman,* and always speak of me with a kind of Wonder, whispering among themselves, that certainly I am somebody in Disguise. By this Means I have been at Liberty to study human Nature, and examine freely the Actions of Mankind." Unable to resist revealing his own craft secrets, Defoe turns the presentation of his new persona into a Boylean relation, explaining the function and use of the technology he is adopting—something Mr. Spectator only did when preparing to bring his experiment to an end. The Universal Spectator pursues his free examination with an eye toward curtailing the freedom of others; he intends to "regulate the Conduct of Mankind," and announces that "from doing this I am not to be affrighted by the tallest Man in Christendom." The means by which the Universal Spectator gains his "Liberty" to "examine freely" are by disguising his body as something ridiculous, laughable, and even monstrous, since it inspires "a kind of Wonder." The reward for such displays of bodily absurdity is supposed to be the right to "regulate . . . Mankind": "free" examination of one's readers facilitates uninhibited experimentation on them.[161] That Defoe wants to replicate Addison and Steele's experiment is clear, but he is unable to get the same results; his frantic insistence on his oddity, and candid explanation of its utility, betrays an artisanal pride that Mr. Spectator would never own. In his eagerness to relate the experiment, Defoe fails to conduct it.

A further reason for the unique success of Mr. Spectator's performance was its relationship to the social performance of Addison, whose modesty and bashfulness were legendary among contemporaries, though which persona influenced which is hard to judge. Anecdotes of Addison's time in Parliament suggest that it was really Mr. Spectator who occupied his seat: on one occasion, he is said to have risen and uttered "Mr. Speaker, I conceive—" three times, leading another member to declare, "Sir, the honourable gentleman has conceived three times, and brought forth nothing."[162] It was not as a rhetor that he could be productive; it was only as a dumb observer that he could make things happen. After his death, Addison was completely collapsed with Mr. Spectator; later in the century, Hugh Blair noted, "He is, in particular, distinguished by a character of modesty, and of politeness, which appears in all his writings," and went on to quote from the *Spectator* itself, as if the "I" speaking were in fact Addison. Quoting Chesterfield's remark that Addison was "the most timorous and aukward man that he ever saw," Johnson pointed out that, for all his bashfulness, he somehow managed to become secretary of state. Like the virtuoso's ingenuous modesty, this diffidence was methodical and "operative," like the new philosophy itself.[163] "Active philosophy" had once sounded like an oxymoron; now

the impossible combination of qualities was a central component of intellectual (and Whig) identity, informing the behavioral aspirations and expectations of a self-identified polite public.[164]

The smartest tactic employed by Tory writers interested in attacking
the *Spectator* was to remind readers of Steele's participation in the project.
Steele's checkered social and romantic history, financial troubles, and disas-
trous alchemical undertakings (through which, as one contemporary joked,
he saw his sense "dissolv'd in Smoke") permitted some "touches," as Defoe
would put it, on at least one of the real people behind the persona of Mr.
Spectator. How could such a flawed person "warn our vagrant Minds, and
fix them right"?[165] The frailties and errors of the man made his use as an
instrument of perception impossible. In *The Character of Richard St–le*,
William Wagstaffe ironically proclaimed, "Behold the Patron of Learning!
the Encourager of Arts and Sciences! the Dispenser of Morality and Philosophy! the Demolisher of Tuckers and Hoop'd-Petticoats! the Terror of
Politicians! and the Debellator of News-Writers! dwindled on a sudden into
an Author below the Character of *Dunton!*" Piling up exclamations of
praise appropriate to Mr. Spectator, Wagstaffe shows them "dwindle" to
the real person behind this mask, an author below even Dunton, just another unsavory coffeehouse projector.[166] But the independent life of this
collective invention was so powerful that even such acts of exposure could
not actually touch Mr. Spectator himself. The *Spectator* duplicated the
methods of the virtuosi whose instruments it appropriated in a very practical sense: as the product of multiple eyes and hands, it was something of
a society. Mr. Spectator's corporate body was constituted not only by Addison and Steele (Steele dropped out in the second series) but Thomas Tick-
ell, Eustace Budgell, John Hughes, and even Alexander Pope. Gathered
together as one man, these contributors added to the aura of the person
who was most identified with the office, an office that their personal foibles
could not disgrace. But this corporate person was not continuous with its
readers in the same way that Dunton's Athenian Society had been; its sovereign body that could not be seen or handled was sacramentally attached
to a particular figure—a virtually sanctified Addison.

Edward Young's *Conjectures on Original Composition* famously presents
Addison's deathbed performance as his most original, and saintly, composi-
tion of all.[167] This composition reprises the last issue of the *Spectator* itself.
Here Mr. Spectator celebrates the sensitive body's ultimate mortification in

death, which provides the decisive escape from the human "Organs" that "in their present Structure, are rather fitted to serve the Necessities of a vile Body, than to minister to his Understanding" (5: 171). The postmortem body, he is certain, will be better suited for "Contemplation"; like the body of an angel, it will be capable of "Intellectual Vision," which is only "somewhat Analogous to the Sense of Seeing." By dying Mr. Spectator will become a spectator indeed: "a Spectator of the long Chain of Events in the natural and moral Worlds"—a spectral spectator across time (5: 171–173). As his body is disciplined, marginalized, effaced, and finally done away with all together, the observer is installed in consummate spectatorial glory. Yet Mr. Spectator declares that even within the parameters of mortal life, "amidst the Darkness that involves human Understanding," occasionally there emerges a genius whose sight is so penetrating that he appears "like one of another Species!" Newton, he claims, is such a genius. By implication, Mr. Spectator is another (171). In the *Spectator*'s last appearance, the fusion of spectatorial authority with the capacity to exhibit oneself as "one of another Species" is complete.

The figure of the dying spectator expresses the old experimentalist ideal even while laying it to rest. Rather than a spectatorial body produced through the disciplining of the sensitive body, we are presented with a textual spectatorial organ unencumbered by any body—a spectator freed from the vile burdens of seeing. That this fantasy settles on the figure of Newton is appropriate, for he offered the age a very different image of what spectatorial authority was. Mr. Spectator is perhaps the last authorial persona in whom Baconian and Newtonian spectatorial bodies resided on something close to equal terms. In terms of subject matter covered, Bacon and Locke, to say nothing of the promoters of nervous physiology, were powerful presences throughout the *Spectator*'s run, and many aspects of the virtuoso's persona were kept up by Mr. Spectator. Boyle, the Christian virtuoso par excellence, had been equally notorious for "swallowing his words," and just as sexless.[168] When praising Addison using rhetoric Mr. Spectator would have appreciated, Johnson described him much as seventeenth-century virtuosi described themselves, making appropriate adjustments for his field of observation. His "rejection and contempt of fiction is rational and manly," Johnson pronounced, suggesting that Addison was much more deeply read in the book of experience than in books themselves: he had "read with critical eyes the important volume of human life," and could see beneath "the surface of affectation"; he had "conversed with many distinct classes of men, had surveyed their ways with very diligent observation"; he "marked with great acuteness the effects of different modes of life . . . quick in discerning whatever was wrong or ridiculous, and not unwilling to expose it." Above all, he "taught innocence not to be ashamed."[169]

Mr. Spectator's Postmortem Body

When the 1381 rebels sought to speak for as well as to others, they assumed generalized titles (Miller, Carter) that could be incorporated into the representative image of the first laborer. Centuries later, experimentalists sought to collect all the experiences comprehended by such "ordinary" callings in an effort to restore that laborer's knowledge.[170] The literature of professional observation is one extension of this massive project; it was by undertaking provisional apprenticeships, and applying artisanal effort to the task of observation, that Fiennes sought to embody an "idea" of the nation. In Mr. Spectator we see the person abandoned almost altogether for the sake of the office, an office that is no longer attached to any bodily work at all. Like his ingenious predecessors, Mr. Spectator laid claim to a representative character, but he went about the task of representation differently: as a service to the public, he personated the public, which could thereby learn how to act in accordance with him. Mr. Spectator's responses to the world expressed unknowable states of mind that no individual member of the public could hope to duplicate internally, but these responses could nonetheless be learned and performed, just as Adam's innocence had been methodically and laboriously reconstructed by the virtuosi. However structurally similar, these projects of imitation were very different. Rather than providing the basis for an ingenious public life, artisanal effort was now required merely to produce oneself as a publicly acceptable person.

If the literature of professional observation was the product of seventeenth-century experimentalism, it is also a medium in which to glimpse its eighteenth-century transformation. As the universities absorbed modern science into their curriculum and science became an acceptable gentlemanly undertaking, aristocratic privilege lost its compulsory identification with ignorance of "things themselves." The knowledge of artisans was no longer exclusive to artisans. The effort to create a commons of knowledge was carried out against the commons, in the absence of any competing Winstanleyan vision—a vision that had been sustained, in ambivalent and reversible forms, by experimentalists and improvers of all kinds. Productive knowledge became consolidated in the figure of the industrial manager. The consolidation of literary authorship as a profession in its own right further detached the intellectual *engagé* from his mimetic obsession with the figure of the artisanal laborer. The hardy emphasis on things themselves and on the grinding labor required to transform them into testimonials was absent from intellectual performances that in the past would have foregrounded such effort. Whereas Ward had bragged that his work of observation among the London crowds required "elbow-labour and much sweating," the "rambles" undertaken by Samuel Johnson in his *Rambler* papers are purely associative intellectual journeys. Mr. Spectator's ambiguous "Rambles, or rather Speculations" mark a transitional moment. The spectatorial metaphors through which the concept of intellectual labor first came into its own endured, but the image of the intellectual as a privileged observer became identified with performances of a more rarefied sort; the signifier remained while its signified passed on, and gradually the signifier changed. Rather than presenting itself as the synthetic product of arduous labor, spectatorial privilege migrated to the sphere of natural, inborn gifts. Writers who looked to the new philosophy (now not so new) as a model for the power that could be exercised through contemplation encountered a very different image of that power. Released from corporate logics and the identification with the artisanal laborer, experimentalist-identified intellectuals could now define themselves in relation to an icon of otherworldly genius.

Newton was elected president of the Royal Society in 1703, the year Hooke died. As Margaret 'Espinasse pointed out long ago, these events were related; the two men hated each other.[171] Although Newton did most of his scientific work in the 1660s and 1670s, in these decades he was not an influential figure. He worked alone and in private, and his infrequent attempts to share his work with the Society always ended in trouble. In 1672, he sent the Society "my poore & solitary endeavours" only to become incensed when Hooke challenged his claims to certainty.[172] Hooke later shared with Newton his hypothesis that the force of gravity was inversely proportional to the square of the distance measured from the center of a gravitating mass; and although Newton provided the quantitative and experimental support to make this hypothesis a theory, his refusal to give

Hooke any credit deepened their animosity.[173] The Society loyally declined to subsidize the publication of the *Principia Mathematica,* having spent their publishing funds on Francis Willoughby and John Ray's *Historia Piscium* instead. But once Hooke died, the "poore & solitary" Newton emerged as the leading light of the Society and set about becoming an international celebrity, sitting for dozens of paintings and busts, of which thousands were reproduced (the Society's portrait of Hooke, in the meantime, went missing).[174] Patricia Fara notes that attaching his name to anything increased its value; Newton became a brand.[175]

Temperamentally unsuited to the collective nature of experimentalist labor, Newton also had little sympathy with descriptive natural history. His effort to reduce surface complexity to what James Thomson called "Laws sublimely simple" was fundamentally at odds with the omnivorous spirit of Baconian induction. By initiating the Society's move to Crane Court a month after Hooke's death, Newton formalized the break with its Greshamite past.[176] Even his account of how he discovered the law of gravity seems to have been a tendentious rewriting of Boyle's own innocent encounter with the forbidden fruit—a calculated challenge to a science that sought to sustain itself on histories of fishes. Newton clearly employed some stagecraft when retailing his own apple story to William Stukeley, bringing his young admirer to the scene of his famous epiphany where "the notion of gravitation came into his mind . . . occasion'd by the fall of an apple, as he sat in a contemplative mood."[177] Boyle's effort to stage an innocent interaction with the forbidden fruit, we recall, required him to dissect it; Newton did not even have to touch it. This, he seems to suggest, was how an occasional meditation was really performed: by sitting in a contemplative mood. Like Boyle, Newton uses the apple to contain the threat it once represented: an apple occasioned the fall, but here, the fall of an *apple* occasions an insight into the omnipresent attractive force of gravity. These two fables of paradise regained—one stressing active physical intervention and the other a purely rational penetration—modeled the difference between mere Adamic ingenuity and the miracle of genius. The virtuoso had sought merely to represent the potential of humanity; Newton was a glorious exception to it.

Gravitational attraction was a nonmechanical force, acting on and through the entire bulk of bodies. Newton found the proposition that gravity was a property inherent in matter appalling: "no Man who has in philosophical Matters a competent Faculty of thinking" could imagine that action at a distance could have its source in "brute Matter." Some contemporaries argued that Newton's action at a distance resurrected the occult forces from which science had just been liberated. As Roger North put it, gravity was "a Simile or rather a Cover for Ignorance . . . If one asks why one thing draws another—It is answered by a certain drawingness it hath": in other words, it was as tautological as the old scholastic concept of form.[178] But Newton's refusal to hypothesize a cause for gravity seemed to contemporaries to be obscurely related to its power: "to us it is enough that gravity does really exist, and act according to the laws which we have explained." Reduced pretensions, it appeared, could elevate a theory above the modest realm of probability—even beyond the realm of debate.[179] The awful simplicity of the inverse square law and the mystery surrounding its central concept thus accrued to the figure of Newton himself. Belief in the magical character of the investigator's "names" could now be restored; the language of nature was the language of mathematics, and Newton spoke it fluently.[180] Then, in the *Opticks,* Newton untwisted the rainbow, recovering from the differently refrangible rays that made up the symbol of God's covenant a beam of white light. The reception of this discovery can be summed up in Pope's famous couplet: "Nature, and Nature's Laws lay hid in Night. / God said, *Let Newton be!* and All was *Light.*" If physico-theology made natural philosophers into priests of nature, Newton as a "second Adam" virtually replaced the Son (whose divinity Newton denied).[181] Thomson imagined Newton as *"pure Intelligence,* whom GOD / To Mortals lent"; Francis Fawkes described Newton as a mediating term between God and man, having "reach'd th'insuperable line, / The nice barrier 'twixt human and divine."[182]

In the Boyle lectures, the boundary between God and his universe became as porous as that between Newton and God. Richard Bentley found in the theory of gravity an "invincible Argument for the Being of God," effectively identifying gravitational attraction as God's "immaterial living Mind" that "doth inform and actuate the dead Matter and support the Frame of the World." Not only did the nonmechanical operation of gravity provide "invincible" proof of a divine being, it was hardly to be distinguished from that being; gravity itself was "the immediate *Fiat* and Finger of God, and the Execution of the Divine Law," a direct manifestation of divine power.[183] The General Scholium described God as "omnipresent, not *virtually* only, but also *substantially* . . . In him are all things contained and moved." In the *Opticks* Newton asked,

> does it not appear from Phaenomena that there is a Being incorporeal, living, intelligent, omnipresent, who in infinite Space, as it were in his Sensory, sees the things themselves intimately, and thoroughly perceives them, and comprehends them wholly by their immediate presence to himself: Of which things the Images only carried through the Organs of Sense into our little Sensoriums, are there seen and beheld by that which in us perceives and thinks.[184]

Few readers could follow Newton's explications, but, reduced to window dressing for revelations like these, they seemed to confer certainty on a vision of a world not only created but actively maintained by an omnipresent, omniscient God.[185] The secrets of creation no longer needed to be pieced together by Sprat's "vulgar hands"; they had been revealed to a man whose sensorium was uniquely continuous with the Creator's. Reprising the biblical proverb "The spirit of man is the candle of the Lord," Newton's big and little sensoria offered scientific evidence that thinking substance, or at least one man's thinking substance, was, as the Cambridge Platonists had imagined, an attribute of the divine.[186] This was no longer the artisanal God, but a dispenser of laws and producer of miracles, much like Newton himself.

The quibble on "Democrit-al" and "democratic" had been an organizing pun of seventeenth-century philosophy; atomists described a world without natural hierarchy or transcendent order—this was a nature in which human agents were intended to intervene. The Newtonian system reduced that world to order. John Theophilus Desaguliers's *Newtonian System of the World, the Best Model of Government* used gravity as a metaphor for the "loose" attraction that linked members of a commonwealth: the attractive forces holding every particle of the universe together were analogous to the ties of sympathy that disposed political subjects to cooperation.[187] Gravitation embodied the politically charged trope of *concordia discors,* suggesting the happy coexistence of sociability and autonomy that characterized a society based on mixed-government and, ultimately, laissez-faire principles, as the *"Fiat* and Finger of God" evolved into the invisible hand.[188]

When reviewing Thomas Burnet's *Sacred Theory of the Earth*, Mr. Spectator had grown wistful: "How pleasing must have been the Specula-tion" of "the Ways of Providence, from the Creation to the Dissolution of the visible World" (2: 76). It was the capacity to "speculate" about invisible operations—as opposed to material operations that could be coaxed into visibility—that Newton, and through him, the figure of the intellectual, increasingly came to embody. This observer offered testimony to what could never be seen: the invisible hand of God in society, ensuring that "Whatever IS, is RIGHT."[189] Mr. Spectator seems to see the invisible hand and "immaterial living Mind" at work during his weepy visit to the Royal Exchange, where the moral expression of gravitational attraction, sociabil-ity, is the surplus created by mutually beneficial self-interested exchanges. While these bodies go about pursuing their private interests, sociability is, as it were, spontaneously generated, sensible only to Mr. Spectator, elevated above the human swarm.[190] The object lesson in human selfishness pro-pounded by Bernard Mandeville's *Fable of the Bees*—a grim inversion of Hartlib's productive hive—becomes an occasion for sentimental reflection and tears. If Mr. Spectator prefigures the lonely sociability of the sentimen-tal author, the spectacle he uncovers is similarly lonely; the bonds of human sympathy are not forged or even directly experienced by any of the partici-pants, only generated from their interactions. This sociability is a subjective feeling without a subjective center, existing only in the "sensorium" of the system as a whole, a sensorium mysteriously continuous with that of Mr. Spectator himself.[191]

Pope, who began his career by contributing numbers to the *Spectator*, clearly benefited from the Addisonian ideal of the author as an inhuman observer whose exceptional perspective granted him the privilege to impose corrective discipline on his readers. As Helen Deutsch has shown, Pope made a virtue out of having a "crazy carcass," turning to account the at-tacks on his "monstrous shape" made by enemies like John Dennis, who declared the poet was "a Creature not of our Original, nor of our Spe-cies."[192] Pope never had to go through what we might regard as the early modern spectator's rite of passage. Initiation in the spectatorial elite had occurred through a sort of ritual humiliation: observers withdrew from sources of authoritative knowledge and social privilege and assumed an exaggerated humility, going so far as to render themselves ugly, ineloquent, even inaudible and invisible. This permitted the observer's status elevation as the culture's designated witness, marked by his reappearance on the scene as a disarmingly likeable monster: an instrument of truth who embodied the inhuman potential of humanity as a whole. Pope did not need to go through this apprenticeship process. Just as his body defied categorization, so his perspective could not be located among those available to the rest of humankind: thus "Tories call me Whig, and Whigs a Tory."[193] We have to see the duncicks through Pope's eyes before we can identify them as dunces, rather than as the accomplished scholars, intellectuals, and actors they seem to be; he provides the needed perspective, and in doing so, he alters their public stature forever. Far from presenting this spectatorial office as the artificial product of pains taken, Pope described it as thrust upon him by nature along with his poetic calling ("I lisp'd in Numbers, for the Numbers came"); readers might benefit from his spectatorial privilege, but they were offered no means of sharing in it. *An Essay on Man* is thus written from the very perspective that it also insists eludes mortal comprehension: that of "The great directing MIND of ALL."[194]

Pope, along with Jonathan Swift and John Arbuthnot, a practicing physician and Royal Society Fellow, were in fact steeped in the experimentalist culture they pretended to deplore; yet it was Newton, not the grubby Baconians, with whom they most sought to identify.[195] Nonetheless, as readers have often remarked, the first two books of *Gulliver's Travels* are the most perfectly realized approximation of the technology of the lens in literature; Swift's mockery of scientists as crazed projectors in the third book is a blatant symptom of anxiety of influence.[196] We are supposed to find the foil to the projectors of Lagado in the commonsensical King of Brobdingnag, who declares that "whoever could make two Ears of Corn, or two Blades of Grass to grow upon a Spot of Ground where only one grew before; would deserve better of Mankind, and do more essential Service to his Country, than the whole Race of Politicians put together." Bacon could not have said it better. Yet of all the ironic praise lavished on the Lilliputians, the modifier Swift uses most damningly is *ingenious:* this society of tiny, malevolent, and mechanically skilled busybodies is a nightmarish version of Hartlib's ingenious public.[197] Pope was happy to versify Locke, attend coffeehouse lectures on physico-theology, and collect curiosities for his grotto, but the experimentalist vision of a knowledge-producing public was exactly what he defined himself against.[198] The Adamic collectivity of truth producers that Milton labored to restore is for Pope a terrifying mob,

mechanically operated by dullness and enthusiasm—a filthy eruption of
Grub Street resembling Cleveland's Adamic rebels: "men sprung from
earth."[199]

The curious eye continued to be cultivated in the eighteenth century:
the amicable *here*'s and *there*'s and *look*'s of the ambling excursion poem
assure us of the poet's presence in the environment he describes: the "ocular
sense" of such verse is conditioned by our confidence that it is the poet
himself, not merely his glance, that moves through the landscape.[200] The
excursion poem's literal and figurative expatiations (the animating pun of
Essay on Man, announced in its fifth line) are above all acts of rendering
visible. In this poetry, rather than ostentatiously wielding the lens (or a
pole), the wanderer silently assumes its powers, revealing, for example, the
"soft Inhabitants" of each "flowery Leaf" (Thomson), "the green myriads in
the peopled grass" (Pope).[201] If their wealth of circumstantial detail qualified these poems as Boylean relations, their periphrases allowed readers to
become virtual witnesses to acts of Adamic naming. Rather than referring
to animals or plants by using their conventional names, constructions like
"The mineral Kinds" provided a nomenclature that revealed the nature of
their being.[202] Like a good trade history, or a physico-theological sermon,
an excursion poem represented a time splice in an ongoing process of "taking notice." Increasingly, however, the effort to look "thro' Nature, up to
Nature's God" strained to give visual expression to what no one could witness: the felicitous, optimal arrangements naturally generated by uncoordinated actors within the newly revealed "system of the world." The elegant
symmetry of the Newtonian universe was not available to even mediated
perception; poets who testified to its beauty expatiated on the limited perspective of humanity as though from a vantage point far beyond it, virtually inhabiting the "CREATIVE WISDOM" that "Exceeds the narrow
Vision" of the human mind. In this way, the invisible hand and the cult of
genius would sustain one another. Just as Newton became identified with
the nonmechanical forces he alone seemed to understand, so in Young's
Night Thoughts the grandeur of absolute space has become "a property of
the self": the night sky is a "Pasture of the *Mind*" where Young "expatiates,
strengthens, and exults."[203]

Seventeenth-century experimentalists had often portrayed themselves
as laboring bodies untouched by the corrupting influence of fancy: the Society was "a *union* of *eyes,* and *hands,*" that would in turn "set many Me-

chanical hands a worke." Through such metonymies they had tried to imagine a collective intellectual life that worked toward the integration of the worker and the thinker. The "mechanical hand" was also what Hooke called "a *sincere Hand*"; it was the token of "a *faithful Eye*" and "philosophical mind." But the corporate production of innocent knowledge had been superseded by the miraculous discovery of a single philosophical mind in "a contemplative mood." A sense of priestly miracle had been restored to the sacrament of knowledge production, revealing a natural order that made paradisal recovery beside the point.

NOTES

Introduction

1. Aquinas made much of Adam's perfections but deemed him relatively ignorant of knowledge gained through experience; see *Summa Theologiae,* 13: 96–97 (1a.94.3). This study follows Solomon's *Objectivity in the Making* in tracing the modern concept of objectivity to Baconian experimentalism, which, as she argues, endowed material particulars with an impersonal and absolute legitimacy traditionally associated with the sovereign. Although Solomon identifies Baconianism with absolutism, I will argue that it was precisely this move—"royalizing the real"—that could make Baconianism a challenge to royal power (Bacon himself had no interest in mounting that challenge; on the difference between Bacon and Baconianism, see note 11 below). On the emergence of objectivity see also Daston, "Baconian Facts"; Daston and Galison, *Objectivity;* Dear, "From Truth to Disinterestedness"; Poovey, *History of the Modern Fact.*

2. The seminal treatments of seventeenth-century England's programs of paradisal restoration are Charles Webster's *Great Instauration* and Hill's *Intellectual Origins,* whose central claims have met with skepticism due to their association with "the Merton thesis" (see Merton, "Science, Technology, and Society," and, for a trenchant discussion of the semantic confusions that have characterized attacks on Merton, Gary Abraham, "Misunderstanding the Merton Thesis"). More recently, Peter Harrison's *The Bible, Protestantism, Natural Science* argues

that literalizing approaches to the Bible made paradisal recovery newly thinkable. Harrison's *Fall of Man*, which appeared after this book was drafted, extends this argument, showing how varying assessments of the fall eventuated in very distinct approaches to restoring Adam's knowledge. Harrison's erudite book covers a much broader historical and geographical range than this study and has different emphases, but see esp. 58, 81, 83, 131–138, and the final two chapters.

    3. The figure of the "veil of ignorance" employed in Rawls's *Theory of Justice* and elaborated by Pogge's *Realizing Rawls* for redistributive ends indicates the political value of this construct. On the relationship of objectivity to intersubjectivity and the task of imagining the world from all possible perspectives, see Bourdieu, *Science of Science and Reflexivity,* and Nagel, *View from Nowhere* and "What Is It Like to Be a Bat?" On the role of origins in constructing early modern intellectual authority, see Snider, *Origin and Authority.*

    4. Arendt, *Human Condition,* 80. My account of how experimentalism exploited the uncertain place of *techne* within these mutually implicating dichotomies is indebted to Pérez-Ramos, *Francis Bacon's Idea of Science*; Whitney, "Paradise Restored"; and Long, *Openness, Secrecy, Authorship.* On how humanist debates over the relative merits of the active and contemplative lives, together with debates over what constituted "true nobility," expanded the category of "active citizens" in England in the decades between the 1580s and the 1620s, see Cust, "The 'Public Man.'"

    5. On the common, see Virno, *Grammar of the Multitude,* which considers the political implications of the collaborative nature of intellectual life, where it is "difficult to say where collective experience ends and individual experience begins" (24). The common is organized by *"Sharing,"* which "is opposed to the *division* of labor—it contradicts that division and causes it to crumble. Of course this does not mean that work loads are no longer subdivided, parceled out, etc.; rather, it means that the segmentation of duties no longer answers to objective 'technical' criteria, but is, instead, explicitly arbitrary, reversible, changeable" (41).

    6. Frederic Jameson has famously challenged academic hagiographies of the intellectual laborer, insisting that we "cannot without intellectual dishonesty assimilate the 'production' of texts . . . to the production of goods by factory workers: writing and thinking are not alienated labor in that sense, and it is surely fatuous for intellectuals to seek to glamorize their tasks . . . by assimilating them to real work on the assembly line" (*Political Unconscious,* 45). One might object that Jameson's corrective entails an equally fatuous identification of "real work" with alienated labor, but his point is clearly that the current division of labor makes production a self-defeating model for intellectual life, which renders the distinction between producers and consumers meaningless: intellectual products require intellectual exertion simply to be valued, thinking is not a

specialized skill, the leisure and work activities of the intellectual are likely to be indistinguishable, and so on. On the challenge that intellectual labor poses to the categories of work and leisure, see Adorno, *Critical Models,* 167–175. On the necessity for the "general exercise of a certain kind of intellectual labor" in a democracy, see Guillory, *Cultural Capital,* 50–53. On professionalization as a means of monopolizing intellectual territory, see Abbott, *System of Professions.*

7. Bradley, *Nosce te Ipsum,* 36.

8. On identification as both the ground and continual disturbance of identity, see Fuss, *Identification Papers.*

9. In distinguishing the calling from a career (in the root sense of a ground over which a competitive race is run), this book takes up the century-long debate over Weber's account of the calling in *Protestant Ethic*—and, more broadly, Marx's characterization of Protestantism as a bourgeois development of Christianity's "*cultus* of abstract man" (*Capital,* 91). I am indebted to Seaver's "Puritan Work Ethic Revisited"—which, taken together with *Wallington's World,* presents a good case against the centrality of the profit motive in early Puritan constructions of godly labor (as many critics of Weber have pointed out, the majority of his examples come from the eighteenth century). See also Breen's "Non-Existent Controversy."

10. On the category of the public or representative person, which is central to this book, see Hill, "Covenant Theology."

11. As Pérez-Ramos points out in *Francis Bacon's Idea of Science,* Bacon's actual scientific writing was embarrassing to many self-described Baconians of the later seventeenth century, not least because of its geocentrism. Despite the many divergences between "Baconianism" and Bacon's own ideas, Pérez-Ramos shows how, functionally, Bacon's reinterpretation of the concept of form did promote "Baconianism"; see esp. 92. Still, as Harkness has shown, every activity Bacon describes taking place in Salomon's House was already being pursued by Elizabethan Londoners; rather than a prophet, Bacon was a man in search of a job "heading up" all this productive activity and reducing it to (a far less democratic) order. Bacon, on this understanding, was far less "Baconian" than many of his later seventeenth-century interpreters. While Harkness focuses on the scheme outlined in *The New Atlantis*—based on "strict hierarchies of knowledge and power, and a complicated division of labor"—my focus will be on the egalitarian potential of Bacon's paradisal myth as it was exploited by his successors (*Jewel House,* 7–8, 251).

12. Marx, *Economic and Philosophical Manuscripts,* 75–77, 129.

13. Blumenberg, *Legitimacy of the Modern Age;* see esp. part III. Blumenberg remarks on the importance of the (apparently false) etymon *cura* to curiosity's rehabilitation at 346; see also Kenny, *Curiosity,* 35–38. In "Ideas above His

Station," Pumfrey discusses the etymon in relation to Hooke's position as Curator of Experiments for the Royal Society. Hooke was repeatedly elected curator until he was finally elected to the office "for perpetuity" (Birch, *History*, 1: 123, 496; 2: 3, 4). *Things themselves* is a signature phrase of experimentalist discourse; see, for example, Petty, *Advice*, 13; Glanvill, *Vanity of Dogmatizing*, 151; Hooke, *Micrographia*, sig. a^v; and Sprat, *History*, 18.

14. Much of the work required to purge *curiosity* of its pejorative connotations happened first on the grounds of *ingenuity;* see Chapters 1 and 3 in this volume. For a word history of curiosity, see Kenny, *Curiosity*.

15. See Zaret, *Origins of Democratic Culture* (although it is not his primary concern, Zaret offers valuable observations on the role of experimental science at 270–275); Norbrook, *Writing the English Republic;* Achinstein, *Milton and the Revolutionary Reader;* Claydon, "The Sermon, the 'Public Sphere' and Political Culture"; Raymond, "The Newspaper, Public Opinion"; Holstun, *Ehud's Dagger*, 106–112; Lake and Pincus, "Rethinking the Public Sphere," which offers a diachronic analysis of England's public sphere(s) from the mid-sixteenth century onward; and the essays in Lake and Pincus, *Politics of the Public Sphere*.

16. Pocock, *Machiavellian Moment*, 335. Although Habermas's construct is generally used by historians of seventeenth-century England as "convenient shorthand for an apparent broadening of political participation" in the period, this usage can discourage us from treating the distribution of intellectual authority as a significant political development in its own right (Claydon, "The Sermon, the 'Public Sphere' and Political Culture," 209). Armstrong and Tennenhouse examine the iconic status of the artisan as it shaped the concept of intellectual labor in *The Imaginary Puritan*, chapter 4.

17. Indeed, the fact that many who appropriated the stereotype of heretic as *illiteratus* were university-trained testifies to the epistemological privilege accorded to experience in the period; see Nicholas McDowell, *English Radical Imagination*. On mechanicks and the mechanical philosophy, see J. A. Bennett, "The Mechanics' Philosophy and the Mechanical Philosophy."

18. The mode of faith that was termed *experimental* was proved by "prophesying," an "act of public verification" that scholars from Nuttall to Charles Webster have related to experiment: see Nuttall, *Holy Spirit*, 8, 38–39, and Webster, *Great Instauration*, xxii, as well as Damrosch, *Sorrows of the Quaker Jesus*, 111; Hill, *Intellectual Origins*, 101–102, 328–329; and Keeble's *Literary Culture of Nonconformity*, 205–206, 284. On the evolution of "prophesyings" from closed clerical exercises, see Collinson, *Elizabethan Puritan Movement*, 168–176. As Collinson argues, prophesyings were instrumental in promoting the ideal of "a unity of belief" based on "assent rather than on ecclesiastical authority" (175). For the evolution of the concept in the seventeenth century, see Nuttall, *Holy Spirit*, esp. chapter 5.

19. For a similar idea, see Almond, *Adam and Eve*, 48.

20. On good conference, see Chapter 1. On the datum versus the fact, and the relationship between "experience" and "experiment," see Eamon, *Science and the Secrets of Nature*, 54–58, and Dear, *Discipline and Experience*, 21–25, 154–155. On experimental Christians, see note 18.

21. For a case study in the convergence of Baconianism and "a republican- ism based on the construction and communication of knowledge" (323), see Johns, *Nature of the Book*, chapter 4.

22. Lake and Pincus note the overlap of classical definitions of active political virtue with hot Protestant notions of godly behavior in "Rethinking the Public Sphere."

23. Hill's *World Turned Upside Down*, with its emphasis on ecstatic self-expression, exhibits this tendency, but in *Intellectual Origins* he put more stress on the role of collaborative empiricism in revolutionizing public life. On the image of the torn mystical body, "rent" by "ranters" and "schismaticks," see Guccr, "Not Heretofore Extant in Print," 82–83, and, as the classic example, Thomas Edwards, *Gangræna*, esp. 162–164.

24. See Macpherson, *Political Theory of Possessive Individualism*. For narra- tives of modernity that bind secularization to individualism (the "atomized" or autonomous self) and disenchantment, see Asad, *Formations of the Secular*, and Shuger, *Renaissance Bible*, esp. 81, 193–194. See also Duffy's influential analysis of the decline of "traditional religion" as a process of social atomization in *Stripping of the Altars*. Joan Bennett critiques the stark contrast between communitarian Catholicism and Protestant individualism in "Asserting Eternal Providence." As Walzer argued long ago, the "study of the Puritans is best begun with the idea of discipline" rather than individualism: "a tense mutual 'watchfulness' . . . radical, ruthless, experimental" ("Puritanism as a Revolutionary Ideology," 79, 64, 89); the commitment to collective discipline is a central concern of this book.

25. Milton, *Complete Prose Works of John Milton* (hereafter *CPW*), 2: 559; Habermas, *Structural Transformation*, 266n62.

26. Milton, *CPW*, 2: 554; Walwyn, *A Parable*, 16. On the nature and limits of toleration in the period, see John Marshall, *John Locke, Toleration*, esp. 281– 334, and Worden, "Toleration and the Cromwellian Protectorate."

27. Winstanley, *Works*, 105. See also Cook, *Monarchy no Creature*, sig. cᵛ.

28. Milton, *CPW*, 1: 871. The "exhilarating" and "heady" character of religious debate in the 1640s reminds David Loewenstein and Morrill of the "rugged individualism" that accompanied "the opening up of the American West" ("Literature and Religion," 664).

29. In a similar vein, Holstun calls attention to the utopian potential that had always resided in the concept of the body politic, which "could never have

served the absolutist project if it had not balanced capital hierarchy with corporal association" (*Ehud's Dagger*, 19).

30. Blumenberg, *Legitimacy of the Modern Age*, 10, 19–20. McKeon asserts that the mystical body was killed along with Charles I in "Parsing Habermas," 276–277. This claim tallies with his understanding of the public sphere as the expression of a modern ontology that eroded the traditional experience of the self as a created part of "a totality that pre-exists individuality" (*Secret History*, 107–108). On the replacement of the sovereign monarch with the sovereign individual, see also chapter 5 of his *Origins of the English Novel*. Rather than challenging McKeon's large-scale narrative, this study dilates a transitional moment within it.

31. Pocock makes this suggestion in "Post-Puritan England," 96.

32. Kahn critiques the tendency to project the "phenomenologically thin subject" of modern social contract theory backward into the seventeenth century in *Wayward Contracts*, 282–283.

33. See Kantorowicz, *King's Two Bodies*, 3–23.

34. Ojakangas, *Philosophy of Concrete Life;* Schmitt, *Roman Catholicism and Political Form*, 14–26; Neumann, *Behemoth*, 469. Schmitt insisted that it was through the exception that "the power of real life breaks through the crust of a mechanism that has become torpid by repetition" (*Political Theology*, 15). Of course, the mechanical repetition of the ritualized miracle was a staple of Protestant controversial literature, but this is not a problem for Schmitt, since he is interested in the possibilities afforded to the state by a *permanent* state of exception; see Benjamin, *Origin of German Tragic Drama*, 65, 69.

35. Schmitt, *Leviathan in State Theory*, 53–55, 95–96. Schmitt is celebrating what William Perkins called "the *propertie of representation*, wherby the Image stands in the stead, place, & room of god" (*Warning against Idolatrie*, 102). For the sovereign as an "Artificiall man" and "*Mortall God*," see Hobbes, *Leviathan*, 9, 132 (introduction and 2.17). In Shulman's account of the process, "prideful creators become the passive subjects of their own sovereign creations": disenchanted machine-building gives way to enchantment through the theatricalization of politics, the process by which subjects "'own' the sovereign as *themselves* 'represented' or 'personated'" ("Metaphor and Modernization," 393, 402). For a different account of how the mortal god relates to the sacrament and the thought of Schmitt, see Kahn's "Hamlet or Hecuba."

36. I am indebted to David Simon for my understanding of this aspect of Hobbes.

37. On private opinion, see esp. Hobbes, *Leviathan*, 453 (3.42).

38. Rubin, "Whose Eucharist?" 199.

39. Boyle, *Works,* 3: 203; on Adam, see 13: 151. As a result, Milton asserted, "we are now justly exempt from paying tithes, to any who claim from *Aaron,* since that priesthood is in us now real, which in him was but a shaddow" (*CPW,* 7: 283). Only half-jokingly, J. Paul Hunter describes the preachers, scientists, and journalists of the later seventeenth century conspiring "to make priests of us all" (*Before Novels,* 198).

40. Funkenstein discusses the threat that secular theology posed to traditional Christological devotion in *Theology and the Scientific Imagination* at 45 and 70–71. See also Agamben's account of modern man who "posits himself, in the productive act, as the origin and nature of man . . . The man who takes on the 'greatest burden' of the redemption of nature is the man of art" (*Man Without Content,* 83, 92).

41. Shuger, *Renaissance Bible,* 89. I believe that the productive sacrament has causal relevance to what Rumrich calls "the wave of antitrinitarian heresy that swept over late seventeenth- and early eighteenth-century England," and a corresponding reduction of respect for kings as Christ's representatives; see "Milton's Arianism," 84, 87, and *Milton Unbound,* 41.

42. See esp. Charleton, *Physiologia,* discussed in Chapter 3. On the gendered nature of the distinction between private and public, see Hughes, "Men, the 'Public' and the 'Private.'"

43. Hill, *Milton and the English Revolution,* 460–461; in this passage Hill invokes the concept of political theology.

44. Baudrillard, *Mirror of Production,* 19, 166. Baudrillard's main contention is that Marxism *"assists the cunning of capital"* by convincing people that they are *"alienated by the sale of their labor power, thus censoring the much more radical hypothesis that they might be alienated as labor power, as the 'inalienable' power of creating value by their labor"* (31). Without censoring this hypothesis, I hope this book offers reason for questioning it. For provocative critiques of employment, see the essays in Richards, *Why Work?*

45. White, *Medieval Technology and Social Change;* the introduction of Whitney's "Paradise Restored" offers a summary of the literature. Long shows how humanists and their patrons, elites who sought to legitimate their power through building programs and other public works, helped to forge an alliance between *techne* and *praxis;* this alliance provided the basis for the joining of *techne* to *episteme* in what later became "disinterested experimental philosophy" (*Openness, Secrecy, Authorship,* 122–129, 250).

46. See note 11 above.

47. Rupert Hall, "Scholar and Craftsman"; see Crombie's response to Hall in the same volume, 66–78. Eamon disputes the notion that Roger Bacon was a proto–Francis Bacon in *Science and the Secrets of Nature,* 82. The literature on the

debt of seventeenth-century experimentalists to the alchemical tradition is vast, but see Henry, "Animism and Empiricism"; Newman and Principe, *Alchemy Tried in the Fire*; and Clucas, "Corpuscular Matter Theory." The terms *alchemy* and *chymistry* were used interchangeably in the period; understood as "the art of transmuting or perfecting everything in its own nature," alchemy was "nothing else but the Art and Knowledge of nature itself" (Lyndy Abraham, *Marvell and Alchemy*, 1, 62).

48. Bacon, *Advancement* (1640 ed.), 40, second pagination; see also Sprat, *History*, 333–334.

49. See Pérez-Ramos, *Bacon's Idea of Science*; Hintikka, "Knowing How, Knowing That, and Knowing What"; and Hacking, *Representing and Intervening*.

50. Whitney, "Paradise Restored," 25, 28. This paragraph is based on chapter 2 of Whitney's "Paradise Restored" and Eamon, *Science and the Secrets of Nature*, esp. 53–58, 82–83.

51. Plato, *The Republic*, 424–425 (10.597a–c). On artisanal epistemology, see Pamela Smith, *Body of the Artisan*.

52. On seventeenth-century science as an attempt to recover literacy in the book of nature, see Bono, *Word of God*; Peter Harrison, *The Bible, Protestantism, Natural Science*; and the introduction to Findlen, *Possessing Nature*.

53. Perkins, *Warning against Idolatrie*, 94; Lady Ranelagh or Katherine Boyle (Robert Boyle's sister) in Boyle, *Correspondence*, 2: 499. I discuss magnification as praise in Chapter 3.

54. Donne, *First Anniversarie*, line 111; this construction of fallen humanity suggests the category of the human as back-formed by the posthuman, which Hayles describes (wrongly, I think) as a distinctly postmodern category in *How We Became Posthuman*.

55. Milton, *CPW*, 8: 554 (this insight is put in the mouth of Moses); Nelson Goodman, *Languages of Art*, 80.

56. Recent theorists of metaphor analyze it not as an extrinsic figure of speech but as the basic transference principle of cognition that enables innovation or "conceptual integration." According to these formulations, the mixed spaces called into being by metaphor combine cognitive domains; the experimentalist Eden is an instance of a mixed space. See Mark Turner, *Literary Mind*, chapter 2; Turner and Fauconnier, "Conceptual Integration and Formal Expression"; and Cacciari, "Why Do We Speak Metaphorically?"; more generally, see Ricoeur, *Rule of Metaphor*, and Max Black, "Metaphor."

57. Because the rule of metaphor extends through literary, visual, and mental representations to govern everyday practice, the mixed spaces or metaphors that "we live by" condition the actual spaces we inhabit (see Lakoff's *Metaphors We Live By*).

58. See Catherine Wilson, *Invisible World,* and Daston, "Language of Strange Facts." On internal contradictions and paradigm shifts, see Kuhn, *Structure of Scientific Revolutions.*

59. Hooke, *Micrographia,* sig. a2.

60. See Tillyard, *Elizabethan World Picture* and Foucault, *Order of Things.* An important study of this kind is John Rogers's *Matter of Revolution.* To the limited degree that the present book imputes a "world picture" to promoters of the new science, it is not one that depends on any particular ideas about matter beyond a commitment to corpuscular theory, which was shared by vitalists and mechanists alike. On the overlapping nature of these two categories, see Henry, "Occult Qualities" and "Robert Hooke," and the essays in Lüthy, Murdoch, and Newman's *Late Medieval and Early Modern Corpuscular Matter Theories,* esp. Newman, "Experimental Corpuscular Theory"; Osler, "How Mechanical Was the Mechanical Philosophy?" and Clucas, "Corpuscular Matter Theory." The matter theories entertained by the Royal Society virtuosi were in any case remarkably heterogeneous.

61. *Virtual witnessing* is a key term of Shapin and Schaffer's *Leviathan and the Air-Pump,* defined at 60–65. Since every reader could not be expected to replicate the findings recorded in experimental relations, guidelines were necessary for accepting textual testimonies in lieu of direct experiential confirmation. Boyle advised aspiring philosophers to be wary of experimental accounts that "are set down only by way of Prescriptions, and not of Relations; that is, unless he that delivers them mentions his doing it upon his own particular knowledge, or upon the Relation of some credible person, avowing it upon his own experience" (*Works,* 2: 209). Credibility is established through the form, rather than the content, of the proposition, since no proposition can be ruled out on prima facie grounds as implausible by a truly unprepossessed observer. Relations differed from prescriptions in two major ways: they recounted in detail the experimental steps that led to the result—so that the reader could relive the experience of discovery—and they offered credible witnesses, witnesses familiar with experimental canons of verification, to attest the validity of the finding. The second half of my book explores the attempt to reinvent reading as an actively curatorial form of virtual witnessing. See also Dear, "Totius in Verba."

62. It might be objected that the model suggested by technologically assisted observation is not strictly identical to that of experimentation (the open-ended explorations of microscopy were often not geared toward the testing of any particular hypothesis), but this distinction was not recognized by the virtuosi; and in fact, microscopists in the period were overwhelmingly concerned with replicating one another's results (see Fournier, *Fabric of Life,* 96–97).

63. Sidney, *Apologie,* sig. B^v; *Old Arcadia,* 3. On the association of poesy with an enclosed space of "play," see Helgerson, *Self-Crowned Laureates,* 37–61.

64. Sidney, *Apologie,* sig. C^v. See Maus, "A Womb of his Own."

65. The "Instrument / Of truth compos'd" is William Browne's epithet for the telescope, which he presents as an alternative to shepherd's pipes, in *Britannia's Pastorals,* 2.1.861–862 (*Whole Works,* 1: 189). See Chapter 5.

66. Sidney, *Apologie,* sig. D; Spenser, Letter to Raleigh, in *Faerie Queene,* 737; Sidney, *Apologie,* 14–15, 28; Spenser, Letter to Raleigh, in *Faerie Queene,* 737.

67. Teskey's account of the modern poet as shaman in *Delirious Milton* uses a different figure to characterize the model of authorship I am describing here. The shaman is like the experimentalist in that he gains his insight from a prosthetic source and imparts a mediated version of that experience to the reader. On the modern genius as a shaman, see also Asad, *Formations of the Secular,* 45–52.

68. On this phrase, see Chapter 1.

69. Despite my opposition of the mirror and the lens, it was through lore about a magic or "imperial" mirror that telescopic vision was imagined long before the telescope made it possible; see Chapter 3 in this volume, and Reeves's *Galileo's Glassworks,* esp. chapter 2.

70. Collini's introduction to *Two Cultures* offers useful context for understanding Snow's apparently simplistic thesis.

71. See part III of *Gulliver's Travels.* Nicolson's work was the great exception, yet it was mostly concerned with how writers mined the new science for content.

72. See, for example, R. F. Jones, "Science and English Prose Style." The old generalizations about the virtuosi's linguistic practice tended to be based on a few programmatic statements made in Sprat's *History* (wrenched from their contexts) rather than on analysis of experimentalist prose, a fact made clear by Starr's analysis of the heavy reliance of seventeenth-century scientific prose on rhetorical devices such as prosopopoeia ("Language of Interpretation").

73. Winn offers a typical assessment of Cowley's ode "To the *Royal Society*" when he claims that "the manner of his poem in praise of Baconian clarity entirely contradicts its matter," a charge that Bacon's prose itself could not escape (*John Dryden,* 132).

74. So Petty: "'tis the Profession of the *Society,* to make Mysterious things plain; to explode and disuse all insignificant and puzling words" (*Discourse,* sig. A5^v; see 4 for an attack on the confusing metaphysics promoted by "*Elderly Divines*").

75. Fish, *Self-Consuming Artifacts,* 377, 380, 381–382.

76. Fish, *Self-Consuming Artifacts,* 378, 380 (quoting Donne, *Sermons,* 2: 282), 381; Godfrey Goodman, *Fall of Man,* 116; Charleton, *Physiologia,* 15.

77. See Fletcher's account of allegory as a "compulsive syndrome" in *Allegory* (esp. 279–303) and the discussions of idolatry throughout Nohrenberg, *Analogy of the Faerie Queene,* and Gross, *Spenserian Poetics.*

78. Godfrey Goodman offers intense rhetorical enactments of this struggle in *Fall of Man,* returning again and again to the refrain is "my tongue is confounded" (292, 310): he can only spread the poison of sin through his sermons, which offer testimony to the effects of the fall (71, 226); Adam's ability to "give a name to every creature, answerable to his propertie" offers the needed foil to a present in which language "cannot significantly expresse" (394, 293). Semiosis is not productive in the experimentalist sense, since it offers only proliferation without "improvement."

79. See Fineman, "Structure of Allegorical Desire."

80. These proliferating signs were now indexical, which altered the structure of romance as it was revived, and reformed, by the erring investigator in the scene of microscopy.

81. Milton, *CPW,* 2:551.

82. This argument is famously made in Keith Thomas, *Religion and the Decline of Magic.*

83. See Philippians 2:12.

84. Milton, *CPW,* 2: 543 (see also 6: 120–122).

85. On this phrase, see Chapter 1.

86. See Shapin's statement in *Scientific Revolution* that there was "no such thing as the Scientific Revolution, and this is a book about it" (1). For a defense of the utility of the term for understanding the civil wars, see Holstun, *Ehud's Dagger,* 9–45.

87. Hill, *Intellectual Origins,* 6; Charles Webster, *Great Instauration,* 88.

88. Mulligan, "Puritans and English Science," 458; for a strong early version of this view, see Purver, *Royal Society.* But see Charles Webster, *Great Instauration,* 499–503.

89. The confusion has been amplified by Sprat's successful efforts to obscure the Parliamentarian connections of many of the Society's members; see Hill, "Puritanism, Capitalism," 95. Sprat's *History* effaces the role of the London group begun by Theodore Haak in the Society's formation, stressing instead the Oxford Philosophical Club (see Michael Hunter, *Science and Society,* 22–23). John Wallis gives this group due consideration in *Defence of the Royal Society,* perhaps a more trustworthy account precisely because it was produced later, after the Society did not need to assert its loyalty to the newly restored monarchy. See also Birch, *History,* 1: 1–3.

90. On Boyle, see Michael Hunter, *Scrupulosity,* 65, and Sargent, *Diffident Naturalist,* 260n9. On Evelyn, see Chapter 4 in this volume. The case of John Beale is equally instructive: to Charles Webster, he is a Republican; to James

Jacob, a royalist Anglican (see references in Leslie, "Spiritual Husbandry," 153n10). In his 1657 inaugural lecture as Gresham professor, Christopher Wren, who would later be a pillar of the Restoration settlement, celebrated England's political and scientific revolutions as a single movement, exulting over the restoration of "Liberty to Philosophy, oppress'd by the Tyranny of the Greek and Roman Monarchies" (quoted in J. A. Bennett, "Wren's Greshamite History," 191). On changing political affiliations, see Charles Webster, *Great Instauration,* 85.

91. Ernst Bloch, *Utopian Function of Art and Literature,* 144.

92. Finlayson, *Historians, Puritanism, and the English Revolution,* 110.

93. See the introduction to Barbour's *English Epicures.* Even apparently theological objections to Laud's Arminianism tended to concern discipline rather than doctrine, since ceremonies could loosely fall under the category of good works; in popular usage, *Arminian* was a term hurled at popish Laudians primarily for reasons of discipline. See Marvell, *Prose Works,* 1: 189, as well as Corns, "Milton's Antiprelatical Tracts," 40–41 and references therein.

94. Hill, *Puritanism and Revolution,* 244; see also his *Intellectual Origins,* 338. Fincham and Lake describe how Laud and his opponents conspired "to reduce the identities available to English Protestants to a stark choice between Laudian orthodoxy and puritan subversion," with consequences for future historiography, in "Popularity, Prelacy and Puritanism," 876. According to Underdown, during the civil wars themselves, "localist neutralism was always more pervasive than either cavalier or roundhead zeal" (*Revel, Riot, and Rebellion,* 276). As Donald Friedman observes, many people were "more profoundly occupied with the question of the right course of action in a revolutionary time" than they were with "siding with one party or the other" (*Marvell's Pastoral Art,* 225).

95. Finlayson, *Historians, Puritanism, and the English Revolution,* 7. Barbara Shapiro has argued that the most dominant ideological strain among the virtuosi was latitudinarianism; see her "Latitudinarianism" and "Science, Politics, and Religion." After the Restoration, the Anglican clergy linked to the Society formally and informally, such as John Wilkins and Gilbert Burnet, tended to be those most interested in comprehension and toleration (see John Marshall, *John Locke: Resistance,* 39–45).

96. Humanism facilitated the elaboration of such originary constructs as the *prisca theologia,* which was central to experimentalist ideology, but the connections between humanism and experimentalism go well beyond a common ideology of restoration. Juan Luis Vives had urged scholars not to be "ashamed to enter into shops and factories, and to ask questions from craftsmen, and to get to know about the details of their work" (*De Tradendis Disciplinis,* 209; see Pamela Smith's discussion in *Body of the Artisan,* 66–67). Rossi remarks on the irony of

Bacon's "violent reaction against classical influence," since when Bacon "turned to the interpretation of classical myths, he saw reflected in them the exact features of his 'new' philosophy" (*Francis Bacon,* 130); see also Eisenstein, "Advent of Printing," 82–84.

97. On Hartlib's salary, see Chapter 1, note 338.

98. *Sylva* (1679 ed.), sig. A3ᵛ, quoted in Michael Hunter, *Science and Society,* 83–84. We can gauge the consequences of the king's failure to support the Society from the bumpy career of the talented naturalist Nehemiah Grew, whom the Society struggled to pay. On Grew and the Society, see Michael Hunter, *Establishing the New Science,* 261–278; for the recommendation that he be "curator to the Society for the anatomy [of] plants" see Birch, *History,* 3: 42.

99. The fact that Grew dedicated his *Anatomy of Plants* to Charles II in the same year that his father Obadiah (a dissenting preacher) was imprisoned for six months gives some indication of the frequently strained relationship between the Fellows and the restored monarchy (Michael Hunter, *Establishing the New Science,* 262). John Ray famously forfeited his position at Trinity College rather than take the oath required by the Act of Uniformity. On "the good old cause," which I am extending beyond any strictly constitutional sense, see Norbrook, *Writing the English Republic,* 16, where he argues that the phrase is effectively a translation of *res publica.* For examples of its use, see Milton, *CPW,* 7: 462, and Marvell, *Prose Works,* 1: 192 (Dzelzainis and Patterson discuss Marvell's identification of the good old cause with "natural causes" at 19–20).

100. Aubrey, *Natural History of Wiltshire,* 5. Aubrey adds an explanatory note: "Experimentall Philosophy was then first cultivated by a club at Oxon." This work was itself part of the movement it begins by describing; although he completed it in 1691, Aubrey started work on it in 1656.

101. Michael Hunter, *Science and Society,* 2–3; Hill, *Nation of Change,* 17. Charles Webster also notes the "remarkable seamlessness between Republic and Restoration" where the scientific community was concerned in *Great Instauration,* xxxi).

102. As Scott puts it, the Restoration is best seen "not as the beginning of a 'long eighteenth century,' but as the second half of the seventeenth century, and a second half peculiarly in the grip of the first" (*England's Troubles,* 4). The suppression of these continuities has had dramatic consequences for literary history; see Damrosch, *God's Plot and Man's Stories,* 3, and Love, *Culture and Commerce,* 8.

103. Pope, "The First Epistle of the Second Book of Horace Imitated," line 108. In *Libertines and Radicals,* James Grantham Turner explores "the upward mobility of abjection" during the Restoration as it shaped aristocratic displays of "bestial" sexuality (158). I explore the court's attempt to shape public life around fallen appetite in Chapter 4.

104. This opens onto the question of female participation in the public sphere, to which this book does not pretend to do justice. Paula McDowell has offered a corrective to the presumption that the late seventeenth-century public sphere was intrinsically masculinist in *Women of Grub Street,* which reveals "the participation of women at virtually every level of the London press" (29). See also Markman Ellis, "Coffee-Women"; Norbrook, "Women, the Republic of Letters, and the Public Sphere"; and the essays in Meehan, *Feminists Read Habermas.*

105. Žižek, *Fragile Absolute,* 89–90. On establishing links between social reality and social thought in the period, see J. C. Davis, "Radicalism in a Traditional Society."

106. Warner, *Publics and Counterpublics,* 185, 167; McKeon, *Secret History,* 74.

107. Shagan, "Pilgrimage of Grace," 33.

108. See Barbara Shapiro, *Culture of Fact.*

109. On thick description, see Geertz, *Interpretation of Cultures,* 3–30. Here Geertz does not so much argue against the concept of the typical as dismiss it as "nonsense"; see esp. 21–22.

110. The ideal type is defined by Weber as a "one-sided *accentuation* of one or more points of view and by the synthesis of a great many diffuse, discrete, more or less present and occasionally absent *concrete individual* phenomena, which are arranged according to those one-sidedly emphasized viewpoints into a unified *analytical* construct. In its conceptual purity, this mental construct cannot be found empirically anywhere in reality. It is a *utopia*" (*Methodology,* 90).

111. As Weber points out, the historian's vocabulary is made up of hundreds of such terms (*Methodology,* 92–93).

112. For an influential critique of Baconian instrumental reason, see the first chapter of Horkheimer and Adorno, *Dialectic of Enlightenment.*

113. See Larrain, *Ideology;* Marx and Engels, *German Ideology,* 47.

114. See Althusser, *Essays,* 36; Barthes, *Mythologies,* 143; Foster, *Recodings,* 3–7, 27, 79–83, 86, and "Postmodernism," x–xi; Mulvey, *Fetishism and Curiosity,* 12–13; and Said, *Representations of the Intellectual.*

115. For the figure of "belonging" as it shaped sixteenth-century literary collectivities, see Phillips, *English Fictions of Communal Identity.*

116. Boyle, *Correspondence,* 2: 329–330.

1. Digging up the *Hortus Conclusus*

1. "Adam lay ibounden," in Davies, *Medieval English Lyrics,* 160–161, lines 9–14. See Lukken, *Original Sin in the Roman Liturgy,* 391. My argument here,

and in the book as a whole, has greatly benefited from Diane McColley's *Gust for Paradise;* see esp. 28–29, 154–159.

2. Adam of Perseigne quoted in Delumeau, *History of Paradise,* 125. Etymologically, paradise is enclosed (*pari* + *daeza* combines *around* and *wall*); see Bremmer, "Paradise." Stanley Stewart's *Enclosed Garden* offers a rich account of the iconography of the Mary-garden, but reaches different conclusions about its relationship to seventeenth-century paradisal reconstructions.

3. Nuttall, *Holy Spirit,* 21.

4. Luke 23:43. The Hebrew word *pardes,* meaning a park, forest, or garden, is used three times in the Old Testament (Ecclesiastes 2:5, Song of Solomon 4:12, and Nehemiah 2:8). The Greek cognate influenced later usages of the word. See Bremmer, "Paradise," and Giamatti, *Earthly Paradise,* 11–15.

5. The atrium where the catechumen waited to be received into the church was also called a paradise (Prest, *Garden of Eden,* 21). On the relationship between paradise and heaven, see Peter Brown, "End of the Ancient Other World," 26–29. In *Heaven,* McDannell and Lang suggest that the conflation of paradise and heaven reflects a mingling of two visions of the afterlife: one based on the postmortem fate of each individual and the other based on the hypothesis of a restored earth after the Last Judgment, when the dead will be resurrected and heaven will come down to earth. A theology in which all the saints ascend to heaven after death has no real need for a restored earth; consequently, as the millennial vision was subordinated to the concern for the fate of the individual soul, the earthly paradise was reconfigured as an antechamber to heaven, a space through which the soul passed on its way to the heavenly city. As I argue below, however, in early modern England the dissolution of purgatory helped to revive the earthly paradise as an object of millennial expectation.

6. See Schiller, *Iconography,* 1: 18; Walther and Wolf, *Codices Illustres,* 95; Prest, *Garden of Eden,* 21.

7. Richard Verstegan, aka Richard Rowland, *Odes,* 26. See Romans 5:12–21 and I Corinthians 15:22. Adam appears in *The Golden Legend* exclusively as a foil to the second Adam: "as the first Adam opened the gates of hell, so the second the gates of paradise" (1: 298; see also 7, 17, 43, 67–68, 208–209, 223–224, and 2: 111; for Mary as the second Eve, see 2: 93–94). The reduction of Adam was frequently literal; in medieval images of the two Adams, Christ often dwarfs his predecessor; see James, *Canterbury Psalter* f. 24; Oakeshott, *Sequence of English Medieval Art,* pl. 39. In representations of Adam under the feet of Christ on the Cross, the first man assumes the position of the wounded serpent: the clear message is that "Christ treads the enemy underfoot" (Schiller, *Iconography,* 2: 130–131). The Mary-garden also generated invidious comparisons between the first and second Eves; see Schiller, *Iconography,* 2: 159–160; Kathryn Smith, *Art,*

Identity and Devotion, 188, 190–191; and Walther and Wolf, *Codices Illustres,* 382–383.

8. Bale, *Tragedie,* sig. A3; Donne, "Twicknam Garden," lines 8–9.

9. Lovelace, "Love Made in the First Age: To *Chloris,*" lines 7, 17–18, 3; Hobbes, *Leviathan,* 97 (1.13).

10. Fish, *Surprised by Sin;* Peyton, *Glasse of Time,* 37. As Michael Wood blithely puts it, we "are not up to" paradise (*Children of Silence,* 5).

11. Hawkins, *Partheneia Sacra,* 10; Beaumont, *Paradise, Psyche, or, Loves mysterie,* 14, 25 (2.10, 2.167).

12. *Lectures on Genesis* in Luther's *Works,* 1: 119–120, 103, 66; see also 68. Luther goes on to suggest that Adam would have labored in this manner "not only without inconvenience but, as it were, in play and with the greatest delight." The moral Luther draws—that the "idle sort of life" of monks and nuns deserves to be condemned—explicitly appeals to the innocent Adam as a relevant model for fallen humanity (102–103). As we will see, Genesis 2:15 could be interpreted to refer to innocent tillage. Imagining Adam as the beneficiary of "infused" knowledge did not necessarily proscribe his use as a model for working philosophers; in many writers, these two concepts of Adam seem to mingle. But the insistence of John Denham, for example, that Adam's knowledge was "Not from experience" seems intended to discourage such a use ("Progress of Learning," line 5); see Aquinas, *Summa Theologiae,* 13: 96–97 (1a.94.3), and Arnold Williams, *Common Expositor,* 80–83.

13. See the clarifying discussion of various understandings of Adamic naming in Leonard, *Naming in Paradise,* 1–22.

14. Bacon, *Advancement* (1640 ed.), 42–43, second pagination. Boyle, for example, denied that the names Adam assigned to the creatures, if understood merely as words, could in themselves be operative or reflective of insight, but he treated Genesis 2:19–20 as the primal scene of experiment (*Works,* 8: 70; 13: 151). For his impatience with a "giddy" sectarian who claimed to speak Adam's language, see *Correspondence,* 1: 105.

15. Although I am stressing how virtuosi used the Adam of Genesis 2:19 to model labor rather than what we would consider magic, the term *natural magic* was often used to refer to what we would consider scientific work. Thus when Elias Ashmole declared that Adam "before his *Fall* was so absolute a *Philosopher,* that he fully understood the true and pure knowledge of *Nature* (which is no other then what we call *Naturall Magick*) in the highest degree of Perfection, insomuch, that by the light thereof, upon the present view of the *Creatures* he perfectly knew their *Natures,*" and was "able to bestow names sutable to their *Qualities* and *Properties,*" he did so precisely in order to remove the taint of "*Necromancy*" from experimental labor: what "common *Custome*" called magic

was really just natural philosophy, and a *"Magus,"* nothing more than *"a studious Observer"* of nature (*Theatrum Chemicum,* 445, 443–444). In this book, where I distinguish between the experimentalist and the magician, it is the latter's identity according to "common *Custome"* to which I am referring. The scholarship on the debt of experimental philosophy to the natural magic tradition is vast, but see Henry, "Occult Qualities" and "Robert Hooke"; on Bacon and natural magic, see Rossi, *Francis Bacon.*

16. Bacon, *Advancement* (1640 ed.), 42, second pagination. In the 1605 edition, it is phrased differently: the "worke of contemplation, that is, when the end of worke is but for exercise and experiment . . . [and] delight in the experiment" (sig. H). Unlike some of his successors, Bacon expressly excludes the sweat of the brow from this work.

17. Findlen discusses the exemplary opposition of the book of nature and books themselves in *Possessing Nature;* see also Bono, *Word of God.*

18. On the reevaulation of curiosity, see Blumenberg, *Legitimacy of the Modern Age;* Kenny, *Curiosity;* Benedict, *Curiosity;* and Chapter 3 in this volume.

19. Bacon, *Works,* 5: 132.

20. Augustine, *Confessions* 2: 175 (10.35); *Essay upon Idleness,* 3; Bacon, *Advancement* (1605 ed.), sig. H. The strongest version of this account of the fall is in Charleton's *Physiologia,* addressed in Chapter 3.

21. Bacon, *Works,* 8: 350. See Low's discussion in *Georgic Revolution,* 140–141.

22. Sprat, *History,* 349–350. I lean heavily on this source throughout this book. Sprat was a spokesperson for the Royal Society rather than an experimenter, but he did not produce the *History* in isolation; a committee was set up for the purpose of reviewing and revising the manuscript, consisting of William Brouncker, Robert Moray, William Petty, and John Wilkins (Birch, *History,* 2: 47). Paul Wood has argued that Wilkins did most of the supervision ("Methodology and Apologetics," 3–4).

23. Hooke, *Micrographia,* 154, sig. a2. Making suggestive use of a homophone, Hooke inserts this speculation in his observations on "the Seeds of *Tyme"* (153).

24. Glanvill, *Vanity of Dogmatizing,* 5; Rabisha, *Adam Unvailed,* 96. Rabisha was a Parliamentary captain; if he was also the author of the decidedly royalist *The Whole Body of Cookery* (1661), he was fabricating an identity that would distance him from his past (*Dictionary of National Biography Online,* hereafter *DNB*).

25. There were two minor grants to the Society, one accruing from the Irish land settlement in 1663, which "proved abortive," and the gift of Chelsea

College, which led to twenty years of "expensive legal wrangling" before the Society was able to sell it back to the king in 1682 (Michael Hunter, *Royal Society,* 16; see also Bluhm, "Royal Society's Finances").

26. On this phrase, see the Introduction, note 99.

27. 1642 Declaration of the Lords and Commons, quoted in Kantorowicz, *King's Two Bodies,* 21. See also Wormuth, *Royal Prerogative,* 108–120. In "Not the King's Two Bodies," Hutson points out that, although Kantorowicz described the doctrine as one that could justify both absolutism and regicide, literary scholarship on the corporate personality has focused single-mindedly on the charisma of the ruler (168). But from Elizabeth's reign onward, MPs saw themselves as embodying a representative identity to which the monarch, for all his or her charisma, could not lay claim. Hirst explores the increased emphasis on the fact of representation under the early Stuarts in *Representative of the People?* 8–9, 157–193. It was in this period that MPs "sent to defend local interests developed a sense of responsibility for the nation as a whole" (Louise Fargo Brown, "Ideas of Representation," 25; see also Arnold, *Third Citizen,* 83–90). The electorate were increasingly thinking in terms of national issues as well—and prepared to regard themselves representatives of the public interest in their own right, as the sphere of extra-parliamentary politics expanded (Hirst, *Representative of the People?* 153, 183–184).

28. Butler, *Transproser Rehears'd,* 97; Overton, *An Appeale From the Degenerate Representative Body of the Commons of England Assembled at Westminster: To the Body Represented, The Free People in General of the several Counties, Cities, Townes, Burroughs, and places within this Kingdome of England, and Dominion of Wales.* On the Army as a representative body, see Haller, *Leveller Tracts,* 11–12, 55, and Massarella, "Politics of the Army," 109.

29. In "The Proceedings of the Councel of State against Richard Overton, now prisoner in the Tower of London," from *The Picture of the Councel of State,* in Haller, *Leveller Tracts,* 231; Overton, *An Appeale,* title page. MPs often appealed to the distinction in their speeches: "I am now no private Person, I am a publick, and a Councellor to the whole State in that place where it is lawful for me to speak my mind freely" (D'Ewes, *Journals,* 241); Overton, along with many others, was extending "that place" of representative speech beyond the House.

30. As Hughes observes, the basic tactic of the Levellers was "to make their own individual 'private' oppression the basis for a generalized, public critique of parliamentary tyranny"; where the distinction between private and public was drawn, it "almost always hinted at the normative or political argument that the general or collective was to be valued above the specific or individual" ("Men, the 'Public' and the 'Private,'" 193).

31. Plowden's *Reports* quoted in Kantorowicz, *King's Two Bodies,* 11, 23. I am not suggesting that a progressive understanding of history was always run through the figure of Adam; on the importance of Antichrist in promoting this understanding, see Hill, *Antichrist,* 160–163.

32. Plowden quoted in Kantorowicz, *King's Two Bodies,* 7; Glanvill, *Vanity of Dogmatizing,* 2. On the phrase "things themselves," see the Introduction, note 13.

33. As a result, I will sometimes quote from material that was published after 1660. Many experimentalist texts published in the 1660s were begun or written during the previous decades; where this is the case, notes will make mention of it.

34. Aylmer observes that at times Winstanley is "capable of making statements about the Norman Conquest which almost suggest that he equated 1066 with the Fall of Man," though in other moods he is happy to make the distinction ("Religion of Gerrard Winstanley," 104). I believe that these apparent conflations are strategic; since appeals to the Norman yoke would have had more traction with some readers than the fall from Eden, Winstanley appeals to both. This is in keeping with his general strategy of semantic transformation through synonymy, discussed below. On Norman yoke theory, see Manning, *English People,* chapter 9, and Hill, *Intellectual Origins,* 361–365.

35. Quoted in Camille, " 'When Adam Delved,' " 265. So William Bloys: "If *Adam* had abode in his integrity . . . all things should have been common, as they were in the beginning of the Gospel" (*Adam in his Innocencie,* 60).

36. For variants and contexts of this proverb, see Horstmann, *Yorkshire Writers,* 1: 173, 367; Albert Friedman, " 'When Adam Delved' "; Hilton, *Bond Men Made Free,* 211–212; and Aston, "Corpus Christi and Corpus Regni," 18.

37. Justice, *Writing and Rebellion,* 108. Indictments of rebels include a sizeable minority of artisans; rural rebels had London allies in groups of organized weavers (Hilton, *Bond Men Made Free,* 179, 195).

38. See Justice, *Writing and Rebellion,* 94, 108–111, 126.

39. Walsingham, *Chronicon,* 321, quoted in Justice, *Writing and Rebellion,* 108–109. Rawls explicates the original position in chapter 3 of *Theory of Justice.* Although he describes it as a "purely hypothetical situation," he also claims that it "helps to explain our having a sense of justice" (104). On how Rawls's construct elicits an argument for economic rights, see Pogge, *Realizing Rawls.*

40. They were seeking a charter by which King Offa had granted their liberty as a reward for their help in building the town, and perhaps "a time of long lost liberties when, according to nature and the law of god, what was brought forth by the earth belonged to all" (Müller, "Aims and Organisation," 15). See also Justice, *Writing and Rebellion,* 47–48. For early modern analogues

to their search for an ancient charter, see Adam Fox, *Oral and Literate Culture,* 281–284.

41. Quoted in Devlin, "Bishop Thomas Brunton," 337.

42. Comito discusses the link of *humilitas* and *humus* in relation to Adam in his valuable essay "Renaissance Gardens," 495.

43. *Apocrypha and Pseudepigrapha,* 2: 16–17; see Isaiah 28: 24–29. For the artisanal God, see Psalm 139:14–15; Pächt, *Rise of Pictorial Narrative,* 24–25; Sheppard, *Giffard Bible,* 150–151 and pl. 157 and 208. The working God had a less certain place in allegorical readings of Genesis, in keeping with the Platonic tradition of contempt for productive knowledge; to support his claim that Eden was merely a symbol for the celestial paradise, Origen asked "who could be found so silly as to believe that God, after the manner of a farmer, planted trees[?]" (quoted in Almond, *Adam and Eve,* 66).

44. See, for example, Galbraith, "Biblical Scenes at Malmesbury Abbey," 42–43; Diane McColley, *Gust for Paradise,* 51; Morgan, *Medieval Painted Glass,* 16–17; Haney, *Winchester Psalter,* pl. 1, 76–77; and Pächt, "Cycle of English Frescoes," 168–169.

45. Galbraith, "Biblical Scenes at Malmesbury Abbey," 42.

46. Hawkins, *Partheneia Sacra,* 14.

47. Camille, "'When Adam Delved,'" 272. The resemblance of Adam in his original sinless state to Christ was a subordinate element in the typological tradition; see Schiller, *Iconography,* 2: 131.

48. In one book of hours, Mary Magdalene presents the divine gardener to King Charles VIII, who kneels to him (fig. 28 in Wieck, *Hours of Henry VIII*). Hildburgh discusses the motif in "Further Miscellaneous Notes"; see pl. 51. According to Leslie, despite its medieval precedents, the iconography of Christ the gardener rarely appears in gardens in the fifteenth and sixteenth centuries; it only reemerges among seventeenth-century Protestant horticulturalists, when "the association of salvation and cultivation resumed its importance" ("Spiritual Husbandry," 156). See also Peter Harrison, *The Bible, Protestantism, Natural Science,* 228.

49. Julian of Norwich, *Writings,* 281–283; Camille, "'When Adam Delved,'" 248–249.

50. Borenius and Tristram, *English Medieval Painting,* 29; see 28–35 generally. The authors consider the influence of *Piers Plowman* on this motif. The diversity of tools depicted is remarkable, extending well beyond agricultural implements to include such tools as scissors and shuttles. See also Hildburgh, "Folk-Life," 259. A fuller consideration of this motif might extend into the representation of saints such as Saint Walstan, who relinquished the crown for a life of hard labor and was normally pictured barefoot, with a crown, ermine, and

scythe; see Duffy, *Stripping of the Altars,* 200–205; James, "Lives of St Walstan"; and Schabacker, "Petrus Christus 'Saint Eloy.'"

51. Reiss, *Sunday Christ,* 2, 11, 32. Protestant Sabbatarianism would continue to focus on recreation. *A Necessary Doctrine and Erudition for any Christen Man,* Henry VIII's guide to religious conduct issued in 1543, warned against being "over scrupulous, or rather supersticious" about abstaining from labor on the Sabbath, especially if such labor was necessary; better that women should spin and men plough than to "lose their tyme in leapinge or dauncinge, and other idell wantonnesse" (sigs. Lviii, M). Indeed, labor could fall under the category of acceptable "pious works" to be performed on the Sabbath; see Hutton, *Rise and Fall of Merry England,* 78.

52. Reiss, *Sunday Christ,* 8. While Reiss may be correct about the intended message of this motif, her discussion of the ways in which these figures inspired identification suggests that their reception was more complex than a strict Sabbatarian reading would allow; see especially 36–38.

53. Borenius and Tristram, *English Medieval Painting,* 32; Reiss, *Sunday Christ,* 7. But see Reiss's counter-reading of this image at 11.

54. Henisch, *Medieval Calendar,* 10–13, 21, 25, 211. This paragraph and the following one are heavily indebted to Henisch's book.

55. Henisch, *Medieval Calendar,* 19. See Isaiah 63:3; Revelation 14:19 and 19:15; Schiller, *Iconography,* 2: 129, 228–229; and Duffy, *Stripping of the Altars,* 218, 251–253. On the Mill of the Host and the mystic winepress, see also Rubin, *Corpus Christi,* 312–316, and Aston, "Corpus Christi and Corpus Regni," 27–31. The motif of the Mill of the Host once decorated the glass in the north transept of Canterbury Cathedral. For thoroughly conventional deployments of the Christ of the winepress topos from the seventeenth century, see Bloys, *Adam in his Innocencie,* 209, and Donne, *Sermons* 9: 65–66.

56. With few exceptions, neither are they seen offering harvest tithes or gathering to witness the priest's blessing of the fields at Rogationtide; see Henisch, *Medieval Calendar,* 16.

57. See Rosser, "Going to the Fraternity Feast," and Farr, *Artisans in Europe,* 251–252. Rubin shows that the "manipulation of the eucharistic symbol" by fraternities and other voluntary associations did not necessarily correlate with an orthodox understanding of it (*Corpus Christi,* 242–243).

58. See Craig, *Reformation, Politics and Polemics,* 154. On the relationship of the ceremonies of the pax and holy bread to priestly prerogative, see Peter Marshall, *Catholic Priesthood,* 65–66.

59. While guilds provided the medium for intensely local connections, they also fostered a culture of mobility among skilled laborers. Early modern England

contained an average of three guilds per parish, forming a nationwide network for workers to move about and earn their livings: this kind of corporate person was far-flung, extending beyond the borders of any single parish. Half the journeyman joiners in 1600–1640 Chester, for example, stayed for less than a year; another 30 percent stayed less than three. See Rosser, "Going to the Fraternity Feast," 431, and Farr, *Artisans in Europe*, 147.

60. Farr, *Artisans in Europe*, 226. Guild rhetoric retained a quasi-ecclesiastical flavor into the early modern period: we learn from Joseph Moxon that "Every *Printing-house* is by the Custom of Time out of mind, called a *Chappel;* and all the Workmen that belong to it are *Members of the Chappel*," while the bookseller Francis Kirkman asserted that the bond between master and apprentice was "as solemn as that of *Matrimony*" (Moxon, *Mechanick Exercises*, 323; Kirkman cited in Johns, *Nature of the Book*, 115). After the Reformation, the upkeep of "brotherly love and verity" within guilds depended on efforts to accommodate members of disparate ideological outlooks—a balance between love and tact much like that later struck in the Royal Society (Joseph Ward, *Metropolitan Communities*, 99–100).

61. See Rosser, "Crafts, Guilds and the Negotiation of Work," 14. Brooks argues that the discourse of charity that shaped the life of guilds in the Middle Ages continued after the Reformation in "Apprenticeship, Social Mobility, and the Middling Sort," 76–77. See also Barry, "Bourgeois Collectivism?" 98. Challenging the habitual contrast between "late medieval unity and early modern fragmentation," Craig offers evidence that moral consensus in "Puritan" towns was rooted in the language of reconciliation; some corporations instituted formal feasts of reconciliation on a monthly basis, which warrant comparison with the love feasts described here (*Reformation, Politics and Polemics*, 155, 180–181).

62. This argument is made in Justice, *Writing and Rebellion*, chapter 4, esp. 168–172, and somewhat differently in Aston, "Corpus Christi and Corpus Regni"; I learned of the detail about the millstone appearing in cross-section as a cross from a conversation with Justice.

63. Cleveland, *Rustick Rampant*, 91.

64. The association of the wafer with the money form is suggestive in this connection. Shell describes the "wafer-god" as "expressly manufactured like a coin" in *Art and Money*, 14–15. The replicability of the eucharist—the fact that it was celebrated "thousands of times every day all over Christendom" with each host holding the same "value"—as well as the fact that the host was in some sense "exchanged" for the payment of tithes, identified the eucharist with the money form and a currency over and above the economy of grace based on the

exchange of blood for sin (Rubin, *Corpus Christi,* 114, 149; see also Aers, "Reflections").

65. Aston, "Corpus Christi and Corpus Regni," 4.

66. Coke cited in Aston, "John Wycliffe's Reformation Reputation," 29; Milton, *CPW,* 2: 553 (see also 2: 231–232). With regard to such issues as the veneration of images, pilgrimages, the mass, intercession, and the vernacular Bible, Coke had a point. Keith Thomas describes Lollardy's "sweeping denial of the Church's claim to manipulate any aspect of God's supernatural power" in *Religion and the Decline of Magic,* 52; see also Lambert, *Medieval Heresy,* 301–304. Peter Marshall discusses Wycliff's attack on intercessory prayer in *Beliefs and the Dead,* 29–30. On Lollard iconoclasm, see Kamerick, *Popular Piety,* esp. 19–27.

67. Lewalski points this out in her *Life,* 590n107. For Milton's Chaucer references, see *CPW,* 1: 560, 570, 579–580. Foxe attributed the Lollard work *Jack up Lande* to Chaucer (see Aston, "Wycliffe's Reformation Reputation," 27n13). See also Milton's approving reference to "the vision and *Creed of Pierce plowman"* at *CPW,* 1: 916.

68. Brian Walker quoted in Keith Thomas, *Religion and the Decline of Magic,* 170. See also Sharpe, *Remapping Early Modern England,* 81.

69. On sixteenth-century conventiclers as "old Lollards" and possible connections to Anabaptist and General Baptist groups, see Watts, *Dissenters,* 7–14. As Watts observes, propagandists like Foxe, eager to suppress the range of dissenting views in the interests of Protestant unity, often overstated and even fabricated the predestinarian commitments of Protestantism's early heroes (12). See also Hill, "From Lollards to Levellers," 50, 58–59, and Collinson, *Birthpangs,* 13, 37.

70. Shagan, *Popular Politics,* 160; his argument that traditional anticlericalism provided a "bridge" to the Reformation, as well as to the more radical "desacralisation of the clergy preached by evangelicals," addresses Lollardy at 134, 139n28, 141n33, and 158.

71. Archer, "Popular Politics," 30; Nuttall, "Lollard Movement after 1384"; Lambert, *Medieval Heresy,* 291–292; Anne Hudson, *Premature Reformation,* 128–133; compare the demographic profile of Quakers in Reay, "Quakerism."

72. Archer, "Popular Politics," 30; in the sphere of print, the Baptist cobbler, Samuel How, became a best-selling author with his *Sufficiencie of the Spirits Teaching* (1640).

73. Burrage, *Early English Dissenters,* 2: 1; see Justice, *Writing and Rebellion,* 94, 124 and references therein; for a characteristic instance of the "experienced Christian" meme, see Sheffield, *Rising Sun,* 286.

74. On *Experience* and *Takeheed* as names, see Underdown, *Fire from Heaven*, 137. On artisanal epistemology, see Pamela Smith, *Body of the Artisan*.

75. *Hamlet*, 5.1.28–29. Shakespeare's Jack Cade appeals to Adam as a gardener (*Henry VI, Part Two*, 4.2.121).

76. This was a much-quoted phrase during the civil wars; Hill explores its scriptural bases in *English Bible*, 156.

77. Basse, *Sword and Buckler*, sigs. C^v, C, C2–C2^v, D4.

78. Bancroft, *Survay*, 8–9.

79. Patterson discusses this fusion in *Shakespeare*, 38–40. See also Matheson, "Peasants' Revolt."

80. Charles I's answer to the Parliament's 19 Propositions, quoted in Hill, "From Lollards to Levellers," 51; *A Declaration of Some Proceedings of Lt. Col. John Lilburn* (an official compilation ordered by the House of Commons in 1648), 25.

81. *Just Reward of Rebels*, sig. B4^v. The poem is an adaptation of the prefatory poem of Samuel Rowlands's *Hell's Broke Loose*, discussed below; although only the Irish rebels are singled out by name, the command to "love your King" is clearly directed to all.

82. Cleveland, *Rustick Rampant*, sig. A3.

83. Milton, *CPW*, 2: 492; Cleveland, *Rustick Rampant*, sig. A4. Dudley Digges used the image to satirize the idea of popular sovereignty: "As for Power inherent in the People, how should we imagine such a thing? . . . like Cadmus his men sprung out of the earth; where none deriving from any pre-existent Parents, had all of them equall originall and power" (cited in Kahn, *Wayward Contracts*, 3). For another riff on the Cadmus topos, see Marvell, *Prose Works*, 1: 45–46.

84. Cleveland, *Rustick Rampant*, 113, 76, 6. He also uses the phrase "Leaguers or *Covenanters*" (84) and imputes to Ball the conviction that "nothing but *Independency* was divine" (9).

85. Cleveland, *Rustick Rampant*, 91, 89–90, 8–9, 121, sig. A4^v.

86. On the uncleanness of dirt residing in the principle of mixture, and its identity as "matter out of place," see Douglas, *Purity and Danger*, esp. 43–50. For another instance of the "sons of earth" motif, see French, "An Unpublished Reply (1659) to Milton's 'Defensio,'" 166. On Adam as a man of earth, see Arnold Williams, *Common Expositor*, 70, 208, 231–232.

87. *Just Reward of Rebels*, sig. A2^v; Cleveland, *Rustick Rampant*, sigs. A5, A3; see also 139.

88. As the ghost of Jack Straw declares in the prologue, the two men agree "in name, and nature . . . wee both were like apoynted, / To take the Sword away from Gods Anoynted"; Rowlands suggests that such rebellious spirits are

vomitted up from hell in every generation (sigs. A2,A3–A3ᵛ, A4). Conversely, William Walwyn spoke of "that lying story of that injured people . . . the Anabaptists of Munster" (quoted in Hill, "From Lollards to Levellers," 50).

89. Rowlands, *Hell's Broke Loose,* sigs. B2–B3.

90. Rowlands, *Hell's Broke Loose,* sig. Bᵛ; see also sig. D3ᵛ.

91. Cleveland, *Rustick Rampant,* 88.

92. *Histrio-Mastix,* sigs. F3ᵛ, F4. The play is traditionally attributed to John Marston. For *Histrio-Mastix* as an Inns of Court play, see Finkelpearl, "John Marston's *Histrio-Mastix*"; on the play as a response to commercialization, see Hawkes, "Idolatry and Commodity Fetishism"; for an argument against Marston's authorship of the play, see Knutson, *"Histrio-Mastix";* for a useful account of Chrisoganus as Jonson, gently parodied but basically respected, see Bednarz, "Representing Jonson."

93. Their other plans include transforming churches into alehouses (sig. F3ᵛ).

94. The liberal arts are joined by a host of personifications, including religion. The play attacks nobles who lack "love and knowledge of the liberall Arts"; Chrisoganus ("golden-born"), the representative of true learning, repeatedly denigrates mechanical learning that is not abstracted from sensible matter while invoking the body politic to illustrate the necessity for the hands to submit to the head (sigs. A3ᵛ, A4, B2, G4). Professional players (the primary butts of satire) are presented as artisans who turn to the stage so that they can ape "Lords and Kings" (sig. B). For an account of the scientific intellectual culture of Elizabethan London and Baconianism as an effort at catch-up (and control), see Harkness, *Jewel House.* On the political self-assertion of craftsmen in the first part of the century, see Manning, *English People,* 212–229.

95. Aubrey, *Observations* in *Three Prose Works,* 319.

96. Winstanley, *Works,* 190. Bradstock provides a useful summary of Winstanley's life and the Digger project in *Faith in the Revolution,* 69–81; his subsequent argument stresses what is specifically Christian about the project; see also his essay "Restoring All Things."

97. Winstanley, *Works,* 315–316. Winstanley is describing his restlessness after publishing *The New Law of Righteousnes* (quoted in the previous sentence) in which he first related his vision. When the Diggers were driven off of George's Hill, they moved to nearby Cobham Heath, where they were well received by the inhabitants and joined by some, before being driven off once again. As Holstun has argued, the assumption that the Digger project failed because of "some sort of interesting internal or tragic flaw" is unwarranted; it was violently suppressed (*Ehud's Dagger,* 406n154, 426). For another instance in which the definition of *declare* is extended to include "Action," see 261.

98. Winstanley, *Works,* 73–74, 413–414. Five of his tracts predate the declaration he made with his spade, two of which clearly anticipate it: *Truth Lifting up its Head Above Scandals* and *The New Law of Righteousnes.* In 1651, after the project was suppressed, he published a plan for the commonwealth, *A Law of Freedom in a Platform,* for Cromwell to implement. Winstanley's writings thus fall into three groups, but I will be treating them all together to expose the experimentalist structure of thought that I believe undergirds the whole corpus.

99. Winstanley, *Works,* 355. The identical argument is made in the first two pages of *Light Shining in Buckinghamshire,* which Hill called a "near-Digger pamphlet" ("The Bible," 90); see also Keith Thomas, "Another Digger Broadside."

100. Winstanley, *Works,* 437. Adam does not have a positive signification in contexts when Winstanley is explicitly distinguishing between the first and second Adams (in *The New Law of Righteousnes* and *Truth Lifting up its Head*). Sometimes the distinction is articulated as one between Adam and Christ, and other times as one between the innocent and fallen Adams; there is no real difference, since both are restored in the working collective. The Diggers also appealed to a New Testament basis for the project, in Acts 2:44 and 4:32 (261); this text was also appealed to by the author of *Light Shining in Buckinghamshire* (616). As Knott observes in *Sword of the Spirit,* Winstanley's basic procedure is to combine references to Genesis with New Testament quotations dealing with "the workings of the Spirit," thus attenuating "the historical role of Christ" (93, 92). However, Knott's claim that Winstanley's concept of innocence was "a profound nostalgia for an idealized life of perfect simplicity" seems to me mistaken (104). When Winstanley celebrates simplicity, it is always in social terms, as forthrightness and freedom from guile, which conduces to collaborative knowledge production.

101. See John Rogers, *Matter of Revolution,* 49–51, 58–60. On kingly power as a tree that must be lopped down, all its roots and branches, see Winstanley, *Works,* 353. For the royal oak, see Herrick's "All Things Decay and Die" and Marvell's *Upon Appleton House,* stanzas 69–70.

102. Winstanley, *Works,* 245. True levelling is defined at 386–391. Kingly power was not restricted to the monarch; it inhered in private property, which was an assault on the true monarch: the internal—and collective—"King of righteousnesse" (see 150 and 264). Aubrey referred to the Diggers as the Levellers, who wanted to turn "the world upside-downe" (Michael Hunter, *John Aubrey,* 153). The identification was understandable; Lilburne similarly described God as having created man as "Lord over the earth," without granting him "dominion over the individuals of Mankind" (*Postcript,* in Aylmer, *Levellers,* 71). Although historians often stress the conservatism of the Levellers relative to the Diggers, the Leveller movement was divided between those who stressed equality

before the law and those who stressed equality enforced by law, as Schenk puts it; thus to a certain extent some Levellers actually *were* levellers (see chapter 4 of *Social Justice,* and Manning, *English People,* 400–402 and *Far Left,* 49–53).

103. On the blurring of human and divine agency in seventeenth-century millenarianism, see Lamont, "Richard Baxter, the Apocalypse, and the Mad Major."

104. Bradstock, "Restoring All Things," 98.

105. Pamela Smith, *Body of the Artisan,* 8.

106. Winstanley, *Works,* 474. In this passage Winstanley is describing the authors of the Bible, but in the following paragraph he identifies these "true Penmen" with living "Mecanicks."

107. Holstun remarks on Winstanley's use of the rhetoric of "guildhall fraternal communalism" and quotes one of its most powerful expressions: the opening of *Watch-word to the City of London,* when Winstanley apostrophizes the city, introducing himself as "one of thy sons by freedome," declaring "I do truly love thy peace; while I had an estate in thee, I was free to offer my Mite into thy publike Treasury Guild-hall, for a preservation to thee, and the whole Land"; see *Ehud's Dagger,* 398, and Winstanley, *Works,* 315.

108. Winstanley, *Works,* 565. The rotating, elective ministry he envisions would not exclude testimonials from those who were not elected: "He who is the chosen Minister for that year to read, shall not be the only man to make Sermons or Speeches: but everyone who hath any experience, and is able to speak of any Art or Language, or of the Nature of the Heavens above, or of the Earth below, shall have free liberty to speak when they offer themselves, and in a civil manner desire an audience, and appoint his day" (564). Hill discusses these services as natural philosophy conferences in *Intellectual Origins,* 109. Abraham Cowley would make a similar recommendation for services at his proposed "philosophical college," where preachers would "only teach God in his just Commandments, and in his wonderful Works" (*Proposition,* 42).

109. See, for example, the Cornish creation play: "I give names to the fishes, / Porpoises, salmons, congers, / All to me obedient they shall be . . . A fish from me shall not escape, / If I honour God perfectly" (Edwin Norris, *Ancient Cornish Drama,* 1: 10–11). Medieval images of the scene of naming emphasize a chain of command rather than a labor of discovery; see Morgan, *Early Gothic Manuscripts* 1: pl. 62; Kathleen Scott, *Later Gothic Manuscripts,* 2: 195; and Green, "Adam and Eve Cycle," 343.

110. Rising is everywhere in Winstanley; see, for example, 264, 477. To state the obvious, this upward movement reverses the fall.

111. Winstanley's attack on imagination—"selfish imaginary power"— occupies the first twenty pages of *Fire in the Bush;* see *Works,* 452–463; see also

243, 329, 377–380. Christopher observes that for many reformers "the flesh had nothing strictly to do with the body . . . 'the flesh' was the principle of the self that set itself up in opposition to God," or "self-sovereignty" (*Milton and the Science of the Saints*, 216–217).

112. *Light Shining in Buckinghamshire* in Winstanley, *Works*, 612.

113. Winstanley, *Works*, 196, 261. "This work to make the Earth a Common Treasury, was shewed us by Voice in Trance, and out of Trance, which words were these, *Work together, Eate Bread together, Declare this all abroad.*" On the following page, the passive voice is used with the indefinite article and no particular people are mentioned at all: we learn merely of what "was heard in a Trance," as if a state of complete freedom from "respect of persons" has been achieved (262).

114. The full title of the official declaration as it appeared in *The True Levellers Standard Advanced* was *A Declaration to the Powers of England, and to all the Powers of the World, shewing the cause why the common people of England have begun, and gives consent to digge up, manure, and sowe corn upon George-Hill in Surrey; by those that have subscribed, and thousands more that gives consent* (251). Other titles followed the declaration's formula, making the appropriate substitutions (see bibliography): e.g., the "Inhabitants of the Town of Wellin[g]borrow" (in *Works*, 649). Compared to Winstanley's "thousands," this latter broadsheet appeals only to "Hundreds more that give Consent"; the manifesto from Iver in Buckinghamshire refers merely to "many more that gives consent." Still, this pamphlet suggests that the movement was more extensive than was once thought, referring to colonies in Barnet, Enfield, Dunstable, Bosworth, and an unspecified part of Nottinghamshire. See Keith Thomas, "Another Digger Broadside."

115. Through "the great restorer of all things . . . we shall become one againe, and never be divided" (243).

116. *Several Pieces*, sig. A2ᵛ, quoted in Corns's interesting essay, "The Road to George Hill," 188; *Mysterie*, A4ᵛ (discussed in Corns, 194). Corns discusses Winstanley's exposure of "interiority" and "the power of self" on 189. The power of self is personally registered without being personal; as Nicola Baxter observes, Winstanley's references to the indwelling spirit are never far from the word *communion* ("Winstanley's Knowledge," 190). A connection can be drawn to what Appelbaum calls the "sliding subjectivities" of Bacon's "I"; see discussion in *Literature and Utopian Politics*, 53–55).

117. Winstanley, *Works*, 81; *England's Spirit Unfoulded*, 13; *Works*, 445.

118. Church, "Propositions," quoted in Hirsch, "Stylistics and Synonymity," 578–579.

119. Winstanley, *Works*, 105, 106, 105. Winstanley's supposed confusion of the fall of the Norman Yoke and the fall itself is another instance of this synony-

mizing strategy, which focuses attention on deep structure rather than on superficial differences that the experienced or experimental eye learns to see through; Winstanley apprentices his reader to this mode of observation through his style.

120. *Monarchy no Creature*, sig. b3ᵛ; Cook remarks that this is a "Poeticall" manner of conveying the idea that the law of England must be grounded on "the Eternall Law of God right reason and pure naturall principles." On Cook's prejudice against landlords in favor of tenants, see *DNB*.

121. Cary, *Little Horns Doom*, 307–308, 310; on Cary, see Capp, "Fifth Monarchists," and Appelbaum, *Literature and Utopian Politics*, 150–153.

122. Locke continues, "Man had a right to a use of the Creatures, by the Will and Grant of God"; see *Two Treatises*, 187, 223 (*First Treatise*, 4.40, 9.86).

123. John Dunn, *Political Thought*, 67; Markley, "'Land Enough in the World,'" 818. In this passage Markley observes that Locke "recast images of the Golden Age" to describe a world that "would remain forever open to appropriation."

124. Locke, *Two Treatises*, 308–309 (*Second Treatise*, 5.32). Reading the treatises as an attempt to promote a coalition capable of armed resistance, Ashcraft argues that property is accorded such prominence in the *Two Treatises* because Locke "needed some means of reconciling the language of equality, natural rights, and the view that all property was originally given to mankind 'in common' with a justification of individual property rights" in order to defend the Whigs against "the accusation of a design to level men's estates, which the Tories repeatedly hurled at them" (*Revolutionary Politics*, 251).

125. John Dunn, *Political Thought*, 232, 23n1, 68, 61, 226. Similarly, Ashcraft argues that while Locke did not advocate "the return of the Diggers . . . his attitude toward property is not so far removed from theirs as is generally assumed"; he "produced a powerful natural law critique of those individuals in society who neither labored nor contributed to the common good" (*Revolutionary Politics*, 272–273; see also 263–264). Ashcraft notes that Locke had access to a comprehensive collection of Leveller and Digger works when he lived with Benjamin Furley (165n145). See also Hoxby, *Mammon's Music*, 6.

126. See Aylmer, "Religion of Gerrard Winstanley," 102. Holstun calls attention to a 1607 manifesto for the Midlands Rising entitled *The Diggers of Warwickshire to all other Diggers* (*Ehud's Dagger*, 372).

127. Winstanley, *Works*, 475; Locke, "Epistle to the Reader," *Essay*, 10.

128. Locke never elaborated a Baconian reading of Genesis 2:19 but he was a strong promoter of the model of knowledge production it was often used to figure; he believed that the names Adam chose for the creatures were arbitrary. Leonard offers an expansive notion of what *arbitrary* meant to Locke's

contemporaries stressing the role of free choice in "arbitratement," in *Naming in Paradise,* 4–6.

129. Boyle, *Works,* 2: 20, 382.

130. Commenting on the dizzying alternation, Marvell's editor throws up his hands: "the frequently varied spelling of this word(s) leaves the editor uncertain as to which to prefer" (*Prose Works,* 1: 381n810).

131. Coles, *An English Dictionary,* sig. T2. Robert Greene discusses Cotes in "Whichcote, Wilkins, 'Ingenuity,' " 229, an article that was very helpful to this section; see also Haskin's incisive discussion in *Milton's Burden,* 42–45. Shapin and Schaffer have a different understanding of how the word functioned in experimentalist circles; see *Leviathan and the Air-Pump,* 129–131.

132. A catchphrase among the virtuosi: see, for example, Sprat, *History,* 54, 342 (where it is associated with "*innocent Works*") and Glanvill, *Philosophia Pia,* 90–91, where it is associated with the growth of "*operative* knowledge" and freedom from violent disputes.

133. The word *intellectual,* in the substantive sense we use it now, did not exist; a being possessed of superior intellectual powers might be called an intellectual, but that being would most likely be an angel or thinking substance itself; see *OED* def. B4. Milton uses the word to describe the thinking part: "the narrow intellectuals of quotationists and common placers" (*CPW,* 2: 230).

134. Sprat, *History,* 33–34. Sprat uses the word at 425, where it appears beside "Inventive" and "Industrious." Marvell agreed that "ingenious persons" were "modest" ones (*Prose Works,* 1: 121). The word appears throughout Marvell's prose; see 1: 418, where Milton is praised for having lived "ingenuously"; ironic uses abound, as in 274; and he is indignant when accused of what he calls "dis-ingenuity" at 267.

135. Quoted in Greene, "Whichcote, Wilkins, 'Ingenuity,' " 233, 241, 233. As a member of Cromwell's committee for the readmission of Jews to England, Whichcote clearly placed great trust in the possibilities of such exchanges. Marvell believed that even a papist endowed with sufficient "ingenuity of spirit" could attain salvation (*Prose Works,* 2: 229). On Locke's admiration for Which-cote, see John Marshall, *John Locke: Resistance,* 78–79, 179.

136. Quotations from Greene, "Whichcote, Wilkins, 'Ingenuity,' " 242, 241, 243–244, 231, 234, 251 (quoting Stephen Geree), 235, 246, 245, 250. Greene notes that he used the word 97 times in 107 sermons (231). For another perspective on their dispute, see Feingold, "Science as a Calling." As Feingold suggests, Tuckney accused Whichcote of keeping company with "ingenious men" and being too enamored of philosophy as opposed to divinity, but it was precisely this distinction that many of the ingenious rejected.

137. Glanvill, *Vanity of Dogmatizing,* 108. Thus Boyle identified "Ingenious Persons" as those who were "unwilling to determine of any important Controversie, without a previous consideration of what may be said on both sides" (*Works,* 2: 208–209).

138. *Mercurius Politicus* 58 (July 10–17, 1651), quoted in Lewalski, *Life,* 256; *Walwyns Just Defence,* 23; see *Vanitie of the Present Churches,* 39. An attack on the pamphlet, *Church-Levellers, or Vanity of Vanities and Certainty of Delusion,* mocked the "ingenuous licenser" who approved it, remarking that the author's "only vertue seems to be his impartiality," since he seemed equally against all organized religions (sigs. A1ᵛ, A2). See also Walwyn's appeal to ingenuity in *A Parable,* sig. A2ᵛ.

139. Bond, *Salvation in a Mystery,* sig. A3ᵛ; Milton, *CPW,* 2: 581, quoted in Greene, "Whichcote, Wilkins, 'Ingenuity,'" 251. The "ingenuous" well understand the primary—original—purpose of matrimony, to gratify an "intellectuall and innocent desire" (*CPW,* 2: 239, 269; see also 249, 252, 286).

140. Cook, *Monarchy No Creature,* 107, 80; Milton, *CPW,* 7: 429.

141. Namely, "Servilenes & Disaffection to reall Learning" (Boyle, *Correspondence,* 1: 190–191). Oldenburg called the Oxford Philosophical Club the "*Embryo* or First Conception of the *Royal Society*" (quoted in Robinson, "Unpublished Letter," 68). On this question, see Hill, "Intellectual Origins of the Royal Society," and Rupert Hall and Marie Boas Hall, "Intellectual Origins of the Royal Society."

142. Evelyn, *Diary,* 3: 416; Wilkins, *Mathematical Magick,* 195. To increase the likelihood of such inventions, he recommended public lectures in the vulgar tongue to inspire "every unlettered ingenious Artificer" (sig. A4ᵛ). Aubrey described Wilkins's own father, a goldsmith, as "a very ingeniose man" with "a very Mechanicall head. He was much for Trying of Experiments, and his head ran much upon the *perpetuall motion*" (*Brief Lives,* 319).

143. Evelyn, *Elysium Britannicum,* 350; Blith, *English Improver Improved,* sig. d3ᵛ, 3–4; the subtitle of the treatise proclaims "*the Improveableness of all Lands.*"

144. Blith thus feels compelled to distinguish himself from the Diggers in his epistle to the reader (*English Improver Improved,* sigs. c2ᵛ–c3). Charles Webster observes that the protégés of Blith and Hartlib "dwelt at length on the intrinsic agricultural merits of enclosure while at the same time pressing for legislation to ensure that this process would not operate to the disadvantage of the poor" (*Great Instauration,* 476–477). Ashcraft makes a similar argument with reference to Locke in *Revolutionary Politics,* 265–266, 281. Holstun takes a harsher view of Blith, and the whole ideology of improvement, in *Ehud's Dagger,* 387–388. But although Holstun identifies improvement with the "instrumental

ethic" of capitalism, he also finds it redeemable, since the Diggers joined it to "an ethic of self-creation through agrarian communism" (377).

145. These assertions come from Evelyn's moralized contrast of the observational styles among different kinds of travelers in *State of France,* sigs. A10–A10ᵛ; see also B3ᵛ–B4.

146. Evelyn, *Sylva* (1670 ed.), 229; *Kalendarium,* 1–2.

147. Evelyn, *Elysium Britannicum,* 29–31 (transcription includes insertions indicated in the notes). The parsley-bed is the "pretended place that babies come from" in the English nursery tradition (*OED,* 2). Evelyn began writing this text around 1657; Parry compares it to other practical books on how to make England "the paradise of the world" published in that decade, books such as Austen's *Treatise of Fruit Trees, with the Spiritual Use of an Orchard* (1653) and John Beale's *Herefordshire Orchards, A Pattern for All England* (1657); see "John Evelyn as Hortulan Saint," 138. For a general treatment of this literature, see Low, *Georgic Revolution,* 142–154. Leslie explores *Elysium Britannicum* as a transitional document between the cultures of the Interregnum and Restoration in "Bringing Ingenuity into Fashion."

148. Evelyn, *Elysium Britannicum,* 33, 350; Glanvill, *Vanity of Dogmatizing,* 108. Glanvill addresses himself to the ingenious reader throughout the book; see sig. Bᵛ, 156.

149. Evelyn, *Elysium Britannicum,* 35, 212. Evelyn cites as his authority Thomas More and the ancients, who only made statues of people who had accomplished something "signal . . . or invented some usefull thing; for so they dignified & made them Noblemen," but it also appears in Winstanley's *Law of Freedom:* "he who findes out any secret in *Nature,* shall have a Title of Honor given him, though he be a young man," though Winstanley further specified that no titles should be granted *except* those won "by industry" or the dignity of age (512).

150. Evelyn, *Elysium Britannicum,* 34. An anecdote about Galileo told by Society Fellow Robert Southwell provides a contrast to continental sensibilities: when a visitor happened upon him working in his garden, he said, "I am asshamed you see me in this clownes habit, I will goe & vestirmi da Pilosopho" (Drake, *Galileo at Work,* xiii).

151. Evelyn, *Elysium Britannicum,* 54; Evelyn appealed to the Earl of Peterborough to become a "Brother of the Spade" (quoted in Douglas Chambers, "'Elysium Britannicum not printed neere ready &c,'" 122).

152. George Fox, *Journal,* 27; see also 51. On exercise and experience see, for example, 25, 62, 75, 277, 340, 378, and 523. We owe our record of this restoration to Fox's amanuensis Thomas Ellwood, who claimed credit for inspiring *Paradise Regain'd,* a poem whose hero, a seeker, shares much in common with

Fox; see Chapter 6. For the contemporary identity of the seeker, see Watts, *Dissenters,* 184–186. Many who called themselves seekers in the mid-seventeenth century became Quakers by the end of it (see Nuttall, *Holy Spirit,* 68 and Schenk, *Social Justice,* 114). As Jonathan Scott argues, " 'Seekers' were not a group but a process of movement" (*England's Troubles,* 241)—agents of a progress. Taxonomizing treatments that follow the example of Thomas Edwards's *Gangræna* underestimate the diachronic element of sectarian multiplicity.

153. Schenk discusses the importance of the sons of Adam topos to the Quakers in *Social Justice,* 122–126. The Diggers famously refused to remove their hats for General Fairfax; see discussion in Manning, *Far Left,* 59–60.

154. George Fox, *Journal,* 27. On "common reason" as "a Relique of that light that was in Adam" see Nuttall, *Holy Spirit,* 36.

155. Evelyn, *Elysium Britannicum,* 34; Winstanley, *Works,* 468.

156. On Winstanley as a possible Quaker, see Alsop, "Gerrard Winstanley's Later Life," and Steven Marx, "The Prophet Disarmed." (On the remarkable spread of Quakerism, which had more adherents than Catholicism at midcentury, see Reay, "Quakerism.") On how the perceived excesses of figures like James Nayler led to a revisionary self-appraisal among Quakers, including Nayler himself, see Nuttall, *James Nayler,* esp. 16–20: Nayler came to believe that "the beginning of the work of a new creature" is "not the work done and finished" (see Nayler, *What the Possession of the Living Faith Is,* 6). On the need for collective discipline and vetting of claims, see Nuttall, *Holy Spirit,* 44–46; Walzer, "Puritanism as a Revolutionary Ideology"; Hill, *Intellectual Origins,* 329; and Damrosch's *Sorrows of the Quaker Jesus.* On the Royal Society's admission of the "enthusiastic quaker" Oliver Hill, see Michael Hunter, *Boyle by Himself,* lxxi, and Hooke, *Diary,* 338.

157. The phrase comes from Burnet's *Theory of the Earth,* 173, second pagination. On Winstanley's "knitting together" topos, see above.

158. See Underdown, *Freeborn People,* 40; Schenk, *Social Justice,* 29; and Hill, *Intellectual Origins,* 228–235. The radical power of Coke's originary myth is evidenced by the famous engraving of John Lilburne defending himself at trial with a copy of Coke's *Institutes* in his hand (reproduced on the cover of Nigel Smith's *Literature and Revolution*). Lilburne explains the "true intent and meaning" of Magna Carta, the "*Customes* of the Realm," and common law in *England's Birth-Right,* 5, 8. Of course, the common law was most often equated with "immemorial custom"; see Davis, "Radicalism in a Traditional Society."

159. See Norbrook, *Writing the English Republic,* 96–98; Underdown, *Freeborn People,* 87; and Zaret, *Origins of Democratic Culture,* 41. On the anniversary of King Charles's death in 1694, Evelyn attended a sermon deriving monarchical government from Adam; he deemed it "excellent" (*Diary,* 5: 165).

160. Peyton, *Glasse of Time,* 69 (misnumbered as 61); Filmer, *Patriarcha,* 1. Of course, adherents of patriarchal theory sought to make hay out of Adam's rule over his family, yet gender subordination was widely understood as a consequence of the fall; see James Grantham Turner, *One Flesh,* esp. chapter 3. Although his most famous tract was not published until 1680, Filmer had some prominence in the 1650s; see Sommerville's introduction to *Patriarcha,* xiv. Anti-royalists traced kingship firmly to Nimrod; see Milton, *PL,* 12.24–37. For background, see Arnold Williams, *Common Expositor,* 160–161.

161. Primogeniture would thus seem to be the necessary cornerstone of Filmer's theory, but he was not particularly attached to it; see *Patriarcha,* xxii, 44.

162. See Salkeld, *Treatise of Paradise,* 101. Compare *The Golden Legend* 1: 68. In "English Protestants," Elizabeth Hudson shows that even in the late sixteenth and early seventeenth centuries, those who were called Puritans steered clear of the *imitatio Christi* theme in contrast to their conservative Protestant counterparts.

163. Pack contends that Adam fell the day he was created and that the fall was indeed fortunate: "in Personal Union with God" Adam's descendants have more holiness "than ever they lost" (*Mystery of the Gospel,* 10).

164. Eachard, *Observations upon an Answer,* 71, 69, 86–87; see also 110. He countered sectarians' objections to hireling priests by pointing out that "certainly there is a labour besides digging," joking that his critics would conclude that "in my heart I was against *Adam*" (*Grounds and Occasions,* 102; *Observations upon an Answer,* 70).

165. Kahn, *Wayward Contracts,* 7, 51–55. As Kahn explains it, prior to the "explosion of the language of contract," the basis of covenant theology as well as social contract theory, "early modern subjects did not so much *consent* to political order as *assent* to a natural order the way we assent to a statement of fact" (2, 9). On covenant theology see Hill, "Covenant Theology," and Perry Miller's *Errand into the Wilderness,* esp. 62–63, 71, 88–89.

166. Evelyn quoted in Douglas Chambers, " 'Elysium Britannicum not printed neere ready &c,' " 120.

167. Thomas Hooker, *Saints Dignitie,* 28; Hooker is specifically describing "*Adam* in innocencie" here. See also Hill, "Covenant Theology," 305.

168. Tuke, *High-way to Heaven,* 56; Keach, *Medium Betwixt Two Extremes,* 12, 14.

169. Robert Harris, *Brief Discourse,* 11. Anthony Burgess described Adam as a "common Person representing all mankind," for "by Gods Covenant we were looked upon, as in him" (*Original Sin,* 2, 46).

170. Burgess, *Original Sin,* 39. Hill discusses the "uneasiness" of this formulation in "Covenant Theology," 309.

171. *Basilikon Doron* in *Political Works of James I,* 12. The association between original sin and the king's power to "bind" his subjects is strikingly presented in Dryden's *Absalom and Achitophel:* "If those who gave the Scepter, / could not tye / By their own deed their own Posterity, / How then coud *Adam* / bind his future Race? / How coud his forfeit on mankind take place? / Or how / coud heavenly Justice damn us all, / Who nere consented to our Fathers fall?" (lines 769–774; see John Marshall, *John Locke: Resistance,* 146). See also Burges, *Two Sermons,* 37.

172. Hill, "Covenant Theology," 310. Observing that the number of contested elections tripled between 1604 and 1624 then doubled again by 1640, Zaret suggests that the electorate was coming to exercise the kind of public reason that was traditionally the province of political representatives alone (*Origins of Democratic Culture,* 79). On contested elections, see Hirst, *Representative of the People?* 216–222.

173. On Locke and original sin, see John Marshall, *John Locke: Resistance,* 145–149. Hill observes that inherited sin "may have begun to lose its immediately obvious inevitability as a contract society grew up within the world of inherited landed property" (*Intellectual Origins,* 340).

174. Bradley, *Nosce Te Ipsum,* 36; Thomas Goodwin, *Christ Set Forth,* 47. Goodwin describes Adam as "a common publique person, not standing singly or alone for himselfe, but as representing all Man-kind to come of him" at 57, and "*All men,* by way of representation" at 59.

175. Seaver, *Wallington's World,* 4. As Seaver puts it, "Nehemiah doubted whether salvation was possible in practice outside the community of saints. And that community was both more extensive and more exclusive—because voluntary and self-selective—than the precinct or parish" (103). Although Wallington was steeped in "the experienced reality of the doctrine of original sin," this did not keep him from seeing the image of his maker in himself, as it had shined in Adam: "in examining myself I see much of God, which doth abound much to the glory of God" (16, 6).

176. Haller and Davies, *Leveller Tracts,* 11. Schenk remarks that Lilburne was gifted with the ability to turn "everything that happened to him into a public event" (*Social Justice,* 22). A new insistence on the individual's ability to turn private experience to public account fostered the cultivation of this gift.

177. Thomas Hooker, *Saints Dignitie and Dutie,* 28; Tuke, *High-way to Heaven,* 56–57.

178. Because the only evidence for the existence of Adamites is the satirical pamphlet literature directed against them, it is hard not to conclude that the "Adamite" existed only as a caricature of sectarians who held antinomian or merely antiformalist beliefs. For the most comprehensive recent study of the

Adamites as "a textual phenomenon," see Cressy, *Transgressions*, 251–280; for a discussion of Adamites in relation to other sectarian "excesses," real and imagined, see John Marshall, *John Locke, Toleration*, 302–311.

179. James Grantham Turner's discussion of the effort to "recover an Adamite relation to the body" fails to register the difference between its Adamitic and Adamic versions (*One Flesh*, 84–88), but the vicious cycle of doing and undoing he describes, of "erotic frenzy" followed by ascetic compensation, is vividly drawn in contemporary antisectarian literature; see also Kristen Poole, *Radical Religion*, 151–169.

180. Accordingly, the term *Adamite* could be used as a virtual synonym for *naked*, as in Vaughan's "I did lye / Pure *Adamite*" ("Upon a Cloke lent him by Mr. *J. Ridsley*," lines 40–41).

181. Couchman, *Adamites Sermon*, 3–4; John Taylor, *Divisions of the Church*, sig. A2ᵛ.

182. Couchman, *Adamites Sermon*, 2. The textile industry's association with religious dissent was so strong that William Cavendish could refer to the "wevers Doctrine" (Strong, *Catalogue of Letters*, 186).

183. John Taylor, *Divisions of the Church*, sig. A2ᵛ.

184. Pinnell, *Word of Prophesy*, sigs. A6ᵛ, 32. This was the opinion of a Mr. Baker, against whom much of the pamphlet is directed.

185. Pinnell, *Word of Prophesy*, 42–43, 37, 56, 58 (misnumbered as 48), 19, 59 (misnumbered as 49).

186. On common features between Pinnell and Boyle, see Michael Hunter, *Scrupulosity*, 49.

187. Horace, *Epistles* 1.13–15, cited in Higgitt, "Why I Don't FRS," 254. One of Evelyn's suggested designs for the Society's coat of arms added *Experiendo* (by experience) to the motto; *Omnia Probate* was another candidate. See J. D. G. D., "Arms of the Society," 38.

188. On contemporary concepts of revolution and progress, see Hill, *Nation of Change*, 82–101.

189. *Trials of Charles the First*, 84; see also 81 (Bradshaw is specifically asserting precedents for the right to try the king). See also Keith Thomas, *Religion and the Decline of Magic*, 430.

190. Blumenberg, *Legitimacy of the Modern Age*, 33; Bacon, *Works*, 8: 27. As Lilley observes in "Robert Recorde and the Idea of Progress," Bacon not only grounds the concept of progress in the cumulative improvement of mechanical arts; he takes the crucial step of applying this concept to his own work: he presents his writings "naked and open, that my errors can be marked and set aside before the mass of knowledge be further infected by them; and it will be easy also for others to continue and carry on my labours" (*Works*, 8: 34). Lilley's

larger claim is that the concept of progress comes not from a comparison of different periods, but from the experience of recognizing one's own participation in a progressive process; he shows that it was only after his contact with artisans that Robert Recorde acquired the habit of presenting his published works as contributions to be improved upon. Lilley's article builds on Zilsel's "Genesis of the Concept of Scientific Progress." Molland's "Medieval Ideas" lends further support to Lilley's account.

191. Blumenberg, *Legitimacy of the Modern Age,* 177; see also chapter 2 of Rossi's *Philosophy, Technology, and the Arts.*

192. Cook, *Monarchy no Creature,* sig. c^v. Whereas in 1613 to "improve" was merely to raise rents, by the middle of the century the word was freely applied to any kind of "thriving" or progress, not least in the area of poor relief; see Slack, *From Reformation to Improvement,* 81.

193. See Kendall, *Calvin and English Calvinism,* esp. 59, 65, 93, 109, 122–123; Cooper, *Fear and Polemic,* chapter 1; Lake, "Serving God," 98–100; Weber, *Protestant Ethic;* and Eaton, *Discovery,* 29, 99–100, 118–120, 191–192, 209, 211, 217.

194. Hill, *Milton and the English Revolution,* 268; Lake, *Boxmaker's Revenge,* 28. Lake criticizes the tendency to interpret apparently Arminian sentiments in the sermons of godly ministers like Stephen Denison as evidence of "subconscious slippage"; rather, appeals to "means" were invitations to experience the fact of election as fully as possible (28). As Como explains, the "strenuous and unremitting application of these means of grace . . . amounted to a conceptual engine whereby human activity—theoretically banished from the realm of right religion by the reformed commitment to faith and predestination—could be reinjected into the soteriological economy"; the insistence on the inseparability of faith and works repeatedly created the opening for an antinomian challenge, revealing antinomianism as the product of a "deep structural instability within puritanism itself" (*Blown by the Spirit,* 124, 131).

195. Burrage, *Early English Dissenters* 2: 1; see Coffey, "A Ticklish Business," 108. While some sects rejected predestination outright, many Puritan styles did not emphasize it; see Hill, *World Turned,* 152–153, passim.

196. Seaver, *Wallington's World,* 104 esp. note 128; Cooper, *Fear and Polemic,* 67; Winstanley, *Works,* 335.

197. Herbert, "Paradise," line 7. Leah Marcus analyzes this ideal of "simple childish obedience" (86) in *Childhood and Cultural Despair.*

198. Comparisons may be drawn to continental examples, but an early owner of this text also saw Milton's Eden in this model for England's betterment, inscribing these lines on the title page: "To Morrow, 'ere fresh Morning streak the East / With first approach of light, we must be risen / and at our pleasant labour to reform / yon flowerey arbours, yonder Allies green, / Our Walk at noon

with branches overgrown." As Comito eloquently puts it, Parkinson's "Letter to the Reader"—like the title of the treatise itself—suggests that what arts repair is not the recalcitrance of postlapsarian matter itself "but simply ignorance, forgetfulness of the possibilities the world continues to offer" ("Renaissance Gardens," 504).

199. While the first illustration (sig. D4ᵛ) is a synopsis of all of sacred history, with Adam and Eve on the far left eating from the tree of knowledge, the illustration of Adam and Eve in the state of innocence (sig. E2ᵛ) offers an abundant variety of flora and fauna.

200. "Where every *Grotte,* and every *Shade,* / Is of a *Tree* of *Knowledge* made, / Which men may *Touch,* and *Tast* without offence, / Secur'd by Thyne Exemplar Innocence" (Evelyn, quoted in Douglas Chambers, "'Elysium Britannicum not printed neere ready &c,'" 120). Thus Beale wrote a tract for Katherine Boyle proving that "scripture, reason & experience sheweth How wee may bee restored to paradyse on Earth" (Charles Webster, *Great Instauration,* 86).

201. Donne, *Sermons,* 9: 64, 69. These sermons were preached at court in 1629.

202. Boyle, *Early Essays,* 245, 244, 248, 247.

203. As Hoxby points out, the commonwealth's interests had traditionally been identified with social harmony; in the seventeenth century, they became identified with productivity (*Mammon's Music,* 3).

204. Phythian-Adams quoted in Collinson, *Birthpangs,* 54. Grossman explores the transformed experience of time from a different, but I think, complementary perspective in *Authors to Themselves;* see esp. 14–15.

205. Hutton uses this term in *Rise and Fall of Merry England,* for example at 134. As a 1948 study of the conflicts engendered by the Book of Sports put it, the whole controversy came down to the question: "'Can I play games on Sunday afternoon?'" The writer continues, "Curiously enough, so it seems today, the man-in-the-street answered 'No!'" (Henderson, *King's Book,* 5). Even so sympathetic a chronicler of festivity as Hutton admits that the 1648 publication of Herrick's *Hesperides,* the most sustained celebration of festivity of the age, was a "non-event" (*Rise and Fall of Merry England,* 173). The book's attitude toward traditional observances predicts its reception; as Marcus observes, Herrick's stage-management of festival registers a melancholy awareness that now, "holiday has to be made to happen" (*Politics of Mirth,* 141). For a summary of Parliament's efforts to pass Sabbatarian legislation in the 1620s, see Hutton, *Rise and Fall of Merry England,* 171–174. Popular anti-Catholic sentiment played an important role in the movement against state-sponsored mirth. As Jensen has discussed, any contemporary needing confirmation of the connection between popery and festival could find it in the Book of Sports itself, which claimed that fostering

traditional pastimes could reconcile those who hankered after the old religion to the reformed church; it was precisely in order to create converts, reformers countered, that the popes had combined idolatrous pagan festivals with Christianity in the first place ("Singing Psalms"; see, for example, Aubrey's comments on festivals in *Three Prose Works,* 133). On anti-popery as a "popular ideology" in the mid-seventeenth century, see Manning, *English People,* chapter 2; Oliver Heywood feared the spread of the "spirit of Atheism" primarily because it served as "a door to popery" (*Diaries,* 2: 216). On the rumor that Laud had actually converted to popery, see Adam Fox, *Oral and Literate Culture,* 356, and Underdown, *Revel, Riot and Rebellion,* 129, 140. Prynne's *Breviate of the Life of William Laud* would lavish attention on Laud's dream that he was "*Reconciled to the Church of Rome*" (10).

206. Duffy, *Stripping of the Altars,* 49–51. For variations, see Needham, "Laudian Marxism" and Michael Stevens, "T. S. Eliot's Neo-Medieval Economics."

207. Howson, *Sermon,* sigs. A2–A2^v.

208. Howson, *Sermon,* sig. A3^v. The term *Merry England* has been traced to John Caius's reference in 1552 to "the old world, when this country was called Merry England"; see Keith Thomas, *Perception of the Past,* 20. Thomas shows how a term that originally connoted prosperity acquired "an increasingly festive connotation."

209. Kenneth Parker, *English Sabbath,* 121, 6; see also 137.

210. Stokes, *REED: Somerset,* 1: 428–429; Thomas Hall, *Funebria Florae,* 17.

211. Collinson et al., *Conferences and Combination Lectures,* xxviii, civ–cv; see also Collinson's *Godly People,* 467–498, and *Birthpangs,* 45–46. For their seventeenth-century evolution, see Nuttall, *Holy Spirit,* chapter 5.

212. Wallis, "Account of Some Passages," 21; Strong, *Catalogue of Letters,* 185.

213. Brigden, "Youth and the English Reformation," 60–61; Earle, *Microcosmographie,* sig. K2^v.

214. Baxter quoted in Manning, *Far Left,* 35; see also Hakewill, *Apologie,* sigs. a3–a3^v; on Evelyn's proof of God, see Frances Harris, *Transformations,* 20.

215. Eliade, *Sacred and Profane,* 178. I refer to Hutton, *Rise and Fall of Merry England,* and Marcus, *Politics of Mirth.* See also Walsham's "Parochial Roots of Laudianism Revisited."

216. Burke, *Popular Culture,* 180–181, 209–210; see Oldenburg's letter to Milton in Milton, *CPW,* 7: 495–496, and his Christmas Eve letter to Boyle in Oldenburg, *Correspondence,* 4: 78. The case is concisely made in Thomas Hall, *Funebria Florae.* As Hutton points out, late-medieval denunciations of popular festivities never made this charge, which was the product of humanist learning, though Lactantius's account of the obscene origins of May Day was an important

source (*Rise and Fall of Merry England,* 71; Marcus, *Politics of Mirth,* 151–152). Polydor Vergil's *De Rerum Inventoribus* (1502) traced Candlemas candles, Shrove Tuesday revelry, Christmas lords and midsummer bonfires to pagan roots; a crucial source for the so-called complaint literature, the book went through thirteen editions over the following century (Hutton, *Rise and Fall of Merry England,* 144–145).

217. See Thomas Hall, *Funebria Florae,* 13–14.

218. Weber, *Protestant Ethic,* 116. See discussion in Marcus, *Politics of Mirth,* 6–7.

219. Laud, who regarded popular challenges to traditional games as an affront to episcopal authority, played an important role not only in reissuing the Book of Sports but in suppressing ministers who refused to read it from the pulpit; see Marcus, *Politics of Mirth,* 14–15; Kenneth Parker, *English Sabbath,* 180.

220. Herrick, "Corinna's Going A-Maying," lines 48–50. For Herrick, "religious duty and festival liberty are joyously one and the same" (Marcus, *Politics of Mirth,* 158). Thomas Peyton's *Glasse of Time* appealed to Corinthians 10:31 to argue that "our sports, our actions, and our playes" are a way of praising God, and that "serious meditations" must be balanced with "honest recreations" (26, misnumbered as 30).

221. Milton, *Maske,* line 807; Strong, *Catalogue of Letters,* 226. On repressive desublimation, see Marcuse, *One-Dimensional Man,* chapter 3, as well as "Repressive Tolerance." Writing after the Restoration, Samuel Parker observed that "*Princes may with less hazard give Liberty to mens Vices and Debaucheries, than to their Consciences*" (*Discourse,* lxv).

222. Perkins, *Foundation of Christian Religion,* sigs. A2–A2ᵛ.

223. Evelyn, *Remaines of Gentilisme and Judaisme,* in *Three Prose Works,* 141–142. For clerics who sought to promote love and fellowship on the alebench, see Collinson, *Birthpangs,* 57; Underdown discusses "cakes and ale" Anglicanism in *Revel, Riot, and Rebellion,* 66–72. This "relaxed 'Anglican' piety," based as much "on the ale bench as the pulpit" did not, of course, characterize all enemies of sectarians; see Lake, "Serving God," 102, 115–116. Clark discusses the connection of the seventeenth-century alehouse with religious and political conservatism in *English Alehouse,* 157–159. On the transfer of "popish reliques" from the church to the alehouse in the century following the Reformation, see Tessa Watt, *Cheap Print,* 178–179, 194–196, 331–332. Of course, given the contemporary paucity of public gathering places, the alehouse cannot be exclusively identified with conservative festive culture; see Hill, "From Lollards to Levellers," 62. Virtuosi tended to harbor negative feelings about alehouses; for typical complaints about the "unreasonable number" of alehouses and their

discouragement of productivity, see Thomas Browne, *Works,* 4: 203, and Evelyn, *Diary and Correspondence,* 624.

224. For Herrick and his pig, see Grossart's introduction to *Complete Poems* 1: xcvii. In addition, "Clark ales" were held to support the salaries of parish clerks (Stokes, *REED: Somerset,* 1: 429). Although there were some clerical attacks on ales in the fourteenth century, by the mid- to late fifteenth century, they had become a regular means of raising parish funds; recovering from the dramatic attack on festive culture during Edward's brief reign, they were going strong during much of Elizabeth's; see Hutton, *Rise and Fall of Merry England,* 113–114. By the seventeenth century, they had become contested affairs. A characteristic instance of the conflicts they generated is the testimony of a John Cornishe, carpenter, against Robert Wolfall, incumbent of Weston, for telling his parishioners to "departe, and followe Robin hoode, according to their aunclent Custome, to the Alle" (*REED: Somerset,* 1: 388–389). In 1633, Bishop William Piers lamented to Laud that church ales had declined: "there are very few of them left: but yet I find, yat by Church-ales heretofore, many poore parishes have cast their Bells, repayred their Towers, Beautyfyed their Churches, and raysed stockes for the poore; and not by the sinnes of the people, (as some Humourists have sayd) but by the Benevolence of people at their honest and harmeless sports and pastimes" (Stokes, *REED: Somerset,* 1: 429).

225. See Clark, *English Alehouse,* 152–153. Richard Rawlidge complained that the decline of "publike sportings on the Sabbath" ("that commendable exercise of shooting, and of Beare-baiting, stoole-ball, foot-ball, wasters, and such like") had left a restive populace with nothing to do but go "Ale-house hunting": with "publike Recreations being laid of[f]," alehouses had multiplied, and with them "drunkennesse and whoring . . . wasting and consuming" (*Monster Late Found Out,* 12–13).

226. Herrick, "The Wake," lines 19–20; Marcus, *Politics of Mirth,* 156.

227. Herrick, "The Wake," line 6. The major difference characterizing the resurrected festivities after the Restoration is that they no longer contributed in any significant way to church finances (see Hutton, *Rise and Fall of Merry England,* 229–231): in this sense, festivities became *less* "profit"-driven (though of course new profit-driven forms of recreation were invented; see Plumb, "Commercialization of Leisure"). Money was raised during festivals, and it went into the parish chest. In some parishes, ales were the church's single largest source of revenue throughout the century (see Phythian-Adams, "Milk and Soot," 92, and Litzenberger, *English Reformation and the Laity,* 19). In Carew's euphemizing description of how ales and games redounded to "the church's profit," the people "lovingly visit one another, and this way frankly spend their money together" (quoted in Judith Bennett, "Conviviality and

Charity," 27: as Moisà points out in her rejoinder to this essay, not everyone was convinced that "the exchange of overpriced ale for cash was charity"; see "Debate," 223).

228. Thomas Hall, *Funebria Florae*, 10; football was itself understood to be "a friendly kind of fight" (quoted in Burke, *Popular Culture*, 212).

229. Strong, *Catalogue of Letters*, 227; Heywood, *Diaries*, 2: 271. On this occasion Heywood witnessed only the destruction of property, but during the Midsummer celebrations the previous June (which elicited a similar comment: "hell seemes broken loose"), he had witnessed a "great tumult, abundance of young men all on an heap . . . striking one another"; a constable attempted to break up the fight but "no good would be done"; he also recorded a rough Easter game that ended in the death of one of the participants (2: 263, 271). In Devon in July 1615, two ales ended in manslaughter (Wasson, *REED: Devon*, 295–296); in 1524, a London "Master of Misrule" was pardoned for murder (Brigden, "Youth and the English Reformation," 50).

230. Žižek, *Looking Awry*, 102–103 (Herrick presents a similar understanding of festival in "The Hock-Cart"); Conway quoted in Underdown, *Freeborn People*, 94; see also Hirst, *Representative of the People?* 6.

231. As Pettitt puts it, seasonal festivity could "function as the vehicle for non-seasonal rebellion" (" 'Here Comes I, Jack Straw,' " 4); Hutton, *Rise and Fall of Merry England*, 89, 9.

232. Winstanley, *Works*, 335. See also the comparison of the "petty-tyrants" (town worthies who sought to drive the Diggers off the land) to "so many fools in a Mid-summer Aile" in *Light in Buckinghamshire* (in Winstanley, *Works*, 620).

233. Stokes, *REED: Somerset*, 1: 347, 351. Townspeople also carried about a board "whereon was paynted the picture of a Caulf" (347).

234. Northbrooke, *Treatise*, 12. Supporters of festival appealed to the importance of callings in the restricted sense, in other words, when it suited them: William Cavendish complained that "Exersisinge & Prophosinge" functioned "to distracte the comon people from their livlyhoode . . . takinge them frome their Calinges as much as the [holy days of] Roman Catholikes doth," and in a much more dangerous manner, for the "Bible in Englishe under everye wevers & Chambermadyes Arme hath dun us much hurte" (Strong, *Catalogue of Letters*, 188).

235. Roberts, *Day of Hearing*, 29, 88, 32, sig. I6, 32–33, sig. A2. A pamphlet attacking May games—*A Godly and Necessary Sermon Against Fleshly Lusts; and against certaine Mischevious May-games, which are the Fruite thereof*—is bound together with *Day of Hearing*.

236. Roberts, *Day of Hearing*, 7, 19. The meme of transcending the examples of fathers was popular among the godly: Wallington kept a shard of broken

glass from his church "to shew to the generation to come what God hath don for us to give us such a reformation that our forefathers never saw the like" (*Notebooks,* 131).

237. On fire-fighting ladders, see Underdown, *Revel, Riot, and Rebellion,* 54, and Hutton, *Rise and Fall of Merry England,* 198. The cutting down of maypoles was a frequent cause of fights; such destruction of maypoles dates back to the Edwardian reformation; see Marcus, *Politics of Mirth,* 151. On the remarkable library put together by the residents of Bury in 1595 in the parish church of St. James, which included a well-thumbed herbal, see Craig, *Reformation, Politics, and Polemics,* 116–121 and appendix 5. The godly of Dorchester contributed globes as well as books on the new science to their library (Underdown, *Fire from Heaven,* 47).

238. Underdown, *Fire from Heaven,* 114–129, and *Revel, Riot and Rebellion,* 41–42. Such "associative solidarity" could also offer pushback to the "localist hegemony of the parish" (Holstun, *Ehud's Dagger,* 35–36, 105).

239. Coffey makes a similar argument in "Ticklish Business"; see esp. 130–131.

240. Denison, *Exposition,* 15–16.

241. Denison, *White Wolfe,* 69 (sig. K3). While Denison promoted intellectual labor among the laity, he also sought to limit its expressions, encouraging magistrates to punish mechanical preachers like John Hethcrington, who had "no lawfull calling" to preach; see *White Wolfe,* sig. A3, 18–19. Lake's *Boxmaker's Revenge* offers an extended treatment of Denison's thought in its social context.

242. Thomas Taylor, *Works,* 411 (sig. Ggg2), whose title page declares the work's publication as having been "earnestly desired by very many experimental CHRISTIANS." Haskin provides a helpful discussion of the affective dimension of experimental reading practices in the first chapter of *Milton's Burden.*

243. Citations to *Grace Abounding* (except from the preface and appended *Relation of the Imprisonment*) are to paragraph number. See also "The Epistle to the Reader" in *Doctrine of the Law and Grace Unfolded* where, bragging that he "never went to School to *Aristotle* and *Plato*," he encourages his reader to imagine herself not reading a book (which might be expected to contain what he calls "whimsical Scholar-like terms") but simply sorting through a "parcel" of "sayings" (sigs. A8ᵛ–B).

244. See, for example, 201. On Bunyan's physical experience of the word and the "disclaiming locutions" through which he presents that experience, see Carlton, "Bunyan: Language, Convention, Authority." On occasions that Bunyan does represent himself reading, it is usually to test a prior experience of the word; when he *simply* reads, the result is unsatisfactory, and he throws down

his book "in a pet" (204); see Luxon's wonderful analysis of this moment in *Literal Figures,* 148.

245. Bunyan, *Doctrine of the Law and Grace Unfolded,* sigs. A6, A3.

246. Bunyan, *Grace Abounding* (preface), 3 (Bunyan specifically identifies these places as sites that "you" have been in, as he has); *Relation of the Imprisonment,* in *Grace Abounding,* 115.

247. See Bunyan, *Grace Abounding,* 63–65 and 262–264. In the first instance, the book from which the passage comes, Ecclesiasticus, is not considered "holy and Canonical," but since it corresponded with his experience, "it was my duty to take the comfort of it." What is particularly interesting about the second instance is its wild imprecision; Bunyan allows the differences between the predicted text and actual text stand unrationalized and unremarked upon, as if they were actually unworthy of comment. The clear message is that to one who reads with an eye to the spirit of the text—the susceptibility of its content to Winstanleyan synonymizing—these discrepancies simply do not matter; experience is all. For an account of the first episode that stresses Bunyan's anxiety, see Haskin, *Milton's Burden,* 231–232. I would argue that for Bunyan anxiety is an aspirational, because productive, state.

248. See Peter Goldman, "Iconoclasm and Beyond." On the process of adequating individual experience to collective norms in the sects, see Carlton, "Bunyan: Language, Convention, Authority"; Walzer, "Puritanism as a Revolutionary Ideology"; McKeon, *Origins of the English Novel,* 299; and Tipson, "English Protestantism." On the soul itself as a "corporation" in Bunyan, see Damrosch, *God's Plot and Man's Stories,* 143–144.

249. The three or four women talking of the things of God riffs on Matthew 18:20: "For where two or three are gathered together in my name, there am I in the midst of them," but once again, the imprecision of experiential translation is part of the point.

250. John Goodwin, *Treatise of Justification,* sigs. b3ᵛ–b4ᵛ; *Glimpse* quoted in Charles Webster, *Great Instauration,* 11 (for Daniel 12:4 as a crucial link between Puritanism and Baconianism in the period see part I generally).

251. Hutton, *Rise and Fall of Merry England,* 208, 259. Hutton argues that this tendency intensified during William and Mary's reign.

252. The Elizabethan church had already trimmed down festival days from 125 to 27 while promoting "historical" holidays like Elizabeth's Accession Day (Cressy, "Protestant Calendar," 34). See also Cressy, *Bonfires and Bells,* 50–56, and Roy Strong, "Popular Celebration of Accession Day." Traditional festival energies could now be channeled in new directions: Gunpowder Treason Day could be seized upon to emphasize the ongoing threat of popery, generating new practices such as the targeted destruction of icons. Outdoor ceremonies to secure

fertility and good weather, such as the blessing of trees on the twelfth day after Christmas, had also been pared away; only the annual perambulation of the parish in Rogation week survived, now serving as a corporate manifestation of the village community rather than an occasion for priestly magic, a distinction Bishop Grindal insisted upon when he asserted that it was "not a procession, but a perambulation"—an opportunity to transmit corporate knowledge of the parish boundaries (see Keith Thomas, *Religion and the Decline of Magic,* 62–63; Davenport, "Elizabethan England's Other Reformation," 260–264; for the adaptation of the ritual to the urban setting, see Berlin, "Reordering Rituals," 57–59).

253. Underdown, *Revel, Riot and Rebellion,* 71. The Lord's Supper had itself become a commemoration of a historical event, as Peter Harrison observes in *The Bible, Protestantism, Natural Science,* 124; see also 131.

254. Seaver, *Wallington's World,* 156; Raymond, *Invention of the Newspaper,* 245. On the transformation of petitioning in the period, see Zaret, *Origins of Democratic Culture.*

255. Evelyn quoted in Frances Harris, *Transformations,* 54. Boyle's practice of occasional meditation as explicated in his 1665 *Occasional Reflections,* a treatise that was largely written during the 1640s (see *Works,* 5: xi–xv), is discussed in Chapter 4. Joseph Hall's *Occasionall Meditations* (1630) provided a model for such meditations, though Boyle went out of his way to deny that he was influenced by it; see chapter 4. Puritans like Isaac Ambrose promoted the practice of diary-keeping in much the same terms as virtuosi like Boyle promoted occasional meditation; see Sachse's introduction to Roger Lowe's *Diary.* Such divinity comprehended private as well as public matters: as Richard Sibbes observed, "If we were well read in the story of our own lives, we might have a divinity of our own, drawn out of the observation of God's particular dealing with us" (*Works,* 1: 277, discussed in Luxon, "'Not I, but Christ,'" 918). See also J. Paul Hunter, *Before Novels,* 198–208, and chapter 12.

256. Wilkins, *Discourse Concerning the Beauty of Providence,* 4, 60–63; see discussion in Hill, "Intellectual Origins," 145.

257. Bunyan, *Book,* 7. Other objects of meditation include a pound of candles falling to the ground and the "Kackling of a Hen" (51, 60). See Marcus's discussion in *Childhood and Cultural Despair,* 52–55. Although it was not published until after his death, it is reasonable to assume that the text was circulated among members of his congregation in some form.

258. *The Proceedings of the Councel of State against Richard Overton, now Prisoner in the Tower of London,* from *The Picture of the Councel of State* in Haller and Davies, *Leveller Tracts,* 216–217, 230, 231, 227, 225.

259. Boyle, *Works,* 3: 239; 13: 170; see also 3: 238 and discussion in Shapin, "House of Experiment," 384. The first quotation comes from *Some Considerations*

Touching the Usefulnesse of Experimental Naturall Philosophy; although this was published in 1663, he had written much of it over a decade earlier (see *Works,* 3: xix–xxiv, 195). The second quotation comes from the 1649–1654 manuscript, "Of the Study of the Booke of Nature," which Boyle mined for *Usefulnesse;* see *Works* 13: xxxvii–xxxviii.

260. Boyle, *Works,* 3: 239; *Correspondence,* 1: 83; *Works,* 3: 204. Boyle offers an extended defense of a physico-theological Sabbath in *Works,* 3: 238–242. On Boyle's Sabbath habits, see Shapin, "House of Experiment," 384 and note 27 (although in his maturity he entered his Pall Mall laboratory immediately after his "morning devotions," he stopped conducting experiments on Sundays in the 1680s; this would be consistent with a suggestion he makes in *Usefulnesse,* of a weekend-long Sabbath, in which Saturday might be devoted to honoring the creation and Sunday to the redemption). See also Derham, *Physico-Theology,* 437–447 (11.6). The physico-theology explosion of the Restoration and early eighteenth century has Interregnum roots: John Ray's *Wisdom of God Manifested in the Works of the Creation* began its long print run in 1691, but it was based on lectures Ray had given in the 50s (Michael Hunter, *Science and Society,* 176).

261. Boyle, *Correspondence,* 1: 83.

262. Hooke, *Micrographia,* sig. g2; see discussion in Michael Hunter, *Science and Society,* 28. On the latitudinarianism of Wilkins and other virtuosi, see Barbara Shapiro, "Latitudinarianism and Science" and *John Wilkins.*

263. Oldenburg quoted in Marie Boas Hall, *Henry Oldenburg,* 89–90.

264. Petty, *Advice,* 23; Salkeld, *Treatise of Paradise,* 145.

265. See Marie Boas Hall, *Henry Oldenburg,* 26–27; Purver, *Royal Society,* 111–112. Eleven out of the twenty-five members of the Rota became Fellows (Michael Hunter, *Establishing the New Science,* 8). On Gresham, see Ames-Lewis, *Sir Thomas Gresham* and Chapter 2 in this volume.

266. Strong, *Catalogue of Letters,* 227.

267. Evelyn, *Sylva* (1670 ed.), 207. The maypole remained the lightning rod for conflict between experimentalist and festive culture during the Restoration. A contemporary remarked that he found "Poles rais'd so high" in the year of Charles's return that "reform'd *London*" had become "Popish *Rome*" (prefatory poem to Thomas Hall's *Funebria Florae,* sig. A2ᵛ). And in the course of presenting the *"Ingenioso* or *Experimenteer"* as a *"despiser* of the *Clergy,"* John Eachard described him as one who "rides up and down the *Country,* and every *Town* he comes at with a *May-Pole,* he wonders what the *Aristotelean Parson* and the *People* mean, that they do not presently cut it down, and set up such a one as is at *Gresham College*" (*Observations,* in *Grounds and Occasions,* 178, second pagination).

268. Thomas Browne, *Works,* 4: 281; Roberts, *Day of Hearing,* sigs. K7–K7ᵛ; Pinnell, *Word of Prophesy,* sig. A6. Aubrey also thought it was a "pity

that they make such a destruction of so fine a tree" (*Remaines of Gentilisme and Judaisme* in *Three Prose Works*, 137).

269. Milton, *CPW*, 2: 545.

270. For a similar contrast, where May Games squelch spiritual blooming in the young who are in the "flower" of their days, see Thomas Hall, *Funebria Florae*, 10.

271. Milton, *CPW*, 7: 408–409.

272. Hutton, *Rise and Fall of Merry England*, 229–231. On festive culture after the Restoration, see Emma Griffin, *England's Revelry*.

273. Boyle, *Works*, 2: 468 (from *Style of the Scriptures*, which, though not published until 1661, was written in the early 1650s; see *Works*, 2: xxv–xxvii, 382, 386, and J. R. Jacob's discussion in *Robert Boyle*, 120–121).

274. From Evelyn's letter to Thomas Browne in Browne, *Works*, 4: 275.

275. See Slack, *From Reformation to Improvement*, 102–104, 110–114. On the Boyle lectures in physico-theology, see Dahm, "Science and Apologetics."

276. Duffy, *Stripping of the Altars*, 8; Rolle, *Lytell Boke*, sig. Aiii^v.

277. Le Goff makes this argument in *Birth of Purgatory* (see esp. 291–292) and Greenblatt expands on it in *Hamlet in Purgatory*, chapter 2. The phrase "temporary fire" appears in the pontifical definition of purgatory made in 1254, cited in Le Goff, *Birth of Purgatory*, 283–284. Gurevich argues that purgatory existed in the popular imagination long before being "invented" by theologians in "Popular and Scholarly Medieval Cultural Traditions." I am arguing that once it was determined that "there are but two places, and there is no third place for any" (Becon, *Displaying of the Popish Masse*, 242), purgatory persisted as a metaphor for the regenerate—and productive—life, but medieval precedents can be found for this continuity; in her *Treatise on Purgatory*, Saint Catherine of Genoa was able to understand what purgatory was like by "Comparing it to the Divine Fire which she Felt in Herself" (17).

278. Gibson, *Election and Reprobation*, 74.

279. Peter Brown, "End of the Ancient Other World," 54. He continues, "A strongly rooted imaginative tradition gave a major place to the operation of 'fire' of some kind."

280. See also 1 Peter 1:7 and 3 Enoch 15:1. For a suggestive treatment of the metaphorics of fire in the urban context, see Nigel Smith, "Making Fire."

281. King's Book of 1543 and Roger Edgeworth quoted in Peter Marshall, *Beliefs and the Dead*, 78; Robert Harris, *Brief Discourse*, 17, 19.

282. Perkins, *Reformed Catholike*, 278.

283. Gibson, *Election and Reprobation*, 107, 14, 102, 109, 74.

284. Roberts, *Day of Hearing*, 18, 23–24, 34.

285. Greenblatt, *Hamlet in Purgatory*, 51–52, pl. 1.

286. The identity of its author, Thomas Savile, is unclear.

287. Savile, *Adams Garden,* sig. A3ᵛ, 1, 14, 22. As I have suggested, this paradise of pains resonates with traditional representations of Adam the delver. *Jacob's Well* presents the work of repentance under the sign of the tool held by Adam, the spade (282–289; see discussion in Reiss, *Sunday Christ,* 37); see also Augustine's *Confessions,* 2: 118–119 (10.16).

288. Salkeld, *Treatise of Paradise,* 33; Greenblatt, *Hamlet in Purgatory,* 38. The ethos of progressive purification was accommodated by reformed orthodoxy: Luther maintained that, although the Christian's imputed righteousness "swallows up all sins in a moment, for it is impossible that sin should exist in Christ," it was nonetheless the case that "alien righteousness is not instilled all at once, but it begins, makes progress, and is finally perfected" (*Two Kinds of Righteousness,* in *Works,* 31: 298–299). Although inspired and led by God, the believer himself was an active agent of this progressive purification; see discussion in Cooper, *Fear and Polemic,* 18. Eventually, progress became imaginable as an attribute of heavenly perfection itself; see Edward Whitaker's *The Future State: or, A Discourse Attempting some Display of the Souls' Happiness in Regard to that Eternally Progressive Knowledge, or Eternal Increase of Knowledge and the Consequences of it, which is amongst the Blessed in Heaven* (1683).

289. The phrase is Clement of Alexandria's, quoted in Constas, "To Sleep, Perchance to Dream," 96. On fire as a symbol of God's ability to transform his own creation, see Peter Brown, "End of the Ancient Other World," 54–55.

290. Bacon, *Works,* 6: 721. Origen taught that, to enter paradise, all souls had to pass through the flaming sword of the cherub and undergo a baptism of fire, but he did not distinguish between eschatological purification and the last judgment, and thus from particular and general judgments, which will result in the restoration of all things in Christ (Hennessey, "Place of Saints and Sinners," 295–303). On connections between the fiery sword and purgatory, see Arnold Williams, *Common Expositor,* 137–138.

291. Hannaway, "Laboratory Design," 585 and note 1; Shapin, "House of Experiment," 377; see also Shapin and Schaffer, *Leviathan and the Air-Pump,* 57n66.

292. Frances Harris, *Transformations,* 24; Boyle, *Correspondence,* 1: 83. The holy use of "Nature's *Vulcan*" to penetrate God's word was an alchemical topos; see, for example, Croll, *Philosophy Reformed,* 5.

293. Boyle, *Correspondence,* 1: 49. When the furnace finally arrived, it was "crumbled into as many pieces, as we into sects"; although his alembics arrived intact, they were "now, through the miscarriage of that grand implement of *Vulcan,* as useless to me, as good parts to salvation without the fire of zeal" (1: 50).

294. It was under this name that Richard Jones served as the addressee of many of Boyle's works. Boyle revealed the identity of this "hopeful Young Gentleman" in an "Advertisement to the Reader" appended to *Certain Physiological Essays* (*Works*, 2: 6).

295. Basse, *Sword and Buckler*, sigs. B, A4ᵛ; John Webster, *Academiarum Examen*, 106, 71. Webster's literacy in Baconian mythology was not accompanied by a firm grasp of experimental practice, and he was attacked by the virtuosi he thought he was defending; see Chapter 5.

296. Shapin and Schaffer, *Leviathan and the Air-Pump*, 174–175, 225.

297. Cowley, "The Garden," stanza 10, from *Several Discourses* in *Works*, 119 (the poem was dedicated to Evelyn; see *Sylva* [1679 ed.], sigs. c–d2); Winstanley, *Englands Spirit*, 13. As he explains elsewhere, "the spirit rose up, and shewed himself, and went to his Father; that is, entred into the Creation, to purge it from the curse; and to spread himselfe in sons and daughters of the Earth" (*Works*, 115). These sons and daughters become instruments of purgation when they act in accordance with "the Spirit Reason, which I call God, the Maker and Ruler of all things . . . the fire that burns up drosse, and so restores what is corrupted" (105, 104).

298. Bradstock, "Restoring all Things," 99; Winstanley, *Works*, 153.

299. Winstanley, *Works*, 394, 87; Cook, *Monarchy no Creature*, 104. In Marvell's *Horatian Ode*, Cromwell is raised up as "The force of angry Heavens flame" that "cast the Kingdome old / Into another Mold" (lines 26, 35–36). John Beale declared himself "very willing to bee an incendiary to inflame the world with the Love of profitable knowledge" (appendix 3 of Leslie and Raylor, *Culture and Cultivation*, 228).

300. Winstanley, *Works*, 446; Evelyn, *Elysium Britannicum*, 101, 103, 69, 195, 148.

301. A point made by James Grantham Turner's *DNB* entry on Austen.

302. Commonplace book remark quoted in Michael Hunter, "John Evelyn in the 1650s," 86; library remark quoted in Mandelbrote, "John Evelyn and his Books," 73.

303. Pettus, *Volatiles*, 27. Pettus was elected to the Royal Society in 1661 (Birch, *History*, 1: 32).

304. Salkeld, *Treatise of Paradise*, 146; Joseph Hall, *Works*, 777; Salkeld, *Treatise of Paradise*, 145; Joseph Hall, *Works*, 777. I quote from Hall to illustrate the dominance of the purgatorial/Adamic paradigm across the ideological spectrum.

305. Salkeld, *Treatise of Paradise*, 144.

306. Bridges, *Defence*, 635; Bacon, *Works*, 3: 381; Becon, *Displaying of the Popish Masse*, 246. This was continuous with Bacon's insistence that paradisal

sovereignty over creation could be restored "by various labours"—not "by disputa-
tions or idle magical ceremonies"; Bacon runs scholastic disputation together with
sacramental magic and opposes both to progressive labor (*Works,* 8: 350).

307. Becon, *Displaying of the Popish Masse,* 233. As Peter Marshall
eloquently puts it, "the lifeblood of the memorializing impulse was a process
of naming and renaming" (*Beliefs and the Dead,* 41). The Protestant attack on
purgatory replicates the attack on ancestor worship through which Judaism
separated itself from polytheistic thought and ritual practice. The reduction in
ritual activity that followed from the firm separation between the living and the
dead consolidated Jewish identity and fed its apocalyptic political vision, focused
on a restored earth under Yahweh's rule. I suggest that the dissolution of
purgatory had similar consequences in early modern England, encouraging the
sacralization of history. See McDannell and Lang, *Heaven,* 7–14; Key, "Concept
of Death"; and Eliade, *Sacred and Profane,* 110–113.

308. This phrase was often used in attacks on the Catholic mass; see, for
example, Barrow, *Plaine Refutation,* 215, and Burnet, *Mystery of Iniquity,* 23.

309. So a late medieval jurist could refer to the "mystical body" of a village;
see Kantorowicz, *King's Two Bodies,* 209–210.

310. See Rosenthal's *Purchase of Paradise.* Peter Marshall describes options
available to less wealthy parishioners, such as obits, but concedes that intercessory
practices operated as a continual challenge to the concept of death as "the great
social leveller" (*Beliefs and the Dead,* 20–21, 33). For a case study in how parish
hierarchy was extended into the afterlife through the distribution of burial
places, see Dinn, "Monuments Answerable to Mens' Worth."

311. Catholic libel quoted in Peter Marshall, *Beliefs and the Dead,* 145;
Willet, *Synopsis Papismi,* 318. On the last becoming first, see Matthew 19:30,
20:16. On chantries operating before the death of their founders, see Duffy,
Stripping of the Altars, 346, and Peter Marshall, *Beliefs and the Dead,* 18n61.

312. Keith Thomas holds the banishment of purgatory partly responsible for
a "more atomistic conception of the relationship in which members of society
stood to each other," permitting each generation to be "indifferent to the spiritual
fate of its predecessor" (*Religion and the Decline of Magic,* 603). In the same vein,
Duffy stresses the traumatic impact that the "casting out of the dead from the
community of the living into a collective anonymity" must have had on parish
life (*Stripping of the Altars,* 494; see also 327–337). Yet the dissolution of the
chantries was carried out with little resistance, and monastic institutions were
often repurposed with popular support; see Cunich, "Dissolution," 174; Whiting,
Local Responses, 20–21; and Shagan, *Popular Politics,* chapter 7. Hoyle argues that
by the time of the dissolutions, "the monastery as a purgatorial institution was
out of fashion" ("Origins of the Dissolution," 276).

313. Perkins, *Reformed Catholike*, 282; Perkins, *Golden Chaine*, 503, cited in Peter Marshall, *Beliefs and the Dead*, 212.

314. Voragine, *Golden Legend*, 2: 289. Founders thus tended to focus on their immediate family (and the royal family): Rosenthal found that only 3 percent of mortmain licenses for chantries of fifteenth-century nobles name all Christian souls as beneficiaries (*Purchase of Paradise*, 22); see also Peter Marshall, *Beliefs and the Dead*, 36–37. Joseph Hall thus had a point when he remarked that "Purgatory can have no rich men in it, but fooles and friendlesse" ("A Serious Disswasive from Poperie," prefixed to *Peace of Rome*, 29).

315. Perkins, *Reformed Catholike*, 282; Peter Marshall, *Beliefs and the Dead*, 229–230. For a characteristic sermon on the bodily resurrection, see Donne, *Sermons*, 4:45–62. Litzenberger's *English Reformation and the Laity* shows that the resurrection came to loom larger in Protestant wills after purgatory's dissolution; see esp. 153.

316. Keith Thomas, *Ends of Life*, 227.

317. Rosenthal, *Purchase of Paradise*, 130; W. K. Jordan, *Charities of London*, 23–24. See also his "Forming of the Charitable Institutions in the West of England." As Jordan suggests, such efforts were part of the process of secularization, but from the perspective of their agents, they were works of faith; see Slack, *From Reformation to Improvement*, esp. chapter 4. On the freeing up of funds for poverty relief, lectureships, hospitals, and other institutions, see Kümin, "Voluntary Religion," 188–189; Tittler, "Reformation, Resources and Authority in English Towns," 198–199; Collinson, *Birthpangs*, 55–56; and Whiting, *Blind Devotion*, 180–182.

318. This trend would bear fruit later in the century in works like Whitaker's *Future State*.

319. Constas, " 'To Sleep, Perchance to Dream,' " 117.

320. Slack, *From Reformation to Improvement*, 79; Cowley, *Works*, 102, seventh pagination; Leslie, "Bringing Ingenuity into Fashion," 151.

321. See Greengrass, Leslie, and Raylor, *Samuel Hartlib*, 16, and Charles Webster, *Samuel Hartlib*, 2. As Raymond points out, Bacon referred to experiments as intelligencers of nature, and newsbooks were also called intelligencers, making Hartlib a human experiment/newspaper (*Invention of the Newspaper*, 159). Masson's profile of Hartlib in *Life of Milton* begins with the statement "Everybody knew Hartlib"; he goes on to complain that the necessary result of trying to paint Hartlib's portrait is that the "canvas becomes rather crowded" with others (3: 193, 199).

322. Comenius quoted in A. C. S., "Notes on the Foundation and History of the Royal Society," 35; letter from John Eliot to Baxter quoted in Slack, *From Reformation to Improvement*, 52.

323. From Evelyn's letter to Thomas Browne in Browne, *Works,* 4: 275; Feingold, "Gresham College," 185. On connections between Hartlib's associates and the Oxford equivalent to the London group, the Oxford Philosophical Club, see Turnbull, "Samuel Hartlib's Influence."

324. Wallis, *Defence of the Royal Society,* 8. For the conversational rules they agreed upon, see 7. A similar version of events is given in Wallis's "Account of some Passages," 39–40. The abstention from ideological disputes, which scholars like Barbara Shapiro have presented as evidence of their latitudinarianism, warrants comparison with the rules developed in guilds after the Reformation to accommodate members of different religious outlooks; see Joseph Ward, *Metropolitan Communities,* chapter 5.

325. Wallis, "Account of some Passages," 39.

326. Birch's introductory "Life" in his edition of Boyle's *Works,* 1: xlii; Mendelsohn, "Alchemy and Politics," 51; Boyle, *Correspondence* 1: 58.

327. It was Syfret who argued that when Boyle described "the corner-stones of the *invisible,* or (as they term themselves) the *philosophical college,*" he was referring to Hartlib's effort to establish a Comenian "Universal College" through the Office of Address (Boyle, *Correspondence,* 1: 46; Syfret, "Origins"; see also Masson, *Life,* 3: 622–666). Then, building on Maddison's suggestion that the term was "a *jeu d'esprit* on the part of Boyle to describe a small group," Charles Webster argued that the invisible college referred very specifically to a fraternity formed by Boyle and Benjamin Worsley, whose other members were drawn from the Anglo-Irish intellectuals associated with Katherine Boyle (Maddison, "Studies," 110; Webster, "New Light on the Invisible College"). Webster suggests that Hartlib made the invisible college less invisible; this is to assume that Boyle was using "invisible" as a synonym for "secret." Perhaps the college was invisible because it was largely constituted by correspondence networks (see Webster, "Benjamin Worsley," 219–220), the fruits of which were to be made public. Thus, when urging Worsley to share his alchemical knowledge, Boyle insisted that "the Minde's Intellectuall Splendor . . . must doubly Joy in that kind Property Diffusion" (*Correspondence,* 1: 48). Webster's larger argument, however, is that the invisible college, Comenius's Universal College, and the Office of Address were cut from the same ideological cloth, promoting experimental knowledge not as "a gentlemanly diversion, but in the spirit of a religious mission"; indeed, he declares that it is "no coincidence that the Levellers, Hartlib's Office of Address and the Invisible College made their appearance simultaneously," nor that the latter two quickly joined forces ("New Light on the Invisible College," 19, 41; see also 24 and Webster's "Benjamin Worsley").

328. Boyle, *Correspondence,* 1: 42, 51; Hartlib, *Considerations,* 51.

329. See Syfret, "Origins," 126.

330. See Charles Webster, *Great Instauration*, 67–77.

331. Hartlib, *Considerations*, 52; Kevin Dunn, "Milton among the Monopolists," 179–181. The Office of Accommodations was to have coordinated the exchange of labor and services,

332. Winstanley, *Works*, 326, 93. Charles Webster notes similarities between the Hartlib circle and the Diggers in *Samuel Hartlib*, 3; Scott-Luckens argues that Winstanley's concept of the world's "treasury" as a "specifically *public* resource, to be unlocked and utilised through human ingenuity and industry" is congruent with Hartlib's ("Providence, Earth's 'Treasury' and the Common Weal," 112).

333. I address the threat that this aim posed to artisans in the following chapter. On the challenge that the utopian chymists associated with Hartlib posed to the "exclusivity of the magus tradition," see Mendelsohn, "Alchemy and Politics," 52,

334. It was through this "great restorer of things" that "we shall become one againe, and never be divided" (Winstanley, *Works*, 105, 243).

335. But see Norbrook, *Writing the English Republic*, 122–124, 282–283; the essays in Greengrass, Leslie, and Raylor, *Samuel Hartlib* ("it was around Hartlib that the perception of knowledge as a public commodity became of central concern for the first time" [18]); and Scott-Luckens, "Providence, Earth's 'Treasury' and the Common Weal."

336. On Hartlib's interest in a street-cleaning project, see Jenner, "'Another Epocha?'"

337. Masson, *Life*, 3: 229–230.

338. Ralph Austen's work on the growing of fruit trees was distributed to members of Parliament (Charles Webster, *Great Instauration*, 478). Hartlib took in a salary of 100 pounds a year for "industry in several public services," which he was paid more consistently than earlier scholars allowed (see Charles Webster, *Great Instauration*, 80–81, and Raylor, "Samuel Hartlib and the Commonwealth of Bees," 95). Peacey explores the degree to which the pamphleteering of the Hartlib circle was undertaken from within the republic's civil service in *Politicians and Pamphleteers*, 105–106.

339. Boyle, *Correspondence*, 1: 218 (Oldenburg was referring to the 1657 naval victory over the Spanish in the Canary Islands); Hartlib describing Johann Rudolf Glauber, quoted in Pamela Smith, *Body of the Artisan*, 168. See discussion in J. R. Jacob, *Robert Boyle*, 124–125.

340. Boyle, *Correspondence*, 1: 46; Evelyn quoted in Michael Hunter, "John Evelyn in the 1650s," 94.

341. *Essay for advancement of husbandry-learning*, 2A. Kevin Dunn discusses Hartlib's use of *luciferous*, with its combined associations of light with lucre, in "Milton among the Monopolists," 180–181.

342. As Appelbaum argues, the literature of the Hartlib circle asks the "general public" to behave "in a quasi-parliamentary, that is, representative fashion" (*Literature and Utopian Politics,* 121).

343. Similarly, Wallington imagined the godly as "a network of concern that stretched to Massachusetts and Connecticut on one side and to France and Germany on the other" (Seaver, *Wallington's World,* 104).

344. See Lynette Hunter's introduction to the *Letters,* which treats the concept of the public at xliii–xlv.

345. Moore, *Letters,* 21, 28–29, 31, 26, 35.

346. Moore, *Letters,* xxii, xxx. In addition to undertaking experiments in distillation with Katherine Boyle, she worked with such experimenters as Thomas Mayerne and Benjamin Worsley (xxx). On Moore's marriage in relation to her calling, see xlv–liv, 53–56, and 69–73; for Dury's account of their "covenant," see 114–117.

347. Boyle, *Correspondence,* 1: 58. Thus Hartlib's grandiose plans for a national laboratory were realized in his kitchen; see Charles Webster, *Great Instauration,* 302–305, and Mendelsohn, "Alchemy and Politics," 51.

348. Milton, *CPW,* 2: 362–363. Milton here defends his assessment of Hartlib as a person sent to England "by some good providence."

349. Hartlib, *Addresses,* sig. A3. The work, which runs from 113 to 150 in the collection, is usually referred to as *An Invitation to Communicativeness.* See Maddison, "The Earliest Published Writing of Robert Boyle." Although Michael Hunter suggests that scholars may have overstressed Hartlib's influence on Boyle, he gives Hartlib credit for turning Boyle's "preoccupation with an almost abstract notion of virtue" into a concern for public service; see *Scrupulosity,* 16, 19, 46–47; see also J. R. Jacob, *Robert Boyle,* 17, 28.

350. As Michael Hunter has stressed, this ideal of "openness" became increasingly problematic to translate into practice as Boyle's scientific career evolved; see *Scrupulosity,* 114, 135–153, 219–221.

351. Hartlib, *Addresses,* 138–139, 148. Boyle also suggests that knowledge gained through direct revelation should be shared; see 147. *Talent* was a popular translation of the Latin *ingenium;* see discussion in Haskin, *Milton's Burden,* 41–42. For similar appeals to the parable of the talents, see Boyle, *Early Essays,* 237; Croll, *Philosophy Reformed,* 2; and Pocock, *Machiavellian Moment,* 373–375.

352. Hartlib, *Considerations,* 10; Moore, *Letters,* 62; Moore was writing in support of Hartlib's payment by Parliament.

353. Moore, *Letters,* 80.

354. From "A Miscellaneous Collection. Begun March the 25th 1648," quoted in J. R. Jacob, *Robert Boyle,* 90.

355. Boyle, *Early Essays,* 132; *Works,* 13: 170 ("Of the Study of the Booke of Nature," on which see note 259). On Boyle's sense during this period that virtue and industry flourished more easily in a commonwealth, see Oster, "Virtue, Providence and Political Neutralism," 28–29.

356. Boyle, *Works,* 2: 468 (from *Style of the Scriptures,* on which see note 273); 1651 letter to John Mallet in *Correspondence,* 1: 105; see also 1: 133 and discussion in J. R. Jacob, *Robert Boyle,* 120–121, and Oster, "Millenarianism and the New Science," esp. 140–141.

357. Quoted in J. R. Jacob, *Robert Boyle,* 125.

358. Walwyn, *A Parable,* 16. Annabel Patterson's 2008 Tanner Lecture at UC Berkeley made mention of uncertainty as a public good in a different context.

359. 1652 letter to Boyle in *Correspondence,* 1: 138 (she refers here to Boyle's belief that the breaking forth of the truth will happen within the next seven years); 1 Corinthians 15: 28, Ephesians 1: 23. See J. R. Jacob, *Robert Boyle,* 124–126, and Milton, *CPW,* 2: 551.

360. See Cooper, *Fear and Polemic,* 28. Philippians 2:12 was the crucial text for such reflections.

361. Thomas Taylor, *Works,* title page, 410 (in *Mirrour of Ingratitude*). As lecturer and curate at St Mary Aldermanbury from 1625 to his death, Taylor was one of the Puritan divines whose parishes effectively modeled "a congregationalist polity within the Established Church" (Seaver, *Puritan Lectureships,* 138).

362. Baxter quoted in Cooper, *Fear and Polemic,* 53; Boyle, *Early Essays,* 239. Baxter's portrait of his wife stressed that "her Religion lay in *doing* more than talk"; he offered her life as an example of the principle that "Gods service lieth more in deeds than in words" (*Breviate,* 99).

363. See Seaver, "Puritan Work Ethic"; Rumrich, *Milton Unbound,* 35.

364. Boyle, *Correspondence,* 2: 474. On Boyle's scruples, see Michael Hunter's *Scrupulosity* and "Disquieted Mind," as well as Chapter 3 in this volume.

365. Mary Evelyn quoted in Wright, "Mary Evelyn and Devotional Practice," 225.

366. Evelyn was particularly proud of the ingenuity of his daugher Susanna, whose "peculiar talent" was for painting. Almost the opposite of the traditional feminine labor of needlepoint, painting was coded as a masculine, artisanal activity undertaken by mechanics. (As discussed in the next two chapters, painters and the virtuosi who imitated them generated findings into the nature of color.) Evelyn once sent her a scolding poem in which he expressed his anxiety that Tunbridge amusements ("Drink, Dresse, & Dice, damned Daunce") would "Thyne Ingenuity all baffle," making her "forget Cromatick pencil": "Fear— better thou hads't learn'd to Spin, / Than ever Tunbridge to have seene" (quoted

in Gibson-Wood, "Susanna and Her Elders," 238–239). Evelyn calls his daughter back from temptation by threatening her with Eve's labor if she does not return to her own properly Adamic pursuit.

367. For an eloquent challenge to the Duffyian view that the Reformation undermined "traditional collective forces," see Barry, "Bourgeois Collectivism?"

368. Pocock, *Machiavellian Moment,* chapter 10 ("Modes of Civic Consciousness before the Civil War," esp. 333–335); see also Hutson's "Not the King's Two Bodies."

369. McKeon, "Parsing Habermas's 'Bourgeois Public Sphere,'" 275–276.

370. McKeon, "Parsing Habermas's 'Bourgeois Public Sphere,'" 276–277; *Secret History of Domesticity,* 557. The second quotation is taken from McKeon's analysis of the role of the "Warming-Pan Scandal" in the events of 1688, whose effect was "to pressure the analogy of the king's two bodies to breaking point" (551). McKeon discusses Parliament's use of the two bodies analogy in *Origins of the English Novel,* 179. While he is obviously correct to call it an "innovative reversal" in practical terms, I am stressing how it realized a potential that had always resided in the doctrine.

2. A Union of Eyes and Hands

1. Oldenburg quoted in Marie Boas Hall, *Henry Oldenburg,* 90.

2. Bacon, *Works,* 3: 297; Genesis 4:17, 4:22. Tubalcain's brothers were also inventors, solidifying the association of technology with the line of Cain; for background, see Arnold Williams, *Common Expositor,* 140–146. As Eliade explains, the opposition between Abel and Cain reflects a primitivist idealization of the life of the nomad over and against agriculturalists and town-dwellers. Cain means smith, a "master of fire": "the first murder is performed by him who in some sort incarnates the symbol of technology . . . Implicitly, all techniques are suspected of magic" (*History of Religious Ideas,* 167–168). On the simultaneously sacred and accursed character of the metal worker, see Girard, *Violence and the Sacred,* 260–262.

3. Joseph Hall, *Contemplations: The First Booke* (1641), in *Works,* 774; Pettus, *Volatiles,* 160, 159, 162–163. Pettus observes that the actual life of a shepherd includes in it "a mixture of the Active life," but he nonetheless describes the question of "which should be best the Contemplative or Active life" as the basis of the brothers' dispute (159, 162).

4. Wilkins, *Mathematical Magick,* 3.

5. Empson refers to the pastoral "pretence" or "trick" throughout *Some Versions of Pastoral.* On this habit, see Dodsworth, "Empson and the Trick of It."

6. And, obviously, the Society's representative identity did not meet Pitkin's criteria for formal or substantive representation (*Concept of Representation*).

7. In the 1680s, the Earl of Angsley worried that appealing directly to "the people" was dangerous since they could "neither meet nor judge"; only through Parliament, he insisted, could the people "meet by representation." Whig pamphleteers, including Locke, ignored such scruples, appealing directly to the people and defending the common right of any man to do the same; see discussion in Ashcraft, *Revolutionary Politics*, 299–331. It is worth noting that Locke sent in natural historical relations to the Society; see Birch, *History*, 3: 220.

8. Michael Hunter, *Establishing the New Science*, x.

9. The texts most associated with the gentlemanly thesis are Shapin and Schaffer, *Leviathan and the Air-Pump*, and Shapin, *Social History of Truth*. For a challenge, see Barbara Shapiro, *Culture of Fact*, 139–143. In the case of Boyle, it is important to keep in mind that his "intellectual proclivities were potentially at odds with the expectations of genteel decorum seen as desirable for a man of his status" (Michael Hunter, *Scrupulosity*, 233); see also Oster, "Scholar and Craftsman," and J. R. Jacob, *Robert Boyle*, 47–57.

10. In the course of rebutting the doctrine, Hakewill suggested that extrapolation from the personal experience of aging helped to account for its popularity (*Apologie*, 26). On the decay of nature controversy, see Victor Harris, *All Coherence Gone;* Williamson, "Mutability, Decay, and Seventeenth-Century Melancholy"; and R. F. Jones, *Ancients and Moderns*, chapter 2. On the frequent interpenetration of cyclical, degenerative, and progressive models of history in the period, see Guibbory, *Map of Time.*

11. Donne, *First Anniversarie*, line 111; in his Whitsunday Sermon of 1625, Donne claims that God has "put into" the world "a reproofe, a rebuke lest it should seem eternall, which is, a sensible decay and age in the whole frame of the world and every piece thereof"; hence the sun is "fainter, and languishing; men lesse in stature, and shorter-lived," and every year discovers "new species of wormes, and flies, and sicknesses, which argue more and more putrefaction of which they are engendred" (*Sermons*, 6: 323). On Donne and decay, see Guibbory, *Map of Time*, 69–104.

12. Hakewill, *Apologie*, title page. First issued in 1627, Hakewill's *Apologie* was enlarged in both 1630 and 1635; it was the likely inspiration for Milton's own "Naturam non pati senium." Appelbaum notes that, after Bacon, the doctrine of progress received no systematic defense in England before Hakewill (*Literature and Utopian Politics*, 117). Hakewill conceded that nature was damaged by the fall but insisted that humanity's knowledge had largely repaired that damage, and would continue to do so; Hill argues for the Baconian basis of this argument in *Intellectual Origins*, 12, 81–82. For Bacon's influence on Hakewill, and Hakewill's reciprocal influence on Baconian thinkers like Wilkins, see also Charles Webster, *Great Instauration*, 19–21, 25, 29. Evelyn

argued that those who believed in the decay of nature were "half Atheists" (*Elysium Britannicum*, 54).

13. Pettus, *Volatiles*, 144–145; on Beale's plans to turn poisons into medicines and "thornes and thickets into Wine and oyle," see Charles Webster, *Great Instauration*, 12; Oldenburg quoted in Marie Boas Hall, *Henry Oldenburg*, 25.

14. Bloys, *Adam in his Innocencie*, 178, 175; see also 63–67. The following chapter explores how virtuosi dealt with this objection to cultivating technological knowledge.

15. An intervening age of heroes further fills out the distance between then and now: *Works and Days*, lines 109–201. See also Ovid's treatment of the golden age in the *Metamorphoses* 1, 89–112. For the influence of the classics on Genesis commentary, see Arnold Williams, *Common Expositor*, chapter 10; for the blending of the golden age with prelapsarian existence, see Giamatti, *Earthly Paradise*, 15–33. Although Lilburne drew on the four ages of man when referring to the *"Iron Norman yoak,"* he described that yoke as an *impediment* to a laboriously productive existence (*Regall Tyrannie*, 25).

16. Boas, *Primitivism and Related Ideas*, 11; Keith Thomas, *Religion and the Decline of Magic*, 161.

17. Brathwaite, *Natures Embassie*, 4.

18. This is the only conspicuously "artful" line in the passage, combining alliteration with internal rhyme.

19. On overseas trade as an impious violation of natural boundaries between sea and land, see Blumenberg, *Shipwreck with Spectator*, 10–11.

20. ". . . nec varios discet mentiri lana colores, / ipse sed in pratis aries iam suave rubenti / murice, iam croceo mutabit vellera luto;/ sponte sua sandyx pascentis vestiet agnos" (lines 42–45).

21. See line 39.

22. Augustine, *City of God*, 3: 374–375 (10.27). Bourne, "Messianic Prophecy," provides a useful overview of readings of the fourth eclogue as a Christian prophecy from Constantine onward; for its impact on English literature, see Stocker, *Apocalyptic Marvell*, 121–124 and references therein. On Virgil as a magician, see Reeves, *Galileo's Glassworks*, 16–17, and Thoms, *Early Prose Romances*, 2: 3–41, where he is an inventor of inextinguishable lamps, a metal serpent, a technology that can render oncomers motionless, and the custodian of a paradisal garden.

23. Paul Alpers, *What Is Pastoral?* 240.

24. Puttenham, *Arte of English Poesie*, 53 (1.18). See discussion in Congleton, *Theories of Pastoral*, 37–51. Patterson's *Pastoral and Ideology* and Montrose's "Gentlemen and Shepherds" are classic modern versions of this approach, whose

"characteristic way of making pastoral interesting," Alpers complains, "is to claim that it undermines or criticizes or transcends itself"; unsurprisingly, Alpers finds that Renaissance accounts of pastoral lack "critical power" (*What Is Pastoral?* 35, 9).

25. Empson, *Some Versions of Pastoral,* 12; Drayton, "To the Reader of his Pastorals," in *Works,* 2: 517.

26. James Richardson has usefully described the pastoral mode in terms of a reduction of the knowledge required to be in the world. This reduction is registered through a restriction of vocabulary; internal deviations from the mode can be measured by the inclusion of terms relating to specialized knowledge of any kind—in which we might include maker's knowledge and what Daston would call "strange facts" (personal communication).

27. This paragraph is a reduction of Whitney's *Paradise Restored,* 26–27. See Seneca, *Ad Lucilium Epistulae Morales* 2: 402–403 (90.13); Plato *Republic,* 597b; *Gorgias,* 491a. As she points out, Augustine's ironic praise of technological advance in *City of God* (22.24) expresses an almost sublime sense of the power of human ingenuity. Putnam discusses the dyeing of wool as a classical emblem of the evils of luxury in *Virgil's Pastoral Art,* 153.

28. Boyle, *Works,* 3: 212; Genesis 30: 31–43.

29. Vaughan, *Magia Adamica,* 35–37; Pettus, *Volatiles,* 44 (see also 38, 58–61). On Pettus's metallurgical Adam, see Charles Webster, *Great Instauration,* 326, and Almond, *Adam and Eve,* 46. On Jacob and his sheep, see also Thomas Browne, *Works,* 3: 12, and Ashmole, *Theatrum Chemicum,* 444. Vaughan's alchemical pursuits did not alienate him from the scientific mainstream; an associate of Hartlib and Boyle, he enjoyed the patronage of Sir Robert Moray after the Restoration (*DNB;* Lyndy Abraham, *Marvell and Alchemy,* 11–12).

30. Birch, *History,* 1: 63, 64; Glanvill, *Vanity of Dogmatizing,* 72. Petty himself, however, was the son of a Romsey clothier.

31. Hakewill, *Apologie,* 366. This passage explicitly links the doctrine to the myth of the four ages. He sounds this theme throughout the *Apologie:* e.g., "I am perswaded that the *fictions* of *Poets* was it which first gave life unto it" (25).

32. Raymond Williams, *Country and the City,* 21. James Grantham Turner's *Politics of Landscape,* in contrast, registers an awareness of this dynamic throughout. What Marx called "the perversion of concepts" that turns "the fertility of the land into an attribute of the landlord" requires the suppression of working knowledge (*Manuscripts of 1844,* 53; see discussion in Turner, *Politics of Landscape,* 161–166).

33. Paul Alpers, *What Is Pastoral?* 39, 93. Alpers borrows the "strength relative to world" formula from Fletcher, who uses it to describe Frye's classification of fictional modes according to "the hero's power of action" (Frye, *Anatomy*

of Criticism, 33; Fletcher, "Utopian History," 34–35); see Alpers's discussion at 49–50.

34. Puttenham, *Arte of English Poesie,* 56 (1.19); Sprat, *History,* 67.

35. Paul Alpers, *What Is Pastoral?* 28. He observes that whereas for Virgil, the pastoral and georgic modes are distinct, the turn of the seventeenth century is when pastoral begins to extend its range, when "the poet need not represent himself as a shepherd in order to sustain the pastoral mode," but he never explains why (185).

36. Alastair Fowler, "Georgic and Pastoral," 84. See also Low, *Georgic Revolution,* esp. chapters 1 and 4.

37. Empson, *Some Versions of Pastoral,* 15.

38. Hooke, *Posthumous Works,* 27; Locke, *Essay,* 296–297 (2.23.3). For a nearly identical formulation in which the mason overtakes Aristotle and his commentators, see Boyle, *Works,* 6: 469. In a similar vein, Gilbert declared that, through the acquisition of mechanical knowledge, "the ingenious mind ascends above the aether" (*De Magnete,* xlviii; "mens ingeniosa, supra aethera scandit" [sig. *ijv in 1600 ed.]). I discuss Locke's treatment of angelic perception in the following chapter. Ashcraft observes that many of Locke's associates were nonplussed by his habit of conversing "freely and willingly" with tradesmen (*Revolutionary Politics,* 372–373).

39. Poggioli, "Oaten Flute," 237. Accounts of the virtuoso's hybrid identity have treated this social type as a blend of scholar and courtier; see Rupert Hall, "Scholar and Craftsman," and Oster, "Scholar and Craftsman."

40. The 1674 memo was written by a Fellow who called himself "A.B." (Amicus Benevolens?), reproduced as Document B in Michael Hunter and Paul Wood, "Towards Solomon's House," reprinted in Michael Hunter, *Establishing the New Science;* the quotation is at 228.

41. *Inpiae rates* is from Horace, *Odes* 1: 3, cited in Blumenberg, *Shipwreck with Spectator,* 11. For commodities in the *Report,* see 4, 7–24, 31; for descriptions of Virginia as both a Golden Age landscape and primitivistic Eden, see 24–25, 31–32, 52, 55–56, 60–61, 74. There is an insistent emphasis on fishing over agriculture: 45–50, 56, 59, 68.

42. The fourth chapter of the first book of *Magnalia Christi Americana,* on the "*Essays* and *Causes*" of the "Second, but Largest Colony of NEW-ENGLAND," is called "Paolo Majora!" (1.15; the phrase is reinvoked at 4.216).

43. Bacon, *Works,* 4: 92; Glanvill, *Vanity of Dogmatizing,* 178–179. The trajectory of Harriot's career encompassed both Americas; after his return to England he devoted himself to experimental optics; see Shirley, *Thomas Harriot.* The Society was interested in gaining access to Harriot's papers (Birch, *History,* 1: 120, 126). On Harriot's use of an early perspective device, see van Helden,

"Invention of the Telescope" and Ronan et al., "Was There an Elizabethan Telescope?"

44. Bacon, *Advancement* (1640 ed.), sig. A2. Montrose describes pastoral as a means of establishing elite community in "Of Gentlemen."

45. Eamon points to John White's *Hocus-Pocus,* "where the hocus-pocus of magic is spelled out in recipes." For many readers, recipe books offered the hope of learning skills without having to join a guild, though given variations in quality and "openness," the degree to which they boosted technical know-how is unclear (*Science and the Secrets of Nature,* 10n12, 132–133). The tug-of-war between secrecy and openness was a feature of late medieval and early modern technical writing generally; inexplicitness offered a means to entice potential patrons; see Long, *Openness, Secrecy, Authorship,* esp. 115, 136, and chapter 4 generally. As Long's book makes clear, "printing by itself should not be credited with the promulgation of the value of openness"; it also promoted the greater circulation of esoterica (175).

46. The resistance of tacit knowledge to verbal communication reinforced its association with secrecy and cunning; for Joseph Moxon, "*Hand-Craft* signifies *Cunning,* or *Sleight,* or *Craft* of the Hand, which cannot be taught by Words, but is only gained by *Practice* and *Exercise.*" This is why, he explains, he could not refer to his text as "*The Doctrine of Handy-Crafts*" (*Mechanick Exercises,* sig. 2). In *Openness, Secrecy, Authorship,* Long explores how words that originally referred to the tacit or unspoken came to be associated with the prohibited and unspeakable; see esp. 7. Bourdieu discusses the "scientific habitus" as a "practical sense," with an "implicit, tacit dimension," even "a conventional wisdom" that can only be communicated through example in *Science of Science,* 37–40. However, by the fifteenth century, writing was increasingly being used to convey knowledge within the crafts (Eamon, *Science and the Secrets of Nature,* 87).

47. See Pamela Smith, *Body of the Artisan,* 86; Eamon, *Science and the Secrets of Nature,* 282; see also Boyle, *Works,* 6: 470.

48. Keith Thomas, *Religion and the Decline of Magic,* 248.

49. Adam Fox, *Oral and Literate Culture,* 174; Charles Butler, *Feminine Monarchie,* sigs. a2–a3. On "old women" and their "rare receipts," see Aubrey, *Observations,* in *Three Prose Works,* 339. Old men were also a rich source of information; at an early meeting, Fellows appealed to the judgment of "an old experienced countryman" of Beale's acquaintance on the effect of "blasts" on cherry blossoms in the course of speculating about the probable results of placing a blossom in the air pump (Birch, *History,* 1: 304).

50. Power's 1649 letter to Thomas Browne, in Browne, *Works,* 4: 259. A doctor working in Halifax, Power collaborated with Robert Townley, but felt he would have made more progress had he had "the noble assistance of such

ingeniosos" as could attend Royal Society meetings regularly (Birch, *History*, 1: 81; see also his 1649 letter to Thomas Browne, *Works*, 4: 260, where he worries that working alone he will make but "lingring progresse"). He corresponded regularly with the Society, however, and was able to make a visit in 1663, when he was elected as a Fellow.

51. Vaughan, *Magia Adamica*, 118. Vaughan's wife Rebecca assisted him in his chymical operations; see Lyndy Abraham, *Marvell and Alchemy*, 11–12; for contemporary descriptions of alchemical processes as cookery, see 76–77. For an example, see Howell's *Hermeticall Banquet, Drest by a Spagiricall Cook for the Better Preservation of the Microscosme*.

52. Michael Hunter, *Science and Society*, 102–103; see discussion of Evelyn's *Panificium* in Birch, *History*, 2: 19–20.

53. Keith Thomas, *Religion and the Decline of Magic*, 271–272 (on male midwives who claimed descent from Adam, see Beier, *Sufferers and Healers*, 34); Sturtevant, *Dibre Adam*, 7.

54. The scholarship on the *prisca theologia* in England is vast, but see D. P. Walker, *Ancient Theology*; Yates, *Rosicrucian Enlightenment*; Sailor, "Moses and Atomism"; and McGuire and Rattansi, "Newton and the Pipes of Pan." The description of Moses in Acts 7:22 as "learned in all the wisdom of the Egyptians" was referred to by defenders of all forms of learning, but especially by defenders of experimental knowledge; see, for example, Bacon, *Works*, 3: 297; Ashmole, *Theatrum Chemicum*, 446; and Milton, *CPW*, 2: 507. On Moses as an alchemist, and a "Maria Prophetissa" who was allegedly Moses's sister, see Lyndy Abraham, *Marvell and Alchemy*, 1, 174–175. On the overlap between Moses and Moschus the Phoenician, see Sailor, "Moses and Atomism."

55. Kantorowicz, *King's Two Bodies*, 304. This distributed subject invites comparison with "the common" described in Virno, *Grammar of the Multitude*.

56. Thomas Browne, *Works*, 2: 52, 42; 4: 202.

57. Aubrey, *Remaines of Gentilisme and Judaisme*, in *Three Prose Works*, 290; Thomas Browne, *Works*, 2: 17, 31. John Beale agreed that many vulgar superstitions derived from "old Tradition, & from true philosophy" (quoted in Leslie, "Spiritual Husbandry," 160).

58. Lowe, *Diary*, 76–77. Aubrey gathered lore on blood staunching in *Observations*, in *Three Prose Works*, 348. *Terra incognita* appears throughout experimentalist literature; see, for example, Glanvill, *Plus Ultra*, 111.

59. Thomas Smith, *De Republica Anglorum*, 65, 73–77; William Harrison, *Description of England*, 117–118. Ironically, the very term *gentleman* was itself being used to obscure social difference in the upper echelons: Petty's list of words that, "by having too many meanings have none at all" included not only words

like *truth* and *duty* but *Yeoman* and *Gentleman (Petty Papers,* 1: 150). Harrison's description of how merchants "often change estate with gentlemen, as gentlemen do with them, by a mutual conversion of the one into the other" suggests that the reality of social fluidity actually worked to reinforce a finicky insistence protecting the term *gentleman* from contamination by work (*Description of England,* 115). As Cressy argues in "Describing the Social Order," the instability of these taxonomies was precisely what made contemporaries so attached to them.

60. Aubrey, *Natural History of Wiltshire,* 6; see Ray's *Collection of English Proverbs.*

61. Aubrey, *Remaines of Gentilisme and Judaisme* in *Three Prose Works,* 290, 255; see also 254; Herrick, "Another to Bring in the Witch," lines 5–6. The preface to the *Remaines of Gentilisme and Judaisme* is arguably more Herrickian: "Old customes, and old wives-fables are grosse things: but yet ought [not] to be quite rejected: there may some truth and usefulnesse be elicited out of them"; but where truth could not be extracted, it was "a pleasure to consider the Errours that enveloped former ages: as also the present" (132). Even here, however, the pleasure taken in considering errors seems related to the notion that progress is being made, however unevenly. J. Paul Hunter presents a thought-provoking account of the relationship between this progress (especially as it relates to the suppression of fairy tales) and the rise of the novel in *Before Novels,* chapter 6.

62. Adam Fox, *Oral and Literate Culture,* 152, 22; Norden, *Surveyors Dialogue,* 173 (a contemporary of Bacon, Norden shared many of his views; see Peltonen, "Francis Bacon," 16).

63. Thomas Browne, *Works,* 2: 38; see also Hooke, *Posthumous Works,* 27.

64. Feingold, "Gresham College," 185; see also Stimson, *Scientists and Amateurs,* 26–30.

65. Wilkins, *Mathematical Magick,* sig. A4^v; Feingold, "Gresham College," 175; Hill, *Intellectual Origins,* 33. See Bacon, *Letters and Life,* 4: 249–254, and Cressy, "Francis Bacon." Feingold suggests that Gresham's unique status as a public space where people united only by shared intellectual interests could gather, anticipated, and was later threatened by, the emergence of the coffee-house, discussed in Chapter 4 ("Gresham College," 175, 185).

66. Hill, *Intellectual Origins,* 49; Wilkins was Cromwell's brother-in-law.

67. Wallis, *Defence of the Royal Society,* 8. As Wallis explains, after Petty left for Ireland, the group met at Wilkins's lodgings in Wadham College. When Wilkins left for Cambridge, the group assembled at the lodgings of Boyle, who rented rooms from an apothecary, John Crosse, who permitted him to use his chemical facilities (see Shapin, "House of Experiment," 380; Purver, *Royal Society,* 118–120; Boyle, *Correspondence,* 1: 193). In "Intellectual Origins," Hill

persuasively argues that this is the most trustworthy contemporary account of the Society's origins because of its late date (1678): the pressure to conceal the group's links to Interregnum figures like Haak (a pressure that has a distorting influence on Sprat's *History*) had to a large extent abated.

68. See, for example, Pepys, *Diary*, 5: 32; 6: 36. On the contemporary sense that Gresham was "virtually indistinguishable" from the Society, see Feingold, "Gresham College," 186; Stimson, *Scientists and Amateurs*, 30; and Hill, *Intellectual Origins*, 112 (Sprat was even known as "the historian of Gresham College").

69. For struggles with the air pump before 1660, see Boyle, *Correspondence*, 1: 382; on the continuity between Hartlib and Oldenburg, see Michael Hunter, *Science and Society*, 49.

70. Marie Boas Hall, *Henry Oldenburg*, 69. See, for example, Birch, *History*, 3: 217. After Oldenburg's death, his duties were taken over by Grew and Hooke, and later Hans Sloane (see Michael Hunter, *Science and Society*, 50–51).

71. Charles's action, undertaken in the summer of 1667, was not entirely unmotivated; Oldenburg's philosophical correspondence with a French virtuoso included exchanges about current events (which were forwarded to Joseph Williamson, Under-Secretary of State), in the course of which he let slip some criticism of the king's handling of the war; see McKie, "Arrest and Imprisonment."

72. The king was "laughing at Sir W Petty . . . and at Gresham College in general. At which poor Petty was I perceive at some loss, but did argue discreetly and bear the unreasonable follies of the King's objections and other bystanders with great discretion" (*Diary*, 5: 32–33, entry from Feb. 1664); Birch, *History*, 2: 463; see discussion in Shapin and Schaffer, *Leviathan and the Air-Pump*, 134. Petty refers testily to the complaint in his *Discourse Made Before the Royal Society*: "Forasmuch as this *Society* has been censured (though without much cause) for spending too much time in matters not directly tending to profit and palpable Advantages (as Weighing of Air and the like)," he offers a discourse on practical matters such as ship sails, water mills, and the labor power of horses, "which are not only gross enough of themselves, but are also as grosly handled in this Exercise, to prevent the further imputation of needless Nicity" (1–2). The only solid assistance the Society received from the king was the grant of Chelsea College in 1669, which Bluhm has called a "white elephant"—the title was unclear and the Society ended up spending over 250 pounds on it, including legal charges; it was eventually surrendered back to the Crown for cash in 1682 (see Bluhm, "Royal Society's Finances," 98; discussion of the grant started in 1664; see Birch, *History*, 1: 391, 419, 432). Charles did present the Society with some objects for which he "expected an account" in return (Birch, *History*, 1: 10,

17; 2: 24, 31). He also accepted gifts from the Fellows—for example, a lunar globe made by Wren (1: 21–22)—and occasionally demanded explanations, of the sensitive plant for example (34). He was always very civil to Hooke; see, for example, Hooke's *Diary,* 336. On the king's personal interest in experimental matters, see D. C. Martin, "Robert Moray."

73. Birch, *History,* 2: 4; 1: 108, 168; 2: 9. For efforts to ingratiate themselves with the king and other fund-raising schemes, see 1: 50, 107, 377, 379. As Johns points out, the only significant investment by the English crown in astronomical research during the whole century went not to the Royal Society but to the creation of an "Astronomer Royal," installed in the Royal Observatory on Greenwich Hill (*Nature of the Book,* 551).

74. At first he "would not agree to take my place there" at all; see Middleton, "What Did Charles II Call the Fellows of the Royal Society?" 14, and "Some Italian Visitors," 160.

75. See Birch, *History,* 1: 268, 271–272, 288–291, 295–296, 312–313, 417. It was because of these preparations that Hooke was first invited to lodge in Gresham College (1: 340–341). For more on the king's projected visit, see Chapter 4.

76. "A.B." (see note 40 above), in Michael Hunter, *Establishing the New Science,* 230.

77. Biagioli, *Galileo's Instruments of Credit,* 52, 45; see also 70n165.

78. Oldenburg, *Correspondence,* 2: 14, 321; 3: 45. To be sure, Oldenburg hoped that if the Fellows offered performances worthy of a Royal Society they would be deemed worthy of royal patronage, but the perpetually deferred realization of this hope may have fostered a semantic drift.

79. Evelyn, *Diary,* 3: 332 (Aug. 20, 1662). Evelyn later presented the Society with a cushion for the mace from Sir Richard Browne (Birch, *History,* 1: 250); see Purver, *Royal Society,* 140.

80. Stubbe, *Censure,* 14. In *Henry Stubbe,* James Jacob argues that Stubbe was in fact only pretending to hold conservative views, but if this was a ruse, his contemporaries were persuaded by it; see Michael Hunter, *Science and Society,* 140.

81. Lilburne, *Declaration,* 25–26, 37.

82. "The Form of Apology and Satisfaction," in Kenyon, *Stuart Constitution,* 35. Indeed, sometimes the Society even concerned itself with Parliamentary business: at a meeting on September 23, 1663, "There was read a petition of the fishmongers, presented to the parliament, concerning the annoyances, whereby the fry and brood of fish is destroyed, and the several ways, whereby the same may be preserved" (Birch, *History,* 1: 305).

83. Michael Hunter, *Establishing the New Science,* 4–5 (quoting Royal Society charter and Sprat, *History,* 79), 21. Hunter offers an indispensable account of the importance of institutionalization at 1–10. Mendelsohn suggests that Charles might have granted a charter to the Society "as a shrewd political move to keep certain dangerous elements under his eye" ("Alchemy and Politics," 74).

84. Evelyn, *Diary,* 3: 332 (August 20, 1662); Sorbière, *Voyage,* 36; Sprat, *History,* 70.

85. Sorbière, *Voyage,* 36. For the Society's stipulations on headgear, see also Birch, *History,* 1: 250, 264 (the president was to remove his hat only when addressing the whole assembly).

86. Shapin, "House of Experiment," 392–393. This essay considers a number of models for the Society's construction of experimental space before fixing on the public rooms of a gentleman's house as the dominant one; see also Johns, *Nature of the Book,* 471. On the public pretensions of the Society in comparison to continental academies, see Michael Hunter, *Royal Society,* 15. A reference in A.B.'s memo to the Council as the "Parliament" of the Society upsets the analogy of the Society as a whole to that body, but sustains the metaphor in a general way (Michael Hunter, *Establishing the New Science,* 228; on A.B., see note 40 above).

87. Neale, *Elizabethan House,* 365; on addressing the speaker bareheaded, see 405. See also Snow, *Parliament,* 164 (for sitting arrangements and the Speaker; an exception was made for London and York representatives), 190–191 (on speaking bareheaded), 173 (on the Sergeant and his mace). The Society's committee structure was also imitative of Parliament (Neale, *Elizabethan House,* 377–379). But see Michael Hunter, *Establishing the New Science,* 24.

88. Shapin, "House of Experiment," 393; Sorbière, *Voyage* (this was published with Sprat's *Observations* thereupon), 35, 164.

89. Biagioli, "Etiquette, Interdependence, and Sociability," 231n117.

90. Sorbière, *Voyage,* 164–165; Michael Hunter, *Establishing the New Science,* 8–9. Aubrey expresses admiration for the Rota in *Brief Lives,* 125.

91. As Biagioli observes, Sprat's response to Sorbière seems to "fit squarely in the anticourt genre" ("Etiquette, Interdependence, and Sociability," 233).

92. See Arnold, *Third Citizen.*

93. Thomas Smith, *De Republica Anglorum,* 79; see also Snow, *Parliament,* 182.

94. D'Ewes, *Journals,* 515, quoted in Arnold, *Third Citizen,* 15.

95. Despite this abundance of body parts, they remained "as it were one body . . . one man" (Snow, *Parliament,* 117, 209); see Arnold, *Third Citizen,* 16–17. In *Origins of Democratic Culture,* Zaret shows that this same argument was employed by the electorate to justify writing to and petitioning Parliament;

see esp. 92–93. Although Hooker insisted that the MPs were to see and judge of "all things," the Earl of Northampton warned the Commons in 1607 that members had "only a local and private wisdom" and were "not fit to examine or determine secrets of state," but MPs took advantage of the ambiguity of the word *country* to extend their representative claims from their own localities to the nation as a whole (Hirst, *Representative of the People?* 158–159).

96. Cited in Arnold, *Third Citizen,* 34, 156 (see D'Ewes, *Journals,* 667, 645–646). For discussion see Louise Fargo Brown, "Ideas of Representation," 29, and Arnold, *Third Citizen,* 34–41, 85–90, 154–159.

97. Sprat, *History,* 85; Birch, *History,* 1: 266; Hooke, *Micrographia,* sig. g.

98. Sprat, *History,* 131, 152, 94, 7, 12.

99. Its run began in 1665. On Parliamentary secrecy, see Neale, *Elizabethan House,* 416–417, and Snow, *Parliament,* 187. On the tension between Parliament's self-identification as a public institution and the privacy of its proceedings, see Lake and Pincus, "Rethinking the Public Sphere," 276. This privacy was constantly violated, of course; see Love, *Culture and Commerce,* esp. 9–22 and 185–186, and Joad, *Invention of the Newspaper,* esp. 101–105.

100. The *terra incognita* to be discovered was often nearby: at one meeting, for example, "Dr. CHARLETON mentioning a peculiar kind of bow, which he thought might be had in Grub-street, was desired to inquire after it, and to obtain the sight of it for the society; which he promised to do" (Birch, *History,* 1: 334).

101. Sprat, *History,* 72. So in an early meeting Fellows heard "a written account of potatoes from [Boyle's] gardiner"; on another occasion, they heard the relations of a bricklayer and his son (Birch, *History,* 1: 216, 276).

102. That said, the Long Parliament House of Commons had perhaps six yeomen among its members, and if one accepts the New Model Army's self-definition as a representative body, the Society was following in its footsteps, since it boasted humbly born men like Edward Sexby and William Allen among its senior officers; see Hirst, *Representative of the People?* 191.

103. Sprat, *History,* 435; Barbara Shapiro, "Natural Philosophy," 309. Michael Hunter's *Royal Society* is the most comprehensive study of the social composition of the Society.

104. Physicians, however, far outnumbered merchants and tradesmen (Michael Hunter, *Royal Society,* 128).

105. Barbara Shapiro, *Culture of Fact,* 140.

106. Michael Hunter, *Royal Society,* 110.

107. Michael Hunter, *Royal Society,* 31; see 110–114. This period saw a broadening of the Society's social composition. In "Reconstructing Restoration Science," the Mulligans argue that Hooke actively used his secretaryship to recruit more humbly born men into the Society, and indeed the proportion of

Fellows who were either plebeian or from the lesser gentry increased during this period (1677–1682). Michael Hunter argues against giving Hooke full credit for this development; see *Establishing the New Science,* 339–355.

108. Boyle, *Correspondence,* 2: 103.

109. Stubbe, *Legends no Histories,* 21; Armytage, "Royal Society and the Apothecaries," 33. See Barbara Shapiro's discussion in *Culture of Fact,* 119–121.

110. The passage appears in a letter by "N.S" at the start of his and Ward's *Vindiciae Academiarum,* 2; Sprat, *History,* 67. In 1647, Boyle had described members of the invisible college in precisely the same way, as men of "so humble and teachable a genius, as they disdain not to be directed to the meanest, so he can but plead reason for his opinion" (*Correspondence,* 1: 46).

111. Birch, *History,* 1: 5; Inwood, *Man Who Knew Too Much,* 28.

112. Waller quoted in Michael Hunter, *Royal Society,* 52; Birch, *History,* 1: 163. On stalled plans to hire more curators, see Michael Hunter, *Establishing the New Science,* 185–222.

113. See, for example, Pumfrey's vigorously argued "Ideas Above his Station." Pumfrey understandably makes much of the following passage: "it was ordered, that Mr. BOYLE should have the thanks of the society for dispensing with him [Hooke] for their use; and that Mr. HOOKE should come and sit amongst them" (Birch, *History,* 1: 124). If the passage seems to identify Hooke as chattel, it also suggests his promotion from the status of a personal servant to a public one. Chapter 8 of Shapin's *Social History of Truth* suggests that Hooke was treated as an "(ambiguous) servant" by his colleagues, someone whose testimony was less trustworthy than that of a gentleman (393). The evidence Shapin provides to support this claim presents what is indeed an ambiguous picture, since he acknowledges that the Society rarely challenged Hooke: "one could hardly imagine how the society could have arranged its affairs if Hooke's testimony had not been generally accepted" (393; see also Barbara Shapiro, *Culture of Fact,* 123, 139–143, and Michael Hunter, *Royal Society,* 237n17).

114. Swann, *Curiosities and Texts,* 89; however, Swann's book also explores the occasions for social levelling promoted by the culture of curiosity (see below and Chapter 4 in this volume).

115. Wren quoted in J. A. Bennett, "Robert Hooke," 33.

116. Pepys, *Diary,* 6: 36–37 (February 15, 1665); Evelyn, *Diary,* 3: 416. Before he settled into his Gresham College quarters, Hooke lived with Lady Ranelagh in Pall Mall, but when he ceased to be a member of the household, he was invited to dine there about thirty times a year. Evelyn threw a dinner party for Hooke, which was attended by Lord Brouncker and others, on March 4, 1664 (Gunther, *Early Science,* 6: 171). Although Hooke's dependent status impresses itself strongly on the consciousness of current scholars, the Society, to its

discredit, sometimes seems to have forgotten it; Hooke was paid irregularly. The surveyorship granted him by the king to help rebuild London after the fire helped, as did Sir John Cutler's stipend for the Cutlerian lectureship. Settling on Hooke fifty pounds a year, this lectureship made it possible for him to accept the position of Curator for thirty pounds a year. Although Fellows hoped that Cutler's generosity would "prove a leading example to others," he was soon following their example instead; Cutler appears throughout Hooke's diary "at his old dog tricks" shirking his financial responsibility (Birch, *History,* 1: 485, 496; Hooke, *Diary,* 269). See 'Espinasse, *Robert Hooke,* 4, 83.

117. *Philosophical Transactions,* 6: 2181. Oldenburg was promoting (and quoting from) Boyle's *Usefulnesse of Experimental Naturall Philosophy;* see *Works,* 6: 402.

118. Bird conceded that interacting with social inferiors was not "pleasant unto our nature, but when Christ commandeth it, that should make it pleasant"; the pleasure promised by intercourse with things themselves was of an entirely different nature (quoted in Craig, *Reformation, Politics and Polemics,* 23).

119. Sprat, *History,* 407.

120. Evelyn, *State of France,* 72, 77, 79, 107, 105. Evelyn expressed alarm that the French king was "inviron'd with men of iron whereever he goes," as if he were leading an invasion against his own people (31).

121. Stimson, "Ballad of Gresham Colledge," 113. The complete ballad, which contains twenty-eight verses, was first published at the end of this 1931 article, at 108–117. Power ascribes the poem to a "W. Glanvill": Stimson argued that Power meant to refer to Joseph Glanvill, but Michael Hunter attributes it to Evelyn's brother-in-law William Glanville (see *Science and Society,* 171).

122. Sprat, *History,* 396.

123. Boyle quoted in Pamela Smith, *Body of the Artisan,* 168.

124. Examples could be multiplied indefinitely, but see Boyle, *Works,* 2: 462, and Evelyn, *Tyrannus,* 16, 24.

125. Boyle, *Correspondence,* 5: 310. Beale was sending Boyle arguments for the Society to use in defense of its activities against "Atheisticall Scoffers" and "Theatricall Buffoons," whom he held to be "more dangerous" than "all the dissenters . . . all our bloody warrs with Forreigners, the greate plauge, & the fireing of London" (303, 299).

126. Swann, *Curiosities and Texts,* 80.

127. Evelyn, *Elysium Britannicum,* 34. For Evelyn's "greate undertaking" with bricks, see *Diary,* 3: 471, 476, 477–478, 495; on the "new fuell," see *Sylva* (98 in 1664 edition, expanded in 1670 edition [189] and in 1679 [210]), and *Diary,* 3: 487–488. On the interest of the Fellows in fuel efficiency, see Ochs, "Royal Society," 139. While Evelyn drew on Sir Hugh Plat's 1603 *A New, Cheape*

and Delicate Fire for his ideas on fuel, Raylor shows that he derived the beekeeping idea from Hartlib, who envisioned an England "filled with thousands of hives tended by conscientious beekeepers"; Hartlib's *Reformed Common-Wealth of Bees* was the product of collective efforts to develop techniques for increased honey production that would "yield massive profits, set the poor to work and turn around the domestic economy" ("Samuel Hartlib and the Commonwealth of Bees," 100, 105). Parry observes that it was the "business of bees" that bought Evelyn into Hartlib's beehive-like "network of communications" in the 1650s ("John Evelyn as Hortulan Saint," 131). See also Scott-Luckens, "Providence, Earth's 'Treasury' and the Common Weal," 115–116.

128. *Account of Philaretus* in Michael Hunter, *Boyle by Himself,* 3.

129. Boyle, *Works,* 2: 215–216. On Boyle's efforts to disguise his debts to hermetic philosophers, see Newman and Principe, *Alchemy Tried in the Fire.* A philosophical anxiety of influence surely played a role in Boyle's attacks on the chymists, but his tone is often that of a frustrated would-be pupil. He attacked chymists on procedural grounds as reluctant dispensers of knowledge, focusing on their "obscure, ambiguous, and almost AEnigmatical Way of expressing what they pretend to Teach" (*Works,* 2: 209).

130. Boyle, *Works,* 2: 221, 216; see 374–376. His victory consists in remaining wisely uncommitted to any doctrine unsupported by experiment; see discussion in Shapin and Schaffer, *Leviathan and the Air-Pump,* 74–75; for Boyle's aims in the treatise, see Sargent, *Diffident Naturalist,* 70–75.

131. See Eamon, *Science and the Secrets of Nature,* 8, and "New Light on Robert Boyle" as well as Boyle, *Works,* 4: 119–122 and 6: 467–469.

132. J. D. G. D., "Arms of the Society," and Wagner, "Royal Society's Coat of Arms," but see also Birch, *History,* 1: 274. On the *venatio* paradigm, see Eamon, *Science and the Secrets of Nature,* chapter 8, and Ginzburg, "Clues." Although the helmet on their coat of arms was a peer's helmet, this design feature was not mentioned in the Charter granted by the king and thus may have been added independently by the engraver; see "Arms of the Society."

133. Stimson, "Ballad of Gresham Colledge," 111.

134. The circumstantial character of experimentalist discourse has been explored from a number of angles; see Dear, "Totius in Verba"; Barbara Shapiro, *Culture of Fact;* Shapin and Schaffer, *Leviathan and the Air-Pump;* and Daston, "Language of Strange Facts."

135. The argument that the credible witness was a gentlemanly one, someone who had "credit," is laid out in Shapin and Schaffer, *Leviathan and the Air-Pump,* and Shapin, *Social History of Truth.* For opposing views, see Sargent, *Diffident Naturalist,* 148–158; Michael Hunter, *Scrupulosity,* 11; and Barbara Shapiro, *Culture of Fact,* 139–143. The miraculous blessing when it "rained

wheat" in Tuchbrooke was believed not only by "the common people" but by the town worthies, whose social standing was not sufficient to make the Fellows credit the report; they required specimens. After examining them, the Fellows concluded that the supposed seeds were merely the droppings of starlings who fed on ivy berries (Birch, *History*, 1: 32–33; see Rollins, "Broadside Ballad," 267 for a late sixteenth-century instance of the miracle). For the alliance between high social standing and credit on the continent as it related to the confirmation of Galileo's telescopic findings, see van Helden, "Telescopes and Authority."

136. Boyle, *Works*, 7: 466–467. See discussions in Poovey, *History of the Modern Fact*, 115–116, and Dear, "From Truth to Disinterestedness," 627.

137. Barbara Shapiro, *Culture of Fact*, 141.

138. Sargent, *Diffident Naturalist*, 152, 193n67; her account of Boyle's collaborative style at 189–193 should be compared with chapter 8 of Shapin's *Social History of Truth*.

139. Stubbe, *Plus Ultra Reduced to a Non Plus*, sig. b3ᵛ, discussed in Johns, *Nature of the Book*, 470n47.

140. Boyle, *Works*, 4: 25. See Sargent's discussion in *Diffident Naturalist*, 132.

141. The poem is printed in Sprat's *History*, sigs. B–B3ᵛ. Cowley was elected into the Society on March 6, 1661, around the time he published his *Proposition for the Advancement of Experimental Philosophy*, which was dedicated to the Society (Birch, *History*, 1: 17).

142. Cowley, "To the *Royal Society*," line 75; A.B. (see note 40 above) in Michael Hunter, *Establishing the New Science*, 227. The context of the quotation is revealing: A.B. is using the guild analogy to promote a sense of belonging on the part of Fellows who were not competent to undertake experiments: one would no more expect every Fellow to be a Curator, he explains, than one would expect "that every Love-Brother of the Company, should know the Trade." (Brothers who "have no genius to prog[ress] in philosophy," however, "may be ready enough to assist with their mony.")

143. The demonstrations performed at meetings usually replicated earlier trials; meetings were thus generally devoted to replicating, or simply discussing, work performed elsewhere, though the exhibition of objects also played an important role (Michael Hunter, *Science and Society*, 42–43, 46).

144. Letter of June 1655 in Oldenburg, *Correspondence*, 1: 75. See Shapin and Schaffer's discussion of this passage in *Leviathan and the Air-Pump*, 299.

145. Although he was supposed to provide "three or four considerable experiments" for each meeting, the overextended Hooke sometimes withheld his labor (Birch, *History*, 1: 123–124; 2: 187, 346 [his salary may have been in arrears; see 343], 418, 452; 3: 70). For Petty's desire that Hooke not be unnecessarily "burthened," see 1: 503; he eventually gained an assistant (2: 206, 289). As

Hooke wrote to Boyle in 1667, "Many other things I long to be at, but I do extremely want time" (Boyle, *Correspondence,* 3: 332).

146. Birch, *History,* 1: 80, 124. This request was made at the same meeting that Hooke was proposed (for the second consecutive meeting) as Curator; for another instance of the title being applied to a nonhireling, see 1: 312–313. The president himself was "desired" to experiment with mercury (1: 301).

147. Michael Hunter, *Royal Society,* 21; A.B. (see note 40 above) in Michael Hunter, *Establishing the New Science,* 226. Boyle attacks the association of experimental knowledge with "the Tricks of Juglers" and "the Pageants that entertain Princes" in *Usefulnesse* (*Works,* 3: 235). Compare Marvell's attack on the popish mass as "the pranks and ceremonies of Juglers and Conjurers" in *Growth of Popery* (*Prose Works,* 2: 228).

148. Quoted in Bluhm, "Royal Society's Finances," 92; see Michael Hunter, *Royal Society,* 18–19.

149. This he refused to do: "Another man brought some vegetable excrescences that had grown on the trunk of a tree. I looked at them attentively and, shrugging my shoulders, said that I did not know what to do with them, nor what to say about them" (quoted in Middleton, "Some Italian Visitors," 160, 162).

150. When Fellows did not embrace his hypothesis concerning a substance "inherent and mixt with the air" that caused combustion, "Mr. HOOKE desired, that some experiments might be suggested, that were thought not solvable by the hypothesis of fire proposed by him" (Birch, *History,* 2: 2, 8).

151. Sprat, *History,* 72, 85; see also 35.

152. See Michael Hunter, *Science and Society,* 57 (non-Fellows would be able to read them after a year's time), and Biagioli, *Galileo's Instruments of Credit,* 66n155. Dunton is discussed in Chapter 4.

153. Johns, *Nature of the Book,* 510, 507, 461, 474.

154. Biagioli, *Galileo's Instruments of Credit,* 117–118. Since Galileo was treated "as an artisan entitled to have proprietary attitudes about the 'secret' of his device," he was able to "develop a monopoly over early observational astronomy" (120, 264).

155. Milton, *CPW,* 2: 551. There is no evidence, however, that anyone actually built an air pump using Boyle's description of it (Shapin and Schaffer, *Leviathan and the Air-Pump,* 229–230).

156. Stimson, "Ballad of Gresham Colledge," 109, 112.

157. Sprat, *History,* 68–69.

158. Sprat, *History,* 69–70.

159. Milton, *CPW,* 2: 366–367, 362. Approximately half were produced between 1647 and 1651, when Hartlib was most active as the parliamentary agent for the advancement of learning: for a list of these writings see Charles Webster,

Samuel Hartlib, 208–211. *Of Education* was certainly more bookish than many of these, though Hill argues that Milton's thoughts on education continued to evolve in an increasingly Hartlibian direction after 1645 (*Milton and the English Revolution,* 147). These schemes had humanist precedents; see, for example, Vives, *Tradendis Disciplinis.* See also Houghton, "History of Trades." A fuller consideration of these continuities would have to consider the Society's relationship to the colleges of experience described in Bacon's *New Atlantis* and Gabriel Plattes's *Macaria;* see Charles Webster, *Great Instauration,* 48–49, and Rattansi, "Intellectual Origins." On the emphasis of Reniassance pedagogy on copying and commonplacing (as opposed to "experience"), see Goldberg, *Writing Matter.*

160. Milton, *CPW,* 2: 406, 413, 393–394.

161. Milton, *CPW,* 2: 412, 375, 369–370, 398, 394, 397, 414.

162. Milton, *CPW,* 7: 492, 490. Locke also complained that "little light" was brought to his understanding at university (quoted in Cranston, *John Locke,* 38).

163. Oldenburg quoted in Lewalski, *Life,* 337.

164. *Aubrey on Education,* 38, 36, 109, 140; I have drawn from Michael Hunter's transcription in *John Aubrey,* 52.

165. Brooks, "Apprenticeship," 79.

166. Aubrey, *Brief Lives,* xxviii, xxxi, xxix; Inwood, *Man Who Knew Too Much,* 155. Similarly, the greatest delight of William Petty growing up was "to be looking upon the artificers . . . smyths, the watchmakers, carpenters, joyners" (quoted in Houghton, "History of Trades," 41). Thomas Gresham himself had undergone an eight-year apprenticeship not out of economic necessity but in order "to come by . . . experience and knowledge" (Blanchard, "Sir Thomas," 13). These pseudo-apprenticeships confirm the justice of Hill's observation that the nearest that many sixteenth- and early seventeenth-century scientists "could get to a laboratory . . . was in the workshops of metalworkers, glass-makers, paper-makers, dyers, brewers, sugar-refiners" (*Intellectual Origins,* 66–67; see also Houghton, "History of Trades," 67). The contrast between the corrupt university and innocent apprenticeship may have been conditioned by the fact that apprenticeships tended to start at an earlier age than university training.

167. Boyle, *Early Essays,* 244. Boyle inverts the remarks of Jack Cade's followers, in *Henry VI Part Two,* that the "nobility think scorn to go in leather aprons" (4.2.10). Boyle may be deliberately inverting "apron" slurs, which were used to belittle popular participation in political and religious discussion; see Manning, *English People,* 127. Marvell expresses disgust with apron slurs in *Rehearsal Transpros'd* (*Prose Works,* 1: 57).

168. Boyle, *Early Essays,* 238–241. Ironically, Boyle's murderous fantasy was itself the fruit of his gentlemanly education; his source was Sextus Julius Frontinus (see *Early Essays,* 241n18). For another outburst against "the busy idleness of

receiving senseless visits," see *Correspondence,* 1: 31, 33–34. These critiques of aristocratic idleness have a prehistory in humanism; see Crane, *Framing Authority.*

169. Evelyn, *Elysium Britannicum,* 35; Fulton, "Honourable Robert Boyle," 132. Boyle did accept an honorary degree as a Doctor of Medicine in 1665 (an honor Hooke himself received in 1691, though his was a Lambeth rather than an Oxford degree) but he refused to serve as president of the Society, most likely because he "recoiled from subscription to the Oaths" (133). Michael Hunter observes that "much of Boyle's life represented a reaction against . . . the mindless social milieu of landed society" in "Robert Boyle: A Suitable Case for Treatment?" 261; see also Oster, "Scholar and Craftsman." On Boyle's efforts to combat Beelzebub with his spade, see Chapter 1.

170. Benedict, *Curiosity;* Stubbe, *Specimen of some Animadversions,* 13. Oldenburg had "read some aphorisms for cider" sent to him by John Beale in a 1662 meeting (Birch, *History,* 1: 144).

171. These compliments are from the dedication of Highmore's *History of Generation,* sigs. 3ᵛ–4.

172. Boyle, *Account of Philaretus,* in Michael Hunter, *Boyle by Himself,* 3, 2. See Shapin, *Social History of Truth,* 147, 130–132, and Canny, *Upstart Earl.* J. Paul Hunter wickedly sums up Boyle's self-fashioning as "the pride of a humble face; he thanked God that he could be like other men" (*Before Novels,* 204).

173. See Justice, *Writing and Rebellion,* 17, and Nicholas McDowell, *English Radical Imagination,* 30, 45.

174. South, *Sermon,* 15; Boyle, *Works,* 8: 170; Sprat, *History,* 82. Hooke's remark that he "dissect[ed] a viper, which gave some good discourses of poison" suggests the serpent itself was compelled to discourse of its poison; experimentalist discourse is not simply about the book of nature but actually squeezed or wrought from it (Gunther, *Early Science,* 6: 209).

175. Hooke, *Posthumous Works,* ii; Aubrey, *Brief Lives,* 165.

176. Aubrey, *Brief Lives,* xxxi.

177. Boyle, *Account of Philaretus* in Michael Hunter, *Boyle by Himself,* 8–10. The parallel to Bunyan's claim, at the start of *Grace Abounding,* that he forgot how to read after being taught is striking; see Chapter 1.

178. Boyle, *Works,* 2: 33, 12–13. Having done so, he was "beginning now to allow my self to read those excellent Books" (13).

179. "Sir Peter Pett's Notes on Boyle," in Michael Hunter, *Boyle by Himself,* 71. But see Principe's "Virtuous Romance" on the relationship between Boyle's early experiments in fiction and his later career.

180. Michael Hunter, *Boyle by Himself,* lxxv; *An Advertisement of Mr. Boyle, about the Loss of many of his Writings: Address'd to Mr.* J. W. [probably his servant John Warr] *to be communicated to those friends of His, that are* Virtuosi, *which may*

serve as a kind of Preface to most of his Mutilated and Unfinish'd Writings, in *Works,* 11: 169–171 (the "mischevious Liquor" was "Oyl of Vitriol" or sulphuric acid [170]).

181. Glanvill, *Vanity of Dogmatizing,* sig. B3. For attacks levelled at scholastic theologians by humanists and reformers, see Rummel, *Humanist-Scholastic Debate.*

182. Drawing on Nicholas of Cusa's *De Docta Ignorancia,* reformers used the phrase *learned ignorance* to describe the acceptance of doctrines beyond human reason; see, for example, Perkins, *Lectures,* 98. By 1660, Prynne was using it as an insult; see *Gospel Plea,* 120. The virtuosi's energetic use of the phrase against the schoolmen may have contributed to the change. The subtitle of Glanvill's *Scepsis Scientifica* contrasted learned ignorance with "Confest Ignorance, the Way to Science": the rhetorical nod to the limits of reason becomes the basis for the trustworthy testing, and subsequent discovery, of things that only seem to be known. See also Locke's *Essay,* 3.10.10, where it is used as a synonym for "artificial Ignorance, and *learned Gibberish*" based on "unintelligible Terms," and contrasted with the knowledge of "the illiterate and contemned Mechanick" (3.10.9); see also 4.12.12, where it is contrasted with a philosophy based on "particular Experiments."

183. Thomas Browne, *Works,* 2: 17, 31; Power, *Experimental Philosophy,* 187; Jager, *Tempter's Voice,* 61–75, 125–126; Glanvill, *Vanity of Dogmatizing,* 152. As Peter Harrison puts it, the fall "could be interpreted as having brought about a reliance upon authority and tradition—the very sources of knowledge which were under attack by reformers in matters of religion and natural philosophy" (*The Bible, Protestantism, Natural Science,* 213).

184. See Boyle, *Works,* 2: 13. On the medieval status of academics as quasi-nobility, see Eamon, *Science and the Secrets of Nature,* 80.

185. This theme will be taken up in Chapter 7.

186. See discussion in Fulton, "Honourable Robert Boyle," 122. In his essay "How Boyle Became a Scientist," Michael Hunter identifies 1649 to 1654 as the crucial transitional period (*Scrupulosity,* 15–57).

187. During this time Petty was also the acting Surveyor-General of Ireland (where he determined the bounds of Boyle's estates); see Fulton, "Honourable Robert Boyle," 122.

188. Petty boasted to Aubrey that "he hath read but little, that is to say, not since 25 aetat . . . had he read much, as some men have, he had not known so much as he does, nor should have made such Discoveries and improvements" (*Brief Lives,* 240–241).

189. Boyle, *Correspondence,* 1: 142–143. However, in the same letter Petty also warned Boyle against the hypochondria that tended to befall beginners in medical and anatomical study.

190. Boyle, *Correspondence,* 1: 167.

191. Locke, "Labour," in *Political Essays,* 326–328. Against the objection that such a scheme would eradicate all social distinctions, he offers a compromise of three hours a day of useful labor for the aristocracy.

192. Justice, *Writing and Rebellion,* 101; Hooke, *Posthumous Works,* 27.

193. Hooke, *Micrographia,* sig. b2.

194. Wallis, "Account of Some Passages," 27; for similar comments on astronomy and geography, see 29–30. Wallis was the first student there to defend the circulation of the blood in a public disputation (29).

195. See Hill, *Intellectual Origins,* 49, and *God's Englishman,* 258–259.

196. See Swann, *Curiosities and Texts,* 50–53.

197. Quoted in Swann, *Curiosities and Texts,* 51.

198. Helpful overviews of this project are provided by Houghton, "History of Trades," and Ochs, "History of Trades Programme."

199. Boyle, *Works,* 6: 476.

200. Farr, *Artisans in Europe,* 21–22; Eamon explores this problem in *Science and the Secrets of Nature,* 341–350.

201. Sprat, *History,* 75 (see also 115), 76, 75. In the meantime, Fellows tried to extend the promise of patents. When Boyle displayed the work of an artisan skilled in "softening wood," he "was desired by the society to let the artist know, how well they were pleased with this skill of his, and that they were willing to assist him in procuring a patent for him, in order that he might enjoy the benefit of his art, upon condition that he should acquaint them with the secret" (Birch, *History,* 1: 219). Secrecy and openness had a paradoxical relationship: while "recurrent proposals for secrecy suggests a principle of exclusivity . . . in fact, secrecy was suggested as a means to attract artisans to divulge their secrets" (Larry Stewart, *Rise of Public Science,* 15). On guilds as the source of early modern notions of intellectual property, see Long, *Openness, Secrecy, Authorship,* esp. 88–96. Hooke himself often expressed an "artisanal" proprietary sense, though he was often happy to share information to those who reciprocated the kindness; see Iliffe, "Material Doubts," 289, 312–314.

202. Boyle, *Correspondence,* 4: 9. Even as he declared himself "a Bungler in Begging," he affirmed that he was "not asham'd to begge" on behalf of the Society and listed the "principall Beggars" as if it were an honor roll (12, 9). The contrast between public-spirited begging and selfish aristocratic habits emerged again and again as active Fellows faced the problem of unpaid arrears, a constant topic of discussion (see, for example, Birch, *History,* 1: 75, 479; 2: 18). During its first sixty years, there was no time that the Society received even half of the subscription fees due to it. But there were examples of individual generosity: John Wilkins bequeathed 400 pounds, and Pepys donated 63 pounds for

the plates of *Historia Piscium* (Bluhm, "Royal Society's Finances," 94–95, 85, 100, 102).

203. Quoted in Pamela Smith, *Body of the Artisan,* 230. See Birch, *History,* 1: 426, 428. The Fellows even made efforts to extract "the Secret" of a "rich dye" from a "poor woman by the sea-side" in Wales; see Aubrey, *Remaines of Gentilisme and Judaisme,* in *Three Prose Works,* 279; see also 356. Iliffe suggests that some craftsmen who were unwilling to reveal their secrets may have been forewarned by enemies of the Society ("In the Warehouse," 31).

204. In "Who was Robert Hooke?" Shapin argues that Hooke operated under artisanal codes rather than those of the Christian virtuoso, and Hunter and Schaffer's introduction to *Robert Hooke: New Studies* suggests that Hooke "was always somewhat wistful" about the lucrative career he might have had as a maker of instruments (14). As an alchemist, Boyle himself was no stranger to the tug-of-war between public service and quasi-artisanal secrecy, and he became increasingly obsessed with the threat of plagiarism in his later career. See Michael Hunter, *Scrupulosity,* 114, 135–153, 219–221; such concerns exemplify the tension within the Society "between Baconian cooperation and individual initiative" (152).

205. Hooke, *Micrographia,* sig. g^v; Iliffe, "In the Warehouse."

206. Evelyn, *Sculptura,* 150. So Boyle: "I have often wish'd, that some ingenious Friends to Experimental Philosophy would take the paines to enquire into the Mysteries, and other practices of Trades, and give us an account, some of one Trade, and some of another." Unadmirably, he goes on to fantasize about planting undercover spies in various workshops as apprentices (*Works,* 6: 476).

207. Boyle, *Correspondence,* 1: 212. This language was recycled in the text of *Sculptura* itself, but here, Evelyn demonstrated his solicitude for the "way of *Engraving*" developed by *Prince Rupert.* Rather than permitting Prince Rupert's secret to be made "vulgar," "prostituted," and "expos'd" by a "naked describing of it," Evelyn would adopt an *"AEnigmatical"* approach, revealing as much as "may suffice to give the hint to all ingenious Persons how it is to be perform'd" (*Sculptura,* 147–148). Evelyn's protectiveness of Prince Rupert seems to restore *vulgar* to its conventional meaning, but elite exclusivity is being reformulated through artisanal know-how (and artisanal mystery). Moreover, behind Rupert lie other noble artists, and one in particular: a "Mr. *Faithorn* . . . himself by Profession a *Graver,* and an excellent *Artist,*" who was preparing a translation of a French treatise on etching that Evelyn had also translated, hoping to append it to his own text; instead, Evelyn appended an advertisement for Faithorn's forthcoming work, yielding to the claims of the master (149–150).

208. See Frances Harris, *Transformations,* 59.

209. Boyle, *Correspondence*, 1: 363; Boyle, *Works*, 6: 467; Evelyn, *Elysium Britannicum*, 32. The charge of caprice suggests that they spoke in riddles or even misled him with false hints; John Ray warned against rustics who "make a shew of knowing strange things" (letter inserted in Aubrey, *Natural History of Wiltshire*, 7).

210. Daston, "Language of Strange Facts," 38. On the expanded role of description in later seventeenth- and eighteenth-century writing, see Wall, *Prose of Things*. Although her emphasis is on consumers rather than producers of things, she discusses the role of experimentalism (and technologically assisted observation) on description's elevation from an "ornamental" to a "*substantive*" role in literature (25); see esp. chapter 3. She also remarks on the inhibiting effect of scholasticism before that time, when the "particular detail" was "the Aristotelian accidental" (2). It is certainly worth stressing that experimentalist curiosity was by no means restricted to the working life; according to the omnivorous spirit of Baconian induction, even a report on the precise dimensions of "a very large herring" was worthy of the Society's attention (Birch, *History*, 1: 271). But exposure to workers' experiences offered new opportunities for becoming intimately acquainted with the real texture of things.

211. Birch, *History*, 1: 60, 61, 60; Boyle, *Works*, 3: 230.

212. In this connection, it is suggestive that the celebration of Petty's trade history in the Ballad of Gresham rhymes *clothing* and *nothing*, as if the Fellows have eyes only for the art of making clothes rather than the surface splendor of clothes themselves.

213. Birch, *History*, 1: 60.

214. See also Boyle's discussion of "Manual Skill" as "Doeing by Physical Knowledge" in *Works*, 6: 489–505.

215. Petty, *Petty Papers*, 2: 172.

216. Evelyn, *Publick Employment*, 13; see also *Aubrey on Education*, 37.

217. Adam Fox, *Oral and Literate Culture*, 154–156. The sixteenth-century mathematical practitioner Leonard Digges made this recommendation to learned readers in *A Prognostication of Right Good Effect*, which was reprinted well into the seventeenth century (sig. Bii^v). Aubrey compiled proverbs "observed by Countrey-people" concerning the weather in his section on "Prognosticks" in *Remaines of Gentilisme and Judaisme* (*Three Prose Works*, 222–223; see 337 for another weather-related "proverbial old ryme . . . observ'd as infallible"). This talent characterized anyone whose work kept them outside: so one Fellow observed that "watermen would prognosticate rainy weather approaching, by a more than ordinary driness in their hands." In this sphere as in others, rural folk wisdom and supernatural wisdom shared a border: Sir Kenelm Digby related that "Dr. DEE, by a diligent observation of the weather for seven years together,

acquired such a prognosticating skill of weather, that he was, on that account, accounted a witch" (Birch, *History*, 1: 334, 300).

218. Hooke presented the hygroscope to the Society in October of 1663 (Birch, *History*, 1: 320); see Observation 27 in *Micrographia*, 147–152. Hooke later found that the cod (i.e., the husk) of a vetch worked better than the beard of the wild oat (see Birch, *History*, 2: 100 and Sprat, *History*, 174). See also J. A. Bennett, "Robert Hooke," 36, and "Hooke's Instruments," 78.

219. Boyle, *Correspondence*, 2: 343. Boyle's *Experimental History of Cold* came out shortly thereafter. That winter, Fellows were encouraged to "make any experiments of cold" that "would make use of this weather" (Birch, *History*, 2: 2).

220. Hooke, *Micrographia*, 242–243. As Inwood dryly remarks, his "imagination added what his eye could not see" (*Man Who Knew Too Much*, 54).

221. Hooke, *Micrographia*, 245; Godwin, *Man in the Moone*, 39; see also 32. The projection of paradise onto the moon had "papist" analogues. In the course of her exploration of how the association between the immaculate Virgin and the moon was destabilized by the latter's "maculate" status, Reeves discusses the attempt of a Jesuit who supported Galileo's theories, Giuseppe Biancani, to give a Marian cast to the opaque and spotted moon by associating lunar craters with the enclosed garden in the Song of Songs (*Painting the Heavens*, 224–225).

222. See Ochs, "Royal Society," 149–150.

223. Tiny microscopes even became a fashion accessory, as charms to dangle from bracelets (see Nicolson's introduction Shadwell's *Virtuoso*, xx). Although Boyle protested that individual experiments were "not sufficient to rob a Tradesman of his Profession" since each trade synthesized numerous operations, he was on firmer ground when he pointed the brisk business in scientific instruments: "these Inventions of ingenious heads doe, when once grown into request, set many Mechanical hands a worke, and supply Tradesmen with new meanes of getting a livelyhood or even inriching themselves" (*Works*, 6: 398–399). See also Michael Hunter, *Science and Society*, 68–69, 84–85, and Jardine, *Ingenious Pursuits*, 45–52 (on the Society's support of engravers, see 83–89).

224. In the years before the publication of *Micrographia*, Hooke was repeatedly charged "to bring in at every meeting one microscopical observation at least" (Birch, *History*, 1: 215, 397). Benedict points out that in the index to the issues of *Philosophical Transactions* from 1665 and 1666, the listing of "Artificial Instruments" occupies more space than almost any other entry (*Micrographia*'s first edition came out in 1665). See *The Philosophical Transactions of Two Years, 1665 and 1666*, and Benedict, *Curiosity*, 66.

225. Boyle, *Correspondence,* 2: 415, 330. See discussion in Michael Hunter, *Royal Society,* 36; see also Cooper, "Hooke's Career," 9.

226. Glanvill, *Scepsis Scientifica,* 209; see also *Vanity of Dogmatizing,* 240.

3. The Productive Eye

1. Sprat, *History,* 51. On philosophers "fruitful of controversies but barren of works," see Bacon, *Works,* 8: 26. Hakewill identified the capacity of the moderns for "deepe speculations" with "*masculine,* and lasting birthes" (*Apologie,* sig. a2ᵛ).

2. Hooke, *Micrographia,* sig. a2. Hooke sometimes referred to them simply as "Organs" or "Engins," as in *Posthumous Works,* 473; "artificial Eys," "artificial helps," and "Mechanical helps" were also common epithets: see Power, *Experimental Philosophy,* sig. c2ᵛ, 82; Glanvill, *Essays,* 17; and Hooke, *Micrographia,* sig. d2.

3. On the old and new man, see Ephesians 4:22–24 and Colossians 3:9–11.

4. See Neaman, "Mystery of the Ghent Bird"; van Helden, "Invention of the Telescope," 15, 19, 23–24. Van Helden explains why, upon hearing of the invention, many individuals believed they had already invented it: they were for all intents and purposes in possession of it. He argues that it was Galileo's improvements that transformed the device into a genuinely scientific instrument (25–26). The compound microscope quickly evolved from the telescope, but the most celebrated microscopes of the period, Antony van Leeuwenhoek's, were simple in their construction, single lenses clamped between plates and held up to the eye; see Ruestow, *Microscope,* 6–11. On problems with the compound microscope preferred by Hooke, see note 162 below.

5. This lore influenced contemporary portrayals of Galileo, protecting Florence, and even a Jesuit outpost on the moon, by immolating enemy ships (*Galileo's Glassworks,* 162–163). While the lore surrounding the Pharo only became widely known in the sixteenth century, Reeves shows that related legends of an imperial glass were current throughout the Middle Ages. The early modern period was characterized by an interest in optical devices of all kinds; for an exploration of the literary and cultural impact of anamorphic images, perspective boxes, and the like, see Gilman, *Curious Perspective.*

6. On Galileo's "noncooperative" attitude in this regard, see Biagioli, *Galileo's Instruments of Credit,* esp. chapters 1 and 2: he exploited the patronage system in an attempt to create a "monopoly." As van Helden remarks, his discoveries were largely accepted on the basis of his personal authority, which was raised "to almost divine proportions," ensuring that Florence and the Medici Court remained the center of telescopic astronomy during his lifetime ("Telescopes and Authority," 16, 25).

7. John Norris, *Reflections,* 132. On the iconic status of the air pump, see Shapin and Schaffer, *Leviathan and the Air-Pump,* esp. 30–40.

8. Hooke, *Micrographia,* sig. d2. By extending the application of such phrases to primitive technologies like fertilizer as well as sophisticated scientific equipment, virtuosi incorporated a wide range of what Oldenburg called "Artificial good things" into an Edenic image repertoire (e.g., "Artificial helps" in Evelyn, *Philosophical Discourse of Earth,* 61).

9. Sterry, *Discourse,* 99. See discussions in Almond, *Adam and Eve,* 66, and Peter Harrison, *The Bible, Protestantism, Natural Science,* 209–211.

10. Sprat, *History,* 349.

11. Sprat, *History,* 349–350. Boyle's celebration of "Man, as the great-High Priest of Nature" from the early 1650s is similarly grounded in an expansive account of Adam's labors of discovery in the garden (*Works,* 13: 151). If experimentation was a "Divine Service," then the *"whole World"* could be considered the *"Temple of God"* (*Works,* 3: 238). This suggests another area of overlap between experimentalist faith and experimental faith: the pursuit of religious experience outside the physical space of the church.

12. The Psalms were also frequently appealed to in support of physico-theology; Psalm 92:5–6 and Psalm 77:11 provided the epigraphs for Aubrey's *Natural History of Wiltshire.* As Catherine Wilson points out, the passage from Romans 1:20 to the effect that the things that are made are to be looked beyond could, in the age of the microscope, be deployed as an apology for assisted observation (*Invisible World,* 22), and in fact Sprat appeals here to this very passage (*History,* 349), as does Sterry (*Discourse,* 99).

13. Aubrey censured the "irreligion" of those who remained ignorant of the "names and virtues" of plants that grew near their dwellings, but the lens could raise devotion to a magnification far beyond the capacity of any simpler (*Aubrey on Education,* 35); see, for example, Evelyn, *Sylva* (1670 ed.), 65.

14. Discussed with references in Kantorowicz, *King's Two Bodies,* 70. See also Almond, *Adam and Eve,* 28–29. This tradition is behind the early modern conviction that, as Sir Walter Raleigh put it, "those of the first Age were of great stature," though Raleigh protests the vulgar error that Adam's shin bones were a thousand fathoms long (*History of the World,* 43). For the influence of the rabbinic tradition on early modern commentaries generally, see Arnold Williams, *Common Expositor,* esp. 11–13.

15. Sprat, *History,* 35, 72.

16. Sprat, *History,* 17, 327. The Latin word *perspicere*—to look through—was strongly associated with enhanced vision and lenses, as an early name for the telescope, *perspicillum,* indicates (Reeves, *Galileo's Glassworks,* 111). On Wycliffite and Protestant objections to the worship of accidents in the popish mass, and the

countertradition of the productive sacrament, see the first two sections of Chapter 1. The "Instrument / Of truth compos'd" is William Browne's epithet for the telescope, an alternative to shepherd's pipes, in *Britannia's Pastorals,* 2.1.861–862 (*Whole Works,* 1: 189), discussed in Chapter 5; on Adam's use of "some such contemplation" analogous to microscopy to name the creatures, see Hooke, *Micrographia,* 154 and below.

17. This phrase occurs everywhere in the discourse of experimental faith and experimentalism alike; see Baxter, *Certainty of Christianity without Popery,* sig. A2; Charleton, *Three Anatomic Lectures,* 24; Ray, *Ornithology,* 359; and Glanvill, *Essays,* 12, sixth pagination (in the context of God's command to "try all things").

18. This association was clinched through the popular pun on Galilee and Galileo. See Reeves, *Painting the Heavens,* 134–135, 224.

19. *Observations,* 178–179, second pagination in *Grounds and Occasions;* see also 78–79, first pagination. When Eachard pilloried the modish clergyman eager to be thought "ingenious"—who exchanged his old library for "a *Wagon full* of *new Philosophy,*" elevated atomists like Gassendi over the church fathers, and sermonized about the man on the moon (even while taking his preface "from *Adam,* though his business lie at the other end of the *Bible*")—he was taking a swipe at one of the Society's most prominent members, who, at the time Eachard was writing, had just been made a bishop: "World in the Moon Wilkins" (Eachard, *Grounds and Occasions,* 78–79, 81, first pagination; 173–174, second pagination; on Wilkins's nickname, see Barbara Shapiro, *John Wilkins,* 84). Wilkins became a bishop two years before the first edition of *The Grounds and Occasions of the Contempt of the Clergy* came out. In *The Discovery of a World in the Moone,* Wilkins had speculated on the possible existence of lunar beings whose postmortem fates were entirely unaffected by Christ's sacrifice on earth, and who perhaps did not stand in need of redemption. It was as if the technology of the lens enabled a glimpse into the distant state it was supposed to restore: a state of innocence embodied not by two individuals but a whole race, one suggestively bearing "some proportion and likenesse to our natures" (*Discovery,* 193). Although it was reissued under his name throughout the century, Wilkins's *Discovery* was initially published anonymously (in 1638) and displayed in the shop of "the most incendiary Puritan bookseller in London, Michael Sparke"; Johns argues that it was the notoriety of Sparke, whose name was prominently displayed on the title page, that fueled Wilkins's conflict with conservative churchman Alexander Ross (*Nature of the Book,* 52). Milton would draw on this exchange for the astronomical discussion between Adam and Raphael in *Paradise Lost.*

20. Milton, *CPW,* 1: 784.

21. For artificial helps, see note 2 above.

22. Aubrey, *Brief Lives*, 36; Boyle, *Correspondence*, 2: 146. See discussion in von Maltzahn, "Laureate," 186.

23. On man as the priest of nature, see Boyle, *Works*, 13: 151; see also Ashmole, *Theatrum Chemicum*, 444. The seminal treatment of this theme in Boyle is Fisch, "Scientist as Priest." In an important article, "Science as a Calling," Feingold argues that university students with scientific interests such as Ray and Derham were effectively forced into careers in the church by the scarcity of endowed positions in the sciences and that the discourse of natural theology they elaborated was a "rationalization" of scientific activity "undertaken for its own sake . . . I do not wish to imply that they did not believe their rhetoric, only that it was not the motivation for the activity" (109). Still, Boyle was under no professional obligation to justify his activities on religious grounds, while Sprat, who seems not to have engaged in scientific activities himself, clearly felt an obligation to promote the ethos of the Christian virtuoso.

24. See Watkins, *Newes from the Dead*, which was a *"True and Exact Narration of the miraculous deliverance of Anne Greene"* (title page); Aubrey mentions the miracle in *Brief Lives*, 238; it also shows up in Derham's *Physico-Theology*, 156–157.

25. Power, *Experimental Philosophy*, sig. a3ᵛ. Power opposes sons of sense to Adam and users of the lens at once.

26. Stubbe, *Censure*, 39–40; see Eamon, *Science and the Secrets of Nature*, 59, and Milton, *PL*, 7.94–96.

27. Ginzburg, "High and Low," 29–30. Thus a warning against moral pride was transformed into a caution against intellectual pride, which was then associated with curiosity.

28. Augustine, *Confessions*, 1: 213 (5.3).

29. Augustine, *Confessions*, 2: 175 (10.35).

30. Augustine, *Confessions*, 2: 181 (10.35). For the *venatio* paradigm, see Ginzburg, "Clues," and Eamon, *Science and the Secrets of Nature*, chapter 8; he discusses the medieval polemic *contra vanam curiositatem* at 58–66; see also Blumenberg, *Legitimacy of the Modern Age*, 279–360. For an account of Chaucer's outriding Monk as a personification of such curiosity, see Olsson's "Grammar, Manhood, and Tears." As Catherine Wilson puts it, the Christian tradition represented self-purifying introspection as "sufficiently absorbing to leave no energy available for external applications of the questioning faculty" (*Invisible World*, 22). There are two alternatives to standing dully besotted with the sights and sounds of the world: turning away from them or using them as the occasion for elevating contemplation through introspection and interpretation; in this sense, all wayward experiences gain retrospective justification by their role in the *Confessions*.

31. On the curious as busybodies, see Quinn, "Polypragmosyne."

32. Kenny's *Curiosity* is the most systematic exploration of the word's seventeenth-century transformation; on the blend of subjective and objective senses, see esp. 15, 189. On curiosity's rehabilitation, see also part III of Blumenberg, *Legitimacy of the Modern Age.* Recent studies that explore the reevaluation of curiosity in a specifically English context include Benedict, *Curiosity,* and Swann, *Curiosities and Texts.*

33. For example, in *Certain Physiological Essays,* Boyle attacks the "curious but groundless structures that men have built up of Opinions alone," then remarks approvingly on an experiment conducted during "an illustrious meeting of Curious Men" that "excited a curiosity among them" (*Works,* 2: 26, 201). Milton was equally skilled at this bait-and-switch, though his usual strategy is to use *curious* in a pejorative sense while celebrating good curiosity as ingenious or, more often, ingenuous. Where curiosity is denounced, it is as an expression of imagination, not investigative desire: so, for example, strict opponents of divorce are "over-curious to strain at *atoms,* and yet to stop every vent and cranny of permissive liberty" because they are victims of a "fals imagination of a strictnes never impos'd from above" (*CPW,* 2: 354; see also 228); in contrast, the "ingenuous" (2: 239, 249, 252) have recovered the primary—original—purpose of matrimony, to gratify an "intellectuall and innocent desire" (269). Where curiosity is praised, it is opposed to imagination, as when the "curious architecture" of the reformed church prophesied in Ezekiel is contrasted with "the devices and imbellishings of mans imagination" (*CPW,* 1: 757). The model again is Bacon, who attacked the schoolmen's "curiosity" as "unprofitable subtility" (*Works,* 3: 286).

34. The proverb shows up in Ben Jonson's *Every Man in his Humour,* 1.4.91–92 (*Jonson,* 3: 317). See Benedict's discussion in *Curiosity,* 122.

35. Derham, *Physico-Theology,* 429–431. Derham caps this passage with Job 36:24.

36. Bacon, *Advancement* (1605 ed.), 31.

37. Thomas Browne, *Religio Medici,* 1.13 in *Works,* 1: 22; see 24 (section 15) where "ruder heads," besotted with elephants and camels, overlook nature's "narrow Engines."

38. Line 143 of Cowley's "To the *Royal Society,*" discussed below.

39. Sprat, *History,* 350.

40. *Il Saggiatore* in Matthews, *Scientific Background,* 56–57. In the *Essay,* Locke describes this disappointing disconnection of our ideas from the world that causes them with vengeful relish: "the *Ideas of primary Qualities* of Bodies, *are Resemblances* of them, and their Patterns do really exist in the Bodies themselves; but the *Ideas, produced* in us *by* these *Secondary Qualities,* have no resem-

blance of them at all. There is nothing like our *Ideas,* existing in the Bodies themselves . . . only a Power to produce those Sensations in us" (2.8.15).

41. Aquinas had argued that it was not possible that anything made of flesh and bone could be nonsensible due to smallness, in part because of Genesis 2:19; see Hutchison, "What Happened to Occult Qualities?" 236.

42. Vaughan, *Magia Adamica,* 29.

43. In his poem to Thomas Harriot celebrating his work with lenses, "To My Admired and Soule-Loved Friend Mayster of all essentiall and true knowledge, *M. Harriots,*" George Chapman had extolled the "perfect eye" and "body absolute" of "True learning," compared to which the fallen body was capable of only "staring ignorance" (lines 41, 63, 85). On the Royal Society's interest in Harriot, see Chapter 2, note 43.

44. Locke, *Essay,* 1.1.2–3, 2.11.15, p. 17 (from Locke's table of contents). Locke is constructing an Adamic fable, one that applies to "the whole course of Men in their several Ages, Countries, and Educations" (2.11.16). In a parallel effort, Bunyan presents the steps of his own progress toward spiritual knowledge as the steps of mankind as a whole: from idolatry, to Judaism, and finally to Christianity, by virtue of his incorporation into a body of believers; see *Grace Abounding,* par. 16–19, 29, 37, 46.

45. Charleton, *Physiologia,* 436 (see also his *Darknes of Atheism,* 10); Petty, *Discourse,* 131. Charleton, like many virtuosi, attributed powers once associated with scholastic form to the atomic particle. When Petty claimed that "Atoms are also *Male* and *Female,*" he meant *"Active* and *Susceptive"* (130). As Rattansi observes, this theory permitted him to dispense with the objection that atoms weren't mentioned in Genesis ("Intellectual Origins," 131).

46. See Newman and Principe, *Alchemy Tried in the Fire,* 18–19.

47. Glanvill, *Vanity of Dogmatizing,* 9. Such speculations extended beyond the virtuosi; Joseph Hall claimed that Adam "saw the inside of all the creatures at first; (his Posterity sees but their skins ever since;)" (*Works,* 776). While Aquinas's Adam had knowledge of universals infused into him, his senses were not more acute; see *Summa Theologia,* 13: 96–99 (1a.94.3).

48. Glanvill, *Vanity of Dogmatizing,* 5–6.

49. Salkeld, *Treatise of Paradise,* 176–177, 135, 205.

50. In early modern formulations, Adam as father and Adam as representative mingle together: speaking of our "first Father *Adam,*" Thomas Hooker declares that "all mankinde was in *Adam,* in his loynes, and *Adam* in innocencie represented all mankind, he stood (as a Parliament man doth for the whole country) for all that should be born of him" (*Saints Dignitie,* 28).

51. Salkeld, *Treatise of Paradise,* 178; Bradley, *Nosce Te Ipsum,* 27, second pagination.

52. Locke, *Reasonableness,* 1–2. Such objections raised the standard for implicit consent in all these contexts.

53. Salkeld, *Treatise of Paradise,* 249, 353; Robert Harris, *Brief Discourse,* 6, 10.

54. Robert Harris, *Brief Discourse,* 11, 16, 11.

55. Bradley, *Nosce te Ipsum,* 36–37, 40–41, 60, 61.

56. Robert Harris, *Brief Discourse,* 1–2; Salkeld, *Treatise of Paradise,* 11, 1–2.

57. Robert Harris, *Brief Discourse,* 5, 6; Thomas Goodwin, *Christ Set Forth,* 47. See also 75, where a "necessary, naturall covenant" made *"Adam* appointed a Common person for us." Although the contrast is with the free covenant made with Christ, I am suggesting that the effort to virtually inhabit Adam in his first estate imbued the natural covenant with choice as well.

58. Robert Harris, *Brief Discourse,* 20; Glanvill, *Vanity of Dogmatizing,* sig. B3.

59. Salkeld, *Treatise of Paradise,* 124; see also 122.

60. Glanvill, *Vanity of Dogmatizing,* sigs. B2^v, B^v, B2, 3, sigs. B2^v, B3–B4.

61. See *OED,* defs. 1–4. Glanvill is eager to make clear that "so severe an intentness" might finally be beyond the capacity of men outside "the Precincts of *Paradise,*" except "He, that came to gain us a better *Eden* then we lost" (112). Christ is not excluded from the experimental imaginary, but he is paradized and made Adamic.

62. Power, *Experimental Philosophy,* 183, 184, sigs. a4–a4^v.

63. Milton, *CPW,* 2: 527; Sprat, *History,* 94. Thus, even as many of his colleagues imagined Adam as more technologically advanced than they were, Boyle thought that the first man would be impressed with the progress his heirs had made in continuing his labors in "the shops of Artificers, the Laboratories of Chymists, and other well-furnished Magazines of Art." Although the experimentalist Eden was often used to figure an America of secrets, Boyle describes a "new world, as it were" into which Adam only glimpsed, created by "the Industry of His Posterity" (*Works,* 3: 212). For an example of Adam's *simultaneous* use as a working model for investigators and an unattainable goal, see Ashmole, *Theatrum Chemicum,* 445–446.

64. Hooke, *Micrographia,* sigs. a2, a.

65. Godfrey Goodman, *Fall of Man,* 115–116, 10, 45, 183. One might say, however, that Goodman's very concessions suggest an incipient experimentalism. In *The Creatures Praysing God,* he concedes that God can be "discerned in the glasse of his Creatures," but only dimly; in contrast, *"sanctifying grace"* operates "like a prospective glasse to discerne" ultimate causes, which the "theatre of the Creatures" can never reveal (14, 17, 16). But even as he insists that "no causes can fully, exactly and totally appeare in their effects" to "sence and sence alone,"

which is "the mother and nurse of idolatry," his own association of grace with technologically assisted vision destabilizes the binary contrast between soul and body, spiritual and carnal knowledge, while his association of grace with knowledge of causes suggest the devotional utility of curiosity as a lever to direct his reader's gaze inward and upward (14, 6).

66. Bloys, *Adam in his Innocencie*, 8, 3, 270, 160.

67. Warning against "excessive delight in planting," Bloys insists that we must work at "amending the barren heart, rather than the barren earth" (78, 175). Bloys also diagnoses the Baconian zeal to "go to and fro" as a specifically Copernican form of giddiness (25–27, 234–235); as in Augustine, curiosity seeks "wholly to please the outward senses of the body" rather than to "strengthen the inward powers and faculties of the soule" (235). Yet even he lauds the book of nature as a source of divine knowledge (9).

68. Bloys, *Adam in his Innocencie*, 270; Glanvill, *Vanity of Dogmatizing*, 15.

69. Hooke, "Cutlerian Lectures," in Gunther, *Early Science*, 8: 1, 3.

70. Charleton, *Physiologia*, 5; Glanvill, *Vanity of Dogmatizing*, 112–113, sig. B2. Charleton's mole-men falsely "fancy themselves to be Eagles" (5).

71. See Fish's discussion of this topos in the first chapter of *Self-Consuming Artifacts*. Wojcik stresses that experimentalists like Boyle justified their empiricism precisely "by appealing to the limits of human understanding," especially those imposed by the body (*Robert Boyle*, xi). On the centrality of reconstructing alien phenomenology to the project of knowledge, see Nagel, "What Is It Like to Be a Bat?" and *View from Nowhere*.

72. Charleton, *Physiologia*, 5.

73. Sprat, *History*, 82; Stubbe, *Censure*, 36–37; [Stubbe], *Reply*, 7. This latter suggestion is ironically made in the negative: "But, methinks, this would be a pritty *Medium* to prove the not-suitableness of experimental Philosophy to a Christian." The paragraph goes on to contrast telescopic and microscopic observation with "wordy Philosophy." Stubbe was on to something; two early Boyle lecturers, Samuel Clarke and William Whiston, were charged with Arianism; see Dahm, "Science and Apologetics," 174. In this connection, see Boyle's rather weak explanation of his failure to treat "the Oeconomy of Man's Salvation by Jesus Christ" at any length in *Of the High Veneration Man's Intellect Owes to God* (*Works*, 10: 179–180).

74. Bourdieu, *Science of Science*, 40, 83; Barbara Shapiro, *Culture of Fact*, 128.

75. Hooke, "Cutlerian Lectures," in Gunther, *Early Science*, 8: 65; Hooke, *Micrographia*, sigs. a2, b2ᵛ; J. A. Bennett, "Hooke's Instruments," 66.

76. Locke, *Essay*, 2.23.11; Power, *Experimental Philosophy*, sig. c2ᵛ; this suggestion also appears in a significantly qualified form in a 1659 letter in Thomas Browne, *Works*, 4: 266. Grew also makes much of the transparency of

objects when viewed under the microscope; the lens user's liberation from *"wanton phansies"* includes the cheat of color (*Idea,* 114, 101).

77. Ginzburg contrasts "the Galilean physicist, professionally deaf to sounds and forbidden to taste or smell," with the physician who sniffed feces and tasted urine ("Clues," 94); the English virtuoso integrated these two personae.

78. Pepys, *Diary,* 7: 239; Birch, *History,* 2: 261. For discussion and the unveiling of a prototype, see Birch, *History,* 2: 255, 261–263, 271; Pepys tried it to his "great content," and believed that it would be "improved to a great heighth" (*Diary,* 9: 146); see also *Micrographia,* sig. b2ᵛ.

79. See Hooke, *Diary,* 233, 146, 414; see also 210 and 245, and Waller, "Life of Dr. Robert Hooke," in Hooke, *Posthumous Works,* iv.

80. The "power of flight always ranked high as a mark of the true adept" in the natural magic tradition (Henry, "Robert Hooke," 174). While Hooke was invoking this tradition, he was also reforming it: the standard medieval and Renaissance view that magic was actually performed by demons whom magicians merely summoned was not utterly banished by the natural magic tradition; see Hutchison, "What Happened to Occult Qualities?" 237–238 and references therein. On Hooke's rejection of magic, see Michael Hunter, *Scrupulosity,* 117.

81. *Leviathan* 132, 9 (2.17, introduction and passim).

82. The result was that "he seems so near to bursting that it excites compassion in the hearer" (Lorenzo Magalotti quoted in Michael Hunter, *Scrupulosity,* 59). Whenever he mentioned God's name, his discourse came to "a visible stop" ("Burnet's Funeral Sermon," in Michael Hunter, *Boyle by Himself,* 48).

83. "John Evelyn's Letters to William Wotton," in Michael Hunter, *Boyle by Himself,* 89.

84. Aubrey, *Brief Lives,* 165; Waller, "Life of Dr. Robert Hooke," in Hooke, *Posthumous Works,* xxvii, xxvi.

85. Aubrey, *Brief Lives,* 165; Waller, "Life of Dr. Robert Hooke," in Hooke, *Posthumous Works,* xxvi (this curvature "increas'd as he grew older, so as to be very remarkable at last"). For similar comments about Francis Willoughby, see Birch, *History,* 3: 66.

86. Beale quoted in von Maltzahn, "Laureate," 146–147.

87. Gilman offers a useful discussion of the influence of perspectivalism on early modern concepts of knowledge in *Curious Perspective.*

88. See *OED,* defs. 1 and 2. Vaughan refers to such an instrument when he remarks that to "give an experienc'd Testimonie of Actions more Ancient than our selves, is a thing impossible for us, unless wee could look into that *Glass,* where all *Occurrences* may bee seen, Past, Present, and to Come" (*Magia Adamica,* 10).

89. "Burnet Memorandum," in Michael Hunter, *Boyle by Himself,* 32. For similar reports, see Aubrey, *Miscellanies,* in *Three Prose Works,* 99–100.

90. "Burnet Memorandum," in Michael Hunter, *Boyle by Himself,* 31–32. Aubrey also relates the lore that the user of such a glass must be "a pure virgin" (*Miscellanies,* in *Three Prose Works,* 100).

91. "John Evelyn's Letters to William Wotton," in Michael Hunter, *Boyle by Himself,* 89.

92. Boyle, *Works,* 8: 57–58; Evelyn, *Acetaria,* 146, quoted in Frances Harris, *Transformations,* 25. On Boyle's relationship to magic, see Michael Hunter, *Scrupulosity,* 93–118.

93. Boyle, *Works,* 8: 58. This passage also invokes the metaphor of reading to express the same point: "the mind is never satisfied till it comes to the end of the Book," but the lot of the individual literatus was "like theirs, that light upon some excellent Romance, of which they shall never see the latter parts." In the meantime, nature's reader and editor, like Milton's first couple, "finds his work to increase daily upon his hands" (57–58).

94. See Michael Hunter, "Robert Boyle: A Suitable Case for Treatment?" 267, his "Disquieted Mind," esp. 93–94, and *Scrupulosity,* esp. 72–118. Burnet noted that Boyle's exactness in experiment was a matter of "Conscience" ("Burnet Memorandum," in Michael Hunter, *Boyle by Himself,* 28).

95. Milton, *PL,* 5.262 (the passage explicitly compares Galileo's telescopic vision to angelic sight); Feyerabend, *Against Method,* 84–102, and esp. note 21; Harold Brown, "Galileo"; Reeves, *Painting the Heavens,* 3–4; van Helden, "Telescopes and Authority," 11–12. Spherical aberration was reduced by larger and flatter lenses with longer focal length, resulting in bigger and more inconvenient telescopes; see "Glass," in Singer, *History of Technology,* 3: 232–233. (On design issues with the microscope, see note 162 below).

96. The topos may have received further motivation from the standard method of measuring the optical power of perspective devices: reading letters from a distance using something like the modern eye-chart (Eileen Reeves, personal communication); see van Helden, "Telescopes and Authority," 26–27. Reciprocally, the association between reading and nearsightedness may have provided motivation for experimentalist caricatures of the text-addled schoolman; myopia became more widespread after the invention of print (van Helden, "Invention of the Telescope," 10).

97. Sprat, *History,* 97. A comparison may be drawn to Bunyan's own boasts of virtual illiteracy, as well as his insistence that he never "went to School to *Aristotle*"; his literacy in God's word was experimental. See Chapter 1.

98. Baker, *Microscope Made Easy,* iv–v; Cowley, "To the *Royal Society,*" line 150 (I quote from the version that prefaces Sprat's *History,* sigs. B–B3ᵛ).

99. R. F. Jones, *Ancients and Moderns,* 7; Pamela Smith, *Body of the Artisan.* But see Hutchison, "What Happened to Occult Qualities?" 240–241, and for the

centrality of the Adamic myth to Paracelsian thought, see Bono, *Word of God,*
129–140.

100. Dear, *Discipline and Experience,* 21–25, 154–155.

101. Croll, *Treatise of Signatures* (bound with *Bazilica Chymica*), sigs. B2,
A2ᵛ, A2, A3. Bono offers a very useful account of how Croll "Calvinizes"
Paracelsus in *Word of God,* 140–166.

102. When Thomas Browne complains that "the Heathens knew better how
to joyne and reade these mysticall letters, than wee Christians, who cast a more
carelesse eye on these common Hieroglyphicks, and disdain to suck Divinity from
the flowers of nature," he is suggesting that these signs are available to our natural
sight *and* that they are saturated with meaning pertaining immediately to human
ends and interests; we just have to overcome our perverse disdain for the natural
world and drink it in (*Religio Medici* 1. 16, in *Works,* 1: 25). See note 117 below.

103. Van Helmont, *Oriatrike,* 29, 35.

104. Ayers, *Locke,* 81–82. The doctrine of preexistence was entertained by
Glanvill, but he offered his Adamic fable as a substitute; see the preface to *Vanity.*
Beale felt that Glanvill required "ballaste . . . from Origenian Platonisme &
Extravagant adventures" to be useful to the Society (Boyle, *Correspondence,* 3: 260).

105. See Hannaway, *Chemists and the Word,* esp. 25–26, and Pamela Smith,
Body of the Artisan, 87.

106. Croll, *Treatise of Signatures,* sig. A3.

107. Foucault, *Order of Things,* 20; Croll, *Treatise of Signatures,* 1–2.

108. Godfrey Goodman, *Fall of Man,* 255, 39. The first quotation appears
in a passage that compares the marriage of man and wife to the union of the soul
and the body, matter and form, and Christ and the Church.

109. Evelyn, *Sylva* (1729 ed.), ix.

110. Hooke, *Micrographia,* sig. a2ᵛ; Charleton, *Physiologia,* 3; Ray, *Wisdom,*
85–86. Charleton had embraced Helmontianism earlier, however; on his
conversion, see Mendelsohn, "Alchemy and Politics."

111. Baker, *Microscope Made Easy,* 299. Baker makes the same argument in
his preface to *The Universe.*

112. Boyle, *Works,* 4: 122, 119, 122. Newton in turn used Boyle's microscopic finding in propounding his theory of color; see Alan Shapiro, "Artists'
Colors and Newton's Colors," 613.

113. Power, *Experimental Philosophy,* sig. c3ᵛ; Hooke, *Posthumous Works,* 449.

114. Hooke, *Micrographia,* sigs. a, g; Hooke, *Posthumous Works,* 338. As a
rebuke to the anthropomorphizing habits Hooke traced to the fall, Ray and
Francis Willoughby's taxonomy of plants was based on their intrinsic structure.
Explicitly departing from the emblematic tradition which was fortified by
signatures, they declared in the preface to their *Ornithology* that "we have wholly

omitted what we find in other Authors concerning . . . *Hieroglyphics, Emblems, Morals, Fables, Presages,* or ought else appertaining to *Divinity, Ethics, Grammar,* or any sort of Humane Learning: And present him [the reader] only with what properly relates to their Natural History" (sig. A4). Through such exclusions, they imparted to their readers a methodological lesson that was also a lesson in humility. It is striking to see divinity in the above list of excluded fields, but although the authors did not meddle in divinity as a discipline, the book claims to serve a devotional purpose: "the illustration of Gods glory, by exciting men to take notice of, and admire his infinite power and wisdom displaying themselves in the Creation of so many *Species*" (sig. A3ᵛ). Divinity as conventionally understood was simply irrelevant to this sacred "illustration" of God. See discussion in Keith Thomas, *Man and the Natural World,* 66–69.

115. Pinnell's preface to Croll, *Philosophy Reformed,* sig. A4.

116. Hooke, *Posthumous Works,* 338. As Sprat declared, Royal Society fellows "promise no Wonders, nor endeavour after them" (*History,* 318). On the relationship between wonder and investigation, see Park and Daston, *Wonders and the Order of Nature.*

117. Lucretius, *De Rerum Natura,* 1.195–197, 2.688–694. See, for example, Boyle, *Works,* 8: 402, where we find twenty-four letters can be "variously combined" to produce all the words in the language; the same analogy is made in Charleton, *Physiologia,* 433. This is not to say that no virtuoso believed in signatures; Thomas Browne was an avid reader of them (see note 102 above). His philosophical correspondence with Power is interesting in this regard; treating Browne as his philosophical mentor and superior, Power begs him for "experimental evacuations," but he also challenges Browne's description of a signature in *The Garden of Cyrus,* pointedly (but ingenuously) confessing his failure to see what Browne describes: "I have narrowly search'd very many yet either my fancy was not so active or else my enquiries not so" (*Works,* 4: 264; for the passage in question, see 1: 207). In treating the decline of form theory and the rise of corpuscularianism, I am condensing a complicated history; my interest is less in theories of matter than the metaphors they generated, and how those metaphors shaped orientations toward the physical world. On how Bacon's reinterpretation of form reveals "conceptual continuity" with particulate theories of matter, promoting a constructivist stance towards nature, see Pérez-Ramos, *Francis Bacon's Idea of Science,* esp. 70, 92, 99. See also Emerton, *Scientific Reinterpretation of Form.*

118. Hooke, *Posthumous Works,* 280, 320; Charleton, *Physiologia,* 129, 433, 427.

119. Grew, *Anatomy of Plants,* 224. When Hooke asserts that he has "discover'd the true form" of objects with the microscope, he makes it clear that for him the term can mean nothing else (*Micrographia,* sig. f2ᵛ).

120. Hooke, *Posthumous Works,* 435.

121. Boyle, *Works,* 8: 397. Bono makes a similar argument in chapter 6 of *Word of God;* hermeneutics gave way to what he calls "deinscription"; he discusses Galileo's influential use of the topos of nature's book at 193–198. On the shift from emblematic to experimental reading see also chapter 2 of Karen Edwards, *Milton and the Natural World,* and Peter Harrison, *The Bible, Protestantism, Natural Science,* esp. 168–169, 194. In chapter 4 of *Galileo's Instruments of Credit,* Biagioli argues that Galileo was backed into the topos by his combat with the theologians and their "book-based regime of truth"; his eventual insistence on the openness of nature's book was intended to contrast with the closed book of scripture, whose interpretation was carefully guarded (see esp. 227, 233, 248). For Baconian experimentalists, in contrast, the topos was continuous with the Protestant insistence on the openness of scripture—and with the practice of experimental Christianity in all its forms. Whereas Galileo uses the topos to insist that creation is "meaning-free," Baconians stressed the virtuoso's ability to invest creation with meaning—relevance to human ends and purposes—through editorial intervention.

122. Power, *Experimental Philosophy,* sig. a3^v, 193.

123. Hooke, *Posthumous Works,* 338. While this description suggests something like a periodic table, Hooke seems to have hoped that the Royal Society Repository itself might perform this function; see Michael Hunter, *Establishing the New Science,* 123–155.

124. Hooke, *Posthumous Works,* 343.

125. Similarly, when Robert South described the "difference between the clear Representations of the understanding then, and the obscure discoveries that it makes now" to the difference between "the Prospect of a Casement, and of a Key-hole," he was not content to describe Adam's expansive scope of perception in exclusively spatial terms. The analogy describes not the visual field simply, but the "Representations of the understanding": the objects of these mental representations are "effects yet unborn, and in the Womb of their Causes." It was by seeing causes, and effects not yet in existence, that Adam's "conjectures" could be described as "improving even to Prophesie, or the certainties of Prediction" (*Sermon,* 9–10, 12).

126. Power, *Experimental Philosophy,* sig. b2^v, 192. On the weakening of the Aristotelian distinction between the artificial and the natural, see Dear, *Discipline and Experience,* chapter 6.

127. Hooke, *Posthumous Works,* 279.

128. Power, *Experimental Philosophy,* sig. b.

129. Hooke, *Micrographia,* sig. a2^v; Baker, *Universe,* 35, 33, 23, and *Microscope Made Easy,* 296–297. For similar reflections on Wilkins's part, see Barbara Shapiro, *John Wilkins,* 236.

130. As Harwood observes with reference to *Micrographia,* the literature of microscopy "made a radical case about familiar sizes, shapes, and textures: such epithets as 'large' and 'small' or 'smooth' and 'coarse', while never very precise, now lost all meaning" ("Rhetoric and Graphics," 136).

131. Baker, *Microscope Made Easy,* 135–136, 117.

132. Baker, *Universe,* 22.

133. Power, *Experimental Philosophy,* 193; Hooke, *Micrographia,* sig. a2ᵛ.

134. The analogical world view was famously elaborated in Tillyard, *Elizabethan World Picture,* and Foucault, *Order of Things;* see also Nicolson, *Breaking of the Circle.*

135. In Edmund Waller's dedicatory poem to Evelyn's translation of Lucretius, for example, an atomized world is a world without any natural kings: "No Monarch Rules the Universe; / But chance and Atomes make *this All* / In Order Democratical, / Where Bodies freely run their course, / Without design, or Fate, or Force" (*Essay on the First Book,* 3).

136. Hooke, *Posthumous Works,* 59; Charleton, *Physiologia,* 126, 431, 432. Although in this passage Charleton dismisses the old notion of the "intestine war" of the elements, he immediately resurrects it in the form of "intestine commotions" among atoms. The word *intestine* shows up nineteen times in the text in similar contexts.

137. For another account of the relationship between atomism and political forms, especially social contract theory, see Charles Taylor, *Philosophy and the Human Sciences,* 190, and Clucas's excellent "Poetic Atomism." For a more general account of the influence of the ancient atomists on seventeenth-century literature, see Charles Harrison, "Ancient Atomists."

138. John Webster, *Academiarum Examen,* 27–28.

139. Power, *Experimental Philosophy,* sig. a3ᵛ, 7. See also Bacon, *Advancement* (1640 ed.), 47, second pagination. For Samuel Johnson's advice (conveyed through the sage Imlac), see chapter 10 of *Rasselas;* see also Johnson, *Works,* 16: 43.

140. Hooke, *Posthumous Works,* 338; Baker, *Universe,* 6; Montagu, *Edward Tyson,* 61.

141. Charleton, *Physiologia,* 6; Milton, *PL,* 9.779.

142. Glanvill, *Vanity of Dogmatizing,* 1. On Eve's absence while Adam named the creatures, see Thomas Browne, *Works,* 2: 345. This attitude toward Eve was not specific to experimentalists; in the course of enumerating Adam's intellectual perfections, Joseph Hall sniffed, "I doe not find, that Man thus framed found the want of an helper" (*Works,* 776).

143. Charleton, *Physiologia,* 6, 7, 6.

144. Charleton, *Physiologia,* 8.

145. Glanvill, *Vanity of Dogmatizing,* 113; Evelyn, *Sylva* (1729 ed.), x–xi.

146. Glanvill, *Vanity of Dogmatizing*, 113.

147. Isaiah 3:17; see Nohrenberg, *Analogy of the Faerie Queene*, 222–277.

148. Charleton, *Physiologia*, 99.

149. Charleton, *Physiologia*, 2; Joseph Hall, *Works*, 778.

150. Evelyn, *Sylva* (1670 ed.), 229; Pepys, *Diary*, 8: 243 (30 May 1667); Evelyn, *Diary*, 3: 478, 482.

151. Evelyn, *Miscellaneous Writings*, xviii.

152. Cowley, "To the *Royal Society*," line 7, and *Proposition*, 40, 35, 15–16; Salkeld, *Treatise of Paradise*, 182.

153. Cowley, "Solitude," from *Several Discourses*, 94 (in *Works*); Evelyn, *Publick Employment*, 58; Marvell, "The Garden," lines 63–64.

154. South, *Sermon*, 28. Salkeld's discussion of the snake thus fluctuates into a meditation on the conquering power of female beauty (*Treatise of Paradise*, 218–219). Salkeld no doubt drew inspiration from the iconographical tradition of the serpent as a reptile with a female face; see Kelly, "Metamorphoses of the Eden Serpent."

155. Bacon, *Masculine Birth of Time*, 72. See Swann's interesting discussion in *Curiosities and Texts*, 67–68.

156. Boyle, *Works*, 1: 64, 128; Hooke, e.g., *Diary*, 24 (for an explanation of his symbol for orgasm, see 3); Waller, "Life of Dr. Robert Hooke," in Hooke, *Posthumous Works*, xxvii.

157. "Burnet's Funeral Sermon," in Michael Hunter, *Boyle by Himself*, 38; Hooke, *Micrographia*, sigs. g2–g2^v.

158. *Poems to the Memory*, 11–12; Milton, *CPW*, 2: 527. See also Sprat, *History*, 327, and Hooke, *Micrographia*, sigs. b2–b2^v.

159. Bacon, *Advancement* (1640 ed.), 40, second pagination.

160. Sprat, *History*, 327; Hooke, *Micrographia*, sig. a2.

161. Evelyn, *Sylva* (1679 ed.), sigs. c–c^v.

162. Grew, *Idea*, 20; Boyle, *Works*, 5: 60. The problem was compounded by the compound microscope itself, which produced chromatic aberration, resulting in colored fringes around the image. Hooke acknowledged the superiority of Leeuwenhoek's single lens design, but he along with most users found it difficult too difficult for the eyes to endure (Ruestow, *Microscope*, 15–19; see *Micrographia*, sig. f^v).

163. Corbet, *Self-Employment in Secret*, 63 (from the section "Notes for My Self"); see Keeble's discussion in *Literary Culture*, 152, 155.

164. Power, *Experimental Philosophy*, 6–7.

165. Power, *Experimental Philosophy*, 59, 25, 3 (see Donne, "The Flea," line 15), 16–18. For Boyle's ecstasies over "little Mites that are bred in mouldy Cheese," see *Works*, 3: 225–226.

166. Boyle, *Correspondence*, 2: 270, 269.

167. Hooke, *Micrographia*, sig. d2.

168. Sprat, *History*, 344.

169. Thomas Browne, *Religio Medici* 2.9, in *Works*, 1: 83; Evelyn, *Sylva* (1670 ed.), 245.

170. It is this version of the poem I will be quoting from, at sigs. B–B3ᵛ.

171. See *Antony van Leeuwenhoek;* for spermatozoa, see esp. 104, 121, 221, 228, 230.

172. Behn, *Emperor of the Moon*, 1.2.8, 62. Behn's depiction of curiosity is suggestively explored in Benedict's *Curiosity*, 59–63.

173. Pope, "The Discovery," in *Twickenham Edition*, 6: 259–264. Todd's *Imagining Monsters* offers a wide-ranging discussion of the Toft hoax; see also Nicolson and Rousseau, *"This Long Disease,"* 109–115. On telescopic length, see note 95 above.

174. Pietz, "Problem of the Fetish."

175. Going naked for a sign could itself be a relatively chaste demonstration, since to be naked could mean to be dressed in a sackcloth, without hats, shoes, or outer garments; see Gowing, *Common Bodies*, 34.

176. Pliny, *Natural History*, 9: 308–309 (35: 65). The association of the fruit with the sacrament was an old motif; see Schiller, *Iconography of Christian Art*, 2: 159–160, and Walther and Wolf, *Codices Illustres*, 382–383.

177. John Norris, *Reflections*, 136, 131, 151; *DNB* entry on Robert South.

178. South quoted in Michael Hunter, *Science and Society*, 171.

179. See discussion in Shapin and Schaffer, *Leviathan and the Air-Pump*, 296, 310–319, 325.

180. Astell, *Essay*, 96–97 (see Houghton, "English Virtuoso," for examples of similar mockery); Sprat, *History*, 76. Johns observes that pastiche was the dominant mode of antiexperimentalist satire in *Nature of the Book*, 456.

181. Hooke, *Diary*, 235, 239. He had already seen one "Atheistical wicked play" by Shadwell, perhaps *The Libertine* (166). The episode is discussed in Everett Jones, "Robert Hooke and *The Virtuoso*."

182. Shadwell, *Virtuoso*, 1.2.11–13; 2.2.84–86.

183. Jardine, "Hooke the Man," 167; see also 'Espinasse, *Hooke*, 51–52. Although Boyle is glanced at in the play, he is most readily identified with Sir Formal, a pretender to eloquence rather than science; see 1.1.213–216, which paraphrases Boyle's *Occasional Reflections* (see *Works*, 5: 60–61).

184. Shadwell, *Virtuoso*, 8 ("Dramatis Personae"), 1.1.1. For further evidence of Gimcrack's bad faith and incompetence, see 3.3.45–50 and 5.2.115.

185. Horne, "Curiosity and Ridicule"; Butler, *Elephant in the Moon*, lines 344, 517–518; Hooke, *Micrographia*, sig. a2.

186. *Hudibras,* 2.3.777–778. This is not to say that Butler did not succeed in making the Fellows self-conscious: Oldenburg confessed to Boyle that he failed to corroborate Charleton's relation of an Irish apothecary who had three testicles because he was "afraid of Hudibras" (Boyle, *Correspondence,* 2: 346). Hooke read the poem; see *Diary,* 327. We first encounter Sidrophel as an astrological conjurer, but by the time Butler composed the "Heroical Epistle of Hudibras to Sidrophel," he was drawing on the *Philosophical Transactions* to associate Sidrophel—not altogether convincingly—with the activities of the "Virtuosi" (line 97); see Wilder's textual introduction, xlvii.

187. Samuel Butler, *Characters and Passages,* 366.

188. Samuel Butler, *Hudibras,* 2.3.377–378, 317–322. On the Society's interest in eels in vinegar, or nematodes, see Harwood, "Rhetoric and Graphics," 129.

189. Samuel Butler, *Characters and Passages,* 357; Svetlana Alpers, *Art of Describing,* 83; Haywood, *Selected Works, Set II,* 3: 85–88. Ladies are even encouraged to send their "fresh Discoveries" to the Royal Society (88–89).

190. Samuel Butler, *Characters and Passages,* 81–82. On experimental philosophy as child's play, see Catherine Wilson, *Invisible World,* 23–24.

191. Power, *Experimental Philosophy,* 193. For a variation, see Charleton, *Physiologia,* 114.

192. See also Hooke, *Posthumous Works,* 135.

193. Samuel Butler, *Hudibras,* 2.3.806.

4. The Culture of Curiosity

1. See Benedict, *Curiosity,* and Swann, *Curiosities and Texts.*

2. Sprat, *History,* 114–115.

3. The primary association of this rhetoric of mystery was with guild mysteries (trade secrets), but this rhetoric was itself sacramental.

4. The preacher Francis Atterbury thematized the changing definition of the category in his eulogy for the Stationer Henry Clements, who had been "a Private, I ought to have said a *Public,* Person, for I am sure in his Station he was a *Public* Good" (quoted in Johns, *Nature of the Book,* 142).

5. James Grantham Turner, *Libertines and Radicals,* 165–166. See also Stallybrass and White's *Politics and Poetics of Transgression,* esp. 100–104, and on the association of the monarch with the May-king, Marcus, *Politics of Mirth,* 166–167. For an admiring overview of libertine hijinks during the Restoration, see John Harold Wilson, *Court Wits of the Restoration,* 3–66.

6. *A Proclamation For the better ordering of those who repair to the Court for their Cure of the Disease called the Kings-Evil* (broadsheet). On how royalists exploited belief in the wonder during the civil war and Restoration, see Marc

Bloch, *Royal Touch*, 208–213; see also Marvell's ironic allusion in *Growth of Popery* (*Prose Works*, 2: 376). Critiquing these gestures toward reviving sacramental kingship, Thomas Hall pointedly remarked that "the Popes Holiness with might and main keeps up his superstitious Festivals as a prime prop of his tottering Kingdome" (*Funebria Florae*, 15).

7. See Sommerville's introduction to *Patriarcha*, xiv–xv. On attempts to revive "old medieval notions" concerning monarchy on the eve of the Restoration, see Reedy, "Mystical Politics," and Edie, "Popular Idea of Monarchy," 356. As Edie shows, however, old tropes were being reworked to accommodate the idea of limited monarchy. Still, in 1701 Defoe found it worth his time to begin work on a 375-page poem attacking the divine right of kings, *Jure Divino* (1706); see discussion in Backsheider, *Daniel Defoe*, 161–194.

8. Wood, *Life and Times*, quoted in Frances Harris, *Transformations*, 50–51.

9. Jonathan Scott, *England's Troubles*, 393 (such forgetfulness was quite literal; in royal proclamations, the years of Charles's reign were calculated from the time of his father's death); Mowry, *Bawdy Politic*.

10. Hill argues that, constitutionally, there was greater continuity between the 1650s and 1660s than between the 1630s and the Restoration period (*Nation of Change*, 21).

11. See Nettleton, *English Drama*, 1–6. The rake's association with court and hell was danced around in many Restoration plays; see, for example, Etherege, *Man of Mode*, 1.1.60, 99–110; 2.2.15–17; 3.3.100–109.

12. See James Grantham Turner, *Libertines and Radicals*, esp. chapter 5; Pepys quoting Bawdy-House rioters on 25 March 1668 (*Diary*, 9: 132); Marvell, *Prose Works*, 1: 103.

13. *Character of a Coffee House* (1665), 6. The term could be used as a synonym for *virtuoso*; see Evelyn, *Numismata*, 208.

14. Quoting Eliot's *Little Gidding*, Schenk observes that enemies during the civil wars sometimes seem "united in the strife which divided them" (*Social Justice*, 27–28); as James Grantham Turner argues in *Libertines and Radicals*, a similar dialectic was at work in Restoration culture.

15. Milton, *PL*, 12.587.

16. *Essay*, 2.3.1. Rather than writing "*if* I may so call it," Locke declares, "*as* I may so call it"; granting himself permission to analogize between the mind and a king's presence room, he modestly asserts the sovereign power of reason he describes.

17. Thomas Hall, *Funebria Florae*, 17. On good fellowship, see Chapter 1 in this volume.

18. As discussed in Chapter 3, the Paracelsian faith in the power of intuition to grasp real essences was entailed by the doctrine of form: the very concept

of innate knowledge was first introduced by Plato's suggestion that the forms were directly apprehended before birth; see Ayers, *Locke,* 81–82.

19. Milton, *CPW,* 2: 528; Hobbes, *Leviathan,* 44 (1.6).

20. Bradley, *Nosce te Ipsum,* 66, 68.

21. Vaughan, *Magia Adamica,* sigs. B2ᵛ–B3ᵛ.

22. Power, *Experimental Philosophy,* 183–184, 65, 71.

23. See William Walker's discussion in *Locke, Literary Criticism,* 31–54; for the development of the wax tablet topos from Plato's *Theaetetus,* see Carruthers, *Book of Memory,* esp. 21–32, 55–57, 72–74.

24. Locke, *Essay,* 2.19.4, 2.11.17, 2.10.5.

25. Locke, *Essay,* 10 ("Epistle to the Reader"). John Marshall discusses John Locke senior's probable participation in the assault, led by Alexander Popham (who would later become Locke's patron), which targeted the windows, organs, fonts, and bishop's seat (*John Locke: Resistance,* 3–4; on Locke's sense of debt to Popham, see 163–164).

26. Locke, *Essay,* 10 ("Epistle to the Reader"), 3.10.9.

27. Locke, *Essay,* 7 ("Epistle to the Reader"), 1.1.1. See also 2.10.7.

28. Shapin and Schaffer, *Leviathan and the Air-Pump,* 58. Given the heterogeneity of the Fellows' metaphysical commitments, consensus on what experiments indicated often lay in the indefinite future. In this very passage Locke seems to allude to the Royal Society motto, describing the would-be philosopher who, because he takes his core beliefs "upon trust" does not have any; "Opiniatrety" is contrasted with "Science," in which "Assent" is the product of collective employment (we "employ our own Reason").

29. On Locke's belief that most people's mental content was second-hand, see John Marshall, *John Locke, Toleration,* 658–659.

30. See Ayers, "Locke's Logical Atomism."

31. Locke was impressed with accounts of Prince Maurice of Nassau's talking and reasoning parrot, about whom he provides a "Relation" taken from Sir William Temple's *Memoires of what Past in Christendom* (2.27.8).

32. Rabisha, *Adam Unvailed,* sig. A5. This was an adaptation of an old topos; see John Skelton's "Speke, parrot." It may also have been a gendered insult, given the association of parrots ("papejays") with female gossips or women; see *MED.* Now the repetitive speech of the parrot becomes a figure for the subject dependent on authority (and, implicitly, perhaps, the ritual repetitions of sacramental religion); the parrot serves as an underhanded portrait of any unimproved person.

33. Hobbes, *Leviathan,* 44 (1.6). See Barnouw, "Hobbes's Psychology of Thought."

34. Milton, *CPW,* 2: 551.

35. Bourdieu, *Science of Science*, 83; Locke, *Reasonableness*, 277. While Lockean principles were often appealed to in defense of an emergent concept of intellectual property, Johns points out that they could also lead one to question whether such property was "conceivable at all" (*Nature of the Book*, 247–248).

36. Howe, *Blessedness of the Righteous*, 91; see Keeble's discussion in *Literary Culture*, 165–166.

37. See Keeble, *Literary Culture*, 13. I believe that Locke's famous phrase (1.1.7) should be understood in similar terms, as a blend of "latitudinarian" and exploratory sentiment. On the overlap between latitudinarian Anglicanism and Puritan concepts of "Christian liberty," see Chernaik, *Poet's Time*, chapter 4.

38. See, for example, Henry More's *Immortality of the Soul*, 83. For discussion, see McGuire and Rattansi, "Newton and the 'Pipes of Pan,'" and McGuire, "Neoplatonism and Active Principles."

39. South, *Sermon*, 38. On this metaphor, see J. Paul Hunter, *Before Novels*, 333.

40. Shaftesbury, *Regimen*, 164, 170, 168. Although I am interested in exploring its basis in Lockean epistemology, the regimen is explicitly based on Stoical principles; see Klein, *Shaftesbury*, 83, and Gill, "Ancient Psychotherapy."

41. Shaftesbury, *Regimen*, 177, 174, 173. "Again thy art . . . Now to be firm . . . No receding; no retreat" (173).

42. Marx and Engels, *German Ideology*, 47.

43. Shaftesbury, *Regimen*, 166, 168. Fancy's "whispers" must be transformed into "plain utterance" (174); see also 176. In *Secret History*, McKeon describes Shaftesbury's regimen as "something like what free association would be for Freud: a utopian technique for making the tacit explicit" (103), which links it to what he calls the "public-sphere technology" of virtual witnessing; see 66–67 and, generally, chapter 2 ("Publishing the Private"). See also Barker-Benfield's analysis of how Shaftesbury's program of self-reformation was designed to produce a subject antithetical to the Restoration rake in *Culture of Sensibility*, 105–119.

44. Locke, *Essay*, 10 ("Epistle to the Reader"); Boyle, *Works*, 2: 20. Sargent discusses the topos in *Diffident Naturalist*, 38n103.

45. Glanvill, *Vanity of Dogmatizing*, 108.

46. On the body absolute of true learning, see Chapter 3, note 43.

47. Glanvill, *Vanity of Dogmatizing*, 111.

48. Boyle, *Works*, 5: 22, 5. All citations from the *Occasional Reflections* are to this volume. In his discussion of occasional meditation, J. Paul Hunter stresses that "knowledge was important, but knowing—the personal experience of discovery—was everything" (*Before Novels*, 199; Hunter offers an account of the practice's relationship to circumstantial narration at 198–208; see also 382n6). In

addition, see Wall, *Prose of Things,* 76–80, and Scott Black, *Of Essays,* 79–85. This genre may owe something to the broadside ballad, in which a circumstantial prose description of a freak of nature—a monstrous pig or fish, or a wheatstorm—was followed by verse stanzas rehearsing the lesson to be extracted from it, combining a news item with an editorial. See Rollins, "Black-Letter Broadside Ballad," 265–272; on how Baconians adapted the genre, see Park and Daston, "Unnatural Conceptions," esp. 43–51.

49. On the medieval emphasis on "vivid mental imagining" of scenes from Christ's life, particularly the crucifixion, during meditation, see Duffy, *Stripping,* 19–20, 238. The classic work on the literary influence of such exercises on Renaissance literature is Martz, *Poetry of Meditation.* For revisionary treatments that stress Protestant departures, see Lewalski, *Protestant Poetics,* esp. chapter 5, and Gilman, *Iconoclasm and Poetry.* Bishop Joseph Hall's *Occasionall Meditations* (1630) may be seen as a transitional document between the two meditative styles being contrasted here, though Boyle went out of his way to deny any influence (see *Works,* 5: 10). Comparing Hall and Boyle's approaches in "Bishop Hall's Meditations," Fisch argues that Boyle is far more interested in "the careful scrutiny and observation of phenomena" and that his approach is more "secular," since he hoped it would generate findings of political, economic, and physical use (22).

50. I am indebted to Freedberg, *Power of Images,* for my understanding of Ignatian meditation and to Collins, *Mind's Eye,* for my understanding of readerly imagining.

51. Quoted in Freedberg, *Power of Images,* 185 (Sucquet's *Road of Eternal Life* ran through twelve editions between 1620 and 1649).

52. Sherlock, *Answer to a Discourse,* 115–116. He specifically disputes the claim that images can recall "wandering thoughts" on this and the following page. For the possible influence of what Yates called the "inner iconoclasm" of Ramism in dismantling this system, see *Art of Memory,* chapter 10, and Peter Harrison, *The Bible, Protestantism, Natural Science,* 118–120.

53. See Charles Webster, *Great Instauration,* xxxiv, and "Burnet Memorandum," in Michael Hunter, *Boyle by Himself,* 33–34.

54. See the actual reflection *"Upon the Sight of the effects of a Burning-glass,"* 178–179. On the imperial glass, discussed in Chapter 3, see Reeves, *Galileo's Glassworks.*

55. Cowley, "To the *Royal Society,*" lines 155–157 (in Sprat, *History,* sigs. B–B3ᵛ); Boyle, *Correspondence,* 2: 600.

56. Boyle specifically rejects the doctrine *"That all Knowledge is but Reminiscence,"* the founding belief of Paracelsian reading (51). Discouragement of intuition could offer a means to avoid the interpretive aporias created by reading providential "signs," since, as J. Paul Hunter puts it, a "storm could mean that

the Whigs were wrong or the Tories"; but in practice occasional meditation never completely divorced itself from this kind of hermeneutic exercise—clearly a risk Boyle found an acceptable one, on the principle that "opening up meaning was more productive than shutting it down" (*Before Novels*, 207).

57. Hooke, *Micrographia*, sig. a2ᵛ.

58. See Wall's incisive analysis of this passage in *Prose of Things*, 78–79; as she puts it, Boyle's engagement with the apple persuades the reader that "I can remake my world by describing it." Oswald Croll also attempted to model an innocent relationship to the apple, regarding it with the "Ingenuity and Knowledge of the Interiour Man" instead of with the "sensual Eye"; see *Bazilica Chymica*, sigs. A2ᵛ, B2ᵛ, second pagination.

59. Milton, *CPW*, 2: 527; on the curious maid topos, see Benedict, *Curiosity*, 71–92; Pope, *Rape of the Lock*, 1.131.

60. On sultry modesty, see Kerrigan and Braden, "Milton's Coy Eve."

61. So Hooke. "And as at first, mankind *fell* by *tasting* of the forbidden Tree of Knowledge, so we, their Posterity, may be in part *restor'd* by the same way, not only by *beholding* and *contemplating*, but by *tasting* too those fruits of Natural knowledge, that were never yet forbidden" (*Micrographia*, sigs. b2–b2ᵛ).

62. Boyle, *Works*, 11: 295.

63. Boyle, *Works*, 2: 16. See Scott Black's useful remarks on Boyle's use of this analogy in *Of Essays*, 75–78.

64. John Dunton paraphrased this sentiment: "When a *Virtuoso* thus seriously reflects on the *Visible World*, (and upon what's Curious in it) he does as 'twere *spiritualize Earthly Things*: He can here make *New Discoveries*, as well as raise his mind from Earth to Heaven" (quoted in J. Paul Hunter, *Before Novels*, 384n17). It is the virtuoso who spiritualizes earthly things, rather than being able to intuit the indwelling spirit in them. And the meaner the objects he spiritualizes—or sets aflame with his reflecting glass—the more impressive his power.

65. Marvell, "The Garden," line 47.

66. Frances Harris, *Transformations*, 54, 179–182. As we learn from Evelyn's *Life of Mrs. Godolphin*, she "fill'd up the whole day, and destin'd almost every minute of it to exercise" and affirmed this resolution in writing: "May the clock, the candle, every thing I see, instruct me"; her "laborious devotions" sometimes caused her to faint (26, 22, 176). Such watchfulness could be exhausting, because there was no object unworthy of it; Seaver makes reference to a 1644 meditation by Ralph Josselin that begins "Stung I was by a bee on my nose" (*Wallington's World*, 184).

67. Her minister Anthony Walker was so impressed by them he printed for the public's benefit after her death under the title of *Eureka, Eureka: The Virtuous Woman Found, Her Loss Bewailed, and Character Exemplifed*. Her usual procedure

is to identify the object of her contemplation and then to declare "Improve this, O my Soul" or "This minds me of" (152, 161). Although the meditation on the phyllerea did not make it into the book (on which see Fell-Smith, *Mary Rich,* 325), the dusty carpet is at 161. See Frances Harris, *Transformations,* 179–180.

68. Wilkins's *A Discourse concerning the Beauty of Providence in all the Rugged Passages of it very Seasonable to Quiet and Support the Heart in these Times of Publick Confusion* appeared in 1649 and was reissued four times thereafter. Boyle's *Reflections* were largely composed in the late 1640s and 1650s (see Boyle, *Works,* 5: xi–xiii and Chapter 1 in this volume).

69. Anthony Walker, *Eureka,* 171.

70. Boyle, *Correspondence,* 2: 148, 473, 476, 475, 477.

71. Boyle, *Correspondence,* 2: 147, 473–474.

72. Herrick, "The Argument of his Book," line 6 (see Chapter 1). A contemporary remarked that he found "Poles rais'd so high" in the year of Charles's return that "reform'd *London*" had become "Popish *Rome*" (prefatory poem to Thomas Hall's *Funebria Florae,* sig. A2ᵛ). In the treatise itself, Hall contrasted festival pastimes with the progress England had made through preaching, praying, and printing: "for us that have had such famous preaching, praying, printing, signal victories, and deliverances continued to us, even to this day; for us to rant and roar, drink Healths, bee drunk and whore, and with the dog to return to our vomit, which for many years wee had left" was such a "high aggravation of our sin, that God will not brook it at our hands" (12).

73. Sprat, *History,* 72.

74. Smart quoted in Winn, *John Dryden,* 21; *Mercurius Britanicus* 12 (November 9–16, 1643), quoted in Nigel Smith, *Literature and Revolution,* 71. On the theatrical metaphor in attacks on the Catholic mass, see Peter Marshall, *Catholic Priesthood,* 35–41.

75. See Keeble, "Why Transpose *The Rehearsal?*" 256.

76. Marvell, *Prose Works,* 1: 196, 189, 134, 55, 150.

77. Marvell, *Prose Works,* 1: 202; 2: 229. Of course such ingenuity would require assistance by "a diviner influence."

78. The contrasts Marvell draws between Parker and his various foils illuminate a more general contrast between "ways of Discoursing" (*Prose Works,* 1: 134).

79. Aubrey, *Brief Lives,* 164; 'Espinasse, *Robert Hooke,* 46.

80. Hopkins's foreword to Hooke's *Diary,* iv; Sprat, *History,* 99. In a meeting on February 10, 1670, "Mr. HOOKE being absent, the society, instead of experiments, was entertained with the reading of some letters"; on December 18, 1672, "Mr. HOOKE, the curator being absent, by reason of sickness, there were no experiments made at this meeting" (Birch, *History,* 2: 418; 3: 70). See also 'Espinasse, *Robert Hooke,* 45.

81. Waller, "Life of Dr. Robert Hooke," in Hooke, *Posthumous Works*, xxviii.

82. Birch, *History*, 1: 288–289. See discussion in Shapin and Schaffer, *Leviathan and the Air-Pump*, 31–32.

83. Hooke, *Diary*, 19 (and see 21), 68, 106, 95. 'Espinasse offers an engaging account of Hooke and Hunt's relationship in *Robert Hooke*, 131–133.

84. See Alan Shapiro, "Artists' Colors and Newton's Colors," esp. 606–607. Techniques for manufacturing and mixing pigments and varnishes were often discussed by the Fellows; see, for example, Birch, *History*, 1: 11–12, 51; Boyle, *Works*, 4: 119–123; and Charleton, *Physiologia*, 196.

85. See 'Espinasse, *Robert Hooke*, 133. These appointments carried a salary of twenty and forty pounds, respectively; on this salary, he was somehow able to lend the Society sums ranging from 200 to 462 pounds (Robinson, "Administrative Staff," 196–197).

86. Hooke, *Diary*, 22, 152.

87. See Swann, *Curiosities and Texts*, 26–27 (but see below). For the continental context, see Eamon, *Science and the Secrets of Nature*, 222–229. On differences between English curiosity cabinets and their continental counterparts, see MacGregor, "Cabinet of Curiosities." Kenny offers some very suggestive remarks on the curiosity cabinet in *Curiosity*, 169–170.

88. Grew, *Musaeum*, 8, 9.

89. Hooke, *Posthumous Works*, 338.

90. Grew, *Musaeum*, sig. A4ᵛ; Swann, *Curiosities and Texts*, 89–90.

91. Swann, *Curiosities and Texts*, 34–37.

92. Despite Ashmole's efforts; see Jardine, *Ingenious Pursuits*, 262.

93. Michael Hunter, *Establishing the New Science*, 135. As it turned out, donors were not even kept track of very well, so that the list of benefactors had to be retroactively created in the eighteenth century using the Society's minutes (141).

94. Grew, *Musaeum*, sigs. A4–A4ᵛ. On the probable contributions of Hunt, Hooke, and Aubrey to Grew's catalogue, see Michael Hunter, *Establishing the New Science*, 141–142.

95. Evelyn, *Diary*, 3: 229. Davenant's performance pieces are discussed in Chapter 5. In a similarly self-critical spirit, the young Shaftesbury wrote to Locke that he was "afraid" that he would enjoy the opera "too well" (*Regimen*, 273). Evelyn was never roused to wonder by theatrical spectacles, but hyperbole came naturally to him when confronted with a work of ingenuity, like a "wonderfull Engine for weaving silk-stockings" (*Diary*, 3: 285).

96. Evelyn, *Diary*, 3: 229, 310.

97. Evelyn, *Diary*, 3: 313, 308, 573, 309. The Duchess of Cleveland is called a "Lady of Pleasure & curse of our nation" (3: 573). For a Prynne-like attack on the innovation of female actors, see 3: 465–466.

98. Evelyn, *Diary,* 3: 590, 596.

99. Evelyn, *Tyrannus,* 11, 29. On Evelyn's uncertainty and "quest for a role" during the Interregnum, see Michael Hunter, "John Evelyn in the 1650s."

100. Evelyn, *Diary,* 3: 464, 463; *Life of Mrs. Godolphin,* 58–59. Evelyn also compared London to Sodom and himself to Lot (*Diary,* 3: 457).

101. Evelyn, *Diary,* 3: 313. When Margaret Blagge informed Evelyn about the court's mockery of the Society, he wrote back furiously: "I have learnd more profitable, and usefull things, from some hours Conversation in that Meeting, than ever I have don from the quintessence and sublimest Raptures of those empty Casks, whose noise you do so admire at Court when they have been declaiming against it" (in Douglas Chambers, " 'Elysium Britannicum not printed neere ready &c,' " 114).

102. Glanvill, *Vanity of Dogmatizing,* 72. Love remarks on the difficulty of finding any "purposive activity" in the Restoration court (*Culture and Commerce,* 208).

103. Pincus's "John Evelyn: Revolutionary" challenges the conventional view of Evelyn as "committed unwaveringly to the monarchy and Church of England" (186). Although Pincus's focus is on Evelyn's relationship to the Glorious Revolution, I believe that my perspective on Evelyn is consistent with his. Since, as Pincus points out, Evelyn copied his diaries over in the 1680s, some of the sentiments analyzed here might have been back-formed.

104. Evelyn, *Diary,* 4: 574; 3: 179, 207–208, 365; see Lewalski, *Life,* 496, and von Maltzahn, "Laureate, Republican, Calvinist," 191.

105. See letter from Hartlib in Evelyn, *Diary and Correspondence,* 598; *Diary,* 3: 162. Evelyn's memorandum for revolutionary change, written in 1688 and discussed by Pincus in "John Evelyn: Revolutionary," calls for the creation of "a standing committee . . . of fit persons to receive and make report of all projects convertible to the public benefit without ridiculing or discouraging the propos-ers" (194): something very like an Office of Address.

106. Evelyn, *Diary,* 3: 80–81, 66. See Bowle, *John Evelyn,* 83.

107. Evelyn, *Diary,* 3: 204, 612. As Frances Harris observes, Evelyn's devoutness "had more than a touch of puritanism" (*Transformations,* 37).

108. Evelyn, *Diary,* 2: 77. See Bowle, *John Evelyn,* 29.

109. Evelyn quoted in Frances Harris, *Transformations,* 58; Evelyn, *Diary,* 3: 546–547, 550. See also 3: 601.

110. Evelyn, *Diary,* 3: 271, 304, 288; see Birch, *History,* 1: 16, 75.

111. Evelyn, *Diary,* 3: 306. The event is recorded in Birch, *History,* 1: 67: "they ordered their thanks to be given him; and in order to make these thanks the more solemn, appointed them to be entered into their journal-book."

112. Of course, Charles had friendly relations with individual members of the Society; Hooke records numerous encounters with the king: far from seeming starstruck, he appears single-mindedly interested in eliciting praise (and a patent) for his spring watch: Hooke, *Diary*, 157, 161, 185.

113. Birch, *History*, 1: 15, 13.

114. Sprat, *History*, 350.

115. See Evelyn, *Miscellaneous Writings*, xviii.

116. Evelyn, *Miscellaneous Writings*, xvii–xviii.

117. Not entirely, however, since he goes on to urge Cowley to write in praise of the Society.

118. Evelyn, *Publick Employment*, 39, 41.

119. Evelyn, *Publick Employment*, 92, 95. Here he is paraphrasing Seneca's criticism of useless pastimes, whose terms he will reverse.

120. Evelyn, *Publick Employment*, 78, 56, 77.

121. Evelyn, *Publick Employment*, 13, 118–119.

122. Evelyn, *Sylva* (1664 ed.), sig. A3.

123. Bacon, *Advancement* (1640 ed.), 40, second pagination; Evelyn, *Diary*, 3: 531–533; Purver, *Royal Society*, 71. For Wallis's account of the proceedings, see Boyle, *Correspondence*, 4: 141–143. See also Michael Hunter, *Science and Society*, 137, 145.

124. Evelyn, *Diary*, 2: 130–131; Kegl, "Politics of Labor," 110–111.

125. Sprat, *History*, 407.

126. The date provided by Anthony Wood is 1650 (see Pincus, "Coffee Politicians Does Create," 811); John Houghton, however, placed the date at 1652 ("Discourse of Coffee," 312); Aytoun Ellis, *Penny Universities*, xiv. The diarist quoted is Thomas Rugg from Pincus, "Coffee Politicians Does Create," 812. This section has drawn a great deal from Pincus's important article; see also Cowan, "Rise of the Coffeehouse" and *Social Life of Coffee*, esp. chapter 4; Dobranski, "'Where Men of Differing Judgements Croud'"; Aytoun Ellis, *Penny Universities*; and Klein, "Coffeehouse Civility."

127. On free discourse, see *Character of a Coffee-House* (1665), 6; Sturtevant, *Dibre Adam*, 7; and Evelyn, *Sylva* (1670 ed.), 229.

128. Habermas, *Structural Transformation*, 30–59; Berry, *Gender, Society, and Print Culture*, 15 (Berry is responding to rather than exhibiting unreflective skepticism on this matter). On St. Paul's, and particularly its churchyard, as London's "transitional public sphere," see Norbrook, *Writing the English Republic*, 74–75; Love, *Culture and Commerce*, 193–194; and Zaret, *Origins of Democratic Culture*, 103–104. Coffeehouses did not exclude women, though they were more likely than men to be present in a professional capacity: see Paula McDowell,

Women of Grub Street, 85, 102–103; Markman Ellis, "Coffee Women"; Pincus, "Coffee Politicians Does Create," 815–816; and Johns, *Nature of the Book,* 112.

129. *Coffee-houses Vindicated,* 4.

130. The effort of the Hartlib circle to extend the concept of a "neighborhood" beyond parish boundaries is discussed in Chapter 1. It is the author of *Character of a Coffee House* (1665) that calls the coffee-drinker a "*Curioso*" (6).

131. *Coffee-houses Vindicated,* 2, 4.

132. *Character of a Coffee House* (1673), 1, 3; *Brief Description* (broadsheet). Ned Ward joked that Lilburne himself might have reconsidered taking up "the Work of Levelling" if he had seen the inside of a coffeehouse (*School for Politicks,* 3, cited in Berry, *Gender, Society, and Print Culture,* 72).

133. Aubrey, *Brief Lives,* cxiii. The information Aubrey gathered resulted in a naked account of seventeenth-century men and manners, on which Anthony Wood was required to "sowe-on some Figge-leaves" (cxiii).

134. *Character of a Coffee-House* (1665), 2.

135. M.P., *Character of Coffee,* 10, 5–6, 7; Butler, *Characters and Passages,* 206.

136. *Cup of Coffee* (broadsheet); *Coffee-houses Vindicated,* 4. Rather than a recreational brutifying of their senses, the interest of coffee drinkers in the physiological effects of the beverage suggests something closer to self-experimentation. Such experimentation is roundly mocked in *A Description of the Academy of the Athenian Virtuosi,* where coffeehouse denizens use the beverage to "put *idaeas* into their heads, that were never there before," and hope to "refine their gross conceptions" even further by "inventing a drink for their own use of Hellebore" (9).

137. M.P., *Character of Coffee,* 4, 5, 9; *Character of a Coffee House* (1665), 6.

138. *Coffee-Houses Vindicated,* 5, 4, 1, 4.

139. *Proclamation for the Suppression of Coffee-Houses* (broadsheet). Charles had commanded Jonathan Goddard to produce a discourse on coffee about a decade before, perhaps in the hopes that it would turn up something negative (Birch, *History,* 2: 9). Unsurprisingly, the proclamation actually worked to cement the coffeehouse's status as "a new realm of public debate . . . which authority could no longer fully police, regulate or control" (Claydon, "The Sermon, the 'Public Sphere' and Political Culture," 210). On the circumstances of the 1675 proclamation, see Cowan, "Rise of the Coffeehouse."

140. As James Grantham Turner observes, "Milton's acoustic portrait of a city terrorized by drunken aristocrats fits Restoration London far better than the Old Testament examples that he cites as 'witness'; Sodom and Gibeah were not noted for their 'Courts and Palaces' " (*Libertines and Radicals,* 153). For a contemporary estimate of the income generated by coffee, see Houghton, "Discourse of Coffee," 316–317.

141. *A Proclamation for the Suppression of Riots*; see also the *Proclamation to Restrain the Spreading of False News and Licentious Talking of Matters and State and Government.*

142. Keith Thomas, *Religion and the Decline of Magic,* 19; Clark, *English Alehouse,* 10, 153, 157, 159.

143. Neale, *Elizabethan House,* 417, 375. J. Paul Hunter recounts an eighteenth-century French visitor's surprise at the sight of "shoeblacks and other persons of that class" discussing matters of state with more interest than they have in their "own affairs," a striking registration of the change undergone by the first person in the period (*Before Novels,* 174). In "Rise of the Coffeehouse," Cowan shows that actual proprietors of coffeehouses legitimized their establishments by appealing to a traditional rhetoric of licensed privilege rather than by emphasizing their role in promoting the sphere of public discussion, which stands to reason given the government's hostility to the latter.

144. In 1656, the Leveller John Wildman bought his own coffeehouse where the Commonwealth club, a forerunner of the Rota, had meetings (see Norbrook, *Writing the English Republic,* 399, and Shapin and Schaffer, *Leviathan and the Air-Pump,* 293); on the Rota, see Aytoun Ellis, *Penny Universities,* 37–42. For the proximity of coffeehouses and bookshops, see Johns, *Nature of the Book,* 111–113.

145. *Cup of Coffee* (broadsheet); Roger North (a hostile observer of this development), quoted in Pincus, "Coffee Politicians Does Create," 813, and in Love, *Culture and Commerce,* 204.

146. "Dialogue between the Two Horses," lines 178, 182; *Character of a Coffee House* (1665), 6.

147. Thomas Jordan, *Triumphs of London,* 23.

148. Milton, *CPW,* 2: 554; Houghton, "Discourse of Coffee," 317; *Coffeehouses Vindicated,* 5.

149. M.P., *Character of Coffee,* 9; Butler, *Transproser Rehears'd,* 48. On the Office of Address, see Chapter 1.

150. *Character of a Coffee-House* (1665), 6.

151. Von Maltzahn has argued for Samuel Butler's authorship of the pamphlet, an attribution accepted by Patterson and Dzelzainis in their edition of Marvell's prose. See his "Samuel Butler's Milton."

152. Samuel Butler, *Transproser Rehears'd,* 33, 36, 41–42. In "Samuel Butler's Milton," von Maltzahn suggests that the author is more eager to engage Milton in argument than the more slippery Marvell.

153. See Achinstein, *Literature and Dissent,* chapter 6, esp. 156–157, 167–171.

154. Samuel Butler, *Transproser Rehears'd,* 48, 147. Regarding the authorship of Marvell's *Growth of Popery,* Roger L'Estrange remarked, "You would have

me guess at the Author . . . I think I may call him *Legion*" (quoted in Chernaik, *Poet's Time*, 96).

155. Samuel Butler, *Transproser Rehears'd*, 16, 112. The author's local objection is to the many roles that Marvell makes "Bayes" play, but the objection necessarily extends to Marvell himself, since his personal boundaries are similarly impossible to fix.

156. Samuel Butler, *Transproser Rehears'd*, 36, 72. The "Kings Personal and Politique Capacity are distinct, and so they fought for his Crown, when they shot at his Person" (97).

157. See Pincus, "Coffee Does Politicians Create." It seems likely that the development of a party system, which made disagreement a permanent feature of civic life, owed something to the coffeehouse's example.

158. Annabel Patterson's 2008 Tanner Lecture at the University of California at Berkeley made mention of uncertainty as a public good.

159. I quote from Clagett's *A Perswasive to an Ingenuous Tryal of Opinions*, a defense of orthodoxy that arguably employed the rhetoric of ingenuity against its ethos.

160. Milton, *CPW*, 2: 555; Lowe, *Diary*, 64. On a similar occasion, Lowe and a John Potter "begann to discourse concerneing the manner of God's worship. He was for Episcopecie and I for Presbittery. The contention had like to have beene hott, but the Lord prevented" (52).

161. Feingold suggests that coffeehouses competed with Gresham "as they became the meeting places of choice for scientific instruction, public demonstrations, and even meetings of the members of the Royal Society" ("Gresham College," 185).

162. For Hooke's clubs, see *Diary*, e.g., 81, 239. For Jonathan's opening night, see 300. See Larry Stewart, "Public Lectures and Private Patronage in Newtonian England," esp. 48, and *Rise of Public Science*, 94–97, 144–146. Don Saltero's was established by James Salter, a onetime servant of Sir Hans Sloane himself. For a contemporary description, see *Tatler* 34 (1: 252) and *A Catalogue of the Rarities to be Seen at Don Saltero's Coffee House in Chelsea*. Richard Blackmore even used Garraway's as an informal office "where he examined and prescribed for patients" (see Bond's note to *Spectator* 138, in 2: 46). The Boyle lectures in physico-theology were the model for these coffeehouse lectures; the coffeehouse in turn provided the model for Steele's "Censorium," an entertainment venue he considered "Newtonian"; see Loftis, *Steele at Drury Lane*, 98–118, and Larry Stewart, *Rise of Public Science*, 94–95, 133–134, 146.

163. M.P., *Character of Coffee*, 10.

164. For good discourse, see *Diary*, 246, 376, 400. For Garaways as a marker of the time, see 133, 237, 246. On another occasion, "It rained hard and I was not at Garaways" (105).

165. Hooke, *Diary*, 208, 205, 84.

166. Hooke, *Diary*, 174, 177, 194, 447. The universal character is referred to in the subsequent entry as a "universall character of Pocket watches" (177).

167. Hooke, *Diary*, 146.

168. See Barbara Shapiro, *Probability and Certainty*.

169. Hobbes insisted that he could see as well through a "common spectacle-glass" as through a thirty-six-foot telescope, "which I confess made me bite my tongue" (Boyle, *Correspondence*, 2: 97). Although Hooke often suffered philosophical impertinence in silence, he did not invariably observe experimental canons of modesty; John Flamsteed complained of Hooke bullying him at Garaways; see Iliffe, "Material Doubts," 316–317. Yet Hooke's *concept* of good discourse excluded such behavior.

170. Shapin and Schaffer, *Leviathan and the Air-Pump*, 322; Shapin, *Social History of Truth*, 199; Boyle, *Boyle on Atheism*, 366; Hooke, *Diary*, 331.

171. This reversal did not preclude the king from continuing to persecute those suspected of spreading "seditious news" in coffeehouses, and trying to turn proprietors into informers; see Love, *Culture and Commerce*, 241–242. As Cowan puts it, "the battle between crown and coffeehouse persisted long after the failure to push through a royal ban" ("Rise of the Coffeehouse," 41); see also chapter 7 of his *Social Life of Coffee*.

172. Berry, *Gender, Society, and Print Culture*, 17.

173. Raymond, *Invention of the Newspaper*, 16, 84.

174. Berry, *Gender, Society, and Print Culture*, 21–22. Dunton is threaded throughout J. Paul Hunter's *Before Novels*, where he emerges almost as the human epitome of the historical and cultural conditions that gave rise to the novel—above all, because of his association with novelty and with a public that would "pay to hear itself puzzle aloud" (13); see esp. 12–18, 99–106.

175. Dunton, *Life and Errors*, 248; Hooke, *Micrographia*, 211.

176. *Athenian Mercury* 1(16) (May 16, 1691); see, for example, 20(10) (June 14, 1697). For Paracelsian rhetoric, see 1(23) (undated). Nonetheless, Aubrey used the periodical as a trusted source; see *Three Prose Works*, 55, 167.

177. *Athenian Gazette* (later *Mercury*) 1(1) (March 17, 1690).

178. *Athenian Gazette* (later *Mercury*) 1(1) (March 17, 1690); *Athenian Mercury* 1(2) (March 24, 1690); see, for example, 1(13) (May 5, 1691) and 1(16) (May 16, 1691). For external evidence that these querists were not fictitious, see Berry, *Gender, Society, and Print Culture*, 43. Letters from angry querists complaining that their questions had not been answered offer internal evidence; see *Athenian Mercury* 11(20) (September 16, 1693) and 12(15) (December 12, 1693). Some readers were nonetheless suspicious; see 15(17) (October 30, 1694).

179. *Athenian Mercury,* 1(12) (May 21, 1691). Dunton admitted in *Life and Errors* that he changed the name to "oblige Authority" (256), no doubt referring to proprietors of the official *London Gazette*; see McEwen, *Oracle of the Coffee House,* 28.

180. Mercuries were also people who sold books wholesale to shops and directly to the public in coffeehouses; a novel presence in the city in the 1640s, they came in "all sexes, sorts and sizes," according to a contemporary (see Johns, *Nature of the Book,* 154–155). Paula McDowell opens the first chapter of *Women of Grub Street* discussing Dunton's decision to dedicate the eleventh volume of the collected *Athenian Gazette* to "the *Worshipfull Society of Mercury-Women in and about the City of* London," noting that Dunton used the term *mercury women* to refer both to itinerant peddlers or "hawkers" of print as well as booksellers (25–26, 55).

181. *Athenian Mercury* 1(2) (March 24, 1690); 10(22) (June 10, 1693). Claydon relates Dunton's participatory model to the public sphere in "Sermon, the 'Public Sphere,' and the Political Culture," 210.

182. *Athenian Mercury,* 1(2) (March 24, 1690).

183. *Athenian Mercury,* 1(14) (May 9, 1691). See also the "Account of our Whole Athenian Project" in the *Supplement to the Fifth Volume of the Athenian Gazette,* 27 (misnumbered as 26).

184. *Athenian Mercury* 1(8) (April 18, 1691).

185. J. Paul Hunter, *Before Novels,* 15. In fact, Dunton enlisted the help of Richard Sault, a mathematician and author of the *Second Spira,* Samuel Wesley, the minister whose children began the Methodist movement (and author of *Maggots,* which was transformed into a predicate of Dunton himself [see J. Paul Hunter, *Before Novels,* 13–14]), and the Anglican clergyman John Norris, ironic given his very public criticisms of the virtuosi (see Chapter 3); Defoe also provided some assistance: see Parks, *John Dunton,* 80–84. However, Hunter's description of Dunton as a single man who pretends to be legion becomes increasingly accurate in Dunton's later appeals to "Athenians"; it seems likely that the waning popularity of his work was a function of the term becoming too closely associated with him personally. Dunton observed that he sold more work under the name of "Anonymous"; clearly, the public wanted to see itself in Dunton (or through Dunton) more than they wanted to see him; see *Before Novels,* 332.

186. *Athenian Mercury* 1(5) (April 7, 1691). See also 15(12) (October 13, 1694) and 16(10) (January 19, 1695). Johns dryly observes that Dunton's imitation Royal Society was in many ways more successful than its prototype (*Nature of the Book,* 457).

187. *Athenian Mercury* 1(15) (May 11, 1691). One reader declared that "*Cambridge* and *Oxford* both abhorr ye"; see 10(22) (June 10, 1693).

188. The ode was printed in the *Supplement to the Fifth Volume of the Athenian Gazette* (1–6); see discussion in Love, *Culture and Commerce,* 298–299.

189. See *Athenian Mercury* 1(13) (May 5, 1691). Gildon's *History of the Athenian Society* (modeled on Sprat's *History*) expanded the membership to twelve: a divine, a philosopher, a physician, a poet, a mathematician, a lawyer, a civilian, a surgeon, an Italian, a Spaniard, a Frenchman, and a Dutchman (13).

190. *Athenian Mercury* 1(15) (May 11, 1691).

191. While the *Ladies Mercury* was short-lived (there were only four issues), there were "Ladies issues" of the *Athenian Mercury,* which explored issues relating to courtship and marriage, but in these issues, female querists did not outnumber the male ones, and even this gesture toward gender segregation was phased out after the fifth volume. See *Athenian Mercury* 2(3) (June 3, 1691), and Berry, *Gender, Society, and Print Culture,* 23, 61, 246.

192. *Athenian Mercury* 1(2) (March 24, 1690).

193. *Athenian Mercury* 1(3) (March 31, 1690).

194. Leonard discusses this Parliamentary convention in *Naming in Paradise,* 80.

195. For the relationship between Boyle's casuistical consultations and his public scruples as an experimenter, see Michael Hunter's *Scrupulosity* and "Disquieted Mind," as well as Chapter 3 in this volume.

196. Dunton, *Life and Errors,* 249. Occasionally, however, Dunton does call attention to the person behind the question; see 14(28) (August 25, 1694). On the casuistical importance of the *Mercury,* see J. Paul Hunter's *Before Novels,* 291–293, and Starr's "From Casuistry to Fiction"; on how the periodical took over functions that had once been restricted to the clergy, see 20–21.

197. Shevelow identifies "the failure of personal connections" as a common thread throughout the letters: writers complain that there is no one for them to consult (*Women and Print Culture,* 74).

198. As Nigel Smith points out, Nedham styled himself against "the 'loyalism' of so many staunch Royalists" (*Literature and Revolution,* 32); as Worden puts it, "he discovered, as did others of his age-group, that the party lines of the 1640s did not yield any single perception of the world to which he could be faithful" (*Literature and Politics,* 29). The first three chapters of Worden's book offer a compelling account of Nedham's career; see 204–215 for his collaboration with Milton on the *Politicus.*

199. *Mercurius Politicus,* 1(33) (June 6–13, 1650), quoted in Jonathan Scott, *England's Troubles,* 15–16. On the queries, see Nigel Smith, *Literature and Revolution,* 60.

200. The Earl of Nottingham saw through a veiled reference to a certain "Decay'd Gentleman" in 7(29) (July 5, 1692); the episode is discussed in McEwen, *Oracle of the Coffee House,* 59–66.

201. Sir John Hoskins, quoted in Michael Hunter, *Establishing the New Science,* 138; Milton, *CPW,* 2: 549. However, occasionally whole issues were devoted to a single topic, and a "Poetical Mercury" was published at intervals; see 5(11) (January 5, 1691). For a complete list of the poetical issues, see McEwen, *Oracle of the Coffee House,* 110n1.

202. Boyle, *Works,* 2: 15. This famous passage from *Certain Physiological Essays* was quoted by Power in his "Preface to the Ingenious Reader," in *Experimental Philosophy,* sigs. c3^v–c4.

203. See Birch, *History,* 1: 463, 491, and Hooke's dedication to the Society (*Micrographia,* sig. A2^v).

204. As Robert South described Adam in relation to his fallen posterity; see *Sermon,* 34.

205. Clarendon quoted in Pincus, "Coffee Politicians Does Create," 827n142 and 832. See also Cowan, "Rise of the Coffeehouse," 36. Within the space of the *Mercury,* the freedom it conferred was even greater and the danger less.

206. Settle, *New Athenian Comedy,* sig. a2^v; *OED,* etymology of *cock-loft.*

207. Settle, *New Athenian Comedy,* 2, sig. a^v, 3. Grub calls it a "full Sessions," as if they were justices of the peace (3).

208. Settle, *New Athenian Comedy,* 5, 28.

209. Settle, *New Athenian Comedy,* 8–10. Although it mutates into a song, it follows the procedure of a Boylean meditation, revealing how "Thoughts can be made to have a Relation to such remote Subjects": Grub uses the "grand Oleo" as an occasion to reflect on the *"Eight Wise Men"* of the Athenian Society itself.

210. Settle, *New Athenian Comedy,* 24; Dunton, *Life and Errors,* 251 (misnumbered as 257).

211. See Hazard, "An Essay to Amplify 'Ornament,'" and Patricia Parker, "Preposterous Events."

212. Dunton, *New Practice,* 37, title page.

213. Power, *Experimental Philosophy,* sig. b2^v.

5. Instruments of Truth

1. For the tradition of "magic glasses" that predates the invention of the microscope and telescope, see Chapter 3, note 5. Current critical thought on the

relationship between texts and lenses in the early modern period is indebted to Nicolson's groundbreaking work on the impact of the new science on the literary imagination (see titles in bibliography). Gilman's *Curious Perspective* explores how optical devices helped to relativize concepts of truth, shaping the "reign of wit" (49). Chapter 3 of Wall's *Prose of Things* explores how technologically assisted observation helped to confer spiritual and intellectual legitimacy on "the practice of seeing depth in surface" and thus on the attempt, not just to see things, but to "see things *oddly*" (71, 81); see her excellent discussion of *Micrographia* at 72–76. Treating a later period, Kevis Goodman's *Georgic Modernity* analyzes the identification of the new perceptual media with sensory discomfort and affective disturbance. I was unable to consult Kalas's fascinating *Frame, Glass, Verse* until I completed the final draft of this book, but see esp. chapter 5, which explores the relationship of real and figurative glass perspectives to a "mode of imaginative perception that . . . discloses the reason extant in the natural order of the temporal world, rather than the musings of the conscious subject" (165).

2. Wilkins, *Discourse concerning a New World*, 195, second pagination. The first half of the sentence summarizes the argument about novelistic verisimilitude made by Gallagher in *Nobody's Story*. Her stronger claim that the concept of fiction did not exist before the novel requires qualification, but seventeenth-century uses of *novel* and *novelist* do tend to slide into what the *OED* calls the "reproachful sense." As McKeon observes, natural philosophers as well as "newsmongers" were often described as novelists; see *Origins of the English Novel*, 47, 68–73, 441n13. On *novel* as a synonym for *news*, see Lennard Davis, *Factual Fictions*, esp. 51, and Paulson, *Beautiful, Novel, Strange*, 61–66.

3. Sidney, *Apologie*, sig. Cᵛ. But on Sidney's effort to "moralize" the imagination, see Guillory, *Poetic Authority*, 10–11.

4. Messina describes the use of the lens in Marvell's *Last Instructions to a Painter* (discussed below) as an instrument of "empiric demythologizing" in "The Heroic Image," 304; Bacon, *Works*, 4: 32.

5. I refer to Milton's "paradise within" (*PL*, 12.587).

6. Coleridge quoted in Abrams, *The Mirror and the Lamp*, 55. Reviving a battery of Neoplatonic metaphors for the mind that stressed emanation, the Romantics adjusted these figures to represent the relationship of the mind to the world as a "bilateral transaction," characterized by "give-and-take" (61).

7. Abrams, *The Mirror and the Lamp*, 62–63, 57.

8. In *Spectator* 413, Addison offers the following gloss of chapter 8 of Book 2 of Locke's *Essay:* "our Souls are at present delightfully lost and bewildered in a pleasing Delusion, and we walk about like the Enchanted Hero of a Romance, who sees beautiful Castles, Woods and Meadows" (3: 546).

9. The phrase is adapted from William Browne's *Britannia's Pastorals,* discussed below.

10. See van Helden, "Galileo and Scheiner on Sunspots." On self-magnification through print, see Keeble, *Literary Culture,* 82–92, and Peacey, *Politicians and Pamphleteers,* 67.

11. Sprat, *History,* 35; Helgerson, *Self-Crowned Laureates,* 227; Sprat, *History,* 99. Experimentalism thus provides one context for understanding Marvell's interest in creating a "poetry of criticism," as Colie called it long ago (*"My Ecchoing Song"*). On the phrase "make a progresse" see Pinnell, *Word of Prophesy,* sig. A6; Locke, *Reasonableness,* 277; and Chapter 1 in this volume.

12. Comenius, *Way of Light,* 189; Milton, *CPW,* 2: 364–366. As Masson observes, this was "barely polite" to Hartlib, though the vehement denunciation of the existing educational system that followed would likely have placated him (*Life,* 3: 235). Jardine observes that Wilkins's *Universal Character* was "obsolete as a venture almost before it was printed" (*Ingenious Pursuits,* 302).

13. Henry Edmundson's *Lingua Linguarum,* a text Fraser cites (*Language of Adam,* 14, 18), appeals to "our great Advancer of Learning" to the effect that "the main business of mankind" is the "redeeming himselfe from those curses which he gained by his sin, the Curse upon the earth by his Fal, which is remedied by Arts, Trades and Professions; and the Curse in the Confusion of Tongues at *Babell*." But his contribution to this cause is nothing more than a Latin textbook: "Till there be a common Language among men (which is to be *wished* and *fancied* rather then *expected* and *hoped*)," Latin will have to do (sigs. A3, a3ᵛ). Although Francis Lodwick worked on developing conceptual symbols, influencing Wilkins's own efforts in that area, the work that appeared in the Society's *Transactions* 16 (126–137)—the "Essay towards an Universal Alphabet"—was merely a phonetic alphabet (on Lodwick, see Salmon, *Study of Language*). Cave Beck's *Universal Character* was modestly designed as "a Mechanicall help for ye unlearnd or such as convers wth unlearned strangers" (Oldenburg, *Correspondence,* 4: 555). Like Latin, it would enable international discussion, thereby assisting trade as well as the sciences: thus the frontispiece features a turbaned man, a black man, a red man, and a white man talking amicably—an Adamic family of man. For a recent summary of the seventeenth-century range of opinion on Adam's language, as well as attempts to "undo Babel," see Almond, *Adam and Eve,* 126–142.

14. But see Thomas Browne, *Religio Medici,* 2.2 in *Works,* 1: 72–73.

15. John Webster, *Academiarum Examen,* 68, 8, sig. B2.

16. John Webster, *Academiarum Examen,* 77, 26, 32. Webster admits there has been some progress in music, but "the mysterious part thereof" remains "untried and unattempted" (42).

17. John Webster, *Academiarum Examen*, 27, 33, 67.

18. See the clarifying discussion of various understandings of Adamic naming in Leonard, *Naming in Paradise*, 1–22. As Leonard points out, Webster does not distinguish a universal language from this paradisal one.

19. Ward and Wilkins, *Vindiciae Academiarum*, 20. But on Boyle's view that mathematics offered an insufficiently experimental basis for truth claims, see Sargent, *Diffident Naturalist*, esp. 37–39, 66–68. On the growing understanding of math as a language, see Funkenstein, *Theology and the Scientific Imagination*, 34–35. See Paul Wood's discussion of the Webster-Ward debate in "Methodology and Apologetics," 17.

20. Cowley, "Of Agriculture," in *Works*, 102, seventh pagination.

21. "An Account of the Life of Mr. Abraham Cowley" (prefaced to Cowley's *Works*), sigs. a2ᵛ, bᵛ, eᵛ, bᵛ. In addition to defending Cowley's devotion to and competence in natural philosophy, Sprat insists that much "useful Knowledge" can be extracted from his "Masculine Works," even *The Mistress;* he also notes that his fatal illness was contracted "by staying too long amongst his Laborers in the Medows" (sigs. e, b2ᵛ, A2ᵛ, b2ᵛ, e2). On Cowley's *Proposition for the Advancement of Experimental Philosophy,* see Chapter 3. Boyle presented Cowley to his brother as a poet "fit to Imitate," though this was largely because Cowley's muse was "Employ'd about such Subjects as may be chosen in the Scripture"; he did, however, call Cowley "Ingenious" (*Works*, 2: 383).

22. Cowley, *Works*, sig. A2; Samuel Johnson, *Lives of the Poets*, 1: 191; Aubrey, *Brief Lives*, 75.

23. Hooke, *Micrographia*, sig. A2ᵛ; Pepys, *Diary*, 6: 18. This entry offers a contrast between the works of ingenuity and the life of the court that is worthy of Evelyn's diary: Pepys had spent a frustrating day at Whitehall where he "saw nothing ordered by judgment."

24. Wall remarks that Hooke's description of the louse "creates a little, coherent, anthropomorphized world busily existing on the human scalp, even before we get to *Gulliver's Travels*" (*Prose of Things*, 74; see also 81, 93, 236, as well as Nicolson, "Microscope," and McKeon, *Secret History*, 400–409).

25. Donne, *Ignatius His Conclave*, 5–7. As I have suggested, Donne's constructions of paradise and Adam were not at all Baconian, but he did not reject the discoveries of the new science; see, for example, *Sermons*, 7: 260, 271.

26. Donne, *Ignatius his Conclave*, 7.

27. Donne, *Ignatius his Conclave*, 7, 9. Donne's source is *Paleotus de Sindone;* see 104.

28. Donne, *Ignatius his Conclave*, 7. See Arnold Williams, *Common Expositor*, 149–151.

29. Sidney, *Apologie,* sig. Cᵛ. For a different assessment of Donne's attitude toward the astronomers, see Hassel, "Ignatius His Conclave." See also Nicolson, "New Astronomy," 453–456.

30. See Burton, *Anatomy of Melancholy,* 2: 33–67 (2.2.3.1). As Barlow observes, the astronomical section of the "Digression of the Ayre" increases by about half, and the new astronomy, which at first the text only entertains, is embraced and elaborated; see his "Infinite Worlds," 292. In this section Burton imagines himself as a "long-winged Hawke . . . still soaring higher and higher"—a pointed contrast to his description of scholars, "mewed up like hawkes all their lives" (2: 33; 1: 307).

31. Barbour, *English Epicures,* 217. Barbour offers a fascinating account of an "anatomy of freedom that runs in fits and starts alongside the anatomy of melancholy," unsettling Stuart authority (68). For melancholy as a result of the fall, see Burton, *Anatomy of Melancholy,* 1: 121–128 (1.1.1.1).

32. Burton, *Anatomy of Melancholy,* 1: 6. This story, taken from the "Letter to Damagetus," was endlessly rehearsed in the period. Lüthy's "Fourfold Democritus" explains how the different traditions surrounding Democritus as "laughing philosopher," moralizing anatomist, alchemist, and magus worked together to pave the way for the acceptance of atomism. Boyle appealed to Democritus's "manifold Dissections of Animals" as a model of what philosophy had been before Aristotle and what it was coming to be again (*Works,* 8: 87; see also 74, 86, 93, and Hakewill, *Apologie,* 272–273).

33. Bacon, *Works,* 5: 5. The miseries of scholars are taken up at 1: 302–327 (1.2.3.15). On Burton's sense of confinement as a scholar and divine, see Nochimson, "Studies in the Life."

34. Burton, *Anatomy of Melancholy,* 1: 74, 78, 79. Burton's term is "Soule, or *intellectus agens.*"

35. Burton, *Anatomy of Melancholy,* 1: 67. Burton elaborates a utopian—really, a Hartlibian—fantasy that includes an ambitious public works program and a social order rather like that imagined by Evelyn, in which anyone who "invents any thing for publike good in any Art or Science" shall be "honoured" (92).

36. But see 1: 426 for one "experiment" he may have performed, discussed in Vicari, *View from Minerva's Tower,* 30 and 215n19.

37. Burton might have derived perverse satisfaction from learning that the very rooms in which he was rumored to have committed suicide would become the residence of the young Robert Hooke (Aubrey, *Brief Lives,* 165). Nochimson objects that Burton was given a proper burial, which would have been denied to a suicide, but his epitaph describing him as "Democritus Junior, to whom Melancholy gave both life and death" lent credit to the rumor (see Nochimson, "Studies in the Life," 108–109).

38. See Fish, *Self-Consuming Artifacts,* chapter 6.

39. Grew, *Idea,* 103. As Lewalski suggests, Milton turned the sonnet into a sort of newsbook by incorporating data from contemporary news reports and his own state letters into "On the Late Massacher in Piedmont" (*Life,* 352).

40. Charleton, *Physiologia,* 267–268.

41. William Browne, *Britannia's Pastorals,* 2.2.15–17 (*Whole Works,* 2: 2). See Alastair Fowler's discussion in "Georgic and Pastoral," 85.

42. William Browne, *Britannia's Pastorals,* 2.1.857–866 (*Whole Works,* 1: 189). See James Grantham Turner's discussion of this passage in "Landscape and the 'Art Prospective,'" 292n25.

43. William Browne, *Britannia's Pastorals,* 2.1.841–843 (*Whole Works,* 1: 189); see van Helden, "Telescopes and Authority," 25–27.

44. Helgerson, *Forms of Nationhood,* 131.

45. William Browne, *Britannia's Pastorals,* 2.1.885–886, 1027–1028, 1043–1044 (*Whole Works,* 1: 190, 194); Puttenham, *Arte of English Poesie,* 53 (1.18). See Chapter 2 in this volume.

46. William Browne, *Britannia's Pastorals,* 2.1.851–856, 887–888 (*Whole Works,* 1: 189, 190). On contemporary depictions of Galileo as a high-flying figure who stole fire from the heavens, see Reeves, *Galileo's Glassworks,* 90–98.

47. On the long-standing habit of associating these two arcana, see Ginzburg, "High and Low." See Achinstein's important discussion of these pamphlets in *Milton and the Revolutionary Reader,* 155–162. Patterson remarks on the literary use of optical instruments for "skeptical political analysis" in "Imagining New Worlds," 259.

48. *A New Invention,* 1, 3, 2, 3. The author predicts that "the Sabbath (if any) shall be free for sports, and he that bows lowest to the Altar be highest in the Bishops favour . . . no more Petitions then" (3).

49. Achinstein, *Milton and the Revolutionary Reader,* 157–158. In this connection, it is perhaps equally important that the review of recent English history offered by the pamphlet takes the form of a series of questions, compelling the reader's active response.

50. *Second Part of the Spectacles,* 3, 5 (misnumbered as 4); see Barbara Shapiro, *Culture of Fact.*

51. *Second Part of the Spectacles,* 8.

52. *Eye Cleard,* 2. Roger L'Estrange said of a later effort, *Eye-Salve for the English Armie,* that it was "a medicine of the same Composition, which (by general report) strook *Milton* Blind" (*Physician Cure Thy Selfe,* 2; see Lewalski, *Life,* 380).

53. Mercurius Melancholicus, *Cuckoo's Nest,* 4; *Great Assises,* 34–35.

54. Biagioli, *Galileo's Instruments of Credit,* 138, 188, 216. On how sunspots made novel demands on forms of scientific communication, see van Helden, "Galileo and Scheiner on Sunspots"; for a comparison of Galileo and Scheiner's approaches to the problem, see Dear, *Discipline and Experience,* 100–107.

55. On periodicity, in addition to Biagioli, *Galileo's Instruments of Credit,* see Sommerville, *News Revolution,* 17–56.

56. This is what Raymond argues in *Invention of the Newspaper,* 210–221, in which he rejects the pamphlet's attribution to George Wither; see also Achinstein, *Milton and the Revolutionary Reader,* 76–77, 171. Holstun draws a suggestive contrast that is relevant to my argument here, between the unveiling of the nobles in the early Stuart court masque and the different sort of *"apokalypsis"* performed by the newsbook's unveiling of "previously unsuspected knowledge" (*Ehud's Dagger,* 109).

57. Bernard, *Looking-Glasse for Rebellion,* sig. A2; see Samuel 15:23. On artisanal epistemology and the public, see Chapter 1.

58. Eachard, *Works,* 3: v. Eachard is speaking of Hobbes, who was often grouped together with other proponents of "the new philosophy," despite his well-documented mistrust of experimental methods.

59. Marvell was fond of tracing this progress from one instrument to the other: see *Prose Works,* 1: 68.

60. For an overview of the event, see P. G. Rogers, *The Dutch in the Medway.* The humiliation, which led to the peace at Breda a month later, presented a dramatic contrast with England's military successes under Cromwell. "Kingdom in a desperate condition," Pepys wrote; he blamed the "horrid effeminacy of the King" (*Diary,* 8: 288–289); see also Evelyn, *Diary,* 3: 484–487.

61. I quote from *The Second Advice to a Painter, for drawing the history of our Naval business, in imitation of Mr Waller,* in Nigel Smith's edition of Marvell, 330. As Rowland observes, the poem "uses the events 'behind' Waller's poem . . . to subvert it" (*Faint Praise and Civil Leer,* 60). On the printing of the painter poems, see Dzelzainis, "Andrew Marvell." For an intricate and sympathetic reading of Waller's poem, see A. B. Chambers, *Marvell and Waller,* 85–107.

62. As Worden puts it, Marvell's "assaults on misgovernment" in this period "belonged to concerted literary campaigns" (*Literature and Politics,* 56). Patterson argues vigorously for Marvell's authorship of (rather than mere participation in) the earlier efforts in "Lady State's First Two Sittings." See also Nigel Smith's introduction to the Advice-to-a-Painter poems in his edition, 321–323.

63. Marvell, *Last Instructions,* line 910. Marvell calls him "dear *Painter*" at lines 390, 511, and 863. All quotations from Marvell's poetry come from Margoliouth's edition.

64. Legouis, *Andrew Marvell*, 168. As Chernaik observes, the "ultimate appeal in Marvell's satiric writings is to a wider audience," since it is only through secrecy that the "ruling cabal is able to maintain its power . . . Truth and justice can be served by stripping the veil of secrecy from the arcana of government" (*Poet's Time*, 71). See also note 56 above.

65. Zwicker, "Virgins and Whores."

66. Marvell, *Last Instructions*, line 652. Douglas dies like a boy going to sleep: "so rests his Head, / As one that's warm'd himself and gone to Bed" (lines 689–690).

67. Messina's "Heroic Image" does address this question. In his view, Marvell's presentation of aristocrats as scientists is intended as an insult to both: debased empiricism and the bed-hopping aristocracy equally represent perversions of natural virtue represented by Douglas, the "noble primitive"; see "The Heroic Image," 303.

68. See Darbishire, *Early Lives*, 74, 175–176, and Brogan, "Marvell's Epitaph." Katherine Boyle's violent dislike for Waller's verse may have been shaped by Marvell's opinions (or vice versa); see Masson, *Life*, 6: 456–457. On Milton and Marvell's friendship, see Hill, "Milton and Marvell."

69. James Grantham Turner, "The Libertine Abject," 217–218.

70. Marvell's clashes with the diehard royalist in Parliament provide the background for this ostensibly disinterested suggestion. At least one of these clashes was literal; after they exchanged blows, Marvell was forced to admit his guilt for having given the "first Provocation" (Legouis, *Andrew Marvell*, 128; see Margoliouth's commentary, 270–271). In Pepys's estimation, Clifford was not "worth a fart" (*Diary*, 8: 289).

71. Zwicker, "Virgins and Whores," 95. On St. Albans, see also Wallace, *Destiny His Choice*, 164–168.

72. See Arnold, *Third Citizen*, and Jennings, *Anecdotal History*, 447. On the house as a degenerate body, see Chapter 1.

73. Patterson, *Marvell and the Civic Crown*, 159. On the "Marvellian tradition" of scribal publication, see Love, *Culture and Commerce*, 238–242, and Dzelzainis, "Andrew Marvell" (which, however, points out that *Last Instructions* had a more restricted circulation than its predecessors). On Marvell's use of multiple printers for single works so that workmen could plausibly claim ignorance of their contents, see Johns, *Nature of the Book*, 100, and Lynch, *"Mr. Smirke,"* esp. 47–48, 63.

74. Marvell, *Prose Works*, 2: 304; Jennings, *Anecdotal History*, 37. See also Patterson, *Marvell and the Civic Crown*, 45–46.

75. Marvell, *Last Instructions*, lines 597–598. On *gallant* as an experimentalist term of abuse, see Chapter 2.

76. Probably Sir Thomas Daniel; see notes in Margoliouth and Nigel Smith's editions.

77. Gearin-Tosh, "The Structure," 54.

78. Marvell, *Last Instructions,* lines 784, 787–788. See Milward, *Diary,* 127.

79. Rochester, "Satyr upon King Charles," line 11; Riebling, "England Deflowered," 139.

80. Marvell, *Last Instructions,* line 943. In lines 377–392, Marvell also compares their joint effort to "represent / In quick *Effigy,* others Faults" to the "Spectacle Innocent" of a Skimmington ride, "a popular festival form tradition-ally independent of established authority and unconnected with the holidays of the church" (Marcus, *Politics of Mirth,* 263); Marvell weaves popular "ancient custom" together with the experimentalist arts of exposure.

81. For contemporary analogizing between Charles and the sun, see Reedy, "Mystical Politics," 28–30.

82. Sunspots were first observed through telescopes in 1610; after 1645, few were recorded: between 1655 and 1660, and again between 1661 and 1671, none were seen at all. See Weiss and Weiss, "Marvell's Spotted Sun," and Eddy, "The Case of the Missing Sunspots."

83. See van Helden, "Invention of the Telescope," 13, and Weiss and Weiss, "Marvell's Spotted Sun," 339.

84. See Weiss and Weiss, "Marvell's Spotted Sun."

85. Kepler quoted in Debus, *Man and Nature,* 96; Evelyn, *Elysium Britan-nicum,* 83.

86. Svetlana Alpers describes Dutch still-life painters following celebrated users of the lens in allowing observation to stand for the self in *Art of Describing,* 90.

87. If the king is to be an "Intelligent Ruler over a Rational People," as Marvell puts it in *Growth of Popery,* the people must take instruction from Marvell's tutorial alongside the painter and Charles himself (*Prose Works,* 2: 226). On Marvellian scribal publication, see note 73 above. For a contemporary account of the coffeehouse reception of Marvell's *Rehearsal Transpros'd,* see Hickeringill, *Gregory, Father-Greybeard,* 5, discussed in *Prose Works,* 1: 3–4.

88. See Kegl, "Politics of Labor," and Low, *Georgic Revolution,* 274–280. Nigel Smith observes in his edition of the poems that Marvell's use of the mower is not unprecedented since mowers or reapers appear in Theocritus; nonetheless, in displacing the shepherd as speaker, Marvell's mower is rightly considered an assault on the pastoral mode as it had developed in the Renaissance (*Poems,* 128; see also Chapter 2 in this volume). What is most relevant for our purposes is that Marvell's mowers explicitly address the challenge of their labor and that they are historically situated speakers; the mower's invective in "The Mower against Gardens," for example, draws on the Diggers' arguments against enclosure (see

Bruce King, "Mower"). Marcus suggests that Marvell's mowers probe the connection between festival sports and violence that the Laudian ideology of sport attempted to suppress (*Politics of Mirth*, 237).

89. Cousins credits Marvell with a "comprehensive rewriting of the country house poem" in "Marvell's *Upon Appleton House*," 54; see also Stocker, *Apocalyptic Marvell*, 66, 161.

90. Marvell exploits the contemporary confusion of Levellers and Diggers in this poem. I will relate the Levellers to the "true Levellers" (i.e., Diggers), whose famous encounter with Fairfax had occurred less than two years earlier (for an account of Fairfax and Winstanley's association, see Wilding, *Dragons' Teeth*, 150–155), but Marvell keeps the scope of reference open. As Hirst and Zwicker observe in their extraordinary account of the poem's relationship to the circumstances of the summer of 1651, Lilburne and Walwyn were organizing enclosure rioters just to the east of Fairfax's estate during these months: Marvell chooses to "vent the *canard* about the levelling aims of the Levellers in one of the very contexts in which Levellers actually were levelling," attacking drainage works ("High Summer," 253n26).

91. James Grantham Turner, *Politics of Landscape*, 61 (here Turner discusses the overlap of the countryhouse and topographical genres); Legouis, *Andrew Marvell*, 78.

92. Eliot, "Andrew Marvell," 170–171, 165, 169; Hodge, *Foreshortened Time*, 61.

93. Marvell, *Upon Appleton House*, line 456, stanza 58.

94. See Carey's witty exploration of the cows passage in "Reversals Transposed," 148. Leishman first made the case for an allusion to Howell's comment that a magnified flea resembles a cow in *Art of Marvell's Poetry*, 222; see Howell, *Epistolae*, 46, third pagination. The reversibility of the lunar and pastoral imagery will be recognized from the telescopic literature glanced at in Chapters 2 and 3.

95. Marvell's interest in the fact conditions his approach to narrative. As Legouis observes, Denham's *Coopers-Hill* sums up the entire history of the English Reformation in fifty lines, while it takes Marvell four times as many to relate a local incident of a territorial dispute between a landowner and the prioress of a nunnery (*Andrew Marvell*, 63). This narrative functions as a case study in the dissolution of the monasteries; the story of the Reformation is "scored out" from the perspective provided by a particular set of circumstances. Chernaik relates the poem's method to occasional meditation in *Poet's Time*, 32, 155–156.

96. See Legouis, *Andrew Marvell*, 48–49; Marvell, *Upon Appleton House*, lines 387, 443, 369–370, 446, 626–628.

97. On contemporary analogies between washing linens and the alchemical purification of matter, see Lyndy Abraham, *Marvell and Alchemy*, 198–200.

Abraham may overstate the poem's interest in allegorizing alchemical processes; I believe that its aim is to appropriate these processes in order to enact a spectatorial alchemy. On the broad use of the term *alchemy* in the period, however, see 1, 62.

98. See stanza 47 and Lovelace's "The Grasse-hopper." I quote from Marcus's account of the grasshoppers, which can hardly be improved on: Marvell here reveals the "traditional structure of society as itself a form of misrule in which authority is determined by accidents of social and economic position. It is the temporary luxuriance of the grass that gives the grasshoppers their advantage. They tower over shrinking men despite their ludicrous smallness because they are placed at the top" (*Politics of Mirth*, 247). See also Stocker, *Apocalyptic Marvell*, 53–54.

99. Marvell, *Upon Appleton House*, line 390, and "The Mower's Song," lines 1–4.

100. See Chapter 3.

101. Marvell, *Upon Appleton House*, lines 444–446. This was the painter Hooke abandoned for a career as an experimentalist.

102. With "Heard," Marvell may be opportunizing orthography to reflect on Davenant's careless confusion of modalities when he describes the Creator's voice represented in a painting; see the final section of this chapter.

103. Marvell, *Upon Appleton House*, lines 452–454. Stocker suggests that the beast is in fact *the* beast of Revelation; see *Apocalyptic Marvell*, 56.

104. A point made by Warnke in "The Meadow Sequence," 238.

105. Hirst and Zwicker suggest that Thestylis is "mocking" Marvell and "speaking out of turn," but she is merely taking her turn; I see no evidence of hostility in this scriptural badinage ("High Summer," 253). But see Grossman, *Story of All Things*, 215–216.

106. At line 369 (I am of course excluding the "I"s spoken by the nun and William Fairfax). Warnke also notices that the first-person singular appears for the first time in the meadow sequence ("The Meadow Sequence," 234). It might seem counterintuitive to argue that the collective authorship comes into its own when we move from "we" to "I," but the "I" Marvell cares about is always a corporate one.

107. Marvell, *Upon Appleton House*, lines 98, 173, 175, 182, 184. Space does not permit a reading of the nunnery episode, but it should be observed that it offers a historical perspective on Fairfax's present predicament, since the stentorian prioress is clearly a stand-in for Lady Fairfax, whose explosive objections to the king's trial created a public spectacle; see Hirst and Zwicker, "High Summer," 260–262. Just as importantly, Marvell's portrayal of the nuns mimics "the politicized Stuart version of the ideal of Christian liberty"—the "cleanly *Wantonnesse*" celebrated by Herrick's *Hesperides* (Marcus, *Politics of Mirth*, 242; "The Argument of his Book," line 6).

108. Marvell, *Upon Appleton House,* lines 385–386. On the "georgic masque," see Low, *Georgic Revolution,* 284–287, 293. As Marcus points out, the harvest imagery of Isaiah and Jeremiah had been appropriated by the Parliamentary forces: "God made them as stubble to our swords" (*Politics of Mirth,* 249). For a more pacifist account of the meadows sequence, see James Grantham Turner, "Marvell's Warlike Studies," 298–300.

109. Marvell, *Upon Appleton House,* lines 394, 424. The cattle become astonished at line 472. On the rail as the king of quails, see Allen, *Image and Meaning,* 209. Allen's identification of the rail with Charles has not won universal acceptance; see Stocker, *Apocalpytic Marvell,* 150.

110. Marvell, *Upon Appleton House,* lines 529, 561. As Patterson puts it, "'Languishing with ease,' 'On Pallets swoln of Velvet Moss,' the 'easie Philosopher' merely thinks he is thinking" (*Marvell and the Civic Crown,* 104; see also Stocker, *Apocalpytic Marvell,* 151–159). By associating easy philosophy with Hermeticism, Marvell may be issuing a gentle corrective to Fairfax, who was absorbed in its mysteries (see Hodge, *Foreshortened Time,* 135). Hirst and Zwicker suggest that Marvell may be reflecting on Fairfax's antinomian sympathies as well, given that 1651 was "the year of the Ranters" ("High Summer," 258).

111. The solipsistic atmosphere results from the dominance of the first-person, which, as Chernaik observes, occurs forty times in the episode (*Poet's Time,* 35). This person, unlike that of the meadows, is lonely and insistent.

112. Marvell, *Upon Appleton House,* lines 650, 654. Walton celebrates fishing as a source of "innocent Mirth" in *The Compleat Angler, or The Contemplative Man's Recreation,* sig. A5ᵛ.

113. Howell, *Epistolae,* 48. See note 94 above for an almost certain borrowing from this source. On occasional reflections, see Chapter 4.

114. Marvell, *Upon Appleton House,* line 726. See Revelation 4:6 and 15:2, and Stocker, *Apocalyptic Marvell,* 60–66.

115. But for Maria and the halcyon, see Lyndy Abraham, *Marvell and Alchemy,* chapter 12.

116. For a vivid account of how this figure shaped astronomical thought, see Reeves, *Painting the Heavens,* chapter 4. Howell uses the figure himself, comparing a handsome woman to the "diaphanous pellucid dainty body" of Venice glass, "which implies *Beuty, but brittlenes withall*" (46).

117. I owe this line of thought to Eileen Reeves; my source is Godfrey, *Development of English Glassmaking;* see 3–7, 82, 157–159, 245. Sprat observed that "the *English* have got a great advantage of late years, by the *Art* of making *Glass,* finer, and more serviceable for *Microscopes,* and *Telescopes,* than that of *Venice*" (*History,* 250, quoted in Godfrey, 248).

118. Challenging conventional understandings of "this word *learning*," Howell insists that "any artisan whatsoever if he know the secret and mystery of his trade may be call'd a learned man," and, indeed, that artisans are "the usefullest sort of learned men" (*Epistolae,* 13, fourth pagination). He also refers to conversations enjoyed at Gresham (9, third pagination).

119. Howell, *Epistolae,* 9, third pagination. For his ambiguous loyalties, see *DNB.*

120. Howell, *Epistolae,* 55–56, third pagination (Howell's addressee was in the Tower). He says later that "This travelling o're of oneself, is one of the paths that leads a man to Paradice" (120, third pagination). Howell also compares the Fleet to "*Noah's Ark,* surrounded with a vast Sea, and huge deluge of calamities, which hath overwhelmd this poor Island"—a possible inspiration for the flooding of the meadows in Marvell's poem (252, second pagination).

121. See their discussion in Marvell, *Prose Works,* 1: 19–20.

122. Marvell, *Upon Appleton House,* lines 763, 762, 768. Marvell's alchemical revision of the estate seems to answer Thomas Vaughan's prayer: "Give me an Art then, that is a perfect intire *Map* of the *Creation,* that can lead me directly to the *Knowledge* of the true *God*" (*Magia Adamica,* 28).

123. Marvell, "The Garden," lines 13–14. There is another echo of Herbert's poem at lines 11–12.

124. On the poem's dating, see Pritchard, "Marvell's 'The Garden,'" discussed below.

125. See Chapter 1. I have benefited from a discussion with Abigail Heald about poetry and narrative responsibility.

126. Published posthumously in 1640, Carew's poetry caused a stir, being named in a petition to the Long Parliament as a grievance to the kingdom; see Ruoff, "Thomas Carew's Early Reputation."

127. Carew, "A Rapture," in *Poems,* 83–89: lines 9–10, 3, 7–9, 20.

128. Carew, "A Rapture," lines 64, 66. Of course the garden is verbally cultivated in opportunistically "occasional" fashion, materializing as snowy alps and bushes as topographically appropriate.

129. Milton, *PL,* 4. 742–743; see Hobbes, *Leviathan,* 98 (1.13) and passim.

130. Although wood pulp was not yet used to make paper, previous chapters have discussed the patristic puns linking foliage to folia. For a contemporary riff on this topos, see the satirical engraving "The World is Ruled and Governed by Opinion" (BM Sat. 272, reproduced on the cover of Sharpe's *Remapping Early Modern England*). The Petrarchan conceit of "scattered leaves" is also operative here; these leaves are now restored to their source.

131. Carew, "Rapture," lines 126–127. I am indebted to the insights of Christine Barrett for my understanding of this part of the poem.

132. Carew, "A Rapture," line 58. For Paula Johnson, "honor wins in the end" and whores are whores ("Dynamics of Fantasy," 155); Schoff agrees, but argues that what has led up to this ending is no harmless fantasy ("Thomas Carew"). In "Beyond Frustration," Braden makes a strong case for the poem as one in which "lust may be said not merely to lose its sinfulness, but indeed to become the agent of a serious kind of moral discipline," as the reader is challenged to reject the established connotations of *whore* (15). Braden's account is the most sensitive to the poem's interest in undertaking an innocent critique of ordinary language.

133. Marvell, "The Garden," line 9. Thus Stocker suggests that in this poem "poetry and eschatology are rendered identical" (*Apocalyptic Marvell,* 254). John Rogers describes a quiet apocalypse, a "process that redeems the fallen natural world and, by extension, the fallen nature of political organization," though he identifies it with a "passive revolution." I see a form of active, innocent, contemplative work closer to what Rogers describes as the Mower's effort "to recover, by means of human labor, a Pauline coalescence with a laboring creation" (*Matter of Revolution,* 98, 65).

134. A point well made by Carpenter, "Marvell's 'Garden,'" 161.

135. A connection can be drawn to Milton's habit of presenting his poems as revisionary preventions, as in the Nativity Ode or "When I Consider."

136. Carew, "A Rapture," lines 79, 105, 120; Marvell, "To his Coy Mistress," line 11.

137. Thomas Browne, *Religio Medici* 2.9, in *Works,* 1: 83. Marvell makes Carew's heterosexual paradise a homosocial one simply by removing *a* woman while asserting collectivity through an Adam called "Man." Although it is not gender-neutral, this man could include anyone.

138. Ellrodt, "Marvell's Mind," 219. This paradox is itself a version of what Stocker calls the "great paradox of renovation—'Annihilating' to make 'green'" (*Apocalpytic Marvell,* 255).

139. Hooke, *Micrographia,* 58, 77–78; Hodge, *Foreshortened Time,* 66–67.

140. Hartman, "Body of Hope," 181.

141. Hooke, *Micrographia,* 58.

142. See Chapter 2.

143. On the reduction to the pristine state, the machined hand, the artificial organ, and this quote, see Chapter 3.

144. Marvell, "The Garden," line 55. Critical disputes center on the cause of the ecstasy rather than the fact of it. Legouis's disagreement with the "eucharistic" reading of the poem offered in chapter 5 of Stanley Stewart's *Enclosed Garden* is instructive in this connection: "That the poet experiences an ecstasy few critics deny . . . but his originality, at that date, is that he communes not with an

allegory but with real, vegetable nature, alone present in the poem" (*Andrew Marvell,* 246).

145. Legouis, *Andrew Marvell,* 64. Empson's estimation is similar: "a graceful finale . . . but not, I think, very important" (*Some Versions of Pastoral,* 118).

146. Hartman describes how the union of faith and works in this passage—one of many instances of "duality overcome"—permits "an unhasty growing of creation into its true body, the redemption of nature with man, of all in all" in "Body of Hope," 194, 185.

147. See Chapter 3. Rajan is instructive here: he suggests that for Marvell "art is a mimesis of the real world," but "it is also a continuing subversion of that mimesis . . . we are not expected to forget the still-persistent force of 'annihilating'" ("Aesthetics of Inconclusiveness," 167). This combination of negative and positive energies is the very condition of sensuous iconoclasm—an attack on false images whose aims are realized through the expansion of the visible world.

148. Norbrook has remarked on the impersonality of Marvell's poetry (*Writing the English Republic,* 165), Ellrodt on its "objective" character ("Marvell's Mind," 224).

149. Indeed, the reduction of that garden dweller to a single bee at the end of "The Garden" may suggest that the "commonwealth of bees" more closely approximates man's happy garden state than any strictly personal relation to nature ever could: one bee is no bee. Although she takes a dimmer view of this transformation, I am indebted to Laura Kolb's unpublished paper "One Bee Is No Bee."

150. Pritchard, "Marvell's 'The Garden,'" 372, 385. Pritchard makes the valuable observation that the traditional dating of "The Garden" was influenced by the "myth" that "the growth of science and rationalism was fatal for lyric poetry" (387). On Cowley and Evelyn's exchange, see Chapter 4.

151. As Pritchard puts it, "Marvell had a special interest both in the most celebrated military retirement of his age and in the most celebrated literary retirement" ("Marvell's 'The Garden,'" 382).

152. Cowley, "The Garden," stanza 10, from *Several Discourses,* 120, in *Works.*

153. Dryden, *Works,* 9: 15. This identification with the virtuoso might have been his way of rationalizing his liberal borrowing from Sprat's *Observations on Mons. de Sorbier's Voyage into England,* however. See the commentary on *An Essay of Dramatick Poesie* in *Works,* 17: 343–346. All quotations from the *Essay* come from this volume. Dryden was proposed as a candidate to the Society by Charleton, and elected, in November 1662 (Birch, *History,* 1: 125), but he was

not a member in good standing, and was one of the first to be expelled. Winn nonetheless makes a case for its influence on him in *John Dryden,* 128–136.

154. Pett quoted in Goldie, "Sir Peter Pett," 265. Pett is referring to religious disputes here.

155. Frye, "Varieties of Eighteenth-Century Sensibility," 161–162.

156. Dryden, *Works,* 17: 15–16. Crites is based on Charles Howard, who became a Royal Society Fellow the same year Dryden did.

157. Dryden's *Essay* was published in 1668; the first edition of *PL* had come out the previous year.

158. It was Davenant, not Milton, who received a laureateship and a Westminster Abbey burial. See Harbage, *Davenant,* 3, 269, and Helgerson, *Self-Crowned Laureates,* 204–205.

159. See *Certain Verses,* 5; Nethercot, *D'Avenant,* 252–254; and Harbage, *Davenant,* 110–111. Aubrey discusses his "ingeniose Designe" to carry weavers with him, culled from Paris prisons, in order to set up textile operations overseas (*Brief Lives,* 87).

160. *Mercurius Politicus* quoted in Nethercot, *D'Avenant,* 271. See Darbishire, *Early Lives,* 30, 271–275; Nethercot, *D'Avenant,* 280–282; and Lewalski, *Life,* 288, 667–668n7. But see also Jacob and Raylor, "Opera and Obedience," 206.

161. Davenant, *First Days Entertainment,* title page; see Harbage, *Davenant,* 121–123. Much of the evening was taken up by a debate between a Parisian and a Londoner on the preeminence of their respective cities. The spy was John Thurloe, whom Susan Wiseman argues had a hand in the drama ("'History Digested,'" 191–193).

162. Harbage, *Davenant,* 126–128; Aubrey, *Brief Lives,* 88. Aubrey credits Davenant with bringing "scenes" into fashion as opposed to having "only a Hanging" (88). This period of license came to an end when Richard Cromwell had him arrested and imprisoned for putting on performances "called Opera, acted, to the scandal of Religion and Government" (Harbage, *Davenant,* 136–137). This sudden change argues for Milton's earlier intervention, since by this time he had lost much of his prior influence; as he told a correspondent, "my influential friends are very few (since I stay nearly always at home—and willingly)" (*CPW,* 7: 507).

163. Davenant, *Proposition,* 11, 14. See Jacob and Raylor, "Opera and Obedience," which views Davenant's scheme and Cavendish's advice to Charles (discussed in Chapter 1) as attempts to formulate a "practical Hobbism" (205). As they point out, the entertainments that Davenant ended up putting on did not realize his aims since (due to a lack of state sponsorship) they were too expensive to reach a wide audience.

164. Spragens, *Politics of Motion;* Hobbes, *Leviathan,* 13 (1.2).

165. Davenant, *Gondibert,* 30–31.

166. See Chapter 3 and the introduction to this volume.

167. For Hobbes's conversion, see Aubrey, *Brief Lives,* 150 (on the encouragement he took from the absence of "sects" in geometry, see Shapin and Schaffer, *Leviathan and the Air-Pump,* 328). For Boyle's account of his conversion experience, see *Account of Philaretus* in Michael Hunter, *Boyle by Himself,* 15–17. See discussion in J. R. Jacob, *Robert Boyle,* 9, 38–42; Rattansi notes that it recapitulates a similar event in Luther's biography ("Intellectual Origins," 134). Shapin and Schaffer discuss the contrast between the two philosophers' conversion experiences in *Leviathan and the Air-Pump,* 318–319.

168. See Shapin and Schaffer, *Leviathan and the Air-Pump,* esp. chapters 1 and 4.

169. See Kahn, *Wayward Contracts.* For an account of the poem as a "Hobbesian deliberation on the artificiality of civil life" (169), see Kroll, *Restoration Drama,* chapter 5.

170. Marvell, *Rehearsal Transpros'd,* in *Prose Works,* 1: 94. See 156 for the sort of passage Marvell is criticizing, and 158–160 for his mockery of efforts to establish a "Universal Language."

171. *Certain Verses,* 4.

172. See part 4 of the *Leviathan,* "Of the Kingdome of Darknesse," esp. chapter 47.

173. Quoted in Harbage, *Davenant,* 23.

174. These statements are excuses for lateness rather than invitations to posterity to carry on his unfinished labors: the work of a "wise Poet" proceeds from "Vigilance and labour," and he cannot "shew his strengths" until they are "in exact government and order" (22). However, the poem was in fact continued a century later by William Thompson, whose *Gondibert and Birtha, A Tragedy* wraps up the plot by permitting Gondibert and Birtha to marry; "Rhodolinda" commits suicide after her attempt to poison Birtha (now merely the "Daughter of a poor Physitian") misfires (336).

175. Cowley, *Poems,* sig. b3ᵛ. On Boyle's approval of Cowley, see note 21 above. Four out of the projected twelve books were published in this 1656 volume, Cowley declaring in the preface that he lacked the *"Appetite* at present to finish the work" (sig. b2). On the "programmatic" nature of both Davenant and Cowley's projects, see Helgerson, *Self-Crowned Laureates,* 220–221.

176. Cowley, *Poems,* sigs. b2ᵛ–b3. He strikes a remarkably millenarian tone here, predicting that the conversion of the Jews and the reformation of poetry will usher in the *"Kingdom of Christ"* (sig. b2ᵛ).

177. Davenant, *Gondibert,* 1.1.46 (see 1.4.27); 3.2.64; 1.1.5 (references are to book, canto, and stanza number). Davenant had set one of his first plays, *The Tragedie of Albovine, King of the Lombards,* in Lombardy, and spread rumors about having a Lombard origin, which were further complicated by his simultaneous claim to being the natural son of Shakespeare. Both were understood as attempts to spruce up humble origins as the son of a vintner. Contemporary satirists mocked his connection to the Lombard Street in Whitefriars, a red-light district where debtors sought safety from the law; references to Lombardy or Lumber are scattered throughout the satirical encomiums to his epic (e.g., *Certain Verses,* 15); see Nethercot, *D'Avenant,* 9–10.

178. Davenant, *Gondibert,* 2.2.66–67; 2.1.44; 2.2.12; see also 2.7.48.

179. The effect may result from his frustration at not being able to write for the stage; it is as if, throughout the poem, he is both putting on a play and trying to direct it (Quint, however, suggests that the real model for this work was aristocratic prose romance; see *Epic and Empire,* 316–317). Kroll observes that the poem is hampered by its "self-reflexive obsession" with "second-order questions" explored in the preface (*Restoration Drama,* 171).

180. *Certain Verses,* 6.

181. Just as the lady Rhodalind's wooers in the corrupt world of Lombardy want to gain her hand only for the political power it confers, so those who woo Birtha are "Hoping for secrets now in Nature's Court" (2.7.13). Despite being a worker in this experimental collective, she is a disruptive presence within it; a "sooty *Chymist,*" seeing her "passing by, / Broke his lov'd Lymbick, through enamour'd haste" (2.7.12). When she falls in love with Gondibert, something similar happens to her: "since he came, my medc'nal Huswiffrie, / Confections, and my Stills, are all forgot" (2.8.14).

182. The word appears at 2.6.22; see *Certain Verses,* 18, 21, 22, 24. He is also mocked for his Baconian use of *Experienc'd* as a term of praise—see 24.

183. Marvell, *Rehearsal Transpros'd,* in *Prose Works,* 1: 201. Perhaps Marvell enjoyed the homophone of *praise* and *prays,* but he also calls attention to the lines in which the power of praise is compared to gunpowder that destroys kingly palaces (2.6.87).

184. Davenant, *Gondibert,* 2.6.53; John Rogers, *Matter of Revolution,* 42. Davenant may be alluding to Pliny's *Natural History* 35: 65, in which the illusion associated with the birds fooled by painted grapes is less powerful than the spectacle of an artist duped by a feigned curtain (9: 310–311).

185. Davenant, *Gondibert,* 2.6.60. Davenant does not use Marvell's punning orthography, which increases the likelihood that Marvell intended to mock the sensory muddle Davenant created here

186. The pointed fusion of sensory modalities at the end of *Last Instructions* could not be more different. Helgerson discusses the poem's anxious grasping after recent discoveries in *Self-Crowned Laureates,* 212–213.

187. The echoes with the texts explored earlier in the chapter will be clear, but this may allude to Donne's *First Anniversarie,* where man, "Loth to goe up the hill, or labor thus / To goe to heaven, we make heaven come to us" (lines 281–282). Telescopes as long as forty-eight feet were common; even telescopes 200-feet-long were tried, in an effort to solve the problem of spherical aberration; see "Glass," in Singer, *History of Technology,* 3: 232–233.

188. However, some books in Astragon's library meet a kinder fate than those of "Truth's Tormentors."

189. Gilman, *Curious Perspective,* 48–49.

190. Compare "the Courts cheap Glasse of outward showe" (2.4.26).

191. "Sir Peter Pett's Notes on Boyle," in Michael Hunter, *Boyle by Himself,* 69.

192. This according to his widow Elizabeth; see Newton's edition of *Paradise Lost,* 1: lvi; see also Samuel Johnson, *Lives of the English Poets,* 1: 275. For Boyle's admiration of Cowley, see note 21 above.

6. Milton and the Paradizable Reader

1. On Milton's lack of sympathy with the *felix culpa* tradition, see Diane McColley's *Gust for Paradise,* esp. 154–159, from which my argument drew much of its inspiration, as well as Danielson, *Milton's Good God,* and Kaufman, *Paradise in the Age of Milton.* Catherine Gimelli Martin's *Ruins of Allegory* argues powerfully for Milton's "liberation of Edenic emblems from their traditional isolation and stasis" (258); see also Low, *Georgic Revolution,* 319–320.

2. "Adam Unparadiz'd" replaced "Adams Banishment," a change that enacts the migration of paradise from place; see French, "Chips from Milton's Workshop," 234.

3. *CPW,* 2: 327. See also 253, 309 ("in some proportion," "in proportion as things now are") and 240, 245. This pamphlet exploits the word *ingenuous* to muddle the distinction between pre- and postlapsarian states, even while acknowledging the difficulty of closing the gap between them; thus the "ingenuous" (239, 249, 252, 286) understand the original, and therefore the true, purpose of matrimony: to gratify an "intellectuall and innocent desire" (269).

4. *CPW,* 2: 250, 328.

5. Eachard, *Grounds and Occasions,* sigs. A4–A4ᵛ. In this respect Milton resembles Lilburne, who, as Schenk observes, made "everything that happened to him into a public event" (*Social Justice,* 22). On the word *occasion* in Milton, see

Radzinowicz, *Toward Samson Agonistes,* 167–170. On occasional reflections see Chapters 1 and 4.

6. See *CPW,* 2: 142–143, 223–226, 418, 479.

7. *Samson Agonistes* (hereafter *SA*), line 1716.

8. *PL,* 12.587. Sommerville, "Conscience, Law, and Things Indifferent," offers a useful overview of the debate over *adiaphora.* For the classic statement of its relevance to Milton, see Fish, "Things and Actions Indifferent." Milton's position was straightforward: "what more free then *indifferency?*" (*CPW,* 1: 585; see also 2: 228). In "Allegory" and *Machiavellian Rhetoric* Kahn argues that Milton enlarges the sphere of indifference in order to expand the realm of interpretive freedom, associated, for Kahn, less with the collective construction of fact than with indeterminacy and rhetorical ambivalence. Although Kahn contends that such indeterminacy characterizes both pre- and postlapsarian states, she still credits Milton with upholding a firm distinction between these states (but see *Machiavellian Rhetoric,* 225).

9. Fish, *Surprised by Sin,* 107. Fish's argument that the reader is "forced to come to terms with his tendency to remake everything in his own sinful image" (104) informs the whole book, but see esp. 100–107. As Kerrigan observes, Fish's approach introduces "a new and unheard-of flaw in the poem: the alarming idea that its mythopoesis is not generative but repetitive," producing a "duplication of discursive meaning" as "tyrannical" as it is endless (*Sacred Complex,* 99); see also Norbrook, *Writing the English Republic,* 437.

10. *PL,* 4.625. Ricks devotes much of *Milton's Grand Style* to expounding usage in which, as he puts it, "the evil meaning is consciously and ominously excluded." He suggests that our only alternative to a proleptic reading of these moments is to imagine that Milton became "strangely absent-minded" or "forgetful" of the connotations of words like *error* while writing about paradise, but I think Milton gives his readers more options than that (110–111). The provocative word choices are also discussed in Stein, *Answerable Style,* 66–67.

11. For the indignation that the apparent discrepancy between title and matter aroused in early readers, see Huttar, "The Passion of Christ," and Wittreich, *Milton's Paradise Regained,* 1. The absence of any extended treatment of the crucifixion in Milton's corpus has been widely noted, but see Hanford and Taaffe, *Milton Handbook,* 115, 194; Christopher, *Science of the Saints,* 223; John Rogers, "Milton and the Heretical Priesthood of Christ"; Wittreich, *Angel of Apocalypse,* 103–146, 233; Rumrich, "Milton's Arianism," and *Milton Unbound,* 67.

12. *PL,* 11.818, 890.

13. I borrow the concept of scoring out from line 15 of Marvell's *Last Instructions* (see Chapter 5 in this volume). I have benefited from a discussion with Abigail Heald about poetry and narrative responsibility.

14. Hutchinson, *Order and Disorder,* 5 ("Preface"). Thus the teasing exchange between God and Adam that leads to the creation of Milton's Eve is replaced with the flat statement, "whether he begged a mate is not known"; Milton's suggestion that Eden's plants grew "promiscuously" offers another instance of the dangers of seeking truth "from men's inventive brains" (3.312, 141, 158).

15. Milton's contempt for this practice is indicated by his mockery of so-called marginal Prynne—"whom ye may know by his wits lying ever beside him in the margent" (*CPW,* 7: 294; see also 1: 910, 945, and Lamont, *Marginal Prynne,* 6).

16. "On Mr. Milton's Paradise Lost," lines 20, 10. See Gross, "'Pardon Me, Mighty Poet'"; for another incisive account of the poem, see McWilliams, "Marvell and Milton's Literary Friendship." Expressing the same anxiety, Defoe complained that the "dull authority, call'd *poetic Licence . . .* will not pass in so solemn an affair as that"; either "we must forbear to give up to Mr. *Milton,* or must set aside part of the sacred Text, in such a manner, as will assist some people to set it all aside" (*History of the Devil,* 74, 73).

17. Hence the decision to incorporate Marvell's dissenting murmur into the project. On how Marvell enacts a model of readerly liberty for us by emphasizing his own personal reading experience and evolving judgment, see Achinstein, *Literature and Dissent,* 174–181.

18. *CPW,* 1: 951.

19. Samuel Johnson, *Lives of the Poets,* 1: 287; Leavis, "Milton's Verse," 50; Eliot, *On Poetry and Poets,* 152.

20. *PL,* 3.55, 12.9; *CPW,* 2: 403.

21. Catherine Gimelli Martin calls Milton "the most Baconian poet of the seventeenth century" in "'What If the Sun,'" 231. Long before the recent explosion of interest in Milton and science, critics associated him with Bacon; see Heron (i.e., Pinkerton), *Letters of Literature,* 72. Although this chapter is concerned with Milton and experimentalism (a term I have extended to experimental Christianity) rather than Milton and science as such, I have benefited from the wealth of studies on that subject. Svendsen's argument in *Milton and Science* that Milton was backward-looking was persuasively challenged by Marjara, *Contemplation of Created Things,* which documents *PL*'s engagement with a wide range of contemporary scientific debates. Subsequent work in this area has largely focused on Milton's ideas about matter, which I engage only incidentally as they relate to a constructivist orientation toward creation. Stephen Fallon's *Milton among the Philosophers* describes Milton's ontology as "a hybrid amalgam of Hobbesian materialism, Galenic-Aristotelian pneumatism, and Aristotelian hylomorphism" (134), and John Rogers's *Matter of Revolution* stresses

the specifically political valences of Milton's representations of matter. More recently, Duran's *Age of Milton* explores the influence of experimentalism as a specifically pedagogical movement, and Karen Edwards's *Milton and the Natural World* addresses Milton's rejection of the emblematic tradition and exploration of the new descriptive possibilities opened up by Baconian natural philosophy. Particular debts to these works will be noted below. William Poole's "Milton and Science" objects to the assumption that Milton would have found the outlook of Gresham congenial, but his suggestion that after the Restoration Milton would have been in sympathy with Stubbe is unconvincing. Even if one were to accept James Jacob's argument in *Henry Stubbe* that Stubbe was merely pretending to be a reactionary defender of orthodoxy (as Poole does), it seems unlikely that Milton would have seen through (or approved of) the ruse. Nonetheless, it is worth stressing that Milton's attraction to the new science was not that of an aspiring virtuoso; experimentalism attracted him as an ideology and as a model of intellectual labor. This did not stop him from occasionally adopting the rhetoric of a natural investigator; see, for example, *CPW*, 2: 507.

22. *CPW*, 4: 614; Masson, *Life*, 1: 566; Lewalski, *Life*, 55. In this passage Milton specifically distinguishes these trips into the city from book-purchasing jaunts. Haak, the driving force behind the philosophical club at Gresham (who would later translate parts of *PL* into German) was a friend; see Hill, "Milton and Marvell," 22.

23. Given this postulate, it follows that one must "inglobe, or incube" this shape, to make it more "squat" (*CPW*, 1: 790–791).

24. Quoted in Lewalski, *Life*, 341. Masson suggests that their friendship dated back to 1646 or 1647 and that by the 1650s she was his most beloved friend; see Masson, *Life*, 3: 658–660; 5: 229–235; 6: 455–458. Long after he surrendered the young Richard Jones to Oldenburg's care, Milton continued to send the young man hectoring letters urging him to display "zeal and indus-try" after the example of "that most excellent woman your mother" (*CPW*, 7: 489).

25. Beale in a letter to Evelyn, quoted and discussed in von Maltzahn, "Laureate, Republican," 183, 186. Milton seems to have discouraged him through the "Friendly conveiyance" of Evelyn (187). See also von Maltzahn's "Royal Society," where he elaborates the context around Royal Society printer James Allestry's publication of Milton's *History of Great Britain,* and the first chapter of Duran, *Age of Milton.*

26. Hill famously describes Milton as "more sociable and clubbable than is often thought" in *Milton and the English Revolution,* 9. Dobranski builds on this assessment in "Where Men of Differing Judgments Crowd," where he suggests Milton was a frequenter of coffeehouses.

27. *CPW,* 1: 240, 244–245, 241, 246–247, 245. His fourth prolusion, against the resolution of substance to first matter, consists largely of ironic complaints about the stupidity of the assignment (1: 249–256).

28. See the Introduction to this volume.

29. *CPW,* 1: 890.

30. *CPW,* 1: 292, 295–296; Rajan, "Simple, Sensuous, and Passionate," 291.

31. *CPW,* 2: 363, 366, 364, 366–369.

32. *Discreet* and *discrete* were often spelled identically. Milton may be describing an expansion of the scope of priestly knowledge since the term was conventionally applied to ecclesiastics (*OED,* def. C).

33. *CPW,* 2: 406, 393–394, 413, 412.

34. *CPW,* 2: 390, 394.

35. *CPW,* 2: 372, 374, 373, 375.

36. *CPW,* 2: 376; *PL,* 3.548–549. The phrase "this World" appears in lines 543 and 554, while line 527 tells us that he is "Just o're" paradise.

37. Bacon, *Works,* 6: 646–648, 720–722; *CPW,* 2: 376, 403. On the association of Orpheus with poetry and the arts that compel matter, see Peter Thomas, "Henry Vaughan, Orpheus, and the Empowerment of Poetry."

38. *CPW,* 1: 522, 520; 2: 379.

39. *CPW,* 1: 874; 2: 412–413. Aubrey agreed that "Young men do much want airing"; his pupils would also "travel at several times over all England," making notes on rock formations as well as "botanics" (*Aubrey on Education,* 35).

40. *CPW,* 2: 385, 415, 551.

41. *CPW,* 2: 492. At one point Milton even tries to imagine himself joining the fray using his pen as a weapon: taking credit for the death of Salmasius, he boasts that he met him "in single combat and plunged into his reviling throat this pen, the weapon of his own choice" (4: 556). A discursive act unites absolutely with a physical one, but the vehicle outstrips the tenor altogether.

42. "Il Penseroso," lines 165, 169, 168, 170–174. For another account of this passage, see Duran, *Age of Milton,* 50–52.

43. *OED* def. 2, 2b. Fish makes the typically reflexive argument that it is just such laborious decipherment that the poem enjoins the reader to undertake ("What It's Like to Read," 131). The *OED* suggests a figurative and poetic meaning of *spell* as "to engage in study or contemplation *of* something" (def. 2, II 6b) but offers this line as the first such usage.

44. *OED* def. 1. In "A Book was writ," customers gazing at the title page of *Tetrachordon* "Stand spelling fals," trying to pronounce the difficult title out loud (line 7).

45. *CPW,* 1: 819, 820.

46. The Elysian fields of "L'Allegro" entomb a sleeping Orpheus and a very different "paradisal" image; Orpheus is woken on a bed of flowers by music in which he hears only the failure of his own (lines 145–150). L'Allegro's deficiencies as an observer are elucidated in Fish's "What It's Like to Read." His illiteracy in the natural world, in particular, is indicated by the famous Sweet-Briar/Eglantine confusion at lines 47–48, which, from a Baconian perspective, tallies with his pastoral effacement of labor (lines 63–74).

47. *PL*, 3.54–55; "Il Penseroso," line 176. On the contemporary association of melancholy with intellectual pursuits, see Klibansky, Panofsky, and Saxl, *Saturn and Melancholy*.

48. Other commentators have asserted a connection between this scene and the end of "Il Penseroso": see esp. Bedford, "Right Spelling." The Puritan attack on festival was examined in Chapter 1 as a positive rather than a purely negative campaign; on festival ideology see above all Marcus, *Politics of Mirth*. While Milton had no interest in legislating traditional pastimes out of existence, he found it "a horror to think" that "men should bee pluck't from their soberest and saddest thoughts . . . instigated by publique Edict, and with earnest indeavour push't forward to gaming, jigging, wassailing, and mixt dancing" (*CPW*, 1: 589). In *A Maske*, The Lady's tendentious substitution of *chastity* for *charity* at line 215 (along with her speech in favor of redistributive justice at lines 765–779) aligns the former virtue with the spirit of resistance to seasonal charity as defenders of festival constructed it.

49. *Maske*, lines 172, 179, 177. Line numbers are from the 1645 version.

50. *Maske*, lines 613, 102–104, 808.

51. *Maske*, lines 73, 77, 76, 619–628.

52. *Maske*, lines 710, 714.

53. *Maske*, lines 629–630, 638. For references, see Adams, "Reading Comus," which comes out strongly against identifying haemony with grace. In "Milton's Haemony," Steadman identifies the herb with knowledge; see also Hunt, "Managing Spenser," 326–330.

54. It is essential, therefore, that the herb does not work as a fetish or mechanically efficacious charm; it must be supplemented by a skilled hand: the hands of Sabrina, whose gifts to the locals include working knowledge, healing arts that are the object of occasional (hence innocent) rural celebration (847–849). It is possible that the shepherds merely take the occasion of traditional festivals to "Carrol her goodnes lowd in rustick layes," but the substance of their celebration is occasional; and its style is temperate, like that of the *"victorious dance / O're sensual Folly, and Intemperance"* that concludes the masque itself (lines 974–975).

55. *Maske,* line 687. The opening dance that plunges the revelers into the menstrual emissions of a "Dragon woom" that "makes one blot of all the ayr" clearly identifies cyclical time (the "swift round" of "Months and Years") with aborted enlightenment (lines 131–133, 114).

56. *CPW,* 7: 460. The academy was originally the garden outside Athens where Plato taught; when Milton refers to "a spatious house and ground about it fit for an *Academy*" in *Of Education* he is perhaps evoking this garden (2: 379). For the patristic notion of paradise as a school, see Jager, *Tempter's Voice,* 26–27.

57. *Lycidas,* line 119. On the phrase's association with "blind bellies," see Kaminski, "Striving with Vergil." In the flower catalogue, itself an autocritique of "lean and flashy" poesy associated with "false surmise," the image reappears in pastoral code as "quaint enameld eyes" that "suck" (lines 123, 153, 139–140). In Milton, *quaint* is associated not only with fussy ornateness but with backwardness: see, for example, stanza 21 in the Nativity Ode and *PL,* 9.35. On the poem's countervailing apocalpytic vision, see Lieb, " 'Yet Once More.' "

58. See *CPW,* 1: 812 and note 79 there.

59. *CPW,* 1: 520–522.

60. *CPW,* 1: 549.

61. *CPW,* 1: 822. For similar sentiments, see Defoe, *Compleat English Gentleman,* 201.

62. *CPW,* 1: 784. See, for example, 1: 616, 819; 2: 491, 547.

63. *CPW,* 2: 543, 557. For "spiritfull exercise," see 2: 274.

64. *CPW,* 1: 664, 670. It might be objected that Milton invokes "strong and sinewy force" in the course of defending the satiric style of his own pamphlet, but he goes on to identify Smectymnuus's "Satyr" with a "liberty of speaking" that delivers the "full insight" associated with the perspective glass— offering "an Anatomie of the shiest, and tenderest particular truths" (669–670).

65. *CPW,* 1: 871, 788. *Schism* was of course a contested term throughout these decades; at stake was precisely the question of what sort of behavior was conductive to the unity of the mystical body. For some, that unity was already achieved by ritual means; for cultivators of the public sphere, it was a goal toward which to work.

66. *CPW,* 1: 569–570. Here as elsewhere scripture does not simply speak for itself; it is an instrument that needs to be "weilded and manag'd" by a skilled user (1: 699).

67. Winstanley, *Works,* 468.

68. Title page; see appendix C in *CPW,* 2: 800–807.

69. Cleveland, *Rustick Rampant,* 10; Boyle, *Examen of Mr. T Hobbs,* in *Works,* 3: 164.

70. *CPW,* 2: 550. Compare Beale's declaration that "all those who call themselves reformed, must ere long bee reformed, and bee newe-modelled before wee bee fit to call in the nations" (quoted in Charles Webster, *Great Instauration,* 15).

71. Thus he heaps scorn on ministers that refuse to move beyond Hercules's pillars (identified with "a warm benefice"); see *CPW,* 2: 546.

72. *CPW,* 2: 554, 559.

73. Johns, *Nature of the Book,* 264.

74. *CPW,* 2: 538. That Milton never met Galileo at all is possible, since it is unclear why he would wait until writing *Areopagitica* to mention it. The debate is summarized in *CPW,* 2: 538n180. The veracity of Milton's account has no real bearing on the issue of Galileo's symbolic importance to Milton.

75. *CPW,* 2: 549. On the control that licensers exerted over texts under Laud's regime and the efforts of the Long Parliament to exert comparable control over printed material, see Peacey, *Politicians and Pamphleteers,* chapter 4.

76. Title page reproduced in *CPW,* 2: 485; Lilburne, *Declaration of Some Proceedings,* 25.

77. Lilburne did the same. In *England's Birth-Right Justified,* addressed to *"all the Free-borne People of* ENGLAND" as his *"Fellow-Commons,"* Lilburne might even be said to appeal to the people *as* Parliament (sig. 1v). It can be assumed that Milton found the Levellers sympathetic; he was invited to attack the Levellers by the Council of State and never did (Hill, *Milton and the English Revolution,* 102). He did write approvingly of the Parliament's courteous reception of petitioners ranging from "the meanest artizans and labourers" to women (*CPW,* 1: 926). As Zaret shows in *Origins of Democratic Culture,* petitioning in the period became a means for the public to address itself, not just Parliament.

78. *CPW,* 2: 554, 535.

79. *CPW,* 2: 488, 493. "[P]rivate persons" become "publick men" from pages 2 to 4 of the original edition.

80. See Woods, "'That Freedom of Discussion Which I Loved,'" 14–15.

81. William Harrison, *Description of England,* 114–115; Joseph Hall, *Quo Vadis,* 533, quoted in Benet, "Escape from Rome," 33. The notion that a visit to Italy precipitated a descent into effeminate idolatry was still current in the eighteenth century; Thomas Newton remarked that "our modern travelers . . . go out boys, and return such as we see, but such as I do not choose to name." Milton, in contrast, made his tour the occasion for "exercise and improvement" ("Life of Milton" prefixed to his edition of *PL,* 1.viii–ix).

82. O'Connell, "Milton and the Art of Italy," 217. Jonathan Richardson was struck by Milton's apparent insensibility: "He does not appear to have Much Regarded what was done with the Pencil; no not even when in *Italy,* in *Rome,* in

the *Vatican*. Neither does it seem Sculpture was Much Esteem'd by him" (Darbishire, *Early Lives*, 212).

83. I adopt Woods's translation ("'That Freedom of Discussion Which I Loved'"). On the Italian academies as a model of paradise, see Haan, "From *Academia* to *Amicitia*," 4–6, 64. (Nardo, in contrast, suggests the academic discussions Milton witnessed in Italy were the model for those of the fallen angels in hell, "in wandring mazes lost"; see "Academic Interludes," 218–220.)

84. *CPW*, 2: 527, 514, 561. Note how Milton introduces the concept of "play" to the negative image of winds in Ephesians 4:14.

85. *CPW*, 1: 809. A select few, including Milton's, were selected for performance; see Haan's "From *Academia* to *Amicitia*," 19–22. On Milton's probable election, see 12–15.

86. Shapin and Schaffer, *Leviathan and the Air-Pump*, 58.

87. *Lycidas*, line 193. Dobranski observes that Milton's Italian recollections are described entirely in terms of the people he met rather than the places he saw (*Milton, Authorship, and the Book Trade*, 69). Dustin Griffin articulates the suspicion of many readers when he remarks that "Milton was primarily delighted with the academies because he had spent much of his youth in solitary study"; he goes on to suggest that "upon his return home he could not expect to find or construct an English equivalent," yet Milton created an imaginative equivalent in his portrait of the English public ("Milton in Italy," 24).

88. Haan, "From *Academia* to *Amicitia*," 35–36, 43–44. On Dati and Galileo, see also Arthos, *Milton and the Italian Cities*, 40–41. Milton may also have met Galileo through his son Vincenzo; see Haan, "From *Academia* to *Amicitia*," 44.

89. See Freedberg, *Eye of the Lynx*, and Eamon, *Science and the Secrets of Nature*, 229–233, 285, 292. On the link between the spotted lynxes of Milton's poem and the academy, see Haan, "From *Academia* to *Amicitia*," 162–163. Wren remarked on the belief that "only to succeeding Lyncei is it granted to add to the discoveries of Galileo" (quoted in van Helden, "Telescopes and Authority," 15); Milton was making his bid. Giovanni Battista Manso was the head of the Neapolitan Accademia degli Oziosi, with whose members Milton may have mingled (Masson, *Life*, 1: 815). Lewalski suggests that Milton also attended meetings of the Florentine Academy, whose discussions covered Galileo's findings as well as Torricelli's experiments (*Life*, 91–92).

90. Dati quoted in Haan, "From *Academia* to *Amicitia*," 46, 50. Haan discusses the parallel with Milton's *Contra Philosophiam Scholasticam*, and a possible nod to Galileo, at 48–50.

91. *CPW*, 2: 538; 1: 810. Haan observes that Milton's experience in the Italian academies "strengthened his belief in the validity of the *vernacular* as a

medium," paradoxically confirming his identity as an English author ("From *Academia* to *Amicitia*," 168).

92. *CPW,* 1: 819. *Discreet* binds the public to the ideal of the priesthood of believers (see note 32 above).

93. *CPW,* 2: 532, 531, 554, 548.

94. *CPW,* 1: 809; 2: 554.

95. *CPW,* 2: 554, 555, 550–551. On the crucial distinction between unity and uniformity in this tract, see David Loewenstein, *Milton and the Drama of History,* 48–49. For another instance of "brotherly" contentions, see 1: 781.

96. *CPW,* 2: 549–550, 553. Norbrook remarks on the "uncharacteristic ritualism" of the famous declaration that "a good Booke is the pretious life-blood of a master spirit, imbalm'd and treasur'd up on purpose to a life beyond life" (2: 493) in *Writing the English Republic,* 122. Here, all the clichés associated with the Immortal body of the sovereign attach to the mystery of authorial presence sustained by print.

97. Perkins, *Warning against Idolatrie,* 107–108.

98. Wittreich's *Shifting Contexts* explores the multiple uses to which the figure of Samsonian England was put in the period. On Samson as a symbol of the good old cause, see Achinstein, *Literature and Dissent,* 113. On Milton's strategic use of Samson in the prose, see Radzinowicz, *Toward Samson Agonistes,* 74–83. See also Hill, *Milton and the English Revolution,* 428–431.

99. Gray, "Severed Hair," 221.

100. *PL,* 4.301–303; *CPW,* 1: 858–859. Adam's locks are of course "manly"; Eve's are famously unruly, which accords with her more private nature (see below). Our introduction to Adam and Eve as appendages to their hair looks ahead to the comparison of the couple to Samson (9.1059–1063).

101. I am working with Lupton's suggestion that Samson's hair in *SA* figures at once "the order of a well-regulated people" and the "energy of the unruly multitude," an observation with relevance to this passage, which is revived in the final simile of the play; but while Lupton identifies the laboring multitude with a prepolitical state, I suggest that the multitude becomes a sovereign public by being put to work; see *Citizen-Saints,* 201. Of course, Samson's hair was allegorized as almost everything; Bishop Jewel declared that "We are *Samson,* the strength of our haires is the knowledge of the will of GOD" (*A Viewe,* 184), while in Burgess, *Treatise of Original Sin,* 91, it is original sin.

102. On Samson's hair as a figure of nonhierarchical organization, see John Rogers, "Secret."

103. See *Additional Discourse* by the Parliamentarian officer Robert Norwood.

104. Perkins, *Treatise of the Vocations,* 5; for the discussion of Samson's vocation, see 9. Samson and Adam are also paired in Robert Harris, *Brief Discourse,* 20.

105. Yule adduces this source in "The Word 'Muing'"; see L. C. Martin's response "'Muing Her Mighty Youth.'"

106. Haan, "From *Academia* to *Amicitia,*" 123. See note 89 above.

107. Calvin's *Institutes of the Christian Religion,* 1.5.12, quoted in Lees-Jeffries, "From the Fountain," 152.

108. I have benefited from Amanda Goldstein's insights into these birds.

109. Ingenuity pervades the pamphlet: see 2: 521, 531, 551.

110. Glanvill, *Vanity of Dogmatizing,* sig. B2 (see also 9).

111. God tends "to dispense and deal out by degrees his beam, so as our earthly eyes may best sustain it" (566).

112. *CPW,* 2: 512, 514, 515. Milton may have associated Galileo and Aretino as daring moderns; Galileo was known to appreciate the pornographer (Reeves, *Painting the Heavens,* 251n35).

113. *CPW,* 2: 527. Indeed, this construction is reformed as soon as it is made, since virtue bred in ignorance is an immaturity of vice rather than a victory over it—"a youngling . . . a blank vertue, not a pure" (515–516).

114. *CPW,* 2: 521, 496. Milton specifically calls this ability an "art" in the latter passage, and his language here blends culinary and metallurgical arts together.

115. As earlier chapters have shown, the commanding gerund-stream is a signature of experimentalist style.

116. *CPW,* 3: 232; 1: 787–788.

117. *CPW,* 3: 601, 342, 601. See also 3: 339: "the blockish vulgar." But see Norbrook, *Writing the English Republic,* 205. On the difficulty of extirpating the "royal image," see Sharpe, *Remapping Early Modern England,* 223–265.

118. *CPW,* 3: 347, 601.

119. *CPW,* 7: 457, 462, 427; 3: 347. See Ezekiel 37. However, see Norbrook's analysis of the optimistic undercurrent of this passage (*Writing the English Republic,* 414–415, 420).

120. The liberty he defends is consistently the "Liberty [that] consists in manly and honest labours" (*CPW,* 1: 588). John Rogers argues that disappointment in "the masses" turned a defender of popular sovereignty into an apologist for rule by a "revolutionary elite" in *Matter of Revolution,* 109–110. Norbrook points out that Milton presents his proposals as "merely a short-term expedience while the crisis defers other possibilities" (*Writing the English Republic,* 421): as Milton puts it, a permanent constitutional solution "may be referrd to time, so we be still going on by degrees to perfection" (7: 444). On the subordination of

constitutional matters to "civil life" in Milton's thought, see Worden, *Literature and Politics,* 161–165.

121. *CPW,* 7: 460.

122. For more on this passage, see Tabor, *Things Unutterable* and McDannell and Lang, *Heaven,* 34n26. Contemporaries explicitly linked Milton's motto to his blindness; see French, *Life Records,* 4: 118–119.

123. *CPW,* 4: 589–590, 587–588; 2: 557.

124. *CPW,* 4: 589; see Eamon, *Science and the Secrets of Nature,* 285.

125. For example, those for whom worship ends in the "customary ey-Service of the body" only have their eyes on things, yet idolators are unable to see "things themselves" (1: 520, 788; see also 850).

126. See Dobranski's exploration of this theme in *Milton, Authorship, and the Book Trade,* 33.

127. *PL,* 1.288.

128. As Patterson observes, the poem's allusions to Galileo "are meant to form a sequence, establishing the astronomer's paradigm as one inseparable from the poem's own development" ("Imagining New Worlds," 259). See also Julia Walker, "Milton and Galileo," 111. The critical literature on the poem's treatment of Galileo is sufficiently vast to render exhaustive citation pointless, but I have been particularly influenced by these two sources and Herz, "'For whom this Glorious Sight?'"

129. Nicolson, "Milton and the Telescope."

130. Since Curry's exploration of Chaos in *Milton's Ontology,* there has been a steady stream of critical treatments of Chaos exploring its association with matter as encountered in the created world. I have particularly benefited from Adams, "A Little Look into Chaos," and Schwartz, "Milton's Hostile Chaos"; although I do not experience Chaos as an enemy force in the way she suggests, her argument at least registers the extremity of Milton's experiment here. In the final chapter of *Milton Unbound,* Rumrich offers an illuminating account of the relationship of Chaos to contingency and indeterminacy, which characterizes life in Eden as well. Catherine Gimelli Martin eloquently relates Chaos to the period between the Copernican revolution and the rise of Newtonianism when "the profound instability of matter provides a powerful source of both expanded speculation and expanded doubt" (*Ruins of Allegory,* 83–84). On Chaos as a psychic state, see Arnold Teskey, *Delirious Milton,* chapter 4. On how Milton's treatment of Chaos departs from earlier commentaries on Genesis, see Arnold Williams, *Common Expositor,* 46–52. For the political dimension of Chaos, see below.

131. *PL,* 5.472. On the new philosophy's challenging of place, see Koyré, *From the Closed World to the Infinite Universe;* Whitman, "Losing a Position";

Nicolson, *Breaking of the Circle;* and Catherine Gimelli Martin, *Ruins of Allegory* (esp. 92–93). The metaphysical challenge gained moral reinforcement from the belief that "it is a practise very idolatrous, to bind adoration to any particular thing, or to any particular place" (Perkins, *Warning against Idolatrie,* 28).

132. Bacon, *Works,* 5: 132.

133. Charles Gildon, "To Mr. T. S.," in Timothy Miller, ed., *The Critical Response,* 35. In this passage, Gildon asserts that Milton would never have been "capable" of these speculations "had he not been altogether depriv'd of his *Outward Sight.*" Even while directing us toward some such understanding, however, Milton also affirms the ability of his insight to penetrate the still-cherished sensuous world—a remarkable balancing act that experimentalism made possible.

134. Samuel Johnson, *Lives of the Poets,* 1: 287.

135. Leavis, "Milton's Verse," 50; see Eliot's "Milton I" (in *On Poetry and Poets,* 138–145); in "Milton II" Eliot suggests that the Civil War should be held responsible rather than Milton himself (*On Poetry and Poets,* 152–153).

136. See Carey and Fowler's edition of the poems, 447.

137. See *PL,* 4.410 and 1.210 and Carey and Fowler's edition of the poems, 431, 434. The reader's constructive labor is the counterpart to the "artificial" quality of secondary epic identified by Lewis in *Preface to Paradise Lost,* 58–60.

138. Grossman's *Authors to Themselves* explores "semantic deferral as narrative form" (ix) in the poem from a different but, I think, complementary perspective.

139. Fletcher, *Allegory,* 279–303.

140. Quoted in Freedberg, *The Power of Images,* 185.

141. Scarry, *Dreaming by the Book,* 77–88.

142. *PL,* 4.590. The beam enables Milton to avoid the awkward task of representing the angel taking off by flapping his wings. In *Spectator* 321 Addison complained that the "Device . . . seems below the Genius of *Milton*" (3: 174). Heron took Addison to task for not being even more critical of this "tinsel" (*Letters of Literature,* 424). Hume was more admiring; anticipating Scarry, he compares the device to Homer's use of the shooting star to suggest the flashing of Achilles's armor when he is motion (*Annotations,* 152–153).

143. Bentley, *Milton's "Paradise Lost,"* 126.

144. See chapter 5 of Collins, *Mind's Eye,* esp. 107–109.

145. He presents his unrhymed verse as an example for a future taken from the past, of liberty restored; the frame he imposes on the poem's formal features is clearly intended to shape our reception of its matter.

146. *PL,* 1.4. In "The Opening," Daiches notes the parenthetical treatment of Eden's loss, seeing a "dark irony" in Milton's apparent casualness; I suggest that Milton challenges us to take this casualness at face value.

147. See Herman, "*Paradise Lost,* the Miltonic 'Or,' and the Poetics of Incertitude." When *or* becomes *and* at 1.17, we land in Milton. The phrase "place of rest" comes from 12.647.

148. Chaos is the matter of paradise in a psychological as well as a physical sense, since, as Teskey puts it, Chaos is "the presence of choices before any choice is made . . . every situation that is left to develop on its own without our decisive intervention" (*Delirious Milton,* 82, 85).

149. *PL,* 8.447–448. I refer to Adam's lengthy criticism of God's handiwork when he finds himself without a mate: "Thus farr to try thee, *Adam,* I was pleas'd'; God explains that he "Knew it not good for Man to be alone," and brought Adam into the garden alone "for trial onely" (8.437, 445, 447).

150. God relates the inner light to "My Umpire *Conscience*" (3.195). As Frye observes, "The heaven of *Paradise Lost,* with God the supreme sovereign and the angels in a state of unquestioning obedience to his will, can only be set up on earth inside the individual's mind. The free man's mind is a dictatorship of reason obeyed by the will without argument: we go wrong only when we take these conceptions of kingship and service of freedom as *social* models" (*Return of Eden,* 111). Collectively extending this internal dictatorship to the matter of the world requires a continual struggle; the only other time "Umpire" appears in the poem it describes Chaos (2.907).

151. I am quoting from *Of Education* (*CPW,* 2: 373); see the first section of this chapter.

152. As Guillory observes, the promise contained in the invocation's puns on *revisit* ("to go to see again") is fulfilled in the "re-versing, re-seeing" that takes place in the second half of the invocation (*Poetic Authority,* 121, 126).

153. Hume, *Annotations,* 100. Hume offers this observation in support of a reckless textual emendation (changing *blanc* to a more appropriately dark *blot*). See Leonard's discussion in *Naming in Paradise,* 70.

154. Kerrigan suggests that, by resisting the temptation of "respectable arguments depreciating physical seeing" that were readily available to him, Milton resisted the common defense against loss (devaluing the object), instead affirming the value of the phenomenal world in *Sacred Complex,* 132–133. Experimentalism deserves some credit for this psychological achievement; see note 133 above.

155. The word appears in Book 9 more often than in other book. Benign uses of the word are rare: 8.258 and 11.845.

156. *PL,* 9.706–708. For the experimentalist contrast between Eve's "degustation" and Adamic production, see Chapter 3.

157. I have benefited here from a conversation with Zena Meadowsong.

158. With "flowrie Brooks," the poem adjusts its preferred spelling, *flour,* to blend floral substance with the river's flow, reiterated in the following line: "warbling flow."

159. *PL,* 3.46–47; Hooke, *Micrographia,* sig. a2ᵛ; see Chapter 3 in this volume. Thomas Peyton's *Glasse of Time* also invokes Urania (sig. A3ᵛ, 4): God, in turn, is her "inspiror" (3)—but even Urania has to be told "be not bold to pry" into God's "secrets" or she will find herself, like Adam and Eve, naked (51–52). Milton's humility, in contrast, does not extend to the source of his inspiration. Peyton also identifies the "wandring minds of curious men" as a result of the fall (34).

160. Power, *Experimental Philosophy,* sig. c2ᵛ; see Chapter 3 in this volume.

161. Defoe, *History of the Devil,* 73, 72. Yet Defoe set great store by dreams as a source of premonitions and divine advice: "when any Notice for Good, or Warning against Evil, is given us in a Dream, I think 'tis no Arrogance at all for us to say, the Angel of the Lord appear'd to us in a Dream (*Vision of the Angelick World,* 16, in *Serious Reflections,* second pagination).

162. Adelman, "Creation and the Place of the Poet," 57.

163. Marvell, *Last Instructions,* line 949; see Chapter 5 in this volume. It is worth noting that, for Milton, *art,* like *descry,* certainly evoked the graphic sense; as Freedberg has shown in *Eye of the Lynx,* the Linceans, like Hooke, regarded illustration as a crucial instrument of knowledge production. In the 1630s, the cultural tourist who deliberately sought out Galileo might well have seen the lunar engravings made by Claude Mellan using Galileo's very own telescope. In Mellan's engraving, the silver disk becomes truly three-dimensional and palpable, like Satan's shield: ponderous, large, and massy, and yet "Ethereal," looming out of "darkness visible." James Grantham Turner points out to me that in an engraving, it is literally true that darkness creates visibility. On illustration as a medium for philosophical discussion, see also Albert van Helden, "Galileo and Scheiner on Sunspots." On the significance of Galileo's use of the words *arte* and *artista,* see Arthos, *Milton and the Italian Cities,* 45n12. Milton may have used the telescope in the garden of Duke of Salviati's villa, which overlooked Fiesole; Dati enjoyed entertaining visitors with the sight of mountains on the moon (see Arthos, *Milton and the Italian Cities,* 40n58).

164. Milton may have been interested in the challenge to Mariolatry posed by the maculate moon, on which see Reeves, *Painting the Heavens,* chapter 4. The woman in Revelation 12:1–4 with the moon at her feet was long identified as the virgin, the moon an emblem of her purity; hence Milton's association of "Heav'ns Queen and Mother" with the "mooned *Ashtaroth*" in the Nativity Ode, lines 200–202.

165. See Herz, "'For Whom this Glorious Sight?'" 149–150. For recent rehabilitations of the so-called Romantic Satan, see Gross, "Satan," and Forsyth, *Satanic Epic,* esp. chapter 2, which explores the relationship of Satan and narration in the opening books.

166. Though his frame of reference is considerably more cosmopolitan, Milton follows Hooke's procedure in *Micrographia* (see Chapter 2 in this volume). As Marjara argues, the image of the moon through glass "is not drawn from everyday experience, but needs to be mentally visualized by readers. Unless the readers are familiar with Galileo's astronomical observations, they will not register the full impact of the image" (*Contemplation of Created Things,* 61–62).

167. *PL,* 1.292–294. See chapter 5. As Helgerson points out, there is also an echo of Cowley's description of Satan's spear in *Davideis* (see *Self-Crowned Laureates,* 234): "His *Spear* the *Trunk* was of a lofty *Tree,* / Which *Nature* meant some tall *ships Mast* should be" (3.394–395).

168. See Collins, *Mind's Eye,* chapter 6.

169. *PL,* 1.63. Further complicating matters is the apparent contradiction between this line and lines 181–183; for an energetic rationalization of the discrepancy, see Jonathan Richardson, *Explanatory Notes,* 21–22.

170. *PL,* 1.201. The metaphor was dismissed by Eliot as "so much extraneous matter" in a passage he later omitted from "Milton II," as Ricks informs us in *Milton's Grand Style,* 6n1.

171. *PL,* 1.227–228. This introduces a further complication, as Milton asks his reader to accept the idea of solid as well as liquid fire (1.229).

172. Thomas Browne, *Works,* 4: 279.

173. Satan exposes his familiarity with Hobbes at 2.19–24, 30–36. Contemporary attacks on Hobbes often figured him as the Leviathan; see Mintz, *Hunting of Leviathan.* It is also possible that Milton was inspired by an event Aubrey describes in his *Miscellanies:* "A little before the Death of Oliver Protector, a Whale came into the River Thames and was taken at Greenwich . . .'Tis said, Oliver was troubled at it" (*Three Prose Works,* 27).

174. Catherine Gimelli Martin remarks that by evoking "a form of sovereign power far superior to that of mere mortals," Job 41:1–4 offered a "warrant for interpreting leviathan not as a mythical *opponent* of divine power but as an exemplum of human weakness and a 'vehicle' for its correction" ("Phoenix," 249). See also Joan Bennett, "Asserting Eternal Providence," 224–225. On Satan as tyrant, see Bennett's analysis of the portrayal of Satan as a "royal portrait," analogous to that undertaken in *Eikonoklastes,* in *Reviving Liberty,* 33–58; for Cromwellian parallels, see Robert Thomas Fallon, *Divided Empire,* 62–71.

175. *PL,* 1.795, 2.391. For "Synod," see also 6.156. Milton refers to the fallen angels as Satan's *peers* in a richly ambiguous sense in the first book; by the second, it is clearly being used by the angels themselves as a title of office; see 1.39, 618, 757, and 2.119, 445; for more particular political references, see Norbrook, *Writing the English Republic,* 452–455. For London as papal Rome, see Thomas Hall, *Funebria Florae,* sig. A2ᵛ; on Pride's Purge and Hell, see Jennings, *Anecdotal History,* 7. Karen Edwards suggests that the smokiness of Pandemonium evokes the London of Evelyn's *Fumifugum* (*Milton and the Natural World,* 194–195).

176. Defoe, *History of the Devil,* 71.

177. *PL,* 2.163–164, 223–224, 169. Ricks discusses Belial's "appalling jauntiness" in *Force of Poetry,* 78.

178. *PL,* 1.501–502, 498, 497, 494–495. See Chapter 2.

179. *PL,* 4.193. Belial gets the longest description in the catalogue of devils. William Hunter argues that Belial was a late insertion, introduced after "the new public moral standards" introduced by the Restoration had become evident to the public ("Belial's Presence," 8). See also Flannagan, "Belial and 'Effeminate Slackness.'"

180. Bradley, *Nosce te Ipsum,* 31–32; *Light Shining,* in Winstanley, *Works,* 614. See also *CPW,* 1: 893; 2: 225.

181. See James Grantham Turner, *Libertines and Radicals,* 153; Thomas Hall, *Funebria Florae,* 4, title page; Robert Harris, *Brief Discourse,* 22, 21.

182. *CPW,* 2: 528.

183. This phrase occurs seventeen times in the *Leviathan;* see Spragens, *Politics of Motion.* Lieb describes how Belial "invokes the world of Chaos" in *Dialectics of Creation,* 21–22.

184. Koyré, *From the Closed World to the Infinite Universe.*

185. John Rogers, *Matter of Revolution,* 109, 131. In God's infusion of "vital warmth" into Chaos Rogers sees an attempt to subsume the foundations of Hobbesianism, though he finds the effort riddled with ambivalence and doubt, due to the "dregs" (132–143).

186. *PL,* 2.226–227. On "private opinion," see esp. Hobbes, *Leviathan,* 453 (3.42). On the "biological inertia" of Hobbesian agents, who share some features of scooting atoms of Lucretius, see Spragens, *Politics of Motion.*

187. Curry, *Milton's Ontology,* 81–82.

188. Hutchinson, *Order and Disorder,* 1.21, 127.

189. Hutchinson, *Order and Disorder* (Preface), 3, 4 and note. Her opinions on Lucretius are discussed in Barbour, "Between Atoms and Spirit." Hutchinson thus avoided what Kerrigan calls the "peculiarly modern obligation" Milton imposed on himself: to be "responsible to the nature of things as well as to the

meaning of Christian history," joining Lucretius to the tradition of Christian epic (*Sacred Complex*, 195).

190. *CPW*, 2: 515; *PL*, 9.341, 336. So Joan Bennett observes in *Reviving Liberty*, 115; see 94–118 on the separation scene in relation to problems of collective agency.

191. Galileo, *The Assayer*, in Matthews, *Scientific Background*, 59. He has just claimed that if "ears, tongues, and noses be taken away, the number, shape, and motion of bodies would remain, but not their tastes, sounds, and odors" (59). The absence of eyes in the first list, and color in the second, is glaring (a list just before this one included both). It is also strategic, given the form of sight he goes on to celebrate.

192. Galileo, *The Assayer*, in Matthews, *Scientific Background*, 61.

193. Milton's own account will retrace the progression, from "vital warmth" to a light filling vast spaces (7.236).

194. Charleton insisted that the "Matter of Bodies is not idle and unactive, as most have dreamt, but uncessantly operative; and that, not by impression, but *Inhaerency*" (*Darknes of Atheism*, 308).

195. Hooke, *Posthumous Works*, 343; see Chapter 3 in this volume.

196. Catherine Gimelli Martin, *Ruins of Allegory*, 75, 27, 72. At 71–72, Martin persuasively relates this mode of vision to Eve's understanding of the fruit; see also Grossman, *Authors to Themselves*, 109 110 and 189–193. In chapter 8 of *Machiavellian Rhetoric*, Kahn associates this episode with a reifying mode of perception that precludes real engagement with the external world; see esp. 216–218.

197. *PL*, 10.312–313.

198. Stephen Fallon, *Milton among the Philosophers*, 182; 2.667. See also Ferry, *Milton's Epic Voice*, chapter 5. If we accept that heavenly events played out in more or less the way Raphael explains them (as 5.574–576 might seem to encourage us to do), then Satan first felt pain during the battle, not during the migraine caused by Sin's supposed birth; as a psychological projection she is reflecting back to him, even as she fables, the pain of rebellion (6.327, 2.752). But the association of rebellion and imagination is even deeper than that, since the war in heaven itself seems a "wild work" of imagination, which, like Satanic imitation, is "tediously parodic," marking the distance between "Milton's poetics and the concept of imagination" (Guillory, *Poetic Authority*, 111). As readers often notice, the phrase "wild work" applies to both the war and Eve's dream (5.112, 6.698). See also Stein, "Milton's War in Heaven."

199. Catherine Gimelli Martin offers a reading of the Paradise of Fools as a satire on the "'superstitious' Ptolemaic cosmos" in "'What If the Sun'"; see esp. 256–261.

200. Addison singled out Satan's "falling into a Cloud of Nitre" for special praise as a specimen of probable description in *Spectator* 309 (3: 120–121).

201. Lucretius, *De Rerum Natura,* 2.62–66; see Clucas, "Poetic Atomism."

202. Lucretius, *De Rerum Natura,* 5.259; *PL,* 2.911, 897, 900, 905, 901–907. It is suggestive that in Lucretius's poem this phrase, as Teskey observes, refers to the earth itself (*Delirious Milton,* 76).

203. *PL,* 1.598–599. See Joan Bennett's discussion of this passage as an attack on the "warped analogical reasoning" characterizing Charles I's own use of the royalist sun symbol (*Reviving Liberty,* 37). Milton is also opportunizing the "sad presage" of the eclipse that occurred the day Charles II was born, and disabling the Christological interpretation Dryden foisted on it to promote sacerdotal kingship; see discussion in Leonard, *Naming in Paradise,* 113–114.

204. As Marvell would suggest through his use of the "bold Tube" in *Last Instructions* (see chapter 5). In *Of Reformation* Milton had mocked those who read "portentous" signs of political developments in the heavens; he, in contrast, consulted the facts on the ground—the actual results of state policies (1: 585). For similar sentiments, see Evelyn's *Diary,* 3: 63, upheld by the 1652 broadsheet *On Bugbear Black-Monday, March 29, 1652. Or, The London-Fright at the Eclipse proceeding from a Natural Cause.*

205. See Lucretius, *De Rerum Natura,* 2.1–332, esp. 216–224 and 288–293, and Don Fowler, *Lucretius on Atomic Motion.*

206. *PL,* 2.989, 1038, 1034–1035, 3.10–12. See Ricks's analysis of the relationship between the end of Book Two and the start of Book Three in *Force of Poetry,* 72–77. While Satan is "prone in flight" as he "Sailes between worlds and worlds," Milton is, as he says to God, "led by thee" (5.266, 268, 7.12). As the analogy between the fallen angels and fallen leaves suggests, they are detached from a life-giving source; but, in his effort to open this physical and cognitive wilderness to exploration, Milton is employing a visual faculty that was "planted" in him by God. Satan benefits from the healing beam of the sun that "sharp'nd his visual ray," but Milton is "Illumin[ed]" by celestial light; and while Satan finds the sun "beyond expression bright," Milton gives expression to that brightness in his inspired art of testimonial, which employs all the latest "arts"— arts that enable him, like the Son, God's "effectual might," to raise paradise in "the wast Wilderness" (3.620, 1.23, 3.591, 170; *PR,* 1.7).

207. Blith, *English Improver Improved,* 3–4. See Diane McColley, *Gust for Paradise,* 85. In *Doctrine and Discipline of Divorce,* Milton had related Chaos to his effort to exert control over his matrimonial life, celebrating divorce as a reenactment of God's first creative act, "the first and last of all his visible works; when by his divorcing command the world first rose out of Chaos, nor can be renew'd again out of confusion but by the separating of unmeet consorts": God's

creative orientation with respect to matter is replicated in Milton's own dissatisfaction with Mary Powell. And in his very first prolusion, he had imagined sight,
the "noblest of the senses," as a property of the "light of the world's eye," without
which there would be no "means of staying the lapse of all things into the
primeval Chaos" (*CPW*, 2: 273; 1: 229–230).

208. *PL*, 3.374, 2.900, 896–897, 922–924. For Milton, forms were
themselves material; see *CPW*, 6: 308.

209. See Chapter 3, note 135. Quint explores the poem's acceptance of "the
contingency that conditions human freedom" in relation to republican thought,
which "creates a space that is *for practical purposes* open-ended" in *Epic and Empire*,
301–302; see also Catherine Gimelli Martin, *Ruins of Allegory*, 44. Norbrook
suggests that by associating Chaos with political disorder, Milton "arouses expectations of a baldly anti-republican reading only to frustrate them": identified with "a
cosmic civil war in which there is as yet no complete resolution," Chaos "highlights
a basic radicalism in the poem, a desire to go back to the simplest components and
start again" (*Writing the English Republic*, 472; see also 491).

210. Boyle, *Works*, 5: 61 (see Chapter 4 in this volume).

211. "'For Whom This Glorious Sight?'" 156. See also Catherine Gimelli
Martin, "'What If the Sun,'" 252. More "anxious" accounts include Guillory,
Poetic Authority, 156–161, and Donald Friedman, "Galileo."

212. *PL*, 2.1048, 3.76; see Charleton, *Physiologia*, 6, and Chapter 3 in this
volume.

213. See, for example, 4.592–596.

214. On Eve's relationship to experience, see the following section.

215. John Phillips justified his own disregard for his uncle's enemy by
pointing out that Salmasius "made use of trite Instances, as that of the Government of Bees, & such like to prove the preeminency of Monarchy" (Darbishire,
Early Lives, 27).

216. For many Hartlibians, this actually did make the beehive a plausibly
modern model for society because of its status as a dynamic—and productive—
system of free but united agents that "work with one consent." See Appelbaum,
Literature and Utopian Politics, 118–121, and, on the reformed use of analogy in
relation to bees and ants, Karen Edwards, *Milton and the Natural World*, 128–138.

217. *PL*, 4.239, 629, and 9.211. In *PL*, however, the only spokesman for this
doctrine is Satan; see 2.16.

218. In *Milton's Burden*, Haskin pillories the reflexive assumption that Adam
and Eve are "always already fallen" (184–189). Haskin's larger argument recovers
interpretive ambiguity for innocent existence; I will be treating Psyche's "incessant
labour" as knowledge production rather than hermeneutics, but these activities are
obviously not separable.

219. *PL*, 4.325; Bentley, *Milton's Paradise Lost*, 118–119.

220. *PL*, 4.631, 628, 9.211. Wildness is insistently paired with Chaos (see lines 541, 588, 910, 951, 1014 in Book Two alone) and the productions of fancy (e.g., 5.112; paradisal plants are themselves called "Fancies . . . Wilde above Rule or Art" at 5.296–297; for "Subjection," see 4.308). See chapter 7 of Haskin's *Milton's Burden*, esp. 223–224, and Rumrich's account of the connections between Eve's excess, the chaotic womb, and Eden in the last two chapters of *Milton Unbound*.

221. *PL*, 4.625, 9.212, 209. Ricks argues that *luxuriant* and *luxurious* cannot be distinguished in paradise, but the first couple is not tolerant of either one; his comparison of the garden's wanton growth to Herrick's "cleanly-wantonesse" is one I believe Milton would resent (*Milton's Grand Style*, 111–112). Those who populate Herrick's world are urged to participate in that wantonness; Adam and Eve display their innocence by exerting themselves as a countervailing force against it. As Diane McColley argues so powerfully in *Gust for Paradise*, they are artists and Eden is their material.

222. As Addison remarked in *Spectator* 273, these are not "Strangers": "the principal Actors in this Poem are not only our Progenitors, but our Representatives" (2: 565). He distinguishes these representatives from "indifferent Persons," but of course what makes them representative, for Milton, is their capacity to personate undifferentiated humanity.

223. Dalila tries to excuse her perfidy by blaming her "Curiosity, inquisitive, importune / Of secrets" (*SA*, lines 775–776); in *PR* Satan first appears to the Son as a country yokel "curious" about "What happ'ns new" in the world, in order to tempt Christ into a demonstration of his power (1.333–334).

224. *PL*, 9.392.

225. See Grant McColley, "Milton's Dialogue," for the evidence that Milton depended much more heavily on Wilkins and Ross than he did on Galileo. McColley's Milton is sympathetic to Ross, but I support Lewalski's claim that this scene is itself a prototype of Galileo's *Dialogue* (*Rhetoric of Literary Forms*, 46–50). As Fowler points out in his edition of the poem, most of the absurdities of astronomical theory Raphael satirizes in this episode are pre-Keplerian.

226. *PL*, 7.91–93, 96–97. Adam's philosophical labors are continuous with prayer, which in the physico-theological religion of paradise, is made up of descriptive praise of God's works.

227. *PL*, 5.438; Hume, *Annotations*, 183. See Grossman's analysis in *Authors to Themselves*, 104–112. John King argues for a parodic understanding of the passage in "Miltonic Transubstantiation."

228. See *OED* (defs. I, II, 7; and III), and Chapter 2; Evelyn, *Acetaria*, 146, quoted in Frances Harris, *Transformations*, 25.

229. *PL*, 7.126, 5.508–512; Salkeld, *Treatise of Paradise*, 120.

230. Schwartz argues that Milton imagines a "transubstantiating universe . . . only to bar us from it in the end. With the disobedient Adam, we are exiled from the paradisal communion," and "Real Presence" becomes "Real Hunger" (*Sacramental Poetics*, 63, 69–70). In her reading, Milton "places the cosmic communion in the lost paradise, and it will only be recovered at the end of time," yet even in paradise, the unity of divinity and humanity is anticipated, not achieved; it is a goal toward which to work (69).

231. Rumrich, *Milton Unbound*, 122.

232. Locke, *Reasonableness*, 277.

233. *Coffee-houses Vindicated*, 4. See Chapter 4 in this volume.

234. *PL*, 7.41; *CPW*, 1: 819. At 8.648–649 Adam supports Milton's assessment, calling Raphael's "condescension" "affable": both easy to be spoken to and easy of speech.

235. Luxon observes that it is this exchange that dominates our virtual experience of paradise, extending from 5.360 to the end of Book 8, and posing a pointed contrast to the two most substantive exchanges Adam has with Eve, about her disturbing dream (5.28–128) and the wisdom of separation (9.205–403); see *Single Imperfection*, 149.

236. Rather than a glutting of the sensitive body, insatiety describes an expansion of its capacities.

237. For example, Adam is given no firm grasp of the sense in which the war in heaven actually happened, given the doctrine of accommodation spelled out at 5.570–574, which seems to be retracted in the following two lines; the interpretive dilemma that results becomes our problem as well (see note 198 above). And, of course, Adam finds much of the categorical instruction he does receive debatable (8.595–613). As Lewalski suggests, Raphael's refusal to provide certain answers on his own "angelic authority" is precisely what enables him to provide Adam (and us) with "a model for scientific inquiry" (*Rhetoric of Literary Forms*, 46).

238. *PL*, 5.452–455, 459. This is the only occurrence of *conference* in the poem: the devils' deliberations are referred to as Parliamentary or ecclesiastical gatherings or consults; the word evokes celebrations of "good conference" discussed in Chapters 1 and 4.

239. *PL*, 8.273–282. He addresses the sun, of course, for the lack of any other interlocutor, but as Quint remarks, Adam does not make the mistake of identifying it as God; he addresses it as a fellow creature (*Epic and Empire*, 288). Eve, in contrast, does not feel herself to be "constitutively lonely" at all when she is first created (Luxon, *Single Imperfection*, 147).

240. Bradley, *Nosce te Ipsum*, 36.

241. *PL*, 4.506. See the analogies to Samson (9.1059–1064) and the laborer (12.629–632). Milton is evoking what Appelbaum calls the "utopia of industriousness" based on "cooperative, collective, and 'experimental' behavior" envisioned decades before in Platte's *Macaria:* "Well, I am imparadised in my minde, in thinking that England may bee made happy, with such expedition and facility" (14); see discussion in *Literature and Utopian Politics,* 123–124.

242. *PL*, 4.629; Sprat, *History,* 85.

243. *PL*, 8.499. Before the fall, Adam's "Bone of my Bone, Flesh of my Flesh, my Self" is thus supplemented by "And they shall be one Flesh, one Heart, one Soule" (8.495, 499), but when Adam feels "The Link of Nature draw" him to eat the fruit, "Flesh of Flesh, / Bone of my Bone" stands without a spiritualizing phrase (9.914–915).

244. Samuel Johnson, *Lives of the Poets,* 1: 290. The state of innocence "comprises neither human actions nor human manners"; Johnson doubts whether "in our present misery, it be possible to conceive" of it (289, 288). The conviction that Adam lacks humanity is a variation on the idea that he is a "child-man" rather than an adult; Damrosch shows how the poem's rejection of this notion ensures that the fall cannot be regarded as a "fall into consciousness" in *God's Plot,* 111–114.

245. See Froula, "When Eve Reads Milton"; Guillory, "Milton, Narcissism, Gender"; and Kerrigan and Braden, "Milton's Coy Eve."

246. As Nyquist argues in "Genesis of Gendered Subjectivity," Eve has "an intimately subjective sense of self," is "associated in a distinctive manner with . . . interiority," and is "almost quintessentially, 'private'" (119). From the reader's perspective, her naming of the flowers never acquires "the precise status of an event" (100).

247. Christopher, *Milton and the Science of the Saints,* 216–217; Winstanley, *Works,* 377.

248. *PL*, 8.460–461, 464, 567–568. Luxon points out that Milton makes it impossible to determine how much Eve overhears of this exchange; see *Single Imperfection,* 153–154. This haziness enhances a symbolic understanding of her exclusion; the private person is virtually removed, held in abeyance, or repressed, but never wholly expunged from the scene of public discussion.

249. As Teskey puts it, Adam sees Eve as "a visible thing that is also an illusion" (*Delirious Milton,* 109).

250. Karen Edwards, *Milton and the Natural World,* 20–21.

251. Rumrich makes quick work of Fish's portrayal of her as a "budding empiricist" during the temptation scene in *Milton Unbound,* 13.

252. On Eve's idolatrous relationship to the fruit, see Catherine Gimelli Martin, *Ruins of Allegory,* 71–72, and Grossman, *Authors to Themselves,* 109–110 and 189–193.

253. *PL*, 9.336. *Trial* is the key word of this debate; see 9.316, 366, 370, 380.

254. *PL*, 5.98, 90, 88, 7.556. This is a literal flight of fancy. Eve's account of her dream borrows from the discourse surrounding the "night-flying" of the witches' Sabbath, right down to Satan's manifestation as a toad, whose shamanistic resonances resulted from the psychotropic properties of toad secretions and the toad mushroom (see Ginzburg, *Ecstasies,* 303–307). The scene thus resonates with the description of the Night-Hag dancing with "*Lapland* Witches" at 2.662–666. As Ginzburg explains, the dreams of women who participated in this ritual were characterized by orgasmic flight and sexual unions with the devil. Anti-Catholic polemic related these imagined flights to fictitious spaces like purgatory (*Ecstasies,* 100, 137–138). That said, it is abundantly clear that, as Wittreich argues, Milton radically deviates from the Eve/Satan typology—which, as he shows, Dryden worked hard to restore in *The State of Innocence;* see "Milton's Transgressive Maneuvers," 248–250. See also Diane McColley's argument that Eve's dream enables her to "experience evil without doing evil" ("Eve's Dream," 28).

255. *PL*, 5.112, 6.698, 9.212. The link between flowers and cultivated vision, which makes the opening of flowers optically suggestive as well, is explored below.

256. Scarry, *Dreaming by the Book,* 40–71, 158–192.

257. See, for example, George Gascoigne's 1573 collection *A Hundreth Sundrie Flowres bounde up in one small poesie;* Herbert, "The Flower," line 39.

258. *PL*, 5.296. The sweetness that the garden pours forth in this line is specifically identified with the imagination: "Virgin Fancies," matter requiring subjection.

259. *PL*, 4.259–260. On the participation of the motor centers in the production of mental imagery, see Collins, *Poetics of the Mind's Eye,* esp. 92–100.

260. The truism that we are restricted to viewing the garden through Satan's eyes is challenged by Ferry, *Milton's Epic Voice,* 52.

261. So Bentley: "*Juppiter* from a Person chang'd into the *Element, Pater Aether impregning the Clouds?* So *Adam* smil'd upon *Eve,* no otherwise than as the *Aether* smiles upon a Cloud. Is not this *Ixion's* Deception, a *Cloud* instead of *Juno?* And then the Clouds, that shed *May-flours?*" (*Milton's Paradise Lost,* 124). Bentley refers to the false Hera Zeus made out of a cloud to fool her attempted seducer Ixion (*Iliad* 14.346–351), whose position is occupied here by Satan, not the reader.

262. *PL*, 4.764. I refer to the topos of paradise as Adam's "workhouse," discussed in Chapter 1; on butterflies as petals, see Scarry, *Dreaming by the Book,* 91, 235.

263. On Aretino and *PL,* see James Grantham Turner, *One Flesh,* 248–249.

264. *PL*, 4.763, 3.52–53. A fuller account of Milton's presentation of this scene would address the supplementary role of radiant ignition.

265. *PL*, 4.311. On the concept of a Puritan art of love, see Haller, "Puritan Art of Love," and James Grantham Turner, *One Flesh*, 73.

266. Through this flower catalogue, Lycidas's flower-strewn coffin becomes Evelyn's "parsly bed" of paradise, and pastoral verse becomes georgic.

267. *PL*, 4.311; Luxon, *Single Imperfection*, 137.

268. *PL*, 8.593–594. Raphael alludes to the *Doctrine and Discipline of Divorce*, where Milton dismisses the suggestion that 1 Corinthians 7:9 refers to the "meer goad of a sensitive desire": "God does not principally take care for such cattel"—rubbish or trash, but also, perhaps, cattle (*CPW*, 2: 251).

269. As Grossman suggests, "we see Adam and Eve not simply acting in accordance with their natures but rather continually creating those natures" (*Authors to Themselves*, 68–69). Grossman is interested in the individual as a potential author of history; although my interest is in the magnified, public self, I believe that my account of the poem is consistent with his.

270. There are thirty-four occurrences of *flour* or *flours*, as compared to five of *flowr* or *flowers* (and none of *flower* at all), and seven occurences of *flourie* as opposed to one of *flowrie*, discussed above. In *Lycidas* and *SA*, flowers are put to very different uses, associated with idolatrous funeral decoration and Dalilan temptation, and *flower* is the dominant spelling.

271. *PL*, 9.425–427. Kristen Poole observes that Eve "almost appears to be wearing the roses" (*Radical Religion*, 176). Poole argues that Milton's incessant covering of the first couple suggests "the inaccessibility of paradise," not its accessibility through cultivated perception (181).

272. *CPW*, 2: 251, 255, 251.

273. *CPW*, 2: 249.

274. On the continuity of Chaos with the garden, see Rumrich, *Milton Unbound*, 132–133.

275. For a discussion of the scene of intercession that has made this moment possible (11.14–44), see John Rogers, "Milton and the Heretical Priesthood." David Loewenstein points out that Adam's reeducation begins with the same laborious ascent that begins the attempt to "repair the ruins of our first parents" in *Of Education* (*Milton and the Drama of History*, 95); Coiro takes note of the parallel in "To Repair the Ruins," which reads the final two books as a darkly parodic rewriting of that treatise.

276. *CPW*, 1: 566. L'Estrange had actually accused Milton of being the author of *Eye-Salve*, "a medicine of the same Composition, which (by general report) strook *Milton* Blind" (*Physician Cure Thy Selfe*, 2). See Lewalski, *Life*, 380.

277. To look through history is to cultivate a historical consciousness, which, as David Loewenstein argues in *Milton and the Drama of History*, is a

continual process of "casting down imaginations" and the traditions with which they are intertwined.

278. *PL,* 11.818, 890. On the dispersal of heroism in Milton's epic, see Norbrook, *Writing the English Republic,* chapter 10. In *Spectator* 327, Addison saw the model of the one just man in Abdiel, remarking that Milton "doubtless, designed it [Abdiel's character] as a Pattern to those who live among Mankind in their present State of Degeneracy and Corruption" (3: 204). As Satan was progressively degraded to bestial status, Abdiel was thrust forward as a figure of sublime singularity, a sort of "artificial help" or methodone for readers addicted to individual heroism—but now his character is dispersed across a series of people. On "Satan and the technique of degradation," see Waldock, *"Paradise Lost" and Its Critics,* chapter 4, esp. 80–87.

279. For Enoch, see 11.700–705.

280. Such porousness anticipates the "all in all" world subject at the end of time, as the poet's own voice does; see, for example, when the song of the angelic chorus seems to become "my Song," which it is (3.413).

281. *PL,* 12.609–625. The spillage of *mee* and *thee* is most pronounced at 614–617, but it is sustained through satellite words like *receav'd, sleep, dreams, seed, Eve,* and Adam's being "Well pleas'd." I refer to Eve's final speech as an exchange, but Adam's contribution is nonverbal; in this moment, a reformed Eve speaks for both of them—cultivating her capacity as a public person, predicated on her incorporation with Adam—and he is pleased.

282. I have benefited from talking with Johnny Hernandez about this point.

283. Gombrich quoted in Owens, "Feminism and Postmodernism," 7.

284. As I suggested above, Milton's labors were not solitary at all. In addition to the collaborations made necessary by his blindness, Milton himself distended into a corporate subject, "male and female," in the process of creation, as suggested by his demand to be *"milkd"* by his amanuenses (Darbishire, *Early Lives,* 33).

285. *PL,* 8.343–354; see also 8.272–273. Raphael's account of the creation dispenses with the event in a single line: "And thou thir Natures know'st, & gav'st them Names, / Needlest [i.e., needless] to thee repeated" (7.493–494), though he makes reference to Adam naming the birds at 6.73–76. Leonard offers an enlightening discussion of the contrast between the sense of abundance in Raphael's account of the creation in Book Seven and the orderly "two by two" procession of Genesis 2:19, which would seem to exclude the "broad Herds." Although there are indications that Raphael is not referring exclusively to the first week of creation, the sense remains that there is just too much to fit into this scene, especially given the Baconian necessity for "calling" to encompass

commanding; as he points out, the snake appears before Eve "uncall'd" at 9.523 (*Naming in Paradise*, 263–265, 273). For Leonard's final, expansive word on all that is involved in naming "experimentally," see 291–292; this virtually requires that Genesis 2:19 be presented as "a comparatively unimportant affair" (32).

286. Rabisha, *Adam Unvailed*, 96.

287. Weber, *Protestant Ethic*, 88.

288. Karen Edwards, *Milton and the Natural World*, 193.

289. *PL*, 4.117. I have benefited from discussion with Richard Johnston on this point.

290. Deleuze and Guattari, *Kafka*, 9, 95n12. To claim Milton as a "minor" author is merely to acknowledge his major poetry as an expression of nonconformist culture (Keeble, *Literary Culture*, 1–24).

291. The great exception is the "flowry valley" passage (4.586–595), but it is swiftly followed by another statement of indifference: "Wandring the Wilderness, whatever place, / Habit, or state, or motion, still expressing / The Son of God"; it is "by vanquishing / Temptation" that the Son has "regain'd lost Paradise" (4.600–602, 607–608).

292. Ellwood, *History of the Life of Thomas Ellwood*, 246–247. I see no reason to disbelieve Ellwood's account: French observes in this connection that no outline of *PR* appears in the Trinity manuscript ("Chips from Milton's Workshop," 242).

293. *PR*, 4.600, 1.192; George Fox, *Journal*, 1, 6, 27. *Seek* looms large throughout the poem, but see esp. 1.335–336, and for the open-ended teleology of such seeking, 2.245–246. The term *seeker* had a broad scope; see Jonathan Scott, *England's Troubles*, 241, and Watts, *Dissenters*, 184–186. For a suggestive discussion of *PR*'s relationship to Quaker thought, see Steven Marx, "Prophet Disarmed."

294. Of course, he had already taken steps to prevent its reification within *PL* by subjecting Galileo's telescope to a floral transformation. Milton is really seeing through Ellwood's misreading of the poem. Duran offers a different account of Satan's use of this technology in *Age of Milton*, 258–261.

295. *PR*, 4.40. The "aerie jaunt" reprises Milton's own flight through matter in the Chaos episode, and the "specular Mount" recalls the "top / Of Speculation" where Adam witnessed the pageant of history (4.402, 236; *PL*, 12.588–589). Nicolson's suggestion that Milton was extrapolating from "vague accounts of the new instrument" of the microscope and "misunderstood its function" seems to me extremely unlikely ("Milton and the Telescope," 11). Svendsen found a possible source in Leonard and Thomas Digges' *Geometrical Practical Treatise;* see his "Milton's Aerie Microscope." I think the reader's primary sense is that the

two technologies Milton had used for the purposes of magnification are now being fused into one misused tool.

296. Fish, "Things and Actions Indifferent."

297. *PR*, 4.572–573; Romans 8:14. "But as many as received him, to them gave he power to become the sons of God" (John 1:12). On "the glorious liberty of the Sons of God," see Nayler, *Possession*, 6, 15. Lewalski discusses the Son's lack of separation from the rest of creation in *Milton's Brief Epic*, 145–148; see also her comments on the significance of Hercules in this simile at 231–232, 241. Samuel's "Regaining of Paradise" also addresses the inclusive character of the Son.

298. Indeed, as Leonard observes, the word had not appeared in Milton's verse since 1646 (*Naming in Paradise*, 103–104). That Milton makes reference to the tragedy *Christ Suffering* in the prefatory note to *SA* makes the word's absence in the poem before it all the more striking; see Knoppers, *Historicizing Milton*, 36.

299. See note 11 above.

300. The pronominal confusion is at line 583; it caused Charles Dunster to "grieve" (Wittreich, *Milton's Paradise Regained*, 260, second pagination). In arguing that the double syntax that unites Satan and the Son might be read straight, I am merely unpacking Frye's suggestion that the poem is a "parody of a dragon-killing romance, or, more accurately, it presents the reality of which the dragon-killing romance is a parody": the threat represented by Satan cannot be represented by—restricted to—a figure named Satan ("Agon and Logos," 136). By the same token, the Messiah cannot be conceived of in the third person singular.

301. *PR*, 4.390, 372. The Son—whom Satan promises to make "a King compleat / Within thy self" will "to pieces dash / All Monarchies" (4.283–284, 149–150).

302. Of course, Satan associates the fire with God's ire. Here Milton's well-known critique of responses to the poem, immortalized by Defoe, is relevant: "Well, I see the Reason plainly, why this Book is not liked so well as the other, for I am sure it is the better Poem of the two, but People have not the same Gust of Pleasure at the regaining Paradise, as they have Concern at the loss of it, and therefore they do not relish this so well as they did the other, tho' it be without Comparison the best Performance." It is precisely our "Concern" in losing paradise, and regaining it through a kingly Christ, that provides the false "Gust of Pleasure" so affectingly evoked by the gentle storm or gust Satan describes (Milton quoted from Defoe's *Review* 63 (August 18, 1711) in Riffe, "Milton on 'Paradise Regained,'" 25).

303. *PR*, 4.634. Nayler observed that "the beginning of the work of a new Creature" is "not the work done and finished" (*Possession*, 5, 6); see discussion in Nuttall, *James Nayler*, 17.

304. See *PL,* 3.341, 6.732; 1 Corinthians 12:6 and 15:28; Ephesians 1:23; and Winstanley, *Works,* 486.

305. *SA,* line 2.

306. Keeble, *Literary Culture,* 224. Although the following account of the play stresses Samson's identity as a corporate intellectual laborer, see Hoxby's *Mammon's Music,* chapter 7 for a meditation on the meanings of his individual physical labor at the mill.

307. At line 1146, the structure is a temple; at 1605, a theater; for the blending of sacrifice and sport, see lines 1612–1614. For antecedents, see Wittreich, *Shifting Contexts,* 96–97. On the structure as both a triumphal arch and a Restoration playhouse, see Jose, *Ideas of Restoration,* 156–157.

308. I refer to the "ev'ning Dragon" pun at line 1692, discussed below.

309. *SA,* lines 580, 205, 420. Of course, Marvell also employed Samson to figure a captive England in *Last Instructions,* lines 731–736.

310. *SA,* lines 1211–1213. For parallels between Milton's Samson and other defenders of the good old cause, see Worden, "Milton, *Samson Agonistes,* and the Restoration."

311. *SA,* lines 31, 94–95. Milton is playing on an old formula for the location of the soul (Arnold Williams, *Common Expositor,* 78). See also Catherine Gimelli Martin, "Phoenix," 258–259.

312. See Guibbory, *Map of Time,* 201, and Low, *Blaze of Noon,* 162–163.

313. *SA,* line 1382. I refer to Samuel Johnson's famous complaint that the play "must be allowed to want a middle, since nothing passes between the first act and the last, that either hastens or delays the death of Sampson" (*Works,* 4: 376; see also *Lives of the Poets,* 1: 292). This supposed missing middle is best understood as an instance of the frequently noted antitheatricality of the play, its insistent emphasis on the capacity of carnal sight to "misrepresent" (line 124).

314. I believe that Samson's association with iconoclasm, the calling, and a knowledge-producing public—and the play's roots in *Areopagitica,* discussed below—provide grounds for a pacifist (but not quietistic) reading of the play. On reading the biblical story "against itself," see Wittreich, *Shifting Contexts,* esp. 193–242. The question Wittreich poses—does Samson act as a public or private person?—is different if we imagine him as a public person in the Adamic sense—that is, as the actual public. I have drawn inspiration from Lupton's analysis of the poem's search for "forms of sovereignty beyond the state" in the final chapter of *Citizen-Saints,* which suggestively explores Samson's hair as a figure for the multitude (184). Her argument builds on Kahn's analysis of Samson's "sovereign decision"; see her "Political Theology" and *Wayward Contracts,* chapter 10. See also note 101 above.

315. See John Rogers, "Secret," and Deleuze and Guattari, *Anti-Oedipus*.

316. Asad, *On Suicide Bombing*, 75.

317. *SA*, lines 566–570. On the allusive irony of "Fathers house," see Haskin, *Milton's Burden*, 143–144, 169–171. For a Weberian analysis of the conflict between Samson's two fathers, see Guillory, "The Father's House."

318. Girard, *Violence and the Sacred*, 305. Although Milton is not terribly interested in remaining true to his Old Testament source, to the degree that Samson can be identified with his biblical counterpart, Milton demonstrates that "the temptation of Christ" long predates his incarnation. Knoppers offers an incisive account of the play's conclusion, which "does not so much make Samson a martyr as it shows how his fellow Israelites do so. The closure invoked by the Chorus is not closure for the reader, who knows that Israel does not 'take hold' upon this occasion . . . The supreme irony is that Samson's act of iconoclasm makes him a kind of idol for his own people" (*Historicizing Milton*, 63). So McLoone: "Drawn to a vicarious empowerment, Manoa and the Danites will celebrate an imaginary figure, a Samson ('Like Samson' 1710)" (*Milton's Poetry of Independence*, 109).

319. *SA*, line 1756. See Lewalski's essential analysis of the importance of "experience" to our understanding of Samson's action in "Milton's *Samson*." In contrast to his other acts of inspired law-breaking, Samson's decision to marry Dalila is based not on any discovery facilitated by experience but mere precedent: experience fossilized as datum (line 231). I have benefited from a discussion with Abraham Stoll on this point.

320. Nayler speaking to the judges at Appleby in 1653, in *Collection*, 12.

321. *SA*, lines 1637–1638; *CPW*, 2: 554.

322. It might seem perverse to argue that the Philistines should recognize their corporate incarnation in an Israelite, but it is Samsonian England that is Milton's concern, not the historical Samson of Judges; when Samson describes "the ends / For which our countrey is a name so dear" to Dalila, he is clearly speaking to her as a fellow citizen (lines 893–894); see Joan Bennett's discussion of these lines in *Reviving Liberty*, 142–143.

323. *SA*, line 1692. Threading *agon* throughout these terms, Milton creates a sonic continuity that makes the razing and subsequent raising of Samson an object of the reader's sensuous experience.

324. I quote from Charles's proclamation against coffeehouses, discussed in Chapter 4.

325. On the dragon, see also David Loewenstein, *Milton and the Drama of History*, 147n59.

326. *SA*, lines 1706–1707. I read "a secular bird" as a parenthetical appositional phrase, so that the fame survives (literally, lives beyond) aeons made up of many lifetimes; as A. J. Church points out, if the sense were that it "outlives the

Phoenix, secular bird though it be, by ages of lives," we would expect a definite article. See his edition of the poem, 95.

327. On secularization, see the introduction. For a provocative reading of the ambiguities of *secular* in this passage, see Coiro, "Fable and Old Song," 144–145; it is, as she says, a "volatile word." Kahn sees the process of secularization in the play's "internalization of judgment" which represents a "historical way station between theology and aesthetics" (*Wayward Contracts*, 276).

328. *CPW*, 2: 566. Wittreich cites Steven Goldsmith's observation that the action begins at line 1640, the year of the Long Parliament, and ends at 1659, right before the Restoration (*Shifting Contexts*, 5).

329. Wittreich, *Shifting Contexts*, 119. Such continual revolution accords with the model of "progressive revelation" that informs what Radzinowicz calls the "free and open-ended theology" of the poem (*Toward Samson Agonistes*, 271, 349).

330. *PR*, 1.185, 188. Locke contrasts the Son's work with priesthood in *Reasonableness*, 214, 256–257.

331. *PR*, 4.638–639. Wilding, among others, has argued that the hero of *PR* is "humble, modest, private," and that Milton has now embraced a "quietist ethic of private moral victories" (*Dragons Teeth*, 257).

332. See *PL*, 2.561.

333. Marvell, *Last Instructions*, lines 949, 974; see Chapter 5 in this volume.

334. Hooke quoted in J. A. Bennett, "Hooke's Instruments," 99. Hooke purchased or borrowed several of Milton's works, including *Areopagitica;* see discussion in William Poole, "Milton and Science," 22–23. For another instance of Samson-as-experimentalist, see Boyle, *Works*, 5: 52.

335. See Haskin's discussion in *Milton's Burden*, 123, 161–162, and Teskey, *Delirious Milton*, 125–128.

7. The Professional Observer

1. The term *professional observation* has also been used by Nablow, who suggests that "the Addisonian tradition" of social observation has given rise to our own "age of 'professional observers'" (*Addisonian Tradition in France*, 15).

2. Power, *Experimental Philosophy*, sig. a3ᵛ (see Chapter 3 in this volume); Ned Ward, *London Spy*, 11, 125, 11, 27. Wall analyzes the shift from a chorography emphasizing fixity toward a topographical literature that depends on "the trope of a guide, briskly leading the reader through the London maze" in *Literary and Cultural Spaces* (102). On the importance of *The London Spy* as a periodical, see Troyer, *Ned Ward*, 30–32.

3. Tom Brown, *Amusements Serious and Comical*, 6; Ned Ward, *London Spy*, 187.

4. Defoe, *Tour,* 1: 167; Fiennes, *Journeys,* 54, 124.

5. See Dekker, *The Dead Terme,* sig. G3, discussed in Conklin, *History of Hamlet Criticism,* 18–19, and Robert Greene's *Defence of Conny-Catching.*

6. Milton, *PL,* 5.898–899; see also *PR,* 1.493, 3.386, 4.109, 4.401.

7. Ross, *New Planet no Planet,* sig. A2ᵛ; on the *sensus communis,* see Shaftesbury, *Characteristicks,* 1: 37–81.

8. To be sure, there already existed a vast conduct literature—literature that did not offer to "present an alternative world" but instructed people in how to navigate this one. As J. Paul Hunter observes, the bossy intrusiveness of this writing does not unsettle because of its assault on the reader's freedom (since there really is no such assault), but rather because of its urgent intimacy (*Before Novels,* 301, 233–234). Registering the voice of a person with whom one might disagree, such literature—in contrast to the *Spectator*—is as much expressive as it is prescriptive.

9. Shevelow's *Women and Print Culture* offers an incisive comparison between the two periodicals, particularly as they relate to the fashioning of female behavior; see esp. 106.

10. Defoe, *Review,* 7 (18): 143 (February 22, 1711); Sprat, *History,* 72, 99 (I quote from Sprat's description of the office of Curator of Experiments; see Chapter 2).

11. This is a conceptual progression rather than one determined by publication date; Fiennes's and Defoe's intellectual roots are in the seventeenth-century dissenting community.

12. Klein, "Gender, Conversation and the Public Sphere," 108. Klein's *Shaftesbury and the Culture of Politeness* treats this culture as a Whiggish construct, pitting an ideal of discursive liberty against Tory loyalism. See also Bryson, *From Courtesy to Civility*; Copley, "Commerce, Conversation and Politeness"; and Paula McDowell, *Women of Grub Street,* 285–301.

13. Fuller, *Medicina Gymnastica,* 187; Cheyne, *English Malady,* 199.

14. A veteran of Cromwell's campaign against the Scots whose mother was killed by royalist forces, Sydenham helped to root out opposition to Parliament within Wadham College. It was under the tutelage of Thomas Coxe, associated with Hartlib's Office of Address, that he became serious about pursuing medicine; throughout the Restoration he was a loud critic of the universities, suggesting, for example, that one could learn more essential lessons about anatomy from butchers (see *DNB*). On Locke's close collaboration with him, see Romanell, *Locke and Medicine,* and Meynell, "John Locke and the Preface to Thomas Sydenham's *Observationes Medicae.*"

15. See Rousseau, "Cultural History in a New Key" and "Nerves, Spirits and Fibres," as well as Barker-Benfield, *Culture of Sensibility,* 6–9. It is clear that

such disorders were indeed identified with refinement during the period, which suggests that the target audience of the therapeutic literature either did not pick up on its savagely critical undertone or was unperturbed by it. It is this criticism that will be my focus. Sena did pioneering work in reconstructing the persona of the nervous, melancholic, or splenetic English; see "Belinda's Hysteria" and "Smollett's Persona." For an account of the therapeutic ambitions of the early novel, see Sill, *Cure of the Passions.*

16. Purcell, *Treatise of Vapours,* 76.

17. Locke, *Essay,* 2.10.7, 2.3.1; Cheyne, *English Malady,* 197.

18. Fuller, *Medicina Gymnastica,* 148, 206.

19. Cheyne, *English Malady,* 14; see also 17. See Guerrini's analysis of this passage in *Obesity,* 132.

20. Cheyne, *English Malady,* 169, 262, 169, 233.

21. Cheyne, *English Malady,* iii, ii; Sydenham, *Entire Works* (1749 ed.), 416 (from a dedicatory epistle); Sydenham, *Entire Works* (1742 ed.), vi ("The Author's Preface"); Cheyne, *English Malady,* 105. See also the preface to Purcell's *Treatise.*

22. Cheyne, *English Malady,* 325–327, 363–364, 370; see also xiii.

23. Fuller, *Medicina Gymnastica,* 153–154, 186; Addison's summary of Fuller's argument in *Spectator* 115 (1: 472), discussed in the fifth section of this chapter.

24. Porter, "Barely Touching," 66; see also Rousseau, "Nerves, Spirits, and Fibres." But Porter's argument in "Consumption" is closer to the one presented here.

25. Flynn, "Running Out of Matter," 154.

26. Fuller, *Medicina Gymnastica,* 36; Cheyne, *English Malady,* 262.

27. Cheyne, *English Malady,* 58, 54, 158, 246.

28. Cheyne, *English Malady,* 367, 246; Fuller, *Medicina Gymnastica,* 206. Cheyne also uses "Delicacy" to describe the actual provisions available at the "Tables of the Rich and the Great," so the shift from man of taste to gluttonous hog is already implicit in the flattery (49).

29. Glanvill, *Vanity of Dogmatizing,* 152; Cheyne, *English Malady,* 303, 231.

30. Fuller, *Medicina Gymnastica,* sigs. a2ᵛ–a3, 24.

31. Cheyne, *English Malady,* 232, 209. Cheyne's emphasis on the movement of spirits clearly serves as a euphemizing means of describing the digestive system as well; Cottom points out that hypochondria itself was a means of referring to digestive problems ("Bowels," 163n11).

32. Fuller, *Medicina Gymnastica,* 35, 145, 25, 16. Fuller uses *rich* in a straight-forwardly economic sense elsewhere (e.g., 245, 254), which confirms the deliberate nature of these figurative inversions.

33. Fuller, *Medicina Gymnastica,* 39, 9, sig. b3ᵛ.

34. Fuller, *Medicina Gymnastica,* 145, 165 (see also 112), 164, 105; see also Cheyne, *English Malady,* 38. For Power's discussion of volatilized reason, see Chapter 4. On how Cheyne's spiritual and moralizing approach provides a bridge from a religious past to "a secularizing present," see Guerrini, *Obesity,* 105, but see also the Methodist forms of discipline examined in Mack, "Dissenters in Enlightenment England," as well as Bryan Turner's "Government of the Body." Bull offers a useful critique and refinement of Turner's thesis in "Secularization and Medicalization," though he treats a later period.

35. Fuller, *Medicina Gymnastica,* 257–258, 262, 144.

36. Fuller, *Medicina Gymnastica,* 186; Hooke, *Posthumous Works,* 27.

37. Fuller, *Medicina Gymnastica,* 137, 152, 253, 153.

38. Fuller, *Medicina Gymnastica,* 137, sig. a7; Locke, "Labour," in *Political Essays,* 327 (see Chapter 2 in this volume).

39. Milton, *CPW,* 1: 784; Fuller, *Medicina Gymnastica,* 147.

40. Cheyne, *English Malady,* 209.

41. Sydenham quoted in Fuller, *Medicina Gymnastica,* 189. Rational judgment leads to physical exertion, which in turn further strengthens the rational faculties.

42. See 'Espinasse, *Robert Hooke,* 117; she refers to "Dancing Shoos: Ambling Sadle" in the RS classified papers and suggests a connection to the "springy saddle" he presented to the Society. The *Diary* offers only hints: he "Received Dancing Shoos" and "Tumbled Down," but on the following day, "Tryd shoos. At Home. Running gallery till I sweat. Experiment succeeded beyond hope. Contrived pacing saddle with waywiser" (80). A later entry offers an intriguing trio: "At Crown, spake of artificiall muscles, swimming and Dancing shoos" (304). He presented his "springy saddle" to the Society in April 1666 and improved versions thereafter; see Birch, *History,* 2: 66, 83, 101, 106.

43. Hooke, *Diary,* 84, 163, 77; Newton's edition of *Paradise Lost,* 1: xlviii; Darbishire, *Early Lives,* 194.

44. Hooke, *Diary,* 233.

45. Hooke, *Diary,* 4 (iron and mercury are designated by symbols; see key on 2–3), 172.

46. Hooke, *Diary,* 28, 39, 26, 15, 34. He also undertook self-experimentation in an official capacity for the Royal Society; see 'Espinasse, *Hooke,* 51–52, and Birch, *History,* 1: 179, 192. Inwood observes that Hooke was more addicted to self-medication than to any drug (*Man Who Knew Too Much,* 146). See also Beier, *Sufferers and Healers,* 151, 167–170.

47. Hooke, *Diary,* 300, 16. This is Jardine's view; see "Hooke the Man."

48. Shapin, *Social History of Truth,* 155.

49. Montagu, *Edward Tyson,* 61; Sprat, *History,* 53.

50. Floyer and Baynard, *Psychrolousia,* sigs. Bv, A8, 234; this text was first published in 1706.

51. Cheyne, *English Malady,* 69; see also 98.

52. Floyer and Baynard, *Psychrolousia,* 265, 306. See Holsinger, *Music, Body, and Desire.*

53. Floyer and Baynard, *Psychrolousia,* sigs. A7ᵛ–A8, A4ᵛ. The papists who miscredited the "demonstrable benefits" of cold water immersion to saints had still been good observers (sigs. A5–A6ᵛ).

54. Floyer and Baynard, *Psychrolousia,* 198.

55. But see Cottom, "Bowels," and Hembry, *The English Spa.* Both studies examine the overlap of "fashion" and science in spa culture and the opportunities it offered for levelling distinctions (as well as reestablishing them).

56. Fuller, *Medicina Gymnastica,* 205, sig. b5ᵛ, 189–190. For identical advice, see Cheyne, *English Malady,* 180–182; Sydenham, *Works,* 452, 554; and Purcell, *Treatise,* 147.

57. Sprat, *History,* 407; Fuller, *Medicina Gymnastica,* 203, 202.

58. Fiennes, *Journeys,* 32.

59. See Charles Webster, *Samuel Hartlib,* 6; Fiennes, *Journeys,* 13. William Fiennes was a strong supporter of the Independents in the House of Lords; see *DNB.* On the scandal surrounding the surrender of her father to the royalists at Bristol in 1643, see Peacey, *Politicians and Pamphleteers,* 116.

60. Willy, *Three Women Diarists,* 10. Fiennes was an extraordinary figure, but by the middle of the eighteenth century this exceptional case had become the norm. Domestic tourism became a serious business—one that, with the rise of spa culture, could hardly be separated from the health industry. See Hembry, *English Spa;* Porter, *Medical History;* and Fabricant, "Literature of Domestic Tourism."

61. Fiennes, *Journeys,* 32–33.

62. A.B. quoted in Michael Hunter, *Establishing the New Science,* 228; Fiennes, *Journeys,* 32.

63. See Mendyk, "Early British Chorography"; Helgerson, *Forms of Nationhood,* 131–139; and Wall, *Literary and Cultural Spaces.* Wall's analysis of Stow's *Survey* shows how even the incorporation of stories associated with various houses function to "fix the structure" in space and time, connecting the present to the past; where change is acknowledged, it is presented as "slow change" (98–99). Cormack's "Good Fences" offers an interesting account of how early modern geography articulated a vision proper to "an expanding globe and an enclosing nation" (640).

64. Leland, *Laboryouse Journey*, sigs. B8, D4ᵛ; Edelen's introduction to William Harrison's *Description of England*, xxi, xx.

65. William Harrison, *Description of England*, 135–137.

66. Nicholson, *Lakers*, 25. On her probable intention to print the *Journeys*, see Morris's introduction and George, *Women*, 247; but see also Love's account of the *Journeys* as an instance of "publication through one copy" in *Culture and Commerce*, 71–72.

67. Fiennes, *Journeys*, 32; Southey, "An Early Tour to the Lakes," quoted in Kaderly, "Southey's Borrowings," 250.

68. Fiennes, *Journeys*, 215, 175. By contrast, the sixteenth-century chorographer "never encounters bad weather, impassible roads, or poor fare"; his trip is "an expository device" rather than "a historical event" (Helgerson, *Forms of Nationhood*, 151).

69. Clark, *Early Modern Town*, 238; Willy, *Three Women Diarists*, 16–17; Morris's introduction to Fiennes, *Journeys*, 26–27. Moir praises both her "naïve, childlike enthusiasm" and "woman's eye" (*Discovery of Britain*, 36). While it would be asinine to argue that she should instead be compared to Joyce or Austen, her artless style is not without design; it serves perfectly her aims and strategies as a traveler and observer. Many of the text's stylistic features may reflect its status as a work in progress, yet her investigative procedure, and her actual "findings," probably would not have been significantly altered in a printed version.

70. Southey, "An Early Tour of the Lakes," quoted in Kaderly, "Southey's Borrowings," 251.

71. Fiennes, *Journeys*, 191. The Royal Society addressed itself to the mystery and concluded that although "the more credulous sort of people," egged on by unscrupulous divines, had been led to imagine divine interference, the effect was explicable by mechanical means (Birch, *History*, 1: 105, 120–123).

72. Fiennes, *Journeys*, 42; see Defoe, *Tour*, 1: 197.

73. The Reformation was still being battled over at these sites; when a man was found dead at the well in 1630 after having mocked its supposed powers, a jury brought in a verdict of death by divine judgment; 1712 saw the publication of the twelfth-century Robert, Prior of Shrewsbury's *Life and Miracles of S Wenefride*, reissued with hostile commentary by William Fleetwood the following year. See Keith Thomas, *Religion and the Decline of Magic*, 70, and, more broadly, Hembry, *English Spa*.

74. Fiennes, *Journeys*, 93, 108; in Hooke's *Diary*, see, for example, 33, 35, 39, 300.

75. Fiennes, *Journeys,* 139. Wall explores Fiennes's interest in interior decoration but agrees that, like Defoe, she was more interested in productive processes and infrastructure. Similarly, Defoe does not bother going inside Chatsworth to provide a room-by-room description; it is the house's role in a larger system that interests him, not the sensual exteriors of consumables inside (*Prose of Things,* 190–191).

76. The *Journeys* was not printed, but the intellectual performances it records were staged in print by others—not, for the most part, by women. In her capacity as "The Female Spectator," for example, Eliza Haywood would make no effort to present herself as the agent of scrupulously innocent observation. Addressing her readers as a contrite woman of experience, a more thoughtful Moll Flanders, she urged her female readership to take up innocent amusements such as microscopy, but such recommendations never settled on her own persona. After retiring this character, Haywood made another incursion into periodical literature in the character of an adventure-prone "Bird of Parts" *(The Parrot):* a prattling gossip reduced to the status of an intelligent beast (perhaps modeled on the Prince of Nassau's parrot whose understanding had so impressed Locke). It was while inhabiting this character—one based on a misogynist stereotype that nonetheless did not settle on her person—that she felt able to present the "Compass of my Observation" as "somewhat extraordinary" (*Selected Works,* set II, 3: 88; 1: 181, 185).

77. See Pat Rogers, *Text of Great Britain,* 20–23.

78. Vickers suggests that it was at Morton's that Defoe "was introduced to the idea that the knowledge of things, not words, made a scholar" (*Defoe and the New Sciences,* 62). See also Cohen, "Compendium Physicae."

79. Defoe, *Review,* 2: 38 (May 31, 1705); see discussions in Richetti, *Life,* 5; and West, *Life,* 110–111.

80. Defoe, *Compleat English Gentleman,* 212, 207. His subsequent discussion of a "little Accademy" (218) based on these principles is clearly a nod to Morton's. See discussion in Vickers, *Defoe and the New Sciences,* 56.

81. Defoe, *Plan of English Commerce,* 7, 9.

82. Defoe, *Tour,* 2: 657; Vickers, *Defoe and the New Sciences,* 159, 67–68.

83. Defoe, *Review,* 1(2): 35 (July 4, 1704); 3(7): 61 (May 21, 1706). Defoe also invented a mythical society, the Scandal Club, to vet errors of other publications; Novak points out that, although Dunton believed that Defoe had stolen this idea from him, it closely resembles the "Parnassus" conceit (*Daniel Defoe,* 214; see also Chapter 5 in this volume).

84. Defoe, *Review,* 9(22): 53 (January 31, 1713).

85. Defoe, *Tour,* 1: 251–252; 2: 664, 595. For his defense of the term, see 1: 5. He claims to have made seventeen circuits in addition to three "general Tours" of England proper (1: 3). As Pat Rogers points out, these circuits were at once

imaginative and imaginary; see *Text of Great Britain*, 20. Parkes suggestively relates Defoe's circuits to cartography in "A True Survey."

86. Defoe, *Tour*, 2: 595; 1: 251, 148, 3, 5; see Fiennes, *Journeys*, 173 (this was by nine o'clock).

87. Defoe, *Tour*, 2: 656, 707, 633; e.g., 1: 331. As Wall argues, in Defoe one feels a strong conviction that the "grammar of space" entails "a grammar of motion" (*Literary and Cultural Spaces*, 111)

88. Defoe, *Tour*, 1: 251. Evelyn eschewed *"Radomontadas"* in his *State of France*, sig. A6.

89. Defoe, *Tour*, 1: 318. See Wall's discussion in *Literary and Cultural Spaces*, 78, 108–111.

90. Pope, *Correspondence*, 1: x, 94.

91. See Pat Rogers, *Text of Great Britain*, 111–116, and Andrews, "Defoe and the Sources," "Case of Plagiarism," and "Defoe's *Tour*."

92. Defoe, *Tour*, 1: 325, 308, 3; see Romans 15:20.

93. Defoe, *Tour*, 1: 223. In his concern to copy England rather than other accounts of it, Defoe seems to miss the point of his own procedure, since a confirmation of previous reports would render them suitable for experimental use, but experimentalist norms are important to him only insofar as they contribute to the construction of a spectatorial authorial persona.

94. Defoe, *Tour*, 1: 148–150. Parkes makes the intriguing suggestion that Defoe is offended by the legend because it discourages viewing the river as part of a larger system ("A True Survey, 406–407).

95. See, for example, 1: 13; 2: 510.

96. Defoe, *Tour*, 1: 105, 15. Compare Birch, *History*, 1: 462.

97. Defoe, *Tour*, 2: 466, 451; 1: 187. These are the Salisbury plains, which Hooke projected onto the face of the moon.

98. Defoe, *Tour*, 2: 745. See Duckworth's discussion of the "Face of Diligence" (1: 61) in "Whig Landscapes," 455.

99. Defoe, *Tour*, 1: 54, 40–45. While the cases of Dunwich and Ipswich are more complex than the examples offered by antiquity, they too are the victims of invasion—of the "encroaching Ocean" in one case and London's economic might in the other.

100. See Hackos, "The Metaphor of the Garden."

101. See Hooke, *Posthumous Works*, 320, and Chapter 3 in this volume.

102. Defoe, *Tour*, 1: 159. Bowers discusses Defoe's "delight" in confusing residences of the wealthy and the great in "Great Britain Imagined," 157–158.

103. Those who are awed by titles are like Power's "sons of Sense"—who "onely gaz'd at the visible effects and last Resultances of things" (*Experimental Philosophy*, sig. a3ᵛ, 193).

104. Defoe, *Tour,* 1: 367. As Defoe argued in *The True-Born Englishman,* the predicate *English* itself imposed a spurious unity on a people "derived" from a heterogeneous mass of Picts, Scots, "*Norwegian* Pirates" and "Buccaneering *Danes*" who, "joined with *Norman-French,* compound the Breed / From whence your *True-Born Englishmen* proceed" (15).

105. Defoe, *Tour,* 1: 338–339, 43. As Duckworth observes, "Defoe cannot be convicted of mystifying his landscapes by applauding the result while concealing the process" ("Whig Landscapes," 454). The tendency to figure London's growth as "monstrous" was deeply rooted: addressing Charles on the occasion of his restoration, William Cavendish had described London as " "thatt greate Leviathan, thatt Monster beinge the heade, & thatt heade so much to bigg for the bodye of the comon wealth off Englande" (Strong, *Catalogue of Letters,* 176).

106. Defoe, *Tour,* 1: 43. It is worth noting, however, that such a nostrum took the form of an "overplus," which could be sold to London wholesalers; see Sill, "Defoe's *Tour.*"

107. Bowers makes some very suggestive remarks on Defoe's sense of Britain's Edenic potential in "Great Britain Imagined," 164-166; see also Hackos, "The Metaphor of the Garden."

108. Defoe, *Tour,* 2: 576. When he approaches anything "recommended to me for a Wonder" later in his journeys, he invokes his Peak experience: "I, who was surfeited with Country Wonders in my passing the *Peak,* was not so easily surprized at the wonderful strangeness of this Part" (2: 619).

109. Defoe, *Tour,* 2: 568. Chapter 7 of Pat Rogers's *Text of Great Britain* explores Defoe's demythologizing crusade in the Peak.

110. He does, however, concede that Elden Hole is a wonder (584–585).

111. Stafford, "Telling One's Arse from a Hole in the Ground." For an excellent account of Defoe's use (and misuse) of his sources in this section, see Hartle, "Defoe and *The Wonders of the Peake.*"

112. The caves were by far the most popular sights in the Peak district; by midcentury "near a hundred" locals were trying to scrape together a living by giving tours of Poole's Hole; see Ousby, *Englishman's England,* 133–137.

113. Baker, *Microscope Made Easy,* 296–297.

114. Baker, *The Universe,* 15, 23.

115. Defoe, *Tour,* 2: 733. Perhaps Defoe was attracted to Harley's offer because being constantly on the move permitted him to escape the detection of creditors and because he believed that Harley, raised in the dissenting tradition like himself, was doing God's work, but the clash between his stated and actual aims is certainly glaring. See discussion in Pat Rogers, *Text of Great Britain,* 20–23, 64, and Novak, *Daniel Defoe,* 196.

116. Defoe, *Letters,* 158–159 (November 26, 1706); in a January 4, 1707, letter to Harley he writes "I have Acted a *True spy* to you" (189).

117. Defoe, *Letters,* 100 (August 14, 1705).

118. Defoe, *Tour,* 2: 641. In addition to offering thirdhand reflections on Marston Moor, he includes a lengthy relation of the siege of Colchester at 1: 18–31.

119. Defoe, *Tour,* 2: 658. He at least does so figuratively in this sentence.

120. Defoe displays a Miltonic ability to identify with Satan in *History of the Devil:* "since his Fall from *Heaven* . . . he is more a Vagrant than a Prisoner . . . confin'd to a vagabond, wandering, unsettl'd Condition . . . without any certain Abode . . . this is certainly part of his punishment, that he is continually hovering over this inhabited Globe of Earth; swelling with the Rage of Envy, at the Felicity of his Rival, Man . . . but extremely limited in Power, to his unspeakable Mortification: This is his present State, without any fix'd Abode, Place, or Space, allow'd him to rest the Sole of his Foot upon" (81). In describing a limited power to act that imprisons the wanderer, Defoe is clearly drawing on his own experience as a prisoner of debt who spent time on the move in order to escape creditors.

121. Defoe, *Letters,* 454 (April 26, 1718). He was writing to Charles De la Faye, Under-Secretary of State; at the time, he was writing for *Mercurius Politicus* as well as the *Weekly Journal,* having been engaged to do so by the Whig ministry (see editor's note). See discussion in Richetti, *Life,* 337–344.

122. See Starr's *Defoe and Casuistry* and "From Casuistry to Fiction."

123. Berry, *Gender, Society, and Print Culture,* xi; Nagel, *The View from Nowhere.* See also J. Paul Hunter, *Before Novels,* 92, 289–294.

124. West, *Life,* 219. Pat Rogers observes that his "anonymity" seems "almost sinister" (*Text of Great Britain,* 61). Andrews remarks on the "not very informative mixture of vagueness and precision" that characterizes all of his autobiographical statements; just as suggestively, Andrews observes that he had a talent for "passing off other people's experiences as his own" ("Defoe and the Sources," 271).

125. This is perhaps clearest in Defoe, since, as Pat Rogers puts it, one of the key functions of the text is "to incorporate Scotland into his system, as the Union had been designed to incorporate it into the British polity" (*Text of Great Britain,* 189–190). Although Fiennes's "idea of England" cannot seem to accommodate Scotland, she makes the same effort Rogers attributes to Defoe: to deflate "ancient particularism" predicated on "local claims to glory" (166). For other accounts of the text as a nation-building project, see Bowers's "Great Britain Imagined," and Parkes, " 'A True Survey.' "

126. Sprat, *History,* 114; Defoe, *The Free-Holder's Plea,* quoted in Richetti, *Life,* 146.

127. Pat Rogers points out that Defoe is similarly disconcerted by Bath, having "little feeling for construction sponsored by leisure pursuits" (*Text of Great Britain,* 187).

128. Similarly, in *Compleat English Gentleman,* Defoe contends that "meer schollers are a kind of mechanicks," dealing in citations as "haberdashers deal in small ware" (201).

129. Milton, *CPW,* 1: 751–754. In this connection, Hoxby makes the interesting suggestion that whatever profits Samson's labor at the mill yield the Philistines, they are "offset by the strength Samson recovers with exercise" (*Mammon's Music,* 217).

130. Tom Brown, *Amusements Serious and Comical,* 6–7.

131. Hooke, *Posthumous Works,* 62.

132. Tom Brown, *Amusements Serious and Comical,* 23.

133. However, for signs of effort (and strain), see 62 and 113; he lets the Indian speak for himself in the form of a letter at 116–118. The London Spy, of course, is provided with a companion who knows all the ways of the town.

134. Ned Ward, *London Spy,* 132–133, 180–181. His comrade praises him for making "rare use" of the show, in pointed contrast to the rest of the audience (192). At the Lord's Mayor pageants, he showcases his anthropological interest by "staring at the spectators much more than the show" (222).

135. See, for example, Ned Ward, *London Spy,* 22–24, 67–75, 135, 281–290.

136. However, John Hughes did compare Bickerstaff to "a Philosophick Surgeon" who could "dissect . . . The Follies of the finest Minds" (1: 446–447), and, like the *Athenian Mercury,* the *Tatler* sought to "gratify the Curiosity of Persons of all Conditions, and of each Sex" (1: 7). References to the *Spectator* and *Tatler* will be to volume and page number of Donald Bond's editions.

137. For example, in 1: 7.

138. But see Scott Black's wonderful discussion of the evolution of Bickerstaff's voice in *Of Essays,* 88–91, as well as Bond, "Isaac Bickerstaff." Shevelow warns against the temptation to regard Steele's *Tatler* as a "dress rehearsal" for the *Spectator*—a temptation to which I have surrendered in this chapter; see *Women and Print Culture,* 215–216n9.

139. Mr. Spectator's "prevailing Passion"—his only passion—is "Curiosity" (2: 111).

140. Samuel Johnson, *Lives of the Poets,* 3: 7.

141. *Spectator,* 4: 370; 1: 4.

142. Manley, *Memoirs of Europe,* 260; *Spy Upon the Spectator,* iii. Manley is more explicitly disgusted by his Whiggery; "Politicks and sordid Interest" have led him away from Helicon. See Smithers's discussion in *Life,* 253.

143. *Spectator,* 1: 4; *Spy Upon the Spectator,* 4–5. Gordon has discussed this pamphlet in an essay that argues that our distance from Mr. Spectator's "threats" has worked to "dissipate the anxiety felt by those in close proximity," but he does not provide evidence that original readers found Mr. Spectator "frightening," though naturally Addison and Steele's Tory opponents were irritated by his cultural influence ("Voyeuristic Dreams," 14, 18).

144. "Oration in Defence of the New Philosophy," 153. Compare *Tatler* 119 and 216.

145. Ketcham also suggests that Mr. Spectator's "visual acuity" seems related to his personal awkwardness in *Transparent Designs,* 11–13.

146. Charleton, *Physiologia,* 5 (see Chapter 3 in this volume).

147. Furtwangler argues that for readers of the *Spectator,* reading and seeing "are finally the same activity . . . The process of reading does not seem like parsing or decoding or interpreting, but like direct perception. Through his eyes, one can practice philosophy, not learn it" ("The Making of Mr. Spectator," 35, 37).

148. *John Tutchin's Ghost,* 3–4. The consumption of the *Spectator* brings to mind Anderson's famous description of the morning newspaper as a mass ceremony conducted privately, a solitary routine undertaken in the knowledge that it is being undertaken simultaneously by thousands of others (*Imagined Communities,* 35). The simultaneous virtual witnessing of the contemporary scene could sustain a consensus about it; see in this connection Ketcham's suggestion that the daily periodical essay form is inherently Lockean— constructed on the understanding that "we process knowledge according to corpuscular moments of experience" (*Transparent Designs,* 162).

149. *Spectator,* 2: 103, 20; 4: 182, 498. See also 1: 33.

150. *Spectator,* 2: 20, 42, 20; 1: 53. Bunyan related suspicions that he was a Jesuit and witch with similar pride; as signs of his difference from conformist ministers, such suspicions evince his "innocence" and "increase my Glory" (*Grace Abounding,* par. 307–308, 311).

151. *Spy upon the Spectator,* 5–6.

152. On the bold tube, see Marvell, *Last Instructions,* line 949, and Chapter 5 in this volume. But see Pollock's provocative essay "Neutering Addison and Steele," which argues that the reformist aims of the paper are dramatized as pyrrhic.

153. On women and the *Spectator,* see Shevelow, *Women and Print Culture,* 132–140; Osell, "Tatling Women"; and Markman Ellis, "Coffee-Women."

154. *Spectator,* 1: 472. In his attack on aristocratic pastimes, Boyle declared that hunters were "as arrant Beasts as those they pursue" (*Early Essays,* 239).

155. Knight expresses a similar idea: if the Spectator's main concern was "telling people what to think," Addison and Steele nonetheless attempted to include their readers in the process of constructing "communicative generalities"

("Generalizing Discourse," 51). In Pollock's view, the fiction that "All will become spectators" masquerades a command to "leave the seeing to us" ("Neutering Addison and Steele," 713); I suggest that the model of technologically assisted observation made it possible to sustain the paradox.

156. As McKeon puts it, "the virtuality of the public sphere was self-consciously exploited" by Addison and Steele to promote "a droll fantasy of imaginary power that also held more than a grain of truth" (*Secret History*, 82–83).

157. The death of Sir Roger occurs in *Spectator* 517; on the strategically sentimental association of Sir Roger with a dying cause, see Lewis, "Addison."

158. *Spectator*, 2: 20, 1. On how the *Spectator* abstracts friendship from persons, see Scott Black, *Of Essays*, 98.

159. Defoe, *Review*, 8(19): 61 (August 14, 1711).

160. Defoe, *Review*, 8(19): 61 (August 14, 1711).

161. *Universal Spectator*, 1: 19, 18, 23, 19. See 4:27 for his ability to "mingle with the Crowd" without being part of it.

162. Jennings, *Anecdotal History*, 94.

163. Blair quoted in Bloom, *Joseph Addison and Richard Steele*, 367; Samuel Johnson, *Lives of the Poets*, 3: 19–20. Johnson compares the project undertaken by the *Tatler* and *Spectator* to the Royal Society at 8.

164. On the Spectator as a Whig organ, see Cowan, "Mr. Spectator."

165. *The British Censor*, 9. On Steele's alchemical venture, see Winton, *Captain Steele*, 51–53.

166. Wagstaffe, *Character*, 10.

167. See Young, *Conjectures*, 99–112.

168. See Chapters 2 and 3. As Paulson points out, the fictional "Fraternity of Spectators" (1: 45) that gathers around Mr. Spectator is also defined by "decidedly unsexual interests" (*Beautiful, Novel, Strange*, 51).

169. Samuel Johnson, *Lives of the Poets*, 3: 24, 20, 22.

170. I refer to Sprat's "extraordinary men, though but of ordinary Trades" (*History*, 67).

171. See 'Espinasse, *Robert Hooke*, 1–2.

172. Newton quoted in Westfall, *Life*, 83. See discussion in Gleick, *Newton*, 79–89. Even Westfall, who is sympathetic toward Newton, characterizes Newton's response to Hooke's objections as "viciously insulting—a paper filled with hatred and rage" (*Life*, 93). Like Galileo, Newton withheld crucial information about the instruments he used in his early experiments; see Schaffer, "Glass Works," and Biaglioli, *Instruments of Credit*, 83n17.

173. See Westfall, *Life*, 152, and Gleick, *Newton*, 120–121.

174. See 'Espinasse, *Hooke,* 10–13. Evidence for the portrait's existence depends on the testimony of a German visitor to the Society in 1710, which may not be reliable; see Chapman, *England's Leonardo,* 1, 262–268.

175. Fara, *Newton,* 30–58.

176. Thomson, *Summer,* line 1562, in *The Seasons.* See 'Espinasse, *Hooke,* 1, 12–13 (the move did not actually take place until 1710), and 16–41 for the sharp contrast between Greshamite and Newtonian styles.

177. Stukeley, *Memoirs of Sir Isaac Newton's Life,* 19–20. On the wide currency this story enjoyed, see Gleick, *Newton,* 55–56.

178. Newton, *Isaac Newton's Papers,* 303, 302; North quoted in Fara, *Newton,* 18. For an explication of the understanding of gravity as an occult quality, see Hutchison, "What Happened to Occult Qualities?" 250–253.

179. Newton, *Principia,* 2: 547.

180. On snobbery toward non-mathematical approaches to science in the wake of Newton, see 'Espinasse, "Decline and Fall." On Boyle's ambivalent relation to mathematics, see Sargent, *Diffident Naturalist,* esp. 37–39, 66–68.

181. Pope, *Poems,* 6: 317. In Westfall's words, the "mere thought of trinitarianism, the 'fals infernal religion,' was enough to fan Newton into a rage" (*Life,* 127).

182. Thomson, *Summer,* lines 1560–1561, in *The Seasons;* Fawkes, *Original Poems,* 136. See Nicolson, *Newton Demands the Muse,* for an overview of the literary reception of Newton's *Opticks;* Nicolson describes it as a kind of "deification" (11). It may have helped that Newton was born on Christmas Day (according to the English calendar).

183. Bentley, *Eight Sermons,* 278, 127.

184. Newton, *Principia,* 2: 545; *Opticks,* 370.

185. For Addison's popularization of this idea, see *Spectator* 565, esp. 4: 532.

186. Proverbs 20:27. See Patrides's introduction to *Cambridge Platonists.*

187. In contrast, the Cartesian scheme, like the French monarchy, subjected all motion to the dead hand of mechanical necessity.

188. See Dobbs and Jacob, *Newton and the Culture of Newtonianism,* 110–123, as well as Arendt, *Human Condition,* 323. On the invisible hand, see Smith, *Wealth of Nations,* 4.2.9. This famous passage condenses several claims: that "uncoordinated actions undertaken by individuals in society contribute functionally to group processes"; that "social systems . . . embody felicitous, optimal arrangements"; and that they do so *"by nature"* (Judith Goldman, "Visible Hand," 2). Goldman's important thesis recovers Smith's invisible hand as a self-reflexive rhetorical figure. I am suggesting that the groundwork for Smith's theory was laid down decades before by Newtonians.

189. Pope, *Essay on Man,* 1.294.

190. *Spectator,* 1: 292–294.

191. The free indirect discourse of the novel takes form within this space. Banfield has described free indirect discourse as originating in a deictic center without a subject—an abstracted version of the "diversified narration" Tom Brown had attempted to formulate. See Banfield, "Describing the Unobserved."

192. Pope quoted in Rousseau, "Et in Arcadia Homo," 53; Dennis, *True Character of Mr. Pope,* 4. Deutsch's *Resemblance and Disgrace* explores how Pope makes "deformity . . . a literary method" (4). Pope was as frequently portrayed as Newton; see chapter 1 of *Resemblance and Disgrace.*

193. Pope, *First Satire of the Second Book of Horace Imitated,* line 68.

194. Pope, "Epistle to Dr. Arbuthnot," line 128; *Essay on Man,* 1.266.

195. See, for example, Arbuthnot, *Usefulness,* 9–10.

196. And even this episode draws heavily on Defoe's *Consolidator,* in which virtuosi from outer space are objects of enthusiastic fantasy (see 15–17).

197. Swift, *Gulliver's Travels,* 124; the Lilliputians are "a most ingenious people," like the architect and doctor he meets in Laputa (19, 168, 175).

198. See Sherburn, "Pope and 'The Great Shew of Nature,'" 306–315; Nicolson and Rousseau, *"This Long Disease,"* 137–156, 251–265; Mack, *Pope,* 232. The famous couplet of his most self-consciously "philosophical" poem, the *Essay on Man,* "Why has not Man a microscopic eye? / For this plain reason, Man is not a Fly" is a Lockean riff (1.193–194).

199. See Chapter 1. Colley Cibber's first speech in the *Dunciad* even identifies the "good old cause" as the cause of Dullness: "Dulness! whose good old cause I yet defend, / With whom my Muse began, with whom shall end" (1.165–166).

200. See Trickett, "Curious Eye," 239, 242. See also Spacks, *Poetry of Vision.*

201. Thomson, *Summer,* lines 296–297, in *The Seasons;* Pope, *Essay on Man,* 1.210.

202. See Arthos, "Poetic Diction"; Thomson, *Summer,* line 134.

203. Pope, *Essay on Man,* 4.332; Thomson, *Summer,* lines 319, 323, in *The Seasons;* Young, *Night Thoughts,* "Introduction," 6, and 9.1039–1040. See note 188.

BIBLIOGRAPHY

Pre-Twentieth-Century Texts

Addison, Joseph. "An Oration in Defence of the New Philosophy. Spoken in the Theatre at Oxford, July 7, 1693, by Mr. Addison." In *A Conversation on the Plurality of Worlds . . . To which is Added, Mr. Addison's Defence of the Newtonian Philosophy.* London, 1769.

Addison, Joseph and Richard Steele. *The Spectator,* ed. Donald F. Bond. 5 vols. Oxford: Clarendon Press, 1965.

Apocrypha and Pseudepigrapha, ed. B. H. Charles. 2 vols. Oxford: Clarendon Press, 1913.

Aquinas, St. Thomas. *Summa Theologiae.* 60 vols. Cambridge: Blackfriars, 1964–1976.

Arbuthnot, John. *An Essay on the Usefulness of Mathematical Learning, in a Letter from a Gentleman in the City to his Friend in Oxford,* 2nd ed. Oxford, 1721.

Ashmole, Elias. *Theatrum Chemicum Britannicum.* London, 1652.

[Astell, Mary.] *An Essay In Defence of the Female Sex. In which are inserted the Characters of A Pedant, A Squire, A Beau, A Vertuoso, A Poetaster, A City-Critick, &c.* London, 1696.

Aubrey, John. *Aubrey on Education: A Hitherto Unpublished Manuscript by the Author of Brief Lives,* ed. J. E. Stephens. London: Routledge and Kegan Paul, 1972.

————. *Aubrey's Brief Lives,* ed. Oliver Lawson Dick. Boston: David R. Godine, 1999.

————. *The Natural History of Wiltshire,* ed. John Britton. London: J. B. Nichols and Son, 1847.

————. *Three Prose Works,* ed. John Buchanan-Brown. Carbondale: Southern Illinois University Press, 1972.

Augustine, St. *The City of God against the Pagans,* trans. Eva Matthews Sanford and William McAllen Green. 7 vols. Cambridge, Mass.: Harvard University Press, 1957–1972.

————. *Expositions on the Book of Psalms,* trans. H. M. Wilkins. 6 vols. Oxford: J. H. Parker, 1847–1857.

————. *Saint Augustine's Confessions,* trans. William Watts. 2 vols. Cambridge, Mass.: Harvard University Press, 1977.

Bacon, Francis. *The Letters and the Life of Francis Bacon,* ed. James Spedding. 7 vols. London: Longmans, 1861–1874.

————. *The Masculine Birth of Time,* trans. Benjamin Farrington. In Farrington, *The Philosophy of Francis Bacon,* pp. 59–72. Liverpool: Liverpool University Press, 1964.

————. *Of the Advancement and Proficience of Learning or the Partitions of Sciences,* trans. Gilbert Wats. Oxford, 1640.

————. *The Twoo Bookes of Francis Bacon. Of the proficience and advancement of Learning, divine and humane.* London, 1605.

————. *The Works of Francis Bacon,* ed. J. Spedding, R. L. Ellis, and D. D. Heath. 14 vols. London: Longman, 1857–1874.

Baker, Henry. *The Microscope Made Easy.* London, 1742.

————. *The Universe. A Poem. Intended to restrain the Pride of Man.* London, 1734.

————. See also Defoe, Daniel.

Bale, John. *A Tragedie or Enterlude, manifesting the chiefe promises of God unto man.* London, 1577.

Bancroft, Richard. *A Survay of the Pretended Holy Discipline.* London, 1593.

Barrow, Henry. *A Plaine Refutation of M.G. Giffardes reprochful booke.* [Dordrecht?], 1591.

Bas[se], William. *Sword and Buckler, Or, Serving-Man's Defence.* London, 1602.

Baxter, Richard. *A Breviate of the Life of Margaret . . . Wife of Richard Baxter.* London, 1681.

————. *The Certainty of Christianity without Popery.* London, 1672.

————. *Reliquiæ Baxterianæ: or, Mr. Richard Baxters Narrative of the Most Memorable Passages of his Life and Times,* ed. Matthew Sylvester. London, 1696.

Baynard, Edward. See Floyer, Sir John.

Beaumont, Joseph. *The Minor Poems of Joseph Beaumont,* ed. Eloise Robinson. Boston: Houghton Mifflin, 1914.

————. *Psyche: or Loves Mysterie in XX. Canto's: Displaying the Intercourse Betwixt Christ and the Soule.* London, 1648.

Beck, Cave. *The Universal Character, By which all the Nations in the World may Understand one anothers Conceptions, Reading out of one Common Writing their own Mother Tongues.* London, 1657.

Becon, Thomas. *The Displaying of the Popish Masse.* London, 1637.

Behn, Aphra. *The Rover and Other Plays,* ed. Jane Spencer. Oxford: Oxford University Press, 1995.

Bentley, Richard. *Eight Sermons Preach'd at the Honourable Robert Boyle's Lecture, in the First Year, MDCXCII,* 5th ed. Cambridge, 1724.

————. see also Milton, John.

Bernard, Nathaniel. *A Looking-Glasse for Rebellion.* Oxford, 1644.

Birch, Thomas, ed. *The History of the Royal Society of London for Improving of Natural Knowledge* (reprint). 4 vols. Hildesheim, Germany: Georg Olms, 1968.

Blith, Walter. *The English Improver Improved or the Survey of Husbandry Surveyed Discovering the Improveableness of all Lands.* London, 1652.

Bloys, William. *Adam in his Innocencie.* London, 1638.

Bond, John. *Salvation in a Mystery: Or a Prospective Glasse for England's Case. As it was laid forth in a Sermon preached at Margarets in Westminster, before the Honourable House of Commons, at their Monthly Fast, March 27, 1644.* London, 1644.

Boyle, Robert. *An Account of Philaretus during his Minority.* In *Robert Boyle by Himself and His Friends with a Fragment of William Wotton's Lost "Life of Boyle,"* ed. Michael Hunter, pp. 1–22. London: William Pickering, 1994.

————. *Boyle on Atheism,* ed. J. J. MacIntosh. Toronto: University of Toronto Press, 2005.

————. *The Correspondence of Robert Boyle,* ed. Michael Hunter, Antonio Clericuzio, and Lawrence M. Principe. 6 vols. London: Pickering and Chatto, 2001.

————. *The Early Essays and Ethics of Robert Boyle,* ed. John T. Harwood. Carbondale: Southern Illinois University Press, 1991.

————. *The Works of Robert Boyle,* ed. Michael Hunter and Edward B. Davis. 14 vols. London: Pickering and Chatto, 1999–2000.

Bradley, Thomas. *Nosce te ipsum, in a Comparison between the First, and the Second Adam.* York, 1668.

Brathwaite, Richard. *Natures Embassie: Or, The Wilde-Mans Measures.* London, 1621.

Bridges, John. *A Defence of the Government Established in the Church of Englande for Ecclesiasticall Matters.* London, 1587.

A Brief Description of the Excellent Vertues of that Sober and Wholesome Drink, Called Coffee. London, 1674.

The British Censor. A Poem. London, 1712.

Brown, Tom. *Amusements Serious and Comical, Calculated for the Meridian of London,* 2nd ed. London, 1702.

Browne, Thomas. *The Works of Sir Thomas Browne,* ed. Geoffrey Keynes. 4 vols. Chicago: University of Chicago Press, 1964.

Browne, William. *William Browne: The Whole Works,* ed. W. Carew Hazlitt. 2 vols in 1. Hildesheim, Germany: Georg Olms, 1970.

Bunyan, John. *A Book for Boys and Girls: or, Country Rhimes for Children.* London, 1686.

———. *The Doctrine of the Law and Grace Unfolded.* London, 1659.

———. *Grace Abounding to the Chief of Sinners,* ed. Roger Sharrock. Oxford: Clarendon Press, 1962.

———. *A Relation of the Imprisonment of Mr. John Bunyan.* In *Grace Abounding to the Chief of Sinners,* ed. Roger Sharrock. Oxford: Clarendon Press, 1962.

Burges, Cornelius. *Two Sermons Preached to the Honourable House of Commons, at two Publike Fasts; The one March 30.1642. the other, April 30.1645.* London, 1645.

Burgess, Anthony. *A Treatise of Original Sin.* London, 1658.

Burnet, Gilbert. *The Mystery of Iniquity Unvailed.* London, 1673.

———. *A Sermon Preached Before the King, at Whitehall, on the Second of December, 1697.* London, 1697.

Burnet, Thomas. *The Theory of the Earth.* London, 1697.

Burton, Robert. *The Anatomy of Melancholy,* ed. Thomas C. Faulkner et al. 6 vols. Oxford: Clarendon Press, 1989–2000.

Butler, Charles. *The Feminine Monarchie or a Treatise Concerning Bees.* Oxford, 1609.

Butler, Samuel. *Characters and Passages from Note-Books,* ed. A.R. Waller. Cambridge: Cambridge University Press, 1908.

———. *Hudibras,* ed. John Wilders. Oxford: Clarendon Press, 1967.

———. *The Poetical Works of Samuel Butler,* ed. John Mitford. 2 vols. Boston: Little, Brown, 1853.

———. [?] *The Transproser Rehears'd: or The Fifth Act of Mr. Bayes's Play.* Oxford, 1673.

Carew, Thomas. *Poems by Thomas Carew Esquire.* London, 1640.

Cary, Mary. *The Little Horns Doom & Downfall: Or A Scripture-Prophesie of King James, and King Charles, and of this present Parliament, Unfolded.* London, 1651.

A Catalogue of the Rarities to be Seen at Don Saltero's Coffee House in Chelsea. To Which is Added a Compleat List of the Donors Thereof. London, 1731.

Catherine of Genoa. *Saint Catherine of Genoa: Treatise on Purgatory, The Dialogue,* trans. Charlotte Balfour and Helen Douglas Irvine. London: Sheed and Ward, 1946.

Cennini, Cennino d'Andrea. *The Craftsman's Handbook: The Italian "Il Libro dell'Arte,"* trans. Daniel V. Thompson Jr. New York: Dover Publications, 1960.

Certain Verses Written by severall of the Authors Friends; to be Re-Printed with the Second Edition of Gondibert. London, 1653.

Chapman, George. *The Poems of George Chapman,* ed. Phyllis Brooks Bartlett. New York: Russell and Russell, 1962.

The Character of a Coffee-House. Wherein is contained a Description of the Persons usually frequenting it, with their Discourse and Humors, as also the Admirable Vertues of Coffee. By an Eye and Ear Witness. London, 1665.

The Character of a Coffee-House, with the Symptomes of a Town-Wit. London, 1673.

Charles II. *By the King. A Proclamation For the better ordering of those who repair to the Court for their Cure of the Disease called the Kings-Evil.* London, 1662.

————. *By the King. A Proclamation for the Suppression of Coffee-Houses.* London, 1675.

————. *By the King. A Proclamation for the Suppression of Riots.* London, 1675.

————. *By the King. A Proclamation to Restrain the Spreading of False News, and Licentious Talking of Matters of State and Government.* London, 1674.

Charleton, Walter. *The Darknes of Atheism Dispelled by the Light of Nature.* London, 1652.

————. *Physiologia Epicuro-Gassendo-Charltoniana: Or A Fabrick of Science Natural, Upon the Hypothesis of Atoms, Founded by Epicurus, Repaired by Petrus Gassendus, Augmented by Walter Charleton.* London, 1654.

————. *Three Anatomic Lectures.* London, 1683.

Cheyne, George. *The English Malady, Or, A Treatise of Nervous Diseases of all Kinds, as Spleen, Vapours, Lowness of Spirits, Hypochondriacal, and Hysterical Distempers, &c.* London, 1733.

Church-Levellers, or, Vanity of Vanities and Certainty of Delusion: Discovered in the Pamphlet, called the Vanity of the Present Churches. London, 1649.

Cleveland, John. *The Idol of the Clownes, Or, Insurrection of Wat the Tyler.* London, 1654.

————. *The Rustick Rampant, or Rurall Anarchy Affronting Monarchy: in the Insurrection of Wat Tiler.* London, 1658.

Coffee-houses Vindicated in Answer to the late Published Character of a Coffee-House Asserting from Reason, Experience, and Good Authors the Excellent Use, and Physical Vertues of that Liquor. With the Grand Conveniency of such Civil Places of Resort and Ingenious Conversation. London, 1673.

Coles, Elisha. *An English Dictionary.* London, 1677.

Comenius, John Amos. *The Way of Light,* trans. E. T. Campagnac. Liverpool: Liverpool University Press, 1938.

Cook, John. *Monarchy no Creature of Gods Making.* Waterford, Ireland, 1652.

Corbet, John. *Self-Imployment in Secret: Containing Evidences Upon Self-Examination. Thoughts upon Painful Afflictions. Memorials for Practice.* London, 1681.

Couchman, Obadiah. *The Adamites Sermon: Containing their Manner of Preaching, Expounding, and Prophesying.* London, 1641.

Cowley, Abraham. *A Critical Edition of Abraham Cowley's "Davideis,"* ed. Gayle Shadduck. New York: Garland Publishing, 1987.

———. *Poems Written by A. Cowley.* London, 1656.

———. *A Proposition for the Advancement of Experimental Philosophy.* London, 1661.

———. *The Works of Mr. Abraham Cowley.* London, 1668.

Croll, Oswald. *Bazilica Chymica, & Praxis Chymiatricæ Or Royal and Practical Chymistry, in Three Treatises.* London, 1670.

———. *Philosophy Reformed and Improved in Four Profound Tractates,* ed. Henry Pinnell. London, 1657.

———. *A Treatise of Oswaldus Crollius of Signatures of Internal Things; Or, A True and Lively Anatomy of the Greater and Lesser World.* London, 1669. Bound with *Bazilica Chymica.*

A Cup of Coffee: or, Coffee in its Colours. London, 1663.

Davenant, Sir William. *The First Days Entertainment at Rutland-House, By Declamations and Musick: After the manner of the Ancients.* London, 1656.

———. *A Proposition for Advancement of Moralitie, by a New Way of Entertainment of the People.* London, 1654. Reproduced in James R. Jacob and Timothy Raylor, "Opera and Obedience: Thomas Hobbes and *A Proposition for Advancement of Moralitie* by Sir William Davenant." *The Seventeenth Century* 6(2) (1991): 205–250 (the *Proposition* is reprinted on pp. 241–248).

———. *Sir William Davenant's Gondibert,* ed. David F. Gladish. Oxford: Clarendon Press, 1971.

Davies, R. T., ed. *Medieval English Lyrics.* Evanston, Ill.: Northwestern University Press, 1964.

Defoe, Daniel. *The Compleat English Gentleman,* ed. Karl D. Bülbring. London: David Nutt, 1890.

———. *The Consolidator: or Memoirs of Sundry Transactions from the World in the Moon.* London, 1705.

————. *Defoe's Review*, ed. Arthur Wellesley Secord. 22 vols. New York: Facsimile Text Society and Columbia University Press, 1938.

————. *The History of the Devil, as well Ancient as Modern: In Two Parts.* London, 1727.

————. *The Letters of Daniel Defoe*, ed. George Harris Healey. Oxford: Clarendon Press, 1955.

————. *A Plan of the English Commerce.* London, 1728.

————. *Serious Reflections During the Life and Surprising Adventures of Robinson Crusoe: with his Vision of the Angelick World.* London, 1720.

————. *A Tour thro' the Whole Island of Great Britain.* 2 vols. London: Frank Cass, 1968.

————. *The True-Born Englishman. A Satyr.* London, 1700.

Defoe, Daniel and Henry Baker, aka "Henry Stonecastle." *The Universal Spectator.* London, 1736.

Dekker, Thomas. *The Dead Terme. Or, Westminsters Complaint for Long Vacations and Short Termes.* London, 1608.

Democritus, "General Reflections." In *The Presocratics*, ed. Philip Wheelwright, pp. 184–186. New York: Macmillan, 1966.

Denham, John. *The Poetical Works of Sir John Denham*, ed. Theodore Howard Banks Jr. New Haven: Yale University Press, 1928.

————. See also *Certain Verses.*

Denison, Stephen. *An Exposition upon the First Chapter of the Second Epistle of Peter.* London, 1622.

————. *The White Wolfe or, A Sermon Preached at Pauls Crosse.* London, 1627.

Dennis, John. *A True Character of Mr. Pope*, 2nd ed. London, 1717.

Derham, William. *Physico-Theology: Or, A Demonstration of the Being and Attributes of God, from his Works of Creation*, 3rd ed. London, 1714.

Desaguliers, John Theophilus. *The Newtonian System of the World, the Best Model of Government: An Allegorical Poem.* Westminster, U.K., 1728.

A Description of the Academy of the Athenian Virtuosi. London, 1673.

D'Ewes, Simonds. *The Journals of all the Parliaments during the Reign of Queen Elizabeth.* London, 1682.

Digges, Leonard. *A Prognostication of Right Good Effect.* London, 1555.

Donne, John. *The Complete Poetry of John Donne*, ed. John T. Shawcross. New York: New York University Press, 1968.

————. *Ignatius His Conclave*, ed. T. S. Healy. Oxford: Clarendon Press, 1969.

————. *Sermons*, ed. George R. Potter and Evelyn M. Simpson. 10 vols. Berkeley: University of California Press, 1953–1962.

Drayton, Michael. *The Works of Michael Drayton*, ed. J. William Hebel. 5 vols. Oxford: Shakespeare's Head and Blackwell, 1931–1934.

Dryden, John. *The Works of John Dryden,* ed. Edward Niles Hooker and H. T. Swedenberg Jr. 20 vols. Berkeley: University of California Press, 1956–2001.

Dunton, John. *The Athenian Gazette.* 20 vols. London, 1691–1697.

———. *The Life and Errors of John Dunton.* London, 1705.

———. *The New Practice of Piety: Writ in Imitation of Dr. Browne's Religio Medici: or, The Christian Virtuoso: Discovering the Right Way to Heaven, Between all Extreams.* London, 1704.

Eachard, John. *The Grounds and Occasions of the Contempt of the Clergy and Religion Enquired into, &c.,* 9th ed. London, 1685.

———. *Some Observations upon the Answer to an Enquiry into the Grounds and Occasions of the Contempt of the Clergy and Religion.* Reissued with separate pagination in *Grounds and Occasions of the Contempt of the Clergy and Religion Enquired into, &c.* London, 1685.

———. *The Works of Dr. John Eachard.* 3 vols. London, 1773–1774.

Earle, John. *Micro-Cosmographie: Or, A Piece of the World Discovered; in Essayes and Characters.* London, 1633.

Eaton, John. *The Discovery of the Most Dangerous Dead Faith.* London, 1641.

Edmundson, Henry. *Lingua Linguarum: The Naturall Language of Languages.* London, 1655.

Edwards, Thomas. *The First and Second Part of Gangræna.* London, 1646.

Ellwood, Thomas. *The History of the Life of Thomas Ellwood,* 2nd ed. London, 1714.

An Essay upon Idleness: Or Chusing to Live without Business. London, 1707.

Etherege, George. *The Man of Mode, or Sir Fopling Flutter,* ed. John Barnard. London: Norton, 1979.

Evelyn, John. *The Diary of John Evelyn,* ed. E. S. De Beer. 6 vols. Oxford: Clarendon Press, 1955.

———. *Elysium Britannicum, or The Royal Gardens,* ed. John E. Ingram. Philadelphia: University of Pennsylvania Press, 2001.

———. *An Essay on the First Book of T. Lucretius Carus De Rerum Natura. Interpreted and Made English Verse.* London, 1656.

———. *Kalendarium Hortense: or, The Gard'ner's Almanac, Directing What he is to do Monthly through-out the Year.* London, 1666.

———. *Life of Mrs. Godolphin,* ed. Edward William Harcourt. London: Sampson Low, Marston, Searle, and Rivington, 1888.

———. *Miscellaneous Writings of John Evelyn,* ed. William Upcott. London: Henry Colburn, 1825.

———. *Numismata. A Discourse of Medals, Antient and Modern.* London, 1697.

———. *A Philosophical Discourse of Earth, Relating to the Culture and Improvement of it for Vegetation, and the Propagation of Plants, &c. as it was presented to the Royal Society, April 29. 1675.* London, 1676.

———. *Publick Employment and an Active Life Prefer'd to Solitude, and all its Appanages, Such as Fame, Command, Riches, Conversation, &c. In Reply to a late Ingenious Essay of a contrary Title.* London, 1667.

———. *Sculptura: or The History, and Art of Chalcography and Engraving in Copper.* London, 1662.

———. *The State of France, As it stood in the IXth yeer of this present Monarch, LEWIS XIIII.* London, 1652.

———. *Sylva, or A Discourse of Forest-Trees, and the Propagation of Timber in His Majesties Dominions.* London, 1664, 1670, 1679, 1729.

———. *Tyrannus or The Mode: in a Discourse of Sumptuary Lawes.* London, 1661.

Everard, William, et al. *The True Levellers Standard Advanced: or, The State of Community Opened, and Presented to the Sons of Men.* London, 1649.

Eye-Salve for the English Armie, and their Assistants. London, 1660.

Fawkes, Francis. *Original Poems and Translations.* London, 1761.

Fiennes, Celia. *The Illlustrated Journeys of Celia Fiennes 1685–c.1712,* ed. Christopher Morris. London: MacDonald, 1982.

Fletcher, Joseph. *The Historie of the Perfect-Cursed-Blessed Man.* London, 1628.

Floyer, Sir John and Edward Baynard. *Psychrolousia: Or, The History of Cold-Bathing: Both Ancient and Modern,* 5th ed. London, 1722.

Fox, George. *The Journal of George Fox,* ed. John L. Nickalls. Cambridge: Cambridge University Press, 1952.

French, J. Milton, ed. *The Life Records of John Milton.* 5 vols. New York: Gordian Press, 1966.

Fuller, Francis. *Medicina Gymnastica: Or, A Treatise Concerning the Power of Exercise, With Respect to the Animal Oeconomy; and the Great Necessity of it in the Cure of Several Distempers,* 3rd ed. London, 1707.

Galilei, Galileo. *Dialogue Concerning the Two Chief World Systems,* trans. Stillman Drake. 2nd rev. ed. Berkeley: University of California Press, 1967.

———. See also Matthews, Michael.

Gibson, William. *Election and Reprobation Scripturally and Experimentally Witnessed unto, &c.* London, 1678.

Gildon, Charles. *The History of the Athenian Society, for the Resolving all Nice and Curious Questions, by a Gentleman, who Got Secret Intelligence of their Whole Proceedings.* London, 1691.

Glanvill, Joseph. *Essays on Several Important Subjects in Philosophy and Religion.* London, 1676.

———. *Philosophia Pia; or, A Discourse of the Religious Temper, and Tendencies of the Experimental Philosophy, Which is profest by the Royal Society.* London, 1671.

———. *Plus Ultra: Or, The Progress and Advancement of Knowledge Since the Days of Aristotle.* London, 1668.

―――. *A Praefatory Answer to Mr. Henry Stubbe.* London, 1671.

―――. *Scepsis Scientifica: Or, Confest Ignorance, the Way to Science,* ed. John Owen. London: Kegan Paul, Tremch, 1885.

―――. *The Vanity of Dogmatizing: Or Confidence in Opinions Manifested in a Discourse of the Shortness and Uncertainty of our Knowledge, and its Causes; With some Reflexions on Peripateticism; and an Apology for Philosophy.* London, 1661; New York: Columbia University for the Facsimile Text Society, 1931.

Godwin, Francis. *The Man in the Moone: A Story of Space Travel in the Early Seventeenth Century.* Hereford, U.K.: Nagrom, 1959.

Goodman, Godfrey. *The Creatures Praysing God: Or, the Religion of dumbe Creatures.* London, 1622.

―――. *The Fall of Man, or the Corruption of Nature, proved by the light of our naturall Reason.* London, 1616.

Goodwin, John. *Imputatio Fidei. Or A Treatise of Justification.* London, 1642.

Goodwin, Thomas. *Christ Set Forth In his Death, Resurrection, Ascension, Sitting at God's right hand, Intercession, As the Cause of Justification, Object of Justifying Faith.* London, 1642.

The Great Assises Holden in Parnassus by Apollo and His Assessours. London, 1645.

Grew, Nehemiah. *The Anatomy of Plants. With an Idea of a Philosophical History of Plants.* London, 1682.

―――. *An Idea of a Phytological History Propounded.* London, 1673.

―――. *Musæum Regalis Societatis: or, A Catalogue and Description of the Natural and Artificial Rarities Belonging to the Royal Society, and Preserved at Gresham Colledge.* London, 1685.

Gunther, R. T, ed. *Early Science in Oxford.* 15 vols. Oxford, 1923–1967.

Hakewill, George. *An Apologie or Declaration of the Power and Providence of God in the Government of the World: Consisting in an Examination and Censure of the Common Errour Touching Natures Perpetuall and Universall Decay,* 3rd ed. Oxford, 1635.

Hall, Joseph. *Occasionall Meditations.* London, 1630.

―――. *The Peace of Rome: Proclaimed to All the world, by her famous Cardinall Bellarmine . . . Whereto is Prefixed a Serious Disswasive from Poperie.* London, 1609.

―――. *The Works of Joseph Hall, Bishop of Norwich.* London, 1647.

Hall, Thomas. *Funebria Floræ: The Downfall of May-Games.* London, 1660.

Haller, William and Godfrey Davies, eds. *The Leveller Tracts 1647–1653.* Gloucester, Mass.: Peter Smith, 1964.

Hammon, George. *A Discovery of the Latitude of the loss of the Earthly Paradise by Original Sin.* London, 1655.

Harriot, Thomas. *A Briefe and True Report of the New Found Land of Virginia: The Complete 1590 Theodor de Bry Edition.* New York: Dover Publications, 1972.

Harris, Robert. *A Brief Discourse of Mans Estate in the First and Second Adam.* London, 1653.

Harrison, William. *The Description of England: The Classic Contemporary Account of Tudor Social Life,* ed. Georges Edelen. Washington, D.C.: Folger Shakespeare Library; New York: Dover Publications, 1994.

Hartlib, Samuel. *Chymical, Medicinal, and Chyrurgical Addresses Made to Samuel Hartlib, Esquire.* London, 1655.

———. *Considerations Tending to the Happy Accomplishment of Englands Reformation in Church and State.* London, 1647.

———. *Englands Thankfulnesse, or An Humble Remembrance.* London, 1642.

———. *An Essay for Advancement of Husbandry-Learning: or Propositions for the Errecting Colledge of Husbandry.* London, 1651.

———. *A further Discoverie of the Office of Publick Addresse for Accommodations.* London, 1648.

[Hawkins, Henry.] *Partheneia Sacra.* Rouen, 1633.

Haywood, Eliza. *Selected Works of Eliza Haywood,* ed. Alexander Pettit et al. 6 vols. London: Pickering and Chatto, 2000–2001.

Helmont, Jan Baptista van. *Oriatrike, or Physick Refined.* London, 1662.

Henry VIII. *A Necessary Doctrine and Erudition for any Christen Man, sette furthe by the kynges majestie of Englande.* London, 1543.

Herbert, George. *The English Poems of George Herbert,* ed. Helen Wilcox. Cambridge: Cambridge University Press, 2007.

Heron, Robert (John Pinkerton). *Letters of Literature.* London, 1785.

Herrick, Robert. *The Complete Poems of Robert Herrick,* ed. Alexander B. Grosart. 3 vols. London: Chatto and Windus, 1876.

———. *The Complete Poetry of Robert Herrick,* ed. J. Max Patrick. New York: Norton, 1968.

Hesiod. *Hesiod: Theogony, Works and Days, Testimonia,* trans. Glenn W. Most. Cambridge, Mass.: Harvard University Press, 2006.

Heywood, Oliver. *The Rev. Oliver Heywood, B.A., 1630–1702: His Autobiography, Diaries, Anecdote and Event Books,* ed. J. Horsfall Turner. 4 vols. Brighouse, England: A. B. Bayes, 1882–1885.

Hickeringill, Edmund. *Gregory, Father-Greybeard, with his Vizard Off.* London, 1673.

Highmore, Nathaniel. *The History of Generation.* London, 1651.

Hobbes, Thomas. *Leviathan.* Oxford: Clarendon Press, 1947.

Hooke, Robert. *The Diary of Robert Hooke, M.A., M.D., F.R.S., 1672–1680,* ed. Henry W. Robinson and Walter Adams. London: Taylor and Francis, 1935.

———. *Micrographia: Or Some Physiological Descriptions of Minute Bodies Made by Magnifying Glasses with Observations and Inquiries thereupon.* London, 1665.

———. *Posthumous Works of Robert Hooke, M.D.S.R.S. Geom. Prof. Gresh. &c. Containing his Cutlerian Lectures, and other Discourses, Read at the Meetings of the Illustrious Royal Society,* ed. Richard Waller. London, 1705.

Hooker, John. See Snow, Vernon F.

Hooker, Thomas. *The Saints Dignitie and Dutie Together with The Danger of Ignorance and Hardnesse.* London, 1651.

Horstmann, C. *Yorkshire Writers: Richard Rolle of Hampole, an English Father of the Church, and his Followers.* 2 vols. London: Swan Sonnenschein; New York: Macmillan, 1895–1896.

Houghton, John. "A Discourse of Coffee, read at a Meeting of the Royal Society, by Mr. John Houghton, F.R.S." *Philosophical Transactions* 21 (1699): 311–317.

Howe, John. *The Blessedness of the Righteous.* London, 1668.

Howell, James. *Epistolæ Ho-Elianæ. Familiar Letters Domestic and Forren; Divided into sundry Sections, partly Historicall, Politicall, Philosophicall, Upon Emergent Occasions.* London, 1650.

———. *A Hermeticall Banquet, Drest by a Spagiricall Cook: for the Better Preservation of the Microcosme.* London, 1651.

Howson, John. *A Sermon Preached at St Maries in Oxford . . . in Defence of the Festivities of the Church of England.* Oxford, 1602.

Hume, Patrick. *Annotations on Milton's "Paradise Lost."* London, 1695.

Hutchinson, Lucy. *Order and Disorder,* ed. David Norbrook. Oxford: Blackwell, 2001.

Jacob's Well: An Englisht Treatise on the Cleansing of Man's Conscience, ed. Arthur Brandeis. London: Kegan Paul, Trench, Trübner, 1900.

James I. *The Political Works of James I,* ed. Charles Howard McIlwain. Cambridge, Mass.: Harvard University Press, 1918.

Jewel, John. *A Viewe of a Seditious Bul sent into Englande.* London, 1582.

Johnson, Samuel. *The Lives of the Most Eminent English Poets; with Critical Observations on their Works,* ed. Roger Lonsdale. 4 vols. Oxford: Clarendon Press, 2006.

———. *The Yale Edition of the Works of Samuel Johnson.* 18 vols. New Haven: Yale University Press, 1958–2005.

John Tutchin's Ghost to Richard St–le, Esq. London, 1714.

Jonson, Ben. *Ben Jonson,* ed. C. H. Herford, Percy Simpson, and Evelyn Simpson. 11 vols. Oxford: Clarendon Press, 1925–1952.

Jordan, Thomas. *The Triumphs of London performed on Friday, Octob. 29, 1675.* London, 1675.

Julian of Norwich. *The Writings of Julian of Norwich: A Vision Showed to a Devout Woman and a Revelation of Love,* ed. Nicholas Watson and Jacqueline Jenkins. University Park: Pennsylvania State University Press, 2006.

The just reward of Rebels, or The Life and Death of Jack Straw, and Wat Tyler. London, 1642.

Keach, Benjamin. *A Medium betwixt Two Extremes.* London, 1698.

Leeuwenhoek, Antony Van. See Dobell, Clifford.

Leland, John. *The Laboryouse Journey [and] Serche of Johan Leylande, for Englandes Antiquitees.* London, 1549.

L'Estrange, Roger. *No Blinde Guides.* London, 1660.

Lilburne, John. *England's Birth-Right Justified Against all Arbitrary Usurpation, whether Regall or Parliamentary, or under what Vizor soever.* London, 1645.

———. *Regall Tyrannie discovered.* London, 1647.

Lilburne, John with George Masterson. *A Declaration of some Proceedings of Lt. Col. Lilburn, and his Associates.* London, 1648.

Little Non-Such: or, Certaine new Questions Moved out of Ancient Truths. London, 1646.

Locke, John. *An Essay Concerning Human Understanding,* ed. Peter H. Nidditch. Oxford: Clarendon Press, 1979.

———. *Locke: Political Essays,* ed. Mark Goldie. Cambridge: Cambridge University Press, 1997.

———. *The Reasonableness of Christianity, As Delivered in the Scriptures.* London, 1695.

———. *Two Treatises of Government,* 2nd ed., ed. Peter Laslett. Cambridge: Cambridge University Press, 1970.

Lod[o]wick, Francis. *Essay Towards an Universal Alphabet.* London, 1686.

Lovelace, Richard. *The Poems of Richard Lovelace,* ed. C. H. Wilkinson. Oxford: Clarendon Press, 1930.

Lowe, Roger. *The Diary of Roger Lowe, of Ashton-in-Makerfield, Lancashire, 1663–74,* ed. William L. Sachse. New Haven: Yale University Press, 1938.

Luther, Martin. *Lectures on Genesis, Chapters 1–5,* trans. George V. Schick. Vol. 1 of *Works,* ed. Jaroslav Pelikan and Helmut Lehmann. 55 vols. St. Louis: Concordia Publishing House; Philadelphia: Fortress, 1955–1986.

Manley, Delariviere. *Memoirs of Europe, towards the Close of the Eighth Century,* 2nd ed. London, 1711.

[Marston, John.] *Histrio-Mastix: Or, The Player Whipt.* [London], 1610.

Marvell, Andrew. *The Poems and Letters of Andrew Marvell,* 2nd ed., ed. H. M. Margoliouth. 2 vols. Oxford: Clarendon Press, 1967.

———. *The Poems of Andrew Marvell,* ed. Nigel Smith. Harlow, U.K.: Pearson Longman, 2003.

————. *The Prose Works of Andrew Marvell,* ed. Annabel Patterson, Martin Dzelzainis, N. H. Keeble, and Nicholas von Maltzahn. 2 vols. New Haven: Yale University Press, 2003.

Mather, Cotton. *Magnalia Christi Americana: or, The Ecclesiastical History of New-England.* London, 1702.

Matthews, Michael R., ed. *The Scientific Background to Modern Philosophy: Selected Readings.* Indianapolis: Hackett Publishing, 1989.

Melancholicus, Mercurius. *The Cuckoo's-nest at Westminster.* London, 1648.

Miller, Timothy C., ed. *The Critical Response to John Milton's "Paradise Lost."* Westport, Conn.: Greenwood Press, 1997.

Milton, John. *The Complete Prose Works of John Milton,* ed. Don M. Wolfe. 8 vols. New Haven: Yale University Press, 1953–1982.

————. *John Milton's Complete Poetical Works* (facsimile ed.), ed. Harris Francis Fletcher. 4 vols. Urbana: University of Illinois Press, 1943–1948.

————. *Milton's "Paradise Lost." A New Edition,* ed. Richard Bentley. London, 1732.

————. *Milton's "Samson Agonistes," with Notes,* ed. A. J. Church. London: Seeley, Jackson, and Halliday, 1872.

————. *Paradise Lost: A Poem, in Twelve Books . . . A New Edition with Notes of Various Authors,* ed. Thomas Newton. 2 vols. London, 1749.

————. *The Poems of John Milton,* ed. John Carey and Alastair Fowler. London: Longmans, 1968.

————. *The Riverside Milton,* ed. Roy Flannagan. Boston: Houghton Mifflin, 1998.

Milward, John. *The Diary of John Milward, Esq.,* ed. Caroline Robbins. Cambridge: Cambridge University Press, 1938.

Moore, Dorothy. *The Letters of Dorothy Moore, 1612–64: The Friendships, Marriage, and Intellectual Life of a Seventeenth-Century Woman,* ed. Lynette Hunter. Aldershot, U.K.: Ashgate Publishing, 2004.

More, Henry. *The Immortality of the Soul, so farre forth as it is demonstrable from the Knowledge of Nature and the Light of Reason.* London, 1659.

Moxon, Joseph. *Mechanick Exercizes: or, the Doctrine of Handy-Works.* London, 1693.

————. *Mechanick Exercises on the Whole Art of Printing,* 2nd ed., ed. Herbert Davis and Harry Carter. New York: Dover Publications, 1978.

M.P. *A Character of Coffee and Coffee-Houses.* London, 1661.

Nayler, James. *A Collection of Sundry Books, Epistles and Papers written by James Nayler, Some of which were never before Printed.* London, 1716.

————[Naylor]. *What the Possession of the Living Faith Is, and the Fruits thereof.* London, 1659.

A New Invention; or, A Paire of Cristall Spectacles, By helpe whereof may be read so small a Print that what twenty sheetes of paper will hardly containe shall be discover'd in one; besides, they have such a speciall vertue in them, that he that makes right use of them though hee hath beene blinde three or foure yeares will recover his sight very perfectly. London, 1644.

Newton, Isaac. *Isaac Newton's Papers and Letters on Natural Philosophy and Related Documents,* ed. I. Bernard Cohen and Robert E. Schofield. Cambridge, Mass.: Harvard University Press, 1958.

———. *Newton's Principia: Motte's Translation Revised,* ed. and trans. Florian Cajori. 2 vols. Berkeley: University of California Press, 1962.

———. *Opticks.* New York: Dover Publications, 1952.

Norden, John. *The Surveyors Dialogue.* London, 1607.

Norris, John. *Reflections upon the Conduct of Human Life: With reference to the Study of Learning and Knowledge.* London, 1690.

Northbrooke, John. *Treatise wherein Dicing, Dau[n]cing, Vaine plaies or Enterludes with other idle pastimes, &c. commonly used on the Sabboth day, are reprooved.* London, 1579.

Norwood, Robert. *An Additional Discourse Relating unto a Treatise lately published by Capt. Robert Norwood.* London, 1653.

Nourse, Timothy. *Campania Fœlix. Or, A Discourse of the Benefits and Improvements of Husbandry.* London, 1700.

Oldenburg, Henry. *Correspondence of Henry Oldenburg,* ed. and trans. A. Rupert Hall and Marie Boas Hall. 13 vols. Madison: University of Wisconsin Press; London: Mansell; London: Taylor and Francis, 1965–1986.

———. *The Philosophical Transactions of Two Years, 1665 and 1666, beginning March 6, 1665. and ending with February 1666; abbreviated in an Alphabetical Table: And also afterwards Digested into a more Natural Method.* London, 1668.

On Bugbear Black-Monday, March 29. 1652. Or, The London-Fright at the Eclipse proceeding from a Natural Cause. London, 1652.

Overton, Richard. *An Appeale From the degenerate Representative Body the Commons of England assembled at Westminster: To the Body Represented The free people in general of the several Counties, Cities, Townes, Burroughs, and places within this Kingdome of England, and Dominion of Wales.* London, 1647.

Pack, Samuel. *The Mystery of the Gospel Unvail'd: Wherein is plainly shewed and proved, That the Man CHRIST JESUS has honoured all the Perfections of GOD more than Adam and all his Posterity could have done, had they continued in their Primitive State of Innocency.* London, 1691.

Paracelsus. *Four Treatises of Theophrastus von Hohenheim, called Paracelsus,* ed. Henry E. Sigerist, trans. C. Lilian Temkin, George Rosen, Gregory Zilboorg, and Henry E. Sigerist. Baltimore: Johns Hopkins University Press, 1941.

Parkinson, John. *Paradisi in Sole Paradisus Terrestris. A Garden of all sorts of pleasant flowers which our English ayre will permitt to be noursed up.* London, 1629.

Pepys, Samuel. *The Diary of Samuel Pepys,* ed. Robert Latham and William Matthews. 11 vols. Berkeley: University of California Press, 1970–1983.

Perkins, William. *The Foundation of Christian Religion, gathered into six Principles.* [London?], 1591.

———. *Lectures upon the Three First Chapters of the Revelation: Preached in Cambridge Anno Dom. 1595.* London, 1604.

———. *A Reformed Catholike.* Cambridge, 1598.

———. *A Treatise of the Vocations, or Callings of men, with the sorts and kinds of Them, and the right use Thereof.* Cambridge, 1603.

———. *A Warning against the Idolatrie of the last times.* Cambridge, 1601.

Pett, Peter. "Sir Peter Pett's Notes on Boyle." In *Robert Boyle by Himself and His Friends with a Fragment of William Wotton's Lost "Life of Boyle,"* ed. Michael Hunter, pp. 58–83. London: William Pickering, 1994.

Pettus, John. *Volatiles from the History of Adam and Eve.* London, 1674.

Petty, William. *The Advice of W.P. to Mr. Samuel Hartlib for the Advancement of Some particular Parts of Learning.* London, 1647.

———. *The Discourse Made Before the Royal Society the 26. of November, 1674.* London, 1674.

———. *The Petty Papers: Some Unpublished Writings of Sir William Petty edited from the Bowood Papers,* ed. Henry, Marquis of Lansdowne. 2 vols. in 1. New York: Augustus M. Kelley, 1967.

Peyton, Thomas. *The Glasse of Time, in the two first Ages.* London, 1620.

Philalethes, Eugenius. See Vaughan, Thomas.

Pinnell, Henry. *A Word of Prophesy, Concerning the Parliament, Generall, and the Army. With A little of the First Adam.* London, 1648.

Plato. *Gorgias,* trans. Walter Hamilton. Harmondsworth, U.K.: Penguin, 1960.

———. *The Republic,* trans. Desmond Lee. Harmondsworth, U.K.: Penguin, 1974.

Pliny. *Pliny: Natural History,* trans. H. Rackham. 10 vols. Cambridge, Mass.: Harvard University Press, 1938–1952.

Plutarch. *Moralia 6:439a–523b,* ed. W. C. Helmbold. Cambridge, Mass.: Harvard University Press, 1957.

Poems to the Memory of that Incomparable Poet Edmond Waller Esquire. By Several Hands. London, 1688.

Pope, Alexander. *The Correspondence of Alexander Pope,* ed. George Sherburn. 5 vols. Oxford: Clarendon Press, 1956.

———. *The Poems of Alexander Pope,* ed. John Butt. 6 vols. London: Methuen; New Haven: Yale University Press, 1951–1969.

Power, Henry. *Experimental Philosophy, in Three Books: Containing New Experiments Microscopical, Mercurial, Magnetical.* London, 1664.

Prynne, William. *A Breviate of the Life of William Laud, Arch-bishop of Canterbury.* London, 1644.

———. *A Gospel Plea (Interwoven with a Rational and Legal) for the Lawfulness and Continuance of the Antient Setled Maintenance and Tenths of the Ministers of the Gospel.* London, 1660.

Purcell, John. *A Treatise of Vapours, or Hysterick Fits.* London, 1702.

Puttenham, George. *The Arte of English Poesie, Contrived into three Bookes: The first of Poets and Poesie, the second of Proportion, the third of Ornament.* London, 1589. Reprinted in *English Reprints,* vol. 4. New York: AMS Press, 1966.

Rabisha, William. *Adam Unvailed, and Seen with open Face: Or, Israel's right way from Egypt to Canaan, Lately Discovered.* London, 1649.

Raleigh, Sir Walter. *The History of the World.* London, 1617.

Rawlidge, Richard. *A Monster Late Found Out and Discovered. Or The scourging of Tiplers, the ruine of Bacchus, and the bane of Tapsters.* Amsterdam, 1628.

Ray, John. *A Collection of English Proverbs.* London, 1670.

———. *The Ornithology of Francis Willughby of Middleton in the County of Warwick Esq., Fellow of the Royal Society.* London, 1678.

———. *Three Physico-Theological Discourses.* London, 1693.

———. *The Wisdom of God Manifested in the Works of the Creation.* London, 1691.

Richardson, Jonathan, Father and Son. *Explanatory Notes and Remarks on Milton's "Paradise Lost."* London, 1734.

R[oberts], H[ugh]. *The Day of Hearing.* London, 1600.

———. *A Godly and Necessary Sermon against fleshly lustes; and against certaine mischevious May-games, which are the fruite thereof.* London. [Printed at Oxford, 1600, bound with *The Day of Hearing.*]

Rochester, John Wilmot. *The Complete Poems of John Wilmot, Earl of Rochester,* ed. David M. Vieth. New Haven: Yale University Press, 1968.

Rolle, Richard. *Here begynneth a lytell boke, that speketh of Purgatorye.* London, 1534.

Ross, Alexander. *The New Planet no Planet: or, The Earth no wandring Star, Except in the wandering heads of Galileans.* London, 1646.

Rowland, Richard. See Verstegan, Richard.

Rowlands, Samuel. *Hell's Broke Loose.* London, 1605.

Salkeld, John. *A Treatise of Paradise.* London, 1617.

Savile, George. *The Complete Works of George Savile, First Marquess of Halifax,* ed. Walter Raleigh. Oxford: Clarendon Press, 1912.

The Second Part of the Spectacles; Or, Rather a Multiplying Glass, fitted for their use, which are not able to see with Spectacles: By the helpe whereof may be discerned many things at distance, which are hardly to be seen otherwise, and not ordinarily taken notice of. London, 1644.

Seneca. *Ad Lucilium Epistulae Morales,* trans. Richard M. Gummere. 3 vols. Cambridge, Mass.: Harvard University Press, 1925–1934.

Shadwell, Thomas. *The Virtuoso,* ed. Marjorie Hope Nicolson and David Stuart Rodes. Lincoln: University of Nebraska Press, 1966.

Shaftesbury, Anthony Ashley Cooper, Third Earl. *Characteristicks of Men, Manners, Opinions, Times,* ed. Philip Ayres. 2 vols. Oxford: Clarendon Press, 1999.

———. *The Life, Unpublished Letters, and Philosophical Regimen of Anthony, Earl of Shaftesbury,* ed. Benjamin Rand. London: Swan Sonnenschein, 1900.

Shakespeare, William. *The Norton Shakespeare,* ed. Stephen Greenblatt, Walter Cohen, Jean E. Howard, and Katharine Eisaman Maus. New York: Norton, 1997.

Sheffield, John. *The Rising Sun: Or The Sun of Righteousness Shining upon the Sons of Unrighteousness, a Theological Sun-Dyal Wherein Is to be seen the Rising, Motion, Influence and Manifold Operations of Christ upon the Soul.* London, 1654.

Sherlock, William. *An Answer to a Discourse Intituled, Papists Protesting against Protestant-Popery.* London, 1686.

Sidney, Philip. *An Apologie for Poetrie.* London, 1595.

———. *The Countess of Pembroke's Arcadia (The Old Arcadia),* ed. Katherine Duncan-Jones. Oxford: Oxford University Press, 1999.

Smith, Adam. *An Inquiry into the Nature and Cause of the Wealth of Nations. The Glasgow Edition of the Works and Correspondence of Adam Smith,* vol. 2, ed. R. H. Campbell and A. S. Skinner. Indianapolis: Liberty Fund, 1976.

Smith, Richard et al. *A Declaration of the Grounds and Reasons why we the Poor Inhabitants of the Town of Wellinborrow, in the County of Northampton, have begun and give consent to dig up, manure and sow Corn upon the Common, and waste ground, called Bareshanke, belonging to the Inhabitants of Wellinborrow, by those that have subscribed, and hundreds more that give Consent.* London, 1650.

Smith, Sir Thomas. *De Republica Anglorum,* ed. Mary Dewar. Cambridge: Cambridge University Press, 1982.

Snow, Vernon F. *Parliament in Elizabethan England: John Hooker's Order and Usage.* New Haven: Yale University Press, 1977.

Sorbière, Samuel. *A Voyage to England . . . As Also Observations on the Same Voyage, by Dr. Thomas Sprat.* London, 1709.

South, Robert. *A Sermon Preached At the Cathedral Church of St. Paul, Novemb. 9. 1662.* London, 1663.

S[outhey, Robert]. "An Early Tour of the Lakes." *Athenaeum: A Magazine of Literary and Miscellaneous Information* 2 (1807): 25–27.

Spedding, James. *The Letters and Life of Francis Bacon.* 7 vols. London: Longman, Green, Longman, and Roberts, 1861–1874.

Spenser, Edmund. *The Faerie Queene,* ed. A. C. Hamilton. London: Longman, 1977.

Sprat, Thomas. *The History of the Royal Society of London, for the Improving of Natural Knowledge.* London, 1667. Reproduced and edited by Jackson I. Cope and Harold Whitmore Jones. St. Louis: Washington University, 1958.

————. See also Sorbière, Samuel.

A Spy Upon the Spectator. London, 1711.

Steele, Sir Richard. *The Tatler,* ed. Donald F. Bond. 3 vols. Oxford: Clarendon Press, 1987.

Sterry, Peter. *A Discourse of the Freedom of the Will.* London, 1675.

Stokes, James, ed. *Records of Early English Drama: Somerset.* 2 vols. Toronto: University of Toronto Press, 1996.

Strong, Sanford Arthur, ed. *A Catalogue of Letters and Other Historical Documents Exhibited in the Library at Welbeck.* London: John Murray, 1903.

Stubbe, Henry. *A Censure upon Certaine Passages Contained in the History of the Royal Society, As being Destructive to the Established Religion and Church of England.* Oxford, 1670.

————. *Legends no Histories: or, A Specimen of some Animadversions Upon The History of the Royal Society.* London, 1670.

————. *A Reply unto the Letter Written to Mr. Henry Stubbe in Defense of the History of the Royal Society.* Oxford, 1671.

————. *A Specimen of some Animadversions upon a Book, Entituled, Plus Ultra.* London, 1670.

Stukeley, William. *Memoirs of Sir Isaac Newton's Life,* ed. A. Hastings White. London: Taylor and Francis, 1936.

Swift, Jonathan. *Gulliver's Travels,* ed. Claude Rawson and Ian Higgins. Oxford World's Classics, 2005.

Sydenham, Thomas. *The Entire Works of Dr. Thomas Sydenham,* 2nd ed., ed. John Swan. London, 1749.

Taylor, John. *The Divisions of the Church of England Crept in at XV Several Doores.* London, 1642.

Taylor, Thomas. *The Works of that Faithful Servant of Jesus Christ, Dr. Thom. Taylor, Sometimes Minister of the Gospel in Aldermanbury, London.* London, 1653.

Thompson, William. *Poems on Several Occasions, To which is added Gondibert and Birtha, A Tragedy.* Oxford, 1757.

Thoms, William J., ed. *A Collection of Early Prose Romances.* 3 vols. London: William Pickering, 1828.

Thomson, James. *The Seasons,* ed. James Sambrook. Oxford: Clarendon Press, 1981.

The Trials of Charles The First, and of some of the Regicides: with Biographies of Bradshaw, Ireton, Harrison, and Others. London: John Murray, 1841.

Tuke, Thomas. *The High-way to Heaven: or, The doctrine of Election, effectuall Vocation, Justification, Sanctification and eternall Life.* London, 1609.

Vaughan, Thomas (Philalethes, Eugenius). *Magia Adamica: or the Antiquitie of Magic, and the Descent thereof from Adam downwards, proved.* London, 1650.

Verstegan, Richard (Richard Rowland). *Odes in Imitation of the Seaven Penitential Psalmes.* Antwerp, 1601.

Virgil. *Virgil,* trans. H. Rushton Fairclough, rev. G. P. Goold. 2 vols. Cambridge, Mass.: Harvard University Press, 1999–2000.

Vives, Juan Luis. *On Education: A Translation of the Tradendis Disciplinis,* trans. Foster Watson. Totowa, N.J.: Rowman and Littlefield, 1971.

Voragine, Jacobus de. *The Golden Legend: Readings on the Saints,* trans. William Granger Ryan. 2 vols. Princeton: Princeton University Press, 1993.

[Wagstaffe, William.] *The Character of Richard St–le, Esq. With some Remarks. By Toby, Abel's Kinsman,* 2nd ed. London, 1713.

Walker, Anthony. *Eureka, Eureka: The Virtuous Woman found, Her Loss Bewailed, and Character Exemplifed in a Sermon.* London, 1678.

Waller, Richard. See Hooke, Robert, *Posthumous Works.*

Wallington, Nehemiah. *The Notebooks of Nehemiah Wallington, 1618–1654: A Selection,* ed. David Booy. Aldershot, U.K.: Ashgate Publishing, 2007.

Wallis, John. "Account of Some Passages in His Own Life." In Christoph J. Scriba, "The Autobiography of John Wallis, F.R.S." *Notes and Records of the Royal Society of London* 25(1) (1970): 17–46.

———. *A Defence of the Royal Society, And the Philosophical Transactions.* London, 1678.

Walton, Izaak. *The Compleat Angler or the Contemplative Man's Recreation.* London, 1653.

Walwyn, William. *A Parable, or Consultation of Physitians upon Master Edwards.* London, 1646.

———. *The Vanitie Of the present Churches, and Uncertainty of their Preaching, discovered.* London, 1649.

———. *Walwyns Just Defence against the Aspertions Cast Upon Him, in a late un-christian Pamphlet entituled, Walwyns Wiles.* London, 1649.

Ward, Ned. *The London Spy,* ed. Paul Hyland. East Lansing, Mich.: Colleagues Press, 1993.

Ward, Seth and John Wilkins. *Vindiciae Academiarum Containing Some briefe Animadversions upon Mr. Websters Book, Stiled the Examination of Academies.* Oxford, 1654.

Wasson, John M., ed. *Records of Early English Drama: Devon*. Toronto: University of Toronto Press, 1986.

Watkins, Richard. *Newes from the Dead. Or A True and Exact Narration of the miraculous deliverance of Anne Greene*. Oxford, 1651.

Webster, John. *Academiarum Examen, Or the Examination of Academies, Wherein is discussed and examined the Matter, Method and Customes of Academick and Scholastick Learning, and the insufficiency thereof discovered and laid open*. London, 1654.

Whitaker, Edward. *The Future State: or, A Discourse Attempting some Display of the Souls Happiness, in regard to that Eternally Progressive Knowledge, or Eternal Increase of Knowledge, and the Consequences of it, which is amongst the Blessed in Heaven*. London, 1683.

Wilkins, John. *A Discourse concerning A New World & Another Planet in 2 Bookes*. London, 1640.

——. *A Discourse concerning the Beauty of Providence In all the rugged passages of it. Very seasonable to quiet and support the heart in these times of publick confusion*. London, 1649.

——. *The Discovery of a World in the Moone. Or, A Discourse Tending to Prove, that 'tis probable there may be another habitable World in that Planet*. London, 1638.

——. *An Essay Towards a Real Character, And a Philosophical Language*. London, 1668.

——. *Mathematical Magick or, the Wonders That may be performed by Mechanicall Geometry*. London, 1648.

Willet, Andrew. *Synopsis Papismi, That is, A Generall Viewe of Papistry*. London, 1592.

Winstanley, Gerrard. *England's Spirit Unfoulded, or An Incouragement to Take the Engagement*. In G. E. Aylmer, "A Newly Discovered Pamphlet by Gerrard Winstanley," *Past and Present* 40 (1968): 3–15, pp. 9–15.

——. *The Mysterie of God, Concerning the whole Creation, Mankinde*. London, 1648.

——. *The Works of Gerrard Winstanley with an Appendix of Documents Relating to the Digger Movement*, ed. George H. Sabine. New York: Russell and Russell, 1965.

Woodward, John. *Brief Instructions for Making Observations in All Parts of the World*. London, 1696.

Young, Edward. *Conjectures on Original Composition. In a Letter to the Author of Sir Charles Grandison*. Leeds: Scolar Press, 1966.

——. *Night Thoughts*, ed. Stephen Cornford. Cambridge: Cambridge University Press, 1989.

Secondary and Modern Texts

Abbott, Andrew. *The System of Professions: An Essay on the Division of Expert Labor.* Chicago: University of Chicago Press, 1988.

Abraham, Gary A. "Misunderstanding the Merton Thesis: A Boundary Dispute between History and Sociology." *Isis* 74(3) (1983): 368–387.

Abraham, Lyndy. *Marvell and Alchemy.* Aldershot, U.K.: Scolar Press, 1990.

Abrams, M. H. *The Mirror and the Lamp: Romantic Theory and the Critical Tradition.* Oxford: Oxford University Press, 1953.

Achinstein, Sharon. *Literature and Dissent in Milton's England.* Cambridge: Cambridge University Press, 2003.

———. *Milton and the Revolutionary Reader.* Princeton: Princeton University Press, 1994.

A.C.S. "Notes on the Foundation and History of the Royal Society." *Notes and Records of the Royal Society of London* 1(1) (1938): 32–36.

Adams, Robert M. "A Little Look into Chaos." In *Illustrious Evidence: Approaches to English Literature of the Early Seventeenth Century,* ed. Earl Miner, pp. 71–89. Berkeley: University of California Press, 1975.

———. "Reading Comus." *Modern Philology* 51(1) (1953): 18–32.

Adelman, Janet. "Creation and the Place of the Poet in *Paradise Lost.*" In *The Author in His Work: Essays on a Problem in Criticism,* ed. Louis L. Martz and Aubrey Williams, pp. 51–69. New Haven: Yale University Press, 1978.

Adorno, Theodor W. *Critical Models: Interventions and Catchwords,* trans. Henry W. Pickford. New York: Columbia University Press, 1998.

———. See also Horkheimer, Max.

Aers, David. "Altars of Power: Reflections on Eamon Duffy's *The Stripping of the Altars: Traditional Religion in England 1400–1580.*" *Literature and History,* 3rd ser. 3 (1994): 90–105.

Agamben, Giorgio. *The Man without Content,* trans. Georgia Albert. Stanford: Stanford University Press, 1999.

Allen, Don Cameron. *Image and Meaning: Metaphoric Traditions in Renaissance Poetry.* Baltimore: Johns Hopkins Press, 1968.

Almond, Philip C. *Adam and Eve in Seventeenth-Century Thought.* Cambridge: Cambridge University Press, 1999.

Alpers, Paul. *What Is Pastoral?* Chicago: University of Chicago Press, 1996.

Alpers, Svetlana. *The Art of Describing: Dutch Art in the Seventeenth Century.* Chicago: University of Chicago Press, 1983.

Alsop, James. "Gerrard Winstanley's Later Life." *Past and Present* 82 (1979): 73–81.

Althusser, Louis. *Essays on Ideology.* London: Verso, 1984.

Anderson, Benedict. *Imagined Communities,* rev. ed. London: Verso, 2006.

Andrews, J. H. "A Case of Plagiarism in Defoe's *Tour.*" *Notes and Queries* 6(10) (1959): 399.

———. "Defoe and the Sources of His 'Tour.'" *The Geographical Journal* 126(3) (1960): 268–277.

———. "Defoe's *Tour* and Macky's *Journey.*" *Notes and Queries* 7(8) (1960): 290–292.

Appelbaum, Robert. *Literature and Utopian Politics in Seventeenth-Century England.* Cambridge: Cambridge University Press, 2002.

Archer, Ian W. "Popular Politics in the Sixteenth and Early Seventeenth Centuries." In *Londinopolis: Essays in the Cultural and Social History of Early Modern London,* ed. Paul Griffiths and Mark S. R. Jenner, pp. 26–46. Manchester: Manchester University Press, 2000.

Arendt, Hannah. *The Human Condition.* Chicago: University of Chicago Press, 1998.

Armstrong, Nancy and Leonard Tennenhouse. *The Imaginary Puritan: Literature, Intellectual Labor, and the Origins of Personal Life.* Berkeley: University of California Press, 1992.

Armytage, W. H. G. "The Royal Society and the Apothecaries 1660–1772." *Notes and Records of the Royal Society of London* 11(1) (1954): 22–37.

Arnold, Oliver. *The Third Citizen: Shakespeare's Theater and the Early Modern House of Commons.* Baltimore: Johns Hopkins University Press, 2007.

Arthos, John. *Milton and the Italian Cities.* London: Bowes and Bowes, 1968.

———. "Poetic Diction and Scientific Language." *Isis* 32(2) (1940): 324–338.

Asad, Talal. *Formations of the Secular: Christianity, Islam, Modernity.* Stanford: Stanford University Press, 2003.

———. *On Suicide Bombing.* New York: Columbia University Press, 2007.

Ashcraft, Richard. *Revolutionary Politics & Locke's "Two Treatises of Government."* Princeton: Princeton University Press, 1986.

Aston, Margaret. "Corpus Christi and Corpus Regni: Heresy and the Peasants' Revolt." *Past and Present* 143 (1994): 3–47.

———. "John Wycliffe's Reformation Reputation." *Past and Present* 30 (1965): 23–51.

Ayers, Michael. *Locke: Epistemology and Ontology.* London: Routledge, 1993.

———. "Locke's Logical Atomism." *Proceedings of the British Academy* 67 (1981): 209–225.

Aylmer, G. E., ed. *The Levellers in the English Revolution.* Ithaca, N.Y.: Cornell University Press, 1975.

———. "The Religion of Gerrard Winstanley." In *Radical Religion in the English Revolution,* ed. J. F. McGregor and B. Reay, pp. 91–119. Oxford: Oxford University Press, 1984.

Banfield, Ann. "Describing the Unobserved: Events Grouped Around an Empty Centre." In *The Linguistics of Writing: Arguments Between Language and Literature,* ed. Nigel Fabb, pp. 265–285. Manchester: Manchester University Press, 1987.

Barbour, Reid. "Between Atoms and Spirit: Lucy Hutchinson's Translation of Lucretius." *Renaissance Papers* (1994): 1–16.

———. *English Epicures and Stoics: Ancient Legacies in Early Stuart Culture.* Amherst: University of Massachusetts Press, 1998.

Barker-Benfield, G. J. *The Culture of Sensibility: Sex and Society in Eighteenth-Century Britain.* Chicago: University of Chicago Press, 1992.

Barlow, Richard G. "Infinite Worlds: Robert Burton's Cosmic Voyage." *Journal of the History of Ideas* 34(2) (1973): 291–302.

Barnouw, Jeffrey. "Hobbes's Psychology of Thought: Endeavours, Purpose, and Curiosity." *History of European Ideas* 10(5) (1989): 519–545.

Barry, Jonathan. "Bourgeois Collectivism? Urban Association and the Middling Sort." In *The Middling Sort of People: Culture, Society and Politics in England, 1550–1800,* ed. Jonathan Barry and Christopher Brooks, pp. 84–112. New York: St. Martin's Press, 1994.

Barthes, Roland. *Mythologies,* trans. Richard Howard. New York: Hill and Wang, 1979.

Baudrillard, Jean. *The Mirror of Production,* trans. Mark Poster. St. Louis: Telos Press, 1975.

Bauman, Zygmunt. *Legislators and Interpreters: On Modernity, Post-modernity and Intellectuals.* Cambridge: Polity Press, 1987.

Baxter, Nicola. "Gerrard Winstanley's Experimental Knowledge of God (The Perception of the Spirit and the Acting of Reason)." *Journal of Ecclesiastical History* 39(2) (1988): 184–201.

Bedford, R. D. "Right Spelling: Milton's *A Masque* and *Il Penseroso.*" *English Literary History* 52(4) (1985): 815–832.

Bednarz, James P. "Representing Jonson: '*Histriomastix*' and the Origin of the Poets' War." *Huntington Library Quarterly* 54(1) (1991): 1–30.

Beier, Lucinda McCray. *Sufferers and Healers: The Experience of Illness in Seventeenth-Century England.* London: Routledge and Kegan Paul, 1987.

Benedict, Barbara M. *Curiosity: A Cultural History of Early Modern Inquiry.* Chicago: University of Chicago Press, 2001.

Benet, Diana Treviño. "The Escape from Rome: Milton's *Second Defense* and a Renaissance Genre." In *Milton in Italy: Contexts, Images, Contradictions,* ed.

Mario A. Di Cesare, pp. 29–49. Binghamton, N.Y.: Medieval and Renaissance Texts and Studies, 1991.

Benjamin, Walter. *The Origin of German Tragic Drama,* trans. John Osborne. London: NLB, 1977.

Bennett, J. A. "Christopher Wren's Greshamite History of Astronomy and Geometry." In *Sir Thomas Gresham and Gresham College: Studies in the Intellectual History of London in the Sixteenth and Seventeenth Centuries,* ed. Francis Ames-Lewis, pp. 189–197. Hampshire, U.K.: Ashgate Publishing, 1999.

———. "Hooke's Instruments." In *London's Leonardo: The Life and Work of Robert Hooke,* ed. Jim Bennett, Michael Cooper, Michael Hunter, and Lisa Jardine, pp. 63–104. Oxford: Oxford University Press, 2003.

———. "The Mechanics' Philosophy and the Mechanical Philosophy." *History of Science* 24(1) (1986): 1–28.

———. "Robert Hooke as Mechanic and Natural Philosopher." *Notes and Records of the Royal Society of London* 35(1) (1980): 33–48.

Bennett, Joan S. "Asserting Eternal Providence: John Milton through the Window of Liberation Theology." In *Milton and Heresy,* ed. Stephen B. Dobranski and John P. Rumrich, pp. 219–243. Cambridge: Cambridge University Press, 1998.

———. *Reviving Liberty: Radical Christian Humanism in Milton's Great Poems.* Cambridge, Mass.: Harvard University Press, 1989.

Bennett, Judith M. "Conviviality and Charity and Medieval and Early Modern England." *Past and Present* 134 (1992): 19–41.

Berlin, Michael. "Reordering Rituals: Ceremony and the Parish, 1520–1640." In *Londinopolis: Essays in the Cultural and Social History of Early Modern London,* ed. Paul Griffiths and Mark S. R. Jenner, pp. 47–66. Manchester: Manchester University Press, 2000.

Berry, Helen. *Gender, Society and Print Culture in Late-Stuart England: The Cultural World of the "Athenian Mercury."* Aldershot, U.K.: Ashgate Publishing, 2003.

Biagioli, Mario. "Etiquette, Interdependence, and Sociability in Seventeenth-Century Science." *Critical Inquiry* 22(2) (1996): 193–238.

———. *Galileo's Instruments of Credit: Telescopes, Images, Secrecy.* Chicago: University of Chicago Press, 2006.

Black, Max. "Metaphor." *Proceedings of the Aristotelian Society* 55 (1954–1955): 273–294.

Black, Scott. *Of Essays and Reading in Early Modern Britain.* Houndmills, U.K.: Palgrave Macmillan, 2006.

Blanchard, Ian. "Sir Thomas and the 'House of Gresham': Activities of a Mercer-Merchant Adventurer." In *Sir Thomas Gresham and Gresham College: Studies in the Intellectual History of London in the Sixteenth and Seventeenth Centuries,* ed. Francis Ames-Lewis, pp. 13–23. Hampshire, U.K.: Ashgate Publishing, 1999.

Bloch, Ernst. *The Utopian Function of Art and Literature: Selected Essays,* trans. Jack Zipes and Frank Mecklenburg. Cambridge, Mass.: MIT Press, 1993.

Bloch, Marc. *The Royal Touch: Sacred Monarchy and Scrofula in England and France,* trans. J. E. Anderson. London: Routledge and Kegan Paul, 1973.

Bloom, Edward A. and Lillian D. Bloom. *Joseph Addison and Richard Steele: The Critical Heritage.* London: Routledge, 1995.

Bluhm, R. K. "Remarks on the Royal Society's Finances, 1660–1768." *Notes and Records of the Royal Society of London* 13(2) (1958): 82–103.

Blumenberg, Hans. *The Legitimacy of the Modern Age,* trans. Robert M. Wallace. Cambridge, Mass.: MIT Press, 1991.

———. *Shipwreck with Spectator: Paradigm of a Metaphor for Existence,* trans. Steven Rendall. Cambridge, Mass.: MIT Press, 1997.

Boas, George. *Primitivism and Related Ideas in the Middle Ages.* Baltimore: Johns Hopkins University Press, 1997.

Bond, Richmond P. "Isaac Bickerstaff, Esq." In *Restoration and Eighteenth-Century Literature: Essays in Honor of Alan Dugald McKillop,* ed. Caroll Camden, pp. 103–124. Chicago: University of Chicago Press, 1963. ["Published for William Marsh Rice University by the University of Chicago Press."]

Bono, James J. *The Word of God and the Languages of Man: Interpreting Nature in Early Modern Science and Medicine.* Madison: University of Wisconsin Press, 1995.

Borenius, Tancred and E. W. Tristram. *English Medieval Painting.* Florence, Italy: Pantheon, 1926.

Bourdieu, Pierre. *Science of Science and Reflexivity,* trans. Richard Nice. Chicago: University of Chicago Press, 2004.

Bourne, Ella. "The Messianic Prophecy in Vergil's Fourth Eclogue." *The Classical Journal* 11(7) (1916): 390–400.

Bowers, Terence N. "Great Britain Imagined: Nation, Citizen, and Class in Defoe's *Tour thro' the Whole Island of Great Britain.*" *Prose Studies* 16(3) (1993): 148–178.

Bowle, John. *John Evelyn and His World: A Biography.* London: Routledge and Kegan Paul, 1981.

Braden, Gordon. "Beyond Frustration: Petrarchan Laurels in the Seventeenth Century." *Studies in English Literature, 1500–1900* 26(1) (1986): 5–23.

———. See also Kerrigan, William.

Bradstock, Andrew. *Faith in the Revolution: The Political Theologies of Müntzer and Winstanley*. London: Society for Promoting Christian Knowledge, 1997.

———. "Restoring All Things From the Curse: Millenarianism, Alchemy, Science and Politics in the Writings of Gerrard Winstanley." In *The Arts of Seventeenth-Century Science: Representations of the Natural World in European and North American Culture,* ed. Claire Jowitt and Diane Watt, pp. 95–108. Aldershot, U.K.: Ashgate Publishing, 2002.

Breen, Timothy Hall. "The Non-Existent Controversy: Puritan and Anglican Attitudes on Work and Wealth, 1600–1640." *Church History* 35(3) (1966): 273–287.

Bremmer, Jan N. "Paradise, from Persia, via Greece, into the Septuagint." In *Paradise Interpreted: Representations of Biblical Paradise in Judaism and Christianity,* ed. Gerard P. Luttikhuizen, pp. 1–20. Leiden: Brill, 1999.

Brigden, Susan. "Youth and the English Reformation." *Past and Present* 95 (1982): 37–67.

Brogan, Hugh. "Marvell's Epitaph on —— ——." *Renaissance Quarterly* 32(2) (1979): 197–199.

Brooks, Christopher. "Apprenticeship, Social Mobility and the Middling Sort, 1550 1800." In *The Middling Sort of People: Culture, Society and Politics in England, 1550–1800,* ed. Jonathan Barry and Christopher Brooks, pp. 52–83. New York: St. Martin's Press, 1994.

Brown, Harold I. "Galileo on the Telescope and the Eye." *Journal of the History of Ideas* 46(4) (1985): 487–501.

Brown, Louise Fargo. "Ideas of Representation from Elizabeth to Charles II." *Journal of Modern History* 11(1) (1939): 23–40.

Brown, Peter. "The End of the Ancient Other World: Death and Afterlife between Late Antiquity and the Early Middle Ages." In *The Tanner Lectures on Human Values,* vol. 20, ed. Grethe B. Peterson, pp. 19–85. Salt Lake City: University of Utah Press, 1999.

Bryson, Anna. *From Courtesy to Civility: Changing Codes of Conduct in Early Modern England*. Oxford: Clarendon Press, 1998.

Bull, Malcolm. "Secularization and Medicalization." *British Journal of Sociology* 41(2) (1990): 245–261.

Burke, Peter. *Popular Culture in Early Modern Europe* (rev. reprint). Aldershot, U.K.: Ashgate Publishing, 2002.

Burrage, Champlin. *The Early English Dissenters in the Light of Recent Research (1550–1641).* 2 vols. Cambridge: Cambridge University Press, 1912.

Cacciari, Cristina. "Why Do We Speak Metaphorically? Reflections on the Functions of Metaphor in Discourse and Reasoning." In *Figurative Language and Thought,* ed. Albert N. Katz, Cristina Cacciari, Raymond W. Gibbs Jr., and Mark Turner, pp. 119–157. Oxford: Oxford University Press, 1998.

Camille, Michael. "'When Adam Delved': Laboring on the Land in English Medieval Art." In *Agriculture in the Middle Ages: Technology, Practice, and Representation,* ed. Del Sweeney, pp. 247–276. Philadelphia: University of Pennsylvania Press, 1995.

Canny, Nicholas P. *The Upstart Earl: A Study of the Social and Mental World of Richard Boyle, First Earl of Cork, 1566–1643.* Cambridge: Cambridge University Press, 1982.

Capp, Bernard. "The Fifth Monarchists and Popular Millenarianism." In *Radical Religion in the English Revolution,* ed. J. F. McGregor and B. Reay, pp. 165–189. Oxford: Oxford University Press, 1984.

Carey, John. "Reversals Transposed: An Aspect of Marvell's Imagination." In *Approaches to Marvell: The York Tercentenary Lectures,* ed. C. A. Patrides, pp. 136–154. London: Routledge and Kegan Paul, 1978.

Carlton, Peter J. "Bunyan: Language, Convention, Authority." *English Literary History* 51(1) (1984): 17–32.

Carpenter, Margaret Ann. "Marvell's 'Garden.'" *Studies in English Literature, 1500–1900* 10(1) (1970): 155–169.

Carruthers, Mary J. *The Book of Memory: A Study of Memory in Medieval Culture.* Cambridge: Cambridge University Press, 1990.

Chambers, A. B. *Andrew Marvell and Edmund Waller: Seventeenth-Century Praise and Restoration Satire.* University Park: Pennsylvania State University Press, 1991.

Chambers, Douglas. "'Elysium Britannicum not printed neere ready &c: The 'Elysium Britannicum' in the Correspondence of John Evelyn." In *John Evelyn's "Elysium Britannicum" and European Gardening,* ed. Therese O'Malley and Joachim Wolschke-Bulmahn, pp. 107–130. Washington, D.C.: Dumbarton Oaks Research Library and Collection, 1998.

Chapman, Allan. *England's Leonardo: Robert Hooke and the Seventeenth-Century Scientific Revolution.* Bristol, U.K.: CRC Press, 2005.

Chernaik, Warren L. *The Poet's Time: Politics and Religion in the Work of Andrew Marvell.* Cambridge: Cambridge University Press, 1983.

Christopher, Georgia B. *Milton and the Science of the Saints.* Princeton: Princeton University Press, 1982.

Clark, Peter. *The English Alehouse: A Social History 1200–1830.* London: Longman, 1983.

Claydon, Tony. "The Sermon, the 'Public Sphere' and the Political Culture of Late Seventeenth-Century England." In *The English Sermon Revised: Religion, Literature and History 1600–1750,* ed. Lori Anne Ferrell and Peter

McCullough, pp. 208–234. Manchester: Manchester University Press, 2000.

Clucas, Stephen. "Corpuscular Matter Theory in the Northumberland Circle." In *Late Medieval and Early Modern Corpuscular Matter Theories,* ed. Christoph Lüthy, John E. Murdoch, and William R. Newman, pp. 181–207. Leiden: Brill, 2001.

———. "Poetic Atomism in Seventeenth-Century England: Henry More, Thomas Traherne and 'Scientific Imagination.'" *Renaissance Studies* 5(3) (1991): 327–340.

Coffey, John. "A Ticklish Business: Defining Heresy and Orthodoxy in the Puritan Revolution." In *Heresy, Literature, and Politics in Early Modern English Culture,* ed. David Loewenstein and John Marshall, pp. 108–136. Cambridge: Cambridge University Press, 2006.

Cohen, I. Bernard. "The *Compendium Physicae* of Charles Morton (1627–1698)." *Isis* 33(6) (1942): 657–671.

Coiro, Ann Baynes. "Fable and Old Song: *Samson Agonistes* and the Idea of a Poetic Career." *Milton Studies* 36 (1998): 123–152.

———. "'To Repair the Ruins of Our First Parents': *Of Education* and Fallen Adam." *Studies in English Literature, 1500–1900* 28(1) (1988): 133–147.

Colic, Rosalie L."*My Ecchoing Song*": Andrew Marvell's Poetry of Criticism. Princeton: Princeton University Press, 1970.

Collins, Christopher. *The Poetics of the Mind's Eye: Literature and the Psychology of Imagination.* Philadelphia: University of Pennsylvania Press, 1991.

Collinson, Patrick. *The Birthpangs of Protestant England: Religious and Cultural Change in the Sixteenth and Seventeenth Centuries.* Houndmills, U.K.: Palgrave, 1988.

———. *The Elizabethan Puritan Movement.* Berkeley: University of California Press, 1967.

———. *Godly People: Essays on English Protestantism and Puritanism.* London: Hambledon Press, 1983.

Collinson, Patrick, John Craig, and Brett Usher, eds. *Conferences and Combination Lectures in the Elizabethan Church: Dedham and Bury St Edmunds 1582–1590.* Woodbridge, U.K.: Boydell Press, 2003.

Comito, Terry. "Renaissance Gardens and the Discovery of Paradise." *Journal of the History of Ideas* 32(4) (1971): 483–506.

Como, David R. *Blown by the Spirit: Puritanism and the Emergence of an Antinomian Underground in Pre-Civil-War England.* Stanford: Stanford University Press, 2004.

Congleton, J. E. *Theories of Pastoral Poetry in England, 1684–1798.* Gainesville: University of Florida Press, 1952.

Conklin, Paul Salisbury. *A History of Hamlet Criticism.* London: Routledge and Kegan Paul, 1957.

Constas, Nicholas. "'To Sleep, Perchance to Dream': The Middle State of Souls in Patristic and Byzantine Literature." *Dumbarton Oaks Papers* 55 (2001): 91–124.

Cooper, Tim. *Fear and Polemic in Seventeenth-Century England: Richard Baxter and Antinomianism.* Aldershot, U.K.: Ashgate Publishing, 2001.

Copley, Stephen. "Commerce, Conversation and Politeness in the Early Eighteenth-Century Periodical." *British Journal for Eighteenth-Century Studies* 18(1) (1995): 63–77.

Cormack, Lesley B. "'Good Fences Make Good Neighbors': Geography as Self-Definition in Early Modern England." *Isis* 82(4) (1991): 639–661.

Corns, Thomas N. "Milton's Antiprelatical Tracts and the Marginality of Doctrine." In *Milton and Heresy,* ed. Stephen B. Dobranski and John P. Rumrich, pp. 39–48. Cambridge: Cambridge University Press, 1998.

———. "The Road to George Hill: The Heretical Dynamic of Winstanley's Early Prose." In *Heresy, Literature, and Politics in Early Modern English Culture,* ed. David Loewenstein and John Marshall, pp. 185–202. Cambridge: Cambridge University Press, 2006.

Cottom, Daniel. "In the Bowels of the Novel: The Exchange of Fluids in the Beau Monde." *NOVEL: A Forum on Fiction* 32(2) (1999): 157–186.

Cousins, A. D. "Marvell's 'Upon Appleton House, to my Lord Fairfax' and the Regaining of Paradise." In *The Political Identity of Andrew Marvell,* ed. Conal Condren and A. D. Cousins, pp. 53–84. Aldershot, U.K.: Scolar Press, 1990.

Cowan, Brian William. "Mr. Spectator and the Coffeehouse Public Sphere." *Eighteenth-Century Studies* 37(3) (2004): 345–366.

———. "The Rise of the Coffeehouse Reconsidered." *The Historical Journal* 47(1) (2004): 21–46.

———. *The Social Life of Coffee: The Emergence of the British Coffeehouse.* New Haven: Yale University Press, 2005.

Craig, John. *Reformation, Politics and Polemics: The Growth of Protestantism in East Anglian Market Towns, 1500–1610.* Aldershot, U.K.: Ashgate Publishing, 2001.

Crane, Mary Thomas. *Framing Authority: Sayings, Self, and Society in Sixteenth-Century England.* Princeton: Princeton University Press, 1993.

Cranston, Maurice William. *John Locke: A Biography.* London: Longmans, Green, 1957.

Cressy, David. *Bonfires and Bells: National Memory and the Protestant Calendar in Elizabethan and Stuart England.* London: Weidenfeld and Nicholson, 1989.

———. "Describing the Social Order of Elizabethan and Stuart England." *Literature and History* 3 (1976): 29–44.

———. "Francis Bacon and the Advancement of Schooling." *History of European Ideas* 2(1) (1981): 65–74.

———. "The Protestant Calendar and the Vocabulary of Celebration in Early Modern England." *Journal of British Studies* 29(1) (1990): 31–52.

———. "Purification, Thanksgiving and the Churching of Women in Post-Reformation England." *Past and Present* 141 (1993): 106–146.

———. *Travesties and Transgressions in Tudor and Stuart England: Tales of Discord and Dissension.* Oxford: Oxford University Press, 2000.

Crombie, A. C. "Commentary on the Papers of Rupert Hall and Giorgio de Santillana." In *Critical Problems in the History of Science,* ed. Marshall Clagett, pp. 66–78. Madison: University of Wisconsin Press, 1959.

Cunich, Peter. "The Dissolution of the Chantries." In *The Reformation in English Towns, 1500–1640,* ed. Patrick Collinson and John Craig, pp. 159–174. Houndmills, U.K.: Macmillan, 1998.

Curry, Walter Clyde. *Milton's Ontology, Cosmogony, and Physics.* Lexington: University of Kentucky Press, 1957.

Cust, Richard. "The 'Public Man' in Late Tudor and Early Stuart England." In *The Politics of the Public Sphere in Early Modern England,* ed. Peter Lake and Steven Pincus, pp. 116–143. Manchester: Manchester University Press, 2007.

D., J. D. G. "The Arms of the Society." *Notes and Records of the Royal Society of London* 1(1) (1938): 37–39.

Dahm, John J. "Science and Apologetics in the Early Boyle Lectures." *Church History* 39(2) (1970): 172–186.

Daiches, David. "The Opening of *Paradise Lost.*" In *The Living Milton: Essays by Various Hands,* ed. Frank Kermode, pp. 55–69. London: Routledge and Paul, 1960.

Damrosch, Leopold, Jr. *God's Plot and Man's Stories: Studies in the Fictional Imagination from Milton to Fielding.* Chicago: University of Chicago Press, 1985.

———. *The Sorrows of the Quaker Jesus: James Nayler and the Puritan Crackdown on the Free Spirit.* Cambridge, Mass.: Harvard University Press, 1996.

Danielson, Dennis. *Milton's Good God: A Study in Literary Theodicy.* Cambridge: Cambridge University Press, 1982.

Darbishire, Helen, ed. *The Early Lives of Milton.* New York: Barnes and Noble, 1965.

Daston, Lorraine. "Baconian Facts, Academic Civility, and the Prehistory of Objectivity." *Annals of Scholarship* 8(3–4) (1991): 337–363.

———. "The Language of Strange Facts in Early Modern Science." In *Inscribing Science: Scientific Texts and the Materiality of Communication,* ed. Timothy Lenoir, pp. 20–38. Stanford: Stanford University Press, 1998.

Daston, Lorraine and Peter Galison. *Objectivity.* New York: Zone Books, 2007.

Daston, Lorraine and Katherine Park. *Wonders and the Order of Nature, 1150–1750.* New York: Zone Books, 1998.

Davenport, Edwin. "Elizabethan England's Other Reformation of Manners." *English Literary History* 63(2) (1996): 255–278.

Davis, J. C. "Radicalism in a Traditional Society: The Evaluation of Radical Thought in the English Commonwealth, 1649–1660." *History of Political Thought* 3(2) (1982): 193–213.

Davis, Lennard J. *Factual Fictions: The Origins of the English Novel.* Philadelphia: University of Pennsylvania Press, 1996.

Dear, Peter. *Discipline and Experience: The Mathematical Way in the Scientific Revolution.* Chicago: University of Chicago Press, 1995.

———. "From Truth to Disinterestedness in the Seventeenth Century." *Social Studies of Science* 22(4) (1992): 619–631.

———. "*Totius in Verba:* Rhetoric and Authority in the Early Royal Society." *Isis* 76(2) (1985): 145–161.

Debus, Allen G. *Man and Nature in the Renaissance.* Cambridge: Cambridge University Press, 1978.

Delany, Paul. "Attacks on Carew in William Habington's Poems." *Seventeenth Century News* 26(2) (1968): 36.

Deleuze, Gilles and Felix Guattari. *Anti-Oedipus: Capitalism and Schizophrenia,* trans. Robert Hurley, Mark Seem, and Helen R. Lane. Minneapolis: University of Minnesota Press, 1983.

———. *Kafka: Toward a Minor Literature,* trans. Dana Polan. Minneapolis: University of Minnesota Press, 1986.

Delumeau, Jean. *History of Paradise: The Garden of Eden in Myth and Tradition,* trans. Matthew O'Connell. New York: Continuum, 1995.

Deutsch, Helen. *Resemblance and Disgrace: Alexander Pope and the Deformation of Culture.* Cambridge, Mass.: Harvard University Press, 1996.

Devlin, Mary Aquinas. "Bishop Thomas Brunton and His Sermons." *Speculum* 14(3) (1939): 324–344.

Dinn, Robert. "'Monuments Answerable to Mens Worth': Burial Patterns, Social Status and Gender in Late Medieval Bury St Edmunds." *Journal of Ecclesiastical History* 46(2) (1995): 237–255.

Dobbs, Betty Jo Teeter and Margaret C. Jacob. *Newton and the Culture of Newtonianism.* Atlantic Highlands, N.J.: Humanities Press, 1995.

Dobel, Clifford, ed. *Anthony van Leeuwenhoek and His "Little Animals."* New York: Harcourt, Brace, 1932.

Dobranski, Stephen B. *Milton, Authorship, and the Book Trade.* Cambridge: Cambridge University Press, 1999.

————. "'Where Men of Differing Judgements Croud': Milton and the Culture of the Coffee Houses." *The Seventeenth Century* 9 (1994): 35–56.

Dodsworth, Martin. "Empson and the Trick of It." *Essays in Criticism* 51(1) (2001): 101–118.

Douglas, Mary. *Purity and Danger: An Analysis of the Concepts of Pollution and Taboo,* 2nd ed. New York: Routledge, 2002.

Drake, Stillman. *Galileo at Work: His Scientific Biography.* Chicago: University of Chicago Press, 1978.

Duckworth, Alistair M. "'Whig' Landscapes in Defoe's *Tour.*" *Philological Quarterly* 61(4) (1982): 453–465.

Duffy, Eamon. *The Stripping of the Altars: Traditional Religion in England, c. 1400–c. 1580.* New Haven: Yale University Press, 1992.

Dunn, John. *The Political Thought of John Locke: An Historical Account of the Argument of the "Two Treatises of Government."* London: Cambridge University Press, 1969.

Dunn, Kevin. "Milton among the Monopolists: *Areopagitica,* Intellectual Property and the Hartlib Circle." In *Samuel Hartlib and Universal Reformation: Studies in Intellectual Communication,* ed. Mark Greengrass, Michael Leslie, and Timothy Raylor, pp. 177–192. Cambridge: Cambridge University Press, 1994.

Duran, Angelica. *The Age of Milton and the Scientific Revolution.* Pittsburgh: Duquesne University Press, 2007.

Dzelzainis, Martin. "Andrew Marvell and the Restoration Literary Underground: Printing the Painter Poems." *The Seventeenth Century* 22(2) (2007): 395–410.

Eamon, William. "New Light on Robert Boyle and the Discovery of Colour Indicators." *Ambix* 27 (1980): 204–209.

————. *Science and the Secrets of Nature: Books of Secrets in Medieval and Early Modern Culture.* Princeton: Princeton University Press, 1994.

Edie, Carolyn A. "The Popular Idea of Monarchy on the Eve of the Stuart Restoration." *Huntington Library Quarterly* 39(4) (1976): 343–373.

Eddy, John A. "The Case of the Missing Sunspots." *Scientific American* 236(5) (1977): 80–92.

Edwards, Karen L. *Milton and the Natural World: Science and Poetry in "Paradise Lost."* Cambridge: Cambridge University Press, 1999.

Eisenstein, Elizabeth L. "The Advent of Printing and the Problem of the Renaissance." *Past and Present* 45 (1969): 19–89.

Eliade, Mircea. *A History of Religious Ideas,* vol. 1: *From the Stone Age to the Eleusinian Mysteries,* trans. Willard R. Trask. Chicago: University of Chicago Press, 1978.

————. *The Sacred and the Profane: The Nature of Religion,* trans. Willard R.
   Trask. New York: Harcourt and Brace, 1959.

Eliot, T. S. "Andrew Marvell." In *Selected Prose of T. S. Eliot,* ed. Frank Kermode,
   pp. 161–171. New York: Harcourt, Brace Jovanovich and Farrar, Straus and
   Giroux, 1975.

————. *On Poetry and Poets.* London: Faber and Faber, 1957.

Ellis, Aytoun. *The Penny Universities: A History of the Coffee Houses.* London:
   Secker and Warburg, 1956.

Ellis, Markman. "Coffee-Women, *The Spectator* and the Public Sphere in the
   Early Eighteenth Century." In *Women, Writing and the Public Sphere,
   1700–1830,* ed. Elizabeth Eger, Charlotte Grant, Clíona Ó Gallchoir, and
   Penny Warburton, pp. 27–52. Cambridge: Cambridge University Press,
   2001.

Ellrodt, Robert. "Marvell's Mind and Mystery." In *Approaches to Marvell: The
   York Tercentenary Lectures,* ed. C. A. Patrides, pp. 216–233. London: Routledge and Kegan Paul, 1978.

Emerton, Norma E. *The Scientific Reinterpretation of Form.* Ithaca, N.Y.: Cornell
   University Press, 1984.

Empson, William. *Some Versions of Pastoral.* Norfolk, Conn.: New Directions,
   1960.

'Espinasse, Margaret. "The Decline and Fall of Restoration Science." *Past and
   Present* 14 (1958): 71–89.

————. *Robert Hooke.* Berkeley: University of California Press, 1962.

Evans, J. M. *"Paradise Lost" and the Genesis Tradition.* Oxford: Oxford University
   Press, 1968.

Fabricant, Carole. "The Literature of Domestic Tourism and the Public Con-
   sumption of Private Property." In *The New Eighteenth Century: Theory, Politics,
   English Literature,* ed. Felicity Nussbaum and Laura Brown, pp. 254–275.
   New York: Methuen, 1987.

Fallon, Robert Thomas. *Divided Empire: Milton's Political Imagery.* University
   Park: Pennsylvania State University Press, 1995.

Fallon, Stephen M. *Milton among the Philosophers: Poetry and Materialism in
   Seventeenth-Century England.* Ithaca, N.Y.: Cornell University Press, 1991.

Fara, Patricia. *Newton: The Making of Genius.* New York: Columbia University
   Press, 2002.

Farr, James R. *Artisans in Europe, 1300–1914.* Cambridge: Cambridge University
   Press, 2000.

Fauconnier, Gilles. See Turner, Mark.

Feingold, Mordechai. "Gresham College and London Practitioners: The Nature
   of the English Mathematical Community." In *Sir Thomas Gresham and*

Gresham College: Studies in the Intellectual History of London in the Sixteenth and Seventeenth Centuries, ed. Francis Ames-Lewis, pp. 174–188. Aldershot, U.K.: Ashgate Publishing, 1999.

———. "Science as a Calling? The Early Modern Dilemma." *Science in Context* 15(1) (2002): 79–119.

Fell-Smith, Charlotte. *Mary Rich, Countess of Warwick (1625–1678): Her Family and Friends.* London: Longmans Green, 1901.

Ferry, Anne Davidson. *Milton's Epic Voice: The Narrator in "Paradise Lost."* Cambridge, Mass.: Harvard University Press, 1967.

Feyerabend, Paul. *Against Method,* rev. ed. London: Verso, 1988.

Fincham, Kenneth and Peter Lake. "Popularity, Prelacy and Puritanism in the 1630s: Joseph Hall Explains Himself." *English Historical Review* 111(443) (1996): 856–881.

Findlen, Paula. *Possessing Nature: Museums, Collecting, and Scientific Culture in Early Modern Italy.* Berkeley: University of California Press, 1994.

Fineman, Joel. "The Structure of Allegorical Desire." In *Allegory and Representation,* ed. Stephen J. Greenblatt, pp. 26–60. Baltimore: Johns Hopkins University Press, 1981.

Finkelpearl, Philip J. "John Marston's 'Histrio-Mastix' as an Inns of Court Play: A Hypothesis." *Huntington Library Quarterly* 29(3) (1966): 223–234.

Finlayson, Michael G. *Historians, Puritanism, and the English Revolution: The Religious Factor in English Politics before and after the Interregnum.* Toronto: University of Toronto Press, 1983.

Fisch, Harold. "Bishop Hall's Meditations." *Review of English Studies* 25(99) (1949): 210–221.

———. "The Scientist as Priest: A Note on Robert Boyle's Natural Theology." *Isis* 44(3) (1953): 252–265.

Fish, Stanley E. *Self-Consuming Artifacts: The Experience of Seventeenth-Century Literature.* Berkeley: University of California Press, 1972.

———. *Surprised by Sin: The Reader in "Paradise Lost."* Cambridge, Mass.: Harvard University Press, 1998.

———. "Things and Actions Indifferent: The Temptation of Plot in *Paradise Regained.*" *Milton Studies* 17 (1983): 163–185.

———. "What It's Like to Read *L'Allegro* and *Il Penseroso.*" In *Is There a Text in this Class? The Authority of Interpretive Communities,* pp. 112–135. Cambridge, Mass.: Harvard University Press, 1980.

Flannagan, Roy. "Belial and 'Effeminate Slackness' in *Paradise Lost* and *Paradise Regained.*" *Milton Quarterly* 19(1) (1985): 9–11.

Fletcher, Angus. *Allegory: The Theory of a Symbolic Mode.* Ithaca, N.Y.: Cornell University Press, 1982.

———. "Utopian History and *The Anatomy of Criticism*." In *Northrop Frye in Modern Criticism,* ed. Murray Krieger, pp. 31–73. New York: Columbia University Press, 1966.

Flynn, Carol Houlihan. "Running out of Matter: The Body Exercised in Eighteenth-Century Fiction." In *The Languages of Psyche: Mind and Body in Enlightenment Thought,* ed. G. S. Rousseau, pp. 147–185. Berkeley: University of California Press, 1990.

Forsyth, Neil. *The Satanic Epic.* Princeton: Princeton University Press, 2003.

Foster, Hal. "Postmodernism: A Preface." In *The Anti-Aesthetic: Essays on Postmodern Culture,* ed. Hal Foster, pp. ix–xvi. Port Townsend, Wash.: Bay Press, 1983.

———. *Recodings: Art, Spectacle, Cultural Politics.* Port Townsend, Wash.: Bay Press, 1985.

Foucault, Michel. *Madness and Civilization: A History of Insanity in the Age of Reason,* trans. Richard Howard. New York: Vintage Books, 1973.

———. *The Order of Things: An Archaeology of the Human Sciences.* New York: Vintage Books, 1973.

Fournier, Marian. *The Fabric of Life: Microscopy in the Seventeenth Century.* Baltimore: Johns Hopkins University Press, 1996.

Fowler, Alastair. "Georgic and Pastoral: Laws of Genre in the Seventeenth Century." In *Culture and Cultivation in Early Modern England: Writing and the Land,* ed. Michael Leslie and Timothy Raylor, pp. 81–88. Leicester, U.K.: Leicester University Press, 1992.

Fowler, Don. *Lucretius on Atomic Motion: A Commentary on De Rerum Natura, Book Two, lines 1–332.* Oxford: Oxford University Press, 2002.

Fox, Adam. *Oral and Literate Culture in England, 1500–1700.* Oxford: Oxford University Press, 2000.

Fraser, Russell. *The Language of Adam: On the Limits and Systems of Discourse.* New York: Columbia University Press, 1977.

Freedberg, David. *The Eye of the Lynx: Galileo, His Friends, and the Beginnings of Modern Natural History.* Chicago: University of Chicago Press, 2002.

———. *The Power of Images: Studies in the History and Theory of Response.* Chicago: University of Chicago Press, 1989.

French, J. Milton. "Chips from Milton's Workshop." *English Literary History* 10(3) (1943): 230–242.

———. "An Unpublished Reply (1659) to Milton's 'Defensio.'" *Modern Philology* 55(3) (1958): 164–169.

Friedman, Albert B. "'When Adam Delved . . .': Contexts of an Historic Proverb." In *The Learned and The Lewd: Studies in Chaucer and Medieval Literature,* ed. Larry D. Benson, pp. 213–230. Cambridge, Mass.: Harvard University Press, 1974.

Friedman, Donald M. "Galileo and the Art of Seeing." In *Milton in Italy: Contexts, Images, Contradictions,* ed. Mario A. Di Cesare, pp. 159–174. Binghamton, N.Y.: Medieval and Renaissance Texts and Studies, 1991.

———. *Marvell's Pastoral Art.* London: Routledge and Kegan Paul, 1970.

Froula, Christine. "When Eve Reads Milton: Undoing the Patriarchal Economy." In *John Milton,* ed. Annabel Patterson, pp. 142–164. London: Longman, 1992.

Frye, Northrop. "Agon and Logos: Revolution and Revelation." In *The Prison and the Pinnacle,* ed. Balachandra Rajan, pp. 135–163. Toronto: University of Toronto Press, 1973.

———. *The Return of Eden: Five Essays on Milton's Epics.* Toronto: University of Toronto Press, 1965.

———. "Varieties of Eighteenth-Century Sensibility." *Eighteenth-Century Studies* 24(2) (1990–1991): 157–172.

Fulton, John F. "The Honourable Robert Boyle, F.R.S. (1627–1692)." *Notes and Records of the Royal Society of London* 15 (1960): 119–135.

Funkenstein, Amos. *Theology and the Scientific Imagination from the Middle Ages to the Seventeenth Century.* Princeton: Princeton University Press, 1986.

Furtwangler, Albert. "The Making of Mr. Spectator." *Modern Language Quarterly* 38 (1977): 21–39.

Fuss, Diana. *Identification Papers.* New York: Routledge, 1995.

Galbraith, K .J "The Iconography of the Biblical Scenes at Malmesbury Abbey." *Journal of the British Archaeological Association,* 3rd ser. 28 (1965): 39–56.

Gallagher, Catherine. *Nobody's Story: The Vanishing Acts of Women Writers in the Marketplace, 1670–1820.* Berkeley: University of California Press, 1994.

Gearin-Tosh, Michael. "The Structure of Marvell's 'Last Instructions to a Painter.'" *Essays in Criticism* 22 (1972): 48–57.

Geertz, Clifford. *The Interpretation of Cultures.* New York: Basic Books, 1973.

George, Margaret. *Women in the First Capitalist Society: Experiences in Seventeenth-Century England.* Urbana: University of Illinois Press, 1988.

Giamatti, A. Bartlett. *The Earthly Paradise and the Renaissance Epic.* New York: Norton, 1966.

Gibson-Wood, Carol. "Susanna and her Elders: John Evelyn's Artistic Daughter." In *John Evelyn and his Milieu,* ed. Frances Harris and Michael Hunter, pp. 233–254. London: British Library, 2003.

Gill, Christopher. "Ancient Psychotherapy." *Journal of the History of Ideas* 46 (1985): 307–325.

Gilman, Ernest B. *The Curious Perspective: Literary and Pictorial Wit in the Seventeenth Century.* New Haven: Yale University Press, 1978.

———. *Iconoclasm and Poetry in the English Reformation: Down Went Dagon.* Chicago: University of Chicago Press, 1986.

Ginzburg, Carlo. "Clues: Morelli, Freud, and Sherlock Holmes." In *The Sign of Three: Dupin, Holmes, Peirce,* ed. Umberto Eco and Thomas A. Sebeok, pp. 81–118. Bloomington: Indiana University Press, 1983.

————. *Ecstasies: Deciphering the Witches' Sabbath,* trans. Raymond Rosenthal. New York: Penguin, 1991.

————. "High and Low: The Theme of Forbidden Knowledge in the Sixteenth and Seventeenth Centuries." *Past and Present* 73 (1976): 28–41.

Girard, René. *Violence and the Sacred,* trans. Patrick Gregory. Baltimore: Johns Hopkins University Press, 1977.

Gleick, James. *Isaac Newton.* New York: Pantheon, 2003.

Godfrey, Eleanor S. *The Development of English Glassmaking, 1560–1640.* Chapel Hill: University of North Carolina Press, 1975.

Goldberg, Jonathan. *Writing Matter: From the Hands of the English Renaissance.* Stanford: Stanford University Press, 1990.

Goldie, Mark. "Sir Peter Pett, Sceptical Toryism and the Science of Toleration in the 1680s." In *Persecution and Toleration: Papers Read at the Twenty-Second Summer Meeting and the Twenty-Third Winter Meeting of the Ecclesiastical History Society,* ed. W. J. Sheils, pp. 247–273. Oxford: Basil Blackwell for the Ecclesiastical History Society, 1984.

Goldman, Judith. "Visible Hand: 'System,' Method, and Suasion in the Human Natural Science of Adam Smith." Unpublished PhD dissertation.

Goldman, Peter. "Living Words: Iconoclasm and Beyond in John Bunyan's *Grace Abounding.*" *New Literary History* 33(3) (2002): 461–489.

Goodman, Kevis. *Georgic Modernity and British Romanticism: Poetry and the Mediation of History.* Cambridge: Cambridge University Press, 2004.

Goodman, Nelson. *Languages of Art: An Approach to a Theory of Symbols.* Indianapolis: Hackett Publishing, 1976.

Gordon, Scott Paul. "Voyeuristic Dreams: Mr. Spectator and the Power of Spectacle." *The Eighteenth Century: Theory and Interpretation* 36(1) (1995): 3–23.

Gowing, Laura. *Common Bodies: Women, Touch, and Power in Seventeenth-Century England.* New Haven: Yale University Press, 2003.

Gray, Erik. "Severed Hair from Donne to Pope." *Essays in Criticism* 47 (1997): 220–239.

Green, Rosalie B. "The Adam and Eve Cycle in the *Hortus Deliciarum.*" In *Late Classical and Mediaeval Studies in Honor of Albert Mathias Friend, Jr.,* ed. Kurt Weitzmann, pp. 340–347. Princeton: Princeton University Press, 1955.

Greenblatt, Stephen. *Hamlet in Purgatory.* Princeton: Princeton University Press, 2001.

Greene, Robert A. "Whichcote, Wilkins, 'Ingenuity,' and the Reasonableness of Christianity." *Journal of the History of Ideas* 42(2) (1981): 227–252.

Greengrass, Mark, Michael Leslie, and Timothy Raylor, eds. *Samuel Hartlib and Universal Reformation: Studies in Intellectual Communication.* Cambridge: Cambridge University Press, 1994.

Griffin, Dustin. "Milton in Italy: The Making of a Man of Letters?" In *Milton in Italy: Contexts, Images, Contradictions,* ed. Mario A. Di Cesare, pp. 19–27. Binghamton, N.Y.: Medieval and Renaissance Texts and Studies, 1991.

Griffin, Emma. *England's Revelry: A History of Popular Sports and Pastimes, 1660–1830.* Oxford: The British Academy and Oxford University Press, 2005.

Gross, Kenneth. " 'Pardon Me, Mighty Poet': Versions of the Bard in Marvell's 'On Mr. Milton's *Paradise Lost.*' " *Milton Studies* 16 (1982): 77–96.

———. "Satan and the Romantic Satan: A Notebook." In *Re-Membering Milton: Essays on the Texts and Traditions,* ed. Mary Nyquist and Margaret W. Ferguson, pp. 318–341. New York: Methuen, 1987.

———. *Spenserian Poetics: Idolatry, Iconoclasm, and Magic.* Ithaca, N.Y.: Cornell University Press, 1985.

Grossman, Marshall. *"Authors to Themselves": Milton and the Revelation of History.* Cambridge: Cambridge University Press, 1987.

———. *The Story of All Things: Writing the Self in English Renaissance Narrative Poetry.* Durham, N.C.: Duke University Press, 1998.

Gucer, Kathryn. " 'Not Heretofore Extant in Print': Where the Mad Ranters Are." *Journal of the History of Ideas* 61(1) (2000): 75–95.

Guerrini, Anita. *Obesity and Depression in the Enlightenment: The Life and Times of George Cheyne.* Norman: University of Oklahoma Press, 2000.

Guibbory, Achsah. *The Map of Time: Seventeenth-Century English Literature and Ideas of Pattern in History.* Urbana: University of Illinois Press, 1986.

Guillory, John. *Cultural Capital: The Problem of Literary Canon Formation.* Chicago: University of Chicago Press, 1993.

———. "The Father's House: *Samson Agonistes* in Its Historical Moment." In *Re-Membering Milton: Essays on the Texts and Traditions,* ed. Mary Nyquist and Margaret W. Ferguson, pp. 148–176. New York: Methuen, 1988.

———. "Milton, Narcissism, Gender: On the Genealogy of Male Self-Esteem." In *Critical Essays on John Milton,* ed. Christopher Kendrick, pp. 194–233. New York: G. K. Hall, 1995.

———. *Poetic Authority: Spenser, Milton, and Literary History.* New York: Columbia University Press, 1983.

Gurevich, A. J. "Popular and Scholarly Medieval Cultural Traditions: Notes in the Margin of Jacques Le Goff's Book." *Journal of Medieval History* 9(2) (1983): 71–90.

Gurney, John. "Gerrard Winstanley and the Digger Movement in Walton and Cobham." *The Historical Journal* 37(4) (1994): 775–802.

Haan, Estelle. "From *Academia* to *Amicitia:* Milton's Latin Writings and the Italian Academies." *Transactions of the American Philosophical Society,* new ser. 88(6) (1998): i–x, 1–208.

Habermas, Jürgen. *The Structural Transformation of the Public Sphere: An Inquiry into a Category of Bourgeois Society,* trans. Thomas Burger and Frederick Lawrence. Cambridge, Mass.: MIT Press, 1999.

Hacking, Ian. *Representing and Intervening: Introductory Topics in the Philosophy of Natural Science.* Cambridge: Cambridge University Press, 1983.

Hackos, Jo Ann T. "The Metaphor of the Garden in Defoe's *Tour thro' the Whole Island of Great Britain.*" *Papers on Language and Literature* 15(3) (1979): 247–262.

Hall, Marie Boas. "The Establishment of the Mechanical Philosophy." *Osiris* 10 (1952): 412–541.

———. *Henry Oldenburg: Shaping the Royal Society.* New York: Oxford University Press, 2002.

———. *Promoting Experimental Learning: Experiment and the Royal Society 1660–1727.* Cambridge: Cambridge University Press, 1991.

———. See also Hall, Rupert.

Hall, Rupert. "The Scholar and the Craftsman." In *Critical Problems in the History of Science,* ed. Marshall Clagett, pp. 3–23. Madison: University of Wisconsin Press, 1959.

Hall, Rupert and Marie Boas Hall. "The Intellectual Origins of the Royal Society: London and Oxford." *Notes and Records of the Royal Society of London* 23(2) (1968): 157–168.

Haller, William and Malleville Haller. "The Puritan Art of Love." *Huntington Library Quarterly* 5(2) (1942): 235–272.

Haney, Kristine Edmondson. *The Winchester Psalter: An Iconographic Study.* Leicester, U.K.: Leicester University Press, 1986.

Hanford, James Holly and James G. Taaffe. *A Milton Handbook,* 5th ed. New York: Appleton-Century-Crofts, 1970.

Hannaway, Owen. *The Chemists and the Word: The Didactic Origins of Chemistry.* Baltimore: Johns Hopkins University Press, 1975.

———. "Laboratory Design and the Aim of Science: Andreas Libavius versus Tycho Brahe." *Isis* 77(4) (1986): 584–610.

Harbage, Alfred. *Sir William Davenant: Poet Venturer, 1606–1668*. New York: Octagon Books, 1971.

Harkness, Deborah E. *The Jewel House: Elizabethan London and the Scientific Revolution*. New Haven: Yale University Press, 2007.

Harris, Frances. *Transformations of Love: The Friendship of John Evelyn and Margaret Godolphin*. Oxford: Oxford University Press, 2004.

Harris, Victor. *All Coherence Gone: A Study of the Seventeenth Century Controversy over Disorder and Decay in the Universe*. London: Frank Cass, 1966.

Harrison, Charles Trawick. "The Ancient Atomists and English Literature of the Seventeenth Century." *Harvard Studies in Classical Philology* 45 (1934): 1–79.

Harrison, Peter. *The Bible, Protestantism, and the Rise of Natural Science*. Cambridge: Cambridge University Press, 1998.

———. *The Fall of Man and the Foundations of Science*. Cambridge: Cambridge University Press, 2007.

Hartle, P. N. "Defoe and *The Wonders of the Peake*: The Place of Cotton's Poem in *A Tour thro' the Whole Island of Great Britain*." *English Studies* 67(5) (1986): 420–431.

Hartman, Geoffrey H. "Marvell, St. Paul, and the Body of Hope." *English Literary History* 31(2) (1964): 175–194.

Harwood, John T. "Rhetoric and Graphics in *Micrographia*." In *Robert Hooke: New Studies,* ed. Michael Hunter and Simon Schaffer, pp. 119–147. Woodbridge, U.K.: Boydell Press, 1989.

Haskin, Dayton. *Milton's Burden of Interpretation*. Philadelphia: University of Pennsylvania Press, 1994.

Hassel, R. Chris, Jr. "Donne's Ignatius His Conclave and the New Astronomy." *Modern Philology* 68(4) (1971): 329–337.

Hawkes, David. "Idolatry and Commodity Fetishism in the Antitheatrical Controversy." *Studies in English Literature, 1500–1900* 39(2) (1999): 255–273.

Hayles, N. Katherine. *How We Became Posthuman: Virtual Bodies in Cybernetics, Literature, and Informatics*. Chicago: University of Chicago Press, 1999.

Hazard, Mary E. "An Essay to Amplify 'Ornament': Some Renaissance Theory and Practice." *Studies in English Literature, 1500–1900* 16(1) (1976): 15–32.

Helgerson, Richard. *Forms of Nationhood: The Elizabethan Writing of England*. Chicago: University of Chicago Press, 1992.

———. *Self-Crowned Laureates: Spenser, Jonson, Milton, and the Literary System*. Berkeley: University of California Press, 1983.

Hembry, Phyllis. *The English Spa, 1560–1815: A Social History*. London: Althone Press, 1990.

Henderson, Robert W. *The King's Book of Sports in England and America.* New York: New York Public Library, 1948.

Henisch, Bridget Ann. *The Medieval Calendar Year.* University Park: Penn State University Press, 2002.

Hennessey, Lawrence R. "The Place of Saints and Sinners after Death." In *Origen of Alexandria: His World and His Legacy,* ed. Charles Kannengiesser and William L. Petersen, pp. 295–312. Notre Dame, Ind.: University of Notre Dame Press, 1988.

Henry, John. "Occult Qualities and the Experimental Philosophy: Active Principles in Pre-Newtonian Matter Theory." *History of Science* 24 (1986): 335–381.

———. "Robert Hooke, the Incongruous Mechanist." In *Robert Hooke: New Studies,* ed. Michael Hunter and Simon Schaffer, pp. 149–180. Woodbridge, U.K.: Boydell Press, 1989.

Herman, Peter C. "*Paradise Lost,* the Miltonic 'Or,' and the Poetics of Incertitude." *Studies in English Literature, 1500–1900* 43(1) (2003): 181–211.

Herz, Judith Scherer. "'For Whom This Glorious Sight?' Dante, Milton, and the Galileo Question." In *Milton in Italy: Contexts, Images, Contradictions,* ed. Mario A. Di Cesare, pp. 147–157. Binghamton, N.Y.: Medieval and Renaissance Texts and Studies, 1991.

Higgit, Rebekah. "Why I Don't FRS My Tail: Augustus de Morgan and the Royal Society." *Notes and Records of the Royal Society* 60(3) (2006): 253–259.

Hildburgh, W. L. "Folk-Life Recorded in Medieval English Alabaster Carvings." *Folklore* 60(2) (1949): 249–265.

———. "Further Miscellaneous Notes on Medieval English Alabaster Carvings." *The Antiquaries Journal* 17 (1937): 181–191.

Hill, Christopher. *Antichrist in Seventeenth-Century England.* London: Oxford University Press, 1971.

———. "The Bible in Seventeenth-Century English Politics." In *The Tanner Lectures on Human Values,* vol. 14, ed. Grethe B. Peterson, pp. 85–107. Salt Lake City: University of Utah Press, 1993.

———. "Covenant Theology and the Concept of 'A Public Person.'" In *The Collected Essays of Christopher Hill,* vol. 3, ed. Christopher Hill, pp. 300–324. Amherst: University of Massachusetts Press, 1986.

———. *England's Turning Point: Essays on Seventeenth Century English History.* London: Bookmarks, 2000.

———. *The English Bible and the Seventeenth-Century Revolution.* London: Allen Lane, 1993.

———. "From Lollards to Levellers." In *Rebels and Their Causes: Essays in Honour of A. L. Morton,* ed. Maurice Cornforth, pp. 49–67. London: Lawrence and Wishart, 1978.

———. *God's Englishman: Oliver Cromwell and the English Revolution.* New York: The Dial Press, 1970.

———. *The Intellectual Origins of the English Revolution Revisited.* Oxford: Clarendon Press, 1997.

———. "The Intellectual Origins of the Royal Society—London or Oxford?" *Notes and Records of the Royal Society of London* 23(2) (1968): 144–156.

———. "Milton and Marvell." In *Approaches to Marvell: The York Tercentenary Lectures,* ed. C. A. Patrides, pp. 1–30. London: Routledge and Kegan Paul, 1978.

———. *Milton and the English Revolution.* New York: Viking Press, 1977.

———. *A Nation of Change and Novelty: Radical Politics, Religion and Literature in Seventeenth-Century England.* London: Routledge, 1990.

———. *Puritanism and Revolution: Studies in Interpretation of the English Revolution of the Seventeenth Century.* New York: St. Martin's Press, 1997.

———. "Puritanism, Capitalism and the Scientific Revolution." *Past and Present* 29 (1964): 88–97.

———. *Society and Puritanism in Pre-Revolutionary England.* New York: Schocken Books, 1964.

———. *The World Turned Upside Down: Radical Ideas during the English Revolution.* London: Penguin, 1975.

Hilton, Rodney. *Bond Men Made Free: Medieval Peasant Movements and the English Rising of 1381.* New York: Viking Press, 1973.

Hintikka, Jaakko. "Knowing How, Knowing That, and Knowing What: Observations on Their Relation in Plato and Other Greek Philosophers." In *Modality, Morality and Other Problems of Sense and Nonsense: Essays Dedicated to Sören Halldén,* ed. Sören Halldén, pp. 1–12. Lund: Gleerup, 1973.

Hirsch, E. D, Jr. "Stylistics and Synonymity." *Critical Inquiry* 1(3) (1975): 559–579.

Hirst, Derek. *The Representative of the People? Voters and Voting in England under the Early Stuarts.* Cambridge: Cambridge University Press, 1975.

Hirst, Derek and Steven Zwicker. "High Summer at Nun Appleton, 1651: Andrew Marvell and Lord Fairfax's Occasions." *The Historical Journal* 36(2) (1993): 247–269.

Hodge, R. I. V. *Foreshortened Time: Andrew Marvell and Seventeenth Century Revolutions.* Ipswich, U.K.: D. S. Brewer, 1978.

Holsinger, Bruce. *Music, Body, and Desire in Medieval Culture: Hildegard of Bingen to Chaucer.* Stanford: Stanford University Press, 2001.

Holstun, James. *Ehud's Dagger: Class Struggle in the English Revolution.* London: Verso, 2000.

Horkheimer, Max and Theodor W. Adorno. *Dialectic of Enlightenment: Philosophical Fragments,* ed. Gunzelin Schmid Noerr, trans. Edmund Jephcott. Stanford: Stanford University Press, 2002.

Horne, William C. "Curiosity and Ridicule in Samuel Butler's Satire on Science." *Restoration: Studies in English Literary Culture, 1660–1700* 7(1) (1983): 8–18.

Houghton, Walter E, Jr. "The History of Trades: Its Relation to Seventeenth-Century Thought: As Seen in Bacon, Petty, Evelyn, and Boyle." *Journal of the History of Ideas* 2(1) (1941): 33–60.

Hoxby, Blair. *Mammon's Music: Literature and Economics in the Age of Milton.* New Haven: Yale University Press, 2002.

Hoyle, R. W. "The Origins of the Dissolution of the Monasteries." *The Historical Journal* 38(2) (1995): 275–305.

Hudson, Anne. *The Premature Reformation: Wycliffite Texts and Lollard History.* Oxford: Clarendon Press, 2002.

Hudson, Elizabeth K. "English Protestants and the *Imitatio Christi,* 1580–1620." *Sixteenth Century Journal* 19(4) (1988): 541–558.

Hughes, Ann. "Men, the 'Public' and the 'Private' in the English Revolution." In *The Politics of the Public Sphere in Early Modern England,* ed. Peter Lake and Steven Pincus, pp. 191–212. Manchester: Manchester University Press, 2007.

Hunt, Maurice. "Managing Spenser, Managing Shakespeare in *Comus.*" *Neophilologus* 88 (2004): 315–333.

Hunter, J. Paul. *Before Novels: The Cultural Contexts of Eighteenth-Century English Fiction.* New York: W. W. Norton, 1990.

Hunter, Michael. "The Disquieted Mind in Casuistry and Natural Philosophy: Robert Boyle and Thomas Barlow." In *Contexts of Conscience in Early Modern Europe, 1500–1700,* ed. Harald E. Braun and Edward Vallance, pp. 82–99. Basingstoke, U.K.: Palgrave Macmillan, 2004.

———. *Establishing the New Science: The Experience of the Early Royal Society.* Woodbridge, U.K.: Boydell Press, 1989.

———. *John Aubrey and the Realm of Learning.* New York: Science History Publications, 1975.

———. "John Evelyn in the 1650s: A Virtuoso in Quest of a Role." In *John Evelyn's "Elysium Britannicum" and European Gardening,* ed. Therese O'Malley and Joachim Wolschke-Bulmahn, pp. 79–106. Washington, D.C.: Dumbarton Oaks Research Library and Collection, 1998.

———. *Robert Boyle, 1621–91: Scrupulosity and Science.* Woodbridge, U.K.: Boydell Press, 2000.

———. "Robert Boyle (1627–91): A Suitable Case for Treatment?" *British Journal for the History of Science* 32(3) (1999): 261–275.

————, ed. *Robert Boyle by Himself and His Friends with a Fragment of William Wotton's Lost "Life of Boyle."* London: William Pickering, 1994.

————. *The Royal Society and Its Fellows, 1660–1700: The Morphology of an Early Scientific Institution.* Chalfont St. Giles, U.K.: British Society for the History of Science, 1982.

————. *Science and Society in Restoration England.* Cambridge: Cambridge University Press, 1981.

Hunter, Michael and Simon Schaffer, eds. *Robert Hooke: New Studies.* Woodbridge, U.K.: Boydell Press, 1989.

Hunter, Michael and Paul B. Wood. "Towards Solomon's House: Rival Strategies for Reforming the Early Royal Society." *History of Science* 24 (1986): 49–108.

Hunter, William B. "Belial's Presence in *Paradise Lost*." *Milton Quarterly* 19(1) (1985): 7–9.

Hutchison, Keith. "What Happened to Occult Qualities in the Scientific Revolution?" *Isis* 73(2) (1982): 233–253.

Hutson, Lorna. "Not the King's Two Bodies: Reading the 'Body Politic' in Shakespeare's Henry IV, Parts 1 and 2." In *Rhetoric and Law in Early Modern Europe,* ed. Victoria Kahn and Lorna Hutson, pp. 167–198. New Haven: Yale University Press, 2001.

Huttar, Charles A. "The Passion of Christ in *Paradise Regained*." *English Language Notes* 19 (1982): 236–260.

Hutton, Ronald. *The Rise and Fall of Merry England: The Ritual Year, 1400–1700.* Oxford: Oxford University Press, 1994.

Iliffe, Rob. "In the Warehouse: Privacy, Property and Priority in the Early Royal Society." *History of Science* 30 (1992): 29–68.

————. "Material Doubts: Hooke, Artisan Culture and the Exchange of Information in 1670s London." *British Journal for the History of Science* 28(3) (1995): 285–318.

Inwood, Stephen. *The Man Who Knew Too Much: The Strange and Inventive Life of Robert Hooke, 1635–1703.* London: Macmillan, 2002.

Jacob, James R. *Henry Stubbe: Radical Protestantism and the Early Enlightenment.* Cambridge: Cambridge University Press, 1983.

————. *Robert Boyle and the English Revolution: A Study in Social and Intellectual Change.* New York: Burt, Franklin, 1977.

Jacob, James R. and Timothy Raylor. "Opera and Obedience: Thomas Hobbes and 'A Proposition for Advancement of Moralitie' by Sir William Davenant." *The Seventeenth Century* 6(2) (1991): 205–250.

Jacob, Margaret C. See Dobbs, Betty Jo Teeter.

Jager, Rick. *The Tempter's Voice: Language and the Fall in Medieval Literature.* Ithaca, N.Y.: Cornell University Press, 1993.

James, M. R. *The Canterbury Psalter.* Canterbury, U.K.: Percy Lund Humphries, 1935.

———. "Lives of St Walstan." *Norfolk Archaeology* 19 (1917): 238–267.

Jameson, Frederic. *The Political Unconscious: Narrative as a Socially Symbolic Act.* Ithaca, N.Y.: Cornell University Press, 1981.

Jardine, Lisa. "Hooke the Man: His Diary and his Health." In *London's Leonardo: The Life and Work of Robert Hooke,* ed. Jim Bennett, Michael Cooper, Michael Hunter, and Lisa Jardine, pp. 163–206. Oxford: Oxford University Press, 2003.

———. *Ingenious Pursuits: Building the Scientific Revolution.* New York: Nan A. Talese, 1999.

Jenner, Mark. " 'Another *epocha*'? Hartlib, John Lanyon and the Improvement of London in the 1650s." In *Samuel Hartlib and Universal Reformation: Studies in Intellectual Communication,* ed. Mark Greengrass, Michael Leslie, and Timothy Raylor, pp. 343–356. Cambridge: Cambridge University Press, 1994.

Jennings, George Henry. *An Anecdotal History of the British Parliament, from the Earliest Periods to the Present Time.* New York: D. Appleton, 1881.

Jensen, Phebe. "Singing Psalms to Horn-Pipes: Festivity, Iconoclasm, and Catholicism in *The Winter's Tale.*" *Shakespeare Quarterly* 55(3) (2004): 279–306.

Johns, Adrian. *The Nature of the Book: Print and Knowledge in the Making.* Chicago: University of Chicago Press, 1998.

Johnson, Mark. See Lakoff, George.

Johnson, Paula. "Carew's 'A Rapture': The Dynamics of Fantasy." *Studies in English Literature, 1500–1900* 16(1) (1976): 145–155.

Jones, Everett. "Robert Hooke and *The Virtuoso.*" *Modern Language Notes* 66(3) (1951): 180–182.

Jones, Richard Foster. *Ancients and Moderns: A Study of the Rise of the Scientific Movement in Seventeenth-Century England.* New York: Dover Publications, 1961.

Jordan, W. K. *The Charities of London, 1480–1660: The Aspirations and the Achievements of the Urban Society.* London: George Allen and Unwin, 1960.

———. "The Forming of the Charitable Institutions of the West of England: A Study of the Changing Pattern of Social Aspirations in Bristol and Somerset, 1480–1660." *Transactions of the American Philosophical Society,* new ser. 50(8) (1960): 1–99.

Jose, Nicholas. *Ideas of the Restoration in English Literature, 1660–71.* Cambridge, Mass.: Harvard University Press, 1984.

Justice, Steven. *Writing and Rebellion: England in 1381.* Berkeley: University of California Press, 1994.

Kaderly, Nat Lewis. "Southey's Borrowings from Celia Fiennes." *Modern Language Notes* 69(4) (1954): 249–253.

Kahn, Victoria. "Allegory and the Sublime in *Paradise Lost*." In *John Milton,* ed. Annabel Patterson, pp. 185–201. London: Longman, 1992.

———. "Hamlet or Hecuba: Carl Schmitt's Decision." *Representations* 83 (2003): 67–96.

———. *Machiavellian Rhetoric: From the Counter-Reformation to Milton.* Princeton: Princeton University Press, 1994.

———. "Political Theology and Reason of State in *Samson Agonistes*." *The South Atlantic Quarterly* 95(4) (1996): 1065–1097.

———. *Wayward Contracts: The Crisis of Political Obligation in England, 1640–1674.* Princeton: Princeton University Press, 2004.

Kalas, Rayna. *Frame, Glass, Verse: The Technology of Poetic Invention in the English Renaissance.* Ithaca, N.Y.: Cornell University Press, 2007.

Kamerick, Kathleen. *Popular Piety and Art in the Late Middle Ages: Image Worship and Idolatry in England, 1350–1500.* New York: Palgrave, 2002.

Kaminski, Thomas. "Striving with Vergil: The Genesis of Milton's 'Blind Mouths.'" *Modern Philology* 92(4) (1995): 482–487.

Kantorowicz, Ernst H. *The Kings Two Bodies: A Study in Mediaeval Political Theology,* rev. ed. Princeton: Princeton University Press, 1997.

Kaufman, U. Milo. *Paradise in the Age of Milton.* Victoria, Canada: University of Victoria Press, 1978.

Keeble, N. H. *The Literary Culture of Nonconformity in Later Seventeenth-Century England.* Athens: University of Georgia Press, 1987.

———. "Why Transprose *The Rehearsal?*" In *Marvell and Liberty,* ed. Warren Chernaik and Martin Dzelzainis, pp. 249–268. Houndmills, U.K.: Macmillan, 1999.

Kegl, Rosemary. "'Joyning My Labour to My Pain': The Politics of Labor in Marvell's Mower Poems." In *Soliciting Interpretation: Literary Theory and Seventeenth-Century English Poetry,* ed. Elizabeth D. Harvey and Katharine Eisaman Maus, pp. 89–118. Chicago: University of Chicago Press, 1990.

Kelly, Hans A. "The Metamorphoses of the Eden Serpent during the Middle Ages and Renaissance." *Viator* 2 (1971): 301–328.

Kendall, R. T. *Calvinism and English Calvinism to 1649.* Carlisle, U.K.: Paternoster Press, 1997.

Kenny, Neil. *Curiosity in Early Modern Europe: Word Histories.* Wiesbaden: Harrassowitz, 1998.

Kenyon, John Philipps. *The Stuart Constitution, 1603–1688: Documents and Commentary.* Cambridge: Cambridge University Press, 1986

Kerrigan, William. *The Sacred Complex: On the Psychogenesis of "Paradise Lost."* Cambridge, Mass.: Harvard University Press, 1983.

Kerrigan, William and Gordon Braden. "Milton's Coy Eve: *Paradise Lost* and Renaissance Love Poetry." In *Modern Critical Interpretations: John Milton's "Paradise Lost,"* ed. Harold Bloom, pp. 133–156. New York: Chelsea House, 1987.

Ketcham, Michael G. *Transparent Designs: Reading, Performance, and Form in the "Spectator" Papers.* Athens: University of Georgia Press, 1985.

Key, Andrew F. "The Concept of Death in Early Israelite Religion." *Journal of Bible and Religion* 32(3) (1964): 239–247.

King, Bruce. "'The Mower against Gardens' and the Levellers." *Huntington Library Quarterly* 33(3) (1970): 237–242.

King, John N. "Miltonic Transubstantiation." *Milton Studies* 36 (1998): 41–58.

Klein, Lawrence E. "Coffeehouse Civility, 1660–1714: An Aspect of Post-Courtly Culture in England." *Huntington Library Quarterly* 59(1) (1996): 30–51.

———. "Gender, Conversation and the Public Sphere in Early Eighteenth-Century England." In *Textuality and Sexuality: Reading Theories and Practices,* ed. Judith Still and Michael Worton, pp. 100–115. Manchester: Manchester University Press, 1993.

———. *Shaftesbury and the Culture of Politeness: Moral Discourse and Cultural Politics in Early Eighteenth-Century England.* Cambridge: Cambridge University Press, 1994.

Klibansky, Raymond, Erwin Panofsky, and Fritz Saxl. *Saturn and Melancholy: Studies in the History of Natural Philosophy, Religion, and Art.* London: Nelson, 1964.

Knight, Charles A. "*The Spectator*'s Generalizing Discourse." In *Telling People What to Think: Early Eighteenth-Century Periodicals from the Review to the Rambler,* ed. J. A. Downie and Thomas N. Corns, pp. 44–57. London: Frank Cass, 1993.

Knoppers. Laura Lunger. *Historicizing Milton: Spectacle, Power, and Poetry in Restoration England.* Athens: University of Georgia Press, 1994.

Knott, John R, Jr. *The Sword of the Spirit: Puritan Responses to the Bible.* Chicago: University of Chicago Press, 1980.

Knutson, Roslyn L. "*Histrio-Mastix:* Not by John Marston." *Studies in Philology* 98(3) (2001): 359–377.

Kolb, Laura. "One Bee Is No Bee." Unpublished paper.

Koyré, Alexandre. *From the Closed World to the Infinite Universe.* Baltimore: Johns Hopkins University Press, 1957.

Kroll, Richard. *Restoration Drama and "The Circle of Commerce": Tragicomedy, Politics, and Trade in the Seventeenth Century.* Cambridge: Cambridge University Press, 2007.

Kuhn, Thomas S. *The Structure of Scientific Revolutions.* Chicago: University of Chicago Press, 1996.

Kümin, Beat. "Voluntary Religion and Reformation Change in Eight Urban Parishes." In *The Reformation in English Towns, 1500–1640,* ed. Patrick Collinson and John Craig, pp. 175–189. New York: St. Martin's Press, 1998.

Lake, Peter. *The Boxmaker's Revenge: "Orthodoxy", "Heterodoxy" and the Politics of the Parish in Early Stuart London.* Stanford: Stanford University Press, 2001.

———. "Serving God and the Times: The Calvinist Conformity of Robert Sanderson." *Journal of British Studies* 27(2) (1988): 81–116.

———. See also Fincham, Kenneth.

Lake, Peter and Steven Pincus, eds. *The Politics of the Public Sphere in Early Modern England.* Manchester: Manchester University Press, 2007.

———. "Rethinking the Public Sphere In Early Modern England." *Journal of British Studies* 45(2) (2006): 270–292.

Lakoff, George and Mark Johnson. *Metaphors We Live By.* Chicago: University of Chicago Press, 1980.

Lambert, Malcolm. *Medieval Heresy: Popular Movements from the Gregorian Reform to the Reformation.* Oxford: Blackwell, 2002.

Lamont, William M. "Richard Baxter, the Apocalypse, and the Mad Major." *Past and Present* 55 (1972): 68–90.

———. *Marginal Prynne, 1600–1669.* London: Routledge and Kegan Paul, 1963.

Lang, Bernhard. See McDannell, Colleen.

Leavis, F. R. "Milton's Verse." In *Revaluation: Tradition and Development in English Poetry,* pp. 42–67. New York: Norton, 1963.

Lees-Jeffries, Hester. "From the Fountain to the Well: Redcrosse Learns to Read." *Studies in Philology* 100(2) (2003): 135–176.

Le Goff, Jacques. *The Birth of Purgatory,* trans. Arthur Goldhammer. Chicago: University of Chicago Press, 1984.

Legouis, Pierre. *Andrew Marvell: Poet, Puritan, Patriot.* Oxford: Clarendon Press, 1968.

Leishman, James B. *The Art of Marvell's Poetry.* London: Hutchinson Press, 1966.

Leonard, John. *Naming in Paradise: Milton and the Language of Adam and Eve.* Oxford: Clarendon Press, 1990.

Leslie, Michael. "'Bringing Ingenuity into Fashion': The 'Elysium Britannicum' and the Reformation of Husbandry." In *John Evelyn's "Elysium Britannicum" and European Gardening,* ed. Therese O'Malley and Joachim Wolschke-Bulmahn, pp. 131–152. Washington: Dumbarton Oaks Research Library and Collection, 1998.

————. "The Spiritual Husbandry of John Beale." In *Culture and Cultivation in Early Modern England: Writing and the Land,* ed. Michael Leslie and Timothy Raylor, pp. 151–172. Leicester, U.K.: Leicester University Press, 1992.

————. See also Greengrass, Mark.

Lewalski, Barbara Kiefer. *The Life of John Milton: A Critical Biography.* London: Blackwells, 2000.

————. *Milton's Brief Epic: The Genre, Meaning, and Art of "Paradise Regained."* Providence, R.I.: Brown University Press, 1966.

————. "Milton's Samson and the 'New Acquist of True [Political] Experience.'" *Milton Studies* 24 (1988): 233–251.

————. *"Paradise Lost" and the Rhetoric of Literary Forms.* Princeton: Princeton University Press, 1985.

————. *Protestant Poetics and the Seventeenth-Century Religious Lyric.* Princeton: Princeton University Press, 1979.

Lewis, C. S. "Addison." In *Essays on the Eighteenth Century Presented to David Nichol Smith in Honour of his Seventieth Birthday,* pp. 1–14. Oxford: Clarendon Press, 1945.

————. *A Preface to "Paradise Lost."* Oxford: Oxford University Press, 1961.

Lieb, Michael. *The Dialectics of Creation: Patterns of Birth and Regeneration in "Paradise Lost."* Amherst: University of Massachusetts Press, 1970.

————. "'Yet Once More': The Formulaic Opening of *Lycidas.*" *Milton Quarterly* 12(1) (1978): 23–28.

Lilley, Samuel. "Robert Recorde and the Idea of Progress: A Hypothesis and Verification." *Renaissance and Modern Studies* 2 (1958): 3–37.

Litzenberger, Caroline J. *The English Reformation and the Laity: Gloucestershire, 1540–1580.* Cambridge: Cambridge University Press, 1997.

Loewenstein, David. *Milton and the Drama of History: Historical Vision, Iconoclasm, and the Literary Imagination.* Cambridge: Cambridge University Press, 1990.

Loewenstein, David and John Morrill. "Literature and Religion." In *Cambridge History of Early Modern English Literature,* ed. David Loewenstein and Janel Mueller, pp. 664–713. Cambridge: Cambridge University Press, 2002.

Loftis, John. *Steele at Drury Lane.* Berkeley: University of California Press, 1952.

Long, Pamela O. *Openness, Secrecy, Authorship: Technical Arts and the Culture of Knowledge from Antiquity to the Renaissance.* Baltimore: Johns Hopkins University Press, 2001.

Love, Harold. *The Culture and Commerce of Texts: Scribal Publication in Seventeenth-Century England.* Boston: University of Massachusetts Press, 1998.

Low, Anthony. *The Blaze of Noon: A Reading of "Samson Agonistes."* New York: Columbia University Press, 1974.

————. *The Georgic Revolution*. Princeton: Princeton University Press, 1985.

Lukken, G. M. *Original Sin in the Roman Liturgy: Research into the Theology of Original Sin in the Roman Sacramentaria and the Early Baptismal Liturgy*. Leiden: E. J. Brill, 1973.

Lupton, Julia Reinhard. *Citizen-Saints: Shakespeare and Political Theology*. Chicago: University of Chicago Press, 2005.

Lüthy, Christoph. "The Fourfold Democritus on the Stage of Early Modern Science." *Isis* 91(3) (2000): 443–479.

Lüthy, Christoph, John E. Murdoch, and William R. Newman, eds. *Late Medieval and Early Modern Corpuscular Matter Theories*. Leiden: Brill, 2001.

Luxon, Thomas H. *Literal Figures: Puritan Allegory and the Reformation Crisis in Representation*. Chicago: University of Chicago Press, 1995.

————. "'Not I, But Christ': Allegory and the Puritan Self." *English Literary History* 60(4) (1993): 899–937.

————. *Single Imperfection: Milton, Marriage and Friendship*. Pittsburgh: Duquesne University Press, 2005.

Lynch, Beth. "Mr. Smirke and 'Mr. Filth': A Bibliographic Case Study in Nonconformist Printing." *The Library* 1(1) (2000): 46–71.

MacGregor, Arthur. "The Cabinet of Curiosities in Seventeenth-Century Britain." In *The Origins of Museums: The Cabinet of Curiosities in Sixteenth- and Seventeenth-Century Europe*, ed. Oliver Impey and Arthur MacGregor, pp. 147–158. Oxford: Clarendon Press, 1985.

Mack, Phyllis. "Religious Dissenters in Enlightenment England." *History Workshop Journal* 49 (2000): 1–23.

Macpherson, C. B. *The Political Theory of Possessive Individualism: Hobbes to Locke*. Oxford: Clarendon Press, 1962.

Maddison, R. E. W. "Studies in the Life of Robert Boyle, F.R.S. Part VI: The Stalbridge Period, 1645–1655, and the Invisible College." *Notes and Records of the Royal Society of London* 18(2) (1963): 104–124.

Mandelbrote, Giles. "John Evelyn and His Books." In *John Evelyn and His Milieu*, ed. Frances Harris and Michael Hunter, pp. 71–94. London: British Library, 2003.

Manning, Brian. *The English People and the English Revolution*, rev ed. London: Bookmarks, 1991.

————. *The Far Left in the English Revolution, 1640 to 1660*. London: Bookmarks, 1999.

Marcus, Leah Sinanoglou. *Childhood and Cultural Despair: A Theme and Variations in Seventeenth-Century Literature*. Pittsburgh: University of Pittsburgh Press, 1978.

————. *The Politics of Mirth: Jonson, Herrick, Milton, Marvell, and the Defense of Old Holiday Pastimes.* Chicago: University of Chicago Press, 1989.

Marcuse, Herbert. *One-Dimensional Man,* 2nd ed. London: Routledge, 2002.

————. "Repressive Tolerance." In Robert Paul Wolff, Barrington Moore Jr., and Herbert Marcuse, *A Critique of Pure Tolerance,* pp. 81–123. Boston: Beacon Press, 1969.

Marjara, Harinder Singh. *Contemplation of Created Things: Science in "Paradise Lost."* Toronto: University of Toronto Press, 1992.

Markley, Robert. " 'Land Enough in the World': Locke's Golden Age and the Infinite Extension of 'Use.' " *South Atlantic Quarterly* 98(4) (1999): 817–837.

Marshall, John. *John Locke: Resistance, Religion and Responsibility.* Cambridge: Cambridge University Press, 1996.

————. *John Locke, Toleration and Early Enlightenment Culture: Religious Intolerance and Arguments for Religious Toleration in Early Modern and "Early Enlightenment" Europe.* Cambridge: Cambridge University Press, 2006.

Marshall, Peter. *Beliefs and the Dead in Reformation England.* Oxford: Oxford University Press, 2002.

————. *The Catholic Priesthood and the English Reformation.* Oxford: Clarendon Press, 1994.

Martin, Catherine Gimelli. "The Phoenix and the Crocodile: Milton's Natural Law Debate with Hobbes Retried in the Tragic Forum of *Samson Agonistes*." In *The English Civil Wars in the Literary Imagination,* ed. Claude J. Summers and Ted-Larry Pebworth, pp. 242–270. Columbia: University of Missouri Press, 1999.

————. *The Ruins of Allegory: "Paradise Lost" and the Metamorphosis of Epic Convention.* Durham, N.C.: Duke University Press, 1998.

————. " 'What If the Sun Be Centre to the World?' Milton's Epistemology, Cosmology, and Paradise of Fools Reconsidered." *Modern Philology* 99(2) (2001): 231–265.

Martin, D. C. "Sir Robert Moray, F.R.S. (1608?–1673)." *Notes and Records of the Royal Society of London* 15 (1960): 239–250.

Martin, L. C. " 'Muing Her Mighty Youth': A Defence." *Review of English Studies* 21(81) (1945): 44–46.

Marx, Karl. *Capital: A Critique of Political Economy,* trans. Samuel Moore and Edward Aveling, ed. Frederick Engels. New York: Random House, 1906.

————. *Economic and Philosophic Manuscripts of 1844.* Moscow: Foreign Languages Publishing House, 1961.

Marx, Steven. "The Prophet Disarmed: Milton and the Quakers." *Studies in English Literature, 1500–1900* 32(1) (1992): 111–128.

Massarella, Derek. "The Politics of the Army and the Quest for Settlement." In *"Into Another Mould": Aspects of the Interregnum,* rev. ed., ed. Ivan Roots, pp. 101–137. Exeter, U.K.: University of Exeter Press, 1998.

Masson, David. *The Life of John Milton: Narrated in Connexion with the Political, Ecclesiastical, and Literary History of His Time.* 7 vols. Reprint, Gloucester, Mass.: Peter Smith, 1965.

Matheson, Lister M. "The Peasants' Revolt through Five Centuries of Rumor and Reporting: Richard Fox, John Stow, and Their Successors." *Studies in Philology* 95(2) (1998): 121–151.

Maus, Katharine Eisaman. "A Womb of His Own: Male Renaissance Poets in the Female Body." In *Sexuality and Gender in Early Modern Europe: Institutions, Texts, Images,* ed. James Grantham Turner, pp. 266–288. Cambridge: Cambridge University Press, 1993.

McColley, Diane Kelsey. "Eve's Dream." *Milton Studies* 12 (1978): 25–45.

———. *A Gust for Paradise: Milton's Eden and the Visual Arts.* Urbana: University of Illinois Press, 1993.

McColley, Grant. "Milton's Dialogue on Astronomy: The Principal Immediate Sources." *Papers of the Modern Language Association* 52(3) (1937): 728–762.

McDannell, Colleen and Bernhard Lang. *Heaven: A History,* rev. ed. New Haven: Yale University Press, 2001.

McDowell, Nicholas. *The English Radical Imagination: Culture, Religion, and Revolution, 1630–1660.* Oxford: Clarendon Press, 2003.

McDowell, Paula. *The Women of Grub Street: Press, Politics, and Gender in the London Literary Marketplace, 1678–1730.* New York: Oxford University Press, 1998.

McEwen, Gilbert D. *The Oracle of the Coffee House: John Dunton's Athenian Mercury.* San Marino, Calif.: Huntington Library, 1972.

McGuire, J. E. "Neoplatonism and Active Principles: Newton and the *Corpus Hermeticum.*" In *Hermeticism and the Scientific Revolution,* ed. Robert S. Westman and J. E. McGuire, pp. 95–142. Los Angeles: William Andrews Clark Memorial Library, 1977.

McGuire, J. E. and P. M. Rattansi. "Newton and the 'Pipes of Pan.'" *Notes and Records of the Royal Society of London* 21(2) (1966): 108–143.

McKeon, Michael. *The Origins of the English Novel, 1600–1740.* Baltimore: Johns Hopkins University Press, 1987.

———. "Parsing Habermas's 'Bourgeois Public Sphere.'" *Criticism* 46(2) (2004): 273–277.

———. *The Secret History of Domesticity: Public, Private, and the Division of Knowledge.* Baltimore: Johns Hopkins University Press, 2005.

McKie, Douglas. "The Arrest and Imprisonment of Henry Oldenburg." *Notes and Records of the Royal Society of London* 6(1) (1948): 28–47.

McLoone, George H. *Milton's Poetry of Independence: Five Studies.* Lewisburg, Penn.: Bucknell University Press, 1999.

McWilliams, John. "Marvell and Milton's Literary Friendship Reconsidered." *Studies in English Literature, 1500–1900* 46(1) (2006): 155–177.

Meehan, Johanna, ed. *Feminists Read Habermas: Gendering the Subject of Discourse.* New York: Routledge, 1995.

Mendelsohn, J. Andrew. "Alchemy and Politics in England 1649–1665." *Past and Present* 135 (1992): 30–78.

Mendyk, Stan. "Early British Chorography." *The Sixteenth Century Journal* 17(4) (1986): 459–481.

Merton, R. K. "Science, Technology and Society in Seventeenth Century England." *Osiris* 4 (1938): 360–632.

Messina, Joseph. "The Heroic Image in *The Last Instructions to a Painter.*" In *Tercentenary Essays in Honor of Andrew Marvell,* ed. Kenneth Friedenreich, pp. 297–310. Hamden, Conn.: Archon Books, 1977.

Meynell, G. G. "John Locke and the Preface to Thomas Sydenham's *Observationes Medicae.*" *Medical History* 50(1) (2006): 93–110.

Middleton, W. E. Knowles. "Some Italian Visitors to the Early Royal Society." *Notes and Records of the Royal Society of London* 33(2) (1979): 157–173.

———. "What Did Charles II Call the Fellows of the Royal Society?" *Notes and Records of the Royal Society of London* 32(1) (1977): 13–16.

Miller, Perry. *Errand into the Wilderness.* Cambridge, Mass.: Harvard University Press, 1984.

Mintz, Samuel I. *The Hunting of Leviathan: Seventeenth-Century Reactions to the Materialism and Moral Philosophy of Thomas Hobbes.* Cambridge: Cambridge University Press, 1962.

Mitchell, Joshua. "Hobbes and the Equality of All under the One." *Political Theory* 21(1) (1993): 78–100.

Moir, Esther. *The Discovery of Britain: The English Tourists, 1540 to 1840.* London: Routledge and Kegan Paul, 1964.

Moisà, Maria. "Debate: Conviviality and Charity in Medieval and Early Modern England." *Past and Present* 154 (1997): 223–234.

Molland, A. G. "Medieval Ideas of Scientific Progress." *Journal of the History of Ideas* 39(4) (1978): 561–577.

Montagu, M. F. Ashley. *Edward Tyson, M.D., F.R.S., 1650–1708, and the Rise of Human and Comparative Anatomy in England.* Philadelphia: American Philosophical Society, 1943.

Montrose, Louis Adrian. "Of Gentlemen and Shepherds: The Politics of Elizabe-
    than Pastoral Form." *English Literary History* 50(3) (1983): 415–459.
Morgan, Nigel. *Early Gothic Manuscripts*. 2 vols. London: Harvey Miller
    Publishers and Oxford University Press, 1982.
———. *The Medieval Painted Glass of Lincoln Cathedral*. London: Oxford
    University Press, 1983.
Mowry, Melissa M. *The Bawdy Politic in Stuart England, 1660–1714: Political
    Pornography and Prostitution*. Aldershot, U.K.: Ashgate Publishing, 2004.
Müller, Miriam. "The Aims and Organisation of a Peasant Revolt in Early
    Fourteenth-Century Wiltshire." *Rural History* 14(1) (2003): 1–20.
Mulligan, Lotte. "Puritans and English Science: A Critique of Webster." *Isis* 71(3)
    (1980): 456–469.
Mulligan, Lotte and Glenn Mulligan. "Reconstructing Restoration Science:
    Styles of Leadership and Social Composition of the Early Royal Society."
    Social Studies of Science 11(3) (1981): 327–364.
Mulvey, Laura. *Fetishism and Curiosity*. Bloomington: Indiana University Press;
    London: British Film Institute, 1996.
Murdoch, John E. See Lüthy, Christoph.
Nablow, Ralph A. *The Addisonian Tradition in France: Passion and Objectivity in
    Social Observation*. Cranbury, N.J.: Associated University Presses, 1990.
Nagel, Thomas. *The View from Nowhere*. New York: Oxford University Press,
    1986.
———. "What Is It Like to Be a Bat?" In *Mortal Questions,* pp. 165–180.
    Cambridge: Cambridge University Press, 1979.
Nardo, Anna K. "Academic Interludes in *Paradise Lost.*" *Milton Studies* 27 (1991):
    209–241.
Neale, J. E. *The Elizabethan House of Commons*. London: Jonathan Cape, 1961.
Neaman, Judith S. "The Mystery of the Ghent Bird and the Invention of
    Spectacles." *Viator* 24 (1993): 189–214.
Needham, Joseph. "Laudian Marxism? Thoughts on Science, Religion, and
    Socialism." *The Criterion* 12(46) (1932): 56–72.
Nethercot, Arthur H. *Sir William D'Avenant, Poet Laureate and Playwright-
    Manager*. New York: Russell and Russell, 1967.
Nettleton, George Henry. *English Drama of the Restoration and Eighteenth
    Century (1642–1780)*. New York: Macmillan, 1914.
Neumann, Franz L. *Behemoth: The Structure and Practice of National Socialism,
    1933–1944*. New York: Octagon Books, 1963.
Newman, William R. "Experimental Corpuscular Theory in Aristotelian
    Alchemy: From Geber to Sennert." In *Late Medieval and Early Modern*

Corpuscular Matter Theories, ed. Christoph Lüthy, John E. Murdoch, and William R. Newman, pp. 291–329. Leiden: Brill, 2001,

Newman, William R. and Lawrence M. Principe. *Alchemy Tried in the Fire: Starkey, Boyle, and the Fate of Helmontian Chymistry.* Chicago: University of Chicago Press, 2002.

Nicholson, Norman. *The Lakers: The Adventures of the First Tourists.* London: Robert Hale, 1955.

Nicolson, Marjorie Hope. *The Breaking of the Circle: Studies in the Effect of the "New Science" upon Seventeenth-Century Poetry.* New York: Columbia University Press, 1960.

———. "The Microscope and the English Imagination." *Smith College Studies in Modern Languages* 16(4) (1935): 1–92.

———. "Milton and the Telescope." *English Literary History* 2(1) (1935): 1–32.

———. *Newton Demands the Muse: Newton's Opticks and the Eighteenth Century Poets.* Princeton: Princeton University Press, 1946.

Nicolson, Marjorie Hope and G. S. Rousseau. *"This Long Disease, My Life": Alexander Pope and the Sciences.* Princeton: Princeton University Press, 1968.

Nochimson, Richard L. "Studies in the Life of Robert Burton." *Yearbook of English Studies* 4 (1974): 85–111.

Nohrnberg, James. *The Analogy of "The Faerie Queene."* Princeton: Princeton University Press, 1976.

Norbrook, David. "Women, the Republic of Letters, and the Public Sphere in the Mid-Seventeenth Century." *Criticism* 46(2) (2004): 223–240.

———. *Writing the English Republic: Poetry, Rhetoric, and Politics, 1627–1660.* Cambridge: Cambridge University Press, 1999.

Norris, Edwin, ed. and trans. *The Ancient Cornish Drama.* 2 vols. Oxford: Oxford University Press, 1859.

Novak, Maximillian E. *Daniel Defoe, Master of Fictions: His Life and Ideas.* Oxford: Oxford University Press, 2001.

Nuttall, Geoffrey F. *The Holy Spirit in Puritan Faith and Experience,* rev. ed. Chicago: University of Chicago Press, 1992.

———. *James Nayler: A Fresh Approach* (Supplement 26 to the *Journal of the Friends' Historical Society*). London: Friends' Historical Society, 1954.

———. "The Lollard Movement after 1384, Its Characteristics and Continuity." *Transactions of the Congregational Historical Society* 12(6) (1935): 243–250.

Nyquist, Mary. "The Genesis of Gendered Subjectivity in the Divorce Tracts and in *Paradise Lost.*" In *Re-Membering Milton: Essays on the Texts and Traditions,* ed. Mary Nyquist and Margaret W. Ferguson, pp. 99–127. New York: Methuen, 1988.

Oakeshott, Walter. *The Sequence of English Medieval Art Illustrated Chiefly from Illuminated Manuscripts, 650–1450.* London: Faber and Faber, 1949.

Ochs, Kathleen H. "The Royal Society of London's History of Trades Programme: An Early Episode in Applied Science." *Notes and Records of the Royal Society of London* 39(2) (1985): 129–158.

O'Connell, Michael. "Milton and the Art of Italy: A Revisionist View." In *Milton in Italy: Contexts, Images, Contradictions,* ed. Mario A. Di Cesare, pp. 215–236. Binghamton, N.Y.: Medieval and Renaissance Texts and Studies, 1991.

Ojakangas, Mika. *A Philosophy of Concrete Life: Carl Schmitt and the Political Thought of Late Modernity.* New York: Peter Lang, 2006.

Olsson, Kurt. "Grammar, Manhood, and Tears: The Curiosity of Chaucer's Monk." *Modern Philology* 76(1) (1978): 1–17.

Osler, Margaret J. "How Mechanical Was the Mechanical Philosophy? Non-Epicurean Aspects of Gassendi's Philosophy of Nature." In *Late Medieval and Early Modern Corpuscular Matter Theories,* ed. Christoph Lüthy, John E. Murdoch, and William R. Newman, pp. 423–439. Leiden: Brill, 2001.

Oster, Malcolm. "Millenarianism and the New Science: The Case of Robert Boyle." In *Samuel Hartlib and Universal Reformation: Studies in Intellectual Communication,* ed. Mark Greengrass, Michael Leslie, and Timothy Raylor, pp. 137–148. Cambridge: Cambridge University Press, 1994.

————. "The Scholar and the Craftsman Revisited: Robert Boyle as Aristocrat and Artisan." *Annals of Science* 49 (1992): 255–276.

————. "Virtue, Providence and Political Neutralism: Boyle and Interregnum Politics." In *Robert Boyle Reconsidered,* ed. Michael Hunter, pp. 19–36. Cambridge: Cambridge University Press, 1994.

Ousby, Ian. *The Englishman's England: Taste, Travel, and the Rise of Tourism.* Cambridge: Cambridge University Press, 1990.

Owens, Craig. "The Discourse of Others: Feminists and Postmodernism." In *The Anti-Aesthetic: Essays on Postmodern Culture,* ed. Hal Foster, pp. 57–82. Port Townsend, Wash.: Bay Press, 1983.

Pächt, Otto. "A Cycle of English Frescoes in Spain." *Burlington Magazine* 103(698) (1961): 166–175.

————. *The Rise of Pictorial Narrative in Twelfth-Century England.* Oxford: Clarendon Press, 1962.

Park, Katherine and Lorraine Daston. "Unnatural Conceptions: The Study of Monsters in Sixteenth- and Seventeenth-Century France and England." *Past and Present* 92 (1981): 20–54.

————. See also Daston, Lorraine.

Parker, Kenneth L. *The English Sabbath: A Study of Doctrine and Discipline from the Reformation to the Civil War.* Cambridge: Cambridge University Press, 1988.

Parker, Patricia. "Preposterous Events." *Shakespeare Quarterly* 43(2) (1992): 186–213.

Parkes, Christopher. "'A True Survey of the Ground': Defoe's *Tour* and the Rise of Thematic Cartography." *Philological Quarterly* 74(4) (1995): 395–414.

Parks, Stephen. *John Dunton and the English Book Trade: A Study of His Career with a Checklist of His Publications.* New York: Garland Publishing, 1976.

Parry, Graham. "John Evelyn as Hortulan Saint." In *Culture and Cultivation in Early Modern England,* ed. Michael Leslie and Timothy Raylor, pp. 130–150. Leicester, U.K.: Leicester University Press, 1992.

Patrides, C. A, ed. *The Cambridge Platonists.* Cambridge: Cambridge University Press, 1969.

Patterson, Annabel. "Imagining New Worlds: Milton, Galileo, and the 'Good Old Cause.'" In *The Witness of Times: Manifestations of Ideology in Seventeenth-Century England,* ed. Katherine Z. Keller and Gerald J. Schifforst, pp. 238–260. Pittsburgh: Duquesne University Press, 1993.

———. "Lady State's First Two Sittings: Marvell's Satiric Canon." *Studies in English Literature, 1500–1900* 40(3) (2000): 395–411.

———. *Marvell and the Civic Crown.* Princeton: Princeton University Press, 1978.

———. *Pastoral and Ideology: Virgil to Valéry.* Berkeley: University of California Press, 1987.

———. *Shakespeare and the Popular Voice.* Oxford: Blackwell, 1989.

Paulson, Ronald. *The Beautiful, Novel, and Strange: Aesthetics and Heterodoxy.* Baltimore: Johns Hopkins University Press, 1996.

Peacey, Jason. *Politicians and Pamphleteers: Propaganda during the English Civil Wars and Interregnum.* Aldershot, U.K.: Ashgate Publishing, 2004.

Peltonen, Markku. "Francis Bacon, the Earl of Northampton, and the Jacobean Anti-Duelling Campaign." *The Historical Journal* 44(1) (2001): 1–28.

Pérez-Ramos, Antonio. *Francis Bacon's Idea of Science and the Maker's Knowledge Tradition.* Oxford: Clarendon Press, 1988.

Pettitt, Thomas. "'Here Comes I, Jack Straw': English Folk Drama and Social Revolt." *Folklore* 95(1) (1984): 3–20.

Phillips, Joshua. *English Fictions of Communal Identity.* New York: Palgrave, 2010.

Phythian-Adams, Charles. "Milk and Soot: The Changing Vocabulary of a Popular Ritual in Stuart and Hanoverian London." In *The Pursuit of Urban History,* ed. Derek Fraser and Anthony Sutcliffe, pp. 83–104. London: Edward Arnold, 1983.

Pietz, William. "The Problem of the Fetish, II: The Origin of the Fetish." *Res* 13 (1987): 23–45.

Pincus, Steven. "'Coffee Politicians Does Create': Coffeehouses and Restoration Political Culture." *Journal of Modern History* 67(4) (1995): 807–834.

———. "John Evelyn: Revolutionary." In *John Evelyn and His Milieu,* ed. Frances Harris and Michael Hunter, pp. 185–219. London: British Library, 2003.

———. "The State and Civil Society in Early Modern England: Capitalism, Causation and Habermas's Bourgeois Public Sphere." In *The Politics of the Public Sphere in Early Modern England,* ed. Peter Lake and Steven Pincus, pp. 213–231. Manchester: Manchester University Press, 2007.

———. See also Lake, Peter.

Pitkin, Hanna Fenichel. *The Concept of Representation.* Berkeley: University of California Press, 1967.

Plumb, J. H. "The Commercialization of Leisure in Eighteenth-Century England." In *The Birth of a Consumer Society: The Commercialization of Eighteenth-Century England,* ed. Neil McKendrick, John Brewer, and J. H. Plumb, pp. 265–285. Bloomington: Indiana University Press, 1982.

Pocock, J. G. A. *The Machiavellian Moment: Florentine Political Thought and the Atlantic Republican Tradition.* Princeton: Princeton University Press, 1975.

———. "Post-Puritan England and the Problem of the Enlightenment." In *Culture and Politics From Puritanism to the Enlightenment,* ed. Perez Zagorin, pp. 91–111. Berkeley: University of California Press, 1980.

Pogge, Thomas W. *Realizing Rawls.* Ithaca, N.Y.: Cornell University Press, 1989.

Poggioli, Renato. "The Oaten Flute." In *Perspectives on Poetry,* ed. James L. Calderwood and Harold E. Toliver, pp. 224–242. New York: Oxford University Press, 1968.

Pollock, Anthony. "Neutering Addison and Steele: Aesthetic Failure and the Spectatorial Public Sphere." *English Literary History* 74(3) (2007): 707–734.

Poole, Kristen. *Radical Religion from Shakespeare to Milton: Figures of Nonconformity in Early Modern England.* Cambridge: Cambridge University Press, 2000.

Poole, William. "Milton and Science: A Caveat." *Milton Quarterly* 38(1) (2004): 18–34.

Poovey, Mary. *A History of the Modern Fact: Problems of Knowledge in the Sciences of Wealth and Society.* Chicago: University of Chicago Press, 1998.

Porter, Roy. "*Barely Touching:* A Social Perspective on Mind and Body." In *The Languages of Psyche: Mind and Body in Enlightenment Thought,* ed. G. S. Rousseau, pp. 45–80. Berkeley: University of California Press, 1990.

———. "Consumption: Disease of the Consumer Society?" In *Consumption and the World of Goods,* ed. John Brewer and Roy Porter, pp. 58–81. London: Routledge, 1993.

————, ed. *The Medical History of Waters and Spas.* London: Wellcome Institute for the History of Medicine, 1990.

Prest, John. *The Garden of Eden: The Botanic Garden and the Re-Creation of Paradise.* New Haven: Yale University Press, 1981.

Principe, Lawrence M. "Virtuous Romance and Romantic Virtuoso: The Shaping of Robert Boyle's Literary Style." *Journal of the History of Ideas* 56(3) (1995): 377–397.

————. See also Newman, William R.

Pritchard, Allan. "Marvell's 'The Garden': A Restoration Poem?" *Studies in English Literature, 1500–1900* 23(3) (1983): 371–388.

Pumfrey. Stephen. "Ideas above His Station: A Social Study of Hooke's Curatorship of Experiments." *History of Science* 29 (1991): 1–44.

Purver, Margery. *The Royal Society: Concept and Creation.* Cambridge, Mass.: MIT Press, 1967.

Putnam, Michael C. J. *Virgil's Pastoral Art.* Princeton: Princeton University Press, 1970.

Quinn, Dennis. "Polypragmosyne in the Renaissance: Ben Jonson." *The Ben Jonson Journal* 2 (1995): 157–169.

Quint, David. *Epic and Empire: Politics and Generic Form from Virgil to Milton.* Princeton: Princeton University Press, 1993.

Radzinowicz, Mary Ann. *Toward Samson Agonistes: The Growth of Milton's Mind.* Princeton: Princeton University Press, 1978.

Rajan, Balachandra. "Andrew Marvell: The Aesthetics of Inconclusiveness." In *Approaches to Marvell: The York Tercentenary Lectures,* ed. C. A. Patrides, pp. 155–173. London: Routledge and Kegan Paul, 1978.

————. "Simple, Sensuous and Passionate." *Review of English Studies* 21(84) (1945): 289–301.

Rattansi, P. M. "The Intellectual Origins of the Royal Society." *Notes and Records of the Royal Society of London* 23(2) (1968): 129–143.

————. See also McGuire, J. E.

Rawls, John. *A Theory of Justice,* rev. ed. Cambridge, Mass.: Belknap Press of Harvard University Press, 1999.

Raylor, Timothy. "Samuel Hartlib and the Commonwealth of Bees." In *Culture and Cultivation in Early Modern England: Writing and the Land,* ed. Michael Leslie and Timothy Raylor, pp. 91–129. Leicester, U.K.: Leicester University Press, 1992.

————. See also Greengrass, Mark.

Raymond, Joad. *The Invention of the Newspaper: English Newsbooks, 1641–1649.* Oxford: Clarendon Press, 1996.

————. "The Newspaper, Public Opinion, and the Public Sphere in the Seventeenth Century." In *News, Newspapers, and Society in Early Modern Britain,* ed. Joad Raymond, pp. 109–140. London: Frank Cass, 1999.

Reay, B. "Quakerism and Society." In *Radical Religion in the English Revolution,* ed. J. F. McGregor and B. Reay, pp. 141–164. Oxford: Oxford University Press, 1984.

Reedy, Gerald. "Mystical Politics: The Imagery of Charles II's Coronation." In *Studies in Change and Revolution: Aspects of English Intellectual History, 1640–1800,* ed. Paul J. Korshin, pp. 19–42. Menston, U.K.: Scolar Press, 1972.

Reeves, Eileen. *Galileo's Glassworks: The Telescope and the Mirror.* Cambridge, Mass.: Harvard University Press, 2008.

————. *Painting the Heavens: Art and Science in the Age of Galileo.* Princeton: Princeton University Press, 1997.

Reiss, Athene. *The Sunday Christ: Sabbatarianism in English Medieval Wall Painting.* Oxford: Archaeopress, 2000.

Richards, Vernon. *Why Work? Arguments for the Leisure Society.* London: Freedom Press, 1997.

Ricks, Christopher. *The Force of Poetry.* Oxford: Clarendon Press, 2001.

————. *Milton's Grand Style.* Oxford: Clarendon Press, 1978.

Ricoeur, Paul. *The Rule of Metaphor: Multi-disciplinary Studies of the Creation of Meaning in Language,* trans. Robert Czerny. Toronto: University of Toronto Press, 1977.

Riebling, Barbara. "England Deflowered and Unmanned: The Sexual Image of Politics in Marvell's 'Last Instructions.'" *Studies in English Literature, 1500–1900* 35(1) (1995): 137–157.

Riffe, Nancy Lee. "Milton on 'Paradise Regained.'" *Notes and Queries* 13(1) (1966): 25.

Robinson, H. W. "The Administrative Staff of the Royal Society, 1663–1861." *Notes and Records of the Royal Society of London* 4(2) (1946): 193–205.

————. "An Unpublished Letter of Dr. Seth Ward Relating to the Early Meetings of the Oxford Philosophical Society." *Notes and Records of the Royal Society of London* 7(1) (1949): 68–70.

Rogers, John. *The Matter of Revolution: Science, Poetry, and Politics in the Age of Milton.* Ithaca, N.Y.: Cornell University Press, 1996.

————. "Milton and the Heretical Priesthood of Christ." In *Heresy, Literature and Politics in Early Modern English Culture,* ed. David Loewenstein and John Marshall, pp. 203–220. Cambridge: Cambridge University Press, 2006.

————. "The Secret of *Samson Agonistes.*" *Milton Studies* 33 (1996): 111–132.

Rogers, P. G. *The Dutch in the Medway.* London: Oxford University Press, 1970.

Rogers, Pat. *The Text of Great Britain: Theme and Design in Defoe's "Tour."*
Newark: University of Delaware Press; London: Associated University Presses,
1998.

Rollins, Hyder E. "The Black-Letter Broadside Ballad." *Papers of the Modern
Language Association* 34(2) (1919): 258–339.

Romanell, Patrick. *John Locke and Medicine: A New Key to Locke.* Buffalo, N.Y.:
Prometheus Books, 1984.

Ronan, Colin A. and G. L'E. Turner, J. Darius, J. Rienitz, D. Howse, and S. D.
Ringwood. "Was There an Elizabethan Telescope?" *Bulletin of the Scientific
Instrument Society* 37 (1993): 2–10.

Rosenthal, Joel T. *The Purchase of Paradise: Gift Giving and the Aristocracy,
1307–1485.* London: Routledge and Kegan Paul, 1972.

Rosser, Gervase. "Crafts, Guilds and the Negotiation of Work in the Medieval
Town." *Past and Present* 154 (1997): 3–31.

———. "Going to the Fraternity Feast: Commensality and Social Relations in
Late Medieval England." *Journal of British Studies* 33(4) (1994): 430–446.

Rossi, Paolo. *Francis Bacon: From Magic to Science,* trans. Sacha Rabinovitch.
London: Routledge and Kegan Paul, 1968.

———. *Philosophy, Technology, and the Arts in the Early Modern Era,* trans.
Salvator Attanasio, ed. Benjamin Nelson. New York: Harper and Row, 1970.

Rousseau, G. S. "Cultural History in a New Key: Towards a Semiotics of the
Nerve." In *Interpretation and Cultural History,* ed. Joan H. Pittock and
Andrew Wear, pp. 25–81. New York: St. Martin's Press, 1991.

———. "*Et in Arcadio Homo:* Opera, Gender, and Sexual Politics in *The Dunciad."* In *"More Solid Learning": New Perspectives on Alexander Pope's "Dunciad,"* ed. Catherine Ingrassia and Claudia N. Thomas, pp. 33–61. Cranbury,
N.J.: Associated University Presses, 2000.

———. "Nerves, Spirits, and Fibres: Towards Defining the Origins of Sensibility." *The Blue Guitar* 2 (1976): 125–153.

———. "Sinews of Science, Medicine, and Art during the Enlightenment."
Eighteenth-Century Studies 26(1) (1992): 77–96.

———. See also Nicolson, Marjorie Hope.

Rowland, Jon Thomas. *Faint Praise and Civil Leer: The "Decline" of Eighteenth-
Century Panegyric.* London: Associated University Presses, 1994.

Rubin, Miri. *Corpus Christi: The Eucharist in Late Medieval Culture.* Cambridge:
Cambridge University Press, 1991.

———. "Whose Eucharist? Eucharistic Identity as Historical Subject." *Modern
Theology* 15(2) (1999): 197–208.

Ruestow, Edward G. *The Microscope in the Dutch Republic: The Shaping of
Discovery.* Cambridge: Cambridge University Press, 1996.

Rummel, Erika. *The Humanist-Scholastic Debate in the Renaissance and Reforma-tion.* Cambridge, Mass.: Harvard University Press, 1995.

Rumrich, John P. "Milton's Arianism: Why It Matters." In *Milton and Heresy,* ed. Stephen B. Dobranski and John P. Rumrich, pp. 75–92. Cambridge: Cambridge University Press, 1998.

———. *Milton Unbound: Controversy and Reinterpretation.* Cambridge: Cambridge University Press, 1996.

Ruoff, J. E. "Thomas Carew's Early Reputation." *Notes and Queries* 202 (1957): 61–62.

Said, Edward. *Representations of the Intellectual.* New York: Random House, 1996.

Sailor, Danton B. "Moses and Atomism." *Journal of the History of Ideas* 25(1) (1964): 3–16.

Salmon, Vivian. *The Study of Language in Seventeenth-Century England.* Amsterdam: John Benjamins, 1979.

Samuel, Irene. "The Regaining of Paradise." In *The Prison and the Pinnacle,* ed. Balachandra Rajan, pp. 111–134. Toronto: University of Toronto Press, 1973.

Sargent, Rose-Mary. *The Diffident Naturalist: Robert Boyle and the Philosophy of Experiment.* Chicago: University of Chicago Press, 1995.

Scarry, Elaine. *Dreaming by the Book.* Princeton: Princeton University Press, 2001.

Schabacker, Peter H. "Petrus Christus' 'Saint Eloy': Problems of Provenance, Sources and Meaning." *Art Quarterly* 35 (1972): 103–120.

Schaffer, Simon. "Glass Works: Newton's Prisms and the Uses of Experiment." In *The Uses of Experiment: Studies in the Natural Sciences,* ed. David Gooding, Trevor Pinch, and Simon Schaffer, pp. 67–104. Cambridge: Cambridge University Press, 1989.

———. See also Shapin, Steven.

Schenk, Werner. *The Concern for Social Justice in the Puritan Revolution.* London: Longmans, Green, 1948.

Schiller, Gertrud. *Iconography of Christian Art,* trans. Janet Seligman. 2 vols. Greenwich, Conn.: New York Graphic Society, 1971–1972.

Schmitt, Carl. *The Concept of the Political,* trans. George Schwab. New Brunswick, N.J.: Rutgers University Press, 1976.

———. *The Leviathan in the State Theory of Thomas Hobbes: Meaning and Failure of a Political Symbol,* trans. George Schwab and Erna Hilfstein. Westport, Conn.: Greenwood Press, 1996.

———. *Political Theology: Four Chapters on the Concept of Sovereignty,* trans. George Schwab. Cambridge, Mass.: MIT Press, 1985.

———. *Roman Catholicism and Political Form,* trans. G. L. Ulmen. Westport, Conn.: Greenwood Press, 1996.

Schoff, Francis G. "Thomas Carew: Son of Ben or Son of Spenser?" *Discourse* 1 (1958): 8–24.

Schwartz, Regina M. "Milton's Hostile Chaos: '. . . And the Sea Was No More.'" *English Literary History* 52(2) (1985): 337–374.

———. *Sacramental Poetics at the Dawn of Secularism: When God Left the World.* Stanford: Stanford University Press, 2008.

Scott, Jonathan. *England's Troubles: Seventeenth-Century English Political Instability in European Context.* Cambridge: Cambridge University Press, 2000.

Scott, Kathleen L. *Later Gothic Manuscripts, 1390–1490.* 2 vols. London: Harvey Miller Publishers, 1996.

Scott-Luckens, Carola. "Providence, Earth's 'Treasury' and the Common Weal: Baconianism and Metaphysics in Millenarian Utopian Texts 1641–55." In *The Arts of Seventeenth-Century Science: Representations of the Natural World in European and North American Culture,* ed. Claire Jowitt and Diane Watt, 109–124. Aldershot, U.K.: Ashgate Publishing, 2002.

Seaver, Paul S. *The Puritan Lectureships: The Politics of Religious Dissent, 1560–1662.* Stanford: Stanford University Press, 1970.

———. "The Puritan Work Ethic Revisited." *Journal of British Studies* 19(2) (1980): 35–53.

———. *Wallington's World: A Puritan Aristan in Seventeenth-Century London.* Stanford: Stanford University Press, 1985.

Sena, John F. "Belinda's Hysteria: The Medical Context of *The Rape of the Lock.*" *Eighteenth-Century Life* 5(4) (1979): 29–42.

———. "Smollett's Persona and the Melancholic Traveler: An Hypothesis." *Eighteenth-Century Studies* 1(4) (1968): 353–369.

Shagan, Ethan H. "The Pilgrimage of Grace and the Public Sphere?" In *The Politics of the Public Sphere in Early Modern England,* ed. Peter Lake and Steven Pincus, pp. 31–58. Manchester: Manchester University Press, 2007.

———. *Popular Politics and the English Reformation.* Cambridge: Cambridge University Press, 2005.

Shapin, Steven. "The House of Experiment in Seventeenth-Century England." *Isis* 79(3) (1988): 373–404.

———. *The Scientific Revolution.* Chicago: University of Chicago Press, 1996.

———. *A Social History of Truth: Civility and Science in Seventeenth-Century England.* Chicago: University of Chicago Press, 1994.

———. "Who Was Robert Hooke?" In *Robert Hooke: New Studies,* ed. Michael Hunter and Simon Schaffer, pp. 253–285. Woodbridge, U.K.: Boydell Press, 1989.

Shapin, Steven and Simon Schaffer. *Leviathan and the Air-Pump: Hobbes, Boyle, and the Experimental Life.* Princeton: Princeton University Press, 1985.

Shapiro, Alan E. "Artists' Colors and Newton's Colors." *Isis* 85(4) (1994): 600–630.

Shapiro, Barbara J. *A Culture of Fact: England, 1550–1720*. Ithaca, N.Y.: Cornell University Press, 2000.

———. *John Wilkins, 1614–1672: An Intellectual Biography*. Berkeley: University of California Press, 1969.

———. "Latitudinarianism and Science in Seventeenth-Century England." *Past and Present* 40 (1968): 16–41.

———. "Natural Philosophy and Political Periodization: Interregnum, Restoration and Revolution." In *A Nation Transformed: England after the Restoration*, ed. Alan Houston and Steve Pincus, pp. 299–327. Cambridge: Cambridge University Press, 2001.

———. *Probability and Certainty in Seventeenth-Century England*. Princeton: Princeton University Press, 1986.

———. "Science, Politics and Religion." *Past and Present* 66 (February 1975): 133–138.

Sharpe, Kevin. *Remapping Early Modern England: The Culture of Seventeenth-Century Politics*. Cambridge: Cambridge University Press, 2000.

Shell, Marc. *Art and Money*. Chicago: University of Chicago Press, 1995.

Sheppard, Jennifer M. *The Giffard Bible: Bodleian Library MS Laud misc. 752*. New York: Garland Publishing, 1985.

Sherburn, George. "Pope and 'The Great Shew of Nature.'" In *The Seventeenth Century: Studies in the History of English Thought and Literature from Bacon to Pope*, ed. Richard Foster Jones, pp. 306–315. Stanford: Stanford University Press, 1951.

Shevelow, Kathryn. *Women and Print Culture: The Construction of Feminity in the Early Periodical*. London: Routledge, 1989.

Shirley, John W., ed. *Thomas Harriot: Renaissance Scientist*. Oxford: Clarendon Press, 1974.

Shuger, Debora Kuller. *The Renaissance Bible: Scholarship, Sacrifice, and Subjectivity*. Berkeley: University of California Press, 1994.

Shulman, George. "Metaphor and Modernization in the Political Thought of Thomas Hobbes." *Political Theory* 17(3) (1989): 392–416.

Sill, Geoffrey M. *The Cure of the Passions and the Origins of the English Novel*. Cambridge: Cambridge University Press, 2001.

———. "Defoe's *Tour*: Literary Art or Moral Imperative?" *Eighteenth-Century Studies* 11(1) (1977): 79–83.

Singer, Charles, E. J. Holmyard, A. R. Hall, and Trevor I. Williams. *A History of Technology*, vol. 3: *From the Renaissance to the Industrial Revolution c. 1500–1750*. Oxford: Clarendon Press, 1957.

Slack, Paul. *From Reformation to Improvement: Public Welfare in Early Modern England.* Oxford: Clarendon Press, 1999.

Smith, Kathryn A. *Art, Identity and Devotion in Fourteenth-Century England: Three Women and Their Books of Hours.* Toronto: University of Toronto Press, 2003.

Smith, Nigel. *Literature and Revolution in England, 1640–1660.* New Haven: Yale University Press, 1994.

———. " 'Making Fire': Conflagration and Religious Controversy in Seventeenth-Century London." In *Imagining Early Modern London: Perceptions and Portrayals of the City from Stow to Strype, 1598–1720,* ed. J. F. Merritt, pp. 273–293. Cambridge: Cambridge University Press, 2001.

Smith, Pamela H. *The Body of the Artisan: Art and Experience in the Scientific Revolution.* Chicago: University of Chicago Press, 2004.

Smithers, Peter. *The Life of Joseph Addison.* Oxford: Oxford University Press, 1968.

Snider, Alvin. *Origin and Authority in Seventeenth-Century England: Bacon, Milton, Butler.* Toronto: University of Toronto Press, 1994.

Solomon, Julie Robin. *Objectivity in the Making: Francis Bacon and the Politics of Inquiry.* Baltimore: Johns Hopkins University Press, 1998.

Sommerville, C. John. *The News Revolution: Cultural Dynamics of Daily Information.* New York: Oxford University Press, 1996.

Sommerville, Johann. "Conscience, Law, and Things Indifferent: Arguments on Toleration from the Vestiarian Controversy to Hobbes and Locke." In *Contexts of Conscience in Early Modern Europe, 1500–1700,* ed. Harald E. Braun and Edward Vallance, pp. 166–179. New York: Palgrave Macmillan, 2004.

Spacks, Patricia Meyer. *The Poetry of Vision: Five Eighteenth-Century Poets.* Cambridge, Mass.: Harvard University Press, 1967.

Spragens, Thomas A., Jr. *The Politics of Motion: The World of Thomas Hobbes.* Lexington: University Press of Kentucky, 1973.

Stafford, David. "Telling One's Arse from a Hole in the Ground: Restoration Peak Discourse." Western Society for Eighteenth-Century Studies Conference Paper, February 14, 1997.

Stallybrass, Peter and Allon White. *The Politics and Poetics of Transgression.* Ithaca, N.Y.: Cornell University Press, 1986.

Starr, G. A. *Defoe and Casuistry.* Princeton: Princeton University Press, 1971.

———. "Defoe's Prose Style: I. The Language of Interpretation." *Modern Philology* 71(3) (1974): 277–294.

———. "From Casuistry to Fiction: The Importance of the *Athenian Mercury*." *Journal of the History of Ideas* 28(1) (1967): 17–32.

Steadman, John M. "Milton's Haemony: Etymology and Allegory." *Papers of the Modern Language Association* 77(3) (1962): 200–207.

Stein, Arnold. *Answerable Style: Essays on "Paradise Lost."* Minneapolis: University of Minnesota Press, 1953.

———. "Milton's War in Heaven—An Extended Metaphor." *English Literary History* 18(3) (1951): 201–220.

Stevens, Michael R. "T. S. Eliot's Neo-Medieval Economics." www.acton.org/files/mm-v2n2-stevens.pdf.

Stewart, Larry. "Public Lectures and Private Patronage in Newtonian England." *Isis* 77(1) (1986): 47–58.

———. *The Rise of Public Science: Rhetoric, Technology, and Natural Philosophy in Newtonian Britain, 1660–1750.* Cambridge: Cambridge University Press, 1992.

Stewart, Stanley. *The Enclosed Garden: The Tradition and the Image in Seventeenth-Century Poetry.* Madison: University of Wisconsin Press, 1966.

Stimson, Dorothy. "Ballad of Gresham Colledge." *Isis* 18(1) (1932): 103–117.

———. *Scientists and Amateurs: A History of the Royal Society.* New York: Henry Schuman, 1948.

Stocker, Margarita. *Apocalyptic Marvell: The Second Coming in Seventeenth-Century Poetry.* Brighton, U.K.: Harvester Press, 1986.

Strong, Roy C. "The Popular Celebration of the Accession Day of Queen Elizabeth I." *Journal of the Warburg and Courtauld Institutes* 21(1–2) (1958): 86–103.

Svendsen, Kester. "Milton's 'Aerie Microscope.'" *Modern Language Notes* 64(8) (1949): 525–527.

Swann, Marjorie. *Curiosities and Texts: The Culture of Collecting in Early Modern England.* Philadelphia: University of Pennsylvania Press, 2001.

Syfret, R. H. "The Origins of the Royal Society." *Notes and Records of the Royal Society of London* 5(2) (1948): 75–137.

Tabor, James D. *Things Unutterable: Paul's Ascent to Paradise in Its Greco-Roman, Judaic, and Early Christian Contexts.* Lanham, Md.: University Press of America, 1986.

Taylor, Charles. *Philosophy and the Human Sciences: Philosophical Papers,* vol. 2. Cambridge: Cambridge University Press, 1985.

Teskey, Gordon. *Delirious Milton: The Fate of the Poet in Modernity.* Cambridge, Mass.: Harvard University Press, 2006.

Thomas, Keith. "Another Digger Broadside." *Past and Present* 42 (1969): 57–68.

———. *The Ends of Life: Roads to Fulfilment in Early Modern England.* New York: Oxford University Press, 2009.

———. *Man and the Natural World: Changing Attitudes in England, 1500–1800.* London: Allen Lane Publishers, 1983.

———. *The Perception of the Past in Early Modern England: The Creighton Trust Lecture.* London: University of London, 1983.

———. *Religion and the Decline of Magic.* New York: Scribner, 1971.

Thomas, Peter. "Henry Vaughan, Orpheus, and the Empowerment of Poetry." In *Of Paradise and Light: Essays on Henry Vaughan and John Milton in Honor of Alan Rudrum,* ed. Donald R. Dickson and Holly Faith Nelson, pp. 218–249. Newark: University of Delaware Press, 2004.

Tillyard, E. M. W. *The Elizabethan World Picture: A Study of the Idea of Order in the Age of Shakespeare, Donne and Milton.* New York: Vintage, 1961.

Tipson, Baird. "A Dark Side of Seventeenth-Century English Protestantism: The Sin against the Holy Spirit." *The Harvard Theological Review* 77(3–4) (1984): 301–330.

Tittler, Robert. "Reformation, Resources and Authority in English Towns: An Overview." In *The Reformation in English Towns, 1500–1640,* ed. Patrick Collinson and John Craig, pp. 190–201. New York: St. Martin's Press, 1998.

Todd, Dennis. *Imagining Monsters: Miscreations of the Self in Eighteenth-Century England.* Chicago: University of Chicago Press, 1995.

Trickett, Rachel. " 'Curious Eye': Some Aspects of Visual Description in Eighteenth-Century Literature." In *Augustan Studies: Essays in Honor of Irvin Ehrenpreis,* ed. Douglas Lane Patey and Timothy Keegan, pp. 239–252. Cranbury, N.J.: Associated University Presses, 1985.

Troyer, Howard William. *Ned Ward of Grubstreet: A Study of Sub-Literary London in the Eighteenth Century.* Cambridge, Mass.: Harvard University Press, 1946.

Turnbull, G. H. "Samuel Hartlib's Influence on the Early History of the Royal Society." *Notes and Records of the Royal Society of London* 10(2) (1953): 101–130.

Turner, Bryan S. "The Government of the Body: Medical Regimens and the Rationalization of Diet." *British Journal of Sociology* 33(2) (1982): 254–269.

Turner, James Grantham. "Landscape and the 'Art Prospective' in England, 1584–1660." *Journal of the Warburg and Courtauld Institutes* 42 (1979): 290–293.

———. "The Libertine Abject: The 'Postures' of *Last Instructions to a Painter.*" In *Marvell and Liberty,* ed. Warren Chernaik and Martin Dzelzainis, pp. 217–248. Houndmills, U.K.: Macmillan, 1999.

———. *Libertines and Radicals in Early Modern London: Sexuality, Politics and Literary Culture, 1630–1685.* Cambridge: Cambridge University Press, 2002.

———. "Marvell's Warlike Studies." *Essays in Criticism* 28(4) (1978): 288–301.

———. *One Flesh: Paradisal Marriage and Sexual Relations in the Age of Milton.* Oxford: Clarendon Press, 1987.

———. *The Politics of Landscape: Rural Scenery and Society in English Poetry, 1630–1660.* Oxford: Blackwell, 1979.

Turner, Mark. *The Literary Mind: The Origins of Thought and Language.* New York: Oxford University Press, 1996.

Turner, Mark and Gilles Fauconnier. "Conceptual Integration and Formal Expression." *Metaphor and Symbolic Activity* 10(3) (1995): 183–203.

Underdown, David. *Fire from Heaven: Life in an English Town in the Seventeenth Century.* London: Yale University Press, 1992.

——— *A Freeborn People: Politics and the Nation in Seventeenth-Century England.* Oxford: Clarendon Press, 1996.

———. *Revel, Riot and Rebellion: Popular Politics and Culture in England, 1603–1660.* Oxford: Oxford University Press, 1985.

Van Helden, Albert. "Galileo and Scheiner on Sunspots: A Case Study in the Visual Language of Astronomy." *Proceedings of the American Philosophical Society* 140(3) (1996): 358–396.

———. "The Invention of the Telescope." *Transactions of the American Philosophical Society,* new ser. 67(4) (1977): 1–67.

———. "Telescopes and Authority from Galileo to Cassini" *Osiris,* 2nd ser. 9 (1994): 8–29.

Vicari, E. Patricia. *The View from Minerva's Tower: Learning and Imagination in "The Anatomy of Melancholy."* Toronto: University of Toronto Press, 1989.

Vickers, Ilse. *Defoe and the New Sciences.* Cambridge: Cambridge University Press, 1996.

Virno, Paulo. *A Grammar of the Multitude for an Analysis of Contemporary Forms of Life,* trans. Isabella Bertoletti, James Cascaito, and Andrea Casson. http://www.generation-online.org/c/fcmultitude3.htm (accessed 1/15/09).

Von Maltzahn, Nicholas. "Laureate, Republican, Calvinist: An Early Response to Milton and *Paradise Lost* (1667)." *Milton Studies* 29 (1992): 181–198.

———. "The Royal Society and the Provenance of Milton's *History of Britain* (1670)." *Milton Quarterly* 32(3) (1998): 90–95.

———. "Samuel Butler's Milton." *Studies in Philology* 92(4) (1995): 482–495.

Waldock, A. J. A. *"Paradise Lost" and Its Critics.* Cambridge: Cambridge University Press, 1966.

Walker, D. P. *The Ancient Theology: Studies in Christian Platonism from the Fifteenth to the Eighteenth Century.* Ithaca, N.Y.: Cornell University Press, 1972.

Walker, Julia M. "Milton and Galileo: The Art of Intellectual Canonization." *Milton Studies* 25 (1989): 109–123.

Walker, William. *Locke, Literary Criticism, and Philosophy.* Cambridge: Cambridge University Press, 1994.

Wall, Cynthia Sundberg. *The Literary and Cultural Spaces of Restoration London.* Cambridge: Cambridge University Press, 1998.

———. *The Prose of Things: Transformations of Description in the Eighteenth Century.* Chicago: University of Chicago Press, 2006.

Wallace, John M. *Destiny His Choice: The Loyalism of Andrew Marvell.* Cambridge: Cambridge University Press, 1968.

Walsham, Alexandra. "The Parochial Roots of Laudianism Revisited: Catholics, Anti-Calvinists and 'Parish Anglicans' in Early Stuart England." *Journal of Ecclesiastical History* 49(4) (1998): 620–651.

Walther, Ingo F. and Norbert Wolf. *Codices Illustres: The World's Most Famous Illuminated Manuscripts 400–1600.* Cologne: Taschen, 2001.

Walzer, Michael. "Puritanism as a Revolutionary Ideology." *History and Theory* 3(1) (1963): 59–90.

Ward, Joseph P. *Metropolitan Communities: Trade Guilds, Identity, and Change in Early Modern London.* Stanford: Stanford University Press, 1997.

Warner, Michael. *Publics and Counterpublics.* New York: Zone Books, 2005.

Warnke, Frank J. "The Meadow-Sequence in *Upon Appleton House:* Questions of Tone and Meaning." In *Approaches to Marvell: The York Tercentenary Lectures,* ed. C. A. Patrides, pp. 234–250. London: Routledge and Kegan Paul, 1978.

Watt, Tessa. *Cheap Print and Popular Piety, 1550–1640.* Cambridge: Cambridge University Press, 1991.

Watts, Michael R. *The Dissenters: From the Reformation to the French Revolution.* Oxford: Clarendon Press, 1985.

Weber, Max. *The Methodology of the Social Sciences,* trans. and ed. Edward A. Shils and Henry A. Finch. New York: The Free Press, 1949.

———. *The Protestant Ethic and the Spirit of Capitalism,* trans. Talcott Parsons. New York: Routledge, 1992.

Webster, Charles. "Benjamin Worsley: Engineering for Universal Reform from the Invisible College to the Navigation Act." In *Samuel Hartlib and Universal Reformation: Studies in Intellectual Communication,* ed. Mark Greengrass, Michael Leslie, and Timothy Raylor, pp. 213–235. Cambridge: Cambridge University Press, 1994.

———. *The Great Instauration: Science, Medicine and Reform, 1626–1660,* rev. ed. Oxford: Peter Lang, 2002.

————. "New Light on the Invisible College: The Social Relations of English Science in the Mid-Seventeenth Century." *Transactions of the Royal Historical Society,* 5th ser. 24 (1974): 19–42.

————. "The Origins of the Royal Society." *History of Science* 6 (1967): 106–128.

————. *Samuel Hartlib and the Advancement of Learning.* London: Cambridge University Press, 1970.

Weiss, J. E. and N. O. Weiss. "Marvell's Spotted Sun." *Notes and Queries* 27(4) (1980): 339–341.

West, Richard. *Daniel Defoe: The Life and Strange Surprising Adventures.* New York: Carroll and Graf, 1988.

White, Lynn, Jr. *Medieval Technology and Social Change.* New York: Oxford University Press, 1966.

Whiting, Robert. *The Blind Devotion of the People: Popular Religion and the English Reformation.* Cambridge: Cambridge University Press, 1989.

————. *Local Responses to the English Reformation.* Basingstoke, U.K.: Macmillan; New York: St. Martin's Press, 1998.

Whitman, Jon. "Losing a Position and Taking One: Theories of Place and *Paradise Lost.*" *Milton Studies* 29 (1992): 21–33.

Whitney, Elspeth. "Paradise Restored: The Mechanical Arts from Antiquity through the Thirteenth Century." *Transactions of the American Philosophical Society,* new ser. 80(1) (1990): 1–169.

Wieck, Roger S., William M. Voelkle, and K. Michelle Hearne. *The Hours of Henry VIII: A Renaissance Masterpiece by Jean Poyet.* New York: George Braziller and Pierpont Morgan Library, 2000.

Wilding, Michael. *Dragons Teeth: Literature in the English Revolution.* Oxford: Clarendon Press, 1987.

Williams, Arnold. *The Common Expositor: An Account of the Commentaries on Genesis, 1527–1633.* Chapel Hill: University of North Carolina Press, 1948.

Williams, Raymond. *The Country and the City.* New York: Oxford University Press, 1973.

Williamson, George. "Mutability, Decay, and Seventeenth-Century Melancholy." *English Literary History* 2(2) (1935): 121–150.

Willy, Margaret. *Three Women Diarists: Celia Fiennes, Dorothy Wordsworth, Katherine Mansfield.* London: Longmans, Green, 1964.

Wilson, Catherine. *The Invisible World: Early Modern Philosophy and the Invention of the Microscope.* Princeton: Princeton University Press, 1995.

Wilson, John Harold. *The Court Wits of the Restoration: An Introduction.* Princeton: Princeton University Press, 1948.

Winn, James Anderson. *John Dryden and His World.* New Haven: Yale University Press, 1987.

Winton, Calhoun. *Captain Steele: The Early Career of Richard Steele.* Baltimore: Johns Hopkins University Press, 1964.

Wiseman, Susan J. "History Digested: Opera and Colonialism in the 1650s." In *Literature and the English Civil War,* ed. Thomas Healy and Jonathan Sawday, pp. 189–204. Cambridge: Cambridge University Press, 1990.

Wittreich, Joseph Anthony, Jr. *Angel of Apocalypse: Blake's Idea of Milton.* Madison: University of Wisconsin Press, 1975.

———. *Milton's "Paradise Regained": Two Eighteenth-Century Critiques.* Gainesville, Fla.: Scholars' Facsimiles and Reprints, 1971.

———. "Milton's Transgressive Maneuvers: Receptions (Then and Now) and the Sexual Politics of *Paradise Lost.*" In *Milton and Heresy,* ed. Stephen B. Dobranski and John P. Rumrich, pp. 244–266. Cambridge: Cambridge University Press, 1998.

———. *Shifting Contexts: Reinterpreting "Samson Agonistes."* Pittsburgh: Duquesne University Press, 2002.

Wojcik, Jan W. *Robert Boyle and the Limits of Reason.* Cambridge: Cambridge University Press, 1997.

Wood, Michael. *Children of Silence: On Contemporary Fiction.* New York: Columbia University Press, 1998.

Wood, Paul B. "Methodology and Apologetics: Thomas Sprat's *History of the Royal Society.*" *British Journal for the History of Science* 13(1) (1980): 1–26.

———. See also Hunter, Michael.

Woods, Susanne. " 'That Freedom of Discussion Which I Loved': Italy and Milton's Cultural Self-Definition." In *Milton in Italy: Contexts, Images, Contradictions,* ed. Mario A. Di Cesare, pp. 9–18. Binghamton, N.Y.: Medieval and Renaissance Texts and Studies, 1991.

Worden, Blair. *Literature and Politics in Cromwellian England: John Milton, Andrew Marvell, Marchamont Nedham.* Oxford: Oxford University Press, 2007.

———. "Milton, *Samson Agonistes,* and the Restoration." In *Culture and Society in the Stuart Restoration: Literature, Drama, History,* ed. Gerald MacLean, pp. 111–136. Cambridge: Cambridge University Press, 1995.

———. "Toleration and the Cromwellian Protectorate." In *Persecution and Toleration: Papers Read at the Twenty-Second Summer Meeting and the Twenty-Third Winter Meeting of the Ecclesiastical History Society,* ed. W. J. Sheils, pp. 199–233. Oxford: Basil Blackwell for the Ecclesiastical History Society, 1984.

Wormuth, Francis D. *The Royal Prerogative, 1603–1649: A Study in English Political and Constitutional Ideas.* Ithaca, N.Y.: Cornell University Press, 1939.

Wright, Gillian. "Mary Evelyn and Devotional Practice." In *John Evelyn and His Milieu,* ed. Frances Harris and Michael Hunter, pp. 221–232. London: British Library, 2003

Wrightson, Keith. "'Sorts of People' in Tudor and Stuart England." In *The Middling Sort of People: Culture, Society, and Politics in England, 1550–1800,* ed. Jonathan Barry and Christopher Brooks, pp. 28–51. New York: St. Martin's Press, 1994.

Yates, Frances A. *The Art of Memory.* Chicago: University of Chicago Press, 1966.
———. *The Rosicrucian Enlightenment.* London: Routledge and Kegan Paul, 1972.

Yule, G. Udny. "The Word 'Muing' in Milton's *Areopagitica.*" *Review of English Studies* 19(73) (1943): 61–66.

Zaret. David. *Origins of Democratic Culture: Printing, Petitions, and the Public Sphere in Early-Modern England.* Princeton: Princeton University Press, 2000.

Zilsel, Edgar. "The Genesis of the Concept of Scientific Progress." *Journal of the History of Ideas* 6(3) (1945): 325–349.

Žižek, Slavoj. *The Fragile Absolute: Or, Why Is the Christian Legacy Worth Fighting For?* London: Verso, 2001.
———. *Looking Awry: An Introduction to Jacques Lacan through Popular Culture.* Cambridge, Mass.: MIT Press, 1991.

Zwicker, Steven N. "Virgins and Whores: The Politics of Sexual Misconduct in the 1660s." In *The Political Identity of Andrew Marvell,* ed. Conal Condren and A. D. Cousins, pp. 85–110. Aldershot, U.K.: Scolar Press, 1990.
———. See also Hirst, Derek.

Reference Works

Dictionary of National Biography Online. www.oxforddnb.com.
Oxford English Dictionary Online. www.oed.com.

ACKNOWLEDGMENTS

In the many years it has taken me to complete this book I have incurred significant debts. I must first thank my teachers Barbara Shapiro, George Starr, and James Grantham Turner, whose footnote about William Browne got me started; George, in particular, tolerated more office hour visits than any professor should have to bear. My colleagues Oliver Arnold, Larry Danson, Kevis Goodman, Steven Justice, Victoria Kahn, Eileen Reeves, David Simon, Nigel Smith, Janet Sorensen, and an anonymous reviewer for Harvard University Press read the manuscript in various states of repair and made many helpful suggestions. I am particularly grateful to Vicky and Eileen for encouraging me and for lending their knowledge to the project.

I thank members of the Berkeley Eighteenth-Century Studies Group, the British and Commonwealth Studies Forum at the University of Memphis, the Northeast Milton Seminar, and the Stanford Humanities Center's Seminar on Enlightenment and Revolution, as well as those foolhardy enough to participate in my 2003 "Prehistory of the Posthuman" conference, sponsored by Princeton's Center for the Study of Religion, for listening to earlier versions of my arguments and for helping me refine them. The project received essential support from the Center for the Study of Religion, the UC Berkeley Division of Arts and Humanities, and the Townsend Humanities Center.

I am grateful for permission to rework material that appeared elsewhere first: "Optical Instruments and the Eighteenth-Century Observer," *Studies in Eighteenth-Century Culture* 29 (2000): 123–153; "Experimentalism in Restoration and Eighteenth-Century England," in *A Concise Companion to the Restoration and Eighteenth Century,* ed. Cynthia Wall (Oxford: Blackwell, 2004), pp. 36–57; "Reforming the Garden: The Experimentalist Eden and *Paradise Lost,*" *English Literary History* 72(1) (Spring 2005): 23–78; "Breaking through the Mode: Celia Fiennes and the Exercise of Curiosity," *Literature Compass* 6(2) (February 2009): 291–313; "The Public Person and the Play of Fact," *Representations* 105(1) (February 2009): 85–132.

The manuscript would not have made its way into print without the expert assistance of Phoebe Kosman and Hannah Wong and the generous vision of Lindsay Waters, who helped me see possibilities in what I thought were obstacles. John Donohue initiated me into the mysteries of copyediting with grace and good humor, and I am grateful to him for his painstaking work.

For inspiration and help of all kinds I thank Julia Bader, Christian Barry, Dan Blanton, Stephen Booth, Eduardo Cadava, Jeff Clark, Jeff Dolven, Craig Dworkin, Talissa Ford, Anne-Lise François, Diana Fuss, Catherine Gallagher, Denise Gigante, Judith Goldman, Michael Goldman, Amanda Goldstein, Erik Gray, Stephen Greenblatt, Kenneth Gross, Richard Halpern, Saskia Hamilton, Kristin Hanson, Martin Harries, Robert Hass, Brenda Hillman, Bruce Holsinger, Christine Hume, Janna Israel, Virginia Jackson, Joseph Jordan, Priya Joshi, Lili Loofbourow, John Marshall, Christopher Mead, Maura Nolan, Julie Park, Jeffrey Perl, James Richardson, Christopher Rovee, Michael Rubenstein, Matthew Seidel, Michael Seidel, Stephen Smith, Batya Ungar-Sargon, Cynthia Wall, Connie You, and especially Joshua Phillips, my comrade in all things early modern.

My greatest thanks go to Geoffrey G. O'Brien. I could not have revised this book or stopped revising it without his help.

INDEX